Contents

◄◄ London Eye ◄ Big Ben

Introduction to

London

What strikes visitors more than anything else about London is the sheer size of the place. Stretching for more than thirty miles on either side of the River Thames, and with an ethnically diverse population of just under eight million, it's Europe's largest city by far. Londoners tend to cope with all this by compartmentalizing the city, identifying with the neighbourhoods in which they work or live, and just making occasional forays "into town" or "up West", to the West End, London's shopping and entertainment heartland.

Despite Scottish, Welsh and Northern Irish devolution, **London** still dominates the national horizon, too: this is where the country's news and money are made, it's where the central government resides and, as far as its inhabitants are concerned, provincial life begins beyond the circuit of the city's orbital motorway. Londoners' sense of superiority causes enormous resentment in the regions, yet it's undeniable that the capital has a unique aura of excitement and success – in most walks of British life, if you want to get on, you've got to do it in London.

For the visitor, too, London is a thrilling place – and after winning the right to stage the Olympics in 2012, the city is also in a relatively buoyant mood. The facelift that the capital has undergone over the last decade or so has seen virtually every one of London's world-class **museums**, **galleries** and **institutions** reinvented, from the Royal Opera House to the British Museum. The city now boasts the world's largest modern art gallery in Tate Modern, the tallest observation wheel in the London Eye, and two fan-

The **Rough Guide** to

London

written and researched by

Rob Humphreys

with additional contributions by

Beth Chaplin, Rebecca Morrill, Sally Schafer,

Helena Smith, Joe Staines and Neville Walker

ROUGH
GUIDES

NEW YORK • LONDON • DELHI

www.roughguides.com

tastic new pedestrian bridges that have helped transform the south bank of the Thames into a magnet for visitors and Londoners alike. And after years of being the only major city in the world not to have a governing body, London now has its own elected assembly, housed in an eye-catching building within sight of Tower Bridge, and a mayor who's determined to try and solve one of London's biggest problems: transport.

▲ Covent Garden market

In the meantime, London's traditional **sights** continue to draw in millions of tourists every year. Monuments from the capital's more glorious past are everywhere to be seen, from medieval banqueting halls and the great churches of Christopher Wren to the eclectic Victorian architecture of the triumphalist British Empire. There is also much enjoyment to be had from the city's quiet Georgian squares, the narrow alleyways of the City of London, the riverside walks, and the quirks of what is still identifiably a collection of villages. Even London's traffic problems are offset by surprisingly large expanses of greenery: Hyde Park, Green Park and St James's Park are all within a few minutes' walk of the West End, while, further afield, you can enjoy the more expansive parklands of Hampstead Heath and Richmond Park.

You could spend days just **shopping** in London, mixing it with the upper classes in Harrods, or sampling the offbeat weekend markets of Portobello Road, Brick Lane, Greenwich and Camden. The **music**, **clubbing** and **gay** and **lesbian** scenes are second to none, and mainstream **arts** are no less exciting, with regular opportunities to catch outstanding theatre companies, dance troupes, exhibitions and opera. **Restaurants** these days are an attraction, too. London has more Michelin-star establishments than Paris, as well as a vast range of low-cost, high-quality Chinese restaurants and Indian curry houses. Meanwhile, the city's **pubs** have heaps of atmosphere, especially away from the centre – and an exploration of the farther-flung communities is essential to get the complete picture of this dynamic metropolis.

What to see

London has grown not through centralized planning but by a process of agglomeration, meaning that though the majority of the city's sights are situated to the north of the **River Thames**, which loops through the centre of the city from west to east, there is no single focus of interest. Villages and urban developments that once surrounded the core are now lost within the amorphous mass of Greater London, leaving London's highlights widely spread, and meaning that visitors should make mastering the public transport system, particularly the Underground (tube), a top priority.

If London has a centre, it's **Trafalgar Square**, home to Nelson's Column and the National Gallery. It's also as good a place as any to start exploring the city, especially as the area to the south of here, **Westminster and Whitehall**, is one of the easiest bits to discover on foot. This was the city's royal, political and ecclesiastical power base for centuries, and you'll find some of London's most famous landmarks here: Downing Street, Big Ben, the Houses of Parliament, **Westminster Abbey** and, across St James's Park, Buckingham Palace. The grand streets and squares of **St James's**, **Mayfair** and **Marylebone**, to the north of Westminster, have been the playground of the rich since the Restoration, and now contain the city's busiest shopping zones: Piccadilly, **Bond Street**, **Regent Street** and, most frenetic of the lot, **Oxford Street**.

East of Piccadilly Circus, **Soho**, **Chinatown** and **Covent Garden** are also easy to walk around and form the heart of the West End entertainment district, where you'll find the largest concentration of theatres, cinemas, clubs, flashy shops, cafés and restaurants. Adjoining Covent Garden to the north, the university quarter of **Bloomsbury** is the traditional home of the publishing industry and location of the ever-popular **British Museum**, a stupendous treasure house that now boasts the largest covered public space in Europe. Welding the West End to the financial district, **Holborn** is a little-visited area, but offers some of central London's most surprising treats, among them the

▲ Gherkin, the City

eccentric Sir John Soane's Museum and the secluded quadrangles of the Inns of Court.

A couple of miles downstream from Westminster, **The City** – or the City of London, to give it its full title – is simultaneously the most ancient and the most modern part of London. Settled since Roman times, the area became the commercial and residential heart of medieval London, with its own Lord Mayor and its own peculiar form of local government, both of which survive (with considerable pageantry) to this day. The Great Fire of 1666 obliterated most of the City, and the resident

▲ Green Park

population has dwindled to insignificance, yet this remains one of the great financial centres of the world, with the most prominent landmarks these days being the hi-tech offices of banks and insurance companies. However, the Square Mile boasts its share of historic sights too, notably the **Tower of London** and a fine cache of Wren churches that includes the mighty **St Paul's Cathedral**.

The **East End** and **Docklands**, to the east of the City, are equally notorious, but in entirely different ways. Impoverished and working-class, the East End is not conventional tourist territory, yet to ignore it is to miss out a crucial element of the real, multi-ethnic London. With its abandoned warehouses converted into overpriced apartment blocks for the city's upwardly mobile, Docklands is the converse of the down-at-heel East End, with the **Canary Wharf** tower, the country's tallest building, epitomizing the pretensions of the 1980s' Thatcherite dream.

The **South Bank**, **Bankside** and **Southwark** together make up the small slice of central London that lies south of the Thames. The South Bank Centre itself, London's little-loved concrete culture bunker, is enjoying a new lease of life – thanks, in part, to the feel-good factor emanating from the graceful London Eye, which hangs over the Thames nearby. Bankside, the city's low-life district from Roman times to the eighteenth century, is also enjoying a millennial renaissance, with a new pedestrian bridge linking St Paul's with the former power station that is now home to the **Tate Modern**, London's extraordinary museum of modern art.

In **Hyde Park** and **Kensington Gardens** you'll find the largest park in central London, a segment of greenery which separates wealthy west

7

London from the city centre. The museums of **South Kensington** – the Victoria and Albert Museum, the Science Museum and the Natural History Museum – are a must; and if you have shopping on your agenda you may well want to investigate the hive of plush stores in the vicinity of Harrods, superstore to the upper echelons.

Some of the most appealing parts of north London are clustered around Regent's Canal, which skirts **Regent's Park** and serves as the focus for the capital's trendiest weekend market, held around **Camden Lock**. Further out, in the chic literary suburbs of Hampstead and Highgate, there are unbeatable views across the city from half-wild **Hampstead Heath**, the favourite parkland of thousands of Londoners. The glory of southeast London is **Greenwich**, with its nautical associations, royal park and observatory

Multi-ethnic London

With around three hundred languages spoken within its confines and all the major religions represented, London is Europe's most ethnically diverse city. First- second- and third-generation **immigrants** make up over thirty percent of the population, while some claim that the majority of white Londoners are in fact descended from French Huguenot refugees. London has, of course, always been a cosmopolitan place. The first well-documented immigrants were invaders like the Romans, Anglo-Saxons, Vikings and Normans, while over the last four centuries, the city has absorbed wave after wave of foreigners fleeing persecution at home, or simply looking for a better life. However, it is the postwar period that stands out as the age of immigration *par excellence*. Initially, people came here from the Caribbean and the Indian subcontinent; today's arrivals are more likely to come from the world's war zones: Somalia, Bosnia, Afghanistan, Iraq.

Though London doesn't have the sort of ghettoization that's widespread in the US, certain areas have become home-from-home for the more established communities. Brixton and Dalston are probably the most prominent Afro-Caribbean and African districts; Dalston and Harringay have the largest Turkish and Kurdish communities; Southall is predominantly Punjabi; Wembley is home to the majority of London's Gujerati population; Acton has a sizable Polish community; Hoxton is a Vietnamese neighbourhood. The East End, London's top immigrant ghetto, has absorbed several communities over the centuries, and is currently the heart of Bengali London, while the Jewish community has more or less abandoned the East End and now has its most significant concentrations in Stamford Hill and Golders Green.

In general, these disparate groups live in peaceful coexistence and the traditions and customs they have brought with them have provided a vibrant contribution to London's cultural life, the most famous manifestation of which is the Notting Hill Carnival (see p.332).

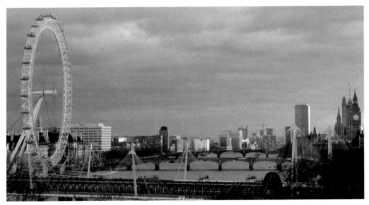
▲ View over the Thames at sunset

(not to mention its Dome). Finally, there are plenty of rewarding day-trips up the Thames from **Chiswick** to **Hampton Court** and, beyond, to **Windsor**, an area that is liberally peppered with the stately homes and grounds of the country's royalty and former aristocracy.

When to go

onsidering how temperate the London **climate** is, it's amazing how much mileage the locals get out of the subject. The truth is that summers rarely get really hot and the winters aren't very cold. In fact, it's impossible to say with any certainty what the weather will be like in any given month. May might be wet and grey one year and gloriously sunny the next; November stands an equal chance of being crisp and clear or foggy and grim. So, whatever time of year you come, be prepared for all eventualities, and bring a pair of comfortable shoes, as, inevitably, you'll be doing a lot of walking.

Average temperatures and monthly rainfall

	Jan	Feb	Mar	Apr	May	June	July	Aug	Sept	Oct	Nov	Dec
Max. temp. (°C)	6	7	10	13	17	20	22	21	19	14	10	7
(°F)	43	44	50	56	62	69	71	71	65	57	50	44
Min. temp. (°C)	2	2	3	6	8	12	14	13	11	8	5	4
(°F)	36	36	37	43	46	53	57	56	52	45	41	39
Rainfall (mm)	54	40	37	37	46	45	57	59	49	57	64	48
(inches)	2.1	1.6	1.5	1.5	1.8	1.8	2.2	2.3	1.9	2.2	2.5	1.9

things not to miss

It's not possible to see everything that London has to offer in one visit – and we don't suggest you try. What follows is a selective taste of the city's highlights; from outstanding art collections and historic architecture to vibrant markets and picturesque parks, all arranged in five colour-coded categories. Each highlight has a page reference to take you straight into the guide, where you can find out more.

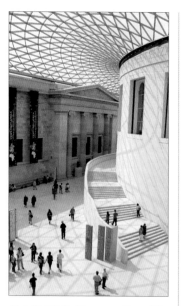

01 British Museum Page **128** • The spectacular Great Court and the renovated Round Reading Room have brought new life to the world's oldest and greatest public museum.

02 Tate Modern Page **270** • One of the world's greatest modern art collections housed in a spectacularly converted riverside power station.

03 The Proms

Page **301** • Annual festival which features top-flight classical concerts night after night at the Royal Albert Hall, with tickets starting at under a fiver.

04

Somerset House Page

168 • Visit the art galleries, chill out by the dancing fountain, or (in winter) skate the night away at this wonderful riverside palace.

05 Shopping in Covent Garden Page 157 • With its

spacious, pedestrianized piazza, covered markets and trendy, offbeat stores, Covent Garden is by far the most enjoyable shopping area in London.

06 Hampstead Heath Page 362 •

Fly kites, look across London and walk over to Kenwood, for fine art, tea and cakes.

07 Highgate Cemetery Page

367 • The city's most atmospheric Victorian necropolis, thick with trees and crowded with famous corpses, with Karl Marx topping the bill.

08 Neasden Temple Page **371** • Perhaps the most remarkable building in the whole of London, the Swaminarayan temple is the largest Hindu temple outside India.

11 National Gallery Page **46** • From the Renaissance to Picasso: one of the world's great art galleries.

09 Sir John Soane's Museum Page **177** • Part architectural set piece, part art gallery, the Soane museum is small and perfectly formed.

10 No. 11 bus Page **39** • Take a ride on the no. 11 bus, a double-decker route, that takes you past Big Ben, Trafalgar Square and St Paul's Cathedral.

12 Greenwich Page **378** • Soak up the naval history at the National Maritime Museum, and climb up to the Royal Observatory to enjoy the view over the river.

13 Wimbledon Lawn Tennis Championships Page 554 •

The only grand-slam tennis tournament that is played on grass, and washed down with strawberries and cream, a quintessentially English experience.

14 London pubs Page 474 •

Have a pint in one of London's many old and historic pubs.

15 St Paul's Cathedral Page 187 •

Christopher Wren's masterpiece remains one of London's greatest landmarks.

16 Imperial War Museum Page 266 •

The former Bedlam lunatic asylum is now home to London's most even-handed military museum and the country's only permanent gallery devoted to the Holocaust.

17 Portobello Market Page 333 •

London's best street market (Friday and Saturday) offers brilliant clothes, bric-a-brac, antiques, and fruit and veg.

18 Tower of London Page **213** •
Bloody royal history, ham Beefeaters,
lots of armour, the Crown Jewels and ravens
– and a great medieval castle.

19 Kew Gardens Page **407** •
Kew boasts three hundred acres
of beautiful botanic gardens by the River
Thames, with the curvaceous Palm House as
its centrepiece.

20 Nightlife Pages **474–496** • From
Hoxton bars to Soho clubs, London's
nightlife is the best in Europe.

21 Hyde Park and Kensington Gardens Page **285** • Two classic London parks joined, where you can mess about in a boat on the Serpentine, or take to two wheels on the many cycle tracks .

22 Clerkenwell and Hoxton bars and galleries Page

222 • Take in some of the city's cutting-edge contemporary art and then trawl the trendy bars of these two fashionable districts.

23 Chinatown Page 118 • Join London's Chinese community for a Sunday lunchtime feast of dim sum.

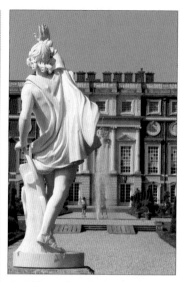

24 Hampton Court Palace

Page **419** • A sprawling red-brick affair on the banks of the Thames, Hampton Court is the finest of London's royal palaces.

25 Houses of Parliament

Page **65** • See the "mother of all parliaments" at work from the public gallery or take a summertime tour.

26 Notting Hill Carnival Page
332 • Free two-day street party featuring decorated floats, eye-catching costumes, thumping sound systems, live bands, good food and massive crowds.

27 London Eye Page 262 •
Londoners have taken to their new landmark, and there is certainly no better view, but book in advance.

28 Victoria and Albert Museum Page 302 •
In terms of sheer variety and scale, the V&A is the greatest applied art museum in the world.

STAGE DOOR →

29 London theatre Page 516 •
Don't leave London without taking in some theatre, anything from a West End musical to an alfresco Shakespeare.

30 Walk along the South Bank Page
258 • Start at the London Eye and stroll along the bank of the Thames, taking in the vista of the north bank, and continue all the way to Tower Bridge.

Basics

Basics

Getting there

Unless you're coming from elsewhere in Britain, or from northwest Europe, the quickest and easiest way to get to London is by plane. The city has five airports (see "Arrival" on p.31 for specific details on each) and is a major destination for most international airlines, so airfares tend to be keenly competitive.

How much you pay to fly to London depends on the **season**, with the highest fares charged from Easter to October, and around Christmas and New Year. Fares will ordinarily be cheaper during the rest of the year, which is considered low season, though some airlines also have a shoulder season – typically April to mid-June and mid-September to October – and a correspondingly shorter high season.

The alternatives to flying are **train** or **bus** (see "Arrival" on p.33 for details).

Booking flights online

Loads of people book tickets online nowadays and good deals can often be found through discount or auction sites, as well as through the airlines' own websites.

Online booking agents and general travel sites

ⓦ **www.cheapflights.com** (US); for Canada ⓦ **www.cheapflights.ca**; for Australia ⓦ **www. cheapflights.com.au**. All the sites offer flight deals, details of travel agents, and links to other travel sites.

ⓦ **www.cheaptickets.com** Hawaii-based discount flight specialists (US only) whose search engine claims to dig up the lowest possible fares worldwide; the one drawback is its cumbersome log-in procedure.

ⓦ **www.etn.nl/discount.htm** A hub of consolidator and discount agent Web links, maintained by the non-profit European Travel Network.

ⓦ **www.expedia.com** (US); for Canada ⓦ **www. expedia.ca**. Discount airfares, all-airline search engine and daily deals.

ⓦ **www.gaytravel.com** US gay travel agent, offering accommodation, cruises, tours and more.

ⓦ **www.hotwire.com** Bookings from the US only.

Last-minute savings of up to forty percent on regular published fares. Travellers must be at least 18 and there are no refunds, transfers or changes allowed. Log-in required. If you're looking for the cheapest possible scheduled flight, this is probably your best bet.

ⓦ **www.lastminute.com.au** (Australia only) Good last-minute holiday package and flight-only deals.

ⓦ **www.priceline.com** Name-your-own-price website that has deals at around forty percent off standard fares.

ⓦ **www.qixo.com** A comparison search that trawls through other ticket sites – including agencies and airlines – to find the best deals.

ⓦ **www.skyauction.com** Bookings from the US only. Auctions tickets and travel packages using a "second bid" scheme, just like eBay. You state the maximum you're willing to pay, and the system will bid only as much as it takes to outbid others, up to your stated limit.

ⓦ **www.travelocity.com** Destination guides, best deals for car rental, accommodation and lodging as well as fares. Provides access to the travel agent system SABRE, the most comprehensive central reservations system in the US.

ⓦ **www.travelshop.com.au** Australian website offering discounted flights, packages, insurance and online bookings.

ⓦ **travel.yahoo.com** Incorporates some Rough Guides material in its coverage of destination countries and cities across the world, with information about places to eat and sleep.

From North America

All major US and Canadian airlines run direct services **from North America to London**, Europe's busiest gateway. Two of London's airports – Heathrow and Gatwick – handle transatlantic flights, and in terms of convenience they're about equal.

Figure on around six hours' **flying time** from New York; it's an hour extra going the other way, due to headwinds. Add three or four hours more for travel from the West Coast. Most eastbound flights cross the Atlantic overnight, arriving the next morning; flying back, departure times tend to be morning or afternoon, arriving in the afternoon or evening of the same day.

Return **fares** (including taxes) from **New York** or Chicago (and even LA) are $400–600 low season, $600–800 high season; from **Toronto** C$600–800 low season, C$800–1000 high season; from **Vancouver** C$900–1000 low season, C$1000–1200 high season.

Major airlines

Aer Lingus ☎1-800/IRISH-AIR, ⓦwww.aerlingus.com
Air Canada ☎1-888/247-2262, ⓦwww.aircanada.com
American Airlines ☎1-800/433-7300, ⓦwww.aa.com
British Airways ☎1-800/AIRWAYS, ⓦwww.ba.com
Continental Airlines ☎1-800/231-0856, ⓦwww.continental.com
Delta Airlines ☎1-800/241-4141, ⓦwww.delta.com
Kuwait Airways ☎212/659-4200, ⓦwww.kuwait-airways.com
Northwest/KLM Airlines ☎1-800/447-4747, ⓦwww.nwa.com, ⓦwww.klm.com
United Airlines ☎1-800/538-2929, ⓦwww.united.com
Virgin Atlantic Airways ☎1-800/862-8621, ⓦwww.virgin-atlantic.com

Discount travel companies

Air Brokers International ☎1-800/883-3273, ⓦwww.airbrokers.com. Consolidator and specialist in round-the-world tickets.
Airtech ☎212/219-7000, ⓦwww.airtech.com. Standby seat broker; also deals in consolidator fares.
Educational Travel Centre ☎1-800/747-5551 or 608/256-5551, ⓦwww.edtrav.com. Low-cost fares worldwide, student/youth discount offers, and Eurail passes, car rental and tours.
New Frontiers ☎1-800/677-0720, ⓦwww.newfrontiers.com. Discount firm, specializing in travel from the US to Europe.
STA Travel US ☎1-800/329-9537, Canada ☎1-888/427-5639, ⓦwww.statravel.com. Worldwide specialists in independent travel; also student IDs, travel insurance, car rental, rail passes, and more.

Student Flights ☎1-800/255-8000 or 480/951-1177, ⓦwww.isecard.com/studentflights. Student/youth fares, plus student IDs and European rail and bus passes.
TFI Tours International ☎1-800/745-8000 or 212/736-1140, ⓦwww.lowestairprice.com. Well-established consolidator with a wide variety of global fares.
Travel CUTS US ☎1-800/592-CUTS, Canada ☎1-888/246-9762, ⓦwww.travelcuts.com. Popular, long-established student-travel organization, with worldwide offers.
Worldtek Travel ☎1-800/243-1723, ⓦwww.worldtek.com. Discount travel agency for worldwide travel.

Tour operators

AESU ☎1-800/638-7640, ⓦwww.aesu.com. Discount airfares and student/low-budget travel.
British Travel International ☎1-800/327-6097, ⓦwww.britishtravel.com. Made-to-measure packages: air tickets, train and bus passes, hotels, and flat and cottage rentals.
Contiki Holidays ☎1-888/CONTIKI, ⓦwww.contiki.com. Specific group tours for people aged 18–35.
Cosmos ☎1-800/276-1241, ⓦwww.cosmosvacations.com. Planned vacation packages with an independent focus.
Euro Vacations ☎1-877/471-3876, ⓦwww.eurovacations.com. Offers BritRail passes plus flight, accommodation and package deals to London.
International Gay Travel Association ☎1-800/448-8550, ⓦwww.iglta.org. Trade group with lists of gay-owned or gay-friendly travel agents, accommodation options and other travel-related services.
Rail Europe ☎1-877/EUROVAC; ⓦwww.raileurope.com. Rail, air, hotel and car reservations in the UK.
Virgin Vacations ☎1-888/YES-VIRGIN, ⓦwww.virgin-vacations.com. Virgin's package-tour division with lots of London breaks on offer.

From Australia and New Zealand

Flight time from Australia and New Zealand to London is at least 22 hours, and can be more depending on routes and transfer times. There's a wide variety of routes, with those touching down in Southeast Asia the quickest and cheapest on average. Given the length of the journey involved, you might be better off including a night's stopover in your itinerary, and indeed some airlines include one in the price of the flight.

The cheapest direct scheduled flights to London are usually to be found on one of the Asian airlines. Average return **fares** (including taxes) from eastern gateways to London are A$1500–2000 in low season, A$2000–2500 in high season. Fares from Perth or Darwin cost around A$200 less. Return fares from Auckland to London range between NZ$2000 and NZ$3000 depending on the season, route and carrier.

Airlines

Air New Zealand Australia ☎13 24 76, ⓦwww .airnz.com.au; New Zealand ☎0800/737 000, ⓦwww.airnz.co.nz

British Airways Australia ☎1300/767 177, New Zealand ☎09/966 9777; ⓦwww.ba.com

Cathay Pacific Australia ☎02/9667 3816, New Zealand ☎09/275 0847; ⓦwww.cathaypacific.com

Delta Australia ☎02/9251 3211, New Zealand ☎09/379 3370; ⓦwww.delta.com

Garuda Indonesia Australia ☎1300/365 330 or 02/9334 9944, New Zealand ☎09/366 1862; ⓦwww.garuda-indonesia.com

KLM Australia ☎1300/303 747, New Zealand ☎09/302 1792; ⓦwww.klm.com

Malaysian Airlines Australia ☎13 26 27, New Zealand ☎0800/777 747 or 649/379 3743; ⓦwww.malaysiaairlines.com

Qantas Australia ☎13 1313, New Zealand ☎09/357 8900 or 0800/808 767; ⓦwww.qantas .com.au

Singapore Airlines Australia ☎13 1011 or 02/ 9350 0262, New Zealand ☎09/379 3209; ⓦwww .singaporeair.com

Sri Lankan Airlines Australia ☎02/9244 2234, New Zealand ☎09/308 3353; ⓦwww.srilankan .aero

Thai Airways Australia ☎1300/651 960, New Zealand ☎09/377 3886; ⓦwww.thaiair.com

Virgin Atlantic Airways Australia ☎02/9244 2747, ⓦwww.virgin-atlantic.com

Flight agents

Flight Centre Australia ☎13 31 33 or 02/9235 3522, ⓦwww.flightcentre.com.au; New Zealand ☎0800/243 544 or 09/358 4310, ⓦwww .flightcentre.co.nz

Holiday Shoppe New Zealand ☎0800/808 480, ⓦwww.holidayshoppe.co.nz

Northern Gateway Australia ☎1800/174 800,

ⓦwww.northerngateway.com.au

STA Travel Australia ☎1300/733 035 or 02/9212 1255, ⓦwww.statravel.com.au; New Zealand ☎0508/782 872 or 09/309 9273, ⓦwww .statravel.co.nz

Trailfinders Australia ☎02/9247 7666 or 1300/780 212, ⓦwww.trailfinders.com.au

www.travel.com.au Australia ☎1300/130 482 or 02/9249 5444; New Zealand ☎0800/468 332, ⓦwww.travel.co.nz

Tour operators

Contiki Australia ☎02/9511 2200, New Zealand ☎09/309 8824; ⓦwww.contiki.com. Frenetic tours for 18–35-year-old party animals.

Explore Holidays Australia ☎13 16 00, ⓦwww .exploreholidays.com.au. Accommodation and package tours to Europe, including all of Britain and Ireland.

From Ireland

Travel from Ireland is easiest by plane, with stiff competition on routes from the North and the Republic keeping prices low. Budget airlines like Ryanair and easyJet offer return tickets from **Dublin**, **Derry**, **Cork** or **Shannon** to London Stansted for as little as €60, depending on availability. From **Belfast** International, easyJet has return fares to London Stansted for £50 or less, if you book far enough in advance; Flybe has similar fares from Belfast City to London Gatwick. A fully flexible fare can cost three or four times that amount, but will allow you to change your ticket or claim a refund.

Airlines

Aer Lingus Northern Ireland ☎0845/084 4444, Republic of Ireland ☎0818/365 000; ⓦwww .aerlingus.ie

bmi Northern Ireland ☎0870/607 0555; ⓦwww .flybmi.com

British Airways Northern Ireland ☎0870/850 9850, Republic of Ireland ☎1800/626 747; ⓦwww.ba.com

easyJet Northern Ireland ☎0871/750 0100, ⓦwww.easyjet.com

Flybe Northern Ireland ☎0870/889 0908, Republic of Ireland ☎1890/925 532; ⓦwww.flybe.com

Ryanair Northern Ireland ☎0871/246 0000, Republic of Ireland ☎0818/303 030; ⓦwww .ryanair.com

Travel agents

Aran Travel International Republic of Ireland ☎091/562 595, ⓦhomepages.iol.ie/~arantvl/aranmain.htm. Good-value flights.

CIE Tours International Republic of Ireland ☎01/703 1888, ⓦwww.cietours.ie. General flight and tour agent.

Go Holidays Republic of Ireland ☎01/874 4126, ⓦwww.goholidays.ie. City breaks and package tours.

Joe Walsh Tours Republic of Ireland ☎01/676 0991, ⓦwww.joewalshtours.ie. Long-established general budget fares and holidays agent.

McCarthy's Travel Republic of Ireland ☎021/427 0127, ⓦwww.mccarthystravel.ie. General flight agent.

Neenan Travel Republic of Ireland ☎01/607 9900, ⓦwww.neenantrav.ie. Specialists in European city breaks.

Premier Travel Northern Ireland ☎028/7126 3333, ⓦwww.premiertravel.uk.com. Discount flight specialists.

Rosetta Travel Northern Ireland ☎028/9064 4996, ⓦwww.rosettatravel.com. Flight and holiday agent.

STA Travel Northern Ireland ☎0870/1600 599, ⓦwww.statravel.co.uk. Worldwide specialists in low-cost flights and tours for students and under-26s, though other customers welcome.

USIT Republic of Ireland ☎01/602 1600, ⓦwww.usitnow.ie. Student, youth and independent travel specialists.

Visas and red tape

Citizens of all European countries – except Albania, Bosnia, Bulgaria, Croatia, Macedonia, Romania, Serbia and Montenegro, and all the former Soviet republics (other than the Baltic states) – can enter Britain with just a passport, for up to three months (indefinitely if you're from the EU). US, Canadian, Australian and New Zealand citizens can stay for up to six months, providing they have a return ticket and adequate funds to cover their stay. Citizens of most other countries require a visa, obtainable from the British consular or mission office in the country of application.

Note that visa regulations are subject to frequent changes, so it's always wise to contact the nearest British embassy or high commission before you travel, or look at the Home Office's website (ⓦwww.homeoffice.gov.uk), from which you can download the full range of application forms and information leaflets. In addition, an independent charity, the Immigration Advisory Service (IAS), County House, 190 Great Dover St, London SE1 4YB (☎020/7967 1200, ⓦwww.iasuk.org), offers free and confidential advice to anyone applying for entry clearance into the UK.

British embassies and high commissions abroad

Australia British High Commission, Commonwealth Ave, Yarralumla, Canberra, ACT 2600 ☎02/6270 6666, ⓦwww.britaus.net

Canada British High Commission, 80 Elgin St, Ottawa, ON K1P 5K7 ☎613/237-1530, ⓦwww.fco.gov.uk

Ireland British Embassy, 29 Merrion Rd, Dublin 4, ☎01/205 3700, ⓦwww.britishembassy.ie

New Zealand British High Commission, 44 Hill St, Wellington ☎04/924 2888, ⓦwww.britain.org.nz

South Africa British High Commission, 255 Hill St, Pretoria, Arcadia 0002 ☎012/421 7500, ⓦwww.britain.org.za

US British Embassy, 3100 Massachusetts Ave, NW, Washington, DC 20008 ☏202/462-1340, ⊛www. britainusa.com

Overseas embassies and high commissions in London

Australian High Commission Australia House, Strand, WC2 ☏020/7379 4334, ⊛www.australia .org.uk
Canadian High Commission Canada House, Trafalgar Square, WC2 ☏020/7528 6533, ⊛www .dfait-maeci.gc.ca
Irish Embassy 17 Grosvenor Place, SW1 ☏020/7235 2171, ⊛www.irlgov.ie
New Zealand High Commission New Zealand House, 80 Haymarket, SW1 ☏020/7930 8422, ⊛www.nzembassy.com
South African High Commission South Africa House, Trafalgar Square, WC2 ☏020/7451 7299, ⊛www.southafricahouse.com
US Embassy 24 Grosvenor Square, W1 ☏020/7499 9000, ⊛www.usembassy.org.uk

Longer stays

For stays of longer than six months, US, Canadian, Australian and New Zealand citizens can apply to the British embassy or high commission (see above) in person or by post for an **Entry Clearance Certificate**. If you want to extend your visa, you should write, before the expiry date given in your passport, to the Immigration and Nationality Dept, Lunar House, 40 Wellesley Rd, Croydon CR9 2BY (☏0870/606 7766).

Working visas

Unless you're an EU resident, you need a **work permit** in order to work legally in the UK, although without the backing of an employer, these can be very difficult to obtain. Persons aged between 17 and 27 may, however, apply for a **Working Holiday-Maker Entry Certificate**, which entitles you to stay in the UK for up to two years, during which it is permissible to undertake work of a casual nature (ie, not in a profession, or as a sportsperson or entertainer). The certificates are only available abroad, from British embassies and high commissions, and when you apply you must be able to convince the officer you have a valid return or onward ticket, and the means to support yourself while you're in Britain. Note, too, that the certificates are valid from the date of entry into the UK – you won't be able to recoup time spent out of the country during the two-year period.

Customs and tax

Travellers coming into Britain directly from another **EU country** do not have to make a declaration to customs at their place of entry. If you've bought the goods in a shop or supermarket within the EU and paid duty, you do not have to declare them. You're allowed to bring as much alcohol and tobacco as you wish for your personal use. However, the guideline limits for what is considered personal use are 90 litres of wine, 20 litres of fortified wine, 10 litres of spirits, 110 litres of beer, 3200 cigarettes or 3kg of tobacco. That said, tobacco restrictions remain in place for eight of the new member states – for more details, contact the HM Revenue & Customs (see below).

If you are travelling from a **non-EU country**, you can still buy tax- or duty-free goods, but not within the EU. The **duty-free allowances** are as follows:

• **Tobacco** 200 cigarettes; or 100 cigarillos; or 50 cigars; or 250g of loose tobacco.

• **Alcohol** 2 litres of still wine, plus 1 litre of spirits or 2 litres of fortified, sparkling or still wine.

• **Perfumes** 60cc of perfume plus 250cc of toilet water.

• **Other goods** to the value of £145.

If you need any clarification on British import regulations, you should contact the **HM Revenue & Customs** on ☏0845/010 9000, ⊛www.hmrc.gov.uk. Pets from countries participating in the **Pet Travel Scheme** (PETS) are allowed into Britain, providing their owners follow certain procedures; for more information, check the government website ⊛www.defra.gov.uk or phone the helpline ☏0870/241 1710.

Most goods in Britain are subject to **Value Added Tax (VAT)**, which increases the cost of an item by 17.5 percent. Visitors from non-EU countries can save money through the Retail Export Scheme (tax-free shopping), which allows a VAT refund on goods taken out of the country. Note that not all shops participate in this scheme (those doing so will display a sign to this effect) and that you cannot reclaim VAT charged on hotel bills or other services.

Costs, money and banks

The strong pound, and the prohibitive cost of accommodation, make London a very expensive place to visit. The minimum expenditure for a couple staying in a budget hotel and grabbing takeaway meals, pizzas or other such basic fare would be in the region of at least £50 per person per day. You only have to add in the odd better-quality meal, plus some major tourist attractions, a few films or other shows, and you're looking at around £75–100 as a daily budget, even in decidedly average accommodation. Single travellers should budget on spending around sixty percent of what a couple would spend (single rooms cost more than half a double). For more details on the costs of accommodation, transport and eating, see p.33 and chapters 25, 26 and 27.

Currency

The basic unit of currency in Britain is the **pound sterling** (£), divided into 100 pence (p). Coins come in denominations of 1p, 2p, 5p, 10p, 20p, 50p, £1 and £2. Notes come in denominations of £5, £10, £20 and £50. The British have an innate mistrust of all high-denomination notes, partly due to the large number of forgeries, and shopkeepers will carefully scrutinize any £50 notes – the best advice is to avoid having to use them. Very occasionally you may receive Scottish banknotes from £1 upwards: they're legal tender throughout Britain, but if you have any problems, go to the nearest bank and get them changed for English currency. At the time of writing, £1 was worth $1.80, €1.50, C$2.30, A$2.40 and NZ$2.60. For the most up-to-date **exchange rates**, contact the useful currency converter websites ⓦwww.oanda.com or ⓦwww.xe.com.

Currency exchange

There are no **exchange controls** in Britain, so you can bring in as much cash as you like and change travellers' cheques up to any amount. Every area of London has a branch of at least one of the big-four high-street **banks**: NatWest, Barclays, Lloyds TSB and HSBC. The opening hours for most are Monday to Friday 9.30am–4.30pm, with some branches in central locations staying open an hour later and some opening on Saturday mornings. Banks tend to give the best rates and charge the lowest commission, and are therefore usually the best places to change money and cheques. Outside banking hours go to a **bureau de change**; these can be found at train stations and airports and in most areas of the city centre. Try to avoid changing money or cheques in hotels, where the rates are normally the poorest on offer.

Carrying money

Credit/debit cards are by far the most convenient way to carry your money. Most hotels, shops and restaurants accept the major credit cards. You can usually withdraw cash on your card from ATMs (widely known as cash machines) – contact your bank to find out which English bank you can use and how much you'll be charged for the service.

Though a lot more hassle, old-fashioned **travellers' cheques** are still the safest way to carry your money. The usual fee for buying them is one or two percent, though this may well be waived if you buy the cheques through a bank where you have an account. It pays to get a selection of denominations. Make sure to keep the purchase agreement and a record of cheque serial numbers safe and separate from the cheques themselves.

A compromise on travellers' cheques and plastic is **Visa TravelMoney** (ⓦinternational.visa.com/ps), a disposable pre-paid debit card with a PIN which works in all ATMs that take Visa cards. You load up your account with funds before leaving home, and when they run out, you simply throw the card away.

Wiring money

Wiring money from home using one of the companies listed below is never convenient or cheap, and should be considered a last resort. It's also possible to have money wired directly from a bank in your home country to a bank in London, although this is somewhat less reliable because it involves two separate institutions. If you go this route, your home bank will need the address of the branch bank where you want to pick up the money and the address and telex number of the head office, which will act as the clearing house; money wired this way normally takes two working days to arrive, and costs around £25 per transaction.

If you're in really dire straits, you can get in touch with your consulate or high commission, who will usually let you make one phone call home free of charge, and will – in worst cases only – repatriate you, but will never, under any circumstances, lend money.

Money-wiring companies

Travelers Express MoneyGram ☎ 0800/6663 9472, ⓦ www.moneygram.com
Western Union ☎ 0800/833 833, ⓦ www .westernunion.com

Tipping

There are no fixed rules for **tipping**. If you think you've received good service, particularly in restaurants or cafés, you may want to leave a tip of ten percent of the total bill (unless service has already been included). It's not normal, however, to leave tips in pubs, although bar staff are sometimes offered drinks, which they may accept in the form of money (the assumption is they'll spend this on a drink after closing time). Taxi drivers, on the other hand, will expect tips on long journeys – add about ten percent to the fare – as will traditional barbers. The other occasion when you'll be expected to tip is in upmarket hotels where, in common with most other countries, porters, bellboys and table waiters rely on being tipped to bump up their often dismal wages.

Youth and student discounts

Once obtained, various official and quasi-official **youth/student ID cards** soon pay for themselves in savings. Full-time students are eligible for the International Student ID Card or **ISIC** (ⓦ www.isiccard.com), which entitles the bearer to special air, rail and bus fares, and discounts at museums, theatres and other attractions. For Americans there's also a health benefit, providing up to $3000 in emergency medical coverage and $100 a day for up to 60 days in hospital, plus a 24-hour hotline to call in the event of a medical, legal or financial emergency. The card costs $22 in the US; C$16 in Canada; A$18 in Australia; NZ$20 in New Zealand; £7 in the UK; and €13 in the Republic of Ireland.

You only have to be 26 or younger to qualify for the **International Youth Travel Card**, which costs the same as the ISIC and carries the same benefits. Teachers qualify for the **International Teacher Card**, offering similar discounts and costing US$22, UK£7, C$16, €13, A$18 and NZ$20. All these cards are available in the US and Canada from STA and Travel CUTS; in Australia and New Zealand from STA; in the UK from STA; and in Ireland from USIT or STA.

Insurance, health and emergencies

Even though EU health-care privileges apply in the UK, you'd do well to take out an insurance policy before travelling to cover against theft, loss and illness or injury. For non-EU citizens, it's worth checking whether you are already covered before you buy a new policy: some all-risks home insurance policies may cover your possessions when overseas, and many private medical schemes include cover when abroad. In Canada, provincial health plans usually provide partial cover for medical mishaps overseas, while holders of official student/teacher/youth cards in Canada and the US are entitled to meagre accident coverage and hospital in-patient benefits. Students will often find that their student health coverage extends during the vacations and for one term beyond the date of last enrolment.

After exhausting the possibilities already mentioned, you might want to contact a **specialist travel insurance company**, or consider the travel insurance deal we offer (see box). A typical travel insurance policy usually provides cover for the loss of baggage, tickets and – up to a certain limit – cash or cheques, as well as cancellation or curtailment of your journey. Many policies can be chopped and changed to exclude coverage you don't need – for example, sickness and accident benefits can often be excluded or included at will. If you do take medical coverage, ascertain whether benefits will be paid as treatment proceeds or only after return home, and whether there is a 24-hour medical emergency number. When securing baggage cover, make sure that the per-article limit – typically under £500/$900 and sometimes as little as £250/$450– will cover

your most valuable possession. If you need to make a claim, you should keep receipts for medicines and medical treatment, and in the event that you have anything stolen, you must obtain an official statement from the police.

Health

Pharmacists (known as chemists in England) can dispense only a limited range of drugs without a doctor's prescription. Most pharmacies are open standard shop hours, though some stay open later: Zafash, 233–235 Old Brompton Rd, SW5 ☎020/7373 2798 (Earl's Court tube) is open 24 hours; while Bliss, at 5–6 Marble Arch, W1 ☎020/7723 6116 (Marble Arch tube), opens from 9am till midnight, seven days a week. To cater for emergencies, every police station keeps a list of all the late-opening pharmacies in its area.

You can get **medical advice** from NHS Direct, the health service's 24-hour helpline (☎0845/4647), or you can turn up at one of the NHS Walk-In Centres: the most central one is at 1 Frith St, W1 (Tottenham Court Rd tube). If your condition is serious enough, you can turn up at the **Accident and Emergency** (A&E) department of local hospitals for complaints that require immediate attention (see p.573 for addresses). Obviously, if it's an absolute emergency, ring for an ambulance (☎999).

Police

Although the traditional image of the friendly British "bobby" has become tarnished over the years by incidences of corruption and racism, in the normal run of events the **police** continue to be approachable and helpful. If you're lost in London, asking a police officer is generally the quickest way

to pinpoint your destination – police officers on street duty wear a distinctive domed hat with a silver tip. Like any other capital, London has its dangerous spots, but these tend to be obscure parts of the city where no tourist has any reason to be. The chief risk on London's streets is pickpocketing, and there are some virtuoso villains at work, especially on the big shopping streets and the Underground (tube). Carry only as much money as you need for the day, and keep all bags and pockets fastened. Should you have anything stolen or be involved in some incident that requires reporting, go to the local police station; the ☎999 number should only be used in emergencies.

Information, websites and maps

If you want to do a bit of research before arriving in London, the British Tourist Authority (BTA) in your home country will happily send you a wealth of free literature, much of it just rose-tinted advertising copy, but some of it extremely useful, especially the maps, guides and event calendars. You can also pick up maps and information from the tourist booths at the airports, ports and in central London. London's most comprehensive listings magazine, *Time Out*, is available from any newsagent. For online information, the Internet has countless sites on London, offering details on just about every aspect of city life.

Tourist offices

The chief BTA office in London is the **London Visitor Centre**, near Piccadilly Circus at 1 Regent St (Mon 9.30am–6.30pm, Tues–Fri 9am–6.30pm, Sat & Sun 10am–4pm; June–Sept same times except Sat 9am–5pm; ⓦwww.visitbritain.com); there's also a tiny information window in the tkts kiosk on Leicester Square (Mon–Fri 8am–11pm, Sat & Sun 10am–6pm; ⓦwww.visitlondon.com).

In addition, some London boroughs run their own tourist information offices, and every London borough has its own tourism/leisure department, which can be consulted via the local council website. The address for Camden is ⓦwww.camden.gov.uk; for other boroughs simply replace Camden with the relevant borough name. The only significant exceptions to the above rule are Kensington & Chelsea, which is ⓦwww.rbkc.gov.uk, and

Hammersmith & Fulham, which is ⓦwww.lbhf.gov.uk.

The most usefully located **borough tourist offices** are: **Greenwich** at Pepys House in the old Royal Naval College (daily 10am–5pm; ☎0870/608 2000); **Richmond** inside the Old Town Hall on Whittaker Avenue (Mon–Sat 10am–5pm; ☎020/8940 9125); and the **Corporation of London** on the south side of St Paul's Cathedral (May–Sept daily 9.30am–5pm; Oct–April Mon–Fri 9.30am–5pm; ☎020/7332 1456).

British Tourist Authority head offices

Australia Level 2, 15 Blue St, North Sydney, NSW 2060 ☎02/9021 4400, ⓦwww.visitbritain.com/au
Canada 5915 Airport Rd, Suite 120, Mississauga, ON L4V 1T1 ☎1-888/VISIT UK, ⓦwww.visitbritain.com/ca
Ireland 18–19 College Green, Dublin 2 ☎01/670 8000, ⓦwww.visitbritain.com/ie
New Zealand ☎0800/700741, ⓦwww.visitbritain.com/nz
South Africa Lancaster Gate, Hyde Park Lane, Hyde Lane, Hyde Park 2196 ☎011/325 0343, ⓦwww.visitbritain.com/za
US 7th Floor, 551 Fifth Ave, New York, NY 10176 ☎1-800/462-2748, ⓦwww.visitbritain.com/us

Listings publications

The most useful London-based publication for visitors is **Time Out**, which comes out every Tuesday and has a virtual monopoly on listings. It carries critical appraisals of all the week's theatre, film, music, exhibitions, children's events and much more besides. If you use the tube on a weekday, you should be able to pick up a copy of London's **free newspaper**, *Metro*, which contains brief news, sport, features and selected listings. It comes from the same stable as *The Evening Standard,* London's only proper daily newspaper, which comes out in several separate editions every weekday, is pretty reactionary, but good for events in the city. Both papers save commuters the trouble of having to talk to one another. In addition, each of the London boroughs has a **local paper**, usually printed twice weekly and filled mostly with news of local crimes and cheap adverts.

Websites

There's a vast quantity of useful London-related information available online. Apart from the aforementioned tourist authority and local borough **websites**, there are some excellent sites on specific areas, such as ⓦwww.london-se1.co.uk and ⓦwww.southbanklondon.com, which both concentrate on the central section of the south bank of the Thames. Most tourist sights have their own website, as do most hotels, B&Bs, shops and restaurants, and we give them in the text. Below are a few of the better general London websites.

ⓦ**www.24hourmuseum.co.uk** A useful national website, with up-to-date information on virtually every single museum, large or small, in London.

ⓦ**www.derelictlondon.co.uk** A pictorial catalogue of the city's abandoned cinemas, pubs, theatres and even toilets, plus other forgotten derelict gems.

ⓦ**www.londonnet.co.uk** A virtual guide to London with useful up-to-date listings on eating, drinking and nightlife.

ⓦ**www.londontown.com** This website is aimed at first-time visitors from abroad, with a basic rundown of the top sights, hotels and restaurants.

ⓦ**www.s-h-systems.co.uk/tourism/london** Short for Smooth Hound Systems, this is a very simply designed and basic tourist info site, which covers London in exhaustive A–Z categories.

ⓦ**www.streetmap.co.uk** Type in the London address or postcode you want and this site will locate it for you in seconds.

ⓦ**www.thegumtree.com** Very useful website aimed at expats living and working in London, particularly those from Down Under.

ⓦ**www.thisislocallondon.co.uk** London's local news website with links to all the capital's local papers.

ⓦ**www.thisislondon.com** Website of *The Evening Standard,* London's only daily newspaper, with constantly updated news and listings.

ⓦ**uk.visitlondon.com** The official LTB website is full of useful information, including an online accommodation service and news about what's new in the city's museums and galleries.

Maps

The **maps** in this book should be adequate for holiday purposes, but you might also want to buy the *Rough Guide London Map*, a comprehensive full-colour, waterproof and non-tearable map detailing restaurants, bars, shops and visitor attractions. Alternatively, the Geographers' A–Z map series produces a whole range of street-by-street maps of London, from pocket-sized foldouts to giant atlases; the Nicholson Streetfinder series is similarly comprehensive. Both series mark and index every street in the city, down to the narrowest alleyway. Virtually every newsagent in London stocks one or the other of them, or you could pick them up from one of the shops listed below. Free maps of the Underground and bus networks can be picked up at tourist offices and Transport for London information offices – see p.33.

Map outlets

UK and Ireland

Stanfords 12–14 Long Acre, London WC2E 9LP ☎020/7836 1321, 🌐www.stanfords.co.uk. Also at 39 Spring Gardens, Manchester ☎0161/831 0250,

and 29 Corn St, Bristol ☎0117/929 9966.
National Map Centre Ireland 34 Aungier St, Dublin ☎01/476 0471, 🌐www.mapcentre.ie

US and Canada

Longitude Books 115 W 30th St #1206, New York, NY 10001 ☎1-800/342-2164, 🌐www .longitudebooks.com
World of Maps 1235 Wellington St, Ottawa, ON K1Y 3A3 ☎1-800/214-8524 or ☎613/724-6776, 🌐www.worldofmaps.com

Australia and New Zealand

Map World (Australia) 371 Pitt St, Sydney ☎02/9261 3601, 🌐www.mapworld.net.au. Also at 900 Hay St, Perth ☎08/9322 5733, Jolimont Centre, Canberra ☎02/6230 4097, and 1981 Logan Rd, Brisbane ☎07/3349 6633.
Map World (New Zealand) 173 Gloucester St, Christchurch ☎0800/627 967, 🌐www.mapworld .co.nz

Communications

You should experience no problems with communications within London or from abroad, the only difficulty being queues at the post office. The mail service is quick and generally efficient, public payphones are numerous, and there are a number of outlets offering Internet access.

Phones

Public **payphones** are operated by a variety of companies, the largest of which is British Telecom (BT) – there should be one less than ten minutes' walk of wherever you're standing. Virtually all pubs have a public phone too, though most eat your money pretty fast. Payphones take all coins from 10p upwards, some take only phonecards and credit cards, and an increasing number take all three. **Phonecards** are available from post offices and newsagents. Resist the temp-

tation to use the phone in your hotel room – telephone surcharges in London hotels are among the most expensive in Europe.

If you're taking your **mobile/cell phone** with you, check with your service provider whether your phone will work abroad and what the call charges will be. Unless you have a tri-band phone, it's unlikely that a mobile bought for use in the US will work outside the States and vice versa. Mobiles in Australia and New Zealand generally use GSM – the same system used by most UK mobile phones – so should work fine.

Costs and codes

The minimum charge for **inland calls** on a BT payphone is 30p, which will give you fifteen minutes' talk time whatever the time of day, anywhere in the UK. **International calls** from BT payphones are generally cheapest between 6pm and 8am on weekdays, and all day at weekends. A cheaper way to call abroad is from one of the number of independent phone centres you'll find around the mainline stations and in many of London's suburbs.

Throughout this guide, London **phone numbers** are prefixed by the area code ☏020, separated from the subscriber number by a forward slash. This code can be omitted if dialling within London. However, some prefixes relate to the cost of calls rather than the location of the subscriber, and should never be omitted: numbers with ☏0800, ☏0808 and ☏0500 prefixes are free of charge; ☏0845 numbers are charged at local rates and ☏0870 up to the national rate, irrespective of where in the country you are calling from in both cases. Beware of premium-rate numbers, which are common for pre-recorded information services – and usually have the prefix ☏0897, ☏0906 or ☏0909; these are charged at anything up to £1.50 a minute.

Operator services

Domestic operator ☏100
International operator ☏155
Domestic directory assistance ☏118 500
International directory assistance ☏118 505

Phoning home

To Australia ☏0061 + area code without the zero + number
To Ireland ☏00353 + area code without the zero + number
To New Zealand ☏0064 + area code without the zero + number
To South Africa ☏0027 + area code without the zero + number
To US and Canada ☏001 + area code + number

One of the most convenient ways of phoning home from abroad is via a **telephone charge card** from your phone company back home. Using a PIN number, you can make calls from most hotel, public and private phones that will be charged to your account. Since most major charge cards are free to obtain, it's certainly worth getting one at least for emergencies; enquire first, though, whether London is covered, and bear in mind that rates aren't necessarily cheaper than calling from a public phone.

Email

A useful way to keep in touch while travelling is using a **free Internet email address** that can be accessed from anywhere, for example YahooMail (🌐www.yahoo.com) and Hotmail (🌐www.hotmail.com). Once you've set up an account, you can use these sites to pick up and send mail from anywhere that provides Internet access – cafés, hotels, libraries etc. You'll find Internet cafés (£2–5 per hour) dotted around the city, though not as many as you might expect given the size of London; easyInternetcafé is the biggest chain with eighteen branches across the city, while some public libraries and hostels offer free access. 🌐www.kropla.com gives useful details of how to plug your laptop in when abroad, phone country codes around the world, and information about electrical systems in different countries.

Mail

Almost all of London's **post offices** are open Monday to Friday 9am–5.30pm, Saturday 9am–noon. The exception is the Trafalgar Square Post Office (24 William IV St, WC2N 4DL ☏020/7930 9580) which is open Monday to Saturday 8am–6.30pm. It's to this office that **poste restante** mail should be sent. Mail is held at the Enquiries Desk and is kept for one month; take a passport or other identification when collecting. In the suburbs you'll find sub-post offices operating out of shops, but these are open the same hours as regular post offices, even if the shop itself is open for longer. To find out your nearest post office, phone ☏0345/223 344.

Stamps can be bought at post office counters, from vending machines outside post offices, or from newsagents and supermarkets, although they usually only sell books of four or ten stamps. A first-class letter to anywhere in the British Isles currently costs 30p and should arrive the next day; second-class letters cost 21p, taking three days. Postcards and airmail letters of less than 10g to the rest of Europe cost 42p; to the rest of the world they cost 47p. For general postal enquiries phone ☎0845/7740 740 (Mon–Fri 8am–7.30pm, Sat 8am–2pm), or visit the website ⓦwww.royalmail.com.

Postcodes

London addresses come with **postcodes** at the end. Each street name is followed by a letter or letters giving the geographical location of the street in relation to the City (E for "east", WC for "west central" and so on) and a number that specifies its location more precisely. Unfortunately, this number corresponds to the position of the first letter of the district in the alphabet, and not to its distance from the centre (as in most cities). So SE5, for example, is closer to the centre of town than SE3, and W5 lies beyond the remote-sounding NW10. Full postal addresses end with a digit and two letters, which specify the individual block, but these are only used in correspondence. Below is a list of some frequently occurring postcodes:

WC1 Bloomsbury
WC2 Covent Garden, Holborn and Strand
EC1 Clerkenwell
EC2 Bank, Barbican and Liverpool Street
EC3 Tower Hill and Aldgate
EC4 St Paul's, Blackfriars and Fleet Street
W1 Mayfair, Marylebone and Soho
W2 Bayswater
W4 Chiswick
W6 Hammersmith
W8 Kensington
W11 Notting Hill
SW1 St James's, Westminster and Belgravia
SW3 Chelsea
SW5 Earl's Court
SW7 Knightsbridge and South Kensington
SW11 Battersea
SW19 Wimbledon
SE1 Lambeth and Southwark
SE10 Greenwich
SE16 Bermondsey and Rotherhithe
SE21 Dulwich
E1 Whitechapel and Wapping
E2 Bethnal Green
E3 Bow
N1 Hoxton and Islington
N5 Highbury
N6 Highgate
NW1 Camden Town
NW3 Hampstead

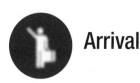

Arrival

The majority of visitors arrive in London at one of its five airports, leaving an expensive trip to the centre. Those arriving by train or bus are dropped right in the middle of the city, with easy access to local transport.

By plane

Flying into London, you'll arrive at: Heathrow, Gatwick, Stansted, Luton or City airport, each of which is less than an hour from the city centre.

Heathrow

Heathrow (☎0870/000 0123, ⓦwww .baa.co.uk) lies around fifteen miles west of

central London, and is the city's busiest airport, with four terminals and two train/tube stations: one for terminals 1, 2 and 3, and a separate one for terminal 4. The fastest way into London is via the high-speed **Heathrow Express** (☎0845/600 1515, ⓦwww.heath rowexpress.com), which takes fifteen minutes from terminals 1, 2 and 3 (eight minutes longer from terminal 4) to reach Paddington station. Trains depart every fifteen minutes between 5am and 11.30pm, tickets cost £14 one way or £26 return (£1 less if you book online or over the phone; £2 extra if you purchase your ticket on board the train), and there are discounts for Family and Disabled Railcard holders. A much cheaper alternative is to take the **Underground's Piccadilly line** (℡020/7222 1234, ⓦwww.tfl.gov.uk/tube), which connects the airport to numerous stations across central London; tickets cost just £3.80, and trains depart at least every five minutes between 5am and 11.30pm, taking about fifty minutes to reach the centre. Note, however, that until September 2006, a **replacement bus service** will run from Hatton Cross to terminal 4. If you plan to spend the rest of your arrival day sightseeing, buy a One-Day Travelcard (Zones 1–6) for £6–12 (see "City transport", p.35).

National Express run **bus services** (℡0870/580 8080, ⓦwww.nationalexpress .com) 24 hours a day from Heathrow direct to Victoria Coach Station (office open daily 6am–9.30pm), which depart every twenty to thirty minutes, take between forty minutes and an hour depending on the traffic, and cost £10 single, £15 return. From midnight, you can take **night bus** #N9 to Trafalgar Square for a bargain fare of £1.20; departures are every thirty minutes and journey time is an hour. Taxis are plentiful, but will set you back between £40 and £70 to central London, and take around an hour (much longer in the rush hour).

Gatwick

Gatwick (℡0870/000 2468, ⓦwww.baa .co.uk) is around thirty miles to the south of London: the non-stop **Gatwick Express** (℡0870/530 1530, ⓦwww.gatwickexpress .co.uk) trains run between the airport's South Terminal and Victoria, taking thirty minutes and costing £13 single, £24 return. Trains run from 5am until 1.35am, and depart every fifteen minutes. A cheaper option is to take a **Southern train service** to Victoria, which costs £9 single, departs every fifteen minutes or so, and takes around forty minutes. **Thameslink** run trains to numerous stations within London, including London Bridge and King's Cross (useful for those heading for north London). Services run roughly every

fifteen to thirty minutes; tickets cost around £10 single and the journey takes thirty minutes to London Bridge. For up-to-date information on all train services from Gatwick, phone National Rail Enquiries (℡08457/48 49 50, ⓦwww.nationalrail.co.uk). A taxi will set you back a ludicrous £90 or more, and take at least an hour.

Stansted

Designed by Norman–Foster, **Stansted** (℡0870/000 0303, ⓦwww.baa.co.uk), London's swankiest international airport, lies roughly 35 miles northeast of the capital. It's served by the **Stansted Express** (℡0870/530 1530, ⓦwww.stanstedexpress .co.uk) to Liverpool Street, which takes 45 minutes and costs £14.50 single, £24 return; trains run every fifteen to thirty minutes from around 5am to 11.30pm. **Airbus** #6 (℡0870/574 7777) runs 24 hours a day, with services every thirty minutes (£10 single, £15 return) to Victoria Coach Station, calling at various places in London en route. Journey time is 1hr 30min (outside rush hour). A taxi will set you back £75 or more, and take at least an hour.

City Airport

Used primarily by business folk, **City Airport** (℡020/7646 0000, ⓦwww.londoncityairport .com) is situated in the Royal Albert Docks, ten miles east of central London, and handles European flights only. The **Docklands Light Railway** (DLR) extension should be up and running by the time you read this, taking you straight into Bank in the City in around 25 minutes; tickets cost around £3. Another option is to take the Silverlink Metro (ⓦwww .silverlink-trains.com), also known as the **North London Line**, which runs every thirty minutes from Silvertown, which is ten minutes' walk from the airport, to Stratford and beyond. A taxi from the airport to the City's financial sector will cost around £20, and take half an hour or so.

Luton

Luton Airport (℡01582/405 100, ⓦwww .london-luton.co.uk) is roughly thirty miles north of London and mainly handles charter flights. A **free shuttle bus** takes five minutes to transport passengers to Luton Airport Parkway station, which is connected by rail to King's Cross St Pancras and other stations in central London. Services are run every ten to twenty minutes by **Thameslink** until 1am; the journey takes around thirty minutes and the single fare is £10.70. **Easybus** (T 0871/417217, W www.easybus.co.uk) run services every 45 minutes from near Baker Street tube for a bargain fare of just £6 single or £2 if you book online. **Green Line** #757 (T 0870/608 7261, W www.greenline.co.uk) runs approximately three buses an hour during the day from Luton to Victoria Station, one or two an hour throughout the evening and night, taking around an hour and a quarter, and costing £9 single, £12.50 return. A taxi will cost in the region of £60 and take at least an hour to central London.

Arriving by train or bus

Eurostar (T 0870/160 6600, W www.eurostar .com) trains arrive at Waterloo International. Trains from the Channel ports arrive at Charing Cross or Victoria, while boat trains from Harwich arrive at Liverpool Street. Arriving by **train** (T 0845/748 4950, W www.nationalrail .co.uk) from elsewhere in Britain, you'll come into one of London's numerous mainline stations, all of which have adjacent Underground stations linking into the city centre's tube network. Coming into London by **coach** (T 0870/580 8080, W www.nationalexpress .com), you're most likely to arrive at Victoria Coach Station, a couple of hundred yards south down Buckingham Palace Road from Victoria train station and tube.

City transport

Thanks to London's mayor, Ken Livingstone, the city's highly complex transport system is finally receiving the attention and investment it badly needs. The controversial congestion charge has reduced traffic by thirty percent within central London, and much of the money has been ploughed into improving the buses. London still has one of the most expensive transport systems in the world, but overall things have definitely improved over the last decade.

Transport for London (TfL) provides excellent free maps and details of bus and tube services, from its **travel information offices**: the main one is at Piccadilly Circus tube station (Mon–Sat 7.15am–9pm, Sun 8.15am–8pm); there are other desks at the arrivals at Heathrow (terminals 1, 2 & 3), Victoria Coach Station plus Euston, King's Cross, Liverpool Street, Paddington and Victoria train stations. There's also a 24-hour phone line for information on all bus and tube services T 020/7222 1234 and a website W www.tfl .gov.uk.

For transport purposes, London is divided into six concentric **zones**, with fares calculated depending on which zones you travel through: the majority of the city's accommodation, pubs, restaurants and sights lie in Zone 1, the central zone. If you cannot produce a valid ticket for your journey, or travel further than your ticket allows, you will be liable for an on-the-spot **Penalty Fare** of £20 (£30 on Tramlink). One word of warning – avoid travelling during the **rush hour** (Mon–Fri 8–9.30am & 5–7pm), when tubes become unbearably crowded (and the lack of air conditioning doesn't help), and some buses get so full they literally won't let you on.

Oyster cards

Since the introduction of the **Oyster card** (☎0870/849 9999, ⓦwww.oystercard .com), London's very own transport smartcard, most Londoners don't bother with paper tickets anymore. You can use an Oyster card in one of two ways: either you can simply store your weekly/monthly/yearly Travelcard, or Pre-Pay – in other words top up your card with money and pay as you go. As you enter the tube or bus, you simply place your card over the card readers – if you're using Pre-Pay, the fare will automatically be taken off your card. Oyster also operates price-capping so that when you've paid the equivalent of a day's Travelcard, it will stop taking money off your card. Note that, as yet, Oyster cards cannot be used on suburban trains. The incentive for Londoners is that Pre-Pay fares are slightly cheaper than normal single fares. Oyster cards are free for those purchasing monthly or yearly tickets; everyone else needs to hand over a £3 deposit.

The tube

Except for very short journeys, the **Under-ground** – or tube, as it's known to London-ers – is by far the quickest way to get about. Eleven different lines cross much of the metropolis, although London south of the river is not very well covered. Each line has its own colour and name – all you need to know is which direction you're travelling in: northbound, eastbound, southbound or westbound (this gets tricky when taking the Circle Line). As a precaution, it's also worth checking the final destination displayed on the front of the train, as some lines, such as the District line, have several different branches.

Services operate from around 5am, Mon-day to Saturday, until 12.30am, and from 7.30am on Sundays, until 11.30pm, and you rarely have to wait more than five minutes for a train between central stations.

Tickets must be bought in advance from automatic machines or from a ticket booth in the station entrance hall. Single fares are outrageously expensive – a journey in the central zone costs an unbelievable £2 – so if you're intending to make more than one jour-ney, a Travelcard (see below) is by far your best option, and if you're staying in London for longer than a few days, then it's probably worth investing in an Oyster card (see box above).

Buses

London's famous red double-decker **buses** (ⓦwww.tfl.gov.uk/buses) are fun to ride on, but sadly often fail to run to their appointed timetable. In central London, and on all the extra-long "bendy buses", you must **buy your ticket before boarding** from one of the bus-stop ticket machines (which don't give out change); elsewhere, you can buy it from the driver. The standard walk-on fare is £1.20. If this is the type of journey you'll be making once or twice a day, then it might be worth buying a block of six Saver tickets for £3.90 for adults, £2.10 for kids. Another option is a One-Day Bus Pass, which costs £3 for adults and £1 for kids and can be used on all buses any time anywhere in London.

Sadly, the old Routemaster double-deck-ers, with their open rear platforms and roving conductors, have virtually all been withdrawn, some replaced by giant bendy buses, others by newer double-deckers. A lot of bus stops are **request stops** (easily recognizable by their red sign), so if you don't stick your arm out to hail the bus you want, it will pass you by, and if you don't ring the bell for the bus to stop, it will just keep on going.

Some buses run a 24-hour service, but most run between about 5am and midnight, with a network of **Night Buses** (prefixed with the letter "N") operating outside this period. Night-bus routes radiate out from Trafalgar Square at approximately twenty- to thirty-minute intervals, more frequently on some routes and on Friday and Saturday nights. Tickets are £1.20 from central London, and Travelcards (see box opposite) are valid until 4.30am. All stops are treated as request stops, so you must signal to get the bus to stop, and press the bell in order to get off.

Suburban trains

Large areas of London's suburbs, particularly in the southeast, are not served by the tube and are impractical to reach by bus. The only way to reach these parts of London is by the **suburban train** network (Travelcards valid), which fans out from the main city termini. Wherever a sight can only be reached by overground train, we've indicated the nearest train station and the central terminus from which trains depart.

A couple of useful train lines that actually cross the capital are the **North London Line** run by Silverlink (ⓦwww.silverlink-trains .com), which connects Richmond and North Woolwich via Hampstead Heath, Camden, Islington and Stratford (Mon–Sat every 15min, Sun every 30min), and the **Thameslink** service (ⓦwww.thameslink.co.uk), which runs north–south via King's Cross, Blackfriars and London Bridge (Mon–Sat every 15min, Sun every 30min).

If you're planning to use the railway network a lot, you might want to purchase a Network Railcard, which is valid for a year, costs £20, and gives you up to a third off fares to destinations in and around the southeast. For information on services, phone National Rail Enquiries on ☎0845/748 4950, or visit ⓦwww.nationalrail.co.uk.

Docklands Light Railway

The **Docklands Light Railway**, or DLR (☎020/7363 9700, ⓦwww.tfl.gov.uk/dlr), runs driverless trains from Bank in the City, or from Tower Gateway (close to Tower Hill tube and the Tower of London) overground to the financial centre of Docklands, plus other areas in the East End and also below ground to Greenwich. Travelcards (see below) are valid, or you can get a variety of DLR-only day passes giving you unlimited travel on certain sections of the network. Tour guides give a free running commentary on DLR trains that set off on the hour from Tower Gateway (daily 10am–3pm), as far as Cutty Sark.

Travelcards

To get the best value out of the public transport system, buy a **Travelcard**. Available from machines and booths at all tube and train stations (and at some newsagents as well – look for the sign), a Travelcard is valid for the bus, tube, Docklands Light Railway (DLR), Tramlink and the suburban rail networks.

Day Travelcards come in two varieties: Off-Peak – which are valid after 9.30am on weekdays and all day during the weekend – and Peak. A Day Travelcard (Off-Peak) costs £4.70 for the central zones 1 and 2, rising to £6 for zones 1–6 (including Heathrow); the Day Travelcard (Peak) starts at £6 for zones 1 and 2. A **3-Day Travelcard** costs £15 for zones 1 and 2, but is obviously only worth it if you need to travel during peak hours; **Weekly Travelcards** are much more economical, beginning at £18.50 for zone 1.

Children under 5 travel free on all forms of transport and under 16s travel free on all buses (under 18s in full-time education will, too, from September 2006), although those aged 14 or over will need to apply for an Oyster card to qualify. Off-Peak Day and Weekend Travelcards for children cost £2 and £3 respectively, however many zones you want. Children aged 14 and 15 must have a Child Rate Photocard to buy any child-rate ticket. However, a better option if you're travelling with kids is to buy a **Family Travelcard**, which costs £3.10 for an adult (zones 1 & 2), rising to £4 (all zones), plus an additional 80p for each child (up to as many as four) on weekdays only; on weekends, the children go free. Despite the name, the adults and children don't have to be related, they just have to travel together, and the restrictions are the same as for Day Travelcards (Off-Peak).

There are further **youth** and **student reductions** available on weekly and monthly Travelcards and passes for 16- and 17-year-olds, and for students. Women over 60 and men over 65, who are London residents, can obtain a yearly Freedom Pass that allows free travel on all services within London; to find out more, contact your local council.

Taxis

Compared to most capital cities, London's metered **black cabs** are an expensive option unless there are three or more of you. The minimum fare is £2.20, and a ride from Euston to Victoria, for example, costs around £12–15 (Mon–Fri 6am–8pm). After 8pm on weekdays and all day during the weekend, a higher tariff applies, and after 10pm, a much higher one. The meter will show two amounts: one calculates distance and time, while the other is a small fixed charge – after these are totalled, a tip is customary. A yellow light over the windscreen tells you if the cab is available – just stick your arm out to hail it. London's cabbies are the best-trained in Europe; every one of them knows the shortest route between any two points in the capital, and they won't rip you off by taking another route. They are, however, a blunt and forthright breed, renowned for their generally reactionary opinions. To order a black cab in advance, phone ☏0871/871 8710, and be prepared to pay an extra £2.

Minicabs look just like regular cars and are considerably cheaper than black cabs, but they cannot be hailed from the street. All minicabs should be licensed and able to produce a Public Carriage Office licence on demand. There are hundreds of minicab firms in the phone book, but the best way to pick is to take the advice of the place you're at, unless you want to be certain of a woman driver, in which case call Ladycabs (☏020/7254 3501), or a gay/lesbian-friendly driver, in which case call Freedom Cars (☏020/7734 1313). Avoid illegal taxi touts, who hang around outside venues alongside licensed cabs, and establish the fare beforehand as minicabs are not metered.

Last, and definitely least, there are usually plenty of **bicycle taxis** available for hire in the West End. The oldest and biggest of the bunch are Bugbugs (☏020/7620 0500, ⓦwww.bugbugs.co.uk), who have over fifty rickshaws operating Monday to Saturday from 7pm until the early hours of the morning. The rickshaws take up to three passengers and fares are negotiable, though they should work out at around £5 per person per mile.

Boats

Boat services on the Thames are much improved, but they still do not form part of an integrated public transport system. As a result fares are quite expensive, with Travelcards currently only giving the holders a 33 percent discount on tickets.

The busiest part of the river is the central section between Westminster and the Tower of London, but boats run direct as far as Greenwich, downstream, and Hampton Court upstream. Look out, too, for the MV *Balmoral* and **paddle steamer** *Waverley*, which make regular visits to Tower Pier over the summer and autumn (☏0845/130 4647, ⓦwww.waverleyexcursions.co.uk).

Typical **fares** are £5.50 single, £7 return Westminster to the Tower or £7 single, £9 return Westminster to Greenwich. If you're heading for Greenwich and/or Docklands, it's worth finding out about **Rail River Rover** passes, a hop-on hop-off ticket for the boats and unlimited travel on the DLR (see p.35). All services are keenly affected by demand, tides and the weather, and tend to be drastically scaled down in the winter months. **Timetables** and services are complex, and there are numerous companies and small charter operators – for a full list pick up the Thames River Services booklet from a TfL information office (see p.33), or phone ☏020/7222 1234 or visit ⓦwww.tfl.gov.uk/river.

Driving

Given the traffic jams, parking hassle and pollution caused, **driving** in London – especially central London – is by far the worst transport option available. However, if you must drive, bear in mind the rules of the road (even if no one else does). Seatbelts are compulsory front and back and the speed limit is 30mph, unless it says otherwise.

Your biggest nightmare as a driver is undoubtedly **parking**. The basic rules are that double red and double yellow lines mean no waiting or stopping, as do the zigzag lines that you'll see near a pedestrian crossing. Single yellow and single red lines mean that you can park on them after 6pm or 7pm, and at the weekends, but times vary from borough to borough, so read the signs before leaving your vehicle. Parking at a meter or **pay-and-display** will cost you £4 an hour or more, up to a maximum of two hours, though again meters are usually free in the evenings and at weekends. Finally, you can go to a **car park** – NCP are the largest operators – which will cost you up to £10 for two hours during the day. If you park your car illegally, you will get a ticket (usually £80), possibly get clamped (another £80) or get towed away (£160 and upwards). If you suspect your vehicle has been towed away, phone the police on ☎020/7747 4747.

The latest attempt to cut down on car usage in London is the **congestion charge**, pioneered by the Mayor of London, Ken Livingstone. All vehicles entering central London on weekdays between 7am and 6.30pm are liable to a congestion charge of £8 per vehicle. Drivers can pay for the charge online, over the phone and at garages and shops, and must do so before 10pm the same day or incur a £5 surcharge. The congestion-charging zone is bounded by Marylebone and Euston roads in the north, Commercial Street and Tower Bridge in the east, Kennington Lane and Elephant & Castle in the south, and Edgware Road and Park Lane in the west. For more details visit ⓦwww.cclondon.com.

Cycling

Despite being a potentially lethal mode of city transport, **cycling** is increasingly popular in London, not least because – in the centre, at least – it's by far the fastest way to get around. If you also use the tubes and suburban trains, it can even be a good way to explore some of the suburbs. There are, however, restrictions on taking **bikes on public transport**: no bikes other than folding bikes are allowed on any part of the system from Monday to Friday between 7.30am and 9.30am, and from 4pm to 7pm. Bikes are also only allowed on the District, Circle, East London, Hammersmith & City and Metropolitan lines, plus certain overground sections of other tube lines. Bicycles are not allowed on the Docklands Light Railway, and restrictions on the suburban trains vary from company to company, so check before you set out.

Bike rental outlets are few and far between. One of the most central is the London Bicycle Tour Company, on the South Bank at 1a Gabriel's Wharf (☎020/7928 6838, ⓦwww.londonbicycle.com), which has bikes for rent at £2.50 an hour or £12 for the first day, £6 per day thereafter. On Your Bike at 52–54 Tooley St, SE1 (☎020/7378 6669, ⓦwww.onyourbike.com) has "street comfort bikes" for rent for around £12 for the first day, £8 thereafter.

Opening hours and sights

Generally speaking, shop opening hours are Monday to Saturday 9am or 10am to 5.30pm or 6pm – with some places in central London staying open till 7pm, and later on Thursdays and Fridays (around 9pm) – and Sundays noon to 6pm. That said, there are still plenty of stores that close completely on Sundays, and numerous family-run corner shops that stay open late every day of the week. The big supermarkets tend to open Monday to Saturday from 8am to 10pm, Sunday 10am or 11am to 4pm or 5pm. Note that many (gas/petrol) service stations in London are open 24 hours and have small shops.

Fee-charging **tourist attractions** and state **museums** are typically open daily 10am to 6pm, occasionally with shorter hours on Sun-

days and public holidays (these are listed on p.574). It's worth noting that most places are closed on December 25 and 26. Several state

The London Pass

If you're thinking of visiting a lot of fee-paying attractions in a short space of time, it's worth considering buying a **London Pass** (Ⓦ www.londonpass.com), which gives you free entry to a mixed bag of attractions including Hampton Court Palace, Kensington Palace, Kew Gardens, London Zoo, London Aquarium, St Paul's Cathedral, the Tower of London and Windsor Castle, plus a whole host of other attractions. You can choose to buy the card with an All-Zone Travelcard thrown in; the extra outlay is relatively small, and this does include free travel out to Windsor. The pass costs around £27 for one day (£18 for kids), rising to £72 for six days (£48 for kids); or £32 with a Travelcard (£20 for kids) rising to £110 (£61 for kids). The London Pass can be bought online or in person from tourist offices and London's mainline train or chief underground stations.

museums now have late-night openings until 9pm or 10pm, typically one or two nights a week. Individual opening hours for all attractions are given in the main text of this guide.

A few of London's historic properties come under the control of the private **National Trust** (Ⓣ0870/458 4000, Ⓦ www .nationaltrust.org.uk), or the state-run **English Heritage** (Ⓣ0870/333 1181, Ⓦ www .english-heritage.org.uk). These properties are denoted in the guide by "NT" or "EH" after the opening times. Both organizations charge an entry fee for the majority of their sites, and these can be quite high (around £5), especially for National Trust sights. Annual membership for each organization is around £35 and allows free entry to their respective properties, though if you're only visiting London for a short time, it's hardly worth it. Many other old buildings, albeit rarely the most momentous structures, are owned by the local authorities, which are generally more lenient with their admission charges, and sometimes allow free access.

Admission to the permanent collections of all national galleries and museums is free (see opposite for a list), although there is an entrance charge to most special exhibitions. By contrast, ticket prices for fee-paying sights continue to increase above the level of inflation. The most shocking entry fees are charged by the royal palaces, each of which now costs over £10. Apart from St Paul's

Cathedral and Westminster Abbey, all religious institutions are open free of charge.

The majority of fee-charging attractions in London offer **reductions** for senior citizens, the unemployed, full-time students and children under 16, with under-5s being admitted free almost everywhere – proof of eligibility will be required in most cases. The entry charges given in the guide are the full adult charges – as a rule, adult reductions are only 25 percent, while reductions for children are closer to 50 percent. A useful website for up-to-date information on London's museums is Ⓦ www.24hourmuseum .co.uk.

Large museums and galleries with free entry

British Museum see p.128.
Imperial War Museum see p.266.
Museum of London see p.199.
National Army Museum see p.321.
National Gallery see p.46.
National Maritime Museum see p.382.
National Portrait Gallery see p.55.
Natural History Museum see p.312.
RAF Museum see p.371.
Science Museum see p.308.
Tate Britain see p.77.
Tate Modern see p.270.
Theatre Museum see p.161.
Victoria & Albert Museum see p.302.

Sightseeing tours and guided walks

Standard sightseeing bus tours are run by several rival companies, their open-top double-deckers setting off every thirty minutes from Victoria station, Trafalgar Square, Piccadilly and other conspicuous tourist spots.

The Original Tour (☏020/8877 1722, ⊛www .theoriginaltour.com) runs several **tour buses** on various routes (daily 9am–5pm; every 10–15min; £16) and you can hop on and off as often as you like. Alternatively, you can climb aboard one of the bright-yellow World War II amphibious vehicles used by London Duck Tours (☏020/7928 3132, ⊛www.london ducktours.co.uk), which offers a combined **bus and boat tour** (daily 9.30am–6pm or dusk; £17.50). After departing from behind County Hall, near the London Eye, you spend 45 minutes driving round the usual sights, before plunging into the river for a half-hour cruise. At the weekend and in the school holidays, it's as well to book ahead.

To save yourself money and an inane commentary, you can hop on a real London **double-decker** – the #11 bus from Victoria station, for example, will take you past Westminster Abbey, the Houses of Parliament, up Whitehall, round Trafalgar Square, along the Strand and on to St Paul's Cathedral.

Walking tours are infinitely more appealing and informative, covering a relatively small area in much greater detail, mixing solid historical facts with juicy anecdotes in the company of a local specialist. Walks on offer range from a literary pub crawl round Bloomsbury to a roam around the remains of the Jewish East End. You'll find most of them detailed, week by week, in *Time Out* (see p.28) magazine (in the "Around Town" section); as you'd imagine, there's more variety on offer in the summer months. Tours cost £5 and take around two hours; normally you can simply show up at the starting point and join.

If you want to plan – or book – walks in advance, contact the most reliable and well-established company, Original London Walks (☏020/7624 3978, ⊛www.walks.com), which offers the widest range.

Travellers with disabilities

London is getting better for disabled travellers, with all new tourist attractions and hotels now obliged to make full provision for wheelchair users. In addition, access to museums, theatres, cinemas and other public places has also greatly improved.

Even **public transport** is very slowly improving, with all buses now wheelchair-accessible. The ancient tube and rail systems, designed, for the most part, in the nineteenth century, are still a problem for those with mobility problems. The only exceptions are the Docklands Light Railway, the new sections of the Jubilee line, Tramlink and the Heathrow Express. For a more detailed rundown, get hold of Transport for London's *Tube Access Guide* or the more detailed **Access to the Underground**, from TfL information offices (see p.33), or by phoning ☏020/7941 4600.

Accommodation poses a similar problem, with modified suites found only at higher-priced establishments and the occasional B&B; one exception is the fully accessible YHA *Rotherhithe Youth Hostel* (see p.439). The London Tourist Board website gives access ratings for all the hotels and B&Bs on their books at ⓦuk.visitlondon.com.

In view of this situation, you might consider approaching one of the growing number of tour operators catering for physically disabled travellers. For more information on these operators and on facilities for the disabled traveller, you should get in touch with **RADAR**, the Royal Association for Disability and Rehabilitation, which publishes its own guide to holidays and travel abroad (see opposite). There's also **Mobility International**, which, among other things, puts out a quarterly newsletter detailing current developments in disabled travel. Similar services are provided in North America, Australia and New Zealand by the organizations listed below. The essential publication for anyone with mobility problems is **Access in London**, a thoroughly researched guide by Couch, Forrester and Irwin, with detailed information and maps covering access to everything from tourist attractions and transport to accommodation, entertainment and sports venues, plus a section on wheelchair-accessible toilets. It's available by post from RADAR (see opposite) or from Amazon. Another valuable service is provided by **Artsline** (☏020/7388 2227, ⓦwww.artsline.org.uk), who can give up-to-date information and advice by phone on access to arts venues and events in London: theatres, cinemas, galleries and concert halls.

Contacts for travellers with disabilities

In the UK

All Go Here ☏01923/840 463, ⓦwww.allgohere.com. Provides information on accommodation suitable for disabled travellers in the UK.
Holiday Care 2nd Floor, Imperial Building, Victoria Rd, Horley, Surrey RH6 7PZ ☏0845/124 9971, minicom ☏0845/124 9976, ⓦwww.holidaycare.org.uk. Provides a free list of accessible attractions in the UK.
RADAR (Royal Association for Disability and Rehabilitation) 12 City Forum, 250 City Rd, London EC1V 8AF ☏020/7250 3222, minicom ☏020/7250 4119, ⓦwww.radar.org.uk. A good source of advice on holidays and travel in the UK.
Tripscope The Vassall Centre, Gill Ave, Bristol BS16 2QQ, ☏0845/758 5641, ⓦwww.tripscope.org.uk. This registered charity provides a national telephone information service offering free advice on UK transport for those with a mobility problem.

In North America

Access-Able ⓦwww.access-able.com. Online resource for travellers with disabilities.
Mobility International USA 451 Broadway, Eugene, OR 97401 ☏541/343-1284, ⓦwww.miusa.org. Information and referral services, access guides, tours and exchange programmes.
Society for the Advancement of Travelers with Handicaps (SATH) 347 5th Ave, New York, NY 10016 ☏212/447-7284, ⓦwww.sath.org. Non-profit educational organization that has actively represented travellers with disabilities since 1976.
Wheels Up! ☏1-888/38-WHEELS, ⓦwww.wheelsup.com. Provides discounted airfare and tour prices for disabled travellers, and publishes a free monthly newsletter.

In Australia and New Zealand

ACROD (Australian Council for Rehabilitation of the Disabled) PO Box 60, Curtin, ACT 2605 ☏02/6282 4333, ⓦwww.acrod.org.au. Provides lists of travel agencies and tour operators for people with disabilities.
Disabled Persons Assembly 4/173–175 Victoria St, Wellington, New Zealand ☏04/801 9100 (also TTY), ⓦwww.dpa.org.nz. Resource centre with lists of travel agencies and tour operators for people with disabilities.

The City

The City

Trafalgar Square

As one of the few large public squares in London, **Trafalgar Square** has been both a tourist attraction and the main focus for political demonstrations for over a century and a half: it was here the first major demo was held in 1848 when the Chartists assembled at the square before marching to Kennington Common, and since then countless demos and rallies have been held. To keep an eye on the proceedings, a police phone box was built into one of the stone bollards in the southeast corner of the square, with a direct link to Scotland Yard.

Nowadays, most folk come here to have a look at **Nelson's Column**, or to visit the **National Gallery** or **National Portrait Gallery**. Each December, the square is graced with a giant Christmas tree covered in fairy lights, donated by Norway in thanks for liberation from the Nazis. And on **New Year's Eve**, thousands of inebriates sing in the New Year, though injuries and fatalities mean that just about everything traditionally associated with the event – drinking, dancing and indiscriminate kissing of police officers – is now officially forbidden.

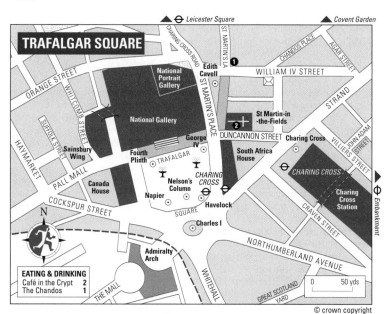

© crown copyright

Finally, on a practical note, Trafalgar Square is the main terminus for London's **night buses**, and so something of a weary and drunken meeting point most nights.

The square

For centuries, Trafalgar Square was the site of the **King's Mews**, established in the thirteenth century by Edward I, who kept the royal hawks and the falconers here (the term "mews" comes from falconry: the birds were caged or "mewed up" there whilst changing their plumage). Chaucer was Clerk of the Mews for a time, and by Tudor times there were stables here, too. During the Civil War they were turned into Parliamentary barracks and later used as a prison for Cavaliers. In the 1760s, George III began to move the mews to Buckingham Palace, and by the time the last horses left in the late 1820s, **John Nash** had already designed the basic layout of the new square (though he didn't live to see his plan executed). The Neoclassical National Gallery filled up the northern side in 1838, followed shortly afterwards by the central focal point, Nelson's Column. The famous bronze lions didn't arrive until 1868 and the fountains – built to deter the gathering of "urban mobs" – finally reached their present shape in the late 1930s. The development of the rest of the square was equally haphazard, though the overall effect is unified by the safe Neoclassical style of the buildings. Today, despite being plagued by scruffy urban pigeons, Trafalgar Square remains one of London's grandest architectural set pieces, and has been given a new lease of life thanks to the pedestrianization of the north side.

Nelson's Column and the statues

Nelson's Column, raised in 1843 and now one of London's best-loved monuments, commemorates the one-armed, one-eyed admiral who defeated the French at the Battle of Trafalgar in 1805, but paid for it with his life. The statue which surmounts the granite column is more than triple life-size but still manages to appear minuscule, and is coated in anti-pigeon gel to try and stem the build-up of guano. The acanthus leaves of the capital are cast from British cannons, while bas-reliefs around the base – depicting three of Nelson's earlier victories as well as his death aboard HMS *Victory* – are from captured French armaments. Edwin Landseer's four gargantuan **bronze lions** guard the column and provide a climbing frame for kids (and demonstrators). If you can, get here before the crowds and watch the Edwin Lutyens' **fountains** jet into action at 9am.

Keeping Nelson company at ground level, on either side of the column, are **bronze statues** of Napier and Havelock, Victorian major generals who helped keep India British; against the north wall are busts of Beatty, Jellicoe and Cunningham, military leaders from the last century. To the right of them are the imperial standards of length – inch, foot and yard – "accurate at 62 degrees Fahrenheit", as the plaque says, and still in common usage by millions of Brits despite all the efforts of the European Union. Above this is an equestrian statue of George IV (bareback, stirrup-less and in Roman garb), which he himself commissioned for the top of Marble Arch, now at the northeast corner of Hyde Park, but which was later erected here "temporarily". The **fourth plinth**, in the northwest corner, was originally earmarked for an equestrian statue of William

IV. In the end, it remained empty until 1999, since when it has been used to display specially commissioned works of modern sculpture (ⓦwww.fourthplinth.co.uk).

Predating the entire square is the **equestrian statue of Charles I**, stranded on a traffic island to the south of the column. It was completed in 1633 and originally intended for a site in Roehampton, only to be confiscated and sold off during the Commonwealth to a local brazier, with strict instructions for it to be melted down. The said brazier, John Rivett, made a small fortune selling bronze mementoes, allegedly from the metal, while all the time concealing the statue in the vaults of St Paul's, Covent Garden (see p.160). After the Restoration, Rivett resold the statue and it was placed on the very spot where eight of

▲ Bronze lion, Trafalgar Square

those who had signed the king's death warrant were disembowelled in 1660, and within sight of the Banqueting House in Whitehall where Charles himself was beheaded (see p.62).

Charles's statue also marks the original site of **Charing Cross**, from where all distances from the capital are measured. The original thirteenth-century cross was the last of twelve erected by Edward I, to mark the overnight stops on the funeral procession of his wife, Eleanor, from Nottinghamshire to Westminster Abbey in 1290. The cross was pulled down by the Puritans, though a Victorian imitation now stands amidst the taxis outside Charing Cross station, at the beginning of the Strand.

South Africa House and Canada House

There's an unmistakable whiff of empire about Trafalgar Square, with **South Africa House** (ⓦwww.southafricahouse.com), erected in 1935 on the east side, complete with keystones featuring African animals, and **Canada House** (Mon–Fri 9am–5pm; free; ☎020/7258 6600, ⓦwww.dfait-maeci.gc.ca), constructed in warm Bath stone, opposite. Canada House was originally built in the 1820s, as a gentlemen's club and home for the Royal College of Surgeons, by Robert Smirke – who also designed the British Museum – and, despite alterations over the years, it retains much of its original Neoclassical interior. You can see the ornate entrance lobby to the south of the building, browse through the Canadian press and then take in the excellent temporary exhibitions. Canadians can also send and receive emails from the folks back home.

St Martin-in-the-Fields

At the northeastern corner of Trafalgar Square stands James Gibbs's church of **St Martin-in-the-Fields** (Mon–Sat 10am–8pm, Sun noon–8pm; ☎020/7766 1100, ⊛www.stmartin-in-the-fields.org), fronted by a magnificent Corinthian portico and topped by an elaborate, and distinctly unclassical, tower and steeple. The first church on this site was indeed built "in the fields", outside the city perimeter, while the present building, completed in 1726, was hemmed in on all sides for more than a century before the surrounding houses were demolished to make way for Trafalgar Square, giving the church a much grander setting. The interior is purposefully simple, though the Italian plasterwork on the barrel vaulting is exceptionally rich; it's best appreciated while listening to one of the church's **free lunchtime concerts**. St Martin's witnessed the marriage of John Constable, the christening of Charles II and the funerals of, among others, the latter's mistress, Nell Gwynne (buried in the former churchyard), the outlaw Jack Sheppard, French sculptor Roubiliac and furniture designer Thomas Chippendale. George I was a church warden (though he seldom turned up for duties), and the present church, as the official parish church for Buckingham Palace, maintains strong royal and naval connections – there's a royal box on the left of the high altar, and one for the admiralty on the right.

The touristy souvenir market along the north wall of the church is just one of St Martin's many money-spinning exercises; more usefully, there's a licensed **café** (Mon–Wed 10am–8pm, Thurs–Sat 10am–11pm, Sun noon–8pm) in the roomy crypt – accessible via steps on the southern side – not to mention a shop, gallery and **brass-rubbing centre** (Mon–Sat 10am–6pm, Sun noon–6pm). The set of steps by the market leads down to a subterranean social care unit and soup kitchen serving the West End homeless, for whom the church has consistently cared since the pioneering work of one of its vicars, Dick Sheppard, among the parish's homeless ex-soldiers following World War I. St Martin's is also the venue for the annual **Costermongers' Harvest Festival** (⊛www .pearlysociety.co.uk) held on the second Sunday in October. Since Victorian times, Cockney market-stallholders and their families have converged on the church from all over London, dressed up in aid of charity as "Pearly Kings and Queens", their clothes studded with hundreds of pearly buttons.

The National Gallery

Taking up the entire north side of Trafalgar Square, the sprawling Neoclassical hulk of the **National Gallery** (daily 10am–6pm, Wed till 9pm; free; ☎020/7747 2885, ⊛www.nationalgallery.org.uk) houses one of the world's greatest art collections. Unlike the Louvre or the Hermitage, the National Gallery is not based on a former royal collection, but was begun as late as 1824 when the government reluctantly agreed to purchase 38 paintings belonging to a Russian émigré banker, John Julius Angerstein. Further paintings were bought by the gallery's wily directors or bequeathed by private individuals in lieu of death duty.

The gallery's years of canny acquisition have produced a collection of more than 2300 paintings, but the collected works' virtue is not so much its size as the range, depth and sheer quality of its contents. A quick tally of the National's **Italian masterpieces**, for example, includes works by Botticelli, Titian, Raphael, Michelangelo and Caravaggio, among others. From Spain there are dazzling pieces by El Greco,

Visiting the gallery

There are **four entrances** to the National Gallery: Wilkins' original portico on Trafalgar Square, the new Getty Entrance to the east, the Sainsbury Wing to the west, and the back entrance on Orange Street. The Getty Entrance and the Sainsbury Wing both have an **information desk**, which hands out free plans, and disabled access, with lifts to all floors. There's a pricey restaurant in the Sainsbury Wing and a less expensive, more informal café by the Getty Entrance.

With over a thousand paintings on permanent display in the main galleries, you'll need visual endurance to see everything in one day. **Audioguides**, with a brief commentary on each of the paintings on display, are available for a "voluntary contribution" of £4, though the commentaries tend to be descriptive rather than interpretive. Much better are the gallery's free **guided tours**, which set off from the Sainsbury Wing foyer (daily 11.30am & 2.30pm, Wed also 6pm & 6.30pm, Sat also 12.30pm & 3.30pm; 1hr). The guides vary enormously in the politics and style of their art criticism and in their choice of paintings, but all try and give you a representative sample. In addition, the information desks have details of the gallery's free lectures, films and talks. If you want to **view the collection chronologically** you should begin with the Sainsbury Wing, which also features a **micro gallery** on the first floor, where you can plan – and print out – your own personalized tour; it's good for learning more about specific paintings and painters and for generally playing around on, but by no means essential.

On any one visit, you're likely to discover at least one or two rooms that are in the process of being re-hung, and will therefore throw our account into confusion. If you're looking for a particular painting, and it has moved, ask the gallery staff. The gallery's reserve collection is also on permanently cramped display in **Lower Gallery A** (closed Wed evening & Sun), accessible from room 15, and more selectively and spaciously in **rooms B–G**, accessible from room 13.

Temporary exhibitions take place in the basement of the Sainsbury Wing but compare unfavourably with those in London's other public art galleries: the rooms are small, have no natural light, and there is sometimes an entrance fee. The temporary displays in the newly expanded **Sunley Room** in the main building, however, are always free; they often focus on the background to one of the gallery's works (and include a video on the subject), and host an annual exhibition by the gallery's artist-in-residence. Look out, too, for the programme of **free concerts** of chamber music, which take place in the Central Hall on Wednesday evenings.

Velázquez and Goya; from the Low Countries, van Eyck, Memlinc and Rubens, and an array of **Rembrandt** paintings that features some of his most searching portraits. Poussin, Claude, Watteau and David are the early highlights of a French contingent that has a particularly strong showing of Cézanne and the **Impressionists**. British art is also represented, with important works by Hogarth, Gainsborough, Stubbs and Turner, though for twentieth-century British art – and many more Turners – you'll need to move on to Tate Britain on Millbank (see p.77). Modern non-British art is at Tate Modern (see p.270).

The National Gallery's original collection was put on public display at Angerstein's old residence, 99 Pall Mall, until today's purpose-built edifice on Trafalgar Square was completed in 1838. A hostile press dubbed the gallery's diminutive dome and cupolas "pepperpots", and poured abuse on the Greek Revivalist architect, William Wilkins, who retreated into early retirement, and died a year later. Subsequent additions to the rear of the building over the next 150 years provoked little comment, but a similar barrage of abuse broke out in the mid-1980s over plans for the new **Sainsbury Wing**, endowed by the supermarket dynasty. The winning design prompted Prince Charles to talk about "a monstrous carbuncle on the face of a much-loved and elegant friend". Planning permission was, of course, refused. Instead, the American husband-and-wife team of Venturi and Scott-Brown were commissioned to produce a softly-softly, postmodern adjunct, which playfully imitates elements of Wilkins' Neoclassicism and even Nelson's Column and, most importantly, got the approval of Prince Charles, who laid the foundation stone in 1988.

The Sainsbury Wing

Chronologically the gallery's collection begins in the **Sainsbury Wing**, which houses the National's oldest paintings dating from 1250 to 1500, mostly early Italian Renaissance masterpieces, with a smattering of early Dutch, Flemish and German works.

Giotto to Fra Filippo Lippi

The gallery's earliest works are displayed in room 52, and include one attributed to **Giotto**, considered, even by his contemporaries, to be "the father of modern painting". He was one of the first painters to develop a softer, more three-dimensional approach to painting after the flat, Byzantine-style paintings that had gone before. **Duccio**, a Sienese contemporary of Giotto, maintained a more iconic approach, but also introduced a new sense of movement and space to his narrative paintings, several of which hang in room 52. The panels are taken from his *Maestà* (a Sienese invention depicting the Madonna enthroned as Queen of Heaven), which was carried in triumph from the artist's studio to the cathedral in 1311 with virtually the whole of Siena looking on.

Room 53 features the extraordinarily vivid **Wilton Diptych**, a portable altarpiece painted by an unknown fourteenth-century artist for the boy king Richard II, who is depicted being presented by his patron saints to the Virgin, Child and assorted angels. Also in this room is a vast altarpiece by **Jacopo di Cione**, whose richly patterned canvases are like gilded jewels, with the figures of Christ and Mary distinguished by their white and gold robes. In room 54, it's worth pausing to admire the surprisingly realistic depiction of old age in the faces of the saints who appear in the panels begun by Masaccio and completed by **Masolino**.

Paolo Uccello's brilliant, blood-free *Battle of San Romano*, which dominates room 55, once decorated a Medici bedroom as part of a three-panel frieze on the same theme. First and foremost, it's a commemoration of a recent Florentine victory over her bitter Sienese rivals, but it's also an early essay in perspective: a foreshortened body, broken lances and pieces of armour are strewn across the foreground to persuade the viewer that the picture is, in fact, three-dimensional. The bucking white charger at the centre of the battle also appears in Uccello's much smaller *St George and the Dragon*, one of the earliest surviving canvas paintings. Another Medici commission is *The Annunciation* by **Fra Filippo Lippi**, a beautifully balanced painting in which the poses of Gabriel and Mary carefully mirror one another, while the hand of God releasing the dove of the Holy Spirit provides the vanishing point.

Jan van Eyck

Room 56 switches to the beginnings of oil painting, which did away with the painstaking overpainting of egg-based tempera and allowed the artist to blend infinite gradations of pigment in the palette. The possibilities of depicting the minutiae of life with oils were explored by the likes of **Rogier van der Wey-**

den in *The Magdalen Reading*, where even the nails in the floor are carefully picked out. But the master of early oil painting was **Jan van Eyck**, whose intriguing *Arnolfini Portrait* is an immensely sophisticated painting despite its seemingly mundane domestic setting: each object has been carefully chosen for its symbolism, from the dog, traditionally a symbol of fidelity, to the status-symbol orange tree that can be glimpsed through the window. The picture has often been interpreted as a depiction of a marriage ceremony, though the theory is now strongly criticized, and the "bride" is thought simply to be fashionably round-bellied, rather than actually pregnant.

Pollaiuolo, Botticelli and Crivelli

It's back to Italian art in room 57, where the **Pollaiuolo** brothers' *Martyrdom of St Sebastian* reads like an anatomical textbook, with the three pairs of archers who surround the saint all striking different poses. Before moving on, don't miss the bloody excesses of **Piero di Cosimo**'s *Fight between the Lapiths and Centaurs*, apparently considered an entertaining subject for a marriage gift.

Also in room 57 are a number of paintings by **Botticelli**, including two of the Nativity. The *Mystic Nativity* is unusual in that it features seven devils fleeing back into the Underworld, while in his *Adoration of the Kings*, Botticelli himself takes centre stage, as the best-dressed man at the gathering, resplendent in bright-red stockings and giving the audience a knowing look. Next door, in room 58, are his much-loved *Tobias and the Angel* and his elongated *Venus and Mars*, depicting a naked and replete Mars in deep postcoital sleep, watched over by a beautifully calm Venus, fully clothed and somewhat less overcome.

In room 59, you'll find one of the most accomplished perspectivist paintings of the period, **Crivelli**'s *Annunciation*. An early exercise in ornamentation and geometry, its single vanishing point is the red hat of the man in the background standing before the window.

Mantegna and Bellini

Room 61 has some fine examples of **Mantegna**'s "cameo" paintings, which imitate the effect of classical stone reliefs, reflecting the craze among fashionable Venetian society for collecting antique engraved marbles and gems. The largest of them (painted to be viewed from below), *The Introduction of the Cult of Cybele*, was the artist's last work, and was commissioned by Francesco Cornaro, a Venetian nobleman who claimed descent from one of the greatest Roman families. Next door, in room 62, hangs one of Mantegna's early works, *The Agony in the Garden*, which demonstrates a convincing use of perspective, with one of the earliest successful renditions of middle distance. Close by, the dazzling dawn sky in the painting on the same theme by his brother-in-law, **Giovanni Bellini**, shows the artist's celebrated mastery of natural light. Also in room 62 is one of Bellini's greatest portraits, *Doge Leonardo Loredan*.

Memlinc, Bermejo, Dürer and della Francesca

Room 63 takes you away from Italy with a jolt. **Memlinc**'s perfectly poised *Donne Triptych*, a portable (though rather heavy) altarpiece features Memlinc himself peering from behind a pillar in the left-hand panel. In the same room, **Bartolomé Bermejo**'s masterly depiction of St Michael trouncing the devil is one of only twenty extant paintings by the Spanish artist. The devil looks like a giant cockroach, while the saint looks utterly resplendent in his shining armour and crumpled cloak – literally dressed to kill – the heavenly city reflected in his jewelled breastplate. Antonio Juan, the Lord of Tous, looks comically unmoved by the whole spectacle, casually leafing through the Book of Psalms, his sword still in its scabbard. Look out, in room 65, for **Dürer**'s sympathetic portrait of his father (a goldsmith in Nuremberg), which was presented to Charles I in 1636 by the artist's home town.

At the far end of the wing, in room 66, it's back to Italy once more for **Piero della Francesca**'s monumental religious paintings, including *The Baptism of Christ*, one of Piero's earliest surviving pictures, dating from the 1450s and a brilliant example of his immaculate compositional technique. Blindness forced Piero to stop painting some twenty years before his death, and to concentrate instead on his equally innovative work as a mathematician.

The main building

The **main building** is nominally divided into east, west and north wings, but you're hardly aware of passing between them. The account below follows the collection chronologically, starting with the sixteenth-century paintings in the west wing, passing through the north wing's seventeenth-century paintings and finishing with the east wing, which takes you right up to 1900, now the official chronological cut-off point between the National and Tate Britain.

Veronese, Titian and Giorgione

The first room you come to from the Sainsbury Wing is the vast Wohl Room (room 9), containing mainly large-scale Venetian works. The largest of the lot is **Paolo Veronese**'s lustrous *Family of Darius before Alexander*, its array of colourfully clad figures revealing the painter's remarkable skill in juxtaposing virtually the entire colour spectrum in a single canvas. Here, too, are all four of Veronese's slightly discoloured *Allegories of Love* canvases, designed as ceiling paintings, perhaps for a bedchamber.

There are more Venetian works in room 10, including **Titian**'s consummate *La Schiavona*, a precisely executed portrait within a portrait. His colourful early masterpiece *Bacchus and Ariadne*, and his much gloomier *Death of Actaeon*, painted some fifty years later, amply demonstrate the painter's artistic development and longevity. The *Madonna and Child* is another typical late Titian, with the paint jabbed on and rubbed in. Also here are two perplexing paintings attributed to the elusive **Giorgione**, a highly original Venetian painter, only twenty of whose paintings survive.

Bronzino, Michelangelo, Raphael and da Vinci

In room 8, **Bronzino**'s strangely disturbing *Venus, Cupid, Folly and Time* is a classic piece of Mannerist eroticism, which suitably enough made its way into the hands of François I, the decadent, womanizing, sixteenth-century French king. It depicts Cupid about to embrace Venus as she, in turn, attempts to disarm him; above them Father Time tries to reveal the face of Fraud as nothing but a mask, while the cherub of Folly gets ready to shower the couple with roses; weirdest of all is the half-animal, half-human Pleasure, whose double-edged quality is symbolized by her honeycomb and the sting in her tail. Here too is **Michelangelo**'s early, unfinished *Entombment*. Unlike earlier, static depictions, this painting shows Christ's body being hauled into the tomb, and has no fixed iconography by which to identify the figures – either of the women could be Mary Magdalene, for example, and it's arguable whether the man in red is John the Evangelist or Nicodemus. The National's major paintings by **Raphael** also hang in this room, ranging from early works such as *St*

Catherine of Alexandria, whose sensuous "serpentine" pose is accentuated by the folds of her clothes, and the richly coloured *Mond Crucifixion*, painted when the artist was a mere 21 years old, to later works like *Pope Julius II* – his (and Michelangelo's) patron – a masterfully percipient portrait of old age, though the gallery's curators thought it was no more than a copy until it was cleaned in 1970.

To continue with the Italians, skip through room 4 to room 2, which boasts **Leonardo da Vinci**'s melancholic *Virgin of the Rocks* (the more famous version hangs in the Louvre) and the "Leonardo Cartoon" – a preparatory drawing of *The Virgin and Child with St Anne and John the Baptist* for a painting which, like so many of Leonardo's projects, was never completed. The cartoon was known only to scholars – that is, until an American tried to buy the picture for £2.5 million in the mid-1960s. In 1987, it gained further notoriety when an ex-soldier blasted the work with a sawn-off shotgun in protest at the political status quo.

Holbein, Cranach, Bosch and Gossaert

Room 4 contains several masterpieces by **Hans Holbein**, most notably his extraordinarily detailed double portrait, *The Ambassadors*. The French duo flank an open cabinet piled high with various objects: instruments for studying the heavenly realm on the upper shelf, those for contemplating the earthly life on the lower. The painting clearly demonstrates the subjects' wealth, power and intelligence, but also serves as an elaborate *memento mori*, a message underlined by the distorted skull in the foreground.

Among the other works by Holbein is his intriguing portrait *A Lady with a Squirrel and a Starling*, painted in 1527 during the artist's first visit to England. Holbein's striking portrait of the 16-year-old Christina of Denmark was part of a series commissioned by Henry VIII when he was looking for a potential fourth wife. The king eventually plumped for Anne of Cleves on the basis of Holbein's flattering portrait (now in the Louvre), though when he saw her in the flesh he was distinctly unimpressed with his "Flanders mare", after which Holbein fell from royal favour.

Holbein's contemporary, **Lucas Cranach the Elder**, made his name from slender, erotic nudes such as the model used for *Cupid Complaining to Venus*, a none-too-subtle message about dangerous romantic liaisons. Venus's enormous

---

Boris Anrep's floor mosaics

One of the most overlooked features of the National Gallery is the mind-boggling **floor mosaics** executed by Russian-born Boris Anrep between 1927 and 1952 on the landings of the main staircase leading to the Central Hall (and now in need of some restoration). The *Awakening of the Muses*, on the halfway landing, features a bizarre collection of famous figures from the 1930s – Virginia Woolf appears as Clio (Muse of History) and Greta Garbo plays Melpomene (Muse of Tragedy). The mosaic on the landing closest to the Central Hall is made up of fifteen small scenes illustrating the *Modern Virtues*: Anna Akhmatova is saved by an angel from the Leningrad Blockade in *Compassion*; T.S. Eliot contemplates the Loch Ness Monster and Einstein's Theory of Relativity in *Leisure*; Bertrand Russell gazes on a naked woman in *Lucidity*; Edith Sitwell, book in hand, glides across a monster-infested chasm on a twig in *Sixth Sense*; and in the largest composition, *Defiance*, Churchill appears in combat gear on the white cliffs of Dover, raising two fingers to a monster in the shape of a swastika.

headgear only emphasizes her nakedness, while the German landscape, to the right, serves to give this mythological morality tale a distinctly "contemporary" edge.

Room 5 contains the National's one and only work by **Hieronymus Bosch**, *Christ Mocked*, in which four manic tormentors (one wearing a dog's collar) bear down on Jesus. Gerard David's *Christ Nailed to the Cross* is iconographically unusual in that Jesus (who shows no outward signs of pain) is being hammered onto his crucifix while flat on the ground. The painting that grabs most folks' attention, however, is **Massys'** caricatured portrait of a grotesque old woman.

Room 12 holds the world's finest collection of works by the Flemish painter **Jan Gossaert**. The tiny *Virgin and Child* was only recently acknowledged as an original after a dendrochronologist dated the wood panel to 1501; it had been in storage for nearly seventy years. One of the greatest portrait specialists of the Italian Renaissance was **Giovanni Moroni**, and several of his likenesses of the fashionably black-clad folk of Brescia and Bergamo can be seen in this room. It has been suggested that Moroni's portrait of *The Tailor* was for services rendered, while Lorenzo Lotto's painting of his landlord and family was executed in lieu of a year's rent.

The gallery's only painting by **Bruegel**, *The Adoration of the Magi*, hangs in room 14, just off room 29, with some very motley-looking folk crowding in on the infant; only the Black Magus looks at all regal.

Vermeer to Ruisdael via Poussin

Tiny room 16 harbours **de Hooch**'s classic *A Woman and her Maid in a Courtyard*, and two typically serene works by **Vermeer**, which provide a counterpoint to one another: each features a *Young Woman at a Virginal*, but where she stands in one, she sits in the other; she's viewed from the right and then the left, in shadow and then in light and so on. Beyond, room 17 contains the seventeenth-century **van Hoogstraten Peepshow**, a box of tricks which perfectly illustrates the Dutch obsession of the time with perspectival and optical devices.

Claude Lorrain's *Enchanted Castle*, in room 19, caught the imagination of the Romantics, supposedly inspiring Keats' *Ode to a Nightingale*, while the English painter **J.M.W. Turner** left specific instructions in his will for two of his Claude-influenced paintings to be hung alongside a couple of the French painter's landscapes. All four now hang in the octagonal room 15, and were slashed by a homeless teenager in 1982 in an attempt to draw attention to his plight. Claude's dreamy classical landscapes and seascapes, and the mythological scenes of **Poussin**, were favourites of aristocrats on the Grand Tour, and made both artists very famous in their time. Nowadays, though Poussin has a strong academic following, his works strike many people as empty and dull. Hardly surprising, then, that rooms 19 and 20, which are given over entirely to these two French artists, are among the quietest in the gallery.

Aelbert Cuyp's landscapes, a number of which hang in room 21, stand out due to the warm Italianate light which suffuses his views of his home town of Dordrecht. In room 22, the eye is drawn to the back wall and one of the finest of all Dutch landscapes, **Hobbema**'s tree-lined *Avenue, Middelharnis*. The market for such landscapes at the time was limited, and Hobbema quit painting at the age of just 30. **Jacob van Ruisdael**, Hobbema's teacher, whose works are on display nearby, also went hungry for most of his life.

Rembrandt and Rubens

Room 23 is dominated by **Rembrandt**'s splendid equestrian portrait of Frederick Rihel, painted to commemorate the entry of William of Orange into Amsterdam in 1660, and the highly theatrical *Belshazzar's Feast*, painted for a rich Jewish patron. Elsewhere in the room, two of Rembrandt's searching self-portraits, painted thirty years apart, regard each other – the melancholic *Self Portrait Aged 63*, from the last year of his life, making a strong contrast with the sprightly early work. Similarly, the joyful portrait of Saskia, Rembrandt's wife, from the most successful period of his life, contrasts with his more contemplative depiction of his mistress, Hendrickje, who was hauled up in front of the city authorities for living "like a whore" with Rembrandt. The portraits of Jacob Trip and his wife are among the most painfully realistic depictions of old age in the entire gallery.

Three adjoining rooms, known collectively as room 29, are dominated by the expansive, fleshy canvases of **Peter Paul Rubens**, the Flemish painter whom Charles I summoned to the English court; a prime example is his *Samson and Delilah*. The one woman with her clothes on is the artist's future sister-in-law, Susanna Fourment, whose delightful portrait became known as *Le Chapeau de Paille* (*The Straw Hat*) – though the hat is actually made of black felt and decorated with white feathers. At the age of 54, Rubens married Susanna's younger sister, Helena (she was just 16), the model for all three goddesses posing in the later version of *The Judgement of Paris*, painted in the 1630s. Also displayed here are Rubens' rather more subdued landscapes, one of which, the *View of Het Steen*, shows off the very fine prospect from the Flemish country mansion Rubens bought in 1635, earning himself the title Lord of Steen.

Velázquez, El Greco, van Dyck and Caravaggio

The cream of the National Gallery's Spanish works are displayed in room 30, among them **Velázquez**'s *Rokeby Venus*, one of the gallery's most famous pictures, painted when Velázquez was court painter to Philip IV, himself the subject of two portraits displayed here. Despite being a religious fanatic, Philip owned several paintings of nudes, though with the Inquisition at its height they were considered a highly immoral subject. Velázquez is nonetheless known to have painted at least four in his lifetime, of which only the *Rokeby Venus* survives, an ambiguously narcissistic image that was slashed in 1914 by suffragette Mary Richardson, who loved the picture but was revolted by the way "men gaped at it all day". Slightly lost in this vast room is the diminutive masterpiece *Christ Driving Traders from the Temple*, by the Cretan painter **El Greco**. Its acidic colouring and angular composition are typical of his highly individual work.

Another Flemish painter summoned by Charles I was **Anthony van Dyck**, whose *Equestrian Portrait of Charles I*, in room 31, is a fine example of the work that made him a favourite of the Stuart court, romanticizing the monarch as a dashing horseman. Adjacent is the artist's double portrait of *Lord John and Lord Bernard Stuart*, two dapper young cavaliers about to set out on their Grand Tour in 1639, and destined to die fighting for the royalist cause shortly afterwards in the Civil War.

Caravaggio's art is represented in the vast room 32 by the typically salacious *Boy Bitten by Lizard*, and the melodramatic *Christ at Emmaus*. The latter was a highly influential painting: never before had biblical scenes been depicted with such naturalism – a beardless and haloless Christ surrounded by scruffy disciples. At the time it was deemed to be blasphemous, and, like many of Caravaggio's religious commissions, was eventually rejected by the customers. One of the most striking paintings in this room is Giordano's *Perseus turning Phineas and his*

Followers to Stone, in which the hero is dramatically depicted in sapphire blue, with half the throng already ossified.

Turner to Tiepolo

Eighteenth-century French art by the likes of Fragonard, Boucher and Watteau is gathered together in room 33. There's a portrait of Louis XV's mistress in an outrageous floral dress and also a spirited self-portrait by the equally well-turned-out Elisabeth Louise Vigée-Lebrun, one of only three women artists in the whole National Gallery collection.

When the Tate Gallery first opened on Millbank in 1897, the vast bulk of the National's British art section was transferred there, leaving a small but highly prized core of works behind. These include a number of superb late masterpieces by **Turner**, two of which herald the new age of steam: *Rain, Steam and Speed* and *The Fighting Temeraire*, in which a ghostly apparition of the veteran battleship from Trafalgar is pulled into harbour by a youthful, fire-snorting tug, a scene witnessed first-hand by the artist in Rotherhithe. Here, too, is **Constable**'s *Hay Wain*, probably the most famous British painting of all time, though it was just one of a series of landscapes that he painted in and around his father's mill in Suffolk, such as the irrepressibly popular *Cornfield*. There are also several works by **Thomas Gainsborough** – landscapes, as well as the portraits at which this quintessentially British artist excelled. The painting of the actress Sarah Siddons is one of his finest "grand ladies", and his feathery, light technique is seen to superb effect in *Morning Walk*, a double portrait of a pair of newlyweds. **Joshua Reynolds**' contribution is a portrait of *Lady Cockburn and her Three Sons*, in which the three boys clamber endearingly over their mother.

There are more works by Gainsborough and Reynolds in the neighbouring room (35), including the only known portrait of the former with his family, painted in 1747 when he was just 20 years old. On the opposite wall are the six paintings from **Hogarth**'s *Marriage à la Mode*, a witty, moral tale that allowed the artist to give vent to his pet hates: bourgeois hypocrisy, snobbery and bad (ie Continental) taste. Where Gainsborough excelled in his "grand ladies", his rival Reynolds was at his best with male sitters – as in the dramatic portrait of the extraordinarily effeminate Colonel Tarleton, displayed in the ornate, domed Central Hall (room 36).

Room 38 features **Canaletto**'s *Stonemason's Yard*, an unusual portrayal of everyday Venetian life compared to his usual glittery vistas of Venice (of which there are also several examples). In room 39, **Guardi**'s postcard snaps of Venice hang rather awkwardly alongside **Goya**'s gloomy portrait of the Duke of Wellington. Close by, in room 40, are examples of the airy draughtsmanship of **Tiepolo**, father and son, seen to best effect in the *Allegory with Venus and Time*, commissioned for the ceiling of a Venetian *palazzo*.

From Ingres to Picasso

In room 41, the austere style of portraiture popular in France after the Revolution is present in **Ingres**'s elegant portrait of a wealthy banker's wife, *Madame Moitessier*, completed when the artist had reached the age of 76, having taken twelve years to finish. **Géricault**'s galvanic *Horse Frightened by Lightning* demonstrates why the artist abandoned his teacher, claiming "one of my horses would have devoured six of his". One of the most eye-catching pictures is **Gustave Courbet**'s languorous *Young Ladies on the Bank of the Seine*, innocent enough to the modern eye, but it caused a scandal when it was first shown in 1857 due to the ladies' "state of undress". Nowadays, the most popular of all the paintings in the room is **Paul Delaroche**'s slick and pretentious *Execution of Lady Jane Grey*, in which the blindfolded, white-robed, 17-year-old queen stoically awaits her fate. In the tiny room 42, there's a sentimental *Winter Landscape* by **Caspar David Friedrich**, one of the few works by the German Romantic painter on public display in Britain.

Five magnificent rooms of Impressionist and early twentieth-century paintings close the proceedings, starring, in room 43, **Manet**'s unfinished *Execution of Maximilian*. This was one of three versions Manet painted of the subject, and was cut into pieces during the artist's lifetime, then bought and reassembled by Degas after Manet's death. The fashionable crowd in Manet's *Music in the Tuileries Gardens* includes the poet Baudelaire and the artist Fantin-Latour. Other major Impressionist works usually displayed here include, in room 44, **Renoir**'s *Umbrellas*, **Monet**'s *Thames below Westminster*, his *Gare St Lazare* (for which he had the entire station cleared of commuters) and one of his many paintings of his beloved garden at Giverny.

Seurat's classic pointillist canvas, *Bathers at Asnières*, in room 44, is one of the National's most reproduced paintings, along with **Pissarro**'s *Boulevard Montmartre at Night*. There are also several townscapes from Pissarro's period of exile, when he lived in south London, having fled Paris before the advancing Prussian army. There's a comprehensive showing of **Cézanne** in room 45, with works spanning the great artist's long life. *The Painter's Father* is one of his earliest extant works, and was originally painted onto the walls of his father's house outside Aix. *The Bathers*, by contrast, is a very late work, whose angular geometry exercised an enormous influence on the Cubism of Picasso and Braque.

Several late canvases by **van Gogh** also hang in room 45: the beguiling *Van Gogh's Chair*, dating from his stay in Arles with Gauguin, and the trademark *Wheatfield with Cypresses*, which typifies the intense work he produced inside the asylum to which he was committed shortly before his suicide. The most famous of the lot, though, his dazzling *Sunflowers*, is just one of seven versions he painted, one of which became the most expensive picture ever sold when it was bought for over £24 million in 1987. Van Gogh himself sold only one painting in his lifetime, and used to dream of finding someone who would pay just £25 for his work.

In room 46, you'll find **Picasso**'s sentimental Blue Period *Child with a Dove*; Vuillard's *Young Girls Walking*, with its deliberately flat, decorative surfaces; and a trio of superb **Degas** canvases: *Miss La-La at the Cirque Fernando*, the languorous pastel drawing *After the Bath* and the luxuriant red-orange *La Coiffure*.

The National Portrait Gallery

Around the east side of the National Gallery lurks the **National Portrait Gallery** (daily 10am–6pm, Thurs & Fri till 9pm; free; ☎020/7312 2463, ⊛www.npg.org.uk), which was founded in 1856 to house uplifting depictions of the good and the great. Though it undoubtedly has some fine works among its collection of ten thousand portraits, many of the studies are of less interest than their subjects. Nevertheless, it's interesting to trace who has been deemed worthy of admiration at any one time: aristocrats and artists in previous centuries, warmongers and imperialists in the early decades of the twentieth century, writers and poets in the 1930s and 1940s. The most popular part of the museum by far is the contemporary section, where the whole thing degenerates into a sort of thinking person's Madame Tussaud's, with photos and very dubious portraits of retired footballers, politicians, and film and pop stars.

The Tudor Galleries

The **Tudor Galleries** on the second floor kick off with a large painting of **Sir Thomas More** (based on an earlier one by Holbein), in which the martyr is surrounded by his soberly dressed ancestors. Beyond, in room 1, there are Tudor portraits of pre-Tudor kings, and a stout **Cardinal Wolsey** looking like the butcher's son he was. Holbein's larger-than-life cartoon of **Henry VIII**, a preparatory drawing for a much larger fresco in Whitehall Palace, shows the king as a macho buck against a modish Renaissance background. The composition is deliberately echoed in the nearby portrait of his sickly young son and heir, **Edward VI**.

The most eye-catching canvas is the anamorphic portrait of the same, syphilitic Edward VI; an illusionistic device, the painting must be looked at from the side to be viewed properly. Nearby hangs the intriguing *Edward VI and the Pope*, in which the boy king is depicted casting down the pontiff and burning religious images. By contrast, the future **Bloody Mary** looks positively benign in a portrait celebrating her reinstatement to the line of succession in 1544.

In room 2 are several classic propaganda portraits of the formidable Elizabeth I and her various favourites. Here, too, is the only known painting of **Shakespeare** from life, a subdued image in which the Bard sports a gold-hoop earring; appropriately enough, it was the first picture acquired by the gallery. Close by is the "rocky face" of his one-time rival playwright, **Ben Jonson**. The exquisite Tudor miniatures in room 3 also deserve attention.

The Stuarts

Leading personalities from the Jacobean court hang in room 4, including an outrageously camp full-length portrait of the **Duke of Buckingham** showing off his lovely long legs. A favourite of James I, he was deeply unpopular with everyone except the king, and was eventually assassinated at the age of just 36.

To keep to the chronology, you must turn left here into room 5, where the quality of the portraiture goes up a notch thanks to the appointment of van Dyck as court painter. Both sides of the Civil War are represented: **Oliver**

Visiting the gallery

There are two **entrances** to the NPG: disabled access is from Orange Street, while the main entrance is on St Martin's Place, opposite the statue of Edith Cavell, the nurse who was accused of spying and shot by the Germans in 1915. Once inside, head straight on for the Ondaatje Wing, where you'll find the main **information desk**. To follow the collection chronologically, as the account below does, take the escalator to the second floor, and work down. The gallery's **special exhibitions** (for which there is often an entrance charge) are well worth seeing – the photography shows, in particular, are often excellent.

You might like to avail yourself of the NPG's **Sound Guide**, which gives useful biographical background on many of the pictures. The service is provided free of charge, though you're strongly invited to give a "voluntary contribution". Before or after viewing the works, you can play around on a CD-ROM of the collection in the mezzanine **IT Gallery**, or simply collapse in the nearby comfy chairs. There's a café in the basement, and a pricey **rooftop restaurant** on the top floor with views over Trafalgar Square.

Cromwell is depicted looking dishevelled but masterful, while the future Charles II, painted at four months old, appears dressed in drag and clutching a toy spaniel. Further on, in room 7, an overdressed, haggard adult Charles hangs alongside his long-suffering Portuguese wife and his most famous mistress, the orange-seller turned actress Nell Gwynne.

There's more romance in room 8, where you can view Queen Anne, her double chin, and her long-term lover, the cocky-looking Duchess of Marlborough.

The Georgian period

The eighteenth century begins in room 9, with members of the Kit-Kat Club, a group of Whig patriots – including Robert Walpole – who met in a pub run by one Christopher Cat. The club was formed to ensure the Protestant succession at the end of William's reign and painted by one of its members, Godfrey Kneller, a naturalized German artist, whose self-portrait can be found in room 10. Keeping company with Kneller is an energetic and determined William Hogarth, depicted in a terracotta bust by Roubiliac, the Duchess of Queensberry, depicted here as a humble milkmaid, a friend of the literati who died of "a surfeit of cherries", according to the caption, and Hogarth's nemesis, Lord Burlington, who strikes an arty pose with his cap and protractor.

Room 11 contains a hotchpotch of visionaries including a juvenile-looking Bonnie Prince Charlie and his saviour, the petite Flora MacDonald. Among the various artists, writers and musicians in room 12 are several fine self-portraits, including a dashing one of the Scot Allan Ramsay, and one each by Angelika Kauffmann and Mary Moser, the gallery's first two women artists.

The subject of room 14 is conquering new worlds and losing them, and features the dramatic death of Pitt the Elder, who collapsed in the House of Lords having struggled in to plead for a tolerant attitude to the rebellious American colonies. Captain Cook can be seen, too, along with the Tahitian warrior, Omai, whom Cook described as "dark, ugly and a downright blackguard", but who nevertheless caused a sensation when he was brought back to England in 1774.

At this point, the first caricatures begin to creep into the collection, led by Gilray and Hogarth, though there are significantly more in room 17, where you'll find a bold likeness of Lord Nelson, along with one of the many idealized portraits painted by the smitten George Romney of Nelson's mistress, Lady Emma Hamilton. Also in room 17 is a portrait of George IV and the twice-widowed Catholic woman, Maria Fitzherbert, whom he married without the consent of his father. His official wife, Queen Caroline, is depicted at the adultery trial in the House of Lords at which she was acquitted. Close by, Caroline is depicted again, with sleeves rolled up ready for her sculpture lessons, in an audacious portrait by Thomas Lawrence, who was called to testify on his conduct with the queen during the painting of the portrait.

The Romantics dominate room 18, with the ailing John Keats painted posthumously by Joseph Severn, in whose arms he died in Rome. Elsewhere, there's Lord Byron in Albanian garb, an open-collared Percy Bysshe Shelley, with his mother-in-law, Mary Wollstonecraft, above it, a naïve sketch of Jane Austen by her sister Cassandra, and a moody image of William Wordsworth by the historical painter Benjamin Haydon. Painted in response to Wordsworth's sonnet on another of Haydon's pictures, this portrait itself became the subject of Elizabeth Barrett Browning's sonnet, *Wordsworth on Helvellyn*.

The Victorians

Down on the first floor are the **Victorians**: mostly stuffy royalty, dour men of science and engineering, and stern statesmen such as those lining the corridor of room 22. Centre stage, in room 21, is a comical statue of **Victoria and Albert** in Anglo-Saxon garb; on the far wall there's the striking sight of rank upon rank of bronze busts of yet more Victorian worthies. Room 24, by contrast, concentrates on the arts, with one deteriorated and oddly affecting group showing the **Brontë sisters** as seen by their disturbed brother Branwell; you can still see where he painted himself out, leaving a ghostly blur between Charlotte and Emily. Nearby are the poetic duo, **Robert** and **Elizabeth Barrett Browning**, looking totally Gothic in their grim Victorian dress.

One of the most notable features on this floor is the emergence of **photography** as an art form, with several great early Victorian photographs displayed throughout the various rooms, including one of engineer **Isambard Kingdom Brunel**, perkily posed in front of colossal iron chains. Before you abandon the Victorians entirely, it's worth popping into room 29, where there are some excellent **John Singer Sargent** portraits, and several works by students of Slade (see p.152): **Augustus John**, looking very confident and dapper at the age of just 22, his sister, **Gwen John**, **Walter Sickert** and **Philip Wilson Steer**, who founded the New English Arts Club, at which the last two portraits were originally exhibited.

The twentieth century

The twentieth-century collection begins in room 30, with a parade of World War I generals. The interwar years are then generously covered in the large room 31, the final one on this floor. The faces on display here are frequently rotated so it's difficult to say with any certainty who will be here. However, there are always one or two genuine works of art, sculptures by Jacob Epstein, self-portraits by **Barbara Hepworth** and her husband **Ben Nicholson**. There's the odd surprise, too, such as the very Deco-ish aluminium bust of **Edith Sitwell** by Maurice Lambert.

Out on the Balcony Gallery, the really popular display of who's who (or was who) in postwar Britain begins in **Britain 1960–90**. Even here, amid the photos of the Swinging Sixties, there are a few genuine works of art by the likes of Leon Kossoff, Andy Warhol, Lucien Freud and Francis Bacon. If you want to find (or skip) the current **Royal Family**, they've been banished to the first-floor landing of the old staircase.

Britain since 1990

The contemporary collection, **Britain since 1990**, on the ground floor, is an unashamedly populist trot through the media personalities of nearly two decades. The displays here are rearranged more often than any others, according to the whims and tastes of the day, making it difficult to predict exactly what will be on show. In addition, much of the space is used for the gallery's excellent temporary exhibitions. Sadly, there are some pretty uninspired paintings here, epitomized by Bryan Organ's obsequious renderings of the great and the good. Amid the welter of publicity photos, you'll find oil paintings of the most unlikely folk, from TV personalities to sporting legends.

Whitehall and Westminster

Political, religious and regal power has emanated from **Whitehall** and **Westminster** for almost a millennium. It was Edward the Confessor (1042–66) who first established Westminster as London's royal and ecclesiastical power base, some three miles west of the commercial City of London. The embryonic English parliament met in the abbey in the fourteenth century, and eventually took over the old royal palace of Westminster when Henry VIII moved out to Whitehall. Whitehall Palace burnt down in 1698 and was slowly replaced by government offices, so that by the nineteenth century Whitehall had become the "heart of the Empire", its ministries ruling over a quarter of the world's population. Even now, though the UK's world status has diminished and its royalty and clergy no longer wield much real power or receive the same respect, the institutions that run the country inhabit roughly the same geographical area: Westminster for the politicians, Whitehall for the ministers and civil servants.

Until the westward expansion of the City of London in the seventeenth century, Westminster was a more or less separate city. Today, the modern borough encompasses a much wider area than that covered in this chapter, including most of the West End and parts of the well-to-do districts of Mayfair and Belgravia, making its council one of the richest in the country. The monuments and buildings covered in this chapter include some of London's most famous landmarks – **Big Ben** and the **Houses of Parliament** and **Westminster Abbey**, plus one of the city's finest permanent art collections, **Tate Britain**. This area is a well-trodden tourist circuit for the most part, though there are only a few shops or cafés and little commercial life to distract you (nearby Soho and Covent Garden are far better areas for this). It's also one of the easiest parts of London to walk round, with all the major sights within a mere half-mile of each other, and linked by one of London's most triumphant – and atypical – avenues, **Whitehall**.

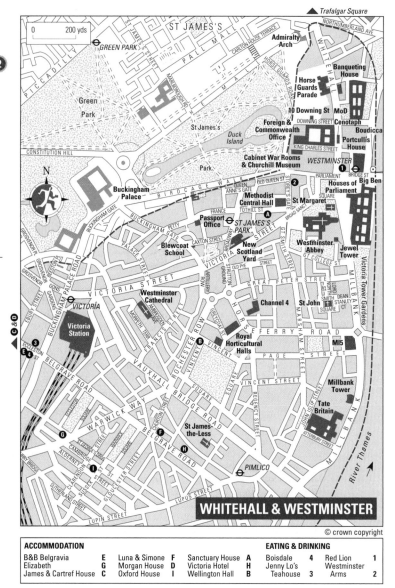

▲ Trafalgar Square

© crown copyright

ACCOMMODATION						EATING & DRINKING			
B&B Belgravia	E	Luna & Simone	F	Sanctuary House	A	Boisdale	4	Red Lion	1
Elizabeth	G	Morgan House	D	Victoria Hotel	H	Jenny Lo's		Westminster	
James & Cartref House	C	Oxford House	I	Wellington Hall	B	Teahouse	3	Arms	2

Whitehall

Whitehall, the unusually broad avenue connecting Trafalgar Square to Parliament Square, is now synonymous with the faceless, pinstriped bureaucracy charged with the day-to-day running of the country. Yet during the sixteenth and seventeenth centuries, as chief London residence of the kings and queens of England, it was synonymous with royalty. The original **Whitehall Palace** started out as the London seat of the Archbishop of York, but was confiscated and greatly extended by Henry VIII after a fire at Westminster Palace forced the king to find alternative accommodation; it was here that he celebrated his marriage to Anne Boleyn in 1533, and here that he died fourteen years later. Described by one contemporary chronicler as nothing but "a heap of houses erected at diverse times and of different models, made continuous", it boasted some two thousand rooms and stretched for half a mile along the Thames. Not much of Whitehall Palace survived the fire of 1698, caused by a Dutch laundry-woman, after which, partly due to the dank conditions in this part of town, the royal residence shifted to St James's and Kensington.

Since then nearly all the key governmental ministries and offices have

The Changing of the Guard and royal parades

The Queen is colonel-in-chief of the seven **Household Regiments** (Ⓦ www.army .mod.uk/ceremonialandheritage): the Life Guards (who dress in red and white) and the Blues and Royals (who dress in blue and white) are the two Household Cavalry regiments; while the Grenadier, Coldstream, Scots, Irish and Welsh guards make up the Foot Guards. The Foot Guards can only be told apart by the plumes (or lack of them) in their busbies (fur helmets), and by the arrangement of their tunic buttons. The three senior regiments (Grenadier, Coldstream and Scots) date back to the time of the Civil War, the Commonwealth and the Restoration, as do the Life Guards and the Blues and Royals, the latter an amalgamation of the Royal Horse Guards (the Blues) and the Royal Dragoons (the Royals). All seven regiments still form part of the modern army as well as performing ceremonial functions such as the Changing of the Guard.

The **Changing of the Guard** takes place at two separate London locations: the Foot Guards hold theirs outside Buckingham Palace (April–July daily 11.30am; Sept–March alternate days; no ceremony if it rains), but the more impressive one is held on Horse Guards Parade, where a squad of twelve mounted Household Cavalry in full livery arrives from Hyde Park to relieve the guards at the Horse Guards building on Whitehall (Mon–Sat 11am, Sun 10am) – alternatively, if you miss the whole thing, turn up at 4pm for the elaborate daily inspection by the Officer of the Guard, who checks the soldiers haven't knocked off early. A ceremony also takes place regularly in Windsor Castle (see p.428).

A considerably grander ceremony is **Trooping the Colour**, when one of the Household battalions presents its colours (flags) to the Queen for inspection, a spectacle memorably described by the Labour politician Peter Mandelson as "lots of chinless wonders with bright scarlet uniforms". This takes place on the Saturday after the Queen's official birthday, June 6, with the Colonel's Review (led by the Duke of Edinburgh) and the Major General's Review taking place on the two preceding Saturdays. The ceremonies take place in Horse Guards Parade, and tickets for a seat in the stands around the parade ground are allocated by ballot; apply in January or February by sending an SAE to the Brigade Major, HQ Household Division, Horse Guards, Whitehall, London SW1A 2AX. Alternatively, you can simply watch the soldiers march to their destination along The Mall.

The other big military display on Horse Guards Parade is the **Beating Retreat**, which takes place on a couple of evenings around the same time in early June. The massed bands of the Household Division beat an hour-long "retreat" on pipes and drums, and tickets for the stands are much easier to get hold of. For tickets and information phone ☏ 020/7839 5323 or visit Ⓦ www.army.mod.uk/ceremonial andheritage.

migrated here, rehousing themselves on an ever-increasing scale, a process which reached its apogee with the grimly bland **Ministry of Defence (MoD)** building, the largest office block in London when it was completed in 1957. Underneath the MoD is the country's most expensive military bunker, Pindar, completed at a cost of over £125 million in 1994. Back above ground, the statues and memorials dotted along Whitehall recall the days when the street stood at the centre of an empire on which the sun never set. Kings and military leaders predominate, starting outside Horse Guards with the 2nd Duke of Cambridge (1819–1904), a man who, as commander-in-chief of the British Army, was so resistant to military reform that he had to be forcibly retired, followed by the 8th Duke of Devonshire (1833–1908), who failed to rescue General Gordon from the Siege of Khartoum. Appropriately enough, Lord Haig (1861–1928), who was responsible for sending thousands to their deaths in the slaughter of World War I, faces the Cenotaph; his horse is famously poised ready for urination.

Banqueting House

The only sections of Whitehall Palace to survive the 1698 fire were Cardinal Wolsey's wine cellars (now underneath the Ministry of Defence and closed to the public) and the **Banqueting House** (Mon–Sat 10am–5pm; £4; ☎0870/751 5178, ⓦwww.hrp.org.uk), the first Palladian building to be built in central London, begun by Inigo Jones in 1619. Opened in 1622 with a performance of Ben Jonson's *Masque of Angers*, the Banqueting House is still used for state occasions (and, as a result, may be closed at short notice). The chief reason for visiting the place is to admire the superlative ceiling paintings, commissioned by Charles I from **Rubens**. A glorification of the divine right of kings, the panels depict the union of England and Scotland, the peaceful reign of James I and, finally, his apotheosis. The information boards posted in the room explain everything you need to know to appreciate the paintings; the video and audioguide are not worth bothering with unless your English history is a bit thin.

The Banqueting House is also a place rich in historical associations. In 1649, **Charles I** walked through the room for the last time and stepped onto the executioner's scaffold from one of its windows. He wore several shirts in case he shivered in the cold, which the crowd would take to be fear; once his head was chopped off, it was then sewn back on again for burial in Windsor – a very British touch. From the Restoration until 1859, "King Charles the Martyr" Holy Day (January 30) was a day of fasting, and his execution is still commemorated here on the last Sunday in January with a parade by the royalist wing of the Civil War Society.

Oliver Cromwell moved into Whitehall Palace in 1654, having declared himself Lord Protector, and kept open table in the Banqueting House for the officers of his New Model Army; he died here in 1658. Two years later **Charles II** celebrated the Restoration here, and kept open house for his adoring public – Samuel Pepys recalls seeing the underwear of one of his mistresses, Lady Castlemaine, hanging out to dry in the palace's Privy Garden. (Charles housed two mistresses and his wife here, with a back entrance onto the river for courtesans.)

Horse Guards

Across the road, where Henry VIII had the palace cockfighting pit, tennis courts and a tiltyard, two mounted sentries of the Queen's Household Cavalry and two horseless colleagues, all in ceremonial uniform, are posted daily from 10am to 4pm. Ostensibly they are protecting the **Horse Guards** building, a modest edifice begun in 1745 by William Kent, originally built as the old palace guard-house, but now guarding nothing in particular. The black dot over the number two on the building's clock face denotes the hour at which Charles I was executed. The mounted guards are changed hourly; those standing have to remain motionless and impassive for two hours before being replaced. Try to time your visit to coincide with the **Changing of the Guard** (see box on p.61), which takes place behind the building on Horse Guards Parade.

Downing Street and the Cenotaph

Further down this west side of Whitehall is London's most famous address, **10 Downing Street** (ⓦwww.number-10.gov.uk), the terraced house that has been the residence of the prime minister, or PM, since it was presented to the First Lord of the Treasury, Robert Walpole, Britain's first PM, by George II in 1732. With no. 11 – home of the Chancellor of the Exchequer since 1806 – and no. 12, home of the government's Chief Whip, it's the only remaining bit of the original seventeenth-century cul-de-sac, though all three are now interconnecting and, having been greatly modernized over the years, house much larger complexes than might appear from the outside. The public have been kept at bay since 1990, when Margaret Thatcher ordered a pair of iron gates to be installed at the junction with Whitehall, an act more symbolic than effective – a year later the IRA lobbed a mortar into the street from Horse Guards Parade, coming within a whisker of wiping out the entire Tory cabinet.

Just beyond the Downing Street gates, in the middle of the road, stands Edwin Lutyens' **Cenotaph**, built in wood and plaster for the first anniversary of the Armistice in 1919, and rebuilt, by popular request, in Portland stone the following year. The stark monument, which eschews any kind of Christian imagery, is inscribed simply with the words "The Glorious Dead" – the lost of World War I, who, it was once calculated, would take three and a half days to pass by the Cenotaph marching four abreast. The memorial remains the focus of the Remembrance Sunday ceremony held on the Sunday nearest November 11. Between the wars, however, a much more powerful, two-minute silence was observed throughout the entire British Empire every year on November 11 at 11am, the exact time of the armistice at the end of World War I.

The Cabinet War Rooms and Churchill Museum

In 1938, in anticipation of Nazi air raids, the basement on the south side of King Charles Street was converted into the **Cabinet War Rooms** (daily 9.30am–6pm; £10; ☎020/7930 6961, ⓦcwr.iwm.org.uk). Though this claustrophobic hideout was fragile in comparison with Hitler's bunker in Berlin (the Führer's refuge was 50ft below ground, whereas the Cabinet War Rooms were protected only by a three-foot-thick concrete slab, reinforced with steel rails and tramlines), it was here that Winston Churchill directed operations and held cabinet meetings for the duration of World War II. By the end of the war, the warren had expanded to cover more than six acres, including a hospital, canteen and shooting range, as well as cramped sleeping quarters; tunnels fan out from the complex to outlying government ministries, and also, it is rumoured, to Buckingham Palace itself, allowing the Royal Family a quick getaway to exile in Canada (via Charing Cross station) in the event of a Nazi invasion.

The rooms have been left pretty much as they were when they were finally abandoned on VJ Day, 1945, and make for an atmospheric underground trot through wartime London. To bring the place to life, avail yourself of the museum's free audioguide, which includes various eyewitness accounts by folk who worked there. When you get to Churchill's secret telephone hotline direct to the American president, signs direct to the excellent new **Churchill Museum**, which begins with his finest moment, when he took over as PM and Britain stood alone against the Nazis. You can hear snippets of Churchill's most famous speeches and check out his trademark bowler, spotted bow tie and half-chewed Havana, not to mention his wonderful burgundy zip-up "romper suit". Fortunately for the curators, Churchill had an extremely eventful life and was great for a soundbite, so there are plenty of interesting anecdotes to keep you engaged.

Back in the Cabinet War Rooms, look out for Winnie's very modest emergency bedroom (though he himself rarely stayed there, preferring to watch the air raids from the roof of the building, or rest his head at the *Savoy Hotel*). Finally, you reach the Map Room, with its rank of multicoloured telephones, copious ashtrays, and floor-to-ceiling maps covering every theatre of war and showing the exact position of the front line on VJ Day.

Parliament Square

Parliament Square was laid out in the mid-nineteenth century to give the new Houses of Parliament and the adjacent Westminster Abbey a grander setting. It has the dubious privilege of being one of the city's first traffic roundabouts, though there are plans to pedestrianize the east side. Meanwhile, statues of notables – Abraham Lincoln, Benjamin Disraeli and Jan Smuts, to name but a few – are scattered amid the swirling cars and buses, and Winston Churchill stoops determinedly in the northeast corner of the central green.

Two other noteworthy statues punctuate nearby **Westminster Bridge**: Boudicca (Boadicea), who led an uprising against the Romans in 60 AD and decimated their London settlement, can be seen keeping her horses and daughters under control without the use of reins – Cowper's boast, "regions Caesar never knew, thy posterity shall sway", adorns the plinth – while on the south side of the bridge stands the Coade Stone Lion, made from a weather-resistant pottery invented in the eighteenth century by Elizabeth Coade. Incidentally, Wordsworth's poem, *Lines Written upon Westminster Bridge* – "Earth has not anything to show more fair. . ." and so on – were addressed to the bridge's predecessor. The current one was only opened in 1862.

▲ Boudicca's statue and Big Ben

Visiting the Houses of Parliament

Debates in the House of Commons – the livelier of the two – begin on Mondays at 2.30pm and end no earlier than 10.30pm; from Tuesday to Thursday they start at 11.30am and finish no later than 7.30pm; and on Friday, they start at 9.30am and finish at 3pm. **Question Time** – when the House is at its most raucous and entertaining – takes place in the first hour (Mon–Thurs); **Prime Minister's Question Time** is on Wednesday from noon until 12.30pm. To attend either Question Time you need a special ticket (see below). The House of Lords kicks off at 2.30pm on Monday, and from 3pm Tuesday to Thursday; if it sits on a Friday, it usually starts at 11am. Recesses (holiday closures) of both Houses occur at Christmas, mid-February, Easter, Whitsuntide and from mid-July to mid-October. If Parliament is in session a Union Jack flag flies from the southernmost tower, the Victoria Tower, and at night there is a light above the clock face on Big Ben. If an MP wants a taxi, a little sign saying "taxi" flashes on the corner railings of Parliament Square.

To watch the proceedings in either the House of Commons or the Lords, simply join the queue for the **public galleries** outside St Stephen's Gate. The public are let in slowly from about 4pm onwards on Mondays, from around 1pm Tuesday to Thursday, and from 10am on Fridays; the security checks are very tight, and the whole procedure can take an hour or more. To avoid the queues, turn up an hour or more later, when the crowds have usually thinned, or on Friday morning, though check first to see if the House is sitting. If you just want to sit in on one of the evidence-taking sessions of the select committees (Mon–Thurs), you can usually go straight in; phone ☏020/7219 4272 for more information or visit the parliamentary websites (🌐www.parliament.uk or 🌐www.explore.parliament.uk). Full explanatory notes on the procedures (and warnings about joining in or causing a disruption) are supplied to all visitors, but if you want to learn more about how Parliament works, pay a visit to the exhibition in the Jewel Tower (see p.69) first.

To see Question Time, you really need to book a **ticket** in advance from your local MP (if you're a UK citizen) or your embassy in London (if you're not). To contact your MP, simply phone ☏020/7219 3000 and ask to be put through. For part of the summer recess (Aug & Sept), there are **guided tours** of Parliament (Mon, Fri & Sat 9.15am–4.30pm, Tues, Wed & Thurs 1.15–4.30pm; Aug also Tues 9.15am–1.15pm; £7), lasting an hour and fifteen minutes. Visitors can book in advance by phoning ☏0870/906 3773, or simply head for the ticket office on Abingdon Green, opposite Victoria Tower. The rest of the year, it's still possible to organize a tour of the building through your MP or embassy. It's also possible to arrange a free guided tour up **Big Ben** (Mon–Fri 10.30am, 11.30am & 2.30pm; no under-11s), again through your MP or embassy. For more information about access requirements, phone ☏020/7219 4862.

Right by Westminster Bridge stands the much criticized **Portcullis House**, designed by Michael Hopkins in 1999 and topped by giant air ducts made to look like Victorian smokestacks. Built at a cost of £250 million to provide MPs with more office space, it's a shame nobody considered the cheapest option: simply cutting the number of MPs from the present 659. The name is unfortunate given the current administration's oft-stated commitment to open government.

Houses of Parliament

The Palace of Westminster, better known as the **Houses of Parliament**, is London's best-known monument. The "mother of all parliaments", it is also the city's finest Victorian building, the symbol of a nation once confident of its

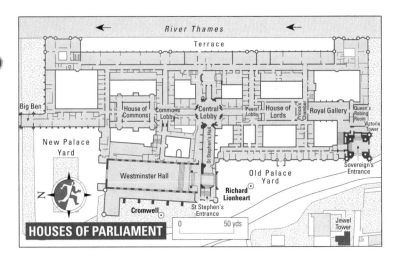

HOUSES OF PARLIAMENT

place at the centre of the world. Best viewed from the south side of the river, where the likes of Monet and Turner once set up their easels, the building is distinguished above all by the ornate, gilded clock tower popularly known as **Big Ben**, at its most impressive when lit up at night. Strictly speaking, "Big Ben" refers only to the thirteen-ton bell that strikes the hour (and is broadcast across the world by the BBC), and takes its name from either the former Commissioner of Works, Benjamin Hall, or a popular heavyweight boxer of the time, Benjamin Caunt.

The original Westminster Palace was built by **Edward the Confessor** in the first half of the eleventh century to allow him to watch over the building of his abbey. Westminster then served as the seat of all the English monarchs until a fire forced Henry VIII to decamp to Whitehall. The Lords had always convened at the palace, but it was only following Henry's death that the House of Commons moved from the abbey's chapter house into the palace's St Stephen's Chapel, thus beginning the building's associations with Parliament.

In 1834, a fire, started by workmen setting alight wooden tally sticks, reduced the old palace to rubble. Save for Westminster Hall, and a few pieces of the old structure buried deep within the interior, everything you see today is the work of **Charles Barry**, whose design had won the competition to create something that expressed national greatness through the use of Gothic and Elizabethan styles. The resulting orgy of honey-coloured pinnacles, turrets and tracery, somewhat restrained by the building's classical symmetry, is the greatest achievement of the Gothic Revival. Inside, the Victorian love of mock-Gothic detail is evident in the maze of over one thousand committee rooms and offices, the fittings of which were largely the responsibility of Barry's assistant, **Augustus Pugin**.

Westminster Hall

Virtually the only relic of the medieval palace is the bare expanse of **Westminster Hall**, on the north side of the complex. First built by William Rufus in 1099, it was saved from the 1834 fire by the timely intervention of the PM,

Lord Melbourne, who had the fire engines brought into the hall itself, and personally took charge of the firefighting. The sheer scale of the hall – 240ft by 60ft – and its huge oak hammerbeam roof, added by Richard II in the late fourteenth century, make it one of the most magnificent secular medieval halls in Europe.

Unless you're on a guided tour, you can only peer down from St Stephen's Porch, en route to the public galleries, at the bare expanse that has witnessed some nine hundred years of English history. Nowadays, the hall is only used for the lying-in-state of members of the Royal Family and a select few non-royals, but until 1821 every royal coronation banquet was held here; during the ceremony, the Royal Champion would ride into the hall in full armour to challenge any who dared dispute the sovereign's right to the throne.

From the thirteenth to the nineteenth centuries the hall was used as the country's highest court of law: Thomas More was convicted of high treason, as was **Guy Fawkes**, the Catholic caught in the cellars trying to blow up the House of Lords on November 5, 1605; he was later hanged, drawn and quartered in Old Palace Yard. **Charles I** was also tried in the hall, but refused to take his hat off, since he did not accept the court's legitimacy. **Oliver Cromwell**, whose statue now stands outside the hall, was sworn in here as Lord Protector in 1653, only to have his head stuck on a spike above the hall after the Restoration – it remained there for several decades until a storm dislodged it. It now resides in a secret location at Cromwell's old college in Cambridge.

St Stephen's Hall and the Central Lobby

From St Stephen's Porch, the route to the parliamentary chambers passes through **St Stephen's Hall**, designed by Barry as a replica of the chapel built by Edward I, where the Commons met for nearly three hundred years until 1834. The ersatz vaulted ceilings, faded murals, statuary and huge wooden doors do their best to conjure up the old medieval atmosphere, but it's still hard to visualize the dramatic events that have unfolded here. It was into this chamber that Charles I entered with an armed guard in 1642 in a vain attempt to arrest five MPs who had made a speedy escape down the river – "I see my birds have flown", he is supposed to have said. Shortly afterwards, the Civil War began, and no monarch has entered the Commons since. St Stephen's also witnessed the only assassination of a prime minister, when in 1812 Spencer Perceval was shot by a merchant whose business had been ruined by the Napoleonic Wars.

After a further wait you're shepherded through the bustling, octagonal **Central Lobby**, where constituents "lobby" their MPs. In the tiling of the lobby Pugin inscribed the Latin motto "Except the Lord keep the house, they labour in vain that build it". In view of what happened to the architects, the sentiment seems like an indictment of parliamentary morality – Pugin ended up in Bedlam mental hospital and Barry died from overwork within months of completing the job.

The House of Commons

If you're going to listen to proceedings in the **House of Commons**, you'll be ushered into a small room where all visitors sign a form vowing not to cause a disturbance; long institutional staircases and corridors then lead to the Public Gallery, rising steeply above the chamber. Everyone is given a guide to the House, which includes explanatory diagrams and notes on procedure, and a Points of Order sheet to help unravel the matters discussed. Protests from the gallery were once a fairly regular occurrence: suffragettes have poured flour, farmers have dumped dung, Irish Nationalists have lobbed tear gas, and lesbians have abseiled down into the chamber. Rigorous security arrangements have for the most part put paid to such antics.

Since an incendiary bomb in May 1941 destroyed Barry's original chamber, what you see now is a rather lifeless postwar reconstruction. Barry's design was modelled on St Stephen's Hall (see p.67), hence the choir-stall arrangement of the MPs' benches. Members of the cabinet (and the opposition's shadow cabinet) occupy the two "front benches"; the rest are "backbenchers". To avoid debates degenerating into physical combat, MPs are not allowed to cross the red lines – which are exactly two swords' length apart – on the floor of the chamber during a debate, hence the expression "toeing the party line". The chamber is at its busiest during Question Time, though if too many of the 659 MPs turn up, a large number have to remain standing, as the House only has 427 seats. For much of the time, however, the chamber is empty, with just a handful of MPs present from each party.

The House of Lords

On the other side of the Central Lobby, a corridor leads to the **House of Lords** (or Upper House), a far dozier establishment peopled by unelected Lords and Ladies, most of whom are appointed by successive PMs, plus a smattering of bishops. Their home boasts much grander decor than the Commons, full of regal gold and scarlet, and dominated by a canopied gold throne where the Queen sits for the state opening of Parliament in November. Directly in front of the throne, the Lord Chancellor runs the proceedings from the scarlet Woolsack, an enormous cushion stuffed with wool, which harks back to the time when it was England's principal export.

Nowadays, the Lords have little real power – they can only advise and review parliamentary bills, although a handful act as the country's final court of appeal. In 1999, the Labour government took the bull by the horns and kicked out all but 92 of the 1000-plus hereditary Lords, who had, until then, the right to vote and debate in the House. The majority of the hereditary Lords were solidly Conservative – over a quarter went to Eton – but rarely bothered to turn up. Nevertheless, they could be (and were) called upon by the Conservatives in emergencies, to ensure a right-wing victory in a crucial vote. The future of the few who now remain in the House is as yet undecided, but their days are surely numbered.

The royal apartments

If the House of Lords takes your fancy, you can see more pomp and glitter by going on a **guided tour** (see p.65). You'll be asked to enter at the **Sovereign's Entrance** below Victoria Tower, where the Queen arrives in her coach for the state opening. Then, after the usual security checks, you'll be allowed up the Royal Staircase to the Norman Porch, every nook of which is stuffed with busts of eminent statesmen.

Next door is the **Queen's Robing Chamber**, which boasts a superb coffered ceiling and lacklustre Arthurian frescoes. As its name suggests, this is the room where the monarch dons the crown jewels before entering the Lords for the opening of Parliament. Beyond here you enter the **Royal Gallery**, a cavernous writing room for the House of Lords, hung with portraits of royals past and present, and two 45-foot-long frescoes of Trafalgar and Waterloo. Before entering the House of Lords itself, you pass through the **Prince's Chamber**, commonly known as the Tudor Room after the numerous portraits that line the walls, including Henry VIII and all six of his wives. The tour then takes you through both Houses, St Stephen's Hall and finally Westminster Hall (all described above), before you leave through New Palace Yard.

Jewel Tower and the Victoria Tower Gardens

The **Jewel Tower** (daily: April–Oct 10am–5pm; Nov–March 10am–4pm; EH; £2.60; ☎020/7222 2219), across the road from the Sovereign's Entrance, is another remnant of the medieval palace. The tower formed the southwestern corner of the original exterior fortifications (there's a bit of moat left, too), and was constructed in around 1365 by Edward III as a giant strongbox for the crown jewels. Nowadays, its three floors house an excellent exhibition on the history of Parliament, including a touch-screen tour of the palace and ending with a video on the procedural rigmarole that still persists there – well worth a visit *before* you enter Parliament. To the south of the Victoria Tower are the leafy **Victoria Tower Gardens**, which look out onto the Thames. Visitors are greeted by a statue of Emmeline Pankhurst, leader of the suffragette movement, who died in 1928, the same year that women finally got the vote on equal terms with men; medallions commemorating her daughter Christabel, and a WPSU Prisoners' Badge, flank the statue. Round the corner, a replica of Rodin's famous sculpture, *The Burghers of Calais*, makes a surprising appearance here, while at the far end of the gardens stands an exotic-looking, badly weathered, neo-Gothic fountain commemorating the abolition of slavery in 1834.

St Margaret's Church

To the north of the Jewel Tower, in the shadow of Westminster Abbey, is **St Margaret's Church** (Mon–Fri 9.30am–3.45pm, Sat 9.30am–1.45pm, Sun 2–5pm; free; ☎020/7222 5152, ⊛www.westminster-abbey.org), which has been the unofficial parliamentary church since the entire Commons tipped up here in 1614 to unmask religious Dissenters among the MPs. St Margaret's has also long been a fashionable church to get married in – Pepys, Milton and Shakespeare were followed in the twentieth century by Churchill and Mountbatten – and it gets a steady stream of visitors simply by dint of being so close to the abbey (and because it's free). The present building dates back to 1523, and its most noteworthy furnishing is the colourful Flemish stained-glass window above the altar, which commemorates the marriage of Henry VIII and Catherine of Aragon (depicted in the bottom left- and right-hand corners). Constructed in 1526, the window was never intended for St Margaret's, and was only bought by the church in 1758 to replace those smashed by the Puritans. The west window commemorates Walter Raleigh, who was beheaded in Old Palace Yard and buried in the old churchyard. Also interred here are the Czech engraver Václav Hollar; John Cleland, author of the saucy *Fanny Hill*; and William Caxton, who audited the parish accounts and set up the country's first printing press in the abbey close in 1476.

Westminster Abbey

The Houses of Parliament dwarf their much older neighbour, **Westminster Abbey**, which squats uncomfortably on the western edge of Parliament Square. Yet this single building embodies much of the history of England: it has been the venue for every coronation since the time of William the Conqueror, and the site of more or less every royal burial for some five hundred years between

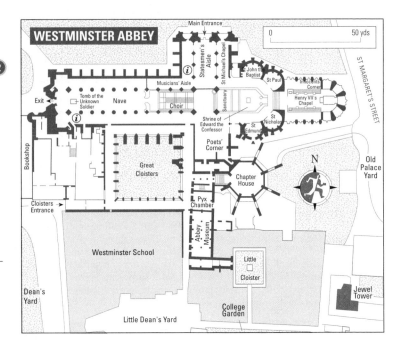

the reigns of Henry III and George II. Scores of the nation's most famous citizens are honoured here, too – though many of the stones commemorate people buried elsewhere – and the interior is cluttered with hundreds of monuments, reliefs and statues.

Legend has it that the first church on the site was consecrated by St Peter himself, who was rowed across the Thames by a fisherman named Edric, who received a giant salmon as a reward. More verifiable is that there was a small Benedictine monastery here by the end of the tenth century, for which **Edward the Confessor** built an enormous church. Nothing much remains of Edward's church, which was consecrated on December 28, 1065, just eight days before his death, though the ground plan is his, as is the crypt. The following January Harold was crowned, and, on Christmas Day, William the Conqueror rode up the aisle on horseback, thus firmly establishing the tradition of royal coronation within the Confessor's church.

It was in Edward's honour that **Henry III** began to rebuild the abbey in 1245, in the French Gothic style of the recently completed Rheims Cathedral, but the vaulting and the whole of the east end had to wait until the reign of **Henry VII**. The monks were kicked out during the Reformation, but the church's status as the nation's royal mausoleum saved it from anything worse. In the early eighteenth century, Nicholas Hawksmoor gave the church its quasi-Gothic twin towers and west front. And in the niches above the west door, you'll find the latest additions: a series of statues representing twentieth-century martyrs, from Dietrich Bonhöffer to Martin Luther King.

Statesmen's Aisle and the north ambulatory

With over 3300 people buried beneath its flagstones and countless others commemorated here, the abbey is, in essence, a giant mausoleum. It has long ceased to be simply a working church, and admission charges are nothing new: Oliver Goldsmith complained about being charged three pence in 1765. A century or so later, so few people used the abbey as a church that, according to George Bernard Shaw, one foreign visitor who knelt down to pray was promptly arrested because the verger thought he was acting suspiciously. Despite attempts to prove otherwise – like the large signs ordering visitors to "Shhhh!" – the abbey is now more a mass tourist attraction than a House of God.

Once you've paid the hefty admission charge, head over to the **information** desk and pick up a free plan. Locating some of the graves is tricky unless your Latin is good, so if you have any questions, ask the vergers in the black gowns or the abbey assistants in the green robes. The north transept, where you enter, is littered with overblown monuments to long-forgotten empire-builders and nineteenth-century politicians, and traditionally known as **Statesmen's Aisle**. Many of those commemorated in the abbey are not, in fact, buried here. **Pitt the Elder** – immediately to the right as you pass the ticket office – is one of the few in the Statesmen's Aisle who is, his statue standing high above his extravagantly expensive tomb, lording it over Britannia and Neptune.

The transept's best funereal art is tucked away in **St Michael's Chapel** to the east, where you can admire the remarkable monument to **Francis Vere** (1560–1609), one of the greatest soldiers of the Elizabethan period, made out of two slabs of black marble, between which lies Sir Francis; on the upper slab, supported by four knights, his armour is laid out, to show that he died away from the field of battle. The most striking grave, by Roubiliac, is that in which **Elizabeth Nightingale**, who died from a miscarriage, collapses in her husband's arms while he tries to fight off the skeletal figure of Death, who is climbing out of the tomb.

From this point, you enter the **north ambulatory**, its two side chapels now containing ostentatious Tudor and Stuart tombs that replaced the altarpieces that had graced them before the Reformation. One of the most extravagant Tudor tombs is that of Lord Hunsdon, which dominates the **Chapel of St John the Baptist**, and, at 36ft in height, is the tallest in the entire abbey. More intriguing, though, are the sarcophagi in the neighbouring **Chapel of St Paul**: one depicts eight "weepers", kneeling children along the base of the tomb – the two holding skulls predeceased their parents – while the red-robed Countess of Sussex has a beautiful turquoise and gold porcupine (the family emblem) as her prickly footrest.

Henry VII's Chapel

Before you enter the main body of the Lady Chapel, better known as **Henry VII's Chapel**, you should pop into the chapel's north aisle, which is virtually cut off from the chancel. Here James I erected a huge ten-poster tomb to his predecessor, **Elizabeth I**. Unless you read the plaque on the floor, you'd never know that Elizabeth's Catholic half-sister, "Bloody Mary", is also buried here, in an unusual act of posthumous reconciliation. The far end of the north aisle, where James I's two infant daughters lie, is known as **Innocents' Corner**: Princess Sophia, who died aged three days, lies in an alabaster cradle, her face peeping over the covers, just about visible in the mirror on the wall; while Princess Mary, who died the following year aged 2, is clearly visible, casually leaning on a cushion. Set into the wall between the two is the Wren-designed urn containing (what are thought to be) the bones of the murdered princes, Edward V and his younger brother, Richard, discovered under a staircase in the Tower of London during Charles II's reign.

Leaving the chapel's north aisle, you enter the **main nave** of Henry VII's chapel, the most dazzling architectural set piece in the abbey. Begun by Henry VII in 1503 as a shrine to Henry VI and as his own future resting place, it represents the final gasp of the English Perpendicular style, with its intricately carved vaulting, fan-shaped gilded pendants and statues of nearly one hundred saints, installed high above the choir stalls. The stalls themselves are decorated with the banners and emblems of the Knights of the Order of the Bath, to whom the chapel was dedicated by George I. **George II**, the last king to be buried in the abbey, lies in the burial vault under your feet, along with Queen Caroline – their coffins were fitted with removable sides so that their remains could mingle. Close by lies the son they both hated, **Frederick Louis**, who died after being hit in the throat by a cricket ball.

Beneath the altar is the grave of Edward VI, the single, sickly son of Henry VIII, while behind lies the chapel's *raison d'être*, the black marble sarcophagus containing **Henry VII** and his spouse – their lifelike gilded effigies, modelled from death masks, are obscured by an ornate Renaissance grille, designed by Pietro Torrigiano, who fled from Italy after breaking Michelangelo's nose in a fight. **James I** is also interred within Henry's tomb, while the first of the apse chapels, to the north, hosts a grand monument by Hubert le Sueur to James's lover, George Villiers, Duke of Buckingham, the first non-royal to be buried in this part of the abbey, who was killed by one of his own soldiers. Le Sueur was also responsible for another overblown monument in the last of the apse chapels, to the south, in which four caryatids, holding a vast bronze canopy, weep for Ludovic Stuart, another of James I's "favourites". The easternmost chapel is dedicated to the RAF, and sports a modern stained-glass window depicting airmen and angels in the Battle of Britain. Beneath it, a plaque marks the spot where Oliver Cromwell rested, briefly, until the Restoration, whereupon his mummified body was disinterred, dragged through the streets, hanged at Tyburn and beheaded.

Before descending the steps back into the ambulatory, squeeze your way around the south aisle of Henry VII's chapel. The first red-robed effigy belongs to the Countess of Lennox, James I's grandmother, followed by James's mother, **Mary Queen of Scots**, whom Elizabeth I had beheaded. James had Mary's remains brought from Peterborough Cathedral in 1612, and paid out significantly more for her extravagant eight-postered tomb, complete with a terrifyingly aggressive red lion, than he had done for Elizabeth's (see above); the 27 hangers-on who are buried with her are listed on the nearby wooden screen. The last of the tombs here is that of **Lady Margaret Beaufort**, Henry VII's mother, her face and hands depicted wrinkles and all by Torrigiano. Below the altar, commemorated by simple modern plaques, lie yet more royals: **William and Mary**, **Queen Anne** and **Charles II**. To the left is a nautically flavoured monument to **General Monck**, who, despite being Cromwell's commander-in-chief, was the man responsible for the restoration of the monarchy in 1660.

The Coronation Chair and the south ambulatory

As you leave Henry VII's Chapel, you're invited to inspect Edward I's **Coronation Chair**, a decrepit oak throne dating from around 1300. The graffiti-covered chair, used in every coronation since 1308, was custom-built to incorporate the **Stone of Scone**, a great slab of red sandstone which acted as the Scottish coronation stone for

▲ Westminster Abbey

centuries before Edward pilfered it in 1296, in a demonstration of his mastery of the north. The stone remained in the abbey for the next seven hundred years, apart from a brief interlude in 1950, when some enterprising Scottish nationalists managed to steal it back and hide it in Arbroath. Then, in a futile attempt to curry favour with the Scots before the 1997 election, the Conservative government returned the stone to Edinburgh Castle, where it now resides.

Behind the chair lies the tomb of **Henry V**, who died of dysentery in France in 1422, and was regarded as a saint in his day. Above him rises the highly decorative H-shaped Chantry Chapel, where the body of Henry's wife, Catherine of Valois, was openly displayed for several centuries – Pepys records kissing her corpse on his 36th-birthday visit to the abbey. The chapel acts as a sort of gatehouse for the **Shrine of Edward the Confessor**, the sacred heart of the building, and site of some of the abbey's finest tombs, now only accessible on a guided tour (see p.71). With some difficulty, you can just about make out the battered marble casket of the Confessor's tomb and the niches in which pilgrims would kneel. From the **south ambulatory** you can admire the six remaining gleaming bronze "weepers" (out of the original fourteen) in the outer recesses of **Edward III**'s tomb.

There are more bombastic Tudor and Stuart tombs in the side chapels of the south ambulatory, and, in the **Chapel of St Edmund**, the second of the two, a very fine effigy of a fourteenth-century knight, which the inscription claims is Bernard Brocas, "who had lands to the value of £400 in Hampshire", and who was beheaded in 1400 for his part in trying to restore the deposed Richard II to the throne. In actual fact, it is his father who is buried in the vault. Close by is the unusual statue of Elizabeth Russell, who died of consumption at the age of just 26, and is depicted seated, "not dead but sleeping" as the Latin inscription has it, with her right foot resting on a skull.

Poets' Corner

Nowadays, the royal tombs have been somewhat upstaged by **Poets' Corner**, in the south transept. The first occupant, **Geoffrey Chaucer**, was buried here in 1400, not because he was a poet, but because he lived nearby. His battered tomb, on the east wall, wasn't built for another 150-odd years. When **Edmund Spenser** was buried here in 1599, his fellow poets – Shakespeare may well have been among them – threw their own works and quills into the grave. But it wasn't until the eighteenth century that this zone became an artistic pantheon, since when the transept has been filled with tributes to all shades of talent.

Among those who are actually buried here, you'll find – after much searching – grave slabs or memorials for everyone from John Dryden and Samuel Johnson to Charles Dickens and Thomas Hardy (though his heart was buried in Dorset). Among the merely commemorated is the dandyish figure of William Shakespeare, erected in 1740 on one of the east walls, and thus starting a trend that looks set to continue well into this century. Even mavericks like Oscar Wilde, commemorated in the Hubbard window, are acknowledged here, though William Blake was honoured by a Jacob Epstein sculpture only in 1957, and Byron was refused burial for his "open profligacy", and had to wait until 1969 for a memorial.

Among the non-poets buried here is the German composer **George Frideric Handel**, depicted by Roubiliac in similar dandyish mode to Shakespeare, and directly opposite the latter. Handel, who spent most of his life at the English court, wrote the coronation anthem, *Zadok the Priest*, which was first performed at George II's coronation, and has been performed at every subsequent one. Further along the same wall, the great eighteenth-century actor **David Garrick** is seen parting the curtains for a final bow. The one illiterate is old Thomas Parr, a Shropshire man who was brought to London as a celebrity in 1635 at the alleged age of 152, but died shortly afterwards, and whose remains were brought here by Charles II.

The sanctuary and the south choir aisle

From the south transept, you can gain access to the central **sanctuary**, site of the coronations. On its north side are three wonderful fourteenth-century gabled tombs featuring "weepers" around their base, but the most precious work of art here is the thirteenth-century Italian **Cosmati floor mosaic**. It depicts the universe with interwoven circles and squares of Purbeck marble, glass, and red and green porphyry, though it's often covered by a carpet to protect it. The richly gilded high altar, like the ornately carved choir stalls, is, in fact, a neo-Gothic construction from the nineteenth century.

There are some excellent memorials to undeserving types in the **south choir aisle**, though you may have to ask a verger to allow you to see them properly. The first is to **Thomas Thynne**, a Restoration rake, whose tomb incorporates a relief showing his assassination in his coach on Pall Mall by three thugs, hired to kill him by his Swedish rival in love. Further along lies **Admiral Clowdisley Shovell**, lounging in toga and wig. One of only two survivors of a shipwreck in 1707, he was washed up alive on a beach in the Scilly Isles, off southwest England, only to be killed by a fisherwoman for his emerald ring. Above Shovell is a memorial to the court portrait painter **Godfrey Kneller**, who declared, "By God, I will not be buried in Westminster . . . they do bury fools there." In the event, he has the honour of being the only artist commemorated in the abbey; the tomb is to his own design, but the epitaph is by Pope, who admitted it was the worst thing he ever wrote – which is just as well, as it's so high up you can't read it.

The cloisters

Doors in the south choir aisle lead to the **Great Cloisters** (daily 8am–6pm; free via Dean's Yard entrance), rebuilt after a fire in 1298 and paved with yet more funerary slabs, including, at the bottom of the ramp, that of the proto-feminist writer **Aphra Behn**, upon whose tomb "all women together ought to let flowers fall", according to Virginia Woolf, "for it was she who earned them the right to speak their minds".

At the eastern end lies the octagonal **Chapter House** (daily 10.30am–4pm; free with abbey ticket), which was built in 1255 for Henry III's Great Council or putative parliament. The House of Commons continued to meet here until 1395, though the monks were none too happy about it, complaining that the shuffling and stamping wore out the expensive tiled floor. Despite their whingeing, the thirteenth-century decorative paving tiles have survived well, as have the remarkable apocalyptic wall-paintings, which were executed in celebration of the eviction of the Commons. Be sure to check out the Whore of Babylon riding the scarlet seven-headed beast from *The Book of Revelation*. The neighbouring **Pyx Chamber**, originally the sacristy of the Confessor's church and subsequently the royal treasury, is currently being refurbished with no date yet set for its reopening.

One of the few surviving Norman sections of the abbey now houses the **Abbey Museum** (daily 10.30am–4pm; free). There's a real mixed bag of exhibits here, from replica coronation regalia used during rehearsals to a second coronation chair, made for Mary II, who was jointly crowned with William III in 1689. The most bizarre items, though, are the bald royal death masks, including those of Edward III and Henry VII, and the wax funeral effigies of Charles II, William III and Mary, and Lady Frances Stuart, model for Britannia on the old penny coin, complete with her pet parrot, which died a few days after she did.

From the cloisters you can make your way via **Little Cloister**, where sick or elderly monks used to live, to the little-known **College Garden** (Tues–Thurs: April–Sept 10am–6pm; Oct–March 10am–4pm; free), a 900-year-old stretch of green, originally used as a herb garden by the monastery's doctor. The garden now provides a quiet retreat and a croquet lawn for pupils of Westminster School; brass band concerts take place here during July and August on Thursdays between 12.30pm and 2pm.

The nave

It's only when you finally leave the cloisters that you get to enter the **nave** itself. Narrow, light and, at over a hundred feet in height, by far the tallest in the country, the nave is an impressive space. The first monument to head for is the **Tomb of the Unknown Soldier**, by the west door, with its garland of red poppies commemorating the million British soldiers who died in World War I. Close by is a large floor slab dedicated to **Winston Churchill**, though he chose to be buried in his family plot in Bladon, Oxfordshire; Neville Chamberlain, his prime ministerial predecessor, lies forgotten in the south aisle.

A tablet in the floor near the Unknown Soldier marks the spot where **George Peabody**, the nineteenth-century philanthropist whose housing estates in London still provide homes for those in need, was buried for a month before being exhumed and removed to his home town in Massachusetts; he remains the only American to have received the privilege of burial in the abbey. On the pillar by St George's Chapel, right by the west door, is a doleful fourteenth-century portrait of **Richard II**, painted at his coronation at the age of just 10, and the oldest known image of an English monarch painted from life. Above the west door, **William Pitt the Younger**, prime minister at just 23, teaches Anarchy a thing or two, while History takes notes.

In the north aisle, **Clement Attlee**, the great prime minister of the postwar Labour government, is buried close to his foreign secretary, **Ernest Bevin**, and **Sidney and Beatrice Webb**, Fabians and founders of the left-wing journal *New Statesman*. Further along the north wall is the grave of poet and playwright **Ben Jonson**, who, despite being a double murderer, was granted permission to be buried here, upright so as not to exceed the eighteen square inches he'd been allowed; his epitaph reads simply, "O Rare Ben Jonson".

The so-called **Musicians' Aisle** lies to the east, beyond a barrier, so you'll need to ask a verger. In fact, just two musicians of great note are buried here: Ralph Vaughan Williams and Henry Purcell, who served as the abbey's organist. Of the statues lining the aisle, only the tireless anti-slavery campaigner William Wilberforce, slouching in his chair, is actually buried in the abbey.

The dried and salted body of the explorer and missionary **David Livingstone** is buried in the centre of the nave – except for his internal organs, which, following the tradition of the African people in whose village he died, were buried in a box under a tree. In an alcove of the gilded neo-Gothic choir screen is a statue of **Isaac Newton**, who, although a Unitarian by faith, would no doubt have been happy enough to be buried in such a prominent position. Other scientists' graves cluster nearby, including non-believer **Charles Darwin**, who, despite being at loggerheads with the Church for most of his life over *On the Origin of Species*, was given a religious burial in the abbey.

In the far corner of the south aisle, are two huge eighteenth-century marble memorials with statues by Roubiliac, one of which – **General Hargrave**'s – has the deceased rising from the grave in response to the Last Trumpet; at the time there was a public outcry that such an undistinguished man – he was Governor of Gibraltar – should receive such a vast memorial.

Methodist Central Hall

In an attempt to avoid the Gothic of the abbey, and the Byzantine style of the Roman Catholic Westminster Cathedral (see p.81), the Methodists opted for the Edwardian beaux-arts style of architecture for their national headquarters, the **Methodist Central Hall** (℡020/7654 3826, ⊛www.c-h-w.com), which opened in 1912 to the northwest of the abbey on Storey's Gate. It's an unusual building for London, looking something like a giant casino, which is hardly appropriate given the Methodists' views on gambling and alcohol. The Great Hall was the venue for the inaugural meeting of the United Nations in 1946, and has been used over the years as much for political meetings as religious gatherings. If there's no event on, you're free to wander round the building and – after donning black gloves – to look at the Historic Roll, a fifty-volume list of the folk who donated a guinea towards the cost of the building. Free guided tours are also available, but if you want to climb up to the stone balustrade atop the reinforced concrete dome, you need to ring ahead (£3). In the cheap cafeteria in the basement (daily 10am–4.30pm), there are occasional exhibitions.

From Millbank to Victoria Street

The area to the south and west of Westminster Abbey, bounded by **Millbank** to the east and St James's Park to the north, is cut off from the noise and pollution which disfigure Parliament Square. The area's proximity to Parliament, and the various governmental ministries that have spread their departmental tentacles across it, mean that property prices are high. Nevertheless, it's a favourite place for MPs to have their London bases, and many of the restaurants and pubs in the area have "division bells", which ring eight minutes before the members are needed for a vote in the House of Commons. As for sights, the area boasts one of London's top public galleries, **Tate Britain**, the Baroque exterior of the church of **St John** and one of its most exotic churches, the Roman Catholic **Westminster Cathedral**.

Millbank

Running south from midway along the Victoria Tower Gardens, the busy riverside road of **Millbank** is dominated by the unprepossessing 1960s Millbank Tower, which reaches a height of 387ft. To the south of it, **Tate Britain** occupies the site of the old Millbank prison, built in the shape of a six-pointed star in 1816, according to the ideas of Jeremy Bentham (see p.152). The prisoners, mostly awaiting transportation to Australia, were kept under constant surveillance, forbidden to communicate with each other for the first half of their sentence and put to work making mailbags and shoes – for its day, an extremely liberal regime. Nevertheless, very little natural light penetrated the three miles of labyrinthine passages, and epidemics of cholera and scurvy were commonplace. The prison closed down in 1890.

The green-and-beige postmodernist ziggurat across the water is the indiscreet headquarters of the foreign arm of the British Secret Intelligence Service, **MI6**. Designed in the early 1990s by Terry Farrell at a cost of £260 million, plus a further £85 million for refurbishment and to build a tunnel under the river to Whitehall. Such conspicuousness comes at a price, however, and in 2000, the building, known as "Legoland" to those who work there, was hit by a rocket attack thought to have been the work of the dissident Irish republican terrorists, the Real IRA. **MI5** (ⓦ www.mi5.gov.uk), the UK's domestic "defensive security intelligence agency", occupies a much more anonymous building on the corner of Horseferry Road and Millbank.

Tate Britain

Originally founded in 1897 with money from Henry Tate, inventor of the sugar cube, **Tate Britain**, on Millbank, is dedicated exclusively to British art from 1500 to the present day. In addition, the gallery has a whole wing devoted to Turner, showcases contemporary British artists and continues to sponsor the **Turner Prize**, the country's most infamous modern-art award. Works by a shortlist of four artists, which can be in any medium, are displayed a month or two prior to the December prize-giving, and the competition is nothing if not controversial, since it tends to rake up all the usual arguments about the value and accessibility of modern conceptual art.

At the moment, the Tate follows a more or less conventional, chronological approach in its permanent displays. Even with over 25 rooms, what you see here is a tiny fraction of the Tate's collection, and from year to year the paintings are

Visiting Tate Britain

Tate Britain (☎020/7887 8000, ⊛www.tate.org.uk) is open daily 10am to 5.50pm and admission is free; the nearest tube is Pimlico. The traditional **entrance** is on Millbank and leads up the steps to a small information desk under the glass-domed rotunda, where you can rent one of the gallery's audioguides for £3. A larger entrance, and **disabled access**, is on nearby Atterbury Street, and leads down to information desks and the cloakroom. The Tate's Clore Gallery extension, which houses the Turner Bequest, can be reached via the modern art galleries, but it also has its own entrance, with its own information desk, to the right of the original gallery entrance.

re-hung. Down the centre of the building are the Duveen galleries, which are used to highlight a particular work; works from 1500 to 1900 occupy the rooms to the left (1–17); to the right are the twentieth-century galleries (18–34). What follows is a general rundown of the artists whose works are usually featured, plus some of the best works the Tate owns, many of which stay on show more or less permanently.

British art from 1500 to 1900

The collection begins with richly bejewelled portraits of the Elizabethan and Jacobean nobility, the most striking being the *Cholmondeley Sisters*, who were born on the same day, married on the same day and "brought to bed" on the same day, but are not now thought to be twins. Despite a smattering of English talent, such as **William Dobson**, whose *Endymion Porter* is usually on display in one of the first few rooms, the Stuarts relied heavily on imported talent such as van Dyck, Peter Lely – several of whose "lovelies" hang here – and Godfrey Kneller, who used to sign himself "Pictor Regis" such was the longevity of his royal patronage.

You can be guaranteed a good selection of works by the first great British artist, **William Hogarth**, including *O the Roast Beef of Old England*, a particularly vicious visual dig at the French, whom Hogarth loathed. **John Constable**'s most famous work, *Hay Wain*, hangs in the National Gallery, though the same location – his native Stour valley in Suffolk – features in many of his paintings. Another painter to look out for is **George Stubbs**, for whom "nature was and always is superior to art", and who portrayed animals – horses in particular – with a hitherto unknown anatomical precision.

Works by **Thomas Gainsborough** and **Joshua Reynolds** are sprinkled throughout the collection. Of the two, Reynolds, first president of the Royal Academy, was by far the more successful, elevating portraiture to pole position among the genres and flattering his sitters by surrounding them with classical trappings. Gainsborough was equally adept at flattery, but rarely used classical imagery, preferring instead more informal settings, and concentrating on colour and light. At the outset of his career, Gainsborough was also a landscape artist, often painting the Stour valley in Suffolk, where he – like Constable – was born.

One room in the gallery is regularly devoted to the visionary works of the poet **William Blake**, who was considered something of a freak by his contemporaries. He rejected oil painting in favour of watercolours, and often chose unusual subject matter which matched his highly personal form of Christianity. He earned a pittance producing illuminated books written and printed entirely by himself, and painted purely from his own visions: "Imagination is My World;

this world of Dross is beneath my notice", as he wrote. From illuminated books he moved on to do a series of twelve large colour prints on the myth of the Creation, now considered among his finest works, several examples of which are normally on display here. Blake's works were originally intended for room 16, which is decorated by Boris Anrep's floor mosaics, accompanied by quotes from Blake's poem *The Marriage of Heaven and Hell*.

The Tate is justifiably renowned for its vast collection of paintings by the **Pre-Raphaelites**, who formed their Brotherhood, the PRB, in 1848 in an attempt to re-create the humble, pre-humanist, pre-Renaissance world. The origins of the name lay in their aim to return to the method and spirit of artists who painted before Raphael. One of the first PRB paintings to be exhibited was **Rossetti**'s *Girlhood of Mary Virgin*, which was well received by the critics, but his *Annunciation*, with its emaciated heroin-chic Virgin, the model for which was his sister, caused outrage. So too did **Millais**'s *Christ in the House of His Parents*; Dickens described the figure of Jesus as "a hideous, wry-necked, blubbering, red-headed boy in a bed-gown". Millais also got into trouble for *Ophelia*, after his model, Elizabeth Siddal, caught a chill from lying in the bath to pose for the picture, prompting threats of a lawsuit from her father. Siddal later married Rossetti, and is also the model in his *Beata Beatrix*, painted posthumously, after she died of an opium overdose in 1862. Other classic PRB paintings in the collection are Arthur Hughes' *April Love*, John William Waterhouse's *The Lady of Shalott*, and Burne-Jones' *King Cophetua and the Beggar Maid*, all inspired by poems by Lord Tennyson.

Throughout Tate Britain, the term "British" is very loosely applied, so you'll find several works by the French artist, **James Tissot**, whose impressionist views of English life (and, in particular, English ladies in frilly frocks) were very popular. Lord Leighton's *Bath of Psyche* is a typical piece of Victorian soft porn, the likes of which made him by far the most successful artist of his generation. Other popular Victorian paintings to look out for include **John Singer Sargent**'s well-known *Carnation, Lily, Lily-Rose* and **Whistler**'s portrait of the precocious *Miss Cecily*, who looks as pissed off as she clearly felt after interminable sittings.

British art from 1900 to the present day

You'll find works by the same twentieth-century and contemporary British artists displayed in both Tate Modern (see pp.270–273) and Tate Britain, which makes it all the more hard to predict what works will be on show here. Sculptors Barbara Hepworth, **Jacob Epstein**, Giacometti and **Henry Moore**, and painters Walter Sickert, **Stanley Spencer** and Francis Bacon are just some of the better-known figures whose works crop up regularly. Vanessa Bell and Duncan Grant, from the Bloomsbury set, are represented, more often than not, and there's usually a good selection of work, too, by living artists such as **Lucien Freud**, R.B. Kitaj, **David Hockney** and Anselm Keifer. Towards the end, you're sure to come across the likes of Rachel Whiteread, Tracey Emin and even Anthony Gormley. Some less well-known artists to look out for include the Vorticist David Bomberg, who forged his own brand of Cubo-Futurism before World War I, and Ivon Hitchens, whose distinctive use of blocks of colour harks back to the late works of Cézanne.

The Clore Gallery: the Turner Bequest

J.M.W. Turner (1775–1851), possibly the greatest artist Britain has ever produced, bequeathed over a hundred oil paintings to the nation, and by the time his relatives had donated their share of the spoils, the total came to three hundred, plus a staggering nineteen thousand watercolours and drawings. Hence the world's largest Turner collection is housed here, in the adjoining Clore Gallery, a strangely childish building designed by James Stirling and opened in 1987.

Turner was an extremely successful artist, exhibiting his first watercolours in the window of his father's barbershop in Maiden Lane, Covent Garden, while still a boy, and at the Royal Academy when he was just 15, becoming an Academician in his twenties. Marine scenes appealed to Turner throughout his life, and one of the finest examples in the Tate is *The Shipwreck*. Natural cataclysms also feature strongly in Turner's works, either for their own sake, as in *Deluge*, or as part of a grand historical painting like *Snow Storm: Hannibal and His Army Crossing the Alps*. Turner's only known self-portrait (he had no pretensions as a portraitist and was rather ashamed of his ruddy complexion) is usually displayed, as are his personal belongings such as his pocket watercolour kit and fishing rod, and his toothless death mask.

The exact location of the paintings in the Turner galleries is difficult to predict, as the works are regularly re-hung to draw out different themes from the artist's life and work, and sometimes even appear in the main galleries. Nevertheless, it's worth seeking out Turner's late works, great smudges of colour that seem to anticipate Monet in their almost total abandonment of linear representation. *Snow Storm – Steam Boat off a Harbour's Mouth* is a classic late Turner, a symbolic battle between the steam age and nature's primeval force. It was criticized at the time as "soapsuds and whitewash", though Turner himself claimed he merely painted what he saw, having been "lashed to a mast" for four hours.

Smith Square to Vincent Square and beyond

Two blocks south of Westminster Abbey lies the fine early Georgian architectural ensemble of **Smith Square**, home to the Conservative Party headquarters and, more importantly, to the church of **St John** (Ⓦwww.sjss.org.uk), a rare slice of full-blown Baroque completed in 1728 by Thomas Archer. With its four distinctive towers topped by pineapples, it was dubbed the "footstool church" – the story being that Queen Anne, when asked how she would like the church to look, kicked over her footstool. Burnt in 1758 and gutted in 1941, it has since been restored as a concert venue, best known for its lunchtime recitals; if the church is not being used for rehearsals or performances, you can have a peek at the bare interior. There is also a good crypt restaurant called *The Footstool*. To complete the Georgian experience, approach the square from Lord North Street, to the north, an almost perfect early eighteenth-century terrace that was built at the same time as the church and square.

Before heading west to Westminster Cathedral, continue two more blocks south and pick up **Page Street**, flanked by Edwin Lutyens' chequerboard council flats, erected in the 1920s – walking between the six-storey blocks is a surreal experience. Page Street brings you, almost, to the playing fields of **Vincent Square**, where the boys from Westminster School play sports, and where the **Royal Horticultural Society** (Ⓦwww.rhs.org.uk) – best known as the organizers of the Chelsea Flower Show (see p.320) – have one of their two exhibition halls (the second is round the corner down Elverton Street). Flower shows are still held here regularly, supplemented by exhibitions on model railways, vintage cars, stamps and so on. To the north of the RHS halls, on Horseferry Road, stands Richard Rogers' **Channel 4** TV headquarters (Ⓦwww.channel4.com), a characteristic mass of shiny neo-industrial tubes, steel cables, external lifts and rust-red iron stanchions.

While you're in these parts, be sure to check out the remarkable High Victorian church of **St James-the-Less** (@www.sjtl.org), designed by George Edmund Street in the 1860s, which lies to the south of Vincent Square, on the far side of Vauxhall Bridge Road, amidst an unprepossessing 1960s housing estate. The red-and-black brickwork patterning on the exterior is exceptional, but is nothing to the red, black, cream and magenta tiling on the interior walls. The capitals of the church's rounded pillars hide biblical scenes amidst the acanthus-leaf foliage, and the font boasts similarly rich adornments, while above the chancel arch there's a wonderfully colourful fresco by G.F. Watts.

Westminster Cathedral

To the west of Vincent Square, just off Victoria Street, you'll find one of London's most surprising churches, the stripy neo-Byzantine concoction of the Roman Catholic **Westminster Cathedral** (Mon–Fri & Sun 7am–7pm, Sat 8am–7pm; free; ☏020/7798 9000, @www.rcdow.org.uk). Begun in 1895, it's one of the last and wildest monuments to the Victorian era: constructed from more than twelve million terracotta-coloured bricks, decorated with hoops of Portland stone, it culminates in a magnificent tapered campanile which rises to 274ft. From the small piazza to the northwest, you can admire the cathedral and the neighbouring mansions on Ambrosden Avenue, with their matching brickwork.

The **interior** is still only half-finished, and the domed ceiling of the nave – the widest in the country – remains an indistinct blackened mass, free of all decoration. To get an idea of what the place will look like when it's eventually completed, explore the series of **side chapels** – in particular the Holy Souls Chapel, the first one in the north aisle – whose rich, multicoloured decor makes use of over one hundred different marbles from around the world. Further down the north aisle is the Chapel of St George and the English Martyrs, where lies the enshrined body of St John Southworth, who was hanged, drawn and quartered as a traitor at Tyburn in 1654. Be sure, too, to check out the striking baldachino (the canopy above the High Altar), held up by mustard-yellow pillars, and the low-relief Stations of the Cross sculpted by the controversial Eric Gill during World War I. The view from the **campanile** is definitely worth taking in as well, especially as you don't even have to slog up flights of steps, but can simply take a lift (April–Nov daily 9.30am–12.30pm & 1–5pm; Dec–March Thurs–Sun 9.30am–12.30pm & 1–5pm; £2); the entrance is in the north aisle.

▲ Westminster Cathedral

North of Victoria Street

In the 1860s, Victorian planners ploughed their way through the slums of Westminster to create **Victoria Street**, a direct link between Parliament and the newly built Victoria train station. The bland 1960s blocks that now line the street give you some idea of what the rest of London might have looked like if the developers had got it all their own way in that iconoclastic decade. The best feature of the street these days is the way in which it perfectly frames the London Eye. One tower block that deserves a special mention, however, is the headquarters of the Metropolitan Police, **New Scotland Yard**, on Broadway opposite the Strutton Ground market. The revolving sign alone should be familiar to many from countless TV detective serials and news reports.

Further down Broadway, at no. 55, is the austere **Broadway House**, home to Transport for London and St James's Park tube station, and the tallest building in London when it was built in 1929 by Charles Holden. It gained a certain notoriety at the time for its nude statues by Jacob Epstein, in particular the boy figure in *Day*, whose penis had to be shortened to appease public opinion. Round the corner, standing on its own in Caxton Street, is the former **Blewcoat School** (Mon–Wed & Fri 10am–5.30pm, Thurs 10am–7pm), a lovely little red-brick building built in 1709 by a local brewer as a charity school for the poor and used as such until 1926. It now serves as a National Trust shop, though a statue of a blue-coated charity boy still stands above the doorway.

There's more delightful Queen Anne architecture just to the north in **Queen Anne's Gate** and **Old Queen Street**, two exquisite streets, originally separated by a wall, whose position is indicated by a weathered statue of Queen Anne. The Labour Party has its headquarters at no. 16 in Old Queen Street, but Queen Anne's Gate is the older and more interesting of the two, each of its doorways surmounted by a rustic wooden canopy with pendants in the shape of acorns. It's worth walking round the back of the houses on the north side to appreciate the procession of elegant bow windows that look out onto St James's Park (see p.83).

St James's

An exclusive little enclave sandwiched between St James's Park and Piccadilly, **ST JAMES'S** was laid out in the 1670s close to the royal seat of St James's Palace. Regal and aristocratic residences overlook nearby **Green Park** and the stately avenue of **The Mall**; gentlemen's clubs cluster along Pall Mall and St James's Street; and jacket-and-tie restaurants and expense-account shops line **Jermyn Street**. Hardly surprising, then, that most Londoners rarely stray into this area. Plenty of folk, however, frequent **St James's Park**, with large numbers heading for the Queen's chief residence, **Buckingham Palace**. If you're not in St James's for the shops, the best time to visit is on a Sunday, when the traffic is quieter, the nearby Mall is closed to traffic, and the royal chapels, plus the one accessible Palladian mansion, are open to the public.

St James's Park

St James's Park is the oldest of London's royal parks, having been drained and enclosed for hunting purposes by Henry VIII and opened to the public by Charles II, who used to stroll through the grounds with his mistresses, and even take a dip in the canal. By the eighteenth century, when some 6500 people had access to night keys for the gates, the park had become something of a byword for robbery and prostitution: diarist James Boswell was among those who went there specifically to be accosted "by several ladies of the town". The park's current landscaping was devised by Nash in the 1820s in an elegant style that established a blueprint for later Victorian city parks.

Today, the banks of the tree-lined lake are a favourite picnic spot for the civil servants of Whitehall (see p.60) and an inner-city reserve for wildfowl. James I's two crocodiles have left no descendants, alas, but the pelicans (which have resided here ever since a pair was presented to Charles II by the Russian ambassador) can still be seen at the eastern end of the lake, and there are exotic ducks, swans and geese aplenty. From the bridge across the lake there's a fine view over to Westminster and the jumble of domes and pinnacles along Whitehall – even the dull facade of **Buckingham Palace** looks majestic from here.

ST JAMES'S

EATING & DRINKING

ICA Bar	4
Inn the Park	5
The Red Lion (Crown Passage)	2
The Red Lion (Duke of York St)	1
Sports Café	3

ACCOMMODATION

The Stafford · A

▲ Spröth Magers Lee Gallery

PICCADILLY CIRCUS

PICCADILLY

BRICK ST

GREEN PARK

The Ritz

ARLINGTON ST

Spencer House

Green Park

QUEEN'S WALK

Lancaster House

CONSTITUTION HILL

Buckingham Palace

Buckingham Palace Gardens

Royal Mews

Queen's Gallery

BUCKINGHAM GATE

SPUR ROAD

Victoria Memorial

THE MALL

Clarence House

St James's Palace

Chapel Royal

Little St.

Cleveland Row

Marlborough Road

Queen Alexandra Memorial

Queen's Chapel

Marlborough House

Schomberg House

St James's Park

BIRDCAGE WALK

Guards' Chapel

Guards Museum

Wellington Barracks

BUCKINGHAM GATE

WILFRED STREET

PALACE STREET

STAG PLACE

BRESSENDEN PLACE

LOWER GROSVENOR PL.

Grosvenor Place ▲

PALL MALL

St James's Square

London Library

DUKE OF YORK ST

DUKE STREET

KING STREET

BURY STREET

Christie's

Carlton Club

Crown Pass.

JERMYN STREET

Fortnum & Mason

Dunhill

PICCADILLY ARCADE

PRINCE'S ARCADE

Hauser & Wirth Gallery

St James's

Bodlle's

White's

Brooks's

ST JAMES'S STREET

BLUEBELL YD.

JAMES'S PL.

ST JAMES'S PLACE

LOWER REGENT STREET

CHARLES II STREET

HAYMARKET

ROYAL OPERA ARCADE

ORANGE STREET

PANTON STREET

WHITCOMBE STREET

SUFFOLK ST.

SUFFOLK PL.

Guards' Crimean Memorial

Travellers' Club

Reform Club

Athenaeum

Institute of Directors

Duke of York's Column

Giro

ICA

WATERLOO PLACE

CARLTON HOUSE TERRACE

PALL MALL EAST

COCKSPUR STREET

TRAFALGAR SQUARE

Admiralty Arch

Horse Guards Parade

Guards' Memorial

HORSE GUARDS ROAD

WHITEHALL

DOWNING ST.

GREAT SCOTLAND YARD

NORTHUMBERLAND AVE.

WHITEHALL PLACE

GREAT SCOTLAND

AVENUE

NORTHUMBERLAND AVE.

0   100 yds

© crown copyright

The Mall

The tree-lined sweep of **The Mall** – London's nearest equivalent to a Parisian boulevard – is at its best on Sundays, when it's closed to traffic. It was laid out in the first decade of the twentieth century as a memorial to Queen Victoria, and runs along the northern edge of St James's Park. The bombastic **Admiralty Arch** was erected to mark the entrance at the Trafalgar Square end of The Mall, while at the other end stands the ludicrous **Victoria Memorial**, Edward VII's overblown 2300-ton marble tribute to his mother: *Motherhood* and *Justice* keep Victoria company around the plinth, which is topped by a gilded statue of Victory, while the six outlying allegorical groups in bronze confidently proclaim the great achievements of her reign. There has been a thoroughfare on the site of The Mall since the Restoration, though its most distinctive building is John Nash's Carlton House Terrace (see p.89), whose graceful cream-coloured Regency facade stretches away into the distance from Admiralty Arch. Among other things, it serves as the unlikely home of the **Institute of Contemporary Arts** or ICA (Mon noon–10.30pm, Tues–Sat noon–1am, Sun noon–11pm; day pass Mon–Fri £1.50, Sat & Sun £2.50; ℡020/7930 3647, ⌨www.ica.org.uk), London's official headquarters of the avant-garde, so to speak, which moved here in 1968 and has put on a programme of regularly provocative exhibitions, films, talks and performances ever since.

The Wellington Barracks, Guards' Chapel and Museum

Named after James I's aviary, which once stood here, Birdcage Walk runs along the south side of St James's Park, with the Neoclassical facade of the **Wellington Barracks**, built in 1833 and fronted by a parade ground, occupying more than half its length. Of the various buildings here, though, it's the modernist lines of the **Guards' Chapel** that come as the biggest surprise. Hit by a V1 rocket bomb on the morning of June 18, 1944 – killing 121 Sunday worshippers – the chapel was rebuilt in the 1960s. Inside, it's festooned with faded military flags, and retains the ornate Victorian apse, with Byzantine-style gilded mosaics, from the old chapel.

In a bunker opposite is the **Guards' Museum** (daily 10am–4pm; £2; ℡020/7414 3271), which displays the glorious scarlet-and-blue uniforms of the Queen's Foot Guards (see box on p.61). The museum also attempts to explain the Guards' complicated history, and gives a potted military history of the country since the Civil War. Among the exhibits here are a lock of Wellington's hair and a whole load of war booty, from Dervish prayer mats plundered from Sudan in 1898 to items taken from an Iraqi POW during the Gulf War. The museum also displays (and sells) an impressive array of toy soldiers.

Buckingham Palace

The graceless colossus of **Buckingham Palace**, popularly known as "Buck House", has served as the monarch's permanent London residence only since the accession of Victoria in 1837. It began its days in 1702 as the Duke of Buckingham's city residence, built on the site of a notorious brothel, and was sold by the duke's son to George III in 1762. The building was overhauled by Nash in the late 1820s for the Prince Regent, and again by Aston Webb in 1913 for George V, producing a palace that's about as bland as it's possible to be.

Visiting the palace

Until relatively recently, unless you were one of the select 30,000 invited to attend one of the Queen's three annual garden parties – the replacements for the society debutantes' "coming out" parties, which ceased to be royally sanctioned in 1958 – you had little chance of ever seeing inside Buckingham Palace. Since 1993, however, the hallowed portals have been grudgingly opened for two months of the year, and like all the royal residences, entrance fees have more or less doubled since then (Aug & Sept daily 9.30am–4.15pm; £13.50; advance booking on ☎020/7321 2233, ⊛www.royal. gov.uk). **Tickets** are sold online or from the marquee-like box office in Green Park; queues vary enormously, and there's a further wait until your allocated visiting time. While you're waiting, take a moment to admire the unusual **Canadian Memorial**, beside the ticket office. Erected in 1994, it's a beautiful abstract work consisting of a huge piece of dark-red granite from Nova Scotia, randomly scattered with maple-leaf patterning and washed over with water.

For ten months of the year there's little to do here, with the Queen in residence and the palace closed to visitors – not that this deters the crowds who mill around the railings all day, and gather in some force to watch the **Changing of the Guard** (see box on p.61), in which a detachment of the Queen's Foot Guards marches to appropriate martial music from St James's Palace (unless it rains, that is). If the Queen is at home, the Royal Standard flies from the roof of the palace; if not, the Union Jack flutters aloft.

The interior

Once inside, it's all a bit of an anticlimax, despite the voyeuristic pleasure of a glimpse behind those forbidding walls: of the palace's 660 rooms you get to see the twenty or so grandest ones, and as the Queen and her family decamp to Scotland every summer, there's little sign of life. The public entrance is via the **Ambassadors' Court** on Buckingham Palace Road, which lets you into the enormous **Quadrangle**, from where you can see the Nash portico, built in warm Bath stone, that looked over St James's Park until it was closed off by Queen Victoria.

Through the courtyard, you hit the **Grand Hall**, decorated like some gloomy hotel lobby, from where Nash's rather splendid winding, curlicued **Grand Staircase**, with its floral gilt-bronze balustrade and white plaster friezes, leads past a range of very fine royal portraits, all beautifully lit by Nash's glass dome. Beyond, the small Guard Room leads into the **Green Drawing Room**, a blaze of unusually bright green silk walls, framed by lattice-patterned pilasters, and a heavily gilded coved ceiling. It was here that the Raphael Cartoons used to hang, until they were permanently loaned to the V&A (see p.303). The scarlet and gold **Throne Room** features a Neoclassical plaster frieze in the style of the Elgin Marbles, depicting the Wars of the Roses. The thrones themselves are disappointingly un-regal – just two pink his 'n' hers chairs initialled ER and P – whereas George IV's outrageous sphinx-style chariot seats, nearby, look more the part.

Nash originally designed a spectacular hammerbeam ceiling for the **Picture Gallery**, which stretches right down the centre of the palace. Unfortunately, it leaked and was eventually replaced in 1914 by a rather dull glazed ceiling. Still, the paintings on show here are excellent and include several van Dycks, two Rembrandts, two Canalettos, a Poussin, a de Hooch and a wonderful Vermeer. Further on, in the East Gallery, check the cherub-fest in the grisaille frieze, before heading into the palace's rather overwrought **Ballroom**. It's here that the

Queen holds her State Banquets, where the annual Diplomatic Reception takes place, and where folk receive their honours and knighthoods.

Having passed through several smaller rooms, you eventually reach the **State Dining Room**, whose heavily gilded ceiling, with its three saucer domes, is typical of the suite of rooms that overlook the palace garden. Next door lies Nash's not very blue, but incredibly gold, **Blue Drawing Room**, lined with flock wallpaper interspersed with thirty fake onyx columns. The room contains one of George IV's most prized possessions, the "Table of the Grand Commanders", originally made for Napoleon, whose trompe l'oeil Sèvres porcelain top features cameo-like portraits of the military commanders of antiquity.

Beyond the domed Music Room with its enormous semicircular bow window and impressive parquet floor, the **White Drawing Room** features yet another frothy gold and white Nash ceiling and a superb Edwardian portrait of

The Royal Family

Tourists may still flock to see London's royal palaces, but the British public have become more critical of the huge tax bill that goes to support the **Royal Family** (Ⓦwww.royal.gov.uk) in the style to which they are accustomed. This creeping republicanism (Ⓦwww.throneout.com) can be traced back to 1992, which the Queen herself, in one of her few memorable Christmas Day speeches, accurately described as her *annus horribilis* ("One's Bum Year", as the *Sun* newspaper headline pithily put it). This was the year that saw the marriage break-ups of Charles and Diana, and Andrew and Fergie, and the second marriage of divorcée Princess Anne.

Matters came to a head over who should pay the estimated £50 million cost of repairs after the **fire at Windsor Castle** (see p.427). Misjudging the public mood, the Conservative government immediately offered taxpayers' money to foot the entire bill. After a furore, it was agreed that at least some of the cost would be raised by opening up Buckingham Palace to the public for the first time (and by cranking up the admission charges on the rest of London's royal palaces). In addition, the Queen also offered to reduce the number of royals paid out of the Civil List, and, for the first time in her life, pay taxes on her personal fortune.

Estimates of the **Queen's wealth** range from a modest £50 million to £6.5 billion. Whatever the truth, she's certainly not hard up, and public subsidy of the richest woman in the world doesn't stop at the Civil List, as millions more are spent by government departments on luxuries such as the Royal Squadron (for air travel) and the Royal Train (cost estimated at an average of £30,000 per trip), not to mention the upkeep of the palaces. Given the mounting public resentment against the Royal Family, it was hardly surprising that public opinion tended to side with Princess Diana rather than Prince Charles during their acrimonious divorce proceedings. Diana's tragic death, in 1997, rid the Royal Family of one of its most vociferous critics.

The Queen's **Golden Jubilee** Year in 2002 was a rare PR success, but there have been plenty of subsequent royal gaffs to keep the tabloids and republicans happy. When the Queen intervened and caused the collapse of the trial of the butler Paul Burrell, accused of stealing Diana's personal possessions, the revelations about the inner workings of the royal household, the offloading of royal gifts and an alleged homosexual rape, saw the palace press officers working overtime to try and minimize the damage. Since then, we've had Princess Anne's conviction for "being in charge of a dog that was dangerously out of control", Prince Harry's choice of an SS uniform as fancy dress for a friend's birthday party, and, of course, the civil wedding of the two divorcés, Charles and Camilla, in Windsor's modest town hall. Yet despite the Royal Family's drop in popularity over the last couple of decades, none of the mainstream political parties currently advocates scrapping the monarchy. The royal soap opera looks safe to run for many years to come.

Queen Alexandra. The White Drawing Room is also the incongruous setting for an annual royal prank: when hosting the reception for the diplomatic corps, the Queen and family emerge from a secret door behind a mirror to greet the ambassadors – nobody seems clear why. Before you leave the palace, be sure to check out the Canova sculptures: *Mars and Venus* at the bottom of the Ministers' Staircase, and the pornographic *Fountain Nymph with Putto* in the Marble Hall. You exit via the palace gardens, the city's largest private gardens, and are finally ejected onto Grosvenor Place.

Queen's Gallery

A Doric portico on the south side of the palace forms the entrance to the **Queen's Gallery** (daily 10am–5.30pm; £7.50; ☏020/7766 7301, ⊛www .royal.gov.uk). The gallery is three times the size it once was (which actually isn't saying much), and puts on temporary exhibitions drawn from the Royal Collection, which includes paintings by Michelangelo, Raphael, Holbein, Reynolds, Gainsborough, Vermeer, van Dyck, Rubens, Rembrandt and Canaletto, as well as the world's largest collection of Leonardo drawings, the odd Fabergé egg and heaps of Sèvres china. The Queen holds the Royal Collection, which is three times larger than the National Gallery, "in trust for her successors and the nation" – note the word order. However, with over 7000 works spread over the numerous royal palaces, the Queen's Gallery, and other museums and galleries around the country, you'd have to pay a king's ransom to see the lot.

Royal Mews

There's more pageantry on show at the **Royal Mews** (March–July & Oct daily except Fri 11am–4pm; Aug & Sept Mon–Sat 10am–5pm; £6; ☏020/7321 2233, ⊛www.royal.gov.uk), further south on Buckingham Palace Road, built by Nash in the 1820s after the old mews were demolished to make way for Trafalgar Square. The horses – or at least their backsides – can be viewed in their luxury stables, along with an exhibition of equine accoutrements, but it's the royal carriages, lined up under a glass canopy in the courtyard, that are the main attraction. The most ornate is the Gold State Coach, made for George III in 1762, smothered in 22-carat gilding, panel paintings by Cipriani, and weighing four tons, its axles supporting four life-size Tritons blowing conches. Eight horses are needed to pull it and the whole experience apparently made Queen Victoria feel quite sick; since then it has only been used for coronations and jubilees. The mews also house the Royal Family's fleet of five Rolls Royce Phantoms and three Daimlers, none of which is obliged to carry numberplates.

Lower Regent Street and Waterloo Place

Lower Regent Street, at the northeastern edge of St James's, was the first stage in John Nash's ambitious plan to link George IV's magnificent Carlton House with Regent's Park (see p.340), though few of today's houses date from that period. Like so many of Nash's grandiose schemes, it never quite came to fruition, as George IV, soon after ascending the throne, decided that Carlton House – the most expensive palace ever to have been built in London – wasn't quite luxurious enough, and had it pulled down. Its Corinthian columns now support the main portico of the National Gallery.

Instead, Lower Regent Street opens into **Waterloo Place**, which Nash was able to extend beyond Pall Mall once Carlton House had been demolished. At the centre of the square stands the **Guards' Crimean Memorial**, fashioned from captured Russian cannons, and commemorating the 2162 Foot Guards who died during the Crimean War – the horrors of battle were witnessed by Florence Nightingale, whose statue graces one of the monument's pedestals, and who has her own museum on the South Bank (see p.264).

Having dodged the traffic hurtling down Pall Mall and cutting the square in two, you come face to face with the two grandest gentlemen's clubs in St James's (see box overleaf): the former **United Services Club** (now the Institute of Directors), to the east, and the **Athenaeum**, to the west. Their almost identical Neoclassical designs are the work of Nash's protégé Decimus Burton: the better-looking is the Athenaeum, its portico sporting a garish gilded statue of the goddess Athena and, above, a Wedgwood-type frieze inspired by the Elgin Marbles, which had just arrived in London from Athens. The Duke of Wellington was a regular at the United Services Club, over the road, and the horse blocks – confusingly positioned outside the Athenaeum – were designed so the duke could mount his steed more easily.

Appropriately enough, that eminently clubbable man, Edward VII – the "Gentleman of Europe", as he was known – sits permanently on his horse between the two clubs, while more statuary hides behind the railings of Waterloo Gardens, including one of Captain Scott, sculpted by the widow he left behind after failing to complete the return journey from the South Pole. Beyond, overlooking St James's Park, is the "Grand Old" **Duke of York's Column**, erected in 1833, ten years before Nelson's more famous one, and paid for by stopping one day's wages of every soldier in the army that he marched "up the hill and down again", in the famous nursery rhyme.

Having pulled his old palace down, George IV had Nash build **Carlton House Terrace**; the monumental facade now looks out onto St James's Park, but the rear is built on a much more human scale. It has long been a sought-after address: the **Royal Society** (Ⓦwww.royalsoc.ac.uk), the scientific body set up by Wren, among others, occupies no. 6; no. 4, by the exquisitely tranquil Carlton Gardens, was given to de Gaulle for the headquarters of the Free French during the last world war; while nos. 7–9, by the Duke of York steps, were the site of the German embassy from 1849 (when it was the Prussian legation) until the outbreak of World War II. Albert Speer redesigned the interior, but the only external reminder of this period is a tiny grave for *ein treuer Begleiter* (a true friend) behind the railings near the column – it holds the remains of **Giro**, the Nazi ambassador's pet Alsatian, accidentally electrocuted in February 1934.

Pall Mall and around

Running west from Trafalgar Square across Waterloo Place, **Pall Mall** is renowned for its gentlemen's clubs, whose restrained Italianate and Neoclassical facades, fronted by cast-iron torches, still punctuate the street. It gets its bizarre name from the game of *pallo a maglio* (ball to mallet) – something like modern croquet – popularized by Charles II and played here and on The Mall. Crowds gathered here in 1807 when it became London's first gas-lit street – the original closely spaced lampposts (erected to reduce the opportunities for crime and prostitution) are still standing – but the heavy traffic that now pounds down it makes Pall Mall no fun to explore.

Instead, once you've passed Waterloo Place, head one block north to **St James's Square**, which had considerable cachet as a fashionable address when it was first laid out in the 1670s. Around the time of George III's birth at no. 31 in 1738, the square could boast no fewer than six dukes and seven earls, and

The gentlemen's clubs

The **gentlemen's clubs** of Pall Mall and St James's Street remain the final bastions of the male chauvinism and public-school snobbery for which England is famous. Their origins lie in the coffee- and chocolate-houses of the eighteenth century, though the majority were founded in the post-Napoleonic peace of the early nineteenth century by those who yearned for the life of the all-male officers' mess; drinking, whoring and gambling were the major features of early club life. **White's** – the oldest of the lot, and with a list of members that still includes numerous royals (Prince Charles held his (first) stag party here), prime ministers and admirals – on St James's Street, was renowned for its high gambling stakes, as was nearby **Brooks's**. Bets were wagered over the most trivial of things to relieve the boredom – "a thousand meadows and cornfields were staked at every throw" – and in 1755 one MP, Sir John Bland, shot himself after losing £32,000 in one night.

In their day, the clubs were also the battleground of sartorial elegance, particularly **Boodle's**, another St James's Street haunt, where the dandy-in-chief Beau Brummell set the fashion trends for the London upper class and provided endless fuel for gossip. It was said that Brummell's greatest achievement in life was his starched neckcloth, and that the Prince Regent himself wept openly when Brummell criticized the line of his cravat or the cut of his coat. More serious political disputes were played out in clubland, too. The **Reform Club** on Pall Mall, from which Phileas Fogg set off on his "Around the World in Eighty Days" trip, was the gathering place of the liberals behind the 1832 Reform Act, and remains one of the more "progressive" – it's one of the few to admit women as members. The Tories, led by Wellington, countered by starting up the **Carlton Club** for those opposed to the Act – it's still the leading Conservative club, and still men-only (Mrs Thatcher had to be made a special member). To become a member of the **Travellers' Club**, founded in 1819 at 106 Pall Mall, you had to prove you'd travelled 500 miles from London; this is the only club where there's even the remotest possibility of joining a guided tour; phone ☎020/7930 8688 for more details.

over the decades it has maintained its exclusive air: no. 10 was occupied in turn by prime ministers Pitt the Elder, Lord Derby and Gladstone; at no. 16 you'll find the silliest-sounding gentlemen's club, the East India, Devonshire, Sports and Public Schools Club; no. 4 was the home of Nancy Astor, the first woman MP to sit in the House of Commons, in 1919; while no. 31 was where Eisenhower formed the first Allied HQ. The narrowest house on the square (no. 14) is home to the **London Library**, the oldest and grandest private library in the country, founded in 1841 by Thomas Carlyle, who got sick of waiting up to two hours for books to be retrieved from the British Library shelves only to find he couldn't borrow them (he used to steal them instead). It's open only to fee-paying members.

The square is no longer residential and, architecturally, nor is it quite the period piece it once was, but its proportions remain intact, as do the central **gardens**, which feature an equestrian statue of William III, depicted tripping over on the molehill that killed him at Hampton Court. In the northeastern corner, across the road from the Astors' pad, there's a small memorial marking the spot where police officer Yvonne Fletcher was shot dead in 1984 during a raid on what was then the Libyan People's Bureau, at no. 5, by Libyan dissidents. It has a quiet dignity that's lacking in most of London's public statuary to the great and (rarely) good.

Two blocks west of the square, down King Street, are the headquarters of **Christie's** (⊛www.christies.com), the auction house originally founded on Pall Mall in 1767, and specializing in fine art; you can visit the gallery for free during viewing times (see p.101). Back on Pall Mall, the unusual seventeenth-century facade of **Schomberg House**, rebuilt in the 1950s, is one of the few to stand out, thanks to its Dutch-style red brickwork and elongated caryatids; it was here in the 1780s that James Graham ran his Temple of Health and Hymen, where couples having trouble conceiving could try their luck in the "grand celestial bed". Next door, at no. 79, Charles II housed Nell Gwynne, so that the two of them could chat over the garden wall, which once backed onto the grounds of St James's Palace. It was from one of the windows overlooking the garden that Nell is alleged to have dangled her 6-year-old, threatening to drop him if Charles didn't acknowledge paternity and give the boy a title, at which Charles yelled out "save the Earl of Burford!"; another, more tabloid-style version of the story alleges that Charles was persuaded only after overhearing Nell saying "Come here, you little bastard", then excusing herself on the grounds that she had no other name by which to call him.

St James's Palace

At the western end of Pall Mall stands **St James's Palace**, built on the site of a lepers' hospital which Henry VIII bought and demolished in 1532. It was here that Charles I chose to sleep the night before his execution, so as not to have to listen to his scaffold being erected, and when Whitehall Palace burnt down in 1698, St James's became the principal royal residence. In keeping with tradition, an ambassador to the UK is still known as "Ambassador to the Court of St James", even though the court moved down the road to Buckingham Palace when Queen Victoria came to the throne. The main red-brick gate-tower, which looks out onto St James's Street, is the most conspicuous reminder of Tudor times, but the rest of the rambling, crenellated complex is the result of Nash's restoration and remodelling, and now provides a home for the Duke and Duchess of Kent, Princess Alexandra, as well as offices for various other royals and the Lord Chamberlain.

St James's Palace is off limits to the public, with the exception of the **Chapel Royal**, which is open for services only (Oct–Good Friday Sun 8.30am & 11.15am; ⓦwww.royal.gov.uk); access is from the Cleveland Row end of the palace. Charles I took Holy Communion in the Chapel Royal on the morning of his execution, and here, too, the marriages of William and Mary, George III and Queen Charlotte, Victoria and Albert, and George V and Queen Mary, took place. One of the few remaining sections of Henry VIII's palace, it was redecorated in the 1830s, though the gilded strap-work ceiling matches the Tudor original erected to commemorate the brief marriage of Henry and Anne of Cleves (and thought to have been the work of Hans Holbein). The chapel's musical pedigree is impressive, with Tallis, Byrd, Gibbons and Purcell all having worked here as organists. Purcell even had rooms in the palace, which the poet Dryden used to use in order to hide from his creditors.

Clarence House

John Nash was also responsible for **Clarence House** (Aug to mid-Oct daily 9.30am–6pm; £6; ☎020/7766 7303, ⓦwww.royal.gov.uk), connected to the southwest wing of St James's Palace and barely visible from Cleveland Row. Built for William IV when he was the Duke of Clarence, it was the royal residence for the seven years of his reign, and was home to the Queen Mother, widow of George VI, who died in 2002 at the age of 101. It now serves as the official London home of Charles and Camilla (ⓦwww.princeofwales.gov.uk)

and a handful of rooms can be visited over the summer when the happy couple are usually in Scotland. Visits are by guided tour only, and the rooms are pretty unremarkable, so apart from a peek behind the scenes in a working royal palace, or a few mementoes of the Queen Mum, the main draw is the selection of twentieth-century British paintings on display by the likes of Walter Sickert and Augustus John. Tours are very popular, so it's best to book ahead.

The Queen's Chapel and Marlborough House

On the other side of Marlborough Road is the **Queen's Chapel**, once part of St James's Palace but now in the grounds of Marlborough House, and open only for services (Easter–July Sun 8.30am & 11.15am). A perfectly proportioned classical church, it was designed by Inigo Jones for the Infanta of Spain, the intended child bride of Charles I, and later completed for his French wife, Henrietta Maria, who was also a practising Catholic. A little further down Marlborough Road, and looking thoroughly forgotten, is the glorious Art Nouveau memorial to **Queen Alexandra** (wife of Edward VII), the last work of Alfred Gilbert (of Eros fame; see p.95), comprising a bronze fountain crammed with allegorical figures and flanked by robust lampposts.

Marlborough House (closed to the public) is hidden from Marlborough Road by a high, spiked, brick wall, and is only partly visible from The Mall. Queen Anne sacrificed half her garden in granting this land to her lover, Sarah Jennings, Duchess of Marlborough, in 1709. The duchess in turn told Wren to design her a "strong, plain and convenient" palace, only to sack him later and finish the plans off herself. The highlight of the interior is the Blenheim Saloon, with its frescoes depicting the first duke's eponymous victory, along with ceiling paintings by Gentileschi transferred from the Queen's House in Greenwich. The royals took over in 1817, though the last one to live here was Queen Mary, wife of George V, who died in 1953 and is commemorated by a plaque. Since 1965, the palace has been the headquarters of the Commonwealth – for a virtual tour, visit their website (ⓦwww.thecommonwealth.org).

▲ Queen Alexandra Memorial

Jermyn Street

Jermyn Street, which runs parallel with Piccadilly, has been, along with Savile Row in Mayfair, the spiritual home of English gentlemen's fashion since the advent of the clubs (see box on p.90). Its window displays and wooden-panelled interiors still evoke an age when mass consumerism was unthinkable, and when it was considered that gentlemen "should either be a work of art or wear a work of art", in the words of Oscar Wilde. The kind of Englishmen for whom these shops originally catered are now a dying breed, and these days Americans and Japanese tend to make up a large proportion of the customers.

The endurance of the cigar as a status symbol is celebrated at Davidoff, on the corner of St James's and Jermyn streets, with nothing so vulgar as a cigarette in the window. Further down Jermyn Street, on the corner with Bury Street, is Turnbull & Asser, who have placed shirts on the backs of VIPs from David Bowie to Ronald Reagan, while *Wilton's*, at no. 55, is a truly Edwardian English restaurant where ties and jackets are required Monday to Saturday. (Men can leave the tie at home on a Sunday.)

Pipe smokers are a dying breed, but they can find solace at the **Dunhill shop** (Wwww.whitespot.co.uk) on the corner of Jermyn and Duke streets, which has an enormous range of pipes (and cigars) for sale on the first floor, and a small **museum** on the ground floor. The best accessories on display are those made by Dunhill Motorities, gadget suppliers to Rolls Royce, whose slogan was "the smartness of the car is in the equipment". There are hip flasks disguised as books and "Bobby Finders" for detecting police cars, but sadly no sign of Mr Dunhill's greatest cigarette inventions: the in-car hookah and the motorist's pipe with a windscreen for open-top toking.

Antiquated epithets are part of the street's quaint appeal: Taylor, a barber's at no. 74, still describe themselves as "Court hairdressers", Foster & Son, a shoe shop at no. 85, style themselves as "Bootmakers since 1840", while Geo. F. Trumper, at no. 20, is billed as a "Gentlemen's Perfumer". Floris, at no. 89, covers up the Royal Family's body odour with its ever-so-English fragrances, and Paxton & Whitfield, at no. 93, boasts an unrivalled selection of English and foreign cheeses. Lastly, at no. 21a, there's Bates the hatters, not quite as famous as Lock & Co at 6 St James's St, where the bowler hat was invented in 1850, but more memorable thanks to Binks, the stray cat which entered the shop in 1921 and never left, having been stuffed and displayed in a glass cabinet inside the shop, sporting a cigar and top hat. Notably, too, the shop has never had anything so vulgar as a sale.

Green Park

To the west of St James's Palace lies **Green Park**, laid out on the burial ground of the old lepers' hospital by Henry VIII; it was left more or less flowerless – hence its name. Nowadays, apart from the springtime appearance of great swaths of daffodils and crocuses, it remains a beautifully peaceful grassy spot, dominated by graceful London plane trees and, in summer, by stripy deckchairs (for which there's a small charge). In its time, however, it was a popular place for duels (banned from neighbouring St James's Park), ballooning and fireworks displays. Of the last, the most famous was the one immortalized by Handel's *Music for the Royal Fireworks*, performed here on April 27, 1749 to celebrate the Peace of Aix-la-Chapelle, which ended the War of the Austrian Succession – over 10,000 fireworks were let off, setting fire to the custom-built Temple of Peace and causing three fatalities. The music was a great success, however.

Along the east side of the park runs the wide, pedestrian-only **Queen's Walk**, laid out for Queen Caroline, wife of George II, who had a little pavilion built nearby. At its southern end, there's a good view of **Lancaster House** (closed to the public), a grand Neoclassical palace built in rich Bath stone in the 1820s by Benjamin Wyatt, and used for government receptions and conferences since

1913. It was here that the end of white rule in Southern Rhodesia was negotiated in the late 1970s.

Just up from Lancaster House a sign in the garden announces Princess Diana's ancestral home, **Spencer House** (Feb–July & Sept–Dec Sun 10.30am–5.45pm; £9, no under-10s; ☎020/7499 8620, ⊛www.spencerhouse.co.uk), one of London's finest Palladian mansions. Erected in the 1750s, its best-looking facade looks out over Queen's Walk onto Green Park, though access is from St James's Place. Inside, tour guides take you through nine of the state rooms, returned to something like their original condition by current owners, the Rothschilds. The Great Room features a stunning coved and coffered ceiling in green, white and gold, while the adjacent Painted Room is a feast of Neoclassicism, decorated with murals in the "Pompeian manner". The most outrageous decor, though, is to be found in Lord Spencer's Room, with its astonishing gilded palm-tree columns. For another £3.50, you can take a tour of the not-very-large restored gardens.

Mayfair

A long with neighbouring St James's and Marylebone, **Mayfair** emerged in the eighteenth century as one of London's first real residential suburbs. Sheep and cattle were driven off the land by the area's big landowners (the largest of whom were, and still are, the Grosvenors) as small farms made way for London's first major planned development: a web of brick-and-stucco terraces and grid-plan streets feeding into grand, formal squares, with mews and stables round the back. Mayfair quickly began to attract aristocratic London away from hitherto fashionable Covent Garden and Soho, and set the westward trend for middle-class migration, which gradually extended to Kensington and Chelsea. (The Queen was born at 17 Bruton St, and then lived at 145 Piccadilly until 1936.)

Nowadays, offices, embassies and lavish hotels outnumber aristocratic pieds-à-terre, yet the social cachet of Mayfair's luxury apartments and mews houses has remained much the same. When London's wealthier consumers moved west, so too did a large section of the city's commerce, particularly the more upmarket shops, which are still a feature of the area. The borders of Mayfair, in particular, remain among London's **prime shopping streets**, catering to all classes and purses. It's here that Londoners mean when they talk of "going shopping up the West End": to **Piccadilly** and **Regent Street**, and to **Bond Street** and **Oxford Street**. Piccadilly was already a fashionable place to shop by the eighteenth century, as was Bond Street, which runs through Mayfair. Regent Street was created in 1812 and took a while to catch on, while Oxford Street, to the north, didn't really come into its own until early last century, though it now surpasses the lot for the sheer mass of people fighting their way down it.

Piccadilly Circus and around

Anonymous and congested it may be, but **Piccadilly Circus** is, for many Londoners, the nearest their city comes to having a centre. A much-altered product of Nash's grand 1812 **Regent Street** plan, and now a major traffic bottleneck, it's by no means a picturesque place, and is probably best seen at night, when the spread of illuminated signs (a feature since the Edwardian era) gives it a touch of Las Vegas dazzle, and when the human traffic flow is at its most frenetic.

As well as being the gateway to the West End, this is also prime tourist territory, thanks mostly to Piccadilly Circus's celebrated aluminium statue, popularly known as **Eros**. The fountain's archer is one of the city's top tourist attractions,

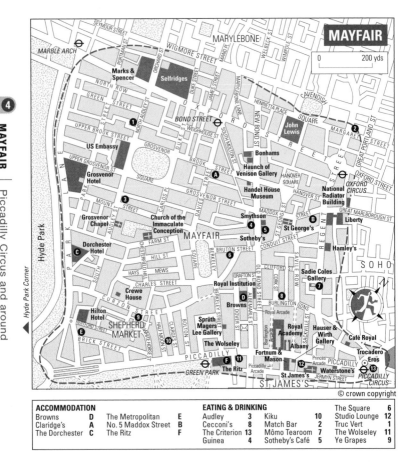

© crown copyright

ACCOMMODATION					EATING & DRINKING						
Browns	**D**	The Metropolitan	**E**		Audley	**3**	Kiku	**10**	The Square	**6**
Claridge's	**A**	No. 5 Maddox Street	**B**		Cecconi's	**8**	Match Bar	**2**	Studio Lounge	**12**
The Dorchester	**C**	The Ritz	**F**		The Criterion	**13**	Mômo Tearoom	**7**	Truc Vert	**1**
					Guinea	**4**	Sotheby's Café	**5**	The Wolseley	**11**
									Ye Grapes	**9**

a status that baffles all who live here – when it was first unveiled in 1893, it was so unpopular that the sculptor, Alfred Gilbert, lived in self-imposed exile for the next thirty years. Despite the bow and arrow, it's not the god of love at all but the *Angel of Christian Charity*, erected to commemorate the Earl of Shaftesbury, a Bible-thumping social reformer who campaigned against child labour.

Eros's plinth stands in front of the **Criterion**, one of London's more elegant theatres, with a sumptuous adjoining restaurant (see p.465). This Art Nouveau building, with its ceiling of glittering gold mosaics was, incredibly, covered over by plastic pizza-chain decor from the 1960s to the 1980s, but is now back to its former glory.

One block east of the Circus, the tacky **Trocadero** (daily 10am–1am; Ⓦwww .londontrocadero.com) stands on the site of a defunct nineteenth-century music hall. Over the past few decades, millions have been poured into this glorified amusement arcade, casino and multiplex cinema, in an unsuccessful attempt to find a winning formula.

Regent Street

Drawn up by John Nash in 1812 as both a luxury shopping street and a triumphal way between George IV's Carlton House and Regent's Park to the north, **Regent Street** was the city's first attempt at dealing with traffic congestion, and was also the first stab at the slum clearance and planned social segregation which would later be perfected by the Victorians. Several unsavoury neighbourhoods were wiped off the map during its construction, and the completed street acted as a barrier separating the disreputable, immigrant Soho from the bourgeois quarters of Mayfair, St James's and Marylebone.

Despite the subsequent destruction of much of Nash's work and its replacement in the 1920s by what one critic described as "neo-fascist Art Deco", it's still possible to admire the stately intentions of his original Regent Street plan, in particular the curve of the **Quadrant** which swerves north from Piccadilly Circus. Sadly the Victorians, who considered Nash's architecture monotonous, tore down the Quadrant's graceful colonnades in 1848 – shopkeepers claimed they obscured their window displays and encouraged prostitution.

Regent Street enjoyed eighty years as Bond Street's nearest rival, before an increase in the purchasing power of the city's middle classes brought the tone of the street "down" and ushered in several heavyweight stores catering for the masses. The only truly bourgeois survivor in the Quadrant itself is the **Café Royal**, at no. 68, focus of the beau monde from the 1890s to the outbreak of World War I, when Oscar Wilde and Aubrey Beardsley presided, along with Walter Sickert, Max Beerbohm, Augustus John and George Bernard Shaw; later, Edward VIII and George VI hung out there (in their days as princes), and in the 1920s, John Betjeman, Stephen Spender and Dylan Thomas were regulars. D. H. Lawrence threw a dinner party here in 1924 to try and persuade his friends to join him on his sojourn in New Mexico.

Of the big stores on the east side of the street, only a couple deserve mention: **Hamley's**, which claims to be the world's largest toy shop, and **Liberty**, the department store that popularized Arts and Crafts designs at the beginning of last century. The Liberty store is divided into two: the older part, which looks onto Regent Street, features a traditional, central roof-lit well, surrounded by wooden galleries carved from the timbers of two old naval battleships; an overhead walkway leads to the eye-catching mock-Tudor extension, added in the 1920s and stretching back along Great Marlborough Street as far as Carnaby Street (see p.124). It's remarkable to think that the striking Art Deco **National Radiator Building**, on the opposite side of Great Marlborough Street, with its sleek black granite facade and gilded "65", is virtually contemporary with Liberty's extension.

Piccadilly

Piccadilly apparently got its name from the ruffs or "pickadills" worn by the dandies who used to promenade here in the late seventeenth century. Despite its fashionable pedigree, it's no place for promenading in its current state, with three lanes of traffic careering down it nose to tail most of the day and night. Infinitely more pleasant places to window-shop are the **nineteenth-century arcades**, originally built to protect shoppers from the mud and horse dung on the streets, but now equally useful for escaping exhaust fumes.

Waterstone's to the Ritz

With the exception of the black modernist 1930s facade of **Waterstone's** flagship bookshop (originally built as Simpson's department store), there's nothing much to distract the eye along the south side of Piccadilly until you reach **St James's Church** (⊛www.st-james-piccadilly.org), Wren's favourite parish church (he built it himself). The church has rich historical associations – Pitt the Elder and William Blake were baptized here – and rich furnishings, with the reredos, organ-casing and font all by the master sculptor Grinling Gibbons. It's a traditional venue for big society weddings, but it also ministers to the homeless (the church's heated interior is an unofficial daytime refuge). In addition, to generate some extra income, St James's runs a daily craft market in the churchyard, and a café at the west end of the church; it also puts on top-class free lunchtime concerts.

Piccadilly may not be the shopping heaven it once was, but there are still several old firms here that proudly display their royal warrants. **Hatchard's Bookshop**, at no. 187, was founded in 1797, when it functioned as something like a cross between a gentlemen's club and a library, with benches outside for customers' servants and daily papers for the gentlemen inside to peruse. Today, Hatchard's is simply a branch of Waterstone's, elegant still, but with its old traditions marked most overtly by a large section on international royalty.

An even older institution, and a favourite with the twinset-and-pearls contingent, is **Fortnum & Mason** (⊛www.fortnumandmason.com), the food emporium at no. 181, which was established in the 1770s by Charles Fortnum, one of George III's footmen. Fortnum's intimate knowledge of the needs of a royal household, together with his partner Hugh Mason's previous work at nearby St James's Market (now defunct), helped make the shop an instant success. Over the main entrance, the figures of its founders bow to each other on the hour as the clock clanks out the Eton school anthem – a rather kitsch addition which dates only from 1964. The store is most famous for its picnic hampers, first introduced as "concentrated lunches" for hunting and shooting parties, and now *de rigueur* for Ascot, Glyndebourne, Henley and other society events. They are, of course, ludicrously priced, but the food hall (the upper floors are for clothes and accessories) has more affordable and individual treats to incite most visitors to open their wallets.

Further along Piccadilly, on the corner of Arlington Street, The **Wolseley** (⊛www.thewolseley.com) is a superb Art Deco building, originally built as a showroom for Wolseley cars in the 1920s. Now converted into a café (see p.454), the interior is still pretty much intact, with zigzag inlaid marble flooring, chinoiserie woodwork and giant red Japanese lacquer columns among the most striking features. Across St James's Street, with its best rooms overlooking Green Park, stands the **Ritz Hotel** (⊛www.theritzhotel.co.uk), a byword for decadence since it first wowed Edwardian society in 1906. The hotel's design, with its two-storey French-style mansard roof and long arcade, was based on the buildings of Paris's rue de Rivoli. For a prolonged look inside, you'll need to be in good appetite, be well dressed and book in advance for the famous afternoon tea in the hotel's *Palm Court* (see box on p.461).

Royal Academy

Across the road from Fortnum & Mason, the **Royal Academy of Arts** (daily 10am–6pm, Fri until 10pm; £5–8; ☏020/7300 8000, ⊛www.royalacademy.org .uk) occupies the enormous Burlington House, one of the few survivors from the ranks of aristocratic mansions that once lined the north side of Piccadilly. Rebuilding in the nineteenth century destroyed the original curved colonnades beyond the main gateway, but the complex has kept much of its Palladian *palazzo* design from the early eighteenth century. The academy itself was the country's first formal art school, founded in 1768 by a group of painters including Thomas Gainsborough and Joshua Reynolds. Reynolds went on to become the academy's first president, and his statue now stands in the courtyard, palette in hand ready to paint the cars hurtling down Piccadilly.

The academy's alumni range from J.M.W. Turner and John Constable to Elisabeth Frink, though the college has always had a conservative reputation for both for its teaching and its shows. More recently, the RA has made an attempt to update its image with the odd, deliberately controversial show, but the record-breaking crowds that flock to the regular exhibitions of impressionist paintings are more typical. Little has changed at the **Summer Exhibition**, too, which opens in June each year and runs until mid-August. It's an odd event: a stop on the social calendar of upper-middle-class England, who are catered for, as at Wimbledon and Ascot, by a Pimm's bar (Pimm's being the classic English summer cocktail). And yet the show itself is, more or less, egalitarian. Anyone can enter paintings in any style, and the lucky winners get hung, in rather close proximity, and sold. An air of gravitas is added by the RA "Academicians", who are allowed to display six of their own works – no matter how awful. The result is a bewildering display, which gets annually panned by highbrow critics.

As well as hosting exhibitions, the RA has a small selection of works from its own collection on **permanent display** in the newly restored white and gold John Madejski Fine Rooms (Tues–Fri 1–4.30pm, Sat & Sun 10am–6pm; free; free guided tours Tues–Fri 1pm). Highlights include a Rembrandtesque self-portrait by Reynolds, plus works by the likes of John Constable, Stanley Spencer and David Hockney. To see the gallery's most valuable asset, Michelangelo's marble relief, the *Taddei Tondo*, head for the glass atrium of Norman Foster's Sackler Galleries, at the back of the building.

Albany and Piccadilly's arcades

Another palatial Piccadilly residence which has avoided redevelopment is **Albany**, a plain, H-shaped Georgian mansion, designed by William Chambers, neatly recessed behind its own iron railings and courtyard to the east of the Royal Academy. Originally built in 1770 for Lord Melbourne, it was divided in 1802 into a series of self-contained bachelor "sets" for members of the nearby gentlemen's clubs too drunk to make it

▲ Burlington Arcade

> ## Monopoly
>
> Although **Monopoly** was invented during the Depression by an American, Charles Darrow, it was the British who really took to the game, and the UK version is now considered the classic. In 1936, to choose appropriate streets and stations for the game, the company director of Waddington's in Leeds sent his secretary, Marjorie Phillips, on a day-trip to London. She came up with an odd assortment, ranging from the bottom-ranking Old Kent Road (still as tatty as ever) to an obscure dead-end street in the West End (Vine Street), and chose only northern train stations. All the properties have gone up in value since the board's inception (six zeros need to be added to most), but Mayfair and Park Lane (its western border), the most expensive properties on the Monopoly board, are still aspirational addresses. The latest UK version – its first revamp in seventy years – includes Canary Wharf and the London Eye.

home. Only those with no connections with trade were permitted to live here, and over the years they have been occupied by such literary figures as Lord Byron, J.B. Priestley, Aldous Huxley and Graham Greene; women have only relatively recently been allowed to lease flats at Albany in their own right.

Along the other side of the Royal Academy runs the **Burlington Arcade**, built in 1819 for Lord Cavendish, then owner of Burlington House, to prevent commoners throwing rubbish into his garden. Today, it's London's longest and most expensive nineteenth-century arcade, lined with mahogany-fronted jewellers, gentlemen's outfitters and the like. Upholding Regency decorum, it's still illegal to whistle, sing, hum, hurry or carry large packages or open umbrellas on this small stretch, and the arcade's beadles (known as Burlington Berties), in their Edwardian frock coats and gold-braided top hats, take the prevention of such criminality very seriously.

Neither of Piccadilly's other two arcades can hold a torch to the Burlington, though they are still worth exploring if only to marvel at the strange mixture of shops. Of the two, the **Piccadilly Arcade** is the finer, an Edwardian extension to the Burlington on the south side of Piccadilly, its squeaky-clean bow windows displaying, among other items, Wedgwood porcelain, Russian icons, model soldiers and Eton collars. The **Princes Arcade**, to the east, exudes a more discreet Neoclassical elegance and contains Prestat (@www.prestat.co.uk), purveyors of hand-made, hand-packed chocolates to the Queen.

North of Piccadilly

Bond Street runs more or less parallel to Regent Street, extending north from Piccadilly all the way to Oxford Street. It is, in fact, two streets rolled into one: the southern half, laid out in the 1680s, is known as Old Bond Street; its northern extension, which followed less than fifty years later, is known as New Bond Street. In contrast to their international rivals, rue de Rivoli or Fifth Avenue, both Bond streets are pretty unassuming architecturally – a mixture of modest Georgian and Victorian town-houses – but the shops that line them are among the flashiest in London. With so many retailers and offices around Piccadilly and Bond Street, Mayfair's residential heart has been pushed westwards into the backstreets north of Piccadilly. This area is dominated by Mayfair's two most grandiose squares, **Berkeley** and **Grosvenor**, named after the district's two big private landowners. Planned as purely residential, both have suffered over the years, and have nothing like the homogeneity of the Bloomsbury squares (see p.145). Nevertheless, they remain impressive urban spaces, and their social lustre has been little tarnished by the encroachment of commerce or the proximity of the masses pouring down Oxford Street.

Bond Street and around

Unlike its overtly masculine counterpart, Jermyn Street (see p.92), **Bond Street** caters for both sexes, and although it has its fair share of old-established names, it's also home to flagship branches of all the leading multinational **designer clothes** outlets like Prada, Versace, Donna Karan, Chanel and so on. This designer madness also spills over into **Conduit Street**, home to Issey Miyake, Mandarina Duck and Moschino, and neighbouring Dover Street, for Comme des Garçons.

In addition to fashion, Bond Street is renowned for its **auction houses** and for its **fine art galleries**. Visiting the auction houses is free and can be fun (see box below), but even if you don't venture in, take a look at the doorway of Sotheby's at 34–35 New Bond St, topped by an Egyptian statue dating from 1600 BC and thus the oldest outdoor sculpture in London. Bond Street's art galleries are actually outnumbered by those on neighbouring **Cork Street**. The main difference between the two locations is that the Bond Street dealers are basically heirloom offloaders, whereas Cork Street galleries sell largely contemporary art. Both have impeccably presented and somewhat intimidating staff, but if you're interested, walk in (or ring the bell to be let in) and look around. They're only shops, after all.

Auction houses

A very Mayfair-style entertainment lies in visiting the area's trio of **auction houses**: **Christie's**, at 8 King St in St James's (☎020/7839 9060, ⊛www.christies.com), which has attracted high society since the days of Garrick, Reynolds and Boswell; **Sotheby's**, at 34–35 New Bond St (☎020/7293 5000, ⊛www.sothebys.com), the oldest of the three, having been founded in 1744 (though its pre-eminence only really dates from the last war); and **Bonhams**, a little more modest, at 101 New Bond St (☎020/7629 6602, ⊛www.bonhams.com).

Viewing takes place from Monday to Friday, and also occasionally at the weekend, and entry to the galleries is free of charge, though without a catalogue (costing £10 or more) the only information you'll glean is the lot number. Thousands of the works that pass through the rooms are of museum quality, and, if you're lucky, you might catch a glimpse of a masterpiece in transit between private collections and therefore only ever on public display in the auction-house galleries. Anyone can attend the auctions themselves, though remember to keep your hands firmly out of view unless you're bidding.

Sotheby's is probably the least intimidating: there's an excellent café, and staff offer free valuations, if you have an heirloom of your own to check out. There's always a line of people unwrapping plastic bags under the polite gaze of valuation staff, who call in the experts if they see something that sniffs of real money. All three, once quintessentially English institutions, are now under foreign control. Business remains buoyant despite the scandals of recent years. In 2002, Sotheby's and Christie's were found guilty of rigging the art market, defrauding sellers out of £290 million: Christie's escaped a fine because it confessed its sins, but Sotheby's was fined £12 million, and its former chairman jailed for a year.

Bond Street also has its fair share of perfumeries and **jewellers**, many of them long-established outlets that have survived the vicissitudes of fashion, and some, like De Beers, relatively recent arrivals. One of the most famous is Asprey & Garrard, at the corner of New Bond Street and Grafton Street, founded in 1781 by a family of Huguenot craftsmen, and now jewellers to the royals. The facade of the store features a wonderful parade of arched windows, flanked by slender Corinthian wrought-iron columns. Close by is a popular double statue of **Winston Churchill and President Roosevelt** enjoying a chat on a park bench.

One Bond Street institution you can feel free to walk into is **Smythson** (ⓦwww.smythson.com), at no. 40 in New Bond Street, the bespoke stationers, founded in 1887, who made their name printing Big Game books for colonialists to record what they'd bagged out in Africa and India. At the back of the shop is a small octagonal museum encrusted with shells and mirrors, and a few artefacts: photos and replicas of the book of condolence Smythson created for JFK's funeral, and the cherry calf-and-vellum diary given to Princess Grace of Monaco as a wedding gift.

Royal Arcade and Albemarle Street

On the west side of Old Bond Street, a garish orange-and-white plasterwork entrance announces the **Royal Arcade**, a full-blown High Victorian shopping mall with tall arched bays and an elegant glass roof, designed so that the wealthy guests of **Brown's** (ⓦwww.brownshotel.com) in Albemarle Street could have a sheltered and suitably elegant approach to the shops on Bond Street. Apart from being a posh hotel opened in the 1830s by James Brown, former butler to Lord Byron, *Brown's* was where the country's first telephone call was placed by **Alexander Graham Bell** in 1876, though initially he got a crossed line with a private telegraph wire, before finally getting through at around 3am to the hotel manager, who was installed at his home in Hammersmith. Also in Albemarle Street, at no. 50, are the offices of John Murray, the publishers of Byron and of the oldest British travel guides. It was here in 1824 that Byron's memoirs were tragically destroyed, after Murray managed to persuade Tom Moore, to whom they had been bequeathed, that they were too scurrilous to publish.

Further up Albemarle Street, at no. 21, is the weighty Neoclassical facade of the **Royal Institution**, a scientific body founded in 1799 "for teaching by courses of philosophical lectures and experiments the application of science to the common purposes of life"; its professors have included Humphry Davy (inventor of the miner's lamp), Michael Faraday and Lord Rutherford. The building's basement was converted into a small **Faraday Museum** (Mon–Fri 9am–6pm; £1; ☎020/7409 2992, ⓦwww.ri.ac.uk) some thirty years ago, and is now well overdue for a bit of refurbishment. Faraday was also instrumental in inaugurating the Royal Institution's six Christmas Lectures, a continuing tradition designed to popularize science among schoolchildren.

Savile Row

Running parallel with New Bond Street, a few blocks to the east, is another classic address in sartorial matters, **Savile Row**, still considered the place to go for made-to-measure suits for those with the requisite £2000 or so to spare. The number of bespoke tailors has declined, but several venerable businesses remain. Gieves & Hawkes (ⓦwww.gievesandhawkes.com), at no. 1, were the first tailors to establish themselves here back in 1785, with Nelson and Wellington among their first customers. Anderson & Sheppard, who've recently moved round the corner to 32 Old Burlington St, make suits for Prince Charles, while Kilgour (ⓦwww.8savilerow.com), at no. 8, famously made Fred Astaire's morning coat for *Top Hat*, helping to popularize Savile Row tailoring in the US. Henry Poole & Co (⊛www.henrypoole.com) at no. 15, has cut suits for the likes of Napoleon III, Dickens, Churchill and de Gaulle and is credited with inventing the short smoking jacket, originally designed for the future Edward VII, and later popularized as the "tuxedo".

Savile Row also has connections with the pop world. **The Beatles** used to buy their suits from Tommy Nutter's House of Nutter established in 1968 at no. 35, and in the same year set up the offices and recording studio of their record label Apple at no.3, until the building's near physical collapse in 1972. On January 30, 1969, The Beatles gave their last live gig on the roof here, stopping the traffic and eventually attracting the attentions of the local police – as captured on film in *Let It Be*.

Handel and Hendrix in Mayfair

Born **Georg Frideric Handel** (1685–1759) to a barber-surgeon in Halle, Saxony, Handel paid his first visit to London in 1711, where he marked his arrival by the composition of *Rinaldo*, which he wrote in fifteen days flat. The furore it produced – not least when Handel released a flock of sparrows for one aria – made him a household name. On his return the following year he was commissioned to write several works for Queen Anne, before becoming the court composer to George I, his one-time patron in Hanover.

London quickly became Handel's permanent home: he anglicized his name and nationality and lived out the rest of his life here, producing all the work for which he is now best known, including the *Water Music*, the *Fireworks Music* and his *Messiah*, which was composed in less than a month and failed to enthral its first audiences, but which is now one of the great set pieces of Protestant musical culture. George III was so moved by the grandeur of the *Hallelujah Chorus* that he leapt to his feet and remained standing for the entire performance. Handel himself fainted during a performance of the work in 1759, and died shortly afterwards in his home (now the Handel House Museum) at 25 Brook St; he is buried in Westminster Abbey.

Today, Handel's birthday is celebrated with a concert of his music given at the Foundling Museum (see p.148), on the site of the hospital he helped to finance, and the London Handel Society organizes an annual Handel festival (⊛www.london-handel-festival.com) around April, centred on St George's Church, Hanover Square (see p.104).

Some two hundred years later, another ground-breaking musician, **Jimi Hendrix** (1942–70), lived on and off for eighteen months in the neighbouring house of no. 23. Both men are currently honoured with blue plaques, Jimi receiving his in 1995 – a first for a rock musician, and only the third black person to be commemorated in such a way. Born Johnny Allen Hendrix in Seattle in 1942, he was persuaded to fly over to London in September 1966 after meeting Chas Chandler, manager and producer of The Animals. Shortly after arriving, he teamed up with two other British musicians, Noel Redding and Mitch Mitchell, and formed The Jimi Hendrix Experience. During the next two years, The Experience toured extensively, releasing three top-selling albums before splitting up in late 1968.

It was at the beginning of 1969 that Hendrix moved into Brook Street with his girlfriend, Kathy Etchingham; apparently he was much taken with the fact that it was once Handel's residence, ordering Kathy to go and buy the albums for him. It was also in London that Hendrix met his untimely death, on September 18, 1970. At around 7am, in a flat below *Samarkand Hotel* in Notting Hill, after a gig at *Ronnie Scott's* in Soho, Hendrix swallowed nine sleeping pills, later vomiting in his sleep and slipping into unconsciousness. He was pronounced dead on arrival at St Mary's Hospital, Paddington and is buried in Seattle.

Hanover Square and the Handel House Museum

Savile Row terminates at Conduit Street, where the funnel-shaped St George Street splays into **Hanover Square**, site of the old Hanover Square Rooms where Bach, Liszt, Haydn and Paganini all performed before the building's demolition in 1900. Halfway up St George Street, and contemporaneous with the square, is the sooty Corinthian portico of **St George's Church**, much copied since, but the first of its kind in London when it was built in the 1720s. Nicknamed "London's Temple of Hymen", it has long been Mayfair's most fashionable church for weddings. Among those who tied the knot here are the Shelleys, Benjamin Disraeli, Teddy Roosevelt and George Eliot, who died a few months afterwards; Handel, a confirmed bachelor, was a warden here for many years and even had his own pew.

Nearby, on the other side of New Bond Street at 25 Brook St, Handel's former home has been converted into the **Handel House Museum** (Tues–Sat 10am–6pm, Thurs till 8pm, Sun noon–6pm; £5; ☎020/7495 1685, ⊛www .handelhouse.org). The composer used the ground floor as a sort of shop where subscribers could buy scores, while the first floor was a rehearsal room. The exhibition contains few original artefacts, but the house has been painstakingly reconstructed and redecorated to how it would have looked in Handel's day. Further atmosphere is provided by the harpsichord in the rehearsal room, which gets played by music students throughout the week, with more formal performances on Thursday evenings from 6pm. Access to the house is via the chic, cobbled yard at the back of the house.

Berkeley and Grosvenor squares

Three blocks west of Old Bond Street, **Berkeley Square** is where, according to the music-hall song, nightingales sing (though it's probable they were, in fact, blackcaps). Laid out in the 1730s, only the west side of the square has any surviving Georgian houses to boast of, and nowadays any birds would have trouble being heard over the traffic. However, the thing that saves the square is its wonderful parade of 200-year-old **London plane trees**. With their dappled, peeling trunks, giant lobed leaves and globular spiky fruits, these pollution-resistant trees are a ubiquitous feature of the city, and Berkeley Square's specimens are among the finest.

Grosvenor Square, to the northwest, is the largest of the three Mayfair squares, and was known during World War II as "Little America" – General Eisenhower, whose statue now stands here, ran the D-Day campaign from no. 20. The American presence is still pretty strong, thanks to the Roosevelt Memorial, the 9/11 memorial garden dedicated to the 67 British victims of the 2001 attack, and to the monstrously ugly **US Embassy**, which occupies the entire west side of the square. Completed in 1960 to designs by Eero Saarinen, the embassy is watched over by a giant gilded eagle plus a small posse of police, as most weeks there's some demonstration or other against US foreign policy – albeit nothing to rank with 1968's violent protests against US involvement in Vietnam. Mick Jagger, so the story goes, was innocently signing autographs in his Bentley as the 1968 riot began, and later wrote *Street Fighting Man*, inspired by what he witnessed.

Eisenhower's initial pied-à-terre was a room painted "whorehouse pink" in **Claridge's**, the hotel for the rich and royal one block east of Grosvenor Square on Brook Street. *Claridge's* also served as the wartime hangout of the OSS, forerunner of the CIA, one of whose representatives held a historic meeting here in 1943 with Szmul Zygielbojm from the Jewish Board of the Polish government-in-exile. Zygielbojm was told that Roosevelt had refused his request to bomb the rail lines leading to Auschwitz; the following day he committed suicide.

American troops stationed over here used to worship at the **Grosvenor Chapel**, two blocks south on South Audley Street, a building reminiscent of early settlers' churches in New England and still popular with the American community. The church's most illustrious occupant is radical MP John Wilkes ("Wilkes and Liberty" was the battle cry of many a mid-eighteenth century riot). Behind the chapel are the beautifully secluded **Mount Street Gardens**, dotted with 200-year-old plane trees and enclosed by nineteenth-century red-brick mansions. At the far eastern end of the gardens is the back entrance to the **Church of the Immaculate Conception**, on Farm Street, the Jesuits' London stronghold, built in ostentatious neo-Gothic style in the 1840s. Every surface is covered in decoration, but the reredos of gilded stone by Pugin (of Houses of Parliament fame) is particularly impressive.

Shepherd Market

Mayfair is named after the infamous fifteen-day fair which was held here in May from the 1680s until 1764 when it was suppressed after the newly ensconced rich residents complained of the "drunkenness, fornication, gaming and lewdness". The site of the old fair, in the southwestern corner of Mayfair, was quickly developed by local builder Edward Shepherd into **Shepherd Market**, a little warren of alleyways and passages now occupied by swanky shops and restaurants, plus a couple of Victorian pubs, all extremely popular in summer.

The village-like area around Shepherd Market still has something of a raffish reputation. It was round the corner at 9 Curzon Place that Cass Elliot (aka Mama Cass) of The Mamas and Papas died in July 1974, and, four years later, Keith Moon, drummer with The Who, died of an overdose. Shepherd Market was also where the Tory fraudster and bestselling author, Jeffrey Archer, met the prostitute, Monica Coghlan. And it was at the *Mirabelle* restaurant on Curzon Street that actors Johnny Depp and Vanessa Paradis spent a cool £17,000 on a meal for two (including £11,000 on a single bottle of burgundy); emerging from the restaurant, Depp lashed out at the paparazzi and ended up in the local police cells.

If you're approaching Shepherd Market from Green Park tube, head west down Piccadilly until you get to **Half Moon Street**, where the fictional Wooster – the perfect upper-class Mayfair resident – and his faithful valet Jeeves of P.G. Wodehouse's novels lived, and where in 1763 the real James Boswell, newly arrived from Edinburgh, took lodgings and wrote his scurrilous diary. At the end of the street, you reach Curzon Street, home to **Crewe House**, originally built by Edward Shepherd, but now a company headquarters and one of the few eighteenth-century Mayfair mansions still standing.

Oxford Street

As wealthy Londoners began to move out of the City during the eighteenth century, in favour of the newly developed West End, so **Oxford Street** (ⓦwww.oxfordstreet.co.uk) – the old Roman road to Oxford – gradually replaced Cheapside (see p.202) as London's main shopping street. Today, despite successive recessions and sky-high rents, this two-mile hotchpotch of shops is still one of the world's busiest streets, its Christmas lights switched on by the briefly famous, and its traffic controllers equipped with loud-hailers to prevent the hordes of Christmas shoppers from losing their lives at the busy road junctions.

East of Oxford Circus, the street forms a scruffy border between Soho and Fitzrovia (see Chapter 6), and features London's two biggest music stores: HMV and Virgin Megastore. **Marks & Spencer** occupies one of the smartest, most historic sites: a black granite 1930s building on the south side of the street at no. 173 called the Pantheon – after the vast rotunda built here in 1772 in the style of Constantinople's St Sophia, and at one time a very fashionable spot. M&S itself started life as a stall run by a Polish Jewish immigrant in Leeds market in 1912 under the slogan "Don't ask the price – it's a penny".

West of Oxford Circus is dominated by more upmarket stores, including the one great landmark, **Selfridge's** (ⓦwww.selfridges.co.uk), a huge Edwardian pile fronted by giant Ionic columns, with the Queen of Time riding the ship of commerce and supporting an Art Deco clock above the main entrance. The store was opened in 1909 by Chicago millionaire Gordon Selfridge, who flaunted its 130 departments with the slogan, "Why not spend a day at Selfridge's?", but was later pensioned off after running into trouble with the Inland Revenue. Selfridge's is credited with selling the world's first television set, as well as introducing the concept of the "bargain basement", the irritating "only ten more shopping days to Christmas" countdown, and the nauseous bouquet of perfumes from the women's cosmetics counters, strategically placed at the entrance to all department stores to entice customers in.

Marylebone

To the north of Oxford Street lies **Marylebone**, once the outlying village of St Mary-by-the-Bourne (the bourne being the Tyburn stream) or St Marylebone (pronounced "marra-le-bun"). Samuel Pepys walked through open countryside to reach its pleasure gardens in 1668 and declared it "a pretty place". During the course of the next century, the gardens were closed and the village was swallowed up as its chief landowners – among them the Portlands and the Portmans – laid out a mesh of uniform Georgian

© crown copyright

ACCOMMODATION					EATING & DRINKING				
Dorset Square	A	Lincoln House	C		Abu Ali	13	Fairuz	12	Patisserie Valerie at Sagne 9
Durrants	E	Palace	F		Ayoush	16	La Galette	5	Paul Rothe & Son	15
Edward Lear	G	Wigmore Court	D		Barley Mow	6	Golden Hind	11	Quiet Revolution	7
Hotel La Place	B				The Chapel	3	O'Conor Don	14	Phoenix Palace	1
					Dover Castle	10	Orrery	2	The Providores	8
					Eat & Two Veg	4			

streets and squares, much of which survives today. Marylebone may not have quite the pedigree and snob value of Mayfair, but it's still a wealthy and aspirational area. It was here that The Beatles took up residence when they moved to London in the 1960s, and more recently Madonna and family moved into the area.

Compared to the brashness of Oxford Street, Marylebone's backstreets are a pleasure to wander, especially the chi-chi village-like quarter around **Marylebone High Street**. The area's more conventional sights include the massively touristed **Madame Tussaud's**, on Marylebone Road, the free art gallery and aristocratic mansion of the **Wallace Collection**, and Sherlock Holmes' old stomping grounds around **Baker Street**.

Langham Place

North of Oxford Circus, Regent Street forms the eastern border of Marylebone, but stops abruptly at **Langham Place**, site of **All Souls**, Nash's simple and ingenious little Bath-stone church, built in the 1820s. The unusual circular Ionic portico and conical spire, which caused outrage in its day, are cleverly designed to provide a visual full stop to Regent Street and a pivot for the awkward twist in the triumphal route to Regent's Park. Behind All Souls lies the totalitarian-looking **Broadcasting House** (closed to the public), BBC radio headquarters since 1931. The figures of Prospero and Ariel (pun intended) above the entrance are by Eric Gill, who caused a furore by sculpting Ariel with overlarge testicles, and, like Epstein a few years earlier at Broadway House (see p.82), was forced in the end to cut the organs down to size. Note that Broadcasting House is the headquarters of BBC radio, and not the BBC TV Centre, which is out in west London, opposite White City tube, and which does offer guided tours (☎0870/603 0304, ⊛www.bbc.co.uk/tours; £8.95).

Opposite Broadcasting House stands the **Langham Hilton**, built in heavy Italianate style in the 1860s, badly bombed in the last war and refurbished at a cost of millions. It features in several Sherlock Holmes mysteries, and its former guests have included Antonín Dvořák (who courted controversy by ordering a double room for himself and his daughter to save money), exiled emperors Napoleon III and Haile Selassie, and the once-famous Ouida (aka Marie Louise de la Ramée), who threw outrageous parties for young Guards officers and wrote many of her bestselling romances in her dimly lit hotel boudoir.

Doctors and dentists

Cavendish Square, just north of Oxford Street, marks the beginning of **Harley Street**, a residential Marylebone street until the nineteenth century when doctors, dentists and medical specialists began to colonize the area in order to serve London's wealthier citizens. Private medicine survived the threat of the postwar National Health Service, and the most expensive specialists and hospitals are still to be found in the streets around here.

For the dentally inclined, the national dental body, the **British Dental Association**, or **BDA** (⊛www.bda-dentistry.org.uk), has its headquarters at nearby 64 Wimpole St. Though dentistry is traditionally associated with pain, it was, in fact, a dentist who discovered the first anesthetic. The BDA museum, which displays the gruesome contraptions of early dentistry, and old prints of agonizing extractions, was at the time of writing closed for refurbishment.

Portland Place

After the chicane around All Souls, you enter **Portland Place**, laid out by the Adam brothers in the 1770s and incorporated by Nash in his grand route. Once the widest street in London, it's still a majestic avenue, lined exclusively with Adam-style houses, boasting wonderful fanlights and iron railings. Several embassies occupy properties here, including the Chinese legation at no. 49, where the exiled republican leader **Sun Yat Sen** was kidnapped and held incognito for several days in 1896, on the express orders of the Chinese emperor. Eventually Sun managed to send a note to one of his British friends, saying "I am certain to be beheaded. Oh woe is me!", though it was only when the press got hold of the story that Sun was finally released; he went on to found the Chinese Nationalist Party and became the first president of China in 1911.

Arguably the finest of all the buildings on Portland Place is the sleek Portland-stone facade of the **Royal Institute of British Architects** or **RIBA** (Mon–Fri 8am–6pm, Tues until 9pm, Sat 8am–5pm; ☎020/7580 5533, ⓦwww .riba.org), built in the 1930s amidst the remaining Adam houses. The highlight of the building is the interior, which you can view en route to the institute's frequent first-floor exhibitions or its elegant café, or during one of the Tuesday-evening lectures held here (£8). The excellent ground-floor bookshop is also worth a browse. The main staircase remains a wonderful period piece, with its etched glass balustrades and walnut veneer, and with two large black marble columns rising up on either side.

At the far end of Portland Place, Nash originally planned a giant "circus" as a formal entrance to Regent's Park (see p.340). Only the southern half – two graceful arcs of creamy terraces known collectively as **Park Crescent** – was eventually completed, and it is now cut off from the park by the busy thoroughfare of Marylebone Road.

The Wallace Collection

Of the three squares immediately north of Oxford Street (Portman and Cavendish being the other two), only minuscule Manchester Square has kept its peaceful Georgian appearance, thanks to its position away from the main traffic arteries. At its head is Hertford House, a miniature eighteenth-century French chateau transplanted to central London, which holds the splendid **Wallace Collection** (daily 10am–5pm; free; ☎020/7563 9500, ⓦwww.wallacecollection .org), a museum-gallery best known for its eighteenth-century French paintings and decorative art. The collection was originally bequeathed to the nation in 1897 by the widow of Richard Wallace, an art collector and the illegitimate son of the fourth Marquess of Hertford. Despite a millennial makeover, the museum remains, at heart, an old-fashioned institution, with exhibits piled high in glass cabinets and paintings covering every inch of wall space. However, it's the combined effect of the exhibits set amidst the period fittings – and a bloody great armoury – that makes the place so remarkable. Labelling can be pretty terse and paintings occasionally move about, so you might considering renting an audioguide (£3).

The ground floor

The ground-floor rooms begin with the **Front State Room**, to the right as you enter, where the walls are hung with several mildly distracting paintings by Reynolds, and Lawrence's typically sensuous portrait of the author and society beauty, the Countess of Blessington, which went down a storm at the Royal

▲ Wallace Collection

Academy in 1822. In the **Back State Room**, you'll find the cream of the house's Sèvres porcelain, and, centre stage, a period copy of Louis XIV's desk, which was the most expensive piece of eighteenth-century French furniture ever made. On the other side of the adjacent Dining Room, you'll find portraits by van Dyck and Velázquez, and more outrageous gilded oak and ebony Boulle furniture in the **Billiard Room**. From the Dining Room, you can cross the glass bridge to the covered courtyard, now home to the *Café Bagatelle*, or head down the stairs to the **Porphyry Court**, named after the eighteenth-century vases displayed there. Off the court, you'll find the **Conservation Gallery**, which reveals the construction techniques that lie behind the expensive furniture and armour in the collection; folk of all ages can also try on some medieval armour. Adjacent, the **Reserve Collection** houses second-division pictures and antique bits and bobs, but also has an interesting section on fakes and forgeries.

In the **Sixteenth-Century Gallery**, there are several interesting medieval and Renaissance pieces, ranging from *pietre dure*, bronze and majolica to Limoges porcelain and Venetian glass. In the **Smoking Room**, a small alcove at the far end survives to give an idea of the effect of the original Minton-tiled decor Wallace chose for this room. The next three rooms house the extensive **Armoury** bought *en bloc* by Wallace around the time of the Franco-Prussian War. (It was in recognition of the humanitarian assistance Wallace provided in Paris during that war that he received his baronetcy.) A fourth room houses Oriental arms and armour, collected by the fourth Marquess of Hertford, including a cabinet of Asante gold treasure and one of the most important Sikh treasures in Britain, the sword of the Maharaja Ranjit Singh. Beyond is the **Housekeeper's Room**, with a group of fine nineteenth-century pictures including several oil paintings by Richard Parkes Bonington, a few by Delaroche, and one by his close friend Delacroix.

The first floor

The most famous paintings in the collection are on the first floor, the tone of which is set by **Boucher**'s sumptuous mythological scenes over the main staircase. In the **Boudoir**, you'll find Reynolds' doe-eyed moppets and Greuze's soft-focus studies of kids. En route to the Study, check out the decorative gold snuffboxes and the silver-gilt Augsburg toilet service for an eighteenth-century lady's *levée*. In the **Study** itself are several portraits by Elisabeth Vigée-Lebrun, one of the most successful portraitists of pre-Revolutionary France. Meanwhile, in the **West Room**, there are more Boucher nudes – the soft porn of the *ancien régime* – and his gloriously florid portrait of Madame de Pompadour, Louis XV's mistress and patron of many of the great French artists of the period.

Among the Rococo delights in the **West Gallery** are some elegiac scenes by Watteau, such as *Halt During the Chase* and *Music Party*, and Fragonard's coquettes, one of whom flaunts herself to a smitten beau in *The Swing*. In addition to all this French finery there's a good collection of Dutch paintings in the **East Galleries** on the other side of the house: de Hooch's *Women Peeling Apples*, oil sketches by Rubens and landscapes by Ruisdael. And in the **Small Drawing Room**, there are contrasting vistas by Canaletto and Guardi, whose works were more or less souvenirs for eighteenth-century Brits doing the Grand Tour.

The **Great Gallery**, the largest room in the house, was specifically built by Wallace to display what he considered to be his finest paintings, including works by Murillo and Poussin, several vast van Dyck portraits, Rubens' *Rainbow Landscape* and **Frans Hals**' *Laughing Cavalier*. Here, too, are *Perseus and Andromeda*, a late work by **Titian**, **Velázquez**'s *Lady with a Fan* and **Rembrandt**'s affectionate portrait of his teenage son, Titus, who helped administer his father's estate after bankruptcy charges and died at the age of just 28. At one end of the room are three portraits of the actress Mary Robinson: one by Romney, one by Reynolds and, best of the lot, **Gainsborough**'s deceptively innocent portrayal, in which she insouciantly holds a miniature of her lover, the 19-year-old Prince of Wales (later George IV).

Marylebone High Street and around

Marylebone High Street, which starts northeast of Manchester Square and finishes at Marylebone Road, is all that's left of the village street that once ran along the banks of the Tyburn stream. It has become considerably more cosmopolitan and upmarket since those bucolic days, though the pace of the street is leisurely by central London standards, and its shops and cafés are mostly small, independent ventures, a pleasant contrast to the big stores on nearby Oxford Street. A couple of shops, in particular, deserve mention: *Patisserie Valerie*, at no. 105, is decorated with the same mock-Pompeian frescoes that adorned it when it was founded in the 1920s (as *Maison Sagne*) by a Swiss pastry-cook; at no. 83 is Daunt, a purpose-built bookshop from 1910, which specializes in travel books, and has a lovely, long, galleried hall at the back, with a pitched roof of stained glass.

Despite its name, **St James's Church**, Spanish Place, is actually tucked away on neighbouring George Street, just off Marylebone High Street. A Catholic chapel was built here in 1791 thanks to the efforts of the chaplain at the Spanish embassy, though the present neo-Gothic building dates from 1890. Designed in a mixture of English and French Gothic, the interior is surprisingly large and richly furnished, from the white marble and alabaster pulpit to the richly gilded heptagonal apse. The Spanish connection continues to this day: Spanish royal heraldry features in the rose window, and there are even two seats reserved for the royals, denoted by built-in gilt crowns high above the choir stalls.

Marylebone Road

At the north edge of Marylebone High Street is **Marylebone Road**, a western extension of Euston Road, built in the 1750s to provide London with its first bypass. It remains one of London's major traffic arteries, and is not a pleasant place along which to stroll. There are, however, a couple of minor sights, such as **St Marylebone Church** and the **Royal Academy of Music**, and one major tourist trap, **Madame Tusssaud's**, that might bring you here. In addition, Marylebone Road is bisected by **Baker Street**, whose associations with the fictional detective Sherlock Holmes are, naturally, fully exploited.

St Marylebone Church

The traffic that pounds down Marylebone Road's six lanes unfortunately cuts off **St Marylebone Church**, built in 1813, from Nash's York Gate, which was designed as an alternative gateway to Regent's Park. The church crypt houses a small chapel, a counselling and healing centre, and a café (Mon–Fri 10am–3pm); the rest of the interior is only open fitfully for services and recitals. But the church's most attractive feature – the gilded caryatids holding up the beehive cupola on top of the tower – is visible from the High Street. It was at this church in 1846 that **Elizabeth Barrett and Robert Browning** were secretly married; various bits and pieces of memorabilia are on display in the Browning Chapel (visit by appointment ☏020/7935 7315). Elizabeth – 40 years old, an invalid and a virtual prisoner in her father's house on Wimpole Street – returned home and acted as if nothing had happened. A week later the couple eloped to Italy, where they spent most of their married life.

Royal Academy of Music

On the other side of Marylebone Road from St Marylebone Church stands the **Royal Academy of Music** (Mon–Fri 12.30–6pm, Sat & Sun 2–5.30pm; free; ☏020/7873 7300, ⊛www.ram.ac.uk), which was founded in 1823, and taught the likes of Arthur Sullivan, Harrison Birtwistle, Evelyn Glennie, Michael Nyman and Simon Rattle. As well as putting on free lunchtime and evening concerts, the academy houses a museum in the York Gate building; to reach it, you must sign in at the main entrance and follow the signs. On the ground floor, you can view John Barbirolli's baton, and Henry Wood's tuning instruments and stopwatch, while upstairs, there are several violins by the likes of Stradivari, Amati and Pressenda, and a series of (mostly English) grand and square pianos. Listening-posts allow you to experience the instruments in live performance, and you can peek into the resident luthier's workshop.

Madame Tussaud's

The wax models at **Madame Tussaud's** (Mon–Fri 9.30am–5.30pm, Sat & Sun 9am–6pm; from £22; ☏0870/400 3000, ⊛www.madame-tussauds.com) have been pulling in the crowds ever since the good lady arrived in London from France in 1802 bearing the sculpted heads of guillotined aristocrats (she herself only just managed to escape the same fate – her uncle, who started the family business, was less fortunate). The entrance fee might be extortionate, the likenesses occasionally dubious and the automated dummies inept, but you can still rely on finding London's biggest queues here – to avoid joining them, book your ticket in advance over the phone or online, and to "save money" whiz round after 5pm when it's cheaper.

The best photo opportunities come in the first section, currently called **Blush** and peppered with contemporary TV, music and sports personalities (one or two of them bafflingly unknown to non-British visitors). The next couple of sections feature more of the same, and eventually lead you down to the **World Stage**, a po-faced gathering of statesmen, clerics, generals and British royalty stretching back to medieval times. As you enter, you're greeted by an elderly and diminutive Madame Tussaud; close by is the oldest of the wax models, Madame du Barry, Louis XV's mistress, who gently respires as Sleeping Beauty – in reality she was beheaded in the French Revolution.

The **Chamber of Horrors**, the most popular section of all, is irredeemably tasteless, and, in an attempt to hype up the hysterics, features live, costumed actors jumping out at you in the dark in the **Chamber Live** section. All the "great" British serial killers are here, and it remains the murderer's greatest honour to be included: Dennis Nilsen, a gruesome killer of young gay men in the 1980s, begged to be allowed to pose for Tussaud's while in prison. There's a reconstruction of John Christie's hanging, a tableau of Marat's death in the bath, and the very guillotine that lopped off Marie Antoinette's head, just for good measure.

The tour of Tussaud's ends with the **Spirit of London**, a manic and irrever-ent five-minute romp through the history of London in miniaturized taxicabs. It begins well, dropping witty visual jokes as it careers from Elizabethan times, the Great Plague, the Great Fire, Wren and Victorian industrialization to the Blitz and Swinging London, ending in a postmodern heritage nightmare (not unlike much of London today) with a cacophony of Beefeaters and Bobbies before shuddering to a halt and disembarking by a slobbering Benny Hill.

Tickets for Madame Tussaud's also allow you to watch a thirty-minute hi-tech presentation, projected onto a vast dome in the adjoining **Auditorium** (formerly known as the London Planetarium). The show changes from time to time, but usually takes you on a journey through the universe, accompanied by New Age music and a cosmic astro-babble commentary.

Baker Street and around

Czech writer Karel Čapek was disappointed to find no trace of Sherlock Hol-mes on **Baker Street**, which cuts across Marylebone Road – "if we briefly touch upon its underground station, we have exhausted everything including our patience," he wrote in the 1930s. Happily, for those on the trail of English literature's languid super-sleuth, who lived at 221b Baker St, London's tourist industry has now rectified all that. First of all, those arriving at Baker Street tube are now confronted with a statue of the pipe-smoking detective, sporting his trademark deerstalker and magnifying glass, as soon as they leave the station. Meanwhile, round the corner, the fans who flock here from all over the world now have a choice of museums dedicated to the man, though neither place has any real connection with the fictional character, nor his creator, Arthur Conan Doyle.

The **Sherlock Holmes Museum** (daily 9.30am–6pm; £6; ☎020/7935 8866, ⊛www.sherlock-holmes.co.uk), at no. 239 (the sign on the door says 221b), is a very competent exercise in period reconstruction, atmospheric and stuffed full of Victoriana and life-size models of characters from the books. You can don a deerstalker and pretend to be the great detective, and it's proved extremely popular with Japanese tourists. On the opposite side of the street at no. 230 is **Sherlock Holmes Memorabilia** (Mon–Sat 10am–5pm, Sun 11am–4pm;

£2.50; ☎020/7486 1426, ⊛www.sh-memorabilia.co.uk), run by a real enthusiast, who has re-created the study from the 1980s British TV series, starring Jeremy Brett, and boasts an impressive collection of first editions.

One last curiosity in this area is **Marylebone Station**, hidden in the backstreets to the north of Marylebone Road on Melcombe Place, where a delicate and extremely elegant wrought-iron canopy links the station to the former *Great Central Hotel* (now *The Landmark*). The last and most modest of the Victorian terminals, this was intended to be the terminal for the Channel tunnel of the 1880s, a scheme abandoned after only a mile or so of digging, when Queen Victoria got nervous about foreign invasions. Marylebone now serves the commuter belt in Buckinghamshire.

6

Soho and Fitzrovia

oho gives you the best and worst of London: the porn joints that proliferated from the 1960s onwards still have a strong presence, but the area also boasts a lively fruit and vegetable market, and a nightlife that has attracted writers and revellers of every sexual persuasion to the place since the eighteenth century. Despite regeneration, it has retained an unorthodox and slightly raffish air, born of an immigrant history as rich as that of the East End, while the area's most recent transformation has seen it become Europe's leading gay centre, with bars and cafés bursting out from the Old Compton Street area.

Bounded by Regent Street to the west, Oxford Street to the north and Charing Cross Road to the east, Soho remains very much the heart of London and one of the capital's most diverse and characterful areas. Conventional sights are few and far between, yet it's a great area for strolling around, with probably more street life than anywhere else in the city – whatever hour you wander through, there's always something going on. Soho's nightlife continues to be the prime attraction, with most folk heading here to visit one of the big movie houses on **Leicester Square**, to knock back a few drinks in the latest trendy bars or to grab a bite to eat at the innumerable cafés and restaurants, ranging from the inexpensive Chinese places that pepper the tiny enclave of **Chinatown**, to exclusive, Michelin-starred establishments in the backstreets.

Fitzrovia, the area immediately to the north, is much quieter than Soho, and has more in common with nearby Bloomsbury. Nevertheless, it has a bohemian pedigree similar to its raunchier southern neighbour, and undoubtedly functions as something of a Soho spillover – in fact, a few years back, there was a failed attempt to rename the area North Soho or "Noho". Tourist sights are again scarce, with just Pollock's Toy Museum and the odd architectural oddity to give you purpose.

Soho

When **Soho** – named after the cry that resounded through the district when it was a hunting ground – was first built over in the seventeenth century, its streets were among the most sought-after addresses in the capital. Princes, dukes and earls built their mansions around Soho and Leicester squares, which became the centre of high-society nightlife, epitomized by Viennese prima donna Theresa Cornelys' wild masquerades, which drew "a riotous assembly of fashionable

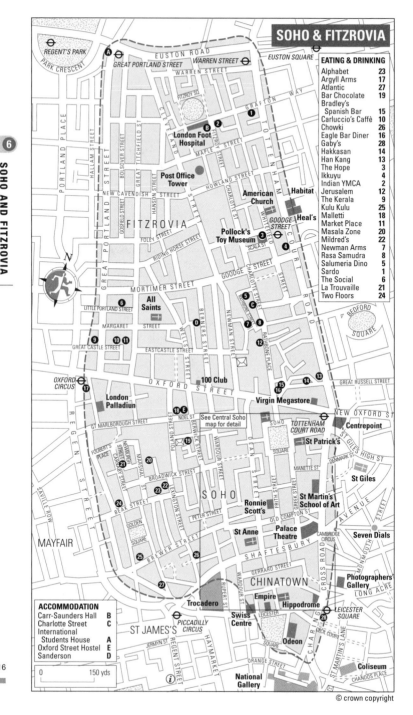

SOHO & FITZROVIA

EATING & DRINKING

Alphabet	23
Argyll Arms	17
Atlantic	27
Bar Chocolate	19
Bradley's Spanish Bar	15
Carluccio's Caffè	10
Chowki	26
Eagle Bar Diner	16
Gaby's	28
Hakkasan	14
Han Kang	13
The Hope	3
Ikkyuy	4
Indian YMCA	2
Jerusalem	12
The Kerala	9
Kulu Kulu	25
Malletti	18
Market Place	11
Masala Zone	20
Mildred's	22
Newman Arms	7
Rasa Samudra	8
Salumeria Dino	5
Sardo	1
The Social	6
La Trouvaille	21
Two Floors	24

ACCOMMODATION

Carr-Saunders Hall	B
Charlotte Street	C
International Students House	A
Oxford Street Hostel	E
Sanderson	D

0   150 yds

SOHO AND FITZROVIA 6

people of both sexes", a traffic jam of hackney chairs and a huge crowd of onlookers. By the end of the eighteenth century, however, the party was over, the rich moved west to Mayfair, and Soho began its inexorable descent into poverty and overcrowding.

Even before the last aristocrats left, Soho had become, along with the East End, the city's main dumping ground for **immigrants**, a place caricatured (albeit much later) by Galsworthy as "untidy, full of Greeks, Ishmaelites, cats, Italians, tomatoes, restaurants, organs, coloured stuffs, queer names, people looking out of upper windows". The first wave of refugees were the French Huguenots, who settled in Bateman Street after fleeing from Louis XIV's intolerant regime, followed later by more French, Italians, Irish and Jews. More recently, Asians, particularly the Chinese, took advantage of Soho's cheap postwar rents for their workshops and restaurants.

For many years, Soho had also been a favourite haunt of the capital's creative bohos and **literati**. It was at the *Turk's Head* coffee shop in 1764, in what is now Chinatown, that Joshua Reynolds founded "The Club", to give Dr Johnson unlimited opportunities for talking. Thomas de Quincey turned up in Soho in 1802, having run away from school, and was saved from starvation by a local prostitute, an incident later recalled in his *Confessions of an English Opium Eater*. Wagner arrived destitute in the neighbourhood in 1839, Marx lived in poverty here after the failure of the revolutionary upheavals of 1848, and Rimbaud and Verlaine escaped to Soho after the fall of the Paris Commune in 1871.

Soho's reputation for tolerance also made it an obvious place of refuge from dour, postwar Britain. Jazz and skiffle venues proliferated in the 1950s, folk and rock clubs in the 1960s, and punk rock at the end of the 1970s. Soho's artistic (and alcoholic) cliques still gather here: the satirical magazine *Private Eye* is based in Carlisle Street and the *Coach and Horses* pub, while writers, publishers and artists hold court at the members-only *Groucho Club* in Dean Street. The area's creative energy is perhaps best expressed in its clubs (both public and private), and the presence of Wardour Street, core of the film and advertising business in Britain, provides a clientele on the doorstep. The attraction, though, remains in the unique mix of people who drift through Soho. There's nowhere else in the city where such diverse slices of London come face to face with each other: businessmen, clubbers, drunks, theatregoers, fashion victims, market-stall-holders, pimps, prostitutes and politicians. Take it all in, and enjoy – for better or worse, most of London is not like this.

Leicester Square

A short hop east of Piccadilly Circus, **Leicester Square** is a popular spot for London's myriad visitors to hang out, with the big cinemas and discos doing good business, and buskers attemping to entertain the crowds. By night it can be one of the most crowded places in London, particularly on a Friday or Saturday, when huge numbers of tourists and half the youth of the suburbs seem to congregate here.

At the centre of the square, situated within the gardens, is a copy of the Shakespeare memorial in Westminster Abbey (see p.74), looked over by a statue of Charlie Chaplin (neither of whom has any connection with the square); around the edge are busts of Sir Isaac Newton, William Hogarth, Joshua Reynolds and a Scottish surgeon, John Hunter – all of whom lived hereabouts in the eighteenth century. At that time, the square was a kind of informal court for the fashionable "Leicester House set", headed by successive princes of Wales who didn't get on with their fathers at St James's.

It wasn't until the mid-nineteenth century that the square began to emerge as an entertainment zone, with Turkish baths, accommodation houses (for prostitutes and their clients), oyster rooms and music halls such as the grandiose Empire and Hippodrome – on the corner of Cranbourn Street, and designed as a variety theatre by Frank Matcham in 1900 – edifices which survive today as cinemas and nightclubs. Movie houses moved in during the 1930s, a golden age evoked by the sleek black lines of the Odeon on the east side, and maintain their grip on the area. **The Empire**, at the top end of the square, is the favourite for the big royal premieres, and, in a rather half-hearted imitation of the Hollywood (and Cannes) tradition, there are handprints visible in the pavement by the southwestern corner of the garden railings.

There are no sights as such on the square, though if you find yourself near the monumentally ugly **Swiss Centre**, you may be assaulted by a five-minute medley played by the centre's wall-mounted **campanole** (Mon–Fri noon, 6–8pm, Sat & Sun noon & 2–8pm) to a surreal procession of cows and peasants. One little-known sight, just off the north side of the square, hidden away in Leicester Place, is the modern Catholic church of **Notre-Dame de France**, heralded by an entrance flanked by two pillars decorated with biblical reliefs. The church's unusual circular plan is derived from the Panorama, a rotunda 90ft in diameter originally built here and decorated with a scenic cylindrical painting by the Irish artist Robert Barker in 1796. The main point of interest, however, is the church's Chapelle du St-Sacrement, which contains a series of simple frescoes by Jean Cocteau from 1960 and a mosaic by Boris Anrep.

Chinatown

Chinatown (@www.china townchinese.com), hemmed in between Leicester Square and Shaftesbury Avenue, and centred on **Gerrard Street**, is a self-contained jumble of shops, cafés and restaurants that makes up one of London's most distinct and popular ethnic enclaves. Few of London's 60,000 Chinese actually live in the three small blocks of Chinatown, yet despite the ersatz touches – telephone kiosks rigged out as pagodas and formal entrances or *paifang* – the area remains a focus for the community, a place to do business or the weekly shopping, celebrate a wedding or just meet up for meals, particularly on Sundays, when the restaurants overflow with Chinese families tucking into dim sum.

The **Chinese New Year** celebrations, instigated here in 1973, are a community-based affair, drawing

▲ Detail of ornamental gateway, Gerrard Street

London's first Chinese immigrants were sailors who arrived here in the late eighteenth and early nineteenth centuries on the ships of the East India Company. A small number settled permanently around the docks at Limehouse (see p.253), which became London's first **Chinatown**, boasting over thirty Chinese shops and restaurants by the turn of the nineteenth century. Predominantly male, this closed community achieved a quasi-mythical status in Edwardian minds as a hotbed of criminal dives and opium dens, a reputation further enhanced by Sax Rohmer's novels (later made into films) featuring the evil Doctor Fu Manchu.

Wartime bomb damage, postwar demolition and protectionist union laws all but destroyed Limehouse Chinatown. At the same time, following the Communist takeover in China, a new wave of predominantly Cantonese refugees arrived via Hong Kong, and began to buy up the cheap and run-down property around Gerrard Street. Western interest in Chinese food provided the impetus for the boom in the catering industry, which to this day remains inexpensive, since it continues to provide for the Chinese community itself.

in thousands of Londoners for the Sunday nearest to New Year's Day (late Jan or early Feb). To a cacophony of fireworks, huge papier-mâché lions dance through the streets devouring cabbages hung from the upper floors by strings pinned with money. The noise is deafening and, if you want to see anything other than the backs of people's heads, you'll need to position yourself close to one of the cabbages around noon and stand your ground.

For the rest of the year, most Londoners come to Chinatown simply to eat – easy and inexpensive enough to do, though the choice of **restaurants** is somewhat overwhelming, especially on Gerrard Street itself. Cantonese cuisine predominates, though there's a smattering of Shanghai and Szechuan outlets. You're unlikely to be disappointed wherever you go – watching where the Chinese themselves eat is the most obvious policy and, if you get offered non-partisan local advice on what to eat and where, take it.

In addition to the restaurants, most of the **shops** in Chinatown are geared towards Chinese trade. If the mood takes you, you can while away several hours sorting through the trinkets, ceramics and ornaments in the various arts and crafts shops. Ying Hwa bookshop, on the corner of Macclesfield Street and Gerrard Street, is a good place to pick up Eastern newspapers in English or Cantonese. If you know what you're looking for, you can amass the right ingredients for a demon stir-fry – with exotic fruits to finish – in the supermarkets on Gerrard Street and Newport Place. Also worth checking out is the big Chinese medicine outlet, Tong Ren Tang, on the corner of Gerrard Place and Shaftesbury Avenue, its window display stuffed with teas, infusions and jars of unmentionables.

Charing Cross Road and Shaftesbury Avenue

The creation in the late 1880s of **Charing Cross Road**, Soho's eastern border and a thoroughfare from Trafalgar Square to Oxford Street, was less disruptive than other Victorian "improvements", though slum clearance was part of its design. The street now boasts the highest concentration of **bookshops** anywhere in London, with one of the first to open here being Foyles (@www

.foyles.co.uk) at no. 119, where De Valera, George Bernard Shaw, Walt Disney and Conan Doyle were all once regular customers. The street retains more of its original character south of Cambridge Circus, where you'll find the capital's main Islamic bookshop, Alhoda, along with a cluster of ramshackle secondhand bookshops, such as Quinto, and swankier outfits like Zwemmer.

One of the nicest places for secondhand-book browsing is **Cecil Court** – the alleyway between the southern end of Charing Cross Road and St Martin's Lane. This short, civilized, paved street boasts specialist bookshops devoted to theatre, Italy, New Age philosophies and the like, plus various antiquarian dealers selling modern first editions, old theatre posters, coins and notes, cigarette cards, maps and stamps. Another place you shouldn't miss, just off Charing Cross Road, is the **Photographers' Gallery** (Mon–Sat 11am–6pm, Sun noon–6pm; free; ☎020/7831 1772, ⓦwww.photonet.org.uk) at nos. 5 and 8 Great Newport Street, established in 1971 as the first of its kind in London, and hosting free temporary exhibitions that are invariably worth a visit, as are the bookshop and café.

As well as being prime bookworm territory, Charing Cross Road is one of the main drags through the West End, flanked by **theatres**, **clubs** and **rock venues**. On Cambridge Circus, the huge terracotta Palace Theatre originally opened in 1891 as the Royal English Opera House, only to fold the following year. Just off Cambridge Circus, hidden away down West Street, is St Martin's Theatre, where Agatha Christie's record-breaking *Mousetrap* has been on non-stop since 1952.

One last venue worth mentioning is the **Coliseum**, at the southern end of St Martin's Lane, parallel with Charing Cross Road, another extravagant work by Frank Matcham, built in 1904 as a variety theatre, where the likes of Lillie Langtry, Sarah Bernhardt and the Ballets Russes all performed. Now home to the English National Opera (ⓦwww.eno.org), it remains London's largest theatre, and following a major refurbishment, the illuminated globe on top of the building is happily revolving once more.

Sweeping northeast towards Bloomsbury from Piccadilly Circus, and separating Soho proper from Chinatown, the gentle curve of **Shaftesbury Avenue** is the heart of mainstream **Theatreland**, with theatres and cinemas along its entire length. Like Charing Cross Road, it was conceived in the late 1870s, ostensibly to relieve traffic congestion but also with the purpose of destroying the slums that lay in its path. Ironically, it was then named after Lord Shaftesbury (of Eros fame; see p.95), whose life had been spent trying to help the likes of those dispossessed by the road scheme.

Central Soho

If Soho has a main drag, it has to be **Old Compton Street**, which runs parallel with Shaftesbury Avenue, linking Charing Cross Road and Wardour Street. The corner shops, peepshows, boutiques and trendy cafés here are typical of the area and a good barometer of the latest Soho fads. One of the few places which have survived the vicissitudes of fashion is the original *Patisserie Valerie* (now with several branches elsewhere), opened by the Belgian-born Madame Valerie in 1926. Several other old stores remain embedded on Old Compton Street, most notably the Algerian Coffee Store, the Italian deli, I Camisa & Son, Capital newsagents, The Vintage House off-licence, which claims to stock over 700 malt whiskies, and Gerry's off-licence, whose spirit-window display is a paean to alcohol and includes a staggering range of Czech absinthe.

The liberal atmosphere of Soho has also made it a permanent fixture on the **gay scene** since the last century: gay servicemen frequented the *Golden Lion*, on Dean Street, from World War II until the end of National Service, while a succession of gay artists found refuge here (and in neighbouring Fitzrovia) during the 1950s and 1960s. Nowadays the scene is much more upfront, with gay bars, clubs and cafés jostling for position on Old Compton Street, and round the corner on Wardour Street. And it doesn't stop there: there's now a gay house-share agency, a gay financial adviser and, even more convenient, a gay taxi service.

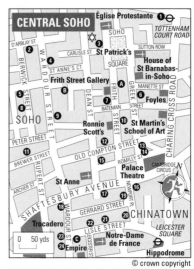

© crown copyright

Greek Street and Frith Street

The streets off Old Compton Street are lined with Soho institutions past and present, starting in the east with **Greek Street**, named after the Greek church that once stood nearby. This and parallel **Frith Street** both lead north to Soho Square (see overleaf).

EATING & DRINKING			
Bar du Marché	5	Mr Kong	21
Bar Italia	10	Patara	6
Beatroot	8	Patisserie Valerie	12
Brasil by Kilo	1	Randall and Aubin	11
Coach & Horses	14	Soho Spice	4
De Hems	16	Spiga	9
Dog & Duck	7	Thai Cottage	2
French House	15	Tokyo Diner	19
Fung Shing	22	The Toucan	3
Imperial China	20	Wong Kei	18
Kopi-Tiam	23		
Lee Ho Fook	17	**ACCOMMODATION**	
Maison Bertaux	13	Hazlitt's	A
Misato	24	Manzi's	C
		Soho Hotel	B

Soho on record

Soho has been a popular meeting point for the capital's up-and-coming pop stars since the late 1950s, when young hopefuls like Cliff Richard, Tommy Steele and Adam Faith used to hang out at the **2 i's coffee bar** at 59 Old Compton St, and perform at the rock'n'roll club in the basement. Marc Bolan, whose parents ran a market stall on Berwick Street, also worked at the café in the early 1960s. The Rolling Stones first met in a pub (since gone) on Broadwick Street in early 1962 and, by the mid-1960s, were playing Soho's premier rock venue, the **Marquee**, which used to be at 90 Wardour St. David Bowie performed there (as David Jones) in 1965, Pink Floyd played their "Spontaneous Underground" sessions the following year, Led Zeppelin had their first London gig there in 1968, and Phil Collins worked for some time as a cloakroom attendant.

In November 1975, The Sex Pistols played their first gig at **St Martin's School of Art** on Charing Cross Road, during which Sid Vicious (in the audience, and not the band, at the time) made his contribution to dance history when he began to "pogo". The classic venue during the heyday of punk in 1976, however, was the **100 Club** on Oxford Street, where the Pistols, The Clash, Siouxsie, The Damned and The Vibrators all played. The Pistols used to rehearse in the studios behind the music shops on **Denmark Street**, London's tame version of New York's Tin Pan Alley, off Charing Cross Road. The Rolling Stones, The Kinks and Genesis all recorded songs there, and Elton John got his first job at one of the street's music publishers in 1963.

SOHO AND FITZROVIA | Central Soho

On Romilly Street, which runs between the two, just south of Old Compton Street, is one of London's landmark restaurants, *Kettner's*, founded back in the 1860s by Napoleon III's personal chef and favoured by Oscar Wilde. It's now part of the *Pizza Express* chain, but retains a smidgen of faded Edwardian elegance in its decor – and a pianist in its champagne bar. Only a little younger is *Maison Bertaux*, opposite at 28 Greek St, founded in 1871; its windows are piled high with patisserie, and there's a wonderful little salon upstairs.

Close by, and also on Greek Street, is the *Coach and Horses*, an ordinary sort of pub that was lorded over for years by the boozy gang of writer Jeffrey Bernard, painter Francis Bacon and jazz man George Melly, as well as the *Private Eye* crew. Jazz connections are in evidence on Frith Street, too, where **Ronnie Scott's** (see p.493), London's longest-running jazz club, was founded in 1958 and still pulls in the big names. Opposite is *Bar Italia*, an Italian café with a big screen for satellite TV transmissions of Italian football games, and late-night hours that ensure its place as an espresso stop on every self-respecting clubber's itinerary. It was in this building, appropriately enough for such a media-saturated area, that **John Logie Baird** made the world's first public television transmission in 1926. Next door, a plaque recalls that the 7-year-old Mozart stayed here in 1763, having wowed George III and London society.

Soho Square

Soho Square is virtually the only patch of green amid the neighbourhood's labyrinth of streets and alleys. It began life as a smart address, surrounded by the houses of the nobility and centred on an elaborate fountain topped by a statue of Charles II. Charles survives, if a little worse for wear, and stands on one of the pathways, but the fountain has made way for an octagonal, mock-Tudor garden shed. As for the buildings around the square, they are a typical Soho mix: 20th Century-Fox; the Victorian Hospital for Sick Women (now a walk-in health centre); Paul McCartney's discreet corporate headquarters, mpl; the British Board of Film Classification; and the Football Association. There are also two square, red-brick churches: the Italianate **St Patrick's**, which serves the Irish, Italian and Chinese communities, and the **Église Protestante** (Protestant Church), sole survivor of London's 23 Huguenot churches, concealed on the north side of the square, whose tympanum relief depicts the French refugees crossing the Channel and being granted asylum by Edward VI.

If you're finding it difficult to imagine Soho ever having been an aristocratic haunt, pay a visit to the **House of St Barnabas-in-Soho**, a Georgian mansion just south of the square on Greek Street – there are regular, though infrequent, guided tours, but it's best to ring ahead to check (Wed 2.30pm & Thurs 11.30am; donation expected; ℡020/7434 2067). Built in the 1740s, the house retains some exquisite Rococo plasterwork on the main staircase and in the Council Chamber, which has a lovely view onto Soho Square. Since 1861 the building has been a Christian charity house for the destitute, so the rest of the interior is much altered and closed off. You can, however, visit the paved garden, whose plane trees inspired Dickens, and whose twisted and gnarled mulberry tree was planted by some silk-weaving Huguenots. On the south side of the garden is a cute little Byzantine-style chapel, built for the residents and used by Serbian refugees during World War I.

Dean Street and Wardour Street

One block west of Frith Street runs **Dean Street**, home of the *Colony Club*, the heart of the postwar bohemian drinking scene, and of the *Groucho Club*, where London's literati and media types preen themselves. Both clubs are members-only, but nearby *The French House*, at no. 49, is an open-to-all bohemian landmark. Once the plain old *York Minster* pub, it was bought by a Belgian, Victor Berlemont, in 1914 and transformed into a French émigré haunt. It was frequented by de Gaulle and the Free French forces during World War II, and has long had a reputation for attracting artists (Salvador Dalí, among others) and writers.

Soho's once-strong Jewish presence is now confined to Dean Street's synagogue. The most famous Jewish immigrant to live in Soho was **Karl Marx**, who in 1850 stayed at no. 64, before moving into two "evil, frightful rooms" further down the street, on the top floor of no. 28, with his wife and maid (both of whom were pregnant by him) and four children, having been evicted from his first two addresses for failing to pay the rent. There's a plaque commemorating his stay (with incorrect dates), and the waiters at *Leoni's Quo Vadis* restaurant, the current occupants, will show diners round the rooms on request.

West again is **Wardour Street** – Soho's longest street, stretching from Coventry Street to Oxford Street, and a kind of dividing line between the trendier, eastern half of Soho and the slightly more porn-prolific western zone. The street is largely given over to the film and TV industry – Warner Bros is based here, along with numerous smaller production companies – though its southern end is part of Chinatown (see p.118). Just north of Shaftesbury Avenue, there's a small park laid out on what used to be **St Anne's Church**, bombed in the last war, with only its tower now standing. The ashes of Dorothy L. Sayers are buried under the tower, and Baron von Neuhoff, a Westphalian adventurer who managed to get himself elected as King of Corsica in 1736, is also interred here. His reign lasted eight months, after which he was forced to flee to try and raise more money and men to fight the Genoese. He lived out his exile on Dean Street and was eventually imprisoned for debt in 1750; when asked what assets he had, he declared "nothing but the Kingdom of Corsica".

Berwick Street, Broadwick Street and around

Despite the council's best efforts, the **vice and prostitution** rackets still have the area immediately west of Wardour Street well staked out. Paul Raymond's Folies Bergères-style *Revue Bar* on Brewer Street has finally closed, no doubt in part due to pressures from the slick lap-dancing clubs leading the new boom in the West End sex industry, though there are still plenty of dodgy video shops and short con outfits operating all over Soho.

In amongst the video shops and triple-X-rated cinemas is the unlikely sight of **Berwick Street Market** (Mon–Sat 9am–6pm), one of the capital's finest (and cheapest) fruit and vegetable markets. The street itself is no beauty spot, but the market's barrow displays are works of art in themselves. On either side of the stalls, you'll find several "hippie" shops and some of London's best specialist record shops (see "Shops and markets", p.530).

The market starts from Peter Street and stops at the crossroads with Broadwick Street, which features a replica of the water pump that caused the deaths of some five hundred Soho residents in the **cholera epidemic** of 1854. Dr John Snow, Queen Victoria's obstetrician, traced the outbreak to the pump, thereby proving that the disease was waterborne rather than airborne, as previously thought. No one believed him, however, until he removed the pump handle and effectively stopped the epidemic. The original pump stood outside the pub now called the *John Snow*, beside which there's a commemorative plaque and a red granite kerbstone.

Soho vice

Prostitution is nothing new to Soho. Way back in the seventeenth and eighteenth centuries, prince and prole alike used to come here (and to Covent Garden) for paid sex. Several prominent courtesans were residents of Soho, their profession recorded as "player and mistress to several persons", or, lower down on the social scale, "generally slut and drunkard; occasionally whore and thief". *Hooper's Hotel*, a high-class Soho brothel which the Prince of Wales frequented, even got a mention in the popular late eighteenth-century book, *The Mysteries of Flagellation*. By Victorian times, the area was described as "a reeking home of filthy vice", where "the grosser immorality flourishes unabashed from every age downwards to mere children". And it was in Soho that Gladstone used to conduct his crusade to save prostitutes – managing "to combine his missionary meddling with a keen appreciation of a pretty face", as one perceptive critic observed.

By World War II, **organized gangs** like the notorious Messina Brothers from Malta controlled a huge vice empire in Soho, later taken over by one of their erstwhile henchmen, Bernie Silver, Soho's self-styled "Godfather". In the 1960s and 1970s, the sex trade threatened to take over the whole of Soho, aided and abetted by the police themselves, who were involved in a massive protection racket. The complicity between the gangs and the police was finally exposed in 1976, when ten top-ranking Scotland Yard officers were charged with bribery and corruption on a massive scale and sentenced to prison for up to twelve years. (Silver himself had been put inside in 1974.) For a while, the combined efforts of the Soho Society and Westminster Council reduced the number of sex establishments, but the area's vice days are by no means over: sex shops and peepshows still dominate large parts of the neighbourhood and the number of lap-dancing clubs continues to grow.

This part of Soho has its fair share of **artistic associations** too. It was on Broadwick Street that William Blake was born in 1757, above his father's hosiery shop, and where, from the age of 9, he had visions of "messengers from heaven, daily and nightly". He opened a print shop of his own next door to the family home, and later moved to nearby Poland Street, where he lived six years with his "beloved Kate" and wrote perhaps his most profound work, *The Marriage of Heaven and Hell*, among other poems. Poland Street was also Shelley's first halt after having been kicked out of Oxford in 1811 for distributing *The Necessity of Atheism*, and Canaletto ran a studio just south on Beak Street for a couple of years while he sat out the Seven Years' War in exile in London.

Carnaby Street and around

Until the 1950s, **Carnaby Street** (ⓦwww.carnaby.co.uk) was a backstreet on Soho's western fringe, occupied, for the most part, by sweatshop tailors who used to make up the suits for nearby Savile Row. Then, in 1954, Bill Green opened a shop called Vince (in neighbouring Newburgh Street), selling outrageous clothes to the gay men who were hanging out at the local baths. He was followed by John Stephen, a Glaswegian grocer's son, who opened His Clothes in nearby Beak Street. In 1960, Stephen opened a branch on Carnaby Street and within a couple of years owned a string of trendy boutiques which catered for the new market in flamboyant men's clothing. By 1964 – the year of the official birth of the Carnaby Street myth – Mods, West Indian Rude Boys and other "switched-on people", as the *Daily Telegraph* noted, had begun to hang out in Carnaby Street. By the time Mary Quant sold her first miniskirt here, the area had become the epicentre of Swinging Sixties' London, and its street sign the capital's most popular postcard.

A victim of its own hype, Carnaby Street quickly declined into an avenue of overpriced tack, and so it remained for the next twenty-odd years. More recently, things have started to pick up again, especially at the top end of the street, and round the corner in Foubert's Place and **Newburgh Street**, where contemporary London fashion now has a firm foothold. Elsewhere, chain clothes stores have moved in, along with the likes of Rugby Scene and Soccer Scene, while shops like The Face flog upmarket Mod clothes.

Fitzrovia

Bounded by Tottenham Court Road to the east, Great Portland Street to the west and the shabbier eastern half of Oxford Street to the south, **Fitzrovia** is a northern extension of Soho. Like its neighbour, it has a raffish, cosmopolitan reputation, and has attracted its fair share of writers and bohemians over the last hundred years or so, including the Pre-Raphaelites and members of the Bloomsbury Group (see p.147). That said, there's a lot less going on here than in Soho, and just two real sights you can visit – the Victorian church on Margaret Street and Pollock's Toy Museum – since the landmark Post Office Tower is closed to the public.

All Saints, Margaret Street

Few London churches are as atmospheric as **All Saints** (@www.allsaints margaretstreet.org.uk), built by William Butterfield in the 1850s, two blocks north of Oxford Street on Margaret Street. Patterned brickwork characterizes the entire ensemble of clergy house, choir school (Laurence Olivier sang here as a boy) and church, set around a small court that's entered from the street through a pointed arch. The church interior, one of London's gloomiest, is best visited on a sunny afternoon when the light pours in through the west window, illuminating the fantastic variety of coloured marble and stone which decorates the place from floor to ceiling. Several of the walls are also adorned with Pre-Raphaelite Minton tile paintings, the east window is a neo-Byzantine quasi-iconostasis with saintly images nestling in gilded niches, and the elaborate pulpit is like the entire church in miniature. Surrounded by such iconographical clutter, you would be forgiven for thinking you were in a Catholic church – but then that was the whole idea of the Victorian High Church movement, which sought to re-Catholicize the Church of England without actually returning it to the Roman fold.

Charlotte Street and around

After All Saints, the place to head for is **Charlotte Street**, Fitzrovia's main street since its heyday in the 1930s. In those days, it was home to the *Tour Eiffel* (official address: 1 Percy St), where Wyndham Lewis and Ezra Pound launched the Vorticist magazine *Blast*; *L'Étoile*, further up, which the likes of Dylan Thomas and T.S. Eliot used to patronize; and *Bertorelli's*, where the Wednesday Club, including Eliot, John Berger and Christopher Isherwood, used to meet in the 1950s. The same crowd would get plastered in the nearby *Fitzroy Tavern* – from which the area got its sobriquet – along with rather more outrageous bohemians, like the hard-drinking Nina Hamnett, the self-styled "Queen of

Bohemia", who used to boast that Modigliani once told her she had the best tits in Europe.

One block east, on Scala Street, is the highly atmospheric, doll's house-like **Pollock's Toy Museum** (Mon–Sat 10am–5pm; £3; ☎020/7636 3452), housed above a wonderful toy shop. Its collections include a fine example of the Victorian paper theatres popularized by Benjamin Pollock, who sold them under the slogan "a penny plain, two pence coloured". The other exhibits range from vintage teddy bears to Sooty and Sweep, and from Red Army soldiers to wax dolls, filling every nook and cranny of the museum's six tiny, rickety rooms and the stairs – be sure to look out for the dalmatian, Dismal Desmond. There are occasionally live performances at the weekend, so phone ahead to check.

Exploring Fitzrovia, it's impossible to ignore the looming presence of the former **Post Office Tower** (officially known as the Telecom Tower these days), a glass-clad pylon designed in the early 1960s by a team of bureaucrats in the Ministry of Works, which sits one block west of Fitzroy Street, the extension of Charlotte Street. It was the city's tallest building until the NatWest Tower topped it in 1981, and is still one of the most obvious landmarks north of the river. Sadly, since an IRA bomb attack in 1971, the tower and its revolving restaurant have been closed to the public.

Fitzroy Square and around

Near the top of Fitzroy Street is **Fitzroy Square**, a Bloomsbury-style square begun by the Adam brothers in the 1790s and faced, unusually, with light Portland stone rather than the ubiquitous dark Georgian brickwork. Traffic is now excluded, but few pedestrians come here either – except those hobbling to the London Foot Hospital – yet it's a square with both artistic and revolutionary associations. The painter **Ford Madox Brown** had fortnightly singsongs at no. 37 with his Pre-Raphaelite chums, and illustrious guests such as Turgenev and Liszt. **Virginia Woolf**'s blue plaque can be seen at no. 29 (a house also lived in by George Bernard Shaw): her Bloomsbury chums considered it a disreputable neighbourhood but she moved here with her brother in 1907, after taking the precaution of checking with the police. Later, in 1913, artist Roger Fry set up his Omega Studios at no. 33, padding the walls with seaweed to keep out the noise. The square enjoyed an even worse reputation in the 1890s when it was home to the International Anarchist School for Children, run by 60-year-old French anarchist Louise Michel. The police eventually raided the building and closed down the school after finding bombs hidden in the basement.

Fitzrovia's radical pedigree has a further presence in **Marie Stopes House**, nearby at 108 Whitfield St, originally opened as the pioneering Mothers' Clinic for Constructive Birth Control in 1921 and kept functioning in the face of numerous legal battles. A qualified paleobotanist, Stopes courted controversy by advocating birth control as an aid to women's sexual pleasure, after her first marriage remained unconsummated for five years. However, her espousal of eugenics – she was keen to reduce the size of working-class families in order to improve the nation's stock, and even invented her own cervical cap called "Pro-racial" – has left a cloud over her reputation.

One last revolutionary of note – the Venezuelan adventurer **General Francisco de Miranda** (1750–1816) – is commemorated with a statue at the eastern corner of the London Foot Hospital situated on the southern side of the square. De Miranda lived nearby for a few years at 58 Grafton Way, and in 1810 he met up in Fitzrovia with fellow revolutionary Simon Bolivar; de Miranda ended his days in a Spanish prison, while Bolivar went on to liberate Venezuela.

Tottenham Court Road

It's been centuries since there was a stately mansion – the original Tottenham Court – at the northern end of **Tottenham Court Road**, which now makes a strong challenge for London's least prepossessing central shopping street. A rash of stores flogging discount-priced stereos, CD players, computers and all sorts of electrical equipment pack out the southern end, while furniture-makers – the street's original vendors – from Habitat and Heal's to cheap sofa outlets, pepper its northern stretch. The London listings magazine *Time Out* has its base here, too. Unless you're desperate for a Sega Megadrive or a pine bed-base, however, you won't lose much by giving this whole street a miss.

The British Museum

The **British Museum** is one of the great museums of the world. With 70,000 exhibits ranged over two and a half miles of galleries, the museum boasts one of the largest and most comprehensive collections of antiquities, prints and drawings to be housed under one roof – seven million at the last count (a number increasing daily with the stream of new acquisitions, discoveries and bequests). Its assortment of Roman and Greek art is unparalleled, its Egyptian collection is the most significant outside Egypt and, in addition, there are fabulous treasures from Anglo-Saxon and Roman Britain, from Africa, China, Japan, India and Mesopotamia – not to mention an enormous collection of prints and drawings, only a fraction of which can be displayed at any one time.

The origins of the BM (as regular visitors call it) lie in the collection of over 80,000 curios – everything from plants and fossils to flamingo tongues and "maggots taken from a man's ear" – belonging to **Hans Sloane**, a wealthy Chelsea doctor who bequeathed them to George II in 1753, in return for £20,000. The king couldn't (or wouldn't) pay, so the collection was finally purchased by an unenthusiastic government to form the kernel of the world's first public secular museum, housed in a mansion bought with the proceeds of a dubiously conducted public lottery. Soon afterwards, the BM began to acquire the antiquities that have given it a modern reputation as the world's largest museum of plundered goods. The "robberies" of Lord Elgin are only the best-known; countless others engaged in sporadic looting throughout the Empire – the Napoleonic Wars provided the victorious Brits with heaps of antiquities pilfered by the French in Egypt – and the BM itself sent out its own archeologists to strip classical sites bare.

As early as 1820 it was clear that more space was needed for all this loot, hence the present structure, built piecemeal over the course of the next thirty years. The overall design was by **Robert Smirke**, whose giant Ionic colonnade and portico, complete with pediment frieze, make this the grandest of London's Greek Revival buildings. Despite the BM's huge size, lack of space continued to be a big problem until the British Library (see p.154) finally moved to St Pancras in the late 1990s, freeing up acres of potential gallery space. In a flurry of millennial construction, the BM's central courtyard, or **Great Court**, was given a startling glass-and-steel curved roof designed by Norman Foster, and opened to the public for the first time since the library's spectacular **Round Reading Room** was plonked in the middle of the courtyard in the 1850s. Boasting one of the largest domes in the world, the Round Reading Room is also open to the public (daily 10am–5.30pm), who can use the reference books on the open

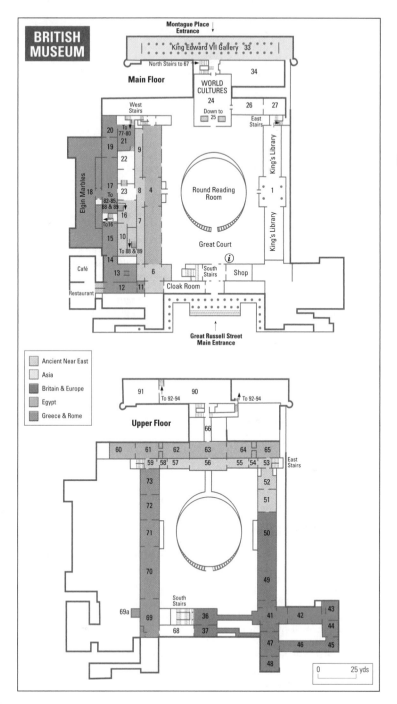

Visiting the British Museum

The BM (℡020/7636 1555, ⓦwww.thebritishmuseum.ac.uk) has **two entrances**, both of which have disabled access and cloakrooms: the main one, on Great Russell Street, brings you straight to the information desk in the Great Court, while the smaller doorway on the north side of the building in Montague Place opens onto the Asian galleries. The nearest tubes are Tottenham Court Road, Holborn or Russell Square. **Opening hours** for the galleries are daily 10am–5.30pm, Thurs & Fri until 8.30pm (note that only a few selected galleries are open on Thurs and Fri evenings), but the Great Court is open daily 9am–6pm, Thurs–Sat until 11pm; **admission** is free.

The BM is keen to sell you a **museum plan**, but you can usually pick one up free from the main information desk in the Great Court. Even equipped with a plan, it's easy enough to get confused, as room numbering is complicated and many sections are spread over more than one floor – don't hesitate to ask the **museum staff**, who are usually extremely helpful and knowledgeable. The BM can get crowded, too, so if you're heading for the major sights, try to get here as early in the day as possible, particularly at weekends. It's a far cry from the museum's beginnings in 1759, when it was open for just three hours a day, entry was by written application only, and tickets for "any person of decent appearance" were limited to ten per hour.

The BM's fourteen-acre site is enough to tire even the most ardent museum lover. J.B. Priestley, for one, wished "there was a little room somewhere in the British Museum that contained only about twenty exhibits and good lighting, easy chairs, and a notice imploring you to smoke". Short of such a place, the best advice is either to see the **highlights** (listed on p.133) and leave the rest for another visit, or to concentrate on one or two sections. Alternatively, you might consider one of the BM's daily **guided tours**: Highlights tours (1hr 30min; £8) are led by professional BM guides, while the eyeOpener tours (50min; free) are led by trained volunteers, and concentrate on just one of the BM's collections. Note that tours can get booked up quickly during high season. Look out, too, for the **Hands-On** desks in some of the galleries (daily 11am–4pm), where you can handle some of the museum's artefacts. Another option is to pick up one of the **audio tours** (£3.50).

The museum's best **café and restaurant** is, in fact, the *Gallery Café* beyond room 12; the *Court Café* in the Great Court itself is more snacky, though it's open longer hours and has a spectacular setting; the *Court Restaurant*, on the upper floor, looks down into the Round Reading Room, and is more formal, pricier and usually best booked in advance (℡020/7323 8990).

stacks, or explore the BM's collections on computer. Of the numerous writers who have studied here, the most famous is Karl Marx, whose *Das Kapital* was reputedly penned at the padded-leather desk O7.

Greece and Rome

The BM's galleries devoted to **Greece and Rome** make up the largest section in the museum and are spread over three floors. The main floor (rooms 11–23) is laid out along broadly chronological lines, starting with the Bronze Age and finishing up in Hellenistic times; highlights include the Elgin Marbles and the Nereid Monument. The upper floors (rooms 69–73) concentrate mostly on Italy before and during the Roman Empire, while the lower floors (rooms 77–85) hold the chaotic Townley Collection of Greek and Roman sculpture.

Classical Greece

From the main entrance, turn left through the cloakroom, and, ignoring the alluring Assyrian sculpture to your right, enter room 11 through the twin half-columns taken from one of the beehive tombs at Mycenae. Beyond, in room 12, lies the **Aegina Treasure** of Minoan gold jewellery, four elaborate earrings, a pendant and other ornaments, dating from before 1500BC. The real highlights of the Classical section, however, are in room 15 onwards, starting with the marble relief from the **Harpy Tomb**, a huge imposing funerary pillar from Xanthos in western Turkey, which originally rose to a height of nearly 30ft. The tomb occupies centre stage in the room, its name derived from the pairs of strange birdwomen, known as harpies, that appear on two sides of the relief, carrying children in their arms. In the purpose-built mezzanine (room 16) is the fifth-century BC marble frieze from the **Temple of Apollo at Bassae**, which would originally have

▲ Great Court

been lodged 50ft up by the roof of the temple, barely visible and poorly lit. Here, you come face to face with naked Greeks battling it out with half-clad Amazons, and inebriated centaurs misbehaving at a Lapith wedding feast, all depicted vigorously in high relief.

Back down the stairs, in room 17, your eyes are drawn to the reconstructed fourth-century BC **Nereid Monument**, a mighty temple-like tomb of a chieftain from Lycia (aka Lykia in the BM), an ancient maritime district of modern-day Turkey, fronted with Ionic columns interspersed with figures once identified as Nereids (sea nymphs), now thought to be Aurae, or wind goddesses. The monument was the most important construction at Xanthos, the Lycian capital, until 1842, when it was carried off by Charles Fellows on the HMS *Beacon*, along with the greater part of the site's moveable art (including the aforementioned Harpy Tomb relief).

Greek vases

The BM boasts an exhausting array of **Greek vases**, starting with the Geometric and early pictorial-style period (ninth and eighth centuries BC) in room 13, and moving on through the unusual Corinthian hybrid-animal vases to more familiar Athenian black-figure vases of the Archaic period (seventh and sixth centuries BC). Among the later red-figure vases from Greece's Classical age (fifth century BC) in rooms 14 and 15, check out the satyrs balancing wine coolers on their erect penises. There are further hoards of early Greek vases in the basement of room 13, and later, mostly red-figure examples in room 19 and the mezzanine room 20a, not to mention the various examples dotted about rooms 68–73 on the upper floors and in the King's Library.

The Elgin Marbles

The large, purpose-built room 18 is devoted to the museum's most famous relics, the **Parthenon sculptures**, better known as the **Elgin Marbles**, after Lord Elgin, who started hacking them off the Parthenon in Athens in 1801. As British ambassador to Constantinople, Lord Elgin claimed he gained permission from the Ottoman authorities (who ruled Greece at the time) to remove "any pieces of stone with figures and inscriptions". He interpreted this as a licence to make off with the majority of the reliefs of the Parthenon frieze and most of its pedimental sculptures, which he displayed in a shed in his Pall Mall garden until he was eventually forced to sell them to the government to settle a debt of £35,000. The government, in turn, passed the marbles on to the BM.

There were justifications for Elgin's action – the Turks' tendency to use Parthenon stones in their limekilns, and the fact that the building had already been partially wrecked in 1687 when a Venetian missile landed on the pile of gunpowder the Turks had thoughtfully stored there – though it was controversial even then and was opposed, notably by Byron. The Greek government has repeatedly requested the sculptures be reunited and have even built a special museum to house them near the Acropolis. The BM's argument that the marbles are in safer hands here in London was seriously undermined when it was disclosed that the gallery has been hired out for parties, and that a cleaning in the last century had actually damaged the sculptures.

Despite their grand setting (and partly due to all the hype), first impressions of the marble friezes, carved between 447 and 432 BC under the supervision of the great sculptor **Pheidias**, can be a little disappointing. After the vigorous high relief of the Bassae frieze, the Parthenon's sculptures can appear flat and lifeless, made up of long, repetitive queues of worshippers. To help prepare you for what you're about to see, first check out the excellent interpretive rooms on either side of the gallery's entrance. In one room, a short, mercifully silent, **video** shows you where the marbles would originally have been situated, which, in the case of the main frieze, was high up and virtually out of sight behind the first set of columns. The video also demonstrates how ingeniously Pheidias dealt with the complex compositional problems of trying to carve groups of people and animals. In the opposite room are casts taken from the pieces of the frieze that remain in Athens, and a useful reminder that the frieze, like most of the classical sculptures in the BM, would originally have been vibrantly picked out in red, blue and gold paint.

The **audioguide** to the marbles (£3.50) helps focus your mind on the sculpture, though it's by no means essential listening, as the explanatory panels are very informative. It's now generally agreed that the main frieze depicts the **Panathenaic Festival**, held every four years to glorify the goddess Athena. One of the most impressive sections is the traffic jam of horsemen on the north frieze, which is better preserved and exhibits superb compositional dexterity – it's worth remembering that the frieze is carved to a maximum depth of only two inches, yet manages to convey a much greater feeling of depth. Another superlative slice stands directly opposite, where the oxen are being led to the gods (said to have inspired Keats to write his *Ode on a Grecian Urn*).

At each end of the room are the freestanding pedimental sculptures: the figures from the east pediment, which depict the extraordinary birth of Athena – she emerged fully grown and fully armed from the head of Zeus – are the most impressive, though most are headless. The surrounding metopes, which vary enormously in quality, derive entirely from the south side of the Parthenon, and depict in high relief the struggle between Centaurs and Lapiths.

The Tomb of Payava and the Mausoleum of Halicarnassus

Beyond the Nereid Monument, in room 19, you come to two of Lord Elgin's less defensible appropriations, looking particularly forlorn and meaningless: a single column and one of the six caryatids from the portico of the **Erechtheion**, also on the Acropolis. Further on, in room 20, is another large relic from Xanthos, the **Tomb of Payava**, built during the incumbent's lifetime in the fourth century BC; the reliefs on the tomb's steep roof (particular to Lycia) would have been out of view of earthbound mortals, and are best viewed from the gallery, known as room 20a, containing the reserve collection of Greek vases.

Room 21 contains fragments from one of the Seven Wonders of the Ancient World: two huge figures, an Amazonian frieze and a marble horse the size of an elephant from the self-aggrandizing tomb of **King Mausolus at Halicarnassus** (source of the word "mausoleum") from the fourth century BC. However, the real gem is the sculpted column drum in room 22, from another Wonder of the World, the colossal **Temple of Artemis at Ephesus**, which is decorated in high relief with scenes from the underworld. The rest of the room is devoted to Hellenistic culture and features a fabulously delicate gold oak wreath with a bee and two cicadas.

The lower floors: Greek and Roman sculpture

From room 21, steps lead down to the **lower-floor** galleries (rooms 77–85). Room 77 is rather like a classical builder's yard, piled high with bits of columns, architraves, entablatures and capitals, much of it gathered from the aforementioned Temple of Artemis, the Mausoleum of Halicarnassus and the Propylaea in Athens. Next comes a room full of classical inscriptions, followed by room after room of Greek and Roman sculpture, arranged in the whimsical manner preferred by the eighteenth-century English collectors who amassed the stuff.

The best pieces come from the **Townley Collection**, bought from dealers in Rome and London between 1768 and 1791 by Charles Townley, for his London house in Queen Anne's Gate. In room 85, there are dozens of portrait busts of emperors and mythological heroes, while in the parallel room 83 there's a monumental marble foot (possibly) from a statue of the Egyptian god Serapis. But the final room (84) houses the most bewildering array of sculpture, much of it modified to Townley's own tastes; here, you'll find two curiously gentle marble greyhounds, a claw-footed sphinx and a chariot-shaped latrine.

One of Townley's last and most famous purchases is a Roman copy of the famous classical Greek bronze of the **Discobolos** (the discus thrower), whose head was positioned facing the wrong way during restoration. (It should be looking at the discus.) The statue is not currently displayed on the lower floors, but is positioned halfway up the south stairs.

The upper floors

The remainder of the Greek and Roman collection is situated on the **upper floors** (rooms 69–73), which you can approach either from the south stairs or from the west stairs – the latter are lined with mosaic pavements from Halicarnassus. Room 69 houses an educative exhibition on daily life in classical times and features a variety of objects grouped under specific themes such as gladiators, music, women and so on. There's a dazzling display of mostly third-century AD silverware from Roman Gaul in room 70, plus an intriguing, warty, crocodile-skin suit of armour worn by a Roman follower of the Egyptian crocodile cult. While you're here, don't miss the first-century AD **Warren Cup**, whose graphic depictions of gay sex were deemed too risqué to be shown to the public until the 1990s. Next to it stands the **Portland Vase**, made from cobalt-blue blown glass around the beginning of the first millennium, and decorated with opaque white cameos. The vase was famously smashed into over two hundred separate pieces by a young Irishman in 1845, for which he was fined £3. The last three rooms (71–73), which round off the Classical section, are of minor interest only, although the finely carved ostrich eggs in room 71, discovered by Napoleon's brother, are worth a look.

Ancient Near East

The collections from the **Ancient Near East** cover all the lands east of Egypt and west of India. The majority of exhibits on the main floor come from the Assyrian Empire, which reached its height in the ninth and eighth centuries BC; upstairs you'll find the Nimrud ivories, rich pickings from Mesopotamia and the Oxus Treasure from ancient Persia.

Assyrian sculpture and reliefs

After passing through the cloakroom, the first gallery you arrive at (room 6) has two attendant gods, their robes smothered in inscriptions, signalling the beginning of the BM's remarkable collection of **Assyrian sculptures and reliefs**. Close by stands a small black obelisk carved with images of foreign rulers paying tribute to Shalmaneser III (858–824 BC), interspersed with **cuneiform inscriptions** – discovered in 1846, these helped significantly in the decoding of this early form of writing. Ahead of you lies the Egyptian sculpture gallery (room 4; see p.136), but to continue with Assyria, turn left and pass between the two awesome five-legged, human-headed winged bulls that once guarded the Temple of Ishtar in Nimrud, built by Ashurnasirpal II (883–859 BC) – two larger ones stand at the entrance to room 10. Beyond is a full-scale reconstruction of the colossal wooden **Balawat Gates** from the palace of Shalmaneser III, which are bound together with bronze strips decorated with low-relief friezes (the originals are displayed close by) depicting the defeat and execution of Shalmaneser's enemies.

The **Nineveh reliefs**, which begin in room 7, were originally brightly coloured, appearing rather like stone tapestries. There are some great snapshots of Assyrian life – a review of prisoners, a bull hunt and so on – but the most memorable scene, located towards the middle of the room, is of the soldiers swimming across the sea on inflated animal bladders. The reliefs in room 9 record the stupendous effort involved in transporting the aforementioned winged bulls from their quarry to the palace; they should be read from left to right, so start at the far end of the room. Evidently the Assyrians moved these huge carved beasts in one piece; not so the British, who cut the two largest winged bulls in the BM into four pieces before transporting them – the joins are still visible on the pair at the entrance to room 10.

Room 10 itself is lined with even more splendid friezes from Assyrian king Sennacherib's palace in Nineveh. On one side is an almost continuous band portraying the chaos and carnage during the Assyrian capture of the Judaean city of Lachish; the friezes were damaged, and Sennacherib's face smashed in by Babylonian soldiers when the Assyrian capital finally fell to its southern neighbours in 612 BC. On the other side are depicted the **royal lion hunts** of Ashurbanipal (668–627 BC), which involved rounding up the beasts before letting them loose in an enclosed arena for the king's sport, a practice which effectively eradicated the species in Assyria; the succession of graphic death scenes features one in which the king slaughters the cats with his bare hands.

Mesopotamia, Ur and the Oxus Treasure

From room 10, it's a convenient trot down into the lower floor (rooms 88 & 89), where there are more friezes and inscriptions on Ashurbanipal's military exploits, and domestic objects, including an iron bathtub decorated with wild goats which was found reused as a coffin. All hail from the **Mesopotamian capital of Ur**, thought to be the first great city on earth, dating from 2500 BC, now in modern-day Iraq.

Up the west stairs in room 59, the upper floor, are the Neolithic **Ain Ghazal statues**, the oldest large-scale representations of humans in the world, dating from the eighth millennium BC. Further on, in room 56, are some more of the BM's oldest artefacts, dating from Mesopotamia in the third millennium BC. The most extraordinary treasures hail from Ur: the enigmatic **Ram in the Thicket**, a deep-blue lapis lazuli and white shell statuette of a goat on its hind legs, peering through gold-leaf branches; the equally mysterious **Standard of Ur**, a small hollow box showing scenes of battle on one side, with peace and banqueting on the other, all fashioned in shell, red limestone and lapis lazuli, set in bitumen; and the **Royal Game of Ur**, one of the earliest known board games.

In room 55, a selection of tablets scratched with infinitesimal cuneiform script includes the **Flood Tablet**, a fragment of the Epic of Gilgamesh, perhaps the world's oldest story, an ancient Sumerian tale written four thousand years ago about the adventures of the King of Uruk (c.2700 BC). Finally, there's the **Oxus Treasure**, in room 52, a hoard of goldwork which appears to have passed from one band of robbers to another until it was eventually bought from the bazaar at Rawalpindi by a British officer. The pieces date from the fifth and fourth centuries BC and are executed in a style used throughout the Persian Empire. The most celebrated are the miniature four-horse chariot and the pair of armlets sprouting fantastical horned griffins.

Egypt

The BM's collection of antiquities from **Egypt**, ranging from Predynastic times to Coptic Egypt, is one of the finest in the world, rivalled only by Cairo's and the New York Met's; the highlights are the Rosetta Stone, the vast hall of Egyptian sculpture and the large collection of mummies.

Egyptian sculpture

On the main floor, just past the entrance to the Assyrian section (see p.134), two black granite statues of **Amenophis III** (c.1417–1379 BC), whose rule coincided with the zenith of Egyptian power, guard the entrance to the BM's large hall of **Egyptian sculpture** (room 4). The name "Belzoni", scratched under the left heel of the larger statue, was carved by the Italian circus strongman responsible for dragging some of the heftiest Egyptian treasures to the banks of the Nile, prior to their export to England. Beyond are a series of **false doors**, richly decorated with hieroglyphs and figures of the deceased, through which, it was believed, the dead person's *ka* (soul) could pass to receive the food offerings laid outside the burial chamber. Further on, a colossal pink-speckled granite head of Amenophis III stands next to his enormous dislocated arm. Nearby are four seated statues of the goddess Sakhmet, the half-lion, half-human bringer of destruction, who was much loved by Amenophis III – each sports solar discs and clutches the *ankh*, the Egyptian symbol of life.

Centre stage in the Egyptian sculpture hall is the **Rosetta Stone**, a black basalt slab found in the Nile delta in 1799 by French soldiers. It was surrendered to the Brits in 1801, but it was a French professor, Champollion, who finally unlocked the secret of Egyptian hieroglyphs, by comparing the stone's three different scripts – ancient hieroglyphs, demotic Egyptian and Greek. North of here, another giant head and shoulders, made of two pieces of different-coloured granite, bears the hole drilled by French soldiers in an unsuccessful attempt to remove it from the Ramesseum, the mortuary temple of Ramses II. Moving towards the end of the room, be sure to check out the colossal granite scarab beetle by the exit.

The mummies and other funerary art

Climbing the west stairs brings you to the popular **Egyptian mummy** collection. In room 61, there's a fascinating array of smaller objects, from signet rings and children's toys to cosmic vessels in the shape of hedgehogs and a rattle to ward off evil spirits. Two of the museum's most popular items can be found here, too: the bronze Gayer-Anderson cat goddess **Bastet**, with gold nose- and ear-rings, and the diminutive glazed turquoise hippo.

In room 62, you'll see numerous mummified corpses, embalmed bodies, and inner and outer **coffins** richly decorated with hieroglyphs. In one display cabinet, there are even mummies of various animals, including cats, apes, crocodiles, falcons and an eel, along with their highly ornate coffins. Also on display

▲ Egyptian mummy

Egyptian mummification

To attain the afterlife, it was necessary that the deceased's name and body continued to exist, in order to sustain the *ka* or cosmic double that was born with every
person. At its height in the New Kingdom (1567–1085 BC), **mummification** entailed
removing the brain (which was discarded) and the viscera (which were preserved in
jars); applying resin to the body and dehydrating the cadaver in salts for about forty
days; packing it to reproduce lifelike contours; inserting artificial eyes and painting
the face or entire body either red (for men) or yellow (for women); wrapping it in
gum-coated linen bandages; and finally cocooning it in mummy-shaped coffins.

are colourful funerary **amulets** which were wrapped with the mummy, and
heart scarabs, which were placed on the chest of the mummy to prevent the
deceased's heart from bearing witness against him or her during the judgement
of Osiris, when the deceased's heart (believed to be the seat of intelligence) was
weighed against Maat's feather of truth. The hearts of the guilty were devoured
by crocodile-headed Ammut, while the righteous were led into the presence of
Osiris to begin their resurrection.

The contents of Egyptian tombs included food, drink, clothing, furniture,
weapons and dozens of **shabti figures** designed to perform any task that the
gods might require in the afterlife. In room 63, there are miniature boats to provide transport in the afterlife, beer brewers, butchers and even an entire model
granary. The last couple of rooms are less interesting, though the 5000-year-old
sand-preserved corpse in room 64 always comes in for ghoulish scrutiny, and
there's a limestone building block from the Great Pyramid of Cheops (Khufu) at
Giza, another of the Seven Wonders of the World.

Britain and Europe

The BM fulfils its less controversial role as national treasure house in the (rather
loosely defined) **Britain and Europe** section on the upper floor (rooms 36,
37 & 41–50), though even here there have been calls for the items to be shared
more with the regional museums.

Prehistoric/Roman Britain

The most spectacular exhibit in room 36, at the top of the south stairs, is the
Bronze Age **Mold cape**, a spectacular embossed gold cape used for ceremonial
purposes. There are some truly intriguing Neolithic finds, too, such as the trio
of precisely carved geometric stone balls and carved limestone drums.

One of the most famous of the treasure hordes here is the fourth-century AD
Mildenhall Treasure, a 28-piece silver tableware set displayed in room 49; the
Great Dish, an outstanding late Roman work, weighs over 8kg and is decorated
with Bacchic images in low relief. Also displayed here are the oldest handwritten documents in Britain, ranging from private letters to official military
documents, all discovered in a rubbish heap in Vindolanda, one of the chief forts
on Hadrian's Wall. Several spectacular finds have been dragged out from the
bottom of the River Thames, too, most notably a bronze head of the Roman
emperor Hadrian. A whole load more are displayed in room 50, including the
Battersea Shield, a bronze-faced Celtic shield from the first century BC.

Room 50 also houses one of the most sensational of the BM's more recent
finds, the leathery half-corpse **Lindow Man**. Clubbed and garrotted during
a Druid sacrificial ceremony (or so it's reckoned), he lay in a hide-preserv-
ing Cheshire bog for 2000 years. There are also some fabulous heavy golden

necklaces, a horned bronze helmet, and fine decorative mirrors and shields. Best of all is the **Snettisham Treasure**, made up mostly of gold and silver torcs (neck-rings), the finest of which is made of eight strands of gold twisted together, each of which is in turn made up of eight wires. Brilliant displays of **Celtic craftwork** follow, two of the most distinctive objects being the French Basse-Yutz wine flagons, made from bronze and inlaid with coral. Showing Persian and Etruscan influences, they are supreme examples of Celtic art, with happy little ducks on the lip and rangy dogs for handles.

Europe: Medieval/Modern

The **Europe: Medieval/Modern** galleries cover well over 1500 years, from the fall of the Roman Empire to the interwar period. Room 41, the first gallery, houses a bewildering array of "Dark Age" treasures from all over the continent, but most visitors come here to see the Anglo-Saxon **Sutton Hoo Treasure**, which includes silver bowls, gold jewellery decorated with inset enamel and an iron helmet bejewelled with gilded bronze and garnets, all buried along with a forty-oar open ship in East Anglia around 625 AD. Discovered by accident in 1939, this enormous haul is by far the richest single archeological find ever made in Britain.

In the Medieval Gallery (room 42) are the thick-set **Lewis chessmen**, wild-eyed twelfth-century Scandinavian figures carved from walrus ivory, which were discovered in 1831 by a crofter in the Outer Hebrides. There are more walrus ivories – mostly chesspieces and religious plaques – from France and Germany elsewhere in the room, as well as a smattering of medieval Russian and Byzantine icons. At the far end of the room is the richly enamelled, fourteenth-century French **Royal Gold Cup**, given by James I to the Constable of Castille, only to find its way back to England in later life.

Room 43 displays tile mosaics and the largest secular tile pavement in the country, but you're likely to get more joy out of the adjacent room (44), which resounds to the tick-tocks and chimes of a hundred or more **clocks**, from pocket watches to grandfather clocks. These range in design from the very simple to the highly ornate, like the sixteenth-century gilded copper and brass clock from Strasbourg, based on the one that used to reside in the cathedral there; its series of moving figures includes the Four Ages of Man, who each strike one of the quarter-hours.

The purple-walled chamber beyond (room 45) contains the **Waddesdon Bequest**, amassed by Baron Rothschild in the nineteenth century: a mixed bag of silver gilt, enamelware, glassware and hunting rifles. The two finest works are a Flemish sixteenth-century boxwood altarpiece, which stands only 6in high and is carved with staggering attention to detail, and the Lyte Jewel, which contains a miniature of James I by Hilliard.

Renaissance and Baroque art fills the long gallery of room 46, with a bafflingly wide range of works from all over Europe (though much of it is of British origin). Highlights to look out for are the Armada Service, a Tudor silver dining set, two pure-gold ice pails that used to belong to Princess Diana's family, Cromwell's wax death mask and a collection of eighteenth-century Huguenot silver. Room 47 brings you into the **European nineteenth-century** section, and reflects the era's eclectic tastes, with all sorts of objets d'art from quasi-medieval jewellery to Neoclassical porcelain vases, much of it inspired by the BM itself. Look out for the Arts and Crafts De Morgan and Minton tiles and Christopher Dresser's outstanding geometric metalwork.

Before you leave, you must pay a visit to room 48, where a small selection of the museum's high-quality **twentieth-century exhibits** are displayed. There are stunning examples of iridescent Tiffany glass, a copper vase by Frank Lloyd Wright and a good selection of Jugendstil and Bauhaus products. A whole case is devoted to Futurist Russian porcelain, including several Suprematist pieces celebrating the 1917 revolution. Perhaps the finest exhibit of all, though, is the chequered oak clock with a mother-of-pearl face, designed by the Scottish architect and designer Charles Rennie Mackintosh.

Money

To get to the BM's **Money Gallery** (room 68), turn sharp right at the top of the south stairs. The displays trace the history of money from the use of grain in Mesopotamia around 2000 BC, to the advent of coins in around 625 BC in Greek cities in Asia Minor, to printed money in China in the tenth century AD. It's an attractive and informative gallery, which features pound-coin moulds and punches, a geometric lathe for old £1 notes and a wonderful turn-of-the-century National Cash Register till designed by Tiffany. The prize for the largest denomination bill goes to the 1993 500,000 million Yugoslav dinar note, but perhaps the most unusual exhibit of all is the 1970s one million dollar note issued by the Hong Kong "Bank of Hell", featuring the face of Harold Wilson, and designed to be burnt as an offering to keep the deceased happy in the afterlife. Room 69a (tucked off room 69) hosts temporary exhibitions drawn from the BM's collection of over 500,000 coins and medals.

The King's Library

The **King's Library** – the oldest section of the building, dating from the 1820s – runs the entire length of the east wing on the main floor and formerly housed George III's library, now the centrepiece of the British Library in St Pancras (see p.154). With its coffered plasterwork ceiling and old-fashioned display cases stuffed with books and artefacts, the library is a period piece from the BM of old, and, appropriately enough, houses an interesting exhibition on the eighteenth-century Enlightenment. Displayed here are some of the museum's earliest acquisitions, brought back from the far reaches of the expanding British Empire: a piece of bark cloth made by Fletcher Christian's Tahitian partner; Tipu Sultan's sword and the ring taken from the finger of his corpse at the Battle of Srirangapatna in 1799; and a whole variety of Javanese puppets, dolls and a model gamelan orchestra, collected by Stamford Raffles. The sheer range and volume of items on display, with their terse (and in some cases non-existent) labels, is a deliberate attempt to illustrate the acquisitive magpie tastes of the eighteenth-century colonial collector, epitomized by Hans Sloane himself, the BM's founder. Sloane's own collection features everything from genuine priapic statuettes to a black obsidian mirror used by the Elizabethan magician, John Dee, to conjure up spirits. And he was not alone in falling for the bizarre and magical to augment his "cabinet of curiosities": the rhino-horn cup which protected the drinker from poison and the Japanese "merman" – a dried monkey sewn onto a fish tail – are typical of some of the items on display here.

World Cultures

The BM's highly successful ethnographic galleries are slowly expanding: the Mexican, North American and African galleries are up and running, along with the Living and Dying section. More are set to open over the course of the next few years.

Mexico and North America

The **Mexican Gallery** (room 27) is a dramatically lit display, covering a huge period of Mexican art from the second millennium BC to the sixteenth century AD. As you enter, you're greeted by an Aztec fire serpent, Xiuhcoatl, carved in basalt. On one side is a collection of Huaxtec female deities in stone, sporting fan-shaped headdresses; on the other are an Aztec stone rattlesnake cleverly lit and mirrored from below, the squatting figure of the sun-god, Xochipili, and the death-cult god, Mictlantecuhtli. A series of limestone Mayan reliefs from Yaxchilan, depicting blood-letting ceremonies, lines one wall and, elsewhere, there are some wonderful jade masks and figurines. Whatever you do, don't miss the brilliant colours of the Mixtec painted screen-fold book made of deerskin.

Next door is the **North American Gallery** (room 26), whose precise exhibits are destined to change over the course of time due to the delicate organic nature of the materials used. However, you can be sure to find feather headdresses, masks, basketry, artefacts carved from walrus ivory and zoomorphic stone pipes, plus intriguing items such as the skin map of Illinois and Indiana from 1775, which reveals the debt the first white cartographers owed to Native Americans. Since Native American culture survives to this day, there are old and new examples of their art, and historic and contemporary photos to accompany them.

Africa

The BM's **Africa** collection, in the series of galleries known as lower-floor room 25, is careful to try and reflect contemporary African culture as well as displaying its rich heritage. To the left, as you enter, there are **woodcarvings** from a whole range of African cultures: everything from a large stool from Cameroon to backrests from the Congo, and a chilling "throne of weapons" from contemporary Mozambique. Further to the left, you'll find the Yoruba royal palace doors, carved in high relief and depicting, among other things, several lazy British imperialists arriving on a litter to collect taxes. You'll also come across a great deal of **military paraphernalia** in this section, including an entire cabinet of throwing knives from the Congo, colourful quilted Sudanese horse armour and a warlike Kenyan cricket shirt.

To the right of the entrance, there's a section on **masquerades**: as well as viewing elaborate crocodile, buffalo, warthog and hippo masks from the last two centuries, you get to examine some of the creations from, and watch a video of, recent initiation ceremonies in Nigeria. Perhaps the most famous of the BM's African exhibits are the **Benin Treasures**, looted when the British took over the country in 1897. Benin was one of the famous gold-producing forest states of West Africa, and some of the exhibits, such as the eye-catching sixteenth-century ivory saltcellar, were actually commissioned by Europeans. The majority of the sculptures, masks and altars displayed here come from the royal court, however, with the single most remarkable exhibit being the beautifully naturalistic brass head from Ife. Equally extraordinary are the ornate brass plaques, nine hundred of which decorated the royal palace in Benin City, and fifty or so of which can be seen here. Also in this section, you'll find some characteristically colourful African fabrics, including one depicting Amílcar Cabral, who fought for the independence of Guinea-Bissau, a Nubian lyre festooned with beads and an antelope-skin helmet decorated with silver and gold.

Asia

The collections from **Asia** cover some of the same geographical area as the museum's ethnographic collections, and also overlap with material in the V&A (see p.302). The Chinese collection is, however, unrivalled in the West, and the Indian sculpture is easily as good as anything at the V&A. The easiest way to approach the Asian galleries (rooms 33–34 & 91–94) is from the Montague Place entrance; from the Great Russell Street entrance, walk across the Great Court and continue up the north stairs.

China

The **Chinese collection** occupies the eastern half of room 33, which is centred on a wonderful marble well that allows you to look down onto the Montague Place foyer. Immediately striking are the pieces of garishly glazed **three-colour statuary**, particularly the central cabinet of horses, camels, kings, officials and fabulous beasts. However, it's the smaller pieces that hold the attention the longest: for example, the central cabinet of miniature landscapes, in cabinet 56, popular among bored Chinese bureaucrats during the Manchu Empire, or the incredible array of **snuff bottles** in the window cabinet, made from extremely diverse materials – lapis lazuli, jade, crystal, tortoiseshell, quartz and amber.

The Chinese invented **porcelain**, and it was highly prized both in China and abroad. The polychrome Ming and the blue-and-white Yuan porcelain became popular in the West from the fifteenth century onwards, as did the brightly coloured cloisonné enamelware, but it's the much earlier unadorned porcelain which steals the show, with its austere beauty and subtle pastel colours, as in the grey-green Ru porcelain and blue-green celadons from the Song dynasty. There's more Chinese chinaware on display in London at the Percival David Foundation; see p.151.

South and Southeast Asia

The other half of room 33 starts with a beautiful gilt-bronze standing statue of Tara, the seventh-century goddess of good fortune, who was born from one of the tears wept by Avalokiteshvara, a companion of the Buddha, who stands on the other side of the well. She heralds the beginning of the **South and Southeast Asian** antiquities, a bewildering array of artefacts from places as far apart as India and Indonesia. There are so many cultures and countries covered (albeit briefly) in this section that it's impossible to do more than list some of the **highlights**: cabinet 54 displays Tibetan musical instruments, with a conch-shell trumpet decorated with gilt and precious stones; the classic Hindu image of **Shiva as Lord of the Dance**, trampling on the dwarf of ignorance, occupies centre stage halfway along the hall; nearby cabinet 39 features a whole set of ivory figures from Kandy, representing the local royal family and officials, including the all-important umbrella-bearer. Look out, too, for Vishnu, depicted in his first incarnation as a fish, carrying a shrine with a tree on it, and Ravana, the ten-headed demon in cabinet 35.

Beyond are larger-scale **Indian stone sculptures**, featuring a bevy of intimidating goddesses such as Durga, depicted killing a buffalo demon with her eight hands. The showpiece of the collection, however, lies behind a glass screen in room 33a, a climatically controlled room of dazzling limestone reliefs, drum slabs and dome sculptures purloined from **Amaravati**, one of the finest second-century Buddhist stupas in southern India. The display is somewhat chaotic, however, and you'll have to consult the accompanying illustrations to get any idea of how it might have looked.

Korea

The centrepiece of the BM's gallery devoted to **Korea** (room 67), up the north stairs from room 33, is a nail-free reconstruction of a *sarangbang* or scholar's study, a wonderfully serene, minimalist space set aside for the gentleman of the house as a study. Among the other exhibits, which range from illuminated Buddhist manuscripts to contemporary Korean objets d'art, look out for the woven horsehair hats and bamboo fans used by dapper Korean gentlemen, the Paduk gaming board (better known in the West as the Game of Go), the seventeenth-century white porcelain "full-moon" jar, admired for both its irregularity and its Confucian austerity, and the heavy gold earrings from the sixth century, worn by both sexes in the leading families of the Silla Kingdom.

Islam

The museum's **Islamic** antiquities, ranging from Moorish Spain to southern Asia, are displayed in room 34, adjacent to the Montague Place entrance. The collection features glass, metalwork and pottery decorated mostly with arabesques and calligraphy (figural representation being forbidden under Islamic law), and **Damascus and Iznik ceramics** in greens, tomato-reds and no fewer than five shades of blue. Some of the best stuff is at the far end of the room, where Moorish lustre pottery resides alongside medieval astrolabes, celestial globes and a **geomantic instrument** from the seventh century, used to discover buried treasure and tell the future. Most unusual of all, though, is a naturalistic **jade terrapin**, discovered in Allahabad in 1600. Other curiosities include a falcon's perch, a back-scratcher and a couple of jade Mughal hookah bases encrusted with lapis lazuli and rubies set in gold.

Bloomsbury

B LOOMSBURY gets its name from its medieval landowners, the Blemunds, who were probably given the estate – described in the Domesday Book as having vineyards and "wood for 100 pigs" – by William the Conqueror. Nothing was built here, though, until the 1660s, when the Earl of Southampton laid out Bloomsbury Square, which John Evelyn thought "a noble square or piazza – a little towne". Through marriage, the Russell family, the earls and later dukes of Bedford, acquired much of the area, and established the other formal, bourgeois squares which remain the main distinguishing feature of Bloomsbury. The Russells named the grid-plan streets after their various titles and estates, and kept the pubs and shops to a minimum to maintain the tone of the neighbourhood.

In the twentieth century, Bloomsbury acquired a reputation as the city's most learned quarter, dominated by the dual institutions of the **British Museum** and **London University** and home to many of London's chief book publishers, but perhaps best known for its literary inhabitants. In its northern fringes, the character of the area changes dramatically, becoming steadily seedier as you near the big main-line train stations of **Euston**, **St Pancras** and **King's Cross**, where cheap B&Bs and run-down council estates have given the area a reputation for prostitution and drug dealing. The area looks set to change in 2007, however, in line with the introduction of the Eurostar trains into St Pancras station.

The British Museum is clearly Bloomsbury's main draw – it has its own chapter (see p.128), and could easily occupy you for an entire day or more – and, in comparison, the other sundry attractions of the area are pretty lightweight, though no less enjoyable for that. The **Dickens Museum** in Doughty Street, at the edge of Holborn, may be the most popular, but the **Foundling Museum** to the north, on the site of an old foundling hospital, has much more to offer, and the museum at the new **British Library**, near St Pancras station, is a definite must. The university museums, scattered about Bloomsbury, are of more specialist interest. Then, of course, there are Bloomsbury's leafy **squares**, which, though no longer the set pieces of Georgian architecture they once were, still provide some of the nicest picnic spots in central London.

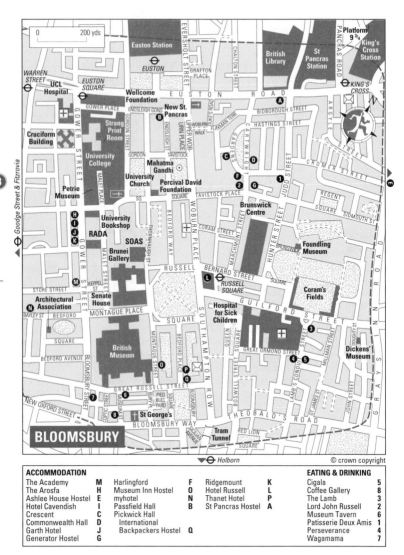

ACCOMMODATION						EATING & DRINKING	
The Academy	M	Harlingford	F	Ridgemount	K	Cigala	5
The Arosfa	H	Museum Inn Hostel	O	Hotel Russell	L	Coffee Gallery	8
Ashlee House Hostel	E	myhotel	N	Thanet Hotel	P	The Lamb	3
Hotel Cavendish	I	Passfield Hall	B	St Pancras Hostel	A	Lord John Russell	2
Crescent	C	Pickwick Hall				Museum Tavern	6
Commonwealth Hall	D	International				Patisserie Deux Amis	1
Garth Hotel	J	Backpackers Hostel	Q			Perseverance	4
Generator Hostel	G					Wagamama	7

South of the British Museum

The grid of Georgian streets **south of the BM** has been threatened with demolition more than once, in order to make space for a more monumental approach to the museum. The parallel streets of Museum Street and Bury Place currently thrive on a mixture of antiquarian and secondhand print and book shops, and cafés and sandwich shops, while just round the corner, it's worth looking in at the window of Jarndyce, the booksellers at 46 Great Russell St, whose left window is renowned for its display of bizarre antiquarian books, with titles such as *Correctly English in Hundred Days* and *The Art of Faking Exhibition Poultry*.

Set back from busy Bloomsbury Way, three blocks south of the BM, is the Church of **St George's Bloomsbury** (Mon–Fri 9.30am–5.30pm; ⓦwww .stgeorgesbloomsbury.org.uk), the westernmost of Hawksmoor's six London churches, built so that Bloomsbury's respectable residents wouldn't have to cross the St Giles rookery (see p.164) in order to attend services at St Giles-in-the-Fields. Its main point of interest is the unusual steeple – Horace Walpole called it "a masterpiece of absurdity" – a stepped pyramid based on Pliny's description of the tomb of Mausolus at Halicarnassus, fragments of which subsequently made their way to the BM (see p.133). The tower is topped by London's only outdoor statue of the unpopular German-speaking monarch, George I, dressed in a Roman toga. Inside the church it's tall and wide, decked out in sky blue and gold, with a large clerestory and great flaming pentecostal tongues on the keystones. The unusual semicircular apse, complete with a gilded scallop-shell recess, served as the original altar until the church's internal realignment in 1781.

The Bloomsbury squares

A little further along Bloomsbury Way, past St George's, is **Bloomsbury Square**, dating from 1665 and the first of the city's open spaces to be officially called a "square". Little remains of its original or later Georgian appearance, and the only reason to venture down Bloomsbury Way is to see **Sicilian Avenue**, an unusually Continental promenade sliced diagonally across the former slums on the corner of Bloomsbury Way and Southampton Row. Separated from the main roads by slender Ionic screens, this simple but effective piece of town planning was created in 1910. On Southampton Row itself, you can see the only **tram lines** left uncovered in central London from what was, between World Wars I and II, the world's largest tram system: to catch a glimpse, you must dodge the traffic and peek over the wrought-iron railings to the tracks as they descend into the former Kingsway Subway.

The most handsome of the Bloomsbury squares is **Bedford Square**, to the west of the BM, up Bloomsbury Street. Some of Bloomsbury's best-known publishing houses – among them Hodder & Stoughton, Bodley Head, Jonathan Cape and Chatto & Windus – had their offices here until the mergers of the 1980s killed off most small independent outfits. Architecturally, however, very little has changed and what you see now is pretty much as it was in the 1770s when it was built by the Russells (who still own it), though the gates which sealed the square from traffic have unfortunately been removed, as have all but one of the mews that used to accommodate the coaches and servants of the square's wealthy inhabitants. Today, it's a perfect example of eighteenth-century symmetry and uniformity: each doorway arch is decorated with rusticated Coade stones; each facade is broken only by the white-stuccoed central houses. The best way to get a look inside one of these Georgian mansions is to head for the **Architectural Association** (opening hours vary; ⓦwww.aaschool.ac.uk) at no. 36, which puts on occasional exhibitions, and has a bookshop in the basement and a studenty café/bar on the first floor, with a roof terrace open in fine weather.

The largest Bloomsbury square – indeed one of the largest in London – is **Russell Square**, to the northeast of the BM. Apart from its monumental scale,

▲ Russell Hotel

little remains of the Georgian scheme, though the gardens, with their gargantuan plane trees, are good for a picnic; you can also grab a hot drink from the café in the north-eastern corner. The figure most closely associated with this square is T.S. Eliot, who worked at no. 24, then the offices of Faber and Faber, from 1925 until his death in 1965. The only architectural curiosity is the *Russell Hotel*, on the eastern side; twice as high as everything around it, it's a no-holds-barred Victorian terracotta fancy, concocted in a bewildering mixture of styles in 1898 by Fitzroy Doll. The hotel's wood-panelled *King's Bar* is worth closer inspection, as are the main foyer and ball-room (the latter hosts an antiquarian and secondhand book fair on the second Sunday of each month; ⓦwww .pbfa.org) – though the nicest touch is the wonder-fully incongruous *Virginia Woolf Burger, Pasta and Grill Restaurant* on the ground floor.

Gordon Square (Mon–Fri 8am–8pm), one block north of Russell Square, with its winding paths and summer profusion of roses, remains one of Bloomsbury's quietest sanctuaries, a favourite with students from the university departments hereabouts. Its one building of note is the strangely towerless neo-Gothic **University Church**, built in 1853 for the Catholic Apostolic sect (who encouraged the congregation to "speak in tongues") in the southwest corner of the square and looking like a miniature cathedral – the unbuilt tower was to have been nearly 300ft high. Gordon Square was once the centre of the Bloomsbury Group (see box, opposite): on the east side, where the Georgian houses stand intact, plaques mark the residences of Lytton Strachey (no. 51) and John Maynard Keynes (no. 46), while another (no. 50) commemorates the Bloomsbury Group as a whole. At no. 53 is the Percival David Foundation of Chinese Art (see p.151).

One block east, and exhibiting almost identical proportions to Gordon Square, is **Tavistock Square**, laid out by Thomas Cubitt in the early part of the nine-teenth century. Though the west side of the square survives intact, the house at no. 52, where the Woolfs lived from 1924 until shortly before Virginia's suicide in 1941, and from which they ran the Hogarth Press, is no longer standing. It was here that Woolf wrote her most famous novels – *To the Lighthouse, Mrs Dalloway, Orlando* and *The Waves* – in a little studio decorated by her sister Vanessa and Duncan Grant. At the centre of the square's gardens is a statue of **Mahatma**

Gandhi, whose presence has transformed the square into something of a garden for peace, with various trees and benches dedicated to the cause. That peace was shattered on the morning of **July 7, 2005** when a suicide bomber blew up bus #30 as it approached the northeast corner of the square, killing at least thirteen people. The blast occurred shortly after the city's tube system had been hit by three other terrorist bombs (see p.592).

A short distance up Upper Woburn Place, not far from where the blast occurred, is the beautifully preserved Georgian terrace of **Woburn Walk**, designed in 1822 by Cubitt as London's first purpose-built pedestrianized shopping street. W.B.Yeats moved into no. 5 in 1895, shortly afterwards losing his virginity at the age of 31 to Olivia Shakespear. He and Olivia had to go to Heal's to order a bed before they could consummate the relationship, and Yeats found the experience (of ordering the bed) deeply traumatic, as "every inch added to the expense". He lived there until 1919, writing some of his greatest poetry while hobnobbing with the likes of Ezra Pound, T.S. Eliot and Rabindranath Tagore. The same address was later occupied by the unrequited love of Yeats' life, Irish nationalist Maud Gonne, reputedly the most beautiful woman in Ireland, with, in Yeats' own words, "the carriage and features of a goddess".

The Bloomsbury Group

The **Bloomsbury Group** were essentially a bevy of upper-middle-class friends who lived in and around Bloomsbury, at that time "an antiquated, ex-fashionable area", in the words of Henry James. The group revolved around Virginia, Vanessa, Thoby and Adrian Stephen, who moved into 46 Gordon Square in 1904, shortly after the death of their father, Leslie Stephen, editor of the *Dictionary of National Biography*. Thoby's Thursday-evening gatherings and Vanessa's Friday Club for painters attracted a whole host of Cambridge-educated snobs who subscribed to Oscar Wilde's theory that "aesthetics are higher than ethics". Their diet of "human intercourse and the enjoyment of beautiful things" was hardly revolutionary, but their behaviour, particularly that of the two sisters (unmarried, unchaperoned, intellectual and artistic), succeeded in shocking London society, especially through their louche sexual practices (most of the group swung both ways).

All this, though interesting, would be forgotten were it not for their individual work. In 1922, Virginia declared, without too much exaggeration, "Everyone in Gordon Square has become famous": Lytton Strachey had been the first to make his name with *Eminent Victorians*, a series of unprecedentedly frank biographies; Vanessa, now married to the art critic Clive Bell, had become involved in Roger Fry's prolific design firm, Omega Workshops; and the economist John Maynard Keynes had become an adviser to the Treasury. (He later went on to become the leading economic theorist of his day.) The group's most celebrated figure, Virginia, now married to Leonard Woolf and living in Tavistock Square, had become an established novelist; she and Leonard had also founded the Hogarth Press, which published T.S. Eliot's *Waste Land* in 1922.

Eliot was just one of a number of writers, such as Aldous Huxley, Bertrand Russell and E.M. Forster, who were drawn to the Bloomsbury set, but others, notably D.H. Lawrence, were repelled by the clan's narcissism and narrow-mindedness. (Virginia Woolf once compared *Ulysses* to a "bell-boy at *Claridges*" scratching his pimples.) Whatever their limitations, the Bloomsbury Group were Britain's most influential intellectual coterie of the interwar years, and their appeal shows little sign of waning – even now, scarcely a year goes by without the publication of the biography or memoirs of some Bloomsbury peripheral.

East of Russell Square

Not many folk wander east of Russell Square, which is hardly surprising as the original Bloomsbury squares and streets here have been bashed about a bit. The chief tourist sight here is **Dickens' House**, the only one of the writer's fifteen London addresses to survive intact. Medical institutions dominate the area, particularly around **Queen Square**, which is popularly known as "hospital square". One of the first to be established here was the Foundling Hospital, on the site of which now stands the excellent **Foundling Museum**, and neighbouring **Coram's Fields**, shelter for London's most central city farm.

The Foundling Museum and Coram's Fields

Halfway along Guilford Street is the old entrance to the **Foundling Hospital**, founded in 1756 by Thomas Coram, a retired sea captain. Coram campaigned for seventeen years to obtain a royal charter for the hospital, having been shocked by the number of dead or dying babies left by the wayside on the streets of London during the gin craze. (At the time, 75 percent of London's children died before they were 5.) All that remains of the original eighteenth-century buildings – which were demolished when the foundation moved to the Home Counties in the 1920s – is the alcove where the foundlings used to be abandoned and the whitewashed loggia which now forms the border to **Coram's Fields**, a wonderful inner-city park for children, with swings and slides, plus a whole host of hens, horses, sheep, pigs and rabbits. Adults are not allowed into the grounds unless accompanied by a child.

At the **Foundling Museum** (Tues–Sat 10am–6pm, Sun noon–6pm; £5; ☎020/7841 3600, ⓦwww.foundlingmuseum.org.uk), just to the north of Coram's Fields, at 40 Brunswick Square, you can learn more about the fascinating story of the hospital. As soon as it was opened, it was besieged, and soon forced to reduce its admissions drastically and introduce a ballot system. After 1801 only illegitimate children were admitted, and even then only after the mother had filled in a questionnaire and given a verbal statement confirming that "her good faith had been betrayed, that she had given way to carnal passion only after a promise of marriage or against her will; that she therefore had no other children; and that her conduct had always been irreproachable in every other respect". Among the most tragic exhibits are the tokens left by the mothers in order to identify the children should they ever be in a position to reclaim them: these range from a heart-rending poem to a simple enamel pot label reading "ale".

One of the hospital's founding governors – he even fostered two of the children – was the artist **William Hogarth**, who decided to set up an art gallery at the hospital to give his fellow artists somewhere to display their works and to attract useful potential benefactors for the hospital. As a result the museum boasts an impressive art collection including works by artists such as Gainsborough and Reynolds, now hung in the eighteenth-century interiors carefully preserved in their entirety from the original hospital.

Hogarth's own *March of the Guards to Finchley*, probably the finest of the pictures, hangs in the Committee Room. Upstairs, the Court Room, where the governors still hold their meetings, has been faithfully reconstructed, with all its fine stuccowork. The fireplace features a wonderful relief depicting the trades of navigation and agriculture, into which the foundling boys were originally apprenticed before being sent out to the colonies. (The girls went into service.)

Charles Dickens

Few cities are as closely associated with one writer as London is with **Charles Dickens** (1812–70). Though not born in London, Dickens spent much of his life here, and the recurrent motifs in his novels have become the clichés of Victorian London – the fog, the slums and alleys, the prisons and workhouses, and of course the stinking river. Drawing on his own personal experience, he was able to describe the workings of the law and the conditions of the poor with an unrivalled accuracy. He also lived through a time of great social change, during which London more than doubled in size, yet in his writing the city remains a surprisingly compact place: only rarely do his characters venture east of the Tower of London, or west of St James's, with the centre of the city hovering somewhere around the Inns of Court, described in detail in *Bleak House*.

Born in Portsmouth to a clerk in the naval pay office, Dickens spent a happy early childhood in London and Chatham, on the Kent coast. This was cut short at the age of 12 when the whole family were imprisoned in Marshalsea debtors' prison, and Charles was forced to work in a rat-infested boot-blacking factory in the old Hungerford Market. The experience, though brief, scarred him for life – he was hurt further by his mother's attempt to force him to keep the job rather than return to school, even after his father's release – and was no doubt responsible for Dickens' strong philanthropic convictions. After two years as a solicitor's clerk at Gray's Inn, he became a parliamentary reporter, during which time he wrote *Sketches by Boz* (Dickens' journalistic pen name) and *The Pickwick Papers*. The publication of these two works propelled him to local fame and comparative fortune in 1836, and in the same year he married Catherine Hogarth and moved to the bourgeois neighbourhood of Doughty Street.

Catherine's younger sister, Mary, also moved into the house after the marriage, and her death in 1837, at the age of just 17, had a profound effect on Dickens. In his will, the author requested that he be buried next to her when he died and wore Mary's ring all his life. Another of Catherine's younger sisters, Georgiana, then moved in with the Dickenses, to help run the household. There followed ten children – "the largest family ever known with the smallest disposition to do anything for themselves", as Dickens later described them – and sixteen novels, each published in monthly (or weekly) instalments, which were awaited with bated breath by the Victorian public. Then in 1857, at the peak of his career, Dickens fell in love with an actress, Ellen Ternan, who was just 18, the same age as his favourite daughter, Kate. His subsequent separation from his wife, and his insistence that she leave the family house (while her sister Georgina and most of the children stayed), scandalized society and forced the author to retreat to his country house in Rochester.

In the last decade of his life, Dickens found an outlet for his theatrical aspirations, and a way of supporting the extended family for which he was now responsible, by touring Britain and America giving dramatic readings of his works. He died at his desk at the age of 58, while working on *The Mystery of Edwin Drood*. According to his wishes, there was no public announcement of his burial, though he was interred in Westminster Abbey (at Queen Victoria's insistence) rather than in Rochester (as he had requested). The twelve people present at the early-morning service were asked not to wear a black bow, long hatband or any other accessories of the "revolting absurdity" of Victorian mourning.

If you're on the Dickens trail, there are one or two other sights worth checking out: the Old Curiosity Shop (see p.176), on Lincoln's Inn Fields, the (possible) inspiration for Dickens' novel of the same name; the atmospheric Inns of Court (see p.173), which feature in several Dickens novels; "Nancy's Steps", where Nancy tells Rose Maylie Oliver's story in *Oliver Twist*, on the west side of London Bridge on the South Bank; and the evocative dockland area of Shad Thames (see p.281), where Bill Sykes has his hide-out.

On the top floor, there's a room dedicated to **George Frideric Handel**, another of the hospital's early patrons, who gave annual charity performances of the *Messiah*, wrote an anthem for the hospital (basically a rehash of the *Hallelujah Chorus*) and donated an organ for the chapel, the keyboard of which survives.

To the south of Coram's Fields is the **Hospital for Sick Children** on Great Ormond Street, which was founded a hundred years after the Foundling Hospital by Charles West, who (like Coram) was appalled by the infant mortality rate in London. Just as Handel had helped out Coram, so Great Ormond Street Hospital was assisted by J.M. Barrie, who donated the copyright (and thus the future royalties) of *Peter Pan* to the hospital in 1929. In 1987, fifty years after Barrie's death, the copyright expired, but the following year an Act of Parliament restored royalty income in perpetuity.

Dickens' House

Despite the plethora of blue plaques marking the residences of local luminaries, the only Bloomsbury address that has been turned into a literary museum is **Dickens' House** (Mon–Sat 10am–5pm, Sun 11am–5pm; £5; ☎020/7405 2127, ⊛www.dickensmuseum.com), southeast of Coram's Fields at 48 Doughty St. Dickens moved here in 1837 – when it was practically on the northern outskirts of town – shortly after his marriage to Catherine Hogarth, and they lived here for two years, during which time he wrote *Nicholas Nickleby* and *Oliver Twist*. Although Dickens painted a gloomy Victorian world in his books, the drawing room here, in which Dickens entertained his literary friends, was decorated (and has since been restored) in a rather upbeat Regency style. Letters, manuscripts and first editions, the earliest known portrait (a miniature painted by his aunt in 1830) and the reading copies he used during extensive lecture tours in Britain and the States are the rewards for those with more than a passing interest in the novelist. There's also a half-hour film of his life.

London University

London has more students than any other city in the world (over half a million at the last count), which isn't bad going for a city that only organized its own **University** (⊛www.lon.ac.uk) in 1826, more than six hundred years after the likes of Oxford and Cambridge. Although the university started life in Bloomsbury, it wasn't until after World War I that it really began to take over the area. Nowadays, the various colleges and institutes have spread their tentacles to form an almost continuous academic swathe from the British Museum all the way to Euston Road, with plenty more further afield. Despite this, the university's piecemeal development has left it with no real focus, just a couple of local landmarks in the form of **Senate House** and **University College** and its attendant hospital. Several of the university departments run their own small, specialist **museums and galleries**, which are fun to visit, not least for the opportunity of wandering around the university.

Senate House and SOAS

Looming behind the British Museum is the skyscraper of **Senate House**, a "bleak, blank, hideous" building, according to Max Beerbohm. Completed by

Charles Holden in 1932 and austerely clad in Portland stone, it's best viewed from Malet Street. During the war it served as the Ministry of Information, where the likes of Evelyn Waugh, Dorothy L. Sayers and George Orwell worked. Orwell later modelled the Ministry of Truth in *1984* on it: "an enormous pyramidal structure of glittering white concrete, soaring up, terrace after terrace, 300 metres into the air".

To the north of Senate House, on Thornhaugh Street, is the **School of Oriental and African Studies** or **SOAS** (ⓦwww.soas.ac.uk), which puts on temporary exhibitions of photography, sculpture and art at the rather snazzy **Brunei Gallery** (Mon–Fri 10.30am–5pm; free), paid for by the immensely rich Sultan of Brunei. There's a bookshop and café on the ground floor, and a secluded Zen-like rooftop garden.

Percival David Foundation of Chinese Art

Tucked away in the southeast corner of Gordon Square, at no. 53, SOAS also runs the **Percival David Foundation of Chinese Art** (Mon–Fri 10.30am–5pm; free; ☎020/7387 3909, ⓦwww.pdfmuseum.org.uk), which contains the finest collection of Chinese ceramics outside the Chinese-speaking world. The majority of the pieces were bequeathed by the collector Percival David, who was born to a wealthy Anglo-Jewish family in Bombay. The museum contains everything from bowls, vases and boxes to incense holders, pipes and birdseed saucers, and begins on the ground floor with ceramics that once belonged to the eighteenth-century emperor Qianlong, who was himself an avid collector. These range from antique Guan ware, from the Song dynasty (960–1279), with its distinctive heavily cracked glaze, to copies of pastiches of Ming-style ceramics produced under Qianlong. Several pieces have inscriptions on them – one even features a poem by the emperor himself – and virtually the whole collection was made for domestic Chinese consumption, not for export. The displays on the two upper floors are more old-fashioned in their layout, but still worth exploring to admire the delicate, pastel-coloured, unadorned Ru, Ding and Yue ware, and the striking purple and blue Jun ware.

University College London

The university's oldest building is William Wilkins' Neoclassical **University College London** or **UCL** (ⓦwww.ucl.ac.uk), on Gower Street, whose Main Building was erected in the 1820s with a handsome Corinthian portico and a fine quadrangle set back (and well hidden) from street. Nicknamed the "godless college" because it was founded for non-Anglican students, who were excluded from both Oxford and Cambridge at the time, UCL also became the first university to accept women as equals in 1878. The Main Building is open to the public and has one or two intriguing sights; the college's museums are spread out across Bloomsbury, but within easy walking distance.

As you enter UCL, behind you, on the opposite side of Gower Street, stands the **Cruciform Building**, a typically striking terracotta and red-brick building designed by Alfred Waterhouse at the end of the nineteenth century as the **University College Hospital** (UCH). Waterhouse planned the teaching hospital with strictly segregated wards so as to prevent the miasma or "foul air" from passing from ward to ward – despite the fact that the discovery of bacterial infection in 1867 had made such precautions redundant. Eric Blair (aka George Orwell) died of tuberculosis here in 1950, shortly after getting married to his second wife, Sonia Brownell, in the hospital ward.

The Main Building

The **Main Building** of UCL is home to the most famous of London's art schools, the **Slade** (℡020/7679 2540, ⓦwww.ucl.ac.uk/slade), which puts on small, but excellent temporary exhibitions drawn from its collection of over 10,000 works of art, by the likes of Dürer, Rembrandt, Turner and Constable, as well as works by former students, such as Stanley Spencer, Paul Nash, Wyndham Lewis, Augustus John and Raymond Briggs. These are held at the **Strang Print Room** (Wed–Fri 1–5pm; free), situated in the south cloister of the main quadrangle.

There's more artwork on display in the octagon underneath UCL's central dome, in an area known as the **Flaxman Gallery** – follow the signs to the library and ask the guards at the barrier to let you through. John Flaxman (1755–1826) made his name producing Neoclassical funerary sculpture – his works feature prominently in both Westminster Abbey and St Paul's – and the walls here are filled with scaled-down, high-relief, plaster models worked on by Flaxman himself for his marble monuments. The gallery's centrepiece is a dramatic full-size plaster model of St Michael overcoming Satan.

Also on display in the cloisters is the philosopher **Jeremy Bentham** (1748–1832), one of the university's founders, who bequeathed his fully-clothed skeleton so that he could be posthumously present at board meetings of the University College Hospital governors, where he was duly recorded as "present, but not voting". Bentham's **Auto-Icon**, topped by a wax head and wide-brimmed hat, is in "thinking and writing" pose as the philosopher requested, and can be seen in a hermetically sealed mahogany booth in the south cloisters of the main building. Close by are a pair of watchful Egyptian lions, reconstructed from several thousand fragments belonging to the Petrie Museum (see below).

Petrie Museum of Egyptian Archeology

The **Petrie Museum of Egyptian Archeology** (Tues–Fri 1–5pm, Sat 10am–1pm; free; ℡020/7504 2884, ⓦwww.petrie.ucl.ac.uk), on the first floor of the D.M.S. Watson Building, down Malet Place, has a couple of rooms jam-packed with antiquities, the bulk of them from excavations carried out in the 1880s by Flinders Petrie, then UCL Professor of Egyptology. To the non-specialist, the first room appears to contain little more than broken bits of pottery (a speciality of Professor Petrie's). Look more closely, however, and you'll also find the world's oldest dress, an understandably ragged pleated garment worn by an Ancient Egyptian teenager around 3000 BC. More intriguing still is the very revealing, erotic bead-net dress made for a 10-year-old, from around 2400 BC, which would have made a seductive rattling sound when worn. In the second room, the cabinets are crammed full of tiny objects including weights and measures, shabti figures (see p.137), combs, bottle stoppers, sandals, legs from a toy table, a mummified bird and a pair of tweezers. Look out, too, for the richly decorated wooden coffin of Nairytisitnefer from 750 BC, and the frog amulets, ivory spoons and bronze cat-goddess Bastet down the back stairs.

Grant Museum of Zoology and Comparative Anatomy

Another room piled high with exhibits – in this case skeletons – can be found in the **Grant Museum of Zoology and Comparative Anatomy** (Mon–Fri 1–5pm; free; ℡020/7679 2647, ⓦwww.grant.museum.ucl.ac.uk), located on the ground floor of the Darwin Building, south of the Main Building on Gower Street. The museum is named after Robert E. Grant (1793–1874), the university's first Professor of Zoology and Comparative Anatomy, a pre-Darwinian transmutationist who always wore full evening dress when delivering lectures and risked his career by teaching evolution at UCL. Among the numerous specimens here, don't miss the walrus's penis bone, the skeletons of a dugong, a dodo, a quagga (an extinct zebra) and a thylacine (an extinct marsupial wolf).

Euston Road

The northern boundary of Bloomsbury is defined by **Euston Road**, laid out in 1756 as the city's first traffic bypass, and now a six-lane traffic jam moving slowly west into Marylebone Road and east towards Islington. Euston Road marked the northern limit of the city until the mid-nineteenth century, and it was here that the rival railway companies built Euston, King's Cross and St Pancras stations, the termini of the lines serving the industrial boom towns of the north of England. Since those days, Euston Road has had some of the city's worst office architecture foisted on it, which, combined with the volume of traffic, makes this an area for selective viewing. The only compelling reason to venture here is to visit the excellent exhibition galleries at the **British Library**, and to admire its neighbour, the **Midland Grand Hotel**, which fronts St Pancras station. However, with the Eurostar trains due to arrive in St Pancras in 2007 (@www.ctrl.co.uk), millions of pounds are currently being poured into regenerating the whole area including the bit behind King's Cross, described in more detail on p.345.

St Pancras New Church to the Wellcome Building

Euston Road's oldest edifice is **St Pancras New Church** (@www.stpancras church.org), built at enormous expense in the 1820s on the corner of Upper Woburn Place. Designed in Greek Revival style, it is notable for its octagonal tower, based on the Tower of the Winds in Athens, and for the caryatids, tacked onto the east end, which are modelled on the Erechtheion on the Acropolis – though the Euston Road ladies had to be truncated at the waist after they were found to be too tall. The best time to visit the interior, which features a dramatically lit Ionic colonnade in the apse, and some lovely Victorian stained glass, is either in the mornings from Wednesdays to Saturdays, or during one of the free Thursday lunchtime recitals. St Pancras Old Church, up Pancras Road towards Camden, is described on p.345.

Amidst all the hubbub of Euston Road, it's easy to miss the depressing modernist hulk of **Euston Station**, descendant of the first of London's great train termini, which was built way back in 1840. This original much-loved landmark was demolished in the face of fierce protests in the 1960s – British Rail claimed it needed the space in order to lengthen the platforms, which it never did – and all that remains of Philip Hardwick's original Neoclassical ensemble are the sad-looking lodge-houses, part of the Euston Arch.

On the other side of the road from Euston station, at no. 183, stands the **Wellcome Building** (@020/7611 8231, @www.wellcome.ac.uk), a Neoclassical block erected in the 1930s by Henry Wellcome, the American-born pharmacist, to accommodate his research laboratories and showcase his collection of artistic and scientific artefacts. Wellcome's collections, ranging from a first edition of Gray's Anatomy to Napoleon's toothbrush, are due to go back on permanent display during 2006, in a new museum housed in the building. The museum will also stage temporary exhibitions and allow access to the Wellcome Library, with its archive of more than 100,000 images. Back across the Euston Road, at no. 210, you can visit the trust's **TwoTen Gallery** (Mon–Fri 9am–6pm; free), which puts on exhibitions exploring the relationship between science and art.

British Library

As one of the country's most expensive public buildings, it's hardly surprising that the £500 million **British Library** came under fire from all sides during its protracted construction. Few readers wanted to move out of the splendid Round Reading Room at the British Museum (see p.129), where the library had been since the 1850s, the number of extra readers' seats was negligible, and the shelving space was already inadequate, thus nullifying the building's original purpose of housing the entire British Library stock in one place.

Architecturally, the charge was led, predictably enough, by Prince Charles, who compared it to an academy for secret policemen. Yet, while it's true that Colin St John Wilson's penchant for red-brick brutalism is horribly out of fashion, and compares unfavourably with its cathedralesque red-brick neighbour, the former *Midland Grand Hotel*, the **interior** of the building has met with general approval, even from His Royal Highness, and the new hi-tech exhibition galleries are an enormous improvement on the noisy, cramped conditions that prevailed in the British Museum.

The new **piazza**, in front of the library, is, it has to be said, redundant as a public space, due to the traffic roaring down Euston Road, though it does feature Paolozzi's giant statue of Isaac Newton bent double over his protractor, inspired by William Blake – just one of a number of specially commissioned works of art on display in the library. Look out, too, for Bill Woodrow's *Book, Ball & Chain* sofa and R.B. Kitaj's unsettling giant tapestry, *If not, not*, both in the main foyer, and Patrick Hughes' optical illusion, *Paradoxymoron*, down in the basement cloakroom.

John Ritblat Gallery

The first of the three exhibition galleries to head for is the dimly lit **John Ritblat Gallery**, where a superlative selection of the BL's ancient manuscripts and precious books are permanently displayed. Closest to the entrance are the library's old **maps**: these change from time to time, but there's usually a Benedictine monk's map of Britain from 1250 and an extract from Mercator's world atlas from the 1560s, drawn by his own

▲ Isaac Newton statue

With the exception of the reading rooms, the library is open to the general public Mon & Wed–Fri 9.30am–6pm, Tues 9.30am–8pm, Sat 9.30am–5pm, Sun 11am–5pm (☏020/7412 7332, ⊛www.bl.uk). Orientation is relatively simple: the excellent bookshop and the entrance to the **exhibition galleries** are to the left as you enter; the cloakroom is in the basement; up the main stairs is the spiritual heart of the BL, a multistorey glass-walled tower housing the vast **King's Library**, collected by George III, and donated to the museum by George IV in 1823; to the side of the King's Library, on the upper ground floor, is the **philatelic collection**; beyond is the café and upstairs is the restaurant. You can sign up for a **guided tour** (Mon, Wed & Fri 3pm, Sat 10.30am & 3pm; £6), but if you want to see the reading rooms, you must come on a Sunday (11.30am & 3pm; £7). In addition to all the above, the library also puts on a wide variety of events, including talks, films and occasional live performances.

8

hand. Beyond are the **sacred texts**, kicking off with the richly illustrated **Lindisfarne Gospels**, begun in 698 AD and seen by many as the apotheosis of Anglo-Saxon art. The artistry displayed in the section and the sheer variety of exhibits are almost overwhelming: as well as numerous illuminated Bibles and Qur'ans (Korans), there are rules for Buddhist monks written on birch bark, a palm-leaf glorification of the Hindu goddess Jagannatha in the shape of a cow and several concertina-style folding books on the life of the Buddha.

One of the exhibition's most appealing innovations is **Turning the Pages**, a small room off the main gallery, where you can turn the pages of various texts – from the Lindisfarne Gospels to Leonardo da Vinci's notebook – "virtually" on a computer terminal, thus allowing you to see much more than the double page displayed in the glass cabinets. In the nearby section on printing, you can see the ninth-century **Diamond Sutra**, an Indian Buddhist text written in Chinese and the world's earliest-dated printed document, along with the **Gutenberg Bible**, from 1454–55, the first Bible printed using moveable type (and therefore capable of being mass-produced).

The most famous of the library's **historical documents** is probably King John's famous letter to his subjects in 1215, better known as the **Magna Carta**. Also displayed here is Thomas More's last letter to Henry VIII, Lady Jane Grey's prayer book given to the Lieutenant of the Tower moments before her execution, Nelson's last letter from the *Victory* setting out his plan for the Battle of Trafalgar and Scott's 1912 polar journal. Along the far wall is a selection of the library's **literary texts**, among them Shakespeare's First Folio from 1623, the original monthly instalments of Dickens' *David Copperfield* and the touchingly beautiful handwritten and illustrated copy of *Alice in Wonderland* given by Lewis Carroll to Alice Liddell. The British Library is also home to the National Sound Archive, so as well as examining James Joyce's maniacally scribbled *Finnegans Wake*, you can also hear Joyce (and several other authors) reading extracts from their works. Similarly, in the **music** section, you can listen to works ranging from Bach and The Beatles to Kalahari bushmen singing a healing dance song.

The other galleries

Situated downstairs from the John Ritblat Gallery is the spacious **Pearson Gallery of Living Words**, which houses temporary exhibitions (for which there is usually an entrance charge), employing more of the library's wonderful texts, supplemented by items on loan from the British Museum. To one side of the Pearson Gallery is the **Workshop of Words, Sounds and Images**, a hands-on exhibition of more universal appeal, where you can listen to Tchaikovsky's *1812 Overture* as it sounded over the course of the twentieth century, from mono wax-cylinder recording to CD. Visitors are also invited to try folding an eighteenth-century chapbook, and to explore a mock-up of a fifteenth-century scribe's studio, including a replica of the kind of wooden hand press used to produce the Gutenberg Bible.

Stamp lovers, meanwhile, should make their way up to the BL's gargantuan **Philatelic Collections**, made up of over eight million items, 80,000 of which are displayed in vertical pull-out drawers just outside the John Ritblat Gallery. The **Tapling Collection** kicks off the proceedings, as it did the collection when it was bequeathed in 1891, and in drawer number one you'll find the famous "Penny Black", the birthmark of modern philately. After that you get a world tour of stamps from long-forgotten mini-kingdoms such as Mecklenburg-Schwerin and Nowanugger. Those with a political interest should head for the **Bojanowicz Collection**, which covers Polish stamps from 1939 to 1946, including ones from the German and Russian occupations, and even POW and displaced persons' camps. The **Kay Collection** consists of stamps from the colonies, but real boffins should head for the **Turner Collection** of railway letter stamps from the likes of the Pembroke & Tenby Railway.

St Pancras and King's Cross stations

The British Library has the misfortune of standing in the shadow of one of the most glorious of London's red-brick Victorian edifices, George Gilbert Scott's **Midland Grand Hotel**. Completed in 1876, the hotel's majestic sweep of lancets, dormers and chimneypots forms the facade of **St Pancras Station**, terminus of the Midland Railway Company, which lies behind it. This masterpiece of neo-Gothic architecture had its heyday in the 1890s when the ratio of staff to guests was 3:1, but with few private bathrooms and no central heating, the hotel couldn't survive long into the modern age. For fifty years from 1935, it languished under the name of **St Pancras Chambers**, as underused British Rail offices, but is due to reopen for business as a hotel in 2008, shortly after the Eurostar finally arrives at the station. In the meantime, you can visit the foyer, the grand staircase and the old coffee lounge, where there's an exhibition on the building and a few remnants of its once lavish interior decor (Mon–Fri 11.30am–3.30pm; free); at the weekend, there are more formal guided tours, lasting an hour (Sat & Sun 11am & 1.30pm; £5; ☎020/7713 6514, ⊛www .lcrproperties.com).

Compared to St Pancras, **King's Cross Station**, opened in 1850 as the terminus for the Great Northern Railway, is a mere shed, though it was simple and graceful enough until British Rail added the modern forecourt. Legend has it that Boudicca's bones lie under platform 10 – the area used to be known as Battle Bridge, and was believed to have been the site of the final set-to between the Iceni and the Romans. More famously, the fictional **Harry Potter** and his wizarding chums leave for school on the Hogwarts Express each term from platform 9¾. The scenes from the films are, in fact, shot between platforms 4 and 5, though a station trolley is now half-embedded in the wall beside the side platforms of 9 and 1, providing a perfect photo opportunity for passing Potter fans.

9

Covent Garden and the Strand

Covent **Garden**'s transformation from a workaday fruit and vegetable market into a fashion-conscious *quartier* is one of the most miraculous and enduring developments of the 1980s. More sanitized and brazenly commercial than neighbouring Soho, it's a far cry from the district's heyday when the piazza was the great playground (and red-light district) of eighteenth-century London. The buskers in front of **St Paul's Church**, the theatres round about, and the **Royal Opera House** on Bow Street are survivors in this tradition, and on a balmy summer evening, **Covent Garden Piazza** is still an undeniably lively place to be. Another positive side effect of the market development has been the renovation of the run-down warehouses to the north of the piazza, especially around the Neal Street area, which now boasts some of the most fashionable shops in the West End, selling everything from shoes to skateboards.

As its name suggests, the **Strand**, just to the south of Covent Garden, once lay along the riverbank; it achieved its present-day form when the Victorians shored up the banks of the Thames to create the Embankment. One show-piece river palace, **Somerset House**, remains, its courtyard graced by a 55-jet fountain, and its chambers home to several museums and galleries, including the Courtauld's superb collection of Impressionist and Post-Impressionist paintings.

Covent Garden

Covent Garden (ⓦ www.coventgardenlife.com) has come full circle: what started out in the seventeenth century as London's first luxury neighbourhood is once more a highly desirable place to live, work and shop. Based around Inigo Jones' piazza – London's oldest planned square – the area had for years been a market centre for fruit, flowers and vegetables. When the flower market closed in 1974, the piazza narrowly survived being turned into an office development.

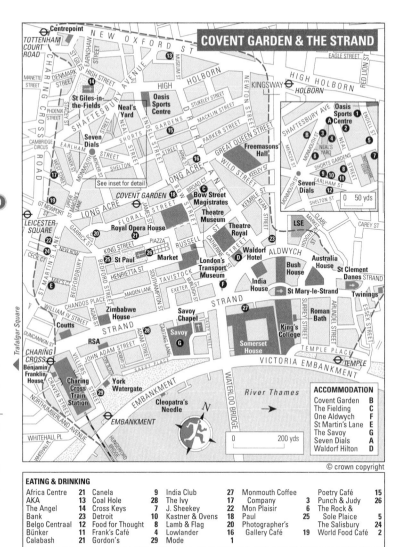

COVENT GARDEN & THE STRAND

© crown copyright

Instead, public protests ensured that the elegant Victorian market hall and its environs were restored to house shops, restaurants and arts-and-crafts stalls.

Boosted by buskers and street entertainers, Covent Garden has since become one of London's major tourist attractions; the area's success has prompted a wholesale gentrification of the streets to the north, particularly on Long Acre, Neal Street and Floral Street, which now boast some of London's trendiest clothes shops, cafés and restaurants. Alongside them, a few tiny pockets of 1970s "alternative" culture survive, left over from the days of squats and cheap rentals, when the whole area was threatened with destruction. London's tourism revenues owe them a considerable debt – it was only their demonstrations, and mass protests, that saved the area.

Most visitors are happy enough simply to wander around watching the street life, having a coffee and doing a bit of shopping, but there are one or two specific sights worth picking out. One of the old market buildings is now occupied by the **Theatre Museum** and **London's Transport Museum**, both highly recommended, and the old Floral Hall has been transformed into the new and very public foyer for the internationally famous **Royal Opera House**, which boasts a great roof terrace overlooking the piazza.

The piazza

Covent Garden's **piazza** was laid out in the 1630s, when the Earl of Bedford commissioned Inigo Jones to design a series of graceful Palladian-style arcades based on the main square in Livorno, Tuscany, where Jones had helped build the cathedral. Initially the development was a great success, its novelty value alone attracting a rich and aristocratic clientele, but over the next century the tone of the place fell as the fruit, vegetable and flower **market**, set up in the earl's back garden, expanded, and theatres, coffee houses and brothels began to take over the peripheral buildings. The historian Macaulay evoked the following scene: "fruit women screamed, carters fought, cabbage stalks and rotten apples accumulated in heaps at the thresholds of the Countess of Berkshire and the Bishop of Durham".

The piazza's status as a centre of entertainment declined with the approach of the nineteenth century. The theatres still drew crowds but the market now occupied most of the area, and the few remaining taverns had become dangerous. However, in the 1830s the piazza was cleaned up, slums were torn down and a proper market hall built in the Greek Revival style. A glass roof was added in the late Victorian era, but otherwise the building stayed unaltered until the closure of the market in 1974 – when trade moved south of the river to Nine Elms in Vauxhall – and its early-1980s renovation as a shopping arcade.

Coffee houses and brothels

By the early eighteenth century **the piazza** was known as "the great square of Venus", with dozens of gambling dens, bawdy houses and so-called "bagnios" in and around the piazza. Some bagnios were plain Turkish baths, but most doubled as brothels, where courtesans stood in the window and, according to one contemporary, "in the most impudent manner invited passengers from the theatres into the houses".

Some of London's most famous **coffee houses** were concentrated here, too, attracting writers such as Sheridan, Dryden and Aphra Behn. The rich and famous frequented places like the *Shakespeare's Head* on the piazza, whose cook made the best turtle soup in town, and whose head waiter, John Harris, even produced a kind of "Who's Who of Whores", revised annually. Russell Street, which leads east from the piazza, was one of the most notorious streets in Covent Garden, and housed the infamous *Rose Tavern*, immortalized in a scene from Hogarth's *Rake's Progress*. This was one of the oldest **brothels** in Covent Garden – Pepys mentions "frigging with Doll Lane" at the *Rose* in his diary of 1667 – and specialized in "Posture Molls", who engaged in flagellation and striptease, and were deemed a cut above the average whore. Food at the *Rose* was apparently excellent, too, and despite the frequent brawls, men of all classes, from royalty to ruffians, made their way there.

St Paul's Church

Of Jones' original piazza, the only remaining parts are the two sections of north-side arcading (one part rebuilt by the Victorians, the other reinstalled by the Royal Opera House) and **St Paul's Church**, facing the west side of the market building. In a now famous exchange, the Earl of Bedford told Jones to make St Paul's no fancier than a barn, to which the architect replied, "Sire, you shall have the handsomest barn in England". The proximity of so many theatres has made it known as the **"Actors' Church"**, and it's filled with memorials to international thespians from Boris Karloff to Gracie Fields. Several famous artists are buried here, too; among them Grinling Gibbons, Peter Lely and satirist Samuel Butler. The cobbles in front of the church's Tuscan portico – where Eliza Doolittle was discovered selling violets by Henry Higgins in George Bernard Shaw's *Pygmalion* – are now a legalized venue for buskers and street performers, who must audition for a slot months in advance. Despite the vetting, the standard of the acts varies enormously, though comedy is the ultimate aim.

The piazza's history of entertainment actually goes back to May 1662, when the first recorded performance of Punch and Judy in England was staged by Italian puppeteer Pietro Gimonde, and witnessed by Pepys. This historic event is now commemorated on the second Sunday in May by a **Punch and Judy Festival**, held in the gardens behind the church, in which numerous booths compete for audiences; for the rest of the year the **churchyard** provides a tranquil respite from the activity outside (access is from King, Henrietta or Bedford streets).

The piazza's markets and shops

The piazza's **market stalls** (daily 10.30am–6.30pm; ⊕www.coventgardenmarket .co.uk) are a victim of their own success, with a captive tourist market all too likely to pick up novelties and "craft" items. However, among the toy clowns, silk ties, jewellery and wooden flowers, there are always a few worthwhile stalls – even the odd clothing designer (knitwear, especially) with imagination and style. And stallholders alternate, often operating on only one or two days, so if you come more than once you may find a different scene. There are in fact two separate market areas: the "Apple Market", inside the old market building, and the tackier Jubilee Hall market, originally opened as the Foreign Flower Market, on the south side of the piazza. The Apple Market specializes in arts and crafts, the Jubilee Hall sells mainly clothes, though both are given over largely to antiques on Mondays.

As for the **shops** in the piazza complex, increased rents have edged out many of the odder and more interesting outlets of the early days in favour of blander franchised fare, including a number of big-name stores, exactly the reverse of the original development plans. A couple of more interesting, smaller outlets, in keeping with the idea of the place, are the Museum Shop, which stocks goods and reproductions from museums across Europe and America, Benjamin Pollock's toyshop, and Mullins & Westley, a "segar & snuff" parlour.

London's Transport Museum

A former flower-market shed on the piazza's east side is now home to the ever-popular **London's Transport Museum** (daily 10am–6pm, Fri opens 11am; £5.95; ⊕020/7565 7299, ⊕www.ltmuseum.co.uk), which is undergoing a thorough refurbishment and won't be open again until 2007. It's impossible to say how the museum will be set out, but among the oldest exhibits is a reconstructed 1829 Shillibeer's Horse Omnibus, which provided the city's first regular horse-bus service. Despite having the oldest underground system in the world, begun in 1863, London was still heavily reliant on horse power at the beginning of the twentieth century – fifty thousand animals worked in the transport system, producing a thousand tons of dung a day. The museum owns several wonderful double-decker electric trams, which, in the 1930s, formed part of the world's largest electric tram system. By 1952 the whole network had been dismantled, to be superseded by trolleybuses, of which the museum has several examples – these, in turn, bit the dust in the following decade. Look out, too, for the lovely 1920s Metropolitan line tube, fitted out in burgundy and green with pretty, drooping lamps, and peep inside the first "tube train", whose lack of windows earned it the nickname "the padded cell". The artistically inclined can buy reproductions of London Transport's stylish maps and posters, many commissioned from well-known artists, at the shop on the way out. While the museum is closed for redevelopment, you might want to visit London Transport's reserve collection in the Depot Museum in Acton (p.402).

Theatre Museum

The rest of the old flower market now houses the **Theatre Museum** (Tues–Sun 10am–6pm; free; ☎020/7943 4700, ⊛www.theatremuseum.org.uk), an outpost of the V&A displaying three centuries of memorabilia from every conceivable area of the performing arts in the western world (the entrance is on Russell Street). The museum's temporary exhibitions have always been consistently engaging, as have the workshops, make-up demonstrations and occasional **live performances**. The V&A's long-term plan is to transform the whole place into a new Museum of Performance, but as yet no dates for this have been set.

Bow Street and around

Covent Garden's once high crime rate was no doubt the reason behind the opening of a new magistrates' office in **Bow Street** in 1748. The first two magistrates were Henry Fielding, author of *Tom Jones*, and his blind half-brother John – nicknamed the "Blind Beak" – who seem to have been exceptional in their honesty and the infrequency with which they accepted bribes (the only income a magistrate could rely on). Finding "lewd women enough to fill a mighty colony", Fielding also set about creating the city's first police force, known as the **Bow Street Runners**. Never numbering more than a dozen, they were employed primarily to combat prostitution, and they continued to exist a good ten years after the establishment of the uniformed Metropolitan Police in 1829. Before it closed in 1989, Bow Street police station had the honour of incarcerating Oscar Wilde after he was arrested for "committing indecent acts" in 1895 – he was eventually sentenced to two years' hard labour. And, in 1928, Radclyffe Hall's lesbian novel *The Well of Loneliness* was deemed obscene by Bow Street magistrates and remained banned in this country until 1949.

The Royal Opera House

The Corinthian portico of the **Royal Opera House** (⊛www.royaloperahouse .org) stands opposite Bow Street magistrates' court. First built as the Covent Garden Theatre in 1732, in a backstreet behind the fruit and vegetable market, it witnessed premieres of Goldsmith's *She Stoops to Conquer* and Sheridan's *The Rivals* before being destroyed by fire in 1809. To offset the cost of building the new theatre, ticket prices were increased; riots ensued for 61 consecutive performances until the manager finally backed down. In 1847 the theatre was

Theatre Royal, Drury Lane

It was at the original **Theatre Royal, Drury Lane**, built in 1663, that women were first permitted to appear on stage in England (their parts having previously been played by boys), but critics were sceptical about their abilities to portray their own gender, and thought their profession little better than prostitution – and, indeed, most had to work at both to make ends meet (as the actress said to the bishop). The women who sold oranges to the audience were even less virtuous, **Nell Gwynne** being the most famous, though she also trod the boards in comic roles. Eventually she became Charles II's mistress, the first in a long line of Drury Lane actresses who made it into royal beds. Sarah Siddons' theatrical success from the 1780s onwards brought a degree of respectability to the female acting profession for the first time; the majority of her female contemporaries, however, were more in the vein of Nancy Dawson, who "danced the jigg to smutty songs" here.

It was at the Theatre Royal that **David Garrick**, as actor, manager and part-owner from 1747, revolutionized the English theatre. Garrick treated his texts with a great deal more reverence than had been customary, insisting on rehearsals and cutting down on improvisations. The rich and privileged, who had previously occupied seats on the stage itself, were confined to the auditorium, and the practice of refunding those who wished to leave at the first interval was stopped. However, an attempt to prevent half-price tickets being sold at the beginning of the third act provoked a riot by disgruntled punters and was eventually withdrawn. Despite Garrick's reforms, the Theatre Royal remained a boisterous and often dangerous place of entertainment: George II and George III both narrowly escaped assassination attempts, and the orchestra often had cause to be grateful for the cage under which they were forced to play. The theatre has one other unique feature: two royal boxes, instigated in order to keep George III and his son, the future George IV, apart, after they had a set-to in the foyer. **Backstage tours** of the theatre are great fun and are led by actors who bring the theatre's history to life through dramatic re-enactment; for more details phone ℡020/7949 5091.

renamed the Italian Royal Opera and soon became the city's main opera house; royal patronage ensured its success, and since the last war it has been home to both the Royal Ballet and Royal Opera.

As part of the opera house's millennial refurbishment, Inigo Jones' arcading was rebuilt in the northeast corner of the piazza and the building opened up to the public as never before. A covered public passageway connects the piazza with Bow Street, and allows access to the ROH box office, from which you're free to head upstairs into the beautifully renovated wrought-iron and glass **Floral Hall** (daily 10am–3pm), once part of the flower market, now the opera house's showcase foyer. Continuing up the escalators, you reach the *Amphitheatre* bar/restaurant, which has a glorious terrace overlooking the piazza. Unfortunately, a by-product of all this redevelopment was the wanton demolition of a Georgian terrace on the north side of Russell Street.

Drury Lane

One block east of Bow Street runs **Drury Lane**, nothing to write home about in its present condition, but in Tudor and Stuart times a very fashionable address. During the Restoration, it became a permanent fixture in London's theatrical and social life, when the first Theatre Royal (see box above) was built in 1663 (the current one dates from 1812 and faces onto Catherine Street). Nell Gwynne was born close by, and Pepys recalls seeing "pretty Nelly standing at her lodgings door in Drury Lane in her smock-sleeves and bodice, looking upon one: she seemed a mighty pretty creature". Like the rest of Covent Garden, Drury Lane had degenerated considerably by the eighteenth century, when Hogarth depicted it in *The Harlot's Progress*. Nowadays, it's something of a backwater, but business certainly prospered for the Sainsbury family, who opened their first shop in 1869 at no. 173, selling dairy products. Meanwhile, Brodie & Middleton, the "scenic colourmen" who established themselves here in the 1840s, are still selling glitters, glues, artificial cobwebs and skinheads from no. 68.

North of the piazza

The network of streets to the north of Covent Garden piazza has been more or less colonized by designer clothes and shoe outlets, and the oddball shops of the sort that once characterized the entire neighbourhood are now few and far between. Neal Street is the area's main street, with Floral Street, Long Acre, Shelton Street and Shorts Gardens all worth exploring, too.

Floral Street and Long Acre

The western half of **Floral Street** is dominated by three adjoining shops run by top-selling British designer Paul Smith, whose tongue-in-cheek window displays are always worth inspecting. Keeping him company are branches of Nicole Farhi, Ted Baker and Joseph, plus a few quirkier outlets, like a shop dedicated purely to Tintin, the Belgian boy-detective. Meanwhile, squeezed beside a very narrow alleyway off the western end of Floral Street is the **Lamb and Flag** pub, where the Poet Laureate, John Dryden, was beaten up in December 1679 by a group of thugs, hired most probably by his rival poet, the Earl of Rochester, who mistakenly thought Dryden was the author of an essay satirizing the earl.

Though it originally specialized in coach manufacture, **Long Acre**, to the north of, and parallel to, Floral Street, was Covent Garden's main shopping street long before the market was converted into a glorified mall. Nowadays, it's dominated by franchises, but there are some survivors of earlier times, most notably **Stanford's**, the world's oldest and largest map shop (see p.29). Look out, too, for **Carriage Hall**, an old stabling yard, surrounded by cast-iron pillars and situated between Long Acre and Floral Street, which was originally used by coachmakers and has now been converted into shops.

Freemasons' Hall

Looking east down the gentle curve of Long Acre, it's difficult to miss the austere, Pharaonic mass of the **Freemasons' Hall** (Mon–Fri 10am–5pm; free; ℡020/7395 9257, ⊛freemasonry.london.museum), built at 60 Great Queen St as a memorial to all the masons who died in World War I. Whatever you may think of this reactionary, secretive, male-only organization, which enjoys a virtual stranglehold over institutions like the police and judiciary, the interior is worth a peek for the Grand Temple alone, whose pompous, bombastic decor is laden with heavy symbolism. To see the Grand Temple, you must sign up for one of the **guided tours** (Mon–Fri usually 11am, noon, 2, 3 & 4pm; free; ℡020/7395 9258) and bring some ID with you. The masonically curious might also take a look at the shop (Mon–Fri 10.30am–5.30pm, Sat 10am–2.30pm) which sells mason merchandise: aprons, wands, rings and books about alchemy and the cabbala, as do the shops of Central Regalia and Toye, Kenning & Spencer, on Great Queen Street.

Neal Street, Neal's Yard and around

Running north from Long Acre, **Neal Street** features some fine Victorian warehouses, complete with stair towers for loading and shifting goods between floors. Once famous for single-theme shops like The Kite Store and The Astrology Shop, the street is now dominated by multinational fashion stores such as Mango, Diesel and O'Neill.

A decade or so ago, the feel of the street was a lot less moneyed and more alternative, but that ambience only really survives in *Food for Thought*, the veggie café that's been here since 1971, and, to a lesser extent, in **Neal's Yard**, a tiny little courtyard off Shorts Gardens, prettily festooned with flower boxes and ivy. Here, you'll find several cafés and takeaway outlets, a remedies shop and

▲ Neal's Yard

a superb cheese shop (out on Shorts Gardens). The complex was set up in the early 1970s by Nick Saunders, one of the leading lights of "alternative London" and the campaign to rescue Covent Garden.

Seven Dials

West of Neal Street is **Seven Dials**, the meeting point of seven streets which make up a little circus, centred on a slender column topped by six tiny blue sundials (the seventh dial is formed by the column itself and the surrounding road). The column has had a chequered history: erected in 1693, it was torn down in 1773 when a rumour went about that treasure was hidden beneath it; it was re-erected in Weybridge, in Surrey, fifty years later, and the replica which now stands in Covent Garden was built in 1989 as a sort of roundabout with seats. **Earlham Street**, which runs through Seven Dials into Charing Cross Road, harbours an old-fashioned ironmonger and a local butcher, and was once a flourishing market street, though only a handful of stalls remain. They include, however, one of London's very best cut-flower stalls – a visual treat at any time of year.

St Giles

Women with scarcely the articles of apparel which common decency requires, with forms bloated by disease, and faces rendered hideous by habitual drunkenness – men reeling and staggering along – children in rags and filth – whole streets of squalid and miserable appearance whose inhabitants are lounging in the public road, fighting, screaming and swearing . . .

Thus Dickens described the old **St Giles rookery**, the predominantly Irish slum area north of Covent Garden, which, less than a hundred years earlier, had provided the setting for Hogarth's *Gin Lane*. Even at its height, St Giles was by no means the most dangerous slum in London (parts of the East End were far worse) but it was the rookery's position at the heart of the West End that scared the daylights out of wealthy Londoners. Here were ten to twelve acres of densely populated hovels which provided "a convenient asylum for the off-scourings of the night-world" – Dickens again. Even after the establishment of the police, few officers could expect to emerge from the maze of brothels and gin shops unscathed; on one occasion a foolhardy evangelist was ejected from the slums stripped and bound, his mouth stuffed with mustard powder.

In the end, the wide new roads of the Metropolitan Board of Works did what no police force or charity organization could manage, by "shovelling out the poor" as one critic put it. Virtually the only reminder of the rookery is the early eighteenth-century church of **St Giles-in-the-Fields** (Mon–Fri 9am–4pm) on the south side of St Giles High Street, last resting place of poet Andrew Marvell, and of the twelve Catholics denounced by Titus Oates as participants in a completely fictitious (as it turned out) Popish plot to murder Charles II. The rest of the slums were demolished to make way for New Oxford Street and the busy interchange of Shaftesbury Avenue, High Holborn and St Giles High Street at the top of Neal Street.

At the western end of the High Street is St Giles Circus, now a godforsaken spot skewered by the hideous 1960s skyscraper called **Centrepoint**, which marks the eastern end of Oxford Street. Designed by Richard Seifert (who was also responsible for the NatWest Tower – aka Tower 42 – in the City), it was built by property tycoon Harry Hyams, who kept it famously empty for more than a decade, a profit-making exercise whose cynicism transcended even the London norms of the time. The tower, which is now a listed building, stands on the site of the gallows where John Oldcastle – the model for Shakespeare's Falstaff and leader of the heretical Lollards – was hanged in chains over a slow fire in 1417.

Strand

The **Strand** – the main road connecting Westminster to the City and forming the southern border of Covent Garden – is a shadow of its former self. From the thirteenth century onwards, the street was famous for its riverside mansions, owned by bishops, noblemen and courtiers, while Nash's improvement to the western end, executed in the 1830s, prompted Disraeli to declare it "perhaps the finest street in Europe". In the 1890s, the Strand boasted more theatres than any other street in London, giving rise to the music-hall song *Let's All Go Down the Strand*. One of the last of the Strand's aristocratic riverside mansions to go was Northumberland House, demolished in the 1870s to make way for Northumberland Avenue, which leads off Trafalgar Square; a hundred years later, the one surviving Nash terrace was chopped in two by the glass frontage of Coutts' Bank. The only surviving Thames palace is now **Somerset House**, which houses several museums and galleries and boasts a wonderful fountain-filled courtyard.

Along the Strand to Aldwych

One of the few buildings worth a mention in the western section of the Strand is the Edwardian-era British Medical Association building – now **Zimbabwe House** – on the corner of Agar Street. Few passers-by even notice the eighteen naked figures by Jacob Epstein that punctuate the second-floor facade, but at the time of their unveiling in 1908, they caused enormous controversy – "a form of statuary which no careful father would wish his daughter and no discriminating young man his fiancée to see", railed the press. When the Southern Rhodesian government bought the building in 1937 they pronounced the sculptures to be "undesirable" and a potential hazard to passers-by, and proceeded to hack at the genitals, heads and limbs of all eighteen, which remain mutilated to this day.

London's largest private bank, at no. 440, is the aforementioned **Coutts & Co** (ⓦwww.coutts.com), whose customers include the Queen. It was founded in 1692, originally on the south side of the Strand, by the Scottish goldsmith, John Campbell; a mock-up of Campbell's premises stands behind a screen in the bank's concrete and marble atrium. Though Coutts is now owned by the Royal Bank of Scotland, today's male employees still sport anachronistic tail-coated suits, but the horse-drawn carriage which used to convey royal correspondence was sadly taken out of service in 1993.

Some way further east on the opposite side of the Strand, the blind side street of Savoy Court – the only street in the country where the traffic drives on the right – leads to **The Savoy** (ⓦwww.savoy-group.co.uk), London's grandest hotel, built in 1889 by Richard D'Oyly Carte on the site of the medieval Savoy Palace. César Ritz was the original manager, Guccio Gucci started out as a dishwasher here, and the list of illustrious guests is endless: Monet and Whistler both painted the Thames from one of the south-facing rooms, Sarah Bernhardt nearly died here, and Strauss the Younger arrived with his own orchestra. It's worthwhile strolling up Savoy Court to check out the hotel's Art Deco foyer and the equally outrageous 1930s fittings of the adjacent **Savoy Theatre**, whose profits helped fund the hotel. The theatre was built in 1881 to stage Gilbert and Sullivan's operas, beginning with *Patience*, which was followed a couple of years later by their biggest hit, *The Mikado*.

Nothing remains of John of Gaunt's medieval Savoy Palace, which was burnt down in the Peasants' Revolt of 1381, though the late-perpendicular **Savoy Chapel** (Tues–Fri 11.30am–3.30pm), hidden round the back of the hotel down Savoy Street, dates from the time when the complex was rebuilt as a hospital for the poor in 1505. The tall belfry has gone, as have most of the interior fittings, but the chapel enjoyed something of a revival as a fashionable venue for weddings when the hotel and theatre were built next door – all three were the first of their kind to be lit by electricity.

Victoria Embankment

To get to the **Victoria Embankment**, from the Strand's western end head down Villiers Street, which slopes sharply down the flank of Charing Cross station. Built between 1868 and 1874, the embankment was the inspiration of French engineer Joseph Bazalgette, whose project simultaneously relieved congestion along the Strand, provided an extension to the underground railway and sewerage systems, and created a new stretch of parkland with a riverside walk – now filled with an eclectic mixture of statues and memorials from Robbie Burns to the Imperial Camel Corps. The 1626 **York Watergate**, in the Victoria Embankment Gardens to the east of Villiers Street, gives you an idea of where the banks of the Thames used to be: the steps through the gateway once led down to the river.

Less evidence remains of the Adam brothers' magnificent riverside development known as the **Adelphi**, from the Greek for "brothers". Built between 1768 and 1772, this featured a terrace of eleven houses supported by massive arches and vaults that opened out onto a newly constructed wharf. The scheme was by no means a success – the houses wouldn't sell (despite having the actor David Garrick among their first residents), the wharf was prone to flooding, and the brothers ended up practically bankrupt – but it was a distinctive feature of the waterfront until 1936, when it was thoughtlessly demolished.

The only surviving Adam houses are between Victoria Embankment Gardens and the Strand: both 1–3 Robert St and 7 Adam St retain the Adams' innovative stucco decoration on their pilasters, and the most elaborate of all, 6–8 John Adam St, is home to the "Royal Society for the encouragement of Arts, Manufactures and Commerce" or **RSA** (⊚www.rsa.org.uk), founded in 1754. On the first Sunday of the month, you can take a look inside the RSA (10am–1pm; free), which contains a small display on the Adelphi and retains several original Adam ceilings and chimneypieces. The Great Room is the highlight, however, due to its sequence of six paintings on *The Progress of Human Knowledge and Culture* begun in 1777 by James Barry, which form a busy, continuous pictorial frieze around the room, punctuated at either end by portraits of two early presidents by Reynolds and Gainsborough.

London's oldest monument, **Cleopatra's Needle**, languishes little-noticed on the Thames side of the busy Victoria Embankment, guarded by two Victorian sphinxes (facing the wrong way). In fact, the 60-foot-high, 180-ton stick of granite has nothing to do with Cleopatra – it's one of a pair erected in Heliopolis in 1475 BC (the other one is in New York's Central Park) and taken to Alexandria by Emperor Augustus fifteen years after Cleopatra's suicide. This obelisk was presented to Britain in 1819 by the Turkish viceroy of Egypt, but nearly sixty years passed before it finally made its way to London. It was erected in 1878 above a time capsule containing, among other things, the day's newspapers, a box of hairpins, a railway timetable and pictures of the country's twelve prettiest women.

The **Benjamin Franklin House** (☏020/7930 9121, ⊚www.rsa.org.uk/franklin) at 36 Craven St, on the other side of Charing Cross station, will probably attract more visitors than Cleopatra's Needle, if the money is ever found to complete the restoration. The tenth son of a candlemaker, Benjamin Franklin (1706–90) had "genteel lodgings" here more or less continuously from 1757 to 1775. Whilst Franklin was espousing the cause of the British colonies (as the US then was), the house served as the first de facto American embassy; eventually, he returned to America to help draft the Declaration of Independence, negotiate the peace treaty with Britain and frame the US Constitution. Franklin was also, rather surprisingly, the inventor of the glass harmonica. At no. 32, two doors up from Franklin's house, a plaque commemorates the German poet **Heinrich Heine**, who stayed here for three unhappy months in 1827, complaining to his friends back home that "no one understands German".

Aldwych

The wide crescent of **Aldwych**, forming a neat "D" with the eastern part of the Strand, was driven through the slums of this zone in the last throes of the Victorian era. A confident ensemble occupies the centre, with the enormous Australia House and India House sandwiching **Bush House**, home of the BBC's World Service (⊚www.bbc.co.uk/worldservice) since 1940. Despite its thoroughly British associations, Bush House was actually built by the American speculator Irving T. Bush, whose planned trade centre flopped in the 1930s. The giant figures on the north facade and the inscription, "To the Eternal Friendship of English-Speaking Nations", thus refer to the friendship between the US and Britain, and are not, as many people assume, the World Service's declaratory manifesto.

Not far from these former bastions of Empire, up Houghton Street, lurks that erstwhile hotbed of left-wing agitation, the **London School of Economics** (@www.lse.ac.uk). Founded in 1895 by, among others, socialists Sidney and Beatrice Webb, the LSE gained a radical reputation in 1968, when a student sit-in in protest against the Vietnam War ended in violent confrontations that were the closest London came to the heady events in Paris that year. Famous alumni include Carlos the Jackal, Cherie Booth (wife of Prime Minister Tony Blair) and Mick Jagger, but the place has been pretty quiet for the last three decades.

Somerset House

South of Aldwych and the Strand stands **Somerset House**, sole survivor of the grandiose river palaces that once lined this stretch of the riverfront, its four wings enclosing a large courtyard rather like a Parisian *hôtel*. However, although it looks like an old aristocratic mansion, the present building was in fact purpose-built from 1776 onwards by William Chambers, to house governmental offices and learned societies. Over the course of the next two centuries, it served as home to, among others, the Navy Board, the Royal Academy of Arts, the Inland Revenue and the General Register of Births, Deaths and Marriages. Nowadays, Somerset House's granite-paved courtyard is a great place to relax thanks to its fab 55-jet **fountain** that spouts straight from the cobbles, and does a little syncopated dance every half-hour. The courtyard is also used for open-air performances, concerts, installations and, in winter, an ice-rink.

The north wing houses the permanent collection of the **Courtauld Institute**, best known for its outstanding Impressionist and Post-Impressionist paintings. The south wing, meanwhile, houses the **Gilbert Collection** of silver and gold objets d'art, and the **Hermitage Rooms**, featuring changing exhibitions – anything from Fabergé eggs to Impressionist masterpieces – drawn from St Petersburg's Hermitage Museum. But before you head off to one of the collections housed here, make sure you go and admire the Royal Naval Commissioners' gilded eighteenth-century barge in the **King's Barge House**, at ground level in the south wing.

Visiting Somerset House

There are **three entrances** to Somerset House (☎020/7845 4600, @www.somerset-house.org.uk): the Strand entrance to the north, the Terrace entrance off Waterloo Bridge and the Great Arch entrance on Victoria Embankment, where folk would once have sailed in off the Thames. All the entrances and the galleries within Somerset House are accessible to wheelchair users. The main courtyard is open daily 10am to 11pm, though the Victoria Embankment entrance is closed after 6pm; the collections are open daily 10am to 6pm. Admission to the courtyard is free; **tickets** to the Courtauld Institute and Gilbert Collection cost £5 each, for the Hermitage Rooms £6. If you visit two collections in one day, you get £1 off; if you visit three, you get £2 off. Note that the Courtauld offers **free admission** on Mondays 10am to 2pm. As for eating, you can grab a snack at the deli in the south wing, or the café in the Courtauld, while more substantial meals can be had at the river terraces alfresco summer café and the excellent but expensive *Admiralty* restaurant, in the south wing (☎020/7845 4646).

Courtauld Institute

Founded in 1931 as part of the University of London, the **Courtauld Institute** (🖳www.courtauld.ac.uk) was the first body in Britain to award degrees in art history as an academic subject. It's much more famous, however, for its priceless art collection, whose virtue is quality rather than quantity. As well as its Impressionist and Post-Impressionist works, the Courtauld also owns a fine array of earlier works by the likes of Rubens, Botticelli, Bellini and Cranach the Elder. More recently, the institute has acquired over one hundred twentieth-century paintings, by the likes of Derain, Vlaminck and Kandinsky, on long-term loan.

The displays currently start on the **ground floor** with a small room devoted to medieval religious paintings from all over Western Europe, including a late, great polyptych by **Bernardo Daddi**, a pupil of Giotto, plus a few enamels and ivories. Next, you ascend the beautiful, semicircular staircase to the **first-floor galleries**, whose exceptional plasterwork ceilings recall their original use as the learned societies' meeting rooms. This is where the cream of the Courtauld's collection is currently displayed: re-hangings have become more frequent, however, so ask if you can't find a particular painting. The Impressionists start off in the first room (2), with **Renoir**'s *La Loge*, **Degas**' *Two Dancers* and a couple of **Monet** landscapes. In room 3, there's a small-scale version of **Manet**'s bold *Déjeuner sur l'herbe*, and his atmospheric *A Bar at the Folies-Bergère*, a nostalgic celebration of the artist's love affair with Montmartre, painted two years before his death. There's a heap of **Cézanne**'s works, including one of his series of *Card Players*, and several magnificent, geometrical but lush landscapes, including, inevitably, one of his beloved *Montagne Sainte-Victoire*. In the same room, **Gauguin**'s Breton peasants *Haymaking* contrasts with his later Tahitian works, including the sinister *Nevermore*. Next door, in room 4, one of **Modigliani**'s celebrated nudes hangs alongside **Van Gogh**'s *Self-Portrait with Bandaged Ear*, painted shortly after his remorseful self-mutilation, following an attack on his housemate Gauguin.

In room 5, there's a large **Botticelli** altarpiece commissioned by a convent and refuge for former prostitutes; hence Mary Magdalene's pole position below the

▲ Manet's *A Bar at the Folies-Bergère*

Cross. Amidst several splendid fifteenth-century Florentine *cassoni* (chests), you can admire the masterful handling of colour and light in **Giovanni Bellini**'s *The Assassination of St Peter Martyr*. Meanwhile, **Lucas Cranach the Elder**'s *Adam and Eve* provides one of the highlights of the collection, with the Saxon painter revelling in the visual delights of Eden. The Courtauld's large collection of works by **Rubens** fills room 6, ranging from oil sketches for church frescoes to large-scale late works and a winningly informal portrait of the family of the son of "Peasant Bruegel", Jan Bruegel.

The **second floor** is used primarily to display the Courtauld's twentieth-century works, which bring a wonderful splash of colour and a hint of modernism to the galleries. Unfortunately, there isn't the space to exhibit the entire collection, so it's impossible to say for definite what paintings will be on show at any one time. Room 8 is home to several small bronze sculptures by **Degas**, and his *After the Bath*, a wonderfully intimate pastel evocation of female domesticity. In room 9, you hit the bright primary colours of the pioneers of **Fauvism**, beginning with **Derain**'s technicolour depictions of London and the Japanese-influenced portrait of his wife by **Matisse**, and continuing in room 10 with the works by **Dufy**.

Beyond, a small room is devoted to **Roger Fry**, who organized the first Impressionist exhibitions in Britain, and went on to found the Omega Workshops in 1913 with Duncan Grant. Fry bequeathed many of the paintings displayed here, including several by Grant, his wife Vanessa Bell, and Fry himself. Before you leave, be sure to check out room 13, which is given over to an outstanding array of works by **Kandinsky**, the Russian-born artist who was 30 when he finally decided to become a painter and moved to Munich. He's best known for his pioneering abstract paintings, such as *Improvisation on Mahogany* from 1910, where the subject matter is still just about discernable in the blocks of colour, and which eventually led to totally abstract works such as *Composition*, a 1922 watercolour essay in off-whites.

Gilbert Collection

The ground floor of the south wing is now given over to the **Gilbert Collection** (⊛www.gilbert-collection.org.uk), a private collection of silver and gold, micromosaics and snuffboxes, gifted to the nation by millionaire Arthur Gilbert. Born in London in 1913 of Polish Jewish ancestry, Gilbert made so much money in the rag trade that he was able to retire to Beverly Hills at the age of just 36, where he amassed even more wealth through real estate. Gilbert began collecting as a hobby in the 1960s, and while there's no denying the craftsmanship of the pieces that attracted his magpie-like attention, the sheer opulence and gaudiness of many of the exhibits may prove too much for some.

After you've picked up your free audioguide and magnifying glass, head off into the **Gilbert shrine**, where a genial wax model of the collector sits at a desk in his slightly vulgar Beverly Hills office. The collection proper kicks off in gallery 1 with a whole series of cabinets, clocks, tables and pictures decorated with **Florentine hard-stone mosaics** or *pietre dure*. An art form invented in the sixteenth century, hard-stone mosaics are made from carefully chosen marbles and minerals, which are cut and fitted together like a stone collage. Technically astounding, the pieces themselves verge on the kitsch, and it comes as something of a relief, therefore, to reach gallery 2, which contains a small collection of **ecclesiastical silver**, including two pairs of spectacular silver-gilt Rococo gates which once formed the central section of an iconostasis presented by Catherine the Great to the monastery church of Pechersk, just outside Kiev.

Gallery 3, on the mezzanine floor above, is a long gallery displaying the bulk of the **silver collection**, everything from flagons and cups to salvers, soup tureens, tea caddies, candelabra and plates. Among the most eye-catching items are a lovely little silver-gilt pomander, from around 1600, that divides into several silver segments, and an outlandish Rococo "epergne", designed to hold fruit and desserts, and looking something like a miniature merry-go-round. Look out, too, for the Monteith Bowl, an unusual piece featuring vigorous battle scenes in relief, and a couple of guys who appear to be fleeing the carnage and attempting to climb into the bowl.

Stairs lead up from the mezzanine to a couple of galleries used for temporary exhibitions, followed by a gallery of Georgian enamel portrait miniatures and numerous snuffboxes. The most decadent snuffboxes are the **gold boxes** in gallery 8, which became a craze in aristocratic circles in eighteenth-century Europe. Fussily decorated with mother-of-pearl reliefs, enamel scenes or gaudy agate figures, the prevalent style is high-kitsch Rococo, and the most over-the-top of the lot are the six boxes made for Frederick the Great.

The final two rooms feature several magnificently ornate **silver-gilt howdahs** (seats for riding elephants), built for Rajasthani rajas in the decadent days of the British Empire, and the sort of bizarre objets d'art that used to grace the "china closets" and *Kunstkammern* (art cabinets) of the European aristocracy: a silver-gilt boat on a stand, a cup made from an ostrich egg, another made from a turban shell and a partridge with mother-of-pearl feathers. And once you've reached the shop, you can start your own little collection of gewgaws.

St Mary-le-Strand to St Clement Danes

Next door to Somerset House, the ugly concrete facade of **King's College** (Ⓦwww.kcl.ac.uk) conceals Robert Smirke's much older buildings, which date from its foundation in 1829. Rather than entering the college itself, stroll down Surrey Street and turn right down Surrey Steps – in the middle of the old *Norfolk Hotel*, whose terracotta facade is well worth admiring. Follow the signs to the **Roman Bath**, and you'll discover a fifteen-foot-long tub (actually dating from Tudor times at the earliest) with a natural spring belching out two thousand gallons a day. Dickens' David Copperfield "had many a cold plunge" here before setting off for a walk in Hampstead. The bath is visible all year round through a window, but you can only get a closer look by appointment (Ⓣ01494/528051; May–Sept Wed 1–5pm; NT; 50p).

Two historic churches survived the Aldwych development, and are now adrift amid the traffic of the Strand. The first is James Gibbs' **St Mary-le-Strand** (Mon–Fri 11am–4pm, Sun 10am–3pm; recitals Wed 1pm; free; Ⓦwww.stmarylestrand.org), his first commission, completed in 1724 in Baroque style and topped by a delicately tiered tower. Even in the eighteenth century, parishioners complained of the noise from the roads, and it's incredible that recitals are still given here. The entrance is flanked by two lovely magnolia trees, and the interior has a particularly rich plastered ceiling in white and gold. It was in this church that Bonnie Prince Charlie allegedly renounced his Roman Catholic faith and became an Anglican, during a secret visit to London in 1750.

In allusion to his own St Mary's, Gibbs placed a 115-foot tower on top of Wren's nearby **St Clement Danes** (daily 8.30am–4.30pm; Ⓦwww.raf.mod.uk), whose bells play out the tune of the nursery rhyme *Oranges and Lemons* each day at 9am, noon, 3pm and 6pm – though St Clement's Eastcheap in the City is more likely to be the church referred to in the rhyme. The church was reduced to a smouldering shell during the Blitz; the vicar died "from the shock and the grief" the following month, and his wife died four months later. In the 1950s, St Clement Danes was handed over to the RAF – who contributed to the restoration costs – and it's now a very well-kept memorial to those killed in the air battles of World War II. Glass cabinets in the west end of the church contain some poignant mementoes, such as a wooden cross carved from a door hinge in a Japanese POW camp. The nave and aisles are studded with over eight hundred squadron and unit badges, while heavy tomes set in glass cabinets record the 120,000 RAF service personnel who died.

In front of the church, the statue of **Gladstone** and his four female allegorical companions is flanked by two air chiefs: to the right, **Lord Dowding**, the man who oversaw the Battle of Britain; to the left, Arthur Harris, better known as "**Bomber Harris**", architect of the saturation bombing of Germany that resulted in the slaughter of thousands of German civilians (and over 55,000 Allied airmen now commemorated on the plinth). Although Churchill was ultimately responsible, most of the opprobrium was left to fall on Harris, who was denied the peerage all the other service chiefs received, while his forces were refused a campaign medal. The decision to honour Harris with this privately funded statue, unveiled by the Queen Mother on May 31, 1992 (the anniversary of the bombing of Cologne), drew widespread protests in Britain and from Germany.

Further east along the Strand are two more architectural curiosities. At no. 216 stands **Twinings** tea shop (Mon–Fri 9.30am–4.30pm; ☎020/7353 3511, ⓦwww.twinings.com), founded in 1706 by Thomas Twining, tea supplier to Queen Anne. Its slender Neoclassical portico features two reclining Chinamen, dating from the time when all tea came from China; there's a small tea museum at the back of the narrow shop. Several doors beyond, at no. 222, **Lloyd's Bank**'s Law Courts branch retains the extravagant decor of the short-lived *Royal Courts of Justice Restaurant*, which was built here in 1883. The foyer features acres of Doulton tiles, hand-painted in blues and greens, and a flying-fish fountain that was originally supplied with fresh water from an artesian well sunk 238ft below the Strand.

Holborn and the Inns of Court

Bounded by Kingsway to the west, the City to the east, the Strand to the south and Theobald's Road to the north, **Holborn** (pronounced "Ho-bun") is a fascinating area to explore. Strategically placed between the royal and political centre of Westminster and the mercantile and financial might of the City, this wedge of land became the hub of the English legal system in the early thirteenth century. Hostels, known as **Inns of Court**, were established where lawyers could eat, sleep and study English Common Law (which was not taught at the universities at the time).

Even today, every aspiring English barrister must study (and eat a required number of dinners) at one of the four Inns – **Inner Temple**, **Middle Temple**, **Lincoln's Inn** and **Gray's Inn** – in order to qualify and be called to the Bar. It's an old-fashioned system of patronage (you need contacts to get accepted at one of the Inns) and one that has done much to keep the judiciary overwhelmingly white, male and Oxbridge-educated to this day.

Hidden away from the general hubbub of London, the Inns are nevertheless open to the public and make for an interesting stroll, their archaic, cobbled precincts exuding the rarefied atmosphere of an Oxbridge college, and sheltering one of the city's oldest churches, the twelfth-century **Temple Church**. Close by the Inns, in Lincoln's Inn Fields, one of the most memorable and enjoyable of London's small museums, the **Sir John Soane's Museum**, is packed with architectural illusions and an eclectic array of curios, while, opposite, the **Hunterian Museum** houses freakish medical curiosities.

Temple

Temple is the largest and most complex of the Inns of Court, consisting of two Inns – **Middle Temple** (ⓦwww.middletemple.org.uk) and **Inner Temple** (ⓦwww.innertemple.org.uk) – both of which lie to the south of the Strand and Fleet Street and, strictly speaking, just within the boundaries of the City of London (see Chapter 11). The demarcation line between these two institutions is not very clear, and few very old buildings survive amidst the soulless neo-Georgian reconstructions that followed the devastation of the Blitz. Still, the maze

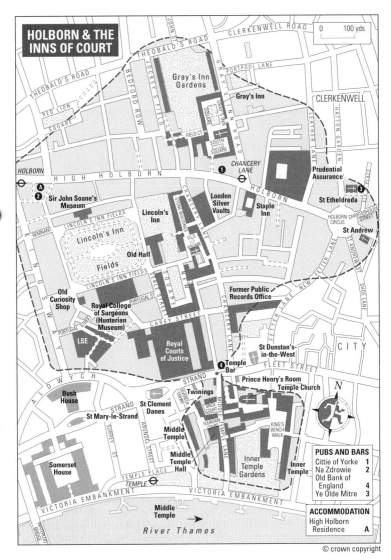

of courtyards and passageways is fun to explore – especially after dark, when the Temple is gas-lit – and it's always a welcome haven from the noise and fumes of central London.

There are several points of access, simplest of which is Devereux Court, which leads south off the Strand. Medieval students ate, attended lectures and slept in the **Middle Temple Hall** (Mon–Fri 10am–noon & 3–4pm; free), across Fountain Court, still the Inn's main dining room. The present building was constructed in the 1560s and provided the setting for many great Elizabethan masques and plays – including Shakespeare's *Twelfth Night*, which is believed to have been premiered here in 1602. The hall is worth a visit for its fine hammer-beam roof, wooden panelling and decorative Elizabethan screen, and the small wooden table said to have been carved from the hatch from Francis Drake's ship, the *Golden Hind*.

The two Temple Inns share use of the complex's oldest building, **Temple Church** (Wed–Sun 11am–4pm, though hours do vary; ☏020/7353 3470, ⊛www.templechurch.com), built in 1185 by the Knights Templar, an order founded to protect pilgrims on the road to Jerusalem that had its base here until 1312, when the Crown took fright at its power and handed the land over to the Knights of St John (for more on whom, see p.228). An oblong chancel was added in the thirteenth century, and the whole building was damaged in the Blitz, but the original round church – modelled on the Church of the Holy Sepulchre in Jerusalem – still stands, with its striking Purbeck marble piers, recumbent marble effigies of medieval knights and tortured grotesques grimacing in the spandrels of the blind arcading. At the northwestern corner of the choir, behind the decorative altar tomb of Edmund Plowden, builder of the Middle Temple Hall, a stairwell leads up to a tiny cell, less than 5ft long, in which disobedient knights were confined. Much of the church was restored in 1682 by Wren (who married his first wife here), although only his carved oak reredos remains today. He was also responsible for the elegant red-brick buildings along the northern side of King's Bench Walk, south of the church in the Inner Temple Court.

A column, to the south of Temple Church, marks the point where the Great Fire of 1666 was extinguished; it's topped by a diminutive statue of two knights sharing a horse, a reference to the fact that Knights Templar were often too poor to have a horse each. **Inner Temple Hall**, to the south of the column, is a postwar reconstruction, as is clear from the brickwork. This was the Inn where Mahatma Gandhi studied law in 1888, living as a true Englishman, dressing as a dandy, dancing, taking elocution lessons and playing the violin, while his close associate Jawaharlal Nehru spent two even wilder years here a decade or so later, gambling, drinking and running up considerable debts. If you're here at the right time, you can also explore the **Inner Temple Garden** (May–Sept Mon–Fri noon–3pm), which slopes down to the Embankment.

Temple Bar and the Royal Courts of Justice

If you walk to the top of Middle Temple Lane, you'll hit the Strand where it ends at **Temple Bar**, the latest in a long line of structures marking the boundary between Westminster and the City of London. It started out in the Middle Ages as a simple chain between two posts but by the 1670s a Wren-designed triumphal arch stood here. The heads of executed traitors (boiled in salt so that birds wouldn't eat them) were displayed on the arch until the mid-eighteenth century – one could even rent a telescope for a closer look. Then, in 1878, the arch was removed to ease traffic congestion, exiled to a park in Hertfordshire, and has recently been re-erected near St Paul's Cathedral (see p.187). The monument that replaced the arch, topped by a winged dragon, marks the spot where the sovereign must ask for the Lord Mayor's permission to enter the City, a tradition that began when Elizabeth I passed through Temple Bar on her way to St Paul's to give thanks for the defeat of the Armada.

Occupying the north side of the Strand before it hits Temple Bar are the **Royal Courts of Justice** (Mon–Fri 9am–4.30pm; ☎020/7947 6000, ⓦwww .hmcourts-service.gov.uk), home to the Court of Appeal and the High Court, where the most important civil cases are tried (criminal cases are heard at the Old Bailey; see p.195). The main portal and steps of this daunting Gothic Revival complex, designed by George Edmund Street in the 1870s, are familiar from innumerable news reports, since this is where many major appeals and libel suits are heard: it was from here that the Guildford Four and Birmingham Six walked to freedom, and it is where countless public figures have battled it out with the tabloids. The fifty-odd courtrooms are open to the public, though you have to go through stringent security checks first (no cameras allowed). Once through those, you're into the intimidating Main Hall, where bewigged barristers are usually busy on their mobiles. The information desk here can equip you with a plan and a short guide to the complex, while the glass cabinets in the centre of the hall list which cases are being heard and where. In the minstrels' gallery, there's a small exhibition on the history of legal dress codes; if you continue heading north, you can leave via the Carey Street exit.

Lincoln's Inn Fields

On the north side of the Law Courts lies **Lincoln's Inn Fields**, London's largest square. Originally simply pasture land and a playground for Lincoln's Inn students, it was used as a place of execution in Tudor times, Anthony Babington and his Catholic accomplices being hanged, drawn and quartered here for high treason in 1586. Laid out as a square in the early 1640s, only no. 59–60, on the west side, survives from that period and is possibly the work of Inigo Jones. On the north side of the gardens is a statue of Margaret MacDonald (wife of the first Labour prime minister Ramsay MacDonald, who died at no. 3), amid a brood of nine children, commemorating her social work among the young.

In the southwest corner of the square is one of London's few surviving timber-framed buildings, the sixteenth-century **Old Curiosity Shop** in Portsmouth Street, which claims to be the inspiration for Dickens' cloyingly sentimental tale of the same name. This seems unlikely, but it is certainly London's oldest shop building. The south side of the square is dominated by the gigantic Royal College of Surgeons, containing the **Hunterian Museum**, a fascinating collection of pickled bits and bobs. Equally unusual is the **Sir John Soane's Museum**, which occupies the house in which the eponymous architect lived on the north side of the square. To the east lies **Lincoln's Inn** itself, the best-preserved of all the Inns of Court.

Hunterian Museum

First opened in 1813 and beautifully refurbished in 2005, the **Hunterian Museum** (Tues–Sat 10am–5pm; free; ☎020/7869 6560, ⓦwww.rcseng.ac.uk), on the first floor of the Royal College of Surgeons building, contains the unique specimen collection of the surgeon-scientist John Hunter (1728–93). Most of the exhibits consist of jars of pickled skeletons and body pieces – from the tibia of a young pig to the human tongue – prepared by Hunter himself and displayed as he wished in a "Crystal Gallery". The museum has even older exhibits, too, such as diarist John Evelyn's anatomical tables from the 1640s, in which arteries and nerves are displayed on wooden boards. Among the prize exhibits are the skeleton of the "Irish giant", Charles Byrne (1761–83), who was seven feet ten inches tall, and, in the adjacent McCrae Gallery, the Sicilian midget Caroline Crachami (1815–24), who stood at only one foot ten and a half inches when she died at the age of 9. Upstairs, in the Science of Surgery gallery, you can have a go at simulated minimal-access surgery, and examine Joseph Lister's cumbersome carbolic-acid spray machine, known as the "donkey engine", with which he pioneered antiseptic surgery, performing operations obscured in a cloud of phenol (he even conducted a foggy operation on Queen Victoria – who had an abscess in the royal armpit – accidentally spraying her in the face in the process).

Sir John Soane's Museum

A group of buildings on the north side of Lincoln's Inn Fields houses **Sir John Soane's Museum** (Tues–Sat 10am–5pm; candlelit first Tues eve of the month also 6–9pm; free. Guided tour Sat 2.30pm; £3; ☎020/7405 2107, ⊛www.soane .org), an unsung glory which many people consider their favourite museum in London. Soane (1753–1837), a bricklayer's son who rose to be architect of the Bank of England, gradually bought up three adjoining Georgian properties here, altering them to serve not only as a home and office, but also as a place to stash his large collection of art and antiquities. No. 13, the central house with the stone loggia, is arranged much as it was in his lifetime, with an ingenious ground plan and an informal, treasure-hunt atmosphere, with surprises in every alcove. Few of Soane's projects were actually built, and his home remains the best example of what he dubbed his "poetry of architecture", using mirrors, domes and skylights to create wonderful spatial ambiguities.

To the right of the hallway, you enter the **dining room**, which adjoins the **library**, bedecked in Pompeiian red and green to give it a Roman feel. Pass through Soane's tiny study and dressing room, little more than a corridor crammed with fragments of Roman marble and loads of cameos and miniatures, and you find yourself in the main colonnaded display hall, built over the former stables. All around are busts and more masonry; below you is the Egyptian sarcophagus (see overleaf); above your head is the wooden chamber on stilts from which Soane used to supervise his students in other rooms. To your right is the **picture room**, whose false walls swing back to reveal another wall of pictures (including original Piranesi studies of the temples at Paestum and architectural drawings of Soane's projects), which itself opens to reveal a window and a balcony looking down onto the

▲ Sir John Soane's Museum

basement. The star paintings are **Hogarth**'s satirical *Election* series and his merciless morality tale *The Rake's Progress*.

A narrow staircase leads down into the flagstoned **crypt**, which features the "monk's parlour", a Gothic folly dedicated to a make-believe padre, Giovanni, complete with tomb (containing Soane's wife's dog, Fanny), cloister and eerie medieval casts and gargoyles. The hushed sepulchral chamber continues the morbid theme with its wooden mummy case, a model of an Etruscan tomb (complete with skeleton), and the tombstones of Soane's wife and son. You then emerge into another colonnaded atrium, where the alabaster **sarcophagus of Seti I**, rejected by the British Museum and bought by Soane, is watched over by rows and rows of antique statuary.

Back on the ground floor, make your way to the **breakfast parlour**, which features all of Soane's favourite architectural features: coloured skylights, a canopied dome and ranks of tiny convex mirrors. The much larger breakfast parlour of no. 12, where the Soanes first lived in the 1790s, has also been restored and is now used for temporary exhibitions. A short stroll up the beautiful cantilevered staircase brings you to the first-floor **drawing rooms**, whose airiness and bright colour scheme come as a relief after the ancient clutter of the downstairs rooms; there's also a startling view of the ground floor's numerous and varied skylights from the north drawing room.

Note that the museum is extremely popular, and on Saturdays, in particular, you need to get there early to avoid queuing. Fascinating hour-long **guided tours** take place each Saturday at 2.30pm, and allow access to the museum's enormous research library of architectural drawings and books, and a room crammed with cork and wood models of Pompeiian and Paestum temples.

Lincoln's Inn

On the east side of Lincoln's Inn Fields lies **Lincoln's Inn** (Mon–Fri 9am–6pm; ☎020/7405 1393, ⊛www.lincolnsinn.org.uk), the first and in many ways the prettiest of the Inns of Court, having miraculously escaped the ravages of the Blitz; famous alumni include Thomas More, Oliver Cromwell and Margaret Thatcher. As you might guess, the oldest buildings are in the Old Buildings courtyard, starting chronologically with the fifteenth-century **Old Hall** (by appointment only), where the lawyers used to live and where Dickens set the case Jarndyce versus Jarndyce, the opening scene in *Bleak House*.

Beyond the Old Hall is the sixteenth-century **gatehouse** – best viewed from Chancery Lane – impressive for its age and bulk, not to mention its faded diamond-patterned brickwork, a decoration repeated elsewhere in the Inn. Adjacent to the gatehouse is the early seventeenth-century **chapel** (Mon–Fri noon–2pm), with its unusual fan-vaulted open undercroft and, on the first floor, the nave, rebuilt in 1880, hit by a Zeppelin in World War I and much restored since, but still boasting its original ornate pews. To the north of the chapel, on the other side of Old Square, lie the Palladian **Stone Buildings**, very different in style to the rest of the Inn and best appreciated from the manicured lawns of the Inn's gardens (Mon–Fri noon–2.30pm); the strange miniature castle near the garden entrance is the gardeners' tool shed, a creation of George Gilbert Scott, designer of London's old red telephone boxes.

Chancery Lane and Gray's Inn

Running along the eastern edge of Lincoln's Inn is legal London's main thoroughfare, **Chancery Lane**, home of the Law Society (the solicitors' regulatory body) and lined with shops where barristers, solicitors and clerks can buy their wigs, gowns, legal tomes, stationery and champagne. The confident piece of mock-Tudor Victorian municipal architecture, just down from Lincoln's Inn's real Tudor gateway, on the opposite side of the street, is now used by King's College, but was originally built to house the Public Records Office, which has since relocated to Kew (see p.409). A little further up, on the same side, are the **London Silver Vaults** (Mon–Fri 9am–5.30pm, Sat 9am–1pm; free; @www .thesilvervaults.com), which began life as the Chancery Lane Safe Deposit for London's wealthy elite, but now house a strange, claustrophobic lair of subterranean shops selling every kind of silverware – mostly antique, mostly English and often quite tasteless.

The last of the four Inns of Court, **Gray's Inn** (Mon–Fri 10am–4pm; ☎020/7458 7800, @www.graysinn.org.uk), lies hidden to the north of High Holborn, at the top of Chancery Lane; the entrance is through an anonymous cream-coloured building next door to the venerable *Cittie of Yorke* pub (see p.480). Established in the fourteenth century, the Inn took its name from the de Grey family, who owned the original mansion used as student lodgings; many more buildings were added during the sixteenth century, but most of what you see today was rebuilt after the Blitz. The **Hall** (by appointment only), with its fabulous Tudor screen and stained glass, is thought to have witnessed the premiere of Shakespeare's *Comedy of Errors* in 1594. Unlike the south side, the north side of the Inn, taken up by the wide green expanse of **Gray's Inn Gardens**, is entirely and impressively visible through its wrought-iron railings from Theobald's Road; the gardens are open to the public weekday lunchtimes.

Holborn Circus

Heading east towards Holborn Circus, it's worth pausing to admire two remarkable buildings. The first, on the right, is **Staple Inn**: not one of the Inns of Court, but one of the now defunct Inns of Chancery, which used to provide a sort of introductory course for those aspiring to the Bar. Its overhanging half-timbered facade and gables date from the sixteenth century and are the most extensive in the whole of London; they survived the Fire, which stopped just short of Holborn Circus, but had to be extensively rebuilt after the Blitz. The second building is the palatial, terracotta-red **Prudential Assurance Building**, begun in 1879 by Alfred Waterhouse, on the opposite side of Holborn (the name of the street at this point). You need to penetrate the inner courtyard to appreciate the magnificent scale of this fortress of Victorian capitalism, with its very own Bridge of Sighs and dramatic memorial to the Prudential men who fell in the two wars. From the Holborn entrance, you can peek through the windows at the original Doulton-tiled interior.

At **Holborn Circus** itself, the traffic swirls around London's politest statue, a cheerful equestrian figure of Prince Albert doffing his hat to passers-by. The nearby church of **St Andrew** (Mon–Fri 8.15am–4.30pm), Wren's largest parish church, marks the beginning of the City (see Chapter 11), which lies to the south and east, over the Holborn Viaduct. Benjamin Disraeli was baptized here by his father, Isaac, in protest at being refused the office of warden at the Bevis Marks Synagogue (see p.210), and Thomas Coram (see p.148) lies at the west end of the church.

Take the first left off Charterhouse Street, which runs northeast from the Circus, and you'll come to **Ely Place**, named after the Bishop of Ely, whose London residence used to stand here. Guarded by a beadle, lodge and wrought-iron gates, this patch is technically still outside the jurisdiction of the London authorities, but all that remains of the bishop's palace is its plain Gothic chapel, now **St Etheldreda's Church**, hidden halfway down this dead-end street on the left. At one time a Roman Catholic chapel to the Spanish ambassador and later used by Welsh non-conformists, St Etheldreda's has been an exclusive Catholic stronghold since 1874, attracting a fair number of worshippers from the City during the week, and foreign diplomats at the weekend. The main body of the church, though much restored, dates back to 1300, and is lined with niches sheltering statues of English martyrs; the atmospherically gloomy crypt contains a model of the pre-Reformation church complex.

The City

THE CITY is where London began. Long established as the financial district, it currently stretches from Temple Bar in the west to the Tower of London in the east – administrative boundaries that are only slightly larger than those marked by the Roman walls and their medieval successors. However, in this Square Mile (as the City is sometimes referred to) you'll find precious few leftovers of London's early days: four-fifths of the area burnt down in the Great Fire of 1666. Rebuilt in brick and stone, the City gradually lost its centrality as London swelled westwards, though it has maintained its position as Britain's financial heartland, home to banking, insurance and other services. What you see on the ground is mostly the product of three fairly recent building phases: the Victorian construction boom of the latter half of the nineteenth century; the overzealous postwar reconstruction following the Blitz; and the building frenzy that began in the 1980s, and which has seen nearly fifty percent of the City's office space rebuilt.

When you consider what has happened here, it's amazing that anything has survived to bear witness to the City's 2000-year history. Wren's spires still punctuate the skyline here and there, and his masterpiece, **St Paul's Cathedral**, remains one of London's geographical and touristic pivots. At the eastern edge of the City, the **Tower of London**, begun shortly after the Norman Conquest, survives (and is covered in Chapter 12). Other relics, such as the City's few existing medieval alleyways, Wren's **Monument** to the Great Fire and London's oldest synagogue and church, are less conspicuous, and even the locals have problems finding the more modern attractions of the **Museum of London** and the **Barbican** arts complex. It's also worth checking out some of the new architecture that has shot up within the Square Mile since the 1980s, most famously the **Lloyd's Building**, a mould-breaking modern construction designed by Richard Rogers, now somewhat overshadowed by the equally unconventional **Gherkin** building by Norman Foster.

Perhaps the biggest change of all, though, has been in the City's **population**. Up until the eighteenth century, the vast majority of Londoners lived and worked in or around the City; nowadays, while more than 300,000 commuters spend the best part of Monday to Friday here, only 5000 people remain at night and at weekends, most of them cooped up in the upmarket apartments of the Barbican complex. The result of this demographic shift is that the City is only fully alive during office hours, making weekdays by far the best time to visit; many pubs, restaurants and even some tube stations and tourist sights close down at the weekend.

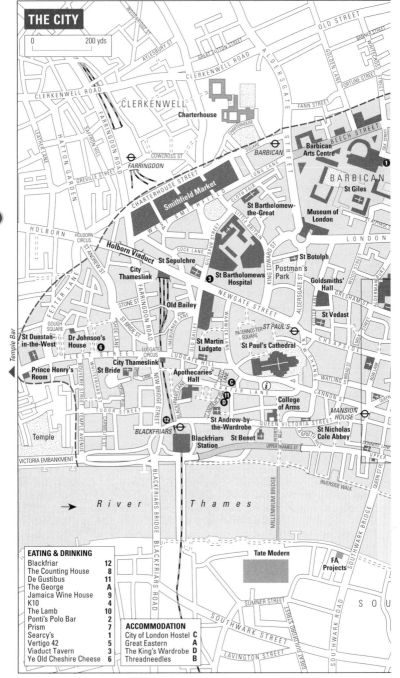

THE CITY

0   200 yds

CLERKENWELL

Charterhouse

BARBICAN

Barbican Arts Centre **1**

St Giles

Smithfield Market

St Bartholomew-the-Great

Museum of London

LONDON

Holborn Viaduct

St Sepulchre

City Thameslink

St Bartholomews Hospital **3**

St Botolph

Postman's Park

Goldsmiths' Hall

Old Bailey

St Vedast

St Dunstan-in-the-West

Dr Johnson's House **6**

St Martin Ludgate

ST PAUL'S

St Paul's Cathedral

City Thameslink

St Bride

Apothecaries' Hall **C** **11** **D**

College of Arms

MANSION HOUSE

Prince Henry's Room

Temple

St Andrew-by-the-Wardrobe **12**

BLACKFRIARS

Blackfriars Station

St Benet

St Nicholas Cole Abbey

VICTORIA EMBANKMENT

Temple Bar

River Thames

Tate Modern

FA Projects

EATING & DRINKING

Blackfriar	12
The Counting House	8
De Gustibus	11
The George	A
Jamaica Wine House	9
K10	4
The Lamb	10
Ponti's Polo Bar	2
Prism	7
Searcy's	1
Vertigo 42	5
Viaduct Tavern	3
Ye Old Cheshire Cheese	6

ACCOMMODATION

City of London Hostel	C
Great Eastern	A
The King's Wardrobe	D
Threadneedles	B

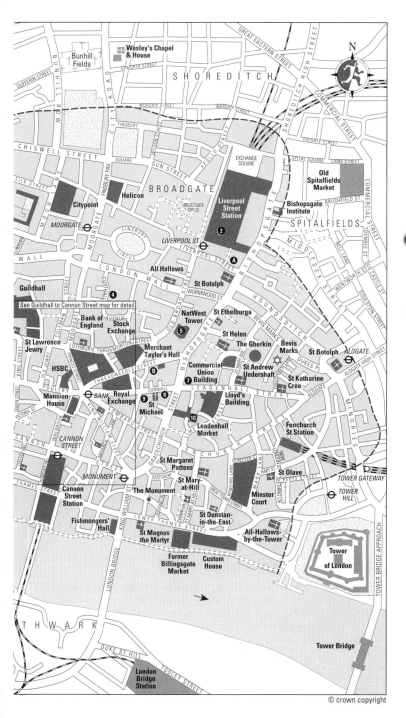

N

Wesley's Chapel & House

Bunhill
Fields

DUFFERIN STREET

BUNHILL ROW

EPWORTH STREET

CITY ROAD

GREAT EASTERN STREET

SHOREDITCH

SHOREDITCH HIGH STREET

COMMERCIAL STREET

CHISWELL STREET

WORSHIP STREET

WORSHIP STREET

FOLGATE STREET

SILK STREET

FINSBURY

SUN STREET

EXCHANGE
SQUARE

SPITAL SQUARE

LAMB STREET

Old
Spitalfields
Market

MOOR LANE

FINSBURY PAV.

SQUARE

BROADGATE

Helicon

Citypoint

BROADGATE
CIRCLE

Liverpool
Street
Station

Bishopsgate
Institute

BRUSHFIELD ST

COMMERCIAL STREET

TOYNBEE ST

MOORGATE

FINSBURY
CIRCUS

LIVERPOOL ST

2

SPITALFIELDS

MIDDLESEX STREET

WALL

MOORGATE STREET

LONDON WALL

LIVERPOOL STREET

A

BISHOPSGATE

HOUNDSDITCH

WENTWORTH STREET

OLD CASTLE ST

BELL LANE

All Hallows

St Botolph

WORMWOOD ST

Guildhall

COLEMAN STREET

4

See Guildhall to Cannon Street map for detail

OLD BROAD STREET

NatWest
Tower

5

St Ethelburga

BEVIS MARKS

St Helen

St Lawrence
Jewry

MOORGATE

LOTHBURY

Bank of
England

THROGMORTON STREET

Stock
Exchange

Merchant
Taylor's Hall

BISHOPSGATE

The Gherkin

Bevis
Marks

St Botolph

ALDGATE

DUKES PL

KING STREET

THREADNEEDLE STREET

Commercial
Union
Building

St Andrew
Undershaft

St Katharine
Cree

ALDGATE HIGH STREET

HSBC

PRINCES STREET

B

7

ST MARY AXE

ALDGATE

QUEEN STREET

Mansion
House

POULTRY

BANK

Royal
Exchange

CORNHILL

9

8

St
Michael

LEADENHALL STREET

Lloyd's
Building

Fenchurch
St Station

MINORIES

VICTORIA ST

WALBROOK

KING WILLIAM STREET

LOMBARD STREET

GRACECHURCH STREET

10

Leadenhall
Market

CANNON
STREET

FENCHURCH STREET

St Margaret
Pattens

St Olave

NEW LONDON STREET

MARK LANE

HART'S LANE

MONUMENT

EASTCHEAP

St Mary-
at-Hill

GREAT TOWER STREET

Minster
Court

SEETHING LANE

PEPYS STREET

TOWER GATEWAY

TOWER
HILL

Cannon
Street
Station

The Monument

ST MARY AT HILL

St Dunstan-
in-the-East

THAMES STREET

Fishmongers'
Hall

LOWER THAMES STREET

PUDDING LANE

All-Hallows-
by-the-Tower

TOWER BRIDGE APPROACH

LONDON BRIDGE

St Magnus
the Martyr

Former
Billingsgate
Market

Custom
House

Tower
of London

SOUTHWARK

DUKE ST HILL

Tower Bridge

TOOLEY STREET

London
Bridge
Station

11

THE CITY

183

© crown copyright

The City of London is crowded with **churches** (⊛ www.cityoflondonchurches.com) – well over forty at the last count, the majority of them built or rebuilt by Christopher Wren after the Great Fire. Prompted by the decline in the City's population, the Victorians demolished a fair few, but there are still a vast number, which now serve the City's working populace as much as the tiny resident population. The **opening times** given in the text should be taken with a pinch of salt, since most churches rely on volunteers to keep their doors open. As a general rule, weekday lunchtimes are the best time to visit the City's churches, many of which put on free lunchtime concerts. On the surface, many of the City churches appear quite similar: plain, light-filled interiors, with white, gold and dark wood furnishings. Below is a list of six of the most varied and interesting within the area:

St Bartholomew-the-Great Cloth Fair. The oldest surviving church in the City and by far the most atmospheric. St Paul's aside, if you visit just one church in the City, it should be this one. See p.197.

St Mary Abchurch Abchurch Lane. Uniquely for Wren's City churches, the interior features a huge, painted, domed ceiling, plus the only authenticated Gibbons reredos. See p.206.

St Mary Aldermary Queen Victoria Street. Wren's most successful stab at Gothic, with fan vaulting in the aisles and a panelled ceiling in the nave. See p.203.

St Mary Woolnoth Lombard Street. Hawksmoor's only City church, sporting an unusually broad, bulky tower and a Baroque clerestory that floods the church with light from its semicircular windows. See p.206.

St Olave Hart Street. Built in the fifteenth century, and one of the few pre-Fire Gothic churches in the City. See p.212.

St Stephen Walbrook Walbrook. Wren's dress rehearsal for St Paul's, with a wonderful central dome and plenty of original woodcarving. See p.205.

The one unchanging aspect of the City is its special status, conferred on the area by William the Conqueror, to appease the powerful burghers, and extended and reaffirmed by successive monarchs and governments ever since. Nowadays, with its own Lord Mayor, its Beadles, Sheriffs and Aldermen, its separate police force and its select electorate of freemen and liverymen, the City is an anachronism of the worst kind. The **Corporation of London** (⊛www.corpoflondon .gov.uk), which runs the City like a one-party mini-state, is an unreconstructed old-boy network whose medievalist pageantry camouflages the very real power and wealth that it holds – the Corporation owns nearly a third of the Square Mile (and several tracts of land elsewhere in and around London). Its anomalous status is all the more baffling when you consider that the area was once the cradle of British democracy: it was the City that traditionally stood up to bullying sovereigns.

Fleet Street and Ludgate Hill

In 1500 a certain Wynkyn de Worde, a pupil of William Caxton, moved the Caxton presses from Westminster to **Fleet Street** to be close to the lawyers of the Inns of Court (who were among his best customers) and to the clergy of St Paul's, who comprised the largest literate group in the city. However, the street really boomed two hundred years later, when in 1702 the now defunct *Daily Courant*, Britain's first daily newspaper, was published here. By the nineteenth century, all the major national and provincial dailies had their offices and printing presses in the Fleet Street district.

This situation prevailed until 1985, when Britain's first colour tabloid, *Today*, appeared, using computer technology that rendered the Fleet Street presses obsolete. It was then left to media tycoon Rupert Murdoch to take on the printers' unions in a bitter year-long dispute that changed the face of the newspaper industry for ever (see p.25). The press headquarters that once dominated this part of town have all now relocated, leaving just a couple of architectural landmarks to testify to five hundred years of printing history. Nonetheless, from Temple Bar, the official gateway to the City from Westminster, Fleet Street offers one of the grandest approaches to the City, thanks to the view across to Ludgate Hill and beyond to St Paul's, the City's number one tourist sight.

Around Temple Bar

Since the Middle Ages, **Temple Bar** (see Chapter 10, p.175), at the top of Fleet Street, has marked the western limit of the Square Mile's administrative boundaries. This western part of the street was spared by the Great Fire, which stopped at the junction with Fetter Lane, just short of **Prince Henry's Room** (Mon–Sat 11am–2pm; free; ☎020/7936 4004, ✆www.cityoflondon.gov.uk/ phr), a fine Jacobean house with timber-framed bay windows on the first floor, and the gateway to Inner Temple at street level. Originally a pub, later a waxworks, the first-floor room now contains material relating to the diarist Samuel Pepys (see box, below), who was born and baptized in the area. Even if you've no interest in Pepys, the wood-panelled room is worth a look – it contains one of the finest Jacobean plasterwork ceilings in London and a lot of original stained glass.

Samuel Pepys

Born to a humble tailor and a laundress in Salisbury Court, off Fleet Street, Samuel Pepys (1633–1703) was baptized in St Bride's (see p.187) and buried in St Olave's, having spent virtually his entire life in London. Family connections secured an education at St Paul's School and Pepys himself earned a top scholarship to Cambridge, followed by a rapid rise through the ranks of the civil service. He served as an MP, rose to the position of Secretary to the Admiralty, and was largely responsible for the establishment of a professional British navy. In 1679 he was imprisoned for six weeks in the Tower on suspicion of treason, but returned to office only to be forced out again in 1689, following the overthrow of James II, after which he withdrew from public life.

Pepys' career achievements are well documented in official archives, but it is his **diaries** that have immortalized him, comprising a million-plus words that record one of the most eventful decades in English history. Written between 1660 and 1669, this rollicking journal includes eyewitness accounts of the restoration of the monarchy, the Great Plague of 1665 and the Great Fire of 1666, giving an unparalleled insight into life in mid-seventeenth-century London. Ultimately, Pepys emerges from the pages, warts and all, as an eminently likeable character, who seems almost imperturbable – he gives as much space to details of his pub meals as he does to the Great Fire, and finishes each day with his catchphrase "and so to bed".

Pepys was also a notorious womanizer, detailing his philanderings in his diary in Spanish so as to avoid detection by his French Huguenot wife. Nevertheless he was caught *in flagrante* with one of her best friends, and his slow reconciliation with his spouse is recorded in a novelist's detail, the diary ending in 1669 as they sail off to the Continent to patch things up. In the event, his wife died later that year and he never remarried. Pepys' later years were largely taken up with compiling his vast library, which he bequeathed along with his manuscripts to his old college in Cambridge. There his diaries lay undiscovered until the nineteenth century, when they were finally transcribed from their shorthand (with the erotic passages omitted) and published for the first time in 1825.

Opposite Prince Henry's Room stands the church of **St Dunstan-in-the-West** (Tues & Fri 9am–3pm, Sun 10am–4pm), whose distinctive octagonal tower and lantern, built in neo-Gothic style, dominate this top end of the street. To the side of the tower is the much earlier clock temple, erected by the parishioners in thanks for escaping the Great Fire; within the temple, the legendary British giants Gog and Magog, in gilded loincloths, nod their heads and clang their bells on the hour. The statue of Queen Elizabeth I, in a niche in the vestry wall, dates from 1586 and is the oldest stone statue of the monarch in existence (it originally stood over the Ludgate entrance into the City and survived the Great Fire). The unusual, octagonal, neo-Gothic interior, built in the 1830s, features a huge wooden iconostasis, for use during the church's regular Romanian Orthodox services.

On the other side of Fleet Street, at no. 37, is **Hoare's Bank** (@www.hoaresbank.co.uk), the only surviving independent private bank in the City, founded by goldsmith Richard Hoare in 1672. The layout of the Fleet Street branch hasn't changed since its refurbishment in 1829, and it's worth peeking inside to admire the flagstone floor and the smell of mahogany. Founded in 1671, following the merger of two goldsmiths, **Child & Company**, at no. 1, was the first bank in Britain (though it's now merely an arm of the Royal Bank of Scotland). The interior retains many of its nineteenth-century fittings, including a case of muskets, kept as a safety measure by many City banks after the Gordon Riots of 1780 (see Contexts, p.586.)

Dr Johnson's House

Numerous narrow alleyways lead off the north side of Fleet Street beyond Fetter Lane, concealing legal chambers and offices. Two such alleys – Bolt Court and Hind Court – eventually open out into Gough Square, a newly cobbled courtyard surrounded, for the most part, by neo-Georgian buildings. Gough Square's one authentic eighteenth-century building is **Dr Johnson's House** (May–Sept Mon–Sat 11am–5.30pm; Oct–April Mon–Sat 11am–5pm; £4.50; @020/7353 3745, @www.drjh.dircon.co.uk), where the great savant, writer and lexicographer lived from 1747 to 1759 while compiling the 41,000 entries for the first dictionary of the English language.

Johnson came to London from Lichfield with the actor David Garrick, the pair taking it in turns to ride the one horse they could afford; Garrick had three halfpennies in his pocket, Johnson was richer by a penny. For several years Johnson lived on little more than bread and water in a garret on Exeter Street, in Covent Garden, before he finally rented the house on Gough Square, paid for with the £1575 advance he received for the dictionary. Despite his subsequent fame, though, Johnson continued to be in and out of debt all his life – his famous philosophical romance, *Rasselas*, was written in less than a week to raise funds for his mother's funeral.

The house itself is filled with portraits and etchings of Johnson, Boswell, his biographer, and other members of their circle, including Johnson's servant Francis Barber, and you get to see the open-plan attic, in which Johnson and his six helpers put together the *Dictionary*, but overall the house is a bit underwhelming.

The press buildings and St Bride's

Two outstanding pieces of architecture bear witness to Fleet Street's heyday. First, at no. 135–141, is the old headquarters of the **Daily Telegraph**. An adventurous building for such a conservative newspaper, it was one of London's first (and few) truly Art Deco edifices, built in a vaguely Greco-Egyptian style in 1928, with a great stone relief above the doorway depicting Mercury's messengers sending news around the world. It was upstaged a few years later, however, by the sleek, black (now former) **Daily Express** building foyer, at no. 127, the city's first glass curtain-wall construction. It's worth a peek inside the cinema-like foyer, which features a silver-leaf sunburst ceiling, ocean-wave floor tiles, shiny silver serpent handrails, and remarkable chrome and gold relief panels extolling the British Empire.

The best source of information about the old-style Fleet Street is the "journalists' and printers' cathedral", the church of **St Bride** (Mon–Fri 9am–5pm, Sat 11am–3pm, Sun for services only; ☎020/7427 0133, ⊛www.stbrides.com), situated behind the former Reuters building on the site of Wynkyn de Worde's sixteenth-century press. The church boasts Wren's tallest and most exquisite spire (said to be the inspiration for the traditional tiered wedding cake), but was extensively damaged in the Blitz. The Nazis' bombs did, however, reveal a crypt containing remains of Roman mosaics, medieval walls and seven previous churches on the site. Nestled among these relics, a little **museum** (same hours as church) of Fleet Street history includes information on the *Daily Courant* and the *Universal Daily Register*, which later became *The Times*, claiming to be "the faithful recorder of every species of intelligence . . . circulated for a particular set of readers only".

Ludgate Circus and Ludgate Hill

Fleet Street terminates at **Ludgate Circus**, which has held onto three of its four original quarter segments, dating from the 1870s. The Circus replaced the bridge crossing the **River Fleet**, which joins the Thames at Blackfriars Bridge. Buried under the roads in the 1760s after a drunken butcher got stuck in the river mud and froze to death, the Fleet marked the western boundary of the Roman city, and was an unmissable feature of the landscape, as the tanneries and slaughterhouses of Smithfield (see p.198) used to turn the water red with entrails.

The western bank of the Fleet was the site of the notoriously inhumane **Fleet Prison**, whose famous incumbents included the poet John Donne, imprisoned here for marrying without his father-in-law's consent. Until the Marriage Act of 1754, Fleet Prison was renowned for its clandestine "**Fleet Marriages**", performed by priests (or impostors) who were imprisoned there for debt. These marriages, in which couples could marry without a licence, attracted people of all classes, and took place in the prison chapel until 1710, when they were banished to the neighbouring taverns, the fee being split between clergyman and innkeeper.

Beyond the Circus, **Ludgate Hill** curves up to St Paul's, the view of the dome punctuated by the lead spire of the church of **St Martin Ludgate** (Mon–Fri 11am–3pm), which still rises above the housetops just as Wren intended. It was originally the church of Ludgate, one of the six City gates, which according to tradition was built by the mythical King Lud in the first century BC; the gate was eventually torn down in 1760. The cruciform interior of the church survived the Blitz intact as did most of the original seventeenth-century furnishings, and the whole place is now crisply maintained by several City guilds and masonic lodges, including the secretive Knights of the Round Table.

St Paul's Cathedral

St Paul's Cathedral, topped by an enormous lead-covered dome that's second in size only to St Peter's in Rome, has been a London icon since the Blitz, when it stood defiantly unscathed amid the carnage (as in the famous wartime propaganda photo). It remains a dominating presence in the City, despite the encroaching tower blocks of the financial sector; its showpiece west facade is particularly magnificent, fronted by a wide flight of steps, a double-storey portico and two of London's most Baroque towers, and is at its most impressive at night when bathed in sea-green arc lights. Westminster Abbey, St Paul's long-standing rival, has the edge when it comes to celebrity corpses, pre-Reformation sculpture, royal connections and sheer atmosphere. St Paul's, by contrast, is a soulless but perfectly calculated architectural set piece, a burial place for captains rather than kings, though it does contain more artists than Westminster Abbey, and continues to serve as a popular wedding church for the privileged few: for better, and as it turned out, for worse, Charles and Diana exchanged their vows here.

Excluding the Temple of Apollo that may have stood here in Roman times, the current building is the fifth church on this site, its immediate predecessor being **Old St Paul's**, a huge Gothic cathedral built by the Normans, whose 489-foot spire was one of the wonders of medieval Europe. By all accounts, Old St Paul's was an unruly place, and home to some obscure cults devoted to the likes of the fictitious St Uncumber, a bearded virgin who could rid women of unwanted husbands in return for pecks of oats. Horse fairs took place here, ball games had to be banned in 1385, and by the close of the sixteenth century it had become a "common passage and thoroughfare . . . a daily receptacle for rogues and beggars however diseased, to the great offence of religious-minded people". During the Commonwealth, the nave became a cavalry barracks, with both men and horses living in the church, and shops were set up in the portico. By the Restoration things had become so bad that St Paul's was dubbed "a loathsome Golgotha" – and on one memorable occasion a circus horse named Morocco performed tricks here, including a quick trot up the stairs to the top of the bell tower.

The **Great Fire** caused irreparable damage to this unlikely centre of iniquity, and Wren was given the task of building a replacement – just one of over fifty church commissions he received in the wake of the blaze. The final design was a compromise solution after several more radical, European-style plans were rejected by the conservative clergy. Hassles over money plagued the project throughout – at one point Parliament withheld half of Wren's salary because they felt the work was proceeding too slowly. Wren remained unruffled and rose to the challenge of building what was, in effect, the world's first Protestant cathedral, completing the commission in 1710 during the reign of Queen Anne, whose statue still stands in front of the west facade.

The interior

Despite the hourly calls for prayer, St Paul's is now a major tourist business, with visitors funnelled through revolving doors towards the ticket booth. Before reaching the till you pass the **Chapel of All Souls** on the left, containing a memorial to Lord Kitchener, the moustachioed figure on the World War I "Your Country Needs You" posters, who was drowned, along with his lover, Captain Fitzgerald (and most of the crew), off the Orkney Islands in 1916.

Once past the ticket office, you can take in the **nave** of the church for the first time. Queen Victoria thought it "dirty, dark and undevotional", though since the destruction of the stained glass in the Blitz, and the recent cleaning and restoration work, it is once again light and airy, as Wren intended. Burials are confined to the crypt, and memorials were only permitted after 1790 when overcrowding at Westminster Abbey had become intolerable. With the onset of the Napoleonic Wars, it was decided to erect a series of expensive monuments to the military commanders who had sacrificed their lives. These overblown funerary monuments are difficult to stomach nowadays: some border on the ludicrous, like the virtually naked statue of Captain Burges, in the south aisle, holding hands with an angel over a naval cannon; others are mildly offensive, such as the nearby monument to Thomas Fanshaw Middleton, first Protestant Bishop of India, depicted baptizing "heathen" locals. The best of the bunch are Flaxman's **Nelson** memorial, in the south transept, with its seasick lion, and, in the north aisle, Alfred Steven's bombastic bronze and marble **Duke of Wellington** monument, begun in 1857 but only topped with the statue of the duke astride his faithful steed, Copenhagen, in 1912.

The best place from which to appreciate the glory of St Paul's is beneath the **dome**, which was decorated (against Wren's wishes) by Thornhill's trompe l'oeil frescoes, rather insipid but on a scale that can't fail to impress. St Paul's most famous work of art, however, hangs in the north transept: the crushingly symbolic *Light of the World* by the Pre-Raphaelite **Holman Hunt**, depicting Christ knocking at the handleless, bramble-strewn door of the human soul, which must be opened from within. The original is actually in Keble College, Oxford, though this copy was executed by the artist himself, some fifty years later in 1900.

By far the most richly decorated section of the cathedral is the **chancel**, in particular the spectacular, swirling, gilded Byzantine-style mosaics of birds, fish, animals and greenery, dating from the 1890s. The intricately carved oak and limewood choir stalls, and the imposing organ case, are the work of Grinling Gibbons, who worked with Wren on many of his commissions. The north choir-aisle contains Henry Moore's *Mother and Child* sculpture and allows you to admire Jean Tijou's pair of ornate black-and-gold **wrought-iron gates** that separate the aisles from the high altar. The latter features an extravagant Baroque baldachin, held up by barley-sugar columns and wrapped round with gilded laurel, and is a postwar creation designed according to a pencil sketch by Wren. Behind the high altar stands the **American Memorial Chapel**, designed in the 1950s in honour of the 28,000 Americans based in Britain who lost their lives in World War II (check out the space rocket hidden in the carved wooden foliage of the far right-hand panel, a tribute to America's space exploration). To leave the chancel, you must pass through the south choir-aisle, where the upstanding shroud of **John Donne**, poet, preacher and one-time Dean of St Paul's, now resides, the only complete effigy to have survived from the previous cathedral.

The galleries

Beginning in the south transept, a series of stairs lead to the dome's three **galleries**, and they're well worth the climb. The initial 259 steps are relatively painless and take you as far as the internal **Whispering Gallery**, so called because of its acoustic properties – words whispered to the wall on one side are distinctly audible over 100ft away on the other, though the place is often so busy you can't hear very much above the hubbub except a ghostly murmur. Another 119 steps up, the broad exterior **Stone Gallery**, around the balustrade at the base of the dome, offers a great view of the City and along the Thames – you should be able to identify the distinctive white facade of Wren's London house, next door to the reconstructed Globe Theatre, from which he

▲ St Paul's Cathedral

was able to contemplate his masterpiece.

The final leg of the climb – 152 spiralling steel steps – takes you inside the dome's very complicated structure: the inner painted cupola is separated from the wooden, lead-covered outer dome by a funnel-shaped brick cone which acts as a support for the lantern, with its **Golden Gallery**, and ultimately the golden ball and cross which top the cathedral. The view from the Golden Gallery is unbeatable, but before you ascend the last flight of stairs be sure to take a look through the peephole in the floor, which looks down onto the monochrome marble floor beneath the dome, a truly terrifying sight.

The crypt

Access to the **crypt** – reputedly the largest in Europe – is immediately on your left as you leave the south choir-aisle. The whitewashed walls and bright lighting, however, make this one of the least atmospheric mausoleums you could imagine – a far cry from the nineteenth century, when visitors were shown around the tombs by candlelight.

You're encouraged to turn right at the entrance to the crypt, thus bringing you to the southern aisle, popularly known as **Artists' Corner**, which boasts as many painters and architects as Westminster Abbey has poets. It became a popular resting place with the arrival of Wren himself; his son composed the famous inscription on his tomb – "*lector, si monumentum requiris, circumspice*" (reader, if you seek his monument, look around). Close to Wren are the grave-slabs of Reynolds, Turner, Millais, Holman Hunt, Lord Leighton and Alma-Tadema; nearby there's a bust of van Dyck, whose monument perished along with Old St Paul's. Over in the north aisle is a modern plaque to the great church reformer John Wycliffe, and the grave of Alexander Fleming, the discoverer of penicillin.

The crypt's two-star tombs are those of **Nelson** and **Wellington**, both occupying centre stage and both with more fanciful monuments upstairs. Wellington's porphyry and granite monstrosity is set in its own mini-chapel, surrounded by later illustrious British field marshals, while Nelson's embalmed body lies in a black marble sarcophagus originally designed for Cardinal Wolsey and later intended for Henry VIII and his third wife, Jane Seymour. As at Trafalgar Square, Nelson lies close to fellow admirals Jellicoe and Beatty – Beatty was the last person to be buried in St Paul's, in 1936. Nearby is a memorial to the hundreds of British soldiers who died in the 1982 **Falklands War**, listed alphabetically, without rank, in an unusually egalitarian gesture.

The **treasury**, situated in the north transept of the crypt, displays church plate, richly embroidered copes and mitres and bejewelled altar crosses; nearby are a couple of damaged marble effigies from the previous cathedral. At the western end of the crypt, you'll find a model of Old St Paul's, the cathedral shop, a café, a licensed restaurant, some toilets and, more importantly, the exit.

The churchyard

St Paul's itself may have survived World War II relatively unscathed, but the area immediately surrounding it, still known optimistically as **St Paul's Churchyard**, was obliterated. From 1500 this district had been the centre of the London book trade; Wynkyn de Worde was among the first to set up shop here, though his main office was on Fleet Street (see p.184). Another feature of the churchyard was **Paul's Cross** – also known as "Pol's Stump" – where proclamations and political speeches were made from a wooden pulpit. Heretics were regularly executed on this spot, and in 1519 Luther's works were publicly burnt here, before Henry VIII changed sides and demanded the "preaching down" of papal authority from the same spot. The cross was finally destroyed by Cromwell and his followers, and is now commemorated by a column erected in 1910, to the northeast of the cathedral. The column is topped by a gilded statue of St Paul and diplomatically inscribed "amid such scenes of good and evil as make up human affairs, the conscience of the church and nation through five centuries found public utterance".

Paternoster Square

The Blitz also destroyed the area immediately to the north of St Paul's, incinerating all the booksellers' shops and around six million books. In their place the City authorities built the brazenly modernist **Paternoster Square**, a grim pedestrianized piazza, surrounded by equally unprepossessing office blocks. In the 1980s, it was decided to tear all that down and, after the first in a long line of architectural interventions from Prince Charles, the Corporation opted for William Whitfield's post-classical office blocks in Portland stone and his Corinthian column topped by a gilded urn. One happy consequence of the square's redevelopment is that **Temple Bar**, the last surviving City gate, found its way back to London after over a hundred years of exile languishing in a park in Hertfordshire. Designed by Wren himself, the triumphal arch used to stand at the top of Fleet Street, and was used to display the heads of traitors (see p.175). Looking weathered but clean, the arch now forms the entrance to Paternoster Square from St Paul's, with the Stuart monarchs, James I and Charles II, and their consorts occupying the niches.

The hundred or so **City Livery Companies** in the Square Mile are descended from the craft guilds of the Middle Ages, whose purpose was to administer apprenticeships and take charge of quality control, in return for which they were granted monopolies. As their powers and wealth grew, the guilds advertised their success by staging lavish banquets and building ever more opulent halls for their meetings and ceremonies. The wealthiest members of each company wore elaborate "livery" (or uniforms) on such occasions, and automatically received the Freedom of the City, entitling them to stand for election to the Court of Common Council, the Corporation's ruling body, and to be appointed to the Court of Aldermen – which was originally responsible for administering the City until the fourteenth century.

Despite various attempts to introduce democracy over the centuries, the organization of the Livery Companies remains deeply undemocratic, but their prodigious wealth – together they own around fifteen percent of the City – has enabled them to fund almshouses, schools and a wide range of other charities, all of which has helped pacify the critics. As in masonic lodges, the elaborate ceremonies serve to hide the very real power that these companies still hold. In spite of the fact that many of the old trades associated with the Livery Companies have died out, liverymen still dominate the Court of Common Council and the Court of Aldermen. What's more, once elected, Aldermen remain in office for life, taking it in turns to be first a Sheriff, and eventually Lord Mayor – a knighthood is virtually guaranteed.

Anyone visiting the City can't fail to notice the numerous signs directing you to the Livery Company halls, many with enticing names such as the Tallow Chandlers and Cordwainers. Few medieval halls survived the Great Fire, fewer still the Blitz, but some are worth a look nonetheless for their ornate interiors. The problem is gaining **admission**. The City of London tourist office (☎020/7332 1456) has tickets to some halls, which they tend to distribute each year in January; other halls will allow you to join a pre-booked group tour for around £5 per person. It's certainly not something you can do on the spur of the moment, though during the City of London Festival (late June to mid-July; ⊛www.colf.org), many events do take place inside the Livery

Blackfriars to Southwark Bridge

The combination of Victorian town planning (which created Queen Victoria Street) and postwar traffic schemes (which are responsible for the thundering dual carriageway and underpass of Upper Thames Street) used to put most people off venturing south of St Paul's. But, with the opening of the **Millennium Bridge** (see p.272) giving access to Tate Modern and Bankside, more folk are traversing the area. However, instead of simply heading for the bridge, it's worth taking time to visit one of the Wren churches, to venture into the backstreets and alleyways, or to go for a peaceful stroll along the **Riverside Walk** which now extends all the way from Blackfriars railway bridge to Tower Bridge.

Blackfriars

The streets to the north and east of **Blackfriars**, where a Dominican monastery stood until the Dissolution, see few tourists nowadays, yet in the seventeenth century this was a fashionable district – Ben Jonson had a house here, as did Shakespeare, who worked in the Blackfriars Theatre, and, later, van Dyck. Thoroughly destroyed in the Great Fire, the area suffered only peripheral damage from wartime bombing, leaving a warren of alleyways, courtyards and narrow streets, which, while holding few specific sights, manage to convey something of the plan of the medieval City before the Victorians, the German bombers and the halls. Below is a selection of the most interesting of the City Livery halls to aim for.

Apothecaries' Hall Blackfriars Lane ☎020/7236 1189, ⓦ www.apothecaries.org. The seventeenth-century courtyard is open to the public, but entry to the magnificent staircase and the Great Hall – with its musicians' gallery, portrait by Reynolds and collection of pharmaceutical gear – is by prior appointment only.

Fishmongers' Hall London Bridge ☎020/7626 3531, ⓦ www.fishhall.co.uk. A prominent Greek Revival building on the riverfront, with a grand staircase hall, a statue of Mayor Walworth and the very dagger with which he stabbed Wat Tyler (see p.198). Open days twice a year; £5.

Goldsmiths' Hall Foster Lane ☎020/7606 7010, ⓦ www.thegoldsmiths.co.uk. One of the easiest to visit as there are occasional public exhibitions offering the chance to see its sumptuous central staircase built in the 1830s. Several open days a year; free.

Merchant Taylors' Hall 30 Threadneedle St ☎020/7450 4440, ⓦ www.merchant taylors.co.uk. The late fourteenth-century crypt chapel here contains more medieval masonry than on any other Livery hall; entry by prior appointment only.

Skinners' Hall 8 Dowgate Hill ☎020/7236 5629, ⓦ www.skinnershall.co.uk. The staircase and courtroom survive from the seventeenth century, while the hall contains a splendid Russian chandelier and a whole series of murals by artist Frank Brangwyn. Open days three times a year; £5.

Tallow Chandlers' Hall 4 Dowgate Hill ☎020/7248 4726, ⓦ www.tallowchandlers .org. Set back from the street around an attractive courtyard, the Candlemakers' Company retains its seventeenth-century courtroom, complete with original seating. Open days twice a year; free.

Vintners' Hall 68 Upper Thames St ☎020/7236 1863, ⓦ www.vintnershall.co.uk. The oldest hall in the City, dating from 1671, with a period-piece staircase with "fabulously elaborate balusters".

1960s brutalists did their worst.

To give some structure to your wanderings, from St Paul's head down Creed Lane and St Andrew's Hill, backstreets to the south of Ludgate Hill, to the least costly of Wren's churches, **St Andrew-by-the-Wardrobe** (Mon–Fri 8.30am–6pm), so called because the royal depot for furniture and armour was situated here before the Great Fire. The nave is usually locked, but you can look through from the vestry at the simple, light interior, with its oak wood-panelling and attractive white plasterwork. To the north, off **Carter Lane**, once a major City thoroughfare, you'll find various unexpected little streets and courtyards – like Wardrobe Place – that present a slice of the pre-Blitz City. At the end of Carter Lane is Ludgate Broadway and the cobbles of Blackfriars Lane. Ahead is the wedding-cake spire of St Bride's (see p.187, viewed across bomb sites that have only recently been redeveloped; to the south is the **Apothecaries' Hall**, one of the prettiest of the City Livery Companies (see box on above), with a tiny doorway leading to a pastel-shaded seventeenth-century court. Round the corner in Blackfriars Court, near the site of the old monastery, is *The Blackfriar*, which boasts a fantastically ornate **Arts and Crafts** pub interior (see p.481).

East to Cannon Street

A short way east along Queen Victoria Street stands the surprising little red-brick mansion of the **College of Arms** (Mon–Fri 10am–4pm; free; ☎020/7248

2762, ⓦwww.college-of-arms.gov.uk), which was built round a courtyard in the 1670s but subsequently opened up to the south with the building of the new road. The Earl Marshal's Court – featuring a gallery, copious wooden panelling and a modest throne – is the only one open to the public, unless you apply to trace your family or study heraldry in the college library. Amid the roar of traffic, Wren's Dutch-looking church of **St Benet** (now a Welsh Church; only open for its Welsh-language services Sun 11am & 2.30pm), opposite, with its distinctive chequered quoins, completes this vignette of seventeenth-century London. Further east stands another prominent Wren church, **St Nicholas Cole Abbey** (Tues 5–6.30pm, Wed & Thurs noon–2pm), which featured prominently in the Ealing comedy *The Lavender Hill Mob*; it's now used by the Free Church of Scotland.

Just down Lambeth Hill is the tower of St Mary Somerset, looking very forlorn, its main body having been destroyed in 1871. Further east still, along Upper Thames Street, is the elegant three-tiered steeple of yet another Wren church, **St James Garlickhythe** (Mon–Fri 10am–4pm; ⓦwww.stjames garlickhythe.org.uk), named after the garlic that used to be sold from the nearby banks of the Thames. Badly damaged in the Blitz, and again in 1991 by a nearby crane which fell through the south rose window into the nave, the interior nevertheless remains much as Wren designed it, with the highest roof in the City after St Paul's, generously lit by clear arched windows in the clerestory, an arrangement which earned it the nickname of "Wren's Lantern".

Continue eastwards, along Skinner's Lane (which runs parallel to Upper Thames Street), to **St Michael Paternoster Royal** (Mon–Fri 8am–5.30pm), another Wren church badly damaged in the war, less remarkable for its architecture than for its modern stained-glass windows, including one of the pantomime character Dick Whittington (see below) with his knapsack and cat. Whittington, the only Lord Mayor of London anyone has ever heard of, was buried in the church and lived next door on College Hill, still an evocative little cobbled street today.

Dick Whittington

The third son of a wealthy Gloucestershire family, **Dick Whittington** was an apprentice mercer, dealing in silks and velvets, who rose to become one of the richest men in the city by the age of just 21. He was an early philanthropist, establishing a library at Greyfriars' monastery and a refuge for single mothers at St Thomas' Hospital, and building one of the city's first public lavatories, a unisex 128-seater known as "Whittington's Night Soil House of Easement". On his deathbed in 1423 he left money to pay half the costs of the Guildhall library, to repair St Bartholomew's Hospital, to refurbish Newgate Prison and to build various almshouses and a college of priests adjacent to St Michael's, who would pray for his soul.

The **pantomime** story appeared for the first time some two hundred years after Whittington's death, though quite how the wealthy Whittington became the fictional ragamuffin who comes to London after hearing the streets are paved with gold, no one seems to know. In the story, Whittington is on the point of leaving London with his knapsack and cat, when he hears the Bow Bells ring out "Turn again, Whittington, thrice Lord Mayor of London" (he was, in fact, mayor on four occasions and was never knighted as the story claims). The theory on the cat is that it was a common name for a coal barge at the time, and Whittington is thought to have made much of his fortune in the coal trade. There's a statue on Highgate Hill commemorating the very spot where Dick allegedly heard the Bow Bells (see p.203).

Newgate to Smithfield

The area to the north of St Paul's is one of the most interesting parts of the City. The financial and business sectors play a more minor role here, the three most important institutions being the criminal court at the **Old Bailey**, which stands on the site of the old **Newgate Prison**; the hospital of **St Bartholomew's**, the only medieval hospital which occupies its original site to the present day; and the meat market at **Smithfield**, one of the last of the ancient London markets within the City.

The Old Bailey

London's Central Criminal Court is more popularly known as the **Old Bailey** (Mon–Fri 10.30am–1pm & 2–4pm; ☎020/7248 3277, ⊛www.cjsonline.org) after the street on which it stands, which used to form the outer wall of the medieval city. The current, rather pompous Edwardian building is distinguished by its green dome, surmounted by a gilded statue of Justice, unusually depicted without blindfold, holding her sword and scales. The Old Bailey's fame, however, rests upon the fact that since 1834 virtually all the country's most serious criminal court cases have taken place here, including the trials of, among others, Oscar Wilde, the Nazi propagandist Lord Haw-Haw, the Kray twins, the Angry Brigade (see p.352), the wrongly convicted Guildford Four and Birmingham Six "IRA bombers", and all Britain's multiple murderers. You can watch the proceedings from the visitors' gallery (no under-14s), but note that no bags, food, drink, cameras, radios, CD players or mobile phones are allowed in, and that there is no cloakroom (the *Viaduct Tavern* (see p.481) across the road will look after your mobile for a small fee). Even if you don't want to sit through a trial, it's worth venturing inside to see the Grand Hall, with its swirling marble floor and walls, succession of domes, and grandiloquent frescoes; the public entrance is on Newgate Street.

Before 1902, the site of the Old Bailey was occupied by **Newgate Prison**, which began life as one of the prisons above the medieval gateways into the City and was burnt down during the Gordon Riots of 1780, only to be rebuilt as "a veritable Hell, worthy of the imagination of Dante", as one of its more famous inmates, Casanova, put it. Earlier well-known temporary residents included Thomas Malory, who wrote *Le Morte d'Arthur* while imprisoned here for murder (among other things); Daniel Defoe, who was put inside for his *The Shortest Way with Dissenters*; Ben Jonson, who served time for murder; Christopher Marlowe, who was on a charge of atheism; and the murderer Major Strangeways, who was "pressed" to death with piles of weights in the courtyard in 1658. (The cellars of the aforementioned *Viaduct Tavern*, opposite the Old Bailey, are thought to be former Newgate cells, and are reputed to be haunted.)

St Bartholomew's Hospital

North of the Old Bailey on Giltspur Street stands the main building of **St Bartholomew's Hospital** (⊛www.bartsandthelondon.nhs.uk) – affectionately known as Bart's. This is the oldest hospital in London, whose departments spread their tentacles across the surrounding area, creating a kind of open-plan medical village. With a couple of notable exceptions (detailed below) the buildings themselves are unremarkable, but the history of the place is fascinating. It began as an Augustinian priory and hospice in 1123, founded by Rahere, court jester to Henry I, on the orders of St Bartholomew, who appeared to him in a

Public executions and body snatchers

After 1783, when hangings at Tyburn were stopped (see box, p.287), **public executions** drew the crowds to Newgate, with more than 100,000 turning up on some occasions. The last public beheading took place here in 1820 when the five Cato Street Conspirators (see p.105) were hanged and then decapitated with a surgeon's knife. It was in hanging, however, that Newgate excelled, and its most efficient gallows could dispatch twenty criminals simultaneously. Unease over the "robbery and violence, loud laughing, oaths, fighting, obscene conduct and still more filthy language" that accompanied public hangings drove the executions inside the prison walls in 1868. Henceforth, a black flag and the tolling of the bell of Old Bailey were the only signs that an execution had taken place. The night before an execution, a handbell was tolled outside the condemned's cell, while the jailer recited the Newgate verse, bellowing the last two lines: "All you who in the condemned hole do lie/Prepare you, for tomorrow you shall die/And when St Sepulchre's bell tomorrow tolls/The Lord have mercy on your souls". The reference was to the "Great Bell of Old Bailey" in the church of **St Sepulchre** (Wed noon–3pm), which tolled the condemned to the scaffold at eight in the morning. The handbell and verse are now displayed inside the church, whose fifteenth-century tower stands diagonally opposite the Old Bailey.

The bodies of the executed were handed over to the surgeons of St Bartholomew's for dissection, but **body snatchers** also preyed on non-criminals buried in the St Sepulchre churchyard. Such was the demand for corpses that relatives were forced to pay a night watchman to guard the graveyard in a specially built watch-house – which still stands to the north of the church – in order to prevent the "Resurrection Men" from retrieving their quarry. If the night watchman proved unsuccessful, however, the stolen stiffs would then be taken up Giltspur Street to the *Fortune of War* tavern, on Pie Corner, at the junction of Cock Lane, where the bodies were laid out for the surgeons. The pub has now gone, but Pie Corner is still marked by a gilded overfed cherub known as **Fat Boy**. He commemorates the "staying of the Great Fire", which, when it wasn't blamed on the Catholics, was ascribed to the sin of gluttony, since it had begun in Pudding Lane and ended at Pie Corner.

vision while he was in malarial delirium on a pilgrimage to Rome. The priory was dissolved by Henry VIII, yet in 1546, as a sick old man with just two weeks to live, Henry agreed to refound the hospital.

There's a statue of Henry VIII in the main gateway, built in 1702, looking out over Smithfield Market; a lame man and a melancholic man sit above the broken pediment. Further along the wall are shrapnel marks left from a 1916 Zeppelin air raid. Immediately on your left as you pass through the gateway stands the church of **St Bartholomew-the-Less** (daily 7am–8pm), sole survivor of the priory's four chapels, where Inigo Jones was baptized. The tower is fifteenth-century, but the octagonal interior was largely rebuilt in neo-Gothic style and reconstructed after the last war. Beyond the church lies three-quarters of the courtyard created for the hospital by James Gibbs in the mid-eighteenth century, including the **Great Hall** and the **staircase**, its walls decorated with biblical murals that were painted free of charge by Hogarth, who was born and baptized nearby and served as one of the hospital's governors.

You can get a glimpse of the staircase from **St Bartholomew's Hospital Museum** (Tues–Fri 10am–4pm; free), situated to the left just before you enter the courtyard. The museum displays the charter granted by Henry VIII on his deathbed, and other medieval documents dating back as far as 1137, but first you get to watch a short video on the foundation of Bart's by Rahere. Among the medical artefacts, there are some fearsome amputation instruments, a pair of leather "lunatic restrainers", some great jars with labels such as "poison – for external use only", and a cricket bat autographed by W.G. Grace, who was a student at Bart's in the 1870s. To see the Great Hall you must go on one of the fascinating **guided tours** (Fri 2pm; £4; ☎020/7601 8152), which take in Smithfield and the surrounding area as well; the meeting point is the hospital gate.

St Bartholomew-the-Great

St Bartholomew-the-Great (Tues–Fri 8.30am–5pm, Sat 10.30am–1.30pm, Sun 8.30am–1pm & 2.30–8pm; mid-Nov to mid-Feb closes 4pm Tues–Fri; ☎020/7606 5171, ⓦwww.greatstbarts.com), hidden away in the backstreets to the north of the hospital, is London's oldest and most atmospheric parish church, and is much beloved of film companies (*Shakespeare in Love* and *Four Weddings and a Funeral* both shot scenes here). Begun in 1123 as the priory's main church, it was partly demolished in the Reformation, and gradually fell into ruins: the cloisters were used as a stable, there was a Nonconformist boys' school in the triforium, a coal and wine cellar in the crypt, a blacksmith's in the north transept and a printing press (where Benjamin Franklin worked for a while) in the Lady Chapel. From 1887, the architect Aston Webb set about restoring what was left of the old church, patching up the chequered patterning and adding the flintwork that now characterizes the exterior.

To get an idea of the scale of the original church, approach it through the half-timbered Tudor **gatehouse**, on Little Britain Street, which was discovered after a Zeppelin raid in World War I. A wooden statue of St Bartholomew stands in a niche, holding the knife with which he was flayed; below is the thirteenth-century arch which once formed the entrance to the nave. The churchyard now stands where the nave itself would have been, and one side of the **cloisters** survives to the south, immediately to the right as you enter the church. The rest is a confusion of elements, including portions of the transepts and, most impressively, the **chancel**, where thick Norman pillars separate the main body from the ambulatory. There are various pre-Fire monuments, the most prominent being Rahere's tomb, which shelters under a fifteenth-century canopy to the north of the altar, with an angel at his feet and two canons kneeling beside him reading from the prophets. Beyond the ambulatory lies the Lady Chapel, mostly Webb's work, though with original stonework here and there; it's now dedicated to the City of London Squadron, hence the RAF standard that hangs here.

Postman's Park

Opposite the former General Post Office building, southeast of Smithfield, on King Edward Street lies **Postman's Park**, one of the most curious and little-visited corners of the City. Here, in 1900, in the churchyard of St Botolph-without-Aldersgate, the painter and sculptor George Frederick Watts paid for a national memorial to "heroes of everyday life", a patchwork of majolica tiles inscribed with the names of ordinary folk who had died in the course of some act of bravery. It exhibits the classic Victorian sentimental fascination with death, and makes for macabre but compelling reading: "Drowned in attempting to save his brother after he himself had just been rescued" or "Saved a lunatic woman from suicide at Woolwich Arsenal station, but was himself run over by the train".

Smithfield

The ground was covered, nearly ankle-deep with filth and mire; a thick steam perpetually rising from the reeking bodies of the cattle, and mingling with the fog.

Charles Dickens, *Oliver Twist*

Blood and guts were regularly spilled at **Smithfield** long before the meat market was legally sanctioned here in the seventeenth century. This patch of open ground outside the City walls (its name is a corruption of "Smooth Field") was used as a horse fair in Norman times, and later for jousts and tournaments. In 1381, the poll-tax rebels under Wat Tyler assembled here to negotiate with the boy-king Richard II. Tyler's lack of respect towards the king gave Lord Mayor Walworth the excuse to pull Tyler from his horse and stab him, after which he was bustled into Bart's for treatment, only to be dragged out by the king's men and beheaded on the spot.

Smithfield subsequently became a venue for **public executions**. The Scottish hero, William Wallace, was dragged behind a horse from the Tower, then hanged, drawn and quartered here in 1305, and the Bishop of Rochester's cook was boiled alive in 1531, but the local speciality was burnings. These reached a peak during the reign of "Bloody" Mary in the 1550s, when hundreds of Protestants were burnt at the stake for their beliefs, in revenge for the Catholics who had suffered a similar fate under Mary's father, Henry VIII, and brother, Edward VI; a plaque on the side of St Bartholomew's Hospital commemorates some of the Protestants who died.

Even more popular than the public executions was the **St Bartholomew's Fair**, a cloth and cattle fair established by Rahere in the twelfth century in order to fund Bart's, and held over three days in late August. Rahere himself used to perform juggling tricks, while Pepys reports seeing a horse counting sixpences and, more reliably, a puppet show of Ben Jonson's play *Bartholomew Fair*. By the sixteenth century, it had become much more than just a cloth fair, with every kind of debauchery and theatrical entertainment laid on, and the Victorians closed it down to protect public morals.

The meat **market**, with which Smithfield is now synonymous, grew up as a kind of adjunct to the fair. Live cattle continued to be herded into central London and slaughtered here until 1852, when the fair was suppressed and the abattoirs moved out to Islington. A new covered market hall, designed by City architect Horace Jones, was erected in 1868, along with the "Winkle", a spiral ramp at the centre of West Smithfield, linked to the market's very own tube station (now a car park). The market tripled in size by 1900, and it remains London's main meat market. If you want to see it in action, you'll need to get here early – the action starts around 4am and is all over by 9am or 10am. The compensation for getting up at this ungodly hour are the early licensing laws which apply to certain local pubs, where you can get a hearty breakfast and an early-morning pint.

London Wall

London Wall is a highway driven through the bomb sites in the north of the City and lined with a phalanx of postwar architectural errors. As the name suggests, it follows the line of the **Roman wall**, portions of which still stand on the north side in St Alphage's Garden and by the Barber Surgeons' Hall; these surviving sections formed part of the Roman fort that was incorporated into the wall system at Cripplegate. If you're interested in tracing the line of the old city walls, you can follow a **trail** that begins outside the nearby Museum of London and extends a mile and a half to the Tower of London, with explanatory panels displayed at intervals along the way.

Barbican

The City's only large residential complex is the **Barbican**, a phenomenally ugly and expensive concrete ghetto built on the heavily bombed Cripplegate area. It's an upmarket urban dystopia, comprising a maze of pedestrian walkways and underground car parks, pinioned by three 400-foot, 42-storey tower blocks – the tallest residential accommodation in Europe when they were built in the 1970s. The great footballer and drinker George Best, a resident in the following decade, described it as "like living in Colditz".

The zone's solitary prewar building is the heavily restored sixteenth-century church of **St Giles-without-Cripplegate** (Mon–Fri 11am–4pm; ☎020/7638 1997, ⓦwww.stgilescripplegate.com), where Oliver Cromwell was married in 1620 and where John Milton is buried. Milton's body was exhumed in 1793, his teeth knocked out as souvenirs and his corpse exhibited to the public until the novelty wore off.

St Giles is now bracketed between a pair of artificial lakes, and lies directly opposite the sole reason for venturing into this depressing complex – the **Barbican Arts Centre** (ⓦwww.barbican.org.uk), the "City's Gift to the Nation", which was formally opened in 1982, nearly thirty years after the first plans were drawn up. Even the arts centre has its drawbacks, not least an obtusely confusing layout that continues to prove user-repellent; just finding the main entrance on Silk Street is quite a feat for most Londoners. Built on nine levels, three of them subterranean, the complex contains a huge concert hall (home of the London Symphony Orchestra), two theatres, a good three-screen repertory cinema, a rooftop garden, a public library and a poorly designed exhibition space, as well as housing the Guildhall School of Music and Drama (ⓦwww.gsmd.ac.uk).

Museum of London

Hidden in the southwestern corner of the Barbican complex is the **Museum of London** (Mon–Sat 10am–5.50pm, Sun noon–5.50pm; free; ☎020/7600 3699, ⓦwww.museumoflondon.org.uk), whose permanent exhibition is basically an educational trot through London's past from prehistory to the present day, illustrated by the city's major archeological finds. This is interesting enough, but the real strength of the museum lies in the excellent temporary exhibitions, gallery tours, lectures, walks and videos it organizes throughout the year .

The permanent displays start on the upper floor (where visitors enter), with a section on **London Before London**, which displays some of the city's oldest archeological artefacts: flint tools from 300,000 BC, a cave bear skull from half a million years ago, not to mention a lion skull and an elephant's foot. Individually, none of the finds is that remarkable, but there's enough hands-on – feel the flint, bone, metal – and touch-screen stuff to keep most people engaged. The **Roman London** section includes gold coins, marble busts from the Temple of Mithras (see p.203), and the Bucklersbury mosaic floor, discovered during the Victorian road-building projects and now displayed in a mock-up of a wealthy Roman dining room.

The **Tudor London** and **Early Stuart London** sections contain, among other things, some excellent models of the great buildings of pre-Fire London: the Royal Exchange, London Bridge, Whitehall Palace, Nonsuch Palace and the Rose Theatre. At the end of the upper floor there's a diorama accompanied by a loop-tape of Pepys' first-hand account of the Great Fire. From here a ramp leads down to the museum's most eye-catching exhibit, the **Lord Mayor's Coach**, which rivals the Queen's in sheer weight of gold decoration. Beyond is the post-Fire section on the lower floor, set around a nursery garden filled with

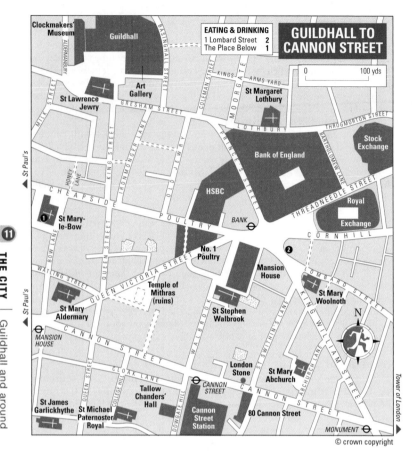

Map labels:

Clockmakers' Museum, Guildhall

EATING & DRINKING
1 Lombard Street 2
The Place Below 1

GUILDHALL TO CANNON STREET

ALDERMANBURY, BASINGHALL STREET, KINGS ARMS YARD, MOORGATE, St Margaret Lothbury

Art Gallery

St Lawrence Jewry

GRESHAM STREET, COLEMAN STREET, LOTHBURY, THROGMORTON STREET

MILK STREET, HONEY LANE, KING STREET, IRONMONGER LANE, OLD JEWRY, PRINCES STREET, BARTHOLOMEW LANE

Stock Exchange

Bank of England

0   100 yds

CHEAPSIDE, POULTRY

HSBC

❶ St Mary-le-Bow

BANK

THREADNEEDLE STREET

Royal Exchange

BOW LANE, QUEEN STREET

WATLING STREET

QUEEN VICTORIA STREET

No. 1 Poultry

CORNHILL

❷

Mansion House

LOMBARD STREET

St Mary Woolnoth

KING WILLIAM STREET

Temple of Mithras (ruins)

St Mary Aldermary

St Stephen Walbrook

WALBROOK

N

MANSION HOUSE

CANNON STREET

London Stone

St Mary Abchurch

SWITHIN'S LANE, ABCHURCH LANE

CLOAK LANE

QUEEN STREET, COLLEGE HILL, DOWGATE HILL

CANNON STREET

Tallow Chandlers' Hall

St James Garlickhythe   St Michael Paternoster Royal

Cannon Street Station

80 Cannon Street

MONUMENT

St Paul's

St Paul's

Tower of London

© crown copyright

THE CITY

11

Guildhall and around

---

plants and flowers typical of various epochs. There are maps of the expanding capital and a reconstructed wood-panelled, late-Stuart interior, followed by a mock prison cell.

In the final gallery, **World City 1789–1914**, you pass Nelson's Sword of Honour, and a pair of Wellington's boots, not to mention his cocked beaver-felt hat with swan-feather plumes, before heading off into the Victorian Walk, a tightly-knit collection of reconstructed nineteenth-century offices, pubs and shops, and then listening to first-hand accounts of the old East End. Rather than have a permanent modern gallery, the museum tends to use its temporary exhibitions to focus on the twentieth century and more contemporary themes.

Guildhall and around

Situated at the geographical centre of the Square Mile, **Guildhall** (May–Sept daily 10am–5pm; Oct–April Mon–Sat 10am–5pm; free; ☎020/7606 3030, ⓦwww.cityoflondon.gov.uk) was the seat of the City administration for over eight hundred years. It remains the headquarters of the Corporation of London, and is still used for many of the City's formal civic occasions. Architecturally, however, it no longer exudes quite the municipal wealth it once did, having been badly damaged in both the Great Fire and the Blitz, and scarred by the early 1970s addition of a concrete cloister and wing.

Nonetheless, the mock-medieval **Great Hall** is worth a visit and is more accessible than it looks – it's entered through the hideous modern extension, not the quasi-Indian porch, which was tacked on in the eighteenth century and is the most striking aspect of the exterior. Venue in 1553 for the high-treason trials of Lady Jane Grey and her husband, Lord Dudley, and Archbishop Cranmer, the Great Hall is still used for meetings of the Court of Common Council and for various state functions. The interior is basically a postwar reconstruction of the fifteenth-century original, complete with a minstrels' gallery from which statues of the pagan giants Gog and Magog look down. The hall is also home to a handful of vainglorious late eighteenth- and early nineteenth-century monuments, replete with lions, cherubs and ludicrous allegorical figures.

The only surviving part of the medieval Guildhall is the **crypt**, which dates from the thirteenth to the fifteenth centuries. Unfortunately, to visit the crypt, you must join up with a group booked in for a guided tour. To find out when the next tour will be, phone the Keeper's Office on the number quoted above.

Guildhall Art Gallery

On the eastern side of Guildhall's main courtyard stands the **Guildhall Art Gallery** (Mon–Sat 10am–5pm, Sun noon–4pm; £2.50, free Fri and daily after 3.30pm; ☎020/7332 3700), a neo-Gothic pastiche purpose-built in 1999 by one of the Gilbert Scott family, nearly sixty years after the original gallery burnt down in the Blitz. As you might expect, there's plenty of pomp and pageantry, especially in the main gallery, where you'll find lots of dull, official portraits of royals, aldermen and mayors. Also hiding up here, now surrounded by a protective glass cabinet, is the marble statue of **Margaret Thatcher**, whose head was knocked off by a protester in 2002. The centrepiece of the entire gallery is the gigantic and very dramatic *Defeat of the Floating Batteries at Gibraltar,* by **John Singleton Copley**, depicting the 1782 Siege of Gibraltar, when the Spanish tried to dislodge the British from the Rock by firing incendiary devices from "unsinkable" floating barges. The picture shows the Brits magnanimously saving the drowning enemy from the flaming barques. Commissioned by the Corporation, poor old Copley had to redo the entire thing when the garrison officers insisted on having more prominence.

More intriguing is the gallery's wide range of paintings depicting London subjects – stretching over several centuries – a small selection of which are hung in the **London rooms**. On the whole, they're interesting as much for what they depict – bygone vistas of old London, postwar bomb sites and so on – as for their artistry. On the same floor, you'll also find a small sample of the 175 oils and 1000 watercolours the gallery owns by the English artist **Matthew Smith** (1879–1959), whose works are heavily influenced by Cézanne's late works and Matisse's Fauvist phase.

Some of the best works are down in the **Victorian galleries**, which are packed floor to ceiling with works by prosperous artists such as G.F. Watts, Alma-Tadema and Lord Leighton. A typical example is *Israel in Egypt* by E.J. Poynter (son of the architect), which was inspired by (and depicts) many exhibits from the British Museum. There are, however, a few exceptional paintings worth seeking out: **Constable**'s full-sized oil sketch of *Salisbury Cathedral*, characterized by loose brushwork and an air of foreboding; **Holman Hunt**'s *The Eve of St Agnes* (inspired by Keats' poem), painted while he was still a student at the RA, and bought by the gallery's first director out of his own pocket; and **Rossetti**'s *La Ghirlandata*, a typically lush portrait, in intense blues and greens, of a model who's a dead ringer for Jane Morris, with whom the artist was infatuated.

During the gallery's construction a **Roman amphitheatre**, dating from around 120 AD, was discovered, and steps lead down from the Victorian galleries to the dramatically-lit archeological remains. The foundations of the amphitheatre's eastern entrance are all you get to see, but they give you a hint of the vast size of the original arena, which would have held up to six thousand spectators. (The outline of the amphitheatre is also marked out on the pavement in the courtyard outside the art gallery.)

Clockmakers' Museum

Round the corner on Aldermanbury hides the **Clockmakers' Museum** (Mon–Fri 9.30am–4.30pm; free; ☎020/7332 1868, ⊛www.clockmakers.org), a collection of timepieces displayed by the Worshipful Company of Clockmakers. You'll find just about every type of device from Tudor pocket watches to grandfather clocks, which ring out in unison on the hour. Some of the more unusual exhibits include an orrery clock, a rolling ball clock (of the kind invented by William Congreve), a water clock and the ghoulish skull watch, once believed to have been given by Mary Queen of Scots to her maid-of-honour. Of particular interest is the collection of marine chronometers belonging to **John Harrison** (1693–1776), including the earliest known clock made by Harrison with his brother when he was only 20, his personal pair-case watch, made under his instructions by one of the guild's apprentices, John Jefferys, and the prototype for the H4 clock that won him half the Longitude Prize money (see p.386). Pride of place, though, goes to H5, which was tested by George III himself at Richmond observatory, and which won Harrison a sum of money almost equivalent to the full prize money. Next door to the clock museum is the Guildhall **library**, which has a small display of antique playing cards, temporary exhibitions of London maps and prints, and the excellent Guildhall **bookshop**.

St Lawrence Jewry

Directly south of Guildhall, across the courtyard, stands Wren's church of **St Lawrence Jewry** (Mon–Fri 7.30am–2pm; recitals 1pm, piano Mon, organ Tues), the splendour of its interior perfectly suited to its role as the official church of the Corporation of London. Opened in 1677 in the presence of Charles II, but gutted during the Blitz, its handsome, wide, open-plan interior has been lovingly restored and is well worth a peek – the richly gilded plasterwork on the ceiling is particularly fine. As the name indicates, this was once the site of London's **Jewish ghetto**. Old Jewry, the street two blocks east, was the nucleus of the quarter, containing a synagogue that was confiscated by the City authorities in 1272, shortly before the bloody expulsion of the entire community by Edward I.

Cheapside and Bow Lane

It's difficult to believe that **Cheapside**, a couple of blocks south of the Guildhall, was once the City's foremost medieval marketplace. Only the names of the nearby streets – Bread Street, Milk Street, Honey Lane, Poultry – recall its former prominence, which faded when the shops and their customers began to move to the West End from the eighteenth century onwards.

Nowadays, the only distinguishing feature on this otherwise bleak parade of postwar office blocks is Wren's church of **St Mary-le-Bow** (Mon–Thurs 6.30am–6pm, Fri 6.30am–4pm; ⊛www.stmarylebow.co.uk), whose handsome tower features each of the five classical orders, a granite obelisk and a dragon weather vane. The tower also contains postwar replicas of the famous "Bow Bells", which sounded the 9pm curfew for Londoners from the fourteenth to the nineteenth centuries, and within earshot of which all true Cockneys are born. The church's interior was totally destroyed in the Blitz and, though rebuilt in the 1950s, contains little of interest. In the church crypt, however, is *The Place Below*, a popular vegetarian café (see p.458).

Down the side of St Mary-le-Bow runs **Bow Lane**, narrow, pedestrianized and jam-packed at weekday lunchtimes with office workers heading for the sandwich bars, but also featuring a butcher's and barber's, not to mention several good pubs. At its southern end, just before you hit Queen Victoria Street, is the church of **St Mary Aldermary** (Mon, Wed & Thurs 11am–3pm; ⊛www .stmaryaldermary.co.uk), whose pinnacled spire suggests a pre-Fire edifice, though it is, in fact, a rare foray into the perpendicular style by Wren, based on the original church – the plaster fan-vaults and saucer domes in the aisles are the highlight.

Just to the east, on the other side of Queen Victoria Street, are the remains of a **Temple of Mithras**, which once stood on the riverbank, discovered in 1954 during the laying of the foundations for the nearby office block. Mithraism was a male-only cult popular among the Roman legions before the advent of Christianity. Its Persian deity, Mithras, is always depicted slaying a cosmic bull, while a scorpion grasps its genitals and a dog licks its wounds – the bull's blood was seen as life-giving, and initiates to the cult had to bathe in it in subterranean tombs. The foundations of the third-century temple, which have been reassembled in the shadow of the office block, give very little impression of what the building would have been like – the rich finds and more substantial reconstruction in the Museum of London (see p.199) offer a slightly better idea.

Bank

Bank is the finest architectural arena in the City. Heart of the finance sector and the busy meeting point of eight streets, it's overlooked by a handsome collection of Neoclassical buildings – among them the Bank of England, the Royal Exchange and Mansion House – each one faced in Portland stone.

By far the most graceful of the trio is the **Royal Exchange**, twice destroyed by fire since it was first built in 1570 at the personal expense of the "King's Merchant", Thomas Gresham (the gilded grasshopper on the roof is his emblem), as a meeting place for City merchants from home and abroad to conduct their business. The current building, fronted by a massive eight-column portico and a very convenient set of steps for lunching office workers, was built in the 1840s by William Tite. Nowadays, it's little more than a glorified designer shopping mall, but it's worth venturing into the inner courtyard, with its beautifully tiled floor, glazed roof and half-columns in three classical orders.

Mansion House, the Lord Mayor's sumptuous Neoclassical lodgings during his or – on only one occasion so far – her term of office, is sadly only open to group tours. However, you might be able to join up with a group if there's space; to do so, though, you'll need to phone several months in advance (☎020/7626

▲ Futures Trader statue, Cannon Street

2500), and then apply in writing. Highlights of the building, which was designed in 1753 by George Dance, include the opulent "Egyptian" Hall, the Lord Mayor's insignia and the vast collection of gold and silver plate.

One magnificent building at Bank that's easy to gain access to is the former Midland Bank headquarters, now a branch of **HSBC** (Mon–Fri 8.30am–5pm), which has its main entrance on Poultry. Built between the wars by Edwin Lutyens, the public banking halls on the ground floor feature magnificent green African verdite square columns, walnut counters, flying-saucer hanging lights and really comfy sofas.

The one blot on Bank's otherwise homogenous surroundings is **No. 1 Poultry**, horizontally striped in sand and salmon colours, and topped by a Swatch-like clock tower, a prime example of 1990s postmodernism by James Stirling. Equally ugly in a very 1970s way is the modern **Stock Exchange** (ⓦwww.londonstockexchange.com), a short way up Threadneedle Street from Bank. Its public gallery has been closed to the public since it was bombed by the IRA in 1990, though in any case the human scrum of share dealing has now been largely replaced by computerized dealing; "open cry", as it's known, is now confined to the London Metal Exchange, 56 Leadenhall St.

London's loos

Down gleaming walls of porc'lain flows the sluice

That out of sight decants the kidney juice

Thus pleasuring those gents for miles around

Who, crying for relief, once piped the sound

Of wind in alleyways . . .

This celebratory ode was composed by Josiah Feable for the opening, in 1855, of the first public flush lavatories, which were situated outside the Royal Exchange. There was a charge of one penny (hence the euphemism) and the toilets were gents-only – ladies had to hold theirs in until 1911, when new lavatories were built.

Bank of England

Established by William III in 1694 to raise funds for his costly war against France, the **Bank of England**, the so-called "Grand Old Lady of Threadneedle Street", wasn't erected on its present site until 1734. During the Gordon Riots of 1780, the bank was attacked by rioters, but successfully defended with the help of some of the bank's clerks who made bullets by melting down their inkwells. Subsequently a detachment of the Foot Guards, known as the Bank Picquet, was stationed outside every night until 1973. Security remains pretty tight at the bank, which, after all, still acts as a giant safe-deposit box, storing the official gold reserves of seventy or so central banks around the world, but not, ironically, of Britain itself. British gold reserves are kept in the Federal Reserve Bank of New York, where they were moved during World War II.

The windowless, outer curtain wall, which wraps itself round the 3.5-acre island site, is pretty much all that remains of the building design on which John Soane (see p.177) spent the best part of his career from 1788 onwards. However, you can view a reconstruction of Soane's Bank Stock Office, with its characteristic domed skylight, in the **museum** (Mon–Fri 10am–5pm; free; ☎020/7601 5545, ◍www.bankofengland.co.uk), which has its entrance on Bartholomew Lane. The permanent exhibition traces the history of the bank, and includes a model of Soane's bank, a Victorian-style diorama of the 1780 siege and, beyond, a reconstruction of Herbert Baker's interwar rotunda (wrecked in the Blitz). Sadly most of the gold bars are fakes, but there are specimens of every note issued by the Royal Mint over the centuries.

St Margaret Lothbury

A couple of blocks east of Guildhall, Gresham Street leads into Lothbury, which runs along the back of the Bank of England. Tucked into the north side of the street is the tiny Wren church of **St Margaret Lothbury** (Mon–Fri 7am–6pm; ◍www.stml.org.uk), whose plain interior harbours some of the finest furnishings of any City church. The most eye-catching is the magnificent screen, designed by Wren (for a different church, as it happens) and consisting of delicate, intertwined spiral columns either side of the main entrance, which features a segmental pediment and a huge eagle. Also worth a closer look is the wonderful hexagonal pulpit and tester, laden with carved putti, birds, fruit and flowers.

Walbrook

Along the west wall of Mansion House runs Walbrook, named after the shallow stream which used to provide Roman London with its fresh water. On the eastern side of Walbrook, behind Mansion House, stands the church of **St Stephen Walbrook** (Mon–Thurs 10am–4pm, Fri 10am–3pm), the Lord Mayor's official church and Wren's most spectacular after St Paul's. Faced with a fairly cramped site, Wren created a church of great space and light, with sixteen Corinthian columns arranged in clusters around a central coffered dome, which many regard as a practice run for the cathedral. The furnishings are mostly original, having been wisely stashed away during the Blitz, but the modern beechwood pews jar, as does Henry Moore's altar, an amorphous blob of Travertine stone – nicknamed "The Camembert" – placed centrally right under the dome. The Samaritans were founded here in 1953, and their first helpline telephone now rests on a plinth in the southwest corner as a memorial.

St Mary Woolnoth to the London Stone

Hidden from the bustle of Bank itself, a short distance down King William Street, stands **St Mary Woolnoth** (Mon–Fri 7.45am–5pm), one of Nicholas Hawksmoor's six idiosyncratic London churches. The main facade is very imposing, with its twin turrets, Doric pillars and heavy rustication, and, as the only City church to come through the war unscathed, the interior is also well worth inspecting. In a cramped but lofty space, Hawksmoor managed to cram in a cluster of three big Corinthian columns at each corner, which support an ingenious lantern lit by semicircular clerestory windows. The most striking furnishing is the altar canopy, held up by barley-sugar columns and studded with seven golden cherubic faces. The church's projecting clock gets a brief mention in T.S. Eliot's *The Waste Land*.

To the north of St Mary Woolnoth, and running east, is **Lombard Street**, focus of London's financial community before the Royal Exchange was built, and named after the region of northern Italy in which most of the bankers and merchants originated. The street contains the head office of Lloyds Bank and also the sign of the golden grasshopper, emblem of Thomas Gresham, who used to live on the site of one of the City's oldest banks, Martin's, founded in 1563. Lombard Street also boasts several old trade signs re-hung for the coronation of Edward VII in 1902. Framed in iron and often as thick as paving stones, these were previously a feature of every commercial street in London, but were banned in 1762 after one fell down and killed four passers-by.

A complete contrast to Hawskmoor's church is provided by Wren's **St Mary Abchurch** (Mon–Thurs 10am–2pm), set in its own courtyard (the paved-over former graveyard) on Abchurch Lane, south off King William Street. Nothing about the dour red-brick exterior prepares you for the interior, which is dominated by a vast dome fresco painted by a local parishioner and lit by oval lunettes, with the name of God in Hebrew centre stage. The lime-wood reredos, festooned with swags and garlands, and decorated with gilded urns and a pelican, is one of the few authenticated works by Grinling Gibbons in the City.

A brief diversion west, via Cannon Street, will take you to one of London's most esoteric sights, the **London Stone**, a small block of limestone lodged behind an iron grille within the exterior wall of the Overseas Chinese Banking Corporation, 111 Cannon St, at the corner of St Swithin's Lane. To some it is London's omphalos, its geomantic centre; to the uninitiated, it looks more like a lump of Roman masonry. Whatever your reaction to this bizarre relic, it has been around for some considerable time, certainly since the 1450 Peasants' Revolt, when the Kentish rebel Jack Cade struck it, declaring himself "Lord of the City". Nearby, on the corner of Walbrook and Cannon Street, is a more recent arrival, a statue of a futures trader on his mobile phone.

Bishopsgate to the Tower

Financial institutions predominate in the easterly section of the Square Mile between Bishopsgate and the Tower, many of them housed in the brashest of the City's new architecture. In fact, the area's two most obvious landmarks are both temples of Mammon: the controversial **Lloyd's Building** and the unmissable **Gherkin**. These, plus the Victorian splendour of **Leadenhall Market**, the oldest **synagogue** in the country, the largest concentration of pre-Fire churches, Wren's famous **Monument** to the Great Fire, and **London Bridge**, make for an especially interesting sector of the City to explore.

Broadgate

The traffic-free piazzas of the **Broadgate** complex, to the west of Bishopsgate, have proved very popular with City workers. The architecture is in the bland US corporate style, but on the plus side Broadgate is adorned with a substantial crop of outdoor sculptures, and is close to the City's busiest train terminal, **Liverpool Street**, with its vibrantly painted wrought-iron Victorian arches. The first sculpture you come face to face with is *Fulcrum*, Richard Serra's rusting steel sheets. To the north lies **Broadgate Circle**, with its circular arena, used as an open-air ice rink in winter and as a performance space in summer. To the west, the gloomy Finsbury Avenue features the dismal sculptural commuters of *Rush Hour*. Continuing north to **Exchange Square**, built above the rail tracks to the north of the station, you'll find a cascading waterfall, the hefty *Broadgate Venus* by Fernando Botero and Xavier Corbero's *Broad Family* of obelisks, one of whose "children" reveals a shoe. The last word, though, goes to the headquarters of the European Bank for Economic Development, on the east side of the square. Set up to provide assistance to the old Eastern Bloc countries, it squandered much of its budget on Italian marble and other luxury fittings for the building.

Bishopsgate

The office blocks on the northern section of **Bishopsgate** look all the more undistinguished when compared with the imaginative faïence facade of the diminutive former **Bishopsgate Institute** across the road from Liverpool Street, a sort of proto-Art Nouveau building designed in 1894 by Harrison Townsend. The institute used to house an excellent reference library specializing in works on the nearby East End, but has recently closed down. Townsend also designed the excellent Whitechapel Art Gallery (see p.240) and the wonderful Horniman Museum (see p.377).

Back on the south side of the train station, the church of **St Botolph-without-Bishopsgate** (Mon–Fri 8am–5.30pm), where John Keats was christened, used to stand just outside the City gates, and is named after the Anglo-Saxon abbot who cared for travellers. It's been restored seven times since the current building was erected in 1728, including when it was damaged by an IRA bomb in the early 1990s, and the church's coved ceiling, with its undersized dome and lantern, added in 1828, currently looks as good as new. The churchyard, with its fountain and tennis court, is a favourite picnic spot for City workers and contains an old charity school building, decorated with a uniformed boy and girl, and a small ceramic and terracotta Turkish bathhouse, now converted into an Italian restaurant.

Further south down Bishopsgate is the City's tallest building (and Britain's tallest building until the completion of Canary Wharf in 1991), the former **NatWest Tower**, designed by Richard Seifert in the shape of the bank's logo, completed in 1971 and over 600ft high. One of the few positive outcomes of the IRA bombing campaign of the early 1990s was the damage inflicted on this colossus, regarded by many as the nadir of postwar City development. Unfortunately, the tower was repaired and renamed **Tower 42** (ⓦwww.tower42 .co.uk) after the number of floors. To appreciate the views you need to head up to the champagne and oyster bar called *Vertigo 42* (ⓣ020/7877 7842, ⓦwww .vertigo42.co.uk) on the top floor; dress smartly and book ahead.

In total contrast to the bombast of the NatWest Tower is the "humble rag-faced front" of the pre-Fire church of **St Ethelburga**, hemmed in by office blocks on the opposite side of Bishopsgate. All but totally destroyed by IRA bombs in the early 1990s, the church has risen from the ashes and now functions as a centre for reconciliation and peace; it's not normally open to the public, but does have open days, usually the first Friday of the month (ⓣ020/7496 1610, ⓦwww.stethelburgas.org).

Another pre-Fire church that suffered extensive damage in the IRA blasts is the late-Gothic church of **St Helen** (Mon–Fri 9am–5pm; ⓦwww.st-helens .org.uk), set back to the east of Bishopsgate. With its undulating crenellations and Baroque bell turret, it's an intriguing building, which incorporates the original Benedictine nunnery church and contains five grand pre-Fire tombs. Its interior has been totally reorganized, the architect Quinlan Terry having raised the floor level, shifted the church screens, added a new organ gallery and rearranged the seating to focus on the pulpit, in keeping with the church's current evangelical bent. It is now by far the best-attended church in the City, with hundreds showing up for the regular Tuesday lunchtime and Sunday services, which feature a rock band on Sunday nights.

The Gherkin and Lloyd's

To the south of St Helen is the giant, bland Commercial Union skyscraper, now thoroughly upstaged by Norman Foster's glass diamond-clad **Gherkin**, officially known as 30 St Mary Axe (ⓦwww.30stmaryaxe.com) and currently headquarters of the reinsurers Swiss Re. Completed in 2003, it occupies the site of the old Baltic Exchange, destroyed by the 1990s IRA bombing campaign. It's obscenely large – at 590ft it's only just surpassed by the NatWest Tower – but most Londoners seem to quite like it for its cheeky shape.

To the south, on St Mary Axe, and dwarfed by the Gherkin, is the medieval church of **St Andrew Undershaft**, which takes its name from the old Cornhill maypole which used to stand outside until it was torn down as an object of pagan idolatry by the curate from neighbouring St Katharine Cree in 1549 (and who died in poverty in 1605). Though less remarkable than St Helen's, it does contain the tomb erected by the widow of John Stow, a humble tailor who wrote the first detailed account of the City in 1598. A memorial service is held here annually in April, during which the Lord Mayor replaces the quill pen in the tailor's hand; at other times, you must ring ahead to arrange a visit (☎020/7283 2231).

To the south of St Andrew Undershaft, on Leadenhall Street, stands the **Lloyd's Building** (ⓦwww.lloyds.com), completed by Richard Rogers in 1984. "A living, breathing machine" of a building, it's a vertical version of Rogers' own Pompidou Centre, a jumble of blue-steel pipes with glass lifts zipping up and down the exterior. It came as something of a surprise that one of the most conservative of all the City's institutions should have decided to build such an avant-garde edifice – the main portico of the

▲ The Gherkin and Lloyd's Building

company's previous, much more sedate building, dating from 1925, can still be seen to the west of Rogers' building. Some things never change, though, and the building is still guarded by porters in antiquated waiters' livery, in recognition of the company's modest origins in a coffee house.

Lloyd's started out in shipping (where it still has major interests) and is now the largest insurance market in the world. The company's famous Lutine Bell in the main office, brought here from a captured French frigate in 1799, is still struck – once for bad news, twice for good. Members of Lloyd's syndicates (known as "Names") pledge their personal fortunes in return for handsome and consistent premiums – that is, they did until the 1990s, when Lloyd's suffered record losses of over £1 billion. One result of the company's financial crisis was the sale of the building to a German financial institution, to which it now pays rent.

Leadenhall Market and Cornhill

Just south of the Lloyd's Building you'll find the picturesque **Leadenhall Market**, whose trading traditions reach back to its days as the centre of the Roman forum. Designed by Horace Jones in 1881, the graceful Victorian cast-ironwork is richly painted in cream and maroon, and each of the four entrances to the covered arcade is topped by an elaborate stone arch. Inside, the traders cater mostly for the lunchtime City crowd, their barrows laden with exotic seafood and game, fine wines, champagne and caviar. The shops and bars remain open until the evening, but to catch the atmosphere, it's best to get here at breakfast or lunchtime.

Across Gracechurch Street from the market, and a short distance down Cornhill stands **St Michael's** (Mon–Fri 8.30am–5pm; ⓦwww.st-michaels.org .uk) – the second, and the more interesting, of the two churches on the street.

Wren-designed, apart from the tower, but drastically "restored" by George Gilbert Scott in the mid-nineteenth century, it's worth venturing inside simply to listen to the terrifyingly loud organ, which is put through its paces during the free Monday lunchtime recitals. Before you leave, make sure you have a look at the remarkable eighteenth-century wooden sculpture of a pelican – a symbol of piety – feeding its young, situated at the west end of the church. While on Cornhill, it's also worth peeking inside the **Union Discount Company of London**'s headquarters, at no. 39, which has a superbly ornate coffered majolica ceiling.

Bevis Marks Synagogue

Hidden away behind a red-brick office block in a little courtyard off Bevis Marks, at the north end of St Mary Axe, is the **Bevis Marks Synagogue** (guided tours Wed & Fri noon, Sun 11.15am; £2; ☎020/7626 1274, ⓦwww .sandp.org). Built in 1701 by Sephardic Jews who had fled the Inquisition in Spain and Portugal, this is the country's oldest surviving synagogue, and its roomy, rich interior gives an idea of just how wealthy the community was at the time. Although it seats over six hundred, it is only a third of the size of its prototype in Amsterdam, where many Sephardic Jews initially settled. Past congregants have included some of the most successful Anglo-Jews, including the Disraeli family and Moses Montefiore, who still has a special seat reserved for him in the front pew. The Sephardic community has since moved out to Maida Vale and Wembley, and the congregation has dwindled, though the magnificent array of chandeliers makes it very popular for candle-lit Jewish weddings.

St Katharine Cree and St Botolph's

Close by Bevis Marks, just past Creechurch Lane, stood the even larger **Great Synagogue** of the Ashkenazi Jews, founded in 1690 but bombed out of existence in 1941, and recalled now only by a plaque. At the southern end of Creechurch Lane is the church of **St Katharine Cree** (Mon–Fri 10.30am–4pm), where Hans Holbein is supposed to have been buried after dying of the plague in 1543. Holbein's grave is now lost, but the church, which was rebuilt in 1630, survived the Great Fire, and remains a rare example of its period. It's a transitional building with classical elements, such as the Corinthian columns of the nave and, above, a Gothic clerestory and ribbing. At the east end is a rare, and very lovely, seventeenth-century stained-glass Catherine-wheel window.

To the east along Aldgate, on the site of the old City gates, is **St Botolph-without-Aldgate** (Mon–Fri 10.30am–3pm; ⓦwww.stbotolphs.org.uk), another unusual church, this time designed in 1741 by George Dance. Its bizarre interior, remodelled last century, features blue-grey paintwork, gilding on top of white plasterwork, some dodgy modern art, a batik reredos and a stunning, modern stained-glass rendition of Rubens' *Descent from the Cross* on a deep-purple background. Situated at the very edge of the East End, this is a famously campaigning church, active on issues like gay priests, the headquarters of the society for promoting Jewish–Christian understanding, and with a crypt used as a day centre for homeless men.

London Bridge and the Monument

Until 1750, **London Bridge** was the only bridge across the Thames. The Romans were the first to build a permanent crossing here, a structure succeeded by a Saxon version that was pulled down by King Olaf of Norway in 1014, an event that gave rise to the popular nursery rhyme *London Bridge is Falling*

Down. It was the medieval bridge, however, that achieved world fame: built of stone and crowded with timber-framed houses, it became one of the great attractions of London. At the centre stood the richly ornate Nonsuch House, decorated with onion domes and Dutch gables, and a small chapel dedicated to Thomas Becket; at the Southwark end was the Great Gatehouse, on which the heads of traitors were displayed, dipped in tar to preserve them. The houses were finally removed in the mid-eighteenth century, and a new stone bridge erected in 1831; that one now stands in the middle of the Arizona desert, having been bought for $2.4 million in the late 1960s by a gentleman who, so the story goes, was under the impression he had purchased Tower Bridge. The present concrete structure, without doubt the ugliest yet, dates from 1972 and is slightly upstream from the site of the previous medieval bridge.

▲ Monument

The only reason to go anywhere near London Bridge is to see the **Monument** (daily 9am–5.30pm; £2; ☎020/7626 2717), which was designed by Wren to commemorate the Great Fire of 1666 (see box, p.584). Crowned with spiky gilded flames, this plain Doric column stands 202ft high, making it the tallest isolated stone column in the world; if it were laid out flat it would touch the site of the bakery where the fire started, east of Monument. The bas-relief on the base, now in very bad shape, depicts Charles II and the Duke of York in Roman garb conducting the emergency relief operation. The 311 steps to the gallery at the top – a favourite place for suicides until a cage was built around it in 1842 – once guaranteed an incredible view; nowadays it is dwarfed by the surrounding buildings.

East to the Tower

Signs from the Monument will point you in the right direction for another Wren edifice, the church of **St Magnus-the-Martyr** (Tues–Fri 10am–4pm, Sun 10am–1pm), whose octagonal spire used to greet travellers arriving across old London Bridge. Now it stands forlorn and battered by the heavy traffic hurtling down Lower Thames Street, though the Anglo-Catholic interior holds, in T.S. Eliot's words, "an inexplicable splendour of Ionian white and gold". In addition, there's a wooden pier from an old Roman wharf in the porch, and a great model of the old London Bridge in the vestry.

Beyond the titanium-blue glass cubes of the nearby Hong Kong and Shanghai Bank, by the river, is old **Billingsgate Market**, London's chief wholesale fish market from Roman times until 1982, when it was moved out to Docklands. It's hard now to imagine the noise and smell of old Billingsgate, whose porters used to carry the fish in towers of baskets on their heads, and whose wives were renowned for their bad language even in Shakespeare's day: "as bad a tongue . . . as any oyster-wife at Billingsgate" (*King Lear*). Next door to Billingsgate stands the **Custom House** (@www.hmce.gov.uk), which has been collecting duties from incoming ships since around 1275. The present undistinguished Neoclassical structure with an Ionic portico dates from 1825.

As an alternative to the riverside walk, which leads you to the Tower, you could cut north from Lower Thames Street up **Lovat Lane**, one of the City's most atmospheric cobbled streets, once renowned for its brothels and known as Love Lane until 1939. Halfway up Lovat Lane, you come to **St Mary-at-Hill** (Mon–Fri 10am–3pm), the old fishermen's church, rebuilt by Wren after the Great Fire – the entrance is to the east, down a passageway in the parallel street of the same name. Having escaped the Blitz unscathed, the church was almost entirely destroyed by fire in 1988, but has since made a phoenix-like recovery. The white-stuccoed dome, held up by four fluted composite columns, has been restored, and the church's remarkable box pews, pulpit and reredos survived, though they have yet to return.

Continuing north up St Mary-at-Hill brings you out onto **Eastcheap**, site of a medieval meat market, along which several admirable Victorian Gothic facades have survived (no. 33 is particularly fancy). If you're looking for a secluded spot, however, you could do worse than the garden in the nave of the ruined church of **St Dunstan-in-the-East**, off St Dunstan's Hill, to the east of St Mary's, which retains its distinctive Wren-designed crown steeple. For a different scale of architecture, cross over Great Tower Street and head down Mincing Lane. Occupying a vast site between here and Mark Lane is **Minster Court**, the London Underwriting Centre, nicknamed "Munster Court" for its Hammer-horror Gothicisms. A stroll under the vast glass atrium guarded by three giant horses will bring you to Dunster Court, and then to **Fenchurch Street station**, a modest little Victorian terminus from the 1850s with a traditional scalloped canopy and a distinctive bow-shaped segmental pediment.

To the south of the station, down New London Street, is the ragstone Gothic church of **St Olave** (Mon–Fri 10am–5pm), or "St Ghastly Grim", as Dickens called it in his *Uncommercial Traveller*, for the skulls and crossbones and vicious-looking spikes adorning the entrance to the graveyard on Seething Lane. Only the outside walls made it through the Blitz, though there are some interesting pre-Fire brasses and monuments. Samuel Pepys lived in Seething Lane for much of his life, and had his own seat in the church's Navy Office pew in the now-demolished galleries; he and his wife, Elizabeth, are both buried here – Elizabeth's monument was raised by Pepys himself; Pepys' own is Victorian.

At the bottom of Seething Lane, on the other side of the noisy highway of Lower Thames Street, stands another pre-Fire church, **All Hallows-by-the-Tower** (Mon–Fri 9am–5.45pm, Sat & Sun 10am–5pm; audioguide £2.50; ℡020/7481 2928, @www.allhallowsbythetower.org.uk). It too was reduced to a burnt-out shell by the Blitz, with only the red-brick tower (from which Pepys watched the Great Fire) remaining intact. The rest of the church is a personal reinterpretation of the Gothic style by the postwar architect Lord Mottistone, and much of it is pretty awful, in particular the concrete nave. Still, the church is full of fascinating furnishings, including lots of maritime memorials, model ships, two wings of a Flemish triptych from around 1500, and, best of all, the exquisitely carved Gibbons lime-wood font cover, sealed in a private chapel in the southwest corner. Close by is an arch from the original church on this site, founded in 675 AD; even older remains of a tessellated Roman pavement can be found in the claustrophobic little crypt. All Hallows also has some superb pre-Reformation brasses, and offers brassrubbing.

12

The Tower of London and around

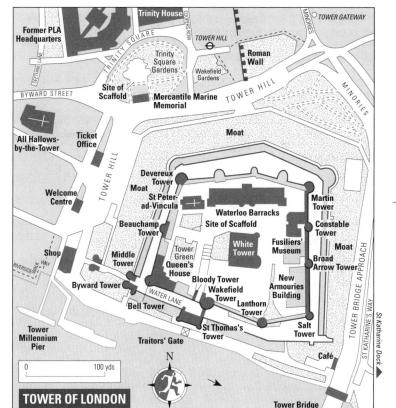

Former PLA Headquarters

Trinity House

TOWER GATEWAY

TRINITY SQUARE

Trinity Square Gardens

TOWER HILL

Roman Wall

Wakefield Gardens

Site of Scaffold

Mercantile Marine Memorial

TOWER HILL

MINORIES

MINORIES

BYWARD STREET

SEETHING LANE

COOPERS ROW

Moat

All Hallows-by-the-Tower

Ticket Office

TOWER HILL

Devereux Tower

Moat

St Peter-ad-Vincula

Welcome Centre

Beauchamp Tower

Waterloo Barracks

Site of Scaffold

Martin Tower

Constable Tower

Fusiliers' Museum

White Tower

Moat

Shop

RIVERSIDE WALK

Middle Tower

Tower Green

Queen's House

Broad Arrow Tower

Byward Tower

WATER LANE

Bloody Tower

Wakefield Tower

Lanthorn Tower

New Armouries Building

Bell Tower

St Thomas's Tower

Salt Tower

TOWER BRIDGE APPROACH

ST KATHARINE'S WAY

St Katharine Dock

Tower Millennium Pier

Traitors' Gate

Café

0   100 yds

N

TOWER OF LONDON

Tower Bridge

© crown copyright

213

The area around Tower Hill is choked with tourists who flock here to see one of London's most famous landmarks, Tower Bridge and the adjacent Tower of London, a superbly fortified castle begun shortly after the Norman Conquest. Despite all the attendant hype and heritage claptrap, the Tower remains one of London's most remarkable buildings, site of some of the goriest events in the nation's history, and somewhere all visitors and Londoners should explore at least once. Sitting beside the river, at the eastern edge of the old city walls, the Tower is chiefly famous as a place of imprisonment and death, yet it has also variously been used as a royal residence, armoury, mint, menagerie, observatory and – a function it still serves – a safe-deposit box for the Crown Jewels. And amidst the crush of tourists and the weight of history surrounding the place, it's easy to forget that the Tower is, above all, the most perfectly preserved medieval fortress in the country.

A brief history

Begun as a simple watchtower, built by **William the Conqueror** to keep an eye on the City, the Tower had evolved into a palace-fortress by 1100. The inner curtain wall, with its numerous towers, was built in the time of Henry III, and a further line of outer fortifications, plus an even wider moat, were added by Edward I, which means that most of what's visible today was already in place by 1307, the year of Edward's death.

The Tower has held some very **famous prisoners**, several of whom were beheaded on Tower Green (see p.218); others like the future Elizabeth I, and Walter Ralegh, were lucky enough to leave alive. The Tower's **first prisoner**, the Bishop of Durham, arrived in 1101, having been found guilty of extortion, and promptly escaped from the window of his cell by a rope, having got the guards drunk. Gruffydd ap Llywelyn, son and rightful heir to the Welsh throne, attempted a similar feat in 1244, with less success: "his head and neck were crushed between his shoulders . . . a most horrid spectacle". Incidentally, the **most famous escapee** from the Tower was the Earl of Nithsdale, imprisoned for his part in the 1715 Jacobite rebellion, who, despite his red beard, managed to get past the guards dressed as a woman, and lived on in exile in Rome for another thirty years.

Following the restoration of the monarchy in 1660, guns were placed along the walls and a permanent garrison stationed in the Tower, which continued to be used as a state prison and an arsenal, as well as housing the Royal Mint, the Record Office and the Royal Menagerie. At the same time, the general public were admitted for the first time to view the coronation regalia and the impressive displays of arms and armour. However, in the 1840s, under the Duke of Wellington, who was convinced revolution was around the corner, the Tower returned to a more military role and the public were excluded.

During the course of the nineteenth century, many of the Tower institutions began to move out, eventually leaving just the Crown Jewels. A programme of "re-medievalization" was begun (though never completed) and a ticket office was set up at the western entrance. By the end of Victoria's reign, the Tower was welcoming half a million visitors annually. Nevertheless, during both world wars, the Tower was still used to hold prisoners. Roger Casement, the Irish nationalist, was held here briefly before his trial and hanging in 1916, and **German spies** would be executed by firing squad; the last execution took place in the Tower on August 14, 1941, when Josef Jakobs, a German spy who had broken his ankle on parachuting into a field in Huntingdonshire, was given the privilege of being seated before the firing squad.

The Tower's **opening times** are March–Oct Mon & Sun 10am–6pm, Tues–Sat 9am–6pm; Nov–Feb closes 5pm; £14.50; ☎0870/756 7070, ⊛www.hrp.org.uk. To save yourself a bit of money, and a bit of queuing, buy your ticket in advance online or by phone. Although you can explore the Tower complex independently, or hire an audioguide (£3), it's a good idea to get your bearings by joining up with one of the free, theatrically irreverent, hour-long **guided tours**, given every thirty minutes by one of the forty-odd, eminently photogenic **Beefeaters** – it's also the only way to get to visit St Peter-ad-Vincula. These self-assured ex-servicemen are best known for their scarlet-and-gold Tudor costumes, but unless it's a special occasion you're more likely to see them in dark-blue "undress". Formed by Henry VIII as a personal bodyguard, they're officially known as Yeoman Warders – the nickname "Beefeaters" was coined in the seventeenth century, when it was a common term of abuse for a well-fed domestic servant. Talking of food, there's a spacious and fairly decent **café** in the New Armouries building, and plenty of benches on which to picnic. Alternatively, you can obtain a re-entry pass and have lunch outside the Tower.

Bell Tower and Traitors' Gate

Visitors today enter the Tower by the twin-towered western gatehouses to the southwest of the building known as the Middle Tower and the Byward Tower, though originally they first had to pass through the Lion Tower (now demolished), where the Royal Menagerie was based until 1834 (see box, p.217). Two of the first victims of the Reformation – Thomas More and John Fisher – were incarcerated nearby in the **Bell Tower**, from whose dinky wooden belfry a bell would toll to signal an execution. More was initially allowed writing materials, but later they were withdrawn; Fisher was kept in even worse conditions ("I decay forthwith, and fall into coughs and diseases of my body, and cannot keep myself in health") and was so weak by the end that he had to be carried to the scaffold on Tower Hill. The 20-year-old future Queen Elizabeth I arrived here via Traitors' Gate in 1554, while her half-sister Queen Mary tried to find incriminating evidence against her. Roman Catholic Mass was performed daily in Elizabeth's cell for the two months of her imprisonment, but she refused to be converted.

In times gone by, most prisoners were delivered through **Traitors' Gate**, on the waterfront, having been ferried down the Thames from the courts at Westminster Hall. The gate forms part of **St Thomas's Tower**, which, along with the Wakefield Tower beyond, has been reconstructed to re-create the atmosphere of Edward I's **Medieval Palace**, with period-clad actors on hand to answer questions. The Aula, where the king ate and relaxed, has a beautiful little oratory in one of the turrets, while the Throne Room, in the Wakefield Tower, contains a gilded and colourful replica of the Coronation Chair (the battered original is in Westminster Abbey), and a huge crown-shaped candelabra depicting the twelve gates of the New Jerusalem. It

▲ Traitors' Gate

was in the Throne Room's oratory that the "saintly but slightly daft" Henry VI was murdered at prayer on the orders of Edward IV in 1471. Not long afterwards, Edward had his brother, the Duke of Clarence, executed for high treason, drowned in a butt of malmsey wine (at his own request).

Bloody Tower

The main entrance to the Inner Ward is beneath a 3.5-ton, 700-year-old portcullis, which forms part of the **Bloody Tower**, so called because it was here that the 12-year-old Edward V and his 10-year-old brother, Richard, were accommodated "for their own safety" in 1483 by their uncle, Richard of Gloucester (later to be Richard III), following the death of their father, Edward IV. Of all the Tower's many inhabitants, few have so captured the public imagination as the **Princes in the Tower**, due in part to Thomas More's detailed account of their murder. According to More, they were smothered in their beds, and buried naked at the foot of the White Tower. In 1674, during repair work, the skeletons of two young children were discovered one on top of the other close to the Tower; they were subsequently buried in Innocents' Corner in Westminster Abbey. Some have contended that Richard III has been the victim of Tudor propaganda, and that several other people in high places were equally keen to dispose of the little dears; the jury is still out on this one.

The Bloody Tower's other illustrious inmate – even more famous in his time than the princes – was **Walter Ralegh**, who spent three separate periods here. His first stay was in 1592, when he incurred the displeasure of Elizabeth I for impregnating one of her ladies-in-waiting; his second and longest spell began in 1603, when his death sentence for suspected involvement in the plot against James I was suspended. In the event, he spent nearly thirteen years here growing and smoking tobacco (his most famous import), writing poetry, concocting various dubious potions in his distillery and completing the first volume of his *History of the World*, which in its day outsold even Shakespeare, despite being banned by James I for being "too saucy in censuring princes". When Ralegh complained that the noise of the portcullis kept him awake at night, he was moved to much worse accommodation. Eventually released in 1616 and sent off to Guyana to discover gold, on condition that he didn't attack the Spanish, he broke his word and was sent straight back to the Tower on his return in 1618. For six weeks he was imprisoned in "one of the most cold and direful dungeons", before being beheaded at Westminster.

Ralegh's study is re-created on the ground floor, while his sleeping quarters upstairs, built especially to accommodate his wife, children and three servants, now house an exhibition on the Princes in the Tower and on the poisoning of the poet **Thomas Overbury**. Confined to the Bloody Tower in 1613 on a flimsy charge by James I, after falling out with one of the king's favourites, Robert Carr, Overbury was slowly poisoned to death with arsenic concealed within the tarts and jellies sent by Carr's wife. Arrested, tried and condemned to death, Carr and his wife were themselves incarcerated in the Tower for five years before being pardoned. The Lieutenant of the Tower was less fortunate, and was hanged for failing to protect his prisoners.

The White Tower

William the Conqueror's central hall-keep, known as the **White Tower**, is the original "Tower", begun in 1076 by the Bishop of Rochester. Whitewashed (hence its name) in the reign of Henry III, it was later returned to its Kentish ragstone exterior by Wren, who added the large windows. Of the tower's four turrets, topped by stylish Tudor cupolas, only three are square: the fourth is rounded in order to encase the main spiral staircase, and for a short while was used by Charles II's royal astronomer, Flamsteed, before he moved to Greenwich. The main entrance to the Tower is the original one, high up in the south wall, out of reach of the enemy, and accessed by a wooden staircase which could be removed during times of siege.

The three floors of arms and armour displayed within the tower represent a mere smidgen of the **Royal Armouries** (the majority of which is now in Leeds, in the north of England), which have been on almost permanent display since the time of Charles II. Even if you've no interest in military paraphernalia, you should at least pay a visit to the first-floor **Chapel of St John**, a beautiful Norman structure completed in 1080, making it the oldest intact ecclesiastical building in London. It was here that Henry VI's body was buried following his murder in 1471; that Henry VII's queen, Elizabeth of York, lay in state surrounded by eight hundred candles, after dying in childbirth; that Lady Jane Grey came to pray on the night before her execution; and that "Bloody Mary" was betrothed by proxy to King Philip of Spain. Today, the once highly decorated blocks of honey-coloured Caen limestone are free of all ecclesiastical excrescences, leaving the chapel's smooth curves and rounded apse perfectly unencumbered.

Among the most striking armour displayed on the first floor are the colossal **Holbein-designed garniture** of 1540 made for Henry VIII, the Japanese armour presented to King James I by the Shogun of Japan and Charles I's unusual gold-leaf suit. Temporary exhibitions are staged on the top floor, along with displays on the Tower's role as an arms store – by around 1600, it housed the largest magazine in the country, comprising nearly 10,000 barrels of gunpowder. Back down on the ground floor, there's yet more weaponry, including the Spanish Armoury, said to have been taken from the Armada, and displayed on and off for the last three hundred years. Other items on show include the **execution block** used for the last public beheading (see box on p.220), a

The Royal Menagerie and the ravens

The **Royal Menagerie** began in earnest in 1235 when the Holy Roman Emperor presented three leopards to Henry III; the leopard keeper was initially paid sixpence a day for the sustenance of the beasts, and one penny for himself. They were put on public display and joined some years later by a polar bear from the King of Norway and an elephant from the King of France. James I was particularly keen on the menagerie, and used to stage regular animal fights on the green, but the practice was stopped in 1609 when one of the bears killed a child. In 1704, six lions, two leopards, three eagles, two Swedish owls "of great bigness", two "cats of the mountains" and a jackal were recorded. Visitors were advised not to "play tricks" after an orang-utan threw a cannonball at one and killed him.

The menagerie was transferred to the newly founded London Zoo in the 1830s, leaving the Tower with just its **ravens**, descendants of early scavengers attracted by waste from the palace kitchens. They have been protected by royal decree since the reign of Charles II, and have their wings clipped so they can't fly away – legend says that the Tower (and therefore the kingdom) will fall if they do, though the Tower was in fact briefly raven-less during the last war after the Tower suffered heavy bombing. While the ravens may appear harmless, they are vicious, territorial creatures best given a wide berth. They live in coops in the south wall of the Inner Ward, have individual names and even have their own graveyard in the dry moat near the ticket barrier.

suit of armour for a man six feet nine inches tall (once thought to have been John of Gaunt) and one for a boy just three feet one and a half inches high (allegedly Richard, Duke of York). Next is the **Line of Kings**, a display first recorded in 1660, depicting the monarchs of England on horseback. Visitors exit via the basement, which contains artillery and the gnarled, melted relics salvaged from the tower after a fire in 1841, some of which were sold to the public immediately afterwards and later made into candelabra and the like.

Tower Green

Being beheaded at Tower Hill (as opposed to being hanged, drawn and quartered) was a privilege of the nobility; being beheaded on **Tower Green**, the stretch of lawn to the west of the White Tower, was an honour conferred on just seven people, whose names are recorded on a brass plate at the centre of the green. It was an arrangement that suited both parties: the victim was spared the jeering crowds and rotten apples of Tower Hill (see p.220), and the monarch was spared bad publicity. The privileged victims were: Lord Hastings, executed (near this spot) immediately after his arrest on the orders of Richard III, who swore he wouldn't go to dinner until Hastings was beheaded; Anne Boleyn (Henry VIII's second wife), accused of incest and adultery, who was dispatched cleanly and swiftly with a French long sword rather than the traditional axe, at her own insistence; Catherine Howard (Henry VIII's fifth wife and Anne's cousin), convicted of adultery and beheaded along with her lady-in-waiting, who was deemed an accomplice; the 70-year-old Countess of Salisbury; the 16-year-old Lady Jane Grey, who was Queen for just nine days; and the Earl of Essex, one-time favourite of Elizabeth I. The bloody, headless corpses of these "traitors", and those of an estimated 1500 other victims executed on Tower Hill, including Thomas More, were all hastily buried in the plain Tudor **Chapel of St Peter-ad-Vincula**, to the north of the scaffold site, accessible only on the Beefeaters' tours.

Close by the chapel is the **Beauchamp Tower**, a relatively plush place which accommodated only the wealthiest of prisoners. The tower also boasts a better class of graffiti: Lord Dudley, husband of the aforementioned Lady Jane Grey, even commissioned a stonemason to carve the family crest on the first floor. On the far side of the green is the **Queen's House** (closed to the public), built in the last years of Henry VIII's reign and distinguished by its swirling timber frames. These were the most luxurious cells in the Tower, and were used to incarcerate the likes of Catherine Howard and Anne Boleyn, who had also stayed there shortly before her coronation. Lady Jane Grey was cooped up here in 1553, and in the following year it was from here she watched the headless torso of her husband, Lord Dudley, being brought back from Tower Hill, only hours before her own execution. In 1688, William Penn, the Quaker and founder of Pennsylvania, was confined to the Queen's House, where he penned his most popular work, *No Cross, No Crown*. The last VIP inmate was **Rudolf Hess**, Hitler's deputy, who flew secretly into Britain to sue for peace in 1941 and was held here for four days; he eventually committed suicide in Berlin's Spandau prison in 1987.

The Crown Jewels

The castellated **Waterloo Barracks**, built to the north of the White Tower during the Duke of Wellington's term as Constable of the Tower, now hold the **Crown Jewels**, perhaps the major reason so many people flock to the Tower. At least some of the Crown Jewels have been kept in the Tower since 1327, and have been on display since Charles II let the public have a look at them (there was a steep entrance charge even then). These days, the displays are efficient and disappointingly swift. While you are queuing, giant video screens inflict a three-minute loop of footage from the last coronation, plus close-up photos of the baubles. Finally, you get to view the actual Jewels, sped along on moving walkways which allow just 28 seconds' viewing during peak periods – at non-peak times, you can usually go back for a second look without queuing once again.

The vast majority of exhibits postdate the Commonwealth (1649–60), when many of the royal riches were melted down for coinage or sold off. The first piece you come to is St Edward's Crown, made in 1661 for Charles II and used in every coronation since; the oldest piece of regalia is the twelfth-century **Coronation Spoon**; the most famous is the **Imperial State Crown**, sparkling with 2868 diamonds, 17 sapphires including one from a ring said to have been buried with Edward the Confessor, 11 emeralds, 5 rubies and 273 pearls. All in all, it's a stunning ensemble, though only a few of the exhibits – Queen Victoria's Small Diamond Crown, for example – could be described as beautiful. Assertions of status and wealth are more important considerations, and the Jewels include the three largest cut diamonds in the world: the 530-carat "First Star of Africa" or Cullinan I, set into the Sceptre with the Cross, the 317-carat "Second Star of Africa" Cullinan II, in the aforementioned Imperial State Crown, and the legendary 105.6-carat **Koh-i-Noor** (Mountain of Light), removed from Queen Mary's Crown and set into the Queen Elizabeth, the Queen Mother's Crown in 1937. Check out, too, the wine cistern at the end, thought to be the heaviest surviving piece of English plate at nearly a quarter of a ton.

Tower ceremonies

The Ceremony of the Keys is a 700-year-old, seven-minute floodlit ceremony which commences at 9.53pm daily. The Chief Yeoman Warder, accompanied by the Tower Guard, locks the Tower gates, and as he attempts to return to the Inner Ward, the following exchange then takes place: "Halt. Who comes there?" "The Keys." "Whose Keys?" "Queen Elizabeth's Keys." "Pass, Queen Elizabeth's Keys. All's well." To obtain tickets to witness this long-running drama, you must send your details and a stamped addressed envelope several months in advance to the Ceremony of the Keys Office, HM Tower of London, London EC3N 4AB.

Gun Salutes are fired by the Honourable Artillery Company (see p.230) at 1pm at Tower Wharf on royal birthdays and other special occasions.

The Constable's Dues occurs around once a year whenever a large Royal Navy ship moors alongside the Tower; the ship's captain and his escort march through the Tower and present a barrel of rum to the Constable of the Tower.

The Ceremony of the Lilies and Roses is carried out every year on May 21 by the provosts of Eton and King's College, Cambridge, who place white lilies and roses (their respective emblems) in the Wakefield Tower – the spot where King Henry VI, founder of both institutions, was murdered in 1471.

The Beating of the Bounds ceremony takes place once every three years on Ascension Day (forty days after Easter), outside the walls of the Tower. It used to be little boys who were beaten, but now it's the 29 stones that mark the limits of the Tower's jurisdiction just outside the Tower that are thrashed with willow wands by local children, while the Chief Yeoman Warder gives the order "Whack it, boys! Whack it!"

The Salt Tower to the Martin Tower

Visitors can now walk along the eastern section of the Tower walls, starting at the **Salt Tower**, which features more prisoners' graffiti, including a stunningly detailed horoscope carved into the walls by Hugh Draper, who was incarcerated in the Tower in 1561 on a charge of sorcery. Further along the walls, the **Broad Arrow Tower** is decked out as it would have been when Simon de Burley – tutor to Richard II and later to be beheaded on Tower Hill – took refuge here during the 1381 Peasants' Revolt.

The **Martin Tower**, at the far end of the wall walk, was previously the home of Henry Percy, the Earl of Northumberland, who moved in here in 1605 having rejected another suite of cells because of their smell and lack of shade. He had good reason to be choosy, since he was serving life imprisonment in the Tower for failing to inform the king of the Gunpowder Plot. One of the richest men in the country, Percy employed his own cook, and paid for a bowling alley as well as for the walls near his cell to be paved for his daily stroll. Like Walter Ralegh (held at the same time in the Bloody Tower; see p.216), Percy brought a library with him, plus three eminent scholars to assist him with his astrological and alchemical studies. When he was finally released in 1621, after paying a large fine, he was given a royal salute from the Tower guns.

The Martin Tower now houses an exhibition entitled **Crowns and Diamonds**, featuring lots of royal crowns without their precious stones or with replicas. The exhibition also relates the most famous attempt to steal the Crown Jewels, which took place in the Martin Tower. Shortly after the Crown Jewels were put on show during the reign of Charles II, "Colonel" **Thomas Blood**, an Irish adventurer, made an attempt to make off with the lot, disguised as a parson. He was caught on the point of escape with the crown under his habit, the orb in one of his accomplices' breeches and the sceptre about to be filed in half. Charles, good-humoured as ever, met and pardoned the felon, and even awarded him a pension and made him welcome at court.

Last, and probably least, there's the **Fusiliers' Museum** (50p), which tells the story of the Royal Fusiliers, who were founded in the 1680s in a desperate attempt by James II to hold on to his throne. The museum trots through the regiment's various campaigns, displays its medals and spoils from across the Empire, and lists its most famous alumni, although it neglects to mention that East End gangsters, the Kray twins, were once Fusiliers.

Tower Hill

Perhaps it's fitting that traffic-blighted **Tower Hill** to the northwest of the Tower should be such a god-awful place, for it was here that 125 "traitors" were executed after being held in the Tower. In 1381, during the Peasants' Revolt, rioters broke into the Tower, dragged out the Chancellor, Robert Hales, and hacked him to death. The first official beheading took place in 1388 and the last in 1747, when the 80-year-old Jacobite Lord Lovat was dispatched. Lovat's beheading drew such a crowd that one of the spectators' stands close to the scaffold collapsed, killing several bystanders, at which Lovat is said to have exclaimed: "the more mischief, the better sport". The Duke of Monmouth, who was beheaded for his attempted rebellion against James II, is credited with suffering the most botched execution, allegedly for failing to pay enough to the infamous executioner, Jack Ketch (who lives on in *Punch & Judy* shows): it took five blows of the axe to sever his head, and even then the job had to be finished off with a surgeon's knife. Hangings continued on this spot for another thirty-odd years, ending with the execution of two prostitutes and a one-armed soldier arrested for attacking a Catholic-run pub in the Gordon Riots of 1780.

The actual spot for the executions, at what was the country's first permanent scaffold, is marked by a plaque on the west side of Trinity Square Gardens, to the northwest of the Tower. Close by stands the **Mercantile Marine Memorial**, an arch designed by Edwin Lutyens, smothered with the names of the 12,000 civilians of the mercantile marine (as the merchant navy was then called) who died in World War I, and subsequently enlarged to commemorate the 24,000 merchant seamen who died in World War II, in a zigzagging sunken section to the north. The marine theme is continued in the buildings overlooking the gardens: the gargantuan temple-like former headquarters of the **Port of London Authority**, an Edwardian edifice that exudes imperial confidence, with Neptune adorning the main tower; and, to the east, the elegant Neoclassical **Trinity House** (⊛www.trinityhouse.co.uk), which oversees the upkeep of the lighthouses of England, Wales, the Channel Islands and Gibraltar – check out the reliefs of mermen, cherubs and lighthouses on the main facade, and the splendid gilded nautical weather vane.

Continuing east, you'll find perhaps the most impressive remaining section of the old **Roman walls** in the forecourt of the *Grange Hotel*, on Coopers Row, and in Wakefield Gardens, close to Tower Hill tube station, along with an eighteenth-century copy of a Roman statue of Emperor Trajan, saved from a Southampton scrapyard by a local vicar.

Tower Bridge

Tower Bridge ranks with Big Ben as the most famous of all London landmarks. Completed in 1894 to a design by Horace Jones, its neo-Gothic towers are clad in Cornish granite and Portland stone, but conceal a frame of Scottish steel, which, at the time, represented a considerable engineering achievement, allowing a road crossing that could be raised to give tall ships access to the upper reaches of the Thames. The raising of the bascules (from the French for "see-saw") remains an impressive sight, and an event that takes place some five hundred times a year – ring ahead to find out when the next raising is (☎020/7940 3984). If you buy a ticket (daily 9.30am–6pm; £5.50; ☎020/7403 3761, ⊛www .towerbridge.org.uk), you get to walk across the elevated walkways linking the summits of the towers (intended for public use but closed from 1909 to 1982 due to their popularity with prostitutes and the suicidal), and visit the Tower's Engine Room, on the south side of the bridge, where you can see the now defunct giant coal-fired boilers which drove the hydraulic system until 1976, and play some interactive engineering games.

13

Clerkenwell and Hoxton

A typical London mix of Georgian and Victorian town-houses, housing estates, old warehouses, loft conversions and art studios, **Clerkenwell** and **Hoxton** lie immediately to the north of the City. Both districts have been transformed over the last decade or so from gently disintegrating inner-city suburbs to fashionable residential enclaves, and though they lie well off the conventional tourist trail, there are a smattering of minor sights and more than enough nightlife to make them worth exploring. Clerkenwell boasts the vestiges of two pre-Fire-of-London priories and has a history of radicalism, exemplified by the **Marx Memorial Library**, where the exiled Lenin plotted revolution. Hoxton, meanwhile, is home to **Wesley's Chapel and House**, the spiritual heart of the Methodist movement, as well as the **Geffrye Museum** of domestic interiors and a whole host of cutting-edge **contemporary art galleries**.

Clerkenwell

Situated slightly uphill from the City and, more importantly, outside its jurisdiction, **Clerkenwell** (pronounced "Clarken-well") began life in the twelfth century as a village serving the local monastic foundations (two of which survive to some extent). Following the Great Plague and the Great Fire, the area was settled by craftsmen, including newly arrived French Huguenots, excluded by the restrictive practices of the City guilds. At the same time, the springs that give the place its name were rediscovered, and Clerkenwell became a fashionable **spa resort** for a century or so.

During the nineteenth century, the district's population trebled, mostly through Irish and Italian immigration; the springs and streams became cholera-infested sewers, and Clerkenwell, then part of the Borough of Finsbury, became an overpopulated **slum area** as notorious in its day as the East End, and the setting for Fagin's Den in *Oliver Twist*. "In its lanes and alleys the lowest debauch – the coarsest enjoyment – the most infuriated passions – the most unrestrained vice – roar and riot", in the words of one contemporary chronicler.

Victorian road schemes and slum clearances, wartime bombing and economic decline all took their toll, though Clerkenwell held on to a residual residential population, even before the latest influx of new wealthier blood – both now live in slightly uneasy proximity. The area's traditional trades, such as locksmithing, clockmaking, printing and jewellery survive here and there, but the overall trend is now towards designer furniture, media companies and fashionable bars and restaurants catering for the area's new loft-dwelling residents.

Hatton Garden

No one would try to pretend that **Hatton Garden**, the street that connects Holborn Circus with Little Italy (see below), is an attractive spot, but as the centre of the city's diamond and jewellery business, it's an intriguing place to visit during the week. As in Antwerp and New York, ultra-orthodox Hasidic Jews are heavily involved in the business here as middlemen (they are catered for by kosher cafés like *The Knosherie* on nearby Greville Street). The diamond trade is, of course, strictly controlled by the all-powerful South African cartel led by **De Beers** (ⓦwww.debeersgroup.com), whose very discreet headquarters are on nearby Charterhouse Street in the City.

Near the top of Hatton Garden, there's a plaque commemorating **Hiram Maxim**, who perfected the automatic gun named after him in the workshops at no. 57. To the east of Hatton Garden, off Greville Street, you'll find **Bleeding Heart Yard**, whose name refers to the gruesome murder of Lady Hatton in 1626, who sold her soul to the devil, so the story goes. One night, during a ball at nearby Hatton House, the devil came to collect, and all trace of her vanished except her heart, which was found bleeding and throbbing on the pavement. Parallel to Hatton Garden, be sure to take a wander through the **Leather Lane Market**, an old Cockney market open weekdays 10.30am–2.30pm, and selling everything from fruit and vegetables to clothes and electrical gear.

Little Italy

In the latter half of the nineteenth century, London experienced a huge influx of Italian immigrants who created their own **Little Italy** in the triangle of land now bounded by Clerkenwell Road, Rosebery Avenue and Farringdon Road; craftsmen, artisans, street performers and musicians were later joined by ice-cream vendors, restaurateurs and political refugees. Between the wars the population peaked at around 10,000 Italians, crammed into overcrowded, insanitary slums. The old streets have long been demolished to make way for council and other low-rent housing, and few Italians live here these days; nevertheless, the area remains a focus for a community that's now spread right across the capital.

The main point of reference is **St Peter's Italian Church**, built in 1863 and still the favourite venue for Italian weddings and christenings, as well as for Sunday Mass. It's rarely open outside of services, though you can view the memorial to the fallen in World War I, situated in the main porch, and, above it, the grim memorial to the seven hundred Anglo-Italian internees who died aboard the *Arandora Star*, a POW ship which sank en route to Canada in 1940. St Peter's is the starting point of the annual Italian Procession, begun in 1883 and now a permanent fixture on the Sunday nearest July 16 (see p.563).

A few old-established Italian businesses survive here, too: the Scuola Guida Italiana driving school at 178 Clerkenwell Rd, and the deli, G. Gazzano & Son, at 169 Farringdon Rd. There's also a plaque to **Giuseppe Mazzini** (1805–72), the chief protagonist in Italian unification, above the Italian barbers at 10 Lay-

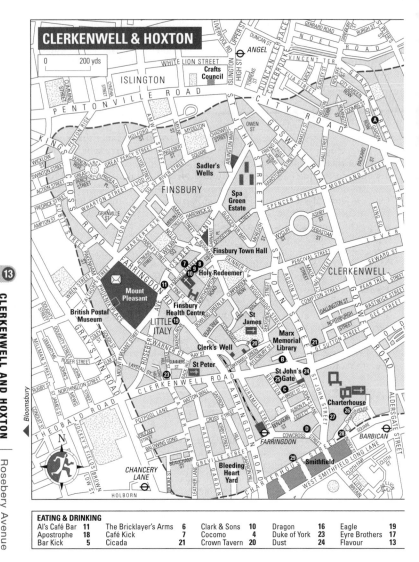

CLERKENWELL & HOXTON

EATING & DRINKING									
Al's Café Bar	11	The Bricklayer's Arms	6	Clark & Sons	10	Dragon	16	Eagle	19
Apostrophe	18	Café Kick	7	Cocomo	4	Duke of York	23	Eyre Brothers	17
Bar Kick	5	Cicada	21	Crown Tavern	20	Dust	24	Flavour	13

stall St. Mazzini lived in exile in London for many years and was very active in the Clerkenwell community, establishing a free school for Italian children in Hatton Garden.

Rosebery Avenue

Halfway up **Rosebery Avenue** – built in the 1890s to link Clerkenwell Road with Islington to the north – stands the **Mount Pleasant Post Office**, Europe's largest sorting office, built on the site of the Coldbath Fields prison.

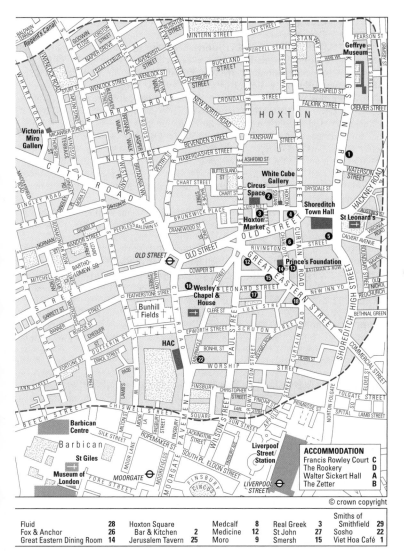

© crown copyright

ACCOMMODATION	
Francis Rowley Court	C
The Rookery	D
Walter Sickert Hall	A
The Zetter	B

Fluid	28	Hoxton Square		Medcalf	8	Real Greek	3	Smiths of
Fox & Anchor	26	Bar & Kitchen	2	Medicine	12	St John	27	Smithfield 29
Great Eastern Dining Room	14	Jerusalem Tavern	25	Moro	9	Smersh	15	Sosho 22
								Viet Hoa Café 1

Over a third of all inland mail passes through this building, some of it once
brought by the post office's own underground railway network, **Mail Rail**
(ⓦwww.mailrail.co.uk). Opened in 1927 and similar in design to the tube, the
railway was fully automatic, sending driverless trucks of mail between London's
sorting offices and train stations at speeds of up to 35mph. Unfortunately, all
23 miles of this two-foot-gauge railway was mothballed in 2003, and there are
no immediate plans to reactivate it. The only consolation for philatelists is the
tiny **British Postal Museum** (Mon–Fri 10am–5pm, Thurs until 7pm; free;
ⓣ020/7239 2570, ⓦwww.postalheritage.org.uk), by the side of the sorting

office on Phoenix Place, which puts on changing exhibitions drawn from its vast archive of stamps and postal memorabilia.

Opposite Mount Pleasant is **Exmouth Market**, now at the epicentre of trendy Clerkenwell. The market has been reduced to a raggle-taggle of tatty stalls and a pie-and-mash shop survives, but the rest of the street has been colonized by modish new shops, bars and restaurants. At the end of the market, to the right, the Spa Field Gardens recall Clerkenwell's days as a fashionable spa, which began in 1683 when Thomas Sadler rediscovered a medicinal well in his garden and established a music house to entertain visitors. The well has since made a comeback at the **Sadler's Wells Theatre** (@www.sadlerswells .com), further up Rosebery Avenue, the fifth theatre on this site and one of the city's main venues for visiting opera and ballet companies. A borehole sunk into the old well now provides all the theatre's non-drinking supplies, helps cool the building and produces 45 gallons of bottled drinking water a day for the punters.

Another building that catches the eye on Rosebery Avenue is the turn-of-the-century **Finsbury Town Hall**, whose name is spelt out in magenta glass on the delicate wrought-iron canopy that juts out into the street. The Borough of Finsbury (incorporating more or less the whole of Clerkenwell) was subsumed into Islington in 1965, but the town hall building is still used as council offices. As the plaque outside states, the district was the first in the country to boast an Asian MP, **Dadabhai Nairoji**, who was elected (after a recount) as a Liberal MP in 1892 with a majority of five.

Later, in keeping with its radical pedigree, the borough elected several Communist councillors and became known popularly as the People's Republic of Finsbury. The council commissioned the Georgian-born Berthold Lubetkin

Lenin in Clerkenwell

Virtually every Bolshevik leader spent at least some time in exile in London at the beginning of the twentieth century, to avoid the attentions of the Tsarist secret police. **Lenin** (1870–1924), whose real name was Vladimir Ilyich Ulyanov, and his wife, Nadezhda Krupskaya, arrived in London in April 1902 and found unfurnished lodgings at 30 Holford Square, off Great Percy Street, under the pseudonyms of Mr and Mrs Jacob Richter. Like Marx, Lenin did his studying in the British Library – L13 was his favourite desk. The couple also entertained numerous other exiles – including Trotsky, whom Lenin met for the first time at Holford Square in October 1902 – but the most important aspect of Lenin's life here was his editing of *Iskra* with Yuli Martov (later the Menshevik leader) and Vera Zasulich (one-time revolutionary assassin). The paper was set in Cyrillic script at a Jewish printer's in the East End and run off on the Social Democratic Federation presses on Clerkenwell Green.

In May 1903, Lenin and Krupskaya left to join other exiles in Geneva, but over the next eight years Lenin visited London on five more occasions, twice for research purposes and three times (his second, third and fifth visit) for congresses of the Russian Social Democratic Labour Party (RSDLP). The second and third congresses were held at secret locations, but the fifth, attended by 330 delegates including Trotsky, Gorky and Stalin, was held openly in the Brotherhood Church on Southgate Road in Islington (since destroyed). Lenin's Holford Square house was destroyed in the war, so the local council erected a (short-lived) monument to Lenin (the bust now resides in Islington Museum). A blue plaque at the back of the hotel on the corner of Great Percy Street commemorates the site of 16 Percy Circus, where Lenin stayed in 1905 for the third RSDLP congress.

to design the modernist **Finsbury Health Centre** on Pine Street, just off Exmouth Market, described by Jonathan Glancey as "a remarkable outpost of Soviet thinking and neo-Constructivist architecture in a part of central London wracked with rickets and TB". Lubetkin's later **Spa Green Estate**, the council flats further north on the opposite side of Rosebery Avenue from Sadler's Wells, featured novelties such as rubbish shutes and an aerofoil roof to help tenants dry their clothes.

Clerkenwell Green and around

Izaak Walton lived on **Clerkenwell Green** – just to the north of Clerkenwell Road and east of Farringdon Road – while he wrote *The Compleat Angler* (1653), but by the following century the Green had long since lost its grass. Poverty and overcrowding were the main features of nineteenth-century Clerkenwell, and it was here that Oliver Twist learnt the tricks of the trade. At this time the Green was known in the press as "the headquarters of republicanism, revolution and ultra-non-conformity" and became a popular spot for **demonstrations**. The most violent of these was the "Clerkenwell Riot" of 1832, when a policeman was stabbed to death during a clash between unemployed demonstrators and the newly formed Metropolitan Police Force. The "blue devils", as they were known, were at the height of their unpopularity, and the coroner reached a verdict of justifiable homicide. London's first **May Day** march set off from here in 1890, and the tradition continues to this day.

The largest building on the Green is the Middlesex Sessions House, once the scene of many a political trial, now in the hands of the Freemasons. The oldest building, at no. 37a, is the former Welsh Charity School, built in 1737 and now home to the **Marx Memorial Library** (Mon–Thurs 1–2pm or by appointment; closed Aug; free; ☎020/7253 1485, ⊛www.marxlibrary.net). Headquarters of the left-wing London Patriotic Society from 1872, and later William Morris' Twentieth Century Press, this is where **Lenin** edited seventeen editions of the Bolshevik paper *Iskra* in 1902–03 (see box, opposite); the poky little back room where Lenin worked is maintained as a kind of shrine – even the original lino survives. The library, situated on the first floor, was founded in 1933 in response to the book burnings taking place in Nazi Germany. You're free to view the Lenin Room, an original copy of *Iskra* produced there, and the library's "workerist" Hastings Mural from 1935, but to consult the unrivalled collection of books and pamphlets on the labour movement you need to become a library member.

Clerkenwell's connections with **radical politics** have a long history and continue to this day: the modern-day Labour Party was founded at a meeting of socialists and trade unionists on Farringdon Road in 1900; the Communist Party had its headquarters at nearby St John Street for many years, and the

▲ Lenin, Marx Memorial Library

Party paper, the *Daily Worker* (later the *Morning Star*), was printed on Farringdon Road, currently home to the *Guardian*, the country's only popular left-leaning daily broadsheet, and its sister paper, *The Observer*, the world's oldest Sunday newspaper, founded in 1791. In fact, you can visit the *Guardian's* **Newsroom** (Mon–Fri 10am–5pm, Sat noon–4pm; ☎020/7886 9898, ⊚www.guardian .co.uk/newsroom), in a former bonded warehouse at no. 60, and pick up a free copy of the paper, take advantage of the café, or visit one of the photographic exhibitions put on here.

The area north of the Green was once occupied by the Benedictine convent of St Mary, founded in the twelfth century. The buildings have long since vanished, though the current church of **St James** (Mon–Fri 10am–6pm; ⊚www .jc-church.org), on Clerkenwell Close, is the descendant of the convent church. A plain, galleried eighteenth-century building decorated in Wedgwood blue and white, its most interesting feature is the twin staircases for the galleries at the west end, both of which were fitted with wrought-iron guards to prevent parishioners from glimpsing any ladies' ankles as they ascended.

The original **Clerk's Well**, which gives the area its name, flowed through the west wall of the nunnery and was "excellently clear, sweet and well tasted" even in 1720, and still in use until the mid-nineteenth century, by which time it had become polluted. It was rediscovered in 1924 and is now visible through the window of 14–16 Farringdon Lane; to get a closer look at it, you need to arrange a visit with the Finsbury Library, 245 St John Street (☎020/7527 7960).

St John's Gate

Of Clerkenwell's three medieval religious establishments, remnants of two survive, hidden away to the southeast of Clerkenwell Green. The oldest is the priory of the Order of St John of Jerusalem, whose Knights Hospitaller, along with the Knights Templar, were responsible for the defence of the Holy Land. The sixteenth-century **St John's Gate**, built in Kentish ragstone on the south side of Clerkenwell Road and originally forming the southern entrance to the complex, is the most visible survivor of the foundation. The twelfth-century priory was sacked by Wat Tyler's poll-tax rebels in 1381, in search of the prior, Robert Hales, who was responsible for collecting the tax; Hales was eventually discovered at the Tower and beheaded on the spot. After the Reformation, the Knights moved to Malta and the Gate housed the Master of Revels, the Elizabethan censor, and later a coffee house run by Richard Hogarth, father of the painter, William.

Today, the gatehouse forms part of a **museum** (Mon–Fri 10am–5pm, Sat 10am–4pm; free; ☎020/7324 4070, ⊚www.sja.org.uk), whose main room traces the development of the Order of St John of Jerusalem before its expulsion in 1540 by Henry VIII. Elsewhere, there are bits of masonry from the old priory, crusader coins and a small collection of arms salvaged from the Knights' armoury on Rhodes, where they were besieged and eventually expelled in 1523. In 1877, the **St John Ambulance** was established, to provide a voluntary first-aid service to the public. It's in this field that the Order is now best known in Britain, and a splendid Time to Care interactive gallery is now devoted to the history of the service. The cabinets of uniforms and pull-out drawers of cigarette cards, badges and medals are interspersed with touch-screen interviews with members past and present. Be sure to check out the Ashford Litter, an early ambulance that was basically a stretcher on wheels with a protective hood.

To get to see the rest of the gatehouse, including the Chapter Hall, which was redesigned in mock-medieval style in the nineteenth century, and to visit the Grand Priory Church over the road, you must take a **guided tour** (Tues, Fri & Sat 11am & 2.30pm; £5 donation requested). Of the original twelfth-century church, all that remains is the **Norman crypt**, which contains two outstanding monuments: a sixteenth-century Spanish alabaster effigy of a Knight of St John, and the emaciated effigy of the last prior, who is said to have died of a broken heart in 1540 after hearing of the Order's dissolution. Above ground, the curve of the church's walls – it was circular, like the Temple Church (see p.175) – is traced out in cobblestones on St John's Square.

Charterhouse

A little to the southeast of St John's Gate lies **Charterhouse**, founded in 1371 as a Carthusian monastery. The public school with which the foundation is now most closely associated moved out to Godalming, Surrey in 1872, but forty-odd pensioners – known as "brothers" – continue to be cared for here. The Carthusians were one of the few religious bodies in London to put up any resistance during the Reformation, for which the prior was hanged, drawn and quartered at Tyburn, and his severed arm nailed to the gatehouse as a warning to the rest of the community, fifteen more of whom were later martyred. This gatehouse on Charterhouse Square, which retains its fourteenth-century oak doors, is the starting point for the exhaustive two-hour **guided tours** (April–Aug Wed 2.15pm; £5; ☎020/7251 5002) that are the only way to visit the site; advance booking is essential.

The monastery was rebuilt as a private mansion in the Tudor period, which is why its architecture is reminiscent of an Oxbridge college rather than a religious institution. Very little remains of the original monastic buildings, which featured a large cloister surrounded by individual monks' cells, each with its own garden. The monks lived on a diet of fish and home-grown vegetables, and were only allowed to speak to one another on Sundays; three of their tiny self-contained cells can still be seen in the west wall of **Preachers' Court**. The larger of the two enclosed courtyards, **Masters' Court**, retains the wonderful Great Hall, which boasts a fine Renaissance carved screen and a largely reconstructed hammerbeam roof, as well as the Great Chamber where Elizabeth I and James I were entertained. The **Chapel**, with its geometrical plasterwork ceiling, is half-Tudor and half-Jacobean, and contains the marble and alabaster tomb of **Thomas Sutton**, whose greyhound-head emblem crops up throughout the building. It was Sutton, deemed "the richest commoner in England" at the time, who bought the place in 1611 and converted it into a charity school for boys and an almshouse for gentlemen.

Hoxton

Until recently, the area called **Shoreditch**, on the northeastern edge of the City, was a none-too-savoury slice of London, an unpleasant amalgam of furniture factories, wholesale clothes and shoe warehouses, striptease pubs and roaring traffic. Vestiges of Shoreditch's former persona survive here and there, but over the last decade or so the area has been regenerated. Moreover, it has been rejacketed: what was once Shoreditch is now **Hoxton**, previously a much smaller neighbourhood confined to the north of Old Street. Whatever its real name, the area is, in actual fact, rich in literary and artistic associations. It was here that James Burbage established the country's first public theatre – called simply the Theatre – in 1576 (he subsequently took it down and reassembled it on Bankside as the Globe). The area became something of an entertainment district, and the subject of a poem, written at the beginning of the seventeenth century, entitled *'Tis a mad world at Hogsdon*.

Despite the area's lack of obvious aesthetic charm, Hoxton has become an increasingly fashionable place to live and work, particularly for London's contemporary art crowd. Rachel Whiteread, Chris Ofili, Anthony Gormley, Tim Noble and Sue Webster have all got studios here, new galleries have opened and several established West End art galleries have relocated or opened up premises, among them Victoria Miro, Jay Jopling's White Cube and Sadie Coles' Hoxton House. The most rewarding activity in Hoxton is cruising the area's **bars** (listed on p.482) and **art galleries** (see p.527), though there are a couple of specific sights: **Wesley's Chapel and House** and the Georgian almshouses that now house the **Geffrye Museum** of period interiors.

Bunhill Fields and the HAC

Just south of the Old Street tube and roundabout – Hoxton's chief transport link with the rest of London – lie **Bunhill Fields** (April–Sept Mon–Fri 7.30am–7pm, Sat & Sun 9.30am–4pm; Oct–March closes 4pm), once a plague pit and later the main burial ground for Dissenters or Nonconformists (practising Christians who were not members of the Church of England). Following bomb damage in the last war, most of the graveyard was fenced off from the public, though you can still stroll through on the public footpaths under a canopy of giant London plane trees. The three most famous graves have been placed in the central paved area: the simple tombstone of poet and artist William Blake stands next to a replica of writer Daniel Defoe's, while opposite lies the recumbent statue of John Bunyan, the seventeenth-century author of *The Pilgrim's Progress*.

The cricket field to the south belongs to the **Honourable Artillery Corps** or HAC (@www.hac.uk.com), whose quasi-medieval barracks, built in 1737, face onto City Road. The oldest regiment in the British army, the HAC is a volunteer unit, formed by Henry VIII in 1537, which now performs ceremonial duties in the City, including the gun salutes that take place outside the Tower of London on special occasions such as royal birthdays.

Wesley's Chapel and House

Directly opposite the entrance to Bunhill Fields, the largely Georgian ensemble of **Wesley's Chapel and House** (Mon–Sat 10am–4pm, Sun noon–1.45pm; free; @020/7253 2262, @www.wesleyschapel.org.uk), set around a cobbled courtyard, strikes an unusual note of calm on busy City Road. A place of pilgrimage for Methodists from all over the world, the chapel was built in 1778 and heralded the coming-of-age of the followers of **John Wesley** (1703–91), who had started out in a small foundry to the east of the present building. The name "Methodist" was first coined as a term of abuse by Wesley's fellow Oxford students, but it wasn't until his "conversion" at a prayer meeting in Aldersgate (marked by a plaque outside the Museum of London) in 1738, and later expulsion from the Anglican Church, that he decided to become an independent field preacher. More verbal and even physical abuse followed – Wesley was accused of being a papist spy and an illegal gin distiller – but by the time of his death there were more than 350 Methodist chapels serving over 130,000 worshippers.

The **chapel**, designed by George Dance the Younger, forms the centrepiece of the complex, though it is uncharacteristically ornate for a Methodist place of worship, with its powder-pink columns of French jasper and its superb, Adam-style gilded plasterwork ceiling, not to mention the colourful Victorian stained glass depicting, among other things, Wesley's night-time conversion, with his brother still in his dressing gown. The chapel has often attracted well-heeled weddings: one Margaret Hilda Roberts got married to divorcé Denis Thatcher here in 1951, and later paid for the new communion rail.

The **Museum of Methodism** (same hours) in the basement tells the story of Wesley and Methodism, and there's even a brief mention of Mrs Mary Vazeille, the 41-year-old, insanely jealous, wealthy widow he married, and who eventually left him. Wesley himself lived his last two years in the Georgian **house** to the right of the main gates, and inside you can see bits of his furniture and his deathbed, plus an early shock-therapy machine with which he used to treat members of his congregation. Wesley's **grave** is round the back of the chapel, in the shadow of a modern office block.

Hoxton Square and around

The geographical focus of Hoxton's transformation is **Hoxton Square**, situated northeast of Old Street tube: a strange and not altogether happy assortment of light industrial units, many of them now converted into artists' studios, arranged around a leafy, formal square. The chief sight here is the **White Cube Gallery** (@www.whitecube.com), which has been likened to a miniature Tate Modern, partly due to the glass roof that tops the building, and partly because it touts the same artists. Another artistic Hoxton enclave lies a couple of blocks west, in the intimate cobbled square of **Hoxton Market**, home to Circus Space (@www.thecircusspace.co.uk), a college for jugglers and acrobats housed in the old Shoreditch power station and refuse destructor.

The area's two architectural landmarks deserve a brief mention. The most prominent is **St Leonard's**, the Neoclassical church at the junction of Old Street, Shoreditch High Street and Kingsland Road. Though usually closed, if you happen to be passing on a Sunday morning, you can take a look inside and admire the memorial to Elizabeth Benson on the southeast wall, which depicts two skeletons tearing at the Tree of Life. A short distance back along Old Street is the former **Shoreditch Town Hall** (@www.shoreditchtownhall.org .uk), a self-confident Victorian edifice, whose tower features Progress, torch and battleaxe in hand, and, in the pediment, Hope and Plenty, reclining beside the Shoreditch motto "More Light, More Power", adopted in recognition of the borough's progressive policy of creating power from rubbish incineration.

Geffrye Museum

In terms of conventional sights, the area has just one to offer: the **Geffrye Museum** (Tues–Sat 10am–5pm, Sun noon–5pm; free; ☏020/7739 9893, @www.geffrye-museum.org.uk), housed in a peaceful little enclave of eighteenth-century ironmongers' almshouses, set back from Kingsland Road. Sold to the London County Council in 1911 at a time when the East End furniture trade was centred on Shoreditch, the almshouses were converted into a museum for the "education of craftsmen". The Geffrye remains, essentially, a furniture museum, with the almshouses rigged out as period living rooms, ranging from the oak-panelled seventeenth century, through refined Georgian to cluttered Victorian. As you pass through the rooms, be sure to take time to admire the original central Georgian **chapel**, with its tiny Neoclassical apse and archetypal stone-coloured wood panelling; round the back of the chapel, an enclosed balcony overlooking the garden serves as a coffee bar.

Hidden behind the almshouses is the museum's **New Gallery Extension**, with four "snapshots in time" from the twentieth century, beginning with an Edwardian drawing room in understated Arts and Crafts style, and finishing off with a minimalist 1990s loft conversion of the type you might well see in today's Hoxton or Clerkenwell. On the lower ground floor, the Geffrye puts on excellent temporary exhibitions and houses a **Design Centre**, where predominantly local artists' work is displayed (and can be bought). Also on the ground floor of the new extension, there's a very pleasant licensed **café–restaurant**, serving inexpensive British food. Out the back, the **gardens** show the transition in horticultural tastes from the seventeenth-century knot gardens to today's patio garden, culminating in a pungent walled **herb garden** (April–Oct only).

To get a feel of what the living conditions in the **almshouses** were like, one of them has been restored to its original condition and can now be visited on the first Saturday of the month, and the first and third Wednesday of the month; numbers are limited, visits are by timed entry only and tickets cost £2.

The East End

> The East End of London is the hell of poverty. Like an enormous, black, motionless, giant kracken, the poverty of London lies there in lurking silence and encircles with its mighty tentacles the life and wealth of the City and of the West End . . .
>
> J.H. Mackay, *The Anarchists* (1891)

Few places in London have engendered so many myths as the **East End** (a catch-all title which covers just about everywhere east of the City, but has its heart closest to the latter). Its name is synonymous with slums, sweatshops and crime, as epitomized by antiheroes such as Jack the Ripper and the Kray twins, but also with the rags-to-riches careers of the likes of Harold Pinter and Vidal Sassoon, and whole generations of Jews who were born in the most notorious of London's cholera-ridden quarters and have now moved to wealthier pastures. Old East Enders will tell you that the area's not

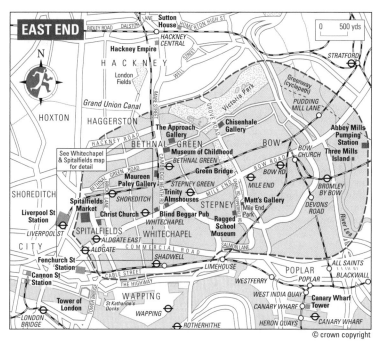

© crown copyright

what it was – and it's true, as it always has been. The East End is constantly changing, as newly arrived **immigrants** assimilate and move out.

The first immigrants were **Huguenots**, French Protestants fleeing from religious persecution in the late seventeenth century – the word "refugee", from the French, *réfugié*, entered the English language at this time. With anti-Catholic feeling running high in London, they were welcomed with open arms by all except the apprentice weavers whose work they undercut, and who attacked them on more than one occasion. Some settled in Soho, but the vast majority settled in Spitalfields, where they were operating an estimated twelve thousand silk looms by the end of the eighteenth century.

Within three generations the Huguenots were entirely assimilated, and the **Irish** became the new immigrant population. Traditionally engaged in the construction industry, Irish labourers, ironically enough, played a major role in building the area's many eighteenth-century Protestant churches, and later were crucial to the development of the docks. The perceived threat of cheap Irish labour provoked riots in 1736 and 1769, and their Catholicism made them easy targets during the Gordon Riots of 1780.

Famine and disease in Ireland brought thousands more Irish over to London in the 1840s and 1850s, but it was the influx of **Jews** escaping pogroms in eastern Europe and Russia that defined the character of the East End in the second half of the nineteenth century. Jewish immigration prompted the Bishop of Stepney to complain in 1901 that his churches were "left like islands in the midst of an alien sea". The same year, the MP for Stepney helped found the first organized racist movement in the East End, the British Brothers League, whose ideology foreshadowed that of the later British Union of Fascists, led by Oswald Mosley and famously defeated at the **Battle of Cable Street** (see p.237).

The area's Jewish population has now dispersed throughout London, though the East End remains a deprived area. Despite the millions that have been poured into the nearby Docklands development, and the proximity of the wealth of the City, little has been done about the perennial unemployment and housing problems of the local population. Unfortunately, racism is still rife in the area, and is directed, for the most part, against the extensive **Bangladeshi** community, who came here from the poor rural region of Sylhet in Bangladesh in the 1960s and 1970s.

Most visitors to the East End come for its famous **Sunday markets**: Petticoat Lane for clothing, **Brick Lane** for bric-a-brac, fashion and cheap curries, Columbia Road for flowers and plants, and **Spitalfields** for crafts and organic food. These apart, the area is not an obvious place for sightseeing, and certainly no beauty spot – Victorian slum clearances, Hitler's bombs and postwar tower blocks have left large areas looking bleak. However, there's a lot of history in the East End, and one or two specific points of interest, including a top-notch **Hawksmoor church**, an old Huguenot grain mill, and a smattering of **museums**, most of them open to the public free of charge. As for the future, one part of the East End that is set to be totally transformed is the lower Lea valley, a run-down industrial area between Bow and Stratford, where the **Olympic Games** are due to be held in 2012 (see p.245).

Whitechapel and Spitalfields

The districts of **Whitechapel**, and in particular **Spitalfields**, within sight of the sleek tower blocks of the financial sector, represent the old heart of the East

WHITECHAPEL & SPITALFIELDS

EATING & DRINKING						ACCOMMODATION	
Arkansas Café	11	Café Spice Namaste	16	Loungelover	6	City Hotel	A
Big Chill Bar	9	E. Pellicci	4	Tayyab's	15		
Brick Lane Beigel Bake	5	Frizzante @ City Farm	1	Ten Bells	12		
Café 1001	10	Jones Dairy	2	Taja	14		
Café Naz	13	Les Trois Garçons	7	Vibe Bar	8		
				Wild Cherry	3		

End, where the French Huguenots settled in the seventeenth century, where the Jewish community was at its strongest in the late nineteenth century, and where today's Bangladeshi community eats, sleeps, works and prays. If you visit just one area in the East End, it should be this zone, which preserves mementoes from each wave of immigration. The further east you venture, the more the damage inflicted on the area during World War II becomes apparent, and the more dispersed the sights, such as they are, become. The best time to visit the area is on a Sunday, when the markets at Petticoat Lane, Spitalfields, Brick Lane and Columbia Road are all up and running.

Petticoat Lane (Middlesex Street) and around

Heavily bombed in the Blitz, **Petticoat Lane** (daily except Sat 9am–2pm) is not one of London's prettiest streets, but it has a rich history: the Huguenots sold the petticoats that gave the market and the street its name; the authorities renamed it Middlesex Street in 1830 to avoid the mention of ladies' underwear (though the original name has stuck) and tried to prevent Sunday trading here until it was finally sanctioned by law in 1936. In the Victorian era the market grew into one of the largest in London, and by the turn of the century it was known as the Jews' Market, and stood at the heart of the Jewish East End, a "stronghold of hard-sell Judaism . . . into which no missionary dared to set foot", according to novelist Israel Zangwill. Nowadays, the stalls are run mostly by Bengalis, Africans and Cockneys, but it remains the city's number one cheap clothes market. A smaller lunchtime version runs throughout the week (though not on Saturdays) on neighbouring Wentworth Street.

To the north of Petticoat Lane are further reminders of the old Jewish community: the **Soup Kitchen for the Jewish Poor**, on Brune Street, which opened in 1902 and finally closed in 1992 (the undulating stone lettering and the Christian and Jewish dates are still clearly visible); the Jewish Free School, which functioned on the corner of Frying Pan Alley, off Bell Lane, from 1821 to 1939, and around 1900 boasted 4300 pupils, making it the largest school in the country; and the **Sandys Row synagogue**, which now struggles to maintain a *minyan* (the minimum of ten male adults needed to perform a service).

The network of narrow streets around Sandys Row is fascinating to walk around – unique survivors that give a strong impression of the old East End. From Sandys Row, walk down Artillery Passage, a mixture of Bengali shops and new, corporate businesses, and on into **Artillery Lane**, which boasts a superb eighteenth-century Huguenot shop front at no. 56. Incidentally, the ballistic connection dates from the reign of Henry VIII, when the Royal Artillery used to hold gunnery practice here.

Old Spitalfields Market and around

To the north of Petticoat Lane lies what's left of **Old Spitalfields Market**, once the capital's premier wholesale fruit and vegetable market, which moved out to

---

The Women's Library

In the 1840s, the Victorians decided it was time to do something about "the great unwashed" and a grandly-named Committee for Promoting the Establishment of Baths and Wash-Houses for the Labouring Classes was set up. One of the plushest public baths was the Goulston Square Wash Houses, opened by Prince Albert himself; "a penny for a cold bath, two for a hot bath for up to four children under eight" were typical charges of the period. The grey-brick facade of the old washhouses survives on Old Castle Street, south of Wentworth Street, but the interior has been transformed into a new home for the **Women's Library**, which puts on excellent exhibitions on a wide range of social issues on the ground floor (Mon–Fri 9.30am–5.30pm, Thurs until 8pm, Sat 10am–4pm; free; ⊛ www.thewomenslibrary.ac.uk). The actual library (Tues–Sat only) was set up by the suffragette Millicent Fawcett in 1926 and has a vast collection of books, pamphlets and periodicals on women's history; it also puts on regular talks and events, and has a café on the first floor.

It was William the Conqueror who invited the first **Jews** to England in 1066. Regarded with suspicion because of their financial astuteness, yet exploited for these very qualities, Jews were banned from numerous professions, but actively encouraged to pursue others, such as moneylending (Christians themselves were banned from lending money for interest, a practice considered sinful by the Church). After a period of relatively peaceful coexistence and prosperity, the small community increasingly found itself under attack, milked by successive monarchs and forced eventually to wear a distinguishing mark or *tabula* on their clothing. The Crusades whipped up further religious intolerance, the worst recorded incident taking place in 1189, when thirty Jews were killed by a mob during the coronation of Richard I. In 1278 Edward I imprisoned the entire community of around six hundred Jews on a charge of "clipping coins" (debasing currency by shaving off bits of silver off coins), executing 267 at the Tower, and finally in 1290 expelling the rest.

For nearly four centuries thereafter, Judaism was outlawed in England. Sephardic (ie Spanish or Portuguese) Jews fleeing the Inquisition began arriving from 1540 onwards, though they had to become, or pretend to be, Christians until 1656, when Oliver Cromwell granted Jews the right to meet privately and worship in their own homes. The Jews who arrived immediately following this **Readmission** were in the main wealthy merchants, bankers and other businessmen. In contrast to conditions in the rest of Europe, Jews in London were self-governing and subject to the same restrictions as all other religious dissenters and foreigners. As a beacon of tolerance and economic prosperity, London quickly attracted further Jewish immigration by poorer Sephardi families and, increasingly, Ashkenazi settlers from eastern and central Europe.

By far the largest influx of **Ashkenazi Jews** arrived after fleeing pogroms that followed the assassination of Tsar Alexander II in 1881. The more fortunate were met by relatives at the Irongate Stairs by Tower Bridge; the rest were left to the mercy of the boarding-house keepers or, after 1885, found shelter in the Jewish Temporary Shelter in Leman Street (later moved to Mansell Street) in the City. They found work in the sweatshops of the East End: cabinetmaking, shoemaking and, of course, tailoring – by 1901, over 45 percent of London's Jews worked in the garment industry.

Perhaps the greatest moment in Jewish East End history was the **Battle of Cable Street**, which took place on October 4, 1936, when Oswald Mosley and 3000 of his black-shirted fascists attempted to march through the East End. More than twice that number of police tried to clear the way for Mosley with baton charges and mounted patrols, but they were met with a barrage of bricks and stones from some 100,000 East Enders chanting the slogan of the Spanish Republicans: "*No pasaran*" (They shall not pass). Barriers were erected along Cable Street and eventually the police chief halted the march – and another East End legend was born. A mural on the side of the old Shadwell town hall on Cable Street commemorates the event.

After World War II, more and more Jews moved out to the suburbs of north London, where the largest Orthodox Jewish communities are now to be found in Golders Green (p.369) and Stamford Hill (p.353). The East End Jewish population, which had peaked at around 130,000 in 1914, is now reduced to a handful of Jewish businesses.

Stratford in 1991. For a decade, the market enjoyed genuine, mixed community use, but following a long – and, it has to be said, fruitless – battle, the western 1920s half of the market was knocked down to make way for yet more boxy, glassy offices, courtesy of Norman Foster. Part of the facade has been retained on Brushfield Street, where you'll also see the signs of the old fruiterers' shops here and there, but the red-brick and green-gabled eastern half of the original building, built in 1893 by rags-to-riches speculator Robert Horner, survives.

You can, on occasion, visit **18 Folgate Street** (☎020/7247 4013, ⊛www.dennissev ershouse.co.uk), to the north of the market, home of the American Artist **Dennis Severs** until his death in 1999. Severs created a theatrical experience which he described as "passing through a frame into a painting". The house is entirely candle-lit and log-fired, and decked out as it would have been two hundred years ago. Visitors are free to explore the ten rooms, and are left with the distinct impression that someone has literally just popped out. The house cat prowls, there's the smell of food, and the sound of horses' hooves on the cobbled street outside. "The Experience" takes place on the first and third Sunday of the month (2–5pm; £8), and on the Mondays (noon–2pm; £5) following those Sundays; plus every Monday, "Silent Night", for which you can book ahead. (April–Sept 8–11pm; Oct–March 6–9pm; £12).

For the moment, that houses a much smaller market (Mon–Fri 10am–4pm, Sun 9am–5am), at its busiest on Sundays, when the stalls specialize in organic food, as well as clothes and jewellery. However, the developers are moving in, and plan to refurbish even this section with glassy partitions, and, of course, up the rent.

The dominant architectural presence in Spitalfields, facing the market from across Commercial Street, is **Christ Church** (Tues 11am–4pm, Sun 1–4pm; ☎020/7247 7202, ⊛www.christchurchspitalfields.org.uk), built between 1714 and 1729 to a characteristically bold design by Nicholas Hawksmoor. Best viewed from Brushfield Street, the church's main features are its huge 225-foot-high broach spire and giant Tuscan portico, raised on steps and shaped like a Venetian window (a central arched opening flanked by two smaller rectangles), a motif repeated in the tower and doors. Inside, there's a forest of giant columned bays, a hexagonal, embossed ceiling, with a lion and a unicorn playing peekaboo on the top of the chancel beam and, opposite, London's largest Georgian organ. The recent, multi-million restoration programme has saved the church from falling down; sadly, it's also removed all the atmosphere the old decaying interior once had.

The church hall, next door, was host in spring 1888 to meetings of the **Bryant & May match girls**, who personified the Dickensian stereotype of the downtrodden East End girl. Some 672 of them went on strike against their miserable wages and work conditions, which gave no protection against "phossy jaw", a deterioration of the jawbone caused by prolonged exposure to yellow phosphorus. Feminist journalist Annie Besant organized a strike committee and galvanized public opinion, and within a fortnight the firm had backed down and met almost all the women's demands.

An outstanding feature of the Spitalfields area is its early Georgian terraced housing. First occupied by **Huguenot silk-weavers** and merchants, many of the houses in the streets around the market retain the original inspection rooms, identifiable by their long windows which gave more light to the weavers' looms. The best examples are to be seen on the north side of **Fournier Street**, most of which have been restored over the last few decades by a fairly well-heeled wave of immigrants – a mix of artists, academics and City workers.

Brick Lane and beyond

Crossing the eastern end of Fournier Street, **Brick Lane**, as its name suggests, was once the main location for the brick kilns that helped rebuild the City after the Great Fire. At the turn of the nineteenth century, many of the streets around here were 100 percent Jewish, making this the high street of the ghetto, but since the 1960s, Brick Lane has been at the heart of the Bengali community. Racism has been a problem for each successive wave of immigrants, but nowadays, it's the developers, who are moving steadily eastwards from the City, that are probably the greatest threat to the community. The southern half of Brick Lane, dubbed "Bangla Town" by the local borough, remains pretty staunchly Bengali: bright-coloured sari fabrics line the clothes-shop windows, the heavy beat of bhangra music emanates from music shops and, in the evening, waiters from the numerous Bangladeshi cafés and restaurants try to cajole you into their establishmens. For the outsider, it's a compelling scene; hidden behind this facade, though, are overcrowded flats and sweatshops that wouldn't look out of place in Victorian times.

The changing ethnic make-up of this part of Brick Lane is most clearly illustrated in the **Jamme Masjid** (Great Mosque) on the corner of Fournier Street. Established in 1743 as a Huguenot church, it became a Wesleyan chapel in 1809, the ultra-Orthodox Spitalfields Great Synagogue in 1897, and since 1976 has served as the main mosque for the area. A little further south is another example of the changing face of Brick Lane: **Christ Church primary school**, still nominally affiliated to the Church of England, though the vast majority of its pupils are Muslim; a hundred years ago they were mainly Jewish, as the Star of David on one of the drainpipes testifies. If you want to dig a bit deeper into the area's past, try to arrange to visit the **Museum of Immigration and Diversity** (occasional open days Sun noon–5pm; free; ☎020/7247 5352, ⊛www.19princeletstreet.org. uk), at 19 Princelet St, where there's a permanent exhibition on Spitalfields' rich history of immigration. The museum is housed in a wonderfully evocative disused synagogue built by Polish Jews in the 1860s, but hidden behind the Georgian facade of an old Huguenot weaver's house.

A red-brick chimney halfway up Brick Lane heralds the **Old Truman Brewery** (⊛www.trumanbrewery.com), which is now a multimedia centre for music, fashion, art and IT. The brewery itself was founded in 1666, and was the world's largest at the end of the nineteenth century, but closed down in 1989. It always acted as a kind of frontier post between the immigrant population to the south and the mostly white population to the north; redeveloped, it now forms the hub of Brick Lane's trendy enclave of clothes and design shops. You can pop into the brewery's popular *Vibe Bar* (⊛www.vibe-bar.co.uk), which offers free Internet access, or the studenty *Café 1001* round the corner in **Dray's Lane**, where the old stables have been turned into shops for designers and artists.

Brick Lane and Columbia Road markets

North of the brewery and railway is the epicentre of **Brick Lane's Sunday market** (8am–2pm) of bric-a-brac. There are in fact virtually no stalls on Brick Lane itself

▲ Columbia Road Flower Market

any more; instead the market extends west along Sclater Street, and east down Cheshire Street. The stalls are a real mixed bag nowadays, selling cheap hardware, fruit and veg, and CDs, and unlocking mobile phones; the shops, though, tend to be more designer accessories and interior furnishings than old-fashioned junk.

Many people combine a visit to Brick Lane with a browse round the lively **Columbia Road flower and plant market** (8am–2pm), which takes place on Sundays amidst the small-scale Victorian terraces to the north. As well as seeds, bulbs, potted plants and cut flowers from the stalls, you can also buy every kind of gardening accessory from the chi-chi shops that line the street, listen to a busker or two and keep yourself sustained with bagels, cakes and coffee. The flower market is the descendant of the market that once occupied a huge cathedralesque Gothic Revival building financed in 1869 by Baroness Burdett-Coutts, who was appalled at the dishonesty of Cockney costermongers. The Archbishop of Canterbury and the Duke of Wellington were present at the grand opening, but the high-handed philanthropy behind the scheme – the great hall was daubed with uplifting inscriptions such as "Speak every man truth with his neighbour" – was resented by the traders; the market flopped and was handed back to the baroness within five years, after which it was let out as workshops and finally pulled down in 1960.

In the nineteenth century, the streets between Columbia Road and Bethnal Green Road formed one of the East End's most notorious slum areas, known as **Old Nichol** (after Old Nichol Street), and fictionalized as the "Jago" in Arthur Morrison's book *Children of the Jago*, published in 1896. On its northern fringe was – in the words of Engels – a "stagnant lake of thickened putrefying matter" which gave off "bubbles of pestilential exhalation". Poverty and disease were the distinguishing features of this slum, cleared away in the 1890s to make way for London's first big municipal housing development, the **Boundary Street Estate**, conceived by the newly formed London County Council. More people were displaced than were rehoused, and few of the original inhabitants could afford the new rents, but the five-storey blocks, centred around the raised garden and bandstand of **Arnold Circus**, became a model for municipal projects throughout Europe. To the modern eye, the rather gloomy red brickwork makes the estate look more like a slum than an ideal home.

Whitechapel Road

Whitechapel Road – along with its extensions, Whitechapel High Street and the Mile End Road – is still the East End's main street, shared by all the many races who live in the Borough of Tower Hamlets. The East End institution that draws in more outsiders than any other is the **Whitechapel Art Gallery** (Tues–Sun 11am–6pm, Thurs until 9pm; free; ℡020/7522 7888, ⊛www .whitechapel.org), a little further up the High Street in a beautiful crenellated 1899 Arts and Crafts building by Charles Harrison Townsend, architect of the similarly audacious Horniman Museum (see p.377). The gallery puts on some of London's most innovative exhibitions of contemporary art, as well as hosting the biennial East End Academy, a chance for local artists to get their work shown to a wider audience; it also has a pleasant café overlooking Angel Alley, with its stainless-steel anarchist portrait gallery, placed there by the Freedom Press (see p.243).

Like the library adjoining it, the gallery was founded by one of the East End's many Victorian philanthropists, **Samuel Barnett**, who was vicar in the worst

The Whitechapel murders

In the space of just eight weeks between August and November 1888, five prostitutes were stabbed to death in and around Whitechapel. Few of the letters received by the press and police, which purported to come from the murderer, are thought to have been genuine (including the one which coined the nickname **Jack the Ripper**), and the murderer's identity remains a mystery to this day. At the time, it was assumed by many that he was a Jew, probably a *shochet* (a ritual slaughterman), since the mutilations were obviously carried out with some skill. The theory gained ground when the fourth victim was discovered outside the predominantly Jewish Working Men's Club in Berner Street (now Henriques Street, off Commercial Road), and for a while it was dangerous for Jews to walk the streets at night for fear of reprisals.

Ripperologists have trawled through the little evidence there is to produce numerous other suspects, none of whom can be conclusively proven guilty. The most celebrated suspect is the Duke of Clarence, eldest son of the future Edward VII, an easy if improbable target, since he was involved in a scandal involving a male brothel and was a well-known homosexual. Another famous suspect is a scholarly cousin of Virginia Woolf, who, it was rumoured, had had an affair with Clarence, and was later committed to an asylum in 1892. Crime writer Patricia Cornwell recently spent more than a million dollars trying (and failing) to prove conclusively that the Ripper was the painter Walter Sickert, who exhibited an unhealthy fascination with the murders during his lifetime. Equally fanciful are the likes of George Chapman, alias Severin Klosowski, a Polish immigrant who poisoned his wife and was hanged for the crime in 1903, and Dr Pedachenko, a junior surgeon from Russia with transvestite leanings who was allegedly sent over by the Tsarist secret police to show up the defects in the British police system. The man who usually tops the lists, however, was a cricket-playing barrister named Druitt whose body was found floating in the Thames some weeks after the last murder, though, as usual, there is no evidence linking him with any of them.

The one positive outcome of the murders was that they focused the attention of the rest of London on the squalor of the East End. Philanthropist Samuel Barnett, for one, used the media attention to press for improved housing, streetlighting and policing to combat crime and poverty in the area. Today, the murders continue to be exploited in gory, misogynistic detail by the likes of Madame Tussaud's and the London Dungeon, while guided walks retracing the Ripper's steps set off every week throughout the year.

parish in Whitechapel in the 1870s. His motives may have been dubious – "the principle of our work is that we aim at decreasing not suffering but sin", he once claimed – but the legacy of his good works is still discernible. Another of Canon Barnett's enduring foundations was **Toynbee Hall** (ⓦ www.toynbeehall .org.uk), founded in 1884 as a residence for Oxbridge volunteers who wished to do social and educational work in the East End. The original nineteenth-century hall survives in a modern courtyard just off Commercial Street.

Barnett's wife, Henrietta, went as far as to propose moving into one of the infamous thieves' dens and brothels to the north of Toynbee Hall. Barnett put his foot down at the suggestion, but he helped set up the East End Dwellings Company, a scheme providing housing for the poor. The Rothschilds followed suit and founded the **Four Per Cent Dwellings Company**, which guaranteed a four percent dividend for the wealthy investors who backed it. The original arch of the scheme survives above the entrance to the modern red-brick Flower and Dean estate, to the north of Wentworth Street, which now stands in its place.

The most visible symbol of the Muslim presence in the East End is the Saudi-financed **East London Mosque** (ⓦ www.eastlondonmosque.org.uk), an enormous gaudy red-brick building a short walk up Whitechapel Road from the art gallery; it stands in marked contrast to the tiny **Fieldgate Street Great Synagogue** (ⓦwww.somethingjewish.co.uk), dating from 1899, which stands behind the mosque. Neither of these buildings is open to the public. Nearby, you can pay a quick visit to the small exhibition in the nearby **Whitechapel Bell Foundry** (Mon–Fri 9am–4.15pm; guided tours occasionally Sat 10am & 2pm; £8; no under-14s; ☎020/7247 2599, ⓦwww.whitechapelbellfoundry .co.uk), part of which occupies the short terrace of Georgian houses on the corner of Fieldgate Street. Big Ben, the Liberty Bell, the Bow Bells and numerous English church bells (including those of Westminster Abbey) all hail from the foundry, established in 1570.

Past Vallance Road, the street widens at the beginning of **Whitechapel Market** (Mon–Sat 8am–6pm), once one of the largest hay markets in London, now given over to everything from nectarines to net curtains, and including a large number of stalls catering for the local Bengali and Somali communities. At the turn of the century, this was where casual workers used to gather to be selected for work in the local sweatshops, earning it the Yiddish nickname *Hazer Mark*, or "pig market". Nearby, on the other side of Vallance Road, stood the Pavilion Theatre, one of several East End theatres that used to put on Yiddish shows for the thousands of newly arrived Jews. Raucous and irreverent, Yiddish theatre was frowned upon by the Anglicized Jews, the *Jewish Chronicle* stating that Yiddish was "a language we should be the last to encourage any efforts to preserve". The sole reminder of those days is the Edward VII monument at the centre of the market, erected by the local Jewish community in 1911.

It was on the Mile End Road that Joseph Merrick, better known as the **Elephant Man**, was discovered in a freak show in 1884 by Dr Treves, and subsequently admitted as a patient to the **Royal London Hospital** on Whitechapel Road. He remained there, on show as a medical freak, viewed by the likes of Princess Alexandra, for four years until his death in 1890, at the age of just 27. The hospital still owns his skeleton, despite an offer of several million pounds some years back from Michael Jackson, though it's not on public display. However, in the **Hospital Museum** (Mon–Fri 10am–4.30pm; free; ⓦwww .medicalmuseums.org), housed beside the red-brick church of St Augustine with St Philip's (now the medical college library) on Newark Street, there's a small section, and an interesting twenty-minute documentary, on Merrick. The museum also covers the history of the hospital and of nursing and medicine in general, with another section on Edith Cavell, who trained here before assisting Allied soldiers to escape from occupied Belgium; she was eventually arrested and shot as a spy by the Germans in 1915.

Just before the point where Whitechapel Road turns into Mile End Road stands the handsome gabled entrance to the former Albion Brewery (now a health centre), where the first bottled brown ale was produced in 1899. Next door lies the **Blind Beggar**, the East End's most famous pub since March 8, 1966, when Ronnie Kray walked into the crowded bar and shot gangland rival George Cornell for calling him a "fat poof". This murder spelt the end of the infamous Kray Twins, Ronnie and Reggie, both of whom were sentenced to life imprisonment, though their well-publicized gifts to local charities created a Robin Hood image that still persists in these parts of town.

Founded in 1886, the **Freedom Press** (Mon–Fri 10.30am–6pm, Sat 11am–5pm; @www.freedompress.org.uk), a small anarchist bookshop and printing press in Angel Alley, by the side of the Whitechapel Art Gallery, is the lone survivor of an East End tradition of radical politics that reached its height at the end of the nineteenth century. East End anarchism found a strong following among the Jewish community especially, and supporters of the *Arbeter Fraint* newspaper staged atheist demonstrations outside Orthodox synagogues on the Sabbath, as well as making other gestures like ostentatiously smoking and eating ham sandwiches. In 1907, delegates to the Fifth Congress of the Russian Social Democratic Labour Party staged a meeting on the corner of Fulbourne Street attended by Lenin, Stalin, Trotsky, Gorky and Litvinov, and the Jubilee Street Anarchist Club later loaned £1700 to the Bolsheviks (paid back in full by the Soviet government after the revolution).

The event for which the anarchists are best remembered, however, is the **Siege of Sidney Street**, which took place in January 1911. A gun battle occurred after a routine police enquiry at the back of a jeweller's on Houndsditch, and left one Russian anarchist and three policemen dead. Over the next few weeks, all but three of the anarchist gang were arrested; following a tip-off, they three were eventually cornered in a building on Sidney Street. A further gun battle ensued: a detachment of Scots Guards and two cannons were deployed, and the Home Secretary, Winston Churchill, arrived on the scene to give orders. By lunchtime the house was in flames, leaving two charred bodies in the burnt-out shell. However, the ringleader, nicknamed Peter the Painter, vanished without trace, to join the likes of Jack the Ripper as an East End legend.

Mile End Road

On Saturdays, the Whitechapel market extends beyond Cambridge Heath Road into the **Mile End Road**, the first section of which is known as the Mile End Waste. It's punctuated at the western end by a bust, and at the eastern by a more dramatic statue, of the most famous of all the East End philanthropists, **William Booth**. It was here one late June evening in 1865 that Booth, moved by the sight of the crowds at the pubs and gin palaces, made his first impromptu public speech. Later on he set up a tent on Vallance Road and began in earnest the missionary work that eventually led to the foundation of the quasi-military **Salvation Army** in 1878. In contrast to many Victorian philanthropists, Booth never accepted the divisive concept of the deserving and undeserving poor – "if a man was poor, he was deserving". Booth preached a simple message of "Heaven in East London for everyone", railing against the laissez-faire economic policies of his era, while at the same time attending to the immediate demands of the poor, setting up soup kitchens and founding hostels, which, by the time of his death in 1912, had spread right across the globe. Booth is buried in Abney Park Cemetery (see p.352).

Another East End philanthropist, **Frederick Charrington**, used to try his best to steer the local inhabitants away from their sinful ways at this very spot. Heir to the eponymous local brewery, Charrington was, rather surprisingly, a tireless temperance campaigner, who in 1886 established a vast Assembly Hall on the Mile End Waste, capable of seating 5000, with a Coffee Palace and a "pure" book salon. He tried unsuccessfully to close down the neighbouring music hall by marching up and down outside with sandwich boards reading "The Wages of Sin is Death" and, more effectively, used to keep vigil outside brothels, threatening to publish the names of those who entered. The Assembly

14

THE EAST END | Mile End Road

Hall was also used for some of the most famous political meetings of the era: the Bryant & May match-girl strikers (see p.238), Eleanor Marx and anarchist Prince Kropotkin, who spoke out against racist trade-union resolutions, and in support of the 1912 dock strikers.

There are two unusual architectural features worth mentioning on the Waste. The biggest surprise is the **Trinity Almshouses**, a quaint courtyard of cottages with a central chapel, built in 1695 for "Twenty-eight decay'd Masters and Commanders and the widows of such", and rebuilt after World War II as a home for the disabled. Further up, on the same side of the street, stands a large Neoclassical former department store, sporting a central domed tower, its facade sliced in two by a small two-storey shop that used to belong to a Jewish watchmaker called **Spiegelhalter**. This architectural oddity is the result of a dispute between Spiegelhalter and his affluent Gentile neighbour, Thomas Wickham, who was forced to build his new store around the watchmaker's shop after he refused to be bought out.

Stepney, Bow and Bethnal Green

Stepney, to the east of Whitechapel, was the site of Edward I's second parliament in 1299, but by Victorian times it was one of the most miserable and crowded districts in the East End. It was here that the first **Ragged School** for the poor was established in 1865 by Dr Barnardo, and today, the museum dedicated to the philanthropist is the area's principal sight (see below). Close by the museum is the **Mile End Park**, a thin slip of a park recently created from bomb sites along the Regent's Canal, and featuring a remarkable "green bridge", designed by Piers Gough, which takes the park (complete with ten trees, a footpath and a cycle track) over the busy Mile End Road.

Further east still lies **Bow**, fringed by the River Lea, along which there developed a milling industry in medieval times, relics of which still survive at **Three Mills Island**. By the second half of the nineteenth century, the East End's relentless expansion had engulfed Bow, which became notorious for its slums and factories, among them the infamous Bryant & May match factory (see p.238). This was the constituency of George Lansbury, who famously resigned his seat in 1912, in order to fight (and, as it turned out, lose) a by-election on the issue of women's suffrage. The following year, Sylvia Pankhurst moved to Bow and set up her radical East London Federation of Suffragettes (ELFS), holding frequent meetings in the area's largest green space, **Victoria Park**.

Once a pleasant country village to the northwest of Stepney, **Bethnal Green** had become one of the poorest parishes in London by Victorian times. Much altered by slum clearances and wartime bombing, the old village green is now the Bethnal Green Gardens centred around the church of St John, built in the 1820s by John Soane, and sporting an unusual square tower topped by a slender stone cupola. The chief sight here is the **Museum of Childhood**, to the north of the gardens, with its celebrated collection of dolls' houses.

Ragged School Museum

To the south of the Mile End Road, on the bombed-out remains of Copperfield Road, the **Ragged School Museum** (Wed & Thurs 10am–5pm, first Sun

Against all the odds, London won the right to stage the **Olympic Games** in 2012. Even more surprisingly, the focus of the games, the Olympic Park, is going to be in the East End, in an unpromising, rundown industrial estate by the River Lea, just north of Three Mills Island and the Abbey Mills Pumping Station, between Hackney Wick and Stratford. The main 80,000-seat Olympic Stadium will be built on Marshgate Lane and will become a 25,000-seat athletics stadium after the games. Close by, there'll be a 20,000-seat aquatic centre, a velodrome and BMX track (alongside the existing Eastway cycling circuit), a hockey complex and, on the site of the former Hackney greyhound stadium, a multi-sports complex for basketball, handball and volleyball. The Olympic village, housing nearly 18,000 athletes will also be here, and will be converted to public housing after the games.

The rest of the events will take place in and around London, mostly in existing venues: Wimbledon will obviously host the tennis and the new Wembley stadium the football, while ExCel, the exhibition centre by Royal Victoria Dock, will be used for boxing, judo, taekwondo, weightlifting and wrestling, and Eton's new rowing centre will serve for some canoeing and kayaking events as well as for skulling. One piece of good news is that the Dome will finally serve a useful purpose by hosting the artistic gymnastics, trampolining and basketball finals, along with a smaller temporary venue for rhythmic gymnastics, table tennis and badminton. Equestrian events are scheduled for Greenwich Park, while Hyde Park will host the triathlon and road cycling and Regent's Park the baseball and softball. Archery will take place at Lord's cricket ground, shooting at the Royal Artillery Barracks in Woolwich and – the one piece of planning that's really grabbed the headlines – beach volleyball will be staged on Horse Guards Parade. Only sailing, mountain biking and the canoeing slalom will take place any great distance from the capital.

The games will certainly generate employment, and provide some badly needed housing for a deprived area, though it's difficult to judge how great the long-term benefits of the games will really be. Despite protestations to the contrary, the environmental costs will be high, and council taxes in London – already among the highest in the country – are set to rise to pay for the privilege. On the positive side, East London's transport infrastructure looks set to improve: trains from Paris will arrive at Stratford in just over two hours from 2007, the East London Line is being extended north into Hackney and south to Crystal Palace, and further extensions are planned for the Docklands Light Railway.

of month 2–5pm; free; ☎020/8980 6405, ⊛www.raggedschoolmuseum.org .uk) occupies a Victorian canalside warehouse. Accommodating more than one thousand pupils from 1877 to 1908, this was the largest of London's numerous Ragged Schools, institutions that provided free education and two free meals daily to children with no means to pay the penny a week charged by most Victorian schools. This particular Ragged School was just one of innumerable projects set up by the East End's most irrepressible philanthropist, the diminutive and devout **Dr Thomas Barnardo**, whose tireless work for the children of the East End is the subject of the ground-floor exhibition. Upstairs, there's a reconstructed Victorian schoolroom, where period-dressed teachers, cane in hand, take today's schoolkids through the rigours of a Victorian lesson. On the top floor you can learn to make a rag rug and take part in wash day; there are also further displays on the nearby docks and local sweatshops, and a canalside café back on the ground floor.

Three Mills Island

The most remarkable vestige of Bow's past is the eighteenth-century architectural ensemble on **Three Mills Island**, an artificial island in the River Lea, which forms the eastern border of Bow (on the other side of the A102 from Bromley-by-Bow tube). Despite its name, there are now only two mills remaining, the most distinctive of which is the Clock Mill, with its conical oasts – kilns used to dry out grain – and its pretty white clock tower. Opposite stands the Dutch-style **House Mill** (May–Oct Sun 2–5pm; £3; ☎020/8980 4626), built in 1776, closed during World War II and now open for guided tours, which take you through the milling process and allow you to see the surviving mill wheels which were driven by the tidal flows from the nearby River Thames. On the first Sunday of the month, from March to December, the mill is open from 11am to coincide with the craft market that takes place on the island (11am–5pm). Beyond the mills are later gin-distillery buildings, most of which have now been converted into television and film studios.

Visible to the northeast of the island is the new **Abbey Mills Pumping Station**, sporting a gleaming metal pitched roof, and, adjacent, its much more famous Victorian predecessor, a glorious Gothic-Italianate edifice nicknamed the "Cathedral of Sewage". The latter was built in the 1860s by Joseph Bazalgette and Edwin Cooper, and was originally flanked by two twin chimneys decorated in Moorish style, which were sadly demolished during World War II. **Guided tours** take place every month; for details phone the Thames Water customer centre (☎0845/9200 800), and remember to book in advance as it's very popular. Visible to the southeast of Three Mills are seven ornate, Grade II–listed wrought-iron **Victorian gasholders**, built on the site of a rocket factory set up in the 1820s by William Congreve.

Bethnal Green Museum of Childhood

The **Bethnal Green Museum of Childhood** (daily except Fri 10am–5.50pm; free; ☎020/8980 2415, ⊛www.museumofchildhood.org.uk), a branch of the V&A, is situated just across Cambridge Heath Road from Bethnal Green tube station. The elegant, open-plan wrought-iron hall was, in fact, part of the original V&A building, and was transported here from South Kensington in the late 1860s in order to bring art to the East End. The emphasis has changed since those pioneering days, and although the wide range of exhibits means that there's something here for everyone, the museum's most frequent visitors are children, and special kids' events are put on here at weekends and during school holidays.

The museum is due to reopen in November 2006 after a major refurbishment, so it's impossible to say exactly how the exhibits will be arranged. However, pride of place will, no doubt, still be reserved for its unique collection of antique dolls' houses dating back to 1673. Among the other curiosities are model trains, cars and rocking horses, wooden models of carcass-hung nineteenth-century butcher's shops, and dolls made from found objects (including a little man made from a lobster claw). There are also a handful of automata – Wallace the Lion gobbling up Albert is always a firm favourite. Elsewhere, there are puppets and a vast doll collection including Native American representations of spirits, stylish flapper dolls carried by the bright young things of the Jazz Age and a macabre Shirley Temple.

Victoria Park

The Victorians were firm believers in parks as instruments of moral and physical improvement, particularly for the working classes. As "sanitary reformer" William Farr maintained, the use of parks would "diminish deaths by several thousands and add years to the lives of the entire population". **Victoria Park** (daily 7am–dusk; bus #277 from Mile End tube or bus #8 from Liverpool Street tube), London's first public park – as opposed to royal park – was opened in the heart of the East End in 1845, after a local MP presented Queen Victoria with a petition of 30,000 signatures.

The only large open space in the area, "Viccy Park" immediately became a favourite spot for political rallies: Chartists congregated here in their thousands in 1848, George Bernard Shaw and William Morris addressed demonstrations, and Suffragette supporters of the ELFS gathered here, under the leadership of Sylvia Pankhurst, who was described by Shaw as "the most ungovernable, self-interested, blindly and deadly wilful little rapscallion-condottiera that ever imposed itself on the infra-red end of the revolutionary spectrum". In 1978, over 100,000 people turned up for an open-air concert organized by the Anti-Nazi League.

The park is divided in two unequal halves by Grove Road. The smaller western section has the largest and nicest of the lakes, complete with a fully functioning fountain, not to mention the **Dogs of Alcibiades**, two snarling sculpted beasts based on the Molossian hounds kept by the Athenian statesman and presented by Lady Regnart in 1912. The much larger eastern section contains an extraordinarily lavish Gothic-cum-Moorish **drinking fountain**, decorated with oversized cherubs and paid for by Baroness Burdett-Coutts in 1861 – it hasn't functioned for years. The **Old English Garden**, laid out to the northeast of the fountain, provides a pleasant haven of flowers and shrubs, while next door there's a small deer enclosure, and a much larger children's playground. The park's **model boat club** meets on most Sunday mornings.

14

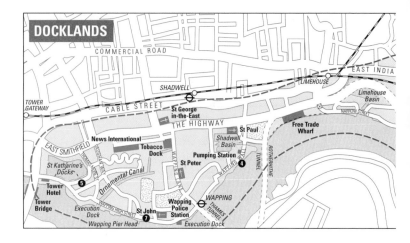

⑮

Docklands

A whole people toil at the unloading of the enormous ships, swarming on the barges, dark figures, dimly outlined, loving rhythmically, fill in and give life to the picture. In the far distance, behind the interminable lines of sheds and warehouses, masts bound the horizon, masts like a bare forest in winter, finely branches, exaggerated, aerial trees grown in all the climates of the globe.

Gabriel Mourey (1865–1943)

The architectural embodiment of Thatcherism according to its critics or a blueprint for inner-city regeneration to its free-market supporters – the **Docklands** development continues to provoke extreme reactions. Despite the catch-all name, however, Docklands is far from homogeneous. **Canary Wharf**, with its Manhattan-style skyscrapers, is only its most visible landmark, and is by no means typical of the area; warehouse conversions, industrial-estate sheds, left-over council housing and Costa del Thames apartments in a whole travesty of styles are more indicative. **Wapping**, the most easily accessible district, and one that you can happily explore on foot, has retained and restored much of its original Victorian warehouse architecture, as has Bermondsey on the south bank (see p.280), while large areas around the Royal Docks, further east, have yet to be fully redeveloped. Travelling through on the overhead **Docklands Light Railway** (DLR), the area comes over as a fascinating open-air design museum, not a place one would choose to live

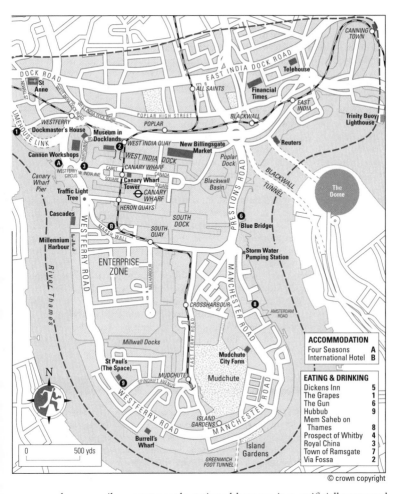

ACCOMMODATION
Four Seasons A
International Hotel B

EATING & DRINKING
Dickens Inn 5
The Grapes 1
The Gun 6
Hubbub 9
Mem Saheb on
Thames 8
Prospect of Whitby 4
Royal China 3
Town of Ramsgate 7
Via Fossa 2

© crown copyright

or work necessarily – most people stationed here see it as artificially removed from the rest of London – but a spectacular sight nevertheless.

From the sixteenth century onwards the **Port of London** was the key to the city's wealth. The "legal quays" – roughly the area between London Bridge and the Tower – were crowded with as many as 1400 seagoing vessels forced to wait for up to six weeks to be unloaded, with some 3500 cutters, barges and punts jostling between their hulls. It was chiefly to relieve such congestion, which worsened with the increased trade from the Empire, that from 1802 onwards London began to construct the largest enclosed **cargo–dock system** in the world. Each dock was surrounded by forty-foot-high walls, patrolled by its own police force and geared towards a specific type of cargo. Casual dockers gathered at the dock gates each morning for the "call-on", a human scrummage to get selected for work. This mayhem was only stopped after World War II, when the Dock Labour Scheme was introduced, and by then it was too late. Since the mid-nineteenth century, competition from the railways had been eroding the river traffic, and with the development of container ships and the movement of the port downriver to Tilbury in the 1960s, the old city docks began to wind down.

Over the course of two decades, the quaysides and the surrounding areas were transformed into a wasteland, beset with high unemployment and a dwindling population, until the **London Docklands Development Corporation** (LDDC) was set up in 1981, with its unfortunate slogan of "Looks like Venice, works like New York". One hundred percent tax relief on capital expenditure, no business rates for ten years and freedom from planning controls were just some of the ploys used to kick-start the project, and were the conditions that allowed Canary Wharf and the Enterprise Zone (EZ) to the south to be built. No one thought the old docks could ever be rejuvenated; the LDDC, on the other hand, predicted a resident population of over 100,000 and a working population twice that, all by the end of the millennium.

In 1998, the LDDC was wound up, having achieved more than many thought possible, but less than it had promised. It's certainly easy to criticize its approach: ad hoc planning; a lack of basic amenities, of open green spaces, of civic architecture or public buildings, and of consultation with the local community. With the onset of recession in the early 1990s, the original developers went bust, offices and flats lay empty and virtually all construction was halted. The real shot in the foot, though, was the government's negligence over basic public transport infrastructure, which meant that the new **Jubilee line extension** to the tube system, linking Canary Wharf with central London, only opened in 1999. The economic situation has since picked up, and construction is once more continuing apace, but the end result is still destined to be, as one critic aptly put it, "a chain of highly polarized ghettos epitomizing the gulf between the rich and poor, home-owner and tenant". For the local community's views on the latest Docklands news, visit ⓦicthewharf.icnetwork.co.uk.

Visiting Docklands

Nothing will convey to the stranger a better idea of the vast activity and stupendous wealth of London than a visit to these warehouses, filled to overflowing with interminable stores of every kind of foreign and colonial products; to these enormous vaults, with their apparently inexhaustible quantities of wine; and to these extensive quays and landing-stages, cumbered with huge stacks of hides, heaps of bales, and long rows of casks . . . Those who wish to taste the wines must procure a tasting-order from a wine merchant. Ladies are not admitted after 1pm. Visitors should be on their guard against insidious effects of "tasting" in the heavy, vinous atmosphere.

Baedeker (1905)

Sadly, visits to the docks are no longer so intoxicating. You can, however, view Docklands from a distance on one of the boats that course up and down the Thames (see p.36). For a close-up you should take the driverless, overhead **Docklands Light Railway** or DLR (see p.35). If you're heading for Greenwich, and fancy taking a boat back into town, it might be worth considering a Rail River Rover ticket (£9.50), which gives you unlimited travel on the DLR and City Cruises services between Greenwich and Westminster. Alternatively, you can now **walk** the two miles from Wapping to Canary Wharf along, or close to, the river bank, by following the Thames Path; there are also several pedestrian bridges linking the different quays around Canary Wharf. Further south, however, walking is not much fun, and you're probably best off exploring by bike – unfortunately bicycles are not allowed on the DLR, though they are allowed to use the Greenwich Foot Tunnel.

Wapping

Once famous for its boatyards and its 36 riverside pubs (a handful of which remain), **Wapping** changed forever with the construction of the enclosed docks in the early nineteenth century. Cut off from the rest of the East End by the high walls of the docks, its inhabitants crowded into insanitary housing, the area became notorious for its thieves, attracted by the opportunities of rolling-drunk sailors and poorly guarded warehouses. With the demise of the docks, Wapping became an early victim of gentrification, though restoration and renovation of existing property rather than demolition and redevelopment has been the rule. Thus something of Wapping's Victorian atmosphere has been preserved, and as it lies just a short walk east of the Tower, this is easily the most satisfying part of Docklands to explore.

St Katharine's Docks

St Katharine's Docks (@www.stkaths.co.uk) were built in the late 1820s immediately east of the Tower – in the process some 11,300 people were made homeless, and the medieval foundations of St Katharine's hospital and church were demolished. Having specialized in luxury goods such as ivory, spices, carpets and cigars, St Katharine's was very badly bombed in the Blitz and became the first phase of the Docklands renewal scheme in the early 1970s, when it was turned into a luxury yacht marina by Taylor Woodrow. First they raised the concrete carbuncle of the *Tower Thistle Hotel*, then the neo-warehouse World Trade Centre (now defunct), which backs onto Tower Bridge Road, and, most recently, Europe House, a typical slice of Docklands architecture – all glassy rooftop penthouses and balconies – designed by Richard Rogers in the docks' northeastern corner.

The docks' redeeming qualities are the old swing bridges, the boats themselves, often beautiful old sailing ships and Dutch barges, and the **Ivory House** warehouse, with its clock tower and wrought-iron colonnade, at the centre of the three basins. Built in 1854, at its peak this warehouse received over 200 tons of ivory annually (that's 4000 dead elephants), plus hippopotamus and walrus teeth and even mammoth tusks from Siberia. On the corner of East Smithfield and Thomas More Street, you can also see the remains of the original dock wall, and the main entrance to the former London Docks, with two Neoclassical Customs and Excise offices from 1805.

St Katharine's proximity to the Tower makes it a popular destination for tour groups and wandering tourists, who tend to head for the *Dickens Inn*. Originally an eighteenth-century timber-framed brewery warehouse, situated several hundred yards east of its present site, much of the current building, including the weatherboarding and galleries, is, in fact, fake. Roughly at the centre of the docks is the ugly **Coronarium chapel** (now a branch of *Starbucks*), built for Queen Elizabeth II's Silver Jubilee, and situated as near as possible to the old church of St Katharine's, which was itself owned by the Crown.

News International to St George-in-the-East

East down the busy Highway lies the headquarters of Rupert Murdoch's **News International**, a complex dubbed "Fortress Wapping", on account of its high walls, barbed wire and security cameras. Murdoch was one of the first capitalist barons to give Docklands his blessing, sacking his entire workforce of printers and journalists when he moved his newspapers – *The Times, Sunday Times, The Sun* and *News of the World* – out here in 1986, thus sparking one of the most bitter trade-union disputes of the Thatcher era. Mounted police engaged in violent skirmishes with protesters for nearly a year – no prizes for guessing who won.

Close by stands **Tobacco Dock**, a huge warehouse built in 1814 and initially used to store tobacco and wine (sheepskin, cork and molasses came later). A fascinating combination of timber and early cast-iron framing, it was converted into a kitsch shopping complex in the 1980s by postmodernist Terry Farrell. Dreams of the East End's answer to Covent Garden evaporated within a matter of years, and the place currently lies empty. The locals would probably prefer another superstore, while the rest of London wouldn't dream of coming out here.

Tobacco Dock is a short distance south of Nicholas Hawksmoor's church of **St George-in-the-East** (daily 9am–5pm), built in 1726 on the north side of the busy Highway. As bold as any of Hawksmoor's buildings, it boasts four "pepperpot" towers above the nave and a hulking west-end tower topped by an octagonal lantern. Within, it comes as something of a shock to find a miniature modern church squatting in the nave, but that's all the parish could come up with following the devastation of the Blitz.

A pleasant feature of this area, which will take you effortlessly back to Wapping High Street, is the tree-lined **canal walk** – all that remains of the huge Western Dock that once stood here – which begins south of Tobacco Dock, where two "pirate" sailing ships are moored.

⑮

Wapping High Street to Shadwell Basin

If you arrive on **Wapping High Street** expecting the usual parade of shops, you're in for a big surprise. Traditionally, the business of Wapping took place on the river; thus tall brick-built warehouses, most now tastefully converted into expensive flats, line the Thames side of the street, while to the north, in a stark contrast typical of Docklands, lie the council estates of the older residents. (Alf Garnett, the bigoted elderly dockworker of the 1960s BBC comedy *Till Death Us Do Part*, lived in Wapping.) Deterred by the swanky riverside housing developments in between, few tourists make it out here, but it's only a ten-minute walk from St Katharine's Dock, and well worth the effort.

Five minutes' walk along the High Street will bring you to **Wapping Pier Head**, the former entrance to the London Docks, now grassed over but still flanked by grand curvaceous Regency terraces built for the officials of the Dock Company. Further east is the unusual neo-Gothic former tea warehouse, **Oliver's Wharf**, a trailblazing apartment conversion from 1972, with a couple of preserved overhead gangways crossing the High Street just beyond. You'll also find one of the few surviving stairways down to the river beside the *Town of Ramsgate* pub; beneath the pub are the dungeons where convicts were chained before being deported to Australia. It was at the *Town of Ramsgate* that **"Hanging" Judge Jeffreys** was captured trying to escape disguised as a collier following the Glorious Revolution of 1688. Jeffreys, Lord Chancellor under James II, was notorious for the harsh sentences he handed down, and was only saved from being lynched by a company of soldiers who took him off to the Tower, where he died a few months later.

Just east of the Pier Head, up Scandrett Street, is the eighteenth-century **St John's Old School**, with Coade stone figures of a boy and girl set in niches. It and its Victorian extension, which features wonderfully exuberant stone swags over the doorways, have been sensitively converted into housing, as has the adjacent parish church, whose tower alone survived the bombs of World War II. Further along the High Street stands **Wapping Police Station**, headquarters of the world's oldest uniformed police force, the Marine Police, founded in the 1790s and now a subdivision of the Met. The current police station is a 1960s building which features funky abstract vertical concrete friezes. Down by the riverside here, at the low-water mark, was **Execution Dock**, where pirates and mutineers were hanged in the conventional manner, after which their bodies were left until three tides had washed over them. The most famous felon to perish here was Captain Kidd, pirate-catcher-turned-pirate, hanged in 1701; the last victims were executed for murder and mutiny in 1830.

Further east, along **Wapping Wall**, beyond Wapping tube station, you'll find the finest collection of nineteenth-century warehouses left in the whole of Docklands, beginning with the gargantuan Metropolitan Wharf, its wrought-iron capstan cranes and pulleys still clearly in evidence. At the far end of Wapping Wall is the venerable *Prospect of Whitby* pub (see p.483), and, opposite, the ivy-clad red-brick **Pumping Station**, built in the 1890s and once chief supplier of hydraulic power to the whole of central London, powering the likes of the bascules of Tower Bridge; it now houses a restaurant and art gallery.

Shadwell Basin, over the swing bridge to the north of the Pumping Station, is one of the last remaining stretches of water that once comprised three interlocking docks, known simply as London Docks and first opened in 1805. Now a water-sports centre, it's enclosed on three sides by new housing finished off in primary reds and blues, a gimmicky touch characteristic of Docklands projects. Rising up majestically behind the houses to the north is **St Paul's Church** (closed except for services), the "sea captains' church", with a Baroque tower.

Limehouse

East of Wapping, **Limehouse** was a major shipbuilding centre in the eighteenth and nineteenth centuries, hub of London's canal traffic and the site of the city's first **Chinatown**, a district sensationalized in Victorian newspapers as a warren of opium and gambling dens, by the likes of Oscar Wilde, Arthur Conan Doyle, Sax Rohmer, and Dickens: "Down by the docks the shabby undertaker's shop will bury you for next to nothing, after the Malay or Chinaman has stabbed you for nothing at all." Wartime bombing and postwar road schemes have all but obliterated Limehouse; the only remnants of the Chinese community are the street names: Canton, Mandarin, Ming and Pekin among them.

If you're heading east from Wapping to Limehouse, you can avoid the busy Highway by taking the Thames Path, which passes below the Legoland ziggurat apartments of **Free Trade Wharf**, eventually bringing you out on **Narrow Street**, Limehouse's sleepy main thoroughfare. Just to the north is one of the playful postmodern portals of the mile-long Limehouse Link tunnel (rumoured to be the world's most expensive piece of road), whose strange sculpture, *Restless Dream*, by Zadok Ben-David, can be admired from the top of Spert Street.

East down Narrow Street, past the giant herring-gull sculpture, several excellent pubs and the entrance to the packed Limehouse Basin, you can see Nicholas Hawksmoor's **St Anne's Church**, rising up beyond the DLR, to the north. Begun in 1714, and dominated by a gargantuan west tower, topped by an octagonal lantern, it boasts the highest church clock in London. The interior was badly damaged by fire in 1850, though it does contain a superb organ built for the Great Exhibition the following year. In the graveyard Hawksmoor erected a strange pyramidal structure carved with masonic symbols, now hopelessly eroded; opposite is a war memorial with relief panels depicting the horrors of trench warfare.

While you're here it's worth walking down Newell Street, to the west, which retains several Georgian houses, while Three Colt Street, to the east, is home to the wonderful Art Nouveau **Limehouse Church Institute**, now converted into flats. Back on the waterfront, the Thames Path continues inexorably towards the Isle of Dogs. A new pedestrian bridge carries the path over the entrance to the tidal inlet of **Limekiln Dock**, overlooked to the north by a picturesque gaggle of listed warehouses, and to the south by the gargantuan Dundee Wharf development, sporting a huge grey free-standing pylon of balconies, which can be accessed by the neighbouring flats. Beyond lies the mock-Egyptian development that houses the *Four Seasons Hotel* (see p.447). The Thames Path will eventually plough its way right round the Isle of Dogs, but for now it's still a bit stop-start once you get past Canary Wharf Pier.

Isle of Dogs

The Thames begins a dramatic horseshoe bend at Limehouse, thus creating the **Isle of Dogs**, a marshy peninsula on which cattle were once fattened for City banquets. The unusual name has prompted various theories as to its origin, from dead dogs washed up on the shore to old royal kennels, though the most plausible is that it's a corruption of the word dyke. In 1802 the peninsula became an island, when a canal was cut to form London's first enclosed trade dock, built to accommodate rum and sugar from the West Indies. With the opening of the Millwall Docks further south, the population rose to 21,000 by the turn of the century. The demise of the docks was slow in coming, but rapid in its conclusion: in 1975, there were 8000 jobs; five years later both docks were closed.

Without doubt, the Isle of Dogs is the geographical and ideological heart of the new Docklands, which reaches its apotheosis in **Canary Wharf**, home to Britain's tallest buildings and, along with West India Quay, the busiest bit of the Isle of Dogs. The rest of the "island" remains surreally lifeless, an uneasy mix of printing works, offices, drab council terraces and 1960s high-rise council estates, encompassed by a horseshoe of new riverside developments – some of them startling, some of them crass, several of them gated. The area's long-term residents continue to see the new developments as a threat rather than a blessing, and a section of them have voiced their discontent in the not-too-distant past by voting for the far-right British National Party.

Canary Wharf

Canary Wharf (ⓦwww.canarywharf.com) – the strip of land in the middle of the former West India Docks, previously a destination for rum and mahogany, later tomatoes and bananas (from the Canary Islands, hence the name) – is the most cohesive and complete Dockland complex. The largest project undertaken by a single developer in Europe, Canary Wharf ran into the ground in the recession of the early 1990s, but has since restarted with a vengeance. Nevertheless, the whole place still feels a bit like a stage-set, a spotlessly clean business quarter with lots of signs to make-believe streets like MacKenzie Walk, Wren Steps and Chancellor Passage.

Canary Wharf's most famous building is Cesar Pelli's landmark tower, now flanked by the glassy HSBC and Citibank towers that stop just short of their older brother, and set to be joined by four more. At 800ft, the Canary Wharf

Tower – officially known as **One Canada Square** – is the highest building in the country. It's also the world's first skyscraper to be clad in stainless steel, and an undeniably impressive sight, both from a distance (its flashing pinnacle is a feature of the horizon at numerous points in London – and out as far as Kent and Essex) and close up. Unless you work here, however – residents include the *Daily Telegraph*, *Daily Mirror* and *Independent* newspapers – there is no public access except to the marble atrium.

Arriving by boat, bus or foot at Canary Wharf, you approach from Westferry Circus, the double-decker roundabout park at the western end of the tree-lined West India Avenue. This, in turn, leads to Cabot Square, centred on a graceful fountain, and, beyond, to the colonnaded offices that terminate at Canada Square.

▲ Canary Wharf

Arriving by DLR at Canary Wharf is even more spectacular, with the rail line cutting right through the middle of the office buildings, spanned by a parabolic steel-and-glass canopy. The station platforms straddle a shopping mall: Cabot Square East features a glass-domed atrium through which you get a great view of Pelli's tower; Cabot Street West gives access to Cabot Square itself. **Arriving by tube**, you get probably the best close-up view of the Pelli tower from the forest of public clocks on West Plaza, right outside Norman Foster's stingray-like entrance to the tube.

West India Quay and around

From Fisherman's Walk, to the north side of Cabot Square, you can cross over a floodlit floating bridge to **West India Quay**, where the last surviving Georgian warehouses of the West India Docks have recently been converted into flats, dockside bars and restaurants. **Warehouse No. 1**, the most impressive of the lot, was built in 1803 for storing rum, sugar, molasses, coffee and cotton and now houses the Museum in Docklands (see below). Out on the water, you can visit one of the boats moored at the quayside, the **SS Robin** (March–Oct Wed–Fri noon–6pm, Sat noon–4pm; free; @www.ssrobin.com), the world's oldest complete steamship, now a photographic gallery and café, but originally launched at the nearby East India Dock in 1890.

Immediately to the west of the warehouses is the old entrance to the West India Docks, heralded by the **Ledger Building** (now yet another *J. D. Wetherspoon* pub), which sports a dinky Doric portico and, round the corner, a splendidly pompous plaque commemorating the opening of the docks from 1800. Opposite, across Hertsmere Road, stands a small, circular, domed building, the surviving one of two guardhouses that flanked the main entrance to the docks; behind it lies the former cooperage, converted in the early 1980s into the **Cannon Workshops**.

To the northeast, behind the Ledger Building, are more little-known remnants of the old docks, among them the stately **Dockmaster's House**, built in 1809 as the Excise Office, later a pub, then a Dock Manager's Office (though never a Dockmaster's) and now an Indian restaurant, with a smart white balustrade. Behind here, on Garford Street, there's a prim row of **Dock Constables' Cottages**, built in pairs in 1802, with the one for the sergeant slightly detached. Before you reach them, you'll pass **Grieg House**, a lovely yellow-and-red-brick building, built in 1903 as part of the Scandinavian Seamen's Temperance Home, with a little cupola and lovely exterior mouldings.

Museum in Docklands

Housed in one of the few original warehouses left on the Isle of Dogs, **Museum in Docklands** (daily 10am–6pm; £5; ✆0870/444 3857, ⊛www.museumin docklands.org.uk) makes a visit to the area well worth the effort. The museum takes a conventional chronological approach, but manages to cover just about every aspect of London's docks, on both sides of the river. Highlights on the top floor include a great model of old London Bridge (see p.210), one side depicting it in 1440, the other around 1600, and the Rhinebeck Panorama, an eight-foot-long watercolour showing the "legal quays" in the 1790s, just before the enclosed docks eased congestion. On the floor below, there are diverse sections on slavery, frost fairs and whaling, a reconstructed warren of late nineteenth-century shops and cobbled streets called "Sailortown", plus mock-ups of a cooperage, a bottling vault and a tobacco-weighing office. Look out for the model of Brunel's *Leviathan*, the excellent wartime film reel and the excellent even-handed coverage of the docks' postwar history. Those with kids should head for Mudlarks, where children can learn a bit about pulleys and ballast, drive a DLR train or simply romp around the soft play area.

Heron Quays and beyond

MacKenzie Walk, on the south side of Cabot Square, is the best place to admire the view over to **Heron Quays**, to the south of Canary Wharf. The modest, low-rise, Swedish-style clapboard buildings were completed way back in 1986, and turned out to be fairly untypical of what was to follow in the rest of the Isle of Dogs. The roundabout to the west sports one of Docklands' more playful monuments: the **Traffic Light Tree**, which features a cluster of traffic signals all flashing madly – a strangely confusing sight for drivers after dark. Impossible to miss, to the southwest, is **Cascades**, a strange wedge of high-rise triangular apartments, erected by CZWG, that's become something of a Docklands landmark. Equally unavoidable is **Millennium Harbour**, a gated development whose weatherboarded top-floor penthouses jut out like air-traffic control towers.

A curved steel footbridge with leaning masts and cables links Heron Quays with **South Quay**, and can swing aside to allow boats to pass through. If you follow dockside walk east from South Quay, you'll eventually reach the **Blue Bridge** that spans the entrance to the South Dock, and gives an unparalleled view of the Millennium Dome (see p.387). You can contemplate the view at more leisure from *The Gun*, an old pub on nearby **Coldharbour**, a street that still retains one or two early nineteenth-century buildings.

Island Gardens and around

Apart from Canary Wharf and its environs, the only other slice of the Isle of Dogs that repays exploration on foot is around **Island Gardens**, Christopher Wren's favourite Thames-side spot, from which he could contemplate his masterpieces, the Royal Naval College and the Royal Observatory, situated across the river in Greenwich and accessible either via the DLR or the 1902 **Greenwich Foot Tunnel**.

If you'd rather explore a little more of Docklands, head west along the river or Westferry Road until you come to **Burrell's Wharf**, a residential development based around the industrial relics of the old Millwall Ironworks, built in the 1830s. The boiler-house chimney survives, as does the Italianate Plate House, where the steel plates for Isambard Kingdom Brunel's 19,000-ton steamship *Leviathan* (later renamed the *Great Eastern*) were manufactured. Built at a cost of £1 million, the *Leviathan* was four times larger than any other ship in the world at the time, but enjoyed a working life of just sixteen years as a passenger liner and cable-layer. The timber piles of the ship's 1857 launching site can still be seen, a little further upstream from Burrell's Wharf.

⑯

The South Bank

For centuries London stopped southwards at the Thames; the **South Bank** was a marshy, uninhabitable place, a popular place for duck-shooting, but otherwise seldom visited. Then, in the eighteenth century, wharves began to be built along the riverbank, joined later by factories, so that by 1905 the *Baedeker* guide book characterized Lambeth (covered in this chapter) and Southwark (covered in the next chapter) as "containing numerous potteries, glass-works, machine-factories, breweries and hop-warehouses". Slums and overhead railway lines added to the grime until 1951, when a slice of **Lambeth**'s badly bombed riverside was used as a venue for the Festival of Britain, the site eventually evolving into the **South Bank Centre**, a concrete arts complex that has never quite managed to win over Londoners.

Since the millennium, however, there has been a concerted effort to regenerate the South Bank. **County Hall**, the old council headquarters, is now home to a variety of tourist attractions from a vast aquarium to a giant amusement arcade. But what really sealed the South Bank's rejuvenation was the arrival of the spectacular **London Eye**, the world's largest observation wheel. At the same time, the British Film Institute built a state-of-the-art **IMAX cinema**; the distinctive **OXO Tower** was turned into homes, workshops and restaurants; and **Hungerford Bridge** was transformed from an overcrowded grimy walkway into a majestic symmetrical double-suspension footbridge.

Suddenly Londoners rediscovered the fact that the South Bank has, in fact, got a lot going for it. Since most of London sits on the north bank of the Thames, the views from the South Bank are the best. Even more importantly, you can happily explore the whole area on foot, free from the traffic noise and fumes that blight so much of central London, and then continue east along the riverside walkway into the regenerated districts of Bankside and Southwark. Only the South Bank Centre itself, first of all these projects, is still undergoing much-needed redevelopment.

Beyond County Hall and the South Bank Centre, there are one or two lesser-known specialist sights worth seeking out, like the **Museum of Garden History**, housed in a deconsecrated church, next door to Lambeth Palace, London residence of the archbishop of Canterbury, and the **Florence Nightingale Museum** within the precincts of St Thomas' Hospital. Larger and more all-encompassing is the **Imperial War Museum**, which includes the country's only permanent exhibition devoted to the Holocaust. To find out about the latest events and exhibitions on the South Bank (and in neighbouring Southwark) visit ⓦwww.london-se1.co.uk.

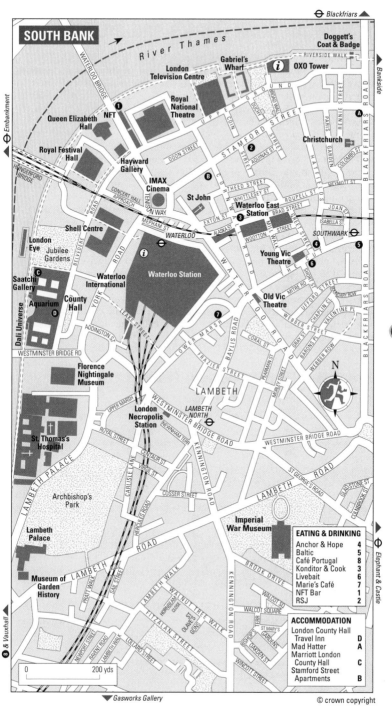

SOUTH BANK

⊖ *Blackfriars* ▲

River Thames

Doggett's
Coat & Badge

Bankside ▶

WATERLOO BRIDGE

London
Television Centre

Gabriel's
Wharf

ℹ OXO Tower

RIVERSIDE WALK

⊖ *Embankment* ◀

Royal
National
Theatre

UPPER GROUND

BRAD STREET

DUCHY STREET

STAMFORD STREET

RENNIE STREET

BLACKFRIARS ROAD

A

FARIS GARDEN

COLOMBO ST

Christchurch

Queen Elizabeth
Hall

❶ NFT

COIN STREET

AQUINAS ST

❷

HATFIELDS

MEYMOTT ST

Royal Festival
Hall

DOON STREET

Hayward
Gallery

THEED STREET

❽

JOAN ST

HUNGERFORD
BRIDGE

CONCERT HALL APPROACH

TENISON WAY

IMAX
Cinema

St John

EXTON ST

WHITTLESEY ST

ROUPELL ST

Waterloo East
Station

❸

WOOTTON

BRAD STREET

CORNWALL ROAD

MILL STREET

GREET STREET

ISABELLA ST

SOUTHWARK ⊖

Shell Centre

MEPHAM ST

WATERLOO

ALASKA ST

❹

❺

London
Eye

Jubilee
Gardens

BELVEDERE ROAD

Waterloo
International

ℹ

Waterloo Station

WATERLOO ROAD

SHORT ST

Young Vic
Theatre

THE CUT

❻

Saatchi
Gallery ❸

YORK ROAD

LEAKE STREET

Old Vic
Theatre

MITRE RD

UFFORD STREET

DIARY ROW

BLACKFRIARS ROAD

Aquarium

County
Hall ❹

ADDINGTON ST

LOWER MARSH

❼

BAYLIS ROAD

WEBBER STREET

GRAY ST

BARONS PL

CHAPLIN C.

VALENTINE PL

WEBBER ROW

Dali Universe

CORAL ST

PEARMAN ST

16

WESTMINSTER BRIDGE RD

FRAZIER STREET

MORLEY STREET

N

Florence
Nightingale
Museum

LAMBETH

WESTMINSTER BRIDGE ROAD

THE SOUTH BANK

UPPER MARSH

London
Necropolis
Station

LAMBETH
NORTH ⊖

NEWNHAM TERR

ST GEORGE'S ROAD

ROYAL STREET

CENTAUR ST

WESTMINSTER BRIDGE ROAD

GLADSTONE ST

St. Thomas's
Hospital

CARLISLE LANE

HERCULES ROAD

TIRRIL ST

COSSER STREET

LAMBETH ROAD

COLNBROOK ST

⊖ *Elephant & Castle* ▶

LAMBETH PALACE ROAD

Archbishop's
Park

Imperial
War Museum

BROOK DRIVE

⊖ & *Vauxhall* ◀

Lambeth
Palace

LAMBETH ROAD

PRATT WALK

SAIL STREET

KENNINGTON ROAD

WALCOT SQ

Museum of
Garden
History

LAMBETH WALK

WALNUT TREE WALK

FITZALAN STREET

HORNGROVE CLOSE

OLAVE'S GDNS

WALCOT SQUARE

ST MARY'S GARDENS

BISHOP'S TERR

DAKDEN ST

259

NEWPORT STREET

RAVEL ROAD

LAMBETH WALK

LOLLARD STREET

KENNINGTON ROAD

WINCOTT STREET

0 ———— 200 yds

▼ *Gasworks Gallery*

© crown copyright

EATING & DRINKING

Anchor & Hope	4
Baltic	5
Café Portugal	8
Konditor & Cook	3
Livebait	6
Marie's Café	7
NFT Bar	1
RSJ	2

ACCOMMODATION

London County Hall Travel Inn	D
Mad Hatter	A
Marriott London County Hall	C
Stamford Street Apartments	B

The South Bank Centre and around

In 1951, the South Bank Exhibition, held on derelict land south of the Thames, formed the centrepiece of the nationwide **Festival of Britain**, an attempt to revive morale postwar by celebrating the centenary of the Great Exhibition (when Britain really did rule over half the world). The most striking features of the site were the ferris wheel (now reincarnated as the London Eye), the saucer-shaped Dome of Discovery (inspiration for the disastrous Millennium Dome), the Royal Festival Hall (which still stands) and the cigar-shaped Skylon tower.

The great success of the festival provided the impetus for the eventual creation of the **South Bank Centre** (◉www.sbc.org.uk), though this failed to capture the imagination of the public in the same way. Instead, the South Bank Centre, comprising the Royal Festival Hall, Queen Elizabeth Hall, the Purcell Room and the Hayward Gallery, became London's much unloved culture bunker, a mess of "weather-stained concrete, rain-swept walkways, urine-soaked stairs", as one critic put it, and the place where the homeless lived out of cardboard boxes in "Cardboard City" in the 1980s.

On the plus side, the South Bank Centre is currently under inspired artistic direction and stands very much at the heart of the capital's arts scene. Its unprepossessing appearance is softened, too, by its riverside location, its avenue of trees, fluttering banners, occasional buskers and skateboarders, and the weekend secondhand bookstalls and café outside the National Film Theatre. There have also been considerable improvements such as better signposting and plans of the area to help punters get around, and further redevelopment is continuing apace.

From the Royal Festival Hall to the Royal National Theatre

The only building left from the 1951 Festival of Britain is the **Royal Festival Hall** or RFH, one of London's main concert venues, which is due to reopen after extensive refurbishment in early 2007. Uniquely, the auditorium is suspended above the open-plan foyer – its curved roof is clearly visible above the main body of the building. The interior furnishings remain fabulously 1950s, and exhibitions and events in the foyer are generally excellent, making this one of the most pleasant South Bank buildings to visit. The outdoor terraces give great views out across the Thames including (from right to left) the Shell-Mex building with its giant clock face, Terry Farrell's postmodern development above Charing Cross station, and the stripy brickwork and pepper pots of Gilbert Scott's former New Scotland Yard building. You can also kill time before a concert in the little-known **Poetry Library** (Tues–Sun 11am–8pm; ◉www.poetrylibrary.org.uk) on Level 5, where you can either browse or, by joining (membership is free), borrow from the library's vast collection of twentieth-century poetry.

> ### Getting to the South Bank
>
> The nearest tube to the South Bank Centre is Waterloo, but the most pleasant way to approach the area is via the rejuvenated Hungerford Bridge from Embankment or Charing Cross tube.

Architecturally, the most depressing parts of the South Bank Centre are the **Queen Elizabeth Hall** (QEH) and the more intimate **Purcell Room**, which share the same foyer and are built in uncompromisingly brutalist 1960s style. The **Hayward Gallery**, which sits behind and on top of all this concrete garbage, is equally repellent from the outside, with the exception of its strange rooftop neon sculpture.

Tucked underneath Waterloo Bridge is the **National Film Theatre**, or NFT (ⓦwww.nft.org.uk), run by the British Film Institute (BFI), which screens London's most esoteric films – some two thousand of them each year – and hosts a variety of talks, lectures and mini-festivals.

On the far side of Waterloo Bridge, looking like a multistorey car park, is Denys Lasdun's **Royal National Theatre** (ⓦwww.nt-online.org) – popularly known as "the National" or NT – an institution first mooted in 1848 but only finally realized in 1976. It contains three separate theatres: the large open-stage Olivier (named after the famous actor, who was also the theatre's first director), the more traditional Lyttelton and the Cottesloe studio theatre. Again, it tends to receive flak from architectural critics, though the theatres themselves are superb, and, in fairness to Lasdun, nobody told him that the concrete exterior would receive a zero maintenance budget. The National offers excellent **backstage tours** around all three theatres (Mon–Sat 3 daily; £5; ☎020/7452 3400) lasting about an hour and a quarter, though you should always ring in advance.

Gabriel's Wharf and the OXO Tower

Beyond the National Theatre, the riverside promenade takes you past another Denys Lasdun building, London Television Centre offices and studios, bringing you eventually to **Gabriel's Wharf** (ⓦwww.gabrielswharf.co.uk), a laid-back collection of lock-up craft shops, brasseries and bars that has a small weekend craft market. It's a pleasant extension to the South Bank Centre's own, rather limited facilities, and one for which the Coin Street Community Builders must be thanked. With the population in this bomb-damaged stretch of the South Bank down from 50,000 at the beginning of the century to 4000 in the early 1970s, big commercial developers were keen to step in and build hotels and office blocks galore. They were successfully fought off, and instead the emphasis has been on projects that combine commercial and community interests.

Coin Street's most high-profile project has been the restoration of the landmark **OXO Tower** (ⓦwww.oxotower.co.uk), an old power station that was converted into a meat-packing factory in the 1930s by Liebig Extract of Meat Company, best known in Britain as the makers of OXO stock cubes. To get round the local council's ban on illuminated advertisements, the company

▲ Gabriel's Wharf

cleverly incorporated the letters into the windows of the main tower, and then illuminated them from within. The building now contains an information centre and contemporary art gallery on the ground floor, plus flats for local residents, sandwiched between a series of retail-workshops for designers on the first and second floors (Tues–Sun 11am–6pm), and a very swanky Harvey Nichols restaurant and brasserie on the top floor. To enjoy the view, however, you don't need to eat or drink here: you can simply take the lift to the eighth-floor **public viewing gallery** (daily 10am–10pm).

Beyond the OXO Tower stands the Seacontainers House, a grotesque 1970s speculative hotel that never came about, now used as offices, and the similarly ugly **Doggett's Coat and Badge** pub. The latter is named after the rowing race from London Bridge to Chelsea, begun in 1715 by an Irish comedian called Thomas Doggett to celebrate the beginning of the Hanoverian dynasty. The race is still held every year in late July, and the winner gets to wear a comical red Hanoverian costume as his prize; for more information, see p.563.

IMAX and Waterloo Station

At the southern end of Waterloo Bridge, the eye-catching glass-drum of the hi-tech **BFI London IMAX Cinema** (⊚www.bfi.org.uk/showing/imax) rises up from the old "Bull Ring" underneath the roundabout. Boasting the largest screen in the country, it's definitely worth experiencing a 3D film here at least once, but as with all IMAX cinemas, it suffers from the fact that very few movies are shot on 70mm film.

On the south side of Hungerford Bridge, overlooking Jubilee Gardens, is the Stalinist-looking **Shell Centre** (officially and poetically entitled the Downstream Building). Built in the 1950s – and the tallest building in London at the time – it's still owned and operated by oil giant Shell, which started life as an East End sea-shell shop in 1833. An overhead walkway leads through the Shell Centre to **Waterloo Station**, originally built in 1848, its grandiose Edwardian facade now lost behind the railway bridge on Mepham Street. Along the western edge of the old station is **Waterloo International**, the main arrival and departure point for Eurostar trains until 2007, when St Pancras will take over as the new terminus. The long, curving platforms are only accessible for passengers about to embark, but you can view the station's snake-like, curving roof, designed by Nicholas Grimshaw, from York Road and from the main station concourse. It was hailed as a major architectural success when it was first unveiled in 1993, but the glass panels have proved unable to withstand the heat, and have since had to be modified.

On the other side of the tracks, at 121 Westminster Bridge Rd, is the turn-of-the-century facade and entrance of the former **London Necropolis Station**, without doubt the city's most bizarre train terminus. It was originally opened in 1854 following one of London's worst outbreaks of cholera, and trains from this station took their hearse-carriages to Brookwood Cemetery in Surrey (at the time, the world's largest cemetery). Brookwood station had separate platforms for Anglicans and Nonconformists and a licensed bar – "Spirits served here", the sign apparently read – but the whole operation was closed down after bomb damage in World War II.

London Eye

London's most prominent new landmark is the **London Eye** (daily: April–Sept 9.30am–10pm; Oct–March 9am–8pm; £12.50; ☎0870/5000 600, ⊚www.ba-londoneye.com), British Airways' magnificently graceful observation wheel which spins slowly and silently over the Thames to the south of the South Bank Centre. Designed by David Marks and Julia Barfield, and standing an incredible 443ft high, it's the largest observation wheel ever built, weighing over 2000 tonnes, yet as simple and delicate as a bicycle wheel. It's constantly in slow motion, which means a full-circle "flight" in one of its 32 pods should take around thirty minutes – that may seem a long time, though in fact it passes incredibly quickly. Unless you know your London landmarks very well, you'll probably need to buy one of the Eye guides (and bring some binoculars if you can). Not surprisingly, you can see right out to the very edge of the city, where the suburbs slip into the countryside – on a good day you can see as far as Windsor – making the wheel one of the few places (apart from a plane window) from which London looks a manageable size. Due to the Eye's popularity, it's advisable to book in advance either over the phone or online; on arrival, you'll still have to queue to be loaded on, but it should only take half an hour maximum.

County Hall

Continuing south, the colonnaded crescent of **County Hall** is the only truly monumental building on the South Bank. Designed to house the London County Council, it was completed in 1933 and enjoyed its greatest moment of fame as the headquarters of the GLC (Greater London Council), under the Labour leadership of Ken Livingstone, or "Red Ken", as the right-wing press loved to call him at the time. The Tories moved in swiftly, abolishing the GLC in 1986, and leaving London as the only European city without an elected authority. In May 2000, Livingstone had the last laugh when he was successfully elected to become London's first mayor, and head of the new Greater London Authority (GLA), which is now housed in City Hall, near Tower Bridge (see p.279). The building is currently home to, among other things, two hotels, several restaurants, a giant aquarium, a glorified amusement arcade called Namco Station and a couple of art galleries. None of the slightly ad hoc attractions that have gravitated here is an absolute must, but they have certainly succeeded in pulling in the crowds, and there are more projects in the pipeline for the near future.

London Aquarium

The basement of County Hall is now home to the **London Aquarium** (daily 10am–6pm or later; £9.75; ☎020/7967 8000, ⓦwww.londonaquarium.co.uk), laid out on two subterranean levels. With some super-large tanks, and everything from dog-face puffers to piranhas, this is an attraction that's pretty much guaranteed to please younger kids. The Touching Pool, where children can actually stroke the (non-sting) rays, is particularly popular. Impressive in scale, the aquarium is fairly conservative in design, though, with no walk-through tanks. Ask at the main desk for the times of the daily presentations.

Dalí Universe

Three giant surrealist sculptures outside County Hall help to advertise the **Dalí Universe** (daily 10am–6pm or later; £9.75; ☎020/7620 2720, ⓦwww.daliuniverse.com), whose entrance lies between the London Eye box office and the London Aquarium. With two museums (in the US and Spain) already devoted to the Catalan artist Salvador Dalí (1904–89), some might question the need for a third. On the other hand, his popularity shows no sign of waning, and as a supreme self-publicist himself – even his moustache was a work of art – he would definitely have approved of the project. The museum has gone out of its way to appear as wacky as its star, but you can't help feeling that he would have done something altogether more outrageous.

There's no denying Dalí was an accomplished and prolific artist, but you'll be disappointed if you come expecting to see his "greatest hits" – those are scattered across the globe. The majority of the works displayed here are little-known bronze and glass sculptures, and various drawings from the many illustrated books which he published, ranging from Ovid to the Marquis de Sade. That said, all his trademark themes are here: melting clocks, lots of Freudian allusions, phalluses and naked Venuses. Aside from these, there's one of the numerous Lobster Telephones which Edward James commissioned for his London home, a copy of his famous Mae West lips sofa and the oil painting from the dream sequence in Hitchcock's movie *Spellbound*.

Saatchi Gallery

County Hall is also home to the **Saatchi Gallery** (Mon–Thurs & Sun 10am–6pm, Fri & Sat 10am–10pm; £8.50; ⊚www.saatchi-gallery.co.uk) of contemporary art, which now occupies the imposing former council chamber on the first floor; its' badly signposted so you may have to ask the way. Charles Saatchi, the Jewish Iraqi-born art collector behind the gallery, was, in fact, the man whose advertising for the Tory government helped topple County Hall's original incumbents, the GLC. Saatchi is perhaps best known as the main promoter of the Young British Artists of the 1990s, who snapped up seminal Turner Prize–nominated works by the likes of Damien Hirst and Tracey Emin. The gallery has no permanent collection, but puts on changing exhibitions drawn from Saatchi's vast collection in this slightly incongruous setting.

Lambeth

South of Westminster Bridge, you leave the South Bank proper behind (and at the same time lose the crowds) and head upstream to what used to be the village of Lambeth (now a borough stretching as far south as Brixton). Vestiges of village atmosphere are notably absent, but there are a few minor sights worth considering, such as **Lambeth Palace** and the **Museum of Garden History**. It's also from this stretch of the riverbank that you get the best views of the Houses of Parliament. Inland, housed in a former lunatic asylum, lies London's most even-handed military museum, the **Imperial War Museum**, which now has a very moving permanent exhibition devoted to the Holocaust.

Florence Nightingale Museum

On the south side of Westminster Bridge, a series of red-brick Victorian blocks and modern accretions make up **St Thomas' Hospital**, which moved here after being ejected from its Georgian premises over by London Bridge in 1862, when the railway came sweeping through Southwark. At the northeastern corner of the hospital, just off Lambeth Palace Road, is the **Florence Nightingale Museum** (Mon–Fri 10am–5pm, Sat & Sun 10am–4.30pm; £5.80; ⊕020/7620

0374, ⑩www.florence-nightingale.co.uk), celebrating the devout woman who revolutionized the nursing profession by establishing the first school of nursing at St Thomas' in 1860 and publishing her *Notes on Nursing*, emphasizing the importance of hygiene, decorum and discipline. The exhibition gives a strictly orthodox and uncritical account, but hits just the right note by putting the two years she spent in the Crimea in the context of a lifetime of tireless social campaigning. Exhibits include the white lantern that earned her the nickname "The Lady with the Lamp", a reconstruction of a Crimean military hospital ward and a slightly disappointing twenty-minute slide show.

Lambeth Palace

A short walk south of St Thomas' stands the imposing red-brick Tudor Gate of **Lambeth Palace** (by appointment Feb–Oct Thurs 11am & 2pm; £5; ☎020/7898 1200, ⑩www.archbishopofcanterbury.org), London residence of the archbishop of Canterbury since 1197. Opened to the general public for the first time ever in 2000, its hour-long guided tours proved so popular that the palace couldn't really cope. At the moment, you have to apply in writing to get on one of the weekly tours, though it's always worth checking beforehand to see if arrangements have changed.

Parts of the newly renovated crypt chapel date back to the original medieval palace, but the most impressive room is, without doubt, the **Great Hall** (now the library), with its oak hammerbeam roof, built after the Restoration by Archbishop Juxon, who made his money in the slave trade, hence the African heads on his coat of arms (and on the bookshelves). On display here are some of the library's most valuable books – a Gutenberg Bible, the Nuremberg Chronicle, "mad" King George III's medical reports – and the grubby leather gloves allegedly handed to Juxon by Charles I on the scaffold. Upstairs, the **Guard Room** boasts an even older, arch-braced timber roof from the fourteenth century, and is the room where Thomas More was brought for questioning before being sent to the Tower (and subsequently beheaded).

Lastly, you get to see the **palace chapel**, where the religious reformer and leader of the Lollards, John Wycliffe, was tried (for the second time) in 1378 for "propositions, clearly heretical and depraved". The door and window frames date back to Wycliffe's day, but the place is somewhat overwhelmed by the ceiling frescoes added in the 1980s, telling the story of the Church of England. Best of all is the fact that you can see the choir screen and stalls put there in the 1630s by Archbishop Laud, and later used as evidence of his Catholic tendencies at his trial (and execution) in 1645.

Museum of Garden History

Just to the south of Lambeth Palace is the Kentish ragstone church of St Mary-at-Lambeth, which retains its fourteenth-century tower but is otherwise a Victorian re-creation. Deconsecrated in 1972, the church now contains a café and an unpretentious little **Museum of Garden History** (daily 10.30am–5pm; free, £3 donation suggested; ☎020/7401 8865, ⑩www.cix.co.uk/~museumgh), which puts particular emphasis on John Tradescant, gardener to James I and Charles I. A tireless traveller in his search for new species, Tradescant set up a museum of curiosities known as "Tradescant's Ark" in Lambeth in 1629. Among the many exhibits were the "hand of a mermaid . . . a natural dragon, above two inches long . . . blood that rained on the Isle of Wight . . . and the Passion of Christ carved very daintily on a plumstone". The less fantastical pieces formed the nucleus of Oxford's Ashmolean Museum, while here you can see a few scant examples: the toothed jaw of a sawfish and a shell-embroidered copy of the habit of Powhatan, "King of Virginia".

A section of the graveyard has been transformed into a small and visually subdued **seventeenth-century garden**, where two interesting sarcophagi lurk among the foliage. The first, which features a sculpted eternal flame, is the resting place of one-time Lambeth resident **Captain Bligh**, the commander of the *Bounty* in 1787 when it set off to transport breadfruit trees from Tahiti to the West Indies for transplanting. On the way home the crew mutinied and set Bligh and eighteen others adrift in a small open boat, with no map and few provisions. Using just a sextant, Bligh navigated the craft 3600 miles to the Indonesian island of Timor, a journey of 48 days. He later became governor of New South Wales, where his subjects once again rebelled, and on his return to England was promoted to vice admiral. The **Tradescant memorial** is more unusual, depicting a seven-headed griffin contemplating a skull, and several crocodiles sifting through sundry ruins flanked by gnarled trees.

Imperial War Museum

From 1815 until 1930, the domed building at the east end of Lambeth Road was the infamous lunatic asylum of Bethlehem Royal Hospital, better known as **Bedlam**. (Charlie Chaplin's mother was among those confined here – the future comedian was born and spent a troubled childhood in nearby Kennington.) When the hospital was moved to Beckenham on the southeast outskirts of London, the wings of the 700-foot-long facade were demolished, leaving just the central building, now home to the **Imperial War Museum** (daily 10am–6pm; free; ☎020/7416 5000, ⊛london.iwm.org.uk), by far the capital's best military museum.

The treatment of the subject is impressively wide-ranging and fairly sober, once you've passed through the Large Exhibits Gallery, with its militaristic display of guns, tanks, fighter planes and a giant V-2 rocket. On the **lower ground floor**, the array of documents and images attesting to the human damage of the last century of war is underlined by a clock which adds two more casualties every minute to its grand total. In addition to the static displays, a good deal of stagecraft is used to convey the misery of combat, with a walk-through World War I trench, and a re-creation of the Blitz in which you wander from an air-raid shelter through bomb-ravaged streets, accompanied by blaring sirens and human voices.

One gallery to head for is **The Children's War**, on the first floor, which focuses on the plight of kids during World War II. With over a million children evacuated to the countryside in September 1939, and some 130,000 losing at least one parent during the course of the war, there are some very moving life stories recounted here. One of the most popular exhibits is the perfectly recreated **1940s House**, a typical two-storey terraced house complete with Morrison shelter in the dining room. Also on the first floor is the **Secret War** gallery, which panders to the popular fascination with the clandestine activities of MI5, MI6 and the SOE (the wartime equivalent of MI6) – expect exploding pencils, trip wires and spy cameras – though it's spoiled by an unrealistically glowing account of the SAS operations in the Gulf War.

Also worth exploring are the museum's **art galleries** on the second floor, which display a changing selection of works by war artists such as Paul Nash, Stanley Spencer, Wyndham Lewis and John Singer Sargent. On the fourth floor, in **Crimes Against Humanity**, a stark minimalist cinema shows a harrowing half-hour film on genocide and ethnic violence in the last century (not recommended for under-16s). Look out, too, for the excellent programme of talks, films, concerts, poetry readings and temporary exhibitions (for which there's usually an admission charge) that the museum puts on.

The Holocaust Exhibition

Many people come to the Imperial War Museum specifically to see the **Holocaust Exhibition** (not recommended for under-14s), which you enter from the third floor. Taking a fairly conventional, sober approach to the subject, the museum has also made a valiant attempt to avoid depicting the victims of the Holocaust as nameless masses, by focusing on individual cases, and interspersing the archive footage with eyewitness accounts from contemporary survivors.

The exhibition pulls few punches, bluntly stating that the pope failed to denounce the anti-Jewish Nuremberg Laws, that writers such as Eliot and Kipling expressed anti-Semitic views, and that the Evian Conference of European powers in 1938 refused to accept any more Jewish refugees. Despite the restrictions of space, there are sections on the extermination of the gypsies, Nazi euthanasia, pre-Holocaust Yiddish culture and the persecution of the Slavs. The genocide, which began with the *Einsatzgruppen* and ended with the gas chambers, is catalogued in painstaking detail, while the problem of "proving" the Final Solution is also addressed, in a room that emphasizes the complexity of the Nazi bureaucracy, which, allied to an ideology of extermination, made the Holocaust not just possible but inevitable.

The centrepiece of the museum is a vast, all-white, scale model of (what is, in fact, only a very small slice of) Auschwitz-Birkenau, showing what happened to the 2000 Hungarian Jews who arrived at the camp from the town of Berehovo in May 1944. The significance of this transport is that, uniquely, photographs, taken by the SS, of the selection process meted out on these particular arrivals managed to survive the war. In the alcoves overlooking the model, which has a pile of discarded possessions from the camps as its backdrop, survivors describe their first impressions of Auschwitz. This section is especially harrowing, and it's as well to leave yourself enough time to listen to the reflections of camp survivors at the end, as they attempt to come to terms with the past.

Southwark

In Tudor and Stuart London, the chief reason for crossing the Thames, to what is now **Southwark** (ⓦwww.visitsouthwark.com), was to visit the disreputable Bankside entertainment district around the south end of London Bridge. Four hundred years on, Londoners have rediscovered the habit of heading for the area, thanks to the wealth of new attractions – with the charge led by the mighty **Tate Modern** on Bankside – that now pepper the riverside from Blackfriars Bridge to Tower Bridge and beyond. Several smaller attractions sit in the shadow of the Tate: the **Millennium Bridge**, central London's first new river crossing for over a century, which provides a wonderful pedestrian link to the City and St Paul's; **Shakespeare's Globe Theatre**, a faithful reconstruction of one of the Elizabethan theatres for which Southwark was once famous; and a couple of specialist museums dedicated to wine, and tea and coffee.

Further east, there's a gruesome museum on the site of the original **Clink Prison**; a replica of Drake's Tudor galleon, the **Golden Hinde**; and, in **South-**

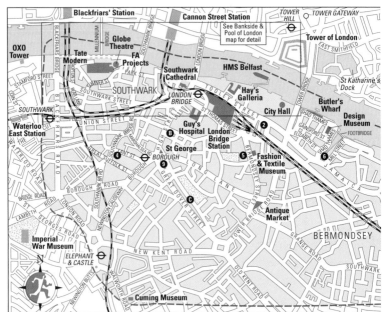

wark Cathedral, some of the city's best-preserved Gothic architecture. At this point, the shops, cafés and stalls of nearby **Borough Market**, which has become something of a gourmet food haven, provide a welcome refuelling stop. East of London Bridge, in what was once the **Pool of London** and the busiest section of the Thames, you'll find the wartime cruiser **HMS Belfast** and, on the riverbank, **City Hall**, Norman Foster's striking new headquarters for London's mayor and assembly. Meanwhile, on Tooley Street, which runs parallel to the river, there are regular queues outside the ever-popular **London Dungeon**.

Bermondsey, to the east of Tower Bridge, marks the beginning of Docklands' south-bank development, which, though less well known than Canary Wharf, contains several interesting warehouse conversions, including a number of commercial art galleries and some of the developers' better stabs at new architecture. **Butler's Wharf**, in particular, is a thriving little warehouse development, centred on the excellent **Design Museum**. Further east, **Rotherhithe** clings onto its old seafaring identity despite the demise of the nearby docks and its subsequent new housing.

Bankside

Bankside has a history as long as that of the City. It started out as a Roman **red-light district**, and its brothels continued to do a thriving illegal trade until 1161, when they were licensed by royal decree. This measure imposed various rules and restrictions on the prostitutes, who could now be fined three

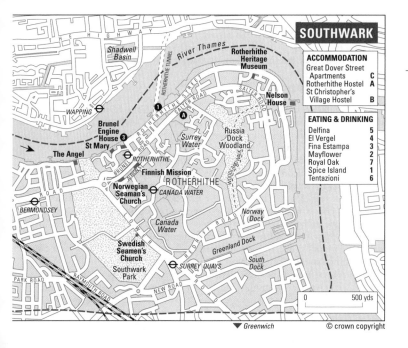

SOUTHWARK

ACCOMMODATION

Great Dover Street Apartments	C
Rotherhithe Hostel	A
St Christopher's Village Hostel	B

EATING & DRINKING

Delfina	5
El Vergel	4
Fina Estampa	3
Mayflower	2
Royal Oak	7
Spice Island	1
Tentazioni	6

0   500 yds

▼ *Greenwich*   © crown copyright

shillings for "grimacing to passers-by", but were given Sunday mornings off in order to attend church. The women wore red-and-white-striped caps and white aprons, and were known as "Winchester Geese", since the land was owned by the bishop of Winchester. The Church made a small fortune out of the rent until Henry VIII, of all people, closed the bawdy houses down. In Elizabethan times, Bankside once more became the most nefarious area in London, known as "Stew's Bank" for its brothels or "stewhouses", and studded with **bull- and bear-pits**. Pepys recalls seeing "some good sport of the bulls tossing of the dogs; one into the very boxes", but opinion was by then inclining towards Evelyn's description of the sport as a "rude and dirty pastime" and in 1682 the last bear garden was closed down.

Theatres – another disreputable institution banned in the City – also flourished on Bankside, with no fewer than four during the reign of James I: the Swan, built in 1587, with Edward Alleyn (founder of Dulwich College) as the lead actor and Christopher Marlowe as its main playwright; the **Rose**, built in 1595, its foundations still extant on Park Street; the Hope, built in 1613, which doubled as a bear garden and theatre; and the **Globe**, the Burbages' theatre (originally built in Shoreditch in 1576, dismantled in 1599 and erected on the south side of Park Street), where Shakespeare put on his greatest plays, now reconstructed on New Globe Walk. The theatres lasted barely half a century before being closed down by the Puritans, who considered them "chapels of Satan". With the Restoration, the focus of the theatre scene, and its accompanying vices, moved to Covent Garden, and Southwark faded from the limelight.

By the nineteenth century, warehouses and factories occupied much of the land closest to the river, while countless houses were demolished during the construction of the new London Bridge and the laying of the train tracks. As a result, little remains above ground to remind you of Southwark's most interesting pre-industrial period. The **Clink Prison Museum** and the rebuilt **Shakespeare's Globe Theatre** go some way towards remedying this, as do **Southwark Cathedral** and the *George Inn*, London's last surviving galleried coaching inn, but the area's biggest attraction by far is the **Tate Modern** gallery, which is housed in the former Bankside power station.

Tate Modern

Architecturally dominating Bankside, the awesome **Tate Modern** is an absolute must for anyone visiting or living in London. Originally designed as an oil-fired power station by Giles Gilbert Scott, this austere, brick-built "cathedral of power" was up and running for just sixteen years, before being closed down in 1980. In the late 1990s, it was transformed by the Swiss architectural duo Herzog & de Meuron into the world's largest modern-art gallery, displaying works by all the major artists of the twentieth century, including Dalí, Duchamp, Giacometti, Matisse, Mondrian, Picasso, Pollock, Rothko and Warhol.

When it comes to **displaying the permanent collection**, Tate Modern's curators have eschewed the old chronological approach, and gone instead for hanging works according to (very broad) themes. Within these, the odd room is devoted to an "-ism", an individual artist, a video or an installation, and, after a short time, you're likely to have forgotten the original theme. The gallery tends to rehang bits of the collection every six months, so it's impossible to say exactly what will be on display; the account below is therefore very selective and specific works may well have returned to storage. The themes, however, are here to stay for the moment.

Visiting Tate Modern

The **opening times** for Tate Modern are daily 10am–6pm, with late-night opening on Friday and Saturday until 10pm; admission to the permanent collection is free (☏020/7887 8000, ⊛www.tate.org.uk). The gallery is worth visiting for its architecture alone, so to appreciate it fully, approach from the Millennium Bridge, since the river crossing gives you an unobstructed view. From the bridge, the nearest entrance is the **North Entrance** underneath the chimney, which brings you out at Level 2. The best way to enter, however, is via the ramp at the **West Entrance**, allowing you to fully appreciate the stupefying enormity of the main **turbine hall**, which sits on Level 1, below the Thames, yet rises to a height of 115ft, and is now used to display large-scale sculptural works. Level 1 is also where you'll find the **information desk**, and, on the opposite side, the museum's **cloakroom** and giant **bookshop**.

Escalators from this floor lead straight up to Level 3, which, along with Level 5, contains the **permanent collection**; Level 4, between the two, is used for large-scale temporary exhibitions, for which there is an entrance fee. **Audioguides** to the permanent collection are available for £2. The galleries themselves are pleasingly varied in size, lighting and colour scheme (though the majority are white). Be warned, however, that you've got to have stamina to wade through more than one or two levels in any one visit, so if there's something you really want to see, go there first before you run out of energy. There are several little alcoves with seating and art books to look at if you need a rest.

It's also worth venturing out onto the **outdoor balconies**, on levels 4 and 6, over-looking the Thames. For the moment, though, the best views of the lot are from Level 7, the lightbeam that sits on top of the power station: as well as the pricey restaurant, there's a bar with a few seats and sofas where you can have a drink and take in the view over St Paul's and the City. The plan is that, one day, you should be able to ascend the building's 325-foot-high central **chimney**.

Level 3

Landscape/Matter/Environment, on Level 3, is as good a place as any to start. The Tate's huge expansion has allowed many works, hitherto seldom seen, to escape from the vaults, but there are also plenty of old favourites, like **Mark Rothko**'s abstract "Seagram Murals". Commissioned by the swanky *Four Seasons* restaurant in New York, they were withheld by Rothko, who decided he didn't wish his art to be a mere backdrop to the recreation of the wealthy, and first exhibited at the Tate shortly after the artist's suicide. Also in this section are several works by **Bonnard**, **Cézanne** and **Vuillard**, a jaunty paper collage by **Matisse**, executed towards the end of his life when he was wheelchair-bound, Yves Klein's blue painting *IKB79* and a smattering of works by the major Surrealists: **Ernst**, **Miró** and **Dalí**. Look out, too, for **Joseph Beuys**, whose bizarre choice of materials derives directly from his wartime experiences, when his plane crashed in the Crimea and he was saved by local Tartars, who cocooned him in felt and fat. If there is a problem with the Tate's mix-and-match approach, it's that the early twentieth-century paintings, some still in their old-fashioned gilded frames, struggle to compete with the attention-grabbing installations; **Monet**'s *Water-lilies*, in particular, would probably be happier back in the National Gallery.

Over in **Still Life/Object/Real Life**, there's a replica of **Marcel Duchamp**'s seminal *Fountain*, a urinal signed "R. Mutt, 1917" which was the first "ready-made", a non-art object which becomes "art" only because it sits in a museum. Taking this idea one stage further, **Kurt Schwitters** put together works such as an "assemblage of discarded rubbish and printed ephemera", for as he himself said, "everything the artist spits is art". A look at **Tony Cragg**'s "stack

Millennium Bridge

Though by no means the only millennial project to run into problems, the sleek, stainless-steel **Millennium Bridge** was the only one to have literally a rocky start. Not finished in time for the official opening by the Queen, the bridge was closed indefinitely, shortly after opening to the public in June 2000, due to the worrying way in which it (and the pedestrians crossing it) bounced up and down. All of which was just a little embarrassing for the high-profile triumvirate who'd helped design it: sculptor Anthony Caro, architect Norman Foster and engineers Ove Arup. Several modifications, and the best part of two years later, London's first new bridge across the Thames since Tower Bridge opened in 1894, and its first-ever designed for pedestrians only, was successfully reopened, allowing folk to cross the Thames from the steps of Peter's Hill, below St Paul's Cathedral, to Tate Modern.

sculptures" of flotsam and jetsam reveals the durability of Dadaism; while one work that has captured a lot of interest is **Michael Craig Martin**'s glass of water on a shelf, called *An Oak Tree*, now exhibited complete with the artist's defence of the work's title.

Level 5

If anything, Level 5 has the edge over Level 3 for sheer variety. In **History/Memory/Society**, pretty much anything (revolutionary) goes, from Soviet graphics and interwar documentaries to neon sculptures and newspaper cuttings. Current highlights include the utopian abstract works of **Mondrian** and the De Stijl movement; **Picasso**'s *Weeping Woman*, which is both a portrait of his lover Dora Maar and a heartfelt response to the Spanish Civil War; and several works by the leading protagonists of **Pop Art**, Andy Warhol and Roy Lichtenstein. The captions, curators' notes and, occasionally, other artists' eulogies that accompany the paintings are by turns revealing, irritating and unintention-

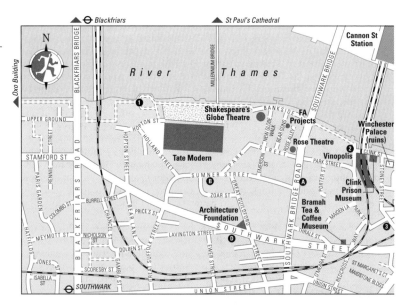

ally hilarious. Confronted by **Lucio Fontana**'s *Spatial Concept "Waiting"*, we are told (without a hint of irony) that "Fontana first slashed his canvases with a razor blade in 1958, although he had been making holes in them since 1949".

In **Nude/Action/Body**, there's some top-class sculpture: an early Cubist bust by Picasso and **Modigliani**'s African-style carved heads. **Stanley Spencer**'s *Double Nude* remains shockingly explicit – had it been publicly exhibited when it was painted, in 1937, it would have almost certainly resulted in criminal prosecution. Equally unsparing in their depiction of the human body are the nude portraits of Britain's leading living painter, **Lucien Freud**.

Shakespeare's Globe Theatre

Dwarfed by the Tate Modern, but equally spectacular in its own way, **Shakespeare's Globe Theatre** (☎020/7902 1400, ⊛www.shakespeares-globe.org) is a more or less faithful 1990s reconstruction of the polygonal playhouse where most of the Bard's later works were first performed. The theatre, which boasts the first new thatched roof in central London since the Great Fire, puts on plays by Shakespeare and his contemporaries, using only natural light and the minimum of scenery. The season runs from mid-May to mid-September, and the performances so far have managed to be both fun, historically authentic, more often than not, critically acclaimed. Plays are regularly performed uncut, sometimes with men playing all the parts, sometimes women, sometimes mixed, and with short intervals between each of the five acts. Seats start at around £13, though you can pick up a "groundling", or standing, ticket for £5; for more details, see p.520.

To find out more about Shakespeare and the history of Bankside, the Globe's stylish **exhibition** (daily: May–Sept 9am–noon & 12.30–5pm; Oct–April 10am–5pm; £9; ☎020/7902 1400), to the west of the theatre, is well worth a visit. It begins by detailing the long campaign by the single-minded American

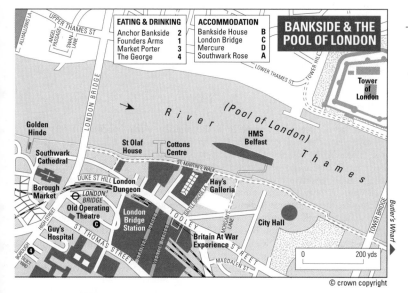

© crown copyright

The discovery of the remains of the **Rose Theatre** (ⓦ www.rosetheatre.org.uk), underneath an office block on Park Street in 1989, helped enormously in the reconstruction of the Globe. After an exhaustive campaign to save the site, the finds have been successfully preserved in the basement of the new building. The outline of the theatre can be clearly traced in the foundations, but most of the remains are currently flooded to preserve them until sufficient funds can be found for a full excavation. Close by the Rose exhibition, there's a plaque showing where the Globe actually stood, before it was destroyed in a fire started by a spark from a cannon during a performance of Shakespeare's *Henry VIII*. Tours of the Rose Theatre form part of the package offered by the Globe exhibition on summer afternoons (May–Sept daily 12.30–5pm; £9).

actor Sam Wanamaker (1919–93) to have the Globe rebuilt, but it's the imaginative interactive exhibits that really hit the spot. You can have a virtual play on period musical instruments such as the crumhorn or sackbut, prepare your own edition of Shakespeare and feel the thatch, hazelnut shell and daub used to build the theatre. There are even booths in which you can record and compare your own rendition of key speeches with those of the stage greats, and the occasional live demo on the exhibition's stage. Visitors also get taken on an informative half-hour **guided tour** round the theatre itself, except in the afternoons during the summer season, when you get to visit the exhibition and the Rose Theatre instead (see box).

⑰ Vinopolis

Housed in the former wine vaults under the railway arches on Clink Street, **Vinopolis** (Mon, Fri & Sat noon–9pm; Tues–Thurs & Sun noon–6pm; £11.50; ☎0870/241 4040, ⓦ www.vinopolis.co.uk) is a strange fish: part wine bar-restaurant, part wine retailers (there's a branch of the excellent Majestic Wines round the back), part museum. The focus of the complex is the "Wine Odyssey", a light-hearted, rather disjointed, trot through the world's wine regions, for which it's pretty much essential to pay the extra £2 for an audioguide. The visual gags – you get to tour round the Italian vineyards on a Vespa – are a bit lame, and tickets are pricey, but do include five wine tastings. The staff diligently use spittoons, but most visitors seem quite happy to get slowly inebriated.

Clink Street

Round the corner from Vinopolis, in the suitably dismal confines of dark and narrow Clink Street, is the **Clink Prison Museum** (daily 10am–6pm or later; £4; ☎020/7403 0900, ⓦ www.clink.co.uk), built on the site of the former Clink Prison, and the origin of the expression "in the clink". The prison began as a dungeon under the bishop of **Winchester's Palace** for disobedient clerics – the rose window of the palace's Great Hall has survived and been restored just east of the prison – and later it became a dumping ground for heretics, debtors, prostitutes and a motley assortment of Bankside lowlife, before being burnt to the ground during the Gordon Riots of 1780. The exhibition features a handful of prison-life tableaux and dwells on the torture and grim conditions within, but, given the rich history of the place, it is a disappointingly, a lacklustre display.

Further east down Clink Street, an exact replica of the **Golden Hinde** (daily

10am–5.30pm, but phone ahead; £3.50; ☎0870/011 8700, ⑩www.golden hinde.co.uk), the galleon in which Francis Drake sailed around the world from 1577 to 1580, nestles in St Mary Overie Dock. This version was launched in 1973, and circumnavigated the world for the next twenty years or so, before eventually settling on a permanent mooring here in Southwark. The ship is surprisingly small and, with a crew of eighty-plus, must have been cramped, to say the least. There's a lack of interpretive panels, so it's worth trying to coincide with one of the regular tours, during which costumed guides show you the ropes, so to speak, and demonstrate activities such as firing a cannon or using the ship's toilet. Always phone ahead, though, to check that a group hasn't booked the place up.

Southwark Cathedral

East of Clink Street, just before London Bridge, stands **Southwark Cathedral** (Mon–Fri 7.30am–6pm, Sat & Sun 8.30am–6pm; free; ⑩www.dswark .org/cathedral), built in the thirteenth century as the Augustinian priory church of St Mary Overie. It's a minor miracle that the church survived the nineteenth century, which saw the east-end chapel demolished to make way for London Bridge, railways built within a few feet of the tower and some very heavy-handed Victorian restoration. As if in compensation, the church was given cathedral status in 1905, and has since gone from strength to strength – if you're feeling peckish, the cathedral refectory serves tasty food.

The cathedral's **interior** has had a lot of money spent on it, its walls now a warm honeyed hue. Of the original thirteenth-century church, only the choir and retrochoir now remain, separated by a beautiful, high, stone Tudor screen; they are probably the oldest Gothic structures left in London and were used by the bishop of Winchester as a court – those sentenced ended up in the Clink (see opposite). The nave was entirely rebuilt in the nineteenth century, though several of the bosses from the original wooden ceiling are displayed against the west wall; among the most interesting is the pelican drawing blood from its breast to feed its young (a symbol of Christ's sacrifice).

The cathedral contains numerous intriguing **monuments**: from a thirteenth-century oak effigy of a knight, to one dedicated to the 51 people who died when the *Marchioness* pleasure boat collided with a barge on the Thames in 1989. Others include the brightly painted tomb of poet John Gower, Chaucer's contemporary, in the north aisle, his head resting on the three

▲ Southwark Cathedral

books he wrote – one in Latin, one in French and one in English. The quack doctor Lionel Lockyer has a humorous epitaph in the north transept, and, nearby, there's a chapel dedicated to John Harvard, who was baptized here in 1607. In the south aisle, an early twentieth-century memorial to Shakespeare (he was a worshipper in the church and his brother is buried here) depicts the Bard in green alabaster lounging under a stone canopy. Above the memorial is a postwar stained-glass window featuring a whole cast of characters from the plays.

Borough Market

Medieval Southwark, also known as **The Borough**, was London's first suburb, clustered round the southern end of London Bridge, London's only bridge over the Thames from Roman times until 1750 (see p.210), and thus the only route south. London Bridge was the most obvious place for the Kent farmers to sell their goods to the City grocers, and there's been a thriving market hereabouts since medieval times. The present **Borough Market** (ⓦwww.boroughmarket .org.uk) is squeezed beneath the railway arches between the High Street and the cathedral. The early-morning wholesale fruit and vegetable market winds up around 9am and is one of the few still trading under its original Victorian wrought-iron shed. It's also recently undergone a transformation from scruffy obscurity to a small foodie haven, with permanent outlets such as Neal's Yard Dairy and Konditor & Cook, joined by gourmet daytime market stalls on Fridays (noon–6pm) and, particularly, Saturdays (9am–4pm).

Bramah Tea and Coffee Museum

Endearingly ramshackle and well worth a visit, the **Bramah Tea and Coffee Museum** (daily 10am–6pm; £4; ☎020/7403 5650, ⓦwww.bramahmuseum .co.uk) is a block or so west of Borough Market at 40 Southwark St. Founded in 1992 by Edward Bramah, whose family have been in the tea business for nearly 250 years, the emphasis is firmly on tea, several varieties of which you can smell and touch. There's an incredibly impressive array of teapots, from Meissen and Chinese porcelain to Clarice Cliff and novelty ones in the shape of planes, camels and even car radiators, plus the largest teapot in the world; ditto, coffee machines, from huge percolator siphons to espresso contraptions spanning the twentieth century.

Tea arrived in London only a decade or two after coffee, but it quickly established itself as the national drink, and remained unchallenged until the 1950s, when the espresso arrived in Soho's trendy cafés. At the same time, the South American coffee producers foisted instant coffee on the unsuspecting public. The tea companies retaliated with tea bags, and the end result is that the British drink the worst tea and coffee in the world. Mr Bramah is quite religious about his mission to try and convert the public to proper tea and coffee, so you can be sure of enjoying a good cup of either beverage at the museum café.

Architecture Foundation

The **Architecture Foundation** (ⓦwww.architecturefoundation.org.uk) is currently building a new headquarters on the corner of Southwark Street and Great Guildford Street, the first London project by the controversial Baghdad-born artist Zaha Hadid. Due to open in 2006, the building will house exhibition and events space, offices and a bar.

Borough High Street

As the main road south out of the City, **Borough High Street** was for centuries famous for its **coaching inns**. Chaucer's Canterbury pilgrims set off from *The Tabard* (in Talbot Yard), but by Dickens' time "these great rambling queer old places", as he called them, were closing down. The only extant coaching inn is the **George Inn**, situated in a cobbled yard east off the High Street, dating from 1677 and now owned by the National Trust. Unfortunately, the Great Northern Railway demolished two of the three original galleried fronts, but the lone survivor is a remarkable sight nevertheless, and is still run as a pub (see p.484).

Opposite Borough tube station, at the southernmost end of Borough High Street, is **St George the Martyr**, built in the 1730s, where Little Dorrit got married in the Dickens novel of the same name, much of which is set in the area. St George's has four clock faces: three white and illuminated at night; one black and pointing towards Bermondsey, whose parishioners refused to give money for the church. Beyond St George's, a wall survives from the **Marshalsea**, the city's main debtors' prison, where Dickens' father was incarcerated for six months in 1824. (It, too, features in *Little Dorrit*.)

Old Operating Theatre Museum and Herb Garret

The most educative and the strangest of Southwark's museums is the **Old Operating Theatre Museum and Herb Garret** (daily 10.30am–5pm; £4; ☎020/7955 4791, ⊛www.thegarret.org.uk) on St Thomas Street. Built in 1821 up a spiral staircase at the top of a church tower, where the hospital apothecary's herbs were stored, this women's operating theatre was once adjacent to the women's ward of St Thomas' Hospital, which has since moved to Lambeth. Despite being entirely gore-free, the museum is as stomach-churning as the nearby London Dungeon, for this theatre dates from the pre-anaesthetic era.

The surgeons who used this room would have concentrated on speed and accuracy (most amputations took less than a minute), but there was still a thirty percent mortality rate, with many patients simply dying of shock, and many more from bacterial infection (about which very little was known). This much is clear from the design of the theatre itself, which has no sink and is made almost entirely of mahogany and pine, which would have harboured bacteria even after vigorous cleaning. Sawdust was sprinkled on the floor to soak up the blood and prevent it dripping onto the heads of the worshippers in the church below. In the herbarium section, you can read up on the medicinal uses of the herbs stored and have a go at making your pills.

Opposite the museum stands **Guy's Hospital**, founded in 1726 by Thomas Guy, a governor of St Thomas' Hospital, with the money he made on the City money markets. As well as occupying a singularly ugly 35-storey tower block, the hospital also retains some of its original eighteenth-century buildings, in particular the courtyard on St Thomas Street, and a pretty little **Hospital Chapel**, built in the 1770s on the west side of the courtyard, with raked balconies on three sides, and cheerful light-blue paintwork throughout. You can wander in to admire the giant marble and alabaster tomb of the founder, who's depicted welcoming a new patient to the hospital, though in fact Guy died a year before the first patients were admitted.

The Pool of London

The central section of the Thames from London Bridge to just past Tower Bridge was known for centuries as the **Pool of London** (⊚www.pooloflondon .co.uk), "the centre from which the commerce of England radiates all over the globe", as *Baedeker* grandly put it in 1905. The stretch of river frontage between London Bridge and Tower Bridge was occupied by Hay's Wharf, the largest of the "sufferance wharves" begun in 1651 to ease the volume of shipping trying to dock at the "legal quays" on the north bank. So much of the city's food – in particular teas, wines, grain, butter, bacon and cheese – was stored here that the area became known as "London's Larder".

Eventually, congestion got so bad, and the ships so big, that London built its own enclosed docks (see p.248) to cut down the traffic within the Pool. Badly bombed in the Blitz, the wharves never really recovered and, for the first time for a millennium or more, there is now very little river traffic in the Pool. Hay's Wharf was eventually rebuilt as offices and shops, most successfully in Hay's Galleria; **HMS Belfast**, the cruiser moored nearby, is the only permanent maritime link. The area's most popular attraction, however, is the Hammer-horror **London Dungeon**, tucked under the railway arches under London Bridge Station.

From London Bridge to Hay's Galleria

London Bridge's proximity to the City made this one of the first targets of the developers, keen to transform the wharves and warehouses into a buzzing new business environment. Redevelopment began inauspiciously in the mid-1980s with the pink granite monstrosity of No. 1 London Bridge, and looks set to go mad with the arrival of the **"Shard of Glass"** (⊚www.londonbridgetower. com), Renzo Piano's tapered tower block, due for completion in 2009 and, at over 1000ft, destined to become Britain's tallest building. Close by, emblazoned with "Hay's Wharf" in giant gold lettering, is **St Olaf House**, a 1930s Art Deco warehouse which boasts a wonderful black and gold mosaic of the Norwegian king, St Olaf, who assisted Ethelred the Unready in his defence of London against the Danes.

Beyond is the Cottons Centre, another spectacularly ugly office development, with mustard-coloured cladding, and **Hay's Galleria**, a shopping precinct built over what used to be Hay's Dock. The idea of filling in the curvaceous dock and covering it with glass and steel barrel-vaulting, while retaining the old Victorian warehouses on three sides, is an effective one. The pastiche of phoney market barrows, *pétanque* pitch, red phone boxes and the gimmicky kinetic sculpture at the centre, however, is less successful. If you've got kids, though, be sure to pop into the Christmas Shop, near the entrance, where it's Christmas all year round.

London Dungeon

The vaults beneath the railway arches of London Bridge train station, on the south side of Tooley Street, are now occupied by the Gothic horrors of the **London Dungeon** (daily: March to mid-July & Sept/Oct 10.30am–5.30pm; mid-July to Aug 9.30am–7.30pm; Nov–Feb 10.30am–5pm; £15.50; ⊙020/7403 7221, ⊚www.thedungeons.com), one of the city's major crowd-pleasers – to avoid the inevitable queue, buy your ticket online. Young teenagers and the credulous probably get the most out of the life-sized waxwork tableaux of folk being hanged, drawn, quartered and tortured, the general hysteria being boosted by actors dressed as top-hatted Victorian vampires, executioners and monks pouncing out of the darkness. Visitors are led into the labyrinth, an old-fashioned mirror maze, before being herded through a series of live action scenarios, starting with an eighteenth-century courtroom, where they're condemned to the "River of Death" boat ride and compelled to endure the "Jack the Ripper Experience", an exploitative trawl through post-mortem photos and wax mock-ups of the victims. And finally it's the "Great Fire of London", in which visitors get to experience the heat and the smell of the plague-ridden city, before being forced to walk through a revolving tunnel of flames.

Britain at War Experience

A little further east along Tooley Street is **Winston Churchill's Britain at War Experience** (daily: April–Sept 10am–6pm; Oct–March 10am–5pm; £8.50; ☎020/7403 3171, ⊛www.britainatwar.co.uk), which, despite its jingoistic name, is an illuminating insight into the stiff-upper-lip London mentality during the Blitz. It begins with a rickety elevator ride down to a mock-up of a tube air-raid shelter (minus the stale air and rats), in which a contemporary newsreel cheerily announces "a great day for democracy" as bombs drop indiscriminately over Germany. This is just a prelude to the museum's hundreds of wartime artefacts, posters and old shop fronts, all looking a bit worn around the edges, but still fascinating. You can sit in an Anderson shelter beneath the chilling sound of the V-1 "doodlebugs", tune in to contemporary radio broadcasts and walk through the chaos of a just-bombed street – pitch-dark, noisy and smoky. As the railway arches are up for redevelopment, the museum is currently set to close in 2008.

HMS Belfast

Permanently moored opposite Southwark Crown Court, the camouflage-painted **HMS Belfast** (daily: March–Oct 10am–6pm; Nov–Feb 10am–5pm; £8; ☎020/7940 6300, ⊛hmsbelfast.iwm.org.uk) was an 11,550-ton World War II cruiser in the Royal Navy. Armed with six torpedoes, and six-inch guns with a range of over fourteen miles, the *Belfast* spent the first two years of the war in the Royal Naval shipyards, after being hit by a mine in the Firth of Forth at the beginning of hostilities. It later saw action in the 1943 Battle of North Cape and assisted in the D-Day landings before being decommissioned after the Korean War, becoming an outpost of the Imperial War Museum (see p.266).

The fun bit, though, is exploring the maze of cabins and scrambling up and down the vertiginous ladders of the ship's seven confusing decks, which could accommodate a crew of over nine hundred. Be sure to check out the punishment cells, in the most uncomfortable part of the ship, and to make it down to the airlocked Boiler Room, a spaghetti of pipes and valves, from which there was very little chance of escape in the event of the boat being hit. If you want to know more about the boat's history, head for the Exhibition Flat in Zone 5; next door, in the Life at Sea room, you can practice your Morse code and knots, and listen to accounts of naval life on board.

City Hall

Developers are currently busy completing the redevelopment of the land east of the *Belfast* to Tower Bridge, with big glassy offices, a stream and a new park on Potters Fields. The centrepiece is, however, Norman Foster's startling glass-encased **City Hall** (Mon–Fri 8am–8pm, plus occasional weekends; ☎020/7983 4000, ⓦwww.london.gov.uk), which looks like a giant car headlight or fencing mask. Headquarters for the Greater London Authority and the mayor of London, it's a "green" building that uses a quarter of the energy a high-specification office would normally use. Visitors are welcome to stroll around the building and watch the London Assembly proceedings from the second floor. On certain weekends, access is also possible to "London's Living Room" on the ninth floor, from which there's a great view over the Thames.

Bermondsey

Famous in the Middle Ages for its Cluniac abbey, and later frequented for its pleasure gardens and spa, **Bermondsey**, to the east of Tower Bridge, changed enormously in the nineteenth century. In 1836, the London and Greenwich Railway – the city's first – was built through the district, supported by 878 brick arches stretching for four miles. At the same time teeming riverside wharves and overcrowded tenements brought some of the worst social conditions in Victorian London, as Charles Kingsley discovered: "O God! What I saw! People having no water to drink but the water of the common sewer which stagnates full of . . . dead fish, cats and dogs."

With the closure of the docks in the 1960s, the streets to the north of Jamaica Road were designated part of the Docklands regeneration scheme. Some areas, like the **Butler's Wharf** warehouse development, were finished pretty quickly, before the money ran out at the end of the 1980s; other sections are only now being redeveloped. The area's prime attraction is the excellent **Design Museum** in Butler's Wharf, along with Zandra Rhodes' new **Fashion and Textile Museum** and the Friday-morning Bermondsey **antique market**, also known confusingly as the New Caledonian Market, since this is the descendant of the prewar flea market that used to take place off Islington's Caledonian Road.

Butler's Wharf

In contrast to the brash offices upstream towards London Bridge, the new developments to the east of Tower Bridge have attempted to retain some semblance of the historical character of the area. This is particularly true of **Butler's Wharf**, one of the densest networks of Victorian warehousing in London, where the policy has been one of restoring the old buildings where possible, while subtly enhancing the area with new modernist and postmodernist constructions. This approach is infinitely preferable to the old scorched-earth policy, and makes this one of the most enjoyable parts of Docklands to explore.

The best place to start is on Tower Bridge itself (for more on which, see p.221), the only place from where you can get a really good view of the old **Anchor Brewhouse**, which produced Courage ales from 1789 until 1982. A cheery, ad hoc sort of building, with a boiler-house chimney at one end and malt-mill tower and cupola at the other, it has been sensitively converted into apartments. Next door is the original eight-storey **Butler's Wharf warehouse**, the largest warehouse complex on the Thames when it was built in 1873. When it closed down in the 1970s, it became London's largest artists' colony, home to everyone from Michael Nyman to Sid Vicious. Nowadays, its flats, shops and restaurants form part of Terence Conran's gastronomic empire, but the wide promenade on the riverfront is open to the public.

Shad Thames, the narrow street at the back of Butler's Wharf, has kept the wrought-iron overhead gangways by which the porters used to transport goods from the wharves to the warehouses further back from the river; it's one of the most atmospheric alleyways in the whole of Docklands. For a totally different ambience, head for **Horsleydown Square**, to the south of Shad Thames, where terracotta-rendered flats, with striking blue balconies, overlook a kind of Continental piazza centred on a fountain encrusted with naked women, whose belongings are sculpted around the edge. Also worth a look, two blocks south on Queen Elizabeth Street, is the **Circle**, CZWG's modern take on the Victorian "circus", its street facades smothered in shiny cobalt-blue tiles.

▲ Porter's gangways, Shad Thames

Design Museum

The big attraction of Butler's Wharf is Terence Conran's superb riverside **Design Museum** (daily 10am–5.45pm, Fri until 9pm; £6; ℡0870/833 9955, ⓦwww.designmuseum.org), at the eastern end of Shad Thames. The stylish white edifice, a Bauhaus-like conversion of an old 1950s warehouse, is the perfect showcase for mass-produced industrial design from classic cars to Tupperware. The museum has no permanent display, but instead hosts a series of temporary exhibitions (up to four at any one time) on important designers, movements or single products. The museum shop is great for design classics and innovations, and the small *Konditor & Cook* coffee bar in the foyer serves delicious cakes and is a great place to relax; there's also a superb but pricey Conran restaurant, the *Blue Print Café*, on the top floor.

St Saviour's Dock and beyond

To the east of the Design Museum, a stainless-steel footbridge takes you across **St Saviour's Dock**, a tidal inlet overlooked by swanky warehouse offices. Incredible though it may seem, it really is still possible to smell the spices – cinnamon, nutmeg and cloves, mostly – which were stored here until the 1970s, especially in the last section of Shad Thames after a shower of rain. The footbridge takes you over to **New Concordia Wharf** on Mill Street, one of the first warehouse conversions in the area, completed in 1984. Next door stands **China Wharf**, designed by CZWG and one of the most photographed postmodernist buildings in Docklands, with its stack of semicircular windows picked out in red.

The area to the east of **Mill Street** was dubbed by the Victorian press "the very capital of cholera". In 1849, the *Morning Chronicle* described it thus:

The **Fashion and Textile Museum** (Tues–Sun 10am–4.45pm; £5; ✆020/7403 0222, ⓦwww.ftmlondon.org) is the lifelong dream of Zandra Rhodes, fashion *grande dame extraordinaire*. Designed by Mexican architect Ricardo Legorreta, and daubed in Rhodes' favourite colours of pink and orange, the FTM (a former cash-and-carry warehouse) is an arresting sight on otherwise drab Bermondsey Street. Rhodes opened her first shop off the King's Road in 1969, and later reached the peak of her popularity during the punk era. Her own sartorial taste hasn't changed much in the intervening years, and although she spent much of the 1990s out in the cold, she's back with a vengeance at the age of sixty. FTM's exhibitions so far have ranged from designer tea cosies to Seventies' fashion, and are often drawn from her own vast collection.

"Jostling with unemployed labourers of the lowest class, ballast heavers, coal-whippers, brazen women, ragged children, and the very raff and refuse of the river, [the visitor] makes his way with difficulty along, assailed by offensive sights and smells from the narrow alleys which branch off." This was the location of Dickens' fictional Jacob's Island, a place with "every imaginable sign of desolation and neglect", where Bill Sikes met his end in *Oliver Twist*.

If you want to continue east on foot to Rotherhithe, you can follow a route alongside the river, stopping en route at **The Angel**, a pub once frequented by Pepys and Captain Cook, which now stands all alone on Bermondsey Wall, with great views over to Wapping. Close by are the foundations of Edward III's moated manor house, begun in 1353, and the "Leaning Tower of Bemondsey", a precariously tilting riverside house downstream from the pub.

⑰

Rotherhithe

Rotherhithe, the thumb of marshy land jutting out into the Thames east of Bermondsey, has always been slightly removed from the rest of London. It was a thriving shipbuilding centre even before the construction of the Surrey Commercial Docks in the nineteenth century, and was described as "chiefly inhabited by sailors, ship-carpenters, coal-heavers and bargemen" at the turn of the century. However, no other set of London dockyards took such a hammering in the Blitz, and the decades until their closure in 1970 were years of inexorable decline. Most of the docks, which took up almost the entire peninsula, have now been reclaimed for new housing estates and more upmarket accommodation. The lack of any relationship between the old Rotherhithe communities, which face the street, and the new ones, which face the water, gives the whole area a strange, dislocated feeling that's typical of Docklands developments.

The area of Rotherhithe worth visiting is the heart of the old eighteenth-century seafaring village around **St Mary's Church**, which stands in its own leafy square just northwest of the tube station. The church itself is unremarkable, but it has rich maritime associations: several of the furnishings are made from the timber of the *Fighting Temeraire*, the veteran of Trafalgar which ended its days in a Rotherhithe breaker's yard (Turner's painting of its last voyage is in the National Gallery), and the master of the *Mayflower* was buried here. The *Mayflower* was pretty much owned and crewed by Rotherhithe, and set off from its mooring outside the *Mayflower* pub in 1620 to transport the Pilgrim Fathers to the New World. (The ship had to call in at Plymouth for repairs after being damaged in the English Channel.) The pub, to the north of the church, is a rickety white weatherboarded building, badly damaged in the last war, and a minor pilgrimage site for Americans.

Brunel Engine House

To the east of St Mary's, down Tunnel Street, you'll find the **Brunel Engine House** (Thurs–Sun 1–5pm; £2; ☎020/7231 3840, ⓦwww.brunelenginehouse .org.uk), a brick-built shed that marks the site of the Thames Tunnel, the world's first under-river tunnel. It was begun in 1825 by Marc Brunel and his more famous son, Isambard, to link Rotherhithe with Wapping, using technology which was invented by Brunel senior and whose basic principles have been used for all subsequent tunnelling. Plagued by periodic flooding, labour unrest, fatalities and lack of funds, the tunnel took eighteen years to construct and was nicknamed "The Great Bore" by the press.

The circular working shaft, which housed an engine to pump water out of the tunnel, survives to the east of the engine house, but funds ran out before the spiral ramps, which would have allowed horse-drawn vehicles actually to use the tunnel, could be built. Instead, in 1843, the tunnel was opened to pedestrians as a tourist attraction, pulling in two million visitors in its first year. It was visited by Queen Victoria herself, who knighted Brunel junior, but soon became the haunt of whores and "tunnel thieves". Since 1869 it has formed part of the East London Railway (now a tube line) and remains the most watertight of all the rail tunnels under the Thames. As well as telling the tunnel's fascinating story, the engine house's museum has some of the old souvenirs sold in Victorian times and a modestly interactive peepshow. Tours of the tunnel itself are occasionally possible – visit the website to find out the latest.

Surrey Docks and Rotherhithe Street

The once marshy land of Rotherhithe peninsula, to the east of the old village, was chosen as the site for London's first wet dock, the Howland Great Dock built in 1696 to take on any extra repair work and refitting emanating from the Royal Dockyards in nearby Deptford (see p.389). Later renamed Greenland Dock, the Rotherhithe dock became part of the network known as **Surrey Commercial Docks**. The main trade was timber, which was piled into stacks up to 80ft high by porters nicknamed "Flying Blondins" (after the tightrope walker), who wore distinctive leather pads on their heads and shoulders to protect them from splinters. The docks took a pounding in the Blitz, and on one particular occasion, 350,000 tons of timber was set ablaze in one of the largest fires ever seen in Britain.

Rotherhithe Street, which hugs the riverbank, is the longest street in London at around a mile and a half. It's mainly residential, a mixture of new Docklands developments and council housing, but the Thames Path, which runs parallel to it for most of the way, is pleasant enough to walk or cycle along, with great views over to Limehouse and Canary Wharf. Halfway along the street, you can learn more about the area's history from the **Rotherhithe Heritage Museum** (Mon–Fri 10am–4pm; free; ℡020/7231 2976, ✆www.thepumphouse.org.uk), which is housed in the old Lavender Pumphouse on Lavender Street. Further along, you can catch a boat back into town or on to Greenwich, from the Nelson Dock Pier beside the *Hilton* hotel. If you've time to kill, check out the three-masted schooner (now a restaurant) built in the 1950s as a training ship for the French navy, and nearby **Nelson House**, a beautiful Georgian house built for one of the wealthy owners of Nelson Dock.

Hyde Park and Kensington Gardens

Londoners tend to see their city as grimy and built-up, but most visitors are amazed at how green and pleasant so much of the centre is, with three royal parks – St James's Park, Green Park and Hyde Park – forming a continuous grassy belt that stretches for four miles. **Hyde Park**, together with its westerly extension, **Kensington Gardens**, is the largest of the trio, covering a distance of a mile and a half from Speakers' Corner in the northeast to Kensington Palace in the southwest. In between, you can jog, swim, fish, sunbathe or mess about in boats on the Serpentine, cross the park on horseback or mountain bike, or view the latest in modern art at the Serpentine Gallery. At the end of your journey, you've made it to one of London's most exclusive districts, the Royal Borough of Kensington and Chelsea, which is covered in the next two chapters.

Hyde Park

Seized from the Church by Henry VIII to satisfy his desire for yet more hunting grounds, **Hyde Park** (daily 5am–midnight; ☎020/7298 2100, ⊛www .royalparks.gov.uk) was first opened to the public by James I, when refreshments available included "milk from a red cow". Under Charles II, the park became a fashionable gathering place for the beau monde, who rode round the circular drive known as the Ring, pausing to gossip and admire each other's equipages. Its present appearance is mostly due to Queen Caroline, an enthusiast for landscape gardens, who spent a great deal of George II's money creating the park's main feature, the **Serpentine** lake.

Hangings, muggings and duels, the Great Exhibition of 1851 and numerous public events have all taken place here – and it's still a popular gathering point or destination for political demonstrations, as well as the location of **Speakers' Corner**, of which more below. For most of the time, however, Hyde Park is simply a leisure ground – a wonderful open space that allows you to lose all sight of the city beyond a few persistent tower blocks. That said, the southeast corner of the park contains two conventional tourist attractions: **Apsley House**, which houses a museum to the Duke of Wellington, and the triumphal **Wellington Arch**, which you can now climb.

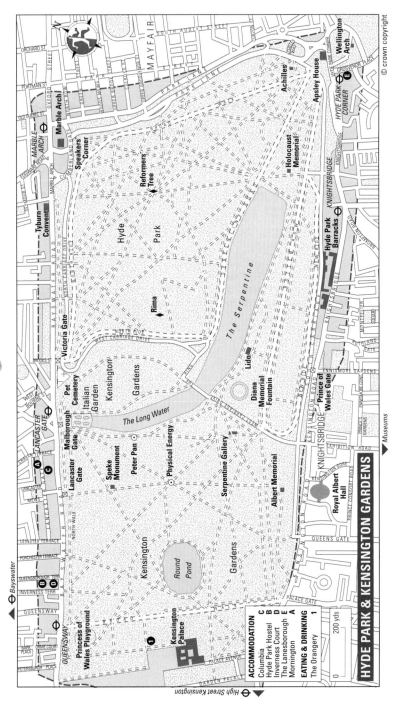

HYDE PARK & KENSINGTON GARDENS

ACCOMMODATION
Columbia   C
Hyde Park Hostel   B
Inverness Court   D
The Lanesborough   E
Mornington   A

EATING & DRINKING
The Orangery   1

0   200 yds

© crown copyright

Marble Arch and Speakers' Corner

Marble Arch, located at the treeless northeastern corner of the park and the west end of Oxford Street, is the most historically charged spot in Hyde Park, as it marks the site of **Tyburn gallows**, the city's main public execution spot until 1783, when the action moved to Newgate (see box below). There's a plaque on the traffic island at the bottom of Edgware Road/Bayswater Road marking the approximate site of the gallows, where around 50,000 lost their lives. Of these, some 105 were Catholics, martyred during the Reformation, in whose memory the **Tyburn Convent** (daily 6.30am–8.30pm; ⓦwww.tyburnconvent .org.uk) was established at 8 Hyde Park Place in 1902. It's run by a group of cloistered French Benedictine nuns who are happy to show visitors round the basement shrine (10am, 3.30pm & 5.30pm; free), which contains a mock-up of the Tyburn gibbet over the main altar, and various pictures and relics of the martyrs. The house next door to (and now part of) the convent, no. 10, is London's smallest, measuring just three and a half feet across.

Tyburn gallows

For nearly five hundred years, **Tyburn** was the capital's main public execution site, with around fifteen victims a month swinging, some of them dispatched for the pettiest of crimes (there were 156 capital offences in eighteenth-century England). "Hanging Matches", as they were known, usually drew huge crowds – up to 200,000 for the execution of a noted criminal – and became something of a show of working-class solidarity, with numerous side-stalls and a large permanent grandstand known as "Mother Proctor's Pews" after the woman who first rented out seats. Dressed in their best clothes, the condemned were processed through the streets in a cart (the nobility were allowed to travel in their own carriages) from Newgate Prison, three miles away, often with the noose already looped in place. They received a nosegay at St Sepulchre, opposite the prison, and then at St Giles-in-the-Fields, and at various taverns along the route they were given a free pint of ale, so that many were blind drunk by the time they arrived at the three-legged gibbet known as the "Tyburn Tree" or the "Triple Tree", which could dispatch over twenty people at one go.

The condemned were allowed to make a speech to the crowd and were attended by a chaplain, though according to one eighteenth-century spectator he was "more the subject of ridicule than of serious attention". The same witness goes on to describe how the executioner, who drove the cart, then tied the rope to the tree: "This done he gives the horse a lash with his whip, away goes the cart and there swings my gentleman kicking in the air. The Hangman does not give himself the trouble to put them out of their pain but some of their friends or relations do it for them. They pull the dying person by the legs and beat his breast to dispatch him as soon as possible."

Not all relatives were so fatalistic, however, and some would attempt to support the condemned in the hope of a last-minute reprieve, or of reviving the victim when they were cut down. Fights frequently broke out when the body was cut down, between the relatives, the spectators hoping to touch the corpse in the belief it had miraculous medicinal qualities, and the surgeons who were allowed ten corpses a year for dissection. The executioner, known as "Jack Ketch" after the famous London hangman who botched the Duke of Monmouth's beheading (see p.220), was allowed to take home the victim's clothes, and made further profit by selling the hanging rope inch by inch. Altogether, an estimated 50,000 were hanged at Tyburn, but following the 1780 Gordon Riots, the powers-that-be took fright at unruly gatherings like Tyburn, and demolished the Tyburn Tree in 1783.

The **Marble Arch** itself has a long and dismal history, and is now stranded on a ferociously busy traffic island. It was designed in 1828 in white Carrara marble by John Nash as a triumphal arch (after the Arch of Constantine in Rome) and was originally positioned in front of Buckingham Palace, for the exclusive use of royalty. The sculpted friezes intended to adorn it ended up on Buck House, while the equestrian statue of George IV, intended to surmount it, was carted off to Trafalgar Square. When the palace was extended in the 1840s, the arch was then moved to form an entrance to Hyde Park, its upper chambers used as a police observation post. During the 1855 riot (described below), a detachment of police emerged, like the Greeks from the Trojan Horse, much to the surprise of the demonstrators.

In 1855 an estimated 250,000 people gathered in the section of the park directly across the road from Marble Arch to protest against the Sunday Trading Bill (Karl Marx was among the crowd and thought it was the beginning of the English Revolution), and ever since then it has been one of London's most popular spots for political demos. In 1866 the Reform League used Hyde Park for its meetings calling for universal suffrage, and there were frequent scuffles with the police. Six years later the government licensed free assembly at **Speakers' Corner** (ⓦwww.speakerscorner.net), a peculiarly English Sunday-morning tradition that continues to this day, featuring an assembly of ranters and hecklers. The largest demonstration in London's history took place here in February 2003 when over a million people turned up to try and stop the war against Iraq.

Hyde Park Corner

A better place to enter the park is at **Hyde Park Corner**, the southeast corner, where **Wellington Arch** (Wed–Sun: April–Oct 10am–5pm; Nov–March 10am–4pm; EH; £3) stands in the midst of another of London's busiest traffic interchanges. Inside, you can view an exhibition on the history of the arch, and of London's outdoor sculpture in general, and take a lift to the top of the monument (once London's smallest postwar police station) where the exterior balconies offer a bird's-eye view of the swirling traffic.

Designed by a youthful Decimus Burton in 1828 to commemorate Wellington's victories in the Napoleonic Wars, the arch originally served as the northern gate into Buckingham Palace grounds. Positioned opposite Burton's delicate Hyde Park Screen, which was intended as a formal entrance into the park, the arch once formed part of a fine architectural ensemble with Apsley House, Wellington's London residence, and St George's Hospital to the west. Unfortunately the symmetry was destroyed when it was repositioned in 1883 to line up with Constitution Hill – whose name derives not from a written constitution, which England has never had, but from the "constitutional" walks that Charles II used to take there. The arch's original statue was an enormous equestrian portrayal of the "Iron Duke" erected in 1846 while he was still alive. The duke was taken down in 1883, and eventually replaced by Peace and her four-horse chariot, erected in 1912.

The replacement statue for Wellington is much smaller, and stands opposite his erstwhile residence, **Apsley House** (see opposite). He is depicted seated astride his faithful steed, Copenhagen, which carried the field marshal for sixteen hours during the Battle of Waterloo; the horse eventually died in 1836 and was buried with full military honours at the duke's country pile in Hampshire. Close by are two powerful war memorials erected in 1925: the first, the **Machine Gun Corps Memorial**, features the naked figure of David leaning on Goliath's sword and the chilling inscription, "Saul hath slain his thousands, but David his tens of thousands"; the larger of the two, the **Artillery Memorial**, includes a 9.2-inch howitzer rendered in Portland stone, realistic relief depictions of the brutality of war, and the equally blunt epitaph, "Here was a royal fellowship of death".

Apsley House: the Wellington Museum

Known during the Iron Duke's lifetime as No. 1, London, **Apsley House** (Tues–Sun: April–Oct 10am–5pm; Nov–March 10am–4pm; EH; £4.95) was once an immensely desirable residence, but nowadays, with traffic roaring past at all hours of the day and night, it would be poor reward for any national hero. The interior isn't what it used to be either, but in this case it's Wellington himself who was to blame. The house was built and exquisitely decorated by Robert Adam in 1771, but after buying the place from his brother in 1817 the duke ordered Benjamin Wyatt to reface the house in Bath stone and replace or modify virtually all of the Adam interiors. As a result, however, the house is very much as it would have been in Wellington's day, and the current duke still lives in the attic.

The Iron Duke

Perhaps if the **Duke of Wellington** had died, like Nelson, at his moment of greatest triumph, he too would enjoy an unsullied posthumous reputation. Instead, he went on to become the epitome of the outmoded reactionary conservative, earning his famous nickname, the "Iron Duke", not from his fearless military campaigning, but from the iron shutters which he had installed at Apsley House after his windows had twice been broken by demonstrators rioting in favour of the 1832 Reform Bill, which gave the vote to almost all members of the middle class, and to which the duke was vehemently opposed.

Born Arthur Wellesley in Dublin in 1769 – the same year as Napoleon – he was educated at Eton and the French military academy at Angers. "Aloof and rather aggressive as a boy", according to one of his contemporaries, he was, by all accounts, a fairly terrifying personality, who barked rather than spoke. He scored his first military victories out in India, defeating Tippoo Sahib, and becoming governor of Mysore. After continued military success in his Napoleonic campaigns, he eventually became Duke of Wellington in 1814, shortly before achieving his most famous victory of all at Waterloo.

Though he had been MP for Trim in Ireland since 1806, and held various political posts throughout his life, it was only with great reluctance that he became prime minister in 1828, "a station, to the duties of which I am unaccustomed, in which I was not wished, and for which I was not qualified . . . I should have been mad if I had thought of such a thing". Despite his own misgivings, his government passed the Catholic Relief Bill – allowing Catholics to sit in Parliament – thus avoiding civil war in Ireland, but splitting the Tory ranks. Accused of popery by the Earl of Winchelsea, Wellington challenged him to a duel in Battersea Park; the duke fired and missed, while the earl shot into the air and apologized for the slur.

Wellington's opposition to the Reform Bill brought down his government and allowed the Whigs to form a majority government for the first time in sixty years. Despite retiring from public life in 1846, he was on hand to organize the defence of the capital against the Chartists in 1848, and strolled across to the Great Exhibition every day in 1851. Something approaching two million people lined the streets for his funeral in 1852 (more than for anyone before or since), and he has more outdoor statues (and pubs named after him) in London than any other historical figure. Despite this, his greatest legacy is, of course, the Wellington boot, originally made of leather, now rubber.

Even if you're no fan of the duke, the house is worth visiting for the **art collection** alone. Wellington acquired the collection in 1813 after the Battle of Vittoria, when he seized the baggage train of Napoleon's brother, who was fleeing for France with 200 paintings belonging to the king of Spain. Wellington offered to return the paintings, but the king of Spain demurred. The best pieces, including works by de Hooch, van Dyck, Goya, Rubens and Murillo, cover the red walls of the **Waterloo Gallery** on the first floor. The most prized of all are a trio by Velázquez – *The Water-Seller of Seville, Portrait of a Gentleman* and *Two Young Men Eating at a Humble Table* – though Wellington preferred Correggio's *Agony in the Garden*, the key for which he used to carry round with him, so he could take the picture out of its frame and dust it fondly.

The room itself was originally hung with yellow satin, which, as one of the duke's friends lamented, "is just the very worst colour he can have for the pictures and will kill the effect of the gilding". It was here that Wellington held his annual veterans' **Waterloo Banquet**, using the 1000-piece silver-gilt Portuguese service, now displayed in the rather lugubrious Dining Room at the other end of the house. Most of the Waterloo portraits are, in fact, hung in the adjacent Striped Drawing Room, which is decorated like a military tent in the manner of Napoleon's Loire chateau, Malmaison.

The famous, more than twice life-sized, **nude statue of Napoleon by Canova** stands at the foot of the main staircase, having been bought by the Prince Regent in 1816 and presented to the duke for services rendered. It was disliked by the sitter, not least for the tiny figure of Victory in the emperor's hand, which appears to be trying to fly away. In the Plate and China Room, also on the ground floor, you can view numerous gifts to the duke, including a 400-piece dinner service decorated with scenes of Wellington's life, and the bizarre Egyptian service, which was originally a divorce present from Napoleon to Josephine; unsurprisingly, she rejected it and Louis XVIII ended up giving it to the duke. In the basement there are various personal effects, medals and a goodly selection of cruel, contemporary caricatures.

Achilles and Rotten Row

Behind Apsley House, a pair of frothy, rather silly, silvery gates – installed in 1993 as a ninetieth birthday present to the Queen Mother – marks the Queen Elizabeth Gate, and the beginning of the park proper. Close by the entrance, overlooking the back of Apsley House, is the 33-ton bronze **Achilles** statue, designed by Richard Westmacott and cast from captured French cannon. It was erected in 1822 on behalf of "the women of Great Britain", who acted as fundraisers for the statue, and commemorates the Duke of Wellington's achievements. As the country's first public nude statue it caused outrage, especially since many thought it a portrait of the duke himself. In actual fact, it isn't meant to represent either the duke or Achilles, but is a copy of one of the horse-tamers from the Monte Cavallo in Rome. William Wilberforce led a campaign to have the statue removed for decency's sake; a fig leaf – still there today – was placed in the appropriate place as a compromise.

From the gates, two roads set off west to Kensington: South Carriage Road, which is open to cars, and **Rotten Row**, thought to be a corruption of *route du roi* (king's way), since it was established by William III as a bridle path linking Westminster and Kensington. William had three hundred lamps hung from the trees to try to combat the increasing number of highwaymen active in the park, thus making Rotten Row the first road in the country to be lit at night. The measure was only partly successful – George II himself was later mugged

Royal Gun Salutes

At noon on February 6, April 21, June 2 and 10, and at 11am on the Queen's official birthday (a variable date in June), the Royal Horse Artillery wheel out cannons and the park resounds to a 41-round Royal Gun Salute.

here. To the south of Rotten Row, the **Hyde Park Barracks** are difficult to miss, thanks to Basil Spence's hideous high-rise design. Early in the morning, you might catch sight of the Household Cavalry exercising in the park, and at around 10.30am daily (Sun 9.30am) they set off for the Horse Guards building in Whitehall for the Changing of the Guard (see p.61).

The Serpentine

Rotten Row remains a bridle path, so pedestrians should wander through the pretty flower gardens to the north instead. Beyond lies the **Serpentine lake**, created in 1730 by damming the Westbourne, a small tributary of the Thames, in order that Queen Caroline might have a spot for the royal yachts to mess about on. A miniature re-enactment of the Battle of Trafalgar was staged here in 1814, and two years later Shelley's pregnant wife, Harriet Westbrook, drowned herself in the lake after the poet had eloped with the 16-year-old Mary Woll-stonecraft. The popular **Lido** (mid-June to mid-Sept daily 10am–6pm; £3.50; ☏020/7706 3422, ⊛www.serpentinelido.com) is situated on the south bank, alongside a café, and rowing boats and pedalos can be rented (March–Oct daily 10am–6.30pm or dusk; £4 per hour; ☏020/7262 1330) from the boathouse on the north bank.

To the west of the Lido is the entrance to the **Diana Memorial Fountain** (March & Oct 10am–6pm; April–Aug 10am–8pm; Sept 10am–7pm; Nov–Feb 10am–4pm; free). Less of a fountain, and more of an oval-shaped mini-moat, the memorial was designed in the shape of a giant oval ring by Kathryn Gustafson and constructed out of white Cornish granite. The intention was to allow children to play in the running water, but, since three people suffered minor injuries, the fountain has been fenced off and supplied with security guards, making it rather less fun for kids, who are now only allowed to dabble their feet in the stream.

To the north of the Sepentine is a Jacob Epstein monument, a relief of **Rima**, the naked spirit of nature, which provoked such hostility when it was unveiled in 1925 that it was tarred and feathered on two separate occasions. The dedicatee of the monument is the naturalist W.H. Hudson, and the area around it is supposed to be a bird sanctuary, though its dribbling fountain and manicured lawn are not the most obvious spot for birds to seek refuge.

Kensington Gardens

The more tranquil half of the park, to the west of Victoria Gate in the north and the Ring (the road that splits the park in half), is known as **Kensington Gardens** (⊛www.royalparks.gov.uk) and is, strictly speaking, a separate entity from Hyde Park, though you hardly notice the change. More exclusive because of the proximity of royalty at Kensington Palace, the gardens were first opened to the public in George II's reign, but only on Sundays and only to those in formal dress, and that didn't include sailors, soldiers or liveried servants. Unrestricted access was only granted in Victoria's reign, by which time, in the view of the Russian ambassador's wife, the park had already been "annexed as a middle-class rendezvous. Good society no longer [went] there except to drown itself."

The Long Water

The upper section of the Serpentine – beyond the bridge – is known as the **Long Water**, and is by far the prettiest section of the lake. It narrows until it reaches a most unlikely sight in an English park: the **Italian Gardens**, a group of five fountains, laid out symmetrically in front of a pumphouse disguised in the form of an Italianate loggia. To the east, by Victoria Gate, lies the odd little **Pet Cemetery**, begun in the 1880s when Mr and Mrs J. Lewis Barnes buried their Maltese terrier, Cherry, here. When the Duke of Cambridge buried his wife's pet hound at the same spot after it had been run over on Bayswater Road, it became the place to bury your pooch; three hundred other miscellaneous cats and dogs followed, until the last burial in 1967. The cemetery – "perhaps the most horrible spectacle in Britain", according to George Orwell – is no longer open to the public, though you can peep over the wall.

The best-known of all Hyde Park's outdoor monuments is **Peter Pan**, the fictional character who enters London along the Serpentine and whose statue stands by the west bank of the Long Water; fairies, squirrels, rabbits, birds and mice scamper round the pedestal. It was in Kensington Gardens that the book's author, J.M. Barrie, used to walk his dog, and it was here that he met the five pretty, upper-class Llewellyn Davies boys, who wore "blue blouses and bright red tam o'shanters", were the inspiration for the "Lost Boys", and whose guardian he eventually became. Barrie himself paid for the statue, which was erected in secret during the night in 1912.

The rough-hewn muscleman struggling with his horse, to the southwest of Peter Pan, is G.F. Watts' **Physical Energy**, a copy of the Rhodes memorial in Cape Town; to the north is a granite obelisk raised to **John Hanning Speke**, who was the first non-African to find the source of the Nile, and who died in 1864 after accidentally shooting himself rather than the partridge he was aiming at. Finally, in the far northwestern corner, is the top-quality **Princess of Wales Playground**, which features a ship stuck in sand, paving gongs and other groovy playthings.

To the south of all this statuary, on the west side of the Ring, stands the **Serpentine Gallery** (daily 10am–6pm; free; ☎020/7298 1515, ⓦwww.serpentinegallery.org), built as a tearoom in 1908 because the park

▲ Peter Pan, Hyde Park

⑱

authorities thought "poorer visitors" might otherwise cause trouble if left without refreshments. Since the 1960s, the tearoom has served as an art gallery, which has a reputation for lively, and often controversial, contemporary art exhibitions, and contains an excellent bookshop. In recent years the gallery has also commissioned a different architect each year to design a temporary **pavilion** for its summer-only teahouse extension.

Albert Memorial

Completed in 1876 by George Gilbert Scott, the **Albert Memorial** (45min guided tours Sun 2pm & 3pm; £4.50; ☎020/7495 0916), on the south side of Kensington Gardens, is as much a hymn to the glorious achievements of Britain as to its subject, Queen Victoria's husband (who died of typhoid in 1861), whose gilded image sits under its central canopy, clutching a catalogue for the Great Exhibition (see box, below). The pomp of the monument is overwhelming: the spire, inlaid with semiprecious stones and marbles, rises to 180ft, a marble frieze

The Great Exhibition and the Crystal Palace

East of the Albert Memorial, opposite Prince of Wales Gate, was the site of the **Great Exhibition** of the Works and Industry of All Nations, held between May 1 and October 15, 1851. The idea originated with Henry Cole, a minor civil servant in the Record Office, and was taken up enthusiastically by Prince Albert despite much opposition from snooty Kensington residents, who complained that it would attract an "invasion of undesirables who would ravish their silver and their serving maids". A competition to design the exhibition building produced 245 rejected versions, until Joseph Paxton, head gardener to the Duke of Devonshire, offered to build his "**Crystal Palace**", a wrought-iron and glass structure some 1848ft long and 408ft wide. The acceptance of Paxton's radical proposal was an act of faith by the exhibition organizers, since such a structure had never been built, and their faith was amply rewarded – a team of two hundred workers completed the building in just four months, and more than six million people came to visit it.

The exhibition was primarily designed to show off the achievements of the British Empire but, with over a third of all the exhibits coming from outside Great Britain, it was also a unique opportunity for people to enjoy the products of other cultures. Thousands of exhibits were housed in the Crystal Palace, including the Koh-i-Noor diamond (displayed in a birdcage), an Indian ivory throne, a floating church from Philadelphia, a bed which awoke its occupant by ejecting him or her into a cold bath, false teeth designed not to be displaced when yawning, a fountain running with eau de Cologne, and all manner of china, fabrics and glass.

To everyone's surprise, the exhibition was even profit-making and the surplus was used to buy 87 acres of land to the south of Kensington Road, for the creation of a "Museumland" where "the arts and sciences could be promoted and taught in a way which would be of practical use to industry and make Britain the leading country of the industrialized world". Much to most people's dismay, the Crystal Palace itself was dismantled after the exhibition and rebuilt in southeast London in 1854, where it served as a concert hall, theatre, menagerie and exhibition space, only to be entirely destroyed by fire in 1936. Its loss has been lamented by Londoners for decades, but so far plans to resurrect the palace – either a full-scale replica (with hotels and other mod cons) at Sydenham or a one-third-size model in Hyde Park itself – have come to nothing.

18

around the pediment is cluttered with 169 life-sized figures (all men) in high relief, depicting poets, musicians, painters, architects and sculptors from ancient Egypt onwards; the pillars are topped with bronzes of Astronomy, Chemistry, Geology and Geometry; mosaics show Poetry, Painting, Architecture and Sculpture; four outlying marble groups represent the four continents; and other statuary pays homage to Agriculture, Commerce and other aspects of imperial economics. Albert would not have been amused: "I can say, with perfect absence of humbug, that I would rather not be made the prominent feature of such a monument . . . it would upset my equanimity to be permanently ridiculed and laughed at in effigy", he once claimed.

Kensington Palace

On the western edge of Kensington Gardens stands **Kensington Palace** (daily: March–Oct 10am–6pm; Nov–Feb 10am–5pm; £11; ☏0870/751 5170, ⊛www .hrp.org.uk), a modestly proportioned Jacobean brick mansion bought as an out-of-town residence by William and Mary in 1689 because the king's asthma and bronchitis were aggravated by Whitehall's damp and fumes. Wren, Hawksmoor and later William Kent were all called in to overhaul and embellish the place, though in the end the palace was the chief royal residence for barely fifty years. The most handsome facade faces south, behind a flamboyant statue of William III, given to Edward VII by the German Kaiser. Most people, however, approach from the Round Pond to the east, where George I used to keep his edible turtles, and the Broad Walk, a favourite local rollerblading avenue; both are overlooked by a flattering statue of Queen Victoria sculpted by her daughter, Princess Louise.

KP, as it's fondly known in royal circles, is, of course, best known today as the place where **Princess Diana** lived up until her death in 1997. It was, in fact, the official London residence of both Charles and Di until the couple formally separated, and Charles moved out to bachelor accommodation in St James's Palace. In the weeks following Diana's death, literally millions of flowers, mementoes, poems and gifts were deposited at the Crowther Gates, and even now Kensington Palace finds itself much busier than it ever used to be. Visitors do get to see some of Diana's dresses, but they don't get to see Diana's rooms, which were situated on the west side of the palace, where the likes of the Duke and Duchess of Kent and the Duke and Duchess of Gloucester all still live.

Royal Ceremonial Dress Collection

You buy your tickets, and can pick up a free audioguide, in the gloomy **Red Saloon** on the east side of the ground floor, where the 18-year-old Victoria held her first Privy Council meeting, just hours after hearing of William IV's death on June 20, 1837.

The **Royal Ceremonial Dress Collection** kicks off with a tableau of a 1920s debutante getting ready to be presented at court, and an ambassador getting kitted out in full court dress. Later on, there's an Edwardian court scene, with the women clothed in flamboyant cream silk dresses designed to accentuate their bust, and the men buttoned up in stiff, military garb. You then get to see a few of the **Queen's dresses**: from the glamorous 1950s ball gowns, smothered in sequins and pearls, to her more suspect later penchant for apricot- and peach-coloured frocks.

After a room used for temporary exhibitions, you get to see a collection of **Princess Diana's dresses**. Although the frocks themselves hail from the top design houses, it's clear from the accompanying photos that it was Diana herself who made them look so glamorous. Lastly, one or two eighteenth-century exhibits can be viewed upstairs in the state apartments, such as the ludicrous **mantua dress** with side hoops, which were eventually dispensed with during the reign of George IV.

State apartments

Little of Wren's work survives in the **King's Apartments**, and the most interesting rooms are mostly designed by William Kent, beginning with the impressive **King's Staircase**, with its Irish black marble steps, its Tijou wrought-iron balustrade and trompe l'oeil crowds of courtiers and yeomen. Another great Kent creation is the "grotesque"-style painting on the ceiling of the **Presence Chamber**, which also features a lovely pear-wood Gibbons overmantle with weeping putti. Two rooms further on, the **Cupola Room**, with its monstrously ugly clock occupying centre stage, features another wonderful trompe l'oeil fresco, which gives the effect of a coffered dome. Another two rooms on, **Queen Victoria's Bedroom** is a bit of a contrast, since it was totally redecorated in 1836. Victoria was born in the decaying palace in 1819, and spent her dull, sad childhood cooped up here with her strict mother, the Duchess of Kent, who even slept in the same room. According to her diary, her best friends were the palace's numerous "black beetles", though it's clear from the Indian clubs that she was also into keep-fit. The grandest room in the palace is the **King's Gallery**, whose red damask walls are hung with paintings by, among others, Tintoretto (the equestrian portrait of Charles I is not, in fact, an original van Dyck). Also of interest is the wind dial above the fireplace, connected to the palace weather vane, built for William III and still fully functioning.

The **Queen's Apartments**, which follow, are, by contrast, much more modest, wood-panelled rooms hung with Dutch works reflecting the tastes of William and Mary – they are also the most dull, since they contain little furniture, and what decoration there was disappeared in the bomb damage of the last war. The best room is the **Queen's Bedchamber**, decked out in deep-blue velvet, with a four-poster bed that belonged to Queen Mary of Modena, James II's second wife, brought here from St James's Palace. It was here that the diminutive Queen Anne died of apoplexy after overeating; the toilet on which George II died of a heart attack, brought on by constipation, is, however, no longer in existence. **Queen Mary's Closet** was the scene of a furious quarrel between Queen Anne and her confidante, the Duchess of Marlborough, after which they never saw each other again. The last room on the tour is **Queen Mary's Gallery**, once magnificently decorated with 154 pieces of Oriental porcelain, now reduced to a mere handful, and lined with royal portraits. At the far end is one by Peter Lely, of Anne Hyde, mistress and later wife of the future James II; they officially married after she was already pregnant, causing something of a royal scandal even in the libidinous Restoration period.

Around the palace

Before you leave the palace grounds, you can peek through the hornbeam hedge at the **Sunken Garden**, created to the east of the palace in 1909 in emulation of the formal gardens laid out by William and Mary. Dwarf cypresses punctuate the garden's oblong pond, with terraced flowerbeds surrounding it, but the prettiest feature is the lime walk. To the north is Nicholas Hawksmoor's exquisite **Orangery** (times as for palace), built for Queen Anne as a summer dining room, where you can now enjoy coffee and snacks while taking in carving and statues by Grinling Gibbons.

Kensington Palace Gardens, the leafy avenue which runs along the edge of Kensington Gardens, was the Millionaires' Row of the Victorian period, flanked by a succession of ostentatious detached mansions set within their own grounds and built by some of the most successful architects of the day, such as Decimus Burton and Sidney Smirke. It remains a private road and an expensive piece of real estate, with most of the houses adopted as embassies or ambassadorial residences.

(18)

South Kensington, Knightsbridge and Chelsea

O ther districts go in and out of fashion, but the Royal Borough of Kensington and Chelsea, particularly the area to the south of Hyde Park, has been in vogue ever since royalty moved into Kensington Palace in the late seventeenth century. Aside from the shops around Harrods in **Knightsbridge**, however, the popular tourist attractions lie in **South Kensington**, where three of London's top free **museums** – the Victoria and Albert, Natural History and Science museums – stand on land bought with the proceeds of the Great Exhibition of 1851. The following half-century saw the entire borough transformed from fields, farms and private estates into street after street of ostentatious Italianate terraces, grandiose red–brick mansions and mews houses. This is prime London real estate (among the world's most expensive) and heartland of the privately educated, wealthy offspring of the middle and upper classes and the rich and famous.

Chelsea, bordering the river to the south, also has royal connections, though these date mostly from Tudor times and have left few tangible remains. Since the nineteenth century, when artists and writers began to move here in significant numbers, Chelsea's character has been more bohemian than its neighbours. In the 1960s, the **King's Road** carved out its reputation as London's catwalk, while in the late 1970s it was the unlikely epicentre of the punk explosion. Nothing so risqué goes on in Chelsea now, though its residents like to think of themselves as rather more artistic and intellectual than the purely moneyed types of Kensington.

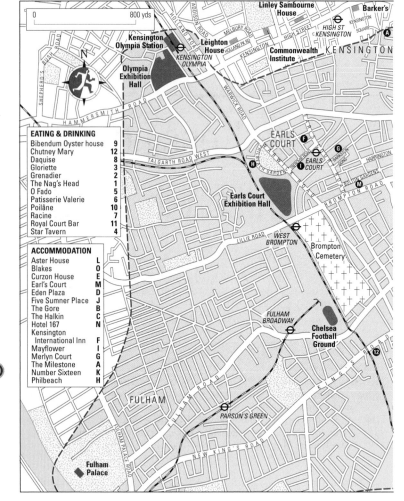

EATING & DRINKING
Bibendum Oyster house	9
Chutney Mary	12
Daquise	8
Gloriette	3
Grenadier	2
The Nag's Head	1
O Fado	5
Patisserie Valerie	6
Poilâne	10
Racine	7
Royal Court Bar	11
Star Tavern	4

ACCOMMODATION
Aster House	L
Blakes	O
Curzon House	E
Earl's Court	M
Eden Plaza	D
Five Sumner Place	J
The Gore	B
The Halkin	C
Hotel 167	N
Kensington International Inn	F
Mayflower	I
Merlyn Court	G
The Milestone	A
Number Sixteen	K
Philbeach	H

19

South Kensington museums

To everyone's surprise, the 1851 Great Exhibition (see box on p.293) was not only an enormous success, but actually yielded a profit of £186,000, with which Prince Albert and his committee bought 87 acres of land in **South Kensington**. Institutions and museums, whose purpose was to "extend the influence of Science and Art upon Productive Industry", were to be established here to form a kind of "Museumland". Albert died of typhoid in 1861 at the age of just 41, and never saw his dream fully realized, but "Albertopolis", with its remarkable cluster of **museums and colleges**, plus the vast

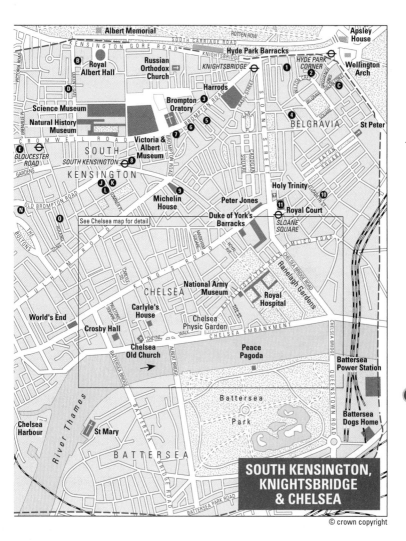

Albert Hall, now stands as one of London's most enlightened examples of urban planning.

With the founding of "Museumland", the surrounding area was transformed almost overnight into one of the most fashionable in town – a status it retains today. The multistorey mansions around the Royal Albert Hall and the grand Italianate houses along Queen's Gate and further south around Onslow Square, one block south of the tube, date from this period. South Ken, as it's known, has acquired further cachet thanks to its **French connections**, with a French school, crèche, bookshop and several genuine patisseries and brasseries clustered around the **Institut Français** (ⓦwww.institut-francais.org.uk) on Queens-

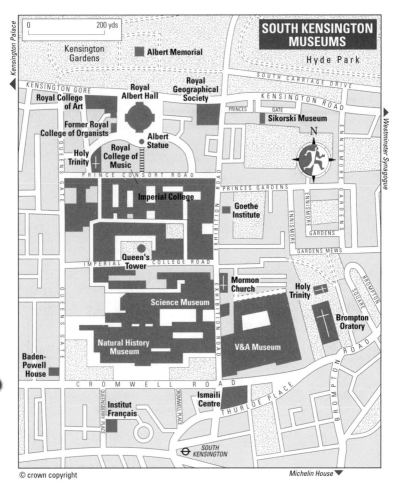

© crown copyright

Michelin House ▼

berry Place, which maintains an interesting programme of theatre, cinema and exhibitions. Over on nearby Exhibition Road, rival German cultural offerings emanate from the **Goethe Institute** (ⓦwww.goethe.de/enindex.htm), while the Islamic world is represented by the **Ismaili Centre** on Cromwell Road.

A further French sight – and one not to be missed while in this part of town – is the gorgeous Art Deco **Michelin House**, a short walk to the south down Brompton Road. Faced in white faïence and decorated with tyres and motoring murals by French artists in 1911, its ground floors now house the shop, café, oyster bar and restaurant of *Bibendum*, all run by Terence Conran (see p.470).

Royal Albert Hall and around

The fresh funds raised to commemorate the Prince Consort on his death in 1861 were squandered on the Albert Memorial (see p.293), and it took considerable effort by Henry Cole, his collaborator on the Great Exhibition, to get funding to complete the **Royal Albert Hall** (☎020/7589 8212, ⓦwww.royalalberthall .com), on Kensington Gore. Plans for this splendid iron- and glass-domed auditorium had been drawn up during the prince's lifetime, with an exter-

▲ Royal Albert Hall

ior of red brick, terracotta and marble that was already the hallmark of South Ken architecture. The hall was finally completed in 1871 by selling seats on 999-year leases – an "ownership" that persists today, though this is also the venue for Europe's most democratic music festival, the Henry Wood Promenade Concerts. Better known as the **Proms** (ⓦwww.bbc.co.uk/proms), these top-flight classical concerts take place from July to September, with standing-only (or sit-on-the-floor) tickets for as little as £4 (see p.510). Daytime **guided tours** (daily except Wed & Thurs 10am–3.30pm; £6) depart from the porch of Door 12 and last around 45 minutes.

Behind the hall, flanked by the monumental **South Steps**, is a memorial to the Great Exhibition, once more featuring the Prince Consort. Predating the Royal Albert Hall (which Albert turns his back on), it originally stood amid the gardens and pavilions of the Royal Horticultural Society, which were replaced in the 1880s by the colossal **Imperial Institute** building. Of this only the 280-foot **Queen's Tower** remains, stranded amid the modern departments of Imperial College, the University of London's science faculty. On the north side of this complex is the neo-Gothic **Royal College of Music**, whose students have included Ralph Vaughan Williams and Benjamin Britten. The college also houses a museum (term-time Wed & Thurs 2–4.30pm; £2; ⓦwww.rcm.ac.uk) containing a collection of over seven hundred instruments, mostly European, dating from the fifteenth to the twentieth centuries.

Several other educational institutions congregate near the Albert Hall, as was Albert's intention. The most striking architecturally is the former **Royal College of Organists** to the west of the Albert Hall, a strange neo-Jacobean confection, designed for free in 1875 by Henry Cole's eldest son and laced with cream, maroon and sky-blue sgraffito. Also on the west side of the Albert Hall is the headquarters of the **Royal College of Art** (ⓦwww.rca.ac.uk), a seven-storey 1960s block which belies its foundation by Prince Albert; student art exhibitions are held during term-time on the ground floor (daily 10am–6pm; free).

To the east of the Albert Hall is the **Royal Geographical Society** (Mon–Fri 10am–5pm; free; ☎020/7591 3000, ⓦwww.rgs.org), a wonderful brick-built complex in the Queen Anne style, with statues of two of the society's early explorers, David Livingstone and Ernest Shackleton, occupying niches along the outer wall. The society hosts exhibitions and lectures, maintains a remarkable library and map room and puts on temporary exhibitions (entrance on Exhibition Road).

There are strong Polish connections in the South Kensington area, as exemplified by the **Sikorski Museum** (Mon–Fri 2–4pm, also first Sat of month

19

10am–4pm; free; ℡020/7589 9249) in the Polish Institute, a little to the east of the Royal Geographical Society at 20 Prince's Gate. This was founded after the war by Polish exiles, whose contribution to the Allied cause was significant, particularly in the RAF. World War II militaria form the bedrock of the museum, along with the personal effects of General Władysław Sikorski, the prewar prime minister who fled to London in 1939, only to die in a mysterious plane accident over Gibraltar in 1943. The absence of a non-Communist leader of Sikorski's standing after the war was lamented by exiled Poles for the next forty years.

Brompton Oratory

London's most flamboyant Roman Catholic church, the **Brompton Oratory** (℗www.bromptonoratory.com), stands just east of the Victoria and Albert Museum. The first large Catholic church to be built since the Reformation, it was begun by the young and unknown Herbert Gribble in 1880 and modelled on the Gesù church in Rome, "so that those who had no opportunity of going over to Italy to see an Italian church had only to come here to see a model of one". The ornate Italianate interior, financed by the Duke of Norfolk, is filled with gilded mosaics and stuffed with sculpture, much of it genuine Italian Baroque from the Gesù church and Siena cathedral, notably the seventeenth-century apostles in the nave and the main altar, and the reredos of the Lady Chapel. The pulpit is a superb piece of neo-Baroque from the 1930s, with a high cherub count on the tester. True to its architecture, the church practises a "rigid, ritualized, smells and bells Catholicism", as one journalist put it, with daily Mass in Latin, and some very high-society weddings throughout the year.

Victoria and Albert Museum (V&A)

In terms of sheer variety and scale, the **Victoria and Albert Museum** (daily 10am–5.45pm, Wed & last Fri of month until 10pm; free; ℡020/7942 2000, ℗www.vam.ac.uk) is the greatest museum of applied arts in the world. The range of exhibits on display at the V&A (as it's popularly known) means that whatever your taste, there's bound to be something to grab your attention: the world's largest collection of Indian art outside India, plus extensive Chinese, Islamic and Japanese galleries; a gallery of twentieth-century objets d'art to rival the Design Museum; more Constable paintings than Tate Britain, plus seven Raphael masterpieces and sizeable collections of miniatures, watercolours and medieval and Renaissance sculpture. As if all this were not enough, the V&A's temporary shows – for which you have to pay – are among the best in Britain, ranging over vast areas of art, craft and technology.

The V&A began life in 1852, under the directorship of **Henry Cole**, as the Museum of Manufactures, a gathering of objects from the Great Exhibition and a motley collection of plaster casts – it being Albert's intention to help bolster Britain's industrial dominance by inspiring factory workers, students and craftspeople with examples of excellence in applied art and design. This notion disappeared swiftly as ancient and medieval exotica poured in from other international exhibitions and from the far corners of the Empire and beyond. By the turn of the century, it was clear that Thomas Cubitt's cast-iron and glass sheds, in which the exhibits were temporarily housed, would have to be replaced with something bigger. Queen Victoria laid the foundation stone of the present, deeply colonial building in 1899 (the last major public engagement of her life); ten years later Aston Webb's imposing main entrance, with its octagonal

Visiting the V&A

As *Baedeker* noted in 1905, "it can hardly be claimed that the arrangements of the [museum] are specially perspicuous". Beautifully but haphazardly displayed across a seven-mile, four-storey maze of halls and corridors, the V&A's treasures are impossible to survey in a single visit. Floor plans from the information desks at the **main entrance** on Cromwell Road and the **side entrance** on Exhibition Road can help you decide which areas to concentrate on – we've listed some of the highlights below. Nevertheless, it's easy to get lost – the room numbering is confusing – so you may prefer to sign up for one of the museum's hourly, free **Introductory Tours** or daily **Gallery Talks**. Those with children in tow should ask about the free "Family Trails", or head for the more interactive British Galleries. The nearest **tube** is South Kensington, from which there's a long, tiled foot-tunnel leading to the V&A and the other South Ken museums.

Highlights

Architecture Level 4, rooms 127–129
British Galleries Level 2, rooms 52–58 & Level 4, rooms 118–126
European Fashion Collection Level 1, room 40
Indian art Level 1, room 41
Photography Gallery Level 1, room 38a
Plaster casts Level 1, rooms 46a & 46b
Poynter, Morris and Gamble rooms Level 1, off rooms 13 & 15
Raphael Cartoons Level 1, room 48a
Twentieth Century Galleries Level 3, rooms 70–74

cupola, flying buttresses and pinnacles, was finished. The side entrance on Exhibition Road into the Henry Cole Wing, originally built in 1873 for the School of Naval Architects and more in the South Ken style, is equally ornate, with its terracotta arcading and Minton tiles.

Raphael Cartoons, Fashion and Musical Instruments

The most famous of the V&A's many exhibits are the **Raphael Cartoons** (room 48a) to the left of the main entrance, beyond the museum shop. The cartoons comprise seven vast, full-colour paintings which are, in fact, designs for tapestries ordered by Pope Leo X for the Sistine Chapel. The pictures – based on episodes from the lives of SS Peter and Paul during the foundation of the early Christian Church (as described in Acts) – were bought by the future Charles I in 1623. They were reproduced in countless tapestries and engravings in the seventeenth and eighteenth centuries – you can view examples of the tapestries at Hampton Court Palace – and during this period were probably more familiar and influential than any of the artist's paintings. Alongside the paintings is an example of one of the tapestries woven at Mortlake in the 1630s, which are considered to be more faithful to the original colours as intended by Raphael than those woven in Brussels for the Vatican.

At the far end of room 48a stands the **Retable of St George**, a huge fifteenth-century gilded altarpiece from Valencia, centred on a depiction of James I of Aragon defeating the Moors at the Battle of Puig in 1237. More alarming, though, are the bloodthirsty side panels, which feature the gross tortures endured by St George, with him having nails driven through his body before being placed in a cauldron of molten lead, dragged naked through the streets and finally beheaded and sawn in half.

Directly opposite the Cartoons room, the V&A uses the dimly lit domed hall of Costume Court to stage special exhibitions drawn from its vast collection of European **Fashion** (room 40). A central flight of stairs leads up to the museum's

---

Future plans

Like most big museums and galleries, the V&A is in a constant state of flux, with galleries opening and closing throughout the year. At the time of writing, the museum was celebrating the opening of its new **Garden**, as well as the **Sacred Silver and Stained Glass** gallery. The **Islamic Middle East** gallery opens during the summer of 2006, with a new **Jewellery** gallery earmarked for 2008, and the completion of the **Medieval and Renaissance** gallery the following year.

(strangely silent) collection of **Musical Instruments** (room 40a), chosen for their decorative rather than musical qualities (you can't actually get to hear any of them being played); it's very often closed due to staff shortages.

South Asia, Islamic Middle East, China and Japan

Back on the ground floor, east of the Costume Court, there follows a string of superb Eastern galleries, kicking off with **South Asia** (room 41), where a fraction of this world-class collection is displayed, much of it derived from London's old East India Company Museum. The most popular exhibit, almost always on display, is **Tippoo's Tiger**, a life-sized wooden automaton of a tiger mauling an officer of the East India Company; the innards of the tiger feature a miniature keyboard which simulates the groans of the dying soldier. It was made for the amusement of the Sultan of Mysore, who was killed when the British took Seringapatam in 1799, and whose watch, telescope, brooch and sword are also displayed here.

One particular exhibit that is highly revered by the Sikh community is the **Golden Throne**, which belonged to **Ranjit Singh**, the last Sikh emperor, and was taken by the British when they annexed the Punjab in 1849. Other treasures at the heart of the gallery include several panels inset with *jalis* (sandstone window screens) and a superb white nephrite-jade wine cup, carved in the shape of a shell, made for the Mogul emperor Shah Jahan.

The new **Islamic Middle East** gallery (room 42), next door, is due to open in late summer 2006. Until then, you must pass straight on to **China** (room 44), which is organized around themes rather than in chronological sequence, with bilingual labelling and touch-screen computers on hand to elucidate. The range of materials, from jade to rhino horn, lacquer to lapis lazuli, is more striking than any individual piece, though the pair of top-hatted gentlemen carved in marble stand out in the parade of Buddhas near the entrance – they are thought to represent Korean envoys.

At the main entrance to the atmospheric adjacent Toshiba Gallery of **Japanese Art** (room 45) is an incredible bronze incense burner, decorated with life-sized peacocks – it was bought by the V&A in 1883 and the price tag of over £1500 was a record at the time. The most intriguing objects, which stand out among a wealth of silk, lacquer and samurai armour, are the tiny, elaborately carved, jade and marble *netsuke* (belt toggles) portraying such quirky subjects as "spider on aubergine" and "starving dog on a bed of leaves". Look out too for the articulated wrought-iron eighteenth-century snake.

Medieval treasures and plaster casts

The gallery (room 46) between the two Cast Courts (see oppposite) is currently used to show off the highlights of the V&A's medieval collection, including the **Gloucester Candlestick**, a Norman masterpiece of gilt bronzework with tiny figures and animals wrapped like ivy round its stem, and the **Thomas Becket**

casket, made of Limoges enamel around 1180 and decorated with scenes of the saint's martyrdom.

On either side are the two enormous **Cast Courts** filled with plaster casts – genuine fakes, as it were, created so that ordinary Londoners would be able to experience the glories of classical and ancient art. Still, with their barrel-vaulted glass roofs and heavy Victorian decor, these little-visited rooms are an astonishing sight, and hark back to the origins of the museum. In the Victorian Court to the west, a copy of the colossal Trajan's Column from the forum in Rome, sliced in half to fit in the room, towers over the rest of the plaster casts, which include the Brunswick Lion, Prague's St George and a full-scale painted replica of the entire portal of the cathedral of Santiago de Compostela, set around the ill-fitting doors of Hildsheim cathedral. In the Italian Court across room 46, a life-sized replica of Michelangelo's *David* (complete with large detachable fig-leaf round the back, used to save visiting royalty from the embarrassing sight of male genitalia) stands opposite Verrocchio's smaller bronze of the same subject in the company of the pulpits of Pisa cathedral and baptistry, and Ghiberti's celebrated bronze doors from the baptistry in Florence, which are framed by the central doorway of Bologna's San Petronio.

Photography and Northern Renaissance

The V&A now has an entire room devoted to **Photography** (room 38a). Given the limited space available, the exhibitions here are likely to change fairly frequently, and are drawn from the museum's vast collection, which was begun by Henry Cole as long ago as 1856 and now numbers over 300,000 works.

Close by are the rooms used for the V&A's special exhibitions, but if you're heading for the Poynter, Morris and Gamble rooms (see below) you need to pass through a whole series of rooms displaying works from **Northern Renaissance 1500–1700** (rooms 25–27), including a very striking simple wooden statue of Christ riding on an ass, a wonderful triptych of St Margaret overcoming a dragon and being boiled alive in pitch, and a German copper tankard designed like a miniature fairy-tale castle.

Poynter, Morris and Gamble rooms

Whatever you do, don't miss the museum's original refreshment rooms at the back of the main galleries (due to reopen in July 2006). Embellished by Edward Poynter with a wash of decorative blue tiling depicting the months and seasons of the year, the eastern **Poynter Room**, where the hoi polloi ate, was originally known as the Grill Room – the grill, also designed by Poynter, is still in place and was in use until 1939. On the other side, the dark-green **Morris Room** – one of Morris & Co's first public commissions – accommodated a better class of diner. The decorative detail is really worth taking in – gilded Pre-Raphaelite panels and Burne-Jones stained glass, embossed olive-branch wallpaper and a running cornice frieze of dogs chasing hares.

The largest and grandest of the rooms lies between the two. The **Gamble Room**, which is now open as a café once more, was designed by the museum's own team of artists and boasts dazzling, almost edible decor, with mustard, gold and cream-coloured Minton tiles covering the walls and pillars from floor to ceiling. Fleshy Pre-Raphaelite nudes hold up the nineteenth-century chimneypiece from Dorchester House, while a ceramic frieze of frolicking cherubs accompanies a quote from Ecclesiastes, spelt out in decorative script around the cornice.

Italy 1400–1500

The Poynter, Morris and Gamble rooms lie off the sprawling, L-shaped series of galleries devoted to the **Renaissance**. The collection begins, confusingly, in room 16, which is devoted to Donatello and contains – among other reliefs – the sculptor's *Ascension*, illustrating his "squashed relief" technique. Room 13 features lots of glazed terracotta works from the workshop of Della Robbia, as does room 12, which has a lovely series of roundels depicting the months and labours of the year, which once decorated the Medici palace in Florence. Room 17 boasts an entire eighteenth-century ceiling fresco, while two rooms on is the Fairfax Cup, an early sixteenth-century Venetian opaque turquoise glass, decorated with enamel scenes from Ovid's *Metamorphoses*. The collection ends in room 20, with an amazing sixteenth-century pear-wood crucifixion scene. Two of the finest works from the period, however, are displayed in room 21 – Giambologna's marble statue *Samson Slaying a Philistine* (not to be confused with Foggini's much later version nearby, *Samson Slaying Two Philistines*) and Michelangelo's two tiny wax models, one for a figure on the tomb of Pope Julius II, the other for a Medici tomb.

British Galleries

The superbly designed **British Galleries** represent the face of the new V&A, and the future looks bright: touch screens, hands-on exhibits, better lighting, colour schemes, subtle labelling, mini-cinemas, plus little puzzles and other imaginative touches combine to make these some of the most enjoyable galleries to visit. On Level 2, for example, you can design your own coat of arms, make a Tudor chair and try on a ruff, while upstairs both male and female visitors can try on a corset and crinoline, or a Sherlock Holmes-style cape.

The first series of rooms covers **Britain 1500–1760** (Level 2, rooms 52–58), and begins with Tudor times. Highlights include a bust of Henry VII by Torrigiani, who went on to design the same king's tomb in Westminster Abbey, Holbein's miniature of Anne of Cleves, with its original ivory case, and the **Howard Grace Cup**, a medieval ivory cup associated with Thomas Becket, but given a Tudor silver-gilt make-over and crowned by a tiny St George and the dragon. At the other end of the scale is the **Great Bed of Ware**, a king-sized Elizabethan oak four-poster in which 26 butchers and their wives are said to have once spent the night, and which gets a mention in William Shakespeare's *Twelfth Night*. Specific items to look out for include the **Dark Jewel** given to Francis Drake by Queen Elizabeth, the tapestries embroidered by **Mary Queen of Scots** during her incarceration, James II's wonderfully camp wedding suit and the amazing high-relief lime-wood *Stoning of St Stephen* by Gibbons.

Among the Spitalfields silks, chinoiserie, Huguenot silver and exquisite marquetry are a number of period interiors saved in their entirety from buildings that have since been demolished. These include a Jacobean panelled room from Bromley-by-Bow, a Georgian parlour from Henrietta Street in Covent Garden and the heavily gilded Rococo Music Room from Norfolk House on St James's Square. Towards the end, you should pass Roubiliac's marble statue of **Handel**, carved in 1738 and the first statue in Europe of a living artist. It originally stood in the then-fashionable Vauxhall Gardens in south London, and caused a great stir in its day, with the composer depicted as Apollo slouching in inspired disarray, one shoe dangling from his foot.

Britain 1760–1900 continues upstairs (Level 4, rooms 118–126), with a Chippendale four-poster made for the actor David Garrick, Canova's *Three*

The Ceramic Staircase and the Leighton Frescoes

Whilst you're on Level 3, make sure you see the spectacular **Ceramic Staircase**, its Minton tile decoration designed by Frank Moody, and intended to be just one of many such splendid stairwells within the museum. Note the ceramic memorial to Henry Cole, the work of his niece, who has rendered her uncle in mosaic with "Albertopolis" in relief above. Look out too for the grandiose **Leighton Frescoes**, which have been cleaned eleven times since World War II in an effort to combat the effects of the damp English climate. They used to look down onto the Cast Courts from on high; now, stuck in the corridor on Level 3 between rooms 107 and 109, you can at least see them close up.

Graces (bought jointly by the V&A and the National Gallery of Scotland in 1994 for £7.6 million) and paintings by Gainsborough and Constable. Again, period interiors are a big feature of the collection: Adam's Venetian-red Glass Drawing Room from Northumberland House and the fan-vaulted Strawberry Room from Lee Priory in Kent, which was inspired by Walpole's Gothic Revival masterpiece in Twickenham, Strawberry Hill (see p.418). You'll also find plenty of outpourings from the **Arts and Crafts movement**, starting with a cabinet painted with medieval scenes by William Morris, inspired by Walter Scott's novels. Other highlights to look out for include *La Belle Iseult*, Morris' only known painting (of his future wife), and a whole room on the Scottish School, including several tables and chairs from Glasgow tearooms designed by Charles Rennie Mackintosh.

Twentieth Century Galleries and Silver

Beyond the British rooms, the attractively designed **Twentieth Century Galleries** (Level 3, rooms 70–74) make a diffident attempt to address contemporary questions of art and design (the original purpose of the V&A). The collection itself is impressive, beginning confusingly with room 74, the first and largest of the galleries, which takes up where the Arts and Crafts room left off. The shift into modernist gear is smoothly effected with furniture by Otto Wagner, Bauhaus and the Wiener Werkstätte co-op. A Frank Lloyd Wright tea and coffee set, Constructivist fabrics and crockery follow, alongside a range of works by Finnish modernist supremo Alvar Aalto. Special exhibitions are staged here too, and the whole parade ends up with a mad melange of veggie Doc Martens, Swatch watches and a bubble-gum-pink vacuum cleaner from Japan, yours in the shops for over £1000.

The **Silver** galleries (Level 3, rooms 65–70) house the national collection of English silver from 1300 to 1800, as well as contemporary works such as a chic chain-mail bolero jacket. The centrepiece, though, is the giant **Jerningham Wine Cooler**, which is smothered with images of Bacchic revelry. It is, in fact, a Victorian copy of an eighteenth-century wine cooler – the world's largest – which took four years to make and now resides in the Hermitage. The nearby "Discovery Area" is the fun section, where you can rub or stamp a hallmark, and flick through the museum's photo store of contemporary artists working in silver. Before you leave, don't miss the three, virtually life-sized silver lions at the far end of the room.

Paintings and Sculpture

The best of the V&A's impressive collection of paintings is now spread out in rooms 81–90 on Level 3. It's difficult to know quite where to start, but the earliest and most varied works are currently "double-hung" in the Victorian style in room 81. Here, you'll find minor works by Corot, Degas, Delacroix, Rembrandt and Botticelli, a study for Ingres' *Odalisque*, a Tiepolo sketch, some Fantin-Latour flowers and several Pre-Raphaelite works, the best of which is Rossetti's verdant, emerald-green *The Day Dream*, one of his last great works. The V&A owns over four hundred works by **John Constable**, bequeathed by his daughter, including famous views of Salisbury Cathedral (in the British Galleries) and Dedham Mill, and full-sized preparatory oil paintings for *The Hay Wain* and *The Leaping Horse*, plus a whole host of his alfresco cloud studies and sketches. There are also several works by **Turner**, including a dreamy view of East Cowes Castle, painted for the castle's owner, John Nash, **Gainsborough's Showbox**, in which he displayed the oil-on-glass landscapes he executed in the 1780s, plus a room of **portrait miniatures** by Holbein, Hilliard and others.

Auguste Rodin donated several sculptures to the V&A in 1914, ranging from fairly straightforward portraits, such as the bust of Balzac, to more expressive and vigorous sculptures like *The Fallen Angel*, a swirling mass of rippling bronze, and the sensuous *Cupid and Psyche*, in which the lovers emerge half-hewn from the white marble. You'll need to ask at the information desk for their whereabouts. There's also a corridor of **small-scale sculpture** in room 111, ranging from medieval religious ivories and alabaster relief panels to images of Christ and the Apostles rendered in lime-wood by German sculptors and a whole collection of works by Gilbert Bayes, who worked at Doulton, the ceramics company. The Art Deco Doulton frieze from the company's headquarters in Lambeth, has also been preserved and is now displayed in room 127 of the Architecture gallery.

Architecture, Glass and Europe and America 1800–1900

Hidden away to the right of the main entrance are a couple of new galleries well worth seeking out. First, there's the V&A's new **Architecture** gallery (Level 4, rooms 127–129), which puts on special exhibitions, but also has a permanent display of architectural models in room 128. It's an eclectic array of realized and unrealized projects – everything from a fifteenth-century mosque, an eighteenth-century British imperial fort, a Le Corbusier villa, Spiral (Daniel Libeskind's now-shelved extension for the V&A), the British Museum's Round Reading Room and contemporary zero-energy housing, to Bluewater, Britain's largest mall.

Beyond lies the small hi-tech **Glass Gallery** (Level 4, room 131) on the second floor, with touch-screen computers and a spectacular modern glass staircase and balustrade. The beauty and variety of the glass on display is staggering, and ranges from the Greek and Roman world to objets d'art by contemporary artists.

Tucked away beneath Glass and Architecture, in the basement, is **Europe and America 1800–1900** (Level 0, rooms 8 & 9). The first room is given over to the kind of over-the-top stuff that packed out the international exhibitions of the 1860s and 1870s – cumbersome neo-Gothic furniture and the like. The small green room at the end contains works from the 1900 Paris Exhibition, which heralded the emergence of Art Nouveau. Tiffany glassware, furniture by Adolf Loos and Otto Wagner, and posters by Toulouse-Lautrec, Hector Guimard and Alfons Mucha are thrown in for good measure.

Science Museum

The **Science Museum** (daily 10am–6pm; free; ☎0870/870 4868, ⊛www .sciencemuseum.org.uk) on Exhibition Road is undeniably impressive, filling seven floors with items drawn from every conceivable area of science, including space travel, telecommunications, time measurement, chemistry, computing, photography and medicine. With the opening of the spectacular, hi-tech **Wellcome Wing**, the museum moved decisively into the twenty-first century, and nearly all the old galleries have now been redesigned and made much more accessible to the non-specialist. The museum also puts on populist special exhibitions (for which you have to pay), often timed to coincide with the latest special-effects movie.

First stop inside should be the **information desk**, where you can pick up a museum plan and find out what events and demonstrations are taking place; you can also sign up for a free **guided tour** on a specific subject. Most people will want to head for the Wellcome Wing at the back of the museum; note, however, that to go on a virtual-reality ride or to see IMAX presentations in the Wellcome Wing, you have to pay and book ahead (see below). The Wellcome Wing is connected to the old museum at each level; touch-screen computers can show you exactly how to get from one section to the other. There's a simple café off the East Hall, and the very funky *Deep Blue Café* in the Wellcome Wing. Those without kids should find out if anything is going on at the museum's **Dana Centre** (☎020/7942 4040, ⊛www.danacentre.org.uk), where free talks, discussions and events aimed at adults take place.

The Energy Hall, Space and the Making of the Modern World

At the time of going to print, the museum was busy redesigning its entrance and the new **Energy Hall**, which focuses on the advent of the Industrial Revolution and features some of the world's first steam engines. Beyond lies the **Space** exhibition, which follows the history of rockets from tenth-century China and Congreve's early nineteenth-century efforts, through the V-1 and V-2 wartime bombs, right up to the Apollo landings. There's a full-size replica of the Apollo 11 landing craft which deposited US astronauts on the moon in 1969, and one of the Viking Landers that reached Mars in the mid-1970s. However, it's obvious from the section on the Hubble Space Telescope on the mezzanine that this gallery is due for a revamp.

The old Transport hall is now **Making the Modern World**, a display of iconic inventions of modern science and technology. These include some of the museum's best-loved exhibits including *Puffing Billy*, the world's oldest surviving steam locomotive, used for hauling coal in 1815, and Robert Stephenson's *Rocket* of 1829, which won the contract for the Manchester to Liverpool passenger service. Other ground-breaking inventions on display include a Ford Model T, the world's first mass-produced car, a gleaming aluminium Lockheed 10A Electra airliner from 1935, which signalled the birth of modern air travel, and the Apollo 10 command module that landed back on earth. Less glamorous discoveries, such as the brain scanner, occupy the sidelines, along with disasters such as the thalidomide drug.

Wellcome Wing

The darkened, ultra-purple **Wellcome Wing** beckons you on, its ground floor dominated by the floating, sloping underbelly of the museum's **IMAX cinema**. If you're interested in visiting the cinema (☎0870/870 4771; £7.50), or having a go at the **SimEx Simulator Ride** (£3.75), you need to buy a ticket from the desk to your right as you enter the wing. To one side is the **Deep Blue Café**, with its enticing underlit perspex tables and flashing pagers that tell you when your table is ready.

The displays on the ground floor, **Antenna** and **Talking Points**, are specifically designed to be changed regularly in order to cover contemporary science issues while they are topical. **Pattern Pod**, meanwhile, is for under-8-year-olds only, and is basically a lot of interactive hi-tech fun. Kids can experiment with water ripples, footprints and the Penrose tessellation, and groove away in the multicoloured human shadow box.

On Floor 1, **Who am I?** is a guaranteed winner, as it concentrates on humans themselves. The gallery features a series of "bloids", large blobs fitted with computers at different levels, where you can morph yourself into the opposite sex, watch a sperm race, and test the gender of your brain. Down the middle of the gallery are traditional static displays and reading matter, which delve more deeply into the issues raised in the bloids.

Floor 2 is home to **Digitopolis**, which attempts to explain the basics of how digital technology works, and its importance in the modern world. Whether it succeeds or not, this is the gallery with the most sophisticated computerized gimmicks – a Sony robot dog, which can actually learn behaviour, is the resident pet. You can make yourself sound like an alien opera singer, make digital music or give yourself a leopard-print skin via a 3D face scanner. The inner workings of these sophisticated tools are on display close by, and there are touch-screen quizzes, snippets of poetry and works of art to keep arts-inclined visitors happy.

Finally, on the third (and uppermost) floor of the Wellcome Wing, **In Future** is a small interactive gallery where several people can gather round and play a series of frivolous but fun multi-player educational games, and vote on contemporary scientific and moral questions, such as "should you be able to choose the gender of your child?"

The basement: hands-on galleries

Throughout the 1990s, the most popular section for those with children was the museum's **Launch Pad**. This lively play area has since been moved to the basement of the Wellcome Wing, and remains riotously popular with kids, though it's due to be redesigned and relocated sometime in the future.

There are two more hands-on galleries and a family picnic area in the rest of the basement. The misleadingly entitled **Garden** is aimed at 3- to 6-year-olds, and there's no denying that they will enjoy themselves – donning waterproofs to experiment with lock gates, and hard hats to play with pulleys.

Beyond the Garden, there's another hands-on gallery, imaginatively entitled **Things**, aimed at the natural curiosity of 7- to 11-year-olds about unidentifiable objects. A longer attention span and a fair bit of reading are involved, and there are the usual problems with crowds at the weekend and with the durability of the exhibits. Lastly, the basement also houses the **Secret Life of the Home**, a static but interesting collection of domestic appliances from the last hundred years, displayed in glass cabinets.

Floor 1

The **Challenge of Materials**, ranged around the balcony on the first floor, is an extremely stylish exhibition – the glass-floored suspension bridge is particularly cool – covering the use of materials ranging from aluminium to zerodur (used for making laser gyroscopes). As well as the excellent hands-on displays, there are aesthetically pleasing exhibits as diverse as a Bakelite coffin and an Axminster-carpet morning gown designed by Vivienne Westwood.

The rest of Floor 1 is relatively old-fashioned. Passing through **Agriculture** with its model ploughs and tractors, followed by displays on surveying and weather, you'll eventually find **Time Measurement**, which stretches from Egyptian water clocks to quartz watches; the medieval clock mechanism from Wells Cathedral booms out over the entire hall every quarter of an hour.

Floor 2

The most popular section on Floor 2 is the new **Energy** gallery, with its "do not touch" electric-shock machine that absolutely fascinates kids. Much of it is thought-provoking stuff – you can play computer games to reduce your carbon emissions – and the rest comprises more conventional, though stylish, static exhibits, everything from a bird oil lamp to a clay stove from contemporary Kenya.

Elsewhere on Floor 2, there are sections on **Computing** and **Mathematics** now renamed "histories", as they were designed some years ago. Taking up quite some space are Charles Babbage's gargantuan Difference Engine 1, the world's first computer built in 1832, and his second version, which was never realized as he ran out of money, but which the museum completed in 1991.

Finally, you reach another little-visited area of the museum, the **Ships** section, with its interminable glass cabinets of model vessels from the *Great Harry* and the *Mayflower* to the *Great Eastern* and the *Cutty Sark*, not to mention Townsend Thoresen's ill-fated *Spirit of Free Enterprise*, which sank in the Zeebrugge disaster of 1987. Look out too for the model of the old London docks, at the point of their demise in the 1960s.

Floor 3

Some exquisitely made scientific instruments, chiefly created by George Adams for George III, provide aesthetic relief in **Science in the 18th Century** on Floor 3, especially the ornate Grand Orrery and Philosophical Table. Close by, the design influence of the Wellcome Institute is evident in the excellent, hi-tech **Health Matters**, which dwells on more modern medical history from the introduction of mass vaccination to the new challenge of finding a cure for HIV. By contrast, the sections on this floor from Optics to Oceanography are very old-fashioned.

Heading west, you pass **On Air**, where over-12s can make a five-minute radio programme in the mock-up studio, and eventually reach the giant hangar of the **Flight** exhibition, festooned with aircraft of every description from a Spitfire to a modern executive jet. Be sure to check out the model of the Montgolfier balloon which recorded the first human flight in 1783, the full-size model of the flimsy contraption in which the Wright brothers made their epoch-making power-assisted flight in 1903, and Vickers' "Vimy", a World War I bomber which completed the first transatlantic flight in 1919.

Floors 4 and 5

On the floor above is a much older Wellcome-sponsored gallery called **Glimpses of Medical History**, a fairly undemanding series of dioramas of medical operations, and larger mock-ups of surgeries and dentists' and chemists' premises through the ages, starting with Neolithic trepanning and finishing up with the gore-free spectacle of an open-heart operation.

The best section here – and arguably of the whole museum – is Wellcome's **Science and Art of Medicine** gallery, all too easily missed on the top floor. Using an anthropological approach, this is a visual and cerebral feast, galloping through ancient medicine, medieval and Renaissance pharmacy, alchemy, quack doctors, royal healers, astrology and military surgery. Offbeat artefacts include African fetish objects, an Egyptian mummified head, numerous masks, an eighteenth-century Florentine model of a female torso giving birth and George Washington's dentures.

Natural History Museum

Alfred Waterhouse's purpose-built mock-Romanesque colossus ensures the status of the **Natural History Museum** (Mon–Sat 10am–5.50pm, Sun 11am–5.50pm; free; ☎020/7942 5000, ⊛www.nhm.ac.uk) as London's most handsome museum. Its vast collections derive from a bequest by Hans Sloane to the British Museum, separated off in the 1860s after a huge power struggle. Charles Darwin, notably, opposed the move, in part for the separation of science from the other arts, in part due to his hatred of the founding director, Richard Owen, an amazing figure who arranged expeditions around the globe to provide everything from butterflies to dinosaurs for the museum's cabinets.

The museum has been massively redeveloped over the last decade or so, and is now, by and large, imaginatively designed, though there are still one or two sections that remain little changed since the original opening in 1881. The museum's dinosaur collection is a real hit with the kids, but its collections are also an important resource for serious zoologists. The **main entrance** is in the middle of the 675-foot terracotta facade and brings you into the **Life Galleries**; if the queues are long (as they can be at the weekend and during school holidays), you're better off heading for the **side entrance** on Exhibition Road, and into what used to be the old Geology Museum, now the museum's **Earth Galleries**.

Life Galleries

The **Central Hall** is dominated by the plaster cast of a **Diplodocus** skeleton, 85ft in length from tip to tail, while the "side chapels" are filled with "wonders" of the natural world – a model of a sabre-toothed tiger, a stuffed Great Bustard, a dodo skeleton and so on. It's worth pausing here to take in the architecture of this vast "nave", whose walls are decorated with moulded terracotta animals and plants.

The redesigning and marketing of the **Dinosaurs** gallery, to the west of the Central Hall, was a stroke of genius by the museum curators. A raised walkway leads straight to the highlight for many kids, the grisly life-sized animatronic tableau of

▲ Central Hall, Natural History Museum

two Oviraptors roosting, while two carnivorous Velociraptors get ready to attack (new fossil discoveries mean that the dinosaurs depicted are now furry). The rest of the displays are less theatrical and more informative, with massive-jawed skeletons and more conventional models.

The other firm favourite with kids is the insect and arthropod room on the other side of the Central Hall, known as **Creepy-Crawlies** (room 33), which is filled with giant models of bugs, arachnids and crustaceans, plus displays on the life cycle of the wasp and other unlovely creatures. It's here that you'll find the only live exhibits in the entire museum, a colony of leaf-cutter ants from Trinidad, which feed on a fungus that they grow on the leaves they've gathered.

A small thicket of reconstructed rainforest, situated opposite the Creepy-Crawlies, forms the entrance to the **Ecology** gallery (room 32), a glass corridor crisscrossed with overhead walkways, which takes you through the basics of green politics – the food chain, recycling, the ozone layer and the greenhouse effect. It's a hi-tech, child-friendly exhibition, with a serious message, only slightly marred by the fact that it's sponsored by British Petroleum.

Down in the basement is an excellent futuristic gallery called **Investigate** (Mon–Sat 10.30am–5pm, Sun 11.30am–5pm; term-time Mon–Fri 2.30–5pm, Sat 10.30am–5pm, Sun 11.30am–5pm), aimed at children aged 7 to 14 years, for which you need to obtain a timed ticket. Kids get to choose a tray of specimens and then play at being scientists, using microscopes, scales, a computer and various tools of the trade to examine and catalogue the items before them. There are one or two simpler hands-on exhibits too, as well as several plant species to look at.

The old-fashioned **Mammals** gallery (rooms 23 & 24), back on the ground floor, is filled with stuffed animals and plastic models and dominated by a full-sized model of a blue whale juxtaposed with its skeleton. It usually goes down well enough with younger children, but it's showing its age somewhat. Upstairs on the first floor, the story of mammals continues with an investigation into the emergence of bipeds among the **Primates**.

Also on the first floor is the old-style **Minerals** gallery (room 102), regimented rows of glass cabinets culminating in a darkened chamber on **Meteorites** – all of which really belongs in the Earth Galleries. If you've made it this far, don't miss the 1300-year-old slice of **Giant Sequoia**, on the second floor, a mere youngster compared to other members of the species that are still standing after more than 3200 years. Whilst you're here, admire the view down onto the Central Hall and the moulded monkeys clinging to the arches.

Darwin Centre

Despite its enormous size, the Natural History Museum has only ever displayed less than a hundredth of its collection, most of which consists of zoological specimens collected from around the world over the last two hundred years and preserved in alcohol. Visitors can now view a few of these zoological bits and bobs in the collections store of the museum's new **Darwin Centre** (closes at 5.30pm, otherwise same hours as main museum). Among the more bizarre items pickled in the glass jars are a 50-year-old piece of algae from Mauritius, a partially digested human head from a sperm whale's stomach and a brown rat found on the Darwin Centre building site.

To see the rest of the Darwin Centre, you need to sign up for a **guided tour** (book ahead either online or by phone ☎020/7942 6128). These set off roughly every half an hour and last about thirty minutes, allowing visitors to get a closer look at the specimens, including the larger ones which have to be preserved in tanks. You also get a look behind the scenes at the laboratories, and even talk to one of the museum's 350 scientists about their work. Phase Two of the Darwin Centre is scheduled to open in winter 2008, and will house the museum's 28 million insect and 6 million plant specimens.

Earth Galleries

Approaching the **Earth Galleries** from Exhibition Road, you enter a vast, darkened hall with the solar system and constellations writ large on the walls, then walk past statues of Medusa, Atlas, Cyclops and an astronaut, before boarding an escalator which takes you through a partially formed globe to **The Power Within**, a big exhibition on volcanoes and earthquakes. The most popular section is the Kobe earthquake simulator, where you enter a mock-up of a Japanese supermarket and see the soy-sauce bottles wobble, while watching an in-store video of the real event. Despite the museum's protestations, the whole thing seems in very poor taste. On the other side of the same floor is **Restless Surface**, an interactive display on the earth's elements, soil and rock erosion and, of course, global warming.

Down one floor is **From the Beginning**, which covers the geological history of the planet from the Big Bang to the present day. The display ends with a crystal ball, which predicts the earth's future (bleak, but probably not within our lifetime). Perhaps the most alluring of the new galleries is the **Earth's Treasury**, a dimly lit display of lustrous minerals and crystals, gemstones and jewels. Exhibits include rocks that shine in UV light, carved artefacts such as a lapis lazuli necklace, and a few serious gems, including a 17-carat diamond worth at least £1 million and an emerald the size of a lemon.

Finally, **Earth Today and Tomorrow** (on the ground floor) is a depressing look at how we are running down the earth's non-renewable natural resources, and polluting the planet in the process. Ironically, one of the chief sponsors is Rio Tinto, the distinctly environmentally unfriendly mining company. More positively, the gallery also explains how the museum dug its own borehole, which provides its washrooms and laboratories with up to half a gallon of water a second.

Adults keen to learn a bit more about UK geology should head for the **Earth Lab** (room 66; daily noon–5pm), where you can (with some professional assistance) play with the museum's microscopes, and identify rock, mineral and fossil samples.

Knightsbridge and Belgravia

Knightsbridge and Belgravia contain some of the most expensive real estate in London (or indeed the world). **Knightsbridge** is irredeemably snobbish, revelling in its reputation as the swankiest shopping area in London, largely thanks to Harrods, one of London's most popular tourist attractions. **Belgravia**, over to the east, was transformed into Regency suburbs in the aftermath of the Napoleonic Wars by the chief landowners, the Grosvenors. Strategically close to Buckingham Palace, which George IV chose as his chief residence, Belgravia had immediate cachet, and still does: it is London's chief embassy land, with at least 25 scattered amongst the grid-plan stuccoed streets.

Harrods

Most people come to Knightsbridge for just one thing: to shop or gawp at **Harrods** (Mon–Sat 10am–7pm or later during the sales; ⊕www.harrods.com) on Brompton Road. Without doubt the most famous department store in London, it started out as a family-run grocery store in 1849, with a staff of two. The current 1905 terracotta building, which turns into a palace of fairy lights at night, is now owned by the Egyptian Mohamed Al Fayed, *bête noire* of the Establishment, and employs in excess of three thousand staff, including several ex-army bagpipers who perform daily. The store occupies four acres, and is made up of more than three hundred departments, a dozen bars and restaurants, and even its own pub, all spread over seven floors.

Tourists flock to Harrods – it's thought to be the city's third top tourist attraction – with some thirty thousand customers passing through each day. Most Londoners limit their visits to the annual sales, with more than 300,000 arriving on the first day of the Christmas give-away bonanza, though the store also has its regular customers, drawn from the so-called "Tiara Triangle" of this very wealthy neighbourhood, who would think nothing of buying dog food at cordon bleu prices. To help keep out the non-purchasing riffraff, a draconian **dress code** is enforced: no shorts, no vest T-shirts, and backpacks to be carried in the hand. Once here, however, make sure you avail yourself of the first-floor "luxury washrooms" where you can splash on a range of perfumes for free.

In truth, you can buy much of what the shop stocks a great deal more cheaply if you can do without the Harrods carrier bag, but the store does have a few sections that are architectural sights in their own right. Chief among these are the **Food Hall**, with its exquisite Arts and Crafts tiling and tempting oyster counter, and the Egyptian Hall, with its pseudo-hieroglyphs and sphinxes, both of which are on the ground floor. The Egyptian Escalator in the centre of the building is an added attraction, especially the **Di and Dodi fountain shrine** at its base. Here, to the strains of Mahler (and the like), you can contemplate photos of the ill-fated couple, and, preserved in a glass pyramid, a dirty wineglass used on the couple's last evening and the engagement ring Dodi allegedly bought for Di the previous day.

Around Knightsbridge

If you want more window-shopping, or you have a wallet equipped for top-range designer clothing shops, **Sloane Street**, which runs due south of Knightsbridge tube, is the obvious next stop. Right on the corner of the street, facing the tube, is **Harvey Nichols**, another palatial department store, whose reputation has spiralled in recent years. Like Harrods, it has a wonderful food hall and a panoply of designer sections, while its fifth-floor café/restaurant is a favourite place to lunch for career shoppers. As you walk down Sloane Street, the names read like a fashion directory, including Giorgio Armani, Chanel, D&G, Christian Dior, Nicole Farhi, Gucci, Katharine Hamnett, Prada, Valentino, Versace and YSL.

For the shopping-surfeited, Knightsbridge's mews and squares are good for a quick stroll. Having been built to house servants and stables, converted mews houses, like those in **Pont Street Mews** immediately behind Harrods, are now among the most sought-after properties in the area. Built on a completely different scale are the red-brick four-, five- and six-storey mansions that flaunt their high Dutch gables off Pont Street proper. The most extreme examples of the "Pont Street Dutch" style are in fact in **Harrington** and **Collingham**

Gardens, to the west of South Kensington tube. They were built by Ernest George, who was fired up after a visit to Holland in the 1870s.

Belgravia

Despite its spacious streets of crisp white stucco, **Belgravia** is a soulless place, and not one in which you're likely to want to spend much time, except perhaps to visit one of its smart pubs (see p.484). If curiosity leads you here, the best approach is to take the tube to Hyde Park Corner and walk along Grosvenor Crescent, which curves round into **Belgrave Square**, a grandiose nineteenth-century set piece with detached villas positioned at three of its four corners. With royalty ensconced in nearby Buckingham Palace, and Queen Victoria's mother temporarily living in the square, the area immediately attracted exactly the sort of clientele that property developer and architect Cubitt had hoped for, with three dukes, thirteen peers and thirteen MPs in residence by 1860. Nowadays, the place bristles with security cameras and police in bulletproof jackets guarding the numerous embassies; few can afford whole houses here, with short-lease apartments alone fetching millions of pounds.

Chelsea, Battersea and Fulham

Until the sixteenth century, **Chelsea** was nothing more than a tiny fishing village on the banks of the Thames. It was Thomas More who started the upward trend by moving here in 1520, followed by members of the nobility, including Henry VIII himself (51 Glebe Place was for a long time thought to be his former hunting lodge). In the eighteenth century, Chelsea acquired its riverside houses along Cheyne Walk, which gradually attracted a posse of literary and intellectual types.

However, it wasn't until the latter part of the nineteenth century that Chelsea began to earn its reputation as London's very own Left Bank, a bohemianism formalized by the foundation of the Chelsea Arts Club in 1891 and entrenched in the 1960s, when Chelsea was at the forefront of "Swinging London", with the likes of David Bailey, Mick Jagger, George Best and the "Chelsea Set" hanging out in Continental-style boutiques and coffee bars. The King's Road was also a fashion parade for hippies, as well as the birthplace of punk.

These days, Chelsea has a more subdued feel, with high rents and house prices keeping things staid, and interior-design shops rather than avant-garde fashion the order of the day. The area's other aspect, oddly enough considering its reputation, is a military one, with the former Chelsea Barracks, the Royal Hospital (home of old soldiers known as the Chelsea Pensioners) and the National Army Museum.

Further west, Chelsea becomes rather more down-to-earth, a transition signalled by the presence of the local football ground, Stamford Bridge. Beyond here lies **Fulham**, whose main point of interest is Fulham Palace, at the very end of the King's Road. To the south, across the river, Chelsea aspirants have, over the past two decades, colonized previously working-class **Battersea**, an area dominated by the brooding presence of Battersea Power Station.

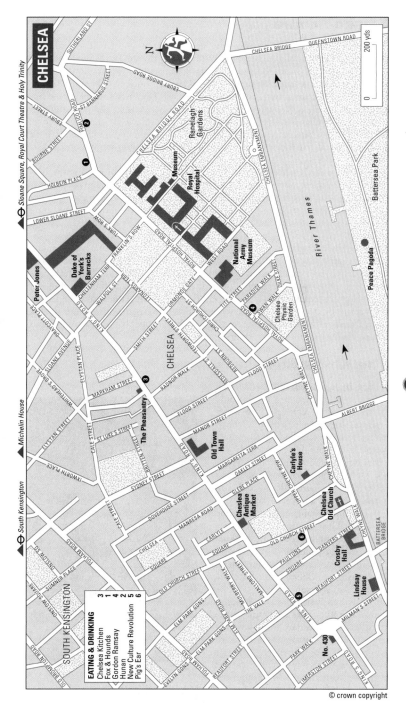

CHELSEA

SOUTH KEN, KNIGHTSBRIDGE AND CHELSEA | Chelsea

EATING & DRINKING
Chelsea Kitchen 3
Fox & Hounds 1
Gordon Ramsay 4
Hunan 2
New Culture Revolution 5
Pig's Ear 6

© crown copyright

Sloane Square

Sloane Square, a leafy nexus on the very eastern edge of Chelsea, takes its name from the wealthy eighteenth-century local doctor Hans Sloane, whose "noble cabinet" of curios formed the basis of the British Museum. In the 1980s, the square gave its name to the "Sloane Rangers", society debutantes whose most famous specimen was Princess Diana herself. The term has since gone out of fashion, but Sloanes – whose natural habitat is here, and in South Kensington and Knightsbridge – still exist, and are easily identifiable by their dress code: blue-and-white pinstriped shirts, cords and brogues for the men; flicked-back hair, pearls and flat shoes for the women; and waxed cotton Barbour jackets for all.

At the head of the square, by the tube, stands the **Royal Court Theatre**, bastion of new theatre writing since John Osborne's *Look Back in Anger* sent tremors through the establishment in 1956, and still going strong. On the opposite side is **Peter Jones**, a popular department store for upper-middle-class wedding lists, housed in London's finest glass-curtain building, built in the 1930s, which curves its way seductively into the King's Road.

Round the corner in Sloane Street is another architectural masterpiece, **Holy Trinity** (Mon–Sat 8.30am–5.30pm, Sun 8.30am–1.30pm; ⊕www.holy-trinitysloanestreet.org), created in 1890, and probably the finest Arts and Crafts church in London. The east window is the most glorious of the furnishings, a vast 48-panel extravaganza designed by Edward Burne-Jones, and the largest ever made by Morris & Co. As with All Saints, Margaret Street (see p.125), Holy Trinity is very High Church, filled with the smell of incense and statues of the Virgin Mary, and even offering confession.

The King's Road

⑲

The **King's Road**, Chelsea's main artery, was designed as a royalty-only thoroughfare by Charles II, in order – so the story goes – to avoid carriage congestion en route to Nell Gwynne's house in Fulham, but more likely as a short cut to Hampton Court. George III used the road to get to Kew, but lesser mortals could do so only on production of a special copper pass – it was finally opened to the public in 1830. This prompted a flurry of speculative building that produced the series of elegant, open-ended squares – Wellington, Markham, Carlyle and Paultons – which still punctuate the road.

The King's Road's household fame, however, came through its role as the unofficial catwalk of the Swinging Sixties. While Carnaby Street cashed in on its past long after its glory days were over, the King's Road managed to move with the times, through the

▲ World's End, King's Road

hippie era, punk and beyond. The "Saturday Parade" of fashion victims is not what it used to be, but posey cafés, boutiques and antiques are still what the King's Road is all about. And the traditional "Chelsea Cruise", when every flash Harry in town parades his customized motor, still takes place at 8.30pm on the last Saturday of the month, though nowadays on the Battersea side of Chelsea Bridge.

If you don't fancy walking down the King's Road, buses #11 and #22 run the length of it, and bus #19 runs partway down and then south across Battersea Bridge. On the south side of the road, a short stroll from Sloane Square, is the **Duke of York's Barracks**, headquarters of the Territorial Army, now transformed into a public piazza with shops and cafés. A little further down on the same side is **Royal Avenue**, the first of the squares that open out onto the King's Road, and where James Bond, Ian Fleming's spy hero, had his London address. Unlike the other squares off the King's Road, this one is rather like a Parisian *place*, with plane trees and gravel down the centre, and was originally laid out in the late seventeenth century as part of William III's ambitious (and unrealized) scheme to link Kensington Palace with the Royal Hospital to the south.

Perhaps the most striking premises along King's Road are **The Pheasantry**, a fine red-brick mansion set back slightly from the road, behind an archway flanked by bronze caryatids and topped by a mini-quadriga. After the pheasants which gave the building its name flew the nest, and the French upholsterers whose wares are still advertised from the stonework upped and left, the house was used by the Russian-born ballet dancer and teacher Princess Stephanie Astafieva as a ballet school. Later it became a drinking club, frequented by the likes of Dylan Thomas and Augustus John; Eric Clapton lived here briefly in the 1960s and, somewhat inevitably, it has now become a branch of *Pizza Express*.

The most famous address of all on the King's Road is **no. 430**, a modest little shop about a mile away from Sloane Square, where the designer Vivienne Westwood and her then-boyfriend Malcolm McLaren opened a teddy-boy revival store called Let It Rock, located, with a neat sense of irony, right next door to the Chelsea Conservative Club. In 1975 they changed tack and renamed the shop Sex, stocking it with proto-punk fetishist gear, with simulated burnt limbs in the window. It became a magnet for the likes of John Lydon and John Simon Ritchie, better known as Johnny Rotten and Sid Vicious – the rest, as they say, is history. Now known as World's End, the shop, with its landmark backward-running clock, continues to flog Westwood's eccentric designer clothes.

Royal Hospital Chelsea

Among the most nattily attired of all those parading down the King's Road are the scarlet- or navy-blue-clad Chelsea Pensioners, the army veterans who live in the nearby **Royal Hospital** (Mon–Sat 10am–noon & 2–4pm, Sun 2–4pm; free; ℡020/7881 5204, ⒲www.chelsea-pensioners.org.uk), founded by Charles II in 1682. Until the Civil War, England had no standing army and therefore no need to provide for its old soldiers; by the time of Charles's reign, all that had changed. Supposedly prompted by Nell Gwynne's encounter with a begging ex-serviceman on the King's Road, but more likely by Louis XIV's Hôtel des Invalides in Paris, Charles II commissioned Wren to provide a suitably grand almshouse for the veterans. The end result – plain, red-brick wings and grassy courtyards, which originally opened straight onto the river – became a blueprint for institutional and collegiate architecture all over the English-speaking world.

19

Wilde about Chelsea

John Singer Sargent, Augustus John, James Whistler and Bertrand Russell all lived at one time or another in Tite Street, which runs alongside the National Army Museum, but by far the street's most famous resident was writer and wit **Oscar Fingal O'Flahertie Wills Wilde** (1856–1900), who moved into no. 1 in 1880 with an old Oxford chum, Frank Miles, only to be asked to leave the following year by the latter (under pressure from his father, Canon Miles), after the hostile reception given to Wilde's recently published poetry. Four years later, Wilde moved back into the street to no. 34, with his new bride Constance Lloyd. By all accounts he was never very good at "playing husband", though he was happy enough to play father to his two boys (when he was there). It was in Tite Street, in 1891, that Wilde first met Lord Alfred Douglas, son of the Marquis of Queensberry and known to his friends as "Bosie", who was to become his lover, and eventually to prove his downfall.

At the height of Wilde's fame, just four days after the first night of *The Importance of Being Earnest*, the marquis left a visiting card for Wilde, on which he wrote "To Oscar Wilde, posing as a somdomite [sic]". Urged on by Bosie, Wilde unsuccessfully sued Queensberry, losing his case when the marquis produced incriminating evidence against Wilde himself. On returning to the *Cadogan Hotel* on Sloane Street, where Bosie had rooms, Wilde was arrested by the police, taken to Bow Street police station, charged with homosexual offences and eventually sentenced to two years' hard labour. Bankrupt, abandoned by Bosie and separated from his wife, he served his sentence in Pentonville, Wandsworth and later Reading jail. On his release he fled abroad, travelling under the pseudonym of Sebastian Melmoth, and died three years later from a syphilitic infection. He was buried in Paris's Père Lachaise cemetery.

The central courtyard, **Figure Court**, is centred on a bronze statue of the founder in Roman attire, by Grinling Gibbons. On Oak Apple Day (May 29), the Pensioners, wearing their traditional tricorn hats, festoon the monarch's statue with oak leaves to commemorate the day after the Battle of Worcester in 1651, when Charles hid in Boscobel Oak to escape his pursuers. On the north side of the courtyard, below the central lantern, a giant Tuscan portico leads to the Octagon Porch. On one side is the austere **chapel**, with a huge barrel vault and a splash of colour in the apse provided by Sebastiano Ricci's *Resurrection*, in which Jesus patriotically bears the flag of St George. Opposite lies the equally grand, wood-panelled **dining hall**, where the four hundred or so Pensioners still eat under portraits of the sovereigns and a vast allegorical mural of Charles II and his hospital by Antonio Verrio. In the Secretary's Office, designed by John Soane, on the east side of the hospital, there's a small **museum** (Mon–Sat 10am–noon & 2–4pm, April–Sept also Sun 2–4pm; free), with Pensioners' uniforms, medals and two German bombs.

The playing fields to the south, from which you get the finest view of the hospital, are the venue for the annual **Chelsea Flower Show**, organized by the Royal Horticultural Society, which takes place during the last week of May (☎0870/906 3781, ⓦwww.rhs.org.uk). To the east is the last remnant of one of London's most famous pleasure gardens, **Ranelagh Gardens**, now a pleasant little landscaped patch used mostly by the Chelsea Pensioners, but open to the general public too. A couple of information panels in the gardens' Soane-designed shelter show what the place used to look like when Canaletto painted it in 1751. The main feature was a giant rotunda, modelled on the Pantheon in Rome, where the beau monde could promenade to musical accompaniment – the 8-year-old Mozart played here. Shortly after it opened in 1742, Walpole reported that "you can't set your foot without treading on a Prince or Duke". Fashion is fickle, though, and the rotunda was eventually demolished in 1805.

National Army Museum

The concrete bunker next door to the Royal Hospital, on Royal Hospital Road, houses the little-visited **National Army Museum** (daily 10am–5.30pm; free; ☎020/7730 0717, ⊛www.national-army-museum.ac.uk). The militarily obsessed are unlikely to be disappointed by the succession of uniforms and medals, but there's not much here for non-enthusiasts. The temporary exhibitions staged on the ground floor are without a doubt the museum's strong point, but overall it's disappointing – you're better off visiting the infinitely superior Imperial War Museum (see p.266).

To follow the museum chronologically, you need to start in the basement with the **Redcoats** (1415–1792), which takes you from Agincourt to the American Revolution, before heading for the **Road to Waterloo**, where you can see the skeleton of Marengo, Napoleon's charger at the battle, the saw used to amputate the Earl of Uxbridge's leg and an audiovisual played out over a large spotlit model of Waterloo (built in the 1830s) where 48,000 lost their lives. Florence Nightingale's supposed lamp and Richard Caton-Woodville's famous painting of *The Charge of the Light Brigade* are among the highlights of the adjacent **Victorian Soldier**, a none-too-critical look at the British Empire, after which you should head across to **From World War to Cold War**, which concentrates on the two world wars.

The **Modern Army** section, on the top floor, starts with a good section on National Service, inviting you to inspect a soldier's kit, learn how to drill and try on a uniform, but overall it's really little more than a propaganda exercise for the armed forces. Next door in the **Art Gallery**, there are some excellent military portraits by the likes of Reynolds, Gainsborough, Romney and Lawrence, not to mention a suave self-portrait by a uniformed Rex Whistler, who died in action shortly after D-Day.

Chelsea Physic Garden

The **Chelsea Physic Garden** (April–Oct Wed noon–5pm, Sun 2–6pm; £6; ☎020/7352 5646, ⊛www.chelseaphysicgarden.co.uk) lies at the western end of Royal Hospital Road. Founded in 1673 by the Royal Society of Apothecaries, this is the oldest botanical garden in the country after Oxford's: the first cedars grown in this country were planted here in 1683, cotton seed was sent from here to the American colonies in 1732, England's first rock garden was constructed here in 1773, and the walled garden contains Britain's oldest olive tree. Unfortunately, it's a rather small garden, and a little too close to Chelsea Embankment to be a peaceful oasis. It's really of most interest to very keen botanists – to learn more, take the free guided walk at 1.30pm. At the entrance (on Swan Walk) you can pick up a map of the garden with a list of the month's most interesting flowers and shrubs, whose labels are slightly more forthcoming than the usual terse Latinate tags. A statue of Hans Sloane, who presented the Society with the freehold, stands at the centre of the garden; behind him there's a teahouse, serving afternoon tea and delicious home-made cakes, with exhibitions on the floor above.

Cheyne Walk

Chelsea Physic Garden marks the beginning of **Cheyne Walk** (pronounced "chainy"), whose quiet riverside locale and succession of Queen Anne and Georgian houses drew artists and writers here in great numbers during the nineteenth century. Since the building of the Embankment and the increase in the volume of traffic, however, the character of this peaceful haven has been lost. Novelist Henry James, who lived at no. 21, used to take "beguiling drives" in his wheelchair along the Embankment; today, he'd be hospitalized in the process. An older contemporary of James, Mary Ann Evans (better known under her pen name George Eliot), moved into no. 4 – the first blue plaque you come to – in December 1880, five months after marrying an American banker 21 years her junior. Three weeks later she died of a kidney disease. In the 1960s, Mick Jagger and Keith Richards graced this section of Cheyne Walk with their presence, at no. 48 and no. 3 respectively.

Perhaps the most famous of all Cheyne Walk's bohemian residents, however, were the trio who lived at the Queen's or Tudor House (no. 16): painter and poet **Dante Gabriel Rossetti**, poet Algernon Charles Swinburne and writer George Meredith. Meredith moved in shortly after the death of his first wife, who had eloped with an artist three years previously. Rossetti too moved in shortly after the death of his first wife, the model Elizabeth Siddall, from an intentional overdose of laudanum in 1862. The "tiny, gesticulating, dirty-minded" Swinburne, as one of his many critics described him, was habitually drunk, but it was Rossetti's back-garden menagerie that really got his neighbours' backs up – an amazing array that included owls, wombats, wallabies, parrots, salamanders, a Brahmin bull, burrowing armadillo, braying jackass and screeching, belligerent peacocks. In 1872 Rossetti tried to commit suicide as his wife had done, but survived to live a progressively more debauched and withdrawn existence until his death in 1882.

Chelsea Old Church and Crosby Hall

At the end of Cheyne Walk's gardens, there's a garish, gilded statue of **Thomas More**, "Scholar, Saint, Statesman", who lived hereabouts and used to worship in nearby **Chelsea Old Church** (Tues–Fri 1.30–5.30pm; ⊛www.chelseaold-church.org.uk), where he built his own private chapel in the south aisle (the hinges for the big oak doors are still visible). More is best known for his martyrdom in 1535, brought about by his refusal to swear the Oath of Succession, which declared Henry VIII's marriage to Anne Boleyn valid, and their children as heirs. However, More was himself known for punishing heretics – he even had some tied to a tree in his Chelsea back garden and flogged; his zeal in dealing with such matters is perhaps another reason why the Catholic Church canonized him in 1935. The church itself was badly bombed in the last war, but an impressive number of monuments were retrieved from the rubble and continue to adorn the interior. Chief among them is Lady Cheyne's memorial (thought to be by Bellini) and More's simple canopied memorial to his first wife, Jane, in which he himself hoped to be buried. In the event, his torso ended up in the Tower chapel, while his head was secretly buried in Canterbury by his daughter, Margaret Roper. More's second wife, Alice, is also buried here.

More's house on Cheyne Walk was destroyed in 1740 by Hans Sloane, but in the 1920s **Crosby Hall**, part of a fifteenth-century wool merchant's house once owned by More, was transferred bit by bit from Bishopsgate in the City and incorporated into the International Hostel of the British Federation of University Women, on the corner of Danvers Street, to the west of the church. The building was once occupied by the Duke of Gloucester (the future Richard III) and features in Shakespeare's *Richard III*. Sadly, it's now a private residence and its fine hammer-beam roof can no longer be viewed. If you're wondering what the twenty-storey pagoda in the distance to the west is, it belongs to **Chelsea Marina**, an exclusive (in a very literal sense) marina and apartment complex completed in 1987.

Beyond Crosby Hall

The western half of Cheyne Walk, beyond Crosby Hall, is no less rich in cultural associations. Mrs Gaskell was born in 1810 at no. 93, while the Brunels, Marc and Isambard, both lived at no. 99. The painter James Whistler, who lived at ten different addresses in the 41 years he spent in Chelsea, lived for a time at no. 96, the house where the Provisional IRA and the British government met secretly in July 1972, to discuss peace, some five months after the Bloody Sunday massacre. The Brunels' and Whistler's old residences form part of **Lindsey House**, the oldest and finest house on Cheyne Walk, built in 1674 on the site of Thomas More's farm. The house was divided into separate homes in 1775, but if you're really keen to have a look inside, it is possible to visit the entrance hall, garden room and gardens by written appointment on four specified Wednesdays of the year; phone the National Trust on ☏01494/528051 for more details (entrance is free). Last but not least, the reclusive J.M.W. Turner lived at no. 118 for the last six years of his life under the pseudonym Booth, and painted many a sunset over the Thames.

Carlyle's House

A short distance inland from Cheyne Walk, at 24 Cheyne Row, is **Carlyle's House** (April–Oct Wed–Fri 2–5pm, Sat & Sun 11am–5pm; NT; £4; ☏020/7352 7087), the Queen Anne house where the historian Thomas Carlyle set up home with his wife, Jane Welsh Carlyle, having moved down from his native Scotland in 1834. Carlyle's full-blooded and colourful style, best illustrated by his account of the French Revolution, brought him great fame during his lifetime – a statue was erected to the "Sage of Chelsea" on Cheyne Walk less than a year after his death in 1881, and the house became a museum just fifteen years later. That said, the intellectuals and artists who visited Carlyle – among them Dickens, Tennyson, Chopin, Mazzini, Browning and Darwin – were attracted as much by the wit of his strong-willed wife, with whom Carlyle enjoyed a famously tempestuous relationship. The house itself is a typically dour Victorian abode, kept much as the Carlyles would have had it – the historian's hat still hangs in the hall. Among the artefacts are an eightieth birthday card signed by the historian's famous chums, a letter from Disraeli offering a baronetcy and Carlyle's reply, refusing it. The top floor contains the garret study where Carlyle tried in vain to escape the din of the street and the neighbours' noisy roosters, in order to complete his final magnum opus on Frederick the Great.

Fulham Palace

One last sight worth visiting in this part of town is **Fulham Palace** (March–Oct Sat & Sun 2–5pm; Nov–Feb Sat & Sun 1–4pm; free; ☏020/7736 3233), stuck in the middle of Bishop's Park, at the far end of the New King's Road by Putney Bridge. Once the largest moated site in England, it was the residence of the bishop of London – third in the Church of England hierarchy – from 704 to 1973. The oldest section of the present-day complex is the modestly scaled Tudor courtyard, patterned with black diamonds; the most recent is William Butterfield's neo-Gothic chapel, which, with the other period interiors, can only be seen on the **guided tours** that take place on selected Sundays at 2pm (£5). At other times, you have to make do with the small **museum** which traces the complex history of the building, and displays a motley collection of archeological finds, including a mummified rat. In the palace grounds there's a lovely herb garden, with a Tudor gateway and a maze of miniature box hedges, but sadly no sign of a moat, since it was filled in 1921.

Battersea

Since the 1980s, aspiring Chelsea types have been colonizing the cheaper terraces and mansions across the river in **Battersea**, otherwise known as "South Chelsea". For the best part of last century, however, Battersea was a staunchly working-class enclave. In 1913 it elected the country's first black mayor, John Richard Archer, and in the 1920s returned Shapurji Saklatvala as its MP – first for the Labour Party, then as a Communist. Saklatvala was always in the news: he was banned from entry into the US and even to his native India. He was also the first person to be arrested during the 1926 General Strike, after a speech in Hyde Park urging soldiers not to fire on striking workers, for which he received a two-month prison sentence.

The poverty in the area was one of the main reasons behind the establishment of **Battersea Park** (ⓦwww.batterseapark.org), opened in 1853 as the capital's second non-royal public park after Victoria Park in the East End, and connected to Chelsea by the Albert Bridge, one of the prettiest to span the Thames, especially when lit at night. The park itself is best known nowadays for its two-tier **Peace Pagoda**, erected in 1985 by Japanese Buddhists. Made from a combination of reconstituted Portland stone and Canadian fir trees, the pagoda shelters four large gilded Buddhas in its niches. To the southeast, there's a small **Children's Zoo** (daily 10am–5pm; £4.95; ⓦwww.batterseaparkzoo. co.uk), established during the 1951 Festival of Britain; you can see monkeys, lemurs, mynah birds, otters and meerkats.

The old village of Battersea was originally centred on **St Mary's Church**, half a mile or so further west by the river. In 1775, when the current church was built, Battersea was a peaceful place with fewer than two thousand inhabitants, among them Catherine Butcher, who went on to marry the poet and visionary William Blake in the church seven years later. Another painter associated with St Mary's is Turner, who used to sit in the oriel vestry window and paint the clouds and sunsets (his favourite chair is now reverently preserved in the chancel).

Most Londoners, though, know Battersea for just two things: its Dogs Home and its Power Station. **Battersea Dogs Home** (Mon–Fri 1–4pm, Sat & Sun 10.30am–4pm; £1; ☎020/7622 3626, ⓦwww.dogshome.org) moved to 4 Battersea Park Rd in 1871 as the "Home for Lost Dogs and Cats"; cats are still catered for, as well as dogs, with over sixteen thousand a year passing through their doors. To the north stands **Battersea Power Station** (ⓦwww.thepowerstation.co.uk), Giles Gilbert Scott's awesome cathedral of power, which looks like an upturned table and features (along with a flying pig) on the Pink Floyd album cover *Animals*. Begun in 1933, it was closed in 1983, but is now going to be resurrected as part of a giant hotel, office and residential complex that will feature a concert venue, shops, bars and restaurants, and a proposed pedestrian footbridge over to the north bank of the Thames.

Earl's Court

Despite displaying the same ostentatious architecture as the rest of Kensington and Chelsea, **Earl's Court** itself is a less moneyed area, with many houses providing cheap bedsits and hotels for young Australians and New Zealanders, earning it the nickname "Kangaroo Valley". In the late 1970s, Earl's Court also became the gay capital of London, a position it has since lost to Soho. Now, it's the (male) leather crowd that predominates here, epitomized by *The Coleherne* on Old Brompton Road, London's oldest leather pub, and by its most famous former resident, **Freddie Mercury**, the flamboyant queen of Queen, whose house, Garden Lodge, 1 Logan Place, has remained a shrine for fans since his death in 1991.

The Earl's Court area is also well known for its two giant exhibition halls (ⓦwww.eco.co.uk). The earlier (and more northern) of the two is the **Olympia Exhibition Hall**, built in 1884 as the National Agricultural Hall, and now hidden behind a severe 1930s facade at the western end of Kensington High Street. It later made its name as a circus venue, but is now firmly established as a show centre, hosting annual events like the Ideal Home Exhibition, and rock concerts by ageing rock bands. Even larger shows are put on at the **Earl's Court Exhibition Hall**, erected in 1937 to the south of Olympia down Warwick Road. Both halls were used during the last war as internment centres for Germans and Italians, many of whom had fled Fascist persecution.

Brompton Cemetery

Close by *The Coleherne* (and consequently a popular cruising area) is **Brompton Cemetery** (daily: summer 8am–8pm; winter 8am–4pm; ⓦwww.royalparks .gov.uk), the least overgrown of London's "Magnificent Seven" Victorian graveyards. It was laid out on a grid plan in 1840 and is now overlooked by the east stand of Chelsea Football Club. The cemetery's leafy central avenue, which leads south to an octagonal chapel, contains the more interesting graves, most notably that of Frederick Leyland, president of the National Telephone Company: designed by Edward Burne-Jones, it's a bizarre copper-green jewel box on stilts, smothered with swirling wrought ironwork. Before you reach the chapel, eerie colonnaded catacombs, originally planned to extend the full length of the cemetery, open out into the Great Circle, a forest of tilted crosses.

Few famous corpses grace Brompton, but enthusiasts might like to seek out Suffragette leader Emmeline Pankhurst; Samuel Sotheby, who founded the famous auction house; Henry Cole, the man behind the Great Exhibition and the V&A; Fanny Brawne, the love of Keats' life; and John Snow, Queen Victoria's anesthetist, whose chloroform-fixes the monarch described as "soothing, quieting and delightful beyond measure". Long Wolf, a Sioux Indian chief, was a temporary resident here, after he died while on tour entertaining the Victorian masses with Colonel "Buffalo Bill" Cody. His body has since been returned to his descendants in America.

20

High Street Kensington to Notting Hill

Despite the smattering of aristocratic mansions and the presence of royalty in Kensington Palace, the village of **Kensington** remained surrounded by fields until well into the nineteenth century, when the rich finally began to seek new stomping grounds away from the West End. The Great Exhibition and its legacy of museums in South Kensington (see p.297) brought further cachet to the area, and prompted a building frenzy that boosted the entire borough's population to over 175,000 by 1901. Kensington village has disappeared entirely now in the busy shopping district around Kensington High Street, and the chief attractions are the wooded **Holland Park** and the former artists' colony clustered around the exotically decorated **Leighton House**.

Once slummy, now swanky, **Bayswater** and **Notting Hill** to the north were for many years the bad boys of the borough, dens of vice and crime comparable to that of Soho. Gentrification has changed them immeasurably over the last forty years – the Blairs even bought a property here in 2004 – though they remain the borough's most cosmopolitan districts, with a strong Arab presence and vestiges of the African-Caribbean community who initiated and still run Notting Hill **Carnival**, London's (and Europe's) largest street festival, which takes place every August Bank Holiday weekend.

Kensington High Street and around

From Anglo-Saxon times onwards, the village of Kensington was centred to the north of today's St Mary Abbots church, and the ridge which extends westwards. It was only when Kensington was transformed into a residential suburb in the nineteenth century that **Kensington High Street** became the area's commercial centre. The street itself is nothing special – the shops on it are the usual franchises – but in the quieter backstreets, you'll find one or two hidden gems like **Holland Park**, the former gardens of an old Jacobean mansion, and **Leighton House**, the perfect Victorian artist's pad.

High Street Kensington

Kensington High Street – better known as **High Street Ken** – is dominated architecturally by the twin presences of George Gilbert Scott's neo-Gothic church of **St Mary Abbots** (whose 250-foot spire makes it London's tallest parish church) and the Art Deco colossus of **Barkers** department store, remodelled in the 1930s. A little-known feature of the High Street is Europe's largest **Roof Gardens** (☎020/7937 7994, ⓦwww.roofgardens.com), which tops the former Derry & Toms department store, another 1930s colossus, situated next door to Barkers. To check the gardens are open, phone ahead; to gain access, you need to sign yourself in at the side entrance on Derry Street and then take the lift to the sixth floor. The nightclub at the centre of the garden is pretty tacky, but the mock-Spanish convent, the formal gardens, the flamingoes and the views across the rooftops are surreal.

On the south side of the High Street lies **Kensington Square**, an early piece of speculative building laid out in 1685. Luckily for the developers, royalty moved into Kensington Palace shortly after its construction, and the square soon became so fashionable that it was dubbed the "old court suburb". By the nineteenth century, the courtiers had moved out and more bohemian residents had moved in: Thackeray wrote *Vanity Fair* at no. 16; the Pre-Raphaelite painter Burne-Jones lived at no. 41 for a couple of years; the actress Mrs Patrick Campbell, with whom George Bernard Shaw was obsessed for most of his life, lived at no. 33; and composer Hubert Parry (of *Jerusalem* fame) gave music lessons to Vaughan Williams at no. 17. John Stuart Mill, philosopher and champion of women's suffrage, lived next door, and it was here that the first volume of Thomas Carlyle's manuscript of *The French Revolution* was accidentally used by a maid to light the fire.

Holland Park

Hidden away in the backstreets to the north of High Street Kensington is the densely wooded **Holland Park**, a spot popular with the neighbourhood's army of nannies and au pairs, who take their charges to the excellent adventure playground. To get there, take one of the paths along the east side of the former **Commonwealth Institute**, a bold 1960s building that's now a conference centre, with a startling tent-shaped Zambian copper roof. The park is laid out in the former grounds of **Holland House** – only the east wing of the Jacobean mansion could be salvaged after World War II, but it gives a fairly good idea of what the place used to look like. A youth hostel is linked to the east wing (see p.439), while a concert tent to the west stages theatrical and musical performances throughout the summer months (ⓦwww.operahollandpark.com), continuing a tradition which stretches back to the first Lady Holland, who put on plays here in defiance of the puritanical laws of Cromwell's Commonwealth. Several formal gardens are laid out before the house, drifting down in terraces to the arcades, Garden Ballroom and Ice House, which have been converted into a café, a restaurant and an art gallery. The most unusual of the formal gardens, which are peppered with modern sculpture, is the Kyoto Garden, a Japanese-style sanctuary to the northwest of the house.

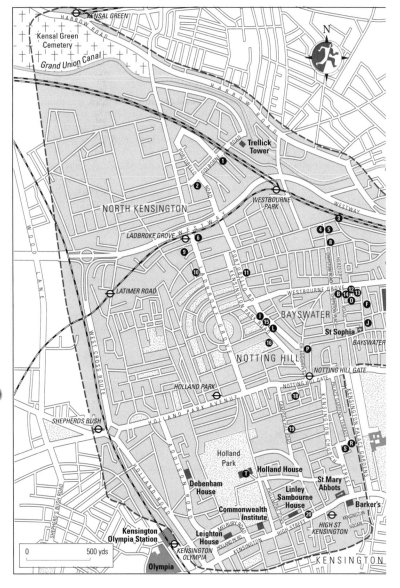

Leighton House

In the second half of the nineteenth century, several of the wealthier artists of the Victorian era rather self-consciously founded an artists' colony around the fringes of Holland Park, and a number of their highly individual mansions are still standing. First and foremost is **Leighton House**, 12 Holland Park

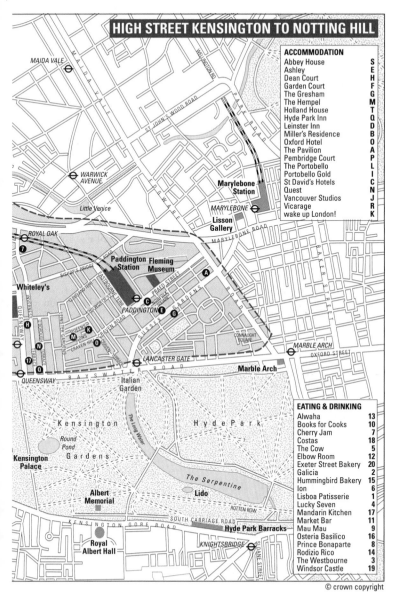

HIGH STREET KENSINGTON TO NOTTING HILL

ACCOMMODATION

Abbey House	S
Ashley	E
Dean Court	H
Garden Court	F
The Gresham	G
The Hempel	M
Holland House	T
Hyde Park Inn	Q
Leinster Inn	D
Miller's Residence	B
Oxford Hotel	O
The Pavilion	A
Pembridge Court	P
The Portobello	L
Portobello Gold	
St David's Hotels	I
Quest	C
Vancouver Studios	N
Vicarage	J
wake up London!	R
	K

EATING & DRINKING

Alwaha	13
Books for Cooks	10
Cherry Jam	7
Costas	18
The Cow	5
Elbow Room	12
Exeter Street Bakery	20
Galicia	2
Hummingbird Bakery	15
Ion	6
Lisboa Patisserie	1
Lucky Seven	4
Mandarin Kitchen	17
Market Bar	11
Mau Mau	9
Osteria Basilico	16
Prince Bonaparte	8
Rodizio Rico	14
The Westbourne	3
Windsor Castle	19

© crown copyright

Rd (daily except Tues 11am–5.30pm; guided tours Wed & Thurs 2.30pm; £3; ☎020/7602 3316, ⓦwww.rbkc.gov.uk/leightonhousemuseum), the "House Beautiful" built by the architect George Aitchison for Frederic Leighton, president of the Royal Academy from 1878 until his death in 1896 and the only artist ever to be made a peer (albeit on his deathbed). "It will be opulence, it will be sincerity", the artist opined before starting work on the house in the 1860s.

The big attraction is its domed Arab Hall, built in 1877: based on the banqueting hall of a Moorish palace in Palermo, it has a central black marble fountain, and is decorated with Saracen tiles, gilded mosaics and latticework drawn from all over the Islamic world. The other rooms are less spectacular in comparison, but are hung with excellent paintings by Lord Leighton and his Pre-Raphaelite friends, Edward Burne-Jones, Lawrence Alma-Tadema and John Everett Millais. Skylights brighten the upper floor, which contains Leighton's vast studio, where he used to hold evening concerts.

Around Leighton House

Leighton's neighbours included artists G.F. Watts and Holman Hunt, Marcus Stone, illustrator of Dickens, and, in the most outrageous house of all, architect William Burges, who designed his own medieval folly, the **Tower House**, at 29 Melbury Rd. Further afield, at 8 Addison Rd, is the Arts and Crafts **Debenham House** (ⓦwww.debenhamhouse.com), designed by Halsey Ricardo in 1906 for the millionaire department store Debenham family. Both houses are closed to the public. The exterior of the latter is covered with peacock-blue and emerald-green tiles and bricks; the interior, which features a wonderful neo-Byzantine domed hall, decorated with a lavish mosaic that features portraits of the Debenham family, and 28 individually tiled fireplaces, is even more impressive – you can usually visit on an Open House weekend.

On the east side of the Commonwealth Institute, two blocks north of Kensington High Street at 18 Stafford Terrace, is **Linley Sambourne House** (guided tours April–Oct Sat & Sun 10 & 11.15am, 1, 2.15 & 3.30pm; £6; ⓣ020/7602 3316, ⓦwww.rbkc.gov.uk/linleysambournehouse), where the highly successful *Punch* cartoonist lived until his death in 1910. A grand, though fairly ordinary stuccoed terrace house by Kensington standards, it's less a tribute to the artist (though it does contain a huge selection of Sambourne's works) and more a showpiece for the Victorian Society, which helps maintain the house in all its cluttered, late-Victorian excess, complete with stained glass, heavy furnishings and lugubrious William Morris wallpaper. The guided tours are great fun, last ninety minutes and are (usually) led by an actor in period garb; there are also occasional evening tours which re-create a night in with the Sambournes.

Bayswater and Notting Hill

It wasn't until the removal of the gallows at Tyburn (see box on p.287) that the area to the north of Hyde Park began to gain respectability. The arrival of the Great Western Railway at Paddington in 1838 further encouraged development, and the gentrification of **Bayswater**, the area immediately north of the park, began with the construction of an estate called Tyburnia. These days Bayswater is mainly residential, and a focus for London's widely dispersed Arab community, who are catered for by some excellent Lebanese restaurants and cafés along the busy Edgware Road.

Much more tangible attractions lie to the west in **Notting Hill**, where London's most popular market, **Portobello Road**, takes place each Saturday, and where the August Bank Holiday weekend sees West Indian London out in force for the annual **Notting Hill Carnival**. The area is now one of the city's trendiest and most affluent multicultural neighbourhoods. Back in the 1950s, when it was among London's poorest neighbourhoods, it was – along with Brixton in south London

– settled by Afro-Caribbean immigrants, invited over to work in the public services. Gentrification in the last two decades has changed the population greatly, but there's still a significant black presence, especially in the northern fringes.

Paddington station and around

Bayswater's combination of classic urban squares, big stuccoed terraces and grand tree-lined avenues gives the district a wealthy and almost Continental feel, but the volume of traffic, as usual, spoils much of the effect. The area's main focus is **Paddington station** on Praed Street, one of the world's great early train stations; designed by Isambard Kingdom Brunel in 1851, the cathedral-scale wrought-iron sheds replaced a wooden structure that was the destination of Victoria and Albert's first railway journey in 1842. The train, pulled by the engine *Phlegethon*, travelled from Slough (near Windsor) at an average speed of 44mph, which the prince consort considered excessive – "Not so fast next time, Mr Conductor", he is alleged to have remarked.

Squeezed between Paddington station and the flyover of the Westway to the north is **Paddington Basin**, built as the terminus of the Grand Union Canal in 1801. Now at the centre of a massive regeneration project known as Paddington Waterside, it's worth exploring if only to have a look at the trio of funky **footbridges** which span the water: Helix Bridge, a twisted tube of perspex; Paddington Bridge, a vast wall of illuminated glass and steel; and Rolling Bridge, a hydraulic gangway that coils up into an octagon rather like a curled-up woodhouse. If you follow the basin to the northwest, you'll reach Little Venice in St John's Wood.

One block east of Paddington up Praed Street is St Mary's Hospital, home of the **Fleming Museum** (Mon–Thurs 10am–1pm; £2; ☎020/7886 6528, ⓦwww.medicalmuseums.org/museums/alex.htm), on the corner of Norfolk Place, where the young Scottish bacteriologist Alexander Fleming accidentally discovered penicillin in 1928. A short video, a small exhibition and a reconstruction of Fleming's untidy lab tell the story of the medical discovery that saved more lives than any other during the last century. Oddly enough, it aroused little interest at the time, until a group of chemists in Oxford succeeded in purifying penicillin in 1942. Desperate for good news in wartime, the media made Fleming a celebrity, and he was eventually awarded the Nobel Prize, along with several of the Oxford team.

Queensway

Bayswater's main drag is **Queensway**, whose rash of cafés, clothes shops and French patisseries keeps buzzing until late in the evening. The renewed prosperity here is due, in large part, to the resurgent Arab community, but to add to the cosmopolitan atmosphere, Queensway also boasts the largest concentration of Chinese restaurants outside Soho's Chinatown. A short distance up Moscow Road, off Queensway, you'll find **St Sophia**, London's ornate Greek Orthodox cathedral, boasting mosaics by Boris Anrep.

One whole block of Queensway is taken up by **Whiteley's** (ⓦwww .whiteleys.com), which opened in 1885 as the city's first real department store or "Universal Provider" with the boast that they could supply "anything from a pin to an elephant". The present building opened in 1907, and in the same year was the scene of the murder of the store's founder, William Whiteley, by a man claiming to be his illegitimate son. Whiteley's also had the dubious distinction of being Hitler's favourite London building – he planned to make it his HQ once the invasion was over. The store closed in 1981, and the building now houses an indoor shopping mall with several restaurants and a multiscreen cinema, but the original wrought-iron staircase, centaurs' fountain and glass-domed atrium all survive.

Notting Hill

The urbanization of **Notting Hill** (⊛www.mynottinghill.co.uk), the area to the north of Holland Park Avenue and west of Queensway, began in the first half of the nineteenth century, when the leafy avenues and majestic crescents of the Norland and Ladbroke estates were laid out. In those days, the area was still known as the Potteries, after the gravel pits and pottery works on Walmer Road (where a kiln survives even today), or the Piggeries, after the district's three-to-one ratio of pigs to people. Along with its fine houses, Notting Hill has always retained its poorer dwellings, and its social status declined in the twentieth century. Some fifty years ago Notting Hill was described as "a massive slum, full of multi-occupied houses, crawling with rats and rubbish", and populated by offshoots of the Soho vice and crime rackets. These insalubrious dwellings – many owned by the infamous vice king and slum landlord Peter Rachman – became home to a large contingent of West Indian immigrants, who had to compete for jobs and living space with the area's similarly downtrodden white residents.

For four days in August 1958, Pembridge Road became the epicentre of the UK's first **race riots**, when busloads of whites attacked West Indian homes in the area. The **Notting Hill Carnival** began unofficially the year after as a response to the riots; in 1965 it took to the streets and has since grown into the world's biggest street festival outside Rio, with an estimated two million revellers turning up on the last weekend of August for the two-day extravaganza of *mas* (costume) parades, steel bands, live music stages and deafening sound systems. In the 1970s and early 1980s, tensions between the black community and the police came to a head at carnival time, but strenuous efforts on both sides have meant that such conflict has generally been avoided in the last two decades. However, there are still plenty of doubters among the area's wealthier and mostly white residents, most of whom switch on the alarm system and leave town for the weekend.

The rest of the year Notting Hill is a lot quieter, though its cafés and restaurants are cool enough to pull in media folk from all over, and thanks to the myths spun about the area in the film *Notting Hill*, there are now significantly more overseas visitors than before. The busiest day of the week is always Saturday, when big crowds of Londoners and tourists alike descend on the mile-long Portobello Road Market.

▲ Portobello Road Market

Notting Hill Carnival

When it emerged in the 1960s, Notting Hill Carnival was little more than a few church-hall events and a carnival parade, inspired by that of Trinidad – birthplace of many of the area's immigrants. Today Carnival, held over the August Bank Holiday weekend, still belongs to West Indians (from all parts of the city), but there are participants too from London's Latin American and Asian communities, and Londoners of all descriptions turn out to watch the bands and parades, and generally hang out.

The main sights of Carnival are the **costume parades**, which take place on the Sunday (for kids) and Monday (for adults) from around 10am until just before midnight. The parade makes its way around a three-mile route, and consists of big trucks which carry the sound systems and *mas* (masquerade) bands, behind which the masqueraders dance in outrageous costumes.

Most of the *mas* bands play a variety of soca music or calypso featuring steel bands – the "pans" of the steel bands are one of the chief sounds of Carnival and have their own contest on the Saturday at Horniman's Pleasance, off Kensal Road by the canal. In addition to those playing *mas*, there are three or four stages for live music – Portobello Green and Powis Square are regular venues – and numerous sound systems where you can catch reggae, ragga, drum'n'bass, jungle, garage, house and much more. A lot of people just mill around the sound systems, dancing as the day progresses, fuelled by cans of Red Stripe, curried goat and Jamaican patties, which are sold by a multitude of weekend entrepreneurs.

Over the last few years, the Carnival has been fairly relaxed, considering the huge numbers of people it attracts. However, this is not an event for you if you're at all bothered by crowds – you can be wedged stationary during the parades – and very loud music. It's worth taking more than usual care with your belongings too: leave expensive cameras and jewellery at home, and bring only enough money for the day, as pickpockets are rife. As for **personal safety**, don't worry unduly about the media's horror stories (a perennial feature, along with pictures of police being kissed by large Caribbean women), as you're in plentiful company. However, the static sound systems are switched off at 7pm each day, and if there's going to be any trouble it tends to come after that point; if you feel at all uneasy, head home early.

Getting to and from the Carnival is quite an event in itself. Ladbroke Grove tube station is closed for the duration, while other stations have restricted hours or are open only for incoming visitors. However, there's a whole network of buses running between most points of London and Notting Hill Gate. For more information, contact Transport for London ☏020/7222 1234, ⊛www.tfl.gov.uk.

Portobello Road Market

Portobello Road Market (see p.549) kicks off at the intersection of Chepstow Road, though this initial stretch, lined with rather junky antique stalls and classier antique shops, is overpriced and geared very much to tourists (⊛www.portobelloroad.co.uk). The market gets a lot more fun and funky after a brief switch to fruit and veg around the **Electric Cinema** (⊛www.the-electric.co.uk), on the corner of Blenheim Crescent, which opened in 1911, had serial killer John Christie as its projectionist during World War II and is now one of London's most expensive and luxurious movie houses. Continuing along Portobello Road, you reach an area under the **Westway** flyover where the emphasis of the market switches to street clothes and jewellery, odd trinkets, records and books.

A wander through the grid between Elgin Crescent and Lancaster Road will take you past art galleries and shops selling contemporary ceramics, old jukeboxes and all manner of exotics and essentials. Blenheim Crescent and adjoining Talbot Road are a good place to start, with the excellent Travel

Bookshop and Books for Cooks on the former, and Rough Trade records on the latter.

Across the Westway, the stalls get progressively cheaper as they swing east into Golborne Road, which sits in the shadow of the awesome **Trellick Tower**, the tallest block of flats in the country when it was built by Ernö Goldfinger in 1973 and, despite its brutalist concrete appearance, still popular with its residents. Golborne Road is really a market of its own, with a constellation of bric-a-brac stalls and Portuguese and Moroccan cafés and shops, giving the road some of the bohemian feel of old Notting Hill, and making it the perfect place to wind up a visit to the market.

Kensal Green Cemetery

Within easy walking distance of Portobello Road, on the other side of the railway tracks, gasworks and the Grand Union Canal, is **Kensal Green Cemetery**, the first of the city's commercial graveyards, opened in 1833 to relieve the pressure on overcrowded inner-city churchyards. Highgate may be the most famous of the "Magnificent Seven" Victorian cemeteries, but Kensal Green has by far the best funerary monuments. It's still owned by the founding company and remains a functioning cemetery, with services conducted daily in the central Greek Revival chapel. **Guided tours** of the cemetery take place every Sunday at 2pm (☎020/8960 1030, ⊛www.kensalgreen.co.uk; £5), and include a visit to the catacombs (bring a torch) on the first and third Sunday of the month.

The graves of the more famous incumbents – Thackeray, Trollope and the Brunels – are less interesting architecturally than those arranged on either side of the Centre Avenue, which leads from the easternmost entrance on Harrow Road. Vandals have left numerous headless angels and irreparably damaged the beautiful Cooke family monument, but still worth looking out for are Major-General Casement's bier, held up by four grim-looking turbaned Indians, circus manager Andrew Ducrow's conglomeration of beehive, sphinx and angels, and artist William Mulready's neo-Renaissance extravaganza. Other interesting characters buried here include Charles Wingfield, who invented lawn tennis; Mary Seacole, the "black Florence Nightingale"; Charles Blondin, the famous tightrope walker; Carl Wilhelm Siemens, the German scientist who brought electric lighting to London; and "James" Barry, Inspector-General of the Army Medical Department, who, it was discovered during the embalming of the corpse, was in fact a woman. The Queen singer, Freddie Mercury, was cremated here, but his ashes were scattered in Bombay.

20

North London: Camden, Regent's Park, Hampstead and beyond

Everything north of the Marylebone and Euston roads was, for the most part, open countryside until the mid-nineteenth century, and is now largely residential, right the way up to the "green belt" created in the immediate postwar period to try and limit the continuing urban sprawl. The area of the city covered in this **north London** chapter is necessarily much smaller, concentrating on just a handful of the satellite villages, now subsumed into the general mass of London. Almost all the northern suburbs are easily accessible by tube from the centre; in fact, it was the expansion of the tube that encouraged the forward march of bricks and mortar in many of the outer suburbs.

The first section of the chapter traces the route of the **Regent's Canal**, which skirts what was, at the beginning of the nineteenth century, the city's northern periphery. Along the way, the canal passes one of London's finest parks, **Regent's Park**, framed by Nash-designed architecture and home to London Zoo. The canal forces its way into Londoners' consciousness only at **Camden**, whose weekend market is one of the city's big attractions – a warren of stalls with an alternative past still manifest in its offbeat wares, street fashion, books, records and ethnic goods.

Few visitors to the capital bother to check out neighbouring **Islington**, which has its own flourishing antiques trade, and **Hackney**, further east, with its huge Turkish, Afro-Caribbean and Hasidic Jewish population, thus missing out on two of north London's defining areas. The real highlights of north London, though, for visitors and residents alike, are **Hampstead** and **Highgate**, elegant, largely eighteenth-century developments which still reflect their village origins. They have the added advantage of proximity to one of London's wild-

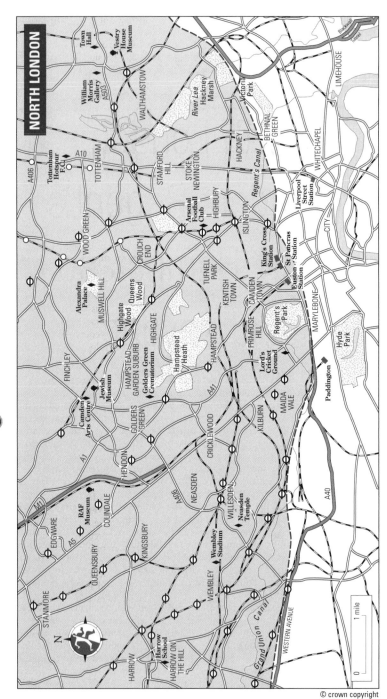

NORTH LONDON

Town Hall

Vestry House Museum

William Morris Gallery A503

WALTHAMSTOW

A10

A406

Tottenham Hotspur F.C.

TOTTENHAM

River Lea Hackney Marsh

Victoria Park

STAMFORD HILL

STOKE NEWINGTON

HACKNEY

BETHNAL GREEN

WHITECHAPEL

CITY

Regent's Canal

Liverpool Street Station

WOOD GREEN

Arsenal Football Club

HIGHBURY

ISLINGTON

CROUCH END

King's Cross Station

St Pancras Station

Euston Station

MARYLEBONE

Alexandra Palace

MUSWELL HILL

Highgate Wood Queens Wood

HIGHGATE

TUFNELL PARK

KENTISH TOWN

CAMDEN TOWN

PRIMROSE HILL

Regent's Park

Hyde Park

FINCHLEY

Hampstead Garden Suburb Golders Green Crematorium

Hampstead Heath

HAMPSTEAD

Lord's Cricket Ground

MAIDA VALE

Paddington

Jewish Museum

Camden Arts Centre

GOLDERS GREEN

CRICKLEWOOD

KILBURN

A41

A1

HENDON

NEASDEN

WILLESDEN

Neasden Temple

RAF Museum

COLINDALE

EDGWARE

A5

QUEENSBURY

KINGSBURY

WEMBLEY

Wembley Stadium

Grand Union Canal

WESTERN AVENUE

A40

A406

M1

STANMORE

N

HARROW

Harrow School

HARROW ON THE HILL

0   1 mile

© crown copyright

est patches of greenery, **Hampstead Heath**, where you can enjoy stupendous views, kite-flying and nude bathing, as well as outdoor concerts and high art in and around the Neoclassical country mansion of **Kenwood House**.

Also covered, at the end of this chapter, are a handful of sights in more far-flung northern suburbs. They include the nineteenth-century utopia of **Hampstead Garden Suburb**; the Orthodox Jewish suburb of **Golders Green**; the **RAF Museum** at Hendon; and the spectacular **Hindu temple** in Neasden.

St John's Wood and Little Venice

The **Regent's Canal**, completed in 1820, was constructed as part of a direct link from Birmingham to the newly built London Docks. Its seemingly random meandering, from the Grand Junction Canal at Paddington to the River Thames at Limehouse, traces the fringe of London's northernmost suburbs at the time. After an initial period of heavy usage it was overtaken by the railway, and never really paid its way as its investors had hoped. By some miracle, however, it escaped being covered over or turned into a rail or road route, and its nine miles, 42 bridges, twelve locks and two tunnels stand as a reminder of another age.

The lock-less run of the canal **between Little Venice and Camden Town** is the busiest, most attractive stretch, tunnelling through to Lisson Grove, skirting Regent's Park, slicing London Zoo in two, and passing straight through the heart of Camden Market. It's also the one section that's served by narrowboats (see box, overleaf). Alternatively, you can cycle, walk or jog along the towpath.

St John's Wood

The Regent's Canal starts out from the west in the smart, residential district of **St John's Wood**, which was built over in the nineteenth century by developers hoping to attract a wealthy clientele with a mixture of semi-detached Italianate villas, multi-occupancy Gothic mansions and white stucco terraces. Edwin Landseer (of Trafalgar Square lions fame), novelist George Eliot and Mrs Fitzherbert, the uncrowned wife of George IV, all lived here, while current residents include knights Richard Branson and Paul McCartney and supermodel Kate Moss.

To catch a canal boat to Camden through the southern borders of this neighbourhood, head for the triangular leafy basin known as **Little Venice**, a nickname coined by one-time resident and poet Robert Browning. The title may be far-fetched, but the willow-tree Browning's Island is one of the prettiest spots on the canal, and the houseboats and barges moored hereabouts are brightly painted and strewn with tubs of flowers. If you're here between November and May, be sure to try and catch a traditional marionette performance on the **Puppet Theatre Barge** (Ⓦwww.puppetbarge.com), moored on the Blomfield Road side of the basin, a unique and unforgettable experience; performances take place every weekend and daily at 3pm throughout the school holidays.

Regent's Canal by boat

Three companies run **boat services** on the Regent's Canal between Camden and Little Venice, passing through the Maida Hill tunnel and stopping off at London Zoo on the way. The narrowboat *Jenny Wren* (℡020/7485 4433) starts off at Camden, goes through a canal lock (the only company to do so) and heads for Little Venice, while Jason's narrowboats (℡020/7286 3428, ⓦwww.jasons.co.uk) start off at Little Venice; the London Waterbus Company (℡020/7482 2660, ⓦwww.londonwaterbus .com) sets off from both places. Whichever you choose, you can board at either end; **tickets** cost around £5–6 one-way (and only a little more return) and journey time is 50 minutes one-way.

Lord's Cricket Ground

The building of the Regent's Canal was bad news for Thomas Lord, who had only recently been forced to shift his cricket ground due to the construction of what is now Marylebone Road. Once more he upped his stumps and relocated, this time to St John's Wood Road, where **Lord's**, as the ground is now known, remains to this day. The ground is owned by the **MCC** (Marylebone Cricket Club), which was founded in 1787 and is the most hallowed institution in the game, boasting a very long members waiting list (unless you're

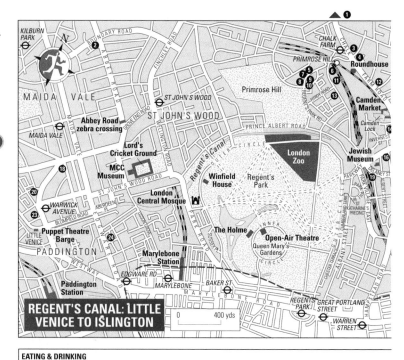

REGENT'S CANAL: LITTLE VENICE TO ISLINGTON

EATING & DRINKING							
Abbey Road Pub &		Bartok	4	Compton Arms	21	The Engineer	13
Dining Room	2	Bar Vinyl	14	Duke of Cambridge	37	King's Head	28
Afghan Kitchen	32	Café Delancey	17	Edinboro Castle	19	Lansdowne	11
Almeida	27	Camden Head	22	Elk in the Woods	35	Lock Tavern	12
Angelic	33	Canonbury Tavern	21	Embassy Bar	29	Mandalay	24

exceptionally famous or rich). Its politics were neatly summed up by Viscount Monckton, who said, "I have been a member of the Committee of the MCC and of a Conservative cabinet, and by comparison with the cricketers, the Tories seem like a bunch of Commies." The MCC only agreed to allow female membership in 1998, after lottery funding was withheld because of the club's exclusively male status – though, of course, the committee denied that this had any effect on their decision.

A match ticket will allow you free access to the **MCC museum**, which traces the history of modern cricket, and features the minuscule pottery urn containing the Ashes (along with the complex tale of this odd trophy), numerous historic balls, bats and bails, and a sparrow which was "bowled out" by Jehangir Khan at Lord's in 1936. If you take one of the **guided tours** (daily except match & preparation days: April–Sept 10am, noon & 2pm; Oct–March noon & 2pm; £8; ☏020/7616 8595, ⊛www.lords.org), you'll also get to see the famous Long Room (from which the players walk onto the pitch), which is otherwise off limits to non-members. The tours set off from the Grace Gates at the southwest corner of the ground, and, in addition to the museum and Long Room, you'll get endless cricketing anecdotes, a tour round Lord's Real Tennis Court and a quick look at the dazzling Mound Stand, designed by Michael Hopkins in the late 1980s, and the futuristic Media Centre, cruelly nicknamed "Cherie Blair's Smile".

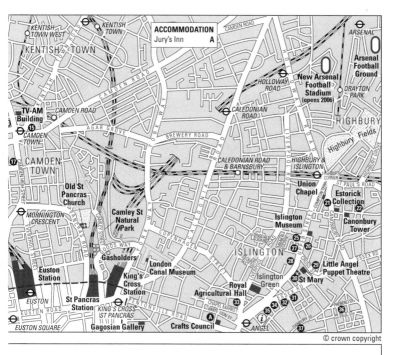

© crown copyright

Mango Room	**15**	Ottolenghi	**26**	Prince Alfred &		Sir Richard Steele	**1**	Viet-Anh Café	**16**
Manna	**5**	Pasha	**30**	Formosa		The Social	**36**	Warrington Hotel	**18**
Marine Ices	**3**	Pembroke Castle	**6**	Dining Rooms	**20**	Trojka	**7**	Warwick Castle	**23**
Medicine	**25**	Primrose		The Queen's	**8**				
Odette's	**10**	Patisserie	**9**	Sausage & Mash Café	**31**				

Since the Fab Four lived in London for much of the 1960s, it's hardly surprising that the capital is riddled with Beatle associations. The prime Beatles landmark is, of course, the **Abbey Road** zebra crossing featured on the album cover, located near the EMI studios, where the group recorded most of their albums. To get there, walk down Grove End Road from St John's Wood tube, and then turn right into Abbey Road – and remember to bring three other friends and someone to take the photos. Incidentally, Paul McCartney still owns the house at 7 Cavendish Ave, two blocks east of the zebra crossing, which he bought in 1966.

One nearby (short-lived) curiosity was the **Apple Boutique**, opened by The Beatles at 94 Baker St, Marylebone, in December 1967 as a "beautiful place where you could buy beautiful things". The psychedelic murals that covered the entire building were whitewashed over after a lawsuit by the neighbours, and eight months later The Beatles caused even more pandemonium when they gave the shop's entire stock away free in the closing-down sale.

Other Beatles locations include the old Apple headquarters in Savile Row, Mayfair, where the 1969 rooftop concert took place (see p.102), while Macca has his current office on Soho Square (see p.122). Real devotees of the group, however, should get hold of a copy of *The Beatles' England* by David Heron and Norman Maslov, which covers every conceivable association. Alternatively, sign up for a Beatles tour, run by The Original London Walks (☎020/7624 3978, ⒲www.walks.com).

Regent's Park

As with almost all of London's royal parks, we have Henry VIII to thank for **Regent's Park** (☎020/7486 7905, ⒲www.royalparks.gov.uk), which he confiscated from the Church for yet more hunting grounds. However, it wasn't until the reign of the Prince Regent (later George IV) that the park began to take its current form – hence it's official title, The Regent's Park – and the public weren't allowed in until 1845 (and even then for just two days of the week). According to the master plan, devised by John Nash in 1811, the park was to be girded by a continuous belt of terraces, blessed with two grand circuses and sprinkled with a total of 56 villas, including a magnificent pleasure palace for the prince himself, which would be linked by Regent Street to Carlton House in St James's (see p.88). Work was halted in 1826 due to lack of funds, and the plan was never fully realized, but enough was built to create something of the idealized garden city that Nash and the Prince Regent envisaged.

The eastern terraces

To appreciate the special quality of Regent's Park, you should take a closer look at the architecture, starting with the Nash terraces, which form a near-unbroken horseshoe of cream-coloured stucco around the Outer Circle. Each one is in a slightly different Neoclassical style, but by far the most impressive is **Cumberland Terrace**, built in 1826–28 and intended as a foil for George IV's private tea pavilion, which never materialized. Its 800-foot-long facade, hidden away on the eastern edge of the park, is punctuated by Ionic triumphal arches, peppered with classical alabaster statues and centred on a Corinthian portico with a pediment of sculptures set against a vivid sky-blue background. In 1936 an angry crowd threw bricks through the windows of no. 16, which belonged to American divorcée Mrs Wallis Simpson, whose relationship with Edward VIII was seen as a national calamity.

Fifty-two more statues depicting British worthies were planned for the even longer facade of **Chester Terrace**, to the south, but Nash decided the ridicule they provoked was "painful to the ears of a professional man" and ditched them. Nevertheless, Chester Terrace is worth walking down if only to take in the splendid triumphal arches at each end, which announce the name of the terrace in bold lettering; the northern one features a bust of Nash. Still further south, facing east onto Albany Street, is Cambridge Gate, built some fifty years later in Bath stone to replace the **Colosseum**, a rotunda built by Decimus Burton in 1829 in the style of the Pantheon. Inside, visitors were treated to a 360-degree view of London, spread out on an acre of canvas, drawn from sketches made by Thomas Hornor from the top of St Paul's Cathedral. A million people visited the panorama in the first year, and further attractions were added, including a hall of mirrors, stalactite caverns and even roller-skating, but it fell into decline and was finally demolished in 1875.

The Inner Circle and the western periphery

Of the numerous villas planned for the park itself, only eight were built, and of those just two have survived around the **Inner Circle**: St John's Lodge, in its own private grounds to the north, and **The Holme**, Decimus Burton's first-ever work (he was 18 at the time), picturesquely sited by the Y-shaped **Boating Lake**. Designed by Nash, and a haven for waterfowl, the lake is fed by the waters of the Tyburn, one of London's "lost" – that is, underground – rivers. Within the Inner Circle is the Open Air Theatre (see p.520), which puts on summer performances of Shakespeare, opera and ballet, and **Queen Mary's Gardens**, by far the prettiest section of the park. A large slice of the gardens is taken up with a glorious rose garden, featuring some four hundred varieties, surrounded by a ring of ramblers.

On the western edge of the park, the curved end wings and quirky octagonal domes of **Sussex Place** stand out among the other, more orthodox, Nash terraces. A further surprise breaks the skyline to the north – the shiny copper dome and minaret of the **London Central Mosque** (☎020/7724 3363, ⓦwww.iccuk.org), an entirely appropriate addition given the Prince Regent's taste for the Orient (as expressed in Brighton Pavilion in East Sussex). Non-Muslim visitors are welcome to look in at the information centre, and glance inside the hall of worship, which is packed out with a diversity of communities for the lunchtime Friday prayers.

A little further up the Outer Circle, there's a trio of modern neo-Nash villas by Quinlan Terry that reflect the conservative tastes of the current Prince of Wales. On the opposite side of

▲ London Central Mosque, Regent's Park

21

the road is **Winfield House**, a dull 1930s replacement for Decimus Burton's Hertford House, built by heiress to the Woolworth chain, Countess Haug-witz-Reventlow (better known as Barbara Hutton), who married Cary Grant in 1942; it's now the US ambassador's residence.

St Katharine's Precinct and Park Village West

To the north of Cumberland Terrace, the neo-Gothic **St Katharine's Pre-cinct** provides a respite from the Grecian surroundings, though not one Nash was at all happy with. The central church now serves the Danish community, who have erected a copy of the imposing tenth-century **Jelling Stone** in an alcove to the right. The original was erected in memory of King Gorm by his son, Harald Bluetooth, the first Danish ruler to convert to Christianity, as the colourful runic inscription and image of Christ hewn into the granite testify.

For proof that Nash could build equally well on a much more modest scale than the Regent's Park terraces, take a stroll round **Park Village West**, which lies in a secluded network of winding streets and culs-de-sac off Albany Street, on the other side of Gloucester Gate, in the northeast corner of the park. The houses, Nash's last work for Regent's Park, feature copious ornamental urns and black lattice pergolas, and range from mock-Athenian cottages to Tudor and Italianate villas.

London Zoo

The lion sits within his cage,
Weeping tears of ruby rage,
He licks his snout, the tears fall down
And water dusty London town.

The Zoo, Stevie Smith

㉑ The northeastern corner of the park, beyond acres of football pitches, is occupied by **London Zoo** (daily: March–Oct 10am–5.30pm; Nov–Feb 10am–4pm; £14; ☎020/7722 3333, ⓦwww.zsl.org/london-zoo). Founded in 1826 with the remnants of the royal menagerie, the zoo has had to change with the times, and now bills itself as an eco-conscious place whose prime purpose is to save species under threat of extinction. It's still not the most uplifting spot for animal-lovers, though the enclosures are as humane as any inner-city zoo could make them, and kids usually love the place. Most are particularly taken by the children's enclosure, where they can actually handle the animals, and the regular "Animals in Action" live shows. The invertebrate house, now known as BUGS, and the new monkey walk-through forest are both guaranteed winners.

The zoo boasts some striking architectural features, too, such as the 1930s modernist, spiral-ramped concrete former penguin pool (where Penguin Books' original colophon was sketched), designed by the Tecton partnership, led by Russian émigré Berthold Lubetkin, who also made the zoo's Round House. The Giraffe House, by contrast, was designed in Neoclassical style by Decimus Burton, who was also responsible for the mock-Tudor Clock Tower. Other landmark features are the mountainous Mappin Terraces, dating from just before World War I, and the colossal tetrahedral aluminium-framed tent of Lord Snowdon's Aviary.

Prince Albert Road and Primrose Hill

Nash intended the Regent's Canal to run right through the middle of the park, but potential residents objected to lower-class canal-faring families ploughing through their well-to-do neighbourhood. Instead, the canal curves its way along the northern periphery, passing right through London Zoo, with the Snowdon Aviary to one side and giraffes and camels to the other. Equally visible from the canal are the millionaire apartment buildings of **Prince Albert Road**, which boast unrivalled views across the park. Nash left the park's north side open so folk might enjoy "the many beautiful views towards the villages of Hampstead and Highgate", and it was left to twentieth-century architects to fill in the gaps with a wild variety of high-rise flats, some clad in Edwardian pomp, others with package-holiday-hotel balconies.

Halfway along Prince Albert Road, the mansions stop to reveal the small northern extension of Regent's Park, known as **Primrose Hill**, which commands a superb view of central London from its modest summit. In the sixteenth century, Mother Shipton prophesied that "When London surrounds Primrose Hill, the streets of the Metropolis shall run with blood", and in May 1829 a Mr Wilson proposed turning the hill into a necropolis, with a lift running down the core of the hill to give access to the various levels. Neither of these calamities came about, and the most unusual thing you're likely to witness is the neo-Druidic ceremony that takes place here occasionally at the equinoxes, and gatherings on the summer solstice as well.

To the east is the much sought-after residential area of Primrose Hill, which has attracted numerous successful literati and artists over the years: H.G. Wells, W.B. Yeats, Friedrich Engels, Kingsley Amis and Morrissey have all lived here. You might catch the present denizens such as Noel Gallagher, Ben Elton, Alan Bennett, Martin Amis or Sam Mendes browsing the bookshops and galleries on **Regent's Park Road**, which skirts Primrose Hill park to the east. Ted Hughes and Sylvia Plath lived in a flat at 3 Chalcot Square, just east of Regent's Park Road, and it was nearby at 23 Fitzroy Rd, in the house that Yeats lived in, that Plath committed suicide in 1963.

Camden Town

Until the canal arrived, **Camden Town** wasn't even a village, but by Victorian times it had become a notorious slum area, an image that it took most of the twentieth century to shed. Over the years, however, it has attracted a fair share of artists, most famously the Camden Town Group formed in 1911 by Walter Sickert, later joined by the likes of Lucien Freud, Frank Auerbach and Leon Kossoff. These days, you're more likely to bump into young foreign tourists heading for the market, and as-yet-unknown bands on the lookout for members of the local music industry.

For all the gentrification of the last twenty years, Camden retains a gritty aspect, compounded by the various railway lines that plough through the area, the canal and the large shelter for the homeless on Arlington Road. Its proximity to three main-line stations has also made it an obvious point of immigration over the years, particularly for the Irish, but also for Greek Cypriots during the 1950s. The **market**, however, gives the area a positive lift, especially at weekends, and is now the district's best-known attribute.

Camden Market

The overabundance of cheap leather, hippie chic, naff jewellery and out-and-out kitsch at **Camden Market** (Ⓦ www.camdenlock.net) is compensated for by the sheer variety of what's on offer: from bootleg tapes to furniture and mountain bikes, along with a mass of clubwear and street fashion that may or may not make the transition to mainstream stores. For all its tourist popularity, and the inevitable encroachment of franchises, this is a market that remains a genuinely offbeat place.

To avoid the crowds, which can be overpowering on a summer Sunday afternoon, you'll need to come either early (before 10am) or late (say, after 4pm), when many of the stalls will be packing up to go. The oldest part of the market is the fruit and vegetable stalls of **Inverness Street** (daily 8.30am–5pm), which have been trading here since the nineteenth century. Opposite, the covered section known as **Camden Market** (daily 9.30am–5.30pm), which backs onto Buck Street, sells clubwear, jewellery and clothes.

The three-storey Victorian **Market Hall**, on the left just past the canal bridge, signals the entrance to the three cobbled yards of **Camden Lock** (daily 10.30am–6pm), enclosed by arty-crafty shops, most of which are densely packed with jewellery and clothing stalls at the weekend. Further up Chalk Farm Road, the **Stables Market** (daily 10.30am–6pm) – made up of an old bonded gin store and a former horse hospital – features lots of vintage and secondhand clothes stalls, plus Goth and clubwear outlets; some places are open daily, but the majority are weekend-only. Another adjunct to the market, which is often overlooked, is the **Camden Canal Market** (Fri–Sun 9.30am–6.30pm), across the High Street from the Market Hall; it's a riot of stalls selling everything from wrought iron to china miniatures.

Camden Market and High Street

Camden Market was confined to Inverness Street until the 1970s, when the focus began to shift towards the disused timber wharf and warehouses around Camden Lock. The tiny crafts market which began in the cobbled courtyard by the lock has since mushroomed out of all proportion, with everyone trying to grab a piece of the action on both sides of Camden High Street and Chalk Farm Road. More than 150,000 shoppers turn up here each weekend and some stalls now stay open all week long, alongside a similarly oriented crop of shops, cafés and bistros. The nearest tube is Camden Town, though this is exit-only at peak times at the weekend; Chalk Farm tube is only ten minutes' walk up Chalk Farm Road from Camden Lock.

Camden Lock to the Roundhouse

If you've seen enough jangly earrings for one day, stand on the bowed iron footbridge by **Camden Lock** itself, and admire the castellated former lock-keeper's house, to the west, and the flight of three locks to the east, which begin the canal's descent to Limehouse to the east of the City. For the boat ride down to Little Venice, you buy tickets on board; the boats leave from the lock inlet, on the north side of the canal (see p.338). Here too are the covered basins of the Interchange Warehouse, which in turn are linked by a disused railway line to the **Camden Catacombs**, built in the nineteenth century as stables for the pit ponies that used to shunt the railway wagons.

The stabling extended as far north as the brick-built **Roundhouse** (Ⓦ www .roundhouse.org.uk), on Chalk Farm Road, built by Robert Stephenson in 1847 as an engine repair shed for 23 goods engines, arranged around a central turntable. Within fifteen years the engines had outgrown the building, and for the next century it was used for storing booze. In 1966, on the initiative of Arnold Wesker, the Roundhouse became a centre for political theatre, rock gigs and other nonconformist happenings, opening with a launch party for the *International Times*, at which Pink Floyd and Soft Machine both performed, and later hosting a Dialectics of Liberation conference organized by R.D. Laing, not to mention performances by the anarchist Living Theatre from New York, which featured a naked cast, and being a regular spot for London's premier psychedelic club *UFO*. The Roundhouse closed down in 1983, but after numerous abortive plans, has recently been given a £28 million facelift and is due to reopen as a youth arts centre and performance venue sometime in 2006.

Camden Town also boasts a few architectural curiosities, from Piers Gough's **Glass Building**, with its undulating bile-green facade on Jamestown Road, to Terry Farrell's corrugated steel-clad former **TV-AM Building**, over the High Street on Hawley Crescent. TV-AM, the country's first breakfast TV station, has long since been replaced by MTV, but the building's best feature, the giant blue-and-white egg cups on the canal facade, remain. Further along the canal are the technologically astonishing **canalside flats** designed by Farrell's former partner, Nicholas Grimshaw. The upper floors feature curved aluminium vertical sliding doors, which allow the dining room to become alfresco; the south side, by contrast, is windowless to cut out noise from the adjacent car park of the Camden Road **Sainsbury's** supermarket, another modernist structure by Grimshaw.

Jewish Museum

Despite having no significant Jewish associations, Camden is home to London's **Jewish Museum** (Mon–Thurs 10am–4pm, Sun 10am–5pm; £3.50; ☏020/7284 1997, ⊛www.jewishmuseum.org.uk), at 129 Albert St, just off Parkway. The purpose-built premises are smartly designed, and the collection of Judaica includes treasures from London's Great Synagogue on Duke's Place in the City, burnt down by Nazi bombers in 1941, and a sixteenth-century Venetian Ark of the Covenant. There's also a video and exhibition explaining Jewish religious practices and the history of the Jewish community in Britain. More compelling are the temporary exhibitions, discussions and occasional concerts put on by the museum. Look out, too, for the excellent temporary exhibitions held in the museum's Finchley branch on East End Road (see p.370).

Old St Pancras to Camley Street Natural Park

By tradition the first parish church built in London, **Old St Pancras Church** lies hidden and neglected behind iron railings on raised ground above Pancras Road, a few minutes' walk east of the bottom of Camden High Street. Parts of the church date from the eleventh century, but the rest was rebuilt in the nineteenth, hence the only real points of interest within are some exposed Norman masonry and the sixth-century Roman altar stone. Unfortunately, since Satanists attacked the church in 1985, access has been difficult outside of services.

The **churchyard**, which backs onto the railway lines and the lugubrious Victorian Hospital for Tropical Diseases, was turned into a public garden in 1877, with the majority of graves being heaped around an ash tree under the supervision of Thomas Hardy. **John Soane's mausoleum** from 1816 – designed initially for his wife, and the inspiration for Giles Gilbert Scott's traditional red phone box – still stands in its original location, to the north of the church. Also buried here was Britain's great protofeminist, **Mary Wollstonecraft Godwin**, who died a few days after giving birth to her daughter, Mary. At the age of 16, the younger Mary was spotted visiting her mother's grave by the poet Percy Bysshe Shelley, who immediately declared his undying love, before eloping with her to Italy – both Marys are now buried in Bournemouth. A list of the graveyard's most prominent dead is inscribed on the monumental sundial erected by Baroness Burdett-Coutts, below which sits a statue of her collie dog, and there's a map of the prominent graves by the entrance.

If you continue down Pancras Road, you'll come to a collection of railway bridges, destined to carry the Eurostar trains into St Pancras station in 2007 (ⓦwww.ctrl.co.uk). The whole area on the east side of the bridges, at the back of King's Cross, is currently undergoing major redevelopment as a result. Despite the engineering works, several of the brooding skeletal **King's Cross Gasholders** are earmarked for survival as they are, in fact, listed buildings. These Victorian monsters hark back to an era when nothing was too lowly to be given Neoclassical decoration, hence the wrought-iron Doric pillars and red triglyphs.

Up Camley Street, past the gasholders, is **Camley Street Natural Park** (summer Mon–Thurs 9am–5pm, Sat & Sun 11am–5pm; winter Mon–Thurs 9am to dusk, Sat & Sun 10am–4pm; free; ☎020/7833 2311, ⓦwww.wildlondon. org.uk), transformed from a rubbish dump into a canalside wildlife haven, and run by the London Wildlife Trust. Pond, meadow and woodland habitats have been re-created and provide a natural environment for birds, butterflies, frogs, newts, toads and even the odd heron, plus a rich variety of plant life.

London Canal Museum

An insight into life on the canals can be gained from the **London Canal Museum** (Tues–Sun 10am–4.30pm; £3; ☎020/7713 0836, ⓦwww.canalmuseum .org.uk), on the other side of York Way, down New Wharf Road. The museum testifies to the hard life boat families had to endure and includes a 1924 film of life on the Regent's Canal. Other exhibits relate to the building itself, which was built as an ice house by Swiss-Italian entrepreneur Carlo Gatti, London's main ice trader in the nineteenth century. Gatti single-handedly popularized ice cream in London, supplying most of the city's vendors, who became known as "Hokey-Pokey Men" – a corruption of the street cry *Ecco un poco*, "Just try a little". Also on view are a restored "butty" (an engine-less narrowboat used for extra storage) and some of the unusual Measham Ware pottery that was popular with canal-boat families.

The Canal Museum stands alongside the **Battlebridge Basin**, which is just about the end of the road if you're walking along the towpath; under the next road bridge the canal enters the Nash-built **Islington Tunnel**, 1000ft long and hard work for the boatmen, who would lie on their backs and push the boat through with their feet. In 1826, a miniature steamboat took over the job, emerging into the light between Vincent Terrace and Noel Road, on the other side of Upper Street (see opposite).

Islington

Islington has acquired something of a reputation as the home of what the British media like to call "the chattering classes" – the liberal, *Guardian*-reading middle class. Local Labour MP Chris Smith is openly gay and the prime minister, Tony Blair, lived in the borough before moving into Number Ten. Parts of Islington have certainly come a long way up the social ladder in the last forty years, since low house prices in the 1960s and 1970s encouraged a lot of arty professionals to buy and renovate the area's dilapidated Regency and early Victorian squares and terraces. In the 1980s this process was accelerated by an influx of far-from-left-leaning yuppies, who snapped up properties in an area attractively convenient for the City.

▲ King's Head pub, Islington

The impact of this gentrification has been relatively minor on the district as a whole, which stretches as far north as Highgate Hill, and Islington remains one of the poorest boroughs in England. On the other hand, the main drag, Upper Street, has changed enormously: the arrival of its antique market, confusingly known as **Camden Passage**, running parallel on the east side, coincided with the new influx of cash-happy customers, and its trendy pubs and ethnic **restaurants**, from Turkish to Thai, Japanese to Lebanese, reflect the wealth of its new residents. For entertainment, there are more **pub-theatres** in Islington than anywhere else, the oldest-established being the *King's Head*, whose better productions transfer to the West End; in addition to these, there's the Almeida – one of London's leading theatres which has attracted the likes of Juliette Binoche, Ralph Fiennes, Kevin Spacey and Liam Neeson – plus several comedy and live-music venues (see "Theatre, comedy and cinema", p.516, for details). All of which makes Islington one of the liveliest areas of north London in the evening – a kind of off-West End.

Upper Street and around

Looking at the traffic fighting its way along **Upper Street**, it's hard to believe that "merry Islington", as it was known, was once a spa resort to which people would flock from the City to drink the pure water and breathe the clean air. Today, the district has fewer green spaces than any other London borough – one of the few being the minuscule **Islington Green**, a short distance along Upper Street from Angel tube (home to Europe's longest escalator). At the apex of the green stands a weathered statue of **Hugh Myddelton**, the Welsh jeweller to James I, who revolutionized London's water supply by drawing fresh water direct from springs in Hertfordshire via an aqueduct known as the **New River**. From 1612 until the late 1980s Myddelton's New River continued to supply most of north London with its water – the succession of ponds to the north-east of Canonbury Road is a surviving fragment of the scheme.

Playwright **Joe Orton** and his lover **Kenneth Halliwell** lived together for sixteen years, spending the last eight years of their lives in a top-floor bedsit at 25 Noel Rd, to the east of Upper Street, where the Regent's Canal emerges from the Islington tunnel. It's ironic that the borough council has seen fit to erect a plaque on the house commemorating the couple, when it was instrumental in pressing for harsh prison sentences after both men were found guilty of stealing and defacing local library books in 1962. (The wittily doctored books are now among the most prized posses-sions of Islington Central Library, up Holloway Road, on the corner of Fieldway Cres-cent; the books themselves are now too delicate to handle, but colour photocopies can be viewed on request.)

Six months in prison worked wonders for Orton's writing, as he himself said: "Being in the nick brought detachment to my writing." It also brought him success, with irreverent comedies like *Loot*, *Entertaining Mr Sloane* and *What the Butler Saw* playing to sell-out audiences in the West End and on Broadway. Orton's meteoric fame and his sexual profligacy drove Halliwell to despair, however, and on August 9, 1967, Halliwell finally cracked – beating Orton to death with a hammer and then killing himself with a drug overdose. Their ashes were mixed together and scattered over the grass at Golders Green Crematorium (see p.370). Apart from the local public toilets, Orton's favourite hangout was the appropriately entitled *Island Queen* pub, at the end of Noel Road.

To the east of the green, a black glass canopy provides shelter for the antique stalls of the **Camden Passage market** (Wed 7am–2pm & Sat 8am–4pm; ⓦwww.camdenpassageislington.co.uk), which began in the 1960s. The antique shops in the market's narrow namesake and the surrounding streets stay open all week, as do the lockups in "The Mall" – in fact a converted tramshed – to the south of the passage. Since many locals are prepared to pay through the nose for antiques, you're unlikely to find bargains here. The perfect antidote, however, is to walk along **Chapel Street market** (Tues–Sun 9.30am–3.30pm, Thurs till 1pm), a short distance up Liverpool Road, on the other side of Upper Street. Selling cheap clothes, fruit and veg and Arsenal football memorabilia, it's a salutary reminder of Islington's working-class roots.

Royal Agricultural Hall and Liverpool Road

On the other side of the green from Camden Passage, the ugly modern glass frontage of the Business Design Centre (ⓦwww.businessdesigncentre.co.uk) hides the former **Royal Agricultural Hall**, built in 1862 and known locally as the "Aggie". As well as hosting annual agricultural and livestock exhibitions, it was in many ways a precursor to the later exhibition halls of Earl's Court and Olympia, hosting the World's Fair, the Grand Military Tournament, Cruft's Dog Show and such marvels as Urbini's performing fleas. During World War II, however, it was requisitioned by the government for use by the Post Office, who remained in residence until 1971. The interior is still magnificent, but the best exterior view is now from **Liverpool Road**, where two large brick tow-ers rise up either side of the roof, rather like a Victorian train station.

Walking along these sections of Upper Street and Liverpool Road, it's impos-sible not to be struck by one of the quirky architectural features of Islington – the raised pavements which protected pedestrians from splattered mud. Such precautions were especially necessary in Islington, which was used as a conve-nient grazing halt for livestock en route to the City markets. The residential streets on either side of Liverpool Road, developed shortly after the completion of the Regent's Canal, are also worth exploring for their wonderful **Georgian and early Victorian squares**. The earliest examples, like Cloudesley Square and Myddelton Square (further south, past Pentonville Road), are in plain Georgian style with early neo-Gothic churches as their centrepieces; Lonsdale Square, with its Tudor styling, and Milner Square, with its parade of giant pilasters, are slightly later Victorian variations on the same theme.

From St Mary's to Highbury Fields

Back on Upper Street, past the green, is **St Mary's Church**, originally built in the 1750s. Only the steeple survived the Blitz, though the light, spacious 1950s interior is an interesting period piece, with six fluted Egyptian-style columns framing the sanctuary. The churchyard opens out into Dagmar Passage, where in 1961 a former temperance hall was converted into the **Little Angel Puppet Theatre** (ⓦwww.littleangeltheatre.com), London's only permanent puppet theatre. The archway at the end of Dagmar Terrace brings you out onto **Cross Street**, Islington's loveliest street, with eighteenth-century houses sloping down to Essex Road and raised pavements on both sides. If you've a penchant for Deco-style buildings, head north up much less lovely Essex Road, where the former **Carlton Cinema** (now a bingo club) was built in 1929 in mock-Egyptian style, using brightly coloured Hathernware tiles.

Back on Upper Street, heading north, you pass **Islington Town Hall**, a handsome 1920s Neoclassical Portland-stone building, whose southernmost entrance is now home to the tiny **Islington Museum** (Wed–Sat 11am–5pm, Sun 2–4pm; free; ⓦwww.islington.gov.uk/leisure), which has a small permanent display on the history of the borough, and puts on exhibitions with a local theme. Continuing north, Upper Street is flanked to the east by Compton Terrace, a standard late-Georgian terrace, interrupted halfway along by the fancifully extravagant **Union Chapel** (ⓦwww.unionchapel.org.uk), built in 1888 at the height of the Congregationalists' popularity. The spacious octagonal interior is designed like a giant auditorium, with raked seating and galleries capable of holding the 1600 rapt worshippers who used to come and listen to the sermons of the local pastor. The number of chapel-goers has since dwindled, and the chapel now doubles as an innovative independent concert venue. To the north of Highbury Corner, at the top of Upper Street, lies the largest open space in the entire borough, **Highbury Fields**, where over 200,000 people gathered in 1666 to escape the Great Fire, and which is now overlooked on two sides by splendid Georgian terraces.

Canonbury Square

East of Compton Terrace is Islington's most perfect Regency set piece, **Canonbury Square**, centred on a beautifully kept flower garden sadly blighted by traffic ploughing up Canonbury Road. In 1928, **Evelyn Waugh** moved into the first floor of no. 17 with his wife Evelyn Gardiner (they called themselves "He-Evelyn" and "She-Evelyn"); in those days, it was a deeply unfashionable place to live, and they moved out after a couple of years. It was precisely the square's squalor that appealed to **George Orwell**, who moved into the top floor of no. 27 in 1944, with his wife and son, having been bombed out of his digs in St John's Wood; he later used it as the prototype for Winston Smith's home in *1984*.

Immediately to the northeast of the square stands the last remaining relic of Islington's bygone days as a rural retreat, the red-brick **Canonbury Tower**, originally part of a Tudor mansion built for the prior of St Bartholomew in the City. The very top floor boasts three Elizabethan interiors, with carved oak panelling and fireplaces carved with Freemasonic and Rosicrucian symbols from when the rooms were used by Renaissance man Francis Bacon. The tower is currently looked after by the nearby Canonbury Academy, who will occasionally show visitors round (☎020/7359 6194, ⊛www.canonbury.ac.uk).

Estorick Collection of Modern Italian Art

Islington's most popular attraction is the **Estorick Collection of Modern Italian Art** (Wed–Sat 11am–6pm, Sun noon–5pm; £3.50; ☎020/7704 9522, ⊛www.estorickcollection.com), housed in a large converted Georgian mansion at 39a Canonbury Square, though the entrance is on Canonbury Road. The collection is the legacy of Eric Estorick, an American sociologist who married Salome Dessau, the wealthy daughter of a Nottingham textile magnate, and became an art dealer. The most exciting works in the gallery are those of the early Italian Futurists, though of course it's impossible to escape the irony of having a museum to a movement whose founding manifesto of 1909, by Filippo Marinetti, urged its followers to "divert the canals to flood the museums!" Marinetti, a rich boy with a penchant for crashing fast cars, was Futurism's mouthpiece and, as evidenced by the photos, had an eye for natty waistcoats, complete with appliqué hands patting the pockets.

The permanent collection, spread out over the two upper floors, ranges from Luigi Russolo's rainbow-coloured *Music*, which is firmly Futurist, to a couple of portraits by Modigliani, and a typically melancholic canvas by Symbolist painter, Giorgio de Chirico. One of the strangest works is Medardo Rosso's wax sculpture *Woman with a Veil*, from 1893, which had a profound influence on several of the movement's artists. Other highlights include Carlo Carrà's *Hand of the Violinist*, a classic Futurist study of movement, speed and dexterity, and Gino Severini's *Dancer*, which is a more or less standard Cubist deconstruction. The gallery also features works by lesser-known Italian artists such as Giorgio Morandi, Massimo Campigli, Mario Sironi and Zoran Music, as well as works by Italy's two leading postwar sculptors, Emilio Greco and Marino Marini. Excellent temporary exhibitions are also held here, and there's a pleasant Italian café that spills out into the back courtyard in good weather.

Hackney and around

The borough of **Hackney** stretches from the East End districts of Hoxton and Shoreditch on the edge of the City (covered in Chapter 13) through the central crossroads of **Dalston** to the north London suburbs of **Stoke Newington** and **Stamford Hill**. With the city's largest Afro-Caribbean community after Brixton, a sizeable Hasidic Jewish population and an even greater number of Turkish/Kurdish inhabitants, this is one of the most ethnically diverse of all London boroughs. It's hardly surprising, then, that the country's longest-serving black woman MP, Diane Abbott, has her constituency in Hackney, or that this was one of the infamous "loony left" councils of the 1980s that the right-wing press loved to hate. The fact that the borough has tourist signposts comes as a surprise to many visitors, yet Hackney repays selective visits: **Ridley Road** boasts one of London's most vibrant multi-ethnic markets, the red-brick Tudor mansion of **Sutton House** hides away on the fringes of Homerton, and

21

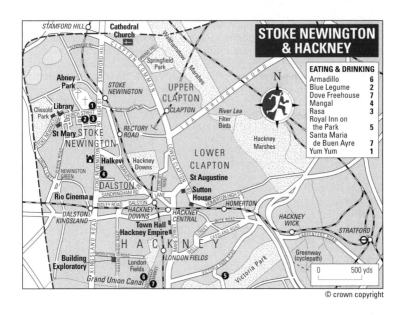

Stoke Newington is a haven of inexpensive Turkish and Indian restaurants and trendy laid-back cafés.

Dalston

In the late 1940s **Dalston** was the scene of battles between Mosley's fascists and supporters of the 43 Club, an organization set up by Jewish ex-servicemen to combat the resurgence of fascism in Britain. Nowadays the different communities of this area have a strong enough presence not to feel threatened by the residual white racism in the borough's southern fringes.

The ethnic diversity of Dalston is best expressed in the **Ridley Road Market** (Mon–Wed 9am–3pm, Thurs till noon, Fri & Sat 9am–5pm): between the Cockney market-stallholders at the Kingsland High Street end and the Turkish/Kurdish supermarket that marks the eastern end (its railings still displaying the Star of David from its original occupants), you'll find West Indian grocers and fishmongers, halal butchers and a bagel bakery – a convenient 24-hour refuelling point. Across the road from the market at 41 Kingsland High St is the *Shanghai* restaurant, formerly F. Cooke, London's best-preserved **eel and pie shop**, founded in 1862 by the Cooke family, its 1910 decor of tiles, marble and glass miraculously intact. A little further north up the High Street stands Dalston's Art Deco **Rio Cinema**, sole survivor of the numerous picture houses that once punctuated the street.

A great way to get to grips with the development of Hackney through the ages is to seek out the **Building Exploratory** (Thurs & Fri 1–5.30pm; free; ☎020/7275 8555, ⒲www.buildingexploratory.org.uk), which is hidden away on Albion Drive, just west of Queensbridge Road, in the south of Dalston. Spread out across a couple of former classrooms on the first floor of an old Victorian school, the interactive displays here cover geology, building techniques, architectural history, and include a giant model of Hackney, a fabulous 3D periodic chart and a model of one of the nearby Holly Street tower blocks, only one of which still stands, including a hundred samples of wallpaper from the flats. The custodians offer free guided tours on Thursday at 4pm and Friday at 2pm.

Stoke Newington

Predominantly rural until the middle of the nineteenth century, the suburb north of Dalston, **Stoke Newington**, was something of a haven for Noncon-formists, who were denied the right to live in the City. When Bunhill Fields (see p.230) became overcrowded, **Abney Park Cemetery** (ⓦwww.abney-park.org.uk), to the north of Church Street, which feeds off west from Stoke Newington High Street, became the "Campo Santo of English non-Conform-ists", in the words of the 1903 brochure. The only really famous grave is that of William Booth, founder of the Salvation Army, by the Church Street entrance, but the romantically overrun cemetery was originally planted as an arboretum, and is now something of an inner-city wildlife reserve (not to mention a gay cruising area). If you want to know more about Abney Park, head for the **vis-itors' centre** (Mon–Fri 9.30am–4.30pm, Sun noon–3pm) housed in one of the Egyptian-style lodges at the main entrance, to the east, at the very top of Stoke Newington High Street.

The most famous Dissenter to live in the village was **Daniel Defoe**, who wrote *Robinson Crusoe* in a house on the corner of what is now Defoe Road and Church Street; his gravestone is displayed in the Hackney Museum (see p.354) – stolen from Bunhill Fields in the 1870s, it was discovered in Southampton in 1940. Dissenters from a later era, the **Angry Brigade**, lived at 359 Amhurst Rd, off Stoke Newington High Street, in the early 1970s. Six members, at the time, of Britain's only home-grown urban terrorist group were arrested here during a dawn raid, and later sentenced to prison for conspiracy to cause explosions. The Angries were blamed for 25 bomb attacks on the homes of Tory politicians and other members of the Establishment; no one was killed.

Back on Stoke Newington Road, just south of Amhurst Road, a former church, built in Moorish/Byzantine style, has, by a judicious twist of fate, been turned into the **Aziziy Mosque**, whose facade is now smothered in Islamic tiles. The mosque lies at the heart of the local Turkish/Kurdish community, whose exclusively male cafés, named after Turkish football clubs, line the street. The various left-wing factions to which most of the community belong join together annually for London's largest May Day march, down the High Street, while the Kurdish New Year (Newroz) is celebrated in April in grand style at **Halkevi**, the Turkish/Kurdish community centre housed in a disused factory built by Simpson's of Piccadilly.

Stoke Newington's two main churches, both dedicated to **St Mary**, are situ-ated halfway down Stoke Newington Church Street, and reflect the changes wrought on this area in the last couple of centuries: the sixteenth-century vil-lage church stands on the north side of the road, opposite a more urbane struc-ture built by George Gilbert Scott in the 1850s, with a spire that outreached all others in London in its day. This pair marks the entrance to **Clissold Park**, founded in 1889 and centred on a porticoed mansion that was built in the 1790s as a country house for London's Quaker Hoare banking family (see "The City" chapter 11), and which now contains the park café. The water in front of the house was once part of the New River, but now serves as a pond for ducks and terrapins; elsewhere there are goats and even deer. To the north, you can just make out the bizarre quasi-medieval turrets and towers of the Stoke Newing-ton pumping station, built in 1856, closed in 1946 and redesigned in the 1990s

㉑

by Nicholas Grimshaw as a popular indoor rock-climbing centre called **The Castle** (@www.castle-climbing.co.uk).

Stamford Hill and the Lea Valley

Stamford Hill, the area northeast of Clissold Park, is home to a tight-knit Yiddish-speaking community of ultra-Orthodox Hasidic Jews, one of Hackney's oldest immigrant populations. The Hasidic movement originated in Poland in the eighteenth century under the charismatic leadership of Baal Shem Tov (often known as the "Besht"), who preached a message of joyful worship, influenced by the mystical teachings of the cabbala. The movement has since rigidified into a much more conservative one, made up of individual dynasties, each of which follows a particular *rebbe* or wise man, whose author-ity is passed from father to son. As such, they have more in common with their brethren in Israel and New York than they do with their Gentile neighbours or even other less orthodox Anglo-Jews. The most visually striking aspect of Stamford Hill's Hasidic Jews is the men's attire – frock coats, white stockings and elaborate headgear – which derives from that worn by the Polish nobility of the period.

The shops on Stamford Hill and Dunsmure Road, running west, are where the Hasidim buy their kosher goods, and on Sundays, large families take the air at **Springfield Park**, a beautifully landscaped space opened in 1905 "to change the habits of the people and to keep them out of the public houses". To get to the park from Stamford Hill, walk across the remnants of Clapton Common, and down Spring Hill. En route, be sure to check out the four winged beasts (char-acters from Revelations) that sit around the base of the spire of the **Cathedral Church of the Good Shepherd** on the corner of Rookwood Road, which was built for the sect of Spiritual Free Lovers known as the Agapemonites in 1892. Six thousand people gathered outside the church in September 1902 to throw rotten tomatoes at the womanizing local vicar who had declared himself the Second Messiah and drive him into the nearby Clapton Pond to see if he could walk on water. The park itself boasts an awesome view east across the Lea Valley, and a decent café down by the River Lea marina, in the park's north-ernmost tip.

On the other side of the river lie the **Walthamstow Marshes**, a valuable stretch of wetland that's alive with butterflies and warblers in the summer. If you follow the river southwards, you will eventually reach the **Middlesex Filter Beds** (Sat & Sun: Easter–Sept 10am–6pm; Oct–Easter 10am–4pm; summer holidays also Mon–Fri 10am–5pm; free), originally built in 1852 on the south side of Lea Bridge Road. Today, drained of most of their water, the filter beds serve as a nature reserve – in the summer check out the noisy frogs in the pond by the main culvert. Beyond, to the south, lie the **Hackney Marshes**, best known as the venue for Sunday League football matches, beyond which is the area earmarked for the London 2012 Olympics (see p.245).

Mare Street and around

The old parish of **Hackney** (as opposed to the modern borough) lies to the east of Dalston, around **Mare Street**, whose main claim to fame is the ornate terracotta **Hackney Empire** (@www.hackneyempire.co.uk), one of the last surviving variety theatres in London, built in typically extravagant style by Frank Matcham in 1899. Next door, set back from Mare Street, stands **Hackney Town Hall**, built in the 1930s in a very restrained Art Deco style.

Opposite stands the equally austere Central Hall, erected between the wars as a 2000-seater Methodist meeting place, refurbished in 2001 as a music venue, but currently closed after going bust in 2004.

The new library, meanwhile, has moved next to the town hall, and houses the **Hackney Museum** (Mon, Tues & Fri 9.30am–5.30pm, Thurs 9.30am–8pm, Sat 10am–5pm; free; ⊛www.hackney.gov.uk/hackneymuseum). The new museum puts on excellent temporary exhibitions, and the permanent displays are full of hands-on stuff, as well as lots of personal accounts from local residents. Specific exhibits to look out for include the "upside-down" map of Dalston and the Saxon log boat found in Springfield Park, thought to have been a ferry for taking folk across the River Lea.

On the north side of the railway bridge, Mare Street is still discernibly a village high street, known, for obvious reasons, as the **Narroway**, and overlooked by the dumpy fifteenth-century tower of the former parish church of **St Augustine**, and next to it, the Old Town Hall originally built in 1802. Head east across the graveyard behind the tower and down the Georgian terrace of Sutton Place and you'll come to **Sutton House** (mid-Jan to mid-Dec Fri & Sat 1–5pm, Sun 11.30am–5pm; NT; £2.50; ☎020/8986 2264), Hackney's prime tourist attraction. In the mid-1980s this mansion was just one of the borough's numerous squats; since then it has been painstakingly restored to a condition that does some justice to its status as the oldest house in the entire East End. Built in 1535 for Ralph Sadleir, a rising star at the court of Henry VIII, it takes its name from Thomas Sutton, founder of Charterhouse (see p.229), who lived in an adjacent building (he is buried at Charterhouse, minus his entrails, which you've just walked over in the graveyard). The National Trust have done their best to adapt to unfamiliar surroundings and have preserved not just the exquisite Elizabethan "linenfold" wooden panelling, but also a mural left by squatters in 1986. In addition to showing its rambling complex of period rooms, the house puts on classical concerts, and hosts contemporary art exhibitions, and even runs a veggie café, all of which are open longer hours (Wed–Sun 11.30am–5pm).

㉑

Walthamstow

"Once a pleasant place enough, but now terribly cocknified and choked up by the jerry builder", according to local boy William Morris, the northeastern suburb of **Walthamstow** (⊛www.walthamforest.gov.uk), east of the River Lea and the marshes, is on few tourists' itineraries, but it's somewhere you could easily spend an afternoon, especially if you've an interest in the work of Morris. Walthamstow is also David Beckham's home manor: he was born and brought up in the borough, and the council website has a Beckham trail you can follow (in English, Spanish and Japanese). Another place to visit is **Walthamstow Market** (Mon–Sat 9am–4pm, Sat till 5pm), which claims to be the longest street market in the country, stretching for well over a mile along the old High Street, north of the tube station. For a traditional East End snack, head for *Manzes*, at no. 76, one of London's finest pie-and-mash shops, with its traditional tiled walls and ceiling.

From the tube, head east down St Mary Road, then Church End, which will take you to the heart of the old village conservation area, a surprising oasis of calm. On your right as you reach the end of Church End is the **Vestry House Museum** (Mon–Fri 10am–1pm & 2–5.30pm, Sat closes 5pm; free; ☎020/8509

1917), built in 1730 and at one time the village workhouse. Later on, it became the police station, and a reconstructed police cell from 1861 is one of the museum's chief exhibits. Pride of place, however, goes to the tiny Bremer car, Britain's first-ever internal combustion engine automobile, designed in 1892 by local engineer Fred Bremer, 20-year-old son of German immigrants. Victorian times are comprehensively covered, and the temporary exhibitions tend to cover contemporary topics. The other point of interest here is the fifteenth-century half-timbered **Ancient House**, a short walk up Church Lane.

Civic Centre and the William Morris Gallery

Walthamstow's two other sights are a five-minute walk north past the concrete-encased church of St Mary's, and up The Drive and its continuation, Hurst Road. First is the local **Civic Centre**, set back from Forest Road (at the top of Hurst Road) around a huge open courtyard. Designed in an unusual Scandinavian style in the 1930s, it is, without doubt, London's grandest town-hall complex. Indeed, there's a touch of Stalinism about the severe classicism of the centre's central portico and in the exhortation above the adjacent Assembly Hall: "Fellowship is life and the lack of fellowship is death." Sadly, construction of the law courts that would have completed the ensemble was interrupted by the war, but this remains one of the most startling public buildings in London.

To the west of the Civic Centre, in front of Lloyd Park along Forest Road, stands a lovely Georgian mansion with two big bay windows, now known as the **William Morris Gallery** (Tues–Sat & first Sun of month 10am–1pm & 2–5pm; free; ☎020/8527 3782, ⓦwww.lbwf.gov.uk/wmg), which became the Morris family home from 1848 until the death of William Morris' father, a successful businessman in the City, in 1856. Poet, artist, designer and socialist, William Morris (1834–96) was one of the most fascinating characters of Victorian London. He was closely associated with both the Pre-Raphaelite and Arts and Crafts movements, and went on to set up Morris & Co, whose work covered all areas of applied art: glasswork, tiles, metalwork, curtains, furniture, calligraphy, carpets, book illumination and (perhaps most famously) wallpaper.

The ground floor of the museum contains a modest array of every kind of work with which Morris got involved, and also hosts temporary exhibitions. Disappointingly, there are only passing references to Morris' stormy personal life: he married Jane Burden, a working-class girl whom Dante Rossetti picked up at the theatre in Oxford and later reclaimed as his lover. Upstairs, there's a small collection of paintings by his later followers and Pre-Raphaelite chums. Edward Burne-Jones shows his mastery of gouache in *St George and the Dragon*, while Ford Madox Brown does the same for pure watercolour in his richly textured portrait, *Jacopo Foscari in Prison*. As is clear from his *Portrait of Alexa Wilding*, Rossetti was so obsessed with Jane Burden that although the model for *The Loving Cup* was a "Chelsea laundry-maid", she looks just like "Janey".

As well as being a successful capitalist – the company's flagship store was on Mayfair's Hanover Square – Morris also became one of the leading political figures of his day, active in the Socialist League with Eleanor Marx, and publishing several utopian tracts, most famously *News from Nowhere*, in which he suggests that the Houses of Parliament be used as "a storage place for manure" (you can buy a copy in the bookshop for the tube journey back). You can see several other works by Morris elsewhere in London: at the V&A (p.305), Holy Trinity Church, off Sloane Square (p.318), and the Red House (p.394).

Hampstead

Perched on a hill to the west of Hampstead Heath, **Hampstead** village (ⓦwww.myhampstead.co.uk) developed into a fashionable spa in the eighteenth century, and was not much altered thereafter. Its sloping site, which deterred Victorian property speculators and put off the railway companies, saved much of the Georgian village from destruction. Later, it became one of the city's most celebrated literary *quartiers* and even now it retains its reputation – just ahead of Islington – as a bolt hole of the high-profile intelligentsia and discerning pop stars. You can get some idea of its tone from the fact that the local Labour MP is currently the actor-turned-politician Glenda Jackson.

The steeply inclined **High Street**, lined with trendy clothes shops and arty cafés, flaunts the area's ever-increasing wealth without completely losing its charm, though the most appealing area is the precipitous network of alleyways, steps and streets north of the tube and west of Heath Street. Proximity to the Heath is, of course, the real joy of Hampstead, for this mixture of woodland, smooth pasture and landscaped garden (see p.362) is quite simply the most exhilarating patch of greenery in London.

Holly Bush to the Admiral's House

If you wander into the backstreets north of Hampstead tube, you will probably end up at the small triangular green on **Holly Bush Hill**, where the white weatherboarded **Romney House** stands (closed to the public). In 1797, painter George Romney converted the house and stables into London's first purpose-built studio house, though he spent only two years there before returning to the Lake District and the wife he had abandoned thirty years earlier. Later, it served as Hampstead's Assembly Rooms, where Constable used to lecture on landscape painting. Several houses are set grandly behind wrought-iron gates, on the north side of the green – the one you can hardly see at all is the late seventeenth-century **Fenton House**, now a museum of musical instruments (see below).

Beyond Fenton House, up Hampstead Grove, is Admiral's Walk, so-called after its most famous building, **Admiral's House**, a whitewashed Georgian mansion with nautical excrescences. Once painted by Constable, it was later lived in by Victorian architect George Gilbert Scott, of Albert Memorial fame. Until his death in 1933 John Galsworthy lived in the adjacent cottage, **Grove Lodge** – "[it] wasn't cheap, I can tell you", he wrote to a friend on arrival – where he completed *The Forsyte Saga* and received the 1932 Nobel Prize, which was presented to him here since he was too ill to travel abroad. Opposite is **The Mount**, a gently sloping street descending to Heath Street, which has changed little since it was depicted in *Work* by Pre-Raphaelite artist (and local resident) Ford Madox Brown – a reproduction is on display in Burgh House (see p.361).

Fenton House

All three floors of **Fenton House** (March Sat & Sun 2–5pm; Easter–Oct Wed–Fri 2–5pm, Sat & Sun 11am–5pm; NT; £4.80; ☎020/7435 3471) are decorated in the eighteenth-century taste and currently house a collection of European and Oriental ceramics bequeathed by the house's last private owner, Lady Binning. The house also contains the superb Benton-Fletcher collection

Over the years, countless writers, artists and politicos have been drawn to Hampstead, which now has more blue plaques commemorating its residents than any other London borough. **John Constable** lived here in the 1820s, trying to make ends meet for his wife and seven children and painting cloud formations on Hampstead Heath, several of which hang in the V&A. **John Keats** moved into Well Walk in 1817, to nurse his dying brother, then moved to a semi-detached villa, fell in love with the girl next door, bumped into Coleridge on the Heath, and in 1821 went to Rome to die; the villa is now a museum (see p.362). In 1856, **Karl Marx** finally achieved bourgeois respectability when he moved into Grafton Terrace, a new house on the south side of the Heath. **Robert Louis Stevenson** stayed here when he was 23 suffering from tuberculosis, and thought it "the most delightful place for air and scenery".

Author **H.G. Wells** lived on Church Row for three years just before World War I. In the same period, the photographer **Cecil Beaton** was attending a local infants' school, and was bullied there by author **Evelyn Waugh** – the start of a life long feud. The composer **Edward Elgar**, who lived locally, became a special constable during the war, joining the Hampstead Volunteer Reserve. **D.H. Lawrence**, and his German wife Frieda, watched the first major Zeppelin raid on London from the Heath in 1915 and decided to leave. Following the war, Lawrence's friend and fellow writer, **Katherine Mansfield**, lived for a couple of years in a big grey house overlooking the Heath, which she nicknamed "The Elephant". Actor **Dirk Bogarde** was born in a taxi in Hampstead in 1921. **Stephen Spender** spent his childhood in "an ugly house" on Frognal, and went to school locally. **Liz Taylor** was born in Hampstead in 1932, and came back to live here in the 1950s during her first marriage to Richard Burton.

In the 1930s, Hampstead's modernist Isokon Flats, on Lawn Road, designed by Hungarian Bauhaus emigré Marcel Breuer, became something of an artistic hangout, particularly its drinking den, the *Isobar*: architect **Walter Gropius**, and artists **Henry Moore**, **Ben Nicholson** and his wife **Barbara Hepworth** all lived there (Moore moved out in 1940 when his studio was bombed and retired to Herefordshire). Another tenant, **Agatha Christie**, compared the exterior to a giant ocean liner; others were less impressed. Local resident **Ian Fleming** even conducted a campaign to stop architect **Ernö Goldfinger** from building his modernist house at 2 Willow Rd (now a National Trust property; see p.361) and named James Bond's adversary after him. **Mohammed Ali Jinnah** abandoned India for Hampstead in 1932, living a quiet life with his daughter and sister, and working as a lawyer. **George Orwell** lived rent-free above Booklovers' Corner, a bookshop on South End Road, in 1934, in return for services in the shop in the afternoon; *Keep the Aspidistra Flying* has many echoes of Hampstead and its characters. **Sigmund Freud** spent the last year of his life in Hampstead, having reluctantly left Austria, following the Nazi Anschluss; his house is now a museum (see p.360). Artist **Piet Mondrian** also escaped to Hampstead from Nazi-occupied Paris, only to be bombed out a year later, after which he fled to New York. **Oskar Kokoschka** was another refugee from Nazi-occupied Europe, who, along with John Heartfield, was given assistance by the Hampstead-based Artists Refugee Committee. **General de Gaulle** lived on Frognal with his wife and two daughters and got some first-hand experience of Nazi air raids.

Ruth Ellis, the last woman to be hanged in Britain in 1955, shot her lover outside the *Magdala Tavern* by Hampstead Heath train station. **Sid Vicious** and **Johnny Rotten** lived in a squat on Hampstead High Street in 1976. **John le Carré** lived here in the 1980s and 1990s and set a murder in *Smiley's People* on Hampstead Heath. Of the current residents, one of the oldest is **Michael Foot**, the former Labour leader, now in his nineties, who lives in a house he bought with his redundancy cheque from Beaverbrook. Actors Hugh Grant, Stephen Fry, Bob Hoskins, chef Jamie Oliver and pop stars Boy George, Robbie Williams, Mel C (aka Sporty Spice) and Emma Bunton (aka Baby), and George Michael all have homes here.

NORTH LONDON | Hampstead

21

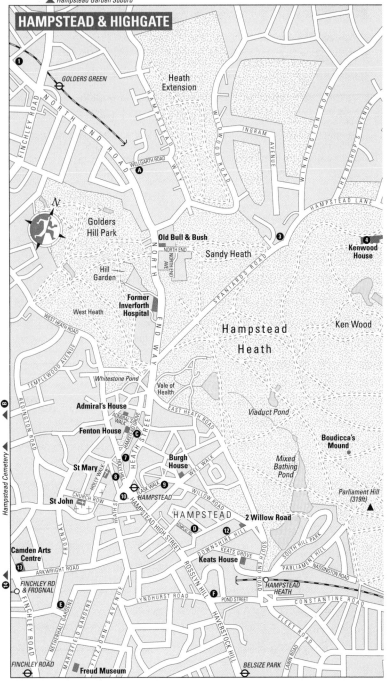

HAMPSTEAD & HIGHGATE

Hampstead Garden Suburb

Heath Extension

GOLDERS GREEN

FINCHLEY ROAD

NORTH END ROAD

HAMPSTEAD WAY

WILDWOOD ROAD

INGRAM

WINNINGTON AVENUE

THE BISHOPS AVENUE

WELLGARTH ROAD

A

HAMPSTEAD LANE

Golders Hill Park

Old Bull & Bush

NORTH END

NORTH END AVE

Sandy Heath

3

4 Kenwood House

Hill Garden

NORTH END WAY

SPANIARDS ROAD

Ken Wood

Former Inverforth Hospital

West Heath

WEST HEATH ROAD

Hampstead Heath

TEMPLEWOOD AVENUE

REDINGTON ROAD

Whitestone Pond

Vale of Health

EAST HEATH ROAD

Viaduct Pond

B

Admiral's House

ADMIRAL'S WALK

HEATH STREET

Boudicca's Mound

Fenton House

C

7

Burgh House

Mixed Bathing Pond

St Mary

HOLLY WALK

8

FLASK WALK

9

WELL WALK

WILLOW ROAD

Parliament Hill (319ft)

10

HAMPSTEAD

St John

CHURCH ROW

HEATH ST

HAMPSTEAD HIGH STREET

HAMPSTEAD

KEMPLAY RD

0

12

2 Willow Road

SOUTH HILL PARK

FROGNAL

DOWNSHIRE HILL

Camden Arts Centre

ARKWRIGHT ROAD

KEATS GROVE

Keats House

SOUTH END ROAD

PARLIAMENT HILL

NASSINGTON ROAD

13

14

FINCHLEY RD & FROGNAL

FINCHLEY ROAD

NETHERHALL GARDENS

MARESFIELD GARDENS

FITZJOHN'S AVENUE

LYNDHURST ROAD

ROSSLYN HILL

HAVERSTOCK HILL

POND STREET

F

HAMPSTEAD HEATH

CONSTANTINE ROAD

FLEET ROAD

E

Freud Museum

FINCHLEY ROAD

LAWN ROAD

BELSIZE PARK

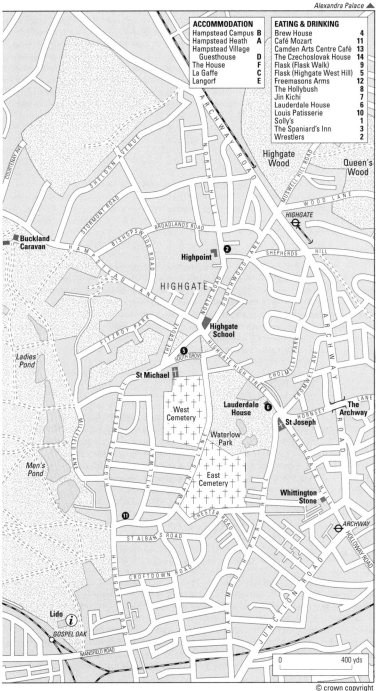

ACCOMMODATION

Hampstead Campus	**B**
Hampstead Heath	**A**
Hampstead Village Guesthouse	**D**
The House	**F**
La Gaffe	**C**
Langorf	**E**

EATING & DRINKING

Brew House	4
Café Mozart	11
Camden Arts Centre Café	13
The Czechoslovak House	14
Flask (Flask Walk)	9
Flask (Highgate West Hill)	5
Freemasons Arms	12
The Hollybush	8
Jin Kichi	7
Lauderdale House	6
Louis Patisserie	10
Solly's	1
The Spaniard's Inn	3
Wrestlers	2

NORTH LONDON | Hampstead

21

0   400 yds

© crown copyright

of **early musical instruments**, chiefly displayed on the top floor – from which you can see right across the Heath. Among the many spinets, virginals and clavichords is an early English grand piano, an Unverdorben lute from 1580 (one of only three in the world) and, on the ground floor, a harpsichord from 1612, on which Handel is thought to have played, though DNA tests have failed to back this up. Experienced keyboard players are occasionally let loose on some of the instruments during the day; **concerts** are also given sometimes in the drawing room on Thursday evenings, although, tickets tend to sell out months in advance; alternatively, sign up for one of the monthly **demonstration tours** (Thurs 2pm; £10). There's very little information within the house, so it's worth buying the briefer of the guides at the entrance. You can also rent a tape of music played on the above instruments (£1), to listen to while you walk round. Don't neglect to take a stroll in the beautiful formal **garden** (£1), which features some top-class herbaceous borders.

St John-at-Hampstead and Hampstead Cemetery

The Georgian terraces of **Church Row**, at the southern end of Heath Street, are the nearest Hampstead comes to an architectural set piece, and the street was where City gents would stay for the week when Hampstead was a thriving spa. Church Row also forms a grand approach to the eighteenth-century church of **St John-at-Hampstead**, which has an attractive Georgian interior and a romantically overgrown cemetery. The chest-tomb of the clockmaker John Harrison is in the churchyard; John Constable is buried in the southeastern corner; Hugh Gaitskill, the Labour Party leader from 1955 to 1963, lies in the Churchyard Extension to the northeast. If you continue up Holly Walk past the extension, you'll come to **St Mary's Church**, whose Italianate facade is squeezed into the middle of a row of three-storey cottages. As this was one of the first Roman Catholic churches to be built in London after the Reformation, the original facade from 1816 was much less conspicuous.

Further Hampstead luminaries are buried in the rather more neatly maintained **Hampstead Cemetery** situated half a mile to the west, on the other side of Finchley Road, and founded in 1876 when the Churchyard Extension was full. The pioneer of antiseptic surgery Joseph Lister, music-hall star Marie Lloyd, children's book illustrator Kate Greenaway, Hollywood actress Lilli Palmer and the Hungarian Laszlo Biro, who invented the ballpoint pen in 1938, are among those buried here. The full-size stone organ monument to the obscure Charles Barritt is the most unusual piece of funerary art, while the most unlikely occupant is Grand Duke Mikhail Mikhailovitch of Russia, uncle to the last tsar, Nicholas II.

Freud Museum

One of the most poignant of London's house museums is the **Freud Museum** (Wed–Sun noon–5pm; £5; ☎020/7435 2002, ⊛www.freud.org.uk), hidden away in the leafy streets of south Hampstead at 20 Maresfield Gardens. Having fled Vienna after the Nazi invasion, **Sigmund Freud** arrived in London in the summer of 1938, and was immediately Britain's most famous Nazi exile. He had been diagnosed as having cancer way back in 1923 (he was an inveterate cigar-smoker) and given just five years to live. He lasted sixteen, but was a semi-invalid when he arrived in London, and rarely left the house except to visit his pet dog, Chun, who was held in quarantine for nearly a year. On September 21, 1939, Freud's doctor fulfilled their eleven-year-old pact and gave his patient a lethal dose of morphine.

The ground-floor study and library look exactly as they did when Freud lived here (they are modelled on his flat in Vienna); the large collection of antiquities and the psychiatrist's couch, sumptuously draped in opulent Persian carpets, were all brought here from Vienna in 1938. Upstairs, where the Freud archive now resides, home movies of the doctor's family life in Vienna are shown continually, while another room is dedicated to his favourite daughter, Anna, herself an influential child analyst, who lived in the house until her death in 1982. Sigmund's architect son, Ernst, designed a loggia at the back of the house so that Freud could sit out and enjoy the garden; it has since been enclosed and serves as the museum shop, which flogs Freudian merchandise such as a "Brainy Beanie" – Freud himself as a cuddly childhood toy – and stocks a superb range of books.

Hampstead Wells

When the healing properties of Hampstead's waters were discovered at the end of the seventeenth century, Hampstead was rapidly transformed from a quiet village into a thriving spa. The assembly rooms and pump room, the standard institutions of any self-respecting spa, have long since been demolished, but there are a few scattered reminders of the days of **Hampstead Wells**, as it was briefly known. Threepenny containers of spring water were sold close to the High Street in the pedestrianized alleyway of **Flask Walk** (hence its name), while bottling took place at *The Flask* on the same street, now one of Hampstead's most popular pubs (see p.487); Flask Walk opens out into **Well Walk**, where the Victorian Chalybeate Well commemorates the springs.

Burgh House

The nearby Queen Anne mansion of **Burgh House** (Wed–Sun noon–5pm; free; ☎020/7431 0144, ⓦwww.london-northwest.com/burghhouse), on New End Square, off Well Walk, dates from the halcyon days of Hampstead Wells, and was at one time occupied by Dr Gibbons, the physician who discovered the spring's medicinal qualities. Surrounded by council housing, its ground floor now serves as an exhibition space, and there's a modest museum upstairs, with special emphasis on such notable locals as Constable and Keats. Other curiosities include a reproduction of Ford Madox Brown's painting *Work* (see p.356), a modernist Isokon plywood chair, found in a Hampstead skip by a local councillor, and the hat from Stanley Spencer's portrait of the artist Daphne Charlton, which was painted at the Charltons' house at 40 New End Square, and now belongs to the Tate. The *Buttery* tearoom (11am–5.30pm) in the basement has outdoor seating in the summer on a lovely terrace.

2 Willow Road

Hampstead's newest attraction is **2 Willow Road** (March & Nov Sat noon–5pm; April–Oct Thurs–Sat noon–5pm; NT; £4.60, £6.60 joint ticket with Fenton House; ☎020/7435 6166), a modernist red-brick terraced house, built in the 1930s by the Hungarian-born architect **Ernö Goldfinger**, best known for his controversial Trellick Tower (see p.334). When Goldfinger moved in, in 1937, this was a state-of-the-art house, its open-plan rooms flooded with natural light and much of the furniture designed by Goldfinger himself.

Strangely for a modernist, Goldfinger changed little in the house in the following sixty years, so what you see is a 1930s avant-garde dwelling preserved in aspic, a house at once both modern and old-fashioned. An added bonus is that the rooms are packed with *objets trouvés* and works of art by the likes of Max Ernst, Marcel Duchamp, Henry Moore and Man Ray. Before 3pm, visits are by hour-long guided tour only (noon, 1 & 2pm), for which you must book in advance; after 3pm the public has unguided, unrestricted access. The house is closed during the day on the first Thursday of the month, but open in the evening instead (5–9pm).

Keats' House

Hampstead's most lustrous figure is celebrated at **Keats' House** (Tues–Sun: April–Oct noon–5pm; Nov–March noon–4pm; £3; ☎020/7435 2062), an elegant, whitewashed Regency double villa on Keats Grove, a short walk south of Willow Road. The consumptive poet moved here in 1818 shortly after his brother Tom had died of the same illness. Inspired by the peacefulness of Hampstead and by his passion for girl-next-door Fanny Brawne (whose house is also part of the museum), Keats wrote some of his most famous works here before leaving for Rome, where he died in 1821. In the pretty front garden, as you approach the house, you pass a deeply uninspiring plum tree, which replaces a much larger specimen in whose shade Keats is said to have sat for two or three hours before composing *Ode to a Nightingale*. The neat, rather staid interior contains books and letters, an anatomical notebook from Keats' days as a medical student at Guy's Hospital, Fanny's engagement ring and the four-poster bed in which the poet first coughed up blood, confiding to his companion, Charles Brown, "that drop of blood is my death warrant". There are regular events – poetry readings, performances and talks – on Wednesday evenings.

Hampstead Heath

Hampstead Heath, north London's "green lung", is the city's most enjoyable public park. Though it may not have much of its original heathland left, it packs in a wonderful variety of bucolic scenery, from the formal **Hill Garden** and rolling green pastures of **Parliament Hill** to the dense woodland of **West Heath** and the landscaped grounds of **Kenwood**. As it is, the Heath was lucky to survive the nineteenth century intact, for it endured more than forty years of campaigning by the Lord of the Manor, Thomas Maryon Wilson, who introduced no fewer than fifteen parliamentary bills in an attempt to build over it. It wasn't until after Wilson's death in 1871 that 220 acres of the Heath passed into public ownership. The Heath now covers over 800 acres, and is currently run by the Corporation of London (🌐www.cityoflondon.gov.uk).

Parliament Hill and the Ponds

Parliament Hill, the Heath's southernmost ridge, is perhaps better known as Kite Hill, since this is north London's premier spot for kite-flying, especially busy at weekends when some serious equipment takes to the air. The parliamentary connection is explained in various ways by historians, so take your pick: a Saxon parliament is thought to have met here; Guy Fawkes' cronies are said to have gathered here with the hope of watching the Houses of Parliament burn; the Parliamentarians placed their cannon here during the Civil War to defend London against the Royalists; and the Middlesex parliamentary elections took place here in the seventeenth century. Whatever the reason for the name, the view over London is rivalled only by the one from Kenwood (see p.364).

The Heath is the source of several of London's lost rivers – the Tyburn, West-bourne and Fleet – and home to some 28 natural ponds, of which the most extensive are the eight **Highgate and Kenwood Ponds**, arranged in steps along a shallow valley on the eastern edge of the Heath. The Highgate Men's Pond (daily 7/8am–9pm or dusk; £2 donation), second from the bottom, is a secluded sylvan spot, popular with nudists, including a strong gay contingent; two ponds up is the cleanest of the lot, the Kenwood Ladies' Pond (times as above), with enough foliage to provide relaxed topless bathing, and similarly popular with lesbians. The Corporation is none too happy with either pond's reputation, but both are preferable to the Mixed Bathing Pond (times as above), which is a bit of a fleshpot, on the Hampstead side of the Heath.

To the Vale of Health

To the northwest of Parliament Hill is a fenced-off tumulus known as **Boudicca's Mound**, where, according to one tradition, Queen Boudicca (Boadicea) was buried after she and 10,000 other Brits had been massacred at Battle Bridge; another legend says that she's buried in King's Cross station (see p.156). Due west lies the picturesque **Viaduct Pond**, named after its red-brick bridge, which is also known as Wilson's Folly. It was built as part of Thomas Maryon Wilson's abortive plans to drive an access road through the middle of the Heath to his projected estate of 28 villas.

Below, to the west, beyond the Viaduct Pond, an isolated network of streets nestles in the **Vale of Health**, an area that was, in fact, a malarial swamp until the late eighteenth century. Literary lion Leigh Hunt moved to this quiet back-water in 1816, after serving a two-year prison sentence for libel, having called the Prince Regent "a fat Adonis of fifty", among other things. Hunt was instru-mental in persuading Keats to give up medicine for poetry, and introduced him to Shelley, Byron and other members of his literary circle. Other artistic residents have included Indian poet and Nobel Prize-winner Rabindranath Tagore, who lived here in 1912, and Stanley Spencer, who stayed here with the Carline family and married their daughter Hilda in the 1920s. D.H. Lawrence spent a brief, unhappy period here in 1915: in September of that year his novel *The Rainbow* was banned for obscenity, and by December, Lawrence and his wife, Frieda von Richthofen, whose German origins were causing the couple immense problems with the authorities, had resolved to leave the country.

North and west of Spaniards Road

The section of the Heath to the northwest of the Vale of Health misses out on the wonderful views of Parliament Hill and Kenwood, but makes up for it with some of the park's best-kept secrets. The place to start is the busy road junction around **Whitestone Pond**, which marks the highest point in north London (440ft). This former horse pond is overlooked by the cream-coloured weatherboarding and castellations of *Jack Straw's Castle*, a pub which, despite appearances, was entirely rebuilt in the 1960s.

To the west of Whitestone Pond is **West Heath**, a densely wooded, boggy area with a thick canopy of deciduous trees sloping down towards Childs Hill; it's a very peaceful place for a stroll and a popular cruising area for gay men. A track leads northwest from *Jack Straw's Castle* across West Heath past **The Hill Garden**, the Heath's most secretive and romantic little gem. It was built as an extension to the grounds of nearby Hill House (formerly the Inverforth Hospital, now converted into flats), and the formal gardens eventually became public property in 1960. Their most startling features are the eccentric balustraded terraces, which look out over West Heath and west to Harrow-on-the-Hill. All along the L-shaped terrace Doric columns support a ruinous pergola, which has been lovingly restored along with the bridge which Lord Lever (who bought the house in 1906) had to build over the public footpath in order to link his two gardens.

The path across West Heath eventually leads to the more formal landscaped gardens of **Golders Hill Park**. The central section of the park is taken up by animal enclosures containing pygmy goats and fallow deer, and a series of impeccably maintained aviaries, home to flamingoes, cranes and other exotic birds; to the north, closer to the entrance, is a beautifully kept walled garden and pond. Before you leave the park, make sure you try some of the café's wonderful Italian ice cream, courtesy of *Arte Gelato*.

Back up North End Road, past the *Old Bull & Bush* pub, a rough track curves its way through another secluded patch of woodland. Halfway along you'll come across a stranded red-brick archway that leads through into **Pitt's Garden**, originally the grounds of Pitt House (destroyed in the last war), home of eighteenth-century statesman William Pitt the Elder. Pitt retreated here on several occasions, most famously in 1767, when "gout in the head", as his bouts of insanity were euphemistically called, rendered him catatonic, upon which he shut himself away and received meals through a hatch.

Past the archway, the track turns into North End Avenue, which joins up with North End, which in turn backs onto Hampstead's sole remaining farmstead, the weatherboarded seventeenth-century **Wyldes Farm**, where William Blake used to stay. In the first decade of the last century, the adjacent farmland was bought from Eton College by Henrietta Barnett to provide land for Hampstead Garden Suburb (see p.369) and also for an eighty-acre addition to the Heath, now known as the **Heath Extension**. Its origins as agricultural pasture land are evident in the surviving hedgerow boundaries, and sheep were grazed here up until the 1930s.

Spaniards Road runs from Whitestone Pond along the eastern edge of **Sandy Heath**, a triangle of oak and beech woodland to the south of the Extension. At the northerneastern end of Spaniards Road, cars struggle to avoid oncoming traffic as the road squeezes between the old tollhouse and the **Spaniards Inn**, an eighteenth-century coaching inn thought to have been used by the highwayman Dick Turpin as a hiding place and vantage point for sizing up the coaches leaving town. The aforementioned Barnetts lived in the white weatherboarded house by the side of the inn.

Kenwood House

The Heath's most celebrated sight is **Kenwood House** (daily: April–Oct 11am–5pm; Nov–March 11am–4pm; EH; free; ☎020/8348 1286), whose beautiful off-white Neoclassical facade faces south to catch the sun. Set in its own magnificently landscaped grounds (daily: summer 8am–8pm; winter 8am–4pm), the house dates from the seventeenth century, but was later remodelled by Robert Adam for the Earl of Mansfield, Attorney-General, Lord Chief Justice and the most powerful jurist in the country. Mansfield, who had sent 102 people to the gallows and sentenced another 448 to transportation, was a deeply unpopular character and one of the prime targets of the Gordon rioters in 1780, who ransacked his Bloomsbury house. A crowd also made their way towards Kenwood, but they were waylaid by the canny landlord of the nearby

Spaniards Inn (an ex-butler of Mansfield's), who plied them with free drink until soldiers arrived to disperse the mob.

Thanks to Kenwood's last private owner, the Earl of Iveagh (head of the Guinness family), the house is now open to the public and home to the **Iveagh Bequest**, a superb collection of seventeenth- and eighteenth-century art from the English, Dutch and French schools. You pass some good examples of Boucher's slightly sickly, flirtatious pastoral scenes, before coming to the Music Room, where you'll find several masterful portraits by **Gainsborough**, including the diaphanous *Countess Howe*, caught up in a bold, almost abstract landscape, plus a whimsical **Reynolds** painting, *Venus Chiding Cupid for Learning to Cast Accounts*. In the Dining Room, a superb **Rembrandt** self-portrait shares space with Franz Hals' *Man with a Cane* and **Vermeer**'s delicate *Guitar Player*, plus works by Van Dyck, Guardi and, once again, Reynolds. Elsewhere, there are canvases by Cuyp, Turner, Romney and Landseer, and several new, long-term loans, among them works by Botticelli and Memlinc.

Of the house's many wonderful period interiors, the most spectacular is Adam's sky-blue and gold **Library**, its book-filled apses separated from the central entertaining area by paired columns. The *pièce de résistance* is a tunnel-vaulted ceiling, decorated by Antonio Zucchi, who fell in love with and married Kenwood's other ceiling painter, Angelica Kauffmann. Upstairs, you can also view the **Suffolk Collection** (11am–4pm), whose highlights include William Larkin's full-length portraits of a Jacobean wedding party, with twin bridesmaids in slashed silver brocade dresses, and the arrogant Richard Sackville, a dissolute aristocrat resplendent in pompom shoes.

Adam was also responsible for landscaping the grounds of Kenwood, creating views across the Heath to St Paul's Cathedral and the Palace of Westminster – vistas that are now obscured by trees. Kenwood has splendid gardens of azaleas and rhododendrons to the west, and a huge grassy amphitheatre to the south, which slopes down to a lake where outdoor **concerts** are held on summer evenings (see p.510) – Handel's *Fireworks Music* has a regular spot on July 4. The grassy lawn is also a favourite picnic spot (and a good place to catch the afternoon rehearsals for free), while the provision-less can head for the excellent coach-house café.

A last and little-known attraction, hidden in a purpose-built hut to the northeast of Kenwood House, is the 1905 Romany-style **Buckland Caravan** (phone ☎020/7973 3893 for times; free), last used in the 1920s, its mahogany and etched glass all now beautifully restored.

21

▲ Kenwood House

Highgate

Northeast of the Heath, and fractionally lower than Hampstead (appearances notwithstanding), **Highgate** lacks the literary cachet of Hampstead, but makes up for it with London's most famous **cemetery**, resting place of, among others, Karl Marx. It also retains more of its village origins, especially around **The Grove**, Highgate's finest row of houses, set back from the road in pairs overlooking the village green, and dating back to 1685. Their most famous one-time resident is Samuel Taylor Coleridge, who lived at no. 3 from 1819, with a certain Dr Gillman and his wife. With Gillman's help, Coleridge reduced his dosage of opium and enjoyed the healthiest, if not necessarily the happiest, period of his life.

Coleridge was initially buried in the local college chapel, but in 1961 his remains were reburied in **St Michael's Church**, in South Grove. Its spire is a landmark, but St Michael's is much less interesting architecturally than the grandiose late seventeenth-century Old Hall next door, or the two tiny ramshackle cottages opposite, which were built for the servants of one of the luxurious mansions that once characterized Highgate. Arundel House, which stood on the site of the Old Hall, was where Francis Bacon, the Renaissance philosopher and statesman, is thought to have died, having caught a chill while trying to stuff a chicken full of ice during an early experiment in refrigeration.

North and south of the High Street

Highgate gets its name from the tollgate – the highest in London and the oldest in the country – that stood where the *Gate House* pub now stands on **Highgate High Street**. The High Street itself, though lined with swanky Georgian shops, is marred by heavy traffic, as is its northern extension, North Road.

If you persevere with North Road, you'll pass **Highgate School**, founded in 1565 for the local poor but long since established as an exclusive fee-paying public school, housed in suitably impressive Victorian buildings. T.S. Eliot was a master here for a while, and famous alumni, known as Cholmleians after the founder Roger Cholmley, include Gerard Manley Hopkins, John Betjeman and Clive Sinclair, creator of the first mass-produced pocket calculator and other, less successful inventions. Further on up North Road, on your left, are the whitewashed high-rises of **Highpoint 1** and **2**, seminal essays in modernist architecture designed by Berthold Lubetkin and his Tecton partnership in the late 1930s. The caryatids that support the entrance to Highpoint 2 are Lubetkin's little joke at the expense of his anti-modernist critics.

In the other direction, Highgate High Street slopes down into **Highgate Hill**, with still more amazing views down towards the City. The steep gradient of Highgate Hill caused enormous problems for horse-drawn vehicles, and in 1813 a tunnel was attempted through neighbouring Hornsey. It collapsed and was replaced by a stone viaduct designed by Nash, in its turn usurped by the current cast-iron **Archway** on Hornsey Lane, a favourite spot for suicide attempts. For the record, you'll find the **Whittington Stone**, with cat, marking the spot where Dick Whittington miraculously heard the Bow Bells chime, towards the bottom of Highgate Hill outside the hospital named after the eponymous mayor (see p.194 for more on Whittington).

The other ecclesiastical landmark in Highgate is the copper dome of "Holy Joe", the Roman Catholic St Joseph's church (www.stjosephshighgate.org)

which stands on Highgate Hill beside **Waterlow Park**. The park is named after Sydney Waterlow, who donated it in 1889 as "a garden for the gardenless", and also bequeathed **Lauderdale House** (⊛www.lauderdalehouse.co.uk), a much-altered sixteenth-century building, which is thought to have been occupied at one time by Nell Gwynne and her infant son. The house, which backs onto the park, is now used to stage children's shows and other events, and contains a decent café and restaurant that spill out into its western terraced gardens. The park itself, occupying a dramatic sloping site, is an amalgamation of several house gardens, and is one of London's finest landscaped parks, providing a through route to Highgate Cemetery.

Highgate Cemetery

Ranged on both sides of Swain's Lane and receiving far more visitors than Highgate itself, **Highgate Cemetery** (☎020/8340 1834, ⊛highgate-cemetery .org) is London's most famous graveyard. Opened in 1839, it quickly became the preferred resting place of wealthy Victorian families, who could rub shoulders here with numerous intellectuals and artists. As long as prime plots were available, business was good and the cemetery could afford to employ as many as 28 gardeners to beautify the place. But as the cemetery filled, funds dried up and the whole place fell prey to vandals. In 1975, the old (west) cemetery was closed completely and was taken under the wing of the Friends of Highgate Cemetery. Unfortunately, the Friends see all visitors as potential vandals, and rarely allow unsupervised wandering, the chief joy of visiting graveyards. You can still wander freely in the newer east cemetery, the less dramatic of the two sites, though even here an entrance fee is now charged.

West Cemetery

The old, overgrown **West Cemetery** (March–Nov Mon–Fri 2pm, Sat & Sun hourly 11am–4pm; Dec–Feb Sat & Sun hourly 11am–3pm; £3; no under-8s) is the ultimate Hammer-horror graveyard, and one of London's most impressive sights, with its huge vaults and eerie statuary. It's a shame you have to follow a tour around it, but even so it's not to be missed, and it must be said that things were pretty seedy before the Friends took over.

Dickens could have been the most famous corpse here, but only his estranged wife and daughter lie in the family tomb – despite the author's wishes to be buried privately and without ostentation, he was posthumously overruled by Queen Victoria, who insisted on his being buried in Westminster Abbey. Instead, the most famous names here are Charles Chubb (of the locks), Charles Cruft (of the Dog Show) and Michael Faraday, who, as a member of the obscure Sandemanian sect, is buried along the unconsecrated north wall. There's no guarantee your tour will cover these tombs, but you're more than likely to be shown the lion that snoozes above the tomb of menagerist George Wombwell, and the faithful and watchful dog (confusingly called Lion) that lies on bare-knuckle fighter Thomas Sayers' grave. Another popular destination is the **Rossetti family tomb**, initiated on the death of Gabriel Rossetti, professor of Italian at King's College, London. Next in the family vault was Elizabeth Siddall, the Pre-Raphaelites' favourite model and wife of Rossetti's artistic son, Dante Gabriel, who buried the only copy of his many love poems along with her. Seven years later he changed his mind and had the poems exhumed and published. The poet Christina Rossetti, Dante's sister, is also buried in the vault.

The cemetery's spookiest section is around **Egyptian Avenue**, entered through an archway flanked by Egyptian half-pillars, known as the "Gateway to the City of the Dead". The avenue slopes gently upwards to the Circle of Lebanon, at the centre of which rises a giant cedar. The circular Egyptian-style sunken catacombs here include the tomb of the lesbian novelist Radclyffe Hall (her lover, Mabel Batten, is also buried here). Above are the **Terrace Catacombs**, and the cemetery's most ostentatious mausoleums, some of which accommodate up to fifteen coffins; the largest – based on the tomb of Mausolus at Halicarnassus – is that of Julius Beer, one-time owner of the *Observer* newspaper.

This section of the cemetery provided inspiration for Bram Stoker's *Dracula*, and was at the centre of a series of bizarre incidents in the early 1970s. Graves were smashed open, cadavers strewn about, and the High Priest of the British Occult Society, Allan Farrant, was arrested here, armed with a stake and crucifix with which he hoped to destroy "the Highgate Vampire". He was eventually sentenced to four years' imprisonment, after being found guilty of damaging graves, interfering with corpses and sending death-spell dolls to two policemen.

East Cemetery

What the **East Cemetery** (April–Oct Mon–Fri 10am–5pm, Sat & Sun 11am–5pm; Nov–March closes 4pm; £2) lacks in atmosphere is in part compensated for by the fact that you can wander at will through its maze of circuitous paths. The most publicized occupant is, of course, **Karl Marx**, who spent more than half his life in London, much of it in bourgeois Hampstead. Marx himself asked for a plain and simple grave topped by a headstone, but by 1954 the Communist movement had decided to move his tomb to a more prominent position and erect the vulgar bronze bust that now surmounts a granite plinth bearing the words "Workers of all lands, unite", from *The Communist Manifesto*. He has been visited here by Khrushchev, Brezhnev and just about every postwar Communist leader in the world.

Buried along with Marx are his grandson, wife and housekeeper, Helene Delmuth, whom he got pregnant. Engels accepted paternity to avoid a bourgeois scandal and only told Marx's daughter, Eleanor, on his deathbed in 1895. Eleanor committed suicide a few years later after discovering her common-law husband had secretly married someone else. Her ashes were finally placed in the family vault in 1954, having been seized from the Communist Party headquarters in London by the police in 1921. Lesser-known Communists such as Yusef Mohamed Dadoo, chairman of the South African Communist Party until his death in 1983, cluster around Marx. Not far away is **George Eliot**'s grave and, behind it, that of her lover, George Henry Lewes.

▲ Highgate Cemetery

Alexandra Palace

Built in 1873 on the commanding heights of Muswell Hill, **Alexandra Palace** (Ⓦwww.alexandrapalace.com) is now London's only surviving example of a Victorian "People's Palace", since its more famous rival, Crystal Palace, burnt down in 1936. However, the history of "Ally Pally" is almost as tragic as that of Crystal Palace. Sixteen days after the official opening, the whole place burnt down and, despite being rebuilt within two years and boasting a theatre, a reading room, an exhibition hall and a concert room with one of the largest organs in the world, it was a commercial failure. During World War I more than 17,000 German POWs passed through its gates, and in 1936 the world's first television transmission took place here. After another devastating fire in 1980 the palace was again rebuilt, and is currently trying to reinvent itself as a multipurpose conference and exhibition venue. In addition to the annual round of shows, there's a pub, the appropriately named *Phoenix Bar*, with great views, a garden centre and an indoor ice rink open daily, as well as a funfair at Easter, Whitsuntide and throughout the summer holidays. There are also historical tours of the palace lasting two hours (occasional Wed & Sun 11.30am & 2pm; £5; ☎020/8365 4199).

Golders Green, Hendon and Neasden

North and west of Hampstead is suburbia good and proper, but there are one or two specific reasons for venturing so far into residential London: **Hampstead Garden Suburb**, an offshoot of Golders Green, is the city's original garden suburb; the **RAF Museum** in Hendon has probably the country's finest collection of military aircraft; the **Hindu temple** in Neasden – the largest outside India – has to be seen to be believed; and finally, there's **Wembley**, the "home of football", whose new stadium is destined to be the world's most expensive.

NORTH LONDON | Golders Green, Hendon and Neasden

㉑

Golders Green

If the East End is the spiritual home of working-class Jews, **Golders Green**, to the northwest of Hampstead, is its middle–class equivalent. Less than a hundred years ago this whole area was open countryside but, like much of suburbia, it was transformed overnight by the arrival of the tube in 1907. Before and after World War II, the area was heavily colonized by Jews moving out of the old East End ghetto around Spitalfields or fleeing as refugees from Europe ahead of the Nazis. Nowadays, Golders Green, along with Stamford Hill, is one of the most distinctive Jewish areas in London. The Orthodox community has a particularly strong presence here and there's a profusion of kosher shops beyond the railway bridge on Golders Green Road, at their busiest on Sundays.

Hampstead Garden Suburb

Much of Golders Green is architecturally bland, the one exception being **Hampstead Garden Suburb** (Ⓦwww.hgs.org.uk), begun in 1907 to the north of the Hampstead Heath Extension. This model housing development was a product of the utopian dream of Henrietta Barnett, wife of the philanthropist who established Toynbee Hall in the East End (see p.241). In the Barnetts' view, the only long-term solution to social reform was to create a mixed social environment where "the poor shall teach the rich, and the rich, let us hope, shall help the poor to help themselves". Yet from the start the suburb was socially segregated, with modest artisan dwellings to the north, middle-class houses to the west and the wealthiest villas overlooking the Heath to the south. As a social engineering experiment it was a failure – the area has remained a thoroughly middle-class ghetto – but as a blueprint for suburban estates it has been enormously influential.

The formal entrance to the suburb is the striking Arts and Crafts gateway of shops and flats on Finchley Road (nearest tube Golders Green). From here, ivy-strewn houses, each with its own garden encased in privet, yew and beech hedges, fan out eastwards along tree-lined avenues towards the deliberately "non-commercial" **Central Square**, laid out by Edwin Lutyens in a neo-Georgian style he dubbed "Wren-aissance". (Pubs, shops, cinemas and all commercial buildings were, and still are, excluded from the suburb.) Lutyens also designed the square's twin churches: the Nonconformist Free Church, sporting an octagonal dome, and the Anglican St Jude's-on-the-Hill, the finer of the two with its steeply pitched roof and spire, and its unusual 1920s murals within. East of the central green is the Lutyens-designed **Institute**, with its clock tower, now occupied by an adult education centre and Henrietta Barnett Girls' School. From the square, you could walk south along cherry-tree-lined Heathgate, which ends at the Heath Extension (see p.364).

Golders Green Crematorium and Jewish Cemetery

To the west of Hampstead Garden Suburb, down Meadway and then Hoop Lane, is the **Golders Green Crematorium** (daily: summer 9am–6pm, winter 4pm), where over 300,000 Londoners have been cremated since 1902. More famous names have been scattered over the crematorium's unromantically named Dispersal Area than have been buried at any single London graveyard: Sean O'Casey, Enid Blyton, Charles Rennie Mackintosh, Ramsay MacDonald, Neville Chamberlain, Kipling, H.G. Wells, Shaw, Stephen Spender, Alexander Fleming, Ralph Vaughan Williams, Gustav Holst, Kathleen Ferrier, Joe Orton, Peter Sellers, Peggy Ashcroft, Joyce Grenfell, Peter Cook, Marc Bolan, Keith Moon, Bram Stoker and T.S. Eliot (who was cremated here though his ashes were scattered in East Coker, Somerset), to name but a few. Finding a particular memorial plaque among this complex of serene red-brick chapels and arcades is no easy task, and if you're keen to trace someone or wish to visit one of the columbaria you should enquire at the office in the main courtyard. The Ernst George Columbarium is where you'll find the ashes of Anna Pavlova; Freud and his wife Martha are contained within one of Freud's favourite Greek red-figure vases in an adjacent room, with their daughter Anna in her own urn close by.

On the opposite side of Hoop Lane is a **Jewish Cemetery** (daily except Sat 8.30am–5pm or dusk), founded in 1895 before the area was built up. The eastern section, to your right, is for Orthodox Sephardic Jews, whose tombs are traditionally laid flat with the deceased's feet pointing towards Jerusalem. To the left are the upright headstones of Reform Jews, including the great cellist Jacqueline du Pré, who died tragically young of multiple sclerosis, and Lord Hore-Belisha, Minister of Transport in the 1930s, who gave his name to "Belisha beacons" (the yellow flashing globes at zebra crossings for pedestrians).

Jewish Museum

To the north of Golders Green, on the other side of the North Circular Road, is the Finchley branch of London's **Jewish Museum** (Mon–Thurs 10.30am–

5pm, Sun 10.30am–4.30pm; £2; ☎020/8349 1143, ⊛www.jewishmuseum.org .uk); the main branch is in Camden (see p.345). Housed within the Sternberg Centre for Judaism, at 80 East End Rd, the museum puts on exceptionally good temporary shows, often focusing on the Holocaust. The museum has a long-term exhibition concentrating on the moving personal account of Londoner Leon Greenman, the only member of his family to survive Auschwitz, who also visits the museum on Sundays to talk to visitors. There's an excellent Jewish bookshop within the museum.

Hendon: the RAF Museum

One of the most impressive collections of historic military aircraft in the world is lodged at the **RAF Museum** (daily 10am–6pm; free; ☎020/8205 2266, ⊛www.rafmuseum.org.uk; Colindale tube), in a godforsaken part of Hendon beside the M1 motorway. The site was an airfield from as early as 1910, and was venue for the RAF Hendon Air Pageants until the 1960s. In the **Main Aircraft Hall**, start your tour at the flimsy biplanes of World War I, with their wooden frames and wicker armchairs. The vast 1920s Southampton reconnaissance flying boat dominates the space ahead, but be sure to check out the Hoverfly, the first really effective helicopter, and, of course, the most famous British plane of all time, the Spitfire. By the exit you'll find a Harrier jump jet, the world's first vertical takeoff and landing aircraft, labelled with a text extolling its role in the Falklands War.

The most chilling section is the adjacent **Bomber Command Hall**, where you're greeted by a colossal Lancaster bomber, a modified version of which was used in Operation Upkeep, the mission carried out by Squadron 617 (and immortalized in the film *The Dambusters*), about which there's a ten-minute documentary. To the museum's credit, the assessment of Bomber Command's wartime policy of blanket-bombing Germany into submission gives both sides of the argument. The video of the so-called "precision bombing" conducted during the 1991 Gulf War is given rather less even-handed treatment. Two other exhibits deserve special mention: the crumbling carcass of a Halifax bomber, recovered from the bottom of a Norwegian fjord, and the clinically white Valiant, the first British aircraft to carry thermonuclear bombs.

Those with children should head for the new hands-on **Fun 'n' Flight** gallery, which teaches the basic principles of flight and airplane construction. Those without children should explore the often overlooked **Display Galleries**, ranged around the edge of the Main Aircraft Hall, which contain an art gallery and an exhibition on the history of flight, accompanied by replicas of some of the deathtraps in which the first aviators risked their lives. Across the car park is the **Battle of Britain Hall**, which contains a huge Sunderland flying boat, a V-1 flying bomb and a V-2 rocket. The focus of the hall, though, is now *Our Finest Hour*, an unashamedly jingoistic fifteen-minute audiovisual of the battle for the skies above Britain fought between the RAF and the Luftwaffe during the autumn of 1940.

Neasden: the Swaminarayan temple

The lotus blooms in splendour, but its roots lie in the dirt.

Hindu proverb

Perhaps the most remarkable building in the whole of London lies just off the North Circular, in the glum suburb of Neasden. Here, rising majestically above the dismal semi-detached houses of the interwar period like a mirage,

Wembley Stadium

A shrine of a different sort – **Wembley Stadium** (ⓦwww.wembleystadium.com) – lies northwest of the Neasden temple. The new 90,000-seater stadium, designed by Norman Foster and featuring a massive steel arch, visible for miles around, is due to be ready for the 2006 FA Cup. Having cost in excess of £750 million to build, it's the most expensive soccer stadium in the world, and will be the football venue for the 2012 Olympic Games (see p.245). The old stadium was the sole survivor of a much larger complex, constructed for the 1924 British Empire Exhibition, and served as the main focus for the 1948 Olympic Games. The most famous features of the old place were the now-demolished "twin towers", forever associated with England's historic victory here in the 1966 World Cup Final. Erected as a mute reference to the old Raj, they were, in fact, only added in 1963, to celebrate the hundredth anniversary of the Football League.

is the **Shri Swaminarayan Mandir** (daily 9am–6pm; free; ☏020/8965 2651, ⓦwww.mandir.org; Neasden tube), a traditional Hindu temple topped with domes and *shikhara*s, erected in 1995 in a style and scale unseen outside of India for over a millennium. The building's vital statistics are incredible: 3000 tons of Bulgarian limestone and 2000 tons of Carrara marble were shipped out to India, carved by over 1500 sculptors, and then shipped back to London and assembled in a matter of weeks. Even more surprising is the fact that Lord Swaminarayan (1781–1830), to whom the temple is dedicated, is a relatively obscure and very recent Hindu deity. There are no more than 10,000 followers in Britain, mostly from Gujarat, and no more than a million worldwide, yet they have dug deep into their pockets and, at an estimated cost of £10 million, erected this fantastic edifice.

To reach the temple, you must enter through the adjacent **Haveli**, or cultural complex, with its carved wooden portico and balcony, and its twin covered, carpeted courtyards. Shoes are the only thing that are sexually segregated inside the temple, so, having placed yours in the appropriate alcove, you can then proceed to the **Mandir** (temple) itself (an audioguide is available for £2.50). The temple is carved entirely out of light-grey Carrara marble from the floor to the dome, with every possible surface transformed into a honeycomb of arabesques, flowers and seated gods. The pillars are intricately decorated with figures of gods and goddesses, while on three sides are alcoves sheltering serene life-sized **Murti** (gods), garish figures in resplendent clothes representing Rama, Sita, Ganesh the elephant god, Hanuman the monkey god, and, of course, Shri Swaminarayan himself. The Murti are only on display from 9am to 11am, and from 4pm to 6.30pm.

Beneath the Mandir, an **exhibition** (daily 9am–6pm; £2) explains the basic tenets of Hinduism through dioramas, extols the virtues of vegetarianism and details the life of Lord Swaminarayan, who became a yogi at the age of 11, and stood naked on one leg for three months amidst snowstorms and "torturing weather". At the end, there's a short video about the history of the building.

Southeast London: Brixton to Greenwich and beyond

Southeast **London** was a confirmed part of rural Kent until the late eighteenth century. Now largely built up into a patchwork of Victorian terraces, one area stands head and shoulders above all the others in terms of sightseeing: **Greenwich**, once home to the Tudor court. Its nautical associations are trumpeted by the likes of the *Cutty Sark* and the National Maritime Museum; its architecture, especially the Old Royal Naval College and the Queen's House, is some of the finest on the river; and its Royal Observatory is renowned throughout the world.

The rest of this chapter is really just a hotchpotch of scattered suburban sights, where, given the distances involved and the dire lack of tube lines south of the river, it pays to be selective. A few areas do, however, stand out: **Dulwich**, whose public art gallery is even older than the National Gallery, and, way out on the very edge of London, the beautiful Arts and Crafts **Red House**, William Morris' former home, the **Chislehurst Caves** and **Down House**, the home of Charles Darwin.

Our account begins with **Brixton** – South London's liveliest neighbourhood, with its large African-Caribbean community and market. Brixton is one of the few areas in southeast London to be served by tube – elsewhere, you'll find details of which overground train to take in the text.

Brixton

Brixton (ⓦwww.mylambeth.co.uk) is a classic Victorian suburb, transformed from open fields into bricks and mortar in a couple of decades following the arrival of the railways in the 1860s. The viaducts still dominate the landscape of

SOUTHEAST LONDON

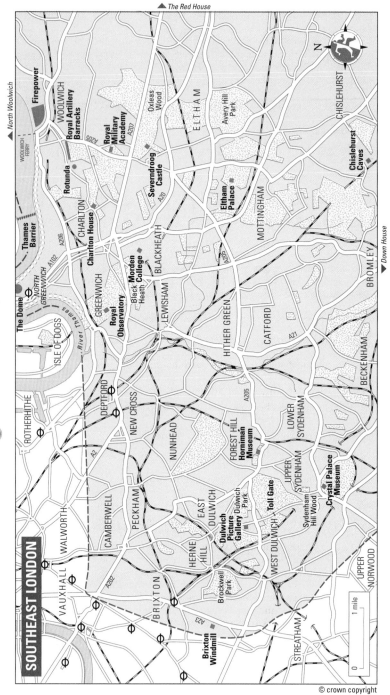

▲ The Red House

N

▲ North Woolwich

WOOLWICH FERRY

Firepower

WOOLWICH

Royal Artillery Barracks

Royal Military Academy

A205

A207

Oxleas Wood

Avery Hill Park

ELTHAM

CHISLEHURST

Rotunda

A206

A102

Thames Barrier

CHARLTON

Charlton House

Severndroog Castle

A20

Eltham Palace

MOTTINGHAM

Chislehurst Caves

NORTH GREENWICH

The Dome

ISLE OF DOGS

River Thames

GREENWICH

Royal Observatory

Black Heath

Morden College

BLACKHEATH

A205

Down House ▼

LEWISHAM

HITHER GREEN

CATFORD

A21

BROMLEY

BECKENHAM

ROTHERHITHE

DEPTFORD

NEW CROSS

A2

NUNHEAD

FOREST HILL

Horniman Museum

LOWER SYDENHAM

A205

Crystal Palace Museum

VAUXHALL

WALWORTH

CAMBERWELL

PECKHAM

A202

EAST DULWICH

Dulwich Park

UPPER SYDENHAM

Sydenham Hill Wood

Dulwich Picture Gallery

WEST DULWICH

Toll Gate

HERNE HILL

Brockwell Park

BRIXTON

A23

STREATHAM

UPPER NORWOOD

Brixton Windmill

0   1 mile

© crown copyright

central Brixton, with shops and arcades hidden under their arches, but it's the West Indian community, who arrived here in the 1950s and 1960s, who now define the character of the place – Notting Hill may have the Carnival, but it's Brixton that has the most upfront African-Caribbean consciousness. Brixton is also still saddled with the reputation for violence it earned during the 1981, 1985 and 1995 riots, when tensions between the police and locals came to a head. Various government initiatives have attempted to get to the root of local discontent, racism and unemployment with limited success, though the visual fabric of the place has definitely improved.

Brixton Market and around

Brixton's main axis is the junction of Brixton Road, Acre Lane and Coldharbour Lane, just to the south of the tube station and overlooked by the slender clock tower of the Edwardian **Lambeth Town Hall**; the dinky neo-Renaissance Tate Library; the Ritzy cinema from 1911; and, on the triangular traffic island, the Neoclassical church of **St Matthew**, with its grandiose Doric portico, its crypt now converted into a trendy bar, restaurant and theatre space.

The commercial lifeblood of Brixton, however, pulses most strongly through **Brixton Market** (Mon–Sat 8am-3pm), whose stalls spread out through the warren of streets and arcades east of Brixton Road. **Electric Avenue** – as in the Eddy Grant song – runs behind the tube station, is solidly fruit and veg (most of it West Indian), and was one of the first London shopping streets to be lit by electricity in the 1880s, hence the name. A network of appealingly shabby interwar arcades runs parallel with the avenue, culminating in the **Granville Arcade**, where you can buy bold African and Asian fabrics, jewellery, all manner of exotic fruit and meat, amazing wigs and much more besides. On the far side of the railway tracks, the market veers eastwards along Brixton Station Road, with stalls selling cheap secondhand clothes to rap and reggae soundtracks from Crystal Records.

The crossroads of Atlantic Road and Coldharbour Lane, to the southeast of the market, marks the beginning of Brixton's so-called "**Front Line**", which, with nearby Railton Road, was the epicentre of the 1981 riots, and still has a drug-dealing reputation. The former *Atlantic* pub on the corner once prided itself on its especially mean reputation, but has since been resurrected as a trendy drinking hole.

Brixton Windmill (@www.brixtonwindmill.org), at the end of Blenheim Gardens, a few stops up Brixton Hill by bus, is a surprising sight. This is about the last place in London that you'd expect to find a windmill, but with its blades intact and a fetching weatherboarded "hood", the 1816 mill makes a splendid sight in a deeply depressing municipal space. In the 1820s, the mill gained another source of power for its corn-grinding: the country's first treadmill, designed by William Cubitt and worked by inmates of nearby **Brixton Prison**. Every year in July, the windmill forms the centrepiece of the community-based Windmill Festival.

Brixton also has a very fine green lung in **Brockwell Park** (daily 8am–dusk), half a mile or so up Effra Road. The park is made up of the former grounds of Brockwell House, a handsome Regency lodge, built by a local glass merchant, that occupies the park's heights and now houses an unremarkable tearoom. There's also a popular 1930s **lido** (mid-May to mid-Sept Mon–Fri 6.45am–6pm or later, Sat & Sun 10am–6pm; £2.50–5; @www.thelido.co.uk), and a beautiful walled garden with yew-hedge snugs and shady arbours.

Dulwich, Forest Hill and Crystal Palace

Dulwich Village is just two stops from Brixton on the overland railway, but light years away in every other respect. This affluent, middle-class enclave is one of southeast London's prettier patches, cut off from most of its suburban neighbours by parkland, playing fields, woods and golfing fairways. The leafy streets boast handsome Georgian houses and even a couple of weatherboarded cottages, while the Soane-designed **Picture Gallery** is one of London's finest small museums. If Dulwich has a fault, it's the somewhat cloying self-consciousness about its "village" status, with its rather twee little shops, rural signposts and fully functioning tollgate – the only one remaining in London.

Nonetheless, Dulwich makes for a pleasant day out south of the river, and can be combined with a visit to the nearby **Horniman Museum**, an enjoyable ethnographic collection, and, for the very curious, the remnants of the old **Crystal Palace**, further south. The green spaces between these sights are also worth exploring. **Dulwich Park**, opposite the Picture Gallery, is a pleasant enough public park, but for something a bit wilder, **Sydenham Hill Wood**, a London Wildlife Trust nature reserve south of Dulwich Common, is the one to head for.

Dulwich Village

Dulwich came to prominence in the 1610s when its lord of the manor, actor-manager Edward Alleyn, founded the **College of God's Gift** (ⓦwww.dulwich .org.uk) as almshouses and a school for poor boys on the profits of his whorehouses and bear-baiting pits on Bankside. The college has long since outgrown its original buildings, which still stand to the north of the Picture Gallery, and is now housed in a fanciful Italianate complex designed by Charles Barry (son of the architect of the Houses of Parliament), south of Dulwich Common; Alleyn is buried in the college chapel. The college is now a fee-paying public school, with an impressive roll call of old boys, including Raymond Chandler, P.G. Wodehouse and World War II traitor Lord Haw-Haw, though they tend to keep quiet about the last of the trio.

Dulwich Picture Gallery

Dulwich Picture Gallery (Tues–Fri 10am–5pm, Sat & Sun 11am–5pm; £4, free on Fri; ☏020/8693 5254, ⓦwww.dulwichpicturegallery.org.uk), on College Road, is the nation's oldest public art gallery. Designed by John Soane in 1814, it houses, among other bequests, the collection assembled in the 1790s by the French dealer Noel Desenfans on behalf of King Stanislas of Poland, who planned to open a national gallery in Warsaw. In 1795, Poland disappeared from the map of Europe, Stanislas was forced to abdicate and Desenfans was left with the paintings. Having failed to persuade either the British government or the Russian tsar to purchase the collection, Desenfans proposed founding a national gallery. In the end it was left to his friend, the landscape painter Francis Bourgeois, and Desenfans' widow, to complete the task and open the gallery in 1817.

Soane, who worked for no fee, created a beautifully spacious building, awash with natural light, and added a tiny **mausoleum** at the centre for the sarcophagi of the Desenfans family and of Francis Bourgeois. Based on an Alexandrian catacomb, it's suffused with golden-yellow light from the mausoleum's coloured glass – a characteristic Soane touch. Originally, Soane had intended

22

to create a new quadrangle, using the old college building to the north. The gallery's gentle new extension by Rick Mather has gone some of the way to realizing that plan, by completing three sides of the courtyard with a glass cloister walk that connects the gallery with the education department and the new café by the entrance.

The gallery itself is crammed with superb paintings – elegiac landscapes by **Cuyp**, one of the world's finest **Poussin** series and splendid works by Hogarth, Murillo and Rubens. There's an unusually cloudy **Canaletto** of Walton Bridge on the Thames, **Rembrandt**'s tiny *Portrait of a Young Man*, a top-class portrait of poet, playwright and Royalist, the future Earl of Bristol, by **van Dyck**, and a moving one of his much lamented kinswoman by marriage, Venetia Stanley, on her deathbed. Among the gallery's fine array of **Gainsborough** portraits are his famous *Linley Sisters*, sittings for which were interrupted by the elopement of one of them with the playwright Sheridan, and a likeness of Samuel Linley that's said to have been painted in less than an hour.

Horniman Museum

To the southeast of Dulwich Park, on the South Circular road, is the wonderful **Horniman Museum** (daily 10.30am–5.30pm; free; ℡020/8699 1872, ⊛www.horniman.ac.uk), purpose-built in 1901 by Frederick Horniman, a tea trader with a passion for collecting. The building itself is a striking edifice designed in warm Doulting stone by Charles Harrison Townsend, architect of the Whitechapel Gallery (see p.240). Its most arresting features are the massive clock tower, with its smoothly rounded bastions and circular cornice, and the polychrome mosaic of allegorical figures in classical dress on the facade. Entry is from the gardens to the west, where you'll find turkeys, goats and hens, a sunken water garden and a graceful Victorian conservatory, brought here from the Horniman mansion in Croydon.

A ramp leads down from the foyer to the **Natural History** collection of stuffed animals and birds – everything from a half-dissected pigeon to an ostrich – and their skeletons; pride of place goes to the Horniman Walrus, lying flat out on a mocked-up iceberg. On the lower ground floor, head first for the dimly lit **Centenary Gallery**, which contains an eclectic ethnographic collection, much of it gathered by Horniman himself, from the precious butterflies that started his obsession at the age of eight to a papier-mâché figure of Kali dancing on Siva. Some of the more recent acquisitions are equally arresting such as the Nigerian puppets of Charles, Di and a British bobby or the "ugly masks" used to chase the winter away in the alps. The **Africa Worlds Gallery** contains a wide-ranging anthropological collection from African masks and vodou altars to Egyptian sarcophagi and Sudanese dung bowls. In the **Music Gallery** you can see and hear more than 1500 instruments including Chinese gongs and electric guitars or have a go at some of the instruments yourself in the hands-on room. An aquarium in the basement is due to open in 2006.

Crystal Palace

In the 1850s, the **Crystal Palace** from the 1851 Great Exhibition (see p.293) was re-erected on the commanding heights of Sydenham Hill, to the south of Dulwich, a site affording spectacular views over London, Kent and Surrey. A fantastic pleasure garden was laid out around this giant glasshouse, with a complex system of fountains, some of which reached a height of 250ft. Exhibitions, funfairs, ballooning, a miniature railway and a whole range of events, including, from 1894 to 1924, the FA Cup Final, were staged here. Despite its initial success, though, the palace soon became a financial liability – then, in 1936, the entire structure burnt to the ground overnight.

All that remains now are the stone terraces, the triumphal staircase, a few sphinxes and a small, uninspiring **museum** on Anerley Hill (Sun 11am–5pm; free; ☎020/8676 0700, ⊛www.crystalpalacefoundation.org.uk) that tells the history of the place. The **park** (daily 7.30am–dusk) is dominated by the TV transmitter, visible from all over London, and the **National Sports Centre**, whose tartan athletics track (Europe's first) was opened in the 1960s and where some 21 world records were set in the following two decades. There are further reminders of the park's Victorian heyday in and around **Lower Lake**, in the southeast corner of the park, whose islands feature around thirty life-sized dinosaurs lurking in the undergrowth, built out of brick and iron by Waterhouse Hawkins in the 1850s and now given the status of listed buildings.

Greenwich

"The most delightful spot of ground in Great Britain", according to Daniel Defoe, **Greenwich** is still one of London's most beguiling places, and the one area in southeast London that draws tourists out from the centre in considerable numbers. At its heart is the outstanding architectural set piece of the **Old Royal Naval College** and the **Queen's House**, courtesy of Christopher Wren and Inigo Jones respectively. Most visitors, however, come to see the **Cutty Sark**, the **National Maritime Museum** and Greenwich Park's **Royal Observatory**, though Greenwich also pulls in an ever-increasing volume of Londoners in search of bargains at its weekend market. With the added attractions of its riverside pubs and walks – plus startling views across to Canary Wharf and Docklands – it makes for one of the best weekend trips in the capital. Greenwich is, of course, also famous as the "home of time", thanks to its status as the **Prime Meridian of the World** from where time all over the globe is measured. It's partly for this reason that Greenwich was chosen as the site for the **Millennium Dome**, visible in the industrial wasteland of North Greenwich, a mile or so northeast of Greenwich town centre.

㉒

Visiting Greenwich

Greenwich is most quickly reached from central London by **train** from Charing Cross, Waterloo East or London Bridge (every 15–30min), although taking a **boat** from one of the piers between Westminster and Tower Bridge is more scenic and leisurely (and more expensive). Another possibility is to take the **Docklands Light Railway** (DLR) from Bank or Tower Gateway direct to Cutty Sark. For the best view of the Wren buildings, though, get out at Island Gardens station to admire the view across the river, and then take the Greenwich Foot Tunnel under the Thames.

The local **tourist information office** (daily 10am–5pm; ☎0870/608 2000), the grandly named Greenwich Gateway Visitor Centre, is located in the Pepys Building by the side of the *Cutty Sark*. Staff there can answer most queries and there's also a little exhibition area, giving a brief outline of the area's history.

GREENWICH

EATING & DRINKING

Cutty Sark	1
Gambardella	7
Goddard's	3
Greenwich Union	6
Richard I	5
Tai Won Mein	4
Trafalgar Tavern	2

ISLE OF DOGS

Greenwich Foot Tunnel

Greenwich Pier

River Thames

The Dome

Gipsy Moth IV

Cutty Sark

CUTTY SARK

Old Royal Naval College

Trinity Hospital

HUSKINS STREET

PARK ROW

Deptford

CREEK ROAD

Chapel

OLD WOOLWICH ROAD

Greenwich Train Station

GREENWICH CHURCH ST

Painted Hall

Greenwich Market

Great Hall

NELSON RD

ROMNEY ROAD

TRAFALGAR ROAD

St Alfege

GREENWICH HIGH RD

National Maritime Museum

MAZE HILL

Queen's House

PARK VISTA

MAZE HILL

Fan Museum

Playground

A

CROOMS HILL

Greenwich Park

N

Vanbrugh Castle

5 & 6

HYDE VALE

Royal Observatory

Roman Remains

MAZE HILL

Planetarium

Tea House

BLACKHEATH AVENUE

CHESTERFIELD WALK

Macartney House

Bandstand

Flower Gardens

Ranger's House

Rose Garden

Wilderness

SHOOTERS HILL ROAD

CHARLTON WAY

Charlton

Black Heath

0   200 yds

© crown copyright

▼ *Blackheath*   ▼ *Blackheath*

SOUTHEAST LONDON | Greenwich

22

379

Greenwich town centre

Greenwich town centre was laid out in the 1820s, hence the Nash-style terraces of Nelson Road, College Approach and King William Walk, now a one-way system plagued with heavy traffic. At the centre of these busy streets, filled with nautical knick-knack shops and bookshops, stands the old covered market, which sold mostly fruit and veg until the late 1980s; you can still see the wonderfully Victorian inscription on one of the archways: "A false balance is abomination to the Lord, but a just weight is his delight." The old market and flanking stables are now part of the new **Greenwich Market** (Thurs–Sun; ⓦwww.greenwich-market.co.uk), a lively antique, crafts and clothes market which spreads far beyond the perimeters of its predecessor at the weekend, spilling out up the High Road, Stockwell Road and Royal Hill (see p.548).

A short distance in from the old covered market, on the opposite side of Greenwich Church Street, rises the Doric portico and broken pediment of Nicholas Hawksmoor's **St Alfege's Church** (Mon–Sat 2–4pm, Sun 10am–4pm; ⓦwww.st-alfege.org). Built in 1712–18 to replace a twelfth-century structure in which Henry VIII was baptized and Thomas Tallis, the "father of English church music", was buried, the church was flattened in the Blitz, but it has been magnificently repaired. Alfege is an unusual saint, in that he wasn't really martyred for his religion. As archbishop of Canterbury he was captured in 1011 by the marauding Danes, and carried off to Greenwich, where they demanded a ransom for him. Alfege refused to allow any ransom to be paid, at which the furious Danes pelted him to death with ox bones. Thorkell the Tall, the one Dane who took pity on him, got an axe in the head for his pains.

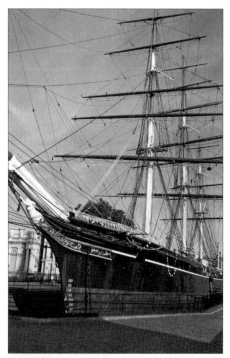

▲ Cutty Sark

Cutty Sark

Wedged in a dry dock by the Greenwich Foot Tunnel is the majestic **Cutty Sark** (daily 10am–5pm; £4.50; ☎020/8858 3445, ⓦwww.cuttysark.org.uk), the world's last surviving tea clipper, which was launched from the Clydeside shipyards in 1869. The *Cutty Sark* lasted just eight years in the China tea trade, and it was as a wool clipper that it actually made its name, returning from Australia in just 72 days. The vessel's name comes from Robert Burns' *Tam O'Shanter*, in which Tam, a drunken farmer, is chased by Nannie, an angry witch in a short Paisley linen dress, or "cutty sark"; the clipper's figurehead shows her clutching the hair from the tail of Tam's horse. Inside, there's little to see beyond the exhibition in the main hold which tells the ship's story from its inception to its arrival in Greenwich in 1954. Before you disembark, don't miss the colourful parade of buxom figureheads in the lower hold.

Old Royal Naval College

It's entirely appropriate that the one London building that makes the most of its riverbank location should be the **Old Royal Naval College** (daily 10am–5pm; free; @www.greenwichfoundation.org.uk), a majestic Baroque ensemble which opens out onto the Thames. Despite the symmetry and grace of the four buildings, which perfectly frame the Queen's House beyond (see p.384), the whole complex has a strange and piecemeal history. John Webb, Inigo Jones' assistant and nephew, began the first of the four blocks in the 1660s as a palace for Charles II, but the money ran out after just five years. William and Mary eschewed the unfinished palace for Hampton Court and decided to turn the Greenwich building into a hospital for disabled seamen, along the lines of the Royal Hospital in Chelsea (see p.319). Wren, working for nothing, then had his original designs vetoed by the queen, who insisted the new development must not obscure the view of the river from the Queen's House – what you see now is Wren's revised plan, augmented by, among others, Hawksmoor and Vanbrugh.

The population of the hospital swelled to over 2500 in the aftermath of the Napoleonic Wars, but charges of cruelty and corruption, coupled with dwindling numbers, forced a move to new premises in 1869. Four years later the vacated buildings were taken over by the Royal Naval College, which later moved to Dartmouth, though specialist training for senior officers continued here until the 1990s. Initially, the government attempted to sell off the historic buildings, but the sale was hampered by the presence of a thirty-year-old nuclear reactor – affectionately known as Jason – in the basement. The buildings now house, among other things, the University of Greenwich and the Trinity College of Music.

The two grandest rooms, situated underneath Wren's twin domes, are well worth visiting. Approaching from King William Walk, you enter via the West Gate, whose gateposts are each topped by a globe: celestial to the left, terrestrial to the right. The **Chapel**, in the east wing, was designed by James "Athenian" Stuart (so called because of his espousal of the Greek Revival style), after a fire in 1779 destroyed its predecessor. However, it is Stuart's assistant, William Newton, whom we have to thank for the chapel's exquisite pastel and sky-blue plasterwork and spectacular decorative detailing, among the finest in London. The altarpiece, by Benjamin West, depicts St Paul wrestling with the viper that leapt out of the fire after he was shipwrecked off Malta.

From here, you descend to the temporary exhibition room, and along the underground Chalk Walk to the licensed café, and then up to the magnificent **Painted Hall**, in the west wing. The hall is dominated by James Thornhill's gargantuan allegorical ceiling painting, which took him nineteen years to complete, and spans several reigns. It depicts William and Mary handing down Peace and Liberty to Europe, with a vanquished Louis XIV clutching a broken sword below them. Equally remarkable are Thornhill's trompe l'oeil fluted pilasters and decorative detailing, while on the far wall, behind the high table, Thornhill himself appears beside George I and family, with St Paul's in the background. Designed as the sailors' dining hall, it was later used for Nelson's lying-in-state in 1806.

The history of Greenwich is replete with royal connections. Edward I appears to have been the first of the English kings to have stayed here, though there was nothing resembling a palace until Henry V's brother, the Duke of Gloucester, built Bella Court in 1426. Henry VI honeymooned here with his new wife, Margaret of Anjou, and eventually took over the place and rebuilt it in her honour. However, it was under the Tudors that Greenwich enjoyed its royal heyday. Henry VII rebuilt it from 1500 onwards, renaming it **Palace of Placentia**. Henry VIII, who was born in Greenwich, made this his main base, pouring even more money into it than into Hampton Court. He added armouries, a banqueting hall and a huge tiltyard, hunted in the extensive grounds and kept a watchful eye over proceedings at the nearby Royal Dockyards in Deptford. His children, Mary and Elizabeth, were both born here.

Edward VI came to Greenwich in 1553 to try to restore his frail health, but died shortly afterwards. Mary came here rarely as queen, and on one of her few visits had the wall of her personal apartment blasted away by a cannonball fired in salute. For Elizabeth, Greenwich was the chief summer residence, and it was here in 1573 that she revived the Maundy Ceremony, washing the feet of 39 poor women (though only after three others had washed them first). The royal palace fell into disrepair during the 1650s Commonwealth, when it was turned into a biscuit factory, and was finally torn down by Charles II to make way for a new edifice, which eventually became the Royal Naval College.

The riverside

A fine vantage point for viewing the Old Royal Naval College is the **Five-Foot Walk**, which squeezes between the college railings and the riverbank. It was here that George I landed to take the throne on September 18, 1714, though it was estimated that 57 other cousins had a better claim. His wife was not with him, having been incarcerated, on George's orders, in a castle in Germany for adultery; she remained there for 32 years. If you're in need of refreshment, drop into the Regency-style **Trafalgar Tavern**, at the east end of the walk. The pub was frequented by Whig politicians and the Victorian literary set – its legendary whitebait suppers inspired Dickens to use the pub as the setting for the wedding breakfast in *Our Mutual Friend*.

Just beyond the pub down Crane Street is the **Trinity Hospital**, founded in 1613 by the Earl of Northampton for 21 pensioners; the entry requirements declared the hospital would admit "no common beggar, drunkard, whore-hunter, nor unclean person . . . nor any that is blind . . . nor any idiot". The cream-coloured mock-Gothic facade and chapel (which contains the earl's tomb) were rebuilt in the nineteenth century, but the courtyard of almshouses remains much as it was at its foundation. Beyond the Trinity Hospital, the Thames Path continues past a power station and a new residential development before emerging at the *Cutty Sark* pub, another great riverside halt. From here you can continue along the river all the way to the Dome (see box on p.387).

National Maritime Museum

The main entrance to the excellent **National Maritime Museum** (daily 10am–5pm, July & Aug closes 6pm; free; ☏020/8858 4422, ☻www.nmm.ac.uk), which occupies the west wing of the former Naval Asylum, is on Romney Road, and brings you out into the spectacular glass-roofed central courtyard. The various themed galleries are ranged over three floors, and are imaginatively designed to appeal to visitors of all ages, with plenty of hands-on stuff to keep children amused. The courtyard, meanwhile, has a new building slap bang in the centre, and several "streets" along the sides, which house some of the museum's largest artefacts, among them the splendid 63-foot-long **Royal Barge**, a gilded Rococo confection designed by William Kent for Prince Frederick, the much-unloved eldest son of George II.

Level 1: Explorers and Passengers

Explorers, on Level 1, takes you from the Vikings to Franklin's attempt to discover the Northwest Passage; on display are the relics recovered from the Arctic by John Rae in 1854, many of which had to be bought from the local Inuit. In the central building, there's footage of the **Titanic**, a ticket belonging to a lucky guy who couldn't go at the last minute and a pocket watch, stopped at 3.07am, retrieved from one of the dead. In **Rank & Style**, you can inspect various marine get-ups from naval uniforms to the survival suit that saved Tony Bullimore's life when his yacht capsized – each one is hidden within a cupboard and accompanied by a brief audioguide. **Maritime London** has displays on the Thames Barrier (see p.390), and gives Lloyds of London a nice opportunity to plug its services as the world's largest marine insurer. **Passengers** relives the glory days of transatlantic shipping, which officially came to an end in 1957 when more people went by air than by sea. To their credit, the displays also touch on the role of shipping in immigration and in transporting refugees. Sponsors P&O get to display their wares at the end, with several huge models of P&O's *Grand Princess*, built in 1998 and, at 109,000 tons and over 950ft in length, at the time the largest passenger vessel ever built.

Level 2: Art, Trade & Empire and Nelson Gallery

On Level 2, there's a large maritime art gallery, **Art & the Sea**, which displays a wide range of works from eighteenth-century oils of historic naval encounters to Art Deco lithographs of submarine life by Admiralty war artist Eric Ravilious. **Trade & Empire** is a gallery devoted to the legacy of the British Empire, warts and all, from the slave trade to the opium wars, while the **Upper Deck**, by the café, is used for special exhibitions. The museum's new **Nelson Gallery** is due to open on this level, displaying a vast collection of Nelson memorabilia, including his grog jug, Bible and the diminutive "undress coat" worn during the Battle of Trafalgar, with a tiny bullet hole made by the musket shot that killed him. Another of the museum's prize possessions is Turner's *Battle of Trafalgar, 21st October, 1805*, his largest work and only royal commission, which was intended for St James's Palace. Look out, too, for the cabinets of nineteenth-century Nelson kitsch: pipes, vinaigrettes, souvenirs made from the timber of HMS *Victory* and, best of all, a set of toy bricks depicting Nelson's funeral procession from Whitehall to St Paul's.

Level 3: Hands-on galleries

Level 3 is the place to head if you've got children, as it boasts two excellent hands-on galleries. **The Bridge** is aimed at all ages, as it really does take some skill to navigate a catamaran, a paddle steamer and a rowing boat to shore. **All Hands** is aimed at a younger audience, and gives kids a taste of life on the seas over the last millennium, loading miniature cargo, firing a cannon, learning to use Morse code and so forth. Also on this level is the **Oceans of Discovery** gallery, which concentrates on the voyages of Cook, Scott and Shackleton. Cook's K1 marine chronometer is here and there's a replica of the *James Caird*, in which Shackleton made the 300-mile journey from Elephant Island to South Georgia, plus lots of Scott memorabilia: his overshoes, his watch, his funky

22

sledging goggles and a basic sketch of his planned route scrawled on some hotel notepaper. Also on Level 3 is **Ship of War**, the museum's collection of model sailing warships from 1650 to 1815, most of them made by the Navy Board at the same time as the ships they represent.

Queen's House

Inigo Jones' **Queen's House**, originally built on a cramped site amidst the Tudor royal palace, is now the focal point of the Greenwich ensemble. As royal residences go, it's an unassuming little Palladian country house, "solid . . . masculine and unaffected" in Jones' own words. Its significance in terms of British architecture, however, is immense. Begun in 1616, it is the earliest example of Renaissance architecture in Britain, and the first classical building in the country since Roman times, signifying a clear break with all that preceded it.

The interior, exterior and setting of the Queen's House have all changed radically since Jones' day, making it difficult to imagine the impact the building must have had when it was built. The house is linked to its neighbouring buildings by open colonnades, added in the early part of the nineteenth century, when the entire complex was converted into a school for the children of seamen. The colonnades follow the course of the muddy road which the H-shaped block originally straddled, thus enabling the queen to pass from the formal gardens to the royal park without sullying her shoes.

The interior is currently used by the National Maritime Museum for temporary exhibitions; nevertheless, one or two features survive (or have been reinstated) from Stuart times. The **Great Hall**, a perfect cube, is galleried and decorated with computer-enhanced copies of Orazio Gentileschi's panel paintings, which were removed to Marlborough House by the Duchess of Marlborough herself during the reign of Queen Anne. The southeastern corner of the hall leads to the beautiful **Tulip Staircase**, Britain's earliest cantilevered spiral staircase, whose name derives from the floral patterning in the wrought-iron balustrade. The only other significant interior decoration is upstairs, in the room intended as the bedchamber of Charles I and Henrietta Maria, which retains its ceiling decoration from the 1630s.

Greenwich Park and the Royal Observatory

Greenwich Park (daily dawn–dusk; ⊛www.royalparks.co.uk) is one of the city's oldest royal parks, having been enclosed in the fifteenth century by the Duke of Gloucester, who fancied it as a hunting ground (its royal title actually came later). Henry VIII was particularly fond of the place, to which he characteristically introduced deer in 1515, as well as archery and jousting tournaments, and sword-fighting contests. André le Nôtre, Louis XIV's gardener at Versailles, seems to have had a hand in redesigning the park after the Commonwealth, though he never actually set foot in Greenwich.

The park was finally opened to the public in the eighteenth century, and after the arrival of the railway in 1838 it began to attract Londoners in great numbers. In 1894 Greenwich Park witnessed one of the more bizarre incidents in London's long history of terrorism: Martial Bourdin, a young French anarchist, was killed when the bomb he was carrying in a brown-paper bag exploded. The questions of whether he was planning to blow up the observatory, and whether he was a police informer, remain unresolved. Joseph Conrad used the episode as the basis of his novel *The Secret Agent*.

The park's chief delight is the view from the steep hill crowned by the Royal Observatory, from which you can see Canary Wharf, the Millennium Dome and much of the City. The most popular place from which to take in the panorama is the statue of **General James Wolfe** (1727–59), who lived at Macartney House at the top of Croom's Hill, close to the Ranger's House (see p.388), and is buried in St Alfege (see p.380). Wolfe is famed for the audacious campaign in which he captured Quebec in 1759, a battle in which he and his opposite number, the French general Montcalm, were both mortally wounded. Victory celebrations took place throughout England, but were forbidden in Greenwich out of respect for Wolfe's mother, who had also lost her husband only a few months previously.

Greenwich Park is also celebrated for its rare and ancient trees, the most famous of which, **Queen Elizabeth's Oak** – not, in fact, an oak, but a sweet chestnut – finally toppled in 1992. For over a hundred years the tree had been reduced to an ivy-covered dead stump, albeit a stump so big that the hollowed-out trunk was at one time used as a lockup by the park police. It was around this oak tree that Henry VIII and Anne Boleyn are said to have danced. Queen Elizabeth was fond of playing in the tree, and it was at a lodge gate close by that, according to tradition, Walter Ralegh earned his knighthood by gallantly throwing down his cloak into the mud for the queen to walk over.

The descendants of Henry's deer are now safely enclosed within **The Wilderness**, a fenced area in the southeast corner where they laze around "tame as children", in Henry James' words; close by is the **Flower Garden**, actually more impressive for its exotic trees than its flowers. If you're in this part of the park, don't miss **Vanbrugh Castle**, halfway down Maze Hill, England's first mock-medieval castle, designed by the architect John Vanbrugh as his private residence in 1726. But don't get too excited by the nearby **Roman Remains**, which are little more than a few floor tiles from a Roman temple. If you're heading for the Ranger's House on the opposite side of the park (see p.388), the best approach is via the semicircular **Rose Garden**, laid out in front of it, which is worth a visit itself from June to August.

The Royal Observatory

The **Royal Observatory** (daily 10am–5pm, July & Aug closes 6pm; free; ☎020/8312 6565, ⊛www.rog.nmm.ac.uk) is the longest-established scientific institution in Britain. Built on the foundations of a medieval outpost of Greenwich Palace, it was established by Charles II in 1675 to house the first Astronomer Royal, John Flamsteed. Flamsteed's chief task was to study the night sky in order to discover an astronomical method of finding the longitude of a ship at sea, the lack of which was causing enormous problems for the emerging British Empire. Astronomers continued to work here at Greenwich until the postwar smog forced them to decamp to Herstmonceux Castle and the clearer skies of Sussex (they've since moved to the Pacific); the observatory, meanwhile, is now a very popular museum.

Greenwich's other great claim to fame is of course as the home of **Greenwich Mean Time** and the **Prime Meridian** – a meridian being any north–south line used as a basis for astronomical observations, and therefore also for the calculation of longitude and time. By the mid-nineteenth century, it was clear that an internationally agreed system of timekeeping was needed. In 1852, Britain adopted "London time", which meant, in effect, Greenwich Mean Time (GMT), though, in fact, this wasn't formally acknowledged until 1880. Three years later the US also adopted Greenwich as the Prime Meridian, and in 1884 persuaded an international convention in Washington DC to agree to make Greenwich the Prime Meridian of the World – in other words, zero longitude. As a result, the entire world sets its clocks in relation to GMT.

The red strip in the main courtyard lies along the Greenwich Prime Meridian, which is still used as an absolute today. However, what the Royal Observatory don't tell you is that, as a result of communications problems encountered during the Vietnam War, the Americans starting using satellites to work out longitude in the 1980s. The global standard for air and sea navigation, and used widely by the military, is now the **Global Positioning System** or GPS, which bases its calculations on the centre of the earth, not the surface, and places the meridian approximately 336ft to the east of the red strip.

Flamsteed House

The oldest part of the observatory is **Flamsteed House**, built by Wren (himself a trained astronomer) "for the observator's habitation and a little for pompe". The northeastern turret sports a bright-red Time-Ball that climbs the mast at 12.58pm and drops at 1pm GMT precisely; it was added in 1833 to allow ships on the Thames to set their clocks. On the house's balcony overlooking the Thames, you can take a look at a **Camera Obscura**, of the kind which Flamsteed used to make safe observations of the sun – the current model gives you a panorama of Greenwich and the Isle of Dogs. Inside, beyond the displays of globes, astrolabes and quadrants, and the restored apartments in which the cantankerous Flamsteed lived, you eventually reach the **Octagon Room**, containing a single eighteenth-century telescope – though, in fact, this room was never used to map the movement of the stars, acting instead as a reception room in which the king could show off. The ceiling plasterwork is all that remains of the original decor, and there are replicas of the precision clocks installed behind the original walnut panelling in 1676, which boast thirteen-foot-long pendulums with a two-second swing.

Longitude

The next gallery focuses on the search for longitude. The displays show you how to use a quadrant in order to measure latitude, and explains the lunar-distance method of calculating longitude. However, before the invention of the seagoing clock, which could tell travellers what time it was back home and therefore how far east or west they'd travelled, longitude was impossible to measure at sea in cloudy weather. The displays reveal some of the crazy ideas that were put forward in order to try to measure longitude and win the £20,000 **Longitude Prize**. Much the most bizarre involved stabbing a number of dogs with the same knife, then taking them off to different countries; at noon in England a man would jab the knife into a mysterious substance called "powder of sympathy", at which point, supposedly, all the dogs would bark simultaneously, thus revealing the time differentials.

▲ Time-Ball, Flamsteed House

The Dome

[A] yellow-spiked Teflon tent... a genetically modified mollusc...The Dome is a blob of correction fluid, a flick of Tipp-Ex to revise the mistakes of nineteenth-century industrialists...a poached egg designed by a committee of vegans.

Iain Sinclair, *Sorry Meniscus*

The Dome is located on contaminated land (formerly one of Europe's largest gas-works) downstream at North Greenwich, and is clearly visible from the riverside at Greenwich and from the royal park. Built at a cost approaching £800 million, and designed by Richard Rogers, it is by far the world's largest dome – over half a mile in circumference and 160ft in height – held up by a dozen, 300-foot-tall yellow steel masts. In 2000, it housed the nation's chief millennium extravaganza: an array of hi-tech sponsor-dominated zones set around a stage, on which a circus-style performance took place to music by Peter Gabriel. Bad reviews and over-optimistic estimates of visitor numbers forced the government to pump in around £150 million of public money just to keep it open. Nevertheless, millions paid £20 each to visit, and millions went away happy.

Entertainment giants, AEG, have now agreed to spend yet more millions to turn the Dome into a six-floor, 23,000-seater music and sports arena, and the O2 mobile company have paid up to rebrand it "the 02". The venue will reopen in 2007, host the 2009 World Gymnastics Championships and be the 2012 Olympic venue for artistic gymnastics, trampolining and basketball. Meanwhile, the land to the southeast is being transformed into the Millennium Village, another conglomeration of riverside flats, plus the mini-wetlands of the Greenwich Peninsula ecology park (Wed–Sun 10am–5pm).

The easiest way to get to the Dome is to take the tube to North Greenwich, as the Dome has its very own, very large, very fancy Jubilee line tube station designed by Will Alsop, with a bus station by Norman Foster. It's also possible to walk or cycle the mile and a half along the riverside pathway from Greenwich, or take bus #188 from Greenwich town centre. The Dome itself is fenced off, but you can walk around the outside and admire the odd work of art: Anthony Gormley's very busy *Quantum Cloud* and Richard Wilson's *Slice of Reality*, the bridge of a boat cut away from its mother ship.

22

The exhibition then progresses to more successful experiments, including the first four marine chronometers designed by **John Harrison**, three of which are still in working order today. Harrison eventually went on to win the prize in 1763 with his giant pocket watch, H4 – the only one that no longer functions – after much skulduggery against his claims, most notably by the Astronomer Royal at the time, Nevil Maskelyne. The story of how Harrison finally won the prize is the subject of the bestselling book *Longitude* by Dava Sobel. The downstairs rooms contain an eclectic collection of timepieces from around the world, including the electrical contacts that used to provide the hourly six pips for the BBC. Among the more unusual exhibits are a delicate Chinese fire clock in the shape of a dragon, which uses a burning incense stick, and an alarm clock from the Cultural Revolution, in which the seconds tick away against a background of women waving Mao's *Little Red Book*.

The Meridian Building and the Planetarium

Flamsteed carried out more than thirty thousand observations – "nothing can exceed the tediousness and ennui of the life" was his dispirited description of the job – in the Quadrant House, which now forms part of the **Meridian Building**, but was originally little more than a brick shed in the garden.

Flamsteed's meridian line is a brass strip in the floor, though it was originally formed by the west wall of his shed. Edmond Halley, who succeeded Flamsteed as Astronomer Royal in 1720, bought more sophisticated quadrants, sextants, spyglasses and telescopes, which are among those displayed in the **Quadrant Room**. With the aid of his eight-foot iron quadrant he charted the comings and goings of the famous comet – though he never lived to see its return – and worked out his own version of the meridian. Next door, the **Bradley Meridian Room** reveals yet another meridian, standard from 1750 to 1850 and still used for Ordnance Survey maps. Finally, you reach a room that's sliced in two by the present-day Greenwich Meridian, fixed by the cross hairs in Airy's "Transit Circle", the astronomical instrument that dominates the room.

The observatory is now in the process of massive redevelopment, which will eventually see the redesigning of the some of the galleries described above and the creation of a state-of-the-art **Planetarium**, housed in the South Building.

Ranger's House

Southwest of the observatory is the **Ranger's House** (Wed–Sun: April–Sept 10am–5pm; EH; £5.30; ☎020/8853 0035), a red-brick Georgian villa which looks out over Blackheath (see opposite). Built as a private residence in the early eighteenth century, it was bought in 1815 by the Crown and became the official residence of the park ranger (hence its name), a sort of top-notch grace-and-favour home. Entrance to the house is either from Croom's Hill, or from the doorway in the wall by the park's Rose Garden.

Pick up an audioguide and head upstairs to find out about **Julius Wernher**, the German-born millionaire Edwardian whose art collection is now displayed in the house. Wernher made his money by exploiting the diamond deposits of South Africa, and at his death in 1912 was one of the world's richest men. His taste in art is eclectic, ranging from medieval ivory miniatures to Iznik pottery, though he was definitely a man who placed technical virtuosity above artistic merit, and despite his Lutheran upbringing, he amassed a vast array of Catholic religious bric-a-brac. Highlights on the top floor include Memlinc's *Virgin and Child*, the jewellery cabinet and the pair of sixteenth-century majolica dishes decorated with mythological scenes for Isabella d'Este, wife of the Marchese of Mantua and a great patron of the arts.

Downstairs, there's a sparkling Reynolds portrait of Lady Caroline Price, a top-notch de Hooch interior, and, in the splendid main gallery with its three bow windows and duck-egg-green coffered ceiling, a whole series of seventeenth-century French tapestries depicting life in the court of the emperor of China. Finally, at the far end of the main gallery is Bergonzoli's striking *Love of Angels*, a highly charged sculpture that, despite weighing two tons, succeeds in appearing light and ethereal.

Fan Museum

At the bottom of Croom's Hill, the twisting road that runs along the western edge of the park and boasts some of Greenwich's finest seventeenth- and eighteenth-century buildings, you'll find the **Fan Museum** (Tues–Sat 11am–5pm, Sun noon–5pm; £3.50; ☎020/8305 1441, ⊛www.fan-museum.org) at no. 12. It's a fascinating little place (and an extremely beautiful house), revealing the importance of the fan as a social and political document. The permanent exhibition on the ground floor traces the history of the materials employed, from peacock feathers to straw, while temporary exhibitions on the first floor explore conditions of production, the fan's link with the Empire and changing fashion. Outside in the garden, there's a kitsch, hand-painted orangery.

Down in Deptford

Deptford, just west of Greenwich, is not an area that immediately springs to mind when thinking of places to visit in London. However, it does have a very rich history, due, in part, to the presence of the **Royal Naval Dockyards** here from 1513 until 1869. It was at Deptford in 1581 that Drake moored the *Golden Hinde* (see p.274) after circumnavigating the globe, had Elizabeth I on board for dinner, and was knighted for his efforts. And, of course, it was in Deptford that the playwright **Christopher Marlowe** was murdered, not after a drunken brawl in a tavern as is often supposed, but in more mysterious circumstances in the company of three men who had links with the criminal underworld and the Elizabethan intelligence service.

All that remains of the old dockyards today are a few officers' quarters hidden in the Pepys housing estate, and the **Master Shipwright's Palace** (☎020/8692 5836), at the bottom of Watergate Street, fifteen minutes' walk west of Cutty Sark DLR or five minutes' walk north of Deptford train station. Originally constructed in Tudor times, the last rebuild, in 1708, was deemed so ridiculously expensive that the building became known as a palace, though in fact it's nothing of the sort. The house is occasionally used for exhibitions and performances, though the idea is to restore it eventually. You can get an idea of how prosperous the area once was just off the High Street at **St Paul's Church** (🌐 www.paulsdeptford.org.uk), the local architectural gem, designed by Thomas Archer in 1720, whose interior Pevsner described as "closer to Borromini and the Roman Baroque than any other English church". Things are looking up, too, if **Laban** (🌐 www.laban.org), Deptford's new centre for contemporary dance at Creekside, east of the High Street, is a sign of things to come. Designed by Tate Modern duo Herzog and de Meuron, it features a colourful corrugated plastic facade.

Blackheath

Immediately south of Greenwich Park lies the well-to-do suburb of **Blackheath** (so called because of the colour of the soil), whose bleak, windswept heath, crisscrossed with busy roads, couldn't be more different from the royal park. Nonetheless, with its pair of century-old pubs, the *Princess of Wales* and *Hare and Billet*, each set beside a pond (on the south side of the heath), it can be quite pleasant on a summer afternoon. The odd fair takes place here on public holidays, and it's south London's premier kite-flying spot.

Blackheath has its historic connections, too, most famously as a plague burial ground – a role which perhaps slowed development. Lying on the main road to Dover, it was also a convenient spot on which to pitch camp, as the Danes did in 1011, having kidnapped St Alfege. Their example was followed during the 1381 Peasants' Revolt by Wat Tyler's rebels, who were treated to a rousing revolutionary sermon by John Bull, which included the famous lines "When Adam delved and Eve span, who was then the gentleman?" The victorious Henry V was welcomed back from the Battle of Agincourt here in 1415, while Henry VII fought a pitched battle on this spot against Cornish rebels in 1497. It was at Blackheath, also, that Henry VIII was so disappointed on meeting his fourth wife, Anne of Cleves, in 1540; he famously referred to her as "the Flanders mare" and filed for divorce after just six months.

The heath's chief landmark is **All Saints' Church**, which nestles in a slight depression in the south corner. Built in rugged Kentish ragstone in 1859, it's at odds with the rest of the architecture bordering the heath, which dates mostly from the area's development in the late eighteenth and early nineteenth centuries. One of the earliest residential developments was **The Paragon**, east of the church, a crescent of four-storey Georgian mansions linked by Doric colonnades. An even earlier foundation, set in its own grounds further to the east, is **Morden College** (not open to the public), the aristocrat of almshouses, built in 1695 not for the deserving poor but for "decayed Turkey merchants" who had lost their fortunes. The quadrangular red-brick building, built by Wren's favourite mason, possibly to a design by the master himself, reflects the lost status of its original inhabitants and is now an old-people's home.

It's worth venturing down the charmingly named Tranquil Vale into the village-like centre of Blackheath, if only to visit the **Reminiscence Centre** (Mon–Fri 10am–5pm, Sat 10am–1.30pm; free; ☎020/8318 9105, ⓦwww.age-exchange.org.uk), situated opposite the train station. A favourite with the older folks of Blackheath, the centrepiece is an old-fashioned shop counter, whose drawers are filled with two-pin plugs, wooden clothes pegs, chalk powder and a whole host of everyday objects now rarely seen. Ask for a demonstration of the shop's rare surviving example of a rapid-wire cash system, via which banknotes could be whizzed from cashier to till worker. Out the back, you can get a cuppa from the museum's period tuck shop, and, if you're lucky, you might even catch an impromptu piano recital.

Woolwich

In 1847, a visitor to **Woolwich** commented that it was the "dirtiest, filthiest and most thoroughly mismanaged town of its size in the kingdom". It's not quite as bad as that, but, with its docks and factories defunct, it remains one of the poorest parts of the old Docklands. The good news is that regeneration is now under way, and will be given a further boost by the arrival of the Docklands Light Railway in 2008. And if you have a fascination for military history, it's definitely worth exploring the old dockyards and arsenal, for their architecture and the **Firepower** artillery museum. The other reason to get the train out to Woolwich is to visit the **Thames Barrier**, an awesome piece of modern engineering and the largest movable flood barrier in the world.

Thames Barrier

The best way to approach the **Thames Barrier** is on a boat from Greenwich, skirting the peninsula that provides a home for the Dome, and gliding between the barrier's gleaming fins. London has been subject to flooding from surge tides since before 1236, when it was reported that in "the great Palace of Westminster men did row with wherries in the midst of the Hall". One of the worst recorded floods took place as recently as 1953, when more than three hundred people were drowned in the Thames Estuary alone. A flood barrier had been advocated as far back as the 1850s, but it wasn't until global warming and rising tides, coupled with the fact that southeast England is sinking slowly into the sea, that the Greater London Council finally agreed to build the present barrier. Built from 1972 to 1984, it's a mind-blowing feat of engineering, with its ten movable steel gates weighing from 400 to 3700 tons.

The **Thames Barrier Information Centre** (daily: April–Sept 10.30am–4pm; Oct–March 11am–3.30pm; £1.50; ☎020/8305 4188, ⓦwww.environment-agency.gov.uk), on Unity Way, is run by the Environment Agency, and has glossy models and macho videos and explains the basic mechanism of the barrier (something which is by no means obvious from above the water). By far the most interesting way to see the Thames Barrier, however, is from the terraced café on the one day a month when it is raised for tests (phone for dates and times). **Boats** from Greenwich to the Thames Barrier are run by Thames Passenger Services (April–Oct only; ☎020/7930 4097). Otherwise it's about a ten-minute walk from either Charlton or Woolwich Dockyard train stations. From the Barrier you can walk inland, mostly through parks, to Charlton House (see p.393), just over a mile to the south.

Military Woolwich

Woolwich, like Deptford, owes its existence to the **Royal Dockyards**, which were established here in 1513 by Henry VIII. The men-of-war that established England as a world naval power were built in these dockyards, starting with the *Great Harry*, the largest ship in the world when it was launched from here in 1514, and Walter Ralegh and Captain Cook set out from Woolwich on their voyages of discovery. Despite costly modernization in the early nineteenth century to enable the dockyards to build and repair steamships, their capacities were quickly outstripped by the much larger iron-clad vessels, and they finally closed in 1869.

The **Royal Arsenal**, for which the area is now famous, grew up alongside the Tudor dockyards. Charles II fortified the area with a sixty-gun battery and sank several ships in the river in preparation for an attack by the Dutch fleet that never materialized. In 1695 the Royal Laboratory for the manufacture of fireworks and gunpowder moved here, and was joined, in 1717, by the main government brass foundry. The complex expanded enormously in the nineteenth century, reaching its heyday during World War I, when it employed nearly 80,000 workers (mostly women). After another boom period during World War II, the ordnance factories were closed altogether in 1967, and council housing built over much of the site. The fine collection of mostly eighteenth-century buildings is now gradually being restored as part of an ambitious programme to turn the whole area into a mixed commercial and residential district.

Royal Arsenal: Firepower

The **Beresford Gateway**, built in 1829 as the arsenal's main entrance, is now freestanding on Beresford Square, very close to Woolwich Arsenal train station, and separated from the rest of the complex to the north by busy Beresford Street/Plumstead Road. From the main gates, you enter **Dial Square**, overlooked by some of the arsenal's most historic buildings: the Main Guard House, with its eighteenth-century Doric portico; Verbruggen's House, opposite, which was begun in 1772, and was the former residence of Jan Verbruggen, the Master Founder; and the Royal Brass Foundry, which is made of wood, but encased in brick, was possibly designed by Vanbrugh in 1717, and is due to house collections from the National Maritime Museum. To the north, the **Dial Arch Block** is distinguished by its central archway, which sports a sundial, pillars and a pile of cannonballs. It was here in 1886 that a group of machinists formed Dial Arch Square Football Club, later Woolwich Arsenal FC, and then just **Arsenal FC**, eventually moving to Highbury in north London (see p.552). The team used to get changed in the toilets of the *Royal Oak* (now the *Pullman*), 27 Woolwich New Rd, right by Woolwich Arsenal train station.

If you head down Number One Street (formerly a continuation of Beresford Street), you'll come to the former bomb factory which now houses **Firepower** (April–July & Sept–Oct Wed–Sun 10.30am–5pm, Aug Tues–Sun 10.30am–

5pm, Nov–March Fri–Sun 10.30am–5pm; £5; ☎020/8855 7755, ⓦwww
.firepower.org.uk), the hi-tech Royal Artillery museum, which used to reside in
the Rotunda (see below). To get the most out of the museum, you do seriously
have to be into guns – lots of them. The main Gunnery Hall features ancient
World War I field guns, old and new howitzers, anti-tank guns, Thunderbird-
style guided-missile launchers and Saracens, familiar from news reports from
Northern Ireland, and allows you to play various war games, fire simulator guns
and watch lots of wartime film clips. Having seduced you with its hardware, the
museum then shows harrowing footage of the human cost of artillery shells in
the Real Weapon side gallery, where there are more hands-on games. The History Gallery above the main hall takes you through the history of artillery and
rocket science, features the gun carriage used in the funeral cortège for Georges
V and VI, and includes the Medals Gallery. Inevitably, there's a propaganda video
on today's Royal Artillery, and a twenty-minute multimedia show, *Field of Fire*,
concentrating on the chief conflicts of the twentieth century.

Royal Artillery Barracks and around

Britain's first two artillery regiments were founded at the arsenal in 1716, and
are now housed in the **Royal Artillery Barracks**, completed in 1802 by James
Wyatt. This stands half a mile to the south of the arsenal, up Grand Depot Road.
Its three-storey Georgian facade, interrupted by stucco pavilions and a central
triumphal arch, runs for an amazing 1080ft, making it one of the longest in
Europe. Appropriately enough, a temporary indoor venue at the barracks will
host the shooting during the 2012 Olympics.

The barracks face south onto the grassy parade ground, to the east of which
lies the abandoned **Garrison Church of St George**, built in neo-Roman-
esque style in 1863. Gutted in the last war, it's now an attractive husk, with
fragments of its colourful interior decor still surviving. Further south still, on
the other side of Woolwich Common, is Wyatt's only slightly less imposing **Old
Royal Military Academy**, built in mock-Tudor style as a foil to the Royal
Artillery Barracks. The 720-foot facade faces north onto a parade ground, with
an imitation of the Tower of London's White Tower as its centrepiece. The academy, known as "The Shop" in the British army, closed in 1948, and is set to be
restored by English Heritage and eventually opened to the public.

To the west of the Royal Artillery Barracks, off Repository Road, stands John
Nash's bizarre Chinese-style **Rotunda** (closed to the public). Originally used
as a marquee in the gardens of Carlton House during the celebrations at the
end of the Napoleonic Wars, it was damaged by a gas explosion, repaired and
re-erected on its present site. It used to house the Royal Artillery's museum,
which has since moved to the old Royal Arsenal (see p.391), and now houses
the museum's reserve collection.

Charlton to Chislehurst and beyond

This final section is a real miscellany of sights, spread between **Charlton** and
Chislehurst and beyond, across considerable tracts of suburbia and countryside.
Unless you're driving, you'll need to be selective in your choices: top targets are
the Tudor **Eltham Palace**, William Morris' **Red House**, the amazing **Chislehurst Caves**, and Charles Darwin's home, **Down House**.

Charlton House to Eltham

A little to the west of Woolwich, on Charlton Road, stands **Charlton House** (Charlton train station from Charing Cross, London Bridge or Victoria) the finest Jacobean mansion in or around London, completed in 1612 as a "nest for his old age" by Adam Newton, tutor to the eldest son of James I, Prince Henry, who died in the same year. It was designed by John Thorpe, architect of Holland House in Kensington, though the Orangery to the north (now a public lavatory) is thought to be the work of Inigo Jones. The house as a whole is currently used as a community centre, which means you're free to roam the place, as long as there are no events going on – call ☎020/8856 3951 to check. Take the wonderful oak staircase to the left of the Great Hall, to appreciate the beautifully carved bulb- and plant-shaped newels and grotesque faces on the balusters. Off the wood-panelled Long Gallery on the top floor, with its strapwork ceiling, is the White Room, which harbours the finest of the house's period fireplaces, adorned with a relief of Perseus and several biblical scenes. The best of the strapwork ceilings, however, is to be found in the Grand Salon, featuring lovely pendants.

A mile or so southeast of Charlton, up Shooters Hill, is a series of ancient woodlands, the most famous of which is the easternmost, **Oxleas Wood**, through which the Tory government were keen to drive a motorway. Coppicing has helped keep the woodland floor a rich floral haven, as well as home to over 200 species of fungi. Jack Wood and Castle Wood, to the west, also feature the odd bit of more formal parkland, and the one point of specific interest, **Severndroog Castle** (closed to the public; ⊛www.severndroogcastle.org.uk), a triangular folly erected in 1784 by Lady James of Eltham in memory of her husband, William, who once attacked a pirate stronghold in the island fortress of Severndroog, off the west coast of India. A mile or so to the south, across Shepherdleas Wood and the odd golf course and playing field, is **Avery Hill Park**, whose Victorian domed Winter Garden (daily 10am–noon & 1–4pm) is, without a doubt, southeast London's finest greenhouse.

Eltham Palace

A mile or so to the south of Oxleas Wood, at the end of Court Yard, lies **Eltham Palace** (Mon–Wed & Sun: April–Oct 10am–5pm; Nov–March 10am–4pm; £7.30, gardens only £4.60; ☎020/8294 2548; Eltham train station from Victoria, London Bridge or Charing Cross), which was one of the country's foremost medieval royal residences and even a venue for Parliament for some two hundred years from the reign of Edward II. All that remains of Eltham's medieval glory now is the fifteenth-century bridge across what used to be the moat, and the **Great Hall**, built by Edward IV in 1479, with a fine hammerbeam roof hung with pendants, and two fan-vaulted stone oriels at the far end. The hall's two original fireplaces are now in Eltham's pubs; the best one, with its sixteenth-century Chinese tiles intact, can be seen in *The Greyhound* on the High Street.

Somewhat incredibly, in the 1930s, the millionaire Stephen Courtauld (of art-collecting fame) got permission to build his own "Wrenaissance"-style **house** onto the Great Hall, and convert the moat into landscaped gardens. Courtauld lavished a fortune on the place, creating a sort of movie star's party palace for his glamorous half-Italian, half-Hungarian wife, Virginia (who sported a risqué tattoo of a snake above one ankle). The house was designed by the duo Seely and Paget, furnished by the best Swedish and Italian designers, and kitted out with all the latest mod cons, including underfloor heating, a centralized vacuum cleaner, a tannoy system and ten en-suite bedrooms. Then, shortly before the end of the war, the family left for Rhodesia, taking most of the house's furniture with them.

Until 1993, the Ministry of Defence used and abused the place; since then, English Heritage has restored the entire house and gardens and replaced lost furnishings. There are acres of exotic veneer, an onyx and gold-plated bathroom, and lots of quirky little Art Deco touches – check out the Alice in Wonderland relief above the door in the circular entrance hall, which is flooded with light from a spectacular glazed dome. The audiotours fill visitors in on the family's various eccentricities, which included keeping a pet ring-tailed lemur called Mah-Jongg, which had its own centrally heated bedroom approached by a bamboo ladder and was notorious for biting disliked male visitors.

Red House

Two miles east of Oxleas Wood, in Bexleyheath on the very outskirts of London, lies the **Red House** (Wed–Sun: Feb & Oct–Dec 11am–4.15pm; March–Sept 11am–5pm; £6), a wonderful red-brick country house designed by Philip Webb in 1859 for his friend **William Morris**, following Morris' marriage to Pre-Raphaelite heart-throb Jane Burden. The details of the house, such as the turreted well-house and the pointed brick arches, are Gothic, but the whole enterprise stands as a landmark in English architecture, and the beginning of the Arts and Crafts movement with which Morris is most closely associated. Edward Burne-Jones and Dante Gabriel Rossetti were among those who helped decorate the interior, and in 1861 they went on to found "The Firm", Morris' famous interior furnishings company. Sadly, after just five years, with "Janey" conducting an affair with Rossetti, the couple left their dream home and moved to Kelmscott in Oxfordshire. The National Trust acquired the property in 2003 and is now in the process of restoring the interior and the garden to its original appearance. To get to the house, walk south from Bexleyheath station (trains from Charing Cross or London Bridge) down Avenue Road, and cross over into Upton Road; Red House Lane is the third street on your right.

Chislehurst Caves

Five miles southwest of Bexleyheath is one of London's more unusual tourist attractions, the **Chislehurst Caves** (Wed–Sun 10am–4pm, daily during school holidays; £4; ☎020/8467 3264, ⊛www.chislehurstcaves.co.uk), prehistoric underground tunnels which stretch for miles and have been used over the centuries by everyone from the Romans, who set up chalk mines, to the locals, who came here to shelter from wartime bombs. **Guided tours** set off on the hour, take around 45 minutes, and are pretty spooky and claustrophobic, as the caves have no lighting and you are taken around by a guide with a lamp. The caves are a short walk north of Chislehurst train station, off Old Hill.

Down House

Down House (Wed–Sun: April–Sept 10am–6pm; Oct 10am–5pm; Nov, Dec, Feb & March 10am–4pm; EH; £6.60; ☎01689/859119), home of the scientist Charles Darwin, is situated another five miles south of Chislehurst in the village of Downe, overlooking the southeastern suburbs of London. Born in Shrewsbury in 1809, Darwin showed little academic promise at Cambridge. It was only after returning from his five-year tour of South America aboard the HMS *Beagle* – in which he stopped off at the Galapagos Islands – that he began work on the theory he would eventually publish in 1859 as *On the Origin of Species*. Darwin moved to Down House in 1842, shortly after his marriage to his cousin Emma Wedgwood, who nursed the hypochondriac scientist here until his death forty years later. The house itself is set in lovely grounds, and is stuffed with Darwin memorabilia, though there's no sign (or smell) of the barnacles which Darwin spent eight years dissecting – he later moved on to the study of orchids (to the relief, no doubt, of his wife and children), several examples of which you can find in the glasshouse. Note that parking is very limited, so English Heritage is trying to encourage folk arriving by car to pre-book timed-entry tickets. If you come by public transport, it's worth knowing that bus #R2 runs every half-hour from Orpington station but not on Sundays, whereas bus #146 runs daily once an hour from Bromley North and Bromley South stations.

(23)

Out West: Hammersmith to Hampton Court

H
ammersmith to **Hampton Court** – a distance of some seven miles overland (more by the river) – takes you from the traffic-clogged western suburbs of London to the touristed royal outpost of **Hampton Court**. In between, London seems to continue unabated, with only fleeting glimpses of the countryside, in particular the fabulous **Kew Gardens** and the two old royal hunting parks, **Richmond** and **Bushy Park** – though, as one nineteenth-century visitor observed, they are "no more like the real untrimmed genuine country than a garden is like a field". Running through the chapter, and linking many of the places described, is the **River Thames**, once known as the "Great Highway of London" and still the most pleasant way to travel in these parts during the summer.

Aside from the river and the parks, the chief attractions are the royal palaces and lordly mansions that pepper the riverbanks: textbook Palladian style at **Chiswick House**, unspoilt Jacobean splendour at **Ham House**, and Tudor and Baroque excess (and the famous maze) at **Hampton Court**. We kick off this chapter at **Hammersmith** – London's gateway to the west, by road or tube – which, with neighbouring **Chiswick**, and **Kew**, **Richmond** and **Twickenham** beyond, has the additional appeal of its riverside walks and pubs.

Hammersmith to Osterley

Most people experience the five-mile stretch of west London between **Hammersmith and Osterley** en route to or from Heathrow airport, either from the above confines of the train or tube (which runs overground at this point) or from the M4, which was driven through areas of parkland in the 1960s. The sights here – former country retreats now surrounded by suburbia – are among the most neglected in this part of the city, receiving nothing like

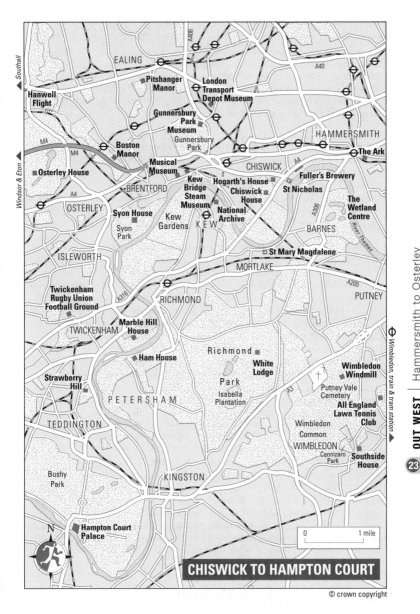

CHISWICK TO HAMPTON COURT

© crown copyright

the number of visitors of Kew and Richmond, on the south bank of the Thames.

The Palladian villa of **Chiswick House** is perhaps the best-known of these attractions, but you'll never see a crowd there and, though nearby Syon Park draws in the locals, most come for the garden centre rather than for the splendid **Syon House**, a showcase for the talents of Robert Adam and Capability Brown. There's yet more of Adam's work at **Osterley House**, another Elizabethan conversion now owned by the National Trust, while **Pitshanger Manor** is a must for fans of John Soane's architecture. The latest attraction in these parts is the remarkable **Wetland Centre**, a purpose-built landscaped haven for water birds and rare wildfowl, across the river from Hammersmith in the sleepy suburb of Barnes.

Hammersmith Bridge to Chiswick Mall

This chapter starts in the hellhole of **Hammersmith**, for several reasons: the nearby tube station, the riverside walk to Chiswick and easy access to Barnes' Wetland Centre. Hammersmith's heart was ripped out in the 1960s when the Hammersmith flyover was built to relieve congestion on the Broadway, the main shopping street. This had the simultaneous effect of making the adjacent roundabout one of the busiest traffic intersections in London, and cutting off Hammersmith from the nearby river. The tube, which lies at the middle of the roundabout, is now enveloped on three sides by a shopping mall and an ugly office building that's home to Coca-Cola's UK headquarters. Squeezed between the flyover and the railway line is Ralph Erskine's **London Ark**, a 1990s ship-shaped office block that was trumpeted as the city's first ecologically sound building.

The riverside walk to Chiswick

The best aspect of Hammersmith is the **riverside walk**, which begins a short way southwest of the roundabout, down Queen Caroline Street. First off, you pass underneath **Hammersmith Bridge**, a graceful suspension bridge from the 1880s that the IRA first bombed in 1939, as part of their attempt to disrupt the British war effort. They tried to destroy the bridge again in 1996, a feat followed up four years later by the splinter group, the Real IRA. From the bridge, you can walk all the way to Chiswick along the most picturesque stretch of riverbank in the whole of London, much of it closed to traffic.

Lower Mall, the section closest to the bridge, is a mixture of Victorian pubs, boathouses, Regency verandas and modern flats. An interesting array of boats huddles around the marina outside the *Dove*, an atmospheric seventeenth-century riverside pub (see p.489). This started out as a coffee house and has the smallest back bar in the country, copious literary associations – regulars have included Graham Greene, Ernest Hemingway and William Morris – and a canopied balcony overlooking the Thames.

It's strange to think that this genteel part of the Thames was once a hotbed of radicals, who used to congregate at **Kelmscott House** (Thurs & Sat 2–5pm; free; ☎020/8741 3735, ⊛www.morrissociety.org), beyond the *Dove* at 26 Upper Mall, where **William Morris** lived and worked from 1878 until his death in 1896. (Morris used to berate the locals from a soapbox on Hammersmith Bridge.) The basement and coach house now contain the original Kelmscott Press and the offices of the William Morris Society, who hold meetings in the

London Wetland Centre

For anyone even remotely interested in wildlife, the **London Wetland Centre** (Mon–Sat: summer 9.30am–6pm, Thurs until 8pm; winter 9.30am–5pm; £6.75; ☏020/8409 4400, ⓦwww.wwt.org.uk) in well-to-do Barnes is an absolute must. Lying across the river from Hammersmith, on the site of four disused reservoirs, the Wildfowl & Wetlands Trust (WWT) has created a hi-tech 105-acre mosaic of wetland habitats. The easiest way to get there is to catch bus #283, the special "Duck Bus" from Hammersmith tube. On arrival – unless it's raining – skip the introductory audiovisual in the theatre, and head straight out to the ponds, which are peppered with all-weather touch-screen computers and information sheets. If the weather's bad, or you've children with you, however, it's definitely worth visiting the **Discovery Centre**, where kids can head upstairs to take part in a swan identification parade, or take a duck's-eye view of the world. You can also look out over the wetlands from the glass-walled **Bird Airport Observatory** next door, or from the tables of the *Water's Edge Café*.

The centre basically serves a dual function: to attract native species of bird to its watery lagoons, and to assist in the WWT's programme of breeding rare wildfowl in captivity. Heading north from the visitor centre, you enter **World Wetlands**, where a network of paths leads you past a variety of extremely rare wildfowl – from White-faced Whistling Ducks to the highly endangered Blue Duck – whose wetland habitats have been re-created in miniature. Beyond, in the **Wildside**, are the reedbeds and pools that attract native species, such as lapwing, tufted ducks, grebes and, if you're lucky, even the odd wintering bittern, all of which you can view from a moss-roofed hide. **Waterlife**, east of the visitor centre, includes a sustainable garden, a chance for younger children to get near some domesticated wildfowl, and, best of all, do some pond-dipping with a WWT volunteer. At the far end is the mother of all hides: a triple-decker octagonal one with a lift, allowing views over the whole of the reserve.

coach house. From 1885 onwards, the Hammersmith branch of the Socialist League and later the Hammersmith Socialist Society used to meet here on a Sunday evening. Keir Hardie (first leader of the parliamentary Labour Party), anarchist Prince Kropotkin, George Bernard Shaw and Fabian founders the Webbs were among the speakers, and their photos now line the walls.

Chiswick Mall

A modern, pedestrianized section of the embankment connects the Upper Mall with **Hammersmith Terrace**, a line of tall Georgian houses built facing the river sometime before 1755. **Chiswick Mall**, which marks the end of Hammersmith, continues for another mile or so to the riverside village of Chiswick. A riotous ensemble of seventeenth- and eighteenth-century mansions lines the north side of the Mall, which cuts them off from their modest riverside gardens. Halfway along, a particularly fine trio ends with **Walpole House**, once the home of Barbara Villiers, Duchess of Cleveland, Countess of Castlemaine and one of Charles II's many mistresses.

Chiswick Mall terminates at the church of **St Nicholas**, built mostly in the nineteenth century, but retaining its original fifteenth-century ragstone tower. The church lay at the heart of the riverside village of **Chiswick** from medieval times until the nineteenth century, when the action moved north to Chiswick High Street, its modern heart. Lord Burlington and his architect friends William Kent and Colen Campbell are all buried in the graveyard, as is the aforementioned Barbara Villiers, though only the painters William Hogarth and James Whistler are commemorated by gravestones, the former enclosed by wrought-iron railings.

Church Lane was the medieval village high street. Its oldest building today is the Old Burlington, originally a sixteenth-century inn, now a private residence. Beyond it lies the huge **Fuller's Griffin Brewery**, dating back to the seventeenth century and still going strong. You can book yourself onto a ninety-minute guided tour (Mon & Wed–Fri 11am, noon, 1 & 2pm; £5; ☎020/8996 2063, ⓦwww.fullers.co.uk), which includes the inevitable tasting session, and also gives visitors the chance to see the country's oldest wisteria, which has clung to the brickwork for over 180 years. To continue on to Chiswick House, head across Powell's Walk (behind the church) to Burlington Lane, which runs along the southeastern edge of the house gardens.

Chiswick House and around

Chiswick House (Wed–Sun: April–Oct 10am–6pm; EH; £3.70; ☎020/8995 0508; Chiswick train station from Waterloo) is a perfect little classical villa, designed by Richard Boyle, third Earl of Burlington, in the 1720s, and set in a beautifully landscaped garden. Like its prototype, Palladio's Villa Rotonda near Vicenza, the house was purpose-built as a "temple to the arts" – here, amid his fine art collection, Burlington used to entertain such friends as Swift, Handel and Pope, who lived in nearby Twickenham.

Guests and visitors (who could view the property on payment of an admission fee even in Lord Burlington's day) would originally have ascended the quadruple staircase and entered the *piano nobile* (upper floor) through the magnificent Corinthian portico. The public entrance today is via the **lower floor**, where the earl had his own private rooms and kept his extensive library. Here, you can pick up an audioguide, watch a short video, and peruse an exhibition on the history of the house and grounds.

Entertaining took place on the **upper floor**, a series of cleverly interconnecting rooms, each enjoying a wonderful view out onto the gardens – all, that is, except the Tribunal, the domed octagonal hall at the centre of the villa, where the earl's finest paintings and sculptures would have been displayed. The Tribunal and other rooms are largely empty, but retain much of their rich decor, in particular the ceilings, designed by William Kent. The most sumptuous is the Blue Velvet Room, decorated in a deep Prussian blue, with eight pairs of heavy gilded brackets holding up the ceiling.

The gardens

If the finer points of classical architecture are a bit lost on you, you'll probably get more pleasure from the house's extensive **gardens** (daily 8am–dusk; free), an intriguing mixture of earlier, formal elements and more "natural" features added under Kent's direction. The gardens span the period in the history of English gardening when tastes fluctuated from the geometrical Versailles-like style to the more "natural" – but equally well-orchestrated – designs perfected by the likes of Capability Brown.

To do a quick circuit of the gardens, head south from the front entrance of the house and cross the canal that provides the setting for England's first **mock ruin**, the Kent-designed cascade. To the west of the lake is one of two *pattes d'oie* (goosefeet) – designs made up of straight-hedged alleyways radiating from a central focal point, in this case the obelisk, at the far end of the nearby terrace. The other goosefoot lies to the northeast of James Wyatt's elegant stone bridge from 1774, and is made up of a network of narrow yew-hedge avenues, each one ending at some diminutive building or statue. One of the most remarkable focal points is the grassy amphitheatre, by the side of the lake, centred on an obelisk in a pond and overlooked by an Ionic temple.

A great place from which to admire the northwest side of the house is the stone benches of the exedra, a set of yew-hedge niches harbouring lions and copies of Roman statuary, and overlooking a smooth carpet of grass, punctuated by urns and sphinxes, that sit under the shadow of two giant cedars of Lebanon. To the north of the villa, beside a section of the gardens' old ha-ha, stands a grand stone gateway designed by Inigo Jones. Beyond the gateway lies a large conservatory which looks out onto the formal **Italian Garden**, laid out in the early nineteenth century by the sixth Duke of Devonshire, who also established a zoo (now sadly gone) featuring an elephant, giraffe, elks and emus.

Hogarth's House

If you leave Chiswick House gardens by the northernmost exit, beyond the conservatory, it's just a short walk (to the right) along the thunderous A4 road to **Hogarth's House** (April–Oct Tues–Fri 1–5pm, Sat & Sun 1–6pm, Nov–March closes one hour earlier; closed Jan; free; ☎020/8994 6757), where the artist spent each summer with his wife, sister and mother-in-law from 1749 until his death in 1764. Nowadays it's difficult to believe Hogarth came here for "peace and quiet", but in the eighteenth century the house was almost entirely surrounded by countryside. After Chiswick House, whose pretentious Palladianism and excess epitomized everything Hogarth loathed the most, the domesticity here comes as some relief. Among the scores of Hogarth's engravings, you can see copies of his satirical series – *An Election, Marriage à la Mode, A Rake's Progress* and *A Harlot's Progress* – and compare the modern view from the parlour with the more idyllic scene in *Mr Ranby's House.*

Gunnersbury Park and around

An even earlier Palladian villa, built by Inigo Jones' son-in-law, John Webb, once stood in **Gunnersbury Park**, a mile or so to the northwest of Chiswick House. In 1801 the villa was demolished and the estate divided (hence the park's two adjacent mansions), only to be reunited under the wealthy Rothschild family in the late nineteenth century. The larger of the mansions is now the **Gunnersbury Park Museum** (April–Oct Mon–Fri 1–5pm, Sat & Sun 1–6pm Nov–March closes 4pm; free; ☎020/8992 1612, ⓦwww.hounslow.info/gunnersburyparkmuseum), with interesting temporary exhibitions on the local boroughs of Ealing and Hounslow, a fully restored set of Victorian kitchens (only viewable at the weekend), and a permanent collection of historical vehicles, including a tandem tricycle and the Rothschilds' own Victorian "chariot". The park itself has been largely given over to sports pitches, but overlooking the boating pond to the west of the museum there's a fine relic of the park's previous existence: a Neoclassical temple erected by George II's daughter Amelia, who used to spend her summers at the aforementioned Palladian villa – it was later used as a private synagogue by the Rothschilds.

Ealing has a large Polish community and **Kensington Cemetery**, which adjoins the park's southeast corner, contains a black marble obelisk erected in 1976 to the 14,500 Polish POWs who went missing in 1940, when the Nazi–Soviet Pact carved up Poland. A mass grave containing 4500 was later discovered by the advancing Nazis at Katyn, near Smolensk, but responsibility for the massacre was denied by the Russians until fifty years later, as a new plaque bitterly records. Fifty yards to the south is the grave of General Komorowski, leader of the Polish Home Army during the ill-fated 1944 Warsaw Uprising, who lived in exile in Britain until his death in 1966. Also buried here is the film director Carol Reed, best known for *The Third Man*. There's no direct access to the graveyard from the park; the main entrance is a quarter of a mile further south down Gunnersbury Avenue.

Depot Museum

London's Transport Museum (see p.160) houses its reserve collection in the purpose-built **Depot Museum** (occasional open weekends Sat & Sun 11am–5pm; £6.95; April–June, Sept & Oct guided tours last Fri of month 11am & 2pm; £10; ☎020/7379 6344, ⓦwww.ltmuseum.co.uk), beside the Piccadilly Track & Signal Operation Centre opposite Acton Town tube. It's a hangar-like building, stuffed full of unlabelled bits and bobs, from old signs and maps to fog repeater signals and the insides of old engines – in other words, a specialist's paradise. However, along with the usual parade of buses and trains, there are one or two sections that have wider appeal, such as the Poster Store, which holds around 16,000 examples of tube artwork, and the LT films shown in the cinema. Also of interest are the various prototypes of projects now consigned to the historical dustbin.

Kew Bridge Steam Museum

Difficult to miss thanks to its stylish tapered Italianate standpipe tower, **Kew Bridge Steam Museum** (daily 11am–5pm; Mon–Fri £4.25, Sat & Sun £5.75; ☎020/8568 4757, ⓦwww.kbsm.org) occupies the former Grand Junction Water Works pumping station, 100yd west of Kew Bridge. At the heart of the museum is the Steam Hall, which contains a green triple-expansion steam engine, similar in date and construction to the one used by the *Titanic*, and four gigantic nineteenth-century Cornish beam engines (one of which was only decommissioned in 1983), while two adjoining rooms house the pumping station's original beam engines, including the world's largest.

The steam engines may be things of great beauty, but they are primarily of interest to enthusiasts. Not so the museum's wonderfully imaginative and educational "Water for Life" gallery, devoted to the history of the capital's water supply. Situated in the basement and overlooked by a vast bank of ancient boilers, baths, sinks, taps and kettles, the exhibition employs plenty of hands-on features to enliven the subject. The section on rats and cockroaches goes down particularly well with kids, while the tales of the Victorian "toshers", who had to work the sewers in gangs of three to protect themselves from rat attacks, will make adults' stomachs turn.

The best time to visit is at weekends, when each of the museum's industrial dinosaurs is put through its paces, and the small narrow-gauge steam railway runs back and forth round the yard (March–Nov Sun). To reach the museum, take a train from Waterloo to Kew Bridge train station, or bus #237 or #267 from Gunnersbury tube or train station.

Musical Museum

Just west of the Steam Museum along a bleak section of Brentford High Street is the superb **Musical Museum** (ⓦwww.musicalmuseum.co.uk), packed with fully functioning musical automata and run by wildly enthusiastic and engaging volunteers. The museum has recently moved into new purpose-built premises and unfortunately is unlikely to reopen until 2007. When it does, it will definitely be worth a visit for the noisy ninety-minute demonstrations, during

23

which you get to hear – and often lend a hand with – every kind of mechanical music-making machine from cleverly crafted music boxes, through badly tuned barrel organs, to the huge orchestrions that were once a feature of London cafés. The museum also boasts one of the world's finest collections of player-pianos, including a "Duo-Art" grand, which can reproduce live performances of the great pianists. In addition, there are fortnightly concerts on Saturday evenings throughout the summer, performed on the museum's enormous Art Deco Wurlitzer, which once graced the Regal cinema in Kingston upon Thames.

Syon Park

Syon Park, directly across the Thames from Kew Gardens (see p.407), is one of the few aristocratic estates left intact in London, with a fantastically lavish stately home at its heart. It has been in the hands of the Percy family since Elizabethan times, although these days it's more of a working commercial concern than a family retreat. It started out as one of the richest monasteries in the country, established by Henry V after the Battle of Agincourt. Dissolved by Henry VIII, who incarcerated his fifth wife, Catherine Howard, here shortly before her execution in 1542, it was eventually granted to the Percys, earls (and later dukes) of Northumberland. It is home to the country's first-ever garden centre (opened in 1965), a trout fishery, an aquatic centre stocked with tropical fish, a mini-zoo and a butterfly house, as well as the old mansion. To get there, take bus #237 or #267 to Brent Lea bus stop from Gunnersbury tube and train station or Kew Bridge train station, or else it's a fifteen-minute walk from Syon Lane train station.

Syon House

From its rather plain castellated exterior, you'd never guess that **Syon House** (April–Oct Wed, Thurs & Sun 11am–5pm; £7.50; ☎020/8560 0881, ⓦwww .syonpark.co.uk) contains the most opulent eighteenth-century interiors in the whole of London. The splendour of Robert Adam's refurbishment is immediately revealed, however, in the pristine **Great Hall**, where you can pick up the excellent audioguide. An apsed double cube with a screen of Doric columns at one end and classical statuary dotted around the edges, the hall has a chequered marble floor that cleverly mirrors the pattern of the coffered ceiling. It was here – or rather, in the hall's Tudor predecessor – that Henry VIII's body lay in state en route to Windsor, and was discovered the next morning surrounded by a pack of hounds happily lapping the blood seeping from the coffin.

From the austerity of the Great Hall you enter the lavishly decorated **Ante Room**, with its florid scagliola floor (made from a mixture of marble-dust and resin) and its green-grey Ionic columns topped by brightly gilded classical statues. Here, guests could mingle before entering the **State Dining Room**, a compromise between the two preceding rooms, richly gilded with a double apse but otherwise calm in its overall effect. The remaining rooms are warmer and softer in tone, betraying their Elizabethan origins much more than the preceding ones. The **Red Drawing Room** retains its original red-silk wall hangings from Spitalfields, upon which are hung portraits of the Stuarts by Lely, van Dyck and others, and features a splendid ceiling studded with over two hundred roundels set within gilded hexagons. Looking out to the Thames, the **Long Gallery** – 136ft by just 14ft – stretches the entire width of the house, decorated by Adam's busy pink and gold plasterwork and lined with 62 individually painted pilasters. It was in the Long Gallery that Lady Jane Grey was formally offered the crown by her father-in-law, John Dudley, the owner of Syon at the time; nine days later they were arrested and later beheaded by "Bloody Mary".

The rest of the house pales in comparison with the first five rooms. However, there are still one or two highlights to look out for: more works by Lely and Van Dyck, as well as Gainsborough and Reynolds in the **Print Room**; a superb Adam fireplace and ornate fan-patterned ceiling, plus portraits by Holbein and Reynolds in the **Green Drawing Room** – still used by the family; and a monster golden Sèvres vase at the foot of the modest principal **staircase**. Upstairs, past the delicate 1000-piece Sèvres dinner service, there are several plush bedrooms, including two refurbished in 1832 for the future Queen Victoria and her mother, the Duchess of Kent, with magnificent canopied beds, blue silk outside and yellow within.

The gardens

While Adam beautified Syon House, Capability Brown laid out its **gardens** (daily 10.30am–5.30pm; £3.75; free with ticket to the house) around an artificial lake, surrounding it with oaks, beeches, limes and cedars. Since then, the gardens have been further enhanced by still more exotic trees, ranging from an Indian bean tree to a pagoda tree. Beside the lake, there's a stretch of lawn overlooked by a Doric column topped by a fibreglass statue of Flora, but the gardens' real highlight is the crescent-shaped **Great Conservatory**, an early nineteenth-century addition which is said to have inspired Joseph Paxton, architect of the Crystal Palace. Those with young children will be compelled to make use of the **miniature steam train** which runs through the park on Sundays from April to October.

▲ Great Conservatory, Syon House

London Butterfly House

Another plus point for kids (and adults) at Syon is the **Butterfly House** (daily: April–Sept 10am–5pm; Oct–March 10am–3.30pm; £5.25; ☏020/8560 0378, ⊛www .londonbutterflyhouse.com), across the car park from the house and gardens. Here, in a small, mesh-covered hothouse, you can walk amid hundreds of exotic butterflies from all over the world, as they flit about the foliage. The largest inhabitant is the Giant Atlas Moth, which only flies at night, but can be admired from close quarters as it sleeps. Displays show the butterfly in its stages of metamorphosis, and an adjoining room houses a collection of iguanas, millipedes, tarantulas and giant hissing Tanzanian cockroaches.

London Aquatic Experience

If your kids show more enthusiasm for life-threatening reptiles than delicate insects, then you could skip the Butterfly House entirely and head for the **London Aquatic Experience** (daily 10am–5.30pm; £5; ☎020/8847 4730, ⓦwww.aquatic-experience.org) instead. The small purpose-built centre, which is adjacent to the Butterfly House, contains a modest but mixed range of aquatic creatures, from the mysterious basilisk, which can walk on water, to the perennially popular piranhas, both vegetarian and carnivorous. Other favourites include several lethal snakes, a few crocodiles, cockatoos and macaws, and some charming, tiny, brightly coloured tree frogs.

Osterley Park

Robert Adam redesigned another colossal Elizabethan mansion three miles northwest of Syon at **Osterley Park** (daily 9am–7.30pm or dusk; free) – one of London's largest surviving estate parks, which still gives the impression of being in the middle of the countryside, despite the presence of the M4 motorway to the north of the house. The main approach, from Osterley tube or by car, is along a splendid avenue of sweet chestnuts to the south, past the National Trust-sponsored farmhouse (whose produce you can buy all year round). From the car park, the driveway curves past the southernmost of the park's three lakes, with a Chinese pagoda at one end. Cedars planted in the 1820s and oaks planted in Victorian times stand between the lake and the house, and to the north are the grandiose Tudor stables of first owner Thomas Gresham, now converted into a café.

Osterley House

Unlike Syon, **Osterley House** (March Sat & Sun 1–4.30pm; Easter–Oct Wed–Sun 1–4.30pm; NT; £4.90; ☎020/8232 5050) was built with mercantile rather than aristocratic wealth: it was erected in 1576 by Thomas Gresham, the brains behind the City's Royal Exchange. Two hundred and fifty years later it was bought by yet another City gent, the goldsmith and banker Francis Child, who appears to have used it merely as a kind of giant safe-deposit box – it was his grandsons who employed Robert Adam to create the house as it is today.

From the outside, Osterley bears some similarity to Syon, the big difference being the grand entrance portico, with a broad flight of steps rising to a tall, Ionic colonnade, which gives access to the central courtyard. From here, you enter Adam's characteristically cool **Entrance Hall**, a double-apsed space decorated with grisaille paintings and classical statuary. The finest rooms are the so-called State Rooms of the south wing, where the nouveaux riches Childs hoped, in vain, to entertain royalty as Gresham had once done. The **Drawing Room** is splendid, with Reynolds portraits on the damask walls and a coffered ceiling centred on a giant marigold, a theme continued in the lush carpet and elsewhere in the house. The **Tapestry Room** is hung with Boucher-designed Gobelin tapestries, while the silk-lined **State Bedchamber** features an outrageous domed bed designed by Adam. Lastly, there's the **Etruscan Dressing Room**, in which every surface is covered in delicate painted trelliswork, sphinxes and urns, a style that Adam (and Wedgwood) dubbed "Etruscan", though it is in fact derived from Greek vases found at Pompeii.

The **Long Gallery** is much broader, taller and plainer than the one at Syon and, like much of the house, features Adam-designed furniture, as well as some fine chinoiserie. Sadly, the Childs' collection of Rubens, van Dyck and Claude pictures no longer hangs here, having been transported to the family's new

23

home in the Channel Islands (where they were destroyed by fire), and replaced instead by second-rank works from the V&A.

The north wing is disappointing after the State Rooms, though the white-washed Library is worth a quick peek. The Neoclassical **Great Staircase**, stuck rather awkwardly halfway along the north wing, has a replica Rubens ceiling painting, the original having been destroyed by fire while being removed by the last owner in 1949. Only a few rooms are open on the first floor, each one pleasant enough but by no means essential viewing.

Pitshanger Manor

Two other country houses worth mentioning are dotted across the suburbs of west London, each within easy walking distance of a tube. To the southeast of Boston Manor tube, down Boston Gardens, is the Jacobean **Boston Manor House** (April–Oct Sat & Sun 2.30–5pm; free; ☏020/8583 4535). Originally built by a wealthy widow who married into the Spencer family, it was bought by James Clitherow, a City merchant, in 1670 and remained in the family until the 1920s. With magnificent cedar trees and ornamental flowerbeds, the grounds (daily dawn–dusk) are well worth a visit, even though the M4 cuts right through the middle. If you come on a weekend afternoon in summer you can also visit the house, the highlight of which is the Drawing Room on the first floor, which retains a sumptuous mantelpiece and an extraordinarily elaborate, original Jacobean plaster ceiling. In an unusual break with protocol, William IV and Queen Adelaide paid a visit to the Clitherows (mere common-ers), and dined in the Dining Room, which also boasts a fine plaster ceiling, in 1834.

A couple of miles north of Boston Manor is Pitshanger Manor, a short walk down the High Street from Ealing Broadway tube, and now rebranded by Ealing council as **PM Gallery & House** (Tues–Fri 1–5pm, Sat 11am–5pm; free; ☏020/8567 1227). Designed in 1770 by George Dance, but later bought and extensively remodelled by John Soane, Pitshanger was superbly restored in the 1980s and is well worth a visit. The balustraded main facade, though small, is magnificent, its bays divided by Ionic pillars topped by terracotta statues. As soon as you enter the narrow vestibule, Soane stops you short with some spa-tial gymnastics by taking a section of the ceiling up through the first floor. To the right is the now book-less Library, which features a cross-vaulted ceiling, decorated with an unusual trelliswork pattern. Soane's masterpiece, though, is the **Breakfast Room**, with caryatids in the four corners and lush red porphyry and grey marbling on the walls.

An unexpected bonus is the **Martinware Gallery**, a display of the idiosyn-cratic stoneware pottery produced around 1900 by the four Martin brothers from the nearby Southall Pottery. Its centrepiece is their Moorish ceramic fire-place, made for the billiard room at Buscot Park, Oxfordshire. The rest of the ware, including face mugs and bird jars, is more of an acquired taste. The man-or's south wing is all that survives from the original house by George Dance (Soane's architectural teacher), the remainder of which Soane demolished. The rooms here are on a much larger scale, providing an interesting contrast to Soane's intimate and highly wrought style, while the Monk's Dining Room in the basement is the precursor of Soane's Monk's Parlour in Lincoln's Inn Fields.

Kew Gardens and around

Kew's **Royal Botanic Gardens** (daily 9.30am–7.30pm or dusk; £10; ℡020/8332 5000, ⊛www.kew.org) manage the extremely difficult task of being both a world leader in botanic research and an extraordinarily beautiful and popular public park at the same time. Kew began as a pleasure garden, created in 1731 by Prince Frederick, eldest son of George II and Queen Caroline, who considered their offspring "the greatest ass, the greatest liar, the greatest canaille and the greatest beast in the whole world". But it was the widow of "Poor Fred", Princess Augusta, who established Kew's first botanic gardens in 1759, with the help of her paramour, the Earl of Bute. Some of the earliest specimens were brought back from the voyages of Captain Cook, instantly establishing Kew as a leading botanical research centre. From its original eight acres Kew has grown into a 300-acre site in which more than 33,000 species are grown in plantations and glasshouses, a display that attracts well over a million visitors every year, most of them with no specialist interest at all.

The glasshouses

The main shop and visitor centre are at the Victoria Gate, as is the distinctive **Campanile**, which originally served as the chimney for the furnaces below the Palm House. Beyond lies the Pond, home to two ten-ton Ming lions, and the best vantage point from which to appreciate the **Palm House**, the first and most famous of Kew's magnificent array of glasshouses. A curvaceous mound of glass and wrought iron, the Palm House was designed by Decimus Burton in the 1840s, predating the Crystal Palace by some three years. Its drippingly humid atmosphere nurtures most of the known palm species, while in the basement there's a small but excellent tropical aquarium. From the Palm House, head north to the diminutive **Waterlily House**, where a canopy of plants and creepers overhangs a circular pond boasting spectacular giant water lilies.

Further north still is the rather less graceful **Princess of Wales Conservatory**, opened in 1987. The cacti collection here is awesome, as are the giant koi fish that swim stealthily beneath the pathways – look out, too, for the bizarre plants in the insectivorous section. Immediately east of the Princess of Wales Conservatory, set amidst Kew's gargantuan Rock Garden, is the new **Alpine House**, a glasshouse shaped like the sail on the back of a dimetrodon.

The largest of all the glasshouses is the **Temperate House**, another of Decimus Burton's innovative structures, to the south (and twice the size) of the Palm House and almost forty years in the making. It contains plants from every continent, including one of the largest indoor palms in the world, the sixty-foot Chilean Wine Palm, first planted in 1846 and currently approaching the roof – and therefore the end of its life.

Visiting Kew

There are four entry points to the gardens, but the vast majority of people arrive at Kew Gardens tube and train station, a few minutes' walk east of the **Victoria Gate**, at the end of Lichfield Road. The only drawbacks with Kew are the hefty entry fee, and the fact that it's on the main flight path to Heathrow. That said, it's a wonderful place with something to see whatever the season, though to get the most out of it, visit sometime between spring and autumn, bring a picnic and stay for the day. On a summer weekend, it's worth getting here early to avoid the queues.

The eighteenth-century gardens

Almost nothing survives of William Chambers' landscape gardening at Kew, but some of the buildings he created in the 1760s for the amusement of Princess Augusta remain dotted about the gardens. The **Orangery** was one of the earliest, and the largest, hothouses in the country when it was built; it now houses a café. The most famous is his ten-storey, 163-foot-high **Pagoda**, Kew's most distinctive landmark, though disappointing close up, since it's lost the eighty enamelled dragons that used to adorn it, and you can't climb it. More fun is the ornate **Japanese Gateway**, a legacy of the 1911 Japanese Exhibition, built in cedar wood and topped by a copper roof, which stands nearby in a sort of miniature tea garden.

To the north of the pagoda, you can walk through Chambers' **Ruined Arch**, purpose-built with sundry pieces of Roman masonry strewn about as if tossed there by barbarian hordes. Close by is Kew's tallest object, a 225-foot-high flagpole fashioned from a single Canadian fir tree and erected in 1959. The rest of Chambers' works are all classical temples, the most picturesque being the **Temple of Aeolus**, situated close to Cumberland Gate on one of Kew's few hillocks, surrounded by a carpet of bluebells and daffodils in the spring.

Capability Brown's work on the gardens at Kew has proved more durable than Chambers': his lake remains a focal point of the Syon vista from the Palm House, and the hidden **Rhododendron Dell** he devised survives to the south

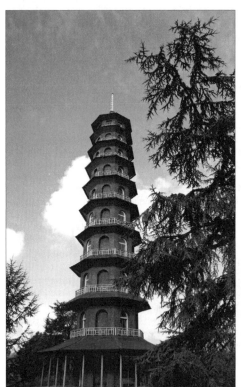
▲ Pagoda, Kew Gardens

of it. This more thickly wooded, southwestern section of the park is the bit to head for if you want to lose the crowds, few of whom ever make it to **Queen Charlotte's Cottage** (April–Sept Sat & Sun 10.30am–4pm; free), a tiny thatched summerhouse built in brick and timber in the 1770s as a royal picnic spot for George III's wife. There's very little to see inside, beyond a room of Hogarth prints and a trompe l'oeil pergola, but the surrounding native woodland is carpeted with bluebells in spring.

Kew Palace

Clearly visible to the west of the Orangery stands the country's smallest royal residence, **Kew Palace** (ⓦwww.hrp.org.uk), a three-storey redbrick mansion measuring a mere 70ft by 50ft, and commonly known as the "Dutch House", after its fancy Flemish-bond brickwork and its curly Dutch gables. It's the sole survivor of the three royal palaces that once stood at Kew and was bought by George II as a nursery for his umpteen children. The only king to live here, though, was George III, who was confined here from 1802 onwards and subjected to the dubious attentions of two doctors who attempted to find a cure for his "madness" by straitjacketing him and applying poultices of mustard and Spanish fly. The palace is scheduled to reopen in 2006 after a lengthy refurbishment. Take time to explore the secluded **Queen's Garden**, behind the palace, set out in a formal eighteenth-century style, with a pleached hornbeam avenue and a lovely sunken nosegay garden.

The museum and art galleries

Kew's Museum No. 1, on the other side of the Pond from the Palm House, and now known as **Plants and People**, provides another excellent wet-weather retreat. Inside, an exhibition shows the myriad uses to which humans have put plants, from food and medicines to clothes and tools. Along with the usual static glass-case displays, there are also touch-screen computers to hand, a scent station and various hands-on exhibits which should keep younger visitors happy.

Kew also boasts two little-known art galleries, some distance from one another along the eastern edge of the gardens. **Kew Gardens Gallery**, the larger of the two, is in the northeastern corner of the gardens in Cambridge Cottage, originally the Earl of Bute's residence but rebuilt in Queen Anne style in 1867. The gallery puts on temporary exhibitions on a wide variety of horticultural themes. To the south of Victoria Gate stands the **Marianne North Gallery**, purpose-built in 1882 to house the prolific output of the self-trained artist Marianne North. Over eight hundred paintings, completed in fourteen years of hectic world travel, are displayed end to end, filling every single space in the gallery.

Kew Green and the National Archives

Kew's majestic **Main Gates**, designed by Decimus Burton, fulfilled their stated function until the arrival of the railway at Kew. Nowadays, you only get to see them if you're walking from Kew Bridge or exploring **Kew Green**, which rivals Richmond's for the accolade of London's prettiest village green. Lined with Georgian houses, the green is centred on the delightful church of **St Anne**, an unusual building sporting a Victorian polygonal clock turret at one end and a peculiar Georgian octagonal cupola at the other; the painters Gainsborough and Zoffany lie in the churchyard.

Hidden in the residential backstreets of Kew is the Public Record Office, a rather nasty-looking beige and green premises housing the **National Archives** (Mon, Wed & Fri 9am–5pm, Tues 10am–7pm, Thurs 9am–7pm, Sat 9.30am–5pm; free; ☎020/8392 5202, ⊛www.nationalarchives.gov.uk). Its research library is full of historians consulting primary source materials, while its exhibition gallery displays a changing rota of fascinating artefacts ranging from the likes of the Domesday Book and the trial record of Charles I, to Queen Victoria's 1851 census return and Elton John's Deed Poll certificate changing his name (wisely) from Reginald Kenneth Dwight.

23

Richmond

Richmond, upstream from Kew, basked for centuries in the glow of royal patronage, with Plantagenet kings and Tudor monarchs frequenting the riverside palace of Shene, as Richmond Palace was then called. In the eighteenth century Richmond enjoyed a brief life as a spa, and its agreeable locale began to attract City merchants, as well as successful artists, actors and writers: Pope, Gainsborough, Garrick and Reynolds are just some of the plaque-worthy names associated with the place. Although most of the courtiers and aristocrats have gone, as has the Tudor palace on the green, Richmond is still a wealthy district, with two theatres and highbrow pretensions. In reality, though, it's been a commuter town since the arrival of the railway in the 1870s. To appreciate its attractions fully, you need to visit the old village green, walk along the riverside to the nearby stately homes of Ham (see p.416) and Marble Hill (see p.417), take in the glorious view from **Richmond Hill** and pay a visit to the vast acreage of **Richmond Park**, the old royal hunting grounds, still wild and replete with deer.

Richmond Green

On emerging from the station at Richmond, you'd be forgiven for wondering why you're here, but the procession of chain stores spread out along the one-way system is only half the story. To see Richmond's more interesting side, take one of the narrow pedestrianized alleyways off busy George Street, a few minutes' walk southwest of the station. Lined with arty shops and tearooms, these will bring you to the wide-open space of **Richmond Green**, one of the finest village greens in London, and no doubt one of the most peaceful before it found itself on the main flight path into Heathrow. Handsome seventeenth- and eighteenth-century houses line the southwest and southeast sides of the green, with the most striking building of all, the flamboyant **Richmond Theatre**, designed by the great Frank Matcham in terracotta and brick in 1899, on Little Green, to the northeast of its larger neighbour.

The southwest side of the green is the site of medieval **Richmond Palace**, built originally in the twelfth century (when it was known as Shene Palace) and acquired by Henry I in 1125. The first king to frequent the place was Edward III, who lay dying here in 1377 while his mistress urged the servants to prise the rings from his fingers. Seventeen years later a grief-stricken Richard II razed the place to the ground after his wife, Anne of Bohemia, died here of plague. Henry V had it restored and Edward IV held jousting tournaments on the green, but it was Henry VII who, in an atypical burst of extravagance, constructed the largest complex of all, renaming it Richmond after his Yorkshire earldom. Henry VIII later granted the palace to his fourth wife, Anne of Cleves, as part of their surprisingly amicable divorce settlement. Queen Mary and Philip of Spain spent part of their honeymoon here and Elizabeth I came here to die in 1603.

A lot of history is attached to the place, but very little of Richmond Palace survived the Commonwealth and even less is visible now. The most obvious relic is the unspectacular **Tudor Gateway**, on the south side of the green; to the left, the building calling itself Old Palace incorporates some of the Tudor brickwork of the outer wall. The gateway, which once led into the palace's outer courtyard, now takes you into **Old Palace Yard**, a sort of miniature village green, and Crown property even today. The palace's furnishings, and over two thousand dresses belonging to Elizabeth I, were once stored in the building on the left – a trio of houses known collectively as the **Wardrobe**.

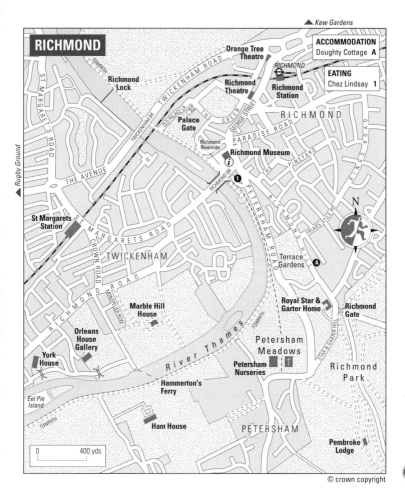

RICHMOND

ACCOMMODATION
Doughty Cottage **A**

EATING
Chez Lindsay **1**

Orange Tree
Theatre

RICHMOND

Richmond
Lock

Richmond
Theatre

Richmond
Station

▲ Rugby Ground

Richmond
Lock

Palace
Gate

R I C H M O N D

Richmond
Riverside

Richmond Museum

St Margarets
Station

TWICKENHAM

Terrace
Gardens

Marble Hill
House

Royal Star &
Garter Home

Richmond
Gate

Orleans
House
Gallery

York
House

Petersham
Meadows

Eel Pie
Island

Hammerton's
Ferry

Petersham
Nurseries

Richmond
Park

Ham House

PETERSHAM

Pembroke
Lodge

0   400 yds

© crown copyright

23

Richmond Riverside

Richmond Riverside is a popular, pedestrianized, terraced development by Quinlan Terry, dating from the late 1980s. To the untrained eye, the Georgian buildings initially look convincing enough, but closer inspection reveals the majority to be a sham: the cupolas conceal air vents, the chimneys are decorative and the facades hide offices and flats. One of the few originals is **Heron House**, a narrow three-storey building where Lady Hamilton and her daughter Horatia came to live shortly after Trafalgar, the battle in which the girl's father died. Steps lead through the house's ground-level arch to the desolate space of Heron Square, which looks like a film set without the extras.

The old town hall, set slightly back from the new development, to the north, now houses the **tourist office** (Mon–Fri 10am–5pm, Easter–Sept also Sat & Sun 10.30am–1.30pm; ☎020/8940 9125, ⓦwww.guidetorichmond.co.uk), a library and, on the second floor, the **Richmond Museum** (Tues–Sat 11am–

5pm, May–Oct also Sun 1–4pm; free; ☎020/8332 1141, ⓦwww.museumof richmond.com). The museum contains a small permanent exhibition on the history of the town, plus the lowdown on (and a model of) the old royal palace; temporary displays tend to focus on Richmond's past luminaries. However, the real joy of the waterfront is **Richmond Bridge** to the south – an elegant span of five arches made from Purbeck stone in 1777, and cleverly widened in the 1930s, thus preserving London's oldest extant bridge. From April to September you can rent rowing boats from the nearby jetties, or take a boat trip to Hampton Court or Westminster. If you continue along the towpath beyond Richmond Bridge, you will eventually come to Ham House – for more on this riverside walk, see p.416.

Richmond Hill

If you're still wondering what's so special about Richmond, take a hike up **Richmond Hill**. To get there, head up Hill Rise from the top of Bridge Street, passing between the eighteenth-century antique shops and tearooms on your left, and the small sloping green on your right. Eventually you come to the **Terrace Gardens**, which stretch right down to the river. The gardens are worth exploring but are most celebrated for the view from the top terrace out across the thickly wooded Thames valley. Turner, Reynolds, Kokoschka and countless other artists have painted this view, which remains relatively unchanged and takes in six counties from Windsor to the North Downs.

Richmond's wealthiest inhabitants have flocked to the hill's commanding heights over the centuries. The future George IV is alleged to have spent his secret honeymoon at **3 The Terrace**, after marrying Mrs Fitzherbert; twice divorced and a Catholic to boot, she was never likely to gain official approval, though she bore the prince ten children. Further along, on the opposite side of the street, William Chambers built **Wick House** in 1772 as a summer residence for the enormously successful Joshua Reynolds. The building currently houses the nurses who work at the nearby **Royal Star & Garter Home**, a rest home for war veterans built shortly after World War I, and now the dominant feature of the hillside.

Richmond Park

Richmond's greatest attraction is the enormous **Richmond Park** (daily: March–Sept 7am–dusk; Oct–Feb 7.30am–dusk; free; ☎020/8948 3209, ⓦwww .royalparks.gov.uk), at the top of Richmond Hill – 2500 acres of undulating grassland and bracken, dotted with coppiced woodland and as wild as anything in London. Royal hunting ground since the thirteenth century (when it was known as Shene Chase), this is Europe's largest city park – eight miles across at its widest point. It's famous for its red and fallow deer, which roam freely – and breed so successfully, they have to be culled twice a year – and for its ancient oaks. Though for the most part untamed, there are a couple of deliberately landscaped plantations which feature splendid springtime azaleas and rhododendrons.

Charles I was the first to formally establish the royal park, appropriating land willy-nilly against the counsel of his advisers, and enclosing his "New Park" with an eight-mile-long wall (still in existence) to keep out trespassers. Equally unpopular with the locals was **Princess Amelia**, youngest daughter of George II, who closed the park off to all but her closest friends shortly after being appointed ranger in 1747. Local opposition – in particular from a Richmond brewer, **John Lewis**, who sued the gatekeeper, Martha Gray, for assault – eventually succeeded in forcing through public access, prompting Amelia's resignation, after which she moved to Gunnersbury (see p.401). Lewis became a local hero, though he was bankrupted by the legal costs and the subsequent flooding of his brewery, and died in poverty.

From Richmond Gate, at the top of Richmond Hill, it's a short walk south along the crest of the hill to **Pembroke Lodge** (originally known as The Molecatcher's), childhood home of the philosopher Bertrand Russell, and now a teahouse with outdoor seating and spectacular views up the Thames. Close by, to the north, is the highest point in the park, known as **King Henry VIII's Mount**, where tradition has it the king waited for the flare launched from the Tower of London, which signalled the execution of his second wife, Anne Boleyn, though historians believe he was in Wiltshire at the time.

For a much longer stroll through the park, head east from Pembroke Lodge into **Sidmouth Wood**, whose sweet chestnuts, oaks and beeches were planted during the nineteenth century. Originally established as pheasant cover, the wood is now a bird sanctuary, and walkers must keep to the central path, known as the Driftway. A little further east lie the **Pen Ponds**, the largest stretches of water in the park and a good spot for bird-watching. To the south is the park's extremely popular **Isabella Plantation**, a carefully landscaped woodland park, with a little rivulet running through it, two small artificial ponds, and spectacular rhododendrons and azaleas in the spring. The round trip from Richmond Gate is about four miles.

The two most important historic buildings in the park are both closed to the public. Of the two, the **White Lodge**, to the east of the Pen Ponds, is the more attractive, a Palladian villa commissioned by George II, and frequented by his wife, Queen Caroline, and their daughter, the aforementioned Amelia. Much altered over the years, it was also the birthplace of the ill-fated Edward VIII, and home to the Duke and Duchess of York (later George VI and the Queen Mother); it currently houses the Royal Ballet School. The **Thatched House Lodge**, in the southernmost corner of the park, was built in the 1670s for the park's rangers, and gets its name from the thatched gazebo in the garden. General Eisenhower hung out in the lodge during World War II, and it's now home to Princess Alexandra died 2004, I believe.

Wimbledon

Wimbledon is a dreary, high, bleak, windy suburb, on the edge of a threadbare heath.

Virginia Woolf

Nowadays, of course, **Wimbledon** is best known for its tennis tournament, the Wimbledon Championships, held every year in the last week of June and the first week of July, on the grass courts of the All England Lawn Tennis and Croquet Club – to give the ground its official title. For the rest of the year, though, Wimbledon's vast **common** is its most popular attraction, worth a visit for its windmill alone, and for the remarkable **Southside House**.

Wimbledon Lawn Tennis Museum

If you've missed the tournament itself (see p.554), the next best thing for tennis fans is a quick spin around the state-of-the-art **Wimbledon Lawn Tennis Museum** (daily 10.30am–5pm; £6; during the championship for ticket-holders only daily 10.30am–8pm; ☎020/8946 6131, ⊛www.wimbledon.org), situated by Gate 4, on the east side of the All England grounds, on Church Road (bus #39 from Southfields tube). The museum traces the history of the game, which is descended from the *jeu de paume* played by the French clergy from the twelfth century onwards. The modern version, though, is considered to have been invented by a Victorian major, who called it "Sphairstike", a name that not surprisingly failed to stick. The new sport was initially seen as a genteel pastime, suitable for both gentlemen and ladies, and its early enthusiasts hailed almost exclusively from the aristocracy and the clergy – the museum's Edwardian dressing room is the epitome of upper-class masculinity. As well as the historical and fashion angles and copious tennis-star memorabilia, there's also plenty of opportunity for watching hours of vintage game-footage. If you're keen for a behind-the-scenes **guided tour** (mid-March to Oct, excluding the championships fortnight; £13.25), you need to phone ahead.

Wimbledon Common

Another reason to visit Wimbledon is **Wimbledon Common** (⊛www.wpcc .org.uk), to the southeast of Richmond Park, which, with neighbouring Putney Heath, is three times larger than Hampstead Heath. With none of the views of Hampstead or Richmond, however, Wimbledon can appear rather bleak: mostly rough grass and bracken punctuated by playing fields and golf courses, and cut through by the busy A3. As at Richmond, the common has been under threat periodically from its blue-blooded landlords, most recently the Spencer family (ancestors of Princess Di), who in 1865 tried unsuccessfully to get a bill through Parliament allowing them to sell off part of the common and enclose the rest. Historically, the common was a popular venue for duelling from at least the seventeenth century. Several prime ministers are recorded as having fought here, including George Canning, who was shot in the leg by another ex-minister, and William Pitt the Younger, who faced the local MP in 1798 – neither was a seasoned marksman, and after two attempts and two misses the duel was called off.

The chief landmark is the **Wimbledon Windmill** (April–Oct Sat 2–5pm, Sun 11am–5pm; £1; ☎020/8947 2825, ⊛www.wimbledonwindmillmuseum. org.uk), situated at the end of Windmill Road in the northern half of the common, with a conveniently placed café nearby. Built in 1817, the mill was closed down in 1864 as part of the Spencer family's plans, and converted into cottages, one of which was home to Baden-Powell when he began writing his *Scouting for Boys* in 1908. Subsequently restored and turned into a museum, the windmill is the last remaining hollow-post flour mill in the country; you can also climb into the first section of the wooden cap and see the giant chain wheel.

Beyond the attractive nearby pool of **Queen's Mere**, just to the west of the windmill, lies **Putney Vale Cemetery**, worth a visit for its wonderful array of Victorian angels and its peaceful Gardens of Remembrance, at their best in early summer. Look out for the nautical grave of Bruce Ismay, *Titanic* survivor and chairman of the ill-fated White Star Line. The cemetery's most illustrious incumbent is Alexander Kerensky, leader of the Russian Revolution of February 1917, which overthrew the tsar. Kerensky's downfall was his failure to bring

23

an end to the war, and he was forced to flee disguised as a Serb during the October Revolution.

In the southeastern corner of the common is **Cannizaro Park**, a small, sheltered, wooded area, made up of the grounds of Cannizaro House (now a hotel frequented by the tennis glitterati), and entered from West Side Common. Within its walls are a lovely stretch of lawn for picnicking, a maze of paths, an aviary, an Italian garden, occasional student art shows, and an open-air theatre and jazz festival every summer. Another peripheral but intriguing sight is the **Wat Buddhapadipa** (Sat & Sun 1–6pm; free; ☎020/8946 1357, ⓦwww .buddhapadipa.org), a white-gabled Thai Buddhist temple east off the common, on Calonne Road, richly decorated in red and gold.

Southside House

Hidden away behind high walls just round the corner from Cannizaro Park in Woodhayes Road is the Dutch-Baroque mansion of **Southside House** (Easter–Sept Wed, Sat & Sun 2, 3 & 4pm; £5; ☎020/8946 7643, ⓦwww.south-sidehouse.com), built in the late seventeenth century, and now hemmed in by Wimbledon's King's College School. The house is currently the headquarters of the School Teachers' Cultural Foundation, and sees few visitors. Yet it's an unforgettable experience, not least because you're guided round, and fed with anecdotes, by the eccentric descendants of the Pennington Mellor Munthe family who first built the house – several of whom still live here in a kind of time warp, using only candles for light and open fires for warmth, surrounded by the house's rich and slowly disintegrating decor, and the family's ancestral hangings, many of which are extremely valuable.

Inside, the house has a ramshackle feel, partly because at heart it's still an old Tudor farmhouse, onto which a Dutch facade has been added, and partly because of bomb damage. Nevertheless, virtually every room is stuffed to the rafters with artworks and other sundry treasures. In the Dining Room alone, there are no fewer than 34, mostly full-length, portraits, including three by Van Dyck, one each by Hogarth and Goya, and a depiction of St George by Burne-Jones. Other treasures on show include the sapphire worn by the last king of Serbia on the day of his assassination, and, in a cabinet of curiosities

Tramlink

23

Wimbledon's newest attraction is its **Tramlink** (ⓦwww.tfl.gov.uk/trams and ⓦwww .croydon-tramlink.co.uk), London's first tram since the whole network was dismantled in the 1950s. Opened in 2000, Tramlink has proved an amazing success, and there are now further plans for trams from Shepherd's Bush to Uxbridge, and from Camden to Brixton. The hub of the Tramlink system is the much maligned southern suburb of Croydon, from which eighteen miles of track – much of it on old railways – fans out to destinations as unlikely as Beckenham, Addington and Wimbledon. A day on the trams might seem a nice idea, especially for those with children; unfortunately, however, there are few conventional sights along the way. The award-winning **Croydon Clocktower** (Mon–Wed & Fri 9am–6pm, Thurs 9.30am–6pm, Sat 9am–5pm, Sun 2–5pm; ☎020/8253 1030) puts on excellent interactive exhibitions, and there's a city farm and bit of National Trust meadow land over in Morden, where Tramlink connects with the tube. However, it's probably the journey itself rather than any particular destination that's the attraction – and, of course, you can visit the **Tramlink shop** at Unit 5, Suffolk House, George St, Croydon (Mon–Fri 9am–5pm; ☎020/8681 8300). Travelcards are valid on the trams, or you can buy tickets from the automatic machines at the stops.

in the royal bedroom upstairs, you can see the pearl necklace worn by Marie Antoinette on the day of her execution. Finally, in the Music Room, there's a portrait of Angelica Kauffmann, a self-portrait by Reynolds, a Fragonard and one of George Romney's famous portraits of Emma, Lady Hamilton, who used to strike her "attitudes" in that very room.

Ham and Twickenham

Ham and **Twickenham** lie on either side of the Thames to the south of Richmond. **Ham House**, slightly off the beaten track, is one of the most appealing of all the historic houses along the river. Twickenham, best known for its rugby – there's a museum if you're really keen (see p.418) – also conceals a cluster of lesser-known sights close to the river, all of which repay a brief visit. It's a pleasant mile-long walk to Ham House from Richmond Riverside, and, weather permitting, **Hammerton's Ferry** will take people (and bicycles) over to the Twickenham side for £1 (Feb–Oct Mon–Fri 10am–6pm, Sat & Sun 10am–6.30pm; Nov–Jan Sat & Sun 10am–6.30pm).

Ham House

The best approach to **Ham House** (April–Oct Mon–Wed, Sat & Sun 1–5pm; £7.50; NT; ☎020/8940 1950) is on foot from Richmond Riverside, heading south along the towpath, which eventually leaves the rest of London far behind. On either side are the wooded banks of the Thames; to the left cows graze on Petersham Meadows, while hidden in the woods some way beyond lies Ham House, home to the earls of Dysart for nearly three hundred years. The first Earl of Dysart was Charles I's childhood whipping boy (he literally received the punishment on behalf of the prince when the latter misbehaved), who was granted a peerage and the estate of Ham for his pains, but it is his ambitious daughter, Elizabeth – at one time Oliver Cromwell's lover – who is most closely associated with the place. With the help of her second husband, the Earl of Lauderdale, one of the most powerful ministers to Charles II, she added numerous extra rooms, "furnished like a great Prince's" according to diarist John Evelyn, and succeeded in shocking even Restoration society with her extravagance.

Elizabeth's profligacy left the family heavily in debt, and the later earls of Dysart could afford to make few alterations, prompting Horace Walpole (who lived across the river at Strawberry Hill) to describe Ham as a "Sleeping Beauty". Restoration has only enhanced this period piece, which boasts one of the finest Stuart interiors in the country. The Great Staircase, to the east of the Central Hall, is stupendously ornate, featuring huge bowls of fruit at the newel posts and trophies of war carved into the balustrade. The rest of the house is equally sumptuous, with lavish plasterwork, silverwork and parquet flooring, Verrio ceiling paintings and rich hangings, tapestries, silk damasks and cut velvets. The Long Gallery, in the west wing, features six "Court Beauties" by Peter Lely, and elsewhere there are works by van Dyck and Reynolds.

Another bonus are the formal seventeenth-century **gardens** (Mon–Wed, Sat & Sun 11am–6pm; £3.50), now restored to something like their former glory. To the east lies the Cherry Garden, laid out with a pungent lavender parterre, and surrounded by yew hedges and pleached hornbeam arbours. To the south, there's a "Wildernesse", where the Lauderdales would display their orange trees, considered the height of luxury at the time. Finally, to the west, you'll find the original kitchen garden (now a rose garden), overlooked by the Orangery, which currently serves as a tearoom.

Marble Hill House

On the Twickenham side of the river, not far from Hammerton's Ferry, is **Marble Hill House** (April–Oct Sat 10am–2pm, Sun 10am–5pm; EH; £4; ☎020/8892 5115), a stuccoed Palladian villa set in rolling green parkland. Unlike Chiswick, this is no architectural exercise, but a real house, built in 1729 for Henrietta Howard, Countess of Suffolk, mistress of George II for some twenty years and, conveniently, also a lady-in-waiting to his wife, Queen Caroline (apparently "they hated one another very civilly"). Her wit and intelligence – though not her beauty – were renowned and she entertained literary figures of the day, such as Alexander Pope, John Gay and Horace Walpole. Another royal mistress, Mrs Fitzherbert, the Prince Regent's unofficial wife, later occupied the house in 1795. Nothing remains of the original furnishings, alas, and the house feels a bit soulless, so it's a good idea to take the audioguide. The principal room is the Great Room on the *piano nobile*, a perfect cube whose coved ceiling carries on up into the top-floor apartments. Copies of van Dycks decorate the walls as they did in Lady Suffolk's day, but the highlight is Lady Suffolk's Bedchamber, with its Ionic columned recess – a classic Palladian device. You can play minigolf in the grounds, and there are open-air concerts on occasional summer evenings.

Orleans House Gallery

Set in a small wood to the west of Marble Hill House is the **Orleans House Gallery** (April–Sept Tues–Sat 1–5.30pm, Sun 2–5.30pm; Oct–March closes 4.30pm; free; ☎020/8831 6000), in what began life as a villa built in 1710 for James Johnston. It was most famously occupied in 1815–17 by the exiled Duc d'Orléans (later to become king of France), and subsequently all but entirely demolished in 1926 – all, that is, except for the **Octagon**. Designed by James Gibbs in 1720 as a garden pavilion, the Octagon was added to the original house by Johnston in honour of a visit by the aforementioned Queen Caroline (see above). The exhibitions staged in the old stables and the modern extension are interesting enough, but it's the Octagon that steals the limelight, an unusually exuberant Baroque confection celebrated for its masterly Italian stucco decoration.

York House and Eel Pie Island

A little further west, towards Twickenham town centre, is **York House**, an early seventeenth-century mansion that now belongs to the local council, though the gardens, laid out by the last private owner, the Indian prince Ratan Tata, are open to the public. The bit to head for is the riverside section – a great picnic spot – that lies beyond the sunken garden, on the other side of the delicate arched bridge spanning the road. Here, in amongst the yew hedges, you'll find the gardens' celebrated "naked ladies", seven larger-than-life marble nymphs frolicking in the water lilies of an Italian fountain, above which Venus rises up at the head of a double-winged horse.

A few yards offshore, near York House, lies **Eel Pie Island**, the only inhabited island in the tidal Thames. Tea dances began at the island's *Eel Pie Hotel* back in

23

the 1920s; bawdy jazz nights were the staple diet in the 1950s; rock and rhythm and blues followed in the 1960s. The hotel burned down in 1972, and the island is now better known for its eccentric community of independent-spirited artisans, among them Trevor Baylis, inventor of the clockwork radio.

Twickenham Museum of Rugby

Sports tourism is a growing industry, and the English rugby fan's number one pilgrimage site is the national stadium at Twickenham. Visits are by **guided tour** only (Tues–Sat 10.30am, noon, 1.30 & 3.30pm, Sun 1 & 3pm; £9; ☎020/8892 8877, ⊛www.rfu.com), and it's best to phone ahead. The tour allows you to see the dressing rooms and walk onto the pitch itself, and also includes a visit to the **Museum of Rugby** (Tues–Sat 10am–5pm, Sun 11am–5pm) in the East Stand. The exhibition is full of video footage and lots of memorabilia from the sport, which was famously invented in 1823, when W. W. Ellis picked up and ran with the ball during a game of football at Rugby School. There's not much here for the non-specialist, however, save for the Calcutta Cup, which is an object of supreme beauty, having been made from 270 silver rupees, with great cobra handles and an elephant lid. Note that on match days the museum is open from 11am until an hour before kickoff (£3 to ticket-holders).

Strawberry Hill

One last oddity well worth making the effort to visit is **Strawberry Hill** (May–Sept Sun 2–3.30pm; £5.50; ☎020/8240 4224, ⊛www.friendsofstrawberryhill.org), to the south of Twickenham and upriver from Eel Pie Island, on Waldegrave Road. In 1747 writer, wit and fashion queen Horace Walpole, youngest son of former prime minister Robert Walpole, bought this "little plaything house . . . the prettiest bauble you ever saw . . . set in enamelled meadows, with filigree hedges", renamed it Strawberry Hill and set about inventing the most influential building in the Gothic Revival. Walpole appointed a "Committee of Taste" to embellish his project with details from other Gothic buildings: screens from Old St Paul's and Rouen cathedrals, and fan vaulting from Henry VII's Chapel in Westminster Abbey.

The house quickly became the talk of London, a place of pilgrimage for royalty and foreign dignitaries alike. Walpole was forced to issue tickets in advance (never more than four and no children) to cut down the number of visitors. Those he wished to meet he greeted dressed in a lavender suit and silver-embroidered waistcoat, sporting a cravat carved in wood by Grinling Gibbons and an enormous pair of gloves that once belonged to James I. When he died in 1797, he left the house to his friend, the sculptor Anne Damer, who continued to entertain in the same spirit, giving lavish garden parties dressed in a man's coat, hat and shoes. The house is now owned and carefully maintained by St Mary's College.

Hampton Court Palace

Hampton Court Palace, a sprawling red-brick ensemble on the banks of the Thames, thirteen miles southwest of London, is the finest of England's royal abodes. The present building began life, however, as an ecclesiastical palace, built in 1516 by the upwardly mobile **Cardinal Wolsey**, Henry VIII's high-powered, fast-living Lord Chancellor. The good times that rolled at Hampton prompted Henry to enquire why the cardinal had built such an extravagant home for himself. Wolsey, in a vain attempt to win back the king's favour, made the fatal reply "to show how noble a palace a subject may offer to his sovereign". In 1529, when Wolsey failed to secure a papal annulment for Henry's marriage to Catherine of Aragon, Henry took him at his word, sacked him and moved into Hampton Court.

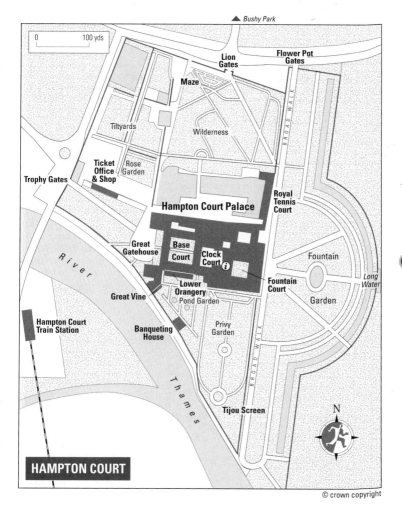

© crown copyright

Visiting Hampton Court

The **opening times** are April to October daily 10am to 6pm; November to March closes 4.30pm (℡0870/752 7777, ⊛www.hrp.org.uk). Trains from Waterloo take around half an hour to reach Hampton Court train station, just across the river from the palace. **Tickets** to the Royal Apartments cost £12 (£11 online or over the phone), and cover entry to everything in the palace and grounds. Those who don't wish to visit the apartments can buy a separate ticket for the gardens (£4) and the Maze (£3.50).

The **State Apartments** are divided into six thematic walking tours, which are numbered and colour-coded. There's not a lot of information in any of the rooms, but **guided tours**, each lasting half an hour or so, are available at no extra charge; all are led by period-costumed historians, who do a fine job of bringing the place to life. In addition, **audioguides** are available (for all except the Wolsey Rooms and the Queen's State Apartments) from the information centre on the east side of Clock Court.

If your energy is lacking – and Hampton Court is a huge complex – the most rewarding sections are **Henry VIII's State Apartments**, the **King's Apartments** (remodelled by William III) and the **Tudor Kitchens**. And be sure not to miss out on the **Maze**.

The **Hampton Court Palace Flower Show** takes place in early July, rivals Chelsea for sheer snob factor, and is likewise organized by the Royal Horticultural Society (⊛www.rhs.org.uk). The **Hampton Court Palace Festival** (⊛www.hamptoncourt festival.com) features stars from the classical and pop music worlds, and takes place each year in June.

Like Wolsey, **Henry VIII** spent enormous sums of money on the palace, enlarging the kitchens, rebuilding the chapel and altering the rooms to suit the tastes of the last five of his six wives. Under Elizabeth I and James I, Hampton Court became renowned for its masques, plays and balls; during the Civil War, it was a refuge and then a prison for Charles I. The palace was put up for sale during the Commonwealth, but, with no buyers forthcoming, Cromwell decided to move in and lived here on and off until his death in 1658. Charles II laid out the gardens, inspired by what he had seen at Versailles, but it was **William and Mary** who instigated the most radical alterations, hiring Christopher Wren to remodel the buildings. Wren intended to tear down the whole palace and build a new Versailles, but contented himself with rebuilding the east and south wings, adding the Banqueting House on the river and completing the chapel for Queen Anne.

▲ Hampton Court Palace

George III eschewed the place, apparently because he associated it with the beatings he received here from his grandfather. Instead, he established grace-and-favour residences for indigent members of the royal household, which still exist today. The palace was opened to the public by Queen Victoria in 1838, and, along with the vast expanse of **Bushy Park**, it's now a major tourist attraction. In March 1986, extensive damage was sustained in a fire started by one such elderly grace-and-favour resident, Lady Gale, who ignited the silk hangings with a bedside candle and died in the blaze.

The Palace

From the train station, it's a short walk across the river through the Trophy Gates, to the Tudor west front, no longer moated but prickly with turrets, castellations, chimneypots and pinnacles. The **Great Gatehouse**, the main entrance to the palace courtyards, would have been twice its present height in Wolsey's day. Before you get stuck into the Royal Apartments, it's worth getting your bearings by walking through the three main courtyards. The first and largest quadrangle, **Base Court**, is reminiscent of an Oxbridge college and features another Tudor gateway known as Anne Boleyn's Gateway, though it too dates from the time of Wolsey. Beyond lies **Clock Court**, which has none of the uniformity of the other two courtyards: to the north rises the Tudor Great Hall, to the south Wren's colonnade, announcing the new State Apartments, and to the east a fairly convincing mock-Tudor gateway by William Kent. Originally centred on a large fountain which was equipped by Elizabeth I with a nozzle that soaked innocent passers-by, the courtyard gets its current name from the **astronomical clock** on the inside of the Anne Boleyn Gateway, made in 1540 for Henry VIII, which was used to calculate the high tide at London Bridge (and thus the estimated time of arrival of palace guests travelling by boat). The last and smallest of the three courtyards is Wren's **Fountain Court**, which crams in more windows than seems possible.

Henry VIII's State Apartments

Henry VIII lavished more money on Hampton Court than on any other palace except Greenwich (which no longer exists). That said, the only major survival from Tudor times is his **Great Hall**, which was completed with remarkable speed in 1534, Henry having made the builders work day and night – a highly dangerous exercise in candlelight. The double hammerbeam roof is exceptionally ornate, and would have originally featured a louvre to allow the smoke to escape from the central hearth. Under Elizabeth I and James I, the hall served as the palace theatre, where theatrical troupes, among them Shakespeare's, entertained royalty. Even Cromwell had an organ installed here so that he and his family could enjoy recitals by John Milton, an accomplished musician as well as poet.

Passing through the Horn Room, you enter the **Great Watching Chamber**. The gilded oak-ribbed ceiling is studded with leather-mâché Tudor insignia, and hung with tapestries that were part of Wolsey's collection. In these surroundings up to eighty yeomen would be stationed at any one time, guarding the principal entrance to the king's private chambers, which William and Mary found "old-fashioned and uncomfortable" and consequently demolished.

From here you come to the **Haunted Gallery**, built by Wolsey to connect his apartments to the chapel, and home to the ghost of Henry's fifth wife, 19-year-old Catherine Howard. The night before her arrest for high treason in November 1541, Catherine is alleged to have run down the gallery in an attempt to make a final plea for mercy to the king, who was praying in the chapel. Henry refused to see her, and she was dragged kicking and screaming back to her chambers – or so the story goes, for it's since been proved that Catherine could not, in fact, have reached the chapel from her rooms via the gallery.

The Haunted Gallery leads into the Royal Pew in the chapel gallery, which was decorated for Queen Anne but has been a feature since Wolsey's day – it was here that Henry VIII was passed the note alleging that Catherine Howard was not in fact a virgin when he married her. From here, you can look down on the **Chapel Royal**, and admire the colourful false-timber vaulting wrought in plaster, heavy with pendants of gilded music-making cherubs – one of the most memorable sights in the whole palace.

The Queen's State Apartments

The **Queen's Apartments** were intended for Queen Mary II, but were completed some years after her death in 1694. The main approach is via the grandiose **Queen's Staircase**, splendidly decorated with trompe l'oeil reliefs and a coffered dome by William Kent.

One of the finest rooms here is the **Queen's Drawing Room**, decorated top to bottom with trompe l'oeil paintings depicting Queen Anne's husband, George of Denmark – in heroic naval guise, and also, on the south wall, riding naked and wigless on the back of a "dolphin". Queen Anne takes centre stage on the ceiling as Justice, somewhat inappropriate given her habit of not paying her craftsmen, including Verrio, the painter of this room. After Anne's death in 1714, the Prince and Princess of Wales (later George II and Queen Caroline) took over the Queen's Apartments, though they hated the trompe l'oeil paintings and hung Mantegna's works over the top of them. In 1717, the couple fell out with the king and moved to Kew; the ceiling painting in the **Queen's Bedroom** by James Thornhill predates the quarrel, with four portraits of a seemingly happy Hanoverian family staring at one another from the coving

The **Queen's Gallery** features one of the most sumptuous marble fireplaces in the palace – originally intended for the King's Bedchamber – with putti, doves and Venus frolicking above the mantelpiece; the walls, meanwhile, are hung with Gobelin tapestries depicting Alexander the Great's exploits. This route ends with **Queen Mary's Closet**, so called because the walls were once hung with needlework by the queen and her ladies, though Mary herself never set foot in the place.

The Georgian Rooms

The **Georgian Rooms** begin with the rooms of the **Cumberland Suite**, lived in by George II before his accession, then by his eldest son, Prince Frederick, and lastly by Frederick's brother, the Duke of Cumberland, better known as "Butcher Cumberland" for his ruthless suppression of the Jacobites in Scotland. The rooms were decorated by Kent, who added Gothic touches to the first two rooms and a grandiose Neoclassical alcove in the bedchamber.

Beyond here you'll find the tiny **Wolsey Closet**, the only remnant of Wolsey's apartments, and a tantalizing glimpse of the splendour of the original palace. It's a jewel of a room – though at 12ft square it's easily missed – with brightly coloured early sixteenth-century paintings set above exquisite linenfold panelling and a fantastic gilded ceiling of interlaced octagons.

Next is the **Communication Gallery**, constructed to link the King's and Queen's apartments, now lined with Lely's "Windsor Beauties", flattering portraits of the best-looking women in the court of Charles II. The **Cartoon**

Gallery itself, designed by Wren for the Raphael cartoons now in the V&A, is hung with seventeenth-century copies – tapestries made from the cartoons are scattered around the Queen's and King's apartments.

The next sequence of rooms is of minor interest, though they do include an excellent Gibbons overmantle in the Queen's Private Bedchamber. Last of all, you enter the **Queen's Private Chapel**, completed for Queen Caroline in 1728 – it's one of the few windowless rooms, hence the octagonal dome and skylight.

The King's Apartments

William III's state apartments are approached via the **King's Staircase**, the grandest of the lot thanks chiefly to Verrio's busy, militaristic trompe l'oeil paintings glorifying the king, depicted here as Alexander the Great. The **King's Guard Chamber** is notable chiefly for its 3000-piece display of arms, arranged as they were laid out in the time of William III. William's rather modest throne still stands in the **King's Presence Chamber**, under a canopy of crimson damask. The sixteenth-century Brussels tapestries in the room were originally commissioned by Henry VIII for Whitehall Palace.

Further on, in the **Privy Chamber**, there's a much grander throne used by William, with a canopy that still retains its original ostrich feathers. The most impressive room here is the **Great Bedchamber**, which boasts a superb vertical Gibbons frieze and ceiling paintings by Verrio – just as you're leaving this floor, you'll catch a glimpse of a splendidly throne-like velvet toilet. Ground-floor highlights include a semi-nude portrait by van Dyck of his mistress Margaret Lemon, in the East Closet, the **Orangery**, built to house the king's orange trees during the winter, and the only room in the palace lockable solely from the inside (a tryst room – highly unusual for the royals' very public life). Past here is the **King's Private Dining Room**, its table laden with pyramids of meringues and fruit and its walls hung with eight full-length portraits of Queen Mary's favourite ladies-in-waiting (known as the "Hampton Court Beauties"), for which the German-born painter Godfrey Kneller received a knighthood.

The Wolsey Rooms and the Renaissance Picture Gallery

The **Wolsey Rooms** comprise four early Tudor rooms, where the only reminders of Wolsey's day are the striking linenfold panelling of the walls and the original gilded strapwork ceilings. The suite is now used to display paintings from the Queen's vast Royal Collection, which kicks off with a wonderfully vibrant *Portrait of a Young Man in Red* by an unknown Tudor artist, and two masterly studies of old age: Holbein's portrait of Johannes Froben, Erasmus's publisher, and Tintoretto's portrait of the Venetian goldsmith Girolamo Pozzo. The grisaille painting, *The Four Evangelists Stoning the Pope*, was specially commissioned by Henry VIII to hang at Hampton Court. Among the portraits in the next room by, among others, Lotto, Titian and Joos van Cleve, the almost photographic *Portrait of a Lady in Green* (possibly by Bronzino) stands out, as does Bellini's terrific *Portrait of a Young Man*, and Raphael's self-portrait, painted at the age of just 23, and presented to George III in 1781. In Cranach's tiny *Judgement of Paris*, the startled Paris looks as though he's been accosted by three naked women whilst riding in the woods, while Pieter Brueghel the Elder's *Massacre of the Innocents* looks more like a village fete, though it was intended as an allegory for the contemporary atrocities committed by the Spanish troops of the Duke of Alba in Holland.

The Tudor Kitchens

After a surfeit of opulent interiors, the workaday **Tudor Kitchens** come as something of a relief. Henry VIII quadrupled the size of the kitchens, large sections of which have survived to this day and have been restored and embellished with historical reconstructions. To make the most of this route, you really do need the audioguide, which evokes the scene with contemporary accounts. Past the Boiling Room and Flesh Larder (not for squeamish vegetarians) you come to the **Great Kitchen**, where a fire is still lit in the main hearth every day. This kitchen is only one of three Henry built to cope with the prodigious consumption of the royal court – six oxen, forty sheep and a thousand or more larks, pheasants, pigeons and peacocks were an average daily total. The tour ends in Henry's vast **Wine Cellar**, where the palace's Rhineland wine was stored. At each main meal, the king and his special guests would be supplied with eight pints of wine; courtiers had to make do with three gallons of beer, which was very weak and drunk as a substitute for what was then a very dodgy water supply.

The Gardens

If you're coming from the State Apartments, you'll probably emerge onto the gardens' magnificent **Broad Walk**, which runs for half a mile from the Thames past Wren's austere east front to the putti-encrusted Flower Pot Gate and is lined with some of the country's finest herbaceous borders. Halfway along the Broad Walk lies the indoor **Royal Tennis Court**, established here by Henry VIII (a keen player of Real Tennis himself), but extensively restored by Charles II. If you're lucky, you might even catch a game of this arcane precursor of modern tennis, though the rules are incredibly tricky.

Fanning out from the Broad Walk is William's **Fountain Garden**, a grand, semicircular parterre, which in William's day featured box hedges, thirteen fountains and dwarf yew trees pruned to look like obelisks. A fair number of these "black pyramids", as Virginia Woolf called them, have been reduced to chubby cone shapes, while a solitary pool stands in place of the fountains, and the box hedges have become plain lawns. A semicircular canal separates the Fountain Garden from the Home Park beyond, its waters feeding Charles II's **Long Water**, Hampton Court's most Versaillean feature, which slices the Home Park in two.

Privy Garden

To the south of the palace lies the formal **Privy Garden**, laid out as it would have been under William III; the twelve magnificent wrought-iron panels at the river end of the garden are the work of Jean Tijou. To the west, you can peek into the **Pond Gardens**, which were originally constructed as ornamental fish ponds stocked with freshwater fish for the kitchens, and feature some of the gardens' most spectacularly colourful flowerbeds. Further along, protected by glass, is the palace's celebrated **Great Vine**, grown from a cutting in 1768 by Capability Brown and averaging about seven hundred bunches of Black Hamburg grapes per year (sold at the palace in September).

Close by stands the **Lower Orangery**, built for William and Mary by Wren and used as a dimly lit gallery for Andrea Mantegna's heroic canvases, *The Triumphs of Caesar*, bought by Charles I in 1629 and kept here ever since. Painted around 1486 for the Ducal Palace in Mantua, Mantegna's home town, these nine richly coloured paintings, depicting the general's victory parade, are among his best works, characterized by his obsessive interest in archeological and historical accuracy. Beyond the South Gardens, beside the river, is William III's dinky little red-brick **Banqueting House**, built for intimate riverside soirees, with castellations and mouldings by Gibbons and exuberant paintings by Verrio.

The Maze

To the north of the palace, Henry VIII laid out a **Tiltyard** with five towers for watching jousting tournaments, one of which survives near the garden restaurant. William III transformed the tiltyard into a **Wilderness** – an informal park of evergreens – which now contains the most famous feature of the palace gardens, the deceptively tricky trapezoidal **Maze**, laid out in 1714. Mazes, or labyrinths as they were called at the time, were used by pilgrims, who used to crawl along on hands and knees reciting prayers, as penance for not making a pilgrimage to the Holy Land. They were all the rage among the eighteenth-century nobility, who used them primarily for amusement, secret conversations and flirtation. The maze was originally planted with hornbeam, but, with the onset of the tourist boom in the 1960s, the hornbeam had to be replaced with yew. Since 2005, the maze has also featured a sound installation, a "speaking maze" in which visitors trigger snippets of laughter, birdsong and the odd snatch of music as they sweep along the paths.

Bushy Park

Beyond the Lion Gates, to the north of the Maze, across Hampton Court Road, lies **Bushy Park**, the palace's semi-wild enclosure of over a thousand acres, which sustains copious herds of fallow and red deer. Wren's mile-long royal road, Chestnut Avenue, cuts through the park, and is at its best in May when the trees are in blossom. The main architectural feature of the park is the **Diana Fountain**, situated a third of the way along the avenue to help break the monotony. The statue – which, in fact, depicts Arethusa – was commissioned by Charles II from Francesco Fanelli and originally graced the Privy Garden; stranded in the centre of this vast pond, she looks ill-proportioned and a bit forlorn.

Off to the west, a little further up the avenue, you'll come upon the **Waterhouse Woodland Gardens**, created in 1949, and at their most colourful each spring when the rhododendrons, azaleas and camellias are in bloom. The crowds are fairly thin even here, compared with the crush around the palace, but if you really want to seek out some of the park's abundant wildlife head for its wilder western section, where few visitors venture.

Windsor and Eton

owering above the town and the Thames on a steep chalk bluff, more than twenty miles west of London, **Windsor Castle** is an undeniably awesome sight, its chilly grey walls, punctuated by mighty medieval bastions, continuing as far as the eye can see. Once there, the small selection of State Rooms open to the public are fairly unexciting, though the magnificent St George's Chapel and the chance to see a small selection of the Queen's private art collection make the trip worthwhile. On a fine day, it pays to put aside some time for exploring Windsor Great Park, which stretches for several miles to the south of the castle.

Though almost as famous as Windsor, **Eton** – the exclusive and inexcusably powerful school founded by Henry VI in 1440 directly across the river from the castle – receives a mere fraction of the tourists. True, there's not so much to see here, but the guided tours give an eye-opening glimpse of life as lived by the offspring of Britain's upper classes, and the Gothic chapel is definitely worth a visit.

Visiting Windsor

Windsor has two **train stations**, both very close to the centre. Direct trains from Waterloo (every 30min; journey time 50min–1hr) arrive at **Windsor & Eton Riverside**, five minutes' walk from the centre; trains from Paddington require a change at Slough (Mon–Fri every 20min, Sat & Sun every 30min; journey time 30–40min), and arrive at **Windsor & Eton Central**, directly opposite the castle. The latter styles itself "Windsor Royal Station", though Queen Victoria herself was very particular to favour neither train station (and therefore company) over the other. Note that you must arrive and depart from the same station, as tickets are not interchangeable. The **tourist office** (daily 10am–5pm, longer hours in summer; ℡01753/743900, ⓦwww.windsor.gov.uk) is at 24 High St, opposite the Guildhall.

Tickets for Windsor Castle (daily: March–Oct 9.45am–5.15pm; Nov–Feb 9.45am–4.15pm; £12.50; ℡020/7766 7304, ⓦwww.royal.gov.uk) include entry to the castle precincts, the St George's and Albert Memorial chapels, the State Apartments, the Drawings Gallery and Queen Mary's Dolls' House. Occasionally, the State Apartments and/or other parts of the castle are closed to the public, in which case the admission will be reduced to reflect this. St George's Chapel is always closed on Sundays, except for those attending one of the services; the chapel closes at 4pm on weekdays, in order to prepare for the daily evensong at 5.15pm. The Changing of the Guard takes place, weather permitting, at 11am Monday to Saturday from April to July, and on alternate days from August to March.

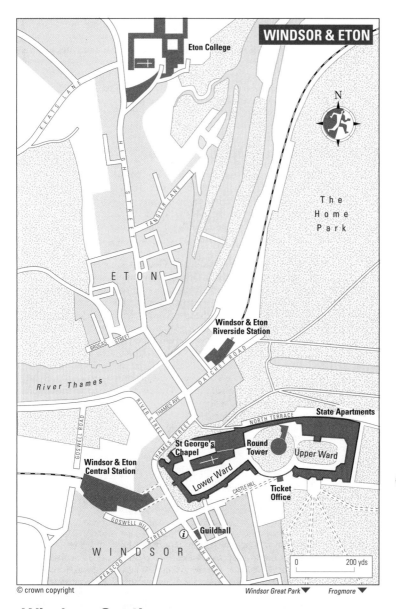

© crown copyright

Windsor Great Park ▼   *Frogmore* ▼

Windsor Castle

Windsor Castle began its life as a wooden keep built by William the Conqueror, and numerous later monarchs also had a hand in its evolution. Henry II tore down the wooden buildings in the thirteenth century and rebuilt the castle in stone, much as you see it now – in plan at least – though George IV in the nineteenth century was mainly responsible for today's rather over-restored appearance.

The most significant event to have befallen the castle in recent years was the devastating **fire** of 1992, which gutted a good number of the State Apartments. Having ignored the advice of various fire officers, and failed to insure the place, the royal family found itself faced with a repair bill of up to £50 million – or rather, the taxpayers did. In an attempt to assuage public opinion, the Queen subsequently offered to foot half the bill, and set about raising some of the money by opening up Buckingham Palace to the public.

The Middle and Upper wards

Leaving the ticket office, you find yourself in the **Middle Ward**, where the flagpole of the **Round Tower** flies the royal standard when the Queen is in residence, and the Union flag at other times. Constructed out of Caen stone in 1170 and heightened 30ft by George IV, the tower is the direct descendant of William the Conqueror's fortress and stands on the original motte-hill; despite its name, the moat below the tower has never held water, as its chalky soil is highly porous.

If you're running late, it's best to head for St George's Chapel first, as it closes at 4pm. If you're here relatively early in the day, head straight for the State Apartments before the tour groups get into their stride – to do so, walk around the Round Tower and pass under the **Norman Tower**. Three kings have been imprisoned in the prison house above the gate: David of Scotland, John of France and James I of Scotland, whose only compensation for his eleven years' incarceration was a glimpse of his future wife, Jane Beaufort, from his cell window.

From here you enter the **Upper Ward** or Quadrangle, where an equestrian statue of Charles II looks across the manicured stretch of lawn where the **Changing of the Guard** takes place when the Queen is at home (April–July Mon–Sat 11am; Aug–March alternate days). The south and east wings contain the Queen's private apartments, where she still hangs out occasionally at the weekend, at Easter, and in June during Ascot. The State Apartments lie to the north: the official state entrance is immediately to your left, but plebs must trot

▲ Windsor Castle

down the passageway and enter from the North Terrace, after admiring the splendid view across to Eton College Chapel, the Mars chocolate factory at Slough, and the Chiltern Hills beyond.

Queen Mary's Dolls' House and the Drawings Gallery

Before entering the State Apartments, most folk pay a quick visit to **Queen Mary's Dolls' House**, a palatial micro-residence designed by the eminent architect Edwin Lutyens for the wife of George V and situated in a dimly lit chamber beneath the royal apartments. The three-storey Neoclassical house features a fully plumbed-in toilet and working electric lights, and contains paintings by eminent artists and handwritten books by Kipling, Hardy and Conan Doyle. If the queue looks bad, however, you may decide to skip the pleasure and walk straight into the **Drawings Gallery** to the left of the main entrance, where you can see exhibitions of prints and drawings culled from Windsor's slice of the royal art collection (which includes the world's finest collection of sketches and notebooks by Leonardo da Vinci).

The State Apartments

The **State Apartments** – originally created for Charles II and his wife, Catherine of Braganza, but much altered since then – receive over a million visitors a year, so it can get crowded in high season. Visitors enter via the **Grand Staircase**, a quasi-medieval stairwell lit by a polygonal lantern – until the 1820s this area was an open courtyard, which once served as the herb garden. To the east lies George III's **Grand Vestibule**, featuring a smaller octagonal lantern, pseudo-Gothic fan vaulting, and floor-to-ceiling displays of arms. There are also several Victorian showcases displaying such treasures as a locket containing the bullet which killed Nelson at Trafalgar, and some wonderful armoury seized from Tippoo Sultan of Mysore when the British took Seringapatam in 1799.

The **Waterloo Chamber**, built to celebrate the defeat of Napoleon, is lined with portraits of wartime worthies and royals, mostly the work of Thomas Lawrence. More interesting is the room's seamless Indian carpet, woven in Agra for the empress of India, Queen Victoria. Most visitors just gape in awe at the monotonous, gilded grandeur of the state rooms, while the real highlights – the paintings from the Royal Collection that line the walls – are rarely given a second glance. In the **King's Drawing Room**, for example, there are no fewer than three works by Rubens over by the fireplace, while the **King's Bed Chamber** features numerous Canalettos and a couple of very fine Gainsborough portraits; the French eighteenth-century domed bed is also rather splendid. The **King's Dressing Room**, meanwhile, despite its small size, contains a feast of art treasures, including a dapper Rubens self-portrait, van Dyck's famous triple portrait of Charles I, and *The Artist's Mother*, a perfectly observed portrait of old age by Rembrandt.

Only three of Verrio's thirteen ceiling paintings have survived the whims of the royals, the first and finest of which is the *Banquet of the Kings* in the rather lush **King's Dining Room**, which is further embellished by fish and fruit festoons courtesy of Grinling Gibbons. The two other surviving works by Verrio are located beyond the Queen's Ballroom, itself lined with portraits of the royals by van Dyck. Sadly the Baroque decor and colourful Gobelin tapestries of these few rooms, which date back to the days of Charles II, give way to yet

24

more neo-Gothicisms in the Queen's Guard Chamber, from which you now enter the part of the palace which suffered most from the 1992 fire.

St George's Hall, in which monarchs from Edward III onwards held banquets for the Knights of the Garter, has been restored more or less to its original 1820s design, though the roof is more steeply pitched and now features brand-new oak hammerbeams. At the far end of the hall you can admire the armour of the Royal Champion, who used to ride into Westminster Hall during the coronation banquet and challenge anyone present to dispute the sovereign's right to the throne. The octagonal **Lantern Lobby** beyond is an entirely new room, replacing Queen Victoria's private chapel which was gutted in the 1992 fire – predictably enough, the royals have again opted for a safe neo-Gothic design.

At this point, those visiting during the winter months are given the privilege of seeing the **Semi-State Rooms**, which are still used in the summer months by the Royal Family. The set of four rooms (and a corridor) were created in the 1820s for George IV, and reflect that monarch's penchant for heavily gilded, pompous decor. If the Semi-State Rooms are closed, visitors pass straight into the **Grand Reception Room**, easily the most stunning of the rooms created by George IV, though the rich helpings of French gilded stuccowork might be a bit much for some. The fantastic chinoiserie clock on the mantelpiece, topped by a peacock and flanked by a Chinese gentleman and lady, was brought here from Brighton Pavilion, while the huge malachite vase managed to survive the fire virtually unscathed, despite being too heavy to move.

The Lower Ward and St George's Chapel

You leave the castle via the sloping **Lower Ward**, site of **St George's Chapel**, a glorious perpendicular structure ranking alongside Henry VII's Chapel in Westminster Abbey (see p.69), and the second most important resting place for royal corpses after the abbey. The chapel was founded by Edward III in 1348 as the spiritual centre for the Order of the Knights of the Garter, the chivalric elite established in the same year; the present edifice, however, was begun by Edward IV but not completed until 1528. If you're interested in visiting only the chapel, you can enter free of charge for the daily services; the 5.15pm evensong is particularly atmospheric thanks to the chapel's excellent boys' choir.

Entrance to the chapel is via the south door, and a one-way system operates; it's worth buying a plan as you enter to locate the graves, which aren't always obvious. What strikes you at once is the superb fan vaulting of the chapel ceiling, the final flowering of English Gothic architecture. The first tomb you come to is the white marble sarcophagus of **Prince Napoleon** (son of Napoleon III), who was speared to death in 1879 during the Zulu War, at the age of just 23. In the Unswick Chantry in the north aisle is the extravagant white marble monument to George IV's only child and heiress to the throne, **Princess Charlotte**, who died in childbirth in 1817; it is said that the doctor who attended to her was so grief-stricken he committed suicide. Shrouded female figures mourn the body of the princess, whose hand emerges dramatically from the folds; meanwhile, her spirit flies heavenwards attended by angels, one of whom is holding her stillborn son. Nearby is a statue of her husband, Leopold, who became the first king of Belgium (and is buried there). **George V** and **George VI** are both buried in the north aisle, the latter in his own memorial chapel along with his wife, the **Queen Mother**.

Continuing up the north choir aisle, it's worth peeking into the tiny **Hastings Chantry**, decorated with brightly coloured sixteenth-century paintings of St

Stephen's martyrdom. More architectural glories lie within the choir itself, with its intricate fifteenth-century three-tier stalls and two exquisite oriel windows side by side – the Gothic **Royal Gallery**, built in wood for Catherine of Aragon, the other in the Renaissance style and carved in stone. Underneath the floor of the choir is the **Queen's Closet**, built for the burial of Jane Seymour, Henry VIII's third wife, who died giving birth to Edward VI; it also contains Henry himself, Charles I and one of the children born to Queen Anne. Edward IV, Henry VI and Edward VII lie either side of the high altar.

The **Albert Memorial Chapel** adjoins St George's Chapel to the east. Built by Henry VII as a burial place for Henry VI, and completed by Cardinal Wolsey for his own burial, it was eventually converted by Queen Victoria into a memorial to her husband, Prince Albert. Albert himself actually lies alongside his wife in the equally extravagant mausoleum in Frogmore (see overleaf). Decorated in the High Victorian style, the vaulted ceiling boasts gold Italian mosaic infill, while the walls are lined with biblical murals in marble. Albert's memorial is upstaged by the centrepiece of the chapel, though: the extraordinary, heavy-duty wrought-iron grille surrounding the tomb of "Eddy", Duke of Clarence and eldest son of Edward VII, who was as dissolute as his father but differed in his sexual preference, and died in 1892, officially from pneumonia, but probably actually from syphilis. Beneath the chapel lies the **Royal Vault**, where George III and Queen Charlotte are buried along with six of their sons, including George IV and William IV.

The foot of the Lower Ward is occupied by the Guard Room, where the Changing of the Guard takes place when the Queen is not in residence. More interesting is the **Horseshoe Cloister**, hidden away to the west of the chapel. These medieval timber-framed houses form an arresting piece of domestic architecture in the otherwise frigid surroundings of the castle, and provide accommodation for members of the chapel choir. When you leave the Lower Ward, be sure to admire the **King Henry VIII Gate**, the castle's main gate: built in 1511, its outer arch is decorated with a panel carved with the Tudor rose and the pomegranate emblem of Henry's first wife, Catherine of Aragon.

Windsor town and Windsor Great Park

Once you've seen the castle, you've covered just about everything worth seeing in Windsor, with the exception of the park (see below). The small network of cobbled streets to the south of the castle is too busy scrambling for every tourist pound to retain any quaintness, and the other so-called "attractions" are well worth skipping. More appealing is the town's **Guildhall**, with a delicate arcaded loggia designed by Wren. The story goes that the town authorities insisted that Wren's initial version, which was supported by only one line of columns, was unstable, so Wren duly added the central row, but placed a one-inch gap at the tops of the columns to prove his point. It was in the Guildhall that divorcés Prince Charles and Camilla Parker-Bowles had a civil marriage in 2005.

Windsor Great Park

At the far end of the Long Walk stands the gargantuan equestrian statue of George III, known as the **Copper Horse**, sculpted by Westmacott and erected by George IV – sixteen people had lunch inside the horse before it was placed on the plinth, or so the story goes. It was here at Windsor that George III lived

The Great Park is a mere fraction of the royal estate, since the Home Park, nearer to the castle, is off limits to the public except for **Frogmore House**, a secluded white-washed mansion at the centre of the Home Park, which can be visited on a few days each year (at least three days in mid-May; £3.50; plus Aug Bank Holiday; £5.50; no under-8s; ☎020/7321 2233). The house was built around 1680, but was bought by Queen Charlotte in the 1790s and converted for use as a royal retreat by architect James Wyatt. With the exception of the Green Pavilion, the decor of the rooms dates from the mid-nineteenth century, when the house was used by the Duchess of Kent, Queen Victoria's crabby mother. The last royal to use the place to any great extent was Queen Mary (of Dolls' House fame), who established a sort of family souvenir and bygones museum.

On the opposite side of the lake from Frogmore House lies the ornate, neo-Roman-esque **Royal Mausoleum**, built by Queen Victoria as a shrine to her husband, Albert, its interior awash with inlaid marble and gilded frescoes after Raphael. Centre stage is Baron Carlo Marochetti's grey granite double sarcophagus, topped by the recumbent marble figures of Victoria and Albert (both carved shortly after Albert's death in 1861). To the southwest of the mausoleum is a royal burial ground containing the graves of three of Victoria's children, plus sundry other royals, including the Duke and Duchess of Windsor (Edward VIII and Mrs Simpson).

out many of his last years, racked by "madness", subsequently diagnosed as por-phyria, a rare metabolic disorder, which gets its name from the purple-coloured urine that characterizes it. It was during one of his attacks at Windsor that George famously leapt from his carriage and addressed an oak tree, believing it to be the king of Prussia.

If you need a focus for your wandering, head for **Savill Garden** (daily: March–Oct 10am–6pm; Nov–Feb 10am–4pm; £3.50–5.50 depending on season; ⊛www.savillgarden.co.uk), a 35-acre patch of woodland on the park's southeastern boundary, a mile or so from the Copper Horse. Begun in 1932, this is one of the finest floral displays in and around London, with magnolias, rhododendrons and camellias galore, plus many other more unusual trees and shrubs. Adjacent, to the southwest, is **Smith's Lawn**, home of the Guards' Polo Club (⊛www.guardspoloclub.com), where you can watch the upper classes at leisure most weekends from May to September.

Eton

Crossing the bridge at the end of Thames Avenue in Windsor brings you to **Eton**, a one-street village lined with bookshops and antique dealers, but famous all over the world for **Eton College** (Easter, July & Aug daily 10.30am–4.30pm; after Easter to June & Sept daily 2–4.30pm; £3.80), a ten-minute walk from the river. When this, Britain's most aristocratic public school, was founded in 1440 by Henry VI, its aim was to give free education to seventy poor scholars and choristers – how times have changed. It would be easier to list Establishment figures who haven't been to Eton than vice versa – Percy Bysshe Shelley, George Orwell and Tony Benn are rare rebels in the roll call. This is the old school of many a Conservative cabinet; it also recently educated princes William and Harry.

Within the rarefied complex, the original fifteenth-century **schoolroom**, gnarled with centuries of graffiti, survives to the north of the first courtyard, but the real highlight is the **College Chapel**, a wonderful example of English perpendicular architecture completed in 1482. The fan vaulting, which was destroyed in the last war, has been completely reconstructed in concrete (though you'd never know from looking at it), but the most remarkable feature of the place is its medieval grisaille wall paintings, the finest in the country, which were whitewashed over by the Victorians and only uncovered in 1923. The small self-congratulatory **Museum of Eton Life** is well worth missing unless you've a fascination with flogging, fagging and bragging about the school's facilities and alumni. If you're thinking of going on a **guided tour** (Easter–Sept daily 2.15 & 3.15pm; £4.90; ☎01753/671177, ⊛www.etoncollege.com), ring ahead to make sure the school isn't closed for some special reason.

Listings

Listings

㉕

Accommodation

T here's no getting away from the fact that **accommodation** in London is expensive. Compared with most European cities, you pay over the odds in every category. The city's hostels are among the most costly in the world, while venerable institutions such as the *Ritz*, the *Dorchester* and the *Savoy* charge guests the very top international prices – from £300 per luxurious night. The city doesn't really have a **low season**, though things do slacken off a little in the months just after Christmas. Book far enough in advance, however, and you should be able to shave £30–50 off room rates at some of the better-healed hotels. You can also often get better rates if you book via the establishment's website.

The cheapest places to stay are the city's **campsites**, some of which also have dormitories, charging as little as £6 a night. A dorm bed in one of the numerous independent **hostels** will cost you double that, while for the official YHA hostels expect to pay upwards of £20. Even the most basic **B&Bs** struggle to bring their tariffs below £45 for a double with shared facilities, and you're more likely to find yourself paying £60 or more. For a decent **hotel** room, you shouldn't expect much change out of £100 a night.

In addition to hotels and B&Bs, there's a growing trend of **apartment complexes**, such as No. 5 Maddox Street, W1 (see p.444); Vancouver Studios, W2 (see p.451); and the King's Wardrobe in the City (see p.447) – suites of rooms including living, sleeping and kitchen areas with concierge and housekeeping facilities included in the rates. Like hotels, they can be booked by the night, but for the price they are generally of a higher standard than other accommodation in the same price band, and are particularly good value for families or groups. Most B&Bs and hotels are housed in former residential properties, which means that rooms tend to be on the small side, and only the more upmarket places have lifts. That said, even the most basic **rooms** tend to have TVs, tea- and coffee-making facilities and telephones, and breakfast is nearly always included in the price. Bear in mind that B&Bs vary widely in quality, from impersonal hostel-like options to comfortable rooms in a family home.

Although many of the places listed below can be booked out months in advance, the sheer size of London means that there's little chance of failing to find a room, even in midsummer, and the tube network makes accommodation in most of the satellite boroughs a feasible option.

We've given phone numbers and websites or email addresses where available for all our listed accommodation, but if you fail to find a bed in any of the places we've recommended, you could turn to one of the various **accommodation agencies**. All London tourist offices (listed on p.27) operate a room-booking service, for which a small fee is levied (they also take the first night's fee in advance).

There are **British Hotel Reservation Centre** (BHRC; Ⓦ www.bhrc.co.uk) desks at Heathrow arrivals terminal, and at both Heathrow underground stations (☎ 020/8564 8808 or 8564 8211), and at both terminals of Gatwick Airport (☎ 01293/502433); there are also four desks in and around Victoria: at the train station (☎ 020/7828 1027), coach station (☎ 020/7824 8232), underground station (☎ 020/7828 2262) and at 13 Grosvenor Gardens, SW1 (☎ 020/7828 2425). Most offices are open daily from 6am till midnight, and there's no booking fee.

You can also book for free **online** at Ⓦ www.londontown.com; payment is made directly to the hotel on checking out and they can offer discounts of up to fifty percent. Other useful websites include Ⓦ www.lastminute.com, Ⓦ www .hotelsengland.com and Ⓦ www.laterooms.com which has great deals if you book right at the last moment.

Where possible, accommodation options have been marked on the chapter maps.

Hostels, student halls and camping

London's seven Youth Hostel Association (YHA) hostels are generally the cleanest, most efficiently run hostels in the capital. However, they charge around fifty percent or more above the rates of private hostels, and tend to get booked up several months in advance. Curfews and character-building daily chores may have been abolished in YHA hostels, but they still exude an institutionalized wholesomeness that isn't to everyone's taste: dorms are segregated, and drinking and smoking are discouraged or forbidden. Members of any association affiliated to Hostelling International have automatic membership of the YHA; non-members can join at any of the hostels. Note that you can book a bed in advance with a credit card either by ringing individual hostels or by logging on to the main website, Ⓦ www.yha.org.uk.

At best, **independent hostels** offer facilities commensurate with those of the YHA but at a lower price and in a less restrictive atmosphere; on the whole, however, they tend to be a little tattier, with facilities that are less reliable. Still, a lot of people find the more relaxed atmosphere ample compensation for the less than salubrious environment. The **St Christopher's Inn** chain (Ⓦ www.st -christophers.co.uk), more often than not attached to a *Belushi's* bar, has six well-maintained hostels in the capital, while the **Astor chain** (Ⓦ www.astorhostels .com) now runs five options in the capital, exclusively for under-30s. A good website for booking independent hostels online is Ⓦ www.hostellondon.com.

Outside term-time, you also have the option of staying in **student halls of residence**. Prices are slightly higher than hostels because you usually get a room to yourself, and some locations are very central and attractive. The quality of the rooms varies enormously, but tends to be fairly basic. Rooms get booked up quickly, especially in July, and can be had on a B&B or self-catering basis – the quads are particularly good value for families.

Finally, London's **campsites** are all out on the perimeters of the city and for committed campers only. Pitches cost £2–4, plus a fee of around £4–6 per person per night, with reductions for children and during the winter months.

Throughout this hostels section, all **prices** quoted are per person for the cheapest beds available in high season or, if available, per room for the cheapest twin/double. Breakfast is not always included in the rate, but will usually only set you back a few pounds.

25

YHA hostels

City of London 36 Carter Lane, EC4 ☎020/7236 4965, ✉city@yha.org.uk; St Paul's tube. See map, p.182. Large 200-bed hostel in a superb location opposite St Paul's Cathedral. Some twins at £53.50 a room, but mostly 4- to 8-bed dorms for £17.20 per person. There's no kitchen, but has a café for lunch and dinner. No groups.

Earls Court 38 Bolton Gardens, SW5 ☎020/7373 7083, ✉earlscourt@yha.org.uk; Earl's Court tube. See map, p.298. Better than a lot of accommodation in Earl's Court, but only offering dorms of mostly 10 beds – the triple bunks take some getting used to. Kitchen, café and patio garden. No groups. £19.50.

Hampstead Heath 4 Wellgarth Rd, NW11 ☎020/8458 9054, ✉hampstead@yha.org .uk; Golders Green tube. See map, p.358. One of the biggest and best-appointed YHA hostels, with its own garden and the wilds of Hampstead Heath nearby. Rooms with 3–6 beds cost £20.40; family rooms with 2–5 beds are also available, starting at £35 for one adult and one child or £45 for two adults.

Holland House Holland Walk, W8 ☎020/7937 0748, ✇www.hollhse.btinternet.co.uk; Holland Park or High Street Kensington tube. See map, p.328. Idyllically situated in the wooded expanse of Holland Park and fairly convenient for the centre, this extensive hostel offers a decent kitchen and an inexpensive café, but tends to be popular with school groups. Dorms only (8–20 beds), at £21.60 per person.

Oxford Street 14 Noel St, W1 ☎020/7734 1618, ✉oxfordst@yha.org.uk; Oxford Circus or Tottenham Court Road tube. See map, p.116. The West End location and modest size (75 beds in rooms of 2, 3 and 4 beds) mean that this hostel tends to be full year-round. No children under 6, no groups, no café, but a large kitchen. From £22.60 per person.

Rotherhithe 20 Salter Rd, SE16 ☎020/7232 2114, ✉rotherhithe@yha.org.uk; Rotherhithe or Canada Water tube. See map, p.268. London's largest purpose-built hostel is located in Rotherhithe's Docklands area, which can feel a little out of things, but is well connected to central London and handy for the sights in the south and east of the city, such as the Tower of London and Greenwich. Often has space when more central places are full. Breakfast, packed lunch and evening meals available. Rooms have 2, 4, 6 or 10 beds and cost from £24.60 per person.

St Pancras 79–81 Euston Rd, NW1 ☎020/7388 9998, ✉stpancras@yha.org.uk; King's Cross or Euston tube. See map, p.144. Housed on six floors of a former police station, directly opposite the British Library, on the busy Euston Road. Beds cost £24.60 per person, and rooms are very clean, bright, triple-glazed and air-conditioned – some even have en-suite facilities. All doubles are en-suite and family rooms are available, all with TVs, from £50.50. No groups.

Private hostels

Ashlee House 261–265 Gray's Inn Rd, WC1 ☎020/7833 9400, ✇www.ashleehouse.co.uk; King's Cross tube. See map, p.144. Clean and friendly hostel in a converted office block near King's Cross station. Internet access, laundry and kitchen facilities are provided. Dorms, which vary in size from 4 to 16 beds, start at £16; there are also a few private singles and twins, starting at £25 per person. Breakfast is included.

Curzon House 158 Courtfield Gardens, SW5 ☎020/7373 6745, ✇www.curzonhousehotel

25

▲ City of London hostel

.co.uk; Gloucester Road tube. See map, p.298. Shared rooms (2-, 3-, 4-, and 8-bed) from just £16, including Continental breakfast and use of a small kitchen and TV lounge, with Internet access. Singles are available from £30, doubles from £44; discounts for longer stays.

Dean Court Hotel 57 Inverness Terrace, W2 ☎020/7229 2961, 🖷7727 1190; Bayswater or Queensway tube. See map, p.328. The first of several good-value but basic places along this street. Dorm beds available plus smaller rooms sleeping 2 to 4 people; 70 beds in total and all rooms have sinks. There's also a kitchen and TV room, and breakfast is included. Dorms £17, rooms from £40.

Generator Compton Place, off Tavistock Place, WC1 ☎020/7388 7666, 🖶www.the-generator .co.uk; Russell Square or Euston tube. See map, p.144. A huge, funky hostel, with over 800 beds, in a converted police barracks, tucked away down a cobbled street. The neon and UV lighting and post-industrial decor may not be to everyone's taste, but with prices starting at just £12.50 a night for a dorm bed and breakfast, this is without doubt the best bargain in this part of town. Facilities include Internet access, games rooms, movie nights, a bar open to residents only (till 2am) and a canteen serving buffet Continental breakfast (included in the room rate) and evening meals from just £3.50. Prices range from £35 for a single, £50 for a double and £60 for a triple. Dorms from £12.50 (12 beds) to £17 (4 beds).

Hyde Park Hostel 2–6 Inverness Terrace, W2 ☎020/7229 5101, 🖶www.astorhostels.com; Bayswater or Queensway tube. See map, p.328. Part of the Astor chain, this grandiose but shabby stucco mansion in Bayswater is situated very close to Hyde Park, with 278 beds (in 2- to 18-bed rooms, which feel pretty crowded), an Internet café, travel and job-search centres. From £11 per person, with reductions for longer stays.

Hyde Park Inn 48–50 Inverness Terrace, W2 ☎020/7229 0000, 🖶www.hydeparkinn.com; Bayswater or Queensway tube. See map, p.328. Cheap and cheerful place with 3- to 12-bed dorms, laundry facilities and Internet access. The larger dorms feel pretty cramped, but the smaller ones are still good value (from £9). Some twins (from £50) and singles (£24).

Leinster Inn 7–12 Leinster Square, W2 ☎020/7229 9641, 🖶www.astorhostels.com; Queensway or Notting Hill Gate tube. See map, p.328. With 360 beds, this is the biggest and liveliest of the Astor hostels, with a party atmosphere, and two bars open until the small hours. Some rooms in all categories have their own shower. Dorm beds (4–8 per room) £14–18 per person, singles £27.50, doubles from £45.

Museum Inn 27 Montague St, W1 ☎020/7580 5360, 🖶www.astorhostels.com; Holborn tube. See map, p.144. In a lovely Georgian house by the British Museum, this is the quietest of the Astor hostels. There's no bar, though it's still a sociable, laid-back place, and well situated. There are 75 beds in dorms of 4 to 10 for £16–20, plus some twins at £50, including breakfast. Decent-sized kitchen and TV lounge, also laundry and Internet access.

Pickwick Hall International Backpackers 7 Bedford Place, WC1 ☎020/7323 4958; Russell Square tube. See map, p.144. Most accommodation is in twin-bed rooms; 3- and 4-bed single-sex dorms are also available, not all of them en-suite. There's a sitting room with cable TV and Internet access, a dining room with kitchen facilities and a laundry. Continental breakfast included. Dorms £20; doubles and twins £44; singles £25.

Quest Hotel 45 Queensborough Terrace, W2 ☎020/7229 7782, 🖶www.astorhostels.com; Queensway tube. See map, p.328. Small, well-worn, but lively Astor hostel. Dorms with 4 to 9 beds from £14, including breakfast. The kitchen is well sized for the hostel's capacity and there's also a TV lounge and Internet access.

St Christopher's Village 161–165 Borough High St, SE1 ☎020/7407 1856, 🖶www.st-christophers .co.uk; London Bridge tube. See map, p.268. Flagship of a chain of independent hostels, with no fewer than three properties on Borough High Street (and branches in Camden, Greenwich and Shepherd's Bush). The decor is upbeat and cheerful, the place is efficiently run and there's a party-animal ambience, fuelled by the neighbouring bar and the rooftop hot tub and sauna. Beds in dorms of 4 to 14 £13–22, twins £44.

Victoria Hotel 71 Belgrave Rd, SW1 ☎020/7834 3077, 🖶www.astorhostels.com; Victoria tube. See map, p.60. One of the original Astor hostels, with the usual lively atmosphere

25

and jobs contacts, plus a great location for sights such as Tate Britain and Westminster Abbey. TV room and Internet access. Some twins (£50); dorms with 5 to 8 beds start at £16, including Continental breakfast. Caters to large groups.

🏃 **wake up! London** 1 Queens Gardens, W2, ☎020/7262 4471, ❀www.wakeuplondon .co.uk; Paddington or Lancaster Gate tube. See map, p.328. New and funky hostel with single-sex 4- to 8-bed dorms, singles and doubles (£50), and great facilities, including an information desk, 24hr reception and a basement bar (with a pool table) that's open daily till 3am. A good choice if you want a party atmosphere. Dorms from £15 (8-bed).

Student halls

Bankside House, London School of Economics (LSE) 24 Sumner St, SE1 ☎020/7633 9877 or 7955 7370, ❀www.lse.ac.uk/collections/vaca-tions; Southwark tube. See map, p.268. Virtually next door to Tate Modern, this place has good-quality singles (from £30), twins (£55), and quads (£74). With the exception of some singles, rooms are en-suite. Available July–Sept.

Carr-Saunders Hall, London School of Economics (LSE) 18–24 Fitzroy St, W1 ☎020/7574 5300 or 7955 7370, ❀www.lse.ac.uk/collections/ vacations; Warren Street tube. See map, p.116. North of Oxford Street, this place looks like nothing more than a 1970s office block. Inside, rooms are clean and comfortable. Twins (£46), some en-suite (£52), and singles (£28) only. Easter & July–Sept only.

Commonwealth Hall, London University 1–11 Cartwright Gardens, WC1 ☎020/7121 7000, ❀www.lon.ac.uk; Russell Square tube. See map, p.144. Basic doubles and singles in a postwar block to the north of Russell Square. Rooms have phones but no sinks, and there are kitchens, a bar and café, plus use of the local tennis courts. Easter & mid-June to mid-Sept. Advance booking neces-sary. From around £20 per person, including Continental breakfast, £25 half-board.

Francis Rowley Court, City University 16 Briset St, EC1 ☎020/7040 5500, ❀www.city .ac.uk/ems; Farringdon tube. See map, p.224. A modern building in trendy Clerkenwell, with self-catering singles from £32, with

TVs in every room and shared facilities throughout. Available year-round.

Great Dover Street Apartments, King's College 165 Great Dover St, SE1 ☎020/7484 1700, ❀www.kcl.ac.uk; Borough tube. See map, p.268. This Victorian building is not far from Bankside, and offers en-suite singles at £35, discounts for students and a shared kitchen. Available July–Sept.

Hampstead Campus, King's College Kidderpore Ave, NW3 ☎020/7435 3564, ❀www.kcl.ac.uk; Finchley Road tube. See map, p.358. A lit-tle tatty around the edges, but perennially popular, this place books up fast. Rooms are in a nice Victorian building on a tree-lined avenue, within walking distance of the Heath. Singles at £25 and twins at £40.50, all with shared facilities. July–Sept.

High Holborn Residence, London School of Economics (LSE) 178 High Holborn, WC1 ☎020/7379 5589 or 7955 7370, ❀www.lse .ac.uk/collections/vacations; Holborn tube. See map, p.174. Rooms in a modern block on this busy street; handy for the West End. Singles (£31), twins (£49), en-suite (£70) and triples (£80). Open July–Sept.

International Students House 229 Great Portland St, W1 ☎020/7631 8300, ❀www.ish .org.uk; Great Portland Street tube. See map, p.116. Hundreds of beds in a vast complex at the southern end of Regent's Park. Single (£33.50), twin (£51), triple (£61.50), quad (£74), and dorm rooms. Open all year.

Passfield Hall, London School of Economics (LSE) Endsleigh Place, WC1 ☎020/7387 7743 or 7955 7370, ❀www.lse.ac.uk/collections/vacations; Euston Square tube. See map, p.144. Compris-ing ten attractive, late-Georgian buildings at the northern reaches of Bloomsbury, Pass-field offers singles (£27) and twins (£48), all with shared facilities. Open July–Sept.

Stamford Street Apartments, King's College 127 Stamford St, SE1 ☎020/7484 1700, ❀www.kcl.ac.uk; Waterloo tube. See map, p.259. A purpose-built block close to the South Bank, with smart en-suite single rooms (£34) and a shared kitchen. July–Sept only.

Walter Sickert Hall, City University Graham Street, N1 ☎020/7040 8822, ❀www.city.ac.uk/ ems; Angel tube. See map, p.224. Just off City Road, this campus has single rooms with shared facilities from £32, upgraded singles with better decor and a TV (£40) plus en-suite twins from £60. Rates include break-fast. Rooms available year-round.

Wellington Hall, King's College 71 Vincent Square, SW1 ☎020/7484 4740, ⊛www.kcl.ac.uk; Victoria tube. See map, p.60. Singles from £30 and twins from £50, all with shared facilities; breakfast is included in the price. Available July–Sept.

Campsites

Abbey Wood Federation Rd, Abbey Wood, SE2 ☎020/8311 7708; Abbey Wood train station from Charing Cross or London Bridge. Enormous, well-equipped Caravan Club site, ten miles southeast of central London. Open all year.

Crystal Palace Crystal Palace Parade, SE19 ☎020/8778 7155; Crystal Palace train station from Victoria or London Bridge. All-year Caravan Club site; some traffic noise.

Lea Valley Leisure Centre Caravan Park Meridian Way, N9 ☎020/8803 6900; Ponders End train station from Liverpool Street. Well-equipped site, situated behind the leisure centre at Pickett's Lock, backing onto a vast reservoir.

Hotels and B&Bs

The following listings indicate some of London's best-value hotels and B&Bs, from palatial establishments patronized by royalty, statesmen and celebs to budget-bracket B&Bs.

The bulk of the recommendations cost between £50 and £100 a double, though a few are considerably more expensive. During the week, the plush hotels tend to charge £300 and over, exclusive of VAT and breakfast. However, when the business types have gone home at the **weekend**, these same places slash their advertised rates to around £200, sometimes even less, with breakfast thrown in, too. Prices given are for the **cheapest double room** during high season (usually, Easter, June–August and Christmas).

Most places take all major **credit cards**, particularly Visa and Access/Master-Card, so in the listings we've simply noted those that don't.

Victoria

The streets south and west of Victoria station harbour dozens of inexpensive and often pretty shabby B&Bs – notably along Belgrave Road and Ebury Street. This area is pretty dead in the evening, but it's generally better value than Earl's Court, is within easy striking distance of the West End, and is very convenient for those taking Continental trains or buses around Britain. Unless otherwise stated, Victoria is the nearest tube.

🏃 **B&B Belgravia** 64–66 Ebury St, SW1 ☎020/7823 4928, ⊛www.bb-belgravia.com.

See map, p.60. A real rarity in this neck of the woods – a B&B with flair, very close to the train and coach station. The 17 rooms are of boutique-hotel quality, with original cornicing and large sash windows and have stylish modern touches – all

▲ B&B Belgravia

25

have flatscreen TVs and funky bathrooms with mosaic tiling. Communal spaces are light and similarly well designed, and staff are welcoming and enthusiastic. Internet access. £94.

Elizabeth Hotel 37 Eccleston Square, SW1 ☏020/7828 6812, ⊛www.elizabeth-hotel.com. See map, p.60. Comfortable old-fashioned hotel, two blocks south of Victoria station and providing mostly en-suites at a decent price. Large TV lounge, and the gardens and tennis courts of Eccleston Square can be used by hotel residents. £98.

James & Cartref House 108 Ebury St, SW1 ☏020/7730 7338 & 129 Ebury St, SW1 ☏020/7730 6167; ⊛www.jamesandcartref .co.uk. See map, p.60. Two clean Georgian B&Bs situated opposite one another, and run by the same owners. Fresh and bright en-suite rooms and ones with shared facilities available. £70.

Luna & Simone Hotel 47–49 Belgrave Rd, SW1 ☏020/7834 5897, ⊛www.lunasimonehotel .com. See map, p.60. Inexpensive B&B with a bright foyer, friendly staff and plain well-maintained rooms with TVs and telephones, most en-suite. Internet access. £75.

Morgan House 107 & 120 Ebury St, SW1 ☏020/7730 2384, ⊛www.morganhouse.co.uk. See map, p.60. An above-average B&B, run by a vivacious couple. Great breakfasts, patio garden, and a fridge for guests to use. Most rooms are en-suite. £66.

Oxford House Hotel 92–94 Cambridge St, SW1 ☏020/7834 6467, ☏7834 0225. See map, p.60. Probably the best-value rooms in the vicinity of Victoria station, though not otherwise distinguished. Showers and toilets are shared, but kept pristine, and full English breakfast is included in the price. £45.

Sanctuary House Hotel 33 Tothill St, SW1 ☏020/7799 4044, ⊛www.fullershotels.co.uk; St James's Park tube. See map, p.60. Run by Fuller's Brewery, situated above a Fuller's pub, and decked out like one too, in gaudy pseudo-Victoriana. Breakfast is extra, and is served in the pub, but the location right by St James's Park is terrific. Ask about the weekend deals. £135.

St James's, Mayfair and Marylebone

St James's and Mayfair contain few choices for lesser mortals. Marylebone is more mixed, with a range of places

on and around Gloucester Place, a convenient but traffic-clogged street running between Regent's Park and Oxford Street.

Brown's 30–34 Albemarle St, W1 ☏020/7493 6020, ⊛www.brownshotel.com; Green Park tube. See map, p.96. An ever-popular, traditionally English hotel situated in Mayfair and dating from the coronation of Queen Victoria, Brown's is renowned as one of the best in its class. It has recently undergone a massive restoration, but rosewood, antiques, stained glass and other fine period details still set the tone. Prices from £375.

Claridge's Brook St, W1 ☏020/7629 8860, ⊛www.savoy-group.com; Bond Street tube. See map, p.96. This famous and glamorous Art Deco Mayfair hotel is the chosen abode of visiting heads of state and media megastars. Twins and doubles start at over £350, but for this you get wardrobes bigger than most bathrooms, showerheads the size of dinner plates and decor as plush as any vacationing potentate could wish for. Gordon Ramsay's Michelin-starred restaurant serves up wonderful modern European cuisine.

The Dorchester 54 Park Lane, W1 ☏020/7629 8888, ⊛www.dorchesterhotel.com; Hyde Park Corner tube. See map, p.96. Rooms here start at around £300 (not including tax and breakfast), for which you get luxuries such as individual buzzers for valet, waiter or maid, and huge bathrooms. Most of the suites overlook Hyde Park, but the hotel won't guarantee park views. Superb British cuisine in the *Grill Room*, afternoon tea amid the marble columns of the *Promenade*, and the *Bar* provides light Italian meals, cocktails and jazz in the evenings. There's also a fabulously equipped spa and gym.

Dorset Square Hotel 39 Dorset Square, NW1 ☏020/7723 7874, ⊛www.slh.com/dorsetsquare; Baker Street or Marylebone tube. See map, p.107. Beautifully appointed on a Marylebone garden square, this relaxing hotel has cheery Regency town-house decor, comfortable doubles and a restaurant in the basement. Breakfast not included. £210.

Durrants Hotel George St, W1 ☏020/7935 8131, ⊛www.durrantshotel.co.uk; Bond Street tube. See map, p.107. Just round the corner from the Wallace Collection and Oxford Street, this Georgian terrace hotel first opened in 1790, and has been run by the same family

25

since 1921. Inside, it's a great exercise in period-piece nostalgia, with doormen, lots of wood panelling and old prints. £165.

Edward Lear Hotel 28–30 Seymour St, W1 ⏀020/7402 5401; Marble Arch tube. See map, **p.107.** Lear's former home enjoys a great location close to Oxford Street and Hyde Park, lovely flower boxes and a plush foyer. Rooms themselves need a bit of a make-over, but the low prices reflect both this and the fact that most only have shared facilities. £66.50.

Hotel La Place 17 Nottingham Place, W1 ⏀020/7486 2323, ⏀www.hotellaplace.com; Baker Street tube. See map, p.107. Just off busy Marylebone Road, this is a small, good-value if rather old-fashioned place; rooms are en-suite and comfortably furnished. £118.

Lincoln House Hotel 33 Gloucester Place, W1 ⏀020/7486 7630, ⏀www.lincoln-house-hotel.co.uk; Marble Arch or Baker Street tube. See map, p.107. Dark wood panelling gives this Georgian B&B in Marylebone a ship's-cabin feel, while all the rooms are en-suite and well equipped. Rates vary according to the size of the bed and length of stay. £79.

The Metropolitan Old Park Lane, W1 ⏀020/7447 1000, ⏀www.metropolitan.co.uk; Green Park or Hyde Park Corner tube. See map, p.96. This terrifyingly trendy hotel near the *Hilton* adheres to the current fad for pared-down minimalism. The Japanese restaurant, *Nobu*, is outstanding, and the famous *Met* bar is members- and residents-only in the evenings. Doubles from around £300.

No. 5 Maddox Street 5 Maddox St, W1 ⏀020/7647 0200, ⏀www.no5maddoxst.com; Oxford Street tube. See map, p.96. With a very discreet entrance, this complex of apartments is all bamboo flooring and trendy minimalist decor. Suites have open fireplaces, workstations, TVs, kitchens and decked balconies, and Muji foldaway bikes are available for guests' use, too. £350.

Palace Hotel 31 Great Cumberland Place, W1 ⏀020/7262 5585; Marble Arch tube. See map, **p.107.** Small but luxurious hotel close to Marble Arch which oozes class, from the hand-painted friezes on the staircase to the four-poster beds in many of the rooms. Continental breakfast included. £70.

The Ritz 150 Piccadilly, W1 ⏀020/7300 2308, ⏀www.theritzhotel.co.uk; Green

Park tube. See map, p.96. In a class of its own among London's hotels, with its extravagant Louis XVI interiors and overall air of decadent luxury. Rooms, which start at around £350 for a double, maintain the opulent French theme, with the west-facing accommodation, overlooking Green Park, in greatest demand. Ask about the special weekend packages, including breakfast and champagne, available throughout the year.

The Stafford Hotel 16–18 St James's Place, SW1 ⏀020/7493 0111, ⏀www.thestafford hotel.co.uk; Green Park tube. See map, p.84. Tucked in a quiet backstreet off St James's Street, *The Stafford* provides high-class rooms in the main building from £230, with more expensive accommodation in the unique Carriage House, a row of eighteenth-century stables luxuriously converted to large guest rooms. The hotel also offers refined dining rooms, while the sporty *American Bar* and its courtyard terrace make a welcome change from the gentlemen's-club norm.

Wigmore Court Hotel 23 Gloucester Place, W1 ⏀020/7935 0928, ⏀www.wigmore-court-hotel.co.uk; Marble Arch or Baker Street tube. See map, p.107. The ruched curtains and floral decor may not be to everyone's taste, but this Georgian town-house in Marylebone is a better-than-average B&B, boasting a high tally of returning clients. Comfortable rooms with en-suite facilities, plus two cheaper doubles with shared facilities. Unusually, there's also a laundry and basic kitchen for guests' use. £89.

Soho, Fitzrovia, Covent Garden and the Strand

Booking into a hotel in Soho or Covent Garden puts you right in the centre of the West End. Hotels tend to be pricey, with just one or two choice places coming in at under £100 a double. Fitzrovia, the area just north of Oxford Street and east of Marylebone, is a little cheaper; while the Strand, very busy with traffic, but offering superb river views from the buildings on its south side, is home to one of the city's most famous luxury hotels, the *The Savoy*.

Charlotte Street Hotel 15–17 Charlotte St, W1 ⏀020/7806 2000, ⏀www.firmdalehotels.com; Goodge Street or Tottenham Court Road tube. **See map, p.116.** Smart but comfortable town-house hotel just north of Oxford Street. Rooms are sumptuously decorated, but resolutely modern in style, with en-suite granite bathrooms complete with, of all things, digital TVs, and retro-style Roberts radios at the bedsides. Doubles from £270.

Covent Garden Hotel 10 Monmouth St, WC2 ⊕020/7806 1000, ✪www.firmdalehotels.com; **Covent Garden tube. See map, p.158.** Stylish conversion of a former French hospital in the heart of the West End. Rooms, which start at around £300 a double, are all stylishly and individually decorated in luxurious and striking furnishings. All mod cons including stereo, video and fax. Bar and brasserie on the ground floor.

The Fielding Hotel 4 Broad Court, Bow St, WC2 ⊕020/7836 8305, ✪www.the-fielding-hotel.co.uk; **Covent Garden tube. See map, p.158.** Quietly and perfectly situated on a traffic-free and gas-lit court, this excellent hotel is one of Covent Garden's hidden gems. Its en-suite rooms are a firm favourite with visiting performers, since it's just a few yards from the Royal Opera House. Breakfast is extra. £100.

Hazlitt's 6 Frith St, W1 ⊕020/7434 1771, ✪www.hazlittshotel.com; **Tottenham Court Road tube. See map, p.116.** Located off the south side of Soho Square, this early eighteenth-century building is a hotel of real character and charm, offering en-suite rooms decorated and furnished as close to period style as convenience and comfort allow. There's a small sitting room, but no dining room (although some of London's best restaurants are a stone's throw away); Continental breakfast (served in the rooms) is available, but isn't included in the rates. £205.

Manzi's 1–2 Leicester St, WC2 ⊕020/7734 0224, ✪www.manzis.co.uk; **Leicester Square tube. See map, p.116.** Set over the Italian and seafood restaurant of the same name, *Manzi's* is one of the very few West End hotels in this price range, although noise might prove to be a nuisance. Continental breakfast is included in the price. £83.

One Aldwych 1 Aldwych, WC2 ⊕020/7300 1000, ✪www.onealdwych.com; **Covent Garden or Temple tube. See map, p.158.** On the outside, this is one of London's few vaguely Art Nouveau buildings, built in 1907 for the *Morning Post*. However, little survives from those days, as the interior of this desper-

ately fashionable luxury hotel firmly follows the minimalist trend. The draws now are the underwater music in the hotel's vast pool, the oodles of modern art about the place and the TVs in the bathrooms of the £335-plus rooms, though check the website for special deals.

St Martin's Lane 45 St Martin's Lane, WC2 ⊕020/7300 5500, ✪www.morganshotelgroup.com; **Leicester Square tube. See map, p.116.** This self-consciously chic "boutique hotel" with a bafflingly anonymous glassed facade is a big hit with the media crowd. The *Light Bar* is the most startling of the hotel's eating and drinking outlets. Rooms currently start at around £250 a double, but rates come down at the weekend.

Sanderson 50 Berners St, W1 ⊕020/7300 1400, ✪www.sandersonhotel.com; **Tottenham Court Road or Oxford Circus tube. See map, p.116.** Set in a listed 1960s Fitzrovia office block. The usual assemblage of objets d'art peppers the white-and-magnolia lobby and the *Long Bar* is all translucent backlit onyx but, like the restaurant, is ludicrously overpriced. 3D "space" lifts take you to the equally bright white rooms (starting at around £280 a double). There's a large gym, steam room, sauna and health club on site.

The Savoy 1 Savoy Hill, Strand, WC2 ⊕020/7836 4343, ✪www.the-savoy.com; **Charing Cross tube. See map, p.158.** Popular with business people and politicians, *The Savoy* is a byword for luxury and service, though in some respects the charisma of the place is what keeps it ahead of many of its rivals. Rooms, which start at around £229 a double (special deals and weekend rates can bring prices down), are decorated in the Art Deco style of the hotel's heyday or in a more classical vein. The *Grill* is justly famed for its excellent cuisine, while the *American Bar* features jazz every night. Breakfasts and afternoon teas are served on the Thames Foyer, which peers through trees onto the river.

Seven Dials Hotel 7 Monmouth St, WC2 ⊕020/7681 0791; ✪www.smoothhound.co.uk/ hotels/sevendials; **Covent Garden tube. See map, p.158.** Pleasant family-run hotel in the heart of theatreland. All rooms are en-suite and have TV, tea/coffee-making facilities and direct-dial phones. £65.

Soho Hotel 4 Richmond Mews, W1 ⊕020/7559 3000, ✪www.sohohotel.com; **Tottenham Court Road tube. See map, p.116.** An ex-NCP

25

car park made over by designer-of-the-moment Kit Kemp. No two areas are the same and the result is eclecticism bordering on schizophrenia, from the Oriental lobby to the camp fuchsia boudoirs and a screening room done out in fake fur and scarlet leather. The penthouse suites (£795 a night anyone?) have wonderful wraparound terraces and rooftop views, and the facilities are, as you'd expect, top-notch. £275.

Waldorf Hilton Aldwych, WC2 ☏020/7836 2400, ⓦ www.lemeridien.com; Holborn or Temple tube. See map, p.158. A stay in the serenely luxurious and recently modernized Edwardian-era *Waldorf* is a memorable experience. The hotel's centrepiece is the Palm Court, which still stages tea dances every Sunday. Published rates start at £279.

Bloomsbury

Bloomsbury is handy for the British Museum and the West End – Oxford Street and Covent Garden are no more than ten minutes' walk away. Unfortunately, the main area for B&Bs is Gower Street, which is plagued by traffic, so make sure you get a room overlooking the gardens at the back. Cartwright Gardens, further north and east, is a much quieter Georgian crescent, and all the B&Bs here have use of the nearby tennis courts. Note that virtually all the hotels in the seedy neighbourhood opposite King's Cross station, north of Bloomsbury, cater for the homeless on welfare.

The Academy Hotel 21 Gower St, WC1 ☏020/7631 4115, ⓦ www.etontownhouse.com; Goodge Street or Tottenham Court Road tube. See map, p.144. Smart if rather chintzy place popular with business folk. Service is excellent, all rooms are air-conditioned, with luxurious bathrooms, and there are two lovely patio gardens to enjoy. £164.

The Arosfa Hotel 83 Gower St, WC1 ☏020/7636 2115, ⓦ www.arosfalondon.com; Goodge Street or Euston Square tube. See map, p.144. Well-maintained, simple B&B with en-suite rooms. Plain furnishings, TVs in all the rooms, with tea and coffee facilities in the lounge area, and a small garden out back. £66.

Hotel Cavendish 75 Gower St, WC1 ☏020/7636 9079, ⓦ www.hotelcavendish.com; Goodge Street tube. See map, p.144. A real bargain, with lovely owners and a walled garden. All rooms have shared facilities, and there are some good-value family rooms, too. £48.

Crescent Hotel 49–50 Cartwright Gardens, WC1 ☏020/7387 1515, ⓦ www.crescenthoteloflondon .com; Euston, King's Cross or Russell Square tube. See map, p.144. Comfortable and clean B&B, with pink furnishings. All doubles are en-suite, but there are a few bargain singles with shared facilities. £93.

Harlingford Hotel 61–63 Cartwright Gardens, WC1 ☏020/7387 1551, ⓦ www.harlingfordhotel .com; Euston or Russell Square tube. See map, p.144. Another good option in this fine Georgian crescent. All rooms are en-suite with TV, the lounge has a real fire, and the breakfast room is bright and cheery. £99.

myhotel 11–13 Bayley St, Bedford Square, WC1 ☏020/7667 6000, ⓦ www.myhotels.co.uk; Tottenham Court Road tube. See map, p.144. The aquarium in the lobby is the telltale sign that this is a feng shui hotel. Despite the positive vibes and Conran-designed look, the double-glazed, air-conditioned rooms are on the small side for the price. Still, there's a gym, a very pleasant library, a restaurant attached, and the location is great for the West End. £270.

Ridgemount Private Hotel 65–67 Gower St, WC1 ☏020/7636 1141, ⓦ www.ridgemounthotel .co.uk; Goodge Street tube. See map, p.144. Old-fashioned, very friendly, family-run place, with small rooms, half with shared facilities, a garden, free hot-drinks machine and a laundry service. A reliable, basic bargain for Bloomsbury. £52.

Hotel Russell Russell Square, WC1 ☏020/7837 6470, ⓦ www.principal-hotels.com; Russell Square tube. See map, p.144. From its grand 1898 exterior to its opulent interiors of marble, wood and crystal, this late-Victorian landmark fully retains its period atmosphere in all its public areas. The rooms live up to the grandeur of the lobby, if not necessarily to its style. Expensive, but various deals are available; check their website. Breakfast is not included. £229.

Thanet Hotel 8 Bedford Place, WC1 ☏020/7636 2869, ⓦ www.thanethotel.co.uk; Russell Square tube. See map, p.144. Small, friendly, family-run B&B close to the British Museum. Rooms are clean, bright and freshly decorated, all with en-suite showers and tea- and coffee-making facilities. £98.

Clerkenwell, the City, Docklands and Whitechapel and Spitalfields

Hotels are few and far between in **Clerkenwell** and, until recently, nonexistent in the **City** and **Docklands**, except within the vicinity of City Airport. However, with areas on the edge of the City, like Clerkenwell, Hoxton and Brick Lane, now replete with bars and restaurants, this is not a bad place to stay.

City Hotel 12 Osborn St, E1 ☎020/7247 3313, ⊕www.cityhotellondon.co.uk; Aldgate East tube. See map, p.235. Spacious and clean, this modern hotel stands on the eastern edge of the City, in the heart of the Bengali East End at the bottom of Brick Lane. The plainly decorated rooms are all en-suite, and many have kitchens, too; 4-person rooms are a bargain for families or small groups. £85.

Four Seasons Hotel Canary Wharf 46 Westferry Circus, E14 ☎020/7510 1999, ⊕www.fourseasons.com; Canary Wharf tube and DLR. See map, p.248. A spectacular riverfront setting, ultra-modern interiors and good links to the City have made this hotel very popular with business folk, but weekend rates, which bring prices down, mean that it's an equally good base for sightseeing. Pool, fitness centre, spa and tennis courts. Several rooms (special offers from £210; £185 at weekends) have superb Thames views. There's also the option of taking a boat into town. £330.

Great Eastern Hotel Liverpool Street, EC2 ☎020/7618 5010, ⊕www.great-eastern-hotel.co.uk; Liverpool Street tube. See map, p.182. This venerable late-nineteenth-century station hotel had a complete Conran makeover, yet manages to retain much of its old-world clubby flavour. The *George* pub boasts a superb mock-Tudor ceiling; the rooms themselves are tastefully furnished; and the fabulous old lobby is now the *Aurora* restaurant. There are three other flash eating options: *Fishmarket*, *Miyabi* and a brasserie, *Terminus*. Doubles start at around £200, but rates are cut at the weekend. £285.

International Hotel Marsh Wall, E14 ☎020/7712 0100, ⊕www.britanniahotels.co.uk; Canary Wharf tube or South Quay DLR. See map, p.248. Within walking distance of Canary Wharf (and thus good transport links south and west as well as into the business district), this is a classic, anonymous, mid-range business hotel. Weekday rates are aimed at the business-account end of the market, but weekend deals and last-minute offers bring prices down considerably. From £99.

Jurys Inn 60 Pentonville Rd, N1 ☎020/7282 5500, ⊕www.jurys.com; Angel tube. See map, p.224. This modern Irish chain hotel is decorated to a high, if bland, standard and geared up for business folk. Located on busy Pentonville Road, close to Angel tube, it's equally convenient for the City and for Islington's and Clerkenwell's trendy bars and restaurants. Service is very friendly, and the fixed room-rate is a bargain for three adults sharing or for those with kids. £134.

The King's Wardrobe 6 Wardrobe Place, Carter Lane, EC4 ☎020/7792 2222, ⊕www.bridgestreet.com; St Paul's tube. See map, p.182. In a quiet courtyard just behind St Paul's Cathedral, this place is part of an international chain that caters largely for a business clientele. The apartments (1- to 3-bed) offer fully equipped kitchens and workstations, a concierge service and housekeeping. Though housed in a fourteenth-century building that once contained Edward III's royal regalia, the interior is unrelentingly modern. £130–160 per night per apartment.

The Rookery 12 Peter's Lane, Cowcross St, EC1 ☎020/7336 0931, ⊕www.rookeryhotel.com; Farringdon tube. See map, p.224. Rambling Georgian town-house on the edge of the City in trendy Clerkenwell that makes a fantastically discreet little hideaway. The rooms start at £245 a double; each one has been individually designed in a deliciously camp, modern take on the Baroque period, and all have super bathrooms with lots of character.

▲ The Rookery

Threadneedles 5 Threadneedle St, EC2 ☎020/7657 8080, ⊛www.etontownhouse .com; Bank tube. See map, p.182. Magnificent former Midland Bank in the heart of the financial district, now converted into the City's first boutique hotel, with every mod con from plasma TV screens to cordless digital telephones. Rooms start at £296 a standard double, but prices often drop below £200 on the weekend.

Zetter Hotel 86–88 Clerkenwell Rd, EC1 ☎020/ 7324 4444, ⊛www.thezetter.com; Farringdon tube. See map, p.224 A warehouse converted with real style and a dash of Sixties glamour. Rooms are simple and minimalist, with fun touches such as lights which change colour and decorative floral panels; ask for a room at the back, overlooking quiet cobbled St John's Square. The attached restaurant serves good modern Italian food, and water for guests is supplied from the *Zetter's* own well, beneath the building. £158.

The South Bank and Southwark

With the resurgence of the South Bank, thanks to the London Eye and Tate Modern, various chain hotels have moved in, and the choices generally are increasing. Neighbouring Southwark and Bankside are also on the up, with a thriving café scene and the additional enticement of Borough food market.

London Bridge Hotel 8–18 London Bridge St, SE1 ☎020/7855 2200, ⊛www.london -bridgehotel.co.uk; London Bridge tube. See map, p.268. Perfectly placed for Southwark and Bankside or the City, this is a tastefully smart hotel right by the station. As it attracts a mainly business clientele, rates go down considerably at the weekend. £159.

London County Hall Travel Inn Belvedere Road, SE1 ☎0870/2383 330, ⊛www.premiertravelinn .com; Waterloo or Westminster tube. See map, p.259. Don't expect river views at these prices, but the location in County Hall itself is pretty good if you're up for a bit of sightseeing. Decor and ambience are functional, but for those with kids, the flat-rate rooms are a bargain. £89.95 (cheaper weekend rates).

Mad Hatter 3–7 Stamford St, SE1 ☎020/7401 9222, ⊛www.fullershotels.co.uk; Southwark or Blackfriars tube. See map, p.268. Situated above a Fuller's pub on the corner of Blackfriars Road, and run by the Fuller's

Brewery. Breakfast is extra on weekdays, and is served in the pub, but this is a great location, a short walk from Tate Modern and the South Bank. Ask about the weekend deals. £125.

Marriott London County Hall Hotel County Hall, SE1 ☎020/7928 5200, ⊛www.marriott. com; Waterloo or Westminster tube. See map, p.259. Historic County Hall, once home to London's government, stands right on the river with over three-quarters of its rooms offering river views, many with small balconies. Prices are from £280. It's all suitably pompous inside, and there's a full-sized indoor pool and well-equipped gym.

Mercure 71–79 Southwark St SE1 ☎020/7902 0800, ⊛www.mercure.com; Southwark tube. See mpa, p.268. A modern and comfortable if rather bland option, in an unbeatable location just a stone's throw from Tate Modern. The gym is free for guests. £165.

Southwark Rose Hotel 43–47 Southwark Bridge Rd, SE1 ☎020/7015 1480, ⊛www. southwarkrosehotel.co.uk; London Bridge tube. See map, p.268 The *Southwark Rose* markets itself as a budget hotel with boutique style; nice design touches raise the rooms several notches above the bland chain hotels in the area. Giant aluminium lamps hover over the lobby, which is lined with funky photographs, while the penthouse restaurant offers breakfast with a rooftop view and free Internet access. £120.

Knightsbridge, Kensington and Chelsea

Adjoining Victoria to the west, the fashionable areas of Belgravia, Knightsbridge and Kensington are full of hotels catering for the sort of customers who can afford to shop in Harrods and other local stores, but there is a scattering of small, independent hotels offering good value for this exclusive neighbourhood. Average prices are slightly lower in South Kensington (site of the Victoria and Albert, Natural History and Science museums), and further south in Chelsea.

Abbey House 11 Vicarage Gate, W8 ☎020/7727 2594, ⊛www.abbeyhousekensington.com; High Street Kensington tube. See map, p.328. Inexpensive Victorian B&B in a quiet street just north of Kensington High Street, maintained to a very high standard by its attentive owners. Rooms are large and bright – prices are kept down by sharing facilities. Full English breakfast, with free tea and coffee available all day. Cash only. £74.

Aster House 3 Sumner Place, SW7 ☏020/7581 5888, ✆www.asterhouse .com; South Kensington tube. See map, p.298. Pleasant, non-smoking and award-winning B&B in a luxurious South Ken white-stuccoed street; there's a lovely garden at the back and a large conservatory, where breakfast is served. Singles with shared facilities start at around £90 a night. Doubles from £140.

Blakes Hotel 33 Roland Gardens, SW7 ☏020/7370 6701, ✆www.blakeshotels.com; Gloucester Road tube. See map, p.298. Blakes' dramatic interior – designed by Anouska Hempel – and glamorous suites have long attracted visiting celebs. A faintly Raffles-esque flavour pervades, with bamboo furniture and old travelling trunks mixing with unusual objects, tapestries and prints. Doubles from £275 are smart but small, the restaurant and bar are excellent, and service is of a very high standard. Singles from £170.

Eden Plaza Hotel 68–69 Queen's Gate, SW7 ☏020/7370 6111, ✆www.crystalhotels.co.uk; Gloucester Road tube. See map, p.298. Part of a fast-growing budget-hotel chain catering for business and leisure clients. Rooms (sleeping up to 4) are small, modern, en-suite and brightly furnished, and there's a bistro and bar on the ground floor; breakfast is included. £85.

Five Sumner Place 5 Sumner Place, SW7 ☏020/7584 7586, ✆www.sumnerplace.com; South Kensington tube. See map, p.298. Discreetly luxurious B&B in one of South Ken's prettiest white-stuccoed terraces. All rooms are en-suite and breakfast is served in the house's delightful conservatory. £130.

The Gore 189 Queen's Gate, SW7 ☏020/7584 6601, ✆www.gorehotel.com; South Kensington, Gloucester Road or High Street Kensington tube. See map, p.298. Popular, privately owned century-old hotel, awash with Oriental rugs, rich mahogany, walnut panelling and other Victoriana. A pricey but excellent bistro restaurant adds to its allure, and it's only a step away from Hyde Park. Rooms, some with four-poster beds, from £190.

The Halkin 5 Halkin St, SW1 ☏020/7333 1000, ✆www.halkin.co.uk; Hyde Park Corner tube. See map, p.298. A luxury hotel that spurns the chintzy country-house theme: elegant, Italian-influenced minimalism prevails in each of the 41 rooms, which cost from £300. The contemporary theme is continued in the cuisine of the restaurant, which offers a mainly Thai menu, served in a room that overlooks a private garden.

Hotel 167 167 Old Brompton Rd, SW5 ☏020/7373 3221, ✆www.hotel167.com; Gloucester Road tube. See map, p.298. Small, stylishly furnished B&B with en-suite facilities, double glazing and a fridge in all rooms. Continental buffet-style breakfast is served in the attractive morning room/reception. £100.

The Lanesborough Hyde Park Corner, SW1 ☏020/7259 5599, ✆www.lanesborough.com; Hyde Park Corner tube. See map, p.298. A former hospital, this early nineteenth-century building has been meticulously restored in Regency style, with all mod cons hidden amid the ornate decor. Proudly offering the most exclusive (read expensive) rooms in London, *The Lanesborough* offers "basic" doubles from £480 and suites for up to a staggering £5000-plus a night.

The Milestone Hotel and Apartments 1 Kensington Court, W8 ☏020/7917 1000, ✆www.redcarnationhotels.com; High Street Kensington tube. See map, p.328. Luxury hotel, situated in two adjoining nineteenth-century town-houses overlooking Kensington Palace and Gardens. Sumptuously decorated in period style, this place feels more like a stately home than a hotel. All mod cons, gym and sauna, too, plus conference facilities. Doubles from around £300.

Number Sixteen 16 Sumner Place, SW7 ☏020/7589 5232, ✆www.numbersixteenhotel .co.uk; South Kensington tube. See map, p.298. A plush but relaxed boutique hotel, prettily furnished in shades of blue, lilac and grey. Rooms are individually decorated and include some singles. Food is served in the light, modern conservatory, which looks onto a secluded garden, where you can dine on wrought-iron chairs under the trees. £170.

Vicarage Private Hotel 10 Vicarage Gate, W8 ☏020/7229 4030, ✆www.londonvicaragehotel .com; Notting Hill Gate or High Street Kensington tube. See map, p.298. Ideally located B&B a step away from Hyde Park. Clean and smart floral rooms with shared facilities, and a full English breakfast included in the rates. Cash or travellers' cheques only. £78.

(25)

Earl's Court

Tariffs take a drastic dive to the west of Kensington in Earl's Court, a network of Victorian terraced streets that's become a recognized backpackers' ghetto. Very few establishments are worth staying in for reasons other than cheapness, but there's a huge concentration of run-of-the-mill B&Bs, some offering dormitory-style accommodation. Earl's Court Road, which bisects this area, is a lively place, full of late-night supermarkets, cheap cafés, gay bars, fast-food joints, money-exchange booths and laundries. The nearest tube for the following places is Earl's Court.

Mayflower Hotel 26–28 Trebovir Rd, SW5 ☏020/7370 0991, ⊛www.mayflower -group.co.uk. See map, p.328. In a street of bog-standard B&Bs, this is a real winner, decked out in bold warm colours and strewn with Indian antiques; there's a stylish water feature in reception and parrots in the lounge. Rooms are en-suite, comfortable and appealing. Singles from £60, and there are also apartments (£130), which are economical if you're in a group. £120.

Merlyn Court Hotel 2 Barkston Gardens, SW5 ☏020/7370 1640, ⊛www.s-h-systems. co.uk/hotels/merlyncourt.html. See map, p.328. Well-appointed and popular B&B in a quiet leafy street close to the tube. Some rooms with en-suite facilities; English breakfast is included. £50.

Paddington, Bayswater and Notting Hill

There's a lot of inexpensive if pretty mundane accommodation in and around Paddington station, especially along Sussex Gardens and in Norfolk Square, where small hotels and B&Bs outnumber residential homes. Proximity to Hyde Park is an added bonus here and in Bayswater, further west. Prices begin to rise, and the choices are more characterful and interesting, in neighbouring Notting Hill, which harbours a faintly bohemian community, as exemplified by the Portobello Road Market.

Ashley Hotel 15 Norfolk Square, W2 ☏020/7723 3375, ⊛www.ashleyhotels.com; Paddington tube. See map, p.328. Three long-established hotels joined into one, just a couple of minutes' walk from Paddington station. All doubles have en-suite facilities, though a few basic singles survive. English breakfast included. If you've got strong legs go for the "Alpine rate": doubles on the fourth floor cost just £65, though there's no lift to get you there.

Columbia Hotel 95–99 Lancaster Gate, W2 ☏020/7402 0021, ⊛www.columbiahotel .co.uk; Lancaster Gate tube. See map, p.328. This large hotel, once five Victorian houses, offers simply decorated rooms, some with views over Hyde Park, a spacious public lounge with a vaguely Art Deco feel, and a cocktail bar. Said to be a rock-star favourite, but surprisingly good value for all that. Rooms are en-suite. £86.

Garden Court Hotel 30–31 Kensington Garden Square, W2 ☏020/7229 2553, ⊛www.garden courthotel.co.uk; Bayswater or Queensway tube. See map, p.328. Presentable, family-run B&B close to Portobello Market; half the rooms are with shared facilities, half are en-suite. English breakfast included. £64, en-suite £92.

The Gresham Hotel 116 Sussex Gardens, W2 ☏020/7402 2920, ⊛www.gresham@renbec .com; Paddington tube. See map, p.328. B&B with a touch more class than many in the area. Rooms are small but tastefully kitted out, and all have TV. Continental breakfast included. £95.

The Hempel 31–35 Craven Hill Gardens, W2 ☏020/7298 9000, ⊛www.the-hempel.co.uk; Lancaster Gate or Queensway tube. See map, p.328. Deeply fashionable minimalist hotel, designed by Anouska Hempel, with a huge and very empty atrium entrance. White-on-white rooms start at £245 for a double, and there's an excellent postmodern Italian/Thai restaurant called I-Thai.

Miller's Residence 111a Westbourne Grove, W2 ☏020/7243 1024, ⊛www.millersuk.com; Bayswater tube. See map on p.328. The address is deceptive – this grandiose and eccentric B&B is accessed from Hereford Road, just round the corner from Westbourne Grove. Every inch is littered with nineteenth-century antiques, from the sumptuous baronial drawing room (much in demand for fashion shoots) to the bedrooms, each named after an English Romantic poet. Some of the rooms are a little small and dark for the price, but the welcome is warm and the ambience unique. £150.

25

The Pavilion Hotel 34–36 Sussex Gardens, W2
☎020/7262 0905, ⊛www.pavilionhoteluk.com;
Paddington tube. See map, p.328. A decadent
rock star's home from home, with outrageously over-the-top decor and every room
individually themed, from "honky tonk Afro"
to "Highland Fling". £100.
Pembridge Court Hotel 34 Pembridge Gardens,
W2 ☎020/7229 9977, ⊛www.pemct.co.uk;
Notting Hill Gate or Holland Park tube. See map,
p.328. A huge town-house close to Portobello Market, with spacious, fully equipped
rooms. Friendly and slightly old-fashioned.
£190.
The Portobello Hotel 22 Stanley Gardens, W1
☎020/7727 2777, ⊛www.portobello-hotel
.co.uk; Notting Hill Gate or Holland Park tube.
See map, p.328. Swish, pretty and secluded
Victorian hotel with individually designed
double rooms, of varying sizes and prices,
the most expensive overlooking the private
gardens. Breakfast is included and there's a
restaurant and 24hr bar for guests. £170.
🏃 Portobello Gold 95–97 Portobello Rd, W1
☎020/7460 4900, ⊛www.portobellogold
.com; Notting Hill Gate or Holland Park tube.
See map, p.328. A fun and friendly option
– six rooms and an apartment above a
cheery modern pub. Rooms are plain
and some are tiny, with miniature en-suite
bathrooms, but all are fairly priced. The
apartment is a brilliant option for a group – it
sleeps 6 (at a bit of a pinch) and costs £150
a night; it has the feel of a cosy, down-
at-heel holiday home, with a dinky Carib-
bean-themed bathroom and a fantastic roof
terrace – the putting green and sweeping
views of London make it the perfect place
to relax with a bottle of wine or two. £70.
St David's Hotels 14–20 Norfolk Square, W2
☎020/7723 3856, ⊛www.stdavidshotels.com;
Paddington tube. See map, p.328. A friendly
welcome is assured at this inexpensive
B&B, famed for its substantial English
breakfast. Most rooms share facilities. The
large rooms make it a good option for families on a budget. £59.
Vancouver Studios 30 Prince's Square, W2
☎020/7243 1270, ⊛www.vancouverstudios
.co.uk; Bayswater tube. See map, p.328. Part
of a growing trend away from standard
hotel accommodation, Vancouver Studios
offers self-contained apartments in a grand
Victorian town-house, with fully equipped
kitchens and hotel-style porterage and maid
service. Decor is to a high standard and

mixes modern trends with traditional period
touches £79.

Hampstead

Hampstead is without doubt one of
the most beguiling London suburbs,
with a real village feel and the Heath
close by, yet it's just twenty minutes by
tube to the West End.

🏃 Hampstead Village Guesthouse 2 Kemplay Rd, NW3 ☎020/7435 8679, ⊛www
.hampsteadguesthouse.com; Hampstead tube.
See map, p.358. Lovely B&B in a freestanding Victorian house on a quiet backstreet
between Hampstead Village and the Heath.
Rooms (most en-suite, all non-smoking)
are wonderfully characterful, crammed
with books, pictures and hand-made and
antique furniture. Cute cabin-like single for
£48, and a self-contained studio for £90.
Meals to order.
The House Hotel 2 Rosslyn Hill, NW3
☎020/7431 8000, ⊛www.the househotel.
co.uk; Hampstead or Belsize Park tube. See
map, p.358. Spacious Victorian mansion on a
busy junction. Newly refurbished in an odd
mix of styles – Victorian and Regency with
some Deco touches – and with all rooms
offering en-suite marble bathrooms. £70.
La Gaffe 107–111 Heath St, NW3 ☎020/7435
8965, ⊛www.lagaffe.co.uk; Hampstead tube.
See map, p.358. Small, warren-like hotel
situated over an Italian restaurant and
bar in the heart of Hampstead Village. All
rooms are en-suite, if a little cramped,
and there's a roof terrace for use in fine
weather. £95.
Langorf Hotel 20 Frognal, NW3 ☎020/7794
4483, ⊛www.langorfhotel.com; Finchley Road
or Hampstead tube. See map, p.358. Pristinely
maintained if rather old-fashioned hotel in a
trio of red-brick Victorian mansions, with a
walled garden. There are also apartments,
sleeping 4 or 5 for £130–150. Doubles from
£98.

Out west: Richmond, Hampton Court and Greenwich

These are good options if you want
a bit of country life in the city.
The Thames is at its most pastoral
as it winds through Richmond and
past mighty Hampton Court, while
Greenwich retains a relaxed small-

25

town feel but has good transport links to the centre of London.

Doughty Cottage B&B 142a Richmond Hill ☎020/8332 9434, ⊛www.doughtycottage.com; Richmond tube. See map, p.411. A walled cottage at the top of Richmond Hill, adjoining a grand eighteenth-century house. The en-suite rooms are extremely comfortable, decked out in ornate Italianate style with some opening onto the little formal garden. Small latticed windows in the upstairs rooms look down to the Thames and Petersham Meadows. £70.

Paddock Lodge The Green, Hampton Court ☎020/8979 5254, ⊛www.paddocklodge.co.uk; Hampton Court train station from Waterloo. A secluded Palladian villa set down a leafy lane amidst wonderful gardens, with luxurious rooms and excellent breakfasts. Four-course dinner available by arrangement. £84.

South Street 81 Greenwich South St, SE10 ☎020/8283 3121, ℮matilda.wade @btopenworld .com; Greenwich DLR or train station from Charing Cross. See map, p.379. Friendly and comfortable B&B in a handsome Georgian house near the centre of Greenwich, with one double room and one single. Guests have their own bathroom and sitting room – decor is traditional but non-chintzy. £60.

26

Cafés and snacks

his chapter covers the full range of **cafés** from unreconstructed "greasy spoons", where you can get traditional fried egg, sausage and bacon English breakfasts, fish and chips, pies and other calorific treats, to the refined salons of London's top hotels, where you can enjoy an afternoon-tea blowout. In between, you'll find bakeries, brasseries, sandwich bars, coffee shops and ice-cream parlours, all of which are open during the day for light snacks or just a drink. We've also included several ethnic eating places where speedy service and low prices are the priority – places perfect for an inexpensive or quick bite before going out to a theatre, cinema or club. Wherever you go, you should be able to fill up for under £10.

If you want to surf while you slurp, you'll find that London has nothing like the number and variety of **Internet cafés** of other capital cities. Your best bet is to head for a branch of *easyInternetcafé* (ⓦwww.easyeverything.com), the no-frills Internet café chain – there's a branch just up the Strand, off Trafalgar Square (8am–11pm). Alternatively, there's the more congenial *Be the Reds!* (ⓣ020/7209

Chain coffeeshops

Whether you like it straight-up, ristretto, frappé, infused with mint syrup or even topped with crushed oreos, you're never far from a cup of coffee in London. A rash of **chain coffeeshops** has emerged in the last few years to meet demand, most with a New York-meets-Milan feel.

Best of the bunch for actual **coffee** is reckoned to be *Café Nero*, with well-trained and friendly baristas, while the ubiquitous *Starbucks*, *Costa Coffee* and *Coffee Republic* offer a wide range of hot and cold drinks and snacks, but have little to choose between them. Bottom of this particular food chain is cheap and cheerful *Benjys*, the builders' choice for their large tea at just 60p. They also dish up breakfast muffins for a quid, hot sarnies, burritos and filling jacket potatoes, as well as the full range of coffee options.

Home-grown chains *Pret a Manger* and *EAT* produce by far the best **lunchtime food**, with great sandwiches and salads made on the premises daily. *Pret*, all flash chrome and zingy service, do their own healthy canned drinks, including the cleansing classic "yoga bunny detox", while *EAT* outlets have a more muted feel and serve good soups, either "simple" (carrot, honey and ginger for example) or "bold" (such as beef and Guinness). *Pret* coffee is Fairtrade or **ethically sourced**, while *EAT* pride themselves on using only organic milk.

No matter where you get your caffeine fix, be sure not to ask for it small, medium or large – variations on primo, medio and massimo are the order of the day.

0984; Mon–Sat 10.30am–2am) at 39 Whitfield St, just off Tottenham Court Road (Goodge Street tube) – a Korean-run place serving *kimbab* and coffee, with billiards in the basement.

Trafalgar Square

Café in the Crypt St Martin-in-the-Fields, Duncannon St, WC2 ☏020/7766 1129; **Charing Cross tube.** The self-service buffet food is nothing special, but there are regular veggie dishes, and the handy (and atmospheric) location – below the church in the crypt – makes this an ideal spot to fill up before hitting the West End. Fortnightly jazz nights (Wed 8pm). Mon–Wed 10am–8pm, Thurs–Sat 10am–11pm, Sun noon–8pm.

Whitehall and Westminster

Jenny Lo's Teahouse 14 Ecclestone St, SW1 ☏020/7259 0399; **Victoria tube.** Bright, bare and utilitarian yet somehow stylish and fashionable too, *Jenny Lo's* serves good Chinese food at low prices. Be sure to check out the therapeutic teas. Mon–Sat noon–3pm & 6–10pm.

Marylebone

Ayoush 77 Wigmore St, W1 ☏020/7935 9839; **Bond Street tube.** Arab-style café off Oxford Street, with pungent hookahs for hire, mint tea to sip, and North African snacks and main courses to sample. Quiet during the day, crammed at night. Daily noon–midnight.

Eat & Two Veg 50 Marylebone High St, W1 ☏020/7258 8595; **Bond Street tube.** A lively and modern veggie restaurant, with some vegan and soya protein choices. The menu is eclectic, with Thai, Greek and Italian dishes. Mon–Sat 9am–11pm, Sun 10am–10pm.

Golden Hind 73 Marylebone Lane, W1 ☏020/7486 3644; **Bond Street tube.** Marylebone's heritage fish-and-chip restaurant, founded in 1914, serves classic cod and chips from around a fiver, as well as slightly fancier fare. Mon–Fri noon–3pm & 6–10pm, Sat 6–10pm.

🏃 **Patisserie Valerie at Sagne 105 Marylebone High St, W1** ☏020/7935 6240; **Bond Street tube.** Founded as Swiss-run *Maison Sagne* in the 1920s, and preserving its wonderful decor from those days, the café is now run by Soho's fab patisserie makers, and is without doubt

Marylebone's finest. Mon–Fri 7.30am–7pm, Sat 8am–7pm, Sun 9am–6pm.

Paul Rothe & Son 35 Marylebone Lane, W1 ☏020/7935 6783; **Bond Street tube.** Old-fashioned deli established in 1900, selling "English & Foreign Provisions" and serving soups, toasties and sandwiches to customers at formica tables inside the shop. Mon–Fri 8am–6pm, Sat 11.30am–5.30pm.

Quiet Revolution 62–64 Weymouth St, W1 ☏020/7487 5683; **Baker Street or Bond Street tube.** Laid-back organic café attached to the Aveda natural cosmetics shop on the corner of Marylebone High Street, serving mostly veggie fare, cakes and fresh juices. Mon–Sat 9am–6pm, Sun 10am–5pm.

Mayfair

Mômo Tearoom 25 Heddon St, W1 ☏020/7434 4040; **Piccadilly Circus tube.** The ultimate Arabic pastiche, and a successful one at that. The adjacent restaurant is pricey, but the tearoom serves delicious snacks and is a great place to hang out, with tables and hookahs spilling out onto the pavement of this little Mayfair alleyway behind Regent Street. Mon–Sat noon–1am, Sun noon–10.30pm.

Sotheby's 34–35 New Bond St, W1 ☏020/7293 5077; **Bond Street tube.** As you might expect, *Sotheby's* café is by no means cheap, but the lunches are exquisitely prepared, and the excellent afternoon teas are a fraction of the price of the nearby hotels (see box, p.101). Mon–Fri 9.30am–4.45pm.

🏃 **The Wolseley 160 Picadilly, W1** ☏020/7499 6996, ⊛www.thewolseley.com; **Green Park tube.** The lofty and stylish 1920s interior of this brasserie/restaurant (built as the showroom for Wolseley cars) is a big draw, service is attentive and non-snooty and the Viennese-inspired food delivers too, and given the glamour levels it's surprisingly affordable too. A great place for breakfast or a cream tea (£7.25). Mon–Fri 7am–midnight, Sat & Sun 11.30am–midnight (Sun 11pm).

(26)

Soho

Bar du Marché 19 Berwick St, W1 ☎020/7734 **4606; Leicester Square or Tottenham Court Road tube.** A weird find in the middle of raucous Berwick Street market: a French café serving quick snacks, brasserie staples and set meals for under £10. Mon–Sat noon–11pm.

 Bar Italia 22 Frith St, W1 ☎020/7437 **4520; Leicester Square tube.** Tiny café that's a Soho institution, serving coffee, croissants and sandwiches more or less around the clock – as it has been since 1949. Popular with late-night clubbers and those here to watch the Italian-league soccer on the giant screen. Nearly 24hr; closed Mon–Fri 4–6am.

Beatroot 92 Berwick St, W1 ☎020/7437 8591; **Piccadilly Circus, Oxford Circus or Tottenham Court Road tube.** Great little veggie café by the market, doling out hot savoury bakes, stews and salads (plus delicious cakes) in boxes of varying sizes – all under £5. Mon–Sat 9am–9pm, Sun noon–7.30pm.

Brasil by Kilo 17 Oxford St, W1 ☎020/7287 **7161; Tottenham Court Road tube.** Basic and friendly refuelling stop on Oxford Street which doles out Brazilian food at £1 per kilo. Go upstairs for the array of hot food and salads, or head for the coffee bar downstairs, which serves traditional snacks and sweets. There's also a juice bar where they claim the fresh juice concoctions (£2.50 each) can combat everything from the common cold to inflammation of the feet. Daily noon–9pm.

Gaby's 30 Charing Cross Rd, WC2 ☎020/7836 **4233; Leicester Square tube.** Busy café and takeaway joint that stays open till late serving a wide range of home-cooked veggie and Middle Eastern specialities. Hard to beat for value or choice – the takeaway falafel is a central London bargain – and it's licensed, too. Mon–Sat 10am–midnight.

Kulu Kulu 76 Brewer St, W1 ☎020/7734 7316; **Piccadilly Circus tube.** Small, friendly *kaiten* (or conveyor belt) sushi restaurant where you simply grab whatever takes your fancy and pay for the number of plates at the end. Mon–Fri noon–2.30pm & 5–10pm, Sat noon–3.45pm & 5–10pm.

 Maison Bertaux 28 Greek St, W1 ☎020/7437 6007; **Leicester Square tube.** Long-standing, old-fashioned and terribly French Soho patisserie, with tables on two floors (and one or two outside). The wonderful offerings here are made on the premises and are among the best in the West End. A loyal clientele keeps the place busy all day long. Daily 8.30am–8pm.

Malletti 26 Noel St, W1 ☎020/7439 4096; **Oxford Circus or Tottenham Court Road tube.** Tiny takeaway serving superior, thin-based *pizza al taglio*, plus risotto or pasta dishes – all for around £2.50 each. Mon–Sat 9am–5pm.

Patisserie Valerie 44 Old Compton St, W1 ☎020/7437 3466; **Leicester Square or Piccadilly Circus tube.** Popular coffee, croissant and cake emporium dating from the 1950s and attracting a loud-talking, arty Soho crowd. Mon–Fri 7.30am–9pm, Sat 8am–9pm, Sun 9.30am–7pm.

▲ Patisserie Valerie

Randall and Aubin 16 Brewer St, W1 ☎020/7287 **4447; Piccadilly Circus tube.** Converted butcher's, now an excellent (but by no means cheap) champagne-oyster bar, rotisserie, sandwich shop and charcuterie, where diners perch at old marble-top counters. Mon–Sat noon–11pm, Sun 4–10.30pm.

Soho and Fitzrovia: Chinatown

Kopi-Tiam 9 Wardour St, W1 ☎020/7434 **1777; Leicester Square tube.** Bright, cheap Malaysian café serving up curries, coconut

London for veggies

Most restaurants in London will make some attempt to cater for **vegetarians**. Below is a list of exclusively vegetarian places recommended in this chapter and in the "Restaurants" chapter.

Beatroot 92 Berwick St, W1 (see p.455).

Eat & Two Veg 50 Marylebone Lane, W1 (see p.454).

Food for Thought 31 Neal St, WC2 (see p.457).

Manna 4 Erskine Rd, NW3 (see p.471).

Mildred's 45 Lexington St, W1 (see p.466).

The Place Below Church of St Mary-le-Bow, Cheapside, EC2 (see p.458).

Rasa 55 Stoke Newington Church St, N1 (see p.472).

Sakonis 127–129 Ealing Rd, Alperton, Middlesex (see p.472).

Wild Cherry 241–247 Globe Rd, E2 (see p.459).

World Food Café 14 Neal's Yard, WC2 (see p.458).

rice, juices and "herbal soups" to local Malays, all for around a fiver. Daily 11am–11pm.

Lee Ho Fook 4 Macclesfield St, W1 ☎0871/332 1572; Leicester Square tube. A genuine Chinese barbecue house – small, spartan and cheap – that is very difficult to find, so here are the directions: on the west side of the street is Dansey Place, and on the corner is a red-and-gold sign in Chinese and a host of ducks hanging on a rack. Daily 11am–midnight, Fri & Sat till 1am.

Misato 11 Wardour St, W1; Leicester Square tube. Modern, canteen-style Japanese café serving stomach-filling rice and noodle dishes for around a fiver, plus miso soup, sushi and bento boxes. Daily noon–3pm & 5–10.30pm.

Tokyo Diner 2 Newport Place, WC2 ☎020/7287 8777; Leicester Square tube. Providing conclusive proof that you don't need to take out a second mortgage to enjoy Japanese food in London, this friendly eatery on the edge of Chinatown shuns elaboration for fast food, Tokyo-style. Minimalist decor lets the sushi do the talking, which – if the number of Japanese who frequent the place is anything to go by – it does fluently. Daily noon–midnight.

Fitzrovia

Carluccio's Caffè 8 Market Place, W1 ☎020/7636 2228; Oxford Circus tube. Snappy, stylish, modern chain of Italian cafés with fresh pastries, excellent coffee, and some full meals on offer, too. Other branches, including in Fenwick, New Bond Street, W1,

on St Christopher's Place, W1, and at 2 Nash Court, E14. Mon–Fri 7.30am–11pm, Sat 10am–11pm, Sun 10am–10pm.

Eagle Bar Diner 3 Rathbone Place, W1 ☎020/7637 1418; Tottenham Court Road tube. Modern and elegant US diner, with cosy leather booths and a long bar serving cocktails, martinis and pick-me-ups. But the real reason to come here is the burgers – Aberdeen Angus beef, chicken, lamb and even emu and ostrich, with brownies and cheesecakes for afters. Mon–Wed noon–11pm, Thurs & Fri noon–1am, Sat 10am–1am, Sun 10am–6pm.

Indian YMCA 41 Fitzroy Square, W1 ☎020/7387 0411; Warren Street tube. Don't take any notice of the signs saying the canteen is only for students – this place is open to all; just press the bell and pile in. The entire menu is portioned up into pretty little bowls; go and collect what you want and pay at the till. The food is great and the prices unbelievably low. Mon–Fri noon–2pm & 7–8.30pm, Sat & Sun 12.30–1.30pm & 7–8.30pm.

Salumeria Dino 15 Charlotte Place, W1 ☎020/7580 3938; Goodge Street tube. Small and authentic Italian café/grocer with outside tables on an appealing pedestrian side street. Daily focaccia and pasta specials, served in generous quantities and with fine ingredients.

Bloomsbury

Coffee Gallery 23 Museum St, WC1 ☎020/7436 0455; Tottenham Court Road

tube. An excellent, small café close to the British Museum, serving mouthwatering Italian sandwiches as well as a few more substantial dishes. Get there early to grab a seat. Mon–Fri 8.30am–5.30pm, Sat 10am–7pm, Sun noon–7pm.

Patisserie Deux Amis 63 Judd St, WC1 ☎020/7383 7029; Euston or King's Cross **tube.** Small, civilized French-style bakery specializing in pastries, filled baguettes and coffee, with a great cheese shop next door – a real find near King's Cross. Mon–Sat 9am–5.30pm, Sun 9am–1.30pm.

🏃 **Wagamama 4 Streatham St, WC1** ☎020/7323 9223; Tottenham Court **Road tube; plus numerous branches.** Much copied since, *Wagamama* was the pioneer when it comes to minimalist canteen-style noodle bars. Diners share long benches and slurp huge bowls of noodle soup or stir-fried plates. Good fresh ingredients, healthy mixed fruit juices and fine ginger cheesecake to round it off. Don't be put off if there's a queue: the rapid turnover means it moves pretty fast even at peak times. Mon–Sat noon–11pm, Sun 12.30–10pm.

Covent Garden and the Strand

Canela 33 Earlham St, WC2 ☎020/7240 6926; **Leicester Square tube.** A little Brazilian/Portuguese café that serves up decent snacks and cakes. Service can be poor, but the high-ceilinged chandeliered interior makes it a nice place for a coffee, or you can sit outside and watch the action on Seven Dials. Mon–Fri 9.30am–10pm, Sat 9.30am–11pm, Sun 9.30am–8pm.

🏃 **Food for Thought 31 Neal St, WC2** ☎020/7836 9072; Covent Garden **tube.** Long-established but minuscule bargain veggie restaurant and takeaway counter – the food is good, with the menu changing twice daily, plus regular vegan and wheat-free options. Expect to queue and don't expect to linger at peak times. Mon–Sat noon–8.30pm, Sun noon–5pm.

Frank's Café 52 Neal St, WC2 ☎020/7836 6345; **Covent Garden tube.** Classic Anglo-Italian café/sandwich bar with easy-going service. All-day breakfasts and plates of pasta and omelettes on offer; come either side of lunch to make sure of a table. Mon–Sat 7am–8pm.

India Club 143 Strand, WC2 ☎020/7836 0650; Covent Garden or Temple **tube.** There's

a very faded period charm to this long-established, inexpensive Anglo-Indian eatery, sandwiched between floors of the cheap *Strand Continental Hotel*, where the chilli bhajis are to be taken very seriously and the set menus are great value. Daily noon–2.30pm & 6–10.50pm.

Kastner and Ovens 52 Floral St, WC2 ☎020/7836 2700; Covent Garden **tube.** Minimalist lunching spot where the emphasis is on top-quality sandwiches and heart-warming savoury bakes, plus a wicked selection of cakes, all cooked on the premises. A few tables inside and lots of takeaway. Mon–Sat 11am–5pm.

Mode 57 Endell St, WC2 ☎020/7240 8085; **Covent Garden tube.** The best things about this stylish Covent Garden café are the Italian sandwiches, the cheeses from nearby Neal's Yard Dairy and the laid-back, funky atmosphere. Mon–Fri 8am–11pm, Sat 9am–10pm.

Monmouth Coffee Company 27 Monmouth St, WC2 ☎020/7645 3561; Covent Garden or **Leicester Square tube; branch at 2 Park St, SE1** ☎020/7645 3585. The marvellous aroma is the first thing that greets you when you walk in. Pick and mix your coffee from a fine selection (or buy the beans to take home), then settle into one of the cramped wooden booths and flick through the daily newspapers on hand. No smoking. Mon–Sat 8am–6.30pm.

Paul 29 Bedford St, WC2 ☎020/7836 3304 **Covent Garden tube; other branches, including 116 Marylebone High St, W1** ☎020/7224 5615, **Bond Street tube.** Seriously French, classy *boulangerie* with a wood-panelled café at the back. Try one of the chewy *fougasses*, quiches or tarts, before launching into the exquisite patisserie. Mon–Fri 7.30am–9pm, Sat & Sun 9am–9pm.

The Photographers' Gallery 5 Great Newport St, WC2 ☎020/7831 1772; Leicester Square **tube.** Bench seats within one of the gallery buildings let you check out the photographs on display whilst tucking into generously filled rolls and tasty cakes. Mon–Sat 11am–5.30pm (Thurs till 7.30pm), Sun noon–5.30pm.

Poetry Café 22 Betterton St, WC2 ☎020/7420 9887; Covent Garden or Holborn **tube.** The ground-floor café is a pleasant place to relax, with salads, quiche and cakes on offer as well as their excellent Portuguese custard tarts; the basement has had some fine poets grace its stage. Mon–Fri 11am–11pm, Sat 6.30–11pm.

The Rock & Sole Plaice 47 Endell St, WC2
T020/7836 3785; **Covent Garden tube.** A no-nonsense traditional fish-and-chip shop in central London. Takeaway, eat in or out at one of the pavement tables. Daily 11.30am–10.30pm.

World Food Café 14 Neal's Yard, WC2
T020/7379 0298; **Covent Garden tube.** First-floor veggie café that comes into its own in summer, when the windows are flung open and you can gaze down upon trendy humanity as you tuck into pricey but tasty dishes from all corners of the globe: Mexican tortillas, Indian thalis or Turkish meze. Bring your own booze, or stick to the fruit juices. Mon–Fri 11.30am–5pm, Sat 11.30am–4.30pm.

The City

De Gustibus 53–55 Carter Lane, EC2
T020/7236 0056; **St Paul's or Blackfriars tube.** Award-winning bakery that creates a wide variety of sandwiches, bruschetta, *croque-monsieur* and quiche to eat in or take away. Mon–Fri 7am–5pm.

K10 20 Copthall Ave, EC2 T020/7562 8510; **Moorgate tube.** Remarkably good, inexpensive City sushi outlet, with busy takeaway upstairs, and a *kaiten* (conveyor-belt) restaurant downstairs. Mon–Fri 11.30am–3pm & takeaway till 6pm.

The Place Below Church of St Mary-le-Bow, Cheapside, EC2 T020/7329 0789; **St Paul's or Bank tube.** Something of a find in the midst of the City – a café serving imaginative vegetarian dishes and delicious breakfast pastries, while the wonderful Norman crypt makes for a very pleasant place in which to dine. Mon–Fri 7.30am–3.30pm.

Ponti's Polo Bar 176 Bishopsgate, Liverpool Street station, EC2 T020/7283 4889; **Liverpool Street tube.** There's nothing in any way special about the *Ponti's* chain of cafés, but they're cheap, filling, vaguely Italian, and this particular branch is open daily 24hr.

Clerkenwell and Hoxton

Al's Café Bar 11–13 Exmouth Market, EC1
T020/7837 4821; **Angel or Farringdon tube.** This is a trendy little spot – a designer greasy spoon with a local media-luvvie clientele, which serves up Italian breads, Mediterranean dishes, nachos, decent

coffee and good soups alongside the chips and grills. In the evening, it's more bar than café. Mon, Tues & Sun 8am–11pm, Wed–Sat 8am–2am.

Apostrophe 42 Great Eastern St, EC2
T020/7739 8412; **Old Street tube.** Modern Hoxton take on the French *boulangerie/patisserie*, serving up delicious sandwiches and coffee, and the legendary Poilâne bread. Mon–Fri 7.30am–6.30pm. The West End branch (23 Barrett St, W1 T020/7355 1001; Bond Street tube) is open Sat & Sun too.

Clark & Sons 46 Exmouth Market, EC1
T020/7837 1974; **Angel or Farringdon tube.** Exmouth Market has undergone something of a trendy transformation, so it's all the more surprising to find this genuine pie-and-mash shop still going strong – this is the most central one in the capital. Mon–Thurs 10.30am–4pm, Fri 10.30am–5.30pm, Sat 10.30am–5pm.

Flavour 35 Charlotte Rd, EC2 T020/7739 5345; **Old Street tube.** Tiny Shoreditch café with just four stools, serving delicious Mediterranean lunch options: big soups, grilled tuna, salads and great pastries all freshly prepared. Mon–Fri 8.30am–4pm, Sat 9am–4pm.

Smiths of Smithfield 67–77 Charterhouse St, EC1 T020/7251 7950; **Farringdon tube.** A big bustling warehouse-style café/bar/restaurant on four levels, with lots of exposed brick and a glam-industrial feel. Not the place for an intimate evening, but the ground-floor café serves up fine all-day breakfasts, hot sarnies, salads, snacks, ice cream and sundaes. Daily 7am–11pm.

The East End: Whitechapel and Spitalfields

Arkansas Café Unit 12, Old Spitalfields Market, E1 T020/7377 6999; **Liverpool Street tube.** American barbecue fuel stop, using only the very best free-range ingredients. Try chef Bubb's own smoked beef brisket and ribs, and be sure to taste his home-made barbie sauce (made to a secret formula). Mon–Fri noon–2.30pm, Sun noon–4pm.

Brick Lane Beigel Bake 159 Brick Lane, E1 T020/7729 0616; **Whitechapel tube.** Classic bagel takeaway shop in the heart of the East End – unbelievably cheap, even for your top-end filling, smoked salmon and cream cheese. Daily 24hr.

Café 1001 1 Dray's Lane, E1 ☎020/7247 9679; **Whitechapel tube.** Off Brick Lane, tucked in by the Truman Brewery, this smoky café has a beaten-up studenty look, with lots of sofas to crash in, and dishes out simple sandwiches and delicious cakes. DJ sets every night. Mon–Wed & Sun 8am–10.30pm, Thurs 8am–11pm, Fri & Sat 8am–midnight.

E. Pellicci 332 Bethnal Green Rd, E2 ☎020/7739 4873; **Bethnal Green tube.** Famous East End caff with original 1940s decor intact, serving great fry-ups and good Anglo-Italian grub at low prices. Mon–Sat 6.15am–5pm.

F. Cooke 9 Broadway Market, E8 ☎020/7254 6458; **bus #55 from Old Street tube.** Great little East End pie-and-mash shop serving meat or veggie-mince versions with mash, and fresh eels too. Mon–Sat 10.30am–7pm.

 Frizzante@City Farm 1a Goldsmith's Row, E2 ☎020/7729 2266; **Bethnal Green tube.** Hackney City Farm's café serves up the best home-made family-friendly breakfasts and lunches this side of Bologna. Generous all-day "Big Farm" or veggie breakfasts, risottos and delicious pizza-like piadinas, all for around a fiver. Tues–Sun 10am–4.30pm.

Jones Dairy 23 Ezra St, E2 ☎020/7739 5372; **Bethnal Green tube.** Take a detour from Sunday's Columbia Road Market (see p.240) to this gorgeous little place, which sells great breads, bagels and fine cheeses. Fri & Sat 9am–3pm, Sun 8am–3pm.

Wild Cherry 241–247 Globe Rd, E2 ☎020/8980 6678; **Bethnal Green tube.** Buddhist veggie restaurant "providing home-cooked meals for the local community", just around the corner from the Museum of Childhood. Mon 11am–3pm, Tues–Fri 11am–7pm.

Docklands

Hubbub 269 Westferry Rd, E14 ☎020/7515 5577; **Mudchute DLR or bus #D7 from Westferry DLR.** A real oasis in the desert of Docklands, this café is housed in a former church, now arts centre, and does decent fry-ups, sandwiches and a few fancier dishes. Weekend brunch till 5pm. Mon–Fri noon–2.30pm & 5.30–10.30pm, Sat & Sun 10am–5pm & 6–10.30pm.

The South Bank and Southwark

Café Portugal 6a Victoria House, South Lambeth Rd, SW8 ☎020/7587 1962; **Vauxhall tube.** One of several Portuguese places stuck out on a limb beyond the traffic nightmare of Vauxhall. Still, this *pastelaria* is worth the trek, and they also serve tapas and hot dishes. Mon–Sat 6.30am–11pm, Sun 9am–10.30pm.

El Vergel 8 Lant St, SE1 ☎020/7357 0057; **Borough tube.** Small, very busy weekday café at the west end of Lant Street, worth the quick stroll from the tube. They do all the usual lunchtime takeaways, but you're really here to sample the Latin American specialities such as their *empanadas*, pasties filled with meat and spices or spinach and feta cheese. Mon–Fri 8.30am–3pm, Sat 10am–3pm.

 Konditor & Cook 22 Cornwall Rd, SE1 ☎020/7261 0456; **Waterloo tube.** Cut above your average bakery, *Konditor & Cook* make the most wonderful cakes and biscuits, as well as offering a choice of sandwiches, coffee and tea. With only a few tables inside, most folk take away. There are branches elsewhere on the south side of the Thames at 10 Stoney St by Borough Market, and in the Design Museum (see p.281). Mon–Fri 7.30am–6.30pm, Sat 8.30am–2.30pm.

Marie's Café 90 Lower Marsh, SE1 ☎020/7928 1050; **Waterloo tube.** As the name doesn't suggest, this is a Thai café – it's basic, cheap and friendly and dishes up tasty red and green curries. Bring your own booze; £1 corkage. Daily 5–10.30pm.

South Kensington, Knightsbridge and Chelsea

Chelsea Kitchen 98 King's Rd, SW3 ☎020/7589 1330; **Sloane Square tube.** A useful cheap café in Chelsea (now a branch of *Stockpot*). Don't expect anything remarkable, just budget stomach-fillers in the form of steaks, spag bol and the like. Daily noon–11pm.

Daquise 20 Thurloe St, SW7 ☎020/7589 6117; **South Kensington tube.** This old-fashioned Polish café right by the tube is something of a South Ken institution, serving Polish home cooking or simple coffee, tea and cakes depending on the time of day. Daily 11.30am–11pm.

Gloriette 128 Brompton Rd, SW7 ☎020/7589 4635; **South Kensington tube.** Long-established Viennese café serving coffee and outrageous cakes as well as

CAFÉS AND SNACKS

26

sandwiches, Wiener schnitzel, pasta dishes, goulash, and fish and chips. Mon–Fri 7am–8pm, Sat 8am–8pm, Sun 9am–6pm.

New Culture Revolution 305 King's Rd, SW3 ☎020/7352 9281; Sloane Square tube. Also branch at 157–159 Notting Hill Gate, W11 ☎020/7213 9688; Notting Hill Gate tube. Great name, great concept – big bowls of freshly cooked noodles in sauce or soup, or dumplings and rice dishes, all offering a one-stop meal at bargain prices in simple, minimalist surroundings. Not a place to linger. Daily noon–11pm.

Patisserie Valerie 215 Brompton Rd, SW7 ☎020/7823 9971; South Kensington tube. From the drool-inducing goodies in the window to the Deco interior, hung with vintage posters, this is an unmissable post-museum stop. Eat at the mirrored bar area, or sit at the back for waiter service. Tasty *croque-monsieur*, as well as fantastic cakes. Mon–Fri 7.30am–9.30pm, Sat 8am–9.30pm, Sun 8am–9pm.

🏃 **Poilâne 46 Elizabeth St, SW1** ☎020/7808 4910; Sloane Square tube. Tiny London outlet of the legendary French *boulangerie*, which produces the city's best Parisian bread, croissants and sourdough. Mon–Fri 7.30am– 7.30pm, Sat 7.30am–6pm.

Books for Cooks 4 Blenheim Crescent, W11 ☎020/7221 1992; Ladbroke Grove or Notting Hill Gate tube. Tiny café/restaurant within London's top cookery bookshop. Conditions are cramped, but this is an experience not to be missed. Just wander in and have a coffee while browsing, or get there in time to grab a table for the set-menu lunch. No smoking. Tues–Sat 10am–3.30pm, closed 3 weeks Aug.

Costas Fish Restaurant Hillgate St, W8 ☎020/7727 4310; Notting Hill tube. One of the best fish-and-chips experiences in London can be had at this old-fashioned Greek-Cypriot caff. Head past the takeaway counter to get a seat. Tues–Sat noon–2.30pm & 5.30–10.30pm.

Exeter Street Bakery 18 Argyll Rd, W8 ☎020/7937 8484; High Street Kensington tube. Tiny bakery (not in Exeter Street) selling unbelievably superb Italian bread, home-made soup plus sweet and savoury pizzas and coffee, stand-up or takeaway. Mon–Sat 8am–7pm, Sun 9am–6pm.

Hummingbird Bakery 133 Portobello Rd, W1 ☎020/7229 6446; Notting Hill tube. A cute and kitsch stop halfway down Portobello Road,

Park cafés

Brew House Kenwood House, Hampstead Lane, NW3 ☎020/8341 5384; Highgate tube or bus #210 from Archway tube. See map, p.358. Everything from full English breakfast to lunches, cakes and teas, all served in the old laundry at Kenwood, or enjoyed in the courtyard or on the terrace overlooking the lake. Daily 9am–6pm.

Burlington's Café Chiswick House, Burlington Lane, W4 ☎020/8987 9431; Chiswick train station from Waterloo or Turnham Green tube. Chiswick House (see p.400) is one of west London's hidden gems, as is its park café, which offers delicious cakes and filling main courses that change daily. Easter–Sept daily 10am–5pm; Oct–Easter Thurs–Sun 10am–4pm.

🏃 **Inn the Park** St James's Park, SW1 ☎020/7451 9999; St James's Park. See map, p.84. The panoramic windows of this curving wooden building look onto the park's lake and the wedding-cake palaces of Whitehall. Produce for the restaurant is sourced only from the UK, while the classy takeaway section provides sandwiches, salads and cakes for a top-notch picnic. Daily 8am–9pm.

Lauderdale House Waterlow Park, Highgate Hill, N6 ☎020/8341 4807; Archway tube. See map, p.358. Lovely café with a terrace overlooking the park, offering full meals as well as exceptional strawberry-and-cream scones on summer weekends. Tues–Sun 8am–6pm.

The Orangery Kensington Palace, Kensington Gardens, W8 ☎020/7376 0239; High Street Kensington or Notting Hill Gate tube. See map, p.286. Very swish café open year-round in Hawksmoor's Orangery, offering great cakes as well as savoury tarts. Daily: March–Oct 10am–6pm; Nov–Feb 10am–5pm.

Afternoon tea

The classic English **afternoon tea** – assorted sandwiches, scones and cream, cakes and tarts, and, of course, lashings of tea – is available all over London. The best venues are the capital's top hotels and most fashionable department stores; a selection of the best is given below. To avoid disappointment it's best to book ahead. Expect to spend £15–30 a head, and leave your jeans and trainers at home – most hotels will expect "smart casual attire", though only *The Ritz* insists on jacket and tie.

Brown's 33–34 Albemarle St, W1 ☎020/7493 6020, ⊕www.brownshotel.com; Green Park tube. Daily 2–6pm.

Claridge's Brook St, W1 ☎020/7629 8860, ⊕www.savoy-group.co.uk; Bond Street tube. Daily 3–5.30pm.

The Dorchester 54 Park Lane, W1 ☎020/7629 8888, ⊕www.dorchesterhotel.com; Hyde Park Corner tube. Daily 3–6pm.

Fortnum & Mason 181 Piccadilly, W1 ☎020/7734 8040, ⊕www.fortnumandmason.com; Green Park or Piccadilly Circus tube. Daily 3–5.30pm.

Lanesborough Hyde Park Corner, SW1 ☎020/7259 5599, ⊕www.lanesborough.com; Green Park tube. Mon–Sat 3.30–6pm, Sun 4–6pm.

The Ritz Piccadilly, W1 ☎020/7493 8181, ⊕www.theritzhotel.co.uk; Green Park tube. Daily 11.30am, 1.30, 3.30 & 5.30pm.

The Savoy Strand, WC2 ☎020/7836 4343, ⊕www.savoy-group.co.uk; Charing Cross tube. Mon–Fri 2–3.30pm & 4–6pm, Sat & Sun noon–1.30pm, 2–3.30pm & 4–6pm.

The Wolseley 160 Picadilly, W1 ☎020/7499 699, ⊕www.thewolseley.com; Green Park tube. Mon–Fri 3–5.30pm, Sat & Sun 3.30–6pm.

selling quality American home baking, from prettily garish cupcakes to sumptuous Brooklyn Blackout Cake. Wrought-iron chairs and tables outside make for great people-watching. Mon–Sat 10am–6pm, Sun 11am–6pm.

🍴 **Lisboa Patisserie 57 Golborne Rd, W10** ☎020/8968 5242; Ladbroke Grove tube. Authentic and basic Portuguese *pastelaria*, with the best *pasteis de nata* (custard tarts) this side of Lisbon – also coffee, cakes and a friendly atmosphere. *Café O'porto* at no. 62a Golborne Rd is a good fall-back if this place is full. Daily 8am–8pm.

Lucky Seven 127 Westbourne Park Rd, W2 ☎020/7727 6771; Ladbroke Grove tube. A small, trendy, but agreeably informal take on the American diner, serving sound enough food at sound enough prices. The fat chips are very good. Mon–Thurs 11am–11pm, Fri & Sat 9am–11pm, Sun 9am–10.30pm.

North London

L. Manze 76 Walthamstow High St, E17 ☎020/8520 2855; Walthamstow Central tube. No longer run by the Manze family, but still boasting its original 1929 decor, this is probably London's finest pie-and-mash

shop, architecturally speaking, and the grub's not bad, too. Mon–Wed 10am–4pm, Thurs–Sat 10am–5pm.

North London: Little Venice to Islington

Afghan Kitchen 35 Islington Green, N1 ☎020/7359 8019; Angel tube. Austere, two-floor café featuring a short menu of spicy stews with rice. Tues–Sat noon–3.30pm & 5.30–11pm.

Café Delancey 3 Delancey St, NW1 ☎020/7387 1985; Camden Town or Mornington Crescent tube. Still probably the best brasserie-style café in Camden, tucked away down a side road off Camden High Street; coffee, croissants, snacks and full meals. Daily 9am–10.30pm.

Marine Ices 8 Haverstock Hill, NW3 ☎020/7482 9000; Chalk Farm tube. Situated halfway between Camden and Hampstead, this is a splendid and justly famous old-fashioned Italian ice-cream parlour; pizza and pasta are served in the adjacent kiddie-friendly restaurant. Mon–Sat 10.30am–11pm, Sun 11am–10pm.

🍴 **Ottolenghi 287 Upper St, N1** ☎020/7288 1454; Angel tube. An elegant light space on fashionable Upper Street, with long white communal tables. A strong emphasis on imaginative and varied salads, such as wild rice and roasted butternut squash, alongside simple but delicious mains that include roast chicken or quiche. It's a fun option for breakfast, with at-table toasters and piles of newspapers, plus there's a hugely tempting takeaway section with exquisite cakes, tarts and pastries. Mon–Sat 8am–10.30pm, Sun 9am–10.30pm.

Primrose Patisserie 136 Regent's Park Rd, NW1 ☎020/7722 7848; Chalk Farm tube. Very popular pastel-pink and sky-blue patisserie in fashionable Primrose Hill, offering superb East European cakes and pastries. Daily 8.15am–6.30pm.

Sausage and Mash Café 4–6 Essex Rd, N1 ☎020/7359 5361; Angel tube. Branches at 268 Portobello Rd, W11 ☎020/8968 8898 and elsewhere. Excellent though pricier-than-usual bangers and mash, with original formica furnishings from its former incarnation, *Alfredo's*. Daily 7.30am–11pm.

North London: Stoke Newington and Hackney

Blue Legume 101 Stoke Newington Church St, N16 ☎020/7923 1303; bus #73 or #476 from King's Cross or Angel tube. Buzzy atmosphere, arty decor, mosaic tables and delicious chocolate cakes, teas and coffee. Good breakfasts too – smoked fish, wild mushrooms on toast and the like. Daily 9.30am–6.30pm.

North London: Hampstead and Highgate

Café Mozart 17 Swains Lane, N6 ☎020/8348 1384; Gospel Oak train station on the North London line. Conveniently located on the southeast side of Hampstead Heath, the best thing about this café is the Viennese cake selection and soothing classical music. Mon–Fri 8am–10pm, Sat & Sun 9am–10pm.

Camden Arts Centre Arkwright Rd, NW3 ☎020/7472 5500; Finchley Road tube. A pleasing light modern space with a Gaggia coffee machine providing excellent brews. Daily lunch specials, soup, snacks and generous slabs of cake. Tues & Thurs–Sun 10am–6pm, Wed 10am–9pm.

Louis Patisserie 32 Heath St, NW3 ☎020/7435 9908; Hampstead tube. Popular Hungarian tearoom serving sticky cakes to a mix of Heath-bound hordes and elderly locals. There's another branch at 12 Harben Parade, Finchley Rd, NW3. Daily 9am–6pm.

Brixton and Clapham

Café Wanda 153 Clapham High St, SW4 ☎020/7738 8760; Clapham Common tube. Clapham has a surfeit of trendified cafés, but *Wanda's* place remains pleasingly unreconstructed, with a piano in the corner and plants strewn everywhere. They dish up Polish specialities such as pork stew with prunes, plus dumplings and meatballs. Great patisserie fare, as well as cocktails and a range of vodkas. Mon–Fri noon–11pm, Sat 11am–11pm, Sun 11am–7pm.

Lounge 56 Atlantic Rd, SW9 ☎020/7733 5229; Brixton tube. Groovy little coffee bar a short way up towards Railton Road, with comfy sofas and snacks with a Middle Eastern twist. Mon–Wed 11am–11pm, Thurs–Sat 11am–midnight, Sun 10am–6pm.

Southeast London: Greenwich

Gambardella 48 Vanbrugh Park, SE3 ☎020/8858 0327; Maze Hill or Blackheath train station from Charing Cross. Good old caff to the southeast of Greenwich Park, serving filling comfort food in a beautiful Art Deco interior with lots of chrome and formica. Mon–Fri 7.30am–5.30pm, Sat 7.30am–2.30pm.

Goddard's 45 Greenwich Church St, SE10 ☎020/8692 3601; Cutty Sark DLR or Greenwich DLR and train station from Charing Cross. Established in 1890, *Goddard's* serves traditional pies (including veggie ones), eels and mash in an emerald-green-tiled interior, with crumble and custard for afters. Mon–Fri 10am–6.30pm, Sat & Sun 10am–7.30pm.

Tai Won Mein 39 Greenwich Church St, SE10 ☎020/8858 1668; Cutty Sark DLR or Greenwich DLR and train station from Charing Cross. Good-quality fast-food noodle bar that gets very busy at weekends. Decor is functional and minimalist; choose between rice, soup or various fried noodles, all for under a fiver. Daily 11.30am–11.30pm.

West London

Café Grove 65 The Grove, W5 ☎020/8810 0364;

Ealing Broadway tube. Polish café serving English fry-ups as well as a whole range of Polish food. Mon–Sat 11am–11pm, Sun 11am–10pm.

Giraffe Chiswick High Rd, W4 ☎020/8995 2100; Turnham Green tube. Branches in Richmond, Hampstead, Islington and elsewhere. Bright decor, dishes from around the world and a reputation for being child-friendly have made this chain very popular. Mon–Fri 8am–11pm, Sat & Sun 9am–11pm.

Petersham Nurseries off Petersham Rd, Petersham, nr Richmond ☎020/8940 5230. A real charmer of a place for lunch or afternoon tea – wooden tables and chairs hide behind exotic ferns, profuse vines and Indian antiques. The food is mainly organic and a little on the pricey side, but well worth the trek. Located a 20min walk from Richmond station: follow the Thames path from Richmond towards Ham House, then take the Capital Ring sign just beyond the public loos across the meadow to Petersham. Lunch Thurs–Sun 12.30–3pm; tea, coffee and cakes Tues–Sat 10am–4.30pm, Sun & Mon 11.30am–4.30pm.

27

Restaurants

London is an exciting – though often expensive – place in which to eat out, and as it's home to people from all over the globe, you can sample pretty much any kind of cuisine here. The city boasts some of the best **Cantonese** restaurants in the whole of Europe, is a noted centre for **Indian and Bangladeshi** food, has some excellent French, Greek, Italian, Japanese, Spanish and Thai restaurants, and also offers more unusual options, with everything from Georgian and Peruvian to Sudanese and Brazilian food available. Traditional and modern **British** food can be found all over town, and some of the best venues are reviewed below.

There are plenty of places to eat around the main tourist drags of the West End – **Soho** has long been renowned for its eclectic and fashionable restaurants – and new eateries appear every month, while **Chinatown**, on the other side of Shaftesbury Avenue, offers value-for-money eating right in the centre of town. Further west, upmarket areas like **Kensington** and **Chelsea** feature many *haute cuisine* restaurants.

To sample the full range of possibilities, it's worth taking time to explore quarters away from the core of the city. Try the Indian, Pakistani and Bangladeshi restaurants of Brick Lane in the **East End** or around **Wembley** and **Southall**, for example, or the bistros and brasseries of **Camden** and **Islington**, a short tube ride away to the north.

Many of the restaurants we've listed will be busy on most nights of the week, particularly Thursday to Saturday. You're best advised to **reserve a table**, and with the most renowned places you'll probably be disappointed unless you plan at least a week ahead.

We've given the **opening hours** for all the restaurants listed in this chapter, but it's always worth calling to check, as things change and some proprietors have a creative attitude towards timekeeping.

As for **prices**, you can pay an awful lot for a meal in London, and if you're used to North American portions you're not going to be particularly impressed by the volume in most places. In the listings, the price ranges we've quoted go from the minimum you can get away with spending (one main course and a drink) to the amount you can expect to pay for a full blowout. For really cheap eats, see the previous chapter, "Cafés and snacks".

Practically everywhere takes major **credit cards**, particularly Visa and Access/ MasterCard – in the listings, we've simply noted those that don't. At most places, **service** is discretionary, but restaurants tend to take no chances, emblazoning their bills with reminders that "Service is NOT included", or even including a ten to fifteen percent service charge on the bill, which they have to announce on the menu, by law. Normally you should, of course, pay service – it's how most of the staff make up their wages – but check to ensure you're not paying twice.

For the **locations** of the recommendations below, see the relevant chapter maps.

Whitehall and Westminster

Boisdale 15 Ecclestone St, SW1 ☎020/7730
6922, ⓦwww.boisdale.co.uk; Victoria tube.
Owned by Ranald MacDonald, son of the
Chief of Clanranald, this restaurant offers
the best of Scottish, in a very gentlemen's-
club and tartan atmosphere. Live jazz
every evening. Mon–Fri noon–1am, Sat
7pm–1am. £15–50.

Mayfair

The Criterion 224 Piccadilly, W1 ☎020/7930
0488; Piccadilly Circus tube. The predominately French food doesn't come cheap at
this Marco Pierre White restaurant (though
lunch is more of a bargain), but it is one
of the city's most beautiful eating places,
situated right by Piccadilly Circus, and with
a sparkling gold mosaic ceiling. Mon–Sat
noon–2.30pm & 5.30–11pm. £28–55.

Kiku Half Moon St, W1 ☎020/7499 4208; Green
Park tube. "Kiku" translates as pricey, but
for top-quality sushi and sashimi, this place
doesn't charge the earth. Take a seat at the
traditional sushi bar and gaze in wonder
at the dexterity of the knife man. Mon–Sat
noon–2.30pm & 6.30–10.15pm, Sun 5.30–
9.45pm. £16–55.

The Square 6–10 Bruton St, W1 ☎020/7495
7100; Green Park tube. Eating at this gra-
cious restaurant is a palate-expanding
experience. *The Square* is very French:
food is terribly important here, and the
head chef – an Englishman – has got it all
so very, very right. Mon–Fri noon–2.30pm
& 6.30–10.45pm, Sat 6.30–10.45pm, Sun
6.30–10pm. £25–110.

Truc Vert 42 North Audley St, W1 ☎020/7491
9988; Bond Street tube. An upmarket but
friendly restaurant, offering quiche, salads,
pâtés, cakes and pastries. The menu
changes daily and begins early with breakfast; you can assemble your own charcuterie and cheese platter and pay by weight,
and corkage is £4.50. Also has a small deli
section. Mon–Sat 7.30am–9.30pm, Sun
1–3pm. £15–40.

Marylebone

Abu Ali 136–138 George St, W1 ☎020/7724
6338; Marble Arch tube. Spartan place that's
the Lebanese equivalent of a northern working men's club, serving honest Lebanese

fare that's terrific value for money, from the
tabbouleh to the kebabs – wash it all down
with fresh mint tea, and then have a go at a
bubble pipe. Daily 9.30am–11pm. Cash or
cheque only. £7–25.

Fairuz 3 Blandford St, W1 ☎020/7486 8108;
Bond Street tube. This is one of London's
most welcoming Middle Eastern restaurants, with an epic list of meze, a selection
of charcoal grills and one or two oven-
baked dishes. Get here early and secure
one of the nook-and-crannyish, tent-like
tables. Mon–Sat noon–11.30pm, Sun
noon–10.30pm. £15–35.

La Galette 56 Paddington St, W1 ☎020/7935
1554, ⓦwww.lagalette.com; Baker Street
tube. Bright modern pancake place, with
a breakfast menu 10am–4pm. The hors
d'oeuvres are very simple and very French,
and the savoury and sweet buckwheat
galettes are generous. Be sure to sample
the range of Breton ciders, too. Mon–Fri
9.30am–11pm, Sat & Sun 10am–11pm.
£7–25.

Orrery 55 Marylebone High St, W1 ☎020/7616
8000, ⓦwww.orrery.co.uk; Baker Street or
Regent's Park tube. Another Conran enterprise, sandwiched between the Conran
shop and the gorgeous Orrery grocery,
and a very good French restaurant indeed.
The service is slick and friendly, the dining
room is beautiful, and the cheeseboard
has won prizes. Mon–Sat noon–3pm &
7–11pm, Sun noon–2.30pm & 7–10.30pm.
£29–90.

Phoenix Palace 3–5 Glentworth St, W1
☎020/7486 3515; Baker Street or Marylebone
tube. The menu here chunters on for over
two hundred dishes into the farthest corners of Chinese chefly imagination, and it's
worth a careful read. Better still, the cooking
is good and the portions large. Mon–Sat
noon–11.30pm, Sun 11am–10.30pm.
£10–55.

The Providores 109 Marylebone High St,
W1 ☎020/7935 6175, ⓦwww.theprovi
dores.co.uk; Baker Street or Bond Street tube.
Outstanding fusion restaurant run by an
amiable New Zealander and split into two:
snacky Tapa Room downstairs and full-on
restaurant upstairs. At both the food, which
may sound like an untidy assemblage on
paper, is original and wholly satisfying.
Mon–Fri 9am–11pm, Sat 10am–11pm, Sun
10am–10pm. £7–22.

Soho and Fitzrovia: Chinatown

Fung Shing 15 Lisle St, W1 ☎020/7437 1539;
Leicester Square tube. You can eat very
cheaply in Chinatown, but if you want to
splash out on some serious Chinese cooking, *Fung Shing* offers really good value. The
food here has that earthy, robust quality that
you only encounter when the chef is absolutely confident of his flavours and textures.
Daily noon–11.30pm. £15–60.

Imperial China White Bear Yard, WC2 ☎020/7734
3388; **Leicester Square tube.** Large restaurant
tucked into a little courtyard off Lisle Street;
fresh and bright, with dim sum that's up
there with the best, service that is "Chinatown brusque", and a menu with eminently
reasonable prices. Mon–Sat noon–11.30pm,
Sun 11.30am–10.30pm. £10–30.

🏃 **Mr Kong 21 Lisle St, WC2** ☎020/7437
7923; **Leicester Square tube.** One of
Chinatown's finest, with a chef-owner who
pioneered many of the modern Cantonese
dishes now on menus all over town. You
may have to be firm with staff if you want
the more unusual dishes – order from the
"Mangager's Recommendations" menu
and don't miss the mussels in black-bean
sauce. If you want to avoid the rather
grungy basement, book ahead. Mon–Sat
noon–2.45am, Sun noon–1.45am. £8–22.

Wong Kei 41–43 Wardour St, W1 ☎020/7437
8408; **Leicester Square tube.** A restaurant
renowned for rudeness may not seem like
much of a recommendation, but if you want
quick, cheap Chinese then this is the place.
The entire ground floor of the Art Noveau
building is given over to lone diners, so you
won't feel silly if you're on your own. Daily
noon–11pm. £6–15.

Soho

Chowki 2–3 Denman St, W1 ☎020/7439 1330;
Piccadilly Circus tube. Large, cheap Indian
restaurant serving authentic home-style
food in stylish surroundings. The menu
changes every month in order to feature
three different areas of India, with the
regional feast great value at £10.95. Daily
noon–11.30pm. £6–15.

La Trouvaille 12a Newburgh St, W1 ☎020/7287
8488, ⊕www.latrouvaille.co.uk; **Oxford Circus
tube.** Here they understand the English need
for really French Frenchness – if you're feeling brave, try the tripe terrine. Mon–Sat
noon–3pm & 6–11pm. £20–50.

Masala Zone 9 Marshall St, W1 ☎020/7287
9966; **Oxford Circus or Piccadilly Circus tube.**
Smart, big restaurant serving modern Indian
food, including lots of veggie options. Kick
off with a plate of "street food", then simply move on to the well-balanced, richly
flavoured curries and thalis. Mon–Fri noon–
3pm & 5.30–11pm, Sat 12.30–11pm, Sun
12.30–3.30pm & 6–10.30pm. £5–18.

🏃 **Mildred's 45 Lexington St, W1**
☎020/7494 1634; **Oxford Circus or Piccadilly Circus tube.** *Mildred's*, tucked away
on a north Soho side street, has a fresher
and more stylish feel than many veggie
restaurants. The stir-fries, pasta dishes
and burgers are wholesome, delicious and
inexpensive. No bookings or credit cards.
Mon–Sat noon–11pm. £8–15.

Patara 15 Greek St, W1 ☎020/7437 1071;
Leicester Square tube. A dimly lit and glamorous place, with orchids on the tables.
Wonderful fresh ingredients and fine Thai
cooking. Set lunch £11.95. Daily noon–3pm
& 6.30–10.30pm. £15–40.

Soho Spice 124–126 Wardour St, W1 ☎020/7434
0808; **Leicester Square or Piccadilly Circus
tube.** Large, busy and very successful
place where the menu features contemporary Indian cuisine. Bookings only taken
for groups of six or more. Mon–Thurs
11.30am–midnight, Fri & Sat 11.30am–3am,
Sun 12.30–10.30pm. £12–35.

Spiga 84–86 Wardour St, W1 ☎020/7734 3444;
Leicester Square tube. A pleasantly casual Ital-
ian affair, with a lively atmosphere, a serious
wood-fired oven and a cool look about it.
Tues noon–midnight, Wed–Sat noon–3am,
Sun noon–10.30pm. £10–35.

Thai Cottage 34 D'Arblay St, W1 ☎020/7439
7099; **Leicester Square tube.** With many cheap
Soho favourites going out of business, it's a
relief to find this tiny and resolutely unfashionable place. The welcome is friendly and
the decor simple, with little lanterns hanging
from the low-beamed ceiling. Follow the
chicken satay with one of their terrific fried-
noodle dishes. The generous set dinner
costs just £11.50. Mon–Wed noon–4pm &
5.30–10.30pm, Thurs 5.30–10.30pm, Fri
noon–4pm & 5.30–11pm, Sat 5.30–11pm.
£8–20.

Fitzrovia

🏃 **Hakkasan 8 Hanway Place, W1**
☎020/7927 7000; **Tottenham Court Road
tube.** The food at this impressively designed

▲ Hakkasan

Chinese restaurant is novel, well presented, fresh, delicious and expensive. The dining area sits inside an elegant and ornate carved wooden cage, and the long cocktail bar, a known posh pulling location, is fashionably crammed. Mon–Wed noon–3pm & 6pm–midnight, Thurs & Fri noon–3pm & 6pm–12.30am, Sat noon–4.30pm & 6pm–12.30am. Thurs–Sat bar open until 2am. £25–100.

Han Kang 16 Hanway St, W1 ☎020/7637 1985; Tottenham Court Road tube. Small nondescript Korean restaurant that serves some of the best Korean food in the capital; the three-course lunch, in particular, is excellent value at £6.50. Mon–Sat noon–3pm & 6–10.30pm. £8–30.

Ikkyu 67a Tottenham Court Rd, W1 ☎020/7636 9280; Goodge Street tube. Busy basement Japanese restaurant, good for a quick lunch or a more elaborate dinner. Either way, prices are infinitely more reasonable than elsewhere in the capital, and the food is tasty and authentic. Mon–Fri noon–2.30pm & 6–9.30pm, Sun 6–9.30pm. £10–40.

The Kerala 15 Great Castle St, W1 ☎020/7580 2125; Oxford Circus tube. Friendly Keralan restaurant, just behind Oxford Circus, that's a contender for bargain of the age. The menu is divided into a number of sections – Syrian Christian specialities, coastal seafood dishes, Malabar biryanis, vegetable curries and special dosas – all well judged and nicely spiced. Daily noon–3pm & 5.30–11pm. £6–22.

Rasa Samudra 5 Charlotte St, W1 ☎020/7637 0222, ⓦwww.rasarestaurants.com; Goodge Street tube. The food served at *Rasa Samudra* would be more at home in Mumbai than in London, consisting as it does of sophisticated Southern Indian fish dishes

– a million miles from curry-house staples. *Rasa* has another branch at 6 Dering St, W1 ☎020/7629 1346 (Bond Street tube), as well as the mother ship in Stoke Newington (see p.116). Mon–Sat noon–3pm & 6–11pm. £10–40.

Sardo 45 Grafton Way, W1 ☎020/7387 2521, ⓦwww.sardo-restaurant.com; Warren Street tube. Sardinian flagship restaurant with a light modern interior and interesting local cuisine, particularly if you concentrate on the specials. Mon–Fri noon–3pm & 6–11pm, Sat 6–11pm. £18–40.

Bloomsbury

Cigala 54 Lamb's Conduit St, WC1 ☎020/7405 1717, ⓦwww.cigala.co.uk; Russell Square tube. Simple dishes, strong flavours, fresh ingredients and real passion are evident at this Iberian restaurant. The menu changes daily and is market-led, which makes for excellent seasonal dishes. There's also a tapas menu. Daily 12.30–10.45pm. £18–60.

Covent Garden and the Strand

Bank 1 Kingsway, WC2 ☎020/7379 9797, ⓦwww.bankrestaurants.com; Covent Garden or Temple tube. The closest London gets to re-creating the all-day buzz and unfussy cuisine of the big Parisian brasseries. *Bank* opens for breakfast, lays on brunch at the weekend, and whatever time of the day, the Modern British food is impressive. Mon–Fri 7am–11.30pm, Sat 11.30am–11pm, Sun 11.30am–9.30pm. £16–60.

Belgo Centraal 50 Earlham St, WC2 ☎020/7813 2233, ⓦwww.belgo-restaurants. com; Covent Garden tube. Massive metal-minimalist cavern off Neal Street, serving excellent kilo buckets of *moules marinière*, with *frites* and mayonnaise, a bewildering array of Belgian beers to choose from, and waffles for dessert. The £6 lunchtime specials are a bargain for central London. Mon–Thurs noon–11.30pm, Fri & Sat noon–midnight, Sun noon–10.30pm. £6–30.

Calabash The Africa Centre, 38 King St, WC2 ☎020/7836 1976; Covent Garden tube. Comfortable, laid-back restaurant in the Africa Centre, serving cheap, unsophisticated, and often spicy and unfamiliar dishes that struggle bravely to give snapshots of the diversity of African cuisine. Mon–Fri 12.30–3pm & 6–11.30pm, Sat 6–11.30pm. £10–25.

The Ivy 1 West St, WC2 ☎020/7836 4751, ⊛www.caprice-holdings.co.uk; Leicester Square tube. Regency-style restaurant built in 1928 that was a theatreland and society favourite throughout the last century – and has never been more so than today, with its focus on good comfort food such as mixed grill with bubble and squeak. The only problem is getting a table; either book months ahead or try at very short notice, make do with a table in the bar area, or go for the bargain £21.50 three-course weekend lunch. Daily noon–3pm & 5.30pm–midnight. £25–60.

J. Sheekey 28–32 St Martin's Court, WC2 ☎020/7240 2565, ⊛www.caprice-holdings .co.uk; Leicester Square tube. *J. Sheekey*'s pedigree goes back to World War I, but the place has been totally redesigned and refurbished since then. The menu is still focused on fish, but in addition to traditional fare such as Dover sole, you're just as likely to find contemporary dishes like braised huss with polenta and gremolata. The weekend lunch menu, at £21.50, is the best value. Mon–Sat noon–3pm & 5.30pm–midnight, Sun 6pm–midnight. £18–70.

🏃 **Mon Plaisir 21 Monmouth St, WC2 ☎020/7836 7243. ⊛www.monplaisir.co.uk; Covent Garden tube.** An atmospheric and sometimes formidably French restaurant with an intimate tiled and wood-panelled interior. Deco posters and a glamorous mirrored bar give a vintage feel, while the classic French meat and fish dishes are reliably excellent. The pre- and post-theatre menu is a bargain at £12.50 for two courses, £14.50 for three. Mon–Fri noon–3pm & 5.45pm–midnight, Sat noon–3pm. £15–65.

The City

1 Lombard Street 1 Lombard St, EC3 ☎020/7929 6611, ⊛www.1lombardstreet.com; Bank tube. This is a brasserie in the City, of the City, by the City and for the City. A long but straightforward spread of dishes delivers on pretty much every front, and the buzzy circular bar sits under a suitably imposing glass dome (a former banking hall). Mon–Fri noon–3pm & 6–10pm. £30–80.

Prism 147 Leadenhall St, EC3 ☎020/7256 3888, ⊛www.harveynichols.com; Bank tube. A very slick expense-account City restaurant in another old banking hall, with the obliga-

tory long bar, the obligatory suave service and a menu comprising well-judged English favourites and modernist influences. The bar menu has Ploughman's and sausage and mash for around a tenner. Mon–Fri 11.30am–3.30pm & 6–10pm. £25–90.

Searcy's Restaurant Level 2, The Barbican Centre, Silk Street, EC2 ☎020/7588 3008, ⊛www. searcys.co.uk; Barbican tube. Hidden within the bowels of the Barbican Centre, *Searcy's* offers modern European cuisine using seasonal produce; mains might include a *ballotine* of guinea fowl with truffle, or sea bass fillet with citrus risotto. Mon–Fri noon–2.30pm & 5.30–10.30pm, Sat 5–10.30pm. £25–55.

Clerkenwell and Hoxton

Cicada 132 St John St, EC1 ☎020/7608 1550, ⊛www.cicada.nu; Farringdon tube. Part bar, part restaurant, *Cicada* offers an unusual pan-Asian menu that allows you to mix and match from small, large and side dishes ranging from fishy tom yum to ginger noodles or sushi. Mon–Fri noon–11pm, Sat 6–11pm. £17–40.

Eyre Brothers 70 Leonard St, EC2 ☎020/7613 5346; Old Street or Liverpool Street tube. Very large, very swish, very elegant restaurant with an atmosphere of comfortable clubbiness. The food is ballsy yet hard to categorize – there are a few Iberian and Italian dishes, a lot of Portuguese specialities and some favourites from Mozambique. There's also a tapas menu. Mon–Fri noon–3pm & 6.30–10.45pm, Sat 7–11pm. £15–50.

Medcalf 40 Exmouth Market, EC1 ☎020/7833 3533, ⊛www.medcalfbar.co.uk; Farringdon or Angel tube. The battered wooden floors and furniture and exposed light bulbs give *Medcalf* a church-hall-meets-cool-minimalism look. Diner-style food for lunch and classy bar grub in the evening, with fresh ingredients, great fish dishes and excellent traditional puds. Mon–Wed & Fri noon–3pm & 6–10pm, Thurs 6–10pm, Sat noon–4pm & 6–10pm, Sun noon–4pm. £12–35.

Moro 34–36 Exmouth Market, EC1 ☎020/7833 8336; Farringdon or Angel tube. Modern, spartan restaurant that typifies the new face of Clerkenwell and attracts a clientele to match. *Moro* is a place of pilgrimage for disciples of the wood-fired oven and those who love food that is both Moorish and more-ish. Mon–Fri 12.30–2.30pm &

7–10.30pm, Sat 7–10.30pm. £18–45.

Real Greek 15 Hoxton Market, N1 ☎020/7739 8212, ⓦwww.therealgreek .com; Old Street tube. Yes, it's run by a real Greek, but this is nothing like your average London Greek-Cypriot joint. Modern and attractive with excellent service and a menu that shows off the authentic dishes of Greece. Set lunch and early-doors dinner are a bargain. Neighbouring *Mezedopolio*, in a sympathetically converted mission building, serves *mezedes* and has a glamorous marble bar. Mon–Sat noon–3pm & 5.30–10.30pm. £10–50.

St John 26 St John St, EC1 ☎020/7251 0848, ⓦwww.stjohnrestaurant.co.uk; Farringdon tube. This minimalist former smokehouse is now a decidedly English restaurant, only a stone's throw from Smithfield meat market and specializing in offal. All those strange and unfashionable cuts of meat that were once commonplace in rural England – brains, bone marrow – are on offer, making this no place for vegetarians. That said, the food is terrific and the service is attentive and informed. Mon–Fri noon–3pm & 6–11pm, Sat 6–11pm. £20–60.

Viet Hoa Café 72–74 Kingsland Rd, E2 ☎020/7729 8293; Old Street tube. Large, light and airy Vietnamese café in a street now heaving with similar places. Try one of the splendid "meals in a bowl", or the noodle dishes with everything from spring rolls to tofu. Be sure, too, to sample the pho soup, a Vietnamese staple that's eaten at any and every meal. Mon–Fri noon–3.30pm & 5.30–11.30pm, Sat & Sun 12.30–11.30pm. £8–18.

The East End: Whitechapel and Spitalfields

Café Naz 46–48 Brick Lane, E1 ☎020/7247 0234; Aldgate East tube. Self-proclaimed contemporary Bangladeshi restaurant that cuts an imposing modern figure on Brick Lane. The menu has all the standards plus a variety of baltis, the kitchen is open-plan, and the prices keen. Daily noon–midnight. £9–22.

Café Spice Namaste 16 Prescott St, E1 ☎020/7488 9242, ⓦwww.cafespice.co.uk; Aldgate East or Tower Hill tube. Very popular East End Indian, where the menu is a touch more varied than in many of its rivals – Goan and Kashmiri dishes are often included – and the tandoori specials, in par-

ticular, are awesome. Weekday lunchtimes are especially busy. Mon–Fri noon–3pm & 6.15–10.30pm, Sat 6.15–10.30pm. £20–50.

Les Trois Garcons 1 Club Row, E1 ☎020/7613 1924; Shoreditch tube. Wildly camp decor is the signature here, with a bejewelled stuffed tiger to greet you at the door, handbags hanging from the ceilings, ornate tiles and glittering engraved mirrors. The opulence is reflected in the menu, with scallops, foie gras and oysters a regular feature. £18–60.

Taja 199a Whitechapel Rd, E1 ☎020/7247 3866; Whitechapel tube. A genuine rarity – an ultra-modern Bangladeshi restaurant in a converted toilet, with a menu that's as rich in veggie dishes as it is in meat ones. Prices are low and standards high. Daily noon–3pm & 5.30pm–midnight. £7–18.

Tayyab's 83–89 Fieldgate St, E1 ☎020/7247 9543, ⓦwww.tayyabs.co.uk; Aldgate East or Whitechapel tube. Opened in 1974, *Tayyab's* has been spruced up lately but, miraculously, they still serve the same straightforward Pakistani fare: good, freshly cooked and served without pretension. Prices have remained low, booking is essential, and service is speedy and slick. Daily noon–11.30pm. £4–15.

Docklands

Mem Saheb on Thames 65–67 Amsterdam Rd, E14 ☎020/7538 3008; Crossharbour DLR. Decent Indian restaurant in the cultural wasteland that is Docklands, with a superb view over the river to the Dome. Mon–Fri noon–2.30pm & 6–11.30pm, Sat & Sun 6–11.30pm. £20–40.

Royal China 30 Westferry Circus, W1 ☎020/7221 2535; Canary Wharf tube; with branches elsewhere. You can eat well from the full menu, but it's the dim sum that is most enticing here: the roast pork puff is famous and this may well be the place to finally take the plunge and try chicken's feet. Mon–Thurs noon–11pm, Fri & Sat noon–11.30pm, Sun 11am–10pm. £14–27.

The South Bank

Livebait The Cut, SE1 ☎020/7928 7211; Waterloo tube. This bustling green- and white-tiled restaurant dishes up seafood galore, from classic fish'n'chips to platters heaped with lobster, crab and prawns. Mon–Sat noon–11pm. £15–£50.

RSJ 13a Coin St, SE1 ☎020/7928 4554, ⓦwww .rsj.uk.com; Waterloo tube. Regularly high standards of Anglo-French cooking make this a good spot for a meal after or before an evening at a South Bank theatre or concert hall. The set meals for around £17 are particularly popular. Mon–Fri noon–2pm & 5.30–11pm, Sat 5.30–11pm. £15–40.

Southwark

Delfina 50 Bermondsey St, SE1 ☎020/7357 0244, ⓦwww.delfina.org.uk; London Bridge tube. This light and spacious adjunct to the Delfina art gallery is a great place to go for lunch. The cooking is "modern eclectic", and the price is beyond café norms, but the quality justifies a bit of a splurge. Mon–Thurs 8am–5pm, Fri 8am–5pm & 7–10pm. £15–40.

Fina Estampa 150 Tooley St, SE1 ☎020/7403 1342; London Bridge tube. One of London's few Peruvian restaurants, which happens to be very good, bringing a little of downtown Lima to London Bridge. The menu is traditional Peruvian; you can kick things off with a Pisco Sour cocktail. Mon–Fri noon–10.30pm, Sat 6.30–10.30pm. £15–30.

Tentazioni 2 Mill St, SE1 ☎020/7237 1100, ⓦwww.tentazioni.co.uk; Bermondsey or Tower Hill tube. Smart busy Italian restaurant serving high-quality peasant fare with strong, rich flavours; try the splendid three-course Tradizione Italiana (£28). Mon & Sat 7–10.45pm, Tues–Fri noon–2.30pm & 7–10.45pm. £10–55.

South Kensington, Knightsbridge and Chelsea

Bibendum Oyster House Michelin House, 81 Fulham Rd, SW3 ☎020/7589 1480, ⓦwww .bibendum.co.uk; South Kensington tube. A glorious tiled affair built in 1911, this former garage is the best place to eat shellfish in London. If you're really hungry, try the "Plateau de Fruits de Mer", which has crab, clams, langoustine, oysters, prawns, shrimps, whelks and winkles. Mon–Sat noon–10.30pm, Sun noon–10pm. £12–30.

Chutney Mary 535 King's Rd, SW10 ☎020/7351 3113, ⓦwww.chutneymary.com; Fulham Broadway tube. Not a cheap restaurant, but it is a good one. The men in the kitchen know their job and turn out refined Indian food. These are the complicated dishes that were developed for the Maharajas: sauces are silky textured, flavours are subtle and the spicing authentic. Mon–Fri 6.30–11pm, Sat noon–3pm & 6.30–11.30pm. £30–90.

Gordon Ramsay 68–69 Royal Hospital Rd, SW3 ☎020/7352 4441, ⓦwww .gordonramsay.com; Sloane Square tube. To order successfully here, just pick a dish or even an ingredient you like and see how it arrives; you won't be disappointed. Gordon Ramsay's Chelsea restaurant is a class act through and through, though you have to book ahead to eat here. Mon–Fri noon–2pm & 6.45–11pm. £40–150.

Hunan 51 Pimlico Rd, SW1 ☎020/7730 5712; Sloane Square tube. Probably England's only restaurant serving Hunan food, a relative of Sichuan cuisine with the same spicy kick to most dishes, and a fair wallop of pepper in those that aren't actively riddled with chillis. Most people opt for the £30.80 "leave-it-to-us feast" which lets the chef, Mr Peng, show what he can do. Mon–Sat noon–2.30pm & 6–11.30pm. £32–60.

O Fado 45–50 Beauchamp Place, SW3 ☎020/7589 3002; Knightsbridge tube. Probably the oldest Portuguese restaurant in London, which speaks volumes for its authenticity. It can get rowdy, what with the live fado ballads (Wed–Sun) and the family parties, but that's half the enjoyment. You'll need to reserve a table. Daily noon–3pm & 7pm–1am. £25–45.

Racine 239 Brompton Rd, SW3 ☎020/7584 4477; Knightsbridge or South Kensington tube. The food here is French – not just any old French, but familiar, delicious, nostalgic dishes from the glory days of French cooking, with friendly service. Booking is imperative. Mon–Fri noon–3pm & 6–10.30pm, Sat noon–3.30pm & 6.30–10pm, Sun noon–3.30pm & 6–10pm. £17–50.

High Street Kensington to Notting Hill

Alwaha 75 Westbourne Grove, W2 ☎020/7229 0806; Bayswater or Queensway tube. Arguably London's best Lebanese restaurant; meze-obsessed, but also painstaking in its preparation of the main-course dishes. Daily noon–midnight. £12–35.

Galicia 323 Portobello Rd, W10 ☎020/8969 3539; Ladbroke Grove or Westbourne Park tube. *Galicia* is a pleasant Spanish restaurant without pretensions. The tapas at the bar are straightforward and good, with a regular

Spanish clientele. Tues–Sat noon–3pm & 7–11.30pm, Sun noon–3pm & 7–10.30pm. £14–35.

Mandarin Kitchen 14–16 Queensway, W2 ☎020/7727 9012; **Bayswater or Queensway tube.** Smart Chinese fish restaurant that purports to sell more lobsters than any other restaurant in Britain. Waiters deftly wheel four-foot-diameter tabletops around like giant hoops as they set up communal tables for parties of Chinese. Daily noon–11.30pm. £15–35.

Osteria Basilico 29 Kensington Park Rd, W11 ☎020/7727 9372; **Ladbroke Grove tube.** A pretty, traditional Italian restaurant on a picturesque street just off Portobello Road. It's a good place for the full Italian monty – antipasto, home-made pasta and then a fish or meat dish – or just for a pizza. Mon–Fri 12.30–3pm & 6.30–11pm, Sat 12.30–4pm & 6.30–11pm, Sun 12.30–3.30pm & 6.30–10.30pm. £10–50.

Rodrizio Rico 111 Westbourne Grove, W11 ☎020/7792 4035; **Notting Hill Gate or Queensway tube.** Eat as much as you like for around £18 a head at this Brazilian churrascaria. Carvers come round and lop off chunks of freshly grilled smoky meats from whichever skewers they are holding, while you prime your plate from the salad bar and hot buffet. Mon–Fri 6pm–midnight, Sat 12–4pm & 6pm–midnight, Sun 12.30–11pm. £18–25.

North London: Little Venice to Islington

Almeida 30 Almeida St, N1 ☎020/7354 4777, ⓦwww.conran-restaurants.co.uk; **Angel or Highbury & Islington tube.** A Conran restaurant, opposite the theatre of the same name, that is a distillation of all that is good about wonderful, old-fashioned, gently familiar French cooking. Mon–Sat noon–2.30pm & 6–11pm, Sun noon–3pm & 5.30–10pm. £18–80.

Elk in the Woods 39 Camden Passage ☎020/7226 3535; **Angel tube.** A stylish little restaurant/bar tucked away on Camden Passage, with distressed wood, floral wallpaper and a stuffed elk looking down on proceedings. Game is a big feature of the menu, with hearty stews, pies and steaks, plus tasty traditional puddings. Daily 10am–11pm. £12–30.

Mandalay 444 Edgware Rd, W2 ☎020/7258 3696; **Edgware Road tube.** Pure and unexpurgated Burmese cuisine – a melange of Thai, Malaysian and a lot of Indian. The portions are huge, the service friendly and the prices

low. Booking essential in the evening. Mon–Sat noon–2.30pm & 6–10.30pm. £6–16.

Mango Room 10–12 Kentish Town Rd, NW1 ☎020/7482 5065; **Camden Town tube.** An engaging, laid-back, Camden-cool Caribbean place whose cooking is consistent and whose presentation is first-class. Tues–Sat noon–3pm & 6pm–midnight, Sun noon–11pm. £12–38.

Manna 4 Erskine Rd, NW3 ☎020/7722 8028, ⓦwww.manna-veg.com; **Chalk Farm tube.** Old-fashioned, casual vegetarian restaurant with 1970s decor, serving large portions of very good food. Mon–Sat 6.30–11pm, Sun 12.30–3pm & 6.30–11pm. £10–45.

Odette's 130 Regent's Park Rd, NW3 ☎020/7586 5486; **Chalk Farm tube.** Charming, picturesque local restaurant idyllically set in pretty Primrose Hill, serving well-judged Modern British food accompanied by warm and delicious olive and walnut bread. Mon–Fri 12.30–2.30pm & 7–11pm, Sat 7–11pm, Sun 12.30–2.45pm. £20–40.

Pasha 301 Upper St, N1 ☎020/7226 1454; **Angel or Highbury & Islington tube.** *Pasha* looks nothing like a traditional Turkish restaurant, with only the odd brass pot hinting at its Ottoman origins. Food is fresh, light and authentic, and the menu easy to decipher. Mon–Thurs noon–3pm & 6–11.30pm, Fri & Sat noon–3pm & 6pm–midnight, Sun noon–11pm. £15–30.

Trojka 101 Regent's Park Rd, NW1 ☎020/7483 3765, ⓦwww.trojka.co.uk; **Chalk Farm tube.** A pleasant neighbourhood restaurant in villagey Primrose Hill, with Russian dolls and samovars stacked to the ceiling. The Eastern European food is filling and tasty: the menu has a whole section on blinis and caviar, plus there are sturdy standbys such as stroganoff, and grills served with *Trojka*'s own tartare sauce. Daily 8am–10.30pm. £7–30.

Viet Anh Cafe 41 Parkway, NW1 ☎020/7284 4082; **Camden Town tube.** Authentic, bright, cheerful café with oilcloth-covered tables run by a young Vietnamese couple. This is a friendly and welcoming place where, if there's anything puzzling or unfamiliar, they'll tell you what and show you how. Daily noon–4pm & 5.30–11pm. £15–40.

North London: Stoke Newington and Hackney

Armadillo 41 Broadway Market, E8 ☎020/7249 3633, ⓦwww.armadillorestaurant.co.uk; **bus #26**

27

or #48 from Liverpool Street tube. Small, neighbourhood restaurant employing unusual combinations of ingredients with a spicy background. The courtyard and balcony are deservedly popular on summer evenings, so book ahead. Tues–Sat 6.30–10.30pm. £18–50.

Mangal 10 Arcola St, E8 ☎020/7275 8981, ⓦwww.mangal1.com; Dalston Kingsland train station. Situated just opposite the Arcola Theatre. Service at this open-grill restaurant is on the brusque side, but if you're after astoundingly filling meaty grills, great breads and lahmacun, and a taste of Istanbul in East London, this is the place to head for. Daily noon–midnight. £8–25.

🏃 **Rasa 55 Stoke Newington Church St, N1 ☎020/7249 0344, ⓦwww.rasarestaurants .com; Stoke Newington train station.** The original *Rasa* features walls the colour of calomine lotion, attentive service and delicious well-priced South Indian vegetarian grub. Round things off with the wonderful fresh-mango sorbet. *Rasa Travancore* across the road specializes in Syrian Christian cooking, serving some meat and fish dishes. £12–30.

🏃 **Santa Maria de Buen Ayre 50 Broadway Market, E8 ☎020/7275 9900, ⓦwww .buenayre.co.uk; bus #26 or #48 from Liverpool Street tube.** An unpretentious neighbourhood place – the only Argentinian restaurant in the UK with a charcoal-fired parrilla (grill). There's quite a wait while the meat cooks but you won't be disappointed – the Argentinian ribeye and sirloin steaks are expertly prepared, tender and delicious. The sausages (hand-made in Walthamstow) are a winner too, and puddings, such as their take on bread pudding, are surprisingly unstodgy. Tues–Fri 6–10.30pm, Sat 11am–10.30pm, Sun 1–10.30pm. £8–40.

Yum Yum 30 Stoke Newington Church St, N16 ☎020 7254 6751, ⓦwww.yumyum.co.uk; Stoke Newington train station. An old Stoke Newington favourite in a new location. Elegantly presented and delicious Thai food and attentive service. Mon–Thurs & Sun noon–3pm & 6–11pm, Fri & Sat noon–3pm & 6–11.30pm.

North London: Hampstead and Highgate

The Czechoslovak House 74 West End Lane, NW6 ☎020/7372 5251; West Hampstead tube. Meat-and-dumpling-dominated meals in a restaurant complete with flock wallpaper and Gambrinus on draught. Set in a lovely house with a garden out back, and very popular with Czech expats – book ahead if you want to come for Sunday lunch. Tues–Fri 6–10pm, Sat & Sun noon–3pm & 6–10pm. Cash or cheque only. £12–26.

Jin Kichi 73 Heath St, NW3 ☎020/7794 6158; Hampstead tube. Eschewing the slick minimalism and sushi-led cuisine of most Japanese restaurants, *Jin Kichi* is cramped, homely and very busy (so book ahead) and specializes in grilled skewers of meat. Tues–Fri 6–11pm, Sat 12.30–2pm & 6–11pm, Sun 12.30–2pm & 6–10pm. £15–30.

Solly's 146–150 Golders Green Rd, NW11 ☎020/8455 2121; Golders Green tube. Downstairs is *Solly's Restaurant*, a small kosher deli specializing in epic falafel; *Solly's Exclusive*, upstairs, is a huge, bustling kosher restaurant. Mon–Thurs 6.30–10.30pm, Sat (winter only) an hour after dusk–1am, Sun 12.30–10.30pm. £17–40.

Wembley

Sakonis 127–129 Ealing Rd, Alperton, Middlesex ☎020/8903 9601; Alperton or Wembley Central tube. Top-notch vegetarian food factory, crowded with Asian families and serving terrific food, especially good dosas, great farari cutlets, deep-fried delights and wonderful juices. Mon–Thurs & Sun 11am–11pm, Fri & Sat 11am–midnight. £5–15.

Brixton

Mo Ca 1st floor, 398 Coldharbour Lane, SW9 ☎020/7733 7515, ⓦwww.mocabrixton.com; Brixton tube. An excellent addition to the Brixton scene, with a Trinidadian chef cooking up fine modern Caribbean food. Follow the "fish, wings and tings" starter with mains such as pan-fried grouper and green banana salad. The petrol-blue dining room is spacious and elegant, with just the distant thud of bass to remind you you're above the *Dogstar* (see p.488). Tues–Sat 6–11pm, Sun noon–6pm. £10–30.

New Fujiyama 7 Vining St, SW9 ☎020/7737 2369, ⓦwww.newfujiyama.com; Brixton tube. With lacquered red walls and a buzzy atmosphere, *Fujiyama* is a good Brixton standby, serving tasty ramen and noodle dishes as well as miso soup. Plenty of vegetarian options. Mon–Fri 11am–4pm & 5pm–1am, Sat & Sun 11am–1am. £8–26.

Satay Bar 450 Coldharbour Lane, SW9 ☎020/7326 5001, ⓦwww.sataybar.co.uk; Brixton

27

tube. Lively, up-for-it bar and restaurant tucked away behind the Ritzy cinema, that plays loud music, serves good Indonesian food and doubles as a local art gallery. Mon–Fri noon–3pm & 6–11.30pm, Sat & Sun noon–midnight. £15–30.

Southall

Gifto's Lahore Karahi 162–164 The Broadway, Southall, Middlesex ☎020/8813 8669; Southall train station. *Gifto's* specializes in freshly grilled, well-spiced meats and exceptionally good breads, backed up by a few curries and one or two odd dishes from Lahore, all done superbly well. Mon–Thurs noon–11.30pm, Fri–Sun noon–midnight. £10–20.
Omi's 1–3 Beaconsfield Rd, Southall, Middlesex ☎020/8571 4831; Southall train station. *Omi's* is a small, no-frills eatery with a kitchen as spacious as the dining area. It may not be prepossessing, but you'll get tasty Punjabi/Kenyan-Asian dishes, lots of rich flavours and great value. Mon–Thurs 11am–10.30pm, Fri & Sat 11am–11pm. £5–12.

Hammersmith to Richmond

Azou 35 King St, W6 ☎020/8563 7266; Stamford Brook or Ravenscourt Park tube. Small, informal and atmospheric North African restaurant where you can enter into the spirit and end up sitting on a cushion on the floor. A warm welcome is assured and the classics – tagines and couscous – are presented with some panache. Mon–Fri noon–2.30pm & 6–11pm, Sat & Sun 6–11pm. £10–30.
Chez Lindsay 11 Hill Rise, Richmond, Surrey ☎020/8948 7473; Richmond tube. Small, bright, authentic Breton creperie, with a loyal local following. The "Cider with Lindsay" fixed menu (£15.75) offers three courses plus a cup of Breton cider. Choose between galettes, crepes or more formal French main courses, including lots of fresh fish and shellfish. Mon–Sat 11am–11pm, Sun noon–10pm. £7–27.

Fish Hoek 6–8 Elliot St, W4 ☎020/8742 0766; Turnham Green tube. Light and airy South African fish restaurant in leafy Chiswick with an impressive menu that changes daily. Most dishes are available in half or full portions. Tues–Sat noon–2.30pm & 6.30–11pm, Sun noon–9pm. £15–60.
The Gate 51 Queen Caroline St, W6 ☎020/8748 6932, ⊛www.gateveg.co.uk; Hammersmith tube. There are ghetto-like vegetarian restaurants and then there are restaurants in a completely different class that, for one reason or another, happen not to use meat or fish in their cooking. *The Gate* is one of the latter, serving excellent and original dishes with intense and satisfying tastes and textures. Located in a converted church with an outside courtyard that's lovely in summer. Mon–Fri noon–3pm & 6–11pm, Sat 6–11pm. £10–40.
La Trompette 5–7 Devonshire Rd, W14 ☎020/8747 1836; Turnham Green tube. A pleasant dining room with a good deal of light oak and chocolate leather on show. The French food is very good, the menu changes on a day-to-day basis and the prix-fixe arrangements (£21.50–£32.50) are straightforward. Their wine list is excellent. Mon–Sat noon–2.30pm & 6.30–10.30pm, Sun 12.30–3pm & 7–10pm. £20–50.
Patio 5 Goldhawk Rd, W12 ☎020/8743 5194; Goldhawk Road or Shepherd's Bush tube. Good, solid Polish food in a friendly, comfortable atmosphere, for a relatively small amount of money. The set menu for around £12 – including a starter, main and a vodka – is the trump card. Mon–Fri noon–3pm & 6pm–midnight, Sat & Sun 6pm–midnight. £13–26.

Pubs and bars

ondon's drinking establishments run the whole gamut from traditional old English alehouses to funky modern bars with resident DJs catering to a pre-club crowd. **Pubs** are one of the country's most enduring social institutions, and have outlived the church and the marketplace as the focal points of communities, with London's fringe theatre, alternative comedy and live-music scenes still pub-based at their roots. At their best, pubs can be as welcoming as their full name, "public house", suggests, offering a fine range of drinks and filling food. At their worst, they're dismal rooms with surly bar staff and rotten snacks. One thing you can be sure of, however, is that most pubs and bars remain smoke-filled places where drinking alcohol is the prime activity.

London's great period of pub building took place in the Victorian era, to which many pubs still pay homage; genuine Victorian interiors, however, are increasingly difficult to find, as indeed are genuinely individual establishments. **Chain pubs** can now be found all over the capital: branches of *All Bar One*, *Pitcher & Piano* and *Slug & Lettuce* are the most obvious, as they all share the chain name, whereas Fuller's, Nicholson and J.D. Wetherspoon pubs do at least vary theirs.

The traditional image of London **pub food** is justifiably dire – a pseudo "ploughman's lunch" of bread and cheese, or a murky-looking pie and chips – but the last couple of decades have seen plenty of improvements. The emergence of **gastropubs**, where the food is as important as the drink, has had a huge impact on the rest of the pub trade. You can get a palatable lunchtime meal at many of the pubs listed in this chapter, decent Thai food in some of them, and at a few you're looking at cooking worthy of restaurant-standard praise and priced accordingly.

Though pubs may be constantly changing hands (and names), the quickest turnover is in **bars**, which go in and out of fashion with incredible speed. These are very different places to your average pub, with designer interiors and drinks; they also tend to be more expensive. We've included a good selection of **club-bars**, too, places which cater for a clubby crowd, which often have resident DJs, along with late opening hours and, more often than not, an entry charge after 11pm.

England's **licensing laws** are changing after almost a century of draconian restrictions, now that the government has finally committed itself to liberalizing opening hours. This will allow many more pubs and bars to stay open way beyond the standard 11pm last orders, so times listed below may well have changed since this book went to press.

Note that this chapter covers pubs, bars and wine bars that are good for drinking in – and, sometimes, eating in. It doesn't include pubs and bars that are primarily live-music venues, which you'll find in Chapter 29, or gay and lesbian pubs and bars, which are covered in Chapter 30.

The **locations** of our recommendations are shown on the corresponding area's chapter map where possible.

Trafalgar Square

The Chandos 29 St Martin's Lane, WC2 ☎020/7836 1401; Leicester Square tube. If you can get one of the booths downstairs, or the leather sofas upstairs in the Opera Room, then you'll find it difficult to leave, especially given the cheap Sam Smith's beer. Mon–Sat 11am–11pm, Sun noon–10.30pm.

Whitehall and Westminster

Red Lion 48 Parliament St, SW1 ☎020/7930 5826; Westminster tube. Good old pub, convenient for Westminster Abbey and Parliament. Popular with MPs, who are called to votes by a division bell in the bar. Mon–Fri 11am–11pm, Sat 11am–9pm, Sun noon–8pm.
Westminster Arms 9 Storey's Gate, SW1 ☎020/7222 8520; Westminster tube. A real parliamentary pub, wall to wall with MPs, and with a division bell in the bar. Mon–Fri 11am–11pm, Sat 11am–6pm, Sun noon–5pm.

St James's

ICA Bar The Mall, SW1 ☎020/7766 1451, ⓦwww .ica.org.uk; Piccadilly Circus or Charing Cross tube. You have to be a member to drink at the *ICA Bar* – but anyone can join on the door (Mon–Fri £1.50, Sat & Sun £2.50). It's a cool drinking venue, with a noir dress code observed by the arty crowd and staff. Occasional club nights. Mon noon–11pm, Tues–Sat noon–1am, Sun noon–10.30pm.
Red Lion 23 Crown Passage, SW1 ☎020/7930 4141; Green Park tube. Not to be confused with the nearby pub of the same name (see below), this is a tiny wood-panelled local with a country-inn feel, hidden away in a passageway off Pall Mall. Mon–Sat 11am–11pm.
Red Lion 2 Duke of York St, SW1 ☎020/7321 0782; Piccadilly Circus tube. Genuine old Victorian gin palace with elegant etched mirrors, polished wood and a great ceiling. Mon–Sat 11.30am–11pm.
Sports Café 80 Haymarket, SW1 ☎020/7839 8300, ⓦwww.thesportscafe.com; Piccadilly Circus tube. A long way from upper-crust St James's, this very central, male-dominated

Beers

The classic English beer is **bitter**, an uncarbonated and dark beverage that should be pumped by hand from the cellar. In the last three decades, **lager** has overtaken bitter in popularity, and every pub will have at least two draught lagers on offer, plus a selection of foreign beers, which go in and out of fashion.

English beer drinkers go almost exclusively for bitter, and take the various brews extremely seriously. A moving force in this camp is **CAMRA** – the Campaign for Real Ale (ⓦwww.camra.org.uk) – which worked hard to keep local beers from dying out amid the big brewery takeovers of the 1970s. Some of the beer touted as good English ale is nothing of the sort (if the stuff comes out of an electric pump, it isn't the real thing), but these days even the big breweries distribute some very good beers.

Smaller operations whose fine ales are available over a wide area include Young's and Fuller's – the two main London breweries – and Wadworth, Adnams, Greene King, Flowers and Samuel Smith's. Regional concoctions from other independent breweries are frequently available, too, at free houses (pubs with no ties to a brewery), and London also has a number of brew-pubs, which produce their own peculiar brand on the premises.

Guinness, a very dark, creamy Irish stout, is also on sale virtually everywhere, and is an exception to the high-minded objection to electrically pumped beers – though purists will tell you that the stuff the English drink does not compare with the home variety.

(28)

Hotel bars

All of London's larger **hotels** have bars open to non-residents, and many of them are spectacular (if pricey) places to sit over a cocktail. Officially, they only serve non-residents during normal pub hours; at other times you may be asked to abstain from alcoholic beverages, or buy some food (which won't come cheap). A few require a jacket and tie for men (they will usually loan the latter), and you'll feel out of place if you don't make some attempt to dress up.

1 Aldwych 1 Aldwych, WC2 ☎020/7300 1070, ⊛www.onealdwych.com; Temple tube. To the left of this classy hotel's main entrance is the achingly smart, minimalist *Lobby Bar*, featuring a stupendously high ceiling and striking modern sculptures. Mon–Sat 8am–midnight, Sun 10am–10.30pm.

Berkeley Wilton Place, SW1 ☎020/7235 6000, ⊛www.the-savoy-group.com/Berkeley; Hyde Park Corner tube. The *Blue Bar* at the *Berkeley* is very blue, but only in the most discreet way, and the cocktails are stupendous even if none of them weighs in at under £10. Mon–Sat 4pm–1am, Sun 3pm–midnight.

Claridge's 49 Brook St, W1 ☎020/7629 8860, ⊛www.the-savoy-group.com; Bond Street tube. This bar has a tasteful Art Deco feel, with terribly English waiters, and splendid, very costly cocktails. Mon–Sat noon–1am, Sun 4pm–midnight.

Dorchester 63 Park Lane, W1 ☎020/7629 8888, ⊛www.dorchesterhotel.com; Hyde Park Corner tube. Wildly over-the-top gilded, mirrored Hollywood decor, big booths to ease into and jolly good cocktails at just under £10 a hit. Mon–Sat noon–11pm, Sun noon–10.30pm.

Lanesborough Hyde Park Corner, SW1 ☎020/7259 5599, ⊛www.lanesborough .com; Hyde Park Corner tube. Very exclusive hotel in a converted hospital; the bar is in the library, and is very, very posh, but also welcoming, with a wicked list of unusual cocktails for around a tenner. Mon–Sat 11am–1am, Sun noon–10.30pm.

Langham Hotel 1 Portland Place, W1 ☎020/7636 1000, ⊛www.langhamhotels .com; Oxford Circus tube. This fantastically ornate nineteenth-century hotel harbours *Tsar's*, a favoured BBC watering hole, replete with over 100 vodkas and a selection of caviars. Mon–Fri noon–midnight, Sat 5pm–midnight.

sports-theme bar is guaranteed to be showing whatever televised sport event is taking place. Mon, Fri & Sat noon–3pm, Tues–Thurs noon–2am, Sun noon–midnight.

Mayfair

Audley 41 Mount St, W1 ☎020/7499 1843; Hyde Park Corner or Marble Arch tube. A grand Mayfair pub, with original Victorian burgundy lincrusta ceiling, chandeliers and clocks. Popular with Americans. Mon–Sat 11am–11pm, Sun noon–10.30pm.

Cecconi's 5a Burlington Gardens, W1 ☎020/7494 1500; Green Park or Piccadilly Circus tube. Little Italian place that has an unstudied upmarket feel, with a long marble bar, leather bench seating and subdued colours. The wine list is forty pages long (don't be afraid to ask for help), and they also serve grappa and limoncello. Mon–Fri 8am–11pm, Sat 10am–11pm, Sun noon–11pm.

Guinea 30 Bruton Place, W1 ☎020/7409 1728; Bond Street or Green Park tube. Pretty, tiny, old-fashioned, flower-strewn mews pub, serving good Young's bitter and excellent steak-and-kidney pies. Mon–Fri 11am–11pm, Sat 6.30–11pm.

Match Bar 37–38 Margaret St, W1 ☎020/7499 3443; Oxford Circus tube. Plenty of tasty cocktails up for grabs in this leather sofa-adorned, wooden-floored bar, tucked away only a stone's throw from the organized chaos of Oxford Street. Mon–Sat 11am–midnight.

Studio Lounge Bar Fifth floor, Waterstone's Piccadilly, 203 Piccadilly, SW1 ☎020/7851 2433; Piccadilly Circus tube. A lounge bar in the sense that you feel as though you're in a particularly stylish front room, albeit one with a panoramic view of London. It's spectacular after dark and makes a good spot for an arty date, or take a pile of books from the shelves to browse. Mon–Sat 10am–10pm, Sun 11am–5pm.

Mandarin Oriental 66 Knightsbridge, SW1 ☎020/7235 2000, ⊛www.mandarin -oriental.com; Knightsbridge tube. The *Mandarin Bar* is one of the most stylish hotel bars in London, a subtle symphony in brown marble and glass, serving superb cocktails. Daily 11am–2am.

The Ritz 150 Piccadilly, W1 ☎020/7493 8181, ⊛www.theritzhotel.co.uk; Green Park tube. The *Rivoli at the Ritz* is a beautiful Art Deco marble bar with Lalique glass where, if dressed correctly, you can sip sumptuous and expensive cocktails. Mon–Sat 11.30am–1.30am, Sun 11.30am–12.30am.

Hotel Russell Russell Square, WC1 ☎020/7837 6470; Russell Square tube. The magnificent high ceilings and wood panelling of this Victorian hotel's *King's Bar* make this a great place in which to luxuriate. It's also a lot less posh – and more fun – than most, and you get free bowls of nibbles. Mon–Sat 7–1am, Sun 7am–midnight.

Sanderson 50 Berners St, W1 ☎020/7300 1400, ⊛www.sandersonhotel.com; Tottenham Court Road or Oxford Circus tube. The *Long Bar* at the *Sanderson Hotel*, is all translucent backlit onyx and, like the rest of the hotel, very self-consciously cool. Mon–Sat 11am–1am, Sun 11am–10.30pm.

The Savoy 1 Savoy Hill, Strand, WC2 ☎020/7836 4343, ⊛www.the-savoy.com; Charing Cross tube. The Savoy's Art Deco *American Bar* is renowned for its cocktails, as it should be since you're paying around £10 a throw. A jazz pianist plays from 7pm. Mon–Sat 2pm–1am.

Soho Hotel 4 Richmond Mews, W1 ☎020/7559 3000, ⊛www.sohohotel.com; Leicester Square tube. *REFUEL*, the hotel's Forties-style bar, has a screamingly colourful mural based on the building's earlier life as a car park, and is the latest, liveliest upmarket drinking spot in Soho. Mon–Fri 8am–midnight, Sun 8am–10.30pm.

The Trafalgar 2 Spring Gardens, SW1 ☎020/7870 2900, ⊛www.trafalgar-london.com; Charing Cross tube. Lounge-lizard minimalism is the feel at the hotel's *Rockwell bar*, with musicians and DJs playing daily and 100 varieties of bourbon behind the bar. In the summer take the lift to the sixth-floor rooftop bar, with stunning views onto Trafalgar Square. Mon–Sat 8am–1am, Sun 9am–10.30pm.

Ye Grapes 16 Shepherd Market, W1 (no phone); Green Park or Hyde Park Corner tube. Busy Victorian free house, with a good selection of beers and an open fire – a great local on a pretty little square in the heart of Mayfair.

Marylebone

Barley Mow 8 Dorset St, W1 ☎020/7935 7318; Baker Street tube. This local pub tucked away in the backstreets of Marylebone has pawnbrokers' snugs and serves a range of real ales. Mon–Sat 11am–11pm.

The Chapel 48 Chapel St, NW1 ☎020/7402 9220; Edgware Road tube. An attractive open-plan gastropub, with vanilla-coloured walls, cast-iron columns and battered wooden floors. The food is very fine, and includes mains such as roast leg of lamb (£12.50) and good puds such as rhubarb *crème brûlée*. Adnams and Greene King IPA on

handpump. Mon–Sat noon–11pm, Sun noon–10.30pm.

Dover Castle 43 Weymouth Mews, W1 ☎020/7580 4412; Regent's Park or Oxford Circus tube. A traditional, quiet boozer hidden away down a labyrinthine and picturesque Marylebone mews. Green upholstery, dark wood and a nicotine-stained lincrusta ceiling add to the atmosphere. Mon–Fri 11.30am–11pm, Sat 12.30–11pm.

O'Conor Don 88 Marylebone Lane, W1 ☎020/7935 9311; Bond Street tube. A stripped bare, stout-loving pub that's a cut above the average, with excellent Guinness, a pleasantly measured pace and Irish food on offer. Closed Sat & Sun.

Soho

Alphabet 61–63 Beak St, W1 ☎020/7439 2190, ⊛www.alphabetbar.com; Oxford Circus tube. *Alphabet* has the feel of two places:

upstairs is light and spacious with decadent leather sofas, a great choice of European beers, and mouthwatering food; downstairs, there are dimmed coloured lights and car seats strewn around. Mon–Fri noon–11pm, Sat 5–11pm.

Argyll Arms 18 Argyll St, W1 ☏ 020/7734 6117; **Oxford Circus tube.** A stone's throw from Oxford Circus, this is a serious find: a great Victorian pub that has preserved many of its original features and serves good real ales. Mon–Sat 11am–11pm, Sun noon–10.30pm.

Atlantic 20 Glasshouse St, W1 ☏ 020/7734 4888; **Piccadilly Circus tube.** The main downstairs bar is located in a wonderfully ornate and spacious Art Deco hall, built as the ballroom of the *Regent Palace Hotel*. A classy venue for a heady cocktail. Mon–Fri noon–3am, Sat 6pm–3am.

Bar Chocolate 27 D'Arblay St, W1 ☏ 020/7287 2823; **Piccadilly Circus tube.** Low-lit café-bar with a check-tiled floor, red art-decked walls, a small corner bar, books, church chairs, large windows and a relaxed clientele. Table service; food available. Mon–Sat 10am–11pm, Sun noon–10.30pm.

Coach & Horses 29 Greek St, W1 ☏ 020/7437 5920; **Leicester Square tube.** Long-standing – and, for once, little-changed – haunt of the ghosts of old Soho, nightclubbers and art students from nearby St Martin's College. 1950s red plastic stools and black formica tables guaranteed. Mon–Sat 11am–11pm, Sun noon–10.30pm.

🏃 **De Hems 11 Macclesfield St, W1** ☏ 020/7437 2494; **Leicester Square tube.** Probably your best bet in Chinatown, this is London's official Dutch pub, and has been since the 1890s; a simple wood-panelled affair with Oranjeboom on tap and Belgian beers in bottles. Mon–Sat noon–midnight, Sun noon–10.30pm.

Dog & Duck 18 Bateman St, W1 ☏ 020/7494 0697; **Leicester Square or Tottenham Court Road tube.** Tiny Soho pub that retains much of its old character, beautiful Victorian tiling and mosaics, a good range of real ales and a loyal clientele that often includes jazz musicians from nearby Ronnie Scott's club. Mon–Sat 11am–11pm, Sun 11am–10.30pm.

French House 49 Dean St, W1 ☏ 020/7437 2799; **Leicester Square tube.** This tiny French pub has been a Soho institution since Belgian Victor Berlemont bought the place shortly before World War I. Free French and literary associations galore, and half-pints only at

the bar (no real ale). Mon–Sat noon–11pm, Sun noon–10.30pm.

The Toucan 19 Carlisle St, W1 ☏ 020/7437 4123, ⊛ www.thetoucan.co.uk; **Tottenham Court Road tube.** Small bar serving excellent Guinness and a wide range of Irish whiskies, plus cheap, wholesome and filling food. So popular it can get mobbed. There's another branch, *Toucan Two*, in Marylebone (94 Wimpole St, W1; Bond Street or Oxford Circus tube). Mon–Fri 11am–11pm, Sat 1–11pm.

Two Floors 3 Kingly St, W1 ☏ 020/7439 1007; **Oxford Circus tube.** Laid-back, designer-style Soho bar, laid out, unsurprisingly, on two floors, attracting a mixed media crowd. Mon–Sat noon–11pm.

Fitzrovia

Bradley's Spanish Bar 42–44 Hanway St, W1 ☏ 020/7636 0359; **Tottenham Court Road tube.** Appealingly unpretentious backstreet bar, set over two very small floors, with a mixed but faithful clientele and an excellent vinyl jukebox full of old favourites. Mon–Sat noon–11pm, Sun noon–10.30pm.

The Hope 15 Tottenham St, W1 ☏ 020/7637 0896; **Goodge Street tube.** Chiefly remarkable for its sausage (veggie ones included), beans and mash lunches, and its real ales. Mon–Sat 11am–11pm, Sun 11.30am–6pm.

Jerusalem 33–34 Rathbone Place, W1 ☏ 020/7255 1120; **Tottenham Court Road tube.** All chandeliers and velvet drapes, this place attracts a more dressed-up crowd enjoying the house DJs who play Thurs, Fri and Sat evenings. Mon noon–11pm, Tues & Wed noon–midnight, Thurs & Fri noon–1am, Sat 7pm–1am.

Market Place 11 Market Place, W1 ☏ 020/7079 2020, ⊛ www.marketplace-london.com; **Oxford Circus tube.** Owned by Cargo, *Market Place* may look more like a sauna than a thriving bar, but it has a varied music policy (with DJs tackling jazz funk, ska, hip-hop and breakbeat) that makes it well worth checking out. The food is above average too. Mon–Wed noon–midnight, Thurs–Sat noon–1am, Sun noon–10.30pm.

Newman Arms 23 Rathbone St, W1 ☏ 020/7636 1127; **Tottenham Court Road or Goodge Street tube.** What *The Hope* is to sausages, the *Newman Arms* is to pies, with every sort from gammon to steak and kidney. Mon–Fri noon–11pm.

🏃 **The Social 5 Little Portland St, W1** ☏ 020/7636 4992, ⊛ www.thesocial.com;

Oxford Circus tube. Industrial club-bar run by the Heavenly record label, with great DJs playing everything from rock to rap, a truly hedonistic-cum-alcoholic crowd and the ultimate snacks – beans on toast and fish-finger sarnies – for when you get an attack of the munchies. Fab music on the upstairs jukebox too. Mon–Fri noon–midnight, Sat 1pm–midnight. Second branch at 33 Linton St, Arlington Square, N1 (☎020/7354 5809; Mon–Fri 5–11pm, Sat noon–11pm, Sun noon–10.30pm).

Bloomsbury

The Lamb 94 Lamb's Conduit St, WC1 ☎020/7405 0713; Russell Square tube. Pleasant Young's pub with a marvellously well-preserved Victorian interior of mirrors, old wood and "snob" screens. Mon–Sat 11am–11pm, Sun 11am–4pm & 7–10.30pm.

Lord John Russell 91–93 Marchmont St, WC1 ☎020/7388 0500; Russell Square tube. Simple, bare-boards pub close to the B&Bs north of Cartwright Gardens, serving a good range of ales and lagers to a truly eclectic crowd, from students to elderly locals. Mon–Sat 11am–11pm, Sun noon–10.30pm.

Museum Tavern 49 Great Russell St, WC1 ☎020/7242 8987; Tottenham Court Road or Russell Square tube. Large and characterful old pub, right opposite the main entrance to the British Museum, and the erstwhile drinking hole of Karl Marx. Mon–Sat 11am–11pm, Sun noon–10.30pm.

Perseverance 63 Lamb's Conduit St, WC1 ☎020/7405 8278; Russell Square tube. Smartened-up old boozer with nasty-but-nice flock wallpaper, stuffed animal heads and chandeliers. Good range of beers and wines and a small upstairs dining room. Mon–Fri 12.30–11pm, Sat 5.30–11pm, Sun 12.30–10.30pm.

Covent Garden and the Strand

Africa Centre 38 King St, WC2 ☎020/7836 1976; Covent Garden tube. Occasionally noisy, convivial basement bar, attracting Africans and Africa-philes. The beer's awful, but that's missing the point. Mon–Sat 6–11pm.

AKA 18 West Central St, WC1 ☎020/7836 0110, ⓦ www.akalondon.com; Tottenham Court Road tube. Minimalist, twenty-first-century-style club-bar, next door to (and owned by) *The End* (see p.495). A chrome balcony overlooks the main floor, which includes a

well-stocked bar where you can also eat such delights as chive and butternut squash soup. Mon–Fri 6pm–3am, Sat 7pm–7am, Sun 9pm–4am.

The Angel 61 St Giles High St, WC2 ☎020/7240 2876; Tottenham Court Road tube. A friendly local in the centre of town, popular with musos. Small courtyard garden, open fires and a loyal crowd. Mon–Fri 11.30am–11pm, Sat noon–11pm, Sun 2–10.30pm.

Bünker 41 Earlham St, WC2 ☎020/7240 0606; Covent Garden tube. Busy, brick-vaulted basement bar with wrought-iron pillars, lots of brushed steel and pricey lagers, some made on the premises – in particular, there's a fine organic brew.

Coal Hole 91 Strand, WC2 ☎020/7379 9883; Charing Cross or Embankment tube. Very popular Edwardian pub next to *The Savoy*, which was once patronized – like many of the pubs in the area – by coal-heavers. There's a nice gallery upstairs, a cellar bar below and real ales. Mon–Sat 11am–11pm, Sun noon–6pm.

Cross Keys 31 Endell St, WC2 ☎020/7836 5185; Leicester Square tube. A wonderfully cluttered old pub, with a good blend of older Covent Garden residents and young workers.

Detroit 35 Earlham St, WC2 ☎020/7240 2662, ⓦ www.detroit-bar.com; Covent Garden tube. Cavernous underground venue with an open-plan bar area, secluded Gaudíesque booths and a huge range of spirits. DJs take over at the weekends, with underground house on Saturdays. Mon–Sat 5pm–midnight.

Gordon's 47 Villiers St, WC2 ☎020/7930 1408; Charing Cross or Embankment tube. Cavernous, shabby, atmospheric wine bar specializing in ports, right next door to Charing Cross Station. The excellent and varied wine list, decent buffet food and genial atmosphere make this a favourite with local office workers, who spill outdoors in the summer. Mon–Sat 11am–11pm, Sun noon–10pm.

Lamb & Flag 33 Rose St, WC2 ☎020/7497 9504; Leicester Square tube. Busy, tiny and highly atmospheric pub, tucked away down an alley between Garrick Street and Floral Street, where John Dryden was attacked in 1679 after scurrilous verses had been written about one of Charles II's mistresses (by someone else as it turned out). Mon–Thurs 11am–11pm, Fri & Sat 11am–10.45pm, Sun noon–10.30pm.

Riverside, canalside and dockland pubs

In summer, the most popular pubs in London are those with a riverside, canalside or dockland view. You can sit outside at any of the places listed below (see main text for reviews); another option is to drink on one of the old **naval and merchant boats** moored on the north bank of the Thames, between Westminster and Blackfriars bridges – there's little to distinguish these, so stroll down and take your pick.

East End and Docklands (see map, p.483)
Dickens Inn
The Grapes
The Gun
Prospect of Whitby
Town of Ramsgate
Via Fossa

Lambeth and Southwark (see map, p.484)
Anchor Bankside
Founders Arms
Mayflower
Spice Island

Greenwich (see map, p.488)
Cutty Sark
Trafalgar Tavern

Hammersmith and Chiswick
Blue Anchor
Dove

Richmond and Twickenham (see map, p.489)
Fox & Grapes
White Cross Hotel
White Swan

Lowlander 36 Drury Lane, WC2 ☏ 020/7379 7446; Covent Garden tube. A lofty, busy bar specializing in hangover-inducing and wallet-bashing Belgian and Dutch beers, many on tap. Table service and deli snacks from the Low Countries, including *moules frites*. Mon–Sat noon–11pm, Sun noon–10pm.

Punch & Judy 40 The Market, WC2 ☏ 020/7379 0923; Covent Garden tube. Horribly mobbed and loud, but this Covent Garden Market pub does boast an unbeatable location with a very popular balcony overlooking the Piazza. Mon–Sat 11am–11pm, Sun noon–10.30pm.

🏃 **The Salisbury** 90 St Martin's Lane, WC2 ☏ 020/7836 5863; Leicester Square tube. One of the most beautifully preserved Victorian pubs in the capital, with etched and engraved windows, bronze figures and a lincrusta ceiling. Mon–Fri 11am–midnight, Sat noon–11pm, Sun noon–10.30pm.

Holborn

🏃 **Cittie of Yorke** 22 High Holborn, WC1 ☏ 020/7242 7670; Chancery Lane tube. A venerable London pub, with a vaulted cellar bar, wood panelling, cheap Sam Smith's beer and grand quasi-medieval wine hall whose cosy cubicles were once the preserve of lawyers and their clients. Mon–Fri 11.30am–11pm, Sat noon–11pm.

Na Zdrowie 11 Little Turnstile, WC1 ☏ 020/7831 9679; Holborn tube. Great Polish bar hidden in an alleyway behind Holborn tube, with a wicked selection of flavoured vodkas and beers, and good cheap Polish food. Mon–Fri 12.30–11pm, Sat 6–11pm.

Old Bank of England 194 Fleet St, EC4 ☏ 020/7430 2255; Temple or Chancery Lane tube. Not the actual Bank of England, but the former Law Courts' branch, this imposing High Victorian banking hall is now a magnificently opulent ale-and-pie pub. Mon–Fri 11am–11pm.

Ye Olde Mitre 1 Ely Court, off Ely Place, EC1 ☎020/7405 4751; **Farringdon tube.** Hidden down a tiny alleyway off Ely Place, this wonderfully atmospheric pub dates back to 1546, although it was actually rebuilt in the eighteenth century. The low-ceilinged, wood-panelled rooms are packed with history and there are some unusual ales on offer. Mon–Fri 11am–11pm.

The City

Blackfriar 174 Queen Victoria St, EC4 ☎020/7236 5474; **Blackfriars tube.** A gorgeous, utterly original pub, with Art Nouveau marble friezes of boozy monks and a highly decorated alcove – all original, dating from 1905. Non-smoking throughout. Mon–Sat 11am–11pm, Sun noon–10.30pm.

The Counting House 50 Cornhill, EC2 ☎020/7283 7123; **Bank tube.** Another Fuller's bank conversion, with fantastic high ceilings, a glass dome, chandeliers and a central oval bar. Mon–Fri 11am–11pm.

The George Bishopsgate, EC2 ☎020/7618 7310; **Liverpool Street tube.** Part of Conran's smoothly-run refurbished *Great Eastern Hotel*, *The George* retains its wonderful original mock-Tudor decor. Mon–Sat 11am–11pm, Sun noon–10.30pm.

Jamaica Wine House St Michael's Alley, EC3 ☎020/7929 6972; **Bank tube.** An old City institution known locally as the "Jam Pot", tucked away down a narrow alleyway. Despite the name, this is really just a pub, divided into four large "snugs" by original high wooden-panelled partitions. Mon–Fri 11am–11pm.

The Lamb Leadenhall Market, EC3 ☎020/7626 2454; **Monument tube.** A great pub right in the middle of Leadenhall Market, serving pricey but excellent roast beef sandwiches at lunchtime. Mon–Fri 11am–9pm.

Vertigo 42 Tower 42, Old Broad St, EC2 ☎020/7877 7842; **Bank or Liverpool St tube.** Rarefied drinking in this champagne bar, 590ft above the City. Each seat has an astounding view of London; drinks prices are correspondingly high, and light meals are on offer. Smart jeans and trainers acceptable; booking essential. Mon–Fri noon–3pm & 5–11pm.

Viaduct Tavern 126 Newgate St, EC1 ☎020/7600 1863; **St Paul's tube.** Glorious gin palace built in 1869 opposite what was then Newgate Prison and is now the

Old Bailey. The walls are adorned with oils of faded ladies representing Commerce, Agriculture and the Arts. Ask staff to show you the old cells downstairs which are said to be haunted. Mon–Fri noon–11pm.

Ye Olde Cheshire Cheese Wine Office Court, 145 Fleet St, EC4 ☎020/7353 6170; **Temple or Blackfriars tube.** A famous seventeenth-century watering hole, with several snug, dark-panelled bars and real fires. Popular with tourists, but by no means exclusively so. Mon–Sat 11am–11pm, Sun noon–3.30pm.

Clerkenwell

Café Kick 43 Exmouth Market, EC1 ☎020/7837 8077, ⊛www.cafekick. co.uk; **Farringdon or Angel tube.** Stylish take on a smoky, local French-style café/bar in the heart of fashionable Exmouth Market, with three busy table-football games to enliven the atmosphere. Mon–Sat noon–11pm, Sun noon–10.30pm. Excellent second branch, *Bar Kick*, at 127 Shoreditch High St, E1 (☎020/7739 8700; Mon–Wed noon–11pm, Thurs–Sat noon–midnight, Sun noon–10.30pm).

Crown Tavern 43 Clerkenwell Green, EC1 ☎020/7253 4973; **Farringdon tube.** Housed in what was once a Victorian concert hall, this large and rambling pub has been pleasantly tarted up and now serves a lively, after-work crowd of media types. Mon–Sat noon–11pm, Sun noon–10.30pm.

Duke of York 156 Clerkenwell Rd, EC1 ☎020/7837 8548; **Chancery Lane tube.** Just the basics you need for a good pub – clear-glass windows, bare boards, bold red and blue paintwork, table football, pool, TV sport, mixed clientele and groovy tunes – and a lot less posey than most of Clerkenwell. Thai food available (Mon–Sat noon–3pm & 6–10pm). Mon–Sat 11am–11pm, Sun noon–10.30pm.

Dust 27a Clerkenwell Rd, EC1 ☎020/7490 5120; ⊛www.dustbar.co.uk; **Farringdon tube.** High-ceilinged bar in a former watchmaker's factory, with the requisite bare boards and art-adorned brick walls. Great cocktails with the bonus of a small dance floor and a late licence at the weekends when quality DJs play house, soul, funk and hip-hop. Tues & Wed 5pm–midnight, Thurs 5pm–2am, Fri & Sat 5pm–4am. £3–5 Fri & Sat.

Eagle 159 Farringdon Rd, EC1 ☎020/7837 1353;

28

Farringdon tube. The first (and still one of the best) of London's pubs to go foody, this place is heaving for lunch and dinner as *Guardian* and *Observer* workers tuck into Mediterranean dishes, but you should be able to find a seat at other times. Mon–Sat noon–11pm, Sun noon–5pm.

Fluid 40 Charterhouse St, EC1 ☎020/7253 3444, ⓦwww.fluidbar.com; Farringdon or Barbican tube. A two-floored, futuristic mix of vintage space-invader machines, low seating, and industrial chic, offering Japanese bottled lagers, Kirin on tap and wasabi martinis, as well as sushi (Mon–Fri). Attracts good DJs playing anything from jazz to electro via breaks nightly. Mon noon–5pm, Tues & Wed noon–midnight, Thurs & Fri noon–2am, Sat 7pm–2am.

Fox & Anchor 115 Charterhouse St, EC1 ☎020/7253 5075; Farringdon or Barbican tube. Handsome Smithfield Market pub famous for its early opening hours and huge breakfasts (served 7–10am). Mon–Fri 7am–9pm.

Jerusalem Tavern 55 Britton St, EC1 ☎020/7490 4281; Farringdon tube. Small, atmospheric converted Georgian coffee house, serving tasty food at lunchtimes, along with an excellent range of draught beers (including organic options) from St Peter's Brewery in Suffolk. Mon–Fri 11am–11pm.

Hoxton

The Bricklayer's Arms 63 Charlotte Rd, EC2 ☎020/7739 5245; Old Street tube. An appealingly ramshackle Shoreditch pub (serving Thai food) that predates the area's trendification, and is therefore all the more popular with its newer arty residents. Mon–Fri 11am–11pm, Sat noon–11pm, Sun noon–10.30pm.

Cocomo 323 Old St, EC1 ☎020/7613 0315; Old Street tube. Trinket-filled and slightly bohemian, *Cocomo* is a great small bar for a cocktail, smoothie, or a draught Red Stripe. DJs Fri and Sat nights. Mon–Sat 5pm–midnight, Sun 5–11pm.

Dragon 5 Leonard St, EC2 ☎020/7490 7110; Old Street tube. Discreetly signed clubby pub with bare-brick walls and crumbling leather sofas, that attracts a mix of local office workers and trendy Hoxtonites. Nightly DJs avoid house and go for a more eclectic mix that covers anything from hip-hop to Sixties. Mon noon–midnight,

Tues, Wed & Thurs noon–1am, Fri & Sat noon–2am, Sun noon–midnight.

Great Eastern Dining Room 54 Great Eastern St, EC2 ☎020/7613 4545; Old Street tube. Wonderful Modern European restaurant and smart bar area upstairs, and the laid-back lounge bar Below 54 downstairs – all sofas, cinema screens, dim lighting and great cocktails. Get there early, if you want to get in. Mon–Wed noon–midnight, Thurs & Fri noon–1am, Sat 6pm–1am.

Hoxton Square Bar and Kitchen 2–4 Hoxton Square, N1 ☎020/7613 0709; Old Street tube. This Blade Runner-esque concrete bar attracts trendy types with its mix of modern European food, kitsch-to-club soundtracks, worn leather sofas, and temporary painting and photography exhibitions. There's a club-like back room, but the bar's best in the summer, when the drinking spills into the square in a carnival spirit. Mon–Thurs & Sun 11am–midnight, Fri & Sat 11am–2am.

Smersh 5 Ravey St, EC2 ☎020/7739 0092, ⓦwww.smershbar.co.uk; Old Street tube. "Smersh", a shortening of Smert Spionam (that marks the inconspicuous entrance), is translated from the Russian as "death to all

▲ The Bricklayer's Arms

spies", referring to the KGB's anti-espionage department. A tiny, tatty but atmospheric basement bar, it has a good range of vodka and a music policy that departs from the usual Hoxton scene with Country & Western, Northern Soul, Mod and reggae DJs Wed to Fri. Mon–Fri 5pm–midnight, Sat 7pm–midnight.

Sosho 2 Tabernacle St, EC2 ☎020/7920 0701, ⓦ www.matchbar.com; **Old Street tube.** Very trendy club-bar with good cocktails and decent food; the ambience is chilled until the very popular DJs kick in at 8.30pm (Wed–Sat), and there's a charge at the weekend. Mon 11.30am–10pm, Tues & Wed 11.30am–midnight, Thurs 11.30am–1am, Fri 11.30am–3am, Sat 7pm–3am.

The East End: Whitechapel and Spitalfields

Big Chill Bar 94 Dray Walk, E1 ☎020/7392 9180, ⓦ www.bigchill.net; **Shoreditch tube.** Spin-off bar of the Big Chill multimedia company, offering quality nightly DJs, cocktails and a general sense of fun. An odd mix of concrete and kitsch, the spacious bar manages to be style-conscious yet relaxed, with punters spilling out onto the tables on funky Dray Walk in warmer weather. Mon–Sat noon–midnight, Sun noon–11.30pm.

Loungelover 1 Whitby St, E1 ☎020/7012 1234, wwww.loungelover.co.uk; **Shoreditch tube.** Behind the unprepossessing facade of this former meat-packing factory lies a bizarre array of opulently camp bric-a-brac, expertly slung together to create a trendy and unique cocktail bar. Drinks are very well executed and deservedly expensive. Reservations (to be made Mon–Fri 10am–6pm, Sat 1–6pm) recommended. Mon–Thurs 6pm–midnight, Fri 6pm–1am, Sat 7pm–1am.

Ten Bells 84 Commercial St, E1 ☎020/7366 1721; **Liverpool Street or Shoreditch tube.** Dating from 1753, this plain and pleasantly ramshackle pub was a hub of nineteenth-century Spitalfields when the area was terrorized by Jack the Ripper (one of his victims was known to drink here). The interior has some great Victorian tiling and the crowd these days is a trendy, relaxed bunch. DJs play Fri–Sun. Mon–Sat noon–11pm, Sun noon–10.30pm.

Vibe Bar Old Truman Brewery, 91–95 Brick Lane, E1 ☎020/7377 2899, ⓦ www.vibe-bar.com;

Shoreditch tube. Trendy bar in an old brewery with free Internet access, good sofas and DJs in the evenings. Great covered beer garden with summer barbecues at weekends. Mon–Thurs & Sun 11am–11.30pm, Fri & Sat 11am–1am.

Docklands

Dickens Inn St Katharine's Way, E1 ☎020/7488 2208; **Tower Hill tube.** Eighteenth-century timber-framed warehouse transported on wheels from its original site, and then much altered. Still, it's a remarkable building, with a great view, but very firmly on the tourist trail. Mon–Sat 11am–11pm, Sun noon–10.30pm.

The Grapes 76 Narrow St, E14 ☎020/7987 4396; **Westferry DLR.** *The Grapes'* fame is assured thanks to a possible connection with Dickens' *Our Mutual Friend*. It has a great riverside balcony out back, standard bar meals and an expensive fish restaurant upstairs. Mon–Fri noon–3.30pm & 5.30–11pm, Sat noon–11pm, Sun noon–10.30pm.

The Gun 27 Cold Harbour, E14 ☎020/7515 5222, ⓦ www.thegundocklands.com; **Canary Wharf tube or South Quay or Blackwall DLR.** Old dockers' pub with a fresh lick of paint and lots of maritime memorabilia, an unrivalled view of the Millennium Dome from its outside deck, and a classy dining area serving Modern European food. Mon–Sat 11am–11pm, Sun noon–10.30pm; open Sat & Sun from 10.30am for brunch but no alcohol.

Prospect of Whitby 57 Wapping Wall, E1 ☎020/7481 1095; **Wapping tube.** London's most famous riverside pub, with a flagstone floor, a cobbled courtyard and great views. Mon–Fri 11am–11pm, Sat noon–11pm, Sun noon–10.30pm.

Town of Ramsgate 62 Wapping High St, E1 ☎020/7264 0001; **Wapping tube.** Dark, narrow, medieval pub located by Wapping Old Stairs, which once led down to Execution Dock. Captain Blood was discovered here with the Crown Jewels under his cloak, "Hanging" Judge Jeffreys was arrested here trying to flee, and Admiral Bligh and Fletcher Christian were regular drinking partners in pre-mutiny days. Mon–Sat noon–11pm, Sun noon–10.30pm.

Via Fossa West India Quay, E14 ☎020/7515 8549; **West India Quay DLR.** Housed in a nineteenth-century warehouse, and accessible from Canary Wharf via a footbridge. If the weather's warm, the south-facing terrace is great to sit out on. Mon–Wed 11am–11pm, Thurs–Sat 11am–midnight, Sun noon–10.30pm.

The South Bank

Anchor & Hope 36 The Cut, SE1 ☎020/7928 9898, Southwark tube. A great addition to this increasingly lively street, the *Anchor* is a welcoming and unfussy gastropub, dishing up truly excellent grub: soups, salads and mains such as slow-cooked pork with choucroute, as well as mouthwatering puds. Extensive wine list. Mon 5–11pm, Tues–Sat 11am–11pm.

Baltic 74 Blackfriars Rd, SE1 ☎020/7928 1111, ⓦwww.balticrestaurant.co.uk; Southwark tube. Very stylish bar (and restaurant) situated opposite Southwark tube in an old Georgian coachworks, serving vodka shots and Baltic snacks. Daily noon–11pm.

NFT Bar South Bank, SE1 ☎020/7928 3535; Waterloo tube. The National Film Theatre's bar is the only one on the South Bank riverfront between Westminster and Blackfriars bridges – worth checking out not only for the views, but also for the food and the congenial crowd. Daily noon–10.30pm.

Southwark

Mayflower 117 Rotherhithe St, SE16 ☎020/7237 4088; Rotherhithe tube. A lot of reconstruction notwithstanding, this pub, in the heart of old Rotherhithe, is steeped in history and has a good view out onto the Thames. Mon–Sat noon–11pm, Sun noon–10.30pm.

Royal Oak 44 Tabard St, SE1 ☎020/7357 7173; Borough or London Bridge tube. Beautiful, lovingly restored Victorian pub that eschews jukeboxes and one-armed bandits and opts simply for serving real ales from Lewes in Sussex. Mon–Fri 11.30am–11pm.

Spice Island 163 Rotherhithe St, SE16 ☎020/7394 7108; Rotherhithe tube. Dramatically sited local boozer housed in a huge modernized wooden warehouse by the Thames, with a large riverside terrace. Mon–Thurs 11am–11pm, Fri & Sat 11am–midnight, Sun noon–10.30pm.

Southwark: Bankside

Anchor Bankside 34 Park St, SE1 ☎020/7407 1577; London Bridge tube. While the rest of Bankside has changed almost beyond all recognition, this pub still looks much as it did when first built in 1770 (on the inside, at least). Good for alfresco drinking by the river. Mon–Sat 11am–11pm, Sun noon–10.30pm.

Founders Arms 52 Hopton St, SE1 ☎020/7928 1899; Southwark or Blackfriars tube. A modern Young's pub, undistinguished except for its position by the river, with outside tables and great views across to the City. Mon–Sat 9am–11pm, Sun 9am–10.30pm.

George Inn 77 Borough High St, SE1 ☎020/7407 2056; Borough or London Bridge tube. London's only surviving coaching inn (see p.277), dating from the seventeenth century and now owned by the National Trust; it also serves a good range of real ales. Mon–Sat 11am–11pm, Sun noon–10.30pm.

Market Porter 9 Stoney St, SE1 ☎020/7407 2495; London Bridge tube. Handsome semicircular pub with early opening hours for workers at Borough Market, and a seriously huge range of real ales. Mon–Sat 6–8.30am & 11am–11pm, Sun noon–10.30pm.

South Kensington, Knightsbridge and Chelsea

Fox and Hounds 29 Passmore St, SW1 ☎020/7730 6367; Sloane Square tube. On a quiet street near Sloane Square, this Young's pub provides a perfect winter retreat. With an open fire, gleaming ranks of faux books and a flagstone floor, as well as plenty of hunting memorabilia, it feels as if you've stumbled into a country squire's manor. Mon–Sat 11am–11pm, Sun noon–10.30pm.

Grenadier 18 Wilton Row, SW1 ☎020/7235 3074; Hyde Park Corner or Knightsbridge tube. Wellington's local (his horse block survives outside) and his officers' mess; the original pewter bar survives, and the Bloody Marys are special. Classy but pricey bar food. Mon–Sat noon–11pm, Sun noon–10.30pm.

The Nag's Head 53 Kinnerton St, SW1 ☎020/7235 1135; Hyde Park Corner or Knightsbridge tube. A convivial, quirky and down-to-earth little pub tucked down a posh cobbled mews, with dark woodpanelling, nineteenth-century china handpumps and old prints on a hunting, fishing and military theme. The unusual sunken back room has a flagstone floor and fires in winter. Mon–Sat 11am–11pm, Sun noon–10.30pm.

The Pig's Ear 35 Old Church St, SW1 ☎020/7352
**2908, ⊛ www.thepigsear.co.uk; Sloane Square
tube.** Deep in Chelsea village, *The Pig's Ear*
is a sympathetically converted and stylish
place. Enjoy a leisurely board game and a
pint of Pig's Ear in the panelled downstairs
bar, where classy pub grub is served, or
head upstairs to the posh dining room
for dishes such as roast monkfish (£15)
and braised pork belly (£12.50). Mon–Sat
noon–11pm, Sun noon–10.30pm

Royal Court Bar Sloane Square, SW1 ☎020/7565
5061; Sloane Square tube. With its concrete
walls, atmospheric downlighting and the
odd splash of luscious red, the downstairs
bar at the Royal Court is much more glamorous than your average theatre bar. A
good place to linger over a drink, as it only
gets really crowded at interval time. Decent
but pricey bar snacks include tomato and
goat's cheese tart and pizza. Mon–Sat
11am–11pm.

Star Tavern 6 Belgrave Mews West, SW1
☎020/7235 3019; **Hyde Park Corner or Knightsbridge tube.** Quiet two-storey mews pub with
a large open sitting room and a murky past:
it was from here that the Great Train Robbery was planned. Fine beer and standard
bar grub. Mon–Sat 11.30am–11pm, Sun
noon–10.30pm.

High Street Ken to Notting Hill

Cherry Jam 52 Porchester Rd, W2 ☎020/7720
9950, ⊛ www.cherryjam.net; Royal Oak tube.
Owned by Ben Watt (house DJ and half
of pop group Everything But The Girl), this
smart, intimate basement place mixes a
decadent cocktail bar with top-end west
London DJs from the broken-beat and
deep-house scenes. Mon–Sat 6pm–2am,
Sun 4pm–midnight.

The Cow 89 Westbourne Park Rd, W2
☎020/7221 5400; **Westbourne Park tube.**
Owned by Tom Conran, son of gastro-mag-
nate Terence, this pub pulls in the beautiful
W11 types, thanks to its spectacular food,
including a daily supply of fresh oysters.
Mon–Sat noon–11pm, Sun noon–10.30pm.

Elbow Room 103 Westbourne Grove, W2
☎020/7221 5211, ⊛ www.elbow-room.co.uk;
Bayswater or Notting Hill Gate tube. *Elbow
Room* redefined the pool pub, with its
designer decor, purple-felt American pool
tables, and better-than-average grilled fast
food and beer. Now, of course, it has a

chain of branches in Islington, Shoreditch
and Swiss Cottage. Mon–Sat noon–11pm,
Sun noon–10.30pm.

Ion 161–165 Ladbroke Grove, W10 ☎020/8960
1702; Ladbroke Grove tube. Retro 1960s feel
to this Mean Fiddler–run bar situated under
the Westway. There's food available on the
mezzanine, DJs (and queues outside) most
nights. Mon–Fri 4pm–midnight, Sat & Sun
4pm–2am.

Market Bar 240a Portobello Rd, W11 ☎020/7229
6472; Ladbroke Grove tube. Relaxed boho pub
with gilded mirrors and weird objets – all
very Notting Hill. Mon–Wed 11am–11pm,
Thurs–Sat 11am–midnight, Sun 11am–
10.30pm.

Mau Mau 265 Portobello Rd, W11 ☎020/7229
8528; Ladbroke Grove tube. A snug but funky
little bar with DJ sets and live music,
popular with a mixed local crowd. Mon–Sat
11am–11pm, Sun noon–10.30pm.

Prince Bonaparte 80 Chepstow Rd, W2
☎020/7313 9491; **Notting Hill Gate or Royal Oak
tube.** Very popular pared-down, trendy, minimalist pub, with acres of space for sitting
and supping while enjoying the bar snacks
or the excellent Brit or Med food in the
restaurant area. Mon–Sat noon–11pm, Sun
noon–10.30pm.

The Westbourne 101 Westbourne Park Villas, W2
☎020/7221 1332; **Westbourne Park tube.** Popular bare-boards Notting Hill gastropub, serving top-notch Brit-Med food. Mon 5–11pm,
Tues–Sat noon–11pm, Sun noon–10.30pm.

Windsor Castle 114 Campden Hill Rd, W8
☎020/7243 9551; **High Street Kensington or Notting Hill tube.** Pretty, popular traditional wood-
panelled English pub with a great courtyard,
that would like to think it's out in the country
rather than tucked away in the backstreets
of one of London's poshest residential
neighbourhoods. Mon–Sat 11am–11pm,
Sun noon–10.30pm.

North London: Little Venice to Islington

**Abbey Road Pub and Dining Room 63 Abbey
Rd, NW8** ☎020/7328 6626; **St John's Wood
tube.** Laid-back, bare-boards gastropub
with adjoining bright restaurant, situated
not far from the famous zebra crossing and
serving up top nosh. Also tables outside.
Mon–Fri noon–11pm, Sat 11am–11pm, Sun
11am–10.30pm.

Angelic 57 Liverpool Rd, N1 ☎020/7278 8433;
Angel tube. A large, bright made-over pub

retaining some original features, popular with an after-work crowd when it can be tricky to bag a seat. The equally agreeable second floor is mostly for those partaking in the posh pub nosh. Mon–Sat noon–11pm, Sun noon–10.30pm.

Bartok 78–79 Chalk Farm Rd, NW1 ☎020/7916 0595; Chalk Farm tube. Stylish bar where punters can sink into a sofa and listen to a varied programme of classical music. Mon–Thurs 5pm–1am, Fri 5pm–2am, Sat noon–2am, Sun noon–midnight.

Bar Vinyl 6 Inverness St, NW1 ☎020/7681 7898; Camden Town tube. Small, funky glass-bricked place with a record shop downstairs (open noon–8pm) and DJs providing a breakbeat, funky house or electro vibe Thurs–Sun. Mon–Sun noon–11pm.

Camden Head 2 Camden Walk, N1 ☎020/7359 0851; Angel tube. In the midst of Islington's antique market on a dainty street, the *Camden Head* is something of an antique too, with engraved glass fittings and mirrors. It also has comedy most nights upstairs, and seating outside. Mon–Sat noon–11pm, Sun noon–10.30pm.

Canonbury Tavern 21 Canonbury Place, N1 ☎020/7288 9881; Highbury & Islington tube. Large and airy, this wood-filled pub is best visited on a sunny day when you can sit outside in its big secluded garden. Mon–Sat noon–11pm, Sun noon–10.30pm; Dec–April Mon & Tues from 4pm.

Compton Arms 4 Compton Ave, N1 ☎020/7359 6883; Highbury & Islington tube. Nice little local, with a great beer garden, hidden away down a sort of mews near Canonbury Square. Mon–Sat noon–11pm, Sun noon–10.30pm.

Duke of Cambridge 30 St Peter's St, N1 ☎020/7359 3066, ⊛www.singhboulton.co.uk; Angel tube. Bright corner pub, all wooden tables and chairs, as the focus here is on the organic food, accompanied by a range of great organic beers, wine and soft drinks. Restaurant seating at the back. Mon–Sat noon–11pm, Sun noon–10.30pm.

Edinboro Castle 57 Mornington Terrace, NW1 ☎020/7255 9651; Camden Town tube. Glammed up and slightly kitsch, this high-ceilinged pub has occasional DJs, but is principally visited for its large, leafy beer garden which hosts summer weekend barbecues. Good selection of international lagers and a couple of bitter options. Mon–Sat noon–11pm, Sun noon–10.30pm.

Embassy Bar 119 Essex Rd, N1 ☎020/7226 0672; Angel tube. Art-school posturing meets pub debauchery in this charismatic, darkened bar. Great music – jazz, funk, soul, deep house and reggae – from the resident DJs (Thurs–Sat). Mon–Thurs 5–11pm, Fri & Sat 5pm–1am, Sun 3–10.30pm.

The Engineer 65 Gloucester Ave, NW1 ☎020/7722 0950, ⊛www.the-engineer.com; Chalk Farm tube. Smart Victorian pub and restaurant for the Primrose Hill posse. The food is excellent though pricey, and it's popular, so get here early to eat in the pub, or book a table in the restaurant or lovely garden out back. Mon–Sat 9am–11pm, Sun 9am–10.30pm.

King's Head 115 Upper St, N1 ☎020/7226 0364, box office t020/7226 1916; Angel tube. The original pub/theatre in the heart of Islington with regular live music and a useful late licence. Mon–Thurs 11am–1am, Fri & Sat 11am–2am, Sun noon–12.30am.

Lansdowne 90 Gloucester Ave, NW1 ☎020/7483 0409; Chalk Farm tube. Big, bare-boards minimalist pub with comfy sofas, in elegant Primrose Hill. Pricey, tasty food. Mon–Sat noon–11pm, Sun noon–10.30pm.

Lock Tavern 35 Chalk Farm Rd, NW1 ☎020/7482 7163, ⊛www.lock-tavern.co.uk; Chalk Farm tube. Part-owned by DJ Jon Carter, this rambling refurbished pub has large battered wooden tables, comfy sofas, a leafy upstairs terrace and beer garden down below, as well as posh pub grub and DJs playing anything from punk funk and electro to rock. Effortlessly cool. Mon–Sat 11am–11pm, Sun 11am–10.30pm.

Medicine 181 Upper St, N1 ☎020/7704 8056, ⊛www.medicinebar.net; Highbury & Islington tube. Very nice if you can get in, this former pub, where comfy couches abound, has DJs playing jazzy tunes as well as rare groove, soul and funk. Mon–Thurs & Sun noon–midnight, Fri & Sat noon–2am. Second very trendy branch at 89 Great Eastern St, EC2 (☎020/7739 5173; Mon–Wed 5–11pm, Thurs & Sat 5pm–2am, Fri 4pm–2am).

Pembroke Castle 150 Gloucester Ave, NW1 ☎020/7483 2927; Chalk Farm tube. Just over the bridge that leads from Chalk Farm into Primrose Hill, the *Pembroke Castle* is a bright, wood-filled boozer with a less pretentious atmosphere than others in the area. Small but sunny beer garden too. Mon–Sat noon–11pm, Sun noon–10.30pm.

Prince Alfred & Formosa Dining Rooms
5a Formosa St, W9 ☏ 020/7286 3027;
Warwick Avenue tube. A fantastic period-piece Victorian pub with all its original 1862 fittings intact, right down to the glazed snob screens that divide the bar into a series of "snugs", which are often reserved. Despite the heritage, the pub manages to pull in a young and funky crowd. The restaurant at the back serves up expensive Modern European food. Mon–Sat 11am–11pm, Sun noon–10.30pm.
The Queen's 49 Regent's Park Rd, NW1
☏ 020/7586 0408; Chalk Farm tube. A light, airy and posh Young's pub in Primrose Hill, with tasteful decor and above-average food for above-average prices. Mon–Sat 11am–11pm, Sun noon–10.30pm.
Sir Richard Steele 97 Haverstock Hill, NW3
☏ 020/7483 1261; Belsize Park or Chalk Farm tube. The cluttered and oddball decor and clientele here make for a fun atmosphere; occasional live music and small beer garden. Mon–Thurs 11am–11pm, Fri & Sat 11am–midnight, Sun 11am–10.30pm.
Warrington Hotel 93 Warrington Crescent, W9
☏ 020/7286 2929; Maida Vale tube. Yet another architectural gem – this time flamboyant Edwardian Art Nouveau – in an area replete with them. The interior is rich and satisfying, as are the draught beers and the Thai food upstairs. Understandably popular, but there are outside tables for the overspill. Mon–Sat 11am–11pm, Sun noon–10.30pm.
Warwick Castle 6 Warwick Place, W9 ☏ 020 7432 1331; Warwick Avenue tube. Pleasant little wood-panelled pub on a quiet side street leading down to the canal, with large etched glass windows and stained-glass touches. The beer's cheap, the food traditional staples and the row of outside tables are complemented by hanging baskets and an impressive iron lamp. Mon–Sat noon–11pm, Sun noon–10.30pm.

North London: Stoke Newington and Hackney

Dove Freehouse 24–28 Broadway Market
☏ 020/7275 7617; bus #26 or #48 from Liverpool Street or London Fields train station. Cosy, low-lit and plant-filled, this characterful pub offers a stupendous selection of draught and bottled Belgian beers. Specially made sausages and burgers, as well as *moules frites*, are highlights of the menu. Mon–Sat noon–11pm, Sun noon–10.30pm.

Royal Inn on the Park 111 Lauriston Rd, E9
☏ 020/8985 3321; bus #277 from Mile End tube. Big, grand Victorian pub with laid-back tunes, real ale, beer garden and, as the name suggests, a location right on the edge of Victoria Park. Mon–Sat noon–11pm, Sun noon–10.30pm.

North London: Hampstead and Highgate

Flask 14 Flask Walk, NW3 ☏ 020/7435 4580;
Hampstead tube. Convivial Hampstead local that retains much of its original Victorian interior, tucked down one of Hampstead's more atmospheric lanes. Mon–Sat 11am–11pm, Sun noon–10.30pm.
Flask 77 Highgate West Hill, N6 ☏ 020/8348 7346; Highgate tube. Ideally situated at the heart of Highgate village green – with a rambling, low-ceilinged interior and a summer terrace – and as a result, very popular. Mon–Sat noon–11pm, Sun noon–10.30pm.
Freemasons Arms 32 Downshire Hill, NW3
☏ 020/7433 6811; Hampstead tube. Big, smart pub close to the Heath, of interest primarily for its large beer garden and its basement skittle alley. Mon–Sat noon–11pm, Sun noon–10.30pm.
The Hollybush 22 Holly Mount, off Holly Hill, NW3
☏ 020/7435 2892; Hampstead tube. A lovely old pub, with a real fire in winter, tucked away in the steep backstreets of Hampstead village, which can get a bit too mobbed at weekends. Mon–Sat noon–11pm, Sun noon–10.30pm.
The Spaniard's Inn Spaniards Rd, NW3
☏ 020/8731 6571; Hampstead tube or bus #210 from Highgate tube. Big sixteenth-century coaching inn near to Kenwood and the Heath, frequented by everyone from Dick Turpin to John Keats. The lovely garden hosts barbecues in good weather. Mon–Sat 11am–11pm, Sun 11am–10.30pm.
Wrestlers 98 North Rd, N6 ☏ 020/8340 4297; Highgate tube. Named after the Beefeaters who came here to wrestle in the seventeenth century, this fine, wood-panelled place has a jovial, mixed clientele and a small but perfectly formed beer garden. Mon–Fri 4.30–11pm, Sat noon–11pm, Sun noon–10.30pm.

Brixton, Kennington and Clapham

Bread & Roses 68 Clapham Manor St, SW4
☏ 020/7498 1779; Clapham Common tube. One good reason for venturing into Clapham,

this Workers' Beer Company pub serves fine ales, holds political events upstairs and is very welcoming to those with kids. Mon–Sat noon–11pm, Sun noon–10.30pm.

Brixtonian Havana Club 11 Beehive Place, SW9 ☏020/7924 9262; **Brixton tube.** Funky, quirky attic bar, hidden away off Brixton Station Road (near the Rec), serving Caribbean food, lots of rum cocktails and a few bottled beers. Tues & Wed noon–1am, Thurs–Sat noon–2am, Sun 4pm–midnight.

Dog Star 389 Coldharbour Lane, SW9 ☏020/7733 7515; **Brixton tube.** At weekends especially, this large wooden pub becomes more like a club complete with full-on techno, house or disco. The vibe is mellower during the week, but the music quality is just as good. Mon–Thurs & Sun noon–2am, Fri & Sat noon–4am.

🏃 **The Effra 38a Kellet Rd, SW2** ☏020/7274 4180; **Brixton tube.** Tucked down a quiet residential street, *The Effra* is the perfect local, with a vibrant cultural/age mix, handsome Victorian looks and great live music, predominately jazz. Their Sunday night gospel singer is a local legend. Daily 3–11.30pm.

South London Pacific 340 Kennington Rd, SE11 ☏020/7820 9189. ⊛www.southlondonpacific .com; **Kennington tube.** From the outlandish exterior to the range of fruity rum cocktails on offer inside, there's no escaping the South Pacific theme at this exuberant little bar/club. Camp cabaret and DJ nights feature regularly. Tues & Wed 6pm–midnight, Thurs 6pm–1am, Fri & Sat 6pm–2am, Sun 6pm–midnight.

Trinity Arms 45 Trinity Gardens, SW2 ☏020/7274 4544; **Brixton tube.** One of Brixton's most attractively located pubs, hidden in the backstreets off Acre Lane. Crowds spill out into the nearby square in summer. Mon–Sat 11am–11pm, Sun noon–10.30pm.

Dulwich

Crown & Greyhound 73 Dulwich Village, SE21 ☏020/8299 4976; **North Dulwich train station from London Bridge.** Grandiose Victorian pub, convenient for the Picture Gallery, with an ornate plasterwork ceiling and a nice summer beer garden. Mon–Sat 11am–11pm, Sun noon–10.30pm.

South London: Greenwich

Cutty Sark Ballast Quay, off Lassell St, SE10 ☏020/8858 3146; **Cutty Sark DLR or Maze Hill**

train station from Charing Cross. This Georgian pub is the nicest place for a riverside pint in Greenwich, and much less touristy than the *Trafalgar Tavern* (it's a couple of minutes' walk further east, following the river). Mon–Sat 11am–11pm, Sun noon–10.30pm.

Greenwich Union 56 Royal Hill, SE10 ☏020/8692 6258; **Greenwich DLR & train station.** A modern laidback place with a youthful feel, good gastro grub and a nice garden. Go for free samples of blonde ale, raspberry beer, chocolate stout or the house Union, before committing yourself to a pint. Mon–Fri 11am–11pm, Sat 10am–11pm, Sun noon–6pm.

Richard I 52–54 Royal Hill, SE10 ☏020/8692 2996; **Greenwich DLR & train station.** Popular Greenwich local tucked away on an attractive street. Good beer and a garden make it an ideal post-market retreat – and if it's too crowded, head for the Greenwich Union next door (see above). Mon–Sat 11am–11pm, Sun noon–10.30pm.

Trafalgar Tavern 5 Park Row, SE10 ☏020/8858 2437; **Cutty Sark DLR or Maze Hill train station from Charing Cross.** Great riverside position and a mention in Dickens' Our Mutual Friend have made this Regency-style inn a firm tourist favourite. Good whitebait and other snacks. Mon–Sat 11.30am–11pm, Sun noon–10.30pm.

Blackheath

The Crown 49 Tranquil Vale, SE3 ☏020/8852 0326; **Blackheath train station from Charing Cross.** Not on the heath, but in the village, this is a pleasingly old-fashioned pub, serving up traditional ale and pies. Mon–Sat 11am–11pm, Sun noon–10.30pm.

Hare & Billet 1a Eliot Cottages, SE3 ☏020/8852 2352; **Blackheath train station from Charing Cross.** A small heathside pub, run by the Hogshead chain, that does good Sunday lunches. Mon–Sat 11am–11pm, Sun noon–10.30pm.

Princess of Wales 1a Montpelier Row, SE3 ☏020/8297 5911; **Blackheath train station from Charing Cross.** Another old heathside pub, on a fine Georgian terrace. Extremely popular in summer, when it's hard to move on the grass outside. Mon–Sat noon–11pm, Sun noon–10.30pm.

Hammersmith and Chiswick

Blue Anchor 13 Lower Mall, W6 ☏020/8748 5774; **Hammersmith or Ravenscourt Park tube.**

First of Hammersmith's riverside pubs, with a boaty theme and a beautiful pewter bar; most people sit outside and enjoy the river, however. Mon–Sat 11am–11pm, Sun noon–10.30pm.

Dove 19 Upper Mall, W6 ℡ 020/8748 5405; Ravenscourt Park tube. Wonderful low-beamed old riverside pub with literary associations, the smallest bar in the UK (4ft by 7ft), and very popular Sunday roast dinners. Mon–Sat 11am–11pm, Sun noon–10.30pm.

Richmond, Twickenham and Wimbledon

Fox & Grapes 9 Camp Rd, SW19 ℡ 020/8946 5599; Wimbledon tube. Right on the edge of Wimbledon Common, with good real ales, this place is great in summer, when you can sit outside on the grass.

White Cross Hotel Water Lane, Richmond ℡ 020/8940 6844; Richmond tube. With a longer pedigree and more character than its rivals, the *White Cross* has a very popular, large garden overlooking the river. Mon–Sat 11am–11pm, Sun noon–10.30pm.

White Swan Riverside, Twickenham ℡ 020/8892 2166; Twickenham train station from Waterloo. Filling pub food, draught beer and a quiet riverside location – except on rugby match days – make this a good halt on any towpath ramble. The excellent summer Sunday barbecues are a big draw. Mon–Sat 11am–11pm, Sun noon–10.30pm.

28

Live music and clubs

L ondon is the nightlife capital of not just Europe, but the world. Since the acid-house explosion and subsequent boom in British-born dance music, the city has never looked back, and a relaxation in the licensing laws has made way for a host of all-night clubs and venues.

This thriving **club scene** offers everything from hip-hop to house, techno to garage, samba to soca and drum'n'bass to R&B on virtually any night of the week.

Live music options are equally varied, encompassing all variations of rock, blues, roots and world music; and although London's jazz clubs are not on a par with those in the big American cities, there's a highly individual scene of home-based artists supplemented by top-name visiting players.

Venues once used exclusively by performing bands now pepper the week with club nights, and you often find dance sessions starting as soon as a band has stopped playing. Bear in mind that there's sometimes an overlap between "live music venues" and "clubs" in the listings below; we've indicated which places serve a double function.

The dance and club scene is, of course, pretty much in constant flux, with the hottest items moving location, losing the plot or just cooling off. Weekly **listings magazines** like *Time Out* give up-to-date details of prices and access, plus previews and reviews.

Live music

Major **bands** on world tours always stop off in London, despite there being no really decent venue for the biggest names to play: Wembley Arena (ⓦwww .whatsonwembleyticket.com) and Earl's Court (ⓦwww.eco.co.uk) have the space, but all the atmosphere of shopping malls. Nonetheless London is hard to beat for its musical mix and smaller venues. Entry prices for gigs run from a couple of pounds for an unknown band thrashing it out in a pub, to up to £80 for major stadium fillers, but £10–15 is the average price for a good night out – not counting expenses at the bar. It's often cheaper to book tickets in advance with a credit card via the Internet, from sites such as ⓦwww.ticketweb.co.uk, ⓦwww.seetickets.com or ⓦwww.gigsandtours.com. We've listed websites for all venues that have them. Radio stations Xfm (ⓦwww.xfm.co.uk) and 6 Music (ⓦwww.bbc.co.uk/6music) are also worth tuning into for gig info.

Club-bars

For **club-bars** and pre-club drinking dens, see Chapter 28; exclusively **gay** clubs and bars are covered in Chapter 30.

General venues

Astoria 157 Charing Cross Rd, WC2 ☏ 020/7434 9592, ⓦ www.meanfiddler.com; Tottenham Court Road tube. One of London's best and most central medium-sized venues, this large, balconied one-time theatre tends to host popular bands from a real variety of genres, usually Mon–Thurs, and club nights Fri & Sat.

▲ Live music at the Astoria

Cargo 83 Rivington St, EC2 ☏ 020/7749 7840, ⓦ www.cargo-london.com; Old Street tube. Small but upmarket club/venue in what was once a railway arch, with an attached restaurant, and bar and garden areas. Hosts a wide variety of interesting live acts, including jazz, Latin, hip-hop, indie and folk, which are often part of their excellent line-up of club nights (see p.495).

Carling Academy Brixton 211 Stockwell Rd, SW9 ☏ 020/7771 2000, ⓦ www.brixton-academy.co.uk; Brixton tube. The *Academy* has seen them all, from mods and rockers to punks to Madonna. Its refurbished Victorian hall, complete with Roman decorations, can hold four thousand and usually does, but still manages to seem small and friendly, probably because no one is forced to sit down. Hosts mainly mid-league bands.

Carling Academy Islington N1 Centre, 16 Parkfield St, N1 ☏ 020/7288 4400, ⓦ www.islington-academy.co.uk; Angel tube. Despite its awful location (in the midst of a modern shopping centre), the Islington *Academy* has some good up-and-coming and mid-level bands, as well as club nights in *Bar Academy* (in the same building). Good views from the

main venue's mezzanine level which opens for well-attended gigs.

Carling Apollo Hammersmith Queen Caroline St, W6 ☏ 020/7416 6022, ⓦ www.carlinglive.com; Hammersmith tube. The former Hammersmith Odeon is a cavernous, theatre-style venue which tends to host safe, middle-of-the-road bands.

Coronet 28 New Kent Rd, SE1 ☏ 020/7701 1500, ⓦ www.coronet-london.co.uk; Elephant and Castle tube. A theatre turned cinema turned music venue, with a gorgeous Deco interior. Live acts, DJ nights and talent shows.

Forum 9–17 Highgate Rd, NW5 ☏ 020/7284 1001, ⓦ www.meanfiddler.com; Kentish Town tube. This is one of the capital's best medium-sized venues – large enough to attract established bands, but also promoting less well-known and interesting ones.

Marquee 1 Leicester Square, WC2 ☏ 020/7336 7326, ⓦ www.themarqueeclub.co.uk; Leicester Square tube. In a labyrinthine industrial building, right on Leicester Square, the *Marquee* boasts mainly newer acts but also some established names.

Mean Fiddler 165 Charing Cross Rd, W1 ☏ 020/7434 9592, ⓦ www.meanfiddler.com; Tottenham Court Road tube. Next door to the *Astoria*, the *Mean Fiddler* has a good line-up of mainly rock and indie bands, with club nights Fri & Sat. The gallery bar is a less frantic place to check out the action.

Shepherds Bush Empire Shepherd's Bush Green, W12 ☏ 020/8771 2000, ⓦ www.shepherds-bush-empire.co.uk; Shepherd's Bush tube. Yet another grand old theatre, the *Empire* now plays host to probably the finest cross-section of mid-league UK and US bands in the capital. Intimate with a great atmosphere downstairs. Upstairs, balconies provide some of the best stage views around.

Spitz Old Spitalfields Market, 109 Commercial St, E1 ☏ 020/7392 9032; Liverpool Street tube. Friendly, small venue in the heart of Spitalfields Market, where you can catch a diverse range of music including jazz, world, indie, folk, blues and electronica. Often puts on new and interesting acts. The downstairs bistro hosts free live music up to four nights a week.

LIVE MUSIC AND CLUBS | Live music

Rock, blues and indie

12 Bar Club Denmark Street, WC2
☏ 020/7209 2248, ⊛ www.12barclub.com;
Tottenham Court Road tube. Tiny, atmospheric
bar, café and venue offering blues, contemporary Country and acoustic folk.

93 Feet East 150 Brick Lane, E2 ☏ 020/7053
2029, ⊛ www.93feeteast.co.uk; Old Street tube.
An intimate live venue during the week and
a club at weekends (see p.494), this is a
good place to catch electronic, punk and
indie gigs.

Amersham Arms 388 New Cross Rd, SE14
☏ 020/8692 2047; New Cross tube or train from
Charing Cross. Students from nearby Goldsmiths' College pack out this indie-oriented
venue.

Barfly 48 Chalk Farm Rd, NW1 ☏ 020/7691 1049;
Chalk Farm tube. Great Camden venue to
catch nightly indie, rock, punk and metal
bands.

Borderline Orange Yard, Manette St, W1
☏ 020/7734 5547, ⊛ www.meanfiddler.com; Tottenham Court Road tube. Small basement joint
with a diverse musical policy, making it a
good place to catch new bands.

Bull & Gate 389 Kentish Town Rd, NW5
☏ 020/7485 5358, ⊛ www.bullandgate.co.uk;
Kentish Town tube. Basic pub venue for currently obscure, but soon to be big, indie
bands.

Dublin Castle 94 Parkway, NW1 ☏ 020/7485
1773; Camden Town tube. Grungy music pub
offering a varied menu of acts.

The Garage 20–22 Highbury Corner, N1
☏ 020/7607 1818, ⊛ www.meanfiddler.com;
Highbury & Islington tube. Modest, mainly indie
place with a good reputation for up-and-coming talent which makes the occasional
excursion into jazz and funk. Two doors
down, *Upstairs at the Garage* is even
smaller with more new acts. Both venues
also have club nights.

Half Moon Putney 93 Lower Richmond
Rd, SW15 ☏ 020/8780 9383, ⊛ www
.halfmoon.co.uk; Putney Bridge tube. Well-respected pub venue – good for blues, rock
and soul and catering for a younger crowd.
Regular acoustic nights on Mondays, and
jazz Sunday afternoons.

Hope and Anchor 207 Upper St, N1 ☏ 020/7354
1312; Angel tube. This cramped venue is
popular with indie acts, many playing their
first gigs here.

Metro 19–23 Oxford St, W1 ☏ 020/7437 0964,

⊛ www.blowupmetro.com; Tottenham Court Road
tube. An intimate venue with a forward-thinking booking policy that makes it a good
place to head to for new bands just before
they get big. Also has club nights Mon–Sat
till late.

Neighbourhood 12 Acklam Rd, W10 ☏ 020/8960
4590, ⊛ www.neighbourhoodclub.net; Ladbroke
Grove tube. Run by Ben Watt of Everything
But the Girl, this is a live-music/club crossover venue in an arch under a flyover, where
the crowd is as trendy as the house-oriented music.

The Social 5 Little Portland St, W1 ☏ 020/7636
4992, ⊛ www.thesocial.com; Oxford Circus tube.
Hosts emerging and established pop, rock
and folk acts on varying week-nights. Free
entry.

Swan 215 Clapham Rd, SW9 ☏ 020/7978
9778, ⊛ www.theswanstockwell.co.uk;
Stockwell tube. Large and very boozy Irish
pub, featuring Celtic-style rock'n'roll and
a plethora of cover and tribute bands,
from The Counterfeit Beatles to Kylie looky-
likies.

Underworld 174 Camden High St, NW1
☏ 020/7482 1932, ⊛ www.theunderworld
camden.co.uk; Camden Town tube. Popular
grungy venue under the World's End pub,
that's a great place to check out metal, hard
core, ska punk and heavy rock bands.

The Venue 2a Clifton Rise, New Cross, SE14
☏ 020/8692 4077, ⊛ www.thevenuelondon.com;
New Cross tube or train from Charing Cross.
Indie bands on a tiny stage, with a club
afterwards. Saturday night is tribute-band
night.

Water Rats 328 Grays Inn Rd, WC1 ☏ 020/7336
7326, ⊛ www.plumpromotions.co.uk; King's
Cross tube. Indie and indie/electronica crossover bands trying to make it big in the biz
can be found thrashing it out in this notoriously high-spirited pub venue.

Jazz

100 Club 100 Oxford St, W1 ☏ 020/7636 0933,
⊛ www.the100club.co.uk; Tottenham Court Road
tube. An unpretentious, inexpensive and fun
jazz venue with an incredible vintage – it's
been going strong for more than sixty years.

606 Club 90 Lots Rd, SW10 ☏ 020/7352 5953,
⊛ www.606club.co.uk; Fulham Broadway tube.
A rare all-jazz venue, located just off the
less trendy end of the King's Road. You can
book a table, and the licensing laws dictate

that if you're a non-member you must eat if you want to drink.

Bull's Head Barnes Barnes Bridge, SW13 ⓣ020/8876 5241, ⓦwww.thebullshead.com; bus #9 from Hammersmith tube or Barnes Bridge train station from Waterloo. This riverside alehouse has been attracting Britain's finest jazz musicians for 45 years. Live music nightly and Sunday lunchtimes.

Dover Street 8–9 Dover St, W1 ⓣ020/7629 9813, ⓦwww.doverst.co.uk; Green Park tube. London's largest jazz restaurant has music and dancing every night until 3am, plus Modern British food. Attracts an older crowd; dress smart.

Jazz after Dark 9 Greek St, W1 ⓣ020/7734 0545, ⓦwww.jazzafterdark.co.uk; Tottenham Court Road tube. A diverse music policy, with jazz often fusing with Latin, blues or funk. It's an intimate little venue in the heart of Soho, with attentive table service.

Jazz Café 5 Parkway, NW1 ⓣ020/7916 6060, ⓦwww.meanfiddler.com; Camden Town tube. Excellent, chilled-out venue with an adventurous booking policy exploring Latin, rap, funk, hip-hop and musical fusions. Restaurant upstairs has a few prime tables overlooking the stage (book ahead if you want one).

Pizza Express 10 Dean St, W1 ⓣ020/7439 8722, ⓦwww.pizzaexpress.co.uk/jazz; Tottenham Court Road tube. Enjoy a good pizza, then listen to the highly skilled guest players: recently these have included Mose Allison and Andy Sheppard.

Pizza on the Park 11 Knightsbridge, Hyde Park Corner, SW1 ⓣ020/7235 5273; Hyde Park Corner tube. Spacious restaurant with upmarket ambience and mainstream jazz acts.

Ronnie Scott's 47 Frith St, W1 ⓣ020/7439 0747, ⓦwww.ronniescotts .co.uk; Leicester Square tube. The most famous jazz club in London: small and smoky and still going strong, even though the great man himself has passed away. The place

for top-line names, who play two sets – one at around 10pm, the other after midnight. Book a table, or you'll have to stand.

The Vortex Jazz Club 11 Gillett St, N16 ⓣ020/7254 4097, ⓦwww.vortexjazz.co.uk; Dalston Kingsland train station or buses #67, #76, #149 & #243 from Liverpool Street. Recently relocated from Stoke Newington and part of the development of Dalston Cultural House, this small venue manages to combine a touch of urban style with a cosy, friendly atmosphere.

West One Four 3 North End Crescent, W14 ⓣ020/7603 7006; West Kensington tube. Pub-like venue with a variety of acts including jazz and folk. There are also club nights.

World music, folk and roots

Barbican Centre Silk St, EC2 ⓣ020/7638 8891, ⓦwww.barbican.org.uk; Barbican tube. The expansive Barbican is a focal point for great world-music bands and orchestras, as well as many other unusual, one-off contemporary music events.

Blackheath Halls 23 Lee Rd, SE3 ⓣ020/8463 0100, ⓦwww.blackheathhalls.com; Blackheath train station from Charing Cross. This medium-sized venue hosts some of the best world, roots and African bands when they come to the capital.

Cecil Sharp House 2 Regent's Park Rd, NW1 ⓣ020/7485 2206, ⓦwww.efdss.org; Camden Town tube. Headquarters of the English Folk Dance and Song Society, with singing and dancing performances as well as workshops and classes.

South Bank Centre South Bank, SE1 ⓣ0870/ 380 0400, ⓦwww.royalfestivalhall.org.uk; Waterloo tube. On the south bank of the Thames, the all-seater Queen Elizabeth Hall, Purcell Room and Royal Festival Hall host imaginative programmes of world music, jazz acts and folk music, as well as classical concerts.

Clubs

A quarter of a century after acid house irreversibly shook up British **clubs**, London remains *the* place to come if you want to party after dark. The sheer diversity of dance music has enabled the city to maintain its status as the world's dance capital and it's a major port of call for DJs from around the globe. The so-called super-clubs may be dying out, but, in their place, there's more variety than ever, both in terms of music being played and the small to mid-sized venues available. The relaxation of late-night licensing laws has encouraged

Dance magazines, record shops and radio stations

Because the club scene changes so fast, one of the best ways to find out about forthcoming nights and guest/resident DJs is either to pick up *Time Out*, one of the specialist **dance magazines** (*DJ*, *Mixmag*, *Jockey Slut*) or to wander around the **dance record shops** in Soho and Covent Garden, which are always full of the latest club flyers. Below is a selection of the best ports of call.

If you have access to a radio, it's also worth tuning into London **dance music stations** like Kiss 100 FM and Choice FM, and to the specialist dance shows on Radio 1 (hosted by Pete Tong, Judge Jules, Gilles Peterson and others), most of which can be found early evenings Friday through to Sunday on 98.8 FM.

Black Market Records 25 D'Arblay St, Soho, W1 ⓦ www.blackmarket.co.uk.
Koobla 17 Berwick St, W1 ⓦ www.koobla.co.uk.
Phonica 51 Poland St, W1 ⓦ www.phonicarecords.co.uk.
Selectadisc Berwick Street, W1
Sister Ray 94 Berwick St, W1 ⓦ www.sisterray.co.uk.
Sounds of the Universe 7 Broadwick St, W1 ⓦ www.souljazzrecords.co.uk.
Uptown Records 3 D'Arblay St, W1 ⓦ www.uptownrecords.com.
Wyld Pytch 51 Lexington St, Soho, W1 ⓦ www.wyldpytch.com.

---

many places to keep serving until 6am or even later, and the resurgence of alcohol in clubland has – much to the relief of the breweries – been echoed by the meteoric rise of the club-bar.

While **dance music** has evolved to now encompass a multitude of sub-genres, London clubs are currently embracing nights that provide a variety of electronic sounds for their punters. That said, **house** still dominates – but the term now covers anything from US garage, deep house and European techno to the home-grown styles of hard house and progressive trance. **Drum'n'bass** and **UK garage** are as popular as ever, the former experiencing a new lease of life thanks to the influx of vocal cuts and Brazilian bossa nova influences. In addition, **reggae**, **ragga** and the US-led fusion of **swing** and **hip-hop** still command a loyal following. **Latin**, **African**, **Indian** and **world music** fans have their own clubs too, and there's also a healthy and vibrant alternative **rock** and **punk** scene. Above all, fun is most definitely back on the agenda.

For nearly all clubs, **opening time** is between 10pm and midnight, with most favouring the 11pm slot. Some are open six or seven nights a week; some keep irregular days; others just open at the weekend – and very often a venue will host a different club on each night of the week. Sunday clubs are increasingly popular: some starting in the wee hours to catch the Saturday-night crew who can't face going home, some featuring a chilled down-tempo and mellow Sunday afternoon vibe, while others are still geared towards the total hedonists who party on until Monday morning.

Admission charges vary enormously, with small midweek nights starting at around £3–5 and large weekend events charging as much as £25; around £10–15 is the average, but bear in mind that profit margins at the bar are even more outrageous than at live-music venues.

Club venues

93 Feet East 150 Brick Lane, E2 ☎ 020/7247 5293, ⓦ www.93feeteast.co.uk; Old Street tube. Weekends see this trendy club/venue (gigs during the week, see p.492), set in part of the Truman Brewery, put on a varied programme playing such delights as electro house, underground beats, hip-hop, breaks and funk. There's an excellent rooftop balcony and courtyard that's well worth a visit in the summer.

333 333 Old St, EC1 ☎ 020/7739 5949, ⓦ www.333mother.com; Old Street tube. One of London's best clubs for new dance music, in the heart of trendy-as-hell Hoxton. Three floors (including the *Mother* bar) of drum'n'bass, twisted disco and breakbeat madness.

Aquarium 256–260 Old St, EC1 ⓣ 020/7251 6136, wwww.clubaquarium.co.uk; **Old Street tube.** The place with the pool – when things get hot and sweaty, you can dive in and cool off. Regular cheesy nights, as well as various promoters' events.

Bar Rumba 36 Shaftesbury Ave, W1 ⓣ 020/7287 6933, ⓦ www.barrumba.co.uk; **Piccadilly Circus tube.** Fun, smallish West End venue with a mix of regular nights ranging from salsa, R&B and dance to popular drum'n'bass night Movement. Pop in during the early evening (when it's free) to sample some cocktails during happy hour.

Café de Paris 3 Coventry St, W1 ⓣ 020/7734 7700, ⓦ www.cafedeparis.com; **Leicester Square tube.** The elegant *Café* ballroom has been restored to its former glory and plays commercial house, garage and disco to a smartly dressed, trendy crowd of wannabes – no jeans or trainers.

Canvas Bagley's Studios, King's Cross Freight Depot, York Way, N1 ⓣ 020/7833 8301, ⓦ www .canvaslondon.net; **King's Cross tube.** Warehouse-style venue that currently hosts the weekly roller-disco but is otherwise used by one-off promoters. Funky, low-beamed foyer bar area.

 Cargo 83 Rivington St, EC2 ⓣ 020/7739 5446, ⓦ www.cargo-london.com; **Old Street tube.** *Cargo* plays host to a variety of excellent and often innovative club nights, from deep house to jazz, and often features live bands (see p.491) alongside the DJs.

The Colosseum 1 Nine Elms Lane, SW8 ⓣ 020/7627 1283, ⓦ www.clubcolosseum .com; **Vauxhall tube.** Huge stomping ground, popular for hard house through to garage. Weekends only.

The Cross Arches 27–31, York Way, London, N1 ⓣ 020/7837 0828, ⓦ www.the-cross.co.uk; **King's Cross tube.** Hidden underneath the arches, the favourite flavours of this renowned club are hard house, house and garage. It's bigger than you imagine, but always rammed with chic clubby types, and there's a cool garden – perfect for those chill-out moments.

Cuba 11–13 Kensington High St, W8 ⓣ 020/7938 4137; **High Street Kensington tube.** Grab a cocktail upstairs in the sociable bar before

heading below for club nights that focus around Latin, salsa and Brazilian bossa nova.

EGG 200 York Way, N7 ⓣ 020/7609 8364, ⓦ www.egglondon.net; **King's Cross tube.** Two exposed-brick, medium-sized rooms, a loft-style bar and a small outdoor chill-out area make up this out-of-the-way club. All kinds of nights including those that bring together techno, funky house and club classics with electro, rock and industrial.

Electric Ballroom 184 Camden High St, NW1 ⓣ 020/7485 9006, ⓦ www.electricballroom .co.uk; **Camden Town tube.** Long-running and large club that hosts rock and disco nights, as well as being an occasional venue for live music.

The End 18 West Central St, WC1 ⓣ 020/7419 9199, ⓦ www.the-end.co.uk; **Tottenham Court Road or Holborn tube.** Owned by Mr C (ex-Shamen MC), this club has been designed for clubbers by clubbers and has one of the best sound systems in the world. Well known for its focus on tech-house (thanks to resident DJs Layo and Matthew "Bushwacka" B) and drum'n'bass at weekends, it's also worth checking out the monthly nights hosted by other clubs or record labels, and for Monday's anything goes Trash, with DJ Erol Alkan.

Fabric 77a Charterhouse St, EC1 ⓣ 020/7336 8898, ⓦ www.fabriclondon .com; **Farringdon tube.** Cavernous, underground, brewery-like space with three rooms, holding 1600 people, as well as a devastating sound system. Fridays are Fabric Live, a mix of drum'n'bass and hip-hop with live acts. Saturdays concentrate on cutting-edge house, techno and electro, played by underground DJs from around the globe. Get there early to avoid a night of queuing.

Fridge Town Hall Parade, Brixton Hill, SW2 ⓣ 020/7326 5100, ⓦ www.fridge.com; **Brixton tube.** Weekends alternate between pumping mixed/gay nights like Saturday's Love Muscle and trance favourites with a psychedelic vibe and plenty of lightstick-waving action.

Herbal 10–14 Kingsland Rd, E2 ⓣ 020/7613 4462, ⓦ www.herbaluk.com; **Old Street or Liverpool Street tube.** An intimate two-floored venue comprising a cool New York-style loft and sweaty ground-floor club. A great place to check out drum'n'bass and breaks.

The Key Lazer Rd, off York Way, King's Cross, N1 ⓣ 020/7837 1027, ⓦ www.thekeylondon.com;

King's Cross tube. Making up the trio of clubs (see also *Canvas* and *The Cross* above) off York Way, *The Key*'s three rooms are often home to cool up-and-coming DJs as well as more renowned names. The club opens late and there's an illuminated dance floor for when you're feeling all John Travolta.

KOKO 1a Camden High St, NW1 ☏09062 100 200, Ⓦ www.koko.uk.com; **Mornington Crescent tube.** Gorgeously revamped theatre that famously hosted gigs as *The Music Machine* in the Seventies and *The Camden Palace* in the Eighties and Nineties. Indie club nights on Fridays, one-off promoter events and live music gigs see the club gaining popularity again.

Ministry of Sound 103 Gaunt St, SE1 ☏020/7378 6528, Ⓦ www.ministryofsound.co.uk; **Elephant & Castle tube.** A vast, state-of-the-art club based on New York's legendary *Paradise Garage*, with an exceptional sound system and the pick of visiting DJs. Corporate clubbing and full of tourists (as well as Sega games machines), but it still draws the top talent. Look out for their excellent, hedonistic Bank Holiday parties – go early or buy a ticket in advance to ensure you get in.

Notting Hill Arts Club 21 Notting Hill Gate, W11 ☏020/7460 4459, Ⓦ www.nottinghillartsclub.com; **Notting Hill Gate tube.** Basement club that's popular for everything from Latin-inspired funk, jazz and disco through to soul, house and garage, and famed for its Sunday late-afternoon into evening deep-house session and "concept visuals".

Pacha London Terminus Place, W1 ☏020/7833 3139, Ⓦ www.pachalondon.com; **Victoria tube.** Don't expect the palm-tree-lined gardens and rooftop bars of the original (and best) *Pacha* in Ibiza. This soulless vast club hasn't really lived up to the hype since opening in 2001, and now draws a mix of Chelsea sloanes, suburban boys and clueless tourists to its Saturday-night house sessions. Even the dancers are lame.

Plastic People 147–149 Curtain Rd, EC2 ☏020/7739 6471, Ⓦ www.plasticpeople.co.uk;

Old Street tube. State-of-the-art sound system and a blend of nights that include an interesting mix of music from punk, funk and rock 'n' roll to Latin, jazz and hip-hop.

Plan B 418 Brixton Rd, SW9 ☏020/7733 0926, Ⓦ www.plan-brixton.co.uk; **Brixton tube.** Slicker and more style-conscious than the average Brixton club, with a good sound system, friendly staff and a great bar. House, hip-hop, funk, psychedelic soul and R&B.

Rhythm Factory 16–18 Whitechapel Road ☏020/7375 3774, Ⓦ www.rhythmfactory.co.uk; **Aldgate East or Whitechapel tube.** This former textile factory turned club houses a bar area serving Thai food and two medium-sized rooms which usually see three live gigs during the week and a range of excellent monthly shenanigans at the weekends, including deep-house night Muak and the funk and hip-hop Breakin' Bread.

Salsa! 96 Charing Cross Rd, WC2 ☏020/7379 3277; **Leicester Square tube.** Funky and fun salsa-based club-cum-restaurant that's a popular choice for birthday bookings: you can book a table to eat as you mambo.

Scala 275 Pentonville Rd, N1 ☏020/7833 2022, Ⓦ www.scala-london.co.uk; **King's Cross tube.** Once a cinema (it was forced to shut down after illegally showing Kubrick's *A Clockwork Orange*), the *Scala* is a sprawling club that holds some unusual one-off nights as well as live bands and the long-running gay/mixed Popstarz (see p.507).

Subterania 12 Acklam Rd, W10 ☏020/8960 4590, Ⓦ www.meanfiddler.com; **Ladbroke Grove tube.** Worth a visit for its diverse club nights at weekends, including the superior hip-hop and R&B-heavy Rotation every Friday.

Turnmills 63b Clerkenwell Rd, EC1 ☏020/7250 3409, Ⓦ www.turnmills.com; **Farringdon tube.** The place to come if you want to sweat from dusk till dawn, with an alien invasion-style bar and funky split-level dance floor in the main room. Trance, house and techno with top-name guest DJs rule Friday's weekly Gallery night, where Tall Paul is resident.

29

Lesbian and gay London

ondon's **lesbian and gay scene** is so huge, diverse and well established that it's easy to forget just how much – and how fast – it has grown over the last few years. Pink power has given rise to the pink pound, gay liberation to gay lifestyle, and the ever-expanding Soho – now firmly established as the homo heart of the city – is vibrant, self-assured and unashamedly commercial. As a result of all this high-profile activity, straight Londoners tend to be a fairly homo-savvy bunch and, on the whole, happy to embrace and even dip into the city's queer offerings.

The wider picture is also positive. The notorious Clause 28 (which forbade the promotion of homosexuality by schools and local authorities) was repealed during the second term of New Labour government at the end of 2003, homophobic hate crime was finally tackled by specific laws in the spring of 2005 and a Civil Partnership Act permitting the registration of same-sex partnerships recently came into force in autumn 2005 – which, whilst falling short of the full marriage rights of lesbians and gay men in Spain, Belgium or the Netherlands, nevertheless represents a very real step forward. Mirroring the way in which **equality** before the law is slowly and surely becoming a reality, the **social acceptance** of lesbians, bisexuals, transgender and gay men has proceeded apace – to the extent that winners of the massively popular reality TV programme *Big Brother* have included both an out gay man and a transsexual.

When it comes to exploring the London scene, **Soho** is the obvious place to start; **Old Compton Street** is, so to speak, its main drag. Here, traditional gay pubs rub alongside cafés and bars selling expensive designer beers and lattes, while hairdressers, letting agencies, sex boutiques and spiritual health centres offer a range of gay-run services. There are clubs to cater for just about every musical, sartorial and sexual taste and, while the bigger ones increasingly congregate just south of the river in **Vauxhall**, there are well-established venues all over the city. Gay men still enjoy the best permanent facilities London-wide, but today's **lesbian scene** is bigger and more eclectic than ever, and the cruisey girl-bars which took up prize pitches on the boys' Soho turf a few years ago look like they're here to stay.

You can also find pockets of queer activity away from the centre in the city's funkier residential areas, most notably Brixton, Islington and, especially for dykes, Stoke Newington and Hackney. Open anti-gay **hostility** is rare but not unknown in London, so it's probably wise not to hold hands or smooch too obviously in areas you don't know well.

Print

Though they carry excellent entertainment listings, most lesbian- and gay-oriented **newspapers and magazines** these days tend towards the glossy and consumerist rather than the overtly political. The titles listed below can be picked up at most major newsagents, in many bookshops (gay and straight), and in the cafés and bars of Soho. In addition to these, listings-based **freesheets** like *Boyz* and *qx* abound in clubs and bars. They're perhaps not the most absorbing reading you'll find, but do give the most up-to-date and accurate club, bar listings and information, with *qx* in particular generally regarded as the London clubber's bible.

Attitude (monthly; £3). Glossy gay men's lifestyle magazine with crossover appeal to style-conscious straight boys and the odd dyke reader. Occasional well-written, offbeat arts pieces and investigative features make it rather more than just a fashion rag.

Axm (monthly; £2.75; ⓦwww.axm-mag.com). This men's glossy describes itself as the ultimate in gay lifestyle, and with celebrity features, fashion, health and fitness, who's to argue?

Bent (monthly; £2.80; ⓦwww.bent.com). Claiming to be the UK's largest circulating gay magazine, *Bent* carries extensive national bar listings spiced up with the odd celebrity interview.

Diva (monthly; £2.99; ⓦwww.divamag.co.uk). Glossy national lifestyle magazine for lesbians, with a middle-brow range of features, news pieces, interviews and arts reviews which aim, perhaps unwisely, to please everyone.

Gay Times (monthly; £3.25; ⓦwww.gaytimes.co.uk). Long-established glossy national aimed primarily at gay men, but also read by lesbians (and edited by one); *GT* offers news, arts and features, listings, reviews and community information.

The Pink Paper (weekly; free; ⓦwww.pinkpaper.com). Recently revitalized by its rescue at the hands of the publishers of *Diva* and *Gay Times*, this weekly forum for community debate is the UK's only serious weekly newspaper addressing lesbian and gay issues.

reFRESH (monthly; £2.99; ⓦwww.refreshmag.co.uk). *reFRESH* claims to be the magazine for fashionably gay men, and it's an occasionally sharp-looking mix of boyz' obsessions, from travel and motoring to property and interior design, plus the inevitable fashion and showbiz bits.

The main **outdoor event** of the year is Pride London in July. Encompassing a rally in Trafalgar Square, a colourful, whistle-blowing march through the city streets, a live cabaret stage and Drag Idol contest in Leicester Square, **Pride London** is the somewhat trimmed-down but perhaps more focused successor to the highly commercialized events of recent years which drew heavy criticism from some sectors of the community. The event is rediscovering its political roots and continues to draw people from all over the country for the largest queer party of the year. For up-to-date information, festival plans and transport information, visit the website ⓦwww.pridelondon.org. Pride London is usually followed at the end of July by a ticket-only music festival, currently labouring under the name **Big Gay Out** (ⓦwww.biggayout.com) and held in north London's Finsbury Park. It's generally judged an improvement on the patchy success of its immediate predecessors. For more information on these events nearer the time, check the weekly *Time Out* and the queer press (see box on above).

London also boasts several gay-oriented **arts events**. In March and April, the

Online

Online information has proliferated over the last few years, which means it's easier than ever to access up-to-date information. The following are the most useful websites, and the only ones to offer more than just an online version of printed publications.

Ⓦ**www.gaytoz.com** For a comprehensive online directory of gay, lesbian, bisexual and TV/TS-friendly organizations and businesses, you can't do better than GAY to Z. A print version is also available, priced £3 from Gay to Z Directories, 41 Cooks Rd, London SE17 3NG.

Ⓦ**www.rainbownetwork.com** Lifestyle e-zine for boys and girls with masses of editorial content. Includes news on the latest events, interviews with scene faces, informative listings and message boards.

Ⓦ**www.gingerbeer.co.uk** Well-designed and regularly updated website for London dykes, offering listings and reviews of bars, clubs and events. Gingerbeer also holds regular women-only club nights – check site for details.

Ⓦ**www.fruitcamp.com** For a slice of London's lesbian and gay life online, fruitcamp provides useful info on flatshares, jobs, the scene and community events.

Ⓦ**www.gaydargirls.com** Online dating for queer girls nationwide. Tempting but often a little disappointing in the flesh, some of the ladies on gaydar girls require careful vetting before you agree to meet up.

Ⓦ**www.gaydar.co.uk** The gaydar revolution has transformed the lives of gay men who prefer to cut to the chase and order a date like they'd order a pizza. If it works for you, it's not a bad place to meet up-for-it guys of all persuasions.

Ⓦ**www.uk.gay.com** British affiliate of the international website for gay men, with regular news stories, features, competitions and scene guide.

Ⓦ**www.transgenderzone.com** Useful, if in part rather medical in tone, this transsexual and transvestite site offers news plus national club and venue listings.

National Film Theatre, Odeon West End and Tate Modern host the annual **Lesbian and Gay Film Festival** (Ⓦwww.llgff.org.uk); the **Pride Festival Fortnight**, staged at venues throughout London, is a mix of theatre, music, opera, dance, sports, film and visual arts that takes place in the run-up to Pride itself.

Elsewhere, queer theatre and arts events take place all year round in the city's many fringe theatres, arts centres, galleries and clubs. If none of this is up your street, there are also a huge number of **gay groups and organizations** which offer everything from ballroom dancing to spanking seminars.

Hotels

Below is a small selection of London's best-known gay accommodation options. They cater mostly for gay men, though all are lesbian-friendly, and a full breakfast is almost always included. The price codes given are for a double room, but singles are often available at reduced rates.

If you'd prefer a self-catering **apartment**, try the gay-run Outlet Gay Accommodation, 32 Old Compton St, W1 (℡020/7287 4244, ⓦwww .outlet4holidays.com) or Clone Zone Apartments, 64 Old Compton St, W1 (℡020/7287 3530; ⓦwww.clonezone.co.uk/apartments.htm); prices start at around £85 per night for two sharing. GAY to Z (see box on p.499) also has comprehensive accommodation listings.

Garth Hotel 69 Gower St, WC1 ℡020/7636 **5761,** ⓦwww.garthhotel-london.com; **Goodge St tube. See map, p.144.** Small, privately owned Bloomsbury hotel. The building itself is a grade II-listed, eighteenth-century, Georgian town-house of historical interest. The *Garth* prides itself on its friendly atmosphere and features many original antiques in its seventeen mostly en-suite bedrooms. From £74.

Kensington International Inn 4 Templeton Place, SW5 ℡020/7370 4333, ⓦwww.kensington internationalinn.com; **Earl's Court tube. See map, p.328.** Tastefully modern hotel in the heart of Earl's Court. All 58 fully refurbished bedrooms are en-suite with tea- and coffee-making facilities, hairdryers, trouser presses, full-sized room safes, satellite tel-

evision. Bar, lounge/conservatory, lift to all floors, 24hr reception, messaging and fax service. £125.

Oxford Hotel 13 Craven Terrace, W2 ℡020/7402 **6860,** ⓦwww.oxfordhotellondon.co.uk; **Paddington or Lancaster Gate tube. See map, p.328.** Friendly and affordable place close to the West End. Basic but neat rooms are en-suite and have tea- and coffee-making facilities. £66.

Philbeach Hotel 30–31 Philbeach Gardens, SW5 ℡020/7373 1244, ⓦwww.philbeachhotel .freeserve.co.uk; **Earl's Court tube. See map, p.328.** London's busiest gay hotel, large and friendly, with room-only or en-suite options, Internet and TV lounge, *Applebys Bar*, and the *Princess Thai* restaurant. £63.

Cafés, bars and pubs

There are loads of lesbian and gay eating and watering holes in London, many of them operating as cafés by day and transforming into drinking dens by night. Lots have cabaret or disco nights and are open until the early hours, making them a fine (and affordable) alternative to the big clubs. Most of these cafés and bars have free admission, though a few levy a charge after 10.30pm (usually £3–5) if there's music, cabaret or a disco.

The places below represent a selective list of the best and most central, from self-consciously minimalist eateries to shabby old pubs. We use "mixed" to mean places for both gays and lesbians, though many "mixed" places are mostly frequented by men.

Mixed cafés, bars and pubs

The Admiral Duncan 54 Old Compton St, W1 ℡020/7437 5300; **Leicester Square tube.** Unpretentious, traditional-style gay bar in the heart of Soho, popular and busy with the post-work crowd, and now fully restored after the blast that ripped through it in 1999.

Balans Café 34 Old Compton St, W1 ℡020/7439 3309; **Leicester Square tube.** This enduringly busy Soho institution never closes. A full restaurant menu including a lengthy brunch section makes it the obvious solution to mid- or post-party wooziness.

Balans Restaurant 60 Old Compton St, W1 ℡020/7439 2183; **Leicester Square tube.** This relaxed, fashionable, reasonably priced

bar-cum-brasserie is quintessential queer Soho – always packed, open late during the week and until 6am Friday and Saturday. In fine weather the big windows are opened and the restaurant spills onto the narrow pavement outside. *Balans* breakfasts are an institution. There's another branch at 239 Old Brompton Rd, SW5 (℡020/7244 8838; Earl's Court tube) and a less overtly gay branch on Kensington High Street.

Bar Aquda 13–14 Maiden Lane, WC2 ℡020/ 7557 9891; **Charing Cross or Covent Garden tube.** Bright, modern and fashionable café-bar with good food. Recently refurbished.

BJs White Swan 556 Commercial Rd, E14 ℡020/7780 9870; **Limehouse DLR.** Busy, late-night East End local with nightly drag, cabaret, trashy disco, infamous amateur stripping contests and legendary Sunday tea dance (see p.508). Mostly men at the weekend.

The Black Cap 171 Camden High St, NW1 ☎020/7428 2721; Camden Town tube. Venerable north London institution offering cabaret of wildly varying quality almost every night. Laugh, sing and lip-synch along, and then dance drunkenly to 80s tunes until the early hours. The upstairs *Mrs Shufflewicks Bar* is quieter, and opens onto the Fong (named after drag legend Regina) Terrace in the summer.

The Box 32–34 Monmouth St, WC2 ☎020/7240 5828; Covent Garden or Leicester Square tube. Popular, bright café-bar serving good food for a gay/straight crowd during the day, and becoming a queerer pre-clubbing crowd as the night goes on.

The Edge 11 Soho Square, W1 ☎020/7439 1313, ⓦwww.edge.uk.com; Tottenham Court Rd tube. Busy, style-conscious and pricey Soho café-bar spread over several floors, although this doesn't seem to stop everyone ending up on the pavement, especially in summer. Food daily, DJs most nights.

Escape 10a Brewer St, W1 ☎020/7734 2626; Piccadilly Circus tube. Trendy DJ bar in the heart of Soho, attracting a young, mixed crowd and open until 3am most nights.

🏃 **First Out** 52 St Giles High St, WC2 ☎020/7240 8042, ⓦwww.firstoutcafe bar.com; Tottenham Court Rd tube. The West End's original gay café-bar, and still permanently packed, serving good veggie food at reasonable prices. Upstairs is airy and non-smoking, downstairs dark and foggy. Girl Friday (Fri) is a busy pre-club session for grrrls; gay men are welcome as guests.

Freedom 60–66 Wardour St, W1 ☎020/7734 0071; Leicester Square or Piccadilly tube. Hip, busy, late-opening place, popular with a straight/gay Soho crowd and recently given a glamorous make-over. The basement transforms itself at night into a funky, intimate basement club, complete with pink banquettes and masses of glitter balls.

G.A.Y. Bar 30 Old Compton St, W1 ☎020/7494 2756; Tottenham Court Rd or Leicester Square tube. Vast, pinky-purple video bar that attracts a young, fashionable, pre-*G.A.Y.* crowd. The basement bar is for women and guests only in the evening.

🏃 **The Green** 74 Upper St, N1 ☎020/7226 8895; Angel tube. Relaxed but stylish

new bar/restaurant fronting Islington Green, with interesting food, wine, beers and classic cocktails. It's open late Thurs–Sat and there's a distinct brunch vibe to Sundays.

Halfway 2 Heaven 7 Duncannon St, WC2 ☎020/7321 2791; Charing Cross tube. Friendly, traditional pub just off Trafalgar Square, featuring occasional cabaret, a regular pub quiz on Wednesdays and karaoke on Sundays. Attracts a largely male crowd, which is slightly older than one that congregates in the Old Compton Street bars.

Joiners Arms 116–118 Hackney Rd, E2 ☎020/7729 9180; Shoreditch or Old St tube. Atmospheric (and smoky) lesbian and gay bar with regular DJs and funky dance floor. Open late at weekends, when it attracts one of the most diverse crowds in London, with everything from East End stalwarts to loft-living trendies.

Kazbar 50 Clapham High St, SW4 ☎020/7622 0070, ⓦwww.kudosgroup.com; Clapham Common or Clapham North tube. Modern, mostly boyz, split-level bar from the team who brought you *Kudos* in the West End, with a video screen playing happy, poppy hits.

King Edward VI 25 Bromfield St, N1 ☎020/7704 0745; Angel tube. Long-established, loud-and-proud 80s style gay bar, with deafening music and a loyal crowd of Islington locals. The *Edward* is particularly popular in fine weather for its garden at the back, and there's a quieter chill-out bar upstairs.

King William IV 75 Hampstead High St, NW3 ☎020/7435 5747; Hampstead tube. Relaxed, traditional and friendly pub with an older crowd of regulars. Great food at lunchtimes.

Ku Bar 75 Charing Cross Rd, WC2 ☎020/7437 4303; Leicester Square tube. Café-bar serving a young, scene-conscious clientele with less attitude than some of the bars in the village. Cheap shots and huge cocktail pitchers make it a good choice for those who don't just want to guzzle beer.

Kudos 10 Adelaide St, WC2 ☎020/7379 4573, ⓦwww.kudosgroup.com; Charing Cross tube. Busy venue, popular amongst smart, besuited post-work boys and London's gay Chinese community, with ground-floor café and a basement video bar.

The Oak 79 Green Lanes, N16 ☎020/7354 2791; Manor House tube. Friendly, spacious local pub with a dance floor and pool table. It hosts a range of club nights and special events (some women-only), including the wildly popular Lower the Tone.

Shops

Most of the major chains (Waterstones, Borders, Books Etc) now have respectable lesbian and gay sections, but it's always worth going to the experts listed below. There are also some specifically lesbian and gay shops catering for most aspects of the rainbow shopping spectrum.

Babes 'n' Horny 57a Redchurch St, E2 ☎020/7538 9838, ⓦwww.babes-n-horny .com; Liverpool Street tube. Sex toys with a difference! Whoever said dildos can't be a work of art has clearly never set foot in this hip Shoreditch emporium. With occasional exhibitions, turntables and design magazines, Babes is way above your average sex shop.

Clone Zone 64 Old Compton St, W1 ☎020/7287 3530; Tottenham Court Road tube, 266 Old Brompton Rd, SW5 ☎020/7373 0598; Earl's Court tube, 23 Islington Green ☎020/7359 0444, ⓦwww.clonezone.co.uk; Angel tube. The world's largest gay retail company stocks a positively cornucopican range of erotic books, photos, magazines and R18 videos and DVDs, as well as clothing, gifts, music, jewellery and a tattooist (Earl's Court).

Expectations 75 Great Eastern St, EC2 ☎020/7739 0292, ⓦwww.expectations .co.uk; Old Street tube. Long-established, large gay men's leather and rubber store with a vast range of clothing, toys and accessories.

Fettered Pleasures 90 Holloway Rd, N7 ☎020/7619 9333 ⓦwww.fetteredpleaures .com; Highbury & Islington tube. Pansexual fetish store with high-quality leather wear, plus eye-poppingly lavish BDSM equipment for the most imaginative scene – body bag or padded, revolving bondage wheel, anyone?

Gay's the Word 66 Marchmont St, WC1 ☎020/7278 7654, ⓦwww.gaystheword .co.uk; Russell Square tube. Long-established, renowned community bookshop, famed for the weekly lesbian discussion groups and readings held in the shop, and offering an extensive collection of lesbian and gay classics, pulps, contemporary fiction and non-fiction, plus cards and calendars.

Prowler Soho 5–7 Brewer St, W1 ☎020/7734 4031, ⓦwww.prowlerstores.co.uk.; Piccadilly Circus tube. Since teaming up in 1999 with the folks from Zipper-Stores and *Gay Times*, Prowler has become a gay and lesbian household name, stocking a great range of literature, art, clothing, postcards and gifts as well as R18 videos and DVDs and fiction. There are smaller branches at 283 Camden High St (Camden Town tube) and at 9 Caledonian Rd (King's Cross tube).

Recoil.557 The Railway Arch, Redcross Way, off Southwark St, SE1 ☎020/7378 0557, ⓦwww.dirtybastards.com. Rubber, skinhead and industrial wear for the kinky or very sleazy, all in suitably dank surroundings. Open Thurs–Sat only.

RoB London 24 Wells St, W1 ☎020/7735 7893, ⓦwww.rob.nl; Oxford Street tube. London outlet of the highly regarded Amsterdam-based leather and fetish wear specialist, in a central location just north of Soho.

Sh! 39 Coronet St, N1 ☎020/7613 5458, ⓦwww.sh-womenstore.com; Old Street tube. Be it leather wear, rubber or lace, sex toys, books or lube, London's original women's erotic emporium is well equipped to whet your sexual appetite.

Silver Moon 3rd Floor at Foyles, 113–119 Charing Cross Rd, WC2 ☎020/7440 1562, ⓦwww.silvermoonbookshop.co.uk; Tottenham Court Road tube. Large, well-stocked women's bookshop boasting the biggest lesbian section in the country, knowledge-able staff and a good selection of magazines, periodicals, cards, T-shirts and other peripherals.

Trax Records 66 Greek St, W1 ☎020/7734 0795, ⓦwww.traxrecords.co.uk; Tottenham Court Road tube. Tiny but legendary record store specializing in gay-oriented dance music, including hi NRG, trance, hard house and club classics.

(30)

Oval House Theatre Kennington Oval, SE11 ☎020/7582 0080, ⊛www.ovalhouse.com; Oval tube. The home-cooked Caribbean and veggie food at this well-loved local theatre has warmed the cockles of many a queer theatregoer's heart.

Retro Bar 2 George Court (off Strand), WC2 ☎020/7321 2811; Charing Cross tube. Friendly, indie/retro bar playing 70s, 80s, goth and alternative sounds, and featuring regular DJs and karaoke.

The Royal Oak 73 Columbia Rd, E2 ☎020/7739 8204; Old Street or Shoreditch tube. In the heart of the famous Columbia Road flower market, this old, comfortable market pub caters for a mixed gay/straight crowd, and offers Sunday breakfasts or Tex-Mex meals at the upstairs restaurant. Open from 8am Sunday.

The Royal Vauxhall Tavern 372 Kennington Lane, SE11 ☎020/7840 0596; Vauxhall tube. A London institution with late opening hours, this huge, disreputable and divey drag and cabaret pub is home to legendary alternative club night, Duckie, on Saturdays, and is packed to the doors on Sunday afternoons for SLAGS with the DE Experience.

Rupert Street 50 Rupert St, W1 ☎020/7292 7140; Piccadilly Circus tube. Smart, trendy bar attracting a mixed after-work crowd on weekdays but with a more obviously pre-club vibe at weekends, when they remove the chairs and tables and it's frequently packed to the rafters.

Sahara Nights 257 Pentonville Rd, N1; King's Cross tube. Happy-go-lucky weekend dance bar with DJs and reliably cheap beer, popular with a young, indie-minded crowd, for whom it's a pit stop on the way to Popstarz.

Shadow Lounge 5 Brewer St, W1 ☎020/7287 7988, ⊛www.theshadowlounge.co.uk; Piccadilly Circus tube. Glitzy gay lounge and members bar (non-members can pay at the door) which attracts an A to Z of celebrity punters. More fag hag than leather lez and, naturally, the boys rule the school.

Ted's Place 305a North End Rd, W14 ☎020/7385 9359; West Kensington or West Brompton tube. Cruisey Fulham local, open weekdays only and exclusively for men, though there is a regular Thursday TV/TS night.

Trash Palace 11 Wardour St, W1; Leicester Square or Piccadilly tube. Alternative, indie/pop/electro bar on two floors, open until 3am Fridays and Saturdays, a popular spot pre-Miss-Shapes or Popstarz.

Two Brewers 114 Clapham High St, SW4

☎020/7498 4971; Clapham Common or Clapham North tube. Big, long-established and popular south London pub, with nightly cabaret in the front bar and a more cruisey dance floor in the back.

Village Soho 81 Wardour St, W1 ☎020/7434 2124; Leicester Square or Piccadilly Circus tube. Elegant three-floor café/bar attracting more pretty boyz than grrrls, recently refurbished with a new look, new DJs and now serving food from 4pm.

The Yard Rupert St, W1 ☎020/7437 2652; Piccadilly Circus tube. Attractive bar with courtyard, loft areas and a laid-back, sociable atmosphere. *The Yard* attracts a 25yr-old-plus crowd and it's still one of the best in Soho for alfresco drinking. Occasional comedy on weekday nights, as well as regular changing artworks.

Lesbian cafés, bars and pubs

Blush 8 Cazenove Rd, Stoke Newington, N16 ☎020/7923 9202; bus #73 from King's Cross or Angel tube. Two floors of fun (one of them smoke-free), with quizzes, live music and a pool bar making this local a popular choice among lesbians north of the city centre.

Candy Bar 4 Carlisle St, WC2 ☎020/7494 4041; Tottenham Court Road tube. Now re-established at its original venue but still with the same crucial, cruisey vibe that made it the hottest girl-bar in central London.

The Drill Hall 16 Chenies St, WC1 ☎020/7307 5061, wwww.drillhall.co.uk; Goodge Street tube. This lesbian-run arts centre offers a good theatrical mix all year round.

Girls Go Down G.A.Y. Bar, 30 Old Compton St, W1; Tottenham Court Road or Leicester Square tube. Women's bar in the basement of the achingly trendy *G.A.Y. Bar* and the only real lesbian venue on Old Compton St.

The Glass Bar West Lodge, Euston Square Gardens, 190 Euston Rd, NW1 ☎020/7387 6184, ⊛www.southopia.com/glassbar; Euston or Euston Square tube. Difficult to find (and hard to forget), this friendly and intimate late-opening women-only members bar (membership is automatic once you're inside) is housed in a listed building and features a wrought-iron spiral staircase which becomes increasingly perilous as the night goes on. Knock on the door to get in. Open from 1pm; no admission after 12.30am on Sat. Closed Sun.

Southopia 146–148 Newington Butts, SE11

📞020/7735 5178, 🖥www.southopia.com; **Kennington or Elephant & Castle tube.** Stylish private members bar for women (men allowed in ground-floor bar as guests). Run by the same company as *The Glass Bar*, with a friendly, grown-up atmosphere. Daily membership £2.

Star at Night 22 Great Chapel St, W1 📞020/7434 3749; **Tottenham Court Rd tube.** Comfortable new venue open from 6pm Tues–Sat, popular with a slightly older crowd who want somewhere to sit, a good glass of wine and good conversation.

Vespa Lounge The Conservatory, Centrepoint House, 15 St Giles High St, WC1 📞020/7836 8956; **Tottenham Court Road tube.** This centrally-located girls' bar gets super busy at weekends. Pool table, video screen, cute bar staff and a predominantly young crowd. Gay men welcome as guests.

Y Bar 142 Essex Rd, N1 📞020/7359 2661; **Angel tube.** Now established as one of the cooler hangouts for gorgeous girls. Mixed, but women-only on Thurs.

Gay men's cafés, bars and pubs

79CXR 79 Charing Cross Rd, WC2 📞020/7734 0769; **Leicester Square tube.** Big, busy, cruisey men-den on two floors, with industrial decor, late licence and a no-messing atmosphere.

BarCode 3–4 Archer St, W1 📞020/7734 3342; **Piccadilly Circus tube.** Busy, stylish cruise and dance bar on two floors, attracting a buff, masculine crowd. On Tuesdays it hosts Comedy Camp, an award-winning gay comedy club.

Brief Encounter 41–43 St Martin's Lane, WC2 📞020/7379 8252; **Leicester Square tube.** Now back with its original name, the West End's longest-running cruise bar is a popular pre-Heaven or post-opera hangout (it's next door to the Coliseum); the upper bar offers regular cabaret, while the lower bar is very, very dark.

Bromptons 294 Old Brompton Rd, SW5 📞020/7370 1344; **Earl's Court tube.** Long-established, leathery and immensely popular late-opening bar-cum-club that's packed at weekends, and features regular cabarets and PAs.

Central Station 37 Wharfdale Rd, N1 📞020/7278 3294; **King's Cross tube.** Award-winning, late-opening community pub on three floors, offering cabaret, cruisey club nights in the basement, and the UK's only gay sports bar. It's also the home of the long-running Gummi rubber fetish night. Not strictly men-only, but mostly so.

The Coleherne 261 Old Brompton Rd, SW5 📞020/7244 5951; **Earl's Court tube.** Famous and permanently packed former leather bar, now popular with a wide range of the gay community and still bristling with history.

Comptons of Soho 53 Old Compton St, W1 📞020/7479 7961; **Leicester Square or Piccadilly Circus tube.** This large, traditional-style pub is a Soho institution, always busy with a butch 25yr-old-plus crowd, but still a relaxed place to cruise or just hang out. The upstairs Club Lounge is more chilled and attracts a younger crowd.

The Kings Arms 23 Poland St, W1 📞020/7734 5907; **Oxford Circus tube.** London's best-known and perennially popular bear bar, with a traditional London pub atmosphere, DJ on Sat and karaoke night Sun.

The Quebec 12 Old Quebec St, W1 📞020/7629 6159; **Marble Arch tube.** Long-established and busy gay venue with downstairs disco and a late licence. Especially popular with the older crowd.

▲ Café life, Old Compton Street

Clubs

London's clubs tend to open up and shut down with surreal frequency, only to pop up again a few months later somewhere entirely different, or in the same place but with a different name. Unless otherwise specified, we've detailed only the longest-running and most popular nights here – check the gay press, listings magazines and individual websites for up-to-date times and prices before you plan your night out.

Somewhere between a café and a club is the institution of the tea dance, a fun and friendly place to try out old-fashioned partner dancing. Traditionally, tea dancing happens on a Sunday, but these days they're just as likely to be on a Saturday. It's best to arrive early, especially if you need a class: ring in advance for details.

Places are listed by club name if this is well known and long-lived, and by venue where there's a variety of changing theme nights, and we've tried to give a London-wide sample of what's on offer (usually clubs are significantly cheaper once you're out of the West End). Entry **prices** start at around £4–5, but are more often between £8 and £15, rising to around £35 or even £50 for special events like New Year's Eve extravaganzas. A few places offer concessions for students and those on benefits, and some extend discounts if you've managed to pick up the right flyer from a bar earlier in the evening. Some clubs, especially the men's, stipulate **dress codes** – mainly leather, rubber, uniform and other fetish wear. We've specified such sartorial regulations, but it's best to check before setting out in your finery.

Most **clubs open** at around 11pm (although some don't get going until the small hours) and close between 3am and 5am, sometimes later. A few of the cafés, bars and pubs listed on pp.500–504 provide a good, cheap alternative to the fully fledged clubs, though they usually close earlier.

Despite their illegality, **drugs** remain an integral part of London's queer clubbing scene; Antidote, 32a Wardour St, W1 (☎020/7437 3523) provides a lesbian, gay, bi and transgender-specific drugs counselling and support service, including a weekly drop-in.

Saunas

London's burgeoning male sauna scene shows no signs of slowing up. The range of places runs from small, intimate affairs with just a steam room and Jacuzzi, to labyrinthine venues with swimming pools and gyms. Some of the best are listed below. They all charge around £10–13.

Chariots Farringdon 57 Cowcross St, EC1 ☎020/7251 5553, ⊛www.gaysauna .co.uk; Farringdon tube. With a fabulous video room, high-power sunbeds, rest rooms and a small, cosy sauna, it's not for nothing that this is called the "City Retreat". Daily 11am–11pm.

Chariots Shoreditch 1 Farechild St, EC2; ☎020/7247 5333, ⊛www.gaysauna .co.uk; Liverpool Street or Old Street tube. London's largest and most fabulous gay sauna features everything you could wish for in the way of hot and sweaty nights indoors. There's a spacious bar too. Daily noon to 9am.

Chariots Streatham Rear of 292 Streatham High Rd, SW16 ☎020/8696 0929, ⊛www.gaysauna.co.uk; Streatham Hill train station. South London sauna with rest rooms and two sauna cabins big enough to fit twenty burly men in each. Mon–Thurs noon to midnight, Fri noon–Sun midnight.

Chariots Waterloo 101 Lower Marsh, SE1 ☎020/7401 8484, ⊛www.gaysauna .co.uk; Waterloo tube. A 40-man steam room, the UK's largest sauna cabin, a maze of private rest rooms, video lounge and Internet café are among the attractions of this air-conditioned club. Open 24hr.

Pleasuredome Sauna Arch 124, Cornwall Rd, SE1 ☎020/7633 9194; Waterloo tube. Facilities here include two saunas, two steam rooms, a chill-out zone and café-bar plus privacy cabins and Jacuzzi. Mixed ages, fast turnover, highly rated. Open 24hr.

The Sauna Bar 29 Endell St, WC2 ☎020/7836 2236; Covent Garden tube. Very central (a skip away from Covent Garden and Soho), this friendly place offers the usual facilities, along with masseurs, a bar, and video entertainment while you lounge in the Jacuzzi. Mon–Fri noon to midnight; open 24hr Sat & Sun.

When it's throwing-out time and you need a guaranteed harassment-free **cab service**, Liberty Cars, 330 Old St, EC1 (☎020/7739 9080) offers a reasonably priced, London-wide, 24-hour ride home; you can order a cab direct from their car marshall in Old Compton Street between *Balans* and *Balans Café*.

Mixed clubs

Beyond *Club Colosseum*, 1 Nine Elms Way, SW8 ☎07905/035682. ⊛www.allthingsorange .com; Vauxhall tube. London's biggest after-hours party kicks off each Sunday morning at 4.30am and carries on until well into the morning. Two massive dance floors, four bars, chill-out areas and funky house music please an eclectic mix of up-for-it clubbers.

Bootylicious *Crash*, 66 Goding St, SE11 ⊛www .bootylicious-club.co.uk; Vauxhall tube. Every second Friday, *Crash* is host to London's only weekend club night devoted to urban dance music. Expect a full-on, sexy vibe with hip-hop, R&B and ragga. For a hot and sweaty dance experience with a beautiful, funky crowd, it doesn't get much better than this.

Club Kali *The Dome*, 1 Dartmouth Park Hill, N19 (no phone); Tufnell Park tube. Held on the first and third Friday of every month, Kali is a huge multi-ethnic extravaganza offering bhangra, Bollywood, Arabic, swing, Hindi and house flavours for a friendly, attitude-free crowd.

Crash 66 Goding St, SE11 ☎020/7793 9262; Vauxhall tube. Four bars, two dance floors, chill-out areas and hard bodies make this weekly Saturday-nighter busy, buzzy, sexy and mostly boyzy. First Saturday of the month is Megawoof! – a testoster-one-fuelled mix of leathermen, bears and muscle boys; last Saturday of the month is Suzy Krueger's mixed fetish night, Hard On (⊛www.hardonclub.co.uk).

DTPM *Fabric*, 77a Charterhouse St, EC1 ☎020/7749 1199, ⊛www.blue-cube.net; Farringdon Road tube. This long-running Sunday-nighter is now well established in *Fabric's* chic, spacious surroundings – the main floor offers the classic DTPM shirts-off experience and some great visuals; the second, a harder electro sound and a live percussionist; and the third, a mellow soulful/oldies mix in the intimate upstairs R&B bar.

Duckie *Royal Vauxhall Tavern*, 372 Kennington Lane, SE11 ☎020/7737 4043, ⊛www.duckie .co.uk; Vauxhall tube. Duckie's modern, rock-based hurdy-gurdy provides a creative and cheerfully ridiculous Saturday night antidote to the dreary forces of gay house domination. Cult DJs The Readers Wives are famed for playing everything from Kim Wilde to The Velvet Underground. Regular live art performances, occasional bouncy castles and theme nights.

Exilio UCL, Houghton St, WC2 ☎07931/374 391; Holborn tube. Every Saturday night, Exilio erupts in a lesbian and gay Latin frenzy, spinning salsa, cumbias and merengue, and also features live acts.

🏃 **Fiction** *The Cross*, King's Cross Freight Depot, off Goods Way, N1 (no phone); King's Cross tube. Brought to you by Blue Cube promotions of *Fabric* fame, Fiction is a mellow but funky Friday night dancefest in a series of brick railway arches, so it manages to be both big and intimate. Music ranges from old skool in the VIP room to classic funky floor-fillers and harder-edged electro sounds. If it gets too sweaty, there are two garden areas in which to chill. Stylish.

G.A.Y. *Astoria*, 157 Charing Cross Rd, WC2 ☎020/7734 6963, ⊛www.g-a-y.co.uk; Tottenham Court Road tube. Widely considered the launch venue for new (and ailing) boy and girl bands, this huge, unpretentious and fun-loving dance night is where the young crowd gather on Mon, Thurs, Fri & Sat. There are lots of cheap entry deals to be had at the G.A.Y. Pink Pounder trash bash – just £1 with flyers found at any gay bar in the West End.

The Ghetto Falconberg Court, W1 ☎020/7287 3726; Tottenham Court Road tube. Late-opening, cruisey club behind the *Astoria* with a range of nights catering for every taste (mainly male) from goth indie to funk. Saturday nights see the very trashy Wig Out.

Heaven *Under the Arches*, Villiers St, WC2 ☎020/7930 2020, ⊛www.heaven-london.com; Charing Cross or Embankment tube. Widely regarded as the UK's most popular gay club, this legendary, 2000-capacity venue continues to reign supreme. Big nights are Mondays (Popcorn), Wednesdays (Fruit Machine) and Saturdays (just Heaven), all with big-name DJs, PAs and shows. More Muscle Mary than Diesel Doris.

Horse Meat Disco *South Central*, 349 Kennington Lane, SE11 ⊛www.horsemeatdisco.co.uk; Vauxhall tube. Freaky, underground disco and electrofunk club for a diverse gay/hetero crowd.

Lower The Tone *The Oak*, 79 Green Lanes, N16 ☎020/7354 2791; Manor House tube. Last Friday monthly. This hugely popular cult club night is the brainchild of painter Sadie Lee and rock star pals Lea Andrews and Jonathan Kemp. Billed as a club for people who don't like clubbing, LTT is a cocktail of sugar-coated hip-hop, classic 1970s pop, sleazy foreign disco and bizarre theme tunes. Mixed, but predominantly women.

Madame Jo-Jos 8–10 Brewer St, W1 t020/7734 3040, ⊛www.madamejojos.com; Piccadilly Circus tube. Lush, louche cabaret club offering a variety of club nights and spectacular drag shows for office girls, gay boys and everyone in between, plus a variety of dance nights. It's not cheap, but good for a special occasion.

Miss-Shapes *The Ghetto*, Falconberg Court, W1 ☎07956/549246, ⊛www.miss-shapes.co.uk; Tottenham Court Road tube. Popular with indie grrrls, this Thursday-nighter is the sister club to Popstarz (see below), playing trash and indie to entice a bevvied and up-for-it grunge-cool crowd. Now with a sister club in New York.

Popstarz *The Scala*, 275 Pentonville Rd, N1 ☎07956/549246, ⊛www.popstarz.org; King's Cross tube. Ground-breaking Friday-night indie club, Popstarz has had to enforce a gay and lesbian majority door policy as its still-winning formula of alternative toons, 70s and 80s trash, cheap beer and no attitude attracts a growing straight, studenty crowd.

🏃 **Queer Nation** *Substation South*, 9 Brighton Terrace, SW9 ☎020/7732 2095, ⊛www.queer nation.org; Brixton tube. Long-running and popular New York-style soulful house and garage nights for funksters; chilled, multi-racial and attitude-free.

Salvation *Café de Paris*, Leicester Square, WC2 ⊛www.salvation-london.com; Leicester Square tube. First Sunday of every month. Recently voted the one club not to miss if you visit London, expect a surfeit of muscled beauties at this glamorous central venue. The fun starts at 5pm and keeps pumping till midnight, ensuring that even the hardest of clubbers get a good night's kip before work on Monday.

WayOut Club at Charlies 9 Crosswall, off Minories, EC3; ℡ 07958/473599; ⓦ www .thewayoutclub.com; Aldgate tube. Long-established Saturday night for gays, straights, cross-dressers, drag queens, TVs, TSs and friends offers a warm welcome, changing rooms, video screen and regular cabaret.

Lesbian clubs

Curves *Agenda*, **Minster Court, 3 Mincing Lane, EC3** ℡ 07947/310967, ⓦ www.curvesclub.net; Tower Hill/Monument tube. First Sat monthly. Recently relaunched dance club in sophisticated new surroundings. Curves offers a plush lounge environment for a sexy, sassy crowd.

Dolly Mixtures *The Candy Bar*, **4 Carlisle St, WC2** ⓦ www.thecandybar.co.uk; Tottenham Court Road tube. DJ Slamma plays house and soul while Crystal gets busy on the mike every Saturday. Friday nights see Grind, with R&B and hip-hop.

Girl Friday *First Out*, **52 St Giles High St, WC2** ℡ 020/7240 8042, ⓦ www.firstoutcafebar.com; Tottenham Court Road tube. This long-standing Friday-nighter is the place to meet girl pals at the end of a busy working week. Expect a packed basement for mingling and pre-club drinking.

Liberte *G Lounge*, **18 Kentish Town Rd, NW1** ℡ 020/7354 2791; Camden Town tube. Last Sat in each month; hugely popular party spinning soulful grooves, reggae and garage for girls who like to smile when they're swinging.

Lyrical Lounge *Battersea Barge*, **Nine Elms Lane, SW8** ⓦ www.gingerbeer.co.uk; Vauxhall tube. Quarterly live-music night showcasing girl talent and organized by the women behind the gingerbeer website; the venue is a candlelit barge on the Thames. Open 7pm–2am. Diva Night is a monthly mixed Sunday-nighter at the same venue.

Rumours *Minories*, **64–73 Minories, EC3** ℡ 07961/158375, ⓦ www.girl-rumours.co.uk; Tower Hill or Aldgate tube. There's room for 500 grrrls at this bi-weekly, women-only Saturday-nighter. Kicking off early at 8pm, this popular and cheap club-night offers two bars, quiet lounges and two dance floors until 2am.

Gay men's clubs

Action Renaissance Rooms, off Miles St, SW8 ℡ 07973/233377, ⓦ www.actionclub.net; Vauxhall tube. Big party-style dance night with mucho muscle, lavish production values and an Ibiza-style outdoor terrace.

Backstreet Wentworth Mews, off Burdett Rd, E3 ℡ 020/8980 8557 or 8980 7880 outside club hours, ⓦ www.thebackstreet.com; Mile End tube. Long-running, traditional leather and rubber club with a strict, very butch, dress code. Open Thurs–Sun.

Fire South Lambeth Rd, Vauxhall, SW8 ℡ 07905/035682, ⓦ www.allthingsorange. com; Vauxhall tube. Vauxhall venue that's the home of a packed line up of dance nights, including the A:M, Rude Boyz & Orange after-hours parties and Sunday afternoon's funky house party, Later.

The Fort 131 Grange Rd, SE1 ℡ 020/8549 4339; London Bridge tube. There's no set dress code at this sleazy, sexy cruise bar but check the free press or phone for details about special themed nights such as the frequent boots-only nights.

The Hoist Railway Arches, 47b-47c South Lambeth Rd, SW8 ℡ 020/7735 9972, ⓦ www.the-hoist.co.uk; Vauxhall tube. London's biggest and best-known leather/dress code bar for men. *The Hoist* also hosts regular skinhead nights, plus SM Gays every third Thursday.

XXL The London Bridge Arches, 53 Southwark St, SE1 ℡ 07812/048574, ⓦ www.xxl-london .com; London Bridge tube. Massively popular Wednesday and Saturday dance club for big, burly men and their fans, attracting a very diverse crowd with its two dance floors, two bars and outside chill-out area.

Tea dances

Original Sunday Tea Dance at BJs White Swan 556 Commercial Rd, E14 ℡ 020/7780 9870; Limehouse DLR. Hosted by popular local DJ Gary Malden, who plays ballroom, cheesy disco and everything in between. Sundays 5.30pm–midnight (tea and sandwiches until 7pm).

Waltzing with Hilda Jacksons Lane Community Centre, 269a Archway Rd, N6 ℡ 07939/072958; Highgate tube. Women-only Latin and ballroom dancing club – with a dash of Country & Western thrown in to keep you on your toes. Beer at pub prices and classes for beginners. Twice monthly on second and last Saturdays, 7.45pm–midnight.

Classical music, opera and dance

W ith the South Bank, the Barbican and Wigmore Hall offering year-round appearances by generally first-rate musicians, and numerous smaller venues providing a stage for less established or more specialized performers, the capital should satisfy most devotees of **classical music**. What's more, in the annual Promenade Concerts at the Royal Albert Hall, London has one of the world's greatest, most democratic music festivals.

Despite its elitist image, **opera** in the capital has an enthusiastic following. While the Royal Opera House (ROH) can attract top international stars to perform there, the downside is the high price of most of the tickets. The nearby English National Opera (ENO) is better value, and can be more adventurous in its repertoire and productions. Apart from the two major companies, there are also outfits like the Almeida Theatre and Battersea Arts Centre that are extending the boundaries of contemporary music theatre in lively and adventurous ways.

The more modest economic demands of **dance** mean that you'll often find a broad spectrum of ambitious work on offer, with some of the world's outstanding companies appearing regularly at Sadler's Wells. Meanwhile, fans of classicism can revel in the Royal Ballet – a company with some of the most accomplished dancers in Europe.

Classical music

London is spoilt for choice when it comes to **orchestras**. On most days you'll be able to catch a concert by either the London Symphony Orchestra, the London Philharmonic, the Royal Philharmonic, the Philharmonia or the BBC Symphony Orchestra, or a smaller-scale performance from the English Chamber Orchestra or the Academy of St Martin-in-the-Fields. There are also more specialized ensembles, like the Orchestra of the Age of Enlightenment, who perform a pre-twentieth-century repertoire on period instruments, and the London Sinfonietta, one of the world's finest contemporary music groups. Unless a glamorous guest conductor is wielding the baton, or one of the world's high-profile orchestras is giving a performance, full houses

Classical music

CLASSICAL MUSIC, OPERA AND DANCE

31

509

are a rarity, so even at the biggest concert halls you should be able to pick up a ticket for around £12 (the usual range is about £5–30), and it's always worth asking about concessions.

Classical music festivals

BBC Henry Wood Promenade Concerts (the "Proms") Royal Albert Hall ☎020/7589 8212, ⊛www.bbc.co.uk/proms/; South Kensington tube. Though the Proms tend to be associated with the raucous "Last Night", when the flag-waving audience sings its patriotic heart out, this jingoistic knees-up is untypical of the season, which from July to September features at least one concert daily in an exhilarating melange of favourites and new or recondite works. You can book a seat as you would for any other concert, but for many the essence of the Proms is the fact that all the stalls seats are removed to create hundreds of standing places costing around £4 and purchased on the day. The upper gallery is similarly packed with people sitting on the floor or standing. The acoustics aren't the world's best – OK for orchestral blockbusters, less so for small-scale works – but the performers are usually outstanding, the atmosphere is great, and the hall is so vast that the likelihood of being turned away if you turn up on the night is slim. A recent innovation is the Proms Chamber Series, a handful of lunchtime concerts held in the recently re-opened Cadogan Hall, just off Sloane Square. These cost £8 with some gallery tickets available at £4 on the day. The annual *Proms Guide*, available at most bookshops from May, gives information on every concert and about additional ticket offers.

City of London Festival Barbican Centre and many venues in and around the City ☎020/7377 0540, ⊛www.colf.org; Barbican or St Paul's tube. An eclectic mix of international soloists, chamber groups, orchestras and choirs perform in a range of venues, including several City churches, livery halls and St Paul's Cathedral, during this month-long arts festival in late June/July.

Kenwood Lakeside Concerts Kenwood House, Hampstead Lane, NW3. Tickets available on ☎0870 890 0146 and ☎0870 333 6206, ⊛www.picnicconcerts.com; bus #210 from Archway tube; shuttle bus from/to East Finchley and Golders Green tubes on concert nights. The grassy amphitheatre in front of Kenwood House is the venue for music every Saturday evening from July to the end of August. These include a few classical concerts of well-known and popular works, which are performed with panache and often end with a fireworks display.

Lufthansa Festival of Baroque Music Various venues, City of Westminster ⊛www .lufthansafestival.org.uk; Piccadilly Circus or Westminster tube. A month-long festival held around May and featuring many outstanding international specialists in Baroque music. Venues usually include St James's, Piccadilly; St John's Smith Square; and Westminster Abbey.

Meltdown South Bank Centre, SE1 ☎08703 808 300, ⊛www.rfh.org.uk/meltdown; Waterloo or Embankment tube. One of the most stimulating musical events in the London calendar, this short festival of cutting edge contemporary music is selected by a different leading musician each year, and held in various parts of the South Bank complex during June.

Spitalfields Festival Christ Church, Spitalfields, E1 ☎020/7377 0287, ⊛www .spitalfieldsfestival.org.uk; Liverpool Street, Aldgate or Aldgate East tube. A varied mix of classical music and community events centred on Hawksmoor's mighty Christ Church, during the area's June arts shindig. There's also a short winter festival in December.

The Proms provide a feast of music at bargain-basement prices (see box), and during the week there are also many **free concerts**, often during lunchtimes, by students or professionals in several London churches, particularly in the City; performances in the Royal College of Music and Royal Academy of Music are of an amazingly high standard, and the choice of work is often a lot riskier than in commercial venues.

Concert venues

Barbican Centre Silk Street, EC2 ☎020/7638 8891, ⓦ www.barbican.org.uk; Barbican or Moorgate tube. With the outstanding resident London Symphony Orchestra, and with top foreign orchestras and big-name soloists in regular attendance, the Barbican is one of the outstanding arenas for classical music. Programming is much more adventurous than it was, and free music in the foyer is often very good. Unfortunately, it's a difficult place to find your way around.

BMIC (British Music Information Centre) Lincoln House, 75 Westminster Bridge Road, SE1 ☎020/7028 1902, ⓦ www.bmic.co.uk; Lambeth North or Waterloo tube. The BMIC exists to promote British contemporary classical music. Its concert series of innovative work, The Cutting Edge, runs on Thursdays during the autumn at The Warehouse, Theed Street.

Cadogan Hall Sloane Terrace, SW1 ☎020/7730 4500; Sloane Square tube. This handsome neo-Byzantine building, originally built in 1901 as a Christian Scientist church, has recently been converted into a 900-seat concert hall with an outstanding acoustic. The London Royal Philharmonic is its resident orchestra and it is also the venue for the Proms short series of chamber concerts (see box opposite).

St Giles Cripplegate Fore Street, Barbican, EC2 ☎020/7638 1997, ⓦ www.stgilescripplegate .com; Barbican or Moorgate tube. Lurking in the midst of the Barbican, this church is regularly used for concerts, especially of choral music, and has a strong connection with the nearby Guildhall School of Music and Drama.

St James Piccadilly, W1 ☎020/7381 0441, ⓦ www.st-james-piccadilly.org; Piccadilly Circus tube. As well as free lunchtime concerts on Mondays, Wednesdays and Fridays, this heavily restored Wren church also hosts fee-paying evening concerts. The restaurant in the crypt is good for before or after.

St John Smith Square, SW1 ☎020/7222 1061, ⓦ www.sjss.org.uk; Westminster tube. This striking Baroque church, situated behind Westminster Abbey, was gutted in 1941 and later turned into a concert hall with a fine acoustic. Its varied musical menu includes orchestral and choral concerts, chamber music and solo recitals, with The Academy of Ancient Music its current resident orchestra. There's a good restaurant in the crypt.

South Bank Centre South Bank, SE1 ☎0870/380 4300, ⓦ www.rfh.org.uk; Waterloo or Embankment tube. The SBC has three concert venues, none of which is exclusively used for classical music. The Royal Festival Hall (RFH) is closed until 2007 for major refurbishment and acoustical enhancement. A gargantuan space, it's tailor-made for large-scale choral and orchestral works, and plays host to some big-name soloists, though only a few can fill it. The Queen Elizabeth Hall (QEH) is the prime location for chamber concerts, solo recitals and contemporary work; while the Purcell Room is the most intimate venue, excellent for chamber music and recitals by up-and-coming instrumentalists and singers.

The Warehouse 13 Theed St, SE1 ☎020/7928 9251; Waterloo tube. The home of the London Festival Orchestra, this multi-purpose commercial space has become one of the best and most exciting venues for contemporary music, with many concerts promoted by the Society for the Promotion of New Music (SPNM).

Wigmore Hall 36 Wigmore St, W1 ☎020/7935 2141, ⓦ www.wigmore-hall.org.uk; Bond Street or Oxford Circus tube. With its near-perfect acoustics, the small Wigmore Hall is a favourite with artists and audiences alike; concerts are best booked well in advance. An exceptional venue for chamber music, it is also well known for its song recitals by some of the world's greatest singers. It stages very popular, fee-paying mid-morning concerts on Sundays.

Classical music | CLASSICAL MUSIC, OPERA AND DANCE

㉛

Free concerts

BBC Maida Vale Concerts Delaware Road, W9 ☎020/8576 1227, Ⓦwww.bbc.co.uk; Warwick Avenue or Maida Vale tube. The BBC Symphony Orchestra hosts free concerts, performed by various BBC ensembles and artists, at the Maida Vale Studios. All concerts are later broadcast. Booking opens six weeks in advance.

Royal Academy of Music Marylebone Road, NW1 ☎020/7873 7373, Ⓦwww.ram.ac.uk; Regent's Park or Baker Street tube. During term time, you can catch at least one lunchtime concert each week (Fri 1pm), and an early evening recital, for which there is usually an entry charge.

Royal College of Music Prince Consort Road, SW7 ☎020/7591 4314, Ⓦwww.rcm.ac.uk; South Kensington tube. During term time, free lunchtime (1pm) concerts are staged at London's top music college on Tuesday, Wednesday and Thursday, and at nearby St Mary Abbots Church, Kensington High Street, on Fridays. There are also occasional evening concerts, for which you need to book, and opera performances, for which there is an entry charge.

St Anne and St Agnes Gresham Street, EC2 ☎020/7606 4986, Ⓦwww.stanneslutheranchurch.org; St Paul's tube. As well as lunchtime recitals (Mon & Fri 1.10pm), this Lutheran place of worship has a small J.S. Bach festival in July.

St Bride Fleet Street, EC4 ☎020/7427 0133, Ⓦwww.stbrides.com; Blackfriars tube. Lunchtime concerts every week (Tues & Fri 1.15pm), usually by professional musicians. A good professional choir sings at two services every Sunday.

St Giles-in-the-Fields St Giles High Street, WC2 ☎020/7240 2532, Ⓦwww.stgilesonline .org; Tottenham Court Road tube. A mixed programme of chamber music and song takes place every Friday in the spring and autumn at 1.10pm. The organ is currently being restored.

St Lawrence Jewry Guildhall, EC2 ☎020/7600 9478; Bank or St Paul's tube. As well as regular organ recitals on an impressive new instrument (Tues 1pm), there is a free lunchtime music festival that runs throughout August.

St Luke Old Street, EC1 ☎020/7382 2556, Ⓦwww.lso.co.uk; Old Street tube. This fine eighteenth-century church has recently been converted into the rehearsal and education centre of the London Symphony Orchestra. There are regular lunchtime concerts and it is also possible to watch the orchestra rehearse.

St Magnus the Martyr Lower Thames Street, EC3 ☎020/7626 4481, Ⓦwww.stmagnusmartyr .org.uk; Monument tube. There's a recital on the 1712 Jordan organ most Tuesdays (1.05pm) as well as a chamber or instrumental concert on Thursdays (1.05pm). A good choir provides sung mass every Sunday (11am).

St Margaret Lothbury, EC2 ☎020/7606 8330, Ⓦwww.stml.org.uk; Bank tube. Lunchtime recitals every Thursday at 1.10pm (except August) on the church's 200-year-old organ.

St Martin-in-the-Fields Trafalgar Square, WC2 ☎020/7839 8362, Ⓦwww.stmartin-in-the -fields.org; Charing Cross or Leicester Square tube. Free lunchtime recitals Monday, Tuesday and Friday (1pm), plus fee-charging concerts in the evenings, sometimes featuring the top-notch orchestra of the Academy of St Martin-in-the-Fields.

St Martin-within-Ludgate Ludgate Hill, EC4 ☎020/7248 6054; St Paul's or Blackfriars tube. This fantastically spired Wren church hosts a varied Wednesday lunchtime recital programme (1.15pm) throughout the year except during August.

St-Mary-le-Bow Cheapside, EC2 ☎020/7248 5139, Ⓦwww.stmarylebow.co.uk; St Paul's tube. A varied programme of mainly chamber and solo recitals every Thursday (1.05pm) except in August and September.

St-Mary-le-Strand Strand, WC2 ☎020/7836 3126, Ⓦwww.stmarylestrand.org; Covent Garden or Temple tube. Every Wednesday (1.05pm) young professional or student musicians provide a respite from the surrounding traffic in this eighteenth-century gem by James Gibbs.

St Michael Cornhill, EC3 ☎020/7248 3826, Ⓦwww.st-michaels.org.uk; Bank tube. Organ recitals take place every Monday (1pm) on an instrument first played by Henry Purcell in 1684.

St Olave Hart Street, EC3 ☎020/7488 4318; Tower Hill tube. Chamber pieces or solo recitals on Wednesday and Thursday (1.10pm) except in August.

St Sepulchre-without-Newgate Holborn Viaduct, EC1 ☎020/7248 3826, Ⓦwww.st-sepulchre .org .uk; Chancery Lane or St Paul's tube. A church with a strong association with musicians, it

holds regular chamber or organ concerts on Wednesdays (1pm) and an outstanding week-long music festival in June.
St Stephen Walbrook Walbrook, EC4 ⊕ 020/7626 8242; **Bank tube.** Friday-lunchtime organ recitals at the earlier than normal time of 12.30pm in one of the finest of all Wren's churches.

The Temple Church Fleet Street, EC4 ⊕ 020/7353 0172, ⊛ www.templechurch.com; **Temple tube.** Wednesday-lunchtime organ recitals (1.15pm), except in August and September, often by leading organists.

Opera

London is extremely well served for **opera**, whether it's the star-studded repertoire standards served up by the Royal Opera House, or the more imaginative, contemporary fare of the annual Almeida Opera Festival. Of the two main companies, the **Royal Opera House** is undergoing a new lease of life since the appointment of a new music director. Meanwhile, **English National Opera** has completely renovated its Edwardian theatre, the vast London Coliseum, while continuing to show what can be achieved with largely home-grown talent and lively, radical productions.

Opera companies and venues

Almeida Theatre Almeida Street, N1 ⊕ 020/7359 4404, ⊛ www.almeida.co.uk; **Angel or Highbury & Islington tube.** The Almeida Opera Festival, held in July, is a brief showcase for contemporary music theatre, and a highlight of the musical year in London. It nearly always includes several world premieres, mostly by British or European composers.
Barbican Centre Silk Street, EC2 ⊕ 020/7638 8891, ⊛ www.barbican.org.uk; **Barbican or Moorgate tube.** Concert performances of operas are frequently performed at the Barbican, usually employing top soloists supported by the resident London Symphony Orchestra.
Battersea Arts Centre Lavender Hill, SW11 ⊕ 020/7223 2223, ⊛ www.bac.org.uk; **Clapham Junction train station.** The BAC is an occasional venue for small-scale, innovative productions of music theatre both ancient and modern, famously the ground-breaking *Jerry Springer – the Opera*. There's also a summer festival, Burst.
English National Opera Coliseum, St Martin's Lane, WC2 ⊕ 020/7632 8300, ⊛ www.eno.org; **Leicester Square or Charing Cross tube.** English National Opera differs from its Royal Opera House counterpart in that all its operas are sung in English, productions tend to be more experimental, and the cost is far less. Ticket prices start at as little as £8, rising to just over £80; day seats are also available to personal callers after 10am on the day of

the performance, with balcony seats going for just £5. It's also worth checking for standbys (tickets that are unsold) which go on sale three hours before a performance at £12.50 to students and £18 to senior citizens and the unemployed. Major restoration work has now been completed and, despite suffering the resignation of its music director, the company continues to produce challenging and often outstanding work.
Holland Park Holland Park, Kensington High Street, W8 ⊕ 0845 230 9769, ⊛ www .operahollandpark.com; **High Street Kensington or Holland Park tube.** Opera takes to the great outdoors in green and pleasant Holland Park during the summer months. Standard repertoire is the order of the day, and productions range unpredictably from the inspired to the workaday. There's a canopy to cover you in case of rain.
Royal Albert Hall Kensington Gore, SW7 ⊕ 020/7589 8212, ⊛ www.royalalberthall.com; **South Kensington tube.** Apart from one or two concert performances of operas that occur as part of the BBC Proms (see box on p.510), the RAH's main operatic claim to fame is the vast spectaculars mounted by the impresario Raymond Gubbay at least once a year. *Aida*, *Carmen* and *Madam Butterfly* have all had the Gubbay treatment, which has proved highly popular, although critics tend to be dismissive.
Royal Opera House Bow St, WC2 ⊕ 020/7304 4000, ⊛ www.royaloperahouse.org; **Covent Garden tube.** Since its 1999 refurbishment,

CLASSICAL MUSIC, OPERA AND DANCE | Opera

the ROH has attempted to make itself more accessible – the Floral Hall foyer is open to the public during the day, there are regular free lunchtime recitals, and more modestly priced, and often more innovative productions in the small Linbury Theatre. As well as this, its dynamic music director, Antonio Pappano, seems keen to rid the company of its conservatism, although the repertoire continues to be pretty standard. However, the ROH still has a deserved reputation for snobbery, and is ludicrously overpriced (over £150 for the very best seats). A small number of day seats (for £30 or under) are put on sale from 10am on the day of a performance – these are restricted to one per person, and you need to get there by 8am for popular shows. Four hours before performances, low-price standbys (subject to availability) can be bought for around £15 by students, senior citizens and the unemployed. In summer, some performances are occasionally relayed live to a large screen in Covent Garden Piazza. All operas are performed in the original language but are discreetly subtitled.

Dance

Dance, in all its myriad forms, has a strong following in London, though it must be said that British companies struggle to keep up with the technical excellence of the best international troupes that frequently visit. For classical ballet lovers, the **Royal Ballet** possesses a number of truly outstanding soloists, while those interested in more cutting edge work can chose between the intimacy of **The Place** or the larger **Sadler's Wells**, both venues for the best contemporary work. London also has a good reputation for international dance festivals showcasing the work of a wide range of companies. The biggest of the annual events is the **Dance Umbrella** (☎020/8741 5881, ⓦwww.danceumbrella.co.uk), a six-week season (Sept–Nov) of often ground-breaking new work at various venues across town.

▲ Darcy Bussell statue, Broad Court

Dance companies and venues

Barbican Centre Silk Street, EC2 ☎020/7638 8891, ⓦwww.barbican.org.uk; Barbican or Moorgate tube. As part of its mixed programming the Barbican regularly stages contemporary dance by top international companies. It's also used as a venue for Dance Umbrella events.
Laban Creekside, SE8 ☎020/8691 8600, ⓦwww.laban.org; Deptford train station from Charing Cross. Named after one of the founding figures of European contemporary dance, Laban has a brand new building designed by Herzog and de Meuron (architects of Tate Modern) which includes the 300-seater Bonnie Bird Theatre. The venue showcases many leading names in contemporary dance as well as work by Laban students.
London Coliseum St Martin's Lane, WC2 ☎020/7632 8300, ⓦwww.eno.org; Leicester Square or Charing Cross tube. The Coliseum (home to English National Opera) is used for dance between breaks in the opera season, most regularly by English National Ballet (ENB). This touring company's frequent performances in London include a regular Christmas slot at the Coliseum, and occasional visits to the Royal Festival Hall and the Royal Albert Hall.
The Place 17 Duke's Road, WC1 ☎020/7387 0031, ⓦwww.theplace.org.uk; Euston tube.

The Place is the base of the Richard Alston Dance Company and home to the London Contemporary Dance School. Its small Robin Howard Dance Theatre presents the work of new choreographers and student performers, and hosts some of the finest small-scale contemporary dance from across the globe.

Riverside Studios Crisp Road, W6 ☎020/8237 1111, ⓦwww.riversidestudios.co.uk; Hammersmith tube. This former TV studio has two performance spaces used for small-scale, often innovative, shows that include dance and performance art.

Royal Ballet Royal Opera House, Bow Street, WC2 ☎020/7304 4000, ⓦwww .royaloperahouse.org; Covent Garden tube. The Royal Ballet is one of the most renowned classical companies in the world, whose outstanding principals include Darcey Bussell, Sylvie Guillem and Carlos Acosta. There are two small performing spaces, the Linbury Theatre and the Clore Studio, where more experimental work can be seen. Prices are almost half of those for the opera, and you should be able to get decent seats

for around £25 if you act quickly, though sellouts are frequent (see Royal Opera House, p.513, for details of day tickets and standbys).

Sadler's Wells Theatre Rosebery Avenue, EC1 ☎0870 737 7737, ⓦwww.sadlers-wells.com; Angel tube. Sadler's Wells Theatre in Islington is home to Britain's best contemporary dance companies, including the Rambert, and many of the finest international companies are also regular visitors. The Lillian Baylis Theatre, tucked around the back, puts on smaller-scale shows, while the Peacock Theatre in the West End is where Sadler's Wells stages more populist dance, including flamenco and tango shows.

South Bank Centre South Bank, SE1 ☎020/7960 4242, ⓦwww.rfh.org.uk; Waterloo or Embankment tube. The South Bank Centre's three venues all stage dance performances, often as part of the Dance Umbrella festival in the autumn. It's also the main venue for Asian dance in the capital, while the Royal Festival Hall (currently closed) is occasionally home to English National Ballet.

Theatre, comedy and cinema

L
ondon has enjoyed a reputation for quality **theatre** since the time of Shakespeare and, despite the continuing dominance of blockbuster musicals and revenue-spinning star vehicles, the city still provides a platform for innovation. The **comedy** scene in London is so big that the capital now boasts more comedy venues than any other city in the world, while comedians who have made the transition to television also stage shows in major theatres.

Cinema is rather less healthy, with arthouse cinemas a dying breed, edged out by the multiscreen complexes and first-run cinemas which show mainstream Hollywood fare some months behind America. Nevertheless, there remain a few excellent independent cinemas, the charge led by the National Film Theatre, which is the focus of the huge and richly varied **London International Film Festival** in November.

Current details of **what's on** can be found in a number of publications, the most comprehensive being the weekly *Time Out*. The *Guardian*'s *The Guide* section (free with the paper on Saturdays) and Friday's *Evening Standard* are other good sources of information. Albemarle of London is a useful online theatre guide at Ⓦ www.albemarle-london.com.

Theatre

The **West End** is the heart of London's "Theatreland", with Shaftesbury Avenue its most congested drag, but the word is more of a conceptual pigeon-hole than a geographical term. West End theatres tend to be dominated by tourist-magnet musicals or similarly unchallenging shows (see box on p.518), but there are more intriguing productions on offer, too. The government-subsidized **Royal Shakespeare Company** and **National Theatre** often put on extremely original performances of mainstream masterpieces, while some of the most exciting work is found in what have become known as the **Off West End** theatres, which consistently stage interesting and frequently challenging productions. Further down the financial ladder still are the **Fringe** theatres, more often than not pub venues, where ticket prices are low, and quality variable.

Tickets under £10 are restricted to the Fringe; the box-office average is closer to £15–25, with £30–40 the usual top price. Tickets for the durable musicals

THEATRES, OPERA HOUSES & CINEMAS

Comedy & Cabaret
Amused Moose — aa
Chuckle Club — bb
Comedy Store — cc

Cinemas
Apollo West End — A
Barbican — B
Odeon Covent Garden — C
Curzon Soho — D
Empire Leicester Square — E
ICA — G
IMAX — 50
Odeon Leicester Square & Mezzanine — J

Odeon Marble Arch — N
NFT — 2
Odeon Panton Street — C
Prince Charles — D
Odeon Tottenham Court Rd — A
UGC Haymarket — G
UGC Shaftesbury Avenue — K
Vue West End — F
Odeon Wardour Street — L

Theatres & Opera Houses

Adelphi	38
Albery	31
Aldwych	19
Apollo Shaftesbury	27
Apollo Victoria	52
Arts	22
Barbican	14
Cambridge	39
Coliseum	40
Criterion	3
Dominion	11
Donmar Warehouse	1
Drill Hall	23
Duchess	35
Duke of York's	12
Fortune	37
Garrick	26
Gielgud	42
Her Majesty's	50
ICA	10
London Palladium	24
Lyceum	30
Lyric Shaftesbury	45
Menier Chocolate Factory	16
New Ambassadors	6
New London	43
New Players	54
Old Vic	5
Open Air	15
Palace	9
Peacock	8
Phoenix	32
Piccadilly	48
Playhouse	13
Prince Edward	36
Prince of Wales	25
Queens	51
Royal Court	47
Royal National Theatre	17
Royal Opera House	20
St Martin's	34
Savoy	4
Shaftesbury	44
Shakespeare's Globe	7
Soho	46
Southwark Playhouse	21
Strand	18
Theatre Royal, Drury Lane	41
Theatre Royal, Haymarket	49
Trafalgar Studios (Whitehall)	33
Vaudeville	28
The Venue	53
Victoria Palace	29
Wyndham's	55
Young Vic	55

200 yds

© crown copyright

32

517

THEATRE, COMEDY AND CINEMA | Theatre

Most overseas visitors to the West End theatres come to see one of the city's big musicals, which became so successful for a while that serious theatre was all but squeezed off the stages. On any given night in the West End there are more people watching musicals than all other forms of theatre put together, and the trend shows no sign of abating, despite the fact that only half the shows actually make money. Below is a list of the established songfests at the time of going to print, along with the three plays that have attained comparable landmark status. All of the shows below are listed on ⓦwww.albemarle-london.com.

Billy Elliot the Musical Victoria Palace Theatre, Victoria St, SW1 ☎0870/895 5577, ⓦwww.billyelliotthemusical.com; Victoria tube. Heart-rending story of a young boy from a mining community who wants to become a ballet dancer.

Blood Brothers Phoenix Theatre, 110 Charing Cross Rd, WC2 ☎0870/060 6629, ⓦwww.theambassadors.com; Tottenham Court Rd or Leicester Square tube. Willy Russell's and Bob Thomson's sentimental, decade-old musical about Scouse (Liverpudlian) twins separated at birth.

Chicago Adelphi Theatre, Strand, WC2 ☎0870/403 0303, ⓦwww.chicagothemusical.com; Charing Cross tube. Cynical tale of two murderesses who escape Death Row for fame and stardom thanks to their scheming lawyer.

Les Misérables Queens Theatre, Shaftesbury Ave, W1 ☎020/7434 5040, ⓦwww.lesmis.com; Leicester Square or Tottenham Court Rd tube. Trevor Nunn's sanitized adaptation of Victor Hugo's classic. Alluring peasants, vicious villains and heart-wrenching musical numbers.

Lion King Lyceum Theatre, Wellington St, WC2 ☎0870/243 9000; Covent Garden or Charing Cross tube. A guaranteed winner with the kids, this stage adaptation of the Oscar-winning Disney film is better than you might fear.

Mamma Mia! Prince of Wales Theatre, Coventry St, W1 ☎0870/850 0393, ⓦwww.mamma-mia.com; Leicester Square tube. Very popular musical with a thin plot padded out with Abba's smash hits.

Mary Poppins Prince Edward Theatre, Old Compton St, W1 ☎0870/850 9191, ⓦwww.marypoppinsthemusical.co.uk; Leicester Square tube. Fantastically English musical set in London that's much better than the famous film.

The Mousetrap St Martin's, West St, WC2 ☎0870/162 8787; Leicester Square tube. Run-of-the-mill Agatha Christie murder mystery that's been running for over fifty years – a world record.

The Phantom of the Opera Her Majesty's Theatre, Haymarket, SW1 ☎0870/160 2878, ⓦwww.thephantomoftheopera.com; Piccadilly Circus tube. Extravagant Lloyd Webber production about a physiognomically challenged subterranean who falls for a beautiful young opera singer.

The Producers Theatre Royal, Drury Lane, WC2 ☎0870/890 1109, ⓦwww.theproducerslondon.com; Covent Garden tube. Mel Brooks's irreverent show about a sure-fire musical flop, *Springtime for Hitler,* which becomes a hit.

The Woman in Black Fortune Theatre, Russell St, WC2 ☎0870/060 6626, ⓦwww.thewomaninblack.com; Covent Garden tube. Susan Hill's effective ghost tale is the longest-running play in this theatre's history.

and well-reviewed plays are like gold dust so try and book ahead. The cheapest way to buy your ticket is to go to the theatre box office in person; if you book over the phone, you're likely to be charged a booking fee. Students, senior citizens and the unemployed can get **concessionary rates** on tickets for most shows, and many theatres offer reductions on standby tickets to these groups.

Whatever you do, avoid the touts and the suspicious-looking ticket agencies

THEATRE, COMEDY AND CINEMA | Theatre

that abound in the West End – there's no guarantee that the tickets are genuine. Ticket agencies such as Ticketmaster (℡020/7344 4444, 🌐www.ticketmaster. co.uk) or First Call (℡020/7420 0000, 🌐www.firstcalltickets.com) can get seats for most West End shows, but add up to ten percent on the ticket price.

The Society of London Theatre (🌐www.officiallondontheatre.co.uk) runs the **Half Price Ticket Booth** in Leicester Square, now known as **tkts** (Mon–Sat 10am–7pm, Sun noon–3.30pm; 🌐www.tkts.co.uk), which sells on-the-day tickets for all the West End shows at discounts of up to fifty percent, though they tend to be in the top end of the price range, are limited to four per person, and carry a service charge of £2.50 per ticket. There's even a branch on platform 4/5 at Canary Wharf DLR station (Mon–Sat 11.30am–6pm).

The venues

What follows is a list of West End theatres which offer a changing roster of good plays, along with the most consistent of the Off West End and Fringe venues. This by no means represents the full tally of London's stages, as there are scores of Fringe places that present work intermittently – the weekly listings magazine *Time Out* provides the most comprehensive and detailed up-to-the-minute survey.

Almeida Almeida St, N1 ℡020/7359 4404, 🌐www.almeida.co.uk; Angel or Highbury & Islington tube. Deservedly popular Off West End venue in Islington that continues to premiere excellent new plays and excitingly reworked classics, and has attracted some big Hollywood names.

Arcola 27 Arcola St, E8 ℡020/7503 1646, 🌐www.arcolatheatre.com; Dalston Kingsland train station. Fringe theatre deep in Dalston/Stoke Newington borders, which has put on some really good, challenging shows.

Barbican Centre Silk St, EC2 ℡020/7638 8891, 🌐www.barbican.org.uk; Barbican or Moorgate tube. The Barbican's two venues – the excellently designed Barbican Theatre and the much smaller Pit – put on a wide variety of theatrical spectacles from puppetry and musicals to new drama works, and of course Shakespeare, courtesy of the Royal Shakespeare Company who perform here (and elsewhere in London) on and off from autumn to spring each year.

Battersea Arts Centre 176 Lavender Hill, SW11 ℡020/7223 2223, 🌐www.bac.org.uk; Clapham Junction train station from Victoria or Waterloo. The BAC is a triple-stage building, housed in an old town hall in south London, and has acquired a reputation for excellent

Fringe productions, from straight theatre to comedy and cabaret.

Bush Shepherd's Bush Green, W12 ℡020/7610 4224, 🌐www.bushtheatre.co.uk; Goldhawk Rd or Shepherd's Bush tube. This minuscule above-pub theatre is London's most reliable venue for new writing after the Royal Court, and it has turned out some great stuff.

Donmar Warehouse Thomas Neal's, Earlham St, WC2 ℡0870/060 6624, 🌐www.donmar -warehouse.com; Covent Garden tube. A performance space that's noted for new plays and top-quality reappraisals of the classics, and whose former artistic director, Sam Mendes, managed to entice several Hollywood stars to take to the stage.

Drill Hall 16 Chenies St, WC1 ℡020/7307 5060, 🌐www.drillhall.co.uk; Goodge St tube. This studio-style venue specializes in gay, lesbian, feminist and all-round politically correct new work.

The Gate The Prince Albert, 11 Pembridge Rd, W11 ℡020/7229 0706, 🌐www.gatetheatre.co.uk; Notting Hill Gate tube. A small pub-theatre noted for its excellent revivals of neglected European classics.

Hampstead Theatre Eton Ave, NW3 ℡020/7722 9301, 🌐www.hampsteadtheatre.com; Swiss Cottage tube. A spanking new zinc-and-glass-fronted theatre in Swiss Cottage (not in Hampstead proper) whose productions often move on to the West End. Such is its prestige that the likes of John Malkovich have been seduced into performing here.

ICA Nash House, The Mall, SW1 ℡020/7930 3647, 🌐www.ica.org.uk; Piccadilly Circus or Charing Cross tube. The Institute of Contemporary Arts attracts the most innovative practitioners in all areas of performance. It also attracts a fair quantity of modish junk, but the hits generally outweigh the misses.

King's Head 115 Upper St, N1 ℡020/7226 1916, 🌐www.kingsheadtheatre.org; Angel or Highbury

& Islington tube. The oldest and probably most famous of London's thriving pub-theatres (with a useful late licence). Adventurous performances in a pint-sized room, at lunchtimes and in the evening.

Menier Chocolate Factory 51–53 Southwark St, SE1 ☏020/7907 7060, ⊛www.menierchocolate factory.com; London Bridge tube. Great name, great new fringe venue in an old Victorian factory; consistently good shows and has a great bar and restaurant attached.

National Theatre South Bank Centre, South Bank, SE1 ☏020/7452 3000, ⊛www.nationaltheatre. org.uk; Waterloo tube. The Royal National Theatre, as it's now officially known, consists of three separate theatres: the 1100-seater Olivier, the proscenium-arched Lyttelton and the experimental Cottesloe. Standards set by the late Laurence Olivier, founding artistic director, are maintained by the country's top actors and directors in a programme ranging from Greek tragedies to Broadway musicals. Some productions sell out months in advance, but twenty to thirty of the cheapest tickets go on sale on the morning of each performance – get there by 8am for the popular shows.

New End Theatre 27 New End, NW3 ☏0870/033 2733, ⊛www.newendtheatre.co.uk; Hampstead tube. Cosy neighbourhood venue in literary-minded Hampstead that offers a reliable programme of Fringe-like fare.

Open Air Theatre Regent's Park, Inner Circle, NW1 ☏0870/060 1811, wwww.openairtheatre. org; Baker St tube. If the weather's good, there's nothing quite like a dose of alfresco drama. This beautiful space in Regent's Park hosts a tourist-friendly summer programme of Shakespeare, musicals, plays and concerts.

Orange Tree 1 Clarence St, Richmond, Surrey ☏020/8940 3633, ⊛www.orangetreetheatre .co.uk; Richmond tube. Consistently good low-budget, period dramas for the wealthy denizens of Richmond and Kew.

Royal Court Sloane Square, SW1 ☏020/7565 5000, ⊛www.royalcourttheatre.com; Sloane Square tube. Newly refurbished, the Royal Court is one of the best places in London to catch radical new writing, either in the proscenium arch Theatre Downstairs, or the smaller-scale Theatre Upstairs studio space.

Shakespeare's Globe New Globe Walk, SE1 ☏020/7401 9919, ⊛www.shakespeares-globe .org; London Bridge, Blackfriars or Southwark tube. This thatch-roofed replica Elizabethan theatre uses only natural light and the minimum of scenery, and currently puts on solid, fun Shakespearean shows from mid-May to mid-September, with "groundling" tickets (standing-room only) for around a fiver.

Soho Theatre 21 Dean St, W1 ☏0870/429 6883, ⊛www.sohotheatre.com; Tottenham Court Rd tube. Great Off West End theatre that specializes in new writing from around the globe, as well as putting on regular comedy acts.

Southwark Playhouse 62 Southwark Bridge Rd, SE1 ☏0870/060 1761, ⊛www.southwarkplay house.co.uk; Borough tube. Tiny but versatile Fringe venue on the Bankside backstreets, which regularly produces the odd gem.

Theatre Royal Stratford East Gerry Raffles Square, E15 ☏020/8534 7374, ⊛www.strat-fordeast.com; Stratford tube. Beautiful, small Victorian theatre in the East End, which puts on community-pleasing shows, including consistently excellent Christmas panto.

The drama schools

The London drama schools each mount as many as ten productions per term, giving you a chance to indulge in a bit of talent-spotting for very little outlay – indeed, plays at the Guildhall are free. The following are the main schools:

Central School of Speech and Drama 64 Eton Ave, NW3 ☏020/7722 8183, ⊛www .cssd.ac.uk; Swiss Cottage tube.

Guildhall School of Music and Drama Silk St, Barbican, EC2 ☏020/7628 2571, ⊛www.gsmd.ac.uk; Barbican or Moorgate tube.

London Academy of Music and Dramatic Art Tower House, 226 Cromwell Rd, SW5 ☏020/7373 9883, ⊛www.lamda.org.uk; Gloucester Rd tube.

Royal Academy of Dramatic Art 62–64 Gower St, WC1 ☏020/7636 7076, ⊛www .rada.org; Goodge St tube.

Tricycle Theatre & Cinema 269 Kilburn High Rd, NW6 ☎020/7328 1000, ⓦwww.tricycle.co.uk; Kilburn tube. One of London's most dynamic fringe venues, showcasing a mixed bag of new plays, often aimed at the theatre's multicultural neighbourhood, and often with a sharp political focus.

Young Vic The Cut, SE1 ☎020/7928 6363, ⓦwww.youngvic.org; Waterloo tube. The Young Vic was built in 1969 as a temporary structure with a five-year lifespan. Now, 36 years later, it has finally been rebuilt from scratch and will open in 2006. Big names have appeared in the main stage over the years and its productions are often very good indeed.

Comedy and cabaret

The **comedy scene** continues to thrive in London, with the leading funnypersons catapulted to unlikely stardom on both stage and screen. The Comedy Store is the best known and most central venue on the circuit, but just about every London suburb has a pub stage giving a platform to young hopefuls (full listings appear on ⓦwww.chortle.co.uk and in *Time Out*) or a nearby purpose-built venue. Note that many venues operate only on Friday and Saturday nights, and that August is a lean month, as much of London's talent heads north for the Edinburgh Festival. Tickets at smaller venues can be had for around £5, but in the more established places, you're looking at £10 or more.

Amused Moose Soho 17 Greek St, W1 ☎020/8341 1341, ⓦwww.amusedmoose.co.uk; Tottenham Court Rd tube. Soho branch of the successful Chalk Farm pub comedy club. Top stand-up, and comedy courses too. Mon & Fri–Sun.

Backyard Comedy Club 231 Cambridge Heath Rd, E2 ☎020/7739 3122, ⓦwww.leehurst .com; Bethnal Green tube. Purpose-built club in Bethnal Green established by comedian Lee Hurst, who has successfully managed to attract a consistently strong line-up. Thurs–Sat.

Banana Cabaret The Bedford, 77 Bedford Hill, SW12 ☎020/8673 8904, ⓦwww.bananacabaret .co.uk; Balham tube. This double-stage pub is one of London's most welcoming comedy venues – well worth the trip out from the centre of town. Fri & Sat from 9pm, followed by a DJ.

Bound & Gagged The Fox, 413 Green Lanes, N13 ☎020/8450 4100, ⓦwww.boundandgagged comedy.com; Palmers Green train station from Moorgate. Swish out-of-town venue with consistently good Friday night line-ups.

Canal Café Theatre The Bridge House, Delamere Terrace, W2 ☎020/7289 6054, ⓦwww .canalcafetheatre.com; Warwick Ave tube. Perched on the water's edge in Little Venice, this venue is good for improvisation acts and is home to the Newsrevue team of topical gagsters; there's usually something going on from Thursday to Sunday.

Chuckle Club Three Tuns Bar, London School of Economics, Houghton St, WC2 ☎020/7476 1672, ⓦwww.chuckleclub.com; Holborn tube.

Student comedy club of some standing, with subsidized bar and a great vibe. Sat from 7.45pm.

Comedy Café 66 Rivington St, EC2 ☎020/7739 5706, ⓦwww.comedycafe.co.uk; Old St tube. Long-established, purpose-built club in Shoreditch/Hoxton, often with impressive line-ups, and free admission for the new-acts slot on Wednesday nights. Wed–Sat.

Comedy Store Haymarket House, 1a Oxendon St, SW1 ☎020/7344 0234, ⓦwww.thecomedystore .co.uk; Piccadilly Circus tube. Widely regarded as the birthplace of alternative comedy, though no longer in its original venue, the Comedy Store has catapulted many a stand-up onto primetime TV. Improvisation by in-house comics on Wednesdays and Sundays, in addition to a stand-up bill; Friday and Saturday are the busiest nights, with two shows, at 8pm and midnight – book ahead.

Ha Bloody Ha Ealing Studios, Ealing Green, St Mary's Rd, W5 ☎020/8566 4067, ⓦwww .headlinerscomedy.biz; Ealing Broadway tube. The famous Ealing Studios are now a comedy club with very strong line-ups and a branch called Headliners over in Chiswick.

Jongleurs Camden Lock, Dingwalls Building, 36 Camden Lock Place, Chalk Farm Rd, NW1 box office ☎020/7564 2500, information ☎0870/787 0707, ⓦwww.jongleurs.com for branches; Camden tube. Jongleurs is the chain store of comedy, doling out pretty high-quality stand-up and post-revelry disco dancing on Fridays. Book well in advance.

Cinema

There are an awful lot of **cinemas** in the West End, but very few places committed to independent films, and even fewer repertory cinemas programming serious films from the back catalogue. November's **London Film Festival** (ⓦ www.lff.org.uk), which occupies half a dozen West End cinemas, is now a huge event, and so popular that many of the films sell out soon after publication of the festival's programme.

Tickets at the major screens in the West End cost £8 and upwards, although afternoon shows are usually discounted. The suburban screens run by the big companies (see *Time Out* for full listings) tend to be a couple of pounds cheaper, as do independent cinemas. Students, senior citizens and the unemployed can get concessionary rates for some shows at virtually all cinemas, usually all day Monday or at other off-peak times on weekdays.

Big screens

Empire Leicester Square, WC2 ☎0871/224 4007, ⓦ www.uci.co.uk; Leicester Square tube. The huge, expensive, hi-tech main auditorium here is London's second largest, and the place where blockbusters tend to premiere, and royalty occasionally turns up.

Odeon Leicester Square Leicester Square, WC2 ☎0871/224 4007, ⓦ www.odeon.co.uk; Leicester Square tube. London's largest cinema, and thus a favourite for celeb-packed premieres. There's just one screen here, so don't mistakenly enter the adjacent Odeon Mezzanine, which crushes five into a far smaller space, or Odeon West End, which is on the south side of the square.

Odeon Marble Arch 10 Edgware Rd, W2 ☎0871/224 4007, ⓦ www.odeon.co.uk; Marble Arch tube. Blockbuster specialist, on account of possessing the city's biggest (normal format) screen, with a sound system to match.

Repertory cinemas

Barbican Silk St, EC2 ☎020/7382 7000, ⓦ www .barbican.org.uk; Barbican or Moorgate tube. Comfy seats, tiny screens and a regular rota of obscure classics, plus the odd mini-festival.

Ciné Lumière 17 Queensberry Place, SW7 ☎020/7073 1350, ⓦ www.institut-francais.org .uk; South Kensington tube. Predominantly, but by no means exclusively, French films, both old and new (sometimes with subtitles), put on by the Institut Français.

Electric 191 Portobello Rd, W11; ☎020/7908 9696, ⓦ www.the-electric.co.uk; Notting Hill Gate or Ladbroke Grove tube. One of the oldest cinemas in the country (opened 1910), the Electric has been filled out with luxury leath-

▲ The Electric Cinema

er armchairs, footstools and sofas. Most seats cost £12.50.

Everyman Hollybush Vale, NW3 ☎020/7431 1777, ⓦ www.everymancinema.com; Hampstead tube. The city's oldest rep cinema, and still one of its best, with strong programmes of classics, cultish crowd-magnets and directors' seasons. Now has two screens and some very plush seating.

Goethe Institut 50 Princes Gate, Exhibition Rd, SW7 ☎020/7596 4000, ⓦ www.goethe.de/london;

South Kensington tube. Sporadic showings of German cinematic masterpieces.

ICA Cinema Nash House, The Mall, SW1 ☎ 020/7930 3647, 🌐 www.ica.org.uk; Piccadilly Circus or Charing Cross tube. Vintage and underground movies shown on one of two tiny screens in the avant-garde HQ of the Institute of Contemporary Arts.

BFI London Imax Centre South Bank, SE1 ☎ 020/7902 1234, 🌐 www.bfi.org.uk/showing /imax; Waterloo tube. The British Film Institute's remarkable glazed drum houses Europe's largest screen. It's stunning, state-of-the-art stuff alright, showing 2D and 3D films on a massive screen, but, like all IMAX cinemas, it suffers from the paucity of good material that's been shot in the format.

National Film Theatre South Bank, SE1 ☎ 020/7928 3232, 🌐 www.bfi.org.uk /showing/nft; Waterloo tube. Known for its attentive audiences and an exhaustive, eclectic programme that includes directors' seasons and thematic series. Around six

films daily are shown in the vast NFT1 and the smaller NFT2 and 3.

Prince Charles 2–7 Leicester Place, WC2 ☎ 020/7494 3654, 🌐 www.princecharlescinema .com; Leicester Square or Piccadilly Circus tube. The bargain basement of London's cinemas (entry for most shows is just £4), with a programme of new movies, classics and cult favourites – the Sing-Along-A-Sound-of-Music (as well as other participatory romps) is a regular.

Riverside Studios Crisp Rd, W6 ☎ 020/8237 1111, 🌐 www.riversidestudios.co.uk; Hammersmith tube. This converted film studio in West London is worth checking out for its mini-festivals and innovative programming.

Watermans 40 High St, Brentford, Middlesex ☎ 020/8232 1010, 🌐 www.watermans.org.uk; Kew Bridge train station from Waterloo or bus #237 or #267 from Gunnersbury tube. Inventive programming at this theatre's rep cinema, but it's a long way from the centre of town.

33

Galleries

The vast collections of the **National Gallery**, the two **Tates** and the **Victoria and Albert Museum**, along with the select holdings of such institutions as the Courtauld Institute and the Wallace Collection, make London one of the world's great repositories of Western art. However, the city is also a dynamic creative centre, boasting undergraduates of the city's many art colleges such as Tracey Emin and Gary Hume through the now established "Young British Artists" (YBAs), to the grandfathers of modern British art, Frank Auerbach, Anthony Caro and Lucien Freud.

London has hundreds of small **commercial galleries** and **artist-run spaces** scattered across the city, pockets of concentrated activity, making it easy to visit several in an afternoon. Mayfair's Cork Street and the surrounding area continues to be the upmarket home of historical and traditional fine arts and antiquities dealers, while the recent growth of spaces exhibiting and trading in contemporary art has dramatically expanded the art map of London, pushing it north and eastwards, to Shoreditch, Hoxton, Bethnal Green and beyond.

An increasing number of competitions offer the chance to see what's (and who's) hot. These include the **Turner Prize** at Tate Britain from October to January for artists under 40 years old working in the UK; **Becks Futures Award** which commences in March until May at the ICA and showcases up and coming artists; and the international **Photography Prize** held at the Photographers' Gallery between January and March. Other annual fixtures include the **Royal Academy's Summer Exhibition**, which takes place from June to August and gives amateur artists a chance to sell the fruits of their labour, and the recently launched **Frieze Art Fair** held in October, when the cream of the international art market descends on Regent's Park to buy, sell, network and party. More exciting than these, however, are the art school **degree shows**, usually in May and June, when the current crop of students put its work on display. The Royal College, Royal Academy, Slade, St Martin's and Goldsmiths' all offer opportunities to talent spot future stars and collect while their prices are still low. Another option for buying original art is at the **Affordable Art Fair**, held twice yearly in Battersea Park, where all prices are under £3,000. For a rundown of the latest exhibitions, pick up a copy of the free **listings** handout *New Exhibitions of Contemporary Art* (ⓦ www.newexhibitions.com) from galleries or the weekly magazine *Time Out*.

Major galleries and public spaces

Expect to pay around £8–10 for entry to one of the exhibitions at the Barbican or Hayward. Similar prices are charged for special shows at the National Gallery, the Tates, the V&A and the Royal Academy. Students, senior citizens and the unemployed are eligible for reductions. Hours vary and many places hold late nights with special events, talks and debates so it's always best to check the website or ring the gallery before setting off.

Barbican Art Gallery Level 1 & 3, Barbican Centre, Silk St, EC2 ☎020/7638 8891, ⓦwww .barbican.org.uk/gallery; Barbican or Moorgate tube. The newly refurbished Barbican Gallery shows major exhibitions of modern and historical art, photography and design. The Curve, the Barbican's free exhibition space, is dedicated to commissioned works by contemporary artists. See p.199.

British Museum Great Russell St, WC1 ☎020/7323 8000, ⓦwww.british-museum .ac.uk; Russell Square or Tottenham Court Rd tube. As well as its world-class collection of antiquities, the BM has outstanding drawings and prints as well as interesting one-off exhibitions. See p.128.

Camden Arts Centre Corner of Arkwright and Finchley roads, NW3 ☎020/7472 5500, ⓦwww.camdenartscentre.org; Finchley Rd tube. Recently renovated by Tony Fretton Architects, Camden Arts Centre is particularly known for its artists-in-residence programmes. Exhibitions by influential and acclaimed artists are shown alongside less established artists. The garden provides a great place for al fresco dining or lazing on a sunny afternoon.

Hayward Gallery South Bank Centre, Belvedere Rd, SE1 ☎020/7960 5226, wwww.hayward .org.uk; Waterloo tube. Part of the huge concrete 1960s South Bank arts complex, the Hayward shows broad ranging thematic exhibitions, and solo shows of major figures such as Douglas Gordon, Paul Klee and Bruce Nauman. It is one of London's most prestigious venues for major touring exhibitions.

ICA Gallery The Mall, SW1 ☎020/7930 3647, ⓦwww.ica.org.uk; Piccadilly Circus or Charing Cross tube. The Institute of Contemporary Arts is housed in an elegant Regency building opposite St James' Park. The multi-purpose venue also benefits from an in-house cinema and trendy café/bar. A day's membership costs £1.50 (Mon–Fri) or £2.50 (Sat & Sun).

Royal Academy Burlington House, Piccadilly, W1 ☎020/7300 8000, ⓦwww.royalacademy.org.uk; Green Park or Piccadilly Circus tube. Alongside extensive non-Western exhibitions such as the Aztecs and Turks, the Royal Academy is well known for its blockbuster one-off art showcases – such as its highly acclaimed Monet show. For the most popular shows, you're advised to pre-book a ticket. See p.98.

Serpentine Gallery Kensington Gardens, Hyde Park, W2 ☎020/7298 1501, ⓦwww .serpentinegallery.org; Lancaster Gate or South Kensington tube. Free exhibitions of dynamic work by new and established artists, as well as a high profile architecture commission each summer which doubles as a café and space for film screenings, talks and music events. See p.292.

South London Gallery 65 Peckham Rd, SE5 ☎020/7703 6120, ⓦwww.southlondongallery .org; bus #36 from Oval tube. Purpose-built gallery, established in Camberwell back in 1891 on socialist principles, the South London Gallery is devoted to contemporary art, with an outstanding A-Z of exhibited artists. Always worth seeing what's on.

Whitechapel Art Gallery 80–82 Whitechapel High St, E1 ☎020/7522 7888, ⓦwww. whitechapel.org; Aldgate East tube. Dubbed by the press as "the Gallery that taught Britain to love Modern Art", the Whitechapel has a critically acclaimed national and international programme of exhibitions. Its biennial summer survey, East End Academy, showcases the work of artists living in the area. Excellent café/bar and late night events including films, music and poetry, as well as high profile talks and lectures. See p.240.

Permanent collections

Unlike most other countries, the national collections of Great Britain, many of which are in London, are free to visit. Some private collections also offer free entry.

Courtauld Institute Somerset House, Strand, WC2 ☎020/7845 4600, ⓦwww .somerset-house.org.uk; Covent Garden or Temple (Mon–Sat only) tube. Excellent collection of Impressionists and Post-Impressionists. See p.169.

Dalí Universe Riverside Building, County Hall, SE1 ☎0870 744 7485, ⓦwww.daliuniverse .com; Westminster tube. Permanent collection of works by Dalí, mostly little-known bronzes and illustrated books. See p.263.

Dulwich Picture Gallery College Rd, SE21 ☎020/8693 5254, ⓦwww.dulwichpicture gallery.org.uk; West Dulwich train station from Victoria. London's oldest public art gallery houses a small but high-quality selection, with notable work from Poussin and Gainsborough to Rembrandt and critically acclaimed loan exhibitions. See p.376.

Estorick Collection 39a Canonbury Square, N1 ☎020/7704 9522, ⓦwww.estorickcollection .com; Highbury & Islington tube. Georgian mansion with a small but interesting collection of twentieth-century Italian art, including Modigliani, di Chirico and the Futurists. See p.350.

Geffrye Museum Kingsland Road, E2, ☎020/7739 9893, ⓦwww.geffrye-museum.org .uk; Old St tube. Furniture, textiles, paintings and decorative arts which represent the quintessential style of English middle-class, displayed in a series of period rooms from 1600 to the present day. See p.231.

Guildhall Art Gallery Guildhall Yard, EC2 ☎020/7332 3700, ⓦwww.cityoflondon.gov.uk; Bank or St Paul's tube. Gallery housing the Corporation of London's collection, which contains one or two exceptional Pre-Raphaelite works by the likes of Rossetti and Holman Hunt. See p.201.

Leighton House 12 Holland Park Rd, W14 ☎020/7602 3316, ⓦwww.rbkc.gov.uk; High St Kensington tube. The house itself is a work of art, and also contains several works by Frederic Lord Leighton and other Pre-Raphaelites. Free entry. See p.328.

National Gallery Trafalgar Square, WC2 ☎020/7747 2885, ⓦwww.nationalgallery.org .uk; Charing Cross or Leicester Square tube.

The country's premier collection; it's difficult to think of a major artist born between 1300 and 1850 who isn't on show here. See p.46.

National Portrait Gallery 2 St Martin's Place, WC2 ☎020 7312 2463, ⓦwww.npg.org.uk; Leicester Square or Charing Cross tube. The collection ranges from paintings of historical figures to photographic portraits of contemporary celebrities, and is supplemented with excellent thematic exhibitions. See p.55.

Queen's Gallery Buckingham Palace Rd, SW1 ☎020/7321 2233, ⓦwww.royal.gov.uk; St James's Park or Victoria tube. Changing exhibitions from the wide-ranging collection of art and treasures held in trust by the Queen for the nation. See p.88.

Saatchi Gallery County Hall, SE1 ☎020/7823 2363, ⓦwww.saatchi-gallery.co.uk; Westminster or Waterloo tube. Charles Saatchi is a major private collector of international contemporary art and his space at County Hall exhibits a selection of his current favourites. See p.264.

Sir John Soane's Museum 12–14 Lincoln's Inn Fields WC2A ☎020/7405 2107, ⓦwww.soane .org; Holborn tube. This eighteenth-century collector rebuilt two neighbouring houses for his ever-expanding collection of art and antiquities. The museum is crammed with gems, displayed in an eccentric and distinctive manner. See p.177.

Tate Britain Millbank, SW1 ☎020/7887 8008, ⓦwww.tate.org.uk; Pimlico tube. The original Tate is now devoted to British art from the sixteenth century onwards. Several galleries display a selection from Turner's immense bequest to the nation. Free entry. See p.77.

Tate Modern Bankside, SE1 ☎020/7887 8008, ⓦwww.tate.org.uk; Southwark tube. Housed in a spectacularly converted power station on the South Bank, the new Tate displays the nation's finest international modern art collection. Free entry. See p.270.

Victoria and Albert Museum Cromwell Rd, SW7 ☎020/7942 2000, ⓦwww.vam.ac.uk; South Kensington tube. The city's principal applied arts museum boasts a scattering of European painting and sculpture, a fine collection of English statuary and two remarkable rooms of casts. See p.302.

Wallace Collection Hertford House, Manchester Square, W1 ⓦ020/7563 9500, ⓦwww .wallacecollection.org; Bond St tube. A

country mansion just off Oxford St, with a small, eclectic collection including fine paintings by Rembrandt, Velázquez, Hals, Gainsborough and Delacroix. Free entry. See p.109.

Commercial galleries

Though they might seem intimidating, they welcome casual visitors and all are free. For opening times, check the website ⓦwww.newexhibitions.com, which lists over two hundred galleries in London alone, or *Time Out* weekly magazine. Many galleries are closed in August.

Central

Frith Street 59–60 Frith St, W1 ☎020/7494 1550, ⓦwww.frithstreetgallery.com; Tottenham Court Rd tube. A particularly strong list of women practitioners are exhibited in the domestic-scale rooms of this fine, if creaky, old Soho building.

Gagosian, 6–24 Brittannia St, WC1X ☎020 7841 9960, ⓦwww.gagosian.com; Kings Cross tube. The Gagosian empire recently opened a new space in a vast warehouse near Kings Cross, and produces museum-quality exhibitions with a portfolio of artists to match.

Haunch of Venison 6 Haunch of Venison Yard, W1 ☎020/7495 5050, ⓦwww.haunchofvenison .com; Bond St tube. In the corner of this wonderfully named yard tucked behind Bond St are three floors of galleries in an eighteenth-century town-house once occupied by Admiral Lord Nelson. Contemporary British talent such as Keith Tyson and Ian Monroe nuzzle between its line up of international stars including Dan Flavin, Robert Ryman and Bill Viola.

Hauser and Wirth 196A Piccadilly, W1 ☎020/7287 2300, ⓦwww.hauserwirth.com; Piccadilly Circus tube. Housed in a magnificent 1920s Edwin Lutyens-designed former bank, and maintaining some original spaces such as the vault, the London branch of the Swiss gallery displays both major figures such as Eva Hesse, Louise Bourgeois and Paul McCarthy, and relative newcomers such as Anri Sala, Martin Creed and Pipilotti Rist, to name but a few.

Lisson Gallery 29 & 52–54 Bell St, NW1 ☎020/7724 2739, ⓦwww.lisson.co.uk; Edgware Rd tube. Now a veteran gallery of the London scene, exhibiting in two spaces, and whose artists – among them Carl

Andre, Anish Kapoor and Rodney Graham – are hugely respected on the international circuit.

Sadie Coles HQ 35 Heddon St, W1 ☎020/7434 2227, ⓦwww.sadiecoles.com; Piccadilly Circus or Oxford Circus tube. Tucked upstairs in an alley off Regent St, Sadie Coles has repeatedly revealed an expert eye, exhibiting some of the most interesting contemporary artists including Sarah Lucas, Jim Lambie and Elizabeth Peyton.

Sprüth Magers Lee 12 Berkeley St, W1 ☎020/7491 0100, ⓦwww.spruethmagerslee .com; Green Park tube. Two successful continental dealers, Monika Sprüth and Philomene Magers, from Munich and Cologne respectively, joined forces with a local lad Simon Lee; the result is this slick gallery in Mayfair. Their impressive line up of international artists includes Jenny Holtzer, Barbara Kruger and Cindy Sherman.

East

The Approach 1st floor, 47 Approach Rd, E2 ☎020/8983 3878, ⓦwww.theapproach.co.uk; Bethnal Green tube. With a reputation for launching the careers of many young and emerging artists, this single storey space is situated above a welcoming Victorian pub frequented by artists.

Chisenhale Gallery 64 Chisenhale Rd, E3 ☎020/8981 4518, ⓦwww.chisenhale.org.uk; Mile End tube. Non-profit exhibition space in a converted East End factory, dedicated to one-person shows by up-and-coming contemporary artists.

Matt's Gallery 42–44 Copperfield Rd, E3 ☎020/8983 1771, ⓦwww.mattsgallery.org; Mile End tube. Long-running and committed industrial style gallery supporting innovative

East End art projects.
Maureen Paley 21 Herald St, E2 ☎ 020/7729 4112, ⊛ www.interimart.net; Bethnal Green tube. One of the first galleries to set up in east London, Maureen Paley has an impressive track record of showing intelligent contemporary artists such as Paul Noble, Wolfgang Tillmans and Gillian Wearing.
Victoria Miro 16 Wharf Rd, N1 ☎ 020/7336 8109, ⊛ www.victoria-miro.com; Angel or Old St tube. This large former factory is one of the most impressive galleries in London. Victoria Miro has helped promote the likes of Doug Aiken, William Egglestone and Chris Ofili.
White Cube 48 Hoxton Square, N1 ☎ 020/7930 5373, ⊛ www.whitecube.com; Old St tube. Major art dealer Jay Jopling has advanced the careers of many of the most collectable YBAs. His popular gallery produces high-quality solo and group exhibitions.

South

FA Projects 1–2 Bear Gardens, SE1 ☎ 020/7928 3228, ⊛ www.faprojects.com; Southwark tube. Neighbour to Tate Modern, this gallery operates a flexible system of collaboration with artists, ranging from one-off projects to exclusive representation, which results in a varied programme of exhibitions.
Gasworks 115 Vauxhall St, The Oval, SE11 ☎ 020/7582 6848, ⊛ www.gasworks.org.uk; Oval or Vauxhall tube. Seminal non-profit gallery and artists' studio complex. Exhibitions profile emerging or mid-career international or UK artists who have had limited previous exposure in London.

Photography

National Portrait Gallery 2 St Martin's Place, WC2 ☎ 020/7306 2463, ⊛ www.npg.org.uk; Leicester Square or Charing Cross tube. The NPG has lots of exceptional photos in its collection, along with temporary photographic exhibitions and an annual photographic portrait award. See p.55.
Photofusion 17a Electric Lane, SW9 ☎ 020/7738 5774, ⊛ www.photofusion.org; Brixton tube. Community-based photo co-op situated in the heart of Brixton that concentrates on social documentary.
Photographers' Gallery 5 & 8 Great Newport St, WC2 ☎ 020/7831 1772, ⊛ www.photonet.org.uk; Leicester Square tube. London's premier photography gallery shows work by new and established British and international photographers, as well as having a print sale gallery. Excellent programme of talks and events, plus a fabulous café. See p.120.
Victoria and Albert Museum Cromwell Rd, SW7 ☎ 020/7942 2000, ⊛ www.vam.ac.uk; South Kensington tube. The V&A now has a permanent gallery devoted to photography showing a small selection from their vast collection. See p.302.

▲ Photographers' Gallery

Architecture and design

The Architecture Gallery, V&A Cromwell Road, SW7 ☎020/7942 2000, @www.vam.ac.uk; **South Kensington tube.** The V&A and RIBA have recently joined forces to show their extraordinary collection of architectural drawings, models and manuscripts.

Crafts Council 44a Pentonville Road, N1 ☎020/7278 7700, @www.craftscouncil .uk; **Angel tube.** Pioneers in promoting quality in craftsmanship, the Crafts Council is Britain's largest crafts gallery and resource for craftspeople. Chelsea Crafts Fair, held in Chelsea Town Hall each autumn, is a fantastic showcase of the finest contemporary international pieces.

Design Museum Butlers Wharf, Shad Thames, SE1 ☎0870 833 9955, @www.designmuseum .org; **London Bridge or Tower Hill tube.** Reborn from an old brick warehouse on Shad Thames, the Design Museum shows several exhibitions concurrently, enabling you to contemplate the best in design, fashion and architecture. The shop sells an eclectic range of well-designed gifts.

Royal Institute of British Architects (RIBA) 66 Portland Place, W1 ☎020/7580 5533, @www .architecture.com; **Oxford Circus or Regent's Park tube.** Regular architectural exhibitions by the leading lights, housed in a beautiful 1930s building, with an excellent café. See p.109.

34

Shops and markets

W hether you've got time to kill or money to burn, London is one big **shopper's playground**. Although chains and superstores predominate along the high streets, you're never too far from the kind of oddball, one-off establishment that makes shopping an adventure rather than a routine. As befits a city of villages, London's **shopping districts** all have their own particular style and flavour, with some known for their specialities and others simply for their location. From the *folie de grandeur* that is Harrods to the frenetic street markets of the East End, there's probably nothing you can't find in some corner of the capital. A full flavour and history of the main shopping districts can be found in earlier chapters, but the brief taster below should help you plan your bag-carrying expeditions. In the sections that follow, we've listed shops according to what they sell, rather than by area.

For shops catering to the gay and lesbian population see p.502.

Where to shop

In the centre of town, **Oxford Street** is the city's hectic chain-store mecca, which, together with **Regent Street**, offers pretty much every mainstream clothing label you could wish for. Just off Oxford Street you can find expensive designer outlets in **St Christopher's Place** and **South Molton Street**, and even pricier designers and jewellers on the very chic **Bond Street**.

Tottenham Court Road is the place to go for stereos, computers, electrical goods and, in its northern section, furniture and design shops, while New Oxford Street has a range of shops selling new and used camera equipment. **Charing Cross Road** is the centre of London's book trade, both new and secondhand. At its north end, and particularly on **Denmark Street** (once the heart of Britain's music industry), you can find music shops selling everything from instruments to sound equipment and sheet music. On the other side of **Charing Cross Road**, and stretching down to Piccadilly, **Soho** offers an offbeat mix of sex boutiques, specialist record shops and fabric stores, while the streets surrounding **Covent Garden** yield art and design shops, mainstream fashion chains, designer wear, camping gear; Neal Street is the place to go to indulge a shoe-shopping habit.

Just off Piccadilly, **St James's** is the natural habitat of the quintessential English gentleman, with **Jermyn Street** in particular harbouring shops dedicated to his grooming. **Knightsbridge**, further west, is home to Harrods, and the big-name fashion stores of **Sloane Street** and **Brompton Road**. A stroll along the South

Bank, east of the National Theatre, will bring you to the craft market of **Gabriel's Wharf** and the appealing design shops of the **OXO Tower**. Less well known, and just a stone's throw from the ugly bustle of Waterloo, **Lower Marsh** harbours a fantastic variety of one-off shops, studios and cafés on either side of the daily local street market, with retro clothes, collectors' records, organic food and designer jewellery rubbing shoulders happily with fruit and veg stalls and greasy-spoon cafés.

Out of the centre, there are a few idiosyncratic shopping streets and areas which are well worth a detour. **Hampstead**, in a luxurious and leafy world of its own to the north of the centre, is a great place to spend an afternoon browsing – just about every upmarket clothing chain has an outlet here. Amongst the fashion stores are deliciously posh delicatessens and patisseries, antiquarian booksellers and shops stocking tasteful accessories, interior fripperies and the like. **Marylebone High Street** is a similar story in the middle of town – a pretty village oasis where you can get all your labels, treats and gifts away from the bustle and in one gentle amble. **Greenwich**, south of the river, has an eclectic range of shops and markets, while **Richmond**, out to the west, has the mainstream staples mixed with little boutiques in a pleasant riverside setting.

When to shop

Opening hours for central London shops are generally Monday to Saturday 9.30am to 6pm, although some stores stay open later, especially on Thursdays and in the weeks leading up to Christmas. Many shops now also open on Sundays, although opening hours tend to be shorter, from around noon to 5pm. If in doubt, it's wise to phone ahead to check.

The cheapest time to shop in London is during one of the two big annual **sale seasons**, centred on January and July, when prices are routinely slashed by anything between twenty and seventy percent. In addition, some shops offer one-off discount events throughout the year: the best place to find details of these is in *Time Out* magazine's "Sell Out" section.

How to pay

Credit cards are almost universally accepted by shops, but travellers' cheques, whether in sterling or other currency, are rarely accepted; change them into cash before hitting the shops. Some stores, notably Marks & Spencer, will take payment in euros, although this is still quite rare. Market stalls tend to take cash only, or personal cheques in sterling (supported by a guarantee card) for more expensive items. Always keep receipts: whatever the shop may tell you, the law

Department stores

Although all of London's **department stores** offer a huge range of high-quality goods under one roof, most specialize in fashion and food. Many of them are worth visiting just to admire the scale, architecture and interior design, and the majority have cafés or restaurants on one floor or another.

Debenhams 334–348 Oxford St, W1 ☎020/7580 3000, ⓦwww.debenhams.com; Oxford Circus or Bond St tube. To shake off its dowdy image, Debenhams has gone a little upmarket and pulled in the help of contemporary fashion and interior designers for its latest collections.

Fortnum & Mason 181 Piccadilly, W1 ☎020/7734 8040, ⓦwww.fortnumandmason .com; Green Park or Piccadilly Circus tube. A beautiful and eccentric store with heavenly murals, cherubs, chandeliers and fountains as a backdrop to its perfectly English offerings. Justly famous for its fabulous, pricey food, it also specializes in the best and most upmarket designer clothes, furniture and stationery.

Harrods 87–135 Brompton Rd, Knightsbridge, SW1 ☎020/7730 1234, ⓦwww .harrods.com; Knightsbridge tube. Put an afternoon aside to visit this enduring landmark of quirks and pretensions – but don't wear shorts, a sleeveless T-shirt or a backpack, or you may fall foul of the draconian dress code. Harrods has everything, but is most notable for its fantastic Art Nouveau tiled food hall, the huge toy department and its range of designer labels.

Harvey Nichols 109–125 Knightsbridge, SW1 ☎020/7235 5000, ⓦwww .harveynichols.com; Knightsbridge tube. Absolutely fabulous, darling, with all the latest designer collections on the fashionable first floor, where even the shop assistants look like models. The gorgeous cosmetics department is frequented by the famous and aspiring, while the fifth-floor food hall offers frivolous goodies at high prices.

House of Fraser 318 Oxford St, W1 ☎0870/160 7258, ⓦwww.houseoffraser.co.uk; Oxford Circus tube. Upmarket store stocking House of Fraser's own-brand home and clothing range, Linea, as well as big-name designer collections. Hip lower-ground-floor department, Therapy, brings in a younger, funkier clientele as does the sleek ground-floor cosmetics department.

John Lewis 278–306 Oxford St, W1 ☎020/7629 7711, ⓦwww.johnlewis.co.uk; Oxford Circus tube. Famous for being "never knowingly undersold", this reliable institution can't be beaten for basics. Every kind of button, stocking, pen and rug can be found here, along with reasonably priced and well-made clothes, furniture and household goods. The staff are knowledgeable and friendly, too.

Liberty 210–220 Regent St, W1 ☎020/7734 1234, ⓦwww.liberty-of-london.com; Oxford Circus tube. A fabulous emporium of luxury, this exquisite store, with its mock-Tudor exterior, is most famous for its fabrics, design and accessories, but is also building an excellent reputation for both mainstream and high fashion. The perfume, cosmetics and household departments are recommended, too.

Marks & Spencer 458 Oxford St, W1 ☎020/7935 7954, ⓦwww.marksandspencer .co.uk; Marble Arch tube. London's largest branch of this everyday British institution offers a huge range of own-brand clothes, food, homeware and furnishings. The underwear is essential, the ready-meals good value, and the clothes well made and reliable.

Selfridge's 400 Oxford St, W1 ☎08708 377 377, ⓦwww.selfridges.com; Bond St tube. This huge, airy mecca of clothes, food and furnishings was London's first great department store and remains its best. The vast mens- and womenswear departments offer mainstream designers and casual lines alongside hipper, younger names and labels. The food hall is impressive, too.

allows a full refund or replacement on purchases which turn out to be faulty. There's no such legal protection if you just decide you don't like something, but most retailers will offer a credit note.

Finally, non-UK visitors can sometimes claim back the value-added tax (VAT) that applies to most goods sold in British shops, although you will need to spend well over £100 for this to be worthwhile. On request, participating stores will issue you with a form that you should hand in to Customs on your way out of the country. There's a six-week wait for reimbursement.

Clothes and shoes

The listings below concentrate on the home-grown rather than the ubiquitous international names, but if it's **designer wear** you're after, bear in mind that nearly all the department stores listed in the box opposite stock lines from both major and up-and-coming names. For designer-style fashion at lower prices, try the more upmarket high street **chain stores** such as Jigsaw and Whistles, while Mango, H&M and Top Shop are a good bet for even cheaper versions of the same. For street, club, secondhand and vintage gear, London's **markets** (see p.547) also have plenty to offer.

Designer

Browns 23–27 South Molton St, W1 ℡020/7514 0000, ⊛www.brownsfashion.com; Bond St tube. London's biggest range of designer wear, with big international names under the same roof as the hip young things, and catering equally well for women and men. Across the way, Browns Labels for Less (50 South Molton St, W1 ℡020/7514 0052) could save you precious pennies.

Burberry 21–23 New Bond St, W1 ℡020/7839 5222, ⊛www.burberry.com; Bond St or Oxford Circus tube. The quintessential British outdoors label successfully relaunched itself as a fashion essential a few years back, with its classic trenchcoat now available in silk – rather less waterproof, but obviously a must-have. Get the traditional stock at a huge discount from Burberry's Factory Shop (29–53 Chatham Place, E9 ℡020/8985 3344; Hackney Central train station from Liverpool St).

Ghost 36 Ledbury Rd, W11, and other branches ℡020/7229 1057, ⊛www.ghost.co.uk; Notting Hill Gate tube. Romantic, floaty and hugely popular modern Victoriana in pastel shades. If you ever regretted chucking out your mum's dirndl skirt, this is where to replace it.

Joseph 23 Old Bond St, W1, and many other branches ℡020/7629 3713, ⊛www.joseph. co.uk; Bond St tube. Classic cuts in imaginative styles, and the only place to go for

perfect trousers for both men and women. The Joseph Sale Shop (53 King's Rd, SW3 ℡020/7730 7562; Sloane Square tube) offers good discounts on womenswear.

🏃 **Koh Samui** 65 Monmouth St, WC2 ℡020/7240 4280, Leicester Square or Covent Garden tube. The leading promoter of young British designers such as Matthew Williamson, this one-stop boutique offers a highly selective range of womenswear with an elegant, eclectic and feminine feel. Also features international names such as Chloe and Missoni, as well as vintage-inspired accessories.

Madeleine Press 90 Marylebone High St, W1 ℡020/7935 9301; Baker St or Bond St tube. The creation of one of the founders of much-missed Press & Bastyan, and with the same emphasis on excellent tailoring. Strongest on the kind of casual "weekend wear" that most of us can only dream of, with well-made and elegant staples in muted colours.

Nicole Farhi 158 New Bond St, W1, and other branches ℡020/7499 8368; Green Park or Bond St tube. Classic designs and cuts for women, mainly in the shades of a chameleon resting on a sandy rock, but no less elegant and popular for that.

Paul Smith Westbourne House, 122 Kensington Park Rd, W11 ℡020/7727 3553, Notting Hill Gate tube, and 40–44 Floral St, WC2 ℡020/7379 7133, Covent Garden tube; ⊛www.paulsmith .co.uk. Both the Covent Garden store, with dark wood and contemporary art on the walls, and the Notting Hill shop-in-a-house are worth a visit in their own right: they're ever so English in Smith's quirky way, and sell the whole range of his well-tailored clothes for men, women and children. The Smith Sale Shop (23 Avery Row, W1 ℡020/7493 1287; Bond St tube) offers huge discounts, and is especially good for blokes.

Souvenir 47 Lexington St, W1 ℡020/7287 9877; Piccadilly Circus tube. A cute north Soho boutique with a Japan meets Cannes feel. Offerings include Anna Sui's delicate and covetable designs and quirky Marc Jacob shoes.

Vexed Generation 3 Berwick St, W1 ℡020/7287 6224, ℠www.thing-is.com; Piccadilly Circus tube. Created in all kinds of new fabrics and coatings, the clothes here are so cool it hurts.

Vivienne Westwood 6 Davies St, W1, and other branches ℡020/7629 3757, ℠www.vivien-newestwood.com; Bond St tube. Revered by the international fashion pack, this quintessentially English maverick is still going strong. The historic World's End branch (430 King's Rd, SW10 ℡020/7352 6551; Sloane Square tube) is the best place to pick up her famous print jeans.

Mid-range and high street

Agnès B 35–36 Floral St, WC2, and other branches ℡020/7379 1992, ℠www.agnesb .com; Covent Garden tube. Sitting with one foot in the designer camp, this French fashion house brings understated Parisian chic to the high street. Classic clothing, a few more adventurous designs, plus hats, bags and other accessories.

Dispensary 8–9 Newburgh St, W1 ℡020/7287 8145; Oxford Circus tube. Located on an alley parallel to Carnaby Street that's great for original fashion, Dispensary has friendly, helpful staff and offers effervescent dressy womenswear with a street edge. Great accessories, too, such as stilettoes made of flip-flop material.

French Connection 396 Oxford St, W1, and many other branches ℡020/7629 7766, ℠www .frenchconnection.com; Oxford Circus tube. A tongue-in-cheek advertising campaign has seen French Connection re-launch itself for a younger, funkier market. Top-quality fabrics and cuts don't come cheap, but for your money you get catwalk styling at a fraction of the cost of the real thing.

H&M 261–271 Regent St, W1, and other branches ℡020/7493 4004, ℠www.hm.com; Oxford Circus tube. Fashion basics for very little outlay – pick up a sparkly party top for under a tenner. Men's clothes, especially shirts, are well cut and amazingly cheap. Also good for bargain accessories.

Joy 432 Coldharbour Lane, SW9, and other branches ℡020/7787 9616, ℠www.joythestore .com; Brixton tube. A joy indeed, and one of the places to be in Brixton. This lively store features fantastic imported designer fashion at high-street prices, from well-cut sassy streetwear to ballgowns. There's a good range of more subdued men's clothes, including Chunk T-shirts, and you can also buy kitsch cards and gifts, including home detox kits and Elvis mouse mats.

The Laden Showroom 103 Brick Lane, E1 ℡020/7247 2431, ℠www.laden.co.uk; Aldgate East tube. This weirdly named emporium showcases over forty independent designers, and is great for exuberant dressers on a budget. You can pick up Indian tunics, handmade customized T-shirts, batik bags and stripey bias-cut frocks. There is a small men's department, but this is really one for the ladies. For similar secondhand gear, check out Rokit next door (see p.536).

Primark Kings Mall, 365–371 Mare St, E8, and other branches ℡020/8748 7119, ℠www .primark.co.uk; Hackney Central train station from Liverpool St. Dubbed "Primarche" by aspiring junior fashion editors who have to look fantastic on a tight budget, Primark provides dirt cheap cutting-edge garments, "inspired" by the catwalk and more established high-street stores. Wide selection of swimming costumes, underwear and nighties, plus cheap, fun handbags for a fiver.

Top Shop 214 Oxford St, W1, and many other branches ℡020/7636 7700, ℠www.topshop.co.uk or ℠www.topman.co.uk; Oxford Circus tube. Proving a big hit with the celebs as well as mere mortals, Top Shop's flagship store is the place to go for this season's must-have item at a snip of the designer prices. Most of the store is given over to women's clothing, with one floor devoted entirely to accessories, another to Top Shop's own-brand stuff and a third to young independent labels. Free personal shopping advisors are on hand to help with styling and sizes.

Street and clubwear

AdHoc/Boy 153 King's Rd, SW3 ☎020/7376 8829; Sloane Square tube. Party gear for exhibitionists: plenty of PVC, lycra, feathers and spangles, with fairy wings and magic wands to set your basics off nicely. There's body-piercing available, too.

Burro 29a Floral St, WC2 ☎020/7240 5120; Covent Garden tube. Funky but with an air of studied nonchalance, this is for boys who really want to look cool but don't want to admit it.

Diesel 43 Earlham St, WC2 ☎020/7497 5543, ⓦwww.diesel.com; Covent Garden tube. Still cool despite the hype, this trippy, industrial-looking store for label-conscious men and women continues to offer the retro-denim look in a dazzling variety of colours and styles.

Dockers Unit 8, North Piazza, Covent Garden Market, WC2 ☎020/7240 7908, ⓦwww .dockers-uk.co.uk; Covent Garden tube. Butch, fashionable American-style workwear for both sexes, featuring basic khakis, a range of heavy-duty, technologically enhanced fabrics, and classic white T-shirts and vests.

Duffer of St George 29 Shorts Gardens, WC2 ☎020/7379 4660, ⓦwww.thedufferofstgeorge .com; Covent Garden tube. Covetable own-label boys' casuals and streetwear, plus a range of other hip labels in the land of jeans, shoes, jackets and so on.

Mambo 39 Shelton St, WC2 ☎020/7438 9800, ⓦwww.mambo.com.au; Covent Garden tube. Iconic surf, skate and graffiti gear, including a range of books, mugs and hats.

Miss Sixty 39 Neal St, WC2 ☎020/7836 3789 and other branches, ⓦwww.misssixty.com; Covent Garden tube. A day-glo store selling skinny girls' clothes with a psychedelic feel.

Urban Outfitters 42–56 Earlham St, WC2 and other branches ☎020/7759 6390, ⓦwww .urbanoutfitters.com; Covent Garden tube. Bedraggled boho style meets streetwear in this large Covent Garden cornerstore. Blokes' clothes include own-brand T-shirts and Levi's. They also stock Sixties-inspired kitschery for the home, such as wiggly plastic cocktail glasses.

Vintage, retro and secondhand

Annie's Vintage Costume & Textiles 10 Camden Passage, N1 ☎020/7359 0796; Angel tube. A tiny and well-stocked shop, draped in shimmering fabrics and specializing in fabulous 1920s and 1930s glamour, from party dresses and embroidered Chinese jackets to handmade shoes and suitcases.

The Antiques Clothing Shop 282 Portobello Rd, W10 ☎020/8964 4830; Ladbroke Grove tube. Lots of treasures in this store, with affordable Victoriana and vintage menswear a speciality.

Beyond Retro 110–112 Cheshire St (off Brick Lane), E2 ☎020/7613 3636; Liverpool St tube. Cavernous warehouse with vintage jeans, Fifties frocks, ranks of cowboy boots and party wigs. In-store bands play on Saturdays.

The Emporium 330–332 Creek Rd, SE10 ☎020/8305 1670; Cutty Sark DLR or Greenwich train station from Charing Cross. Elegant retro store specializing in 1940s to 1960s clothes for men and women, and featuring kitsch and well-preserved bras, stockings, compacts and cigarette-holders in its beautiful glass-fronted cases.

John Savva 6 Windmill St, W1 ☎020/7636 1826; Goodge St tube. The friendly John Savva is a skilled tailor who cuts good suits far cheaper than Savile Row; if you need a perfect fit for your second-hand gear, he can also make any alterations for you.

Laurence Corner 62–64 Hampstead Rd, NW1 ☎020/7813 1010; Warren St tube. London's oldest and most eccentric army surplus shop, which also stocks catering uniforms, thermals, military greatcoats, heavy-duty waterproofs and many kinds of hats. Upstairs are floors and floors of theatrical costumes, for rental only, to suit any conceivable fancy-dress theme.

The Loft 35 Monmouth St, WC2 ☎020/7240 3807, ⓦwww.the-loft.co.uk; Covent Garden tube. A huge array of secondhand designer clothes for men and women. Many are sourced from film shoots or the catwalk, so are in good nick. Labels include Miu Miu, Joseph and Vivienne Westwood.

Modern Age Vintage Clothing 65 Chalk Farm Rd, NW1 ☎020/7482 3787; Chalk Farm tube. Splendid clobber (mostly menswear) for lovers of 1940s and 1950s American-style gear. The best bargains are on the rails outside: inside, the very lovely cashmere and leather coats are a bit pricier.

Old Hat 43a & 66 Fulham High St, SW6 ☎020/7610 6558; Putney Bridge tube. Tailored men's suits (ex-Savile Row) feature high in this largely-for-men vintage clothing store. Some womenswear, mostly Seventies kitsch, but some classics too.

Rokit 105–107 Brick Lane, E1 ☎020/7375 3864, ⊛www.rokit.co.uk; Aldgate East tube. If you want to dress like one of the local asymetrical studenty types, this is the place. Clothes are stylishly presented, with no fusty secondhand smells – you'll find sparkly knits, jeans, legwarmers and 1970s shades the size of dinnerplates, plus baseball caps for the boys.

Steinberg & Tolkien 193 King's Rd, SW3 ☎020/7376 3660; Sloane Square tube. Claims to be London's largest collection of vintage and retro gear and accessories. Clothing is displayed by designer, which says a lot for the quality of the stock. Prices are reasonable given the designer cache, but don't expect to pick up a Westwood original for a fiver.

Still 61d Lancaster Rd, W11 ☎020/7243 2932; Ladbroke Grove tube. Boutique-style layout and a small but select stock make this a great place to start for the faint-hearted vintage shopper. Some designer labels and prices to match.

Underwear

Agent Provocateur 6 Broadwick St, W1 ☎020/7439 0229, Oxford Circus tube, and 16 Pont St, SW1 ☎020/7235 0229, Knightsbridge tube; ⊛www.agentprovocateur.com. Essential for any girl with an interest in the kitsch, sexy and glamorous. Offering a beautifully displayed range of lingerie and shoes, this is the place to get the leopardskin-print bra and knickers you've always wanted, or those Hollywood-style fluffy mules with the marabou trim.

Coco de Mer 23 Monmouth St, WC2 ☎020/7836 8882, ⊛www.coco.de.mer.co.uk. Covent Garden tube. Upmarket sex shop for women, with an inviting boudoir feel. The undies are floaty and feminine and mostly surprisingly demure, in shades of lilac and pistachio as well as more racy scarlet numbers. Pick up a feather tickler and an erotic fortune cookie while you're here.

Coco Ribbon 21 Kensington Park Rd, W1 ☎020/7229 4904; Ladbroke Grove tube. A temple to femininity, with lots of dressing-table fripperies, plus "Love Kylie" undies, Elle Macpherson "Intimates", silicone bra inserts and "nipple concealer adhesives". Also some stunning boho-chic dresses in jade green, fuschia and gold, starting from around £150.

Design Also 101 St Paul's Rd, N1 ☎020/7354 0035; Highbury & Islington tube. Lingerie, hosiery and corsetry galore, not to mention hats and accessories to die for, are all packed into this wonderful one-woman Islington enterprise. Owner Yvonne Lyddon can tell your correct bra size before you've even entered the shop, and offers an excellent fitting service.

Rigby & Peller 2 Hans Rd, SW3 ☎020/7589 9293, Knightsbridge tube, and 22a Conduit St, W1 ☎020/7491 2200, Oxford Circus tube; ⊛www.rigbyandpeller.com. Corsetières to HM the Queen, if that can be counted as a recommendation, this old-fashioned store stocks a wide range of lingerie and swimwear, including designer names and its own range, for all shapes and sizes. Take a ticket and wait for an assistant for a personal fitting.

Shoes

Aldo 3–7 Neal St, WC2 ☎020/7836 7692, and other branches, ⊛www.aldoshoes.com; Covent Garden tube. A Canadian store providing high-fashion, high-quality and really rather sexy shoes for men and women at very reasonable prices They also have a sale shop at 231–233 Camden High St, NW1 (☎020/7284 1982).

Birkenstock 37 Neal St, WC2 ☎020/7240 2783, ⊛www.birkenstock.co.uk; Covent Garden tube. Comfortable, classic sandals and shoes in leather, suede, nubuck and vegan styles.

Buffalo Boots 47–49 Neal St, WC2 ☎020/7379 1051, ⊛www.buffalo-boots.com; Covent Garden tube. Everything from the practical to the clubby via spike-heeled boots and platform shoes.

Camper 39 Floral St, WC2, and many other branches ☎020/7399 8678, ⊛www.camper.es; Covent Garden tube. A Spanish store selling well-made, colourful and quirky shoes; their peace sandals feature a dove for one foot and an olive branch for the other.

Clarks 476 Oxford St, W1, and other branches ☎020/7629 9609, ⊛www.clarks.co.uk; Marble Arch tube. Clarks are being rediscovered by the twenty-something generation thanks to some clever marketing and great new lines. Some of the range still looks more dedicated to comfort than style, but the quality is high and the prices relatively low.

Jones the Bootmaker 15 Foubert's Place, W1, and other branches ☎020/7734 2351, ⊛www

.jonesbootmaker.com; Oxford Circus tube. Mid-range prices but high-quality footwear are the hallmarks of this store. Classic men's and women's styles plus the latest fashion lines.

L.K. Bennett 130 Long Acre, WC2, and other branches ℡020/7379 1710, Ⓦwww.lkbennett.com; Covent Garden tube. Girlie shoes galore: kitten heels, pointy boots and strappy sandals in a wide range of colours. Well made, very stylish and with a price tag to boot.

Manolo Blahnik 49–51 Old Church St, SW3 ℡020/7352 3833; Sloane Square tube. This secluded store on a leafy street off the King's Road is perfect for some fantasy window shopping, with the slender footwear worshipped by *Sex in the City*'s Carrie dramatically downlit and framed by Grecian-style friezes.

Natural Shoe Store 21 Neal St, WC2, and other branches ℡020/7836 5254, Ⓦwww.thenaturalshoestore.com; Covent Garden tube.

Well-made, stylish, comfortable and sometimes strange shoes. Good value, although not cheap.

Office 57 Neal St, WC2, and many other branches ℡020/7379 1896, Ⓦwww.officelondon.co.uk; Covent Garden tube. Good, broad range of basics, including many own-label creations, at reasonable prices, and some more frivolous fashion moments, too.

Shellys 266–270 Regent St, W1, and many other branches ℡020/7287 0939, Ⓦwww.shellys.co.uk; Oxford Circus tube. Offering pretty much everything from the sensible to the silly and with a good deal in between, this madly busy store has a huge range over several floors and at every price, for both men and women.

Sole Trader 72 Neal St, WC2 ℡020/7836 6777, Ⓦwww.sole-trader.co.uk; Covent Garden tube. Walking and running shoes, plus a wide range of fashion trainers from all the big-name designer brands.

Hairdressers

London has plenty of big-name salons, where they put more energy into selling their own products than cutting your hair, and then charge you upwards of sixty quid for the privilege. The options below are either cheaper than this, or worth splashing out on. Bear in mind that as these are the more central and popular crop spots in town, you're unlikely to get seen on spec: usually you'll need to make an **appointment** a week or so in advance. Unless otherwise stated, all cater for both men and women. Most **barber shops** will also cut women's hair if it's short and simple enough – and for a fraction of the price of a salon.

Fish 30 D'Arblay St, W1 ℡020/7494 2398, Ⓦwww.fishweb.co.uk; Oxford Circus or Tottenham Court Rd tube. Once a fishmonger's, now a high-fashion hair emporium catering for twenty-something Soho sophisticates. Good-quality cuts, starting from £32 for men and £38 for women.

George F. Trumper 9 Curzon St, W1 ℡020/7499 1850; Green Park tube. Gentlemen's gentlemen offering a Victorian barbershop experi-

---

You can get yourself a **bargain haircut** from a top hairdressing salon by making yourself available as a model at one of their training schools. Call ahead for prices and appointment times.

L'Oréal International Academy 255 Hammersmith Rd, W6 ℡020/8762 4200, Ⓦwww.loreal.com; High St Kensington tube. Especially good for colour.

Toni & Guy Advanced Academy 75 New Oxford St, W1 ℡020/7836 0606, Ⓦwww.toniandguy.co.uk; Tottenham Court Rd tube. Great for the latest styles at bargain prices. Women only.

Vidal Sassoon School 56–58 Davies Mews, W1 ℡020/7318 5205, Ⓦwww.vidalsassoon.co.uk; Bond St tube. Both classic and wildly imaginative cuts – although you can also just get a trim if you insist.

Vision 8 Dray Walk, The Old Truman Brewery, Brick Lane, E1 ℡020/7247 6842; Aldgate East tube. Funky street-cuts are the order of the day here. Cuts, colours, extensions and dreadlocks all for next to nothing.

ence. They'll even teach you how to shave properly. Shampoo and cut from around £32.

John Frieda 75 New Cavendish St, W1, and other branches ☎ 020/7636 1401; **Great Portland St or Oxford Circus tube.** Good, classic and stylish cuts from a well-established, well-regarded salon; cuts are around £60. Defrizzing a speciality.

Mr Topper's 14a Moor St, W1 ☎ 020/7434 4088; **Leicester Square tube.** Remarkably cheap and surprisingly good dos (£6 for men/£10 for women) in a down-to-earth and friendly Soho salon.

Pacific Hair Artists 16 Beauchamp Place, SW3 ☎ 020/7584 5565; **Knightsbridge tube.** Unisex salon which specializes in hair extensions,

from £50 per section.

Sadlers Wells Barbers Shop 110 Rosebery Ave, EC1 ☎ 020/7833 0556; **Angel tube.** This good, old-fashioned, no-messing barber's will sort you out a good-quality short-back-and-sides, a traditional hot-towel shave, or any variation thereof, for a mere £7.50.

Windle 41 Shorts Gardens, WC2 ☎ 020/7497 2393, ⓦ www.windlehair .com; **Covent Garden tube.** The approachable-yet-cool stylists at Windle take hair very seriously. The salon itself is relaxed, funky and particularly good for straight hair – Windle himself invented the sharp razor-cutting method. Cuts from £45.

Pharmacies and cosmetics

As well as dispensing a large range of over-the-counter drugs and offering everything from photographic developing to ear piercing, London's **pharmacies** are major retailers of **perfumes and cosmetics** – in fact Boots (Britain's main high-street pharmacy chain) accounts for the lion's share of UK cosmetics sales. The big **department stores** – especially Harvey Nichols, Selfridges and Harrods – also house excellent ranges of perfumes and cosmetics.

The Body Shop 374 Oxford St, W1, and many other branches ☎ 020/7409 7868, ⓦ www.the-body-shop.com; **Bond St tube.** One of the first to pioneer and market cruelty-free products, and still going strong after all these years, with new aromas and raw materials emerging regularly alongside old favourites. The make-up range is good, too.

Farmacia 169 Drury Lane, WC2 ☎ 020/7831 0830, ⓦ www.farmacia123.com; **Covent Garden tube.** This pharmacy-cum-herbalist store is staffed by knowledgeable folk who can advise on a wide range of herbal treatments as well as provide more conventional remedies should you so wish. Brands stocked include Dr Hauschka and Burt's Bees; treatments – which should usually be booked in advance – include allergy screening, massage and homoeopathy.

Lush Units 7 & 11, The Piazza, Covent Garden, WC2 ☎ 020/7240 4570, ⓦ www.lush.co.uk; **Covent Garden tube.** Natural, mostly organic products packaged with fun and imagination – deli-counter style fresh facemasks, fizzing bath bombs and body scrubs all prepared and labelled individually.

MAC Cosmetics 109 King's Rd, SW3, and several other branches ☎ 020/7349 0022, ⓦ www.

maccosmetics.com; **Sloane Square tube.** The UK's first professional make-up range, aimed mostly at models, but promoting a nicely subversive take on fashion and beauty, and offering some genuinely excellent products to back up the hype.

Neal's Yard Remedies 15 Neal's Yard, WC2 ☎ 020/7379 7222, ⓦ www.nealsyardremedies .com; **Covent Garden tube.** Fabulously scented, beautifully presented, entirely efficacious herbal cosmetics, toiletries and therapies, plus a whole range of holistic reference books and accessories.

Nelson Pharmacy 73 Duke St, W1 ☎ 020/7629 3118; **Bond St tube.** This famous Victorian homoeopathic pharmacy dispenses its own reputable range of highly effective lotions and potions for every ailment imaginable, as well as a full range of aromatherapy products, essential oils and Bach flower remedies.

Pak Cosmetic Centre 25–27 Stroud Green Rd, N4 ☎ 020/7263 2088; **Finsbury Park tube.** All the Afro hair and skincare products you might ever need, plus a huge range of cosmetics, accessories and appliances. They also manage the hair salon at nos 34–36.

Penhaligon's 41 Wellington St, WC2, and several

other branches ☎ 020/7836 2150, ⓦ www
.penhaligons.co.uk; Covent Garden tube. Wonderfully traditional old perfumery carrying a
great range of colognes, potions and powders – including the famous Penhaligon's
Love Potion No. 9. Great for (rather pricey)
gifts and special occasions.

SPACE.NK 37 Earlham St, WC2 ☎ 020/7379
7030, ⓦ www.spacenk.com; Covent Garden
tube. Stocks its own range of beauty products and a great collection of fashionable
brands too. Not cheap, but the quality
brands and minimalist decor provide the
right tone.

Books

As well as the big-name chain bookstores, most of which have branches
throughout the city, London is blessed with a wealth of local, independent and
specialist bookshops. Listed below are some of the most central, best known or
just most interesting.

General interest

Blackwell's 100 Charing Cross Rd, WC2
☎ 020/7292 5100, ⓦ www.bookshop.blackwell
.co.uk; Tottenham Court Rd or Leicester Square
tube. The London flagship of Oxford's best
academic bookshop is bigger than it looks
and has a much wider range than you might
expect. Its academic stock is, unsurprisingly, excellent, but so too is its range of
computing, travel and fiction titles.

Books Etc 26 James St, WC2, and many other
branches ☎ 020/7236 0398, ⓦ www.booksetc
.co.uk; Covent Garden tube. Laid-back and
user-friendly chain, with a wide and well-
stocked range of mainstream and specialist
titles. Especially good on contemporary
fiction.

Borders Books & Music 203 Oxford St, W1, and
other branches ☎ 020/7292 1600, ⓦ www
.borders.co.uk; Oxford Circus tube. Enormous
London flagship of the American import,
boasting four floors of books alongside a
huge range of CDs and magazines. Good
range of titles, with staff recommendations
and reviews, a solid children's section, regular readings and a coffee bar.

Foyles 113–119 Charing Cross Rd, WC2
☎ 020/7437 5660, ⓦ www.foyles.co.uk; Tottenham Court Rd tube. Long-established,
huge and famous London bookshop with a
big feminist section (Silver Moon) and Ray's
Jazz Shop and café on the first floor.

Hatchards 187 Piccadilly, W1 ☎ 020/7439 9921,
ⓦ www.hatchards.co.uk; Piccadilly Circus
tube. A little overshadowed by the colossal
Waterstone's down the road, Hatchards
nevertheless holds its own when it comes
to quality fiction, biography, history and
travel. The regal interiors are all you'd

expect of a bookseller by appointment to
HM the Queen.

Waterstone's 203–206 Piccadilly, W1, and other
branches ☎ 020/7851 2400, ⓦ www
.waterstones.co.uk; Piccadilly Circus tube.
This flagship bookstore – Europe's largest
– occupies the former Simpson's department store building and boasts a café, bar,
gallery and events rooms as well five floors
of books.

Independent and specialist

Africa Book Centre 38 King St, WC2 ☎ 020/7240
6649, ⓦ www.africabookcentre.com; Covent
Garden tube. Wide variety of African and Caribbean fiction, non-fiction and poetry on the
ground floor of the Africa Centre.

Al-hoda 76–78 Charing Cross Rd, WC2
☎ 020/7240 8381, ⓦ www.alhodanet.com;
Leicester Square tube. Specializing in Islamic
art and culture, with a strong Arabic section.

Arthur Probsthain Oriental & African Bookseller
41 Great Russell St, WC1 ☎ 020/7636 1096,
ⓦ www.oriental-african-books.com; Tottenham
Court Rd tube. Connected to the nearby
School of Oriental and African Studies,
this impressive academic store covers all
relevant aspects of art, history, science and
culture.

Atlantis Bookshop 49a Museum St, WC1
☎ 020/7405 2120, ⓦ www.theatlantisbook-
shopⓦ.com; Tottenham Court Rd tube. Splendid occult-oriented place, with the perfect
ambience for browsing through books and
magazines covering spirituality, psychic phenomena, witchcraft and the like.

Bookmarks 1 Bloomsbury St, WC1 ☎ 020/7637
1848, ⓦ www.bookmarks.uk.com; Tottenham
Court Rd tube. Leftist and radical fare in the

heart of Bloomsbury, with a wide range of political biography, history, theory and assorted political ephemera. There's even a children's section.

Books for Cooks 4 Blenheim Crescent, W11 ☏020/7221 1992, ⊛www.booksforcooks.com; **Ladbroke Grove tube.** Literature on anything and everything to do with food can be found on the shelves of this wonderful new and secondhand bookshop, which also has a tiny café (see p.460) offering cookery demonstrations, coffee for browsers and lunch (ring ahead to book).

The Calder Bookshop 51 The Cut, SE1 ☏020/7620 2900, ⊛www.calderpublications. com; **Waterloo tube.** A fine little bookshop specializing in foreign fiction in translation, owned by the publisher and Beckett scholar John Calder. A high-powered weekly programme of talks and play- and poetry-readings (Thurs 6.45pm; £5) draws a loyal audience of intellectual groupies.

Daunt Books 83–84 Marylebone High St, W1, and other branches ☏020/7224 2295; **Bond St or Baker St tube.** Wide and inspirational range of travel literature as well as the usual guidebooks, presented by expert staff in the beautiful, galleried interior of this famous shop.

European Bookshop 5 Warwick St, W1 ☏020/7734 5259, ⊛www.esb.co.uk; **Piccadilly Circus tube.** This place has an excellent range of European-language books, and very helpful staff.

Forbidden Planet 179 Shaftesbury Ave, WC2 ☏020/7420 3666, ⊛www.forbiddenplanet.com; **Tottenham Court Rd tube.** Two permanently packed floors of all things science fiction- and fantasy-related, ranging from comics and graphic novels to books, games and ephemera.

Gosh! 39 Great Russell St, WC1 ☏020/7636 1011; **Tottenham Court Rd tube.** All kinds of comics for all kinds of readers, whether you're the casually curious or the serious collector. Check out the Cartoon Gallery in the basement.

Helter Skelter 4 Denmark St, WC2 ☏020/7836 1151, ⊛www.helterskelterbooks.com; **Tottenham Court Rd tube.** Every kind of music book, but especially strong on rock history and biographies. Plenty of printed ephemera, too.

Housmans 5 Caledonian Rd, N1 ☏020/7837 4473; **King's Cross tube.** Old, dilapidated and friendly store specializing in black, lesbian

and gay fiction, plus socialism, anarchism and ecology. A good secondhand basement lurks at the bottom of creaky, dusty stairs.

ICA Bookshop The Mall, SW1 ☏020/7766 1452, ⊛www.ica.org.uk; **Piccadilly Circus or Charing Cross tube.** Worth a visit whether you're exploring the rest of the ICA's offerings or not. Hip and artsy, with a strong style bent and lots of funky magazines, postcards and book imports.

Index Bookcentre 16 Electric Ave, SW9 ☏020/7274 8342, ⊛www.indexbooks.co.uk; **Brixton tube.** Small but packed and friendly bookseller with some general stock, but specializing in a good range of black-oriented fiction and non-fiction.

Intermediate Technology Bookshop 103–105 Southampton Row, WC1 ☏020/7436 9761, ⊛www.developmentbookshop.com; **Russell Square tube.** Everything connected with issues in the developing world, from agriculture to healthcare and beyond, plus a small selection of gifts and crafts.

Murder One 76–78 Charing Cross Rd, WC2 ☏020/7734 3483; **Leicester Square or Tottenham Court Rd tube.** As you'd expect, crime fiction galore, from the traditional murder mystery to modern urban noir, with the odd foray into other genres.

Offstage Theatre & Cinema Bookshop 37 Chalk Farm Rd, NW1 ☏020/7485 4996; **Camden Town or Chalk Farm tube.** Excellent, well-stocked shop covering all aspects of stage and screen craft, plus theory, criticism, scripts and biographies.

Persephone Books 59 Lamb's Conduit St, WC1 ☏020/7242 9292, ⊛www .persephonebooks.co.uk; **Russell Square tube.** A true one-off – the attractive bookshop of a publishing house which specializes in neglected early twentieth-century fiction, poetry, biography and cook books, mostly by women. The books are beautifully produced with dove-grey soft covers, all with endpapers in a textile from the relevant period (£10 each or £27 for 3). For an extra £2 you can buy your book of choice and have it giftwrapped with a matching bookmark.

Politico's 8 Artillery Row, SW1 ☏020/7828 0010, ⊛www.politicos.co.uk; **St James's Park tube.** Mainstream political fare, both new and secondhand, with plenty of big biographies. A cosy café, board games and irreverent window displays give it a more frivolous edge.

Stanford's Map and Travel Bookshop 12–14 Long Acre, WC2 ☏020/7836 1321, ⓦwww. stanfords.co.uk; Leicester Square or Covent Garden tube. The world's largest specialist travel bookshop, this features pretty much any map of anywhere, plus a huge range of books and guides.

Zwemmer Arts & Architecture 24 Litchfield St, WC2 ☏020/7240 4158, ⓦwww.zwemmer.com; Leicester Square tube. Specialist art bookstore with a fantastic and expert selection. Zwemmer Media Arts, nearby (80 Charing Cross Rd, WC2 ☏020/7240 4157; Leicester Square tube), specializes in film, design and photography.

Secondhand and antiquarian

In addition to the places listed below, secondhand books are available at Riverside Walk; see "Markets", p.550.

Any Amount of Books 56 Charing Cross Rd, WC2 ☏020/7240 8140, ⓦwww.anyamountofbooks.com; Leicester Square or Charing Cross tube. Wonderful, sprawling secondhand bookshop stocking everything from obscure fifty-pence bargains to rare and expensive first editions. Especially strong on fiction, the arts and literary biography.

Fisher & Sperr 46 Highgate High St, N6 ☏020/8340 7244; Archway or Highgate tube. A little out of the way but well worth a visit, this fabulous old building at the top of Highgate Hill is a literary tardis. Several rooms, one entirely dedicated to books about London, plus a few expensive antiquarian jewels and a wide range of titles covering travel, literature, history and philosophy.

Halcyon Books 1 Greenwich South St, SE10 ☏020/8305 2675, ⓦwww.halcyonbooks. co.uk; Greenwich DLR or train station from Charing Cross. A little stuffy, but packed with treasures for the scholarly minded. Lots on military history, travel and languages. Also stocks some cheap paperback fiction.

Unsworths Booksellers 12 Bloomsbury St, WC1 ☏020/7436 9836; Tottenham Court Rd tube. Good for bargains, including recent and just-out-of-print novels and academic titles. Specializes in the arts and humanities, and features an interesting antiquarian selection.

World's End Bookshop 357 King's Rd, SW3 ☏020/7352 9376; Sloane Square tube. Outside are piles of cheap books, proceeds from the sale of which go to charity. Inside, the shop is piled high with books on just about every subject you can think of, with a few rare editions, but mostly inexpensive secondhand books.

Crafts, design and jewellery

London has a huge number of young **craft designers** whose work you can find in shops and workshops all over the capital. There are also hundreds of outlets catering for craft-type hobbies, and plenty of places specializing in unusual gifts or homewares. The **Crafts Council** (44a Pentonville Rd, N1 ☏020/7278 7700, ⓦwww.craftscouncil.org.uk) is an excellent information centre for all matters craft- and design-related. What follows is a small selection of places to start.

@work 156 Brick Lane, E1 ☏020/7377 0597, ⓦwww.atworkgallery.com; Aldgate East tube. A combined jewellery store and workshop that's perfect for an original gift, with everything from chunky urbanwear such as plastic cuffs and rings with Warhol-esque prints, to outlandish necklaces made from bottle tops and dainty modern takes on the charm bracelet. Prices start at just a tenner, but you can also splash out on commissioned pieces.

The Bead Shop 21a Tower St, WC2 ☏020/7240 0931; Covent Garden tube. Every shape and size of bead, in wood, plastic, glass and any

other material you can think of, plus wire, accessories and a range of semi-precious stones.

Ceramica Blue 10 Blenheim Crescent, W11 ☏020/7727 0288, ⓦwww.ceramicablue.co.uk; Ladbroke Grove tube. A vast and colourful array of multi-ethnic, hand-painted ceramics, at some surprisingly affordable prices.

Contemporary Ceramics William Blake House, 7 Marshall St, W1 ☏020/7437 7605, econtemporary.ceramics@virgin.net; Oxford Circus tube. You can get anything and everything by and for ceramicists at this fascinating gallery-cum-shop, which is also the showcase and retail outlet for the Craft Potters' Association.

Dinny Hall 292 Upper St, N1 ☎020/7704 1543, ⓦwww.dinnyhall.com; Angel tube. Classic modern jewellery, with highly faceted and highly coloured gems in elegant settings.

Flow gallery 1–5 Needham St, W11 ☎020/7243 0782, ⓦwww.flowgallery.co.uk; Notting Hill Gate tube. Showing the work of mainly British artists, Flow excels in well-crafted pieces, including as jewellery, fabrics and sculpture.

Laura Lee 42 Monmouth St, WC2 ☎020/7379 9059, ⓦwww.lauraleejewellery.com; Covent Garden tube. Delicate and colourful jewellery made on the premises. A signature design is gold and silver pieces for men and women, based on the theme of gambling and luck.

Oxo Tower Bargehouse St, SE1 ⓦwww.oxotower. co.uk. An absorbing collection of shops – jewellers, textile-makers and design stores – most selling one-off creations. Look out for Bodo Sperlein's outlet, showcasing his simple and stylish porcelain bowls and lamps.

Sports clothing and equipment

In addition to the following, see also the department stores listed in the box on p.532.

Black's 10–11 Holborn, EC1, and other branches ☎020/7404 5681; Holborn tube. A good range of outdoor equipment, from clothing and boots to tents and camping accessories, all at very competitive prices.

Cyclefit 11–13 Macklin St, WC2 ☎020/7430 0083, ⓦwww.cyclefit.co.uk; Covent Garden tube. If you're serious about cycling, this is the place to head. Sells, repairs and services bikes, and stocks a full range of equipment and accessories. Also offers coaching and cardiovascular testing.

Ellis Brigham 3–11 Southampton St, WC2 ☎020/7636 0696, ⓦwww.ellis-brigham.co.uk; Covent Garden tube. Caters for most outdoor pursuits, but with particular emphasis on skiing, snowboarding and rock climbing.

Evans 178 High Holborn, W1, and other branches ☎0845/070 3737, ⓦwww.evanscycles.co.uk; Holborn tube. With eighty years' experience serving cyclists, this is a friendly and approachable store for the general customer.

JJB Sports 120 Oxford St, W1, and other branches ☎020/7409 2619, ⓦwww.jjb.co.uk; Oxford Circus tube. Masses of trainers and

labelled clothing make this store popular with sport-fashion kids. Not the place to come for serious equipment, but fine for clothing basics.

The Kite Store 48 Neal St, WC2 ☎020/7836 1666, ⓦwww.kitestore.uk.com; Covent Garden tube. One of the few remaining individual shops on a street which is increasingly dominated by chain stores. Kites for kids/ beginners and the more adventurous, plus some other quirky flying gadgets.

Lillywhite's 24–36 Lower Regent St, SW1 ☎020/7930 3181; Piccadilly Circus tube. With the feel of a department store, complete with grand old staircase, this place stocks anything and everything sports related. All the labels are here, too, so whether it's serious sporting equipment you're after or some Tommy Hilfiger clothing, this is the place to head for.

The Lord's Shop Lord's Cricket Ground, St John's Wood Rd, NW8 ☎020/7432 1021; St John's Wood tube. Lord's and MCC souvenirs plus a full range of cricket gear, from pads and helmets to bats.

Food and drink

As you'd expect of a city that has some of the best restaurants in the world, London offers great shopping for even the most discerning of food buffs. In the centre of town, **Soho and Covent Garden**, in particular, are a gourmand's delight: the former replete with Chinese supermarkets and Italian delicatessens, the latter harbouring **Neal's Yard**, a haven for the health-conscious. For more basic requirements, there are numerous **supermarkets** in the high street of nearly every residential area with the two biggest, Tesco and Sainsbury's, also making

Eccentricities

The listings below are a small selection of shops which don't really fit into any particular category, or which are just interesting to visit.

Anything Left-Handed 57 Brewer St, W1 ☎020/7437 3910, ⊛www.anythingleft-handed.co.uk; Piccadilly Circus tube. As the name suggests, the place to go for all kinds of left-handed tools, implements and gifts.

Button Queen 19 Marylebone Lane, W1 ☎020/7935 1505, ⊛www.thebuttonqueen.co.uk; Bond St tube. Located on a quiet corner, this little shop looks like it hasn't changed since the Tahiti pearl buttons in the window were fashioned in 1900. It's piled high with boxes, offering everything from Victorian pressed horn to 1920s Bakelite, alongside jazz-themed gold numbers and 1940s parachute-regiment cufflinks.

Davenport's Magic Shop 7 Charing Cross Underground Arcade, Strand, WC2 ☎020/7836 0408; Charing Cross or Embankment tube. The world's oldest family-run magic business, stocking marvellous tricks for amateurs and professionals.

The Elvis Shop 400 High St North, E12 ☎020/8552 7551; East Ham tube. A little off the beaten track, but essential for any serious disciple of the King. Everything Elvis-related you can imagine is sold in this majestically obsessive and splendid shop: CDs, vinyl, videos, books, magazines, postcards and international memorabilia, dating from the 1950s right up to yesterday.

James Smith & Sons 53 New Oxford St, WC1 ☎020/7836 4731; Tottenham Court Rd tube. A survivor from an earlier time (it was established in 1830), this beautiful and venerable shop purveys hip-flasks, portable seats and canes, but its main trade is in umbrellas. Of the hundreds on display, the most enduringly popular is the man's classic city umbrella (£47).

Mysteries 9–11 Monmouth St, WC2 ☎020/7240 3688; Covent Garden tube. This huge, crowded, lurid and compulsive shop stocks just about every occult-related book, magazine, accessory, crystal and piece of ephemera you can imagine, for the serious esoteric shopper as well as the casual browser. Psychic readings are on offer, too.

Radio Days 87 Lower Marsh, SE1 ☎020/7928 0800; Waterloo tube or train. A fantastic collection of memorabilia and accessories from the 1930s to the 1970s, including shoes, shot-glass collections, cosmetics and vintage magazines. A huge stock of well-kept ladies' and men's clothing from the same period fills the back room.

G. Smith & Sons 74 Charing Cross Rd, WC2 ☎020/7836 7422; Leicester Square tube. Exactly what an old English tobacconist's ought to look and smell like. Every variety of tobacco, including some of the shop's own creations, plus a huge range of snuff and a walk-in humidor featuring some very classy cigars.

Story 4 Wilkes St, E1 ☎020/7377 0313; Liverpool St tube. Located in a modern industrial space on a street of Huguenot houses, this is an exquisitely tasteful and eclectic shop. The unifying theme is that practically everything – art, textiles, furniture, clothing – is in shades of white or cream, the only colour being provided by scattered mother-of-pearl shells, a coral necklace or the odd dove-grey or turquoise vintage garment. There's a whiff of Miss Haversham about the fading lace and Venetian mirrors, but you can pick up surprisingly useful items such as cheap white towels.

forays into the city centre; all of them offer a good range of groceries and fresh foods, plus inexpensive ready-made sandwiches and an increasingly impressive selection of upmarket gourmet and organic fare. **Marks & Spencer** food halls are also an excellent source of fresh foods and good-quality ready-meals, as are those in the major department stores (see box, p.532). But although the supermarkets are hard to beat for convenience, and many now have late (and even 24hr) opening hours, you still can't beat the satisfaction of food shopping in **specialist stores**, and in London's many local **food markets** (see "Markets", p.547).

The specialist beer, wine and spirits outlets listed are the pick of central London's numerous retailers, but you'll also find ever-improving ranges in the main **supermarkets**, for whom budget wine is a highly competitive area. Relaxed **licensing laws** mean that outlets no longer have to close between 3pm and 7pm on Sundays, although some – usually local, family-run places – still do.

Bakeries and patisseries

Berwick Street Bread Stall Berwick St, W1 (no phone); Piccadilly Circus tube. Fresh, good-quality breads at bargain prices, supplied by bakers from all over London; Italian breads, bagels and croissants are the specialities.

Louis' Patisserie 32 Heath St, NW3 ℡020/7435 9908; Hampstead tube. This fabulous-looking Hungarian patisserie doesn't seem to have changed much since it opened in 1963. Breads, pastries and creamy European cakes galore, plus a very splendid tearoom.

Maison Bertaux 28 Greek St, W1 ℡020/7437 6007; Leicester Square tube. Popular Soho hangout, selling fancy cakes, tartlets, croissants and the like, as well as some savoury snacks.

Patisserie Valerie 44 Old Compton St, W1 ℡020/7437 3466, ⓦwww.patisserie-valerie.co.uk. This well-known Soho establishment dates back to the 1920s and still sells croissants, mousses and gooey cakes to die for.

Cheese

International Cheese Centre Unit 5, Marylebone Station, NW1, and several other branches ℡020/7724 1432; Marylebone tube or train. A huge and frequently changing stock of cheeses from all over Europe, with an especially good selection of French and English varieties.

La Fromagerie 30 Highbury Park, N5 ℡020/7359 7440, Highbury & Islington tube, and 2–4 Moxon St, W1 ℡020/7935 0341, Baker St or Bond St tube; ⓦwww.lafromagerie.co.uk. Quality cheeses sourced direct from small farm producers in Britain and across Europe. Also stocks wines, sausages, breads and quiches.

Neal's Yard Dairy 17 Shorts Gardens, WC2 ℡020/7240 5700; Covent Garden tube. Quality cheeses from around the British Isles, with a few exceptionally good ones from further afield. A huge selection and you can taste before you buy.

Paxton & Whitfield 93 Jermyn St, SW1 ℡020/7930 0259, ⓦwww.paxtonandwhitfield.co.uk; Green Park or Piccadilly tube. Quintessentially English, two-hundred-year-old cheese shop offering a very traditional range of English and European varieties, plus a good selection of fine wines and ports.

Coffee and tea

In addition to the places listed below, the shop and café at the Bramah Museum of Tea and Coffee (see p.276) are worth a visit.

Algerian Coffee Stores 52 Old Compton St, W1 ℡020/7437 2480, ⓦwww.algocoffee.co.uk; Leicester Square tube. Every kind of coffee, every kind of coffee-making apparatus and every kind of coffee connoisseur's accessory, all crammed into this great and abiding Soho institution.

Drury Tea & Coffee Company 3 New Row, WC2 ℡020/7836 1960, ⓦwww.drury.uk.com; Leicester Square tube. Thirty different coffees and nearly two hundred types of tea are available at this estimable tea and coffee shop.

Monmouth Coffee Company 27 Monmouth St, WC2 ℡020/7379 3516; Covent Garden or Leicester Square tube. A wonderful range of coffees, all roasted on the premises, and served up with delicious chocolate-coated coffee beans in the strictly non-smoking sampling room at the back of the shop.

R. Twining & Co 216 Strand, WC2 ℡020/7353 3511, ⓦwww.twinings.com; Temple tube. The oldest established tea company in Britain has traded from these premises since the beginning of the eighteenth century. It stocks the full Twinings range and also hosts a small museum on the history of the company.

▲ Neal's Yard Dairy

The Tea House 24 Neal St WC2 ⓣ020/7240 7539; **Covent Garden tube.** The distinctive red-tiled facade conceals two floors of teas – traditional English, green and caffeine-free – as well as a wealth of accessories including infusers, teapots and cosies.

Whittard 209 Kensington High St, W8, and many other branches ⓣ020/7938 4344, ⓦ www.whittard.com; **High St Kensington tube.** Another long-established tea merchant, Whittard these days makes as much from its merchandizing as it does from its teas: cups, teapots, cafetières, plus gift-wrapped tea and coffee boxes.

Confectionery

Charbonnel et Walker 1 The Royal Arcade, 28 Old Bond St, W1 ⓣ020/7491 0939, www .charbonnel.co.uk; **Green Park or Piccadilly Circus tube.** It might sound French, but this is a very English affair dating from 1875, offering beautifully presented chocolates, truffles and peppermint creams.

Godiva 247 Regent St, W1, and many other branches ⓣ020/7495 2845, ⓦ www.godiva.com; **Oxford Circus or Piccadilly Circus tube.** Upmarket chain offering seriously sexy Belgian chocolates – at a price.

Thorntons 254 Regent St, W1, and many other branches ⓣ020/7434 2483, ⓦ www.thorntons .co.uk; **Oxford Circus tube.** Massively popular chain selling good-quality chocolates, truffles, fudges and the like at surprisingly affordable prices.

Delicatessens

The Delicatessen Shop 23 South End Rd, NW3 ⓣ020/7435 7315; **Belsize Park tube or Hampstead Heath train.** Small shop stuffed to the rafters with all manner of delights. Sells handmade chocolates and freshly made sandwiches alongside the cheeses and olives.

Pont de la Tour 36d Shad Thames, SE1 ⓣ020/7403 4030; **Tower Hill tube, London Bridge tube or train.** This upmarket old warehouse complex, just behind the waterfront, is home to Pont de la Tour, which offers an excellent range of deli fare; next door is their elegant wine merchants.

Villandry 170 Great Portland St, W1 ⓣ020/7631 3131, ⓦ www.villandry.com; **Great Portland St tube.** Fresh bread, fruit, veg and fish vie with the groceries for attention in this appealing store. An international range of fare, but with an emphasis on the French.

Health and organic

Brixton Wholefoods Transatlantic 59 Atlantic Rd, SW9 ⓣ020/7737 2210; **Brixton tube.** A splendid institution, offering everything you'd expect from a reliable local wholefood store: fresh bread, groceries, organic fruit and veg, and a wonderful range of herbs and spices.

Fresh and Wild 69–75 Brewer St, W1, and other branches ⓣ020/7434 3179; **Piccadilly Circus tube.** Pricey but mouthwatering organic produce; also has deli counter, café and book section.

Planet Organic 42 Westbourne Grove, W2, and other branches ⓣ020/7221 7171; **Bayswater tube.** Striking a healthy balance between quality and affordability, Planet Organic stocks fresh fruit and veg, plus a wide range of dried and canned goods, dairy produce, meats and food supplements.

Chinese

Loon Fung Supermarket 42–44 Gerrard St, W1 ⓣ020/7437 7332; **Piccadilly Circus tube.** This warren of a supermarket in the heart of Chinatown offers every kind of Chinese food item you can imagine, and probably some you can't. There's also a huge range of foods and groceries in the shops of neighbouring Newport St, Newport Place and Lisle St.

Wing Yip 395 Edgware Rd, NW2 ⓣ020/8450 0422, ⓦ www.wingyip.com; **Kilburn tube.** A Chinese superstore offering everything under one roof, and all helpfully labelled in English.

French

Fileric 57 Brompton Rd, SW7 ⓣ020/7584 2967; **South Kensington tube.** A beautiful French food shop without the extravagant prices you might imagine. Oils, preserves, meats, terrines, cheeses and wines, plus dishes to take away.

Indian

Dokal & Sons 133–135 The Broadway, Southall ⓣ020/8574 1647, ⓦ www.dokalandsons.co.uk; **Southall train station.** Order online or visit in person this store in London's most famous Asian shopping district. Piles of spices, chutneys, pulses, breads, and exotic fruit and veg.

London Oriental Foods 122 Drummond St, NW1

⊤020/7387 3740; Euston or Euston Square tube. Excellent Bengali food store in London's most central Asian shopping and eating enclave; check out the rest of the street for more good Indian food stores.

Taj Stores 112 Brick Lane, E1 ⊤020/7377 0061; **Aldgate East tube.** Big South Asian food store offering everything from halal meats, herbs and spices to fish, fruit and vegetables.

Italian

I. Camisa & Son 61 Old Compton St, W1 ⊤020/7437 7610; **Leicester Square tube.** The whole classic Italian deli range packed into one small Soho space. Excellent cheeses, salamis, pastas and dried foods, plus all the essential wines and spirits.

Carluccio's 28a Neal St, WC2 ⊤020/7240 1487, Ⓦwww.carluccios.com; **Covent Garden tube.** Quality Italian goodies: pastas, olive oils, wild mushrooms, truffles, tarts, cakes and quiches – all stamped with the chef's own label. They also do great summer picnic boxes.

 G. Gazzano & Son 167–169 Farringdon Rd, EC1 ⊤020/7837 1586; **Farringdon tube.** This fabulous Clerkenwell establishment has been keeping the area in Italian fare for a century, and the old wooden cabinets are still holding up under the weight of all that good-quality food.

Wine, beer and spirits

The Beer Shop 14 Pitfield St, N1 ⊤020/7739 3701, Ⓦwww.pitfieldbeershop.co.uk; **Old St tube.** Beers from all over the world in bottles and barrels, and everything you need to make your own.

Berry Bros & Rudd 3 St James's St, SW1 ⊤020/7396 9600, Ⓦwww.bbr.com; **Green Park tube.** This well-stocked, 300-year-old establishment houses a huge range of fine wines, and the friendly and helpful staff know pretty much everything there is to know on the subject.

Bloomsbury Wine & Spirit Company 3 Bloomsbury St, WC1 ⊤020/7436 4763; **Tottenham Court Rd tube.** Wide range of whiskies, brandies, gins and other spirits, with an emphasis on the quality end of the range. Fine wines and ports, too, none of which come cheap.

Gerry's 74 Old Compton St, W1 ⊤020/7734 4215; **Leicester Square tube.** The best, most eclectic and sometimes downright weird range of spirits you'll find anywhere in London; vodka is a speciality.

Majestic Wines Vinopolis, 1 Bank End, SE1 ⊤020/7940 8313; **London Bridge tube.** Vinopolis (see p.274) has a branch of Majestic Wines, a wine warehouse with a mighty brick-arched ceiling and a detailed description of each wine on offer.

Oddbins 141 Notting Hill Gate, W11, and many other branches ⊤020/7229 4082, Ⓦwww .oddbins.com; **Notting Hill Gate tube.** This unswervingly excellent chain offers great wines at good prices, and is especially strong on New World names. There are plenty of good beers, too. Staff are enthusiastic, unpretentious and always ready to help.

The Vintage House 42 Old Compton St, W1 ⊤020/7437 2592, Ⓦwww.vintagehouse.co.uk; **Leicester Square tube.** Wines, brandies and more than seven hundred whiskies line the shelves of this family-run drinker's paradise. To add to the pleasure, the staff know their stuff inside out.

Music

There are hundreds of mainstream, independent and specialist **music shops** in London, catering equally well for the CD bulk-buyer and the obsessive rare-vinyl collector. This is a selection of the best and best known. Bear in mind that London's markets, especially Camden, are also good sources of vinyl (see "Markets", opposite).

Megastores

FOPP 1 Earlham St, WC2 ⊤020/7379 0883, Ⓦwww.fopp.co.uk; **Covent Garden tube.** Three floors of music, at prices that generally undercut its competitors. Lots of DVDs and classic albums for under a fiver. New releases for as little as £10.

HMV 150 Oxford St, W1 ⊤020/7631 3423, Ⓦwww.hmv.co.uk; **Oxford Circus tube.** All the latest releases, as you'd expect, but also an impressive backlist, a reassuring amount of vinyl and a good classical section downstairs. Dance music is also a strength.

MDC Classic Music 437 Strand, WC2, and many other branches ☎020/7240 2157, ⓦwww .mdcmusic.co.uk; Charing Cross tube. Big and brassy, this central chain store has an impressive range of stock, and is known for its special offers and cut-price CDs.
Virgin Megastore 14–16 Oxford St, W1, and many other branches ☎020/7631 1234, ⓦwww.virgin-mega.co.uk; Tottenham Court Rd tube. The main-stream floor here is better stocked than the specialist sections; the bias is rock-heavy, but there's a little of everything else, and plenty of books, magazines, T-shirts and assorted music ephemera.

Independent and specialist

Dub Vendor 274 Lavender Hill, SW11 ☎020/7223 3757, ⓦwww.dubvendor.co.uk; Clapham Junction train station from Victoria or Waterloo. Essential reggae outlet, with up-to-the-minute imports and good advice.
Eukatech 49 Endell St, WC2 ☎020/7240 8060; Covent Garden tube. House, techno and trance on two floors, both vinyl and CD.
Gramex 25 Lower Marsh, SE1 ☎020/7401 3830; Waterloo tube. A splendid find for clas-sical-music lovers, this new and second-hand record store features CDs and vinyl, and offers comfy leather armchairs to sam-ple or discuss your finds at leisure.
Honest Jon's 278 Portobello Rd, W10 ☎020/8969 9822, ⓦwww.honestjons.co.uk; Ladbroke Grove tube. Jazz, soul, funk, R&B, rare groove, dance and much more: a DJ essential and a browser's delight, with cur-rent releases, secondhand finds and reis-sues on vinyl and CD.
Mole Jazz 2 Great Marlborough St, WC1 ☎020/7437 8800, ⓦwww.molejazz.com; Oxford Circus tube. CDs, vinyl, books and ephemera for the jazz purist, with a good range of recent and classic vinyl and CDs and some nice collector's items.
Mr Bongo 44 Poland St, W1 ☎020/7287 1887, ⓦwww.mrbongo.com; Oxford Circus tube. Good on 12" singles, and on hip-hop, jazz,

funk, Latin American and Brazilian sounds.
Rough Trade 130 Talbot Rd, W11, and other branches ☎020/7229 8541, ⓦwww.roughtrade .com; Ladbroke Grove tube. Indie specialist with knowledgeable, friendly staff and a dizzying array of wares, from electronica to hardcore and beyond.
Sister Ray 94 Berwick St, W1 ☎020/7287 8385, ⓦwww.sisterray.co.uk; Oxford Circus or Pic-cadilly Circus tube. Up-to-the-minute indie sounds, with lots of electronica and some forays into the current dance scene, most on vinyl as well as CD.
Stern's African Record Centre 293 Euston Rd, NW1 ☎020/7387 5550; Euston Square tube. World famous for its global specialities, this expert store has an unrivalled stock of African music and excellent selections from pretty much everywhere else in the world, too.

Secondhand

Cheapo Cheapo Records 53 Rupert St, W1 ☎020/7437 8272; Piccadilly Circus tube. Not everything here is totally cheapo cheapo – but there's a lot that is. CDs, vinyl and most musical tastes catered for.
Music & Video Exchange 38 Notting Hill Gate, W11, and other branches ☎020/7243 8573, ⓦwww.mveshops.co.uk; Notting Hill Gate tube. This enduring, expanding and always busy secondhand and collectors' chain almost always has some unexpected treasure in store.
Reckless Records 26 & 30 Berwick St, W1 ☎020/7434 3362 or 7437 4271, ⓦwww .reckless.co.uk; Piccadilly Circus tube. Neigh-bouring, famously hip secondhand CD and vinyl emporia in the heart of Soho. Good-quality stock, though not always as cheap as you might hope.
Steve's Sounds 20–20a Newport Court, WC2 ☎020/7437 4638; Leicester Square tube. Quick-moving stock of CDs and vinyl from rock and pop to dance, jazz, world and classical music. Irresistible prices.

Markets

London's **markets** are more than just a cheap alternative to high-street shop-ping: many of them are significant remnants of communities endangered by the heedless expansion of the city. You haven't really got to grips with London unless you've rummaged through the junk at Brick Lane on a Sunday morning, or haggled over a leather jacket at Camden. Do keep an eye out for **pickpock-ets**: the weekend markets provide them with easy pickings.

Bermondsey (New Caledonian) Bermondsey St and Long Lane, SE1; London Bridge tube. Fri 5am–2pm. Huge, unglamorous but highly regarded antique market offering everything from obscure nautical instruments to attractive but pricey furniture. The real collectors arrive at dawn to pick up the bargains; you need to get here at least before midday to ensure you don't go home empty-handed.

Berwick Street Berwick St and Rupert St, W1; Piccadilly Circus tube. Mon–Sat 9am–6pm. This famous and chaotic fruit and veg market is a piece of living London history, with ferociously fast vendors working the crowds like showmen. There's bread, fish, cheese and herbs, too, and you can pick up produce for next to nothing after 4pm. You'll also find cheap clothes, tapes and CDs aplenty along Berwick Street's southerly extension, Rupert Street.

Borough 8 Southwark St, SE1 ☎020/7401 7300, ⑩www.borough market.org.uk; **London Bridge or Borough tube. Fri noon–6pm, Sat 9am–4pm.** Fine-food heaven – suppliers from all over the UK converge here to sell piles of organic veg, venison, fish, wines and home-baked goodies. The Victorian structure itself, with its slender grass-green wrought-iron columns, is well worth a look as well.

Brick Lane Brick Lane, Cygnet and Sclater streets, E1; Bacon, Cheshire and Chilton streets, E2; Aldgate East, Shoreditch or Liverpool St tube. Sun 8am–2pm. Huge, sprawling, cheap and frenzied, this famous East End market is well worth getting up early for. Fruit and veg, household goods, clothes, antique furniture, scratched records and broken spectacles – it's hard to say what you can't find here, and most of it is going for a song.

Brixton Electric Ave, Pope's, Brixton Station and Atlantic roads, SW9; Brixton tube. Mon–Sat 8am–3pm. Based in the arcades just off Atlantic Rd, but spilling out along nearly all of the neighbouring streets, this huge, energetic market is the centre of Brixton life, offering a vast range of African and Caribbean foods, hair and beauty products, records, clothes, a dazzling range of African fabrics and even triple-fast-action spiritual cleanser-cum-floor-wash.

Camden Camden High St to Chalk Farm Rd, NW1; Camden Town tube. A conglomeration of markets, all with a different emphasis. Camden Market (Camden High St, on the junction of Buck St; Thurs–Sun 9.30am–5.30pm) offers a good mix of new, secondhand, retro and young designer clothes, as well as records and ephemera, while the Electric Market (Camden High St, just before the junction of Dewsbury Terrace; Sat & Sun 10am–5.30pm) and Camden Canal Market (just over Camden Lock bridge; Fri–Sun 9.30am–6.30pm) offer cheap fashion, hippiewear, smoking paraphernalia and souvenir knick-knacks. Camden Lock (Camden Lock Place, off Chalk Farm Rd; daily 10am–6pm; outdoor stalls Sat & Sun 10am–6pm) offers mainly arts, crafts and clothes stalls, with the shops adding a few hip designers, antique dealers and booksellers to the mix. The Stables Yard (leading off from Camden Lock or from Chalk Farm Rd; Sat & Sun 10.30am–6pm) is a sprawling adventure of clubwear, more young designers, furniture, retro design, trinkets and antiques.

Camden Passage off Upper St, N1; Angel tube. Antiques and bric-a-brac Wed 7am–2pm, Sat 8am–4pm; books Thurs 7am–4pm. Narrow, flag-stoned walkway, lined with antique furniture shops and designer jewellery stores, that fills on Wednesday and Saturday with bric-a-brac stalls and antiques vendors. Largely a lot of old tat, tarted up and sold at inflated prices to the nouveaux riches – but you might pick up the odd bargain.

Columbia Road Columbia Rd, E2; Shoreditch tube or Liverpool St tube then bus #26 or Old St tube then bus #55. Sun 8am–2pm. Fabulous flower market in the heart of the East End, with bargains galore for the serious plant-lover. Get here early, have breakfast in one of the many cafés, and take the time to check out the increasingly funky shops while you're at it. Hang around till 1pm, and you'll pick up armfuls of flowers for a few quid.

Covent Garden Apple Market, The Piazza; and Jubilee Market, off Southampton St, WC2; Covent Garden tube. Daily 10.30am–6.30pm. The Apple Market offers handmade, rather twee craft stalls, while Jubilee Market displays endless cheap T-shirts, jewellery, souvenirs and so on. On Mondays, Jubilee is taken over by an antiques market which has some more enjoyable stalls (closes 3pm).

Greenwich Greenwich High Rd, Stockwell St, and College Approach, SE10; Greenwich train station from Charing Cross or Cutty Sark DLR. Another conglomeration, but in a rather more scenic setting than Camden, and

Farmers' markets

An increasing interest in organic produce and mistrust of intensive farming have led to a boom in traditional **farmers' markets** in the last few years. Traders are generally from small operations and are non-factory and organic in orientation. Everything that is sold should have been reared, caught, pickled, preserved and processed by the stallholder and, most importantly, be organic. A few of London's best and most central are listed below; for more information see ⓦ www.farmersmarkets.net.

Blackheath Farmers' Market Blackheath station car park, SE3; Blackheath train station. Sun 10am–2pm.

Islington Farmers' Market Islington Green, Essex Rd, N1; Angel tube. Sun 10am–2pm.

Marylebone Farmers' Market Cramer St car park, off Marylebone High St, E1; Baker St or Bond St tube. Sun 10am–2pm.

Notting Hill Farmers' Market Kensington Palace car park, W8; High St Kensington tube. Sat 9am–1pm.

---

offering a relaxing day out. The covered Crafts Market on College Approach sells mostly twentieth-century antiques on a Thursday (7.30am–5pm) and handmade goods, clothes and gifts from Friday to Sunday (9.30am–5.30pm), while the Central Market, off Stockwell Street (indoor Fri & Sat 10am–5pm, Sun 10am–6pm; outdoor Sat 7am–6pm, Sun 7am–5pm), hosts funky secondhand clothes, bric-a-brac and furniture. The surrounding streets, and the shops inside the covered market, offer obscure maritime devices new and old, plus lots of secondhand books and retro clothes.

Petticoat Lane Middlesex St and around, E1; Liverpool St tube. Mon–Fri and Sun 9am–2pm. Cheap, cheerful and heaving, this famous clothes and bric-a-brac market is much like any other local offering – but much, much bigger. It is worth checking out for the cheap underwear, make-up, leather and electronic goods.

Portobello Road Portobello and Golborne roads, W10 and W11; Ladbroke Grove or Notting Hill Gate tube. Antique market Sat 4am–6pm; general market Mon–Wed 8am–6pm, Thurs 9am–1pm, Fri & Sat 7am–7pm; organic market Thurs 11am–6pm; Golborne Rd market Mon–Sat 9am–5pm. Still a great day out, probably the best way to approach Portobello is from the Notting Hill end, working your way through the antiques and bric-a-brac down to the fruit and veg stalls, and then under the Westway to the seriously hip new and secondhand clothes stalls and shops, around which local style vultures circle and swoop.

Friday is better than Saturday to pick up a bargain here. Still further up again, beyond Portobello Green, the secondhand becomes pure boot-sale material, laid out on rugs on the road. The Golborne Road market is cheaper and less crowded, with some very attractive antique and retro furniture, and other bits and pieces.

Ridley Road Ridley Rd, E8; Dalston Kingsland train station or Marble Arch tube then bus #30, or Old St tube then bus #67, #76, #149 or #236. Mon–Wed 9am–3pm, Thurs 9am–noon, Fri & Sat 9am–5pm. A great food and clothes market in the heart of Hackney, Ridley Rd,

▲ Greenwich Road Market

SHOPS AND MARKETS | Markets

like Brixton Market, is worth travelling to for the sheer diversity of goods on display. African and Caribbean fruit, veg and fish predominate, but there are also Turkish and Asian staples and a long line of shops offering fabrics, hair and beauty products, old gospel albums, cheap shoes and clothes, and much else.

Riverside Walk beneath Waterloo Bridge on the South Bank, SE1; Waterloo or Embankment tube. Sat & Sun 10am–5pm, and occasionally midweek. An attractive book market by the Thames, offering everything from current and recent fiction to obscure psychology textbooks, film theory, modern European poetry and pulp science fiction – most of it reasonably priced, although rarely a complete bargain.

Spitalfields Commercial St, between Brushfield and Lamb streets, E1; Liverpool St tube. Main market Mon–Fri 10am–4pm, Sun 9am–5pm; food market 10am–4pm. The East End's historic Victorian fruit and veg hall now houses an organic food, crafts and second-hand goods market. A hippie delight, with lots of tasty food stalls and a fabulous selection of gift ideas.

Sport

As a quick glance at the national press will tell you, **sport** in Britain is a serious matter. Many of the crucial international fixtures of the **football, rugby and cricket** seasons take place in the capital, and London also hosts one of the world's greatest tennis tournaments, the **Wimbledon** championships. London is also set to host the **2012 Olympic** Games, using several of the capital's existing venues such as Wembley, Wimbledon, Lord's and the Dome, as well as a number of new arenas built specifically for the Games in the Olympic Park in East London, including an athletics stadium, an aquatic centre and a velodrome, all of which should help to improve the city's less-than-brilliant sporting facilities. On the domestic front, **football** (soccer) is the most popular sport, and London's Chelsea and Arsenal are among England's top clubs. The rest of the sporting calendar is chock-full of other quality events, ranging from the sedate pleasures of **county cricket** to the thrills of **horse racing** on Epsom Downs. For up-to-the-minute details of sporting events in London, check *Time Out* or the *Evening Standard*, or contact the London Sportsline (℡08458/508 508, Ⓦwww.sportengland.org).

For those who'd rather compete than spectate, London offers reasonable facilities: council-run leisure centres and parks provide inexpensive access to **swimming pools, gyms, aerobics classes, tennis courts** and so forth, while a host of private establishments cater for everyone from the pool-hall shark to the amateur canoeist – even **golf** enthusiasts can find a course within the city limits.

Spectator sports

In this section we've listed details of each of the main **spectator sports** in London, including a run-through of venues. For the top international events, it can be almost impossible to track down a ticket without paying over the odds through a ticket agency, but for many fixtures you can make credit-card bookings by ringing the numbers we've given.

Should you be thwarted in your attempts to gain admission, you can often fall back on **television or radio coverage**. BBC Radio 5 Live (909 & 685 Mhz) has live commentaries on almost all major sporting events, while one of the TV channels nearly always carries live transmission of the big international rugby and cricket matches. To watch live Premiership (and some international) football, you'll need to find a TV that has the Sky satellite stations – many pubs show Sky games (sometimes on big screens) to draw in custom.

Football

English **football** (or **soccer**) is passionate, and if you have the slightest interest in the game, then catching a league or FA Cup fixture is a must. The season runs from mid-August to early May, when the **FA Cup Final** rounds things off. There are four league divisions: at the top is the twenty-club Premiership, followed by the Championship and leagues one and two. There are London clubs in every single division, with around five or six in the Premiership at any one time.

The battle between **Manchester United** and **Arsenal**, London's most successful club, provided high drama at the top of the Premiership over the last decade. However, another London club, **Chelsea**, lifted the title for the first time in fifty years in the 2004–05 season. With countless millions at their disposal thanks to their new owner, Russian oil tycoon Roman Abramovich, and the tactical acumen of manager Jose Mourinho, Chelsea look set to dominate for the foreseeable future. Tickets for most Premiership games start at £20–25 and are virtually impossible to get hold of on a casual basis: you need to book in advance, or try and see one of the European or knock-out cup fixtures. The most passionate "derby" fixture in the capital is between North London rivals Arsenal and **Tottenham Hotspur**.

The highlights of the day's best games are shown on the BBC's *Match of the Day* on Saturday and Sunday nights. Premiership fixtures usually kick off at 3pm on Saturday, though there are also one or two on Sunday (kick-off between 2 and 4pm), plus Monday and occasionally Wednesday (kick-off around 8pm); all matches apart from the Saturday kick-offs are broadcast live on Sky TV.

Since the introduction of all-seater Premiership stadiums, top-flight games have lost their reputation for tribal violence, and there's been a striking increase in the number of women and children watching the "beautiful game". Nonetheless, it's an intense business, with a lot of foul language, and being stuck in the middle of a few thousand West Ham supporters as their team goes down is not one of life's most uplifting experiences.

Major football stadiums and clubs

Arsenal 2005–06: Highbury Stadium Avenell Rd, N5 2006–07: Emirates Stadium Ashburton Grove, N7 ☏ 020/7704 4040, ⓦ www.arsenal.com; Arsenal tube.

Charlton Athletic The Valley, Floyd Rd, SE7 ☏ 020/8333 4010, ⓦ www.charlton-athletic .co.uk; Charlton train station from Charing Cross.

Chelsea Stamford Bridge, Fulham Rd, SW6 ☏ 0870/300 1212, ⓦ www.chelseafc.com; Fulham Broadway tube.

Fulham Craven Cottage, Stevenage Rd, SW6 ☏ 0870/442 1222, ⓦ www.fulhamfc.com; Putney Bridge tube.

Tottenham Hotspur White Hart Lane Stadium, High St, N15 ☏ 0870/420 5000, ⓦ www.spurs .co.uk; White Hart Lane train station from Liverpool St.

Wembley Stadium Wembley Way, Middlesex ⓦ www.wembleystadium.com; Wembley Park or Wembley Central tube. Rebuilt in 2006 at enormous expense, Wembley is the traditional venue for the FA Cup and England's home internationals.

West Ham United Upton Park, Green St, E13 ☏ 0870/112 2700, ⓦ www.whufc.co.uk; Upton Park tube or Stratford train station from Liverpool St, then bus #104.

Cricket

In the days of the Empire, the English took **cricket** to the colonies as a means of instilling the gentlemanly values of fair play while administering a sound thrashing to the natives. It hasn't quite gone according to plan in more recent times although, that said, the current England side is one of the more successful. To see the game at its best you should try to get tickets for one of the **Test matches** between England and the summer's touring team. These international matches are played in the middle of the cricket season, which runs from April to September. Two of the matches are played in London – one at **Lord's**, the home of English cricket (and the MCC – see p.338) in St John's Wood, the other at **The Oval** in Kennington. In tandem with the full-blown five-day Tests, there's also a series of **one-day internationals**, two of which are usually held in London.

Getting to see England play one of the big teams can be difficult unless you book months in advance, and tickets cost around £20–25. If you can't wangle your way into a Test, you could watch it live on television, or settle down to an inter-county match, either in the **county championship** (these are four-day games) or in one of the fast and furious **one-day competitions** – tickets cost around £10. An even more frenetic innovation, which is a great introduction to cricket, is the **Twenty20 Cup**, in which each team gets to bowl twenty overs each, over the course of just three hours. Two county teams are based in London: **Middlesex**, who play at Lord's, and **Surrey**, who play at The Oval.

Cricket grounds

Lord's St John's Wood, NW8 ☏ 020/7432 1000, ⓦ www.lords.org; St John's Wood tube.
The Oval Kennington Oval, SE11 ☏ 020/7582 6660, ⓦ www.surreycricket.com; Oval tube.

(MCC – see p.338)

Rugby

Rugby gets its name from Rugby public school, where the game mutated from football in the nineteenth century. A rugby match may at times look like a bunch of weightlifters grappling each other in the mud – as the old joke goes, rugby is a hooligan's game played by gentlemen, while football is a gentleman's game played by hooligans – but it is in reality a highly tactical and athletic sport. England's rugby team tends to represent the country with rather more success than the cricket squad, winning the World Cup in Rugby

Union as recently as 2003.

There are two types of rugby played in Britain. Thirteen-a-side **Rugby League** is a professional game played almost exclusively in the north of England. The Super League features the big-name northern clubs and one London club, the former London Broncos, now known as the **Harlequins**, who play at the Stoop Memorial Ground in Twickenham. The season runs from March to September, and games traditionally take place on Sundays at 3pm, but there are also matches on Friday and Saturday nights.

In London, however, virtually all rugby clubs play fifteen-a-side **Rugby Union**, which has upper-class associations and only became a professional sport in 1995. Two Premiership teams play in London – **Harlequins**, who play at the same stadium as their Rugby League namesake, and the more successful of the two, **Wasps**, who play in Acton. The season runs from September until May, finishing off with the Challenge Cup final. International matches are played at **Twickenham Stadium**, but unless you're affiliated to one of the one thousand clubs of the Rugby Football Union, or willing to pay well over the odds at a ticket agency, it's tough to get a ticket. A better bet is to go and see a Wasps league game, where there's bound to be an international player or two on display – you can usually get in for around £10–15.

Major rugby stadiums and clubs

Harlequins Stoop Memorial Ground, Craneford Way, Twickenham ☏ 020/8410 6000, ⓦ www .quins.co.uk; Twickenham train station from Waterloo.
London Wasps Twyford Avenue, Acton, London, W3 ☏ 020/8993 8298, ⓦ www.wasps.co.uk; Ealing Common tube.
Saracens Vicarage Rd, Watford ☏ 01923/475222, ⓦ www.saracens.com; Watford Junction or Watford High St from Euston.
Twickenham Stadium Whitton Rd, Twickenham ☏ 020/8831 6666, ⓦ www.rfu.com; Twickenham train station from Waterloo.

Tennis

Tennis in England is synonymous with **Wimbledon**, the only Grand Slam tournament to be played on grass; winning it is for many players the ultimate goal of their careers. The Wimbledon championships last a fortnight, in the last week of June and the first week of July. Most of the **tickets**, especially seats for the main show courts (Centre and No. 1), are allocated in advance to the Wimbledon Tennis Club's members, other clubs and corporate sponsors, as well as by public ballot (see below); by the time these have taken their slice there's not a lot left for the general public.

On weekdays, queues start to form around dawn – if you arrive by around 7am, you have a reasonable chance of securing one of the limited number of Centre and No. 1 court tickets held back for sale on the day. If you're there by around 9am, you should get admission to the outside courts (where you'll catch some top players in the first week of the tournament). Either way, you then have a long wait until play commences at noon. Avoid the middle Saturday, when thousands of people camp overnight – so many, in fact, numbers have now been restricted.

If you want to see big-name players in London, an easier opportunity is the Stella Artois Men's Championship at **Queen's Club** in Hammersmith, which finishes a week before Wimbledon. Many of the male tennis stars use this tournament to acclimatize themselves to British grass-court conditions. As with Wimbledon, you have to apply for tickets in advance, although there are a limited number of returns on sale at 10am each day.

For the unlucky, there's the consolation of TV coverage, which is pretty all-consuming for Wimbledon.

Tennis clubs
All England Lawn Tennis and Croquet Club
PO Box 98, Church Rd, Wimbledon, SW19

☎020/8971 2473, ⓦwww.wimbledon.com; **Southfields or Wimbledon Park tube.** For public-ballot tickets, you have to send a stamped addressed envelope to the club for an application form (available from the September preceding the championship) and return it by December 31.
Queen's Club Palliser Rd, Hammersmith, W14 ☎020/7385 3421, ⓦwww.queensclub.co.uk; **Barons Court tube.** For public-ballot tickets to the Stella Artois Championships, phone Queen's Club for the address you need in order to apply for an application form – this needs to be done by September 30 at the latest.

Horse racing

There are five **horse racecourses** within easy reach of London: **Kempton Park**, near Sunbury-on-Thames; **Sandown Park**, near Esher in Surrey; and **Windsor**, in Berkshire, which hold top-quality races on the flat (April–Sept) and over jumps (Aug–April). Not much further afield are **Ascot**, in Berkshire, and **Epsom**, in Surrey, which are the real glamour courses, hosting major races of the flat-racing season every June.

Thousands of Londoners have a day out at Epsom on Derby Day, which takes place on the first or second Saturday in June. **The Derby**, a mile-and-a-half race for three-year-old thoroughbreds, is the most prestigious of the five classics of the April to September English flat season, and is preceded by another classic, **The Oaks**, which is for fillies only. The three-day Derby meeting is as much a social ritual as a sporting event, but for sheer snobbery, nothing can match the **Royal Ascot** week in mid-June, when the Queen and selected members of the royal family are in attendance, along with half the nation's bluebloods. The best seats are the preserve of the gentry, who get dressed up to the nines for the day, but as is the case at most racecourses, the rabble are allowed into the public enclosure for a mere £5.

Racecourses

Ascot High St, Ascot, Berkshire ☎ 01344/876 876, ⓦ www.ascot.co.uk; Ascot train station from Waterloo. The jewel in the crown of English racecourses. The week-long Royal Meeting in mid-June is the one to attend and to dress up for – especially on Ladies' Day, when media attention turns to the extravagant headgear sported by the more flamboyant female spectators. The racecourse hosts less glamorous meetings throughout the rest of the year.

Epsom Epsom Downs, Surrey ☎ 01372/726311, ⓦ www.epsomderby.co.uk; Epsom Downs train station from Waterloo, London Bridge or Victoria. Derby week, in the first week of June, is when Epsom really comes alive. There are very few meetings at other times, except evening meetings at the end of June and July, and a two-day event at the end of August.

Kempton Park Staines Rd East, Sunbury-on-Thames ☎ 01932/782292, ⓦ www.kempton.co.uk; Kempton Park train station from Waterloo. This popular course has excellent facilities, including covered enclosures for inclement meetings. The majority of fixtures are run on the flat. Racing takes place all year, with evening meetings in April and from June to August. A highlight is the very popular two-day Christmas Festival, which starts on Boxing Day with the King George VI Stakes.

Sandown Park The Racecourse, Esher Station Rd, Esher ☎ 01372/463072, ⓦ www.sandown.co.uk; Esher train station from Waterloo. Hugely popular, well-equipped venue that has been frequently voted Racecourse of the Year. The annual highlight is the Whitbread Gold Cup towards the end of April, and the Coral-Eclipse Stakes in early June.

Windsor Maidenhead Rd, Windsor ☎ 01753/498400, ⓦ www.windsor-racecourse.co.uk; Windsor & Eton Riverside train station from Waterloo or Windsor Central from Paddington (change at Slough). Great location by the Thames, with Windsor Castle in view, a shuttle-boat service from central Windsor, and an unusual figure-of-eight course.

Greyhound racing

A night out at the **dogs** is still a popular pursuit in London. It's an inexpensive, often boozy spectacle: a grandstand seat costs less than £5, and all the London stadiums have one or more restaurants, some surprisingly good. Indeed, the sport has become so popular that you'd be advised to book in advance if you want to watch the races from a restaurant table, particularly around Christmas. Meetings usually start around 7.30pm and finish at 10.30pm, and generally include around a dozen races. The easiest stadium to get to is **Wimbledon**, in South London, though **Walthamstow**, in the northeast, is probably the most famous.

Greyhound tracks

Walthamstow Chingford Rd, E4 ☎ 020/8498 3300, ⓦ www.wsgreyhound.co.uk; Walthamstow tube, then bus #97.

Wimbledon Plough Lane, SW17 ☎ 0870/880 1000, ⓦ www.wimbledonstadium.co.uk; Wimbledon Park tube or Haydons Rd train station from Blackfriars.

Motorsport

The only forms of motorsport in London itself are stock–car and banger races at **Wimbledon** stadium, held every other Sunday from late August to May. The nearest track for top-class motorsport is **Brands Hatch** in Kent, which holds about eighteen big meetings between February and December, usually on Sundays and bank holidays. Brands Hatch hasn't held a Formula One race since 1986 and is unlikely to do so in future, as the regulations appear to have ruled the circuit out of contention. The track is, however, host to the **World Superbikes** series, and the **British Touring Car Championships**, which attract crowds of some thirty-five thousand, second only to the British Grand Prix at Silverstone (near Northampton).

Tracks and stadiums

Brands Hatch Fawkham, Longfield, Kent ☎ 01474/872331, ⓦ www.motorsportvision.co.uk/brands-hatch; Swanley train station from Charing Cross then taxi.

Wimbledon Stadium Plough Lane, SW17
℡ 0870/840 8905, ⓦ www.wimbledonstadium

.co.uk; Wimbledon Park tube or Haydons Rd
train station from Blackfriars.

Participating sports

The following section lists most of the **sporting activities** possible in the capital. As a rule, the most reasonably priced facilities are provided by council leisure and sports centres, all of which have membership schemes that allow you to use the facilities for free or give discounts to regular users. A year's membership tends to work out at around £30 per month (private clubs charge around twice that), but if you're only here for a short time it's unlikely to be a sensible investment, unless you intend using the gym or swimming pool twice every day. Jogging in the parks and along the embankment is free and, in good weather, very popular.

Golf

Not the most obvious urban sport, it is, nevertheless, quite possible to have a round of **golf** within the city limits. At most places, you don't need to be a member – a pay-and-play round usually costs in the region of £15 – but it's often advisable to book ahead if you're playing at the weekend. There are also a few places closer to the city centre, where you can hone your driving and putting for considerably less. In addition, two of the country's most famous golf courses lie within easy reach of London – **Sunningdale**, near Ascot, and **Wentworth**, in Surrey. Below is a selection of the city's golf courses; for more information visit ⓦ www.londongolf.info.

Lee Valley Golf Course Picketts Lock Lane, N9 ℡ 020/8803 3611; Ponders End train station from Liverpool St. Eighteen-hole course.

Regent's Park Golf School Outer Circle, Regent's Park, NW1 ℡ 020/7724 0643, ⓦ www.rpgts. co.uk; Baker St tube. Driving range, putting practice, plus lessons with the club professional.

Richmond Park Roehampton Gate, Richmond Park, SW15 ℡ 020/8876 3205; Barnes train station from Waterloo, bus #371 or #65 from Richmond tube or bus #85 from Putney Bridge tube. Two eighteen-hole courses.

Sunningdale Ridgemount Rd, Sunningdale, Ascot, Berkshire ℡ 01344/621681, ⓦ www. sunningdale-golfclub.co.uk; Sunningdale train station from Waterloo.

Wentworth Wentworth Drive, Virginia Water, Surrey ℡ 01344/842201, ⓦ www.wentworthclub. com; Virginia Water train station from Waterloo.

Ice-skating

From October to March, there's the Broadgate **outdoor ice rink** (see below), supplemented in the Christmas and New Year period with outdoor rinks at Somerset House (ⓦ www .somerset-house.org.uk) and numerous other locations around London, such as Marble Arch, the Tower of London and Hampton Court Palace. Prices for these rinks tend to be pretty high (£10 or more for a one-hour session) and advance booking absolutely essential. Otherwise, London has just one centrally located **indoor ice rink**, in Bayswater. Session times tend to vary quite a lot, but generally last for around two to three hours and cost between £5 and £7.

Alexandra Palace Ice Rink Wood Green, N22 ℡ 020/8365 4386, ⓦ www.alexandrapalace .com; Alexandra Palace train station from King's Cross. Great location high above the city in Ally Pally.

Broadgate Ice Rink Broadgate Circus, Eldon St, EC2 ℡ 020/7505 4068, ⓦ www.broadgateice .co.uk; Liverpool St tube. A little circle of ice open Oct–March. It's fun (in fine weather), but can get crowded during the weekend. Mon–Wed evenings are for "broomball" matches.

Lee Valley Ice Centre Lea Bridge Rd, E10 ℡ 020/8533 3154, ⓦ www.leevalleypark.org.uk; Clapton train station from Liverpool St. Excellent ice rink in the Walthamstow Marshes.

Leisurebox 17 Queensway, W2 ℡ 020/7229 0172; Queensway or Bayswater tube. The whole family can skate at this rink, which has ice-discos on Friday and Saturday evenings.

▲ Horse riding in Hyde Park

Horse riding

Strange though it might seem, there are places in the metropolis where you can **saddle up**, though at quite a price – £25 per hour is the average. It's usually possible to borrow a hard hat, but you must wear shoes or boots with a heel.

Hyde Park Stables 63 Bathurst Mews, W2 ☎020/7723 2813, ⊛www.hydeparkstables. com; Lancaster Gate tube. The only stables in central London, situated on the north side of Hyde Park. An hour's ride or lesson in a group costs £40–45, or £50–60 for a private lesson.

Lee Valley Riding Centre 71 Lea Bridge Rd, E10 ☎020/8556 2629, ⊛www.leevalleypark.org.uk; bus #48, #55 or #56. Stables over in northeast London by the River Lea. A one-hour class will cost £24, whereas private lessons cost from £25 upwards for half an hour.

Wimbledon Village Stables 24 High St, SW19 ☎020/8946 8579, ⊛www.wvstables.com; Wimbledon tube. Hack over the wilds of Wimbledon Common and Richmond Park for £35–40 per hour. Private lessons available from British Horse Society–approved instructors at £55–60 per hour. Closed Mon.

Boating and watersports

Although the Thames is a dangerously tidal river, and can look unappealingly dirty to boot (despite being one of the cleanest metropolitan rivers in the world), the city does offer a few opportunities for messing around on the water. You can rent a variety of rowing **boats** upstream at Richmond, where you'll find slightly calmer river waters (except either side of high tide). Local recreation areas with lakes, such as Hyde, Regent's and Battersea parks, also rent out small boats during the summer. Quite close to the centre of town, there are also non-tidal basins in the former docks, where you can indulge in a surprising variety of **watersports**. During the summer, these places can get very busy – it's always best to book ahead rather than just turn up.

Docklands Sailing & Watersports Centre West-ferry Rd, Millwall Docks, E14 ☎020/7537 2626, ⊛www.dswc.org; Crossharbour DLR. Dinghy sailing, canoeing, rowing and dragon-boat racing within sight of Canary Wharf. May–Sept daily; Oct–April Sun.

Royal Docks Waterski Club Gate 16, King George V Dock, E16 ☎020/7511 2000, ⊛www .waterskilondon.com; Silvertown train station. Waterskiing or wake-boarding at around £20 a tow, while watching the planes land at London City Airport. Phone in advance.

Tennis courts

The most reasonably priced **tennis courts** in London are those in council-run parks, which should cost £5–9 an hour outdoors, twice that for indoors; the downside is that they are rarely maintained to perfect standard. If you want to book a court in advance, you sometimes have to join the local borough's registration

35

Pool and snooker

Pool has replaced darts as the most popular pub sport in London. There are scores of pubs offering small-scale pool tables, even in the centre of the city where space is at a premium. In some places you may find it hard to get a game, as the regulars tend to monopolize the tables, but in theory the way to get a game is to lay down the fee, usually £1, on the side of the table, and then wait your turn. Some pubs operate a "winner stays on" policy, which generally means you end up paying for the privilege of being slaughtered by the local champ. Generally more pleasurable is to go to one of the city's trendy pool bars with some friends, and hire a much larger **American pool** table by the hour (£5–10). There are also much more serious **snooker halls**, which usually have both American pool and **snooker** tables, the equivalent British game. Below are a couple of friendly pool halls, plus one central establishment in the Centrepoint building where the subtle skills of snooker still prevail.

Centrepoint New Oxford St (corner of Charing Cross Rd), WC1 ☎020/7240 6886; Tottenham Court Rd tube. Very central, licensed snooker and pool club. It's a members club (£30 a year), but you can get in for £3 if the place isn't full. Tables are around £5 per hour (American pool £7 per hour). Daily 11am–6am.

Elbow Room 103 Westbourne Grove, W2 ☎020/7221 5211, ⓦwww.elbow-room.co.uk; Bayswater or Notting Hill Gate tube. The capital's trendiest pool club by far, with designer decor, purple-felt American pool tables, and better-than-average grilled fast-food and beer. There's no membership fee; you simply pay £6–10 per hour for use of the tables, depending on the time of day – get there early if you want a table. Branches in Islington, Shoreditch and Swiss Cottage. Mon–Sat noon–11pm, Sun 1–10.30pm.

The Pool 104–108 Curtain Rd, EC2 ☎020/7739 9608; Old St tube. There are just three pool tables at this retro Hoxton bar on busy Curtain Road. Table hire is £6–8 an hour – free on Sundays – and it's best to book in advance. Mon noon–11pm, Tues–Thurs noon–1am, Fri noon–2am, Sat 5.30pm–2am, Sun noon–midnight.

Ritzy's Pool Shack 16 Semley Place, SW1 ☎020/7823 5817; Victoria tube. Situated behind Victoria coach station, Ritzy's has become one of the city's trendier pool clubs, with a cocktail bar and American-style diner. It's £5 per hour for pool; membership for the 24hr snooker club downstairs is £5. Daily 11am–11.30pm.

---

scheme (£10–20 per year); we've given the phone numbers for the courts in the main central London parks. However, during the day it's generally possible to simply turn up and get a court within half an hour or so, except during July and August, when the Wimbledon tournament spurs a mass of couch potatoes into activity.

Council courts

Battersea Park SW11 ☎020/8871 7542; Battersea Park train station from Victoria.
Bishop's Park SW6 ☎020/7736 1735; Putney Bridge tube.
Highbury Fields N1 ☎020/7226 2334; Highbury & Islington tube.
Holland Park W8 ☎020/7602 2226; High St Kensington tube.

Hyde Park W2 ☎020/7262 3474; Lancaster Gate tube.
Islington Tennis Centre Market Rd, N7 ☎020/7700 1370; Caledonian Rd tube. Outdoor and indoor courts.
Paddington Recreation Ground W9 ☎020/7641 3642; Maida Vale tube.
Regent's Park NW1 ☎020/7486 4216; Regent's Park or Baker St tube.

Swimming pools, gyms and fitness centres

Below is a selection of the best-equipped and most central of London's multipurpose **fitness centres**. We haven't given the addresses of the city's many council-run swimming pools, virtually all of which now have fitness classes and gyms. Wherever you go, however, a swim will usually cost

Climbing walls

Indoor climbing centres are run by serious climbers, but as a beginner you don't need any specialist equipment since you can hire helmet, harness and footwear when you get there; you must be either a registered climber or supervised one to partake, although courses are available for beginners. Climbing has become pretty hip and trendy nowadays, nowhere more so than at the ever-popular **Castle, Green Lanes**, N4 (℡020/8211 7000, ⊛www.castleclimbing.co.uk), which is housed in an old Victorian waterboard building that looks like a hammer horror Gothic castle. Another large-scale operation is the **Westway Climbing Centre**, Crowthorne Rd, W10 (℡020/8969 0992, ⊛www.westway.org/sports/wsc/climbing), with over a hundred climbs on offer. There's also the smaller **Mile End Climbing Centre**, Haverfield Rd, E3 (℡020/8980 0289, ⊛www.mileendwall.org.uk), housed in an old pipe-bending factory in the East End.

you around £3. If you fancy an alfresco dip, then the Serpentine Lido in Hyde Park (see p.291) or the **open-air pools** on Hampstead Heath (see p.363) are your best bet.

Ironmonger Row Baths Ironmonger Row, EC1 ℡020/7253 4011; Old St tube. An old-fashioned kind of place that attracts all shapes and sizes, with a steam room, sauna, small plunge pool, masseurs, a lounge area with beds, and a large pool. Admission for a three-hour weekday morning session is a bargain at around £7 (Mon–Fri) or £11.50 (weekends). Men: Tues, Thurs & Sat 9am–6.30pm; women: Wed, Fri & Sun 10am–6.30pm. Mixed Mon.

Oasis Sports Centre 32 Endell St, WC2 ℡020/7831 1804; Covent Garden tube. Oasis has two pools, one of which is the only heated outdoor pool in central London, open in all weather. Other facilities include a gym, a health suite with sauna and sunbed, massage and squash courts. Pools: Mon–Fri 6.30am–9.30pm, Sat & Sun 9.30am–5pm.

Porchester Spa 225 Queensway, W2 ℡020/7792 3980; Bayswater or Queensway tube. Built in 1926, the Porchester is one of only two Turkish baths in central London, and is well worth a visit for the Art Deco tiling alone. Admission is around £20, and entitles you to use the saunas, steam rooms, plunge pool, Jacuzzi and swimming pool. Men: Mon, Wed & Sat 10am–10pm; women: Tues, Thurs & Fri 10am–10pm, Sun 10am–4pm. Mixed: Sun 4–10pm.

The Sanctuary 12 Floral St, WC2 ℡0870/770 3350, ⊛www.thesanctuary.co.uk; Covent Garden tube. For a day of serious self-indulgence, this women-only club in Covent Garden is the place to go for a real treat: the interior is filled with lush tropical plants and you can swim naked in the pool. It's a major investment at £40–75 for day/eve membership, but your money gets you unlimited use of the pool, Jacuzzi, sauna and steam room, plus one sunbed session. Mon, Tues, Sat & Sun 9.30am–6pm, Wed–Fri 9.30am–10pm.

36

Festivals and special events

The his chapter is simply a rundown of the principal **festivals** and **annual events** in the capital, ranging from the rituals of Royal Ascot to the sassy street party of the Notting Hill Carnival, plus a few oddities like Horseman's Sunday. Our listings cover a pretty wide spread of interests, but they are by no means exhaustive; London has an almost endless roll call of ceremonials and special shows, and for daily information, it's well worth checking *Time Out* or the *Evening Standard*.

January 1

London Parade ☎ 020/8566 8586, ⓦ www.londonparade.co.uk. To kick off the new year, a procession of floats, marching bands, clowns, American cheerleaders and classic cars wends its way from Parliament Square at noon, through the centre of London, to Berkeley Square, collecting money for charity from around one million spectators en route. Admission charge for grandstand seats in Piccadilly, otherwise free.

January 30

Commemoration of Charles the Martyr In a ceremony marking the execution of Charles I in 1649, a platoon of royalists in period costume from the Civil War Society retraces the monarch's final steps from St James's Palace to Banqueting House, placing a wreath on the spot once occupied by the scaffold (see p.62).

Late January

London International Mime Festival ☎ 020/7637 5661, ⓦ www.mimefest.co.uk. Annual mime festival that takes place in the last two weeks of January on the South Bank, and in other funky venues throughout London. It pulls in some very big names in mime, animation and puppetry.

Late January or early February

Chinese New Year Celebrations ⓦ www.chinatown-online.org.uk. Soho's Chinatown explodes in a riot of dancing dragons and firecrackers on the night of this vibrant annual celebration, and the streets and restaurants are packed to capacity.

First Sunday in February

Clowns Service ☎ 020/7254 5062. Special church service for clowns, commemorating the great Joey Grimaldi, at Holy Trinity Church, Beechwood Road E8 (Dalston Kingsland station), with a clown show afterwards in the church hall.

Shrove Tuesday (late February or early March)

Great Spitalfields Pancake Day Race ☎ 020/7375 0441. Erstwhile Spitalfields wholesale fruit and veg market is the arena for this annual bout of absurd athleticism, when anyone armed with a frying pan and pancakes is allowed to run the short but frantic course.

Late March

Head of the River Race ⓦ www.horr.co.uk. Less well known than the Oxford and Cambridge race, but much more fun, since there are over four hundred crews setting off at ten-second intervals and chasing each other from Mortlake to Putney.

Late March or early April

Oxford and Cambridge Boat Race ⓦ www .theboatrace.org. Since 1845 the rowing teams of Oxford and Cambridge universities have battled it out on a four-mile, upstream course on the Thames, from Putney to Mortlake. It's as much a social as a sporting event, and the pubs at prime vantage points pack out early. Alternatively, you can catch it on TV.

Around Easter

Oranges and Lemons Children's Service ⓣ 020/7242 8282. Thanks are given for the restoration of the bells of St Clement Dane's Church in the Strand and local children are given an orange and lemon each. The bells are rung at 9am, noon and 6pm.

Easter Monday (March or April)

London Harness Horse Parade ⓣ 01733/234451. Heavy horses pull a variety of old carriages and carts around Battersea Park, from 10am onwards; there's a bank holiday fun-fair, too.

Second/Third Sunday in April

London Marathon ⓣ 020/7902 0189, ⓦ www .london-marathon.co.uk. The world's most popular marathon, with over forty thousand masochists sweating the 26.2 miles from Greenwich Park to Westminster Bridge. Only a handful of world-class athletes enter each year; most of the competitors are club runners and obsessive flab-fighters. There's always someone dressed up as a gorilla, and you can generally spot a fundraising celebrity or two.

May Bank Holiday weekend

IWA Canal Cavalcade ⓦ www.waterways.org.uk. Lively celebration of the city's inland water-ways, held at Little Venice (near Warwick Avenue tube), with scores of decorated narrow boats, Morris dancers and lots of children's activities.

Sunday nearest to May 9

May Fayre and Puppet Festival ⓣ 020/7375 0441, ⓦ www.alternativearts.com. The garden of St Paul's Church in Covent Garden is taken over by puppet booths to commemo-rate the first recorded Punch and Judy show in England, seen by diarist Samuel Pepys in 1662.

Sunday nearest to May 11

Chestnut Sunday ⓣ 020/8979 1586, ⓦ www .royalparks.gov.uk. Parade of antique bicycles and carriages along Chestnut Avenue, with the trees in full blossom, held in Bushy Park, near Hampton Court Palace.

Sunday in mid-May

Baishakhi Mela (Bangla New Year) ⓦ www .baishakhimela.com. A colourful Bangla New Year Festival held in Brick Lane with street entertainment, fun fairs and lots of food.

Third or fourth week in May

Chelsea Flower Show ⓣ 0870/906 3781, ⓦ www.rhs.org.uk. Run by the Royal Horti-cultural Society, the world's finest horticul-tural event transforms the normally tranquil grounds of the Royal Hospital in Chelsea for four days, with a daily inundation of up to fifty thousand gardening gurus and amateurs. It's a solidly bourgeois event, with the general public admitted on the last two days only, and charged an exorbitant fee for the privilege. Tickets must be bought in advance.

Last week of May

Festival of Mind, Body and Spirit ⓣ 020/7371 9191, ⓦ www.mbsfestival.com. New Agers and the cosmically inclined gather at the Royal Horticultural Halls for this hippie hap-pening. Massage, aromatherapy, Chinese

FESTIVALS AND SPECIAL EVENTS

May 29

Oak Apple Day ☎020/7730 5282. The Chelsea Pensioners of the Royal Hospital honour their founder, Charles II, by wearing posh uniforms and decorating his statue with oak leaves, in memory of the oak tree in which the king hid after the Battle of Worcester in 1651.

Late May or early June

Beating Retreat ☎020/7414 2271. This annual display takes place on Horse Guards' Parade over three evenings, and marks the old military custom of drumming and piping the troops back to base at dusk. Soldiers on foot and horseback provide a colourful, very British ceremony which precedes a floodlit performance by the Massed Bands of the Queen's Household Cavalry.

May to September

Coin Street Festival ⓦwww.oxotower.co.uk. Hugely varied free festival, including music, dance and performance, that takes place in and around the OXO Tower, just east of the South Bank Centre.

First or second Saturday in June

Derby Day ☎01372/726311, ⓦwww .epsomderby.co.uk. Run at the Epsom race-course in Surrey, the Derby is the country's premier flat race and the beast that gets its snout over the line first is instantly worth millions. Admission prices reflect proximity to the horses and to the watching nobility. The race is always shown live on TV.

Early June

Greyhound Derby ☎020/8946 8000, ⓦwww .wimbledondogs.co.uk. Wimbledon Stadium, Plough Lane, SW17. This evening meeting is the culmination of the greyhound-racing year with optional posh black-tie dinner afterwards.

Early June

Spitalfields Festival ☎020/7377 1362, ⓦwww .spitalfieldsfestival.org.uk. Music recitals held over three weeks in Hawksmoor's Christ Church, the parish church of Spitalfields, and other venues in and around the area.

Second Saturday in June

Trooping the Colour This celebration of the Queen's official birthday (her real one is on April 21) features massed bands, gun salutes, fly-pasts and crowds of tourists and patriotic Britons paying homage. For ticket information, see p.61. Otherwise, the royal procession along the Mall allows you a glimpse for free, and there are rehearsals (minus Her Majesty) on the two preceding Saturdays.

Mid-June

Royal Ascot ☎01344/622211, ⓦwww.ascot .co.uk. A highlight of the society year, held at the Ascot racecourse in Berkshire, this high-profile meeting has the Queen and sundry royals completing a crowd-pleasing lap of the track in open carriages prior to the opening races. The event is otherwise famed for its fashion statements, especially on Ladies' Day, and there's TV coverage of both the races and the more extravagant headgear of the female racegoers.

Early June to mid-August

Royal Academy Summer Exhibition ☎020/7300 8000, ⓦwww.royalacademy.org.uk. Thousands of prints, paintings, sculptures and sketches, most by amateurs and nearly all of them for sale, are displayed at one of the city's finest galleries.

Last week in June and first week in July

Wimbledon Lawn Tennis Championships ☎020/8946 2244, ⓦwww.wimbledon.org. This Grand Slam tournament attracts the cream of the world's professionals and is one of the highlights of the sporting and social calendar. For information on how to get hold of tickets, see p.554.

Late June to mid-July

City of London Festival ☎020/7377 0540, ⓦwww.colf.org. For nearly a month, churches (including St Paul's Cathedral), livery halls and corporate buildings around the City play host to classical and jazz musicians, theatre companies and other guest performers.

June to early September

Kenwood Lakeside Concerts ⓦ www
.picnicconcerts.com. Classical concerts every
Saturday from June to early September,
held in the grounds of Kenwood House (see
p.364).

Early July

Hampton Court Flower Show ⓣ 020/8854 1317,
ⓦ www.rhs.org.uk/hamptoncourt. Organised
by the Royal Horticultural Society in the
palace grounds, this five-day international
flower extravaganza is beginning to eclipse
its sister show in Chelsea. RHS members
only on the first two days.

End June to mid-July

Greenwich & Docklands International Festival
ⓣ 020/8858 7755, ⓦ www.festival.org. Ten-day
festival of fireworks, music, dance, theatre,
art and spectacles at venues on both sides
of the river, plus a village fayre in neighbouring Blackheath.

July to August

Test Cricket Matches ⓦ www-uk.cricket
.org. The English cricket team usually plays
a series of at least five international Test
matches at home over the summer, the
second of which always takes place at
Lord's in north London (see p.553). The
best views are from the award-winning
Mound Stand, but this is generally the
domain of blazer-wearing MCC (Marylebone
Cricket Club) members; the less decorous,
more entertaining enthusiasts tend to occupy the open stands. The other four Tests
take place at a variety of venues with The
Oval, in south London, being used for the
last Test. There's always live TV coverage of
all of them.

Mid-July to mid-September

BBC Henry Wood Promenade Concerts
ⓣ 020/7589 8212, ⓦ www.bbc.co.uk/proms.
Commonly known as the Proms, this series
of nightly classical concerts at the Royal
Albert Hall is a well-loved British institution.

Mid-July

Doggett's Coat and Badge Race ⓣ 020/7361
2826, ⓦ www.watermenshall.org/dogget_race

.htm. World's oldest rowing race from
London Bridge to Chelsea, established by
Thomas Doggett, an eighteenth-century
Irish comedian, to commemorate George
I's accession to the throne. The winner
receives a Hanoverian costume and silver
badge.

Sunday nearest July 16

**Italian Procession (Festival of Our Lady of
Mount Carmel)** ⓣ 020/7235 1461. Big, boisterous Italian Catholic parade, which starts
from St Peter's Italian Church on Clerkenwell Road and roams the streets of what
used to be London's very own Little Italy
(see p.223).

Third week in July

Swan Upping ⓣ 01628/523030, ⓦ www.royal
.gov.uk. Five-day scramble up the Thames,
from Sunbury to Pangbourne, during which
liveried rowers search for swans, marking
them (on the bill) as belonging to either
the Queen, the Dyers' or the Vintners' City
liveries. At Windsor, all the oarsmen stand
to attention in their boats and salute the
Queen.

Late July

Lambeth Country Show ⓦ www.lambeth.gov.uk.
A traditional country show comes to Brixton's Brockwell Park, with traction engines,
best jam competitions, farm animals and a
cider tent.

Late July or early August

Cart Marking ⓦ www.cityoflondon.gov.uk.
Recalling a 1681 Act which restricted to
421 the number of horse-drawn carts
allowed in the City, this arcane ceremony
involves vintage vehicles congregating at
11am in Guildhall Yard in a branding ceremony organized by the Worshipful Company of Car Men.

Early August

Great British Beer Festival ⓣ 01727/867201,
ⓦ www.camra.org.uk. A five-day binge at
Olympia hosted by the Campaign for Real
Ale (CAMRA). With five hundred brews to
sample, the entrance fee is a small price to
pay to drink yourself silly.

Last bank holiday weekend in August

Notting Hill Carnival The two-day free festival in Notting Hill is the longest-running, best-known and biggest street party in Europe. Dating back forty years, Carnival is a tumult of imaginatively decorated floats, eye-catching costumes, thumping sound systems, live bands, irresistible food and huge crowds.

Saturday in early to mid-September

Great River Race ⓦ www.greatriverrace.co.uk. Hundreds of boats are rowed or paddled from Ham House, Richmond, down to Island Gardens on the Isle of Dogs. Starts are staggered and there are any number of weird and wonderful vessels taking part.

Third Sunday in September

Horseman's Sunday ☎ 020/7262 1732. In an eccentric 11.30am ceremony at the Hyde Park church of St John and St Michael, a vicar on horseback blesses a hundred or so horses; the newly consecrated beasts then parade around the neighbourhood before galloping off through the park, and later taking part in show-jumping.

Third weekend in September

Open House ⓦ www.londonopenhouse.org. A once-a-year opportunity to peek inside over four hundred buildings around London, many of which don't normally open their doors to the public. You'll need to book in advance for some of the more popular places.

First Sunday in October

Costermongers' Pearly Harvest Festival Service ☎ 020/7930 0089, ⓦ www.pearlysociety.co.uk. Cockney fruit and vegetable festival at St Martin-in-the-Fields Church. Of most interest to the onlooker are the Pearly Kings and Queens who gather at around 3pm in their traditional pearl–button–studded outfits.

First Monday in October

Judges' Service To mark the opening of the legal year the judiciary, in full regalia, attends a service at 10am in Westminster Abbey.

Afterwards they process to the House of Lords for their "Annual Breakfast".

Sunday nearest October 21

Trafalgar Day Parade ⓦ www.sea-cadets.org. Parade of sea cadets and marching bands at 11am, to commemorate the 1805 Battle of Trafalgar, culminating in wreath-laying at the foot of Nelson's Column.

Late October

Return to Camden Town ☎ 020/7916 7272, ⓦ www.returntocamden.org. Ten-day festival of traditional Irish music, song and dance featuring a great line-up of performers as well as talks and workshops.

Late October or early November

State Opening of Parliament ☎ 020/7219 3000, ⓦ www.parliament.uk. The Queen arrives by coach at the Houses of Parliament at 11am accompanied by the Household Cavalry and gun salutes. The ceremony itself takes place inside the House of Lords and is televised; it also takes place whenever a new government is sworn in.

November

London Film Festival ☎ 020/7928 3232, ⓦ www .bfi.org.uk or ⓦ www.lff.org.uk. A three-week cinematic season with scores of new international films screened at the National Film Theatre and some West End venues.

Early November

London Jazz Festival ☎ 020/7405 9900, ⓦ www.bbc.co.uk/radio3. Big ten-day international jazz fest held in all London's jazz venues, large and small, in association with BBC Radio 3.

First Sunday in November

London to Brighton Veteran Car Run ⓦ www .vccofgb.co.uk/lontobri. In 1896 Parliament abolished the Act that required all cars to crawl along at 2mph behind someone waving a red flag. Such was the euphoria in the motoring community that a rally was promptly set up to mark the occasion, and more than a century later it's still going strong. Classic cars built before 1905 set

▲ State Coach, Lord Mayor's Show

off from Hyde Park at 7.30am and travel the 58 miles to Brighton along the A23 at the heady maximum speed of 20mph.

November 5

Bonfire Night ☎ 020/8365 2121. In memory of Guy Fawkes – executed for his role in the 1605 Gunpowder Plot to blow up King James I and the Houses of Parliament – effigies of the hapless Fawkes are burned on bonfires all over Britain. There are council-run fires and firework displays right across the capital; Alexandra Palace (see p.369) provides a good vantage point from which to take in several displays at once.

Second Saturday in November

Lord Mayor's Show ⓦ www.cityoflondon.gov .uk. The newly appointed Lord Mayor begins his or her day of investiture at Westminster, leaving there at around 9am for Guildhall. At 11.10am, the vast ceremonial procession, headed by the 1756 State Coach, begins its journey from Guildhall to the Law Courts in the Strand, where the oath of office is taken at 11.50am. From there the coach and its train of 140-odd floats make their way back towards Guildhall, arriving at 2.20pm. Later in the day there's a fireworks display from a barge tethered between Waterloo and Blackfriars bridges, and a small funfair on Paternoster Square, by St Paul's Cathedral.

Nearest Sunday to November 11

Remembrance Sunday A day of nationwide commemorative ceremonies for the dead and wounded of the two world wars and other conflicts. The principal ceremony, attended by the Queen, various other royals and the prime minister, takes place at the Cenotaph in Whitehall, beginning with a march-past of veterans and building to a one-minute silence at the stroke of 11am.

Mid-November to early January

Christmas lights Assorted celebrities flick the switches, and Bond, Oxford and Regent streets are bathed in festive illumination from dusk to midnight until January 6. The lights along Oxford Street are invariably tacky, but Regent Street usually puts on a tasteful show, and there are other, less ostentatious displays in St Christopher's Place, Kensington High Street and Carnaby Street. Shop windows are dressed up for the occasion, too, with the automated displays of the big stores such as Selfridge's, Liberty and Fortnum & Mason a major seasonal attraction. Also, each year since the end of World War II, Norway has acknowledged its gratitude to the country that helped liberate it from the Nazis with the gift of a mighty spruce tree that appears in Trafalgar Square in early December. Decorated with lights, it becomes the focus for carol singing versus traffic noise each evening until Christmas Eve.

Christmas Day

Serpentine Swim Brave (or foolhardy) members of the Serpentine Swimming Club have taken an icy plunge in the Serpentine Lido every year since 1864.

December 31

New Year's Eve The New Year is welcomed en masse in Trafalgar Square as thousands of inebriated revellers stagger about and slur Auld Lang Syne at midnight. Transport for London runs free public transport all night, sponsored by various public-spirited breweries.

37

Kids' London

On first sight, London seems a hostile place for children, with its crowds, incessant noise and constant traffic. English attitudes towards children can be discouraging as well, particularly if you've experienced the more indulgent approach of the Mediterranean countries. London's restaurateurs, for example, tend to regard children as if they were one step up the evolutionary scale from rats, although the more entrepreneurial realize the power of the family/kids pound. Similarly, pubs still operate under very archaic laws meaning it's not easy to enjoy a brew if you have young ones in tow. Yet, if you pick your place carefully, even central London can be a delight for the pint-sized, and it needn't overly strain the parental pocket.

Covent Garden's buskers and jugglers provide no-cost entertainment in a car-free setting. Another great area to head for is the **South Bank** and Southwark, which are connected by a traffic-free riverside walk that stretches from the **London Eye** to Tower Bridge. And if you don't fancy the walk, there are now plenty of passenger **boats** stopping off at piers along the way.

Right in the centre of the city, there are plentiful green spaces, such as **Hyde Park** and **Regent's Park**, providing playgrounds and ample room for general mayhem, as well as a diverting array of city wildlife. If you want something more unusual than ducks and squirrels, head for one of London's several **city farms**, which provide urbanites with a free taste of country life.

Don't underestimate the value of London's **public transport** as a source of fun, either. The mere idea of an underground train gives a buzz to a lot of kids, and you can get your bearings while entertaining your offspring by installing them in the front seats on the top deck of a **red double-decker bus**. The #11 from Victoria, for instance, will trundle you past the Houses of Parliament, Trafalgar Square and the Strand on its way to St Paul's Cathedral and kids now travel free on all buses. The driverless **Docklands Light Railway** is another source of amusement, too – grab a seat at the front of the train and pretend to be driver; at Island Gardens, you can take the foot tunnel under the river to Greenwich. Another alternative is to have a ride on one of South London's trams (see p.415).

Museums are another, more obvious diversion. The good news is that admission is free to the likes of the **Science Museum**, the **Natural History Museum** and the **National Maritime Museum**. These, and other museums, have hi-tech, hands-on sections that will keep young kids busy for hours, and they might even learn something while they're at it. There are museums, too, devoted to childhood and toys, while teenage horror fans will, of course, demand to visit the **London Dungeon** and **Madame Tussaud's** Chamber of Horrors – among the most expensive sights in the entire city.

The spread of **shows** on offer – from puppet performances to specially commissioned plays – is at its best during school holidays, when even the biggest theatres often stage family entertainment. This is also the case at Christmas, when there's a glut of traditional British **pantomimes**, stage shows based on folk stories or fairy tales, invariably featuring a showbiz star or two, and often with an undercurrent of innuendo aimed at the adults. If that's too passive for you, there are plenty of indoor **play centres** where children can burn off some excess energy. The weekly listings magazine *Time Out* has details of the latest **kids' events**, and also produces *Kids Out*, a monthly listings magazine aimed at those with children.

Major attractions

Listed below are the sights that should appeal to most children. All museums contain at least something of interest for kids; the ones we've picked should evoke more than just the usual enthusiasm – some are covered in more detail in the main part of our guide, and are cross-referenced accordingly. Look out, too, for the child-oriented programmes of workshops, educational story trails, special shows and suchlike offered during school holidays.

Legoland Windsor, Berkshire ☏0870/504 0404, ⊛www.legoland.co.uk; Windsor & Eton Central train station from Paddington (change at Slough) or Windsor & Eton Riverside from Waterloo. Very expensive but enjoyable and relatively tasteful theme park with gentle rides – perfect for five- to eight-year-olds. More adventurous stuff for older kids, including Lego Racers 4D interactive experience. Easter–Oct & Christmas more or less daily 10am–5pm or later – phone to check; adults £24, children 3–15 £22.

London Aquarium County Hall, SE1 ☏020/7967 8000, ⊛www.londonaquarium.co.uk; Westminster or Waterloo tube. London's largest aquarium is on the South Bank, and is very popular with kids. There are over 350 species from sharks and piranhas to clown fish and rays. Daily dives and feeding routines to watch along with regular talks and interactive events. Daily 10am–6pm or later; adults £8.75–9.75, children 3–14 £5.25–6.25. See p.263.

London Eye South Bank, SE1 ☏0870/5000 600, ⊛www.ba-londoneye.com; Westminster or Waterloo tube. All children who don't suffer from vertigo will love the London Eye. Advance booking is recommended (though some queuing is still inevitable) and take some binoculars. Daily: April–Sept 9.30am–10pm; Oct–March 9am–8pm; adults £12.50, children 5–16 £6.50. See p.262.

London Zoo Regent's Park, NW1 ☏020/7722 3333, ⊛www.zsl.org/london-zoo; bus #274 from Camden Town or Baker Street tube, bus #C2 from Camden or Oxford Circus. Smaller kids love the children's enclosure, where they can actually handle the animals, and the regular "Animals in Action" live shows. The invertebrate house, known as BUGS, is also a guaranteed winner, as it has lots of creepy-crawlies and hands-on stuff. Daily: March–Oct 10am–5.30pm; Nov–Feb 10am–4pm; adults £14, children 3–15 £10.75. See p.342.

Syon House and Gardens Brentford, Middlesex ☏020/8560 0881, ⊛www.syonpark.co.uk; bus #237 or #267 from Gunnersbury tube. The stately home itself may not tempt the kids, but with the Butterfly House (see p.404) and the Aquatic Experience (see p.405), plus a weekend miniature steam railway in the house's lovely gardens, it's a good place for a day out. One of the most popular attractions is the Snakes and Ladders indoor play area. Daily 10am–6pm; adults free, under-5s £3–4, over-5s £4–5.

Tower of London Tower Hill, EC3 ☏0870/756 7070, ⊛www.hrp.org.uk; Tower Hill tube. The Tower is the best of the royal properties for those with kids. It's a real, moated (albeit dry) medieval castle with the Crown Jewels, ravens, and lots of arms and armour. The Beefeaters are good value, too, theatrically wallowing in the bloody history. March–Oct Mon & Sun 10am–6pm, Tues–Sat 9am–6pm; Nov–Feb closes 5pm; adults £14.50, children 5–15 £9.50. See p.213.

Big museums

Kids with an open mind will find something of interest at almost any of London's many museums. The following is a brief overview of the ones that should appeal more than most to younger visitors.

London's Transport Museum Covent Garden Piazza, WC2 ☏ 020/7565 7299, ⓦ www.ltmuseum.co.uk; Covent Garden tube. Closed for refurbishment until 2007, when the old buses, trams and tubes will form part of a thoroughly renovated museum. Daily 10am–6pm, Fri opens from 11am; adults £5.95, children under 16 free. See p.160.

National Maritime Museum Romney Road, SE10 ☏ 020/8858 4422, ⓦ www.nmm.ac.uk; Cutty Sark DLR. Most galleries are superbly designed to appeal to visitors of all ages. In addition, Level 3 boasts two hands-on galleries, "The Bridge" and "All Hands", both specifically aimed at kids. Daily 10am–5pm; free. See p.382.

Natural History Museum Cromwell Road, SW7 ☏ 020/7942 5000, ⓦ www.nhm.ac.uk; South Kensington tube. Animated dinosaurs, stuffed animals, live ants, an earthquake simulator and lots of rocks, fossils, crystals and gems keep the young ones entertained, while older kids might enjoy going behind

the scenes and meeting the scientists at the Darwin Centre. Mon–Sat 10am–5.50pm, Sun 11am–5.50pm; free. See p.312.

RAF Museum Grahame Park Way, NW9 ☏ 020/8205 2266, ⓦ www.rafmuseum.org.uk; Colindale tube. Most kids will enjoy the vast collection of planes here, as well as the hands-on Aeronauts; or explore the often overlooked display galleries, ranged around the edge of the Main Aircraft Hall, which contain an art gallery and an exhibition on the history of flight, accompanied by replicas of some of the death-traps of early aviation. Daily 10am–6pm; free. See p.371.

Science Museum Exhibition Road, SW7 ☏ 0870/870 4868, ⓦ www.sciencemuseum.org.uk; South Kensington tube. There's plenty for everyone here: hands-on fun for the little ones in the "Garden" or the "Launch Pad" in the basement, and more hi-tech gadgetry for older kids in the Wellcome Wing. The daily demonstrations are excellent, too. Daily 10am–6pm; free. See p.308.

Smaller museums

The following is a selection of the city's smaller museums that go out of their way to keep children engaged and amused.

Bethnal Green Museum of Childhood Cambridge Heath Road, E2 ☏ 020/8980 2415, ⓦ www.vam.ac.uk; Bethnal Green tube. The museum is famous for its collection of historic dolls' houses and toys, and puts on lots of weekend/holiday events and activities – it will be closed for refurbishment until November 2006. Daily except Fri 10am–5.50pm; free. See p.246.

Hackney Museum 1 Reading Lane, E8 ☏ 020/8356 3500, ⓦ www.hackney.gov.uk/hackneymuseum; Hackney Central train station. There are lots of fun, interactive displays at this modern local museum which explores the borough's diverse multicultural population. Mon, Tues, Fri 9.30am–5.30pm, Thurs 9.30am–8pm, Sat 10am–5pm; free. See p.354.

Horniman Museum London Road, SE23 ☏ 020/8699 1872, ⓦ www.horniman.ac.uk; Forest Hill train station from Victoria or London Bridge. An ethnographic and musical instrument museum primarily, but with lots to interest kids, including a new aquarium (due to open in 2006), a natural history section and lovely grounds. Daily 10.30am–5.30pm; free. See p.377.

Kew Bridge Steam Museum Green Dragon Lane, Brentford, TW8 ☏ 020/8568 4757, ⓦ www.kbsm.org; Kew Bridge train station from Waterloo or bus #237 or #267 from Gunnersbury tube. Best visited at weekends, when the engines are in steam and the miniature railway is in operation. The Water for Life gallery features plenty of grimy details on the capital's water and sewerage network that should appeal to kids. Daily 11am–5pm; adults Mon–Fri £4.25, Sat & Sun adults £5.75; children free. See p.402.

City farms

Free fun is available at the city's various working farms, the majority of them located in London's East End. The website ⊛www.farmgarden.org.uk is also worth a visit for details of other, smaller gardens and wildlife havens in London.

Brooks Farm Skelton's Lane Park, Leyton, E10 ⊕020/8539 4278; Leyton tube. Very much a community resource, this farm has pigs, Shetland ponies, llamas and more, its own allotments and an adventure playground. Daily: April–Oct 9.30am–12.30pm & 1.30–5.30pm; Nov–March closes 4.30pm.

Freightliners Farm Sheringham Road, N7 ⊕020/7609 0467, ⊛www .freightlinersfarm.org.uk; Highbury & Islington or Holloway Road tube. Small farm with cows, pigs, goats, hens, ducks, geese, sheep and giant rabbits. Tues–Sun 10am–1 & 2–4.45pm; winter closes 4pm.

Hackney City Farm 1a Goldsmith's Row, E2 ⊕020/7729 6381, ⊛www .hackneycityfarm.co.uk; Bethnal Green tube. Converted brewery that's now a small city farm, with cows, sheep, pigs, hens, turkeys, rabbits, butterflies and a donkey; also has an organic garden. Weekend kids' activities. Tues–Sun 10am–4.30pm.

Kentish Town City Farm 1 Cressfield Close, Grafton Road, NW5 ⊕020/7916 5421, ⊛www.aapi.co.uk/cityfarm; Chalk Farm or Kentish Town tube. Five acres of farmland with cows, horses, pigs, goats, sheep and chickens. Tues–Sun 9.30am–5pm.

Mudchute City Farm Pier Street, E14 ⊕020/7515 5901, ⊛www.mudchute.org; Mudchute, Crossharbour or Island Gardens DLR. Covering some 35 acres, this is London's largest city farm, with farmyard animals, llamas, pets' corner, study centre and café. Fantastic location with great views of Canary Wharf. Daily 9am–4pm.

Spitalfields Community Farm Weaver Street, E1 ⊕020/7247 8762, ⊛www. spitalfieldscityfarm.org; Shoreditch tube. Another tiny East End farm with sheep, donkeys, goats, pigs, ducks, geese, rabbits and guinea pigs. Also runs a propagation scheme and organic vegetable garden. Tues–Sun: April–Sept 10am–4.30pm; Oct–March 10am–4pm.

Stepping Stones Farm Stepney Way, E1 ⊕020/7790 8204; Stepney Green tube. A rural haven in the East End, with cows, pigs, goats, sheep, rabbits, ferrets, donkeys and guinea pigs. Also has a nature trail and toddlers play area. Tues–Sun 9.30am–dusk.

Surrey Docks Farm Rotherhithe Street, SE16 ⊕020/7237 6525; Surrey Quays tube. A corner of southeast London set aside for goats, sheep, donkeys, chickens, pigs, ducks and bees in hives. Tues–Thurs 10am–5pm, Sat & Sun 10am–1pm & 2–5pm.

Vauxhall City Farm Tyers Street, SE11 ⊕020/7582 4204; Vauxhall tube. Little city farm with sheep, pigs, ducks, ponies and donkeys. Activities at weekends and on holidays. Tues–Thurs & Sat–Sun 10.30am–4pm.

Livesey Museum 682 Old Kent Rd, SE15 ⊕020/7639 5604, ⊛www.liveseymuseum.org .uk; bus #53 or #63 from Elephant & Castle **tube.** A series of child-centred interactive exhibitions are put on at this small local museum, usually with an educational aspect to them, such as Making Maths Fun or Energy in our Daily Lives. Phone ahead to check it's open. Tues–Sat 10am–5pm; free.

Pollock's Toy Museum 1 Scala St, W1 ⊕020/7636 3452; Goodge Street **tube.** Housed above a unique toyshop specializing in toy theatres, the museum's impressive collec- tion includes a fine example of the Victorian paper theatres sold by Benjamin Pollock. Mon–Sat 10am–5pm; adults £3, children £1.50. See p.126.

Ragged School Museum Copperfield Road, E3 ⊕020/8980 6405, ⊛www.raggedschoolmuseum.org.uk; Mile End **tube.** The reconstructed Victorian school- room staffed by a Victorian schoolmistress makes kids realize what an easy life they have these days. Wed & Thurs 10am–5pm, first Sun in month 2–5pm; free. See p.244.

Parks

London is especially well endowed with open, green spaces in which children can run off some excess energy. The parks listed below are those which have additional attractions – from above-average playgrounds to animal enclosures – that should go down well with the kids.

Battersea Park Albert Bridge Road, SW11 ☎020/8871 7539 (playground), ⓦwww.batterseapark.org; Battersea Park or Queenstown Road train station from Victoria. The park has an excellent free adventure playground, a boating lake and a children's zoo (ⓦwww.batterseaparkzoo.co.uk). Playground: term time Tues–Fri 3.30pm–7pm; holidays and weekends 11am–6pm. Zoo: daily 10am–5pm; adults £4.95, children 3–12 £3.75. See p.324.

Coram's Fields 93 Guilford St, WC1 ☎020/7837 6138; Russell Square tube. Very useful, centrally located playground with lots of water and sand play plus mini-farm with ducks, sheep, rabbits, goats and chickens. Adults admitted only if accompanied by a child. Daily 9am–dusk. Free. See p.148.

Hampstead Heath NW3 ☎020/7485 4491; Hampstead tube, Gospel Oak or Hampstead Heath train station. Nine hundred acres of grassland and woodland, with superb views of the city. Excellent kite-flying potential, too, and plenty of playgrounds, sports facilities, music events and fun days throughout the summer. Open daily 24hr. See p.362.

Hyde Park/Kensington Gardens W8 ☎020/7298 2100, ⓦwww.royalparks.gov.uk; Hyde Park Corner, Knightsbridge, Lancaster Gate or Queensway tube. Hyde Park is central London's main open space and now features the Diana Fountain in which the kids can dip their feet; in Kensington Gardens, adjoining its western side, you can find the famous Peter Pan statue and a groovy playground also dedicated to Princess Diana Daily dawn–dusk. See p.285.

Kew Gardens Richmond, Surrey ☎020/8332 5000, ⓦwww.kew.org; Kew Gardens tube. Come here for the edifying open spaces, though the glasshouses usually go down well too, and there's a small aquarium in the basement of the Palm House. Daily 9.30am–7.30pm or dusk; adults £10, children under 16 free. See p.407.

Richmond Park Richmond, Surrey ☎020/8948 3209, ⓦwww.royalparks.gov.uk; Richmond tube or train station from Waterloo. A fabulous stretch of countryside, with opportunities for duck-feeding, deer-spotting, mushroom-hunting and cycling. Playground situated near Petersham Gate or toddlers play area near Kingston Gate. Daily: March–Sept 7am–dusk; Oct–Feb 7.30am–dusk. See p.412.

Theatre, puppetry and circuses

Shows that appeal to children play in the West End all the time. What follows is a pretty selective rundown of theatre, puppetry and circuses that are consistently aimed at kids. For the latest listings, check out the "Children" section of *Time Out*.

Half Moon Young People's Theatre 43 Whitehorse Road, E1 ☎020/7709 8900, ⓦwww.halfmoon.org.uk; Limehouse DLR, Stepney Green tube. Well-established theatre that hosts touring youth shows, puts on its own productions, and runs a programme of workshops and theatre sessions for over-5s. Saturday shows at 11.30am & 2pm; adults £5, under-18s £3.50.

Little Angel Theatre 14 Dagmar Passage, off

▲ Little Angel Theatre

Music

There are plenty of **free music** options worth looking out for: the Barbican (see p.511) puts on excellent weekend foyer concerts; the Royal Festival Hall (see p.511) and the National Theatre (see p.520) run regular seasonal festivals where you can catch some world-class music. In addition, most of the established orchestras run special **children's concerts**: look out for the London Philharmonic Orchestra (ⓦwww.lpo .org.uk), London Symphony Orchestra (ⓦwww.lso.co.uk) and National Children's Orchestra.

Cross Street, N1 ⓣ020/7226 1787, ⓦwww .littleangeltheatre.com; Angel tube. London's only permanent puppet theatre, with shows usually on Saturdays and Sundays at 11am and 2pm. Extra performances during holidays. No babies are admitted. Adults £7.50–8.50, children £5–6.

Polka Theatre 240 The Broadway, SW19 ⓣ020/8543 4888, ⓦwww.polkatheatre.com; Wimbledon or South Wimbledon tube. Aimed at kids aged up to around 12, this is a specially designed junior arts centre, with two theatres, a playground, a café and a toy-shop. Storytellers, puppeteers and mimes make regular appearances. Tickets £5–14 for children and adults alike.

Puppet Theatre Barge Little Venice, W2 ⓣ020/7249 6876 or 0836/202745, ⓦwww .puppetbarge.com; Warwick Avenue tube. Wonderfully imaginative marionette shows on a fifty-seater barge moored in Little Venice from November to May, then at various points along the Thames (including Richmond). Shows usually start at 3pm at weekends and in the holidays. Adults £7.50, children £7.

Tricycle Theatre 269 Kilburn High Rd, NW6 ⓣ020/7328 1000, ⓦwww.tricycle.co.uk; Kilburn tube. High-quality children's shows Sept–June Saturdays at 11.30am & 2pm. Budding thespians can also attend drama and dance workshops after school and during the holidays; for toddlers, a performance workshop/playgroup. Tickets for shows £5.

Unicorn Theatre Tooley St, SE1 ⓣ08700/ 534 534, ⓦwww.unicorntheatre.com; London Bridge. The oldest professional children's theatre in London has moved to new purpose-built premises near City Hall in Southwark. Shows run the gamut from story-telling sessions and traditional plays to creative writing workshops and mime and puppetry.

Zippo's Circus ⓣ0871/210 2100, ⓦwww .zipposcircus.co.uk. Zippo's Circus perform in and around London for most of the year. It's a totally traditional, big-top circus offering a variety of standard acts from clowning and tightrope walking to acrobatic budgies and equine tricks, compered by an old-fashioned ringmaster.

Indoor adventure play centres and swimming pools

Most local leisure centres offer "soft play" sessions for pre-school toddlers during the week. Listed below are some of the bigger operations which also cater for older children.

Bramley's Big Adventure 136 Bramley Rd, W10 ⓣ020/8960 1515, ⓦwww.bramleysbig.co.uk; Latimer Road or Ladbroke Grove tube. Indoor play centre with sophisticated equipment suitable for older and younger children and magazines for bored adults. Mon–Fri unlimited play, Sat & Sun 2hr sessions: £2.50–4.80. Daily 10am–6.30pm.

Discover 1 Bridge Terrace, E15 ⓣ020/8536 5555, ⓦwww.discover.org.uk; Stratford tube. A hands-on interactive play centre with a great outdoor play garden, aimed at story-

building for under 9s. Tues–Thurs, Sat & Sun 10am–5pm; school hols Tues–Sun 10am–5pm; £3.50.

Snakes & Ladders Syon Park, Brentford, Middlesex ⓣ020/8847 0946, ⓦwww.snakes-and -ladders.co.uk/brentford; bus #237 or #267 from Gunnersbury tube. Indoor play centre, with a giant play frame, that forms part of the great Syon Park commercial extravaganza (see p.403). Two-hour session £2–5. Daily 10am–6pm.

Spike's Madhouse Crystal Palace National Sports Centre, Anerley Hill, Upper Norwood, SE19 ☎020/8778 0131, ⓦwww.gll.org; Crystal Palace train from Victoria or London Bridge. Indoor play centre/crèche within the Crystal Palace sports complex. For 2 to 10-year-olds. £2 per hour-long session. Sat & Sun 10am–5pm.

Waterfront Leisure Centre High Street, Woolwich, SE18 ☎020/8317 5000, ⓦwww.gll.org; Woolwich Arsenal train station from Charing Cross. Massive Wild and Wet adventure swimming pool with 100ft-plus slide, wave machine, waterfall and all the usual aquatic high-jinks. Under-3s free, 3–16 from £3.35, adults £4.85. Mon–Thurs 4–8pm, Fri 4–6pm, Sat & Sun 9am–5pm.

Directory

AIDS Helpline ☎0800/567123, ⓦwww.playingsafely.co.uk.

Airport enquiries Gatwick ☎0870/000 2468, ⓦwww.baa.co.uk; Heathrow ☎0870/000 0123, ⓦwww.baa.co.uk; London City Airport ☎020/7646 0000, ⓦwww.londoncityairport.com; Luton ☎01582/405100, ⓦwww.london-luton.com; Stansted ☎0870/000 0303, ⓦwww.baa.co.uk.

Cultural institutes Austrian Cultural Forum, 28 Rutland Gate, SW7 ☎020/7584 8653, ⓦwww.austria.org.uk; Czech Centre, 13 Harley St, W1 ☎020/7307 5180, ⓦwww.czechcentres.cz/london; French Institute, 17 Queensberry Place, SW7 ☎020/7073 1350, ⓦwww.institut-francais.org.uk; Goethe Institute, 50 Princes Gate, Exhibition Rd, SW7 ☎020/7596 4000, ⓦwww.goethe.de; Hungarian Cultural Centre, 10 Maiden Lane, WC2 ☎020/7240 6162, ⓦwww.hungary.org.uk; Instituto Cervantes, 102 Eaton Square, SW1 ☎020/7235 0353, ⓦwww.londres.cervantes.es; Italian Cultural Institute, 39 Belgrave Square, SW1 ☎020/7235 1461, ⓦwww.italcultur.org.uk.

Dentists Emergency treatment: Guy's Hospital, St Thomas St, SE1 ☎020/7188 0511 (Mon–Fri 9am–5pm); London Bridge tube.

Doctor Walk-in consultation: Great Chapel Street Medical Centre, Great Chapel St, W1 ☎020/7437 9360 (phone for surgery times).

Electricity Electricity supply in London conforms to the EU standard of approximately 230V.

Emergencies For police, fire and ambulance services, call ☎999.

Hospitals For 24hr accident and emergency: Charing Cross Hospital, Fulham Palace Rd, W6 ☎020/8846 1234; Chelsea & Westminster Hospital, 369 Fulham Rd, SW10 ☎020/8746 8000; Royal Free Hospital, Pond St, NW3 ☎020/7794 0500; Royal London Hospital, Whitechapel Rd, E1 ☎020/7377 7000; St Mary's Hospital, Praed St, W2 ☎020/7886 6666; University College London Hospital, Grafton Way, WC1 ☎020/7387 9300; Whittington Hospital, Highgate Hill, N19 ☎020/7272 3070.

Left luggage

Airports Gatwick: North Terminal ☎01293/502013 (daily 5am–9pm); South Terminal ☎01293/502014 (24hr). Heathrow: Terminal 1 ☎020/8745 5301 (daily 6am–11pm); Terminal 2 ☎020/8745 4599 (daily 5.30am–11pm); Terminal 3 ☎020/8759 3344 (daily 5am–11pm); Terminal 4 ☎020/8897 6874 (daily 5.30am–11pm). London City ☎020/7646 0000 (daily 6am–9pm). Stansted ☎0870/000 0303 (24hr).

Train stations Charing Cross ☎020/7402 8444 (daily 7am–11pm); Euston ☎020/7387 1499 (daily 7am–11pm); Victoria ☎020/7963 0957 (daily 7am–midnight); Waterloo International ☎020/7401 8444 (daily 7am–10pm).

Library Westminster Central Reference Library, 35 St Martin's St, WC2 ☎020/7641 1300, ⓦwww.westminster.gov.uk; Leicester Square tube. Mon–Fri 10am–8pm, Sat 10am–5pm.

Lost property

Airports Gatwick ☎01293/503162 (Mon–Sat 8am–7pm, Sun 8am–4pm); Heathrow ☎020/8745 7727 (daily 8am–4pm); London City ☎020/7646 0000 (Mon–Sat 5.30am–9pm, Sun 10am–9pm); Stansted ☎0870/000 0303 (daily 6am–midnight).

Buses ☎020/7222 1234, ⓦwww

.londontransport.co.uk (24hr).

Heathrow Express ☎0845/600 1515, ⓦwww.heathrowexpress.co.uk (daily 8am–4pm).

Taxis (black cabs only) ☎020/7833 0966 (Mon–Fri 9am–4pm).

Train stations (ⓦwww.networkrail. co.uk): Euston ☎020/7387 8699 (Mon–Fri 9am–5.30pm); King's Cross ☎020/7278 3310 (Mon–Sat 9am–5pm; Liverpool St ☎020/7247 4297 (Mon–Fri 9am–5.30pm); Paddington ☎020/7313 1514 (Mon–Fri 9am–5.30pm); Victoria ☎020/7963 0957 (daily 7am–11pm); Waterloo ☎020/7401 8444 (Mon–Fri 7am–11pm).

Tube Transport for London ☎020/7486 2496, ⓦwww.tfl.gov.uk.

Motorbike rental Raceways, 201–203 Lower Rd, SE16 ☎020/7237 6494 (Surrey Quays tube) and 17 The Vale, Uxbridge Rd, W3 ☎020/8749 8181 (Shepherds Bush tube), ⓦwww.raceways.net. Mon–Sat 9am–5pm.

Police Central police stations include: Charing Cross, Agar St, WC2 ☎020/7240 1212; Holborn, 10 Lambs Conduit St, WC1 ☎020/7704 1212; Marylebone, 1–9 Seymour St W1 ☎020/7486 1212; West End Central, 27 Savile Row, W1 ☎020/7437 1212, ⓦwww.met.police.uk; City of London Police, Bishopsgate, EC2 ☎020/7601 2222 ⓦwww.cityoflondon.police.uk

Public holidays You'll find all banks and offices closed on the following days (while everything else pretty much runs to a Sunday schedule): New Year's Day (January 1); Good Friday (late March/early April); Easter Monday (late March/early April); Spring Bank Holiday (first Monday in May); May Bank Holiday (last Monday in May); August Bank Holiday (last Monday in August); Christmas Day (December 25); Boxing Day (December 26). Note that if January 1, December 25 or December 26 falls on a Saturday or Sunday, the holiday falls on the following weekday.

Rape crisis ☎020/8683 3300, ⓦwww .rapecrisis.co.uk; Mon–Fri noon–2.30pm & 7–9.30pm, Sat & Sun 2.30–5pm.

Samaritans Drop-in at 46 Marshall St, W1 ☎020/7734 2800 (24hr) or ☎08457/909090, ⓦwww.samaritans.org; daily 9am–9pm.

Time Greenwich Mean Time (GMT) is used from the end of October to the end of March; for the rest of the year the country switches to British Summer Time (BST), one hour ahead of GMT.

Train enquiries For national rail enquiries, call ☎08457/484950, ⓦwww.nationalrail.co.uk.

Travel agents STA Travel, 33 Bedford St, WC2 ☎020/7240 9821, ⓦwww.statravel .co.uk; Trailfinders, Lower Ground Floor,

Contexts

Contexts

History

The citizens of London are universally held up for admiration and renown for the elegance of their manners and dress, and the delights of their tables...The only plagues of London are the immoderate drinking of fools and the frequency of fires.

William Fitzstephen, companion of Thomas Becket

Conflagrations and drunkenness certainly feature strongly in London's complex two-thousand-year history. What follows is a highly compressed account featuring riots and revolutions, plagues, fires, slum clearances, lashings of gin, Ken Livingstone and the London people. For more detailed histories, see p.603.

Legends

Until Elizabethan times, most Londoners believed that London had been founded around 1000 BC as New Troy or *Troia Nova* (later corrupted to Trinovantum), capital of Albion (aka Britain), by the Trojan prince **Brutus**. At the time, according to medieval chronicler Geoffrey of Monmouth, Britain was "uninhabited except for a few giants", several of whom the Trojans subsequently killed. They even captured one called Goemagog (more commonly referred to as Gogmagog), who was believed to be the son of Poseidon, Greek god of the sea, and whom one of the Trojans, called Corineus, challenged to unarmed combat and defeated.

For some reason, by late medieval times, Gogmagog had become better known as two giants, **Gog and Magog**, whose statues can still be seen in the Guildhall (see p200) and on the clock outside St Dunstan-in-the-West (see p186). According to Geoffrey of Monmouth's elaborate genealogical tree, Brutus is related to Leir (of Shakespeare's *King Lear*), Arthur (of the Round Table) and eventually to **King Lud**. Around 70 BC, Lud is credited with fortifying New Troy and renaming it *Caer Ludd* (Lud's Town), which was later corrupted to Caerlundein and finally London.

So much for etymology and mythology. Archeologists and historians tell a different story, and though there is evidence of scattered Celtic settlements along the Thames, no firm proof exists to show that central London was permanently settled before the arrival of the Romans.

Roman Londinium

Julius Caesar led several small cross-Channel incursions in 55 and 54 BC, but it wasn't until nearly a century later, in **43 AD**, that a full-scale invasion force of some forty thousand Roman troops landed in Kent. Britain's rumoured mineral wealth was certainly one motive behind the Roman invasion, but the immediate spur was the need of the emperor Claudius, who owed his power to the army, for an easy military triumph. The Romans defeated the main Celtic tribe of southern Britain, the Catuvellauni, on the Medway, southeast of London, crossed the Thames and then set up camp to await the triumphant arrival of the emperor Claudius, his elephants and the Praetorian Guard.

It's now thought that the site of this first Roman camp was, in fact, in Westminster – the lowest fordable point on the Thames – and not in what is now the City. However, around 50 AD, when the Romans decided to establish the permanent military camp of **Londinium** here, they chose a point further downstream, building a bridge some 50 yards east of today's London Bridge. London became the hub of the Roman road system, but it was not the Romans' principal colonial settlement, which remained at **Camulodunum** (modern Colchester) to the northeast.

In 60 AD, the East Anglian people, known as the Iceni, rose up against the invaders under their queen **Boudicca** (or Boadicea) and sacked Camulodunum, slaughtering most of the legion sent from Lindum (Lincoln) and making their way to the ill-defended town of Londinium. According to archeological evidence, Londinium was burnt to the ground and, according to the Roman historian, Tacitus, whose father-in-law was in Britain at the time (and later served as its governor), the inhabitants were "massacred, hanged, burned and crucified". The Iceni were eventually defeated, and Boudicca committed suicide (62 AD).

In the aftermath, Londinium emerged as the new commercial and administrative (though not military) capital of Britannia, and was endowed with an imposing basilica and forum, a governor's palace, temples, bathhouses and an amphitheatre (see p.202). Archeological evidence suggests that Londinium was at its most prosperous and populous from around 80 AD to 120 AD, during which time it is thought to have evolved into the empire's fifth largest city north of the Alps.

Between 150 AD and 400 AD, however, London appears to have sheltered less than half the former population, probably due to economic decline. Nevertheless, it remained strategically and politically important and, as an imperial outpost, actually appears to have benefited from the chaos that engulfed the rest of the empire during much of the third century. In those uncertain times, fortifications were built, three miles long, 15ft high and 8ft thick, with a large fort, whose ragstone walls can still be seen near today's Museum of London (see p.199), home to many of the city's most significant Roman finds. From 260 AD London formed part of the breakaway "Empire of the Gauls", while from 287 AD to 296 AD it became the capital of the short-lived British Empire, first under Emperor Carausius, and then by his assassin, Allectus.

In the fourth century, London found itself, once again, at the heart of various military revolts by would-be emperors, most notably Magnus Maximus, who in 383 AD led a rebellion in Britain, and marched off to eventual defeat some five years later. In 406 AD, the Roman army in Britain mutinied for the last time and invaded Gaul under the self-proclaimed Emperor Constantine III. The empire was on its last legs, and the Romans were never in a position to return, officially abandoning the city in 410 AD (when Rome was sacked by the Visigoths), and leaving the country and its chief city at the mercy of the marauding Saxon pirates, who had been making increasingly persistent raids on the coast since the middle of the previous century.

Saxon Lundenwic and the Danes

Roman London appears to have been more or less abandoned from the first couple of decades of the fifth century until the ninth century. Instead, the **Anglo-Saxon** invaders, who controlled most of southern England by the sixth century, appear to have settled, initially at least, to the west of the Roman city. When Augustine was sent to reconvert Britain to Christianity, the Saxon city of **Lundenwic** was considered important enough to be granted a bishopric, in 604, though it was Canterbury, not London, that was chosen as the seat of the Primate of England. Nevertheless, trade flourished once more during this period, as attested by the Venerable Bede, who wrote of London in 730 as "the mart of many nations resorting to it by land and sea".

In 841 and 851 London suffered Danish Viking attacks, and it may have been in response to these raids that the Saxons decided to reoccupy the walled Roman city. By 871 the **Danes** were confident enough to attack and established London as their winter base, but in 886 Alfred the Great, King of Wessex, recaptured the city, rebuilt the walls and formally re-established London as a fortified town and a trading port. After a lull, the Vikings returned once more during the reign of Ethelred the Unready (978–1016), attacking unsuccessfully in 994, 1009 and 1013. The following year, the Danes, under Swein Forkbeard, finally recaptured London, only for Ethelred to reclaim it later that year, with help from King Olaf of Norway. In 1016, following the death of Ethelred, and his son, Edmund Ironside, the Danish leader Cnut (or Canute), son of Swein, became King of All England, and made London the national capital (in preference to the Wessex base of Winchester), a position it has held ever since.

Danish rule lasted only 26 years, and with the death of Cnut's two sons, the English throne returned to the House of Wessex, and to Ethelred's exiled son, **Edward the Confessor** (1042–66). Edward moved the court and church upstream to Thorney Island (or the Isle of Brambles), where he built a splendid new palace so that he could oversee construction of his "West Minster" (later to become Westminster Abbey). Edward was too weak to attend the official consecration and died just ten days later: he is buried in the great church he founded, where his shrine has been a place of pilgrimage for centuries. Of greater political and social significance, however, was his geographical separation of power, with royal government based in **Westminster**, while the **City of London** remained the commercial centre.

1066 and all that

On his deathbed in the new year of 1066, the celibate Edward made Harold, Earl of Wessex, his appointed successor. Having crowned himself in the new abbey – establishing a tradition that continues to this day – Harold went on to defeat his brother Tostig (who was in cahoots with the Norwegians), but was himself defeated by **William of Normandy** (aka William the Conqueror) and his invading army at the Battle of Hastings. On Christmas Day of 1066, William crowned himself king in Westminster Abbey. Elsewhere in England, the Normans ruthlessly suppressed all opposition, but in London, William granted the City a charter guaranteeing to preserve the privileges it had enjoyed under Edward. However, as an insurance policy, William also built three forts in the city, of which the sole remnant is the White Tower, now the nucleus of the **Tower of London**. As a further precaution, he also established another castle, a day's march away at **Windsor** and, like his predecessor, Edward, based the court at Westminster.

Over the next few centuries, the City waged a continuous struggle with the monarchy for a degree of self-government and independence. After all, when there was a fight over the throne, the support of London's wealth and manpower could be decisive, as **King Stephen** (1135–54) discovered, when Londoners attacked his cousin and rival for the throne, Mathilda, daughter of Henry I, preventing her from being crowned at Westminster. Again, in 1191, when the future **King John** (1199–1216) was tussling with William Longchamp over the kingdom during the absence of Richard the Lionheart (1189–99), it was the Londoners who made sure Longchamp remained cooped up in the Tower. For this particular favour, London was granted the right to elect its own sheriff, or lord mayor, an office that was officially acknowledged in the Magna Carta of 1215.

Occasionally, however, Londoners backed the wrong side, as they did with Simon de Montfort, who was engaged in civil war with **Henry III** (1216–72) during the 1260s. As a result, the City found itself temporarily stripped of its privileges. In any case, London was chiefly of importance to the medieval kings as a source of wealth, and traditionally it was to the Jewish community, which arrived in 1066 with William the Conqueror, that the sovereign turned for a loan. By the second half of the thirteenth century, however, the Jews had been squeezed dry, and in 1290, after a series of increasingly bloody attacks, **London's Jews** were expelled by Edward I (1272–1307), who turned instead to the City's Italian merchants for financial assistance.

From the Black Death to the Wars of the Roses

London backed the right side in the struggle between Edward II (1307–27) and his queen, Isabella, who, along with her lover Mortimer, succeeded in deposing the king. The couple's son Edward III (1327–77) was duly crowned, and London enjoyed a period of relative peace and prosperity, thanks to the wealth generated by the wool trade. All this was cut short, however, by the arrival of the Europe-wide bubonic plague outbreak, known as the **Black Death**, in 1348. This disease, carried by black rats and transmitted to humans by flea bites, wiped out something like two-thirds of the capital's 75,000 population in the space of two years. Other epidemics followed in 1361, 1369 and 1375, creating a volatile economic situation that was worsened by the financial strains imposed on the capital by having to bankroll the country's involvement in the Hundred Years' War with France.

Matters came to a head with the introduction of the poll tax, a head tax imposed in the 1370s on all men regardless of means. During the ensuing **Peasants' Revolt** of 1381, London's citizens opened the City gates to Wat Tyler's Kentish rebels and joined in the lynching of the archbishop, plus countless rich merchants and clerics. Tyler was then lured to meet the boy-king Richard II at Smithfield, just outside the City, where he was murdered by Lord Mayor Walworth, who was subsequently knighted for his treachery. Tyler's supporters were fobbed off with promises of political changes that never came, as Richard unleashed a wave of repression and retribution.

Parallel with this social unrest were the demands for clerical reforms made by the scholar and heretic **John Wycliffe**, whose ideas were keenly taken up by Londoners. His followers, known as **Lollards**, made the first translation of the Bible into English in 1380. Another sign of the elevation of the common language was the success enjoyed by Geoffrey Chaucer (c.1340–1400), a London wine merchant's son, whose *Canterbury Tales* was the first major work written in English and was later one of the first books to be printed.

After the Peasants' Revolt, the next serious disturbance was **Jack Cade's Revolt**, which took place in 1450. An army of 25,000 Kentish rebels – including gentry, clergy and craftsmen – defeated King Henry VI's forces at Sevenoaks, marched to Blackheath, withdrew temporarily and then eventually reached Southwark in early July. Having threatened to burn down London Bridge, the insurgents entered the City and spent three days wreaking vengeance on their enemies before being ejected. A subsequent attempt to enter the City via London Bridge was repulsed, and the army was dispersed with yet more false promises. The reprisals, which became known as the "harvest of heads", were as harsh as before – Cade himself was captured, killed and brought to the capital for dismemberment.

A decade later, the country was plunged into more widespread conflict during the so-called **Wars of the Roses**, the name now given to the strife between the rival noble houses of Lancaster and York. Londoners wisely tended to sit on the fence throughout the conflict, only committing themselves in 1461, when they opened the gates to the Yorkist king Edward IV (1461–70 and 1471–83), thus helping him to depose the mad Henry VI (1422–61 and 1470–71). In 1470, Henry, who had spent five years in the Tower, was proclaimed king once more, only to be deposed again a year later, following Lancastrian defeats at the battles of Barnet and Tewkesbury.

Tudor London

The **Tudor** family, which with the coronation of **Henry VII** (1485–1509) emerged triumphant from the mayhem of the Wars of the Roses, reinforced London's pre-eminence during the sixteenth century, when the Tower of London and the royal palaces of Whitehall, St James's, Richmond, Greenwich, Hampton Court and Windsor provided the backdrop for the most momentous events of the period. At the same time, the city's population, which had remained constant at around 50,000 since the Black Death, increased dramatically, trebling in size during the course of the century.

One of the crucial developments of the century was the English **Reformation**, the separation of the English Church from Rome, a split initially prompted not by doctrinal issues, but by the failure of Catherine of Aragon, first wife of **Henry VIII** (1509–47), to produce a male heir. In fact, prior to his desire to divorce Catherine, Henry, along with his lord chancellor, Cardinal Wolsey, had been zealously persecuting Protestants. However, when the Pope refused to annul Henry's marriage, Henry knew he could rely on a large amount of popular support, as anti-clerical feelings were running high. By contrast, Henry's new chancellor, Thomas More, wouldn't countenance divorce, and resigned in 1532. Henry then broke with Rome, appointed himself head of the English Church and demanded both citizens and clergy swear allegiance to him. Very few refused, though More was among them, becoming the country's first Catholic martyr with his execution in 1535.

Henry's most far-reaching act, by far, though, was his **Dissolution of the Monasteries**, a programme commenced in 1536 in order to bump up the royal coffers. The Dissolution changed the

▲ The Globe Theatre c. 1812

entire fabric of both the city and the country: previously dominated by its religious institutions, London's property market was suddenly flooded with confiscated estates, which were quickly snapped up and redeveloped by the Tudor nobility.

Henry may have been the one who kickstarted the English Reformation, but he was, in fact, a religious conservative, and in the last ten years of his reign he succeeded in executing as many Protestants as he did Catholics. Religious turmoil only intensified in the decade following Henry's death. First, Henry's sickly son, **Edward VI** (1547–53), pursued a staunchly anti-Catholic policy. By the end of his short reign, London's churches had lost their altars, their paintings, their relics and virtually all their statuary. After an abortive attempt to secure the succession of Edward's Protestant cousin, Lady Jane Grey, the religious pendulum swung the other way for the next five years with the accession of "**Bloody Mary**" (1553–58). This time, it was Protestants who were martyred with abandon at Tyburn and Smithfield.

Despite all the religious strife, the Tudor economy remained in good health for the most part, reaching its height in the reign of **Elizabeth I** (1558–1603), when the piratical exploits of seafarers Walter Ralegh, Francis Drake, Martin Frobisher and John Hawkins helped to map out the world for English commerce. London's commercial success was epitomized by the millionaire merchant Thomas Gresham, who erected the **Royal Exchange** in 1572, establishing London as the premier world trade market.

The 45 years of Elizabeth's reign also witnessed the efflorescence of a specifically **English Renaissance**, especially in the field of literature, which reached its apogee in the brilliant careers of **Christopher Marlowe**, **Ben Jonson** and **William Shakespeare**. The presses of **Fleet Street**, established a century earlier by William Caxton's apprentice Wynkyn de Worde, ensured London's position as a centre for the printed word. Beyond the jurisdiction of the City censors, in the entertainment district of Southwark, whorehouses, animal-baiting pits and theatres flourished. The carpenter-cum-actor James Burbage designed the first purpose-built playhouse in 1576, eventually rebuilding it south of the river as the **Globe Theatre**, where Shakespeare premiered many of his works (the theatre has since been reconstructed; see p.273).

From Gunpowder Plot to Civil War

On Elizabeth's death in 1603, James VI of Scotland became **James I** (1603–25) of England, thereby uniting the two crowns and marking the beginning of the **Stuart dynasty**. His intention of exercising religious tolerance after the anti-Catholicism of Elizabeth's reign was thwarted by the public outrage that followed the **Gunpowder Plot** of 1605, when Guy Fawkes and a group of Catholic conspirators were discovered attempting to blow up the king at the state opening of Parliament. James, who clung to the medieval notion of the divine right of kings, inevitably clashed with the landed gentry who dominated Parliament, and tensions between Crown and Parliament were worsened by his persecution of the Puritans, an extreme but increasingly powerful Protestant group.

Under James's successor, **Charles I** (1625–49), the animosity between Crown and Parliament came to a head. From 1629 to 1640 Charles ruled without the services of Parliament, but was forced to recall it when he ran into problems in Scotland, where he was attempting to subdue the Presbyterians. Faced with extremely antagonistic MPs, Charles attempted unsuccessfully to arrest several of their number at Westminster. Acting on a tip-off, the MPs fled by river to the City, which sided with Parliament. Charles withdrew to Nottingham, where he raised his standard, the opening military act of the **Civil War**.

London was the key to victory for both sides, and as a Parliamentarian stronghold it came under attack almost immediately from Royalist forces. Having defeated the Parliamentary troops to the west of London at Brentford in November 1642, the way was open for Charles to take the capital. Londoners turned out in numbers to defend their city, some twenty-four thousand assembling at Turnham Green. A stand-off ensued, Charles hesitated and in the end withdrew to Reading, thus missing his greatest chance of victory. A complex system of fortifications was thrown up around London, but was never put to the test. In the end, the capital remained intact throughout the war, which culminated in the execution of the king outside Whitehall's Banqueting House in January 1649.

For the next eleven years England was a **Commonwealth** – at first a true republic, then, after 1653, a Protectorate under **Oliver Cromwell**, who was ultimately as impatient of Parliament and as arbitrary as Charles had been. London found itself in the grip of the Puritans' zealous laws, which closed down all theatres, enforced observance of the Sabbath and banned the celebration of Christmas, which was considered a papist superstition.

Plague and fire

Just as London proved Charles I's undoing, so its ecstatic reception of **Charles II** (1660–85) helped ease the **Restoration** of the monarchy in 1660. The "Merry Monarch" immediately caught the mood of the public by opening up the theatres, and he encouraged the sciences by helping the establishment of the **Royal Society** for Improving Natural Knowledge, whose founder members included **Christopher Wren**, **John Evelyn** and **Isaac Newton**.

The Great Fire

In the early hours of September 2, 1666, the **Great Fire** broke out at Farriner's, the king's bakery in Pudding Lane. The Lord Mayor refused to lose any sleep over it, dismissing it with the line "Pish! A woman might piss it out." Pepys was also roused from his bed, but saw no cause for alarm. Four days and four nights later, the Lord Mayor was found crying "like a fainting woman", and Pepys had fled, having famously buried his Parmesan cheese in the garden: the Fire had destroyed some four-fifths of London, including 87 churches, 44 livery halls and 13,200 houses. The medieval city was no more.

Miraculously, there were only nine recorded fatalities, but 100,000 people were made homeless. "The hand of God upon us, a great wind and a season so very dry", was the verdict of the parliamentary report on the Fire, but Londoners preferred to blame Catholics and foreigners. The poor baker eventually "confessed" to being an agent of the pope and was executed, after which the following words, "but Popish frenzy, which wrought such horrors, is not yet quenched", were added to the Latin inscription on the Monument, and only erased in 1831.

The good times that rolled in the early period of Charles's reign came to an abrupt end with the onset of the **Great Plague** of 1665. Epidemics of bubonic plague were nothing new to London – there had been major outbreaks in 1593, 1603, 1625, 1636 and 1647 – but the combination of a warm summer and the chronic overcrowding of the city proved calamitous in this instance. Those with money left the city (the court moved to Oxford), while the poorer districts outside the City were the hardest hit. The extermination of the city's dog and cat population – believed to be the source of the epidemic – only exacerbated the situation by allowing the flea-carrying rat population to explode. In September, the death toll peaked at twelve thousand a week, and in total an estimated hundred thousand lost their lives.

A cold snap in November extinguished the plague, but the following year London had to contend with yet another disaster, the **Great Fire** of 1666. As with the plague, outbreaks of fire were fairly commonplace in London, whose buildings were predominantly timber-framed, and whose streets were narrow, allowing fires to spread rapidly.

Within five years, nine thousand houses had been rebuilt with bricks and mortar (timber was banned), and fifty years later **Christopher Wren** had almost single-handedly rebuilt all the City churches and completed the world's first Protestant cathedral, **St Paul's**. Medieval London was no more, though the grandiose masterplans of Wren and other architects had to be rejected due to the legal intricacies of property rights within the City. The **Great Rebuilding**, as it was known, was one of London's most remarkable achievements – and all achieved in spite of a chronic lack of funds, a series of very severe winters and continuing wars against the Dutch.

Religious differences once again came to the fore with the accession of Charles's Catholic brother, **James II** (1685–88), who successfully put down the Monmouth Rebellion of 1685, but failed to halt the "Glorious Revolution" of 1688, which brought the Dutch king William of Orange to the throne, much to most people's relief. **William** (1689–1702) and his wife **Mary** (1689–95), daughter of James II, were made joint sovereigns, having agreed to a Bill of Rights defining the limitations of the monarch's power and the rights of his or her subjects. This, together with the Act of Settlement of 1701 – which among other things barred Catholics, or anyone married to one, from succession to the throne – made Britain the first country in the world to be governed by a **constitutional monarchy**, in which the roles of legislature and executive were separate and interdependent. A further development during the reign of **Anne** (1702–14), second daughter of James II, was the Act of Union of 1707, which united the English and Scottish parliaments.

Georgian London

When Queen Anne died childless in 1714 (despite having given birth seventeen times), the Stuart line ended, though pro-Stuart or Jacobite rebellions continued on and off until 1745. In accordance with the Act of Settlement, the succession passed to a non-English-speaking German, the Duke of Hanover, who became **George I** (1714–27) of England. As power leaked from the monarchy, the king ceased to attend cabinet meetings (which he couldn't understand anyway), his place being taken by his chief minister. Most prominent among these chief ministers or "prime ministers", as they became known, was **Robert Walpole**, the first politician to live at **10 Downing Street**, and effective ruler of the country from 1721 to 1742.

Meanwhile, London's expansion continued unabated. The shops of the newly developed **West End** stocked the most fashionable goods in the country, the volume of trade more than tripled, and London's growing population – it was by now the largest city in the world, with a population rapidly approaching one million – created a huge market for food and other produce, as well as fuelling a building boom. In the City, the **Bank of England** – founded in 1694 to raise funds to conduct war against France – was providing a sound foundation for the economy. It could not, however, prevent the mania for financial speculation that resulted in the fiasco of the **South Sea Company**, which in 1720 sold shares in its monopoly of trade in the Pacific and along the east coast of South America. The "bubble" burst when the shareholders took fright at the extent of their own investments, and the value of the shares dropped to nothing, reducing many to penury and almost wrecking the government, which was saved only by the astute intervention of Walpole.

Wealthy though London was, it was also experiencing the worst mortality rates since records began in the reign of Henry VIII. Disease was rife in the overcrowded immigrant quarter of the East End and other slum districts, but the real killer during this period was **gin**. It's difficult to exaggerate the effects of the gin-drinking orgy which took place among the poorer sections of London's population between 1720 and 1751. At its height, gin consumption was averaging two pints a week for every man, woman and child, and the burial rate exceeded the baptism rate by more than 2:1. The origins of this lay in the country's enormous surplus of corn, which had to be sold in some form or another to keep the landowners happy. Deregulation of the distilling trade was Parliament's answer, thereby flooding the urban market with cheap, intoxicating liquor, which resulted in an enormous increase in crime, prostitution, child mortality and general misery among the poor. Papers in the Old Bailey archives relate a typical story of the period: a mother who "fetched her child from the workhouse, where it had just been 'new-clothed', for the afternoon. She strangled it and left it in a ditch in Bethnal Green in order to sell its clothes. The money was spent on gin." Eventually, in the face of huge vested interests, the government was forced to pass an Act in 1751 that restricted gin retailing and brought the epidemic to a halt.

Policing the metropolis was an increasing preoccupation for the government. It was proving a task far beyond the city's three thousand beadles, constables and nightwatchmen, who were, in any case, "old men chosen from the dregs of the people who have no other arms but a lantern and a pole", according to one French visitor. As a result, crime continued unabated throughout the eighteenth century, so that, in the words of Horace Walpole, one was "forced to travel even at noon as if one was going into battle". The government imposed draconian measures, introducing capital punishment for the most minor misdemeanours. The prison population swelled, transportations began, and 1200 Londoners were hanged at Tyburn's gallows.

Despite such measures, and the passing of the Riot Act in 1715, rioting remained a popular pastime among the poorer classes in London. Anti-Irish riots had taken place in 1736; in 1743 there were further riots in defence of cheap liquor; and in the 1760s there were more organized mobilizations by supporters of the great agitator **John Wilkes**, calling for political reform. The most serious insurrection of the lot, however, were the **Gordon Riots** of 1780, when up to fifty thousand Londoners went on a five-day rampage through the city. Although anti-Catholicism was the spark that lit the fire, the majority of the rioters' targets were chosen not for their religion but for their wealth. The most dramatic incidents took place at Newgate Prison, where thousands of inmates were freed, and at the Bank of England, which was saved only by the intervention of the military – and John Wilkes, of all people. The death toll was in excess of three hundred, 25 rioters were subsequently hanged, and further calls were made in Parliament for the establishment of a proper police force.

Nineteenth-century London

The **nineteenth century** witnessed the emergence of London as the capital of an empire that stretched across the globe. The world's largest enclosed **dock system** was built in the marshes to the east of the City, Tory reformer **Robert Peel** established the world's first civilian **police force**, and the world's first public transport network was created, with horse-buses, trains, trams and an underground railway.

The city's population grew dramatically from just over one million in 1801 (the first official census) to nearly seven million by 1901. **Industrialization** brought pollution and overcrowding, especially in the slums of the East End. Smallpox, measles, whooping cough and scarlet fever killed thousands of working-class families, as did the cholera outbreaks of 1832 and 1848–49. The **Poor Law** of 1834 formalized **workhouses** for the destitute, but these failed to alleviate the problem, in the end becoming little more than prison hospitals for the penniless. It is this era of slum life and huge social divides that Dickens evoked in his novels.

Architecturally, London was changing rapidly. **George IV** (1820–30), who became Prince Regent in 1811 during the declining years of his father, George III, instigated several grandiose projects that survive to this day. With the architect **John Nash**, he laid out London's first planned processional route, Regent Street, and a prototype garden city around **Regent's Park**. The Regent's Canal was driven through the northern fringe of the city, and Trafalgar Square began to take shape. The city already boasted the first secular public museum in the world, the **British Museum**, and in 1814 London's first public art gallery opened in the suburb of Dulwich, followed shortly afterwards by the National Gallery, which was founded in 1824. London finally got its own university, too, in 1826.

The accession of **Queen Victoria** (1837–1901) coincided with a period in which the country's international standing reached unprecedented heights, and as a result Victoria became as much a national icon as Elizabeth I had been. Though the intellectual achievements of Victoria's reign were immense – typified by the publication of Darwin's *The Origin of Species* in 1859 – the country saw itself above all as an imperial power founded on industrial and commercial prowess. Its spirit was perhaps best embodied by the great engineering feats of **Isambard Kingdom Brunel** and by the **Great Exhibition** of 1851, a display of manufacturing achievements from all over the world, which took place in the Crystal Palace, erected in Hyde Park.

Despite being more than twice the size of Paris, London did not experience the political upheavals of the French capital – the terrorists who planned to wipe out the cabinet in the **1820 Cato Street Conspiracy** were the exception (see p.105). Mass demonstrations and the occasional minor fracas preceded the passing of the **1832 Reform Act**, which acknowledged the principle of popular representation (though few men and no women had the vote), but there was no real threat of revolution. London doubled its number of MPs in the new parliament, but its own administration remained dominated by the City oligarchy.

The **Chartist movement**, which campaigned for universal male suffrage (among other things), was much stronger in the industrialized north than in the capital, at least until the 1840s. Support for the movement reached its height in the revolutionary year of 1848. In March, some ten thousand Chartists occupied Trafalgar Square and held out against the police for two days. Then, on April 10, the Chartists organized a mass demonstration on Kennington Common. The government panicked and drafted in eighty thousand "special constables" to boost the capital's four thousand police officers, and troops were garrisoned around all public buildings. In the end, London was a long way off experiencing a revolution: the demo took place, but the planned march on Parliament was called off.

The birth of local government

The first tentative steps towards a cohesive form of metropolitan government were taken in 1855 with the establishment of the **Metropolitan Board of Works** (MBW). Its initial remit only covered sewerage, lighting and street maintenance, but it was soon extended to include gas, fire services, public parks and slum clearance. The achievements of the MBW – and in particular those of its chief engineer, **Joseph Bazalgette** – were immense, creating an underground sewer system (much of it still in use), improving transport routes and wiping out some of the city's more notorious slums. However, vested interests and resistance to reform from the City hampered the efforts of the MBW, which was also found to be involved in widespread malpractice.

In 1888 the **London County Council** (LCC) was established. It was the first directly elected London-wide government, though as ever the City held on jealously to its independence (and in 1899, the municipal boroughs were set up deliberately to undermine the power of the LCC). The arrival of the LCC coincided with an increase in working-class militancy within the capital. In 1884, 120,000 gathered in Hyde Park to support the ultimately unsuccessful London Government Bill, while a demonstration held in 1886 in Trafalgar

Square in protest against unemployment ended in a riot through St James's. The following year the government banned any further demos, and the resultant protest brought even larger numbers to Trafalgar Square. The brutality of the police in breaking up this last demonstration led to its becoming known as "Bloody Sunday".

In 1888 the Bryant & May matchgirls won their landmark **strike action** over working conditions, a victory followed up the next year by further successful strikes by the gasworkers and dockers. Charles Booth published his seventeen-volume *Life and Labour of the People of London* in 1890, providing the first clear picture of the social fabric of the city and shaming the council into action. In the face of powerful vested interests – landlords, factory owners and private utility companies – the LCC's Liberal leadership attempted to tackle the enormous problems, partly by taking gas, water, electricity and transport into municipal ownership, a process that took several more decades to achieve. The LCC's ambitious housing programme was beset with problems, too. Slum clearances only exacerbated overcrowding, and the new dwellings were too expensive for those in greatest need. Rehousing the poor in the suburbs also proved unpopular, since there was a policy of excluding pubs, traditionally the social centre of working-class communities, from these developments.

While half of London struggled to make ends meet, the other half enjoyed the fruits of the richest nation in the world. Luxury establishments such as The Ritz and Harrods belong to this period, which was personified by the dissolute and complacent Prince of Wales, later **Edward VII** (1901–10). For the masses, too, there were new entertainments to be enjoyed: music halls boomed, public houses prospered, and the circulation of populist newspapers such as the *Daily Mirror* topped one million. The first "Test" cricket match between England and Australia took place in 1880 at the Kennington Oval in front of twenty thousand spectators, and during the following 25 years nearly all of London's professional football clubs were founded.

From World War I to World War II

Public patriotism peaked at the outbreak of **World War I** (1914–18), with crowds cheering the troops off from Victoria and Waterloo stations, convinced the fighting would all be over by Christmas. In the course of the next four years London experienced its first aerial attacks, with Zeppelin raids leaving some 650 dead, but these were minor casualties in the context of a war that destroyed millions of lives and eradicated whatever remained of the majority's respect for the ruling classes.

At the war's end in 1918, the country's social fabric was changed drastically as the voting franchise was extended to all men aged 21 and over and to women of 30 or over. The tardy liberalization of women's rights – largely due to the radical **Suffragette** movement led by Emmeline Pankhurst and her daughters – was not completed until 1928, the year of Emmeline's death, when women were at last granted the vote on equal terms with men.

Between the wars, London's population increased dramatically, reaching close to nine million by 1939, and representing one-fifth of the country's population. In contrast to the nineteenth century, however, there was a marked shift in population out into the **suburbs**. Some took advantage of the new "model dwellings" of LCC estates in places such as Dagenham in the east, though far more settled in "Metroland", the sprawling new suburban districts that followed the extension of the Underground out into northwest London.

In 1924 the **British Empire Exhibition** was held, with the intention of emulating the success of the Great Exhibition. Some 27 million people visited the show, but its success couldn't hide the tensions that had been simmering since the end of the war. In 1926, a wage dispute between the miners' unions and their bosses developed into the **General Strike**. For nine days, more than half a million workers stayed away from work, until the government called in the army and thousands of volunteers to break the strike.

The economic situation deteriorated even further after the crash of the New York Stock Exchange in 1929, with unemployment in Britain reaching over three million in 1931. The Jarrow Marchers, the most famous protesters of the Depression years, shocked London on their arrival in 1936. In the same year thousands of British fascists tried to march through the predominantly Jewish East End, only to be stopped in the so-called **Battle of Cable Street** (see p.237). The end of the year brought a crisis within the Royal Family, too, when Edward VIII abdicated following his decision to marry Wallis Simpson, a twice-divorced American. His brother, **George VI** (1936–52), took over.

There were few public displays of patriotism with the outbreak of **World War II** (1939–45), and even fewer preparations were made against the likelihood of aerial bombardment. The most significant step was the evacuation of six hundred thousand of London's most vulnerable citizens (mostly children), but around half that number had drifted back to the capital by the Christmas of 1939, the midpoint of the "phoney war". The Luftwaffe's bombing campaign, known as the **Blitz** lasted from September 1940 to May 1941. Further carnage was caused towards the end of the war by the pilotless V-1 "doodlebugs" and V-2 rockets, which caused another twenty thousand casualties.

The Blitz

The Luftwaffe bombing of London in World War II – commonly known as the **Blitz** – began on September 7, 1940, when in one night alone some 430 Londoners lost their lives, and over 1600 were seriously injured. It continued for 57 consecutive nights, then intermittently until the final and most devastating attack on the night of May 10, 1941, when 550 planes dropped over 100,000 incendiaries and hundreds of explosive bombs in a matter of hours. The death toll that night was over 1400, bringing the total killed during the Blitz to between 20,000 and 30,000, with some 230,000 homes wrecked. Along with the East End, the City was particularly badly hit: in a single raid on December 29 (dubbed the "Second Fire of London"), 1400 fires broke out across the Square Mile. Some say the Luftwaffe left St Paul's standing as a navigation aid, but it came close to destruction when a bomb landed near the southwest tower; luckily the bomb didn't go off, and it was successfully removed to the Hackney marshes where the 100ft-wide crater left by its detonation is still visible.

The authorities were ready to build mass graves for potential victims, but were unable to provide adequate air-raid shelters to prevent widespread carnage. The corrugated steel **Anderson shelters** issued by the government were of use to only one in four London households – those with gardens in which to bury them. Around 180,000 made use of the tube, despite initial government reluctance, by simply buying a ticket and staying below ground. The cheery photos of singing and dancing in the Underground which the censors allowed to be published tell nothing of the stale air, rats and lice that folk had to contend with. And even the tube stations couldn't withstand a direct hit, as occurred at Bank in January 1941, when over a hundred died. The vast majority of Londoners – some sixty percent – simply hid under the sheets and prayed.

Postwar London

The end of the war in 1945 was followed by a general election, which brought a landslide victory for the Labour Party under **Clement Attlee**. The Attlee government created the **welfare state**, and initiated a radical programme of **nationalization**, which brought the gas, electricity, coal, steel and iron industries under state control, along with the inland transport services. London itself was left with a severe accommodation crisis, with some eighty percent of the housing stock damaged to some degree. In response, prefabricated houses were erected all over the city, some of which were to remain occupied for well over forty years. The LCC also began building huge housing estates on many of the city's numerous bombsites, an often misconceived strategy which ran in tandem with the equally disastrous New Towns policy of central government.

To lift the country out of its gloom, the **Festival of Britain** was staged in 1951 on derelict land on the south bank of the Thames, a site that was eventually transformed into the South Bank Arts Centre. Londoners turned up at this technological funfair in their thousands, but at the same time many were abandoning the city for good, starting a slow process of population decline that has continued ever since. The consequent labour shortage was made good by mass **immigration** from the former colonies, in particular the Indian subcontinent and the West Indies. The first large group to arrive was the 492 West Indians aboard the SS *Empire Windrush*, which docked at Tilbury in June 1948. The newcomers, a large percentage of whom settled in London, were given small welcome, and within ten years were subjected to **race riots**, which broke out in Notting Hill in 1958.

The riots are thought to have been carried out, for the most part, by "Teddy Boys", working-class lads from London's slum areas and new housing estates, who formed the city's first postwar youth cult. Subsequent cults, and their accompanying music, helped turn London into the epicentre of the so-called **Swinging Sixties**, the Teddy Boys being usurped in the early 1960s by the "Mods", whose sharp suits came from London's Carnaby Street. Fashion hit the capital in a big way, and, thanks to the likes of The Beatles, The Rolling Stones and Twiggy, London was proclaimed hippest city on the planet on the front pages of *Time* magazine.

Life for most Londoners, however, was rather less groovy. In the middle of the decade London's local government was reorganized, the LCC being supplanted by the **Greater London Council** (GLC), whose jurisdiction covered a much wider area, including many Tory-dominated suburbs. As a result, the Conservatives gained power in the capital for the first time since 1934, and one of their first acts was to support a huge urban motorway scheme that would have displaced as many people as did the railway boom of the Victorian period. Luckily for London, Labour won control of the GLC in 1973 and halted the plans. The Labour victory also ensured that the Covent Garden Market building was saved for posterity, but this ran against the grain. Elsewhere, whole swathes of the city were pulled down and redeveloped, and many of London's worst tower blocks were built.

Thatcherite London

In 1979 **Margaret Thatcher** won the general election for the Conservatives, and the country and the capital would never be quite the same again. Thatcher went on to win three general elections, steering Britain into a period of ever greater social polarization. While taxation policies and easy credit fuelled a consumer boom for the professional classes (the yuppies of the 1980s), the erosion of the manufacturing industry and weakening of the welfare state created a calamitous number of people trapped in long-term unemployment, which topped three million in the early 1980s. The Brixton riots of 1981 and 1985 and the Tottenham riot of 1985 were reminders of the price of such divisive policies, and of the long-standing resentment and feeling of social exclusion rife among the city's black youth.

Nationally, the Labour Party went into sharp decline, but in London the party won a narrow victory in the GLC elections on a radical manifesto that was implemented by its youthful new leader **Ken Livingstone**, or "Red Ken" as the tabloids dubbed him. Under Livingstone, the GLC poured money into projects among London's ethnic minorities, into the arts and, most famously, into a subsidized fares policy which saw thousands abandon their cars in favour of inexpensive public transport. Such schemes endeared Livingstone to the hearts of many Londoners, but his popular brand of socialism was too much for the Thatcher government, who, in 1986, abolished the GLC, leaving London as the only European capital without a directly elected body to represent it.

Abolition exacerbated tensions between the poorer and richer boroughs of the city. Rich Tory councils like Westminster proceeded to slash public services and sell off council houses to boost Tory support in marginal wards. Meanwhile in impoverished Labour-held Lambeth and Hackney, millions were being squandered by corrupt council employees. **Homelessness** returned to London in a big way for the first time since Victorian times, and the underside of Waterloo Bridge was transformed into a "Cardboard City", sheltering up to two thousand vagrants on any one night. Great efforts were made by non-governmental organisations to alleviate homelessness, not least the establishment of a weekly magazine, the *Big Issue*, which continues to be sold by the homeless right across London, earning them a small wage.

At the same time as homelessness and unemployment were on the increase, the so-called "**Big Bang**", which abolished a whole range of restrictive practices on the Stock Exchange, took place. The immediate effect of this deregulation was that foreign banks began to take over brokers and form new, competitive conglomerates. The side effect, however, was to send stocks and shares into the stratosphere, shortly after which they inevitably crashed, ushering in a recession that dragged on for the best part of the next ten years.

The one great physical legacy of the Thatcherite experiment in the capital is the **Docklands** development, which came about as a direct result of the Big Bang. Aimed at creating a new business quarter in the derelict docks of the East End, Docklands was hampered from the start by the Tories' blind faith in "market forces" and their refusal to help fund proper public-transport links. Unable to find tenants for more than fifty percent of the available office space in the Canary Wharf development, the Canadian group Olympia & York had to call in the receivers just as the recession began to bite. Docklands finally got its tube in 1999 and, with the recession over, is now gradually being completed (see p.254).

Thatcher's greatest folly, however, was the introduction of the **Poll Tax**, a head tax levied regardless of means, which hit the poorest sections of the community hardest. The tax also highlighted the disparity between the city's boroughs. In wealthy, Tory-controlled Wandsworth, Poll Tax bills were zero, while those in poorer, neighbouring, Labour-run Lambeth were the highest in the country. In 1990, the Poll Tax provoked the first full-blooded riot in central London for a long, long time, and played a significant role in Thatcher's downfall later that year.

Twenty-first century London

On the surface at least, **twenty-first-century London** has come a long way since the bleak Thatcher years. Funded by money from the National Lottery and the Millennium Commission, the face of the city has certainly changed for the better: a new pedestrian bridge now links the City with Tate Modern, the British Museum boasts a new covered courtyard, both opera houses have been totally refurbished, Somerset House features a stunning new public fountain and each one of the national museums has totally transformed themselves into state-of-the-art visitor attractions. Less successful were the millennial celebrations focused on the Dome, built and stuffed full of gadgetry for £750 million, but a critical and commercial failure.

The most significant political development for London has been the creation of the **Greater London Assembly** (GLA), along with an American-style Mayor of London, both elected by popular mandate. The Labour government, which came to power on a wave of enthusiasm in 1997, did everything they could to prevent the election of the former GLC leader Ken Livingstone, but, despite being forced to leave the Labour Party and run as an independent, he won a resounding victory in the 2000 mayoral elections.

The mayor has continued to grab the headlines, not always for the right reason, but, once again, the greatest impact he has had is on **transport**. As well as creating more bus routes, introducing bendy buses and backing new tram projects, he managed to push through the introduction of a **congestion charge** for every vehicle entering central London (see p.37). In a bold move that many thought would finish his political career, he achieved a significant reduction in traffic levels in central London, and confounded his many critics. The congestion charge hasn't solved all London's problems, but at least it showed that, with a little vision and perseverance, something concrete could be achieved.

The mayor was also instrumental in helping London win the **2012 Olympics** (see p.245). The bid emphasized its regenerative potential for a deprived, multicultural area of London's East End and, against all the odds, beat Paris in the final head-to-head vote. For a moment, London celebrated wildly. Unfortunately, the euphoria was all too brief. A day after hearing the news about the Olympics, on **July 7, 2005**, London was hit by four **suicide bombers** who killed themselves and over fifty innocent commuters in four separate explosions: on tube trains at Aldgate, Edgware Road and King's Cross and one on a bus in Tavistock Square. Two weeks later a similar attack was unsuccessful after the bombers' detonators failed. The response of Londoners was typically stoical, though in private many sought alternative means of transport and an air of uncertainty entered the capital. It remains to be seen whether these are isolated incidents, or the beginning of a concerted campaign.

London in film

As early as 1889 Wordsworth Donisthorpe made a primitive motion picture of Trafalgar Square, and since then London has been featured in countless films. The chronological selection below ranges from studio re-creations of a city that never existed, to films shot on location from Soho to the suburbs. The cinema may not always have reflected London's diversity, but it has been capable of giving fresh life to some old myths, and of showing some of the lesser-known sides and unexpected sights of the city.

Broken Blossoms (D.W. Griffith, 1919). Limehouse melodrama about a peace-loving Chinaman (Richard Barthelmess), the girl who loves him (Lillian Gish) and her brutal prizefighter father (Donald Crisp). Remarkable for its display of Griffith's technique and for Gish's incandescent performance.

The Lodger (Alfred Hitchcock, 1926). "The first true Hitchcock movie" (according to Hitchcock), and one of the first of many variations on a Jack-the-Ripper theme, here given the "wrong man" twist much favoured by the director.

Piccadilly (E.A. Dupont, 1929). British potboiler made with Germanic style, with Anna May Wong caught in the East–West divide as she moves from Chinatown poverty to clubland luxury.

Underground (Anthony Asquith, 1929). Technically innovative pre-talkie, set on and around the Northern Line and culminating with a fight in Battersea Power Station.

Die Dreigroschenoper (G.W. Pabst, 1931). An un-Brechtian treatment of Brecht and Weill's update of *The Beggar's Opera*, featuring the legendary Lotte Lenya and a stylized re-creation of turn-of-the-century London. The film retained enough political bite to be banned on its initial British release.

Dr Jekyll and Mr Hyde (Rouben Mamoulian, 1931). Still the best version of this oft-filmed story, with Fredric March in the title parts. Set in Paramount's chiaroscuro re-creation of a repressive Victorian London, and made with an assured cinematic style.

Death at Broadcasting House (Reginald Denham, 1934). A conventional but clever whodunit given curiosity value on account of being set at the heart of the BBC.

The Man Who Knew Too Much (Alfred Hitchcock, 1934). Witty and pacy thriller about assassination-plotting anarchists, with Peter Lorre in fine, villainous form, and a nice use of settings (an East End mission house, the Royal Albert Hall). Hitchcock directed a glossier remake in 1956.

Drôle de Drame (Marcel Carné, 1936). A French attempt to poke fun at the British love of detective stories, set in a peculiar London designed by art director Alexander Trauner. Also known, appropriately enough, as *Bizarre, Bizarre*.

They Drive by Night (Arthur Woods, 1938). An atmospheric tale set in a world of Soho clubs and Great North Road transport caffs. Emlyn Williams stars as a petty thief on the run; Ernest Thesiger excels as a sinister sex-murderer.

The Adventures of Sherlock Holmes (Alfred Werker, 1939). The Baker Street Detective has made countless screen appearances, but Basil Rathbone remains the most convincing incarnation. Here Holmes and Watson (Nigel Bruce) are pitted against Moriarty (George Zucco), out to steal the Crown Jewels.

Fires Were Started (Humphrey Jennings, 1942). A re-creation of a day in a firefighter's life during the Blitz. One of several vivid and highly individual films documenting English life in wartime, made by Jennings in his too-brief career.

This Happy Breed (David Lean, 1944). Interwar saga of Clapham life taken from Noël Coward's play, with the emphasis on community values and ordinary, British decency. Enormously popular in its day.

Waterloo Road (Sidney Gilliat, 1944). Worried about his wife's infidelity, a soldier goes AWOL. South-of-the-river melodrama with realist touches, and John Mills and Stewart Granger literally fighting out their differences.

Hangover Square (John Brahm, 1945). Not an address listed in the streetfinder, and having next to nothing to do with the Patrick Hamilton novel it was nominally based on, but an atmospheric Hollywood thriller, in which Laird Cregar plays a schizophrenic composer living in gas-lit Chelsea.

London Town (Wesley Ruggles, 1946). A big-budget Technicolor musical that brought music-hall comedian Sid Field to the screen and aimed to bring Hollywood style to postwar Britain. It ended up a commercial and critical disaster.

Hue and Cry (Charles Crichton, 1947). Boys' Own adventure story featuring Jack Warner as a dubious Covent Garden trader, Alistair Sim as a timid writer of blood-and-thunder stories, and hoards of juvenile crime-fighters. Good use is made of the bomb-damaged locations.

It Always Rains on Sunday (Robert Hamer, 1947). An escaped convict (John McCallum) hides out in the Bethnal Green home of his former girlfriend (Googie Withers). Tense, fatalistic drama with a strong sense of place.

Oliver Twist (David Lean, 1948). An effective distillation of key elements of the Dickens novel, featuring Alec Guinness as a caricaturist's Fagin and a stylized re-creation of early nineteenth-century London from art director John Bryan.

Passport to Pimlico (Henry Cornelius, 1948). The quintessential Ealing Comedy, in which the inhabitants of Pimlico, discovering that they are actually part of Burgundy, abolish rationing and closing time. Full of all the usual eccentrics, among them Margaret Rutherford in particularly fine form as an excitable history don.

Spring in Park Lane (Herbert Wilcox, 1948). One of a series of refined romances directed by Wilcox, and pairing his real-life wife Anna Neagle (austerity Britain's most popular star) with Michael Wilding, here playing an impoverished nobleman who takes a job as a footman.

The Blue Lamp (Basil Dearden, 1949). Metropolitan police drama introducing genial PC Dixon (Jack Warner) and charting the hunt for his killer (bad boy Dirk Bogarde). Now seems to come from another world, but its location photography was ground-breaking at the time.

Dance Hall (Charles Crichton, 1950). An evocative melodrama centred round the life and loves of four working-class women who spend their Saturday nights at the Chiswick Palais dancing to the sound of Ted Heath and his music.

Night and the City (Jules Dassin, 1950). London-set film noir, with Richard Widmark as a hustler on the run in an expressionistic city. Made when Dassin was himself escaping from McCarthyite America, and probably his best film.

Seven Days to Noon (Robert Boulting, 1950). Nightmares about the arms race lead a scientist (Barry Jones) to threaten to blow up London.

Tense Cold War drama that gives an eerie view of the evacuated city.

Limelight (Charles Chaplin, 1952). Chaplin's final American film was a return to his London roots – a sentimental re-creation of poverty and music-hall life. Claire Bloom features as the ballerina whose career is promoted by Calvero (Chaplin), and there's a cameo from Buster Keaton.

The Ladykillers (Alexander Mackendrick, 1955). Delightfully black comedy set somewhere at the back of King's Cross (a favourite location for film-makers). Katie Johnson plays the nice old lady getting the better of Alec Guinness, Peter Sellers and assorted other crooks.

Every Day Except Christmas (Lindsay Anderson, 1957). Short, lyrical and somewhat idealized documentary about work and the workers at Covent Garden.

Nice Time (Claude Goretta, Alain Tanner, 1957). An impressionistic view of Piccadilly Circus on a Saturday night, made by two Swiss film-makers and released, like Anderson's film, under the banner of "Free Cinema".

Beat Girl (Edmond Gréville, 1959). Also known as *Wild for Kicks*, this dated drama of teen rebellion marks Adam Faith's film debut and contains an early glimpse of Oliver Reed's smouldering skills. Notable for a wild party scene in Chislehurst Caves.

Expresso Bongo (Val Guest, 1959). A musical "comedy" in which smooth-talking agent Johnny Jackson (Laurence Harvey) takes "Bongo Herbert" (Cliff Richard) all the way from the coffee bars of Soho to the dizzy heights of fame.

Sapphire (Basil Dearden, 1959). A body discovered on Hampstead Heath is revealed to be that of a black woman passing for white. A worthy but fascinating "problem picture" that takes on rather more (black subculture, white racism and sexual repression) than it can deal with.

Peeping Tom (Michael Powell, 1960). A timid London cameraman (Carl Boehm) films women as he murders them. A discomforting look at voyeurism, sadism and watching movies; reviled on its original release, but latterly recognized as one of the key works of British cinema.

The Day the Earth Caught Fire (Val Guest, 1961). London swelters as the earth edges towards the sun following nuclear tests. A solidly British science-fiction film based around the (then) Fleet Street headquarters of the *Daily Express*.

Gorgo (Eugene Lourié, 1961). A creature from the ocean floor is exhibited at Battersea Funfair, until its mother comes to take it home, knocking down assorted London monuments on her way. An enjoyably tacky variation on the old monster-in-the-city theme.

One Hundred and One Dalmatians (Wolfgang Reitherman, Hamilton S. Luske, Clyde Geromini, 1961). Disney's classic of animal liberation, in which the eponymous dogs do Scotland Yard's work, unmasking an unfriendly plot to turn puppies into fur coats. Villainess Cruella de Vil still manages to steal the show.

Sparrers Can't Sing (Joan Littlewood, 1962). Chirpy, cheeky, Cockney comedy set in the East End in which merchant seamen (James Booth) comes home to find his wife (Barbara Windsor) living with another man.

It Happened Here (Kevin Brownlow, Andrew Mollo, 1963). A shoestring production, filmed in and around London, that imagines Britain in 1944 after a successful German invasion. An anti-fascist film that refused to see people in terms of simple heroes and villains.

The Pumpkin Eater (Jack Clayton, 1964). Pinter-scripted story of middle-class, midlife crisis unravelling in St John's Wood, Regent's Park Zoo and Harrods. Anne Bancroft is excellent as the mother of eight cracking under the strain.

Bunny Lake is Missing (Otto Preminger, 1965). Laurence Olivier plays a policeman searching the city for Carol Lynley's daughter. An accomplished psychological thriller with a creepy cameo from Noël Coward.

Four in the Morning (Anthony Simmons, 1965). This film started out as a documentary about the Thames, but evolved into a low-key drama about relationships and marital breakdown in the small hours of the morning.

The Ipcress File (Sidney J. Furie, 1965). An attempt to create a more down-to-earth variety of spy thriller, with Michael Caine as bespectacled Harry Palmer, stuck in a London of offices and warehouses rather than the exotic locations of the Bond films.

Repulsion (Roman Polanski, 1965). A study of the sexual fears and mental disintegration of a young Belgian woman left alone in a Kensington flat. Polanski's direction and Catherine Deneuve's performance draw the audience into the claustrophobic nightmares of the central character.

Alfie (Lewis Gilbert, 1966). Cockney wide boy Alfie Elkins (Michael Caine) has assorted affairs, and talks about them straight to the camera. An un-feminist comedy taken from Bill Naughton's play.

Blow-Up (Michelangelo Antonioni, 1966). Swinging London and some less obvious backgrounds (notably Maryon Park, Charlton) feature in this metaphysical mystery about a photographer (David Hemmings) who may unwittingly have recorded evidence of a murder.

The Deadly Affair (Sidney Lumet, 1966). Downbeat adaptation of a John Le Carré novel concerning an investigation into the supposed suicide of a Foreign Office diplomat. One of a number of thrillers portraying London as a city of repressed secrets.

Georgy Girl (Silvio Narizzano, 1966). A comedy of mismatched couples enlivened by excellent performances from Lynn Redgrave (as plain but loveable Georgy) and Charlotte Rampling (as her beautiful but cold flatmate).

Morgan, A Suitable Case for Treatment (Karel Reisz, 1966). A schizophrenic artist (David Warner) with a gorilla fixation attempts to win back his divorced wife (Vanessa Redgrave). The "madman as hero" message is rather swamped by the modish, 1960s humour.

Tonite Let's All Make Love in London (Peter Whitehead, 1967). Documentary on the "Swinging London" phenomenon, including music from The Animals, an interview with Allen Ginsberg and a happening at Alexandra Palace. Of its time.

Up the Junction (Peter Collinson, 1967). Middle-class Polly (Suzy Kendall) moves from Chelsea to ungentrified Battersea. Adapted from Nell Dunn's novel, this well-intentioned attempt to put working-class London on the big screen lacked the commitment and vitality of Ken Loach's earlier television version.

One Plus One (Jean-Luc Godard, 1968). A deliberately disconnected mix of footage of The Rolling Stones, assorted Black Power militants in a Battersea junkyard and "Eve Democracy" talking about culture and revolution. Also released as *Sympathy for the Devil*, with a complete version of the Stones number; Godard wasn't pleased.

The Strange Affair (David Greene, 1968). Made at the sour end of the 1960s, and set in a London of office blocks and multistorey car parks, this effectively gloomy police thriller stars

Michael York as an innocent police-man in a corrupt world.

Leo the Last (John Boorman, 1969). Whimsical, sometimes striking fantasy set in a crumbling Notting Hill terrace, where stateless prince Marcello Mastroianni gradually begins to identify with his neighbours.

Performance (Nicolas Roeg, Donald Cammell, 1969). A sadistic gangster (James Fox) finds shelter and begins to lose his identity in another Notting Hill residence, this one belonging to a reclusive rock star (Mick Jagger). An authentic piece of psychedelia, and a cult movie that just about lives up to its reputation.

Deep End (Jerzy Skolimowski, 1970). At the public baths a naive teenager (John Moulder-Brown) becomes obsessed by his older work-mate (Jane Asher). Excellent bleak comedy: set in an unglamorous Lon-don, made by a Polish director, and mainly shot in Munich.

A Clockwork Orange (Stanley Kubrick, 1971). A violent satire about violence, recently shown on British screens for the first time since the 1970s, which used some stylized

▲ *A Clockwork Orange*

sets and Thamesmead locations to convey Kubrick's vision of a soulless near-future.

Death Line (Gary Sherman, 1972). Effectively seedy horror film about cannibalistic ex-navvies lurking in the tunnels around Russell Square Underground station. Most of the sympathy is reserved for the monsters.

Frenzy (Alfred Hitchcock, 1972). Hitchcock's final return to London, adapted from the novel *Goodbye Pic-cadilly, Farewell Leicester Square*, and filmed in and around Covent Gar-den. Displays all his old preoccupa-tions (violence, sex, food) with added graphic detail.

The Satanic Rites of Dracula (Alan Gibson, 1973). At one point known as *Dracula is Alive and Well and Living in London*, this Hammer Horror uses the neat premise of a vampire property developer, but is otherwise unremarkable.

Moon over the Alley (Joseph Despins, 1975). Kitchen sink musi-cal by Gail (Hair) MacDermot set in and around Portobello Road (pre *Notting Hill*), stuffed with offbeat characters and humour.

Punk in London (Wolfgang Büld, 1977). An earnest piece of German anthropology, featuring perform-ances and interviews with the likes of The Sex Pistols, The Jam and X-Ray Specs.

Jubilee (Derek Jarman, 1978). Jar-man's angry punk collage, in which Elizabeth I finds herself transported to the urban decay of late twentieth-century Deptford. Features Jordan as Amyl Nitrate, Little Nell as Crabs, Adam Ant as Kid and Jenny Runacre as the Queen.

The Long Good Friday (John Mackenzie, 1979). An East End gang boss (Bob Hoskins) has plans for the Docklands but finds himself fighting the IRA. A violent, contemporary thriller, looking towards the Thatch-erite 1980s.

Babylon (Franco Rosso, 1980). Attempting to win a sound-system contest, Blue (Brinsley Forde) finds himself up against street crime, racism and police brutality. A sharp South London drama with a fine reggae soundtrack.

The Elephant Man (David Lynch, 1980). The story of John Merrick (John Hurt), exhibited as a fairground freak before being lionized by society. Freddie Francis's black-and-white photography brings out the beauty and horror of Victorian London. Much of the film was shot in Shad Thames, on the south side of Tower Bridge.

The Falls (Peter Greenaway, 1980). Long, strange, ornithologically obsessed pseudo-documentary, supposedly setting out to provide 92 biographies for the latest edition of the *Standard Dictionary of the Violent Unexplained Event*. The locations include Goldhawk Road and Bird-cage Walk.

An American Werewolf in London (John Landis, 1981). Comic horror movie with state-of-the-art special effects about an innocent abroad who gets bitten. Required viewing for all American backpackers.

The Chain (Jack Gold, 1984). The "chain" of the title is a property-buying chain as seven different sets of people move house on the same day, each one representing one of the seven deadly sins.

Dance with a Stranger (Mike Newell, 1984). A well-groomed re-creation of the repressive 1950s, carried by Miranda Richardson's intense impersonation of Soho nightclub hostess Ruth Ellis, the last woman to be hanged in Britain.

Defence of the Realm (David Drury, 1985). Political thriller about state secrecy and newspaper ethics, with Gabriel Byrne, the always excellent Denholm Elliott and some

atmospheric London locations.

My Beautiful Laundrette (Stephen Frears, 1985). A surreal comedy of Thatcher's London, offering the unlikely combination of an entrepreneurial Asian, his ex-National Front boyfriend and a launderette called Powders. Frears and scriptwriter Hanif Kureishi worked together again on *Sammy and Rosie Get Laid* (1987): set in riot-torn Ladbroke Grove, it lacked the magic of their first collaboration, but was at least better than *London Kills Me* (1991), which Kureishi directed.

Absolute Beginners (Julien Temple, 1986). Musical version of the Colin MacInnes book, attempting to create a bold, stylized version of late 1950s Soho and Napoli (Notting Hill), but ending up as a confused mix of pastiche and pop promo.

84 Charing Cross Road (David Jones, 1986). Touching film version of Helene Hanff's novel about her epistolary relationship with Marks & Co, a London bookshop. Anthony Hopkins plays the shy bookshop man and Anne Bancroft the feisty Ms Hanff.

Mona Lisa (Neil Jordan, 1986). A small-time crook (Bob Hoskins) falls for a high-class call-girl (Cathy Tyson) and helps search for her missing friend. Strikingly realized story of vice and betrayal, with great performances from the leads, and a view of King's Cross at its most infernal.

Hidden City (Stephen Poliakoff, 1987). Interesting piece of paranoia about an ill-matched couple (Charles Dance and Cassie Stuart) literally delving beneath the surface of the city. The plot treads fairly familiar territory, but the subterranean locations reveal a decidedly unfamiliar aspect of London.

Little Dorrit (Christine Edzard, 1987). Two-part adaptation (running to six hours in total) of Dickens' novel of Victorian greed and deprivation. Faithful to the complexities of the original, but put together with almost too much loving care.

Dealers (Colin Buckley, 1989). A risk-taking city trader with a private plane discovers that there's more to life than making money. A film as slick and empty as the characters it portrays.

Melancholia (Andi Engel, 1989). Intelligent thriller about a London-based German art critic (Jeroen Krabbe) whose radical past is brought back to him when he's asked to assassinate a Chilean torturer. An effective portrait of urban angst.

Queen of Hearts (Jon Amiel, 1989). Family life and troubles in Little Italy, London. This genial mix of fantasy and realism comes complete with a talking pig, a beautifully shiny espresso coffee machine and a jumbled sense of time and place.

I Hired a Contract Killer (Aki Kaurismäki, 1990). Jean-Paul Léaud decides to end it all by hiring a hitman, and then changes his mind. A typically wry film from this Finnish director, featuring such lesser-known landmarks such as the *Honolulu* (a Docklands bar) and *Vic's Café* (in Hampstead Cemetery).

The Krays (Peter Medak, 1990). A chronicle of the life of Bethnal Green's gangland twins (played by Gary and Martin Kemp) that portrays them both as violent antiheroes and as damaged mother's boys. Billie Whitelaw plays the strong-willed mother.

Life is Sweet (Mike Leigh, 1990). Comic, poignant and acutely observed picture of suburban life and eating habits, with Leigh's semi-improvisational approach drawing fine performances from Alison Steadman, Jim Broadbent, and just about everyone else.

Riff-Raff (Ken Loach, 1990). A young Glaswegian works on a dodgy East End building site and shares a squat with a hopeful singer from Belfast. Less didactic and more comic than much of the director's work, Loach's film is good at conveying the camaraderie of the workers, but less convincing in its story of love found and lost.

Naked (Mike Leigh, 1993). David Thewlis is brilliant as the disaffected and garrulous misogynist who goes on a tour through the underside of what he calls "the big shitty" – life is anything but sweet in Leigh's darkest but most substantial film.

London (Patrick Keillor, 1994). Paul Scofield is the sardonic narrator of this "fictional documentary", describing three pilgrimages to little-visited tourist sights: the first to Strawberry Hill, Twickenham, the second in search of Edgar Allan Poe's old school in Stoke Newington, and the third along the River Brent. A witty, erudite and highly original film essay that looks at both London's literary past and its political present.

The Madness of King George (Nicholas Hytner, 1994). Excellent film version of the play by Alan Bennett, with Nigel Hawthorne in the lead role, Helen Mirren as his long-suffering consort and Rupert Everett as the Prince Regent. Cleverly shot in various locations in and around London, including Syon House, Windsor and Eton.

Beautiful Thing (Hettie Mac-Donald, 1996). Feel-good film, set, somewhat surprisingly, on the grim Thamesmead housing estate in southeast London. Glen Berry leads a cast of newcomers as teenager Jamie, coming to terms with his sexuality, starting with a crush on his best friend.

Restoration (Michael Hoffman, 1996). Flawed but atmospheric evocation of life in London under Charles II, seen through the eyes of a young doctor (Robert Downey Jr), whose career takes off after he restores the monarch's dog to health.

Richard III (Richard Loncraine, 1996). 1930s Britain, torn by civil war and sliding into fascism, is the setting for this pared-down and fast-paced version of Shakespeare's play, in which Ian McKellen gives a compelling performance in the title role. The inventively used locations include St Pancras Station (standing in as the entrance to the Royal Palace) and Bankside Power Station (as the exterior of the Tower of London).

Secrets and Lies (Mike Leigh, 1996). Palme d'Or-winning, heart-rending tale of a young black woman who sets off in search of her natural mother, who turns out to be a sad, white alcoholic, living a miserable life with her catatonic daughter.

Mrs Dalloway (Marleen Goris, 1997). Very straightforward film version of Virginia Woolf's bi-vocal book, intertwining a day in the life of a society hostess, played by Vanessa Redgrave, and the paranoid thoughts of a World War I shell-shock victim.

Sliding Doors (Peter Howitt, 1997). Tricksy romantic comedy of parallel realities, set in London. Helen, played by Gwyneth Paltrow, discovers her boyfriend in bed with her best friend and dumps him; meanwhile, in an alternative reality, she remains blissfully ignorant of his infidelity.

Shooting Fish (Stefan Schwarz, 1997). Light, quirky romantic comedy, featuring two con men living in a London gasholder, who see themselves as modern-day Robin Hoods.

Spice World (Bob Spiers, 1997). The famous five (as they were then) cavort around London in a Union Jack double-decker. The plot is wafer thin, but there are lots of panoramic shots of London and plenty of cameos by famous actors and musicians. Of its time, already.

Lock, Stock & Two Smok-

ing Barrels (Guy Ritchie, 1998). Mostly famous for being directed by Madonna's beau, and featuring the acting debut of Vinnie Jones, former Wimbledon footballing hard man, this is a quick-fire Cockney rebel film about four lads hoping to make some fast money (to pay off their gambling debts) through a drugs deal.

End of the Affair (Neil Jordan, 1999). Not entirely successful film version of wartime Graham Greene novel about a passionate affair between a writer (Ralph Fiennes) and a civil servant's wife (Julianne Moore). Fiennes fans won't be disappointed, however, and there's lots of Catholic guilt to lap up.

Notting Hill (Roger Michell, 1999). Predictable but slick (and occasionally funny) romantic comedy in which Hugh Grant plays a posh and slightly useless bookshop owner, while Julia Roberts pretends to be a famous film actress, and the myth of happy, multicultural Notting Hill is fed to the audience.

Wonderland (Michael Winterbottom, 1999). A long, lively weekend in the life of a typically dysfunctional 1990s South London family, featuring runaway sons, single mums and children born out of wedlock.

24 Hours in London (Alexander Finbow, 2000). Another London gangster movie: the year is 2009, and a bunch of criminals controls the city (so what's changed?). Convoluted plot, over-the-top acting, led by Gary Olsen, and intentionally comic set pieces.

Gangster No. 1 (Paul McGuigan, 2000). Story of a young thug called Gangster, who becomes right-hand man to London crime king Freddy Mays in the late 1960s, only to betray him and see him sent to prison for thirty years. Violent, rather nasty piece of work, starring Malcolm McDowell and David Thewlis.

Last Orders (Fred Schepisi, 2001).

Star-studded adaptation of Graham Swift's affectionate, but unsentimental novel about four dodgy South London geezers taking their mate's ashes to Margate Pier.

28 Days Later (Danny Boyle, 2002). Modern apocalyptic, zombie horror flick, shot on digital video, and set in an eerily (almost) deserted London, a month after a deadly virus has wiped out most of the population.

About a Boy (Chris Weitz, Paul Weitz, 2002). Romantic comedy based on Nick Hornby's book and set in North London, starring Hugh Grant as a wealthy, carefree bachelor who gets involved with a single mum and (more importantly) her adolescent kid.

Dirty Pretty Things (Stephen Frears, 2002). Entertaining romantic thriller set in London's asylum-seeking, multicultural underbelly, shot through with plenty of humour and lots of pace.

The Hours (Stephen Daldry, 2002). David Hare screen version of Michael Cunningham's book, inspired by *Mrs Dalloway*, one-third of which features an Oscar-winning performance of Nicole Kidman wearing a prosthetic nose and pretending to be Virginia Woolf.

Spider (David Cronenberg, 2002). Oedipal drama based on a Patrick McGrath novel, which follows schizophrenic Spider (played by Ralph Fiennes), recently released from a mental hospital, as he revisits his childhood haunts to search for the truth about his mother's murder.

Bullet Boy (Saul Dibb, 2004). Highly credible portrayal of life on a Hackney estate for two young black guys who find themselves involved in a trivial argument that ends in gun violence.

Wimbledon (Richard Loncraine, 2004). Deeply unchallenging romantic tennis drama shot on location, with plenty of tourist board-approved London backdrops.

Creep (Christopher Smith, 2005). Slightly ludicrous, definitely derivative, and yet nevertheless very nasty movie featuring a German woman trapped in the Tube after the last train has gone.

33 x Around the Sun (John Hardwick, 2005). Low budget, independent movie version of Orpheus and Eurydice set in and around a Brick Lane full of East End low life character.

Vera Drake (Mike Leigh, 2005). Critically acclaimed drama set in wonderfully re-created London in 1950 about a woman (Imelda Staunton) who performs illegal backstreet abortions for free.

Books

Given the enormous number of books on London, the list below is necessarily a selective one, with books marked 🎭 being particularly recommended.

London's bookshops are covered in detail on p.539–541. The best known online bookshop is ⓦwww.amazon.com, but if you're looking for a particular book in the UK, ⓦwww.bookbrain.co.uk will tell you which online bookshop is selling it for the cheapest price.

Travel, journals and memoirs

Paul Bailey (ed) *The Oxford Book of London.* Large anthology of musings on London, arranged in chronological order from twelfth-century monks via Dostoevsky and Van Gogh to Hanif Kureishi and Angela Carter.

Julian Barnes *Letters from London.* Witty letters written between 1990 and 1995 for a regular column in the *New Yorker* magazine.

John Betjeman *Betjeman's London.* A selection of writings and poems by the then Poet Laureate, who spearheaded the campaign to save London's architectural heritage in the 1960s.

James Boswell *London Journal.* Boswell's diary, written in 1792–93 when he was lodging in Downing Street, is remarkably candid about his frequent dealings with the city's prostitutes, and is a fascinating insight into eighteenth-century life.

John Evelyn *The Diary of John Evelyn.* In contrast to his contemporary, Pepys, Evelyn gives away very little of his personal life, but his diaries cover a much greater period of English history and a much wider range of topics.

Ford Madox Ford *The Soul of London.* Experimental, impressionist portrait of London.

Tarquin Hall *Salaam Brick Lane: A Year in the New East End.* The stories of a colourful cast of immigrant characters, met by the author when living above a sweatshop in Brick Lane.

Louis Heron *Growing Up Poor in London.* Well-written account of growing up in an East End slum in 1919.

Doris Lessing *Walking in the Shade 1949–62.* The second volume of Lessing's autobiography, set in London in the 1950s, deals with the writing- and theatre-scenes and party politics, including her association with the Communist Party, with which she eventually became disenchanted.

George Orwell *Down and Out in Paris and London.* Orwell's tramp's-eye view of the 1930s, written from firsthand experience. The London section is particularly harrowing.

Samuel Pepys *The Shorter Pepys; The Illustrated Pepys.* Pepys kept a voluminous diary while he was living in London from 1660 until 1669, recording the fall of the Commonwealth, the Restoration, the Great Plague and the Great Fire, as well as describing the daily life of the nation's capital. The unabridged version is published in eleven volumes; Penguin's *Shorter Pepys* is abridged (though still massive); *The Illustrated Pepys* is made up of the choicest extracts accompanied by contemporary illustrations.

Mike Phillips *London Crossings.* A series of snapshots of the city (and elsewhere), full of sensitivity and insight, by a writer who arrived in London from Guyana as a teenager some 45 years ago.

Iain Sinclair *Lights Out for the Territory; Liquid City;* and *London Orbital.* Sinclair is one of the most original (and virtually unreadable) London writers of his generation. *Lights Out* is a series of ramblings across London starting in Hackney; *Liquid City* contains beautiful photos and entertaining text about London's hidden rivers and canals; and *London Orbital* is an account of his walk round the M25, delving into obscure parts of the city's periphery.

History, society and politics

Peter Ackroyd *Dickens*; *Blake*; *Sir Thomas More*; and *London: The Biography*. Few writers know quite as much about London as Ackroyd does, and London is central to all three of his biographical subjects – the result is scholarly, enthusiastic and eminently readable. *London: The Biography* is the massive culmination of a lifetime's love affair with a living city and its intimate history.

Angus Calder *The Myth of the Blitz*. A timely antidote to the backs-against-the-wall, "London can take it" tone of most books on this period. Calder dwells instead on the capital's internees – Communists, conscientious objectors and "enemy aliens" – and the myth-making processes of the media of the day.

Patricia Cornwell *Portrait of a Killer: Jack the Ripper – Case Closed*. Leading US crimewriter Cornwell attempts to pin the crime on the painter Walter Sickert – it's an interesting read, but the evidence is simply not there.

Clive Emsley *The Newgate Calendar*. Grim and gory account of the most famous London criminals of the day – Captain Kidd, Jack Sheppard, Dick Turpin – with potted biographies of each victim, ending with an account of his execution. Starting out as a collection of papers and booklets, *The Newgate Calendar* was first published in 1828 and was second in popularity only to the Bible at the time of publication, but is now difficult to get hold of.

William J. Fishman *The Streets of East London*. Accessible social history of the East End, from Victorian times to the present day, by Jewish East Ender and scholar. Accompanied by black-and-white photos, old and new.

Jonathan Glancey *London Bread and Circuses*. In this small, illustrated book, the *Guardian*'s architecture critic extols the virtues of the old LCC and visionaries like Frank Pick, who transformed London's transport in the 1930s, discusses the millennium projects (the "circuses" of the title), and bemoans the city's creaking infrastructure.

Ed Glinert *The London Compendium*. Glinert dissects every street, every park, every house and every tube station and produces juicy anecdotes every time. Only let down by its index.

Sarah Hartley *Mrs P's Journey: The Remarkable Story of the Woman Who Created the A–Z Map*. The tale of Phyllis Pearsall, the indomitable woman who survived a horrific childhood and went on to found London's most famous mapmaking company – you won't feel the same about the A–Z again.

Rachel Lichtenstein and Iain Sinclair *Rodinsky's Room*. A fascinating search into the Jewish past of the East End, centred on the nebulous figure of David Rodinsky.

Peter Linebaugh *The London Hanged*. Superb, Marxist analysis of crime and punishment in the eighteenth century, drawing on the history of those hanged at Tyburn.

Jack London *The People of the Abyss*. The author went undercover in 1902 to uncover East End poverty.

Henry Mayhew *London Labour and the London Poor*. Mayhew's pioneering study of Victorian London, based on research carried out in the 1840s and 1850s.

Roy Porter *London: A Social History*. This immensely readable history is one of the best books on London published since the war. It is particularly strong on the continuing saga of the capital's government and includes an impassioned critique of the damage done by Thatcher.

Winston G. Ramsey (ed) *The East End Then and Now*. Massive tome full of black-and-white photos of the East End before and after the Blitz – it covers all the legends from the Ripper to the Krays.

Maude Pember Reeves *Round About a Pound a Week*. From 1909 to 1913, the Fabian Women's Group, part of the British Labour Party, recorded the daily budget of thirty families in Lambeth living in extreme poverty. This is the accompanying comment, which is both enlightening and enlightened.

Donald Rumbelow *The Complete Jack the Ripper*. Of all the books exploiting this sordid tale of misogyny, Rumbelow's stands head and shoulders above the rest, trashing most previous accounts as sensationalist, and concluding that there is insufficient evidence to pin the crime on any suspect.

John Stow *A Survey of London*. Stow, a retired tailor, set himself the unenviable task of writing the first-ever account of the city in 1598, for which he is now revered, though at the time the task forced him into penury.

Judith R. Walkowitz *City of Dreadful Delight: Narratives of Sexual Danger in Late-Victorian London*. Weighty feminist tract on issues such as child prostitution and the Ripper murders, giving a powerful overview of the image of women in the fiction and media of the day.

Maureen Waller *1700: Scenes from London Life*. Fascinating minutiae of the crazy, everyday life of eighteenth-century London, meticulously researched.

Ben Weinreb & Christopher Hibbert *The London Encyclopaedia*. More than a thousand pages of concisely presented information on London past and present, accompanied by the odd illustration. The most fascinating book on the capital.

Philip Ziegler *London at War 1939–45*. A wide-ranging and even-handed account of life in the capital during the war years, from the Phoney War to the doodlebugs.

Art, architecture and archeology

Ken Allinson & Victoria Thornton *A Guide to London's Contemporary Architecture*. Comprehensive gazetteer to the new buildings, great and small, erected all over Greater London in the 1980s and 1990s, with a black-and-white photo for each entry.

Felix Barker & Ralph Hyde *London As It Might Have Been*. A richly illustrated book on the weird and wonderful plans that never quite made it off the drawing board.

Felix Barker & Peter Jackson *The History of London in Maps*. A beautiful volume of maps, from the earliest surviving chart of 1558 to the new Docklands, with accompanying text explaining the history of the city and its cartography.

Bill Brandt *London in the Thirties*. Brandt's superb black-and-white photos bear witness to a London lost in the Blitz.

Samantha Hardingham *London: A Guide to Recent Architecture*. Wonderful pocket guide to the architecture of the last ten years or so, with a knowledgeable, critical text and plenty of black-and-white photos.

Elaine Harwood & Andrew Saint *London*. Part of the excellent Exploring England's Heritage series, sponsored by English Heritage. It's highly selective, though each building is discussed at some length and is well illustrated.

Edward Jones & Christopher Woodward *A Guide to the Architecture of London*. Straightforward illustrated catalogue of London's 1920s buildings, each one accompanied by a black-and-white photo, and with useful maps at the beginning of each chapter.

Derek Kendall *The City of London Churches.* A beautifully illustrated book, comprised mostly of colour photos, covering the remarkable City churches, many of them designed by Wren after the Great Fire.

Nikolaus Pevsner and others *The Buildings of England.* Magisterial series, started by Pevsner, to which others have added, inserting newer buildings but generally respecting the founder's personal tone. The latest of the London volumes (there are now five in the series) is a paperback edition devoted to London Docklands.

John Schofield *The Building of London.* A copiously illustrated architectural and archeological guide to pre-Fire London, stretching from the Norman Conquest to the Great Fire itself.

Richard Trench & Ellis Hillman *London under London.* Fascinating book revealing the secrets of every aspect of the capital's subterranean history, from the lost rivers of the underground to the gas and water systems.

London in fiction

Peter Ackroyd *English Music; Hawksmoor; The House of Doctor Dee; The Great Fire of London* and *Dan Leno and the Limehouse Golem.* Ackroyd's novels are all based on arcane aspects of London, wrapped into thriller-like narratives, and conjuring up kaleidoscopic visions of various ages of English culture. *Hawskmoor,* about the great church architect, is the most popular and enjoyable.

Monica Ali *Brick Lane.* Acute, involving and slyly humorous debut novel about a young Bengali woman who comes over with her husband to live in London's East End.

Martin Amis *London Fields; Yellow Dog.* Short sentences and cartoon characters, Amis's novels tend to provoke extreme reactions in readers. Love 'em or hate 'em, these two are set in London.

J.G. Ballard *Concrete Island; High Rise; The Drowned World.* Wild stuff. In *Concrete Island,* a car crashes on the Westway, leaving its driver stranded on the central reservation, unable to flag down passing cars. In *High Rise,* the residents of a high-rise block of flats in East London go slowly mad. *The Drowned World,* Ballard's first novel, is set in a futuristic, flooded and tropical London – if only.

Neil Bartlett *Mr Clive and Mr Page.* Strange, erotic and romantic story which ranges from the 1920s to the 1950s and reveals the homophobia of those years.

Samuel Beckett *Murphy.* Nihilistic, dark-humoured vision of the city, written in 1938, and told through the eyes of antihero Murphy.

Elizabeth Bowen *The Heat of the Day.* Bowen worked for the Ministry of Information during World War II, and witnessed the Blitz first-hand from her Marylebone flat; this novel perfectly captures the dislocation and rootlessness of wartime London.

Anthony Burgess *A Dead Man in Deptford.* Playwright Christopher Marlowe's unexplained murder in a tavern in Deptford provides the background for this historical novel, which brims over with Elizabethan life and language.

Peter Carey *Jack Maggs.* Set in 1837, this is the dark tale of a convict who returns secretly from Australia and gets involved in mystery and mesmerism.

Angela Carter *The Magic Toyshop;*

Wise Children. The Magic Toyshop was Carter's most celebrated 1960s novel, about a provincial woman moving to London, while *Wise Children* was published in 1992, the year of her untimely death.

G.K. Chesterton *The Napoleon of Notting Hill.* Written in 1904, but set eighty years in the future, in a London divided into squabbling independent boroughs – something prophetic there – and ruled by royalty selected on a rotational basis.

Liza Cody *Bucket Nut; Monkey Wrench; Musclebound.* Feisty, would-be female wrestler of uncertain sexuality, with a big mouth, in thrillers set in lowlife London.

J.M. Coetzee *Youth.* Claustrophobic, semi-autobiographical novel by South African Booker Prize-winner, centred on a self-obsessed colonial, struggling to find the meaning of life and become a writer in London in the 1960s.

Arthur Conan Doyle *The Complete Sherlock Holmes.* Deerstalkered sleuth Sherlock Holmes and dependable sidekick Dr Watson penetrate all levels of Victorian London, from Limehouse opium dens to millionaires' pads. *A Study in Scarlet* and *The Sign of Four* are based entirely in London.

Joseph Conrad *The Secret Agent.* Conrad's wonderful spy story, based on the botched anarchist bombing of Greenwich Observatory in 1894, and exposing the hypocrisies of both the police and the anarchists.

Daniel Defoe *Journal of the Plague Year.* An account of the Great Plague seen through the eyes of an East End saddler, written some sixty years after the event.

Charles Dickens *Bleak House; A Christmas Tale; Little Dorrit; Oliver Twist.* The descriptions in Dickens' London-based novels have become the clichés of the Victorian city: the fog, the slums and the stinking river. *Little Dorrit* is set mostly in Borough and contains some of his most trenchant pieces of social analysis. Much of *Bleak House* is set around the Inns of Court that Dickens knew so well.

Nell Dunn *Up the Junction; Poor Cow.* Perceptive and unsentimental account of the downside of south London life in the 1950s after the hype of the Festival of Britain.

Buchi Emecheta *Second-Class Citizen; Head above Water.* Based on her experiences in the 1960s, these tell the story of a young Nigerian woman struggling to survive in North London.

George Gissing *New Grub Street.* Classic 1891 story of intrigue and jealousy among London's Fleet Street hacks.

Graham Greene *The Human Factor; It's a Battlefield; The Ministry of Fear; The End of the Affair.* Greene's London novels are all fairly bleak, ranging from *The Human Factor*, which probes the underworld of the city's spies, to *The Ministry of Fear*, which is set during the Blitz.

Patrick Hamilton *Hangover Square; Twenty Thousand Streets Under the Sky.* The first is a story of unrequited love and violence in Earl's Court in the 1940s, while the latter is a trilogy of stories set in seedy 1930s London.

Neil Hanson *The Dreadful Judgement.* A docu-fiction account in which modern scientific methods and historical knowledge are applied to the Fire of London so vividly you can feel the heat.

Nick Hornby *High Fidelity.* Hornby's extraordinarily successful second book focuses on the loves and life of a thirty-something bloke who lives in North London.

Aldous Huxley *Point Counter Point.* Sharp satire of London's high-society wastrels and dilettantes of the Roaring Twenties.

Robert Irwin *Exquisite Corpse.* Tale of obsessive love set in the Surrealist circles of postwar London (and elsewhere).

Henry James *The Awkward Age.*

Light, ironic portrayal of London high society at the turn of the century.

Hanif Kureishi *The Buddha of Suburbia*; *The Black Album*; *Love in a Blue Time*. *The Buddha of Suburbia* is a raunchy account of life as an Anglo-Asian in late 1960s suburbia, and the art scene of the 1970s. *The Black Album* is a thriller set in London in 1989; while *Love in a Blue Time* is a collection of short stories set in 1990s London.

John Lawton *Black Out*. Thriller set in wartime London which begins with the discovery of a German found murdered in the bomb-torn East End.

Andrea Levy *Small Island*. A warm-hearted novel in which postwar London struggles to adapt to the influx of Jamaicans who in turn find that the land of their dreams is full of prejudice.

Colin MacInnes *Absolute Beginners*; *Omnibus*. *Absolute Beginners*, a story of life in Soho and Notting Hill in the 1950s (much influenced by Selvon – see below), is infinitely better than the film of the same name. *Omnibus* is set in 1957, in a Victoria station packed with hopeful black immigrants; white welfare officer meets black man from Lagos with surprising results.

Somerset Maugham *Liza of Lambeth*. Maugham considered himself a "second-rater", but this book on Cockney lowlife is packed with vivid local colour.

Ian McEwan *Saturday*. On a day of a protest march against the war in Iraq, the main character is forced to consider his attitude to this and many other issues. Captures the mood of London post 9/11.

Timothy Mo *Sour Sweet*. Very funny and very sad story of a newly arrived Chinese family struggling to understand the English way of life, written with great insight by Mo, who is himself of mixed parentage.

Michael Moorcock *Mother London*.

A magnificent, rambling, kaleido-scopic portrait of London from the Blitz to Thatcher by a once-fashion-able, but now very much underrated, writer.

Iris Murdoch *Under the Net*; *The Black Prince*; *An Accidental Man*; *Bruno's Dream*; *The Green Knight*. *Under the Net* was Murdoch's first, funniest and arguably her best novel, published in 1954 and starring a hack writer living in London. Many of her subsequent works are set in various parts of middle-class London and span several decades of the second half of the twentieth century. *The Green Knight*, her last novel, is a strange fable mixing medieval and modern London, with lashings of the Bible and attempted fratricide.

George Orwell *Keep the Aspidistra Flying*. Orwell's 1930s critique of Mammon is equally critical of its chief protagonist, whose attempt to rebel against the system only con-demns him to poverty, working in a London bookshop and freezing his evenings away in a miserable rented room.

Jonanthan Raban *Soft City*. An early work from 1974 that's both a portrait of, and paean to, metropoli-tan life.

Derek Raymond *Not till the Red Fog Rises*. A book which "reeks with the pervasive stench of excrement" as Iain Sinclair (see below) put it, this is a lowlife spec-tacular set in the seediest sections of the capital.

Ruth Rendell *The Keys to the Street*. The mystery centres on the homeless who are being spiked on the railings around rich Regent's Park.

Edward Rutherford *London*. A big, big novel (perhaps too big) that stretches from Roman times to the present and deals with the most dra-matic moments of London's history. Masses of historical detail woven in with the story of several families.

Samuel Selvon *The Lonely Londoners*. "Gives us the smell and feel of this rather horrifying life. Not for the squeamish", ran the quote from the *Evening Standard* on the original cover. This is, in fact, a wry and witty account of the Afro-Caribbean experience in London in the 1950s.

Hanan al-Shaykh *Only in London*. A dryly comic account of the difficulties encountered by Arab women attempting to blend into London life.

🏃 **Iain Sinclair** *White Chappell, Scarlet Tracings; Downriver; Radon Daughters*. Sinclair's idiosyncratic and richly textured novels are a strange mix of Hogarthian caricature, New Age mysticism and conspiracy-theory rant. Deeply offensive and highly recommended.

Gillian Slovo *Death by Analysis; Death Comes Staccato; Catnap*. Private detective Kate Beier generally sleuths around Hackney, but sometimes finds herself in richer haunts.

Stevie Smith *Novel on Yellow Paper*. Poet Stevie Smith's first novel takes place in the publishing world of 1930s London.

🏃 **Zadie Smith** *White Teeth*. Highly acclaimed and funny first novel about race, gender and class in the ethnic melting pot of North London.

John Sommerfield *May Day*. Set in the revolutionary fervour of the 1930s, this novel is "as if Mrs Dalloway was written by a Communist Party bus driver", in the words of one reviewer.

Muriel Spark *The Bachelors; The Ballad of Peckham Rye*. Two London-based novels written one after the other by the Scots-born author, best known for her *The Prime of Miss Jean Brodie*.

Graham Swift *Last Orders*. Four friends recall the East End as it was during the war, in an unsentimental view of Cockney life.

Edith Templeton *Gordon*. A tale of sex and humiliation in postwar London, banned in the 1960s when it was published under a pseudonym (Louisa Walbrook).

Sarah Waters *Affinity; Fingersmith; Tipping the Velvet*. Racy modern novels set in Victorian London. *Affinity* is set in the spiritualist milieu, *Fingersmith* focuses on an orphan girl, while *Tipping the Velvet* is about lesbian love in the music hall.

Evelyn Waugh *Vile Bodies*. Waugh's target, the "vile bodies" of the title, are the flippant rich kids of the Roaring Twenties, as in Huxley's *Point Counter Point* (see p.606).

Patrick White *The Living and the Dead*. Australian Nobel Prize – winner's second novel is a sombre portrait of family life in London at the time of the Spanish Civil War.

Angus Wilson *The Wrong Set*. A collection of short stories written in 1949 satirizing contemporary upper-middle-class characters in Knightsbridge and Kensington.

P.G. Wodehouse *Jeeves Omnibus*. Bertie Wooster and his stalwart butler, Jeeves, were based in Mayfair, and many of their exploits take place with London showgirls and in the Drones gentlemen's club.

🏃 **Virginia Woolf** *Mrs Dalloway*. Woolf's novel relates the thoughts of a London society hostess and a shell-shocked war veteran, with her "stream-of-consciousness" style in full flow.

Specialist guides

Felix Barker & Denise Silvester-Carr *The Black Plaque Guide to London*. An alternative to the official *Blue Plaque Guide*, cataloguing dens of vice, abodes of love and the homes of the disreputable.

Judi Culbertson & Tom Randall *Permanent Londoners*. An illustrated guide to the finest of London's cemeteries, from Westminster Abbey and

St Paul's to the Victorian splendours of Highgate and Kensal Green. Very good on biographical histories of the deceased, too.

Andrew Duncan *Secret London.* With boundless enthusiasm, Duncan takes you along the lost rivers, unmasks the property tycoons, exposes dead tube stations and uncovers just about every undiscovered nook and cranny in the city.

Bob Gilbert *The Green London Way.* This hundred-mile walk (also cyclable) circles the capital, taking in favourites like Greenwich and Kew Gardens, but also covering more unusual urban landscapes such as the Northern Outfall Sewerway. Politically astute and ecologically sound text, too.

The Handbook Guide *Rock & Pop London.* Rock and pop tourism is on the increase, though this unimaginative, rather dry book is unlikely to inspire too many folk, even if it casts its net fairly wide.

Ian McAuley *Guide to Ethnic London.* A fine, accessible outline of the major ethnic communities in present-day London, with useful practical tips and a good all-round bibliography.

Jean Moorcroft Wilson *Virginia Woolf's London.* A book of place, tracing Woolf's connections with Kensington, Bloomsbury and Richmond, and the footsteps of some of her characters.

Christian Wolmar *The Subterranean Railway.* A fascinating history of the Tube, the world's first underground railway.

Glossary of architectural terms

Aedicule Small decorative niche formed by two columns or pilasters supporting a gable.

Aisle Clear space parallel to the nave of a church, usually with lower ceiling than the nave.

Altar Table at which the Eucharist is celebrated, at the east end of a church. (When the church is not aligned to the geographical east, the altar end is still referred to as the "east" end.)

Ambulatory Passage behind and around the chancel.

Apse The curved or polygonal east end of a church.

Arcade Row of arches on top of columns or piers, supporting a wall.

Ashlar Dressed building stone worked to a smooth finish.

Bailey Area enclosed by castle walls.

Baldachin Canopy over an altar.

Barbican Defensive structure built in front of main gate fortress.

Barrel vault Continuous rounded vault, like a semi-cylinder.

Blue plaque English Heritage plaques placed on a building associated with a prominent figure (who must have been dead for at least 25 years).

Boss A decorative carving at the meeting point of the lines of a vault.

Box pew Form of church seating in which each bench is enclosed by high, thin wooden panels.

Broach spire Octagonal spire rising straight out of a square tower.

Buttress Stone support for a wall; some buttresses are wholly attached to the wall, others, known as "flying buttresses", take the form of a tower with a connecting arch.

Capital Upper section of a column or pier, usually carved.

Chancel Section of a church where the altar is located.

Chantry Small pre-Reformation chapel in which masses were said for the soul of the person who financed its construction.

Choir Area in which the church service is conducted; next to or same as chancel.

Clerestory Upper storey of nave, containing a line of windows.

Coffering Regular recessed spaces set into a ceiling.

Corbel Jutting stone support, often carved.

Crenellations Battlements with square indentations.

Crossing The intersection of a church's nave and transepts.

Decorated Middle Gothic style; about 1280–1380.

Dogtooth Form of early Gothic decorative stonework, looking like raised "X"s.

Dormer Window raised above the main roof.

Early English First phase of Gothic architecture in England; about 1150–1280.

Fan vault Late Gothic form of vaulting, in which the area between walls and ceiling is covered with stone ribs in the shape of an open fan.

Finial Any decorated tip of an architectural feature.

Flushwork Kind of surface decoration in which tablets of white stone alternate with pieces of flint; very common in East Anglia.

Gallery A raised passageway.

Gargoyle Grotesque exterior carving, usually a decorative form of waterspout.

Hammerbeam Type of internal roofing in which horizontal beams support vertical timbers that connect to and support the roof.

Keep Main structure of a castle.

Lady chapel Chapel dedicated to the Virgin, often found at the east end of major churches.

Lancet Tall, narrow, plain window with pointed arch.

Lantern Structure on top of a dome or tower, often glazed to let in light.

Listed building A building which has been put on English Heritage's protected list; buildings are classed (in descending order of importance) Grade I, Grade II★ and Grade II.

Lunette Window or panel shaped like a half-moon.

Misericord Carved ledge below a tip-up seat, usually in choir stalls.

Motte Mound on which a castle keep stands.

Mullion Vertical strip between the panes of a window.

Nave The main part of a church on the other (usually western) side of the crossing from the chancel.

Ogee Double curve; distinctive feature of Decorated style.

Oriel Projecting window.

Palladian Eighteenth-century classical style adhering to the principles of Andrea Palladio.

Pediment Triangular space above a window or doorway.

Perpendicular Late Gothic style; about 1380–1550.

Pier Massive column, often consisting of several fused smaller columns.

Pilaster Flat column set against a wall.

Reredos Painted or carved panel at the back of an altar.

Rood screen Wooden screen supporting a crucifix (or rood), separating the choir from the nave; few survived the Reformation.

Rose window Large circular window, divided into vaguely petal-shaped sections.

Sedilia Seats for the participants in the church service, usually on the south side of the choir.

Stalls Seating for clergy in the choir area of a church.

Tracery Pattern formed by narrow bands of stone in a window or on a wall surface.

Transept Sections of the main body of a church at right angles to the choir and nave.

Tympanum Panel over a doorway, often carved in medieval churches.

Vault Arched ceiling.

Glossary of British terms

Bill	Restaurant check	**Jumble sale**	Yard sale
Biscuit	Cookie or cracker	**Jumper**	Sweater
Bonnet	Car hood	**Lager**	Beer
Boot	Car trunk	**Lay-by**	Road shoulder
Caravan	Trailer	**Leaflet**	Pamphlet
Car park	Parking lot	**Lift**	Elevator
Cheap	Inexpensive	**Lorry**	Truck
Chemist	Pharmacist	**Motorway**	Highway
Chips	French fries	**Off-licence**	Liquor store
Coach	Bus	**Pants**	Underwear
Crisps	Potato chips	**Petrol**	Gasoline
Dodgy	Suspect or unreliable	**Pudding**	Dessert
Dual carriageway	Divided highway	**Queue**	Line
Dustbin	Trash can	**Quid**	Pound (money)
First floor	Second floor	**Return ticket**	Round-trip ticket
Fiver	Five-pound note	**Roundabout**	Rotary interchange
Flat	Apartment	**Single carriageway**	Non-divided highway
Fortnight	Two weeks		
Ground floor	First floor	**Single ticket**	One-way ticket
High Street	Main Street	**Stalls**	Orchestra seats
Hire	Rent	**Stone**	Fourteen pounds (weight)
Jam	Jelly		
Jelly	Jell-O		

611

Cockney rhyming slang

The term Cockney originally meant cock's egg or misshapen egg such as a young hen might lay, in other words, a lily-livered townie as opposed to a strong country-man. From the seventeenth century, it was used as a pejorative term for any Londoner, but was later appropriated by Londoners to describe themselves (and their accent). As for Cockney rhyming slang, it's basically a coded language, where a word is replaced by two or more words, the last one of which rhymes with the original. For example, instead of the word "stairs" you have "apples and pears"; a piano (pronounced "pianner") is a "Joanna"; and pinch becomes "half-inch".

The general theory is that it evolved in the criminal underworld of the East End as a secret means of communication, and many folk nowadays think of Cockney rhyming slang as a bit of a joke. In actual fact, it's alive and well, you just need to know a few basic rules. For a start, Londoners often don't use the bit of the phrase which rhymes with the original at all. In other words, rather than say "butcher's hook" (for "look"), they say "have a butcher's at that"; instead of "loaf of bread" (for "head"), you hear use your loaf!", and when it's cold, it's "taters" not "potatoes in the mould". Rhyming slang is constantly evolving, too, with public figures providing rich pickings: Brad Pitt (shit), Posh & Becks (specs) and inevitably Tony Blair (hair). For the latest rhyming slang, and all the old favourites, visit ® www.cockneyrhymingslang.co.uk.

Subway	Pedestrian passageway	**Torch**	Flashlight
Sweets	Candy	**Trainers**	Sneakers
Tap	Faucet	**Trousers**	Pants
Tenner	Ten-pound note	**Tube/Underground**	Subway (train)
Tights	Pantyhose	**Vest**	Undershirt

Travel store

Rough Guides travel...

UK & Ireland
Britain
Devon & Cornwall
Dublin DIRECTIONS
Edinburgh DIRECTIONS
England
Ireland
Lake District
London
London DIRECTIONS
London Mini Guide
Scotland
Scottish Highlands & Islands
Wales

Europe
Algarve DIRECTIONS
Amsterdam
Amsterdam DIRECTIONS
Andalucía
Athens DIRECTIONS
Austria
Baltic States
Barcelona
Barcelona DIRECTIONS
Belgium & Luxembourg
Berlin
Brittany & Normandy
Bruges DIRECTIONS
Brussels
Budapest
Bulgaria
Copenhagen
Corfu
Corsica
Costa Brava DIRECTIONS
Crete
Croatia
Cyprus
Czech & Slovak Republics
Dodecanese & East Aegean
Dordogne & The Lot
Europe
Florence & Siena
Florence DIRECTIONS
France

French Hotels & Restos
Germany
Greece
Greek Islands
Hungary
Ibiza & Formentera DIRECTIONS
Iceland
Ionian Islands
Italy
Italian Lakes
Languedoc & Roussillon
Lisbon
Lisbon DIRECTIONS
The Loire
Madeira DIRECTIONS
Madrid DIRECTIONS
Mallorca & Menorca
Mallorca DIRECTIONS
Malta & Gozo DIRECTIONS
Menorca
Moscow
Netherlands
Norway
Paris
Paris DIRECTIONS
Paris Mini Guide
Poland
Portugal
Prague
Prague DIRECTIONS
Provence & the Côte d'Azur
Pyrenees
Romania
Rome
Rome DIRECTIONS
Sardinia
Scandinavia
Sicily
Slovenia
Spain
St Petersburg
Sweden
Switzerland
Tenerife & La Gomera DIRECTIONS
Turkey
Tuscany & Umbria

Venice & The Veneto
Venice DIRECTIONS
Vienna

Asia
Bali & Lombok
Bangkok
Beijing
Cambodia
China
Goa
Hong Kong & Macau
India
Indonesia
Japan
Laos
Malaysia, Singapore & Brunei
Nepal
The Philippines
Singapore
South India
Southeast Asia
Sri Lanka
Taiwan
Thailand
Thailand's Beaches & Islands
Tokyo
Vietnam

Australasia
Australia
Melbourne
New Zealand
Sydney

North America
Alaska
Boston
California
Canada
Chicago
Florida
Grand Canyon
Hawaii
Honolulu
Las Vegas DIRECTIONS
Los Angeles
Maui DIRECTIONS

Miami & South Florida
Montréal
New England
New Orleans DIRECTIONS
New York City
New York City DIRECTIONS
New York City Mini Guide
Orlando & Walt Disney World DIRECTIONS
Pacific Northwest
Rocky Mountains
San Francisco
San Francisco DIRECTIONS
Seattle
Southwest USA
Toronto
USA
Vancouver
Washington DC
Washington DC DIRECTIONS
Yosemite

Caribbean & Latin America
Antigua & Barbuda DIRECTIONS
Argentina
Bahamas
Barbados DIRECTIONS
Belize
Bolivia
Brazil
Cancùn & Cozumel DIRECTIONS
Caribbean
Central America
Chile
Costa Rica
Cuba
Dominican Republic
Dominican Republic DIRECTIONS
Ecuador
Guatemala
Jamaica

...music & reference

Mexico
Peru
St Lucia
South America
Trinidad & Tobago
Yúcatan

Africa & Middle East
Cape Town & the
  Garden Route
Egypt
The Gambia
Jordan
Kenya
Marrakesh
  DIRECTIONS
Morocco
South Africa, Lesotho
  & Swaziland
Syria
Tanzania
Tunisia
West Africa
Zanzibar

Travel Theme guides
First-Time Around the
  World
First-Time Asia
First-Time Europe
First-Time Latin
  America
Travel Online
Travel Health
Travel Survival
Walks in London & SE
  England
Women Travel

Maps
Algarve
Amsterdam
Andalucia & Costa
  del Sol
Argentina
Athens
Australia
Baja California
Barcelona
Berlin
Boston

Brittany
Brussels
California
Chicago
Corsica
Costa Rica & Panama
Crete
Croatia
Cuba
Cyprus
Czech Republic
Dominican Republic
Dubai & UAE
Dublin
Egypt
Florence & Siena
Florida
France
Frankfurt
Germany
Greece
Guatemala & Belize
Hong Kong
Iceland
Ireland
Kenya
Lisbon
London
Los Angeles
Madrid
Mallorca
Marrakesh
Mexico
Miami & Key West
Morocco
New England
New York City
New Zealand
Northern Spain
Paris
Peru
Portugal
Prague
Rome
San Francisco
Sicily
South Africa
South India
Sri Lanka
Tenerife
Thailand

Toronto
Trinidad & Tobago
Tuscany
Venice
Washington DC
Yucatán Peninsula

Dictionary Phrasebooks
Croatian
Czech
Dutch
Egyptian Arabic
European Languages
  (Czech, French,
  German, Greek,
  Italian, Portuguese,
  Spanish)
French
German
Greek
Hindi & Urdu
Hungarian
Indonesian
Italian
Japanese
Latin American
  Spanish
Mandarin Chinese
Mexican Spanish
Polish
Portuguese
Russian
Spanish
Swahili
Thai
Turkish
Vietnamese

Music Guides
The Beatles
Bob Dylan
Cult Pop
Classical Music
Elvis
Frank Sinatra
Heavy Metal
Hip-Hop
Jazz
Opera
Reggae

Rock
World Music (2 vols)

Reference Guides
Babies
Books for Teenagers
Children's Books, 0–5
Children's Books, 5–11
Comedy Movies
Conspiracy Theories
Cult Fiction
Cult Football
Cult Movies
Cult TV
The Da Vinci Code
Ethical Shopping
Gangster Movies
Horror Movies
iPods, iTunes & Music
  Online
The Internet
James Bond
Kids' Movies
Lord of the Rings
Macs & OS X
Muhammad Ali
Music Playlists
PCs and Windows
Poker
Pregnancy & Birth
Sci–Fi Movies
Shakespeare
Superheroes

Unexplained
  Phenomena
The Universe
Weather
Website Directory

Football
Arsenal 11s
Celtic 11s
Chelsea 11s
Liverpool 11s
Newcastle 11s
Rangers 11s
Tottenham 11s
Man United 11s

Shakespeare's Globe
Theatre Tour and Exhibition

*Let us
on your
imaginary
forces work*

Bankside - London
T: 020 7902 1500
F: 020 7902 1515
E: exhibit@shakespearesglobe.com
www.shakespeares-globe.org

Small print and
Index

A Rough Guide to Rough Guides

In the summer of 1981, Mark Ellingham, a recent graduate from Bristol University, was travelling round Greece and couldn't find a guidebook that really met his needs. On the one hand there were the student guides, insistent on saving every last cent, and on the other the heavyweight cultural tomes whose authors seemed to have spent more time in a research library than lounging away the afternoon at a taverna or on the beach.

In a bid to avoid getting a job, Mark and a small group of writers set about creating their own guidebook. It was a guide to Greece that aimed to combine a journalistic approach to description with a thoroughly practical approach to travellers' needs – a guide that would incorporate culture, history and contemporary insights with a critical edge, together with up-to-date, value-for-money listings. Back in London, Mark and the team finished their Rough Guide, as they called it, and talked Routledge into publishing the book.

That first *Rough Guide to Greece*, published in 1982, was a student scheme that became a publishing phenomenon. The immediate success of the book – with numerous reprints and a Thomas Cook prize shortlisting – spawned a series that rapidly covered dozens of destinations. Rough Guides had a ready market among low-budget backpackers, but soon also acquired a much broader and older readership that relished Rough Guides' wit and inquisitiveness as much as their enthusiastic, critical approach. Everyone wants value for money, but not at any price.

Rough Guides soon began supplementing the "rougher" information about hostels and low-budget listings with the kind of detail on restaurants and quality hotels that independent-minded visitors on any budget might expect, whether on business in New York or trekking in Thailand.

These days the guides – distributed worldwide by the Penguin Group – offer recommendations from shoestring to luxury and cover more than 200 destinations around the globe, including almost every country in the Americas and Europe, more than half of Africa and most of Asia and Australasia. Our ever-growing team of authors and photographers is spread all over the world, particularly in Europe, the USA and Australia.

In 1994, we published the *Rough Guide to World Music* and *Rough Guide to Classical Music*; and a year later the *Rough Guide to the Internet*. All three books have become benchmark titles in their fields – which encouraged us to expand into other areas of publishing, mainly around popular culture. Rough Guides now publish:

- Travel guides to more than 200 worldwide destinations
- Dictionary phrasebooks to 22 major languages
- History guides ranging from Ireland to Islam
- Maps printed on rip-proof and waterproof Polyart™ paper
- Music guides running the gamut from Opera to Elvis
- Restaurant guides to London, New York and San Francisco
- Reference books on topics as diverse as the Weather and Shakespeare
- Sports guides from Formula 1 to Man Utd
- Pop culture books from *Lord of the Rings* to Cult TV
- World Music CDs in association with World Music Network

Visit **www.roughguides.com** to see our latest publications.

SMALL PRINT

Rough Guide credits

Text editors: Karoline Densley, Helen Marsden and Clifton Wilkinson
Layout: Diana Jarvis and Link Hall
Cartography: Katie Lloyd-Jones
Picture editor: Jj Luck
Production: Julia Bovis
Proofreader: Derek Wilde and Susannah Wight
Cover design: Chloë Roberts
Photographer: Mark Thomas
....
Editorial: **London** Kate Berens, Claire Saunders, Geoff Howard, Ruth Blackmore, Polly Thomas, Richard Lim, Alison Murchie, Andy Turner, Ella O'Donnell, Keith Drew, Edward Aves, Nikki Birrell, Alice Park, Sarah Eno, Joe Staines, Duncan Clark, Peter Buckley, Matthew Milton; **New York** Andrew Rosenberg, Richard Koss, Steven Horak, AnneLise Sorensen, Amy Hegarty, Hunter Slaton, April Isaacs
Design & Pictures: **London** Simon Bracken, Dan May, Mark Thomas, Harriet Mills, Chloë Roberts; **Delhi** Madhulita Mohapatra, Umesh Aggarwal, Ajay Verma, Jessica Subramanian, Amit Verma, Ankur Guha
Production: Julia Bovis, Sophie Hewat, Katherine Owers

Cartography: **London** Maxine Repath, Ed Wright; **Delhi** Manish Chandra, Rajesh Chhibber, Jai Prakash Mishra, Ashutosh Bharti, Rajesh Mishra, Animesh Pathak, Jasbir Sandhu, Karobi Gogoi
Online: **New York** Jennifer Gold, Kristin Mingrone; **Delhi** Manik Chauhan, Narender Kumar, Shekhar Jha, Rakesh Kumar, Chhandita Chakravarty
Marketing & Publicity: **London** Richard Trillo, Niki Hanmer, David Wearn, Demelza Dallow, Louise Maher; **New York** Geoff Colquitt, Megan Kennedy, Katy Ball; **Delhi** Reem Khokhar
Custom publishing and foreign rights: Philippa Hopkins
Manager India: Punita Singh
Series editor: Mark Ellingham
Reference Director: Andrew Lockett
PA to Managing and Publishing Directors: Megan McIntyre
Publishing Director: Martin Dunford
Managing Director: Kevin Fitzgerald

Publishing information

This sixth edition published November 2005 by
Rough Guides Ltd,
80 Strand, London WC2R 0RL
345 Hudson St, 4th Floor,
New York, NY 10014, USA
14 Local Shopping Centre, Panchsheel Park,
New Delhi 110017, India
Distributed by the Penguin Group
Penguin Books Ltd,
80 Strand, London WC2R 0RL
Penguin Putnam, Inc.
375 Hudson Street, NY 10014, USA
Penguin Group (Australia)
250 Camberwell Road, Camberwell
Victoria 3124, Australia
Penguin Books Canada Ltd,
10 Alcorn Avenue, Toronto, Ontario,
Canada M4V 1E4
Penguin Group (New Zealand)
Cnr Rosedale and Airborne Roads
Albany, Auckland, New Zealand

Typeset in Bembo and Helvetica to an original design by Henry Iles.
Printed in Italy by LegoPrint
© Rob Humphreys 2005

652pp includes index
A catalogue record for this book is available from the British Library
ISBN 1-84353-461-4

1   3   5   7   9   8   6   4   2

Help us update

We've gone to a lot of effort to ensure that the sixth edition of **The Rough Guide to London** is accurate and up to date. However, things change – places get "discovered", opening hours are notoriously fickle, restaurants and rooms raise prices or lower standards. If you feel we've got it wrong or left something out, we'd like to know, and if you can remember the address, the price, the time, the phone number, so much the better.

We'll credit all contributions, and send a copy of the next edition (or any other Rough Guide if you prefer) for the best letters. Everyone who writes to us and isn't already a subscriber will receive a copy of our full-colour thrice-yearly newsletter. Please mark letters: "**Rough Guide London Update**" and send to: Rough Guides, 80 Strand, London WC2R 0RL, or Rough Guides, 4th Floor, 345 Hudson St, New York, NY 10014. Or send an email to **mail@roughguides.com**

Have your questions answered and tell others about your trip at
www.roughguides.atinfopop.com

Acknowledgements

Rob: thanks to Val for the biblio and to her and Gordon for the odd foray, to Josh for company and to the wonderful Karoline and the man in the shadows, Mr CW.

Helena: Thanks to the following people, for their extraordinary dedication in visiting London's pubs, bars, clubs and restaurants with me: Ed, Clifton, Ruth, Ella, Claire, Gavin, Dan, Matthew, Lisa, Lorna and Markie. Also to co-author Sally and editor Karoline, for being cool, well-organized and fun to be with.

Sally: Although it wasn't difficult finding willing volunteers to help test out London's drinking holes, a great big thanks goes to those who ensured that I never got drunk alone, namely: Helena, Katy, Hayden, Freya, James, Jinny, John, Christina, Ed, Cliff, Keith and Ella; and thanks to Tim and Alice for their expert insider info. Most importantly thanks to Chris and Kate who jointly win the prize for being the best, and most enduring, nightlife voyeurs, as well as great company.

Readers' letters

Thanks to all the readers who have taken the time to write in with comments and suggestions (and apologies if we've inadvertently omitted or misspelt anyone's name):

Dr Leon Allen, Laura Boggs, Megan Bollman, A. Brodie, Sergio Burns, Charlotte Stewart Clark, John Collins, Russ & Jane Davison, Paul Deneve, John Fisher, Dean Fox, Ron Fry, Angela Greenfield, Chihiro Goddard, Jan Hamilton, Ming Wei Hui, Amy Jackson, Andrew Kleissner, Maria Kleissner, Nathaniel Koschmann, Jim Lyons, Miss C A Mumford, Paul Nicol, Joan Nikelsky, Harley Nott, Christelle Passuello, Candice Pettifer, Debbie Porter, Lorraine Rainbow, Irmgard Rathmacher, H H Saffery, Sasha from E13, Caroline Schubert, Pete Tenerelli, Mr A C Wells, Jim Young, Ellen Zimmerman

Photo credits

All photos © Rough Guides except the following:

Cover
Main front picture: Guards marching © Getty
Small front top picture: Holland Park © Alamy
Small front lower picture: London phone boxes © Mark Thomas
Back top picture: Somerset House © Mark Thomas
Back lower picture: London Eye © Alamy

Title page
London Eye © Ian Cumming/Axiom

Introduction
Covent Garden © Network Photographers/Alamy
View over the Thames at sunset © Mark Thomas

Things not to miss
02 The Weather Project by Olafur Eliasson © Brian Harris/Alamy
03 The Proms © Lebrecht Music and Arts Photo Library /Alamy
04 Water jets at Somerset House © Paul Panayiotou/Alamy
09 Sir John Soane's Museum © Sir John Soane's Museum
10 No.11 bus © Mark Thomas
11 *Saint George and the Dragon* by Paolo Uccello © National Gallery Collection; by kind permission of the Trustees of the National Gallery, London/Corbis
13 Venus Williams, Wimbledon Championships © Kieran Doherty/Reuters/Corbis
14 Pub, Soho © Art Kowalsky/Alamy
15 St Paul's Cathedral © Mark Thomas
20 Freud Bar © Naki Kouyioumtzis/Axiom
21 Hyde Park and Kensington Gardens © Mark Thomas
23 Chinatown © Mark Thomas
26 Notting Hill Carnival © Westend61/Alamy
28 Morris Room at the V&A Museum © Massimo Listri/Corbis
29 London theatre © Mark Thomas

Black and whites
p.99 Burlington Arcade © Mark Thomas
p.136 Egyptian mummy, British Museum © Network Photographers/Alamy
p.154 Isaac Newton statue © Mark Thomas
p.169 *A Bar at the Folies-Bergère*, Edouard Manet © The Samuel Courtauld Trust, Courtauld Institute of Art Gallery, London
p.177 Sir John Soane's Museum © Sir John Soane's Museum
p.211 Flaming urn on monument © Mark Thomas
p.215 Traitor's Gate © David Crausby/Alamy
p.261 Studio 6, Gabriel's Wharf © Robert Harding Picture Library Ltd/Alamy
p.318 World's End, King's Road © Mark Thomas
p.365 Kenwood House © Mark Thomas
p.404 The Great Conservatory, Syon House © Robert Harding Picture Library Ltd/Alamy
p.428 Windsor Castle © The Travel Selection/Alamy
p.442 Clock in lounge © B&B Belgravia
p.447 Henry Bennett-Smith room, The Rookery Hotel © The Rookery Hotel
p.467 Hakkasan © Hakkasan
p.482 Bricklayers Arms © Vicki Couchman/Axiom
p.491 Astoria © Mark Thomas
p.504 Old Compton Street © Alex Segre/Alamy
p.522 Electric Cinema sign © Mark Thomas
p.528 Photographers' Gallery © courtesy of The Photographers' Gallery
p.557 Riders, Hyde Park © Network Photographers/Alamy
p.565 The Lord Mayor's Show © Corporation of London
p.570 Little Angel Theatre © Little Angel Theatre
p.582 The Globe Theatre engraving © Stapleton Collection/Corbis
p.597 Poster for *A Clockwork Orange*, 1971 © Pictorial Press/Alamy

Index

Map entries are in colour.

P

INDEX

Map symbols

maps are listed in the full index using coloured text

– – –	Chapter division boundary	⌂	Mosque
═══	Motorway	⚇	Gardens/fountain
══	Main road	🏛	Stately home
══	Minor road	◔	Cave
- - - -	Tunnel	○	Train station
▨▨▨	Pedestrianized street	⊖	Tube station
- - - -	Footpath	✡	Synagogue
━━	Railway	⊠	Post office
▨▨▨	River/canal	ⓘ	Tourist information
— —	Ferry route	♦	Places of interest
= = = =	Walkway	⊞	Hospital
▤▤▤	Steps	■	Building
———	Wall	⊞	Church
♟	Museum	▨	Park
⊙	Statue	⊞	Cemetery

0800 LONDON®
LONDON'S FREE TELEPHONE BOOKING SERVICE

You can now call **FREE** on **0800 LONDON** to book discounted rates for London hotels, theatre, sightseeing and airport transfers. From outside the UK call **+44 800 LONDON**.

Advisors available every day from 8am to midnight.

0800 LONDON
London's Free Telephone Booking Service.

London Information Centre™
LEICESTER SQUARE

Free information and half price hotels. Every day.

Visit us in person in the centre of Leicester Square or call us on **020 729 22 333**
From outside the UK call **+44 20 729 22 333**

London Information Centre,
Leicester Square, London.
Open every day from 8am to 11pm.

.com™

The number one internet site for London offers essential information to help organise the perfect visit to London. Guaranteed lowest rates on London's leading hotels and information on 15,000 reviewed and quality assessed London products and services.

You can now also book over the phone on 0207 437 4370.
From outside the UK call +44 207 437 4370.

 The **#1 Internet Site** for **London**™
Over 30 million customers served

Key bus routes and tourist attractions in central London

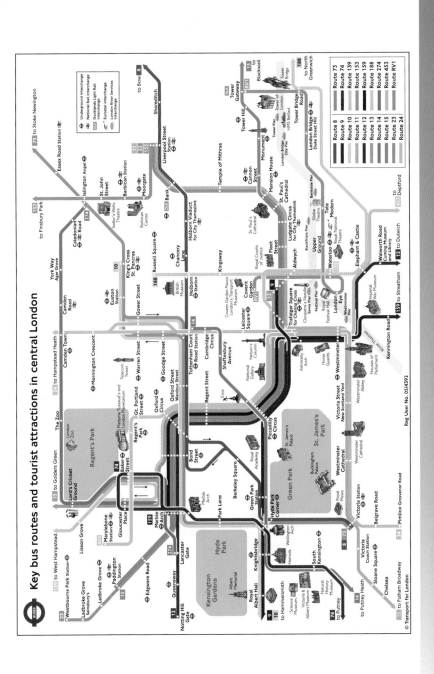

© Transport for London

Reg User No. 05/4392

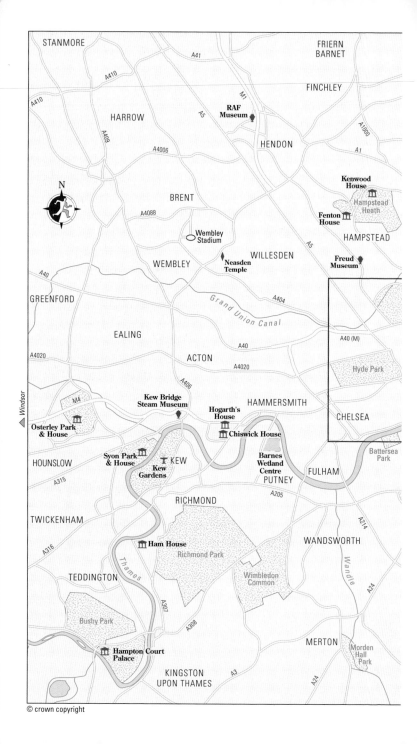

© crown copyright

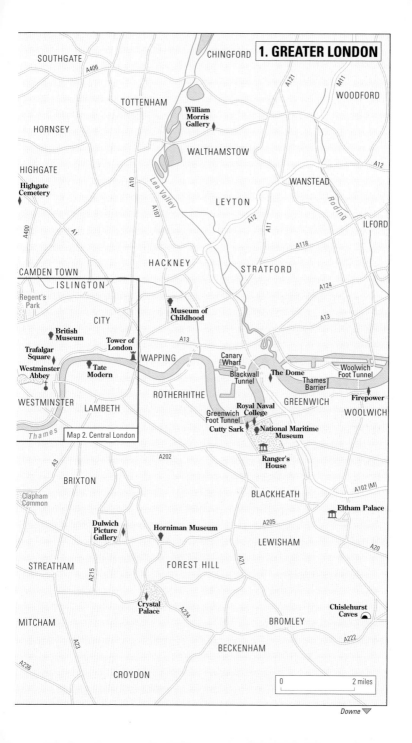

1. GREATER LONDON

SOUTHGATE

CHINGFORD

A406

WOODFORD

TOTTENHAM

M11

A121

HORNSEY

William Morris Gallery

WALTHAMSTOW

A12

HIGHGATE

WANSTEAD

Highgate Cemetery

A10

A107

Lea Valley

LEYTON

Roding

A12

ILFORD

A400

A1

A11

A118

HACKNEY

STRATFORD

A124

CAMDEN TOWN

ISLINGTON

Regent's Park

A13

Museum of Childhood

CITY

British Museum

Tower of London

A13

Canary Wharf

Woolwich Foot Tunnel

Trafalgar Square

WAPPING

Blackwall Tunnel

The Dome

Westminster Abbey

Tate Modern

Thames Barrier

Firepower

ROTHERHITHE

Royal Naval College

GREENWICH

WOOLWICH

WESTMINSTER

LAMBETH

Greenwich Foot Tunnel

Cutty Sark

National Maritime Museum

Thames

Map 2. Central London

A202

Ranger's House

A3

BRIXTON

A102 (M)

Clapham Common

BLACKHEATH

Eltham Palace

Dulwich Picture Gallery

Horniman Museum

A205

LEWISHAM

A20

STREATHAM

A215

FOREST HILL

A21

MITCHAM

Crystal Palace

A234

Chislehurst Caves

BROMLEY

A222

A23

BECKENHAM

A236

CROYDON

0   2 miles

Downe ▽

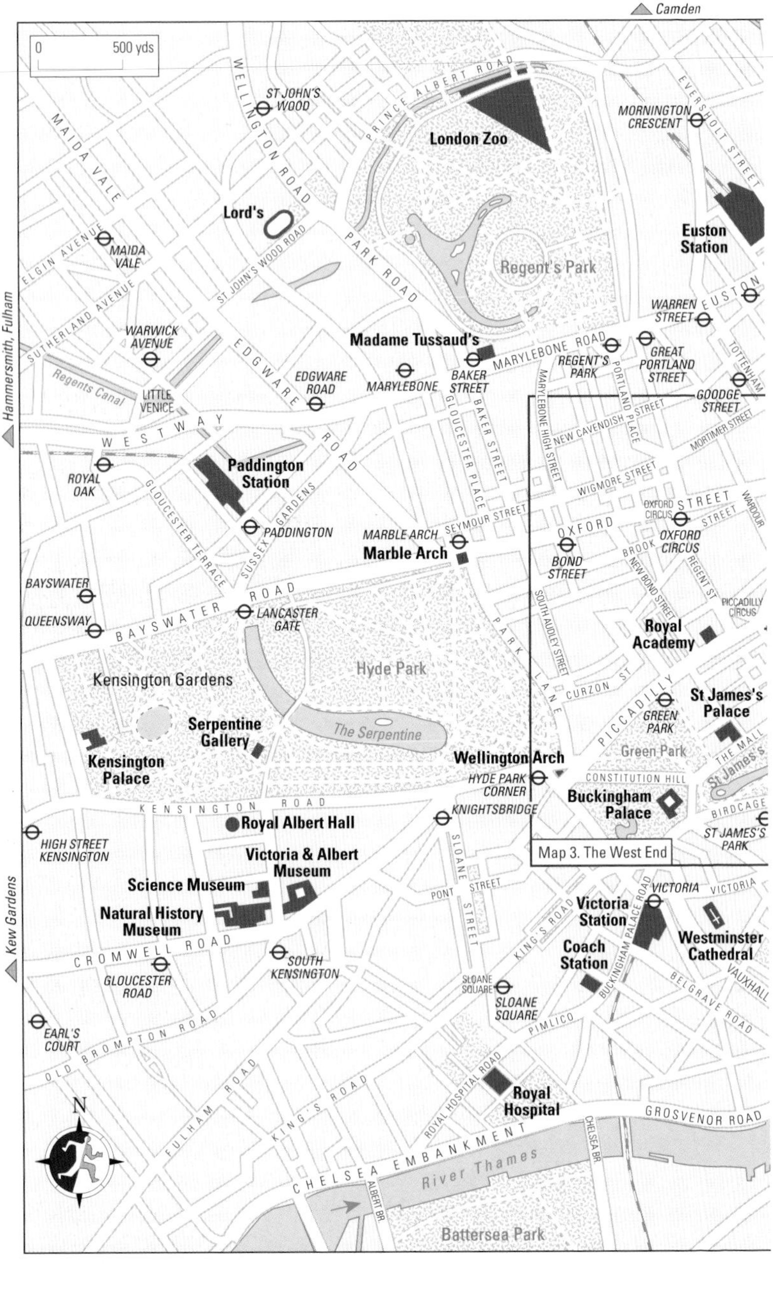

△ Camden

0 ——— 500 yds

WELLINGTON ROAD

ST JOHN'S
WOOD

PRINCE ALBERT ROAD

London Zoo

MORNINGTON
CRESCENT

EVERSHOLT STREET

MAIDA VALE

ST JOHN'S WOOD ROAD

Lord's

PARK ROAD

Regent's Park

**Euston
Station**

ELGIN AVENUE

MAIDA
VALE

SUTHERLAND AVENUE

WARREN
STREET

EUSTON

Hammersmith, Fulham ▽

WARWICK
AVENUE

Regents Canal

EDGWARE ROAD

Madame Tussaud's

MARYLEBONE ROAD

REGENT'S
PARK

GREAT
PORTLAND
STREET

TOTTENHAM COURT

LITTLE
VENICE

WESTWAY

EDGWARE
ROAD

MARYLEBONE

BAKER
STREET

NEW CAVENDISH STREET

PORTLAND PLACE

GOODGE
STREET

MORTIMER STREET

ROYAL
OAK

GLOUCESTER TERRACE

SUSSEX GARDENS

**Paddington
Station**

MARYLEBONE HIGH STREET

GLOUCESTER PLACE

BAKER STREET

WIGMORE STREET

WARDOUR

PADDINGTON

MARBLE ARCH

SEYMOUR STREET

OXFORD STREET

OXFORD
CIRCUS

REGENT STREET

BAYSWATER

ROAD

Marble Arch

OXFORD

BOND
STREET

BROOK

NEW BOND STREET

PICCADILLY
CIRCUS

QUEENSWAY

BAYSWATER

LANCASTER
GATE

Hyde Park

PARK LANE

SOUTH AUDLEY STREET

**Royal
Academy**

Kensington Gardens

**Serpentine
Gallery**

The Serpentine

CURZON ST

GREEN
PARK

**St James's
Palace**

**Kensington
Palace**

KENSINGTON ROAD

Wellington Arch
HYDE PARK
CORNER

CONSTITUTION HILL

Green Park

THE MALL

St James's

HIGH STREET
KENSINGTON

● **Royal Albert Hall**

KNIGHTSBRIDGE

**Buckingham
Palace**

BIRDCAGE

ST JAMES'S
PARK

**Victoria & Albert
Museum**

SLOANE STREET

Map 3. The West End

Science Museum

PONT STREET

VICTORIA

**Victoria
Station**

VICTORIA

**Natural History
Museum**

CROMWELL ROAD

SOUTH
KENSINGTON

**Westminster
Cathedral**

Kew Gardens ▽

GLOUCESTER
ROAD

SLOANE
SQUARE

**Coach
Station**

BUCKINGHAM PALACE ROAD

BELGRAVE ROAD

VAUXHALL

EARL'S
COURT

OLD BROMPTON ROAD

KING'S ROAD

PIMLICO

N

FULHAM ROAD

KING'S ROAD

ROYAL HOSPITAL ROAD

**Royal
Hospital**

GROSVENOR ROAD

CHELSEA BR

CHELSEA EMBANKMENT

ALBERT BR

River Thames

Battersea Park

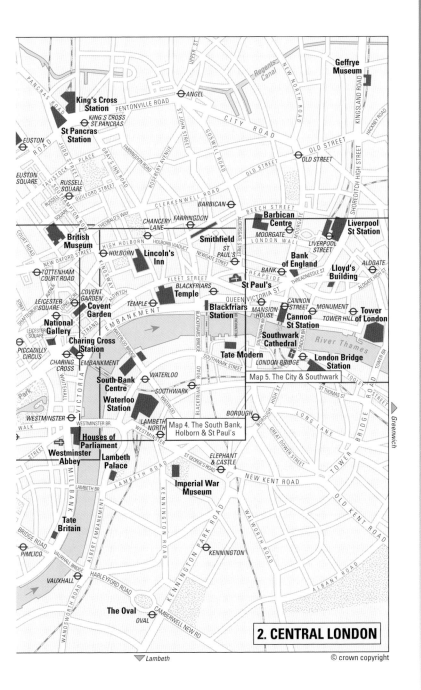

2. CENTRAL LONDON

Geffrye Museum

King's Cross Station
PENTONVILLE ROAD

ANGEL

PANCRAS ROAD

Regents Canal

NEW NORTH ROAD

KINGSLAND ROAD

HACKNEY ROAD

ST JOHN STREET

CITY ROAD

GOSWELL ROAD

King's Cross St Pancras

St Pancras Station

EUSTON ROAD

EUSTON SQUARE

TAVISTOCK PLACE

JUDD STREET

GRAY'S INN ROAD

FARRINGDON ROAD

ROSEBERY AVENUE

OLD STREET

OLD STREET

SHOREDITCH HIGH STREET

RUSSELL SQUARE

GUILFORD STREET

SOUTHAMPTON ROW

CLERKENWELL ROAD

BARBICAN

BEECH STREET

Barbican Centre

Liverpool St Station

COURT ROAD

THEOBALD'S WAY

CHANCERY LANE

FARRINGDON

ALDERSGATE STREET

MOORGATE

LONDON WALL

MOORGATE

LIVERPOOL STREET

British Museum

HIGH HOLBORN

HOLBORN

HOLBORN VIADUCT

Smithfield

ST PAUL'S

NEWGATE STREET

Lincoln's Inn

Bank of England

CHEAPSIDE

THREADNEEDLE ST

Lloyd's Building

ALDGATE

ALDGATE HIGH STREET

NEW OXFORD STREET

TOTTENHAM COURT ROAD

KINGSWAY

FLEET STREET

St Paul's

BANK

COVENT GARDEN

LEICESTER SQUARE

ALDWYCH

BLACKFRIARS

Temple

QUEEN VICTORIA ST

CANNON STREET

MONUMENT

Tower of London

TOWER HILL

Covent Garden

TEMPLE

Blackfriars Station

MANSION HOUSE

Cannon St Station

National Gallery

LEICESTER SQUARE

STRAND

EMBANKMENT

BLACKFRIARS BRIDGE

SOUTHWARK BRIDGE

Southwark Cathedral

River Thames

PICCADILLY CIRCUS

Charing Cross Station

CHARING CROSS

EMBANKMENT

WATERLOO BRIDGE

SOUTHWARK BRIDGE

Tate Modern

LONDON BRIDGE

London Bridge Station

TOWER BR.

WHITEHALL

VICTORIA

South Bank Centre

WATERLOO

SOUTHWARK STREET

Map 5. The City & Southwark

TOOLEY ST

Park

WESTMINSTER

SOUTHWARK

BLACKFRIARS ROAD

ST THOMAS ST

WALK

WESTMINSTER BR.

Waterloo Station

WATERLOO

LAMBETH NORTH

BOROUGH

BOROUGH HIGH STREET

LONG LANE

TOWER BRIDGE ROAD

Greenwich

Houses of Parliament

Map 4. The South Bank, Holborn & St Paul's

WESTMINSTER

STREET

Westminster Abbey

Lambeth Palace

ST GEORGE'S ROAD

ELEPHANT & CASTLE

NEW KENT ROAD

GREAT DOVER STREET

MILLBANK

LAMBETH BR.

LAMBETH ROAD

KENNINGTON ROAD

Imperial War Museum

WALWORTH ROAD

OLD KENT ROAD

BANK

ALBERT EMBANKMENT

Tate Britain

BRIDGE ROAD

PIMLICO

VAUXHALL BRIDGE

KENNINGTON PARK ROAD

KENNINGTON

KENNINGTON NEW RD

ALBANY ROAD

VAUXHALL

WANDSWORTH ROAD

HARLEYFORD ROAD

The Oval

OVAL

CAMBERWELL NEW RD

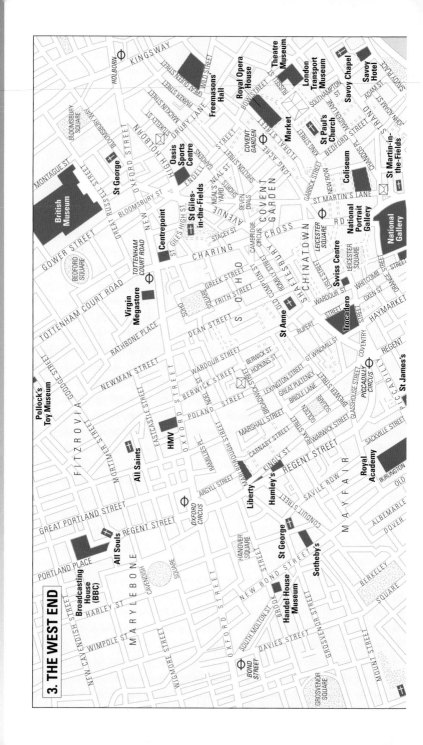

3. THE WEST END

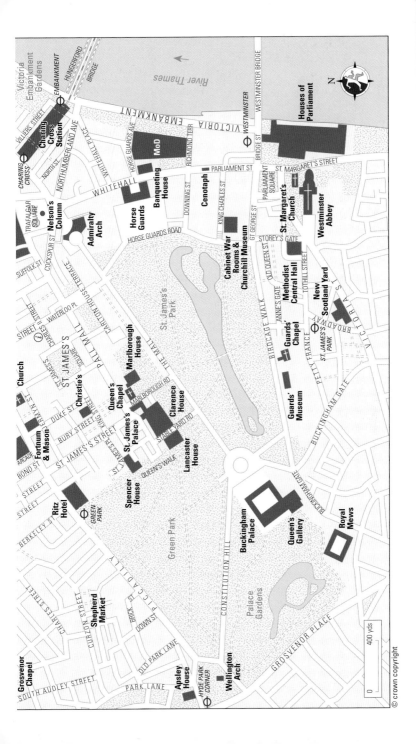

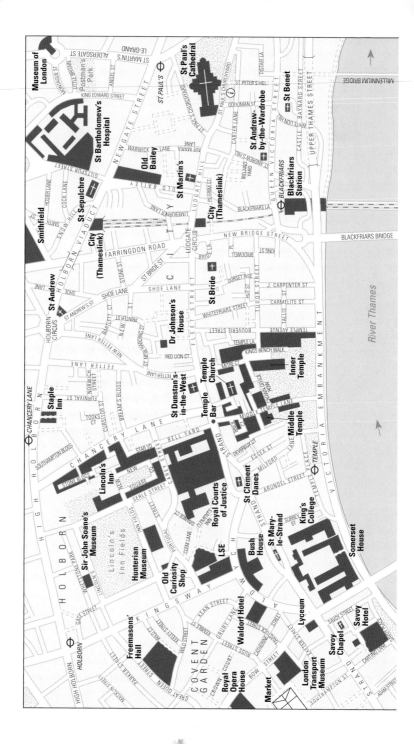

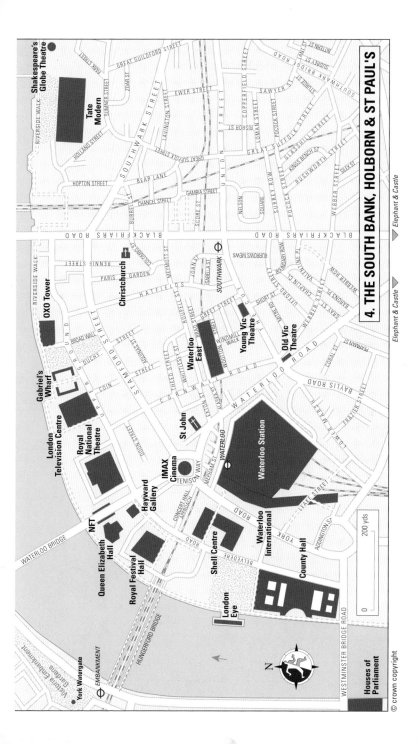

4. THE SOUTH BANK, HOLBORN & ST PAUL'S

© crown copyright

Shakespeare's Globe Theatre

Tate Modern

OXO Tower

Christchurch

Gabriel's Wharf

London Television Centre

Royal National Theatre

Waterloo East

Young Vic Theatre

Old Vic Theatre

St John

NFT

Hayward Gallery

IMAX Cinema

Queen Elizabeth Hall

Royal Festival Hall

Shell Centre

Waterloo Station

Waterloo International

County Hall

London Eye

Houses of Parliament

York Watergate

Victoria Embankment Gardens

Elephant & Castle

Elephant & Castle

0   200 yds

N

Streets

GREAT GUILDFORD STREET
PARK STREET
SUMNER STREET
ZOAR ST
EWER STREET
SAWYER ST
COPPERFIELD STREET
SOUTHWARK BRIDGE ROAD
SUDREY ST
BITTERN ST
SURREY ST ST
RISBORO ST
LOMAN STREET
POCOCK STREET
SUFFOLK STREET
GREAT SUFFOLK STREET
GLASSHILL STREET
KINGS BENCH ST
RUSHWORTH STREET
SILEX ST
WEBBER STREET
SOUTHWARK STREET
HOLLAND STREET
LAVINGTON STREET
UNION STREET
HOPTON STREET
BEAR LANE
GAMBIA STREET
CHANCEL STREET
SCORE ST
BURRELL ST
NELSON SQUARE
SURREY ROW
POCOCK STREET
WEBBER ROW
BLACKFRIARS ROAD
RIVERSIDE WALK
RENNIE STREET
PARIS GARDEN
HATFIELDS
MEYMOTT ST
JOAN ST
ISABELLA ST
SOUTHWARK
COLOMBO ST
BURROWS MEWS
BOUNDARY ROW
GRAY ST
CHAPLIN CL
BARONS PL
UFFORD STREET
CHAPLIN CT
VALENTINE PL
SHORT ST
GROUND
BROAD WALL
DUCHY STREET
STAMFORD STREET
UPPER
COIN STREET
THEED STREET
WHITTLESEY ST
ROUPELL STREET
WOOTTON STREET
WINDMILL WALK
MEAD ROW
WEBBER ROW
BAYLIS ROAD
CORAL ST
PEARMAN ST
CORNWALL ROAD
ALASKA ST
EXTON ST
WATERLOO ROAD
LOWER MARSH
FRAZIER STREET
LEAKE STREET
WATERLOO
MEPHAM ST
TENISON WAY
CONCERT HALL APPROACH
BELVEDERE ROAD
YORK ROAD
ADDINGTON ST
WESTMINSTER BRIDGE ROAD
WATERLOO BRIDGE
EMBANKMENT
HUNGERFORD BRIDGE
RIVERSIDE WALK

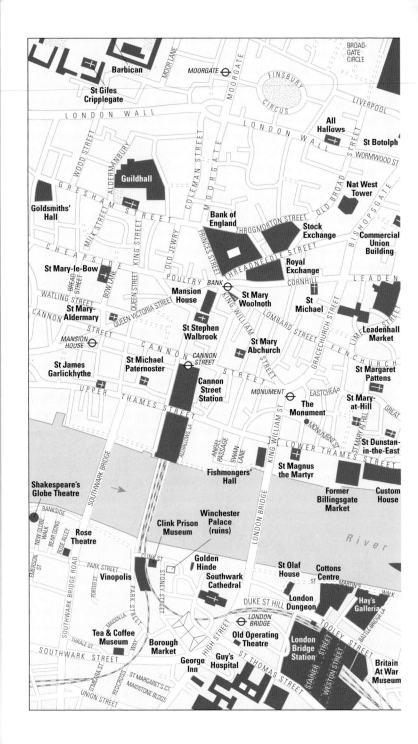

Columbia Road ▲

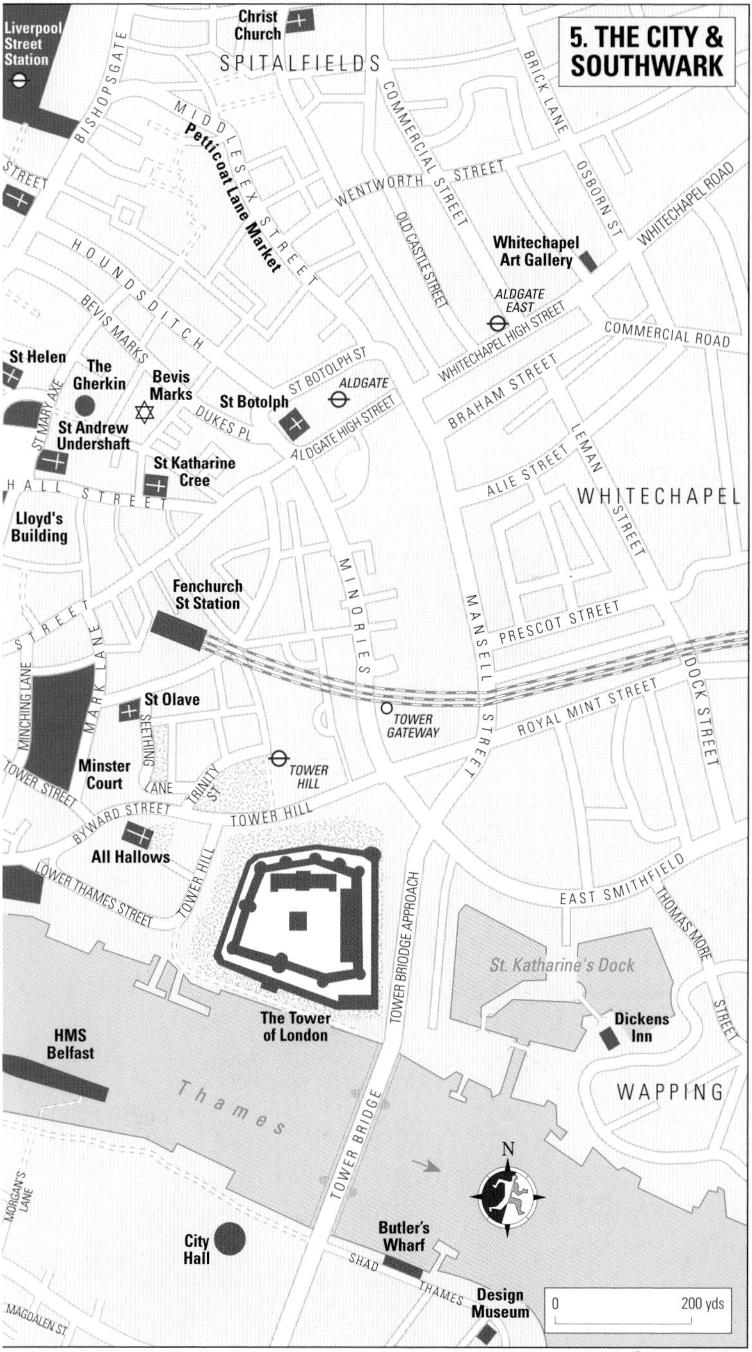

5. THE CITY & SOUTHWARK

Liverpool Street Station

Christ Church

SPITALFIELDS

BISHOPSGATE

MIDDLESEX STREET

Petticoat Lane Market

STREET

COMMERCIAL STREET

BRICK LANE

WENTWORTH STREET

OLD CASTLE STREET

OSBORN ST

WHITECHAPEL ROAD

HOUNDSDITCH

BEVIS MARKS

Whitechapel Art Gallery

ALDGATE EAST

WHITECHAPEL HIGH STREET

COMMERCIAL ROAD

St Helen

The Gherkin

Bevis Marks

ST BOTOLPH ST

St Botolph

ALDGATE

BRAHAM STREET

ST MARY AXE

St Andrew Undershaft

DUKES PL

ALDGATE HIGH STREET

LEMAN STREET

St Katharine Cree

ALIE STREET

WHITECHAPEL

HALL STREET

Lloyd's Building

STREET

MINORIES

MANSELL STREET

PRESCOT STREET

Fenchurch St Station

DOCK STREET

MARK LANE

MINCHING LANE

St Olave

SEETHING

ROYAL MINT STREET

TOWER GATEWAY

TOWER STREET

Minster Court

BYWARD STREET

TRINITY ST

LANE

TOWER HILL

TOWER HILL

All Hallows

LOWER THAMES STREET

TOWER HILL

EAST SMITHFIELD

THOMAS MORE STREET

St. Katharine's Dock

TOWER BRIDGE APPROACH

Dickens Inn

HMS Belfast

The Tower of London

STREET

WAPPING

Thames

TOWER BRIDGE

N

MORGAN'S LANE

City Hall

Butler's Wharf

SHAD

MAGDALEN ST

THAMES

Design Museum

0   200 yds

© crown copyright

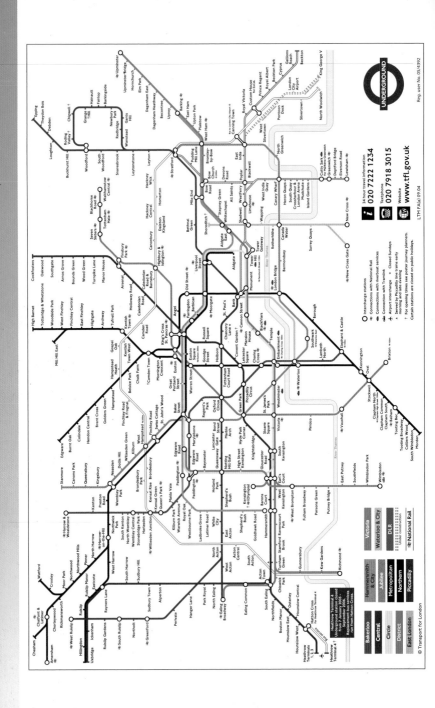